Contents

Managing Editor, Kris Valencia Graef
Editorial Assistants: Michelle Arab,
    Wendy McLeod
Field Editors and Advertising Representa-
    tives: Earl L. Brown, Lynn Owen,
    Jerrianne Lowther, Judy Parkin
Production Manager, Barton R. Vernon
Advertising and Production Coordinator,
    Miyuki Zybura
Production Staff: Marilyn Do, Lou
    Helmick, Jennifer Ring, Trevor Vernon
Art Director, David L. Ranta
Page Designer, Pam Smith
Graphic Designer, Sisi Mereness
Pre-press Supervisor, Glen Jasmer
Fulfillment Manager, Tina L. Boyle
Fulfillment Assistant, Tina Do
Associate Publisher, Michele Andrus Dill
Publisher, Geoffrey P. Vernon

Copyright © 1997
Vernon Publications Inc.

ISSN 0361-1361   ISBN 1-878425-29-3
Key title: The Milepost
Printed in U.S.A. on recycled stock.

COVER: Bull moose in autumn beneath
Mount McKinley, Denali National Park.
(© Leo Keeler 1997)
Matted prints of this cover photo are
available for purchase; see below for
ordering information.
COVER INSETS: Upper left: Gold
stampeders in the Dyea Canyon, AK,
Klondike Gold Rush 1897. (Courtesy of Alaska
State Library, Winter&Pond, #87-682)
Center right: View of cruise ship docked
at Seward harbor. (© Bruce M. Herman)
Center left: RV on the Alaska Highway in
northern British Columbia. (Earl L. Brown, staff)
Cover Design David L. Ranta

**Additional photo credits (column
insets):** Earl L. Brown, pages 3, 68, 211,
259, 725, 734, 735; Roy M. Corral, page
3; Michael N. Dill, page 657; Blake
Hanna, pages 20, 25, 26; Jerrianne
Lowther, pages 182, 292, 317; Sharon
Nault, pages 3, 190, 579, 659, 674; Judy
Parkin, pages 60, 220, 238, 707; Rollo
Pool, pages 663, 664, 670, 686;
Soldotna Historical Society, page 528.

Vernon Publications Inc.
3000 Northup Way, Suite 200
Bellevue, WA 98004
(206) 827-9900 until April 1997
(425) 827-9900 after April 1997
1-800-726-4707
Fax (206) 822-9372 (425) after April 1997
E-mail: books@alaskainfo.com
Internet address: www.alaskainfo.com

Publishers of:
The MILEPOST®
ALASKA A to Z
NORTHWEST MILEPOSTS®
The ALASKA WILDERNESS GUIDE
The MILEPOST® Souvenir Logbook
Alaska Roadhouse Recipes

Vernon Publications Inc.
Geoffrey P. Vernon,
Chairman & CEO
Michele Andrus Dill, Vice President
Judy Vernon, Secretary
Bill R. Vernon, Chairman Emeritus

The MILEPOST® Trip Planner

The first thing to think about in planning your trip North is how you wish to travel—by highway, by ferry, by cruise ship, by airplane, by rail, on your own or with a tour. You may want to use more than one form of transportation, such as driving the Alaska Highway one way and taking the Alaska Marine Highway (the state ferry system) the other way.

Regardless of how you travel, *The MILEPOST®* works the same way. Information in *The MILEPOST®* is organized into sections: Highways, Major Attractions, Railroads, Marine Access Routes, Inside Passage and General Information. All sections are listed on the Contents page.

If you are driving from Anchorage to Denali National Park, for example, turn to the George Parks Highway section for the log of the highway and the Denali National Park section for a description of the park and its facilities. Pertinent sections are always cross-referenced in capital letters in the log at the appropriate junction: When you reach the turnoff for Denali National Park on the George Parks Highway, for example, the log entry reads "see DENALI NATIONAL PARK section for details." The quickest way to find another section is to refer back to the Contents page. Place names and highways are also indexed in the back of the book.

The second thing to consider in planning your trip North is your itinerary. Deciding what you want to see and do will help narrow down the choices on what routes to take. Pull out the Plan-A-Trip map for an overview of the North Country and the access routes leading north. Begin a list of places or activities you want to include on your trip.

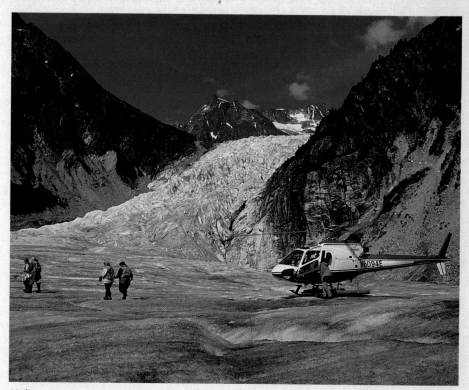

Helicopter tour on an icefield in Southeast Alaska. (Earl L. Brown, staff)

(Remember, you can find specific places by checking the index in the back of the book.) Thumb through the pages of *The MILEPOST®* for photos, advertisements and features on attractions, destinations and activities. Enhance your trip by taking a tour off the beaten path; there are many to choose from.

If you are driving the Alaska Highway, consult one of the 2 access routes to the Alaska Highway logged in *The MILEPOST®*

and the ALASKA HIGHWAY section. If you are taking the water route to Alaska, refer to the MARINE ACCESS ROUTES section for cruise ship and ferry information; read the descriptions of communities accessible by ferry in the INSIDE PASSAGE section; and refer to the HAINES HIGHWAY and KLONDIKE HIGHWAY 2 logs for road connections for ferry travelers. For an overview of the ferry and cruise ship routes, see the maps in the MARINE

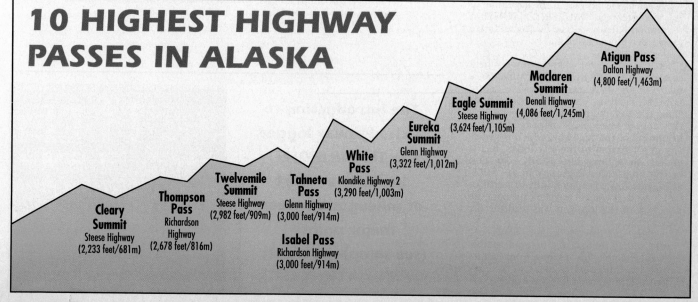

10 HIGHEST HIGHWAY PASSES IN ALASKA

Cleary Summit
Steese Highway
(2,233 feet/681m)

Thompson Pass
Richardson Highway
(2,678 feet/816m)

Twelvemile Summit
Steese Highway
(2,982 feet/909m)

Isabel Pass
Richardson Highway
(3,000 feet/914m)

Tahneta Pass
Glenn Highway
(3,000 feet/914m)

White Pass
Klondike Highway 2
(3,290 feet/1,003m)

Eureka Summit
Glenn Highway
(3,322 feet/1,012m)

Eagle Summit
Steese Highway
(3,624 feet/1,105m)

Maclaren Summit
Denali Highway
(4,086 feet/1,245m)

Atigun Pass
Dalton Highway
(4,800 feet/1,463m)

ACCESS ROUTES section. For a detailed look at the Inside Passage, study the maps on pages 649–653.

Highlights of—and hints about—each method of transportation are discussed in the following pages. Becoming familiar with what's available by highway, by air, by water, by packaged tour and by rail is critical to planning your trip North.

By Highway

For highway travelers, The MILEPOST® includes mile-by-mile logs and detailed maps of all highways in Alaska and northwestern Canada. The highway logs include campgrounds, businesses offering food, gas, lodging and other services, attractions, fishing spots, and the geography and history of the land. Descriptions of highway communities are included in the highway logs.

The Key to Highways map on the opposite page shows you what highways are covered in The MILEPOST®. How to Read a Highway Log below gives a detailed explanation of the highway logging system.

How to Read a Highway Log

To the right is an abbreviated version of part of the George Parks Highway log, keyed to help you understand how to read all highway logs in The MILEPOST®.

1. A boldface paragraph appears at the beginning of each highway log in The MILEPOST® that explains what beginning and ending destinations are used, and what boldface letters represent those destinations. In this log **A** represents **Anchorage, F** is **Fairbanks.**

2. In the log, the boldface numbers represent the distance in miles from the beginning and ending destinations, and the lightface numbers are the metric equivalent in kilometers (unless otherwise noted). For example, the entrance to Denali National Park and Preserve is 237.3 miles, or 381.9 kilometers, from Anchorage.

3. References to other sections in The MILEPOST® are always uppercased. In this example, the DENALI NATIONAL PARK section is referenced. Refer to the Contents page to quickly find other sections.

4. Display advertisements are keyed in the log by a boldface entry at their highway locations, followed by the words "See display ad this section." Their advertisement will appear near this entry.

5. "Log" advertisements are classified-type advertisements that appear in the text. These are identified by the boldface name of the business at the beginning of the entry and "[ADVERTISEMENT]" at the end. These log advertisements are written by the advertisers.

It may also help you to know how our field editors log the highways. The MILEPOST® field editors drive each highway, taking notes on facilities, features and attractions along the way and noting the mile at which they appear. Mileages are measured from the beginning of the highway, which is generally at a junction or the city limits, to the end of the highway, also usually a junction or city limits. Most highways in The MILEPOST® are logged either south to north or east to west. If you are traveling the opposite direction of the log, you will read the log back to front.

To determine driving distance between 2 points, simply subtract the first mileage figures. For example, the distance from Crabb's Crossing at **Milepost A 231.3** to the park entrance at **Milepost A 237.3** is 6 miles.

George Parks Highway Log

1 —

ALASKA ROUTE 1
Distance from Anchorage (A) is followed by distance from Fairbanks (F).

A 231.3 (372.2 km) **F 126.7** (203.9 km) Crabb's Crossing, second bridge northbound over the Nenana River.

A 233.1 (375.1 km) **F 124.9** (201 km) Gravel turnout to east.

A 234.1 (376.7 km) **F 123.9** (199.4 km) Double-ended turnout with litter barrels to east; scenic viewpoint. No overnight parking or camping. Mount Fellows (elev. 4,476 feet/1,364m) to the east. The constantly changing shadows make this an excellent camera subject.

A 235.1 (378.4 km) **F 122.9** (197.8 km) *CAUTION: Railroad crossing.*

2 —
A 237.2 (381.7 km) **F 120.8** (194.4 km) Riley Creek bridge.

A 237.3 (381.9 km) **F 120.7** (194.2 km) Entrance to Denali National Park and Preserve (formerly Mount McKinley National Park) to west. Fresh water fill-up hose and dump station 0.2 mile/0.3 km from junction on Park Road; Visitor Center is 0.5 mile/0.8 km from the highway junction. See DENALI NATIONAL PARK section for details. — 3

A 238 (383 km) **F 120** (193.4 km) Third bridge northbound over the Nenana River.

A 238.1 (383.2 km) **F 119.9** (193 km) **Denali Raft Adventures.** See display ad this section. — 4

A 238.3 (383.5 km) **F 119.7** (192.6 km) Kingfisher Creek.

A 238.5 (383.8 km) **F 119.5** (192.3 km) **McKinley/Denali Steakhouse and Salmon Bake.** Satisfy that hearty Alaskan appetite at a real home-style barbecue restaurant. Rustic heated indoor seating with majestic view of mountains. Free shuttle from all local hotels. Sourdough breakfasts. Large selection of postcards in our upstairs gift shop. T-shirts, sweatshirts and ice for sale. Pay phone. Open daily 5 A.M. to 11 P.M. in summer. [ADVERTISEMENT]

5

The introduction to each highway logged in The MILEPOST® includes a chart of mileages between major points (see sample at right)

	Anchorage	Denali Park	Fairbanks	Talkeetna	Wasilla
Anchorage		237	358	113	42
Denali Park	237		121	153	195
Fairbanks	358	121		245	316
Talkeetna	113	153	245		71
Wasilla	42	195	316	71	

Key to Highways in *The MILEPOST* ®

*Circled letters on map
identify highways as listed below:*

When planning your trip, read the introduction to each highway section for a general description of the road. Major attractions, highest pass or steepest grade, surfacing, season, and a chart of mileages between major points, are prominently displayed at the beginning of each highway section. Additional information and history on the highway is found by reading the introduction.

For a mile-by-mile look at the road, read through the log. Depending on where you want to stop and how much time you have to spend, you can count on driving anywhere from 150 to 500 miles a day! On most roads in the North, you can figure on comfortably driving 250 to 300 miles a day.

Log mileages are keyed on the highway strip maps which accompany each highway section. Use the mileage boxes on these maps to calculate mileages between points (or refer to the mileage box at the beginning of the highway). You can also approximate mileages for your trip by referring to the Mileage Chart on the back

GAS PRICE AVERAGES SUMMER 1996

Alaska Location	Per Gallon U.S. Funds		Canada Location	Per Liter Canadian Funds*
Anchorage	$1.35		Atlin, BC	$.75
Big Lake	1.28		Contact Creek, BC	.67
Chitina	1.55		Dawson City, YT	.79
Cordova	1.82		Dawson Creek, BC	.59
Eagle	1.75		Destruction Bay, YT	.72
Fairbanks	1.41		Fort Nelson, BC	.66
Glennallen	1.65		Fort St. John, BC	.59
Soldotna	1.38		Grande Prairie, AB	.55
Tok	1.56		Teslin, YT	.69
Valdez	1.47		Watson Lake, YT	.70
			Whitehorse, YT	.68

*See chart below for equivalent cost in U.S. funds for 1 gallon

GAS COST IN U.S. FUNDS PER GALLON

If the Canadian Exchange rate is: $1.00 U.S. equals Canadian funds:	20% $1.20	25% $1.25	30% $1.30	35% $1.35	40% $1.40
$.55	$1.73	$1.67	$1.60	$1.54	$1.49
.56	1.77	1.70	1.63	1.57	1.51
.57	1.80	1.73	1.66	1.60	1.54
.58	1.83	1.76	1.69	1.63	1.57
.59	1.86	1.79	1.72	1.65	1.60
.60	1.89	1.82	1.75	1.68	1.62
Canadian .61	1.92	1.85	1.78	1.71	1.65
Price .62	1.96	1.88	1.81	1.74	1.68
Per Liter .63	1.99	1.91	1.83	1.77	1.70
.64	2.02	1.94	1.86	1.79	1.73
.65	2.05	1.97	1.89	1.82	1.76
.66	2.08	2.00	1.92	1.85	1.78
.67	2.11	2.03	1.95	1.88	1.81
.68	2.14	2.06	1.98	1.91	1.84
.69	2.18	2.09	2.01	1.93	1.87

For example: If gas costs $0.60 Canadian per liter and the current exchange rate is 30% ($1.00 U.S. equals $1.30 Canadian), using the above chart, the equivalent to 1 U.S. gallon of gas costs $1.75 U.S.

of the Plan-A-Trip map for mileages between principal points via most direct route.

Once you have figured the number of driving miles in your itinerary, you can calculate approximate gas cost using the Gas Price Averages chart above. (Keep in mind that 1997 prices may vary from 1996 summer averages.) U.S. motorists factor in the exchange rate for Canadian prices using the accompanying conversion chart. Also see Driving in the GENERAL INFORMATION section for more information on driving in the North.

By Air

Slightly more than half of all visitors to Alaska arrive by air. Air travel is also one of the most common forms of transportation in the North. You can fly just about anywhere. If there is no scheduled service, you can charter a plane. A list of scheduled air operators to and within the North is found under Air Travel in the GENERAL INFORMATION section. Also read the information on air transportation in each community description in *The MILEPOST®*. A chart of Flight Times Between Selected Cities appears on the opposite page.

Travelers flying into one of Alaska's hub cities can rent a car or motorhome, join a packaged land tour, or just keep flying. Check the advertisements in the communities and along the highways throughout *The MILEPOST®* for airlines and charter services offering something to meet every interest or need: an afternoon of flightseeing Mt. McKinley/Denali, drop-off and pickup at a remote river, a day tour to Barrow, or an overnight to Kotzebue or Nome. Also check the advertisements in Anchorage, Fairbanks, Whitehorse and other hub cities for car and motorhome rentals. (Keep in mind that renting a vehicle in Canada and dropping it off in Alaska is prohibitively expensive.)

Highway logs in Alaska and northwestern Canada also include information on airstrips for private pilots.

By Water

Travel to and within Alaska by water is described in *The MILEPOST®* in the MARINE ACCESS ROUTES section. Major water carriers are the Alaska State ferries, BC Ferries and cruise ships. Descriptions of each—ports-of-call, schedules and fares—are covered in detail, starting on page 621.

Both ferries and cruise ships use the Inside Passage to Alaska, and each offers a uniquely different experience. Which method to use—ferry or cruise ship—is a personal preference. More than 25 percent of the visitors arriving in Alaska arrive by cruise ship. If you know you like cruising, read through the list of cruise ships on pages 644–645 and see the chart on page 646 to get a general idea of the itineraries available. You'll need to work with a travel agent or contact the cruise line for more details on cruise ship itineraries, land tour options and add-ons, airfares from gateway cities, deck plans and cruise pricing.

There is great variety in the cruise options available (see also By Packaged Tour this section). You can cruise the entire length of the Inside Passage plus cruise across the Gulf of Alaska to Prince William Sound, or cruise just part of the Inside Passage. You can sail on large cruise ships that carry a thousand passengers or more, or go on 90-passenger yachts. You can stay on the cruise ship for the entire trip or cruise one way and fly the other. There is a cruise to suit every taste.

The Alaska Marine Highway through the Inside Passage is the transportation

Relaxing aboard the Alaska state ferry MV Columbia. *(© Crystal Images)*

choice of many independent travelers to Alaska, especially those with vehicles. Travelers may embark at either Bellingham, WA, or Prince Rupert, BC, and connect with the Alaska Highway from either Skagway, AK, via Klondike Highway 2, or Haines, AK, via the Haines Highway. If you get off at Skagway, it is 507 miles/815 km to Tok, AK, and you will drive through Whitehorse, YT. If you get off at Haines, it is 449 miles/722 km from Haines to Tok. (From Tok, it is 206 miles/331 km to Fairbanks, or 328 miles/528 km to Anchorage.)

Bellingham, WA, is about a 1½-hour drive north of Seattle. Train and bus service is available from Seattle to Bellingham's Fairhaven Station. Prince Rupert is served by BC Ferries out of Port Hardy, on the north end of Vancouver Island, and is also accessible via Yellowhead Highway 16 from Prince George. It is approximately 1,033 driving miles/1,662 km from Seattle, WA, to Prince Rupert, BC.

Alaska's ferry system also provides transportation to communities in the Southcentral and Southwest regions of the state. If you wish to visit Cordova,

Kodiak or Seldovia, for example, you'll need to take a ferry (unless you fly). These systems are described in detail in the MARINE ACCESS ROUTE section.

Familiarize yourself with the sights of the Inside Passage by reading the descriptions of communities in southeastern Alaska (beginning on page 647).

An important part of planning your trip by water is making ferry reservations as early as possible. Inside Passage ferries fill up quickly for the summer months.

FLIGHT TIMES BETWEEN SELECTED CITIES

Between	Time	Between	Time	Between	Time
Anchorage—Bethel	1 hr. 15 min.	Anchorage—Valdez	40 min.	Juneau—Haines	35 min.
Anchorage—Cordova	45 min.	Anchorage—Wrangell	2 hrs. 20 min.	Juneau—Ketchikan	50 min.
Anchorage—Dutch Harbor	2 hrs. 5 min.	Fairbanks—Barrow	1 hr. 20 min.	Juneau—Seattle, WA	2 hrs. 10 min.
Anchorage—Fairbanks	50 min.	Fairbanks—Delta Junction	35 min.	Juneau—Sitka	35 min.
Anchorage—Juneau	1 hr. 35 min.	Fairbanks—Kotzebue	2 hrs. 10 min.	Juneau—Skagway	45 min.
Anchorage—King Salmon	1 hr.	Fairbanks—Nome	2 hrs. 20 min.	Juneau—Whitehorse, YT	1 hr.
Anchorage—Kodiak	55 min.	Fairbanks—Northway	1 hr.	Juneau—Yakutat	45 min.
Anchorage—Kotzebue	1 hr. 30 min.	Fairbanks—Prudhoe Bay	1 hr. 25 min.	Ketchikan—Sitka	50 min.
Anchorage—Nome	1 hr. 30 min.	Fairbanks—Whitehorse, YT	3 hrs. 35 min.	Nome—Kotzebue	40 min.
Anchorage—Petersburg	2 hrs.	(1 stop in Dawson City)		Whitehorse—Dawson City	1 hr. 40 min.
Anchorage—Seattle, WA	3 hrs. 15 min.	Juneau—Glacier Bay	25 min.	Yakutat—Cordova	45 min.

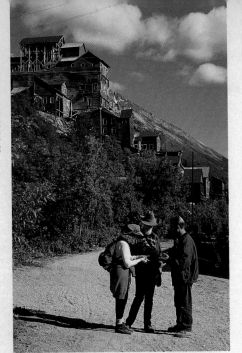

Sightseeing Kennicott mine near McCarthy, AK. (© Ruth von Spalding)

By Packaged Tour

Tours have become so popular in recent years, the visitor industry has designed packages to meet the interests and requirements of almost anyone. A packaged tour takes the worry and planning out of arranging for accommodations and transportation, but you still have to choose which packaged tour you want.

When planning your trip, decide which areas you wish to see, your preference for mode of travel and what will fit your pocketbook and calendar, then check what the tour companies have to offer. For the longer, all-inclusive tours, you'll need to carefully read through the tour company brochures for details on itineraries, dates and prices. Brochures are available from travel agents or by contacting the company. Even on the shorter day tours or overnight trips, check on cancellation policies, additional fees or restrictions and double-check departure dates and times.

Major Alaska tour companies—like Alaska Sightseeing/Cruise West, Princessss Tours and Holland America Westours—offer all-inclusive cruisetour packages.. These include a cruise and land tour portion, and usually range from 7 to 14 days. Cost for the high end 2-week cruisetours ranges anywhere from $4,000 (minimum category stateroom, May departure) to $6,500 (deluxe stateroom, July departure) and up, per person double-occupancy. Airfare from gateway cities is additional.

A sample itinerary for one of the 14-day cruise tours would be: Board cruise ship in Seattle; spend 7 days exploring Inside Passage; jet from Juneau to Anchorage; sightsee Anchorage and area attractions, such as Portage Glacier; motorcoach to Denali National Park for overnight and park wildlife tour; take the train to Fairbanks for sightseeing and stern-wheeler cruise; depart for home by air. See Cruise Lines in the MARINE ACCESS ROUTES section for a list of cruise ships operating in Alaska this year.

Often the major tour companies will offer portions of their tours to independent travelers if space is available. For example, an independent traveler might purchase rail passage on the private railcars operated by Princess Tours or Westours on the Alaska Railroad between Anchorage, Denali Park and Fairbanks (see ALASKA RAILROAD section).

Remember that tours come in all shapes and sizes. There are many 1-day and overnight or longer tours available from dozens of companies—most of them local to the North—for a variety of destinations and activities. Among the choices for independent travelers: Spend the day or 2 days exploring Prince William Sound by tour boat out of Whittier and Valdez; fly to the Arctic Circle, Barrow or Prudhoe Bay for the day, or visit a Native fish camp, from Fairbanks; take a 2-day fly/cruise package to Glacier Bay from *(Continues on page 13)*

Vernon
Publications Inc.

Home Back Forward

Address: http://www.alaskainfo.com

Key Links:

Frequently Asked Questions

What's the Big Deal About Alaska?

Alaska Highway Trivia

Special Delivery for Online Customers

FREE Catalog or To Order

To E-mail Us

Resources:

Campgrounds & RV Parks

Fishing

Gas Stations & Motor Vehicle Services

Gifts & Souvenirs

Guides & Outfitters

Lodgings

Publications & Videos

Restaurants

Tourist Activities & Attractions

Tourist Services

Travel Agencies

Visitor Bureaus & Chambers of Commerce

(Resources are representative.)

Can You Surf Alaska?

Yes ... with the Editors of The MILEPOST®.

The experts on Alaska and Northwestern Canada now have an Internet site, too, and it's a great place to visit. Grab a keyboard and ride a friendly electronic wave to

www.alaskainfo.com

Surf by and check out our Frequently Asked Questions section; our "What's the Big Deal about Alaska?" story; our Alaska Highway Trivia page; our Resources section, and more.

E-mail us from the road, or when you get back, and let us know how your trip went. Or, share a tip or two. And, if you're trying to convince friends and family they should see Alaska, or answer some of their questions, invite them to surf our site.

They, and you, will find interesting information on everything from wildlife you're likely to see, to average temperatures for key cities, to length of the famous Alaska Highway, to major attractions along the Inside Passage cruiseship and ferry lanes.

Alaskainfo.com is designed to complement The MILEPOST® family of print publications, so you'll need to have your print version of The MILEPOST® to plan and take your trip. But for various facts, interesting tidbits, answers to commonly asked questions, quotes from the media about The MILEPOST®, information summaries all at one site, and the opportunity to e-mail us, you'll enjoy alaskainfo.com.

Come visit our site whenever you want. We're looking forward to seeing you!

Internet address: http://www.alaskainfo.com
E-mail: books@alaskainfo.com
Phone: 1-800-726-4707

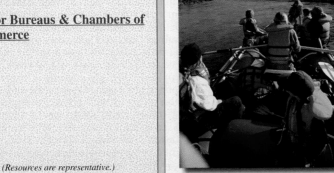

Link: http://www.alaskainfo.com

H1196208

KLONDIKE GOLD RUSH CENTENNIAL 1897-1997

Gold stampeders at the summit of Chilkoot Pass, winter 1897. *(Courtesy of Alaska State Library, Winter&Pond, #87-712)*

The gold strike that set in motion the great Klondike Gold Rush was made on Aug. 16, 1896, on Rabbit Creek in the Klondike River region of the Yukon. But it was the following spring, when the S.S. *Portland* sailed into the port of Seattle carrying "a ton of gold," that word of the strike finally reached the the outside world. If 1896 was the year of discovery, 1897 was the year the gold rush got started.

An estimated 100,000 stampeders set off for the Klondike, most during the winter of 1897–98. There was no single route to the Klondike gold fields, and there was no easy route. Many turned back or perished on ill-chosen routes, like the all-Canadian route from Edmonton. But most made their way up the Inside Passage by steamer to Skagway, AK, then by trail over either the Chilkoot Pass or the White Pass to Bennett and Lindeman lakes. There, the stampeders had to build boats, and then navigate their makeshift crafts down 500 miles of the treacherous Yukon River to Dawson City and the Klondike gold fields (see "Dawson City's Heyday" on page 277).

The Chilkoot Trail

The Chilkoot Trail was the shortest route to the Klondike from tidewater. It started at Dyea, near Skagway, and the summit was less than 20 miles from town. But it was also 3,739 feet above sea level. An easy trail at its start, it slowly became steeper until it reached treeline at Sheep Camp, 13 miles from Dyea. At Mile 16 was The Scales, a weighing place for goods hoisted or packed over the pass. From there, stampeders made the final half-mile ascent to the summit: a 45-degree climb called the "Golden Stairs." In winter, steps were chopped into the snow. In late summer, the route crossed large boulders. Stampeders bringing in their "ton of goods" that winter had to make between 20 and 30 trips to get their outfits across the pass.

For those who could afford it, Chilkoot Indian packers were available for hire, charging up to a dollar a pound. Two steam-operated tram lines were also operating in 1897; they charged 5¢ to 35¢ per pound.

From the summit, it was a 10-mile trek to Lake Lindeman, head of navigation on the water route to the Klondike gold fields. Here, stampeders built boats and prepared for their water journey across Lake Lindeman and Lake Bennett, then down the Yukon River to Dawson.

After 1898, as the gold rush waned, use of the Chilkoot Trail diminished. With completion of the White Pass & Yukon Route Railway over White Pass in 1900, Dyea became a ghost town.

The White Pass Trail

The White Pass Trail from Skagway was 15 miles longer than the Chilkoot Trail, but at 2,885 feet it was not as high nor as steep as the Chilkoot, with the resulting advantage that pack animals could negotiate the pass. Unfortunately, the White Pass Trail's advantage was a disaster for the horses, dogs, mules and oxen that were shipped in by the thousands to carry supplies over the pass. Over-loaded pack animals were killed in falls, dropped dead from exhaustion or starved to death. Their owners then went back to Skagway and bought more. This continuous cruelty is one of the horrors of the gold rush. Dead Horse Gulch, immortalized by author Jack London, was named for the estimated 3,000 pack animals that died there during the gold rush.

Like the Chilkoot Trail, the armies of stampeders were met at the White Pass summit by Canada's North West Mounted Police, who also acted as customs officers. Here they were searched for contraband liquor, paid what duty was necessary and continued on to Lakes Lindeman and Bennett.

A Ton of Goods

It could be argued that shopkeepers outfitting miners headed for the Klondike ended up making more money than the miners. Local merchants from Edmonton, AB, to Seattle, WA, advertised for sale entire miner's outfits for the Klondike. The *Seattle Post-Intelligencer*, in their July 17, 1897 edition, advised, "Although most of the passengers [on board the *Portland*] are returning home with plenty of gold, they all advise and urge people who contemplate going to the Yukon not to think of taking less than one ton of grub and plenty of clothes."

The remoteness of the Klondike goldfields, and the scarcity and high cost of food and supplies in Dawson City, could quickly overwhelm the unprepared miner. The desperate condition of many men arriving in the Klondike led the North West Mounted Police to require anyone entering Canada to have a year's supply of food and equipment.

The one year's outfit for one miner illustrated here (see box opposite page) is an actual order placed at the Alaska Commercial Store in Dawson in June 1897. It is not a complete inventory of a typical miner's outfit. Items this miner might already have purchased would include blankets, shirts, trousers, and other clothing; cooking pots, utensils, cups and plates; gold pan, axes, picks, and other tools; canvas tent, bucket, compass, etc. A miner could spend up to $2,000 in Seattle and elsewhere for a complete outfit. At today's prices, that same miner's outfit would cost about $10,000.

There is a display of the recommended year's supplies for miners at both the Klondike Gold Rush National Historical Park's Skagway unit and Seattle unit. The Skagway unit also has details on hiking the Chilkoot Trail; check with the visitor center at the old Railroad Depot on 2nd Avenue and Broadway (phone 907/98-2921). The Seattle unit, at 117 South Main Street, between First Avenue and Occidental Street (phone 206/553-7220), also offers an overview of Seattle's role as a gold rush staging area in 1897–98.

The "Ton of Gold"

A highlight event this Klondike Gold Rush Centennial year is the re-enactment of the first ton of gold's journey from the Klondike to Seattle.

In Seattle, the "ton of gold" arrives on Pier 57 at 10 A.M. on July 19, 1997, on board the *Spirit of '98* (portraying the *Portland*). The family-oriented "Ton of Gold" weekend in Seattle will include: a ceremony welcoming the *Spirit of '98* and its passengers; an exhibit of Klondike gold; Gold Rush exhibits and displays; period band concerts; a sourdough pancake breakfast; and a ball honoring the stampeders who went North. A detailed schedule of the "Ton of Gold" weekend, and information on other centennial events around Puget Sound, may be obtained from the Klondike Gold Rush Centennial Committee of Washington, 1301 5th Ave., Seattle, WA 98101; phone (206) 389-7240; Internet www.klondike.org.

A "Ton of Gold–Ton of Fun" Festival takes place in Whitehorse, YT, July 11–13, 1997. This entertainment for the whole family will be held at Rotary Park.

Check with the Klondike Visitors Assoc. in Dawson City and the National Park Service visitor center in Skagway about local events in these communities related to the "Ton of Gold" and the Klondike Gold Rush Centennial.

[This article is based in part on material researched and written by Ken Spotswood. Reed Jarvis was also a contributor.]

The White Pass railway was completed in 1900. *(Courtesy of Alaska State Library, Case&Draper, #PCA 39-373)*

(Continued from page 10)
Juneau, Haines or Skagway; take a rail/motorcoach trip between Skagway, AK, and Whitehorse, YT.

Packaged and custom trips are available for fishing, wilderness lodges, flightseeing, bear viewing, whale watching, glacier viewing, Native heritage, gold panning, etc. You can go by small plane, helicopter, horseback, rail, motorcoach, boat or even dogsled. The tour can last a day or a week. Look through the pages of *The MILEPOST®* for advertised tours. There is something for everyone.

By Railroad

Although no railroads connect Alaska or the Yukon with the Lower 48, travel by rail can be combined with other methods of transportation in your itinerary.

If you arrive by ferry or air in Skagway, AK, the White Pass & Yukon Route offers passenger through-service from Skagway to Whitehorse, YT, via rail and motorcoach. Or you can simply enjoy a round-trip rail excursion out of Skagway to White Pass. See the WHITE PASS & YUKON ROUTE section for details.

The Alaska Railroad offers passenger service between Anchorage, Denali Park, Fairbanks and Seward, and shuttle service for passengers and vehicles from the Seward Highway to Whittier, port for Alaska state ferries crossing Prince William Sound. Travelers can easily combine a rail trip with their air or highway itinerary. Rail travel is also included on many packaged tours. See the ALASKA RAILROAD section for details.

ONE YEAR'S OUTFIT FOR ONE MINER

500 lbs. flour	5 lbs. black tea
80 lbs. beans	5 lbs. chocolate
25 lbs. peas	2 bottles lime juice
25 lbs. rolled oats	6 bottles Worcestershire sauce
15 lbs. corn meal	30 lbs. lard
1 case condensed milk (4 dozen 1-lb. cans)	1 12-lb. box macaroni
1 case cabbage (2 dozen 2-lb. cans)	12 lbs. mincemeat
1 case roast beef (1 dozen 2-lb. cans)	2 pairs rubber boots
1 case corned beef (1 dozen 2-lb. cans)	2 36-lb. tins assorted cakes
1 case sausage meat (2 dozen 2-lb. cans)	4 boxes candles (120 to the box)
1 case turkey (2 dozen 2-lb cans)	1 case baking powder (2 dozen 1/2-lb. cans)
1 case tomatoes (2 dozen 2 1/2-lb. cans)	6 bars washing soap
1 case string beans (2 dozen 2-lb. cans)	5 bars toilet soap
75 lbs. bacon	15 lbs. salt
50 lbs. ham	1 case (10 gals.) coal oil
25 lbs. dried apples	2 lamp chimneys
25 lbs. dried prune	100 feet rope, 3/4 or 7/8 (45 lbs.)
25 lbs. dried peaches	1 5-foot bull saw
25 lbs. dried apricots	2 bull-saw files
25 lbs. raisins or grapes	1 pair arctic overshoes
100 lbs. granulated sugar	2 pairs felt boots
1 keg (5 gals.) pickles	4 pairs woolen socks
1 keg (5 gals.) sauerkraut	2 pairs moccasins
5 gals. maple syrup	2 pairs water boots
25 lbs. evaporated potatoes	6 pairs skin mittens
15 lbs. cheese	
20 lbs. Arbuckle's coffee	Cost (in Dawson City): $550.25

Welcome to the North Country

Fishing the Turnagain Arm of Alaska's Cook Inlet at sunset. (© Bruce M. Herman)

The North Country is the land north of 51° 16' latitude. Geographically, it encompasses Alaska, Yukon Territory, western Northwest Territories, northern British Columbia and Alberta. Following are some facts and figures about each of these areas.

Alaska

Capital: Juneau
Population: 550,043
Area: 587,878 square miles/
1,522,596 square km

Alaska was purchased by the U.S. from Russia in 1867. It became the 49th state on January 3, 1959. Alaska is the largest state in the union in area (twice the size of Texas), but ranks 49th in population, based on the 1990 census. (Only Wyoming has fewer residents.) Approximately 15 percent of the population is Native: Eskimo, Aleut and Indian (Athabascan, Tlingit, Haida, Tsimshian).

Alaska has 17 of the 20 highest mountains in the United States, including the highest peak in North America—Mount McKinley (Denali). Chief industries are fishing, timber, tourism and mining (oil and gas). Geographically, the state falls into roughly 6 distinct natural regions: Southeastern, Southcentral, the Interior, Southwestern, Western and the Brooks Range/Arctic.

Southeastern Alaska is a moist, luxuriantly forested panhandle extending some 500 miles/805 km from Dixon Entrance south of Ketchikan to Icy Bay on the Gulf of Alaska coast. This narrow strip of coast, separated from the mainland and Canada by the Coast Mountains, and the hundreds of islands of the Alexander Archipelago, form the Inside Passage water route used by ships and ferries. Cruise ships bring thousands of passengers through the Inside Passage each summer.

The Southcentral region of Alaska curves 650 miles/1,046 km north and west from the Gulf of Alaska coast to the Alaska Range. This region's tremendous geographic variety includes the Matanuska–Susitna river valleys, the Chugach and Wrangell–St. Elias mountain ranges, the Kenai Peninsula and the glaciers of Prince William Sound. Anchorage, the state's largest city, is the hub of Southcentral.

The MILEPOST

1998 LEATHERBOUND COLLECTOR'S EDITION
CELEBRATE 50 YEARS!

The MILEPOST® 1998 Leatherbound Collector's Edition

The 1998 edition of The MILEPOST® will mark half-a-century of publishing this remarkable travel guide. To celebrate this golden anniversary, a limited number of 1998 editions will be available leatherbound, with The MILEPOST® embossed in gold on the cover.

Whether you are a long-time "Mileposter" or a more recent fan of this great travel guide to the North Country, the special leatherbound edition will be a collector's item you'll use and treasure for many years to come. It also makes a great gift!

The leatherbound gold-embossed edition of The MILEPOST® 50th edition costs $50 each. (You can also gold emboss your name on the cover for just $10 more.) Reserve a copy now by filling out and mailing the reservation form below. Quantities are limited. Leatherbound books will be shipped in March 1998.

The First MILEPOST® Published in 1949, was 72 pages and cost $1.00

Please reserve _____ copies of the leatherbound 50th edition of The 1998 MILEPOST® at $50 per copy plus $6 each for shipping. (❑ Add $10 for monogramming your name in gold.) I understand that if I'm paying by credit card, I will not be charged until the books are shipped in March 1998.

$ _____ No. of copies at $50 each

$ _____ Monogram at $10 each. *(For multiple orders, attach additional names.)*

❑❑❑❑❑❑❑❑❑❑❑❑❑❑❑❑❑❑❑❑❑❑❑❑❑❑

$ _____ Shipping at $6 each book

$ _____ **Total cost**   Check enclosed ❑

Credit Card: ❑ *VISA*   ❑ MasterCard   Card No. _____   Signature: _____
(We cannot process a charge without your signature)

Name _____   Phone _____

Address _____   City _____   State _____ Zip _____

Mail orders to: The MILEPOST® 1998 Leatherbound Edition, 3000 Northup Way, Suite 200, P.O. Box 96043, Bellevue, WA 98009-9643
Phone orders to: 1-800-726-4707 • **Fax orders to:** (206) 822-9372

Vintage photos: William A. Wallace Collection

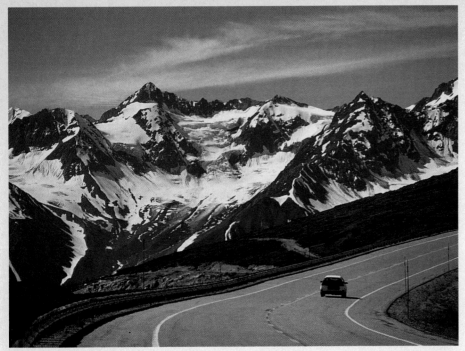

The Haines Highway leads from Haines, AK, over Chilkat Pass in British Columbia, and down into Haines Junction, YT. (© Harry M. Walker Photo)

Interior Alaska lies cradled between the Brooks Range to the north and the Alaska Range to the south, a vast area that drains the Yukon River and its tributaries. It is a climate of extremes, holding both the record high (100°F at Fort Yukon) and the record low (-80°F at Prospect Creek). Fairbanks is the hub of the Interior and a jump-off point for bush communities in both the Interior and Arctic.

Southwestern Alaska takes in Kodiak Island, the Alaska Peninsula and Aleutian Islands. Kodiak, less than an hour's flight from Anchorage and about 10 hours by ferry from Homer, is the largest island in Alaska. Kodiak was Russian Alaska's first capital city. Brown bear viewing is an attraction on Kodiak and at Katmai National Park and Preserve near King Salmon. The Southwest ferry system provides service from Kodiak to Unalaska/Dutch Harbor.

Western Alaska stretches from the head of Bristol Bay north along the Bering Sea coast to the Seward Peninsula near the Arctic Circle. This region extends inland from the coast to encompass the Yukon-Kuskokwim Delta. Nome is perhaps one of the best known destinations in Western Alaska.

Arctic Alaska lies above the Arctic Circle, between the Brooks Range to the south and the Arctic sea coast to the north, and from the Canadian border to the east westward to Kotzebue. Arctic day and overnight trips to destinations such as Kotzebue, Barrow and Prudhoe Bay are popular packages offered out of both Anchorage and Fairbanks.

If you include the Marine Highway, all regions of Alaska are connected by highway with the exception of Western Alaska. And that region's hub cities—Bethel and Nome—are less than 2 hours from Anchorage by air.

Bush travel in all regions of Alaska is covered in detail in our companion guide,

The ALASKA WILDERNESS GUIDE. For ordering information, see page 4.

State symbols include the willow ptarmigan (bird), forget-me-not (flower) and Sitka spruce (tree).

Yukon Territory

Capital: Whitehorse
Population: 27,797
Area: 186,661 square miles/
483,450 square km

Shaped somewhat like a right triangle, Yukon Territory is bordered on the west by Alaska at 141° longitude; on the north by the Beaufort Sea/Arctic Ocean; on the south by British Columbia at latitude 60°; and on the east by the western Northwest Territories.

Yukon Territory is larger than all the New England states combined. Canada's highest peak, Mount Logan (elev. 19,524 feet/5,951m), is located in Yukon's St. Elias Mountains.

First Nations peoples of the Yukon belong to the Athapaskan and Tlingit language families. These are Gwitchin, Han, Northern Tutchone, Southern Tutchone, Kaska, Tagish, Tlingit and Upper Tanana.

The Yukon was made a district of the Northwest Territories in 1895 and became a separate territory in June of 1898. The territory's first capital was Dawson City, site of the great Klondike gold rush, which brought thousands of gold seekers to the Yukon and Alaska in 1897–98. The Klondike gold rush began celebrating its centennial in 1996—marking the discovery of gold on Bonanza Creek on August 16, 1896—and continues the celebration in 1997 (see pages 12–13).

At the height of the gold rush, an estimated 40,000 people lived in Dawson City. By 1903, as other gold stampedes drew off much of Dawson's population, the city's boom days were over, although mining continued to support the community for many years. On March 31, 1953, Whitehorse—on the railway and the highway, with a large airport—replaced

Beautiful Emerald Lake, also called Rainbow Lake, on Klondike Highway 2.
(Earl L. Brown, staff)

Dawson City as capital.

Today, Yukon's chief industries are mining (zinc, gold, lead, silver) and tourism. Territorial symbols include fireweed (flower) and the raven (bird).

Western Northwest Territories

Capital: Yellowknife (until 1999)
Population: 40,000
Area: 550,000 square miles/
1.4 million square km

On April 1, 1999, Northwest Territories will be divided into 2 territories. Passed by popular vote in 1982 and approved by the Canadian Parliament in 1993, this division will create Nunavut, and its capital, Iqaluit on Baffin Island, in what is now the eastern half of Northwest Territories.

Northwest Territories comprises about a third of Canada. Western Northwest Territories is about the size of Alaska. Western Northwest Territories' Wood Buffalo National Park is the second largest national park in the world.

A majority of the population of Northwest Territories is Native. Aboriginal

Coral Falls on the Mackenzie Highway in Northwest Territories. (© Lyn Hancock)

groups are the Dene, Inuvialuit, Inuit, Gwich'in, Dogrib and Metis.

Access to western Northwest Territories is from Alberta via the Mackenzie Highway system, from British Columbia via the Liard Highway, and from Yukon Territory via the Dempster Highway. A major road-building project in the 1960s constructed most of the highway system in western Northwest Territories. Road improvement is ongoing, with paving under way on much of the remaining gravel road.

Chief industries are mining (gold, petroleum, zinc and diamonds), manufacturing and fishing.

The mountain avens is the official flower of the Northwest Territories.

British Columbia

Capital: Victoria
Population: 3,282,061
Area: 365,900 square miles/ 947,800 square km

Canada's most westerly—and 3rd largest—province, British Columbia stretches 813 miles/1,300 km from its southern border with the United States to the north boundary with Yukon Territory. It is bounded on the east by Alberta and on the west by the Pacific Ocean. The province encompasses the Queen Charlotte Islands and Vancouver Island, site of the capital city of Victoria. Approximately half the province's population resides in the Victoria–Vancouver area.

British Columbia entered the Dominion of Canada on July 20, 1871, as the 6th province. An important region in the early fur trade, expansion of the province came with the 1860s Cariboo gold rush followed by the completion of Canada's first transcontinental railway—the Canadian Pacific. Today, the province has a diverse economy based on agriculture, fishing, forestry, manufacturing, mining and services.

Mile Zero of the Alaska Highway is located in Dawson Creek, BC (not to be confused with Dawson City, YT), in the northeastern corner of the province.

Alberta

Capital: Edmonton
Population: 2,545,553
Area: 255,287 square miles/
661,190 square km

More than half of Alberta's population lives in its 2 largest cities—Calgary and Edmonton. Alberta provides most of Canada's natural gas and some 80 percent of its petroleum. The province also grows more barley and oats than any other province or state, and is a leading producer of beef cattle and rye.

Alberta has both the world's largest shopping center (West Edmonton Mall),

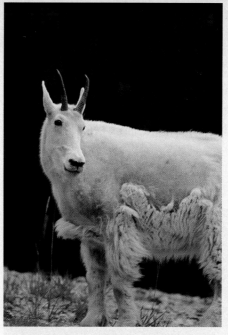

Mountain goat in Alberta's Jasper National Park. (© David Creith/Sahtu)

and the world's largest Easter egg (at Vegreville), made of aluminum and measuring 26 feet long. Alberta became a province on September 1, 1905.

The wild rose is the floral emblem of the province.

Alaska Highway via
EAST ACCESS ROUTE ⑮ ⟨2⟩ ⟨3⟩ ⟨4⟩ ⟨34⟩ ⟨43⟩

Connects: Great Falls, MT, to Dawson Creek, BC   **Length:** 866 miles
Road Surface: Paved   **Season:** Open all year
Major Attractions: Waterton Lakes National Park, Fort Edmonton Park
(See maps, pages 21–22)

	Calgary	Dawson Creek	Edmonton	Great Falls	Lethbridge	Valleyview
Calgary		548	181	318	140	395
Dawson Creek	548		367	866	688	153
Edmonton	181	367		499	321	214
Great Falls	318	866	499		178	713
Lethbridge	140	688	321	178		535
Valleyview	395	153	214	713	535	

Waterton Lakes National Park is easily accessible to East Access Route travelers.
(Blake Hanna, staff)

The East Access Route is logged in *The MILEPOST®* as one of the 2 major access routes (the other is the West Access Route) to the Alaska Highway.

When the Alaska Highway opened to civilian traffic in 1948, this was the only access route to Dawson Creek, BC, the start of the highway. At that time the route led from Great Falls, MT, through Alberta to Edmonton. From Edmonton, it continued north through the province to Clyde and from there to Athabasca via Highway 2 or Smith via Highway 44. At Triangle, the junction of Highways 2 and 2A (then Highway 34), motorists either headed north to McLennan and Peace River, or south via Valleyview to Grande Prairie, AB. In late 1955, Highway 43 was completed connecting Edmonton and Valleyview via Whitecourt.

Highways on this route are all paved primary routes, with visitor services readily available along the way. Total driving distance from Great Falls, MT, to Dawson Creek, BC, is approximately 867 miles/1394 km.

INTERSTATE HIGHWAY 15
The East Access Route begins in **GREAT FALLS** (pop. 55,097; elev. 3,333 feet/1,016m), Montana's second largest city. Head north through northcentral Montana on Interstate 15. From Great Falls to the Canadian border it is 117 miles/188.3 km. *The MILEPOST®* log begins at the Canadian border.

East Access Route Log

ALBERTA HIGHWAY 4
The East Access Route log is divided into 2 sections: Canadian border to Edmonton, and Edmonton to Dawson Creek.

This section of the log shows distance from the Canadian border (CB) followed by distance from Edmonton (E).

CB 0 E 382.2 (615 km) U.S.–Canada border, **COUTTS** border crossing; customs and immigration open 24 hours a day. Food, gas and lodging at border. Duty-free shop.

Altan Duty Free Shops Ltd. See display ad this section.

J.T.'s R.V. Park. Gateway to Alberta. Located on the 49th. 12 pull-through stalls, full hookups with cable TV. $10 per night. Picnic tables, tent sites, laundromat, convenience store, washrooms, currency exchange, open year-round. Phone (403) 344-3802. Your host, James Thiessen. Box 250, Coutts, AB, Canada T0K 0N0. [ADVERTISEMENT] ▲

CB 0.8 (12.9 km) **E 374.2** (602.1 km) **Junction** with Secondary Road 501, which leads west 67 miles/108 km to **CARDSTON** (pop. 3,502), located at the junction of Highways 2, 5 and 501, just 25 miles/40.2 km east of Waterton Lakes National Park. Known for its dramatic lake and mountain scenery, Waterton Lakes park adjoins Glacier National Park in Montana, and the 2 parks together are known as the Waterton–Glacier International Peace Park.

Cardston was established in 1887 by Mormon pioneers from Utah and is the site of the Alberta Temple, the first Mormon temple constructed outside of the continental United States, and a designated historic building. The temple is closed to the public, but there is a visitor centre.

The Remington–Alberta Carriage Centre in downtown Cardston features one of the world's foremost collections of horse-drawn vehicles, with more than 200 vehicles ranging from elegant carriages to stagecoaches. The 20-acre site includes an 80-seat theatre, gift shop, cafeteria, working stable, blacksmith/restoration shop and tackroom. A provincial tourist infocentre is also located here.

CB 11.7 (18.9 km) **E 370.5** (596.2 km) Milk River Travel Information and Interpre-

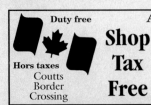

EAST ACCESS ROUTE

Great Falls, MT, to Edmonton, AB

(map continues next page)

To Slave Lake

43

To Jasper
(see YELLOWHEAD HIGHWAY 16 section)
16

16 To Saskatoon

Edmonton

Chip Lake

Wabamun Lake

60

CB-377.9/608.2km Whitemud Creek Golf and RV Park

J-10.2/16.4km Devon Lions Club Campground

19

Devon

Leduc

**DC-367/591km
E-0
CB-382/615km**

39

2

Ponoka

Lacombe

**E-91/146km
CB-291/469km**

Red Deer

Innisfail

Bowden

Olds

Red Deer River

Drumheller

ROCKY

BRITISH COLUMBIA
ALBERTA

Red Deer River

Carstairs

Crossfield
72
Airdrie

Balzac

To Revelstoke
Golden

95

93

Banff

Bow River

1

Calgary

CB-200.8/323.1km Calgary West KOA C

To Regina

CB-188.6/303.5km Pine Creek RV Campground C

**E-181/292km
CB-201/323km**

MOUNTAINS

Columbia River

Kootenay River

Sheep River

High River

Nanton

CB-96.1/154.7km Municipality of Fort MacLeod
Sunset Motel L

Columbia Lake

Willow Creek

Stavely

CB-63/101.4km Chinook Country Tourist Association
Lethbridge RV Parks C

**E-319/514km
CB-63/101km**

95

93

Crowsnest Pass
4,534 ft./1,825m

Claresholm

CB-100.4/161.6km
Roger's RV Park CD
West Wind Crafts

Keho Lake

Oldman R.

Frank

Oldman River

2
Monarch
3

3

To Regina

Lethbridge

Cranbrook

3

785

6

Fort Macleod

5

4
Stirling

52
New Dayton

To Hope
3
Kingsgate

BRITISH COLUMBIA | CANADA
IDAHO | UNITED STATES

Eastport

Lake Koocanusa

Waterton Lakes
National Park

Raymond

Warner

2

Cardston

Milk River ?

CB-0 Altan Duty Free Shops, Ltd.
J.T.'s RV Park CD

5
Waterton
Park

501
Coutts

ALBERTA
MONTANA

Sweetgrass

**E-382/615km
CB-0**

89

95

2

37

93

**Glacier
National
Park**

89

Browning

2

Shelby
2
To Medicine
Hat

To Spokane
Sandpoint

2

Kalispell

Lake
Francis

Conrad

Brady

To Medicine
Hat

89
87

15

CB-117/188km

Great Falls

15

87

To Helena

To Billings

N
W   E
S

Principal Route		Key to Advertiser Services	Scale	Key to mileage boxes

Principal Route

Paved ▬▬▬   Unpaved ▭▭▭

Other Roads

Paved ▬▬   Unpaved ▭▭

Ferry Routes ••••••   **Hiking Trails** ••••••

⚠ Refer to Log for Visitor Facilities
? Visitor Information   🎣 Fishing
⛺ Campground   ✈ Airport   ✈ Airstrip

Key to Advertiser Services

C -Camping
D -Dump Station
d -Diesel
G -Gas (reg., unld.)
I -Ice
L -Lodging
M -Meals
P -Propane
R -Car Repair (major)
r -Car Repair (minor)
S -Store (grocery)
T -Telephone (pay)

Scale

0   20   Miles
0   20   Kilometres

Key to mileage boxes

miles/kilometres
miles/kilometres   from:

CB- Canadian Border
E- Edmonton
DC- Dawson Creek

Map Location

EAST ACCESS ROUTE *Edmonton, AB, to Dawson Creek, BC*

Scale

Key to mileage boxes
miles/kilometres from:
miles/kilometres
CB- Canadian Border
E- Edmonton
DC- Dawson Creek

Map Location

To Fort McMurray

Athabasca

Clyde

DC-367/591km
E-0
CB-382/615km
Edmonton

Smith

Westlock

Onoway

Spruce Grove

Stony Plain

E-10/16km Glowing Embers Travel Centre CS

(map continues previous page)

Northern Woods & Waters Route

Slave Lake

Grizzly Trail

Lesser Slave Lake

Joussard

Swan Hills

Whitecourt
E-80.6/129.7km Rochfort Bridge Trading Post M
E-37.9/61km Gunn General Store and Campground CDdGIMPST

Sangudo

Mayerthorpe

Chip Lake

E-24/38.7km Wabamun Lake Bears & Bedtime Mfg.

High Prairie

Winagami Lake

McLennan

Triangle

Little Smoky
E-192/309km Little Smoky Motel & Campground CL
E-186.4/300km Sands Wilderness Campground and RV Park C

DC-153/246km
E-214/344km

DC-205/330km
E-162/261km

DC-255/411km
E-112/180km

Fox Creek

Valleyview

Edson

Peace River

Nampa

Donnelly

Calais

Crooked Creek

Sturgeon
Smoke Lake

Forestry Trunk Road

Little Smoky River

Athabasca River

To Yellowknife
(see MACKENZIE ROUTE section)

Grimshaw

Fairview

Debolt
E-262/421.6km West Smoky RV Campsite CD
E-230/370.1km Cosy Cove Campground & Marina CDST

Bezanson

M O U N T A I N S

To Jasper
(see YELLOWHEAD HIGHWAY 16 section)

Hines Creek

Dunvegan

Rycroft

Sexsmith

Grande Prairie

Spirit River
Bear River

Woking

Key to Advertiser Services
C - Camping
D - Dump Station
d - Diesel
G - Gas (reg., unld.)
I - Ice
L - Lodging
M - Meals
P - Propane
R - Car Repair (major)
r - Car Repair (minor)
S - Store (grocery)
T - Telephone (pay)

To Fort St. John
(see ALASKA HIGHWAY section)

Fort St. John

To Chetwynd
(see WEST ACCESS ROUTE section)

Peace River

Swan Lake

DC-0
E-367/591km
Dawson Creek

Pouce Coupe
E-361/581km The Pouce Coupe Museum

Wembley

Hythe

Beaverlode
E-311/500.5km Town of Beaverlodge

DC-83/134km
E-284/457km

Demmitt

Tupper

Grande Cache

R O C K Y

Big Horn Highway

Waptti River

ALBERTA

BRITISH COLUMBIA

Heritage Highway

Principal Route
Paved
Other Roads
Paved
Unpaved
Unpaved
Ferry Routes

Hiking Trails

🏛 Refer to Log for Visitor Facilities
ℹ Visitor Information
▲ Campground ✈ Airport/Airstrip ♦ Fishing

tive Centre; picnic tables, dump station, souvenir shop, ice cream shop and travel information. The large dinosaur model on display here makes a good photo subject. Dinosaur fossil sites in Alberta include Devil's Coulee and the Badlands.

CB 13 (21 km) E 369.2 (594.1 km) MILK RIVER (pop. 900) has food, gas, stores, lodging and a small public campground (6 informal sites; no hookups). The 8 flags flying over the campground represent 7 countries and the Hudson's Bay Co., all of which once laid claim to the Milk River area. Grain elevators are on the west side of the highway, services are on the east side. ▲

CB 13.5 (21.7 km) E 368.7 (593.3 km) Junction with Secondary Road 501 east to Writing-on-Stone Provincial Park, 26 miles/42 km; camping, Indian petroglyphs.

CB 16.3 (26.3 km) E 365.9 (588.8 km) Stop of interest sign about Milk River Ridge.

CB 24.4 (39.2 km) E 357.8 (575.8 km) Road west to community of WARNER (pop. 434); store, gas, restaurant. Warner is the gateway to Devil's Coulee Dinosaur Egg Site, where dinosaur eggs, and fossilized fish and reptiles were discovered in 1987. Still under excavation, visits to Devil's Coulee are by tour bus only. The tour buses leave the Dinosaur Egg Interpretive Centre in Warner from June to mid-September.

CB 24.6 (39.6 km) E 357.6 (575.5 km) Junction with Highway 36A north to Taber, centre of Alberta's sugar beet industry.

CB 36.8 (59.2 km) E 345.4 (555.8 km) Small community of New Dayton.

CB 41.5 (66.8 km) E 340.7 (548.3 km) Junction at Craddock elevators with Highway 52 west to Raymond (10 miles/16 km),

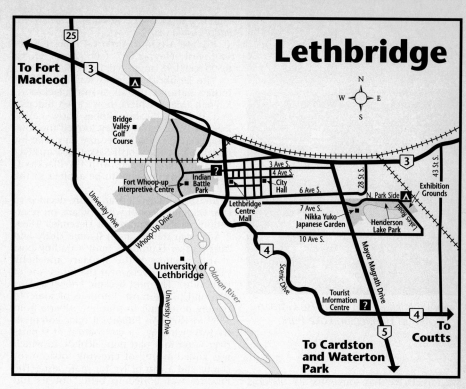

Lethbridge

site of the annual Stampede and Heritage Days; Magrath (20 miles/32 km); Cardston (46 miles/74 km); and Waterton Lakes National Park (74 miles/119 km).

CB 46.1 (74.2 km) E 336.1 (540.9 km) Small community of Stirling to west; municipal campground with 15 sites, some with power and water, dump station, showers and tennis court. Grain elevators and rail yards alongside highway. Stirling is the oldest, best-preserved Mormon settlement in Canada and a National Historic Site. ▲

CB 46.6 (75 km) E 335.6 (540 km) Junction with Highway 61 east to Cypress Hills.

CB 57.2 (92.1 km) E 325 (523 km) Stop of interest sign on west side of road describes how large-scale irrigation began in this area in 1901.

CB 62.9 (101.3 km) E 319.3 (513.8 km) Junction with Highway 5 south to Cardston (48 miles/77 km south) and Waterton Park in Waterton Lakes National Park. Mayor Magrath Drive to north provides access to Lethbridge motels, hotels and Henderson Lake Park (see city description following). Continue west on Scenic Drive for access to Indian Battle Park (via Whoop-Up Drive) and junction with Crowsnest Highway 3.

Alberta's Waterton Lakes National Park (also accessible from Milepost CB 0.8) is actually one large lake broken into 3 sections—Lower, Middle and Upper Waterton lakes. Lower Waterton Lake extends down into Montana. Waterton Park townsite, the tourist centre for the park, is approximately 81 miles/131 km from this junction.

Chinook Country Tourist Information Centre, on the north side of the intersection of Highways 4, 5 and Mayor Magrath Drive, has RV parking, restrooms, picnic shelter, dump station and dumpster; open year-round.

Lethbridge

CB 63 (101.4 km) E 319.2 (513.7 km) **Population:** 65,000. **Elevation:** 3,048 feet/929m. **Emergency Services:** Phone 911 for police, ambulance and fire department. **Hospital:** Lethbridge Regional Hospital, phone (403) 382-6111.

Visitor Information: Chinook Country Tourist Association, on the north side of the intersection of Highways 4, 5 and Mayor

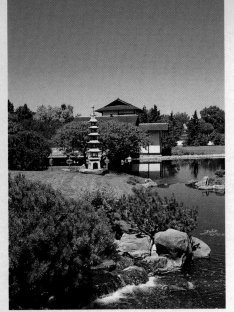

Tranquil Nikka Yuko Japanese Garden is located in Henderson Lake Park.

(Blake Hanna, staff)

Magrath Drive, has souvenirs, RV parking, restrooms, picnic shelter, dump station and dumpster; open year-round. Phone 1-800-661-1222 and ask for operator 48 (while in the area call 320-1222) for information on attractions and facilities in southwest Alberta. A tourist information centre is also located at Highway 3 at the west entrance to the city next to the Brewery Gardens; open

March 1 to Oct. 31. **Newspaper:** *The Lethbridge Herald* (daily).

Private Aircraft: Airport 4 miles/6.4 km southeast; elev. 3,047 feet/929m; length 6,500 feet/1,981m; paved, fuel 100, jet. FSS.

The Lethbridge region was home to 3 Indian nations: the Sik-si-kah (Blackfoot), Kai'nah (Many Chiefs, now called Bloods), and Pi-ku'ni (Scabby Robes, now called Peigans). Collectively, they formed the Sow-ki'tapi (Prairie People). Because European fur traders along the North Saskatchewan River first came into contact with the Blackfoot, that tribal name came to be applied to the entire confederacy.

In 1869, the American Army decided to stop trade in alcohol with Indians on reservations across Montana. In December 1869, 2 American traders, John Jerome Healy and Alfred Baker Hamilton, built a trading post at the junction of the St. Mary and Belly (now Oldman) rivers, near the future site of Lethbridge. The post became known as Fort Whoop-Up, the most notorious of some 44 trading posts built in southern Alberta from 1869 to 1874. An important trade commodity was "whiskey," a concoction of 9 parts river water to 1 part pure alcohol, to which was added a plug of chewing tobacco for colour and a can of lye for more taste. The mixture was boiled to bring out its full flavour, and well deserved the Indian name "firewater."

Alarmed by the activities of the whiskey traders, Prime Minister Sir John A. Macdonald formed the North West Mounted Police (NWMP), now the Royal Canadian Mounted Police, to bring law and order to the West. The NWMP reached Fort Whoop-Up on

Oct. 9, 1874, and immediately put a stop to the whiskey trade.

Early development of Lethbridge commenced in 1874 with the arrival of Nicholas Sheran in search of gold. The gold, in fact, turned out to be black gold—coal—and by the late 1870s a steady coal market and permanent settlement had developed. Elliot Galt, working with his father, Sir Alexander Galt, helped pioneer coal shipments on the Oldman River and later a narrow-gauge railway that connected to the mainline of the Canadian Pacific Railway.

The climax of the early development of Lethbridge came with the CPR construction of the high level rail bridge in 1909, that today carries freight shipments by rail westward through Crowsnest Pass to Vancouver, and onward by ship to the Pacific Rim. The "Bridge"—with a mile-long span and 300-foot elevation—is still the longest and highest bridge of its kind in the world.

Today, Lethbridge is Alberta's third largest city. It has a strong agricultural economy. In late June and early July, bright yellow fields of canola surround the highways leading into the city. Other fields, both irrigated and dryland, produce wheat, sugar beets, potatoes, corn and a variety of other crops.

Lethbridge is southwest Alberta's service and shopping centre, with several malls and a variety of retail businesses. There is a wide choice of restaurants, hotel/motel accommodations, and bed and breakfasts.

There are 2 campgrounds in the city: Henderson Lake campground and Bridgeview campground. ▲

Henderson Lake Park also holds several of

the city's attractions, including the Nikka Yuko Japanese Garden, a golf course, swimming pool, picnic area and rose gardens. The Lethbridge Black Diamonds professional baseball team also plays at the park.

An extensive trail system leads to Indian Battle Park in the beautiful Oldman River valley. Indian Battle Park showcases a replica of Fort Whoop-Up, the Helen Schuler Coulee Centre, the Sir Alexander Galt Museum and the High Level Bridge.

Lethbridge hosts the Ag-Expo in March and the Lethbridge International Airshow and Whoop-Up Days in August.

There is a wealth of attractions located within a short drive from the city. The Alberta Birds of Prey Centre, a 10-minute drive east of Lethbridge, is a 70-acre working conservation centre featuring hawks, falcons, eagles and owls from around the world. Live flying shows with hawks and falcons are presented, weather permitting. Open May 1 to early October, 10:30 A.M. to 5 P.M.; admission fee charged.

Waterton Lakes National Park, a UNESCO World Heritage Site, is located about an hour's drive away in the Rocky Mountains and offers spectacular scenery and recreation opportunities. Another UNESCO World Heritage Site is Head-Smashed-In Buffalo Jump Interpretive Centre located outside of Fort Macleod (see **Milepost CB 100.4**).

Other sites of interest in southern Alberta include the Remington–Alberta Carriage Centre and Alberta Temple in Cardston (see **Milepost CB 0.8**) and the Frank Slide Interpretive Centre at Crowsnest Pass (see **Milepost CB 99**).

Chinook Country Tourist Association. See display ad this section.

Lethbridge R.V. Parks. Lethbridge has 2 beautiful RV parks. Bridgeview, on the banks of the Oldman River, has 100 serviced sites, a brand new 10,000-square-foot clubhouse which includes a registration office, large laundromat and bright, clean washrooms. A new Olympic-sized heated pool, lots of pull-throughs, shade and easy access from Highway 3. Phone (403) 381-2357. Henderson Lake RV Park is centrally located in the city, has 100 sites, close to shopping, restaurants, golf. Phone (403) 328-5452. At both parks you will receive a sampling of friendly Alberta hospitality. [ADVERTISEMENT] ▲

East Access Route Log
(continued)

CB 66.6 (107.2 km) **E 315.6** (507.9 km) Junction with Crowsnest Highway 3. Tourist information centre beside Brewery Gardens.

CROWSNEST HIGHWAY 3
CB 69.5 (111.8 km) **E 312.7** (503.2 km)

Junction with Highway 25. Access to **Park Lake** Provincial Park (9 miles/14 km north); 53 campsites, swimming, boat launch, fishing, playground. ◂▲

CB 72 (115.9 km) **E 310.2** (499.2 km) Community of Coalhurst just north of highway; gas station.

CB 73.5 (118.3 km) **E 308.7** (496.8 km) CPR marshalling yards at Kipp.

CB 80.3 (129.2 km) **E 301.9** (485.8 km) Junction with Highway 23 north. Continue west on Highway 3 for Fort Macleod.

CB 81.5 (131.2 km) **E 300.7** (483.9 km) Community of Monarch; hotel, gas.

Westbound, the highway enters Oldman River valley. Good view west of the Rockies on a clear day.

CB 96.1 (154.7 km) **E 286.1** (460.4 km) Junction with Highway 2 south to the U.S. border and access to Waterton Lakes and Glacier national parks.

Highway 3 continues through **FORT MACLEOD** (pop. 3,100; elev. 3,300 feet/1,006m). Fort Macleod, built in 1874, was the first outpost of the North West Mounted Police (later the RCMP) in western Canada.

There are several hotels and motels, campgrounds, restaurants, shopping facilities and gas stations. This community's Main Street is a designated historic site; walking tours are offered. The main attraction in Fort Macleod is the Fort Museum, which features the history of the Mounted Police, local Native cultures and early pioneers, in a fort setting. During July and August, the museum features a local re-creation of the official RCMP Musical Ride: Youth in NWMP uniforms execute drills on horseback in a colorful display. The museum is open daily from May to mid-October; open weekdays the rest of the year (closed Dec. 24 to March 1) ▲

Municipality of Fort Macleod. See display ad this section.

The Sunset Motel, winner of 9 Alberta Tourism Housekeeping Awards, 2 Diamond AAA/CAA rated, and an Alberta Best property, emphasizes clean, comfortable rooms, friendly service and reasonable prices. They offer air-conditioned 1-, 2-, and 3-room units, free toast and coffee, refrigerators, kitchenettes, remote control cable televisions, free movies, direct dial touch-tone phones, free local calls and Native crafts shop. Laundromat, convenience store, gas and fast food adjacent. Full U.S. exchange. Off-season rates Oct. 1 to May 15. 104 Highway 3 West. Phone (403) 553-4448. [ADVERTISEMENT]

CB 99 (159.4 km) **E 283.2** (455.8 km) Junction with Highway 2 north to Calgary and Edmonton.

Highway 3 (Crowsnest) continues 600 miles/965.6 km west to Hope, BC. The highway takes its name from Crowsnest Pass (elev. 4,534 feet/1,382m), one of the lowest passes in the Rockies, which Highway 3 crosses 65.5 miles/105.5 km west of here. East of the pass (52.8 miles/85 km west of Fort Macleod) is the Frank Slide Interpretive Centre. The centre features the history of the Crowsnest Pass coal mining industry, the railway, and the catastrophic rock slide, which killed 70 people in April 1903, when millions of tons of limestone from Turtle Mountain engulfed the coal mining town of Frank.

ALBERTA HIGHWAY 2
CB 100 (160.8 km) **E 282.2** (454.1 km) **Oldman River** bridge. Alberta government campground to southwest with 10 campsites, dump station, playground, fishing and swimming. North of the river is the largest turkey farm in Alberta. ◂▲

CB 100.4 (161.6 km) **E 281.8** (453.5 km) Junction with Highway 785, which leads 10 miles/16 km to Head-Smashed-In Buffalo Jump, a UNESCO World Heritage Site. The 1,000-foot/305-m-long cliff, where Plains peo-

To Edmonton

To Banff

Calgary

with Secondary Road 533, which leads west to Chain Lakes Provincial Park. ▲

CB 146.8 (236.3 km) **E 235.4** (378.8 km) NANTON (pop. 1,700); all visitor facilities. Nanton is famous for its springwater, which is piped from Big Spring in the Porcupine Hills, 6 miles/10 km west of town, to a large tap located in town centre. Springwater tap operates mid-May to September. WWII Lancaster bomber on display at Centennial Park.

CB 151.1 (243.2 km) **E 231.1** (371.9 km) **Junction** with Highway 2A, which parallels Highway 2 northbound.

CB 162.8 (262 km) **E 219.4** (353.1 km) **Junction** with Highway 23 west to **HIGH RIVER** (pop. 6,600) located on Highway 2A. All visitor facilities. Once the centre of a harness-making industry, High River has elegant sandstone buildings and the Museum of the Highwood (open in summer).

CB 164 (264 km) **E 218.2** (351.1 km) Stop of interest commemorating Spitzee Post, built in 1869.

CB 170 (273.6 km) **E 212.2** (341.5 km) Stop of interest sign about cattle brands.

CB 171.6 (276.1 km) **E 210.6** (338.9 km) **Junction** at Aldersyde with Highways 2A and 7 to Okotoks, Black Diamond and Turner Valley (18.5 miles/30 km). Stop of interest commemorating the Turner Valley oil fields.

CB 173.3 (278.9 km) **E 208.9** (336.2 km) Sheep Creek bridge. **Sheep Creek** Provincial Park has a picnic area, playground, swimming and fishing. ●

CB 183 (294.5 km) **E 199.2** (320.6 km) Junction with Highway 2A to **OKOTOKS** (5 miles/8 km west), which has a general store, RV repair and a tea room. Near Okotoks is Spruce Meadows Equestrian Center, which hosts the International Horse Show, June to September; phone (403) 974-4200.

CB 184.6 (297.2 km) **E 197.6** (318 km) Gas station to east with diesel and propane.

CB 188.6 (303.5 km) **E 193.6** (311.6 km) Calgary southern city limits. Private RV park to east. ▲

Pine Creek R.V. Campground. See display ad this section. ▲

NOTE: To bypass downtown Calgary, exit at Marquis of Lorne Trail and continue to Highway 2 (Deerfoot Trail) north.

CB 196.5 (316.2 km) **E 185.7** (298.8 km) Exit for Glenmore Trail, the southwest bypass route that connects with Trans-Canada Highway 1 west to Banff and Vancouver, BC.

Calgary

CB 200.8 (323.1 km) **E 181.4** (291.9 km) Located at the confluence of the Bow and Elbow rivers. **Population:** 767,059. **Elevation:** 3,440 feet/ 1,049m. **Emergency Services:** Phone 911 for emergency services. **Hospitals:** Bow Valley Centre, 841 Centre Ave. NE; Foothills, 1403 29th St. NW; Rockyview, 7007 14th St. SW; Peter Lougheed Center, 3500 26th Ave. NE.

Visitor Information: In the downtown area at the base of Calgary Tower, and at the Calgary Airport; both are open year-round. A visitor centre at Canada Olympic Park is

ples stampeded buffalo to their deaths for nearly 6,000 years, is one of the world's oldest, largest and best-preserved buffalo jumps. The site was named, according to legend, for a young brave whose skull was crushed when he tried to watch the stampede from under a protective ledge which gave way. An interpretive centre houses artifacts and displays describing the buffalo hunting culture. First Nations interpretive guides available on site. Guided walks available twice daily during July and August. Open year-round; 9 A.M. to 7 P.M., June 1 to Labour Day; 9 A.M. to 5 P.M., Labour Day through May; closed major holidays. Admission fee charged.

Roger's RV Park. Enjoy our open vistas and quiet serene location. 15–30 amp power and water, some with sewer hook-up, unserviced sites. Rates $9 to $15. Free hot showers and dump station. Firewood, laundromat available. Located along Highway 785, 4 km east of World Heritage site: Head-Smashed-In Buffalo Jump. (403) 553-2592, P.O. Box 1798, Monarch, Alberta, Canada T0L 1Z0.
[ADVERTISEMENT]

West Wind Crafts, at Buffalo Junction—Highway 2 and Highway 785. Gifts and souvenirs hand-crafted by some of Alberta's finest crafters. Native art and crafts. Hard ice cream, soft drinks, chips, ice, picnic tables, washrooms. Open April to snowfall from 9 A.M., 7 days a week. One-half mile go-cart track open May to September. RV accessible.
[ADVERTISEMENT]

CB 111.2 (179 km) **E 271** (436.1 km) Road east to Granum, a small settlement dominated by grain elevators. Recreation park in town with 41 campsites. ▲

CB 116.2 (187 km) **E 266** (428 km) Community of Woodhouse.

CB 121.8 (196 km) **E 260.4** (419.1 km) CLARESHOLM (pop. 3,500), a prosperous ranching centre with all visitor facilities. The old railway station houses a museum. Camping at Centennial Park; 15 sites, dump station, playground. ▲

CB 125.9 (202.6 km) **E 256.3** (412.5 km) Stop of interest sign commemorating The Leavings, a stopping place on the Fort Macleod–Calgary trail in 1870.

CB 131.3 (211.3 km) **E 250.9** (403.8 km) Community of Stavely to the east.

CB 132.1 (212.6 km) **E 250.1** (402.5 km) Access road west to **Willow Creek** Provincial Park; 150 campsites, swimming, fishing. ●◄▲

CB 138.4 (222.8 km) **E 243.8** (392.3 km) Small settlement of Parkland.

CB 145.9 (234.8 km) **E 236.3** (380.3 km) Nanton campground (75 sites) at junction open in summer only. Or call Calgary Convention & Visitors Bureau at (403) 263-8510 or 1-800-661-1678 (toll-free in North America).

Private Aircraft: Calgary International Airport, 4 miles/6.4 km northeast; elev. 3,557 feet/1,084m; 3 runways. See Canadian Flight Supplement.

This bustling city is one of Alberta's 2 major population and business centres. A great influx of homesteaders came to Calgary with the completion of the Canadian Pacific Railway in 1883. It grew as a trading centre for surrounding farms and ranches. Oil and gas discovered south of the city in 1914 contributed to more growth.

Perhaps the city's best-known attraction is the annual Calgary Stampede, which takes place at the Exhibition Grounds, July 4–13, 1997. The 10-day event includes a parade and daily rodeo; phone 1-800-661-1260 for Stampede information and tickets.

Some other major attractions are: Calgary Science Centre, 11th Street and 7th Avenue; the Glenbow Museum, which presents a lively journey into the heritage of the Canadian West, 130 9th Avenue SE; the Eau Claire Market, adjacent to Prince's Island in the downtown area; the Calgary Chinese Cultural Centre, 197 1st St. SW; the Energeum, at the Energy Resources Bldg., 640 5th Ave. SW; Fort Calgary Interpretive Centre, 750 9th Ave. SE; Calgary Zoo Botanical Garden and Prehistoric Park, off Memorial Drive, has a prehistoric park with life-sized replicas of dinosaurs; and Heritage Park, west of 14th Street and Heritage Drive SW, a re-creation of Calgary's pioneer eras. Visitors may recognize the distinctive Saddledome, located at the Exhibition Grounds, which was the site of the 1988 Winter Olympics skating and hockey events. Canada Olympic Park (site of ski jumping, luge and bobsled) is on Trans-Canada Highway 1, west of Sarcee Trail.

Calgary has large shopping malls, department stores, restaurants, and many hotels and motels. Most lodging is downtown or on Highway 2 south (Macleod Trail), Trans-Canada Highway 1 north (16th Avenue) and Alternate 1A (Motel Village). There are several campgrounds in and around the city. ▲

Calgary West KOA. See display ad this section. ▲

Calgary is one of Alberta's 2 major population and business centres. *(Brian Stein)*

East Access Route Log
(continued)

CB 211.3 (340 km) **E 170.9** (275 km) Calgary northern city limits.

Highway 2 from Calgary to Edmonton bypasses most communities. Except for a few service centres built specially for freeway traffic, motorists must exit the freeway for communities and gas, food or lodging.

CB 211.9 (341 km) **E 170.3** (273 km) Exit to community of **BALZAC**. Private RV park with dump station. ▲

CB 217.9 (350.7 km) **E 164.3** (264.4 km) Road west to **AIRDRIE** (pop. 13,000). Visitor facilities include hotels and motels.

CB 225 (362 km) **E 157.2** (253 km) Dickson–Stephensson Stopping House on Old Calgary Trail; rest area, tourist information.

CB 232.2 (373.6 km) **E 150** (241.4 km) **Junction** with Highway 2A west to Crossfield and Highway 72 east to Drumheller, 60 miles/97 km, site of Alberta's Badlands. The Badlands are famous for the dinosaur fossils found there. Fossil displays at world-renowned Tyrrell Museum of Paleontology in Drumheller.

CB 232.6 (374.4 km) **E 149.6** (240.7 km) Stop of interest sign about the buffalo that once darkened the prairies here. Gas and restaurant at turnout.

CB 235.1 (378.3 km) **E 147.1** (236.7 km) Exit to **CROSSFIELD**; gas, hotel, food.

CB 243.1 (391.2 km) **E 139.1** (223.9 km) Exit west for **CARSTAIRS** (pop. 1,725), a farm and service community with tourist information centre and campground. The campground has 28 sites, electric hookups, hot showers and dump station. Services here include groceries, liquor store, banks, a motel, propane and gas stations. ▲

CB 252.7 (406.6 km) **E 129.5** (208.4 km) **Junction** with Highway 27 west to **OLDS** (pop. 4,888); all visitor facilities, museum and information booth.

CB 268.8 (432.5 km) **E 113.4** (182.5 km) **Junction** with highway west to Bowden and Red Lodge Provincial Park (8.5 miles/14 km); 110 campsites, playground, swimming and fishing. **BOWDEN** (pop. 1,000) is the site of a large oil refinery and Alberta Nurseries and Seeds Ltd., a major employer. Most visitor services available. ▲

Heritage rest area with 24 campsites, dump station and tourist information booth at highway junction. ▲

CB 276 (444 km) **E 106.2** (171 km) **Junction** with Highway 54 west to **INNISFAIL** (pop. 6,000); all visitor facilities. South of Innisfail 3 miles/5 km is the RCMP Dog Training Centre, the only one in Canada; open to the public daily year-round from 9 A.M. to 4 P.M.

CB 278.8 (448.7 km) **E 103.4** (166.4 km) Stop of interest sign about explorer Anthony Henday.

CB 290 (466.8 km) **E 92.2** (148.3 km) Tourist service area with gas stations and restaurants.

CB 291.4 (468.9 km) **E 90.8** (146.1 km) **Junction** with Highway 2A (Gaetz Avenue) east to **RED DEER** (pop. 60,000). **Emergency Services:** Phone 911. **Visitor Information:** At Heritage Ranch, adjacent Highway 2 at **Milepost CB 295** (watch for signs). Heritage Ranch has a staffed visitor centre (open daily year-round) with a gift shop and snack bar, ample parking and access to Waskasoo Park. Phone 1-800-215-8946 or (403) 346-0180.

Private Aircraft: Airport 6 miles/9.6 km southwest; elev. 2,968 feet/905m; length 5,528 feet/1,685m; fuel 100, jet. FSS.

Located midway between Edmonton and Calgary, Red Deer is in the centre of cattle ranching and grain growing, with a burgeoning oil and gas industry and nearby ethylene plants.

Red Deer is often called the "city within a park," referring to the extensive Waskasoo Park system that stretches through the city along the banks of the Red Deer River. The park has more than 46.5 miles/75 km of walking and cycling trails connecting a variety of popular attractions.

The major annual event in Red Deer is Westerner Days in mid-July.

All visitor facilities available, including major chain motels and retail outlets. Camping at Lions Municipal Campground on Riverside Drive; from Highway 2 exit to 67th Street or 32nd Street. Open May to September, 127 sites (88 full-service), dump station, laundry, picnic area, playground. ▲

CB 298 (479.6 km) **E 84.2** (135.5 km) **Junction** with Highway 11 to Sylvan Lake (10 miles/16 km), a popular watersports

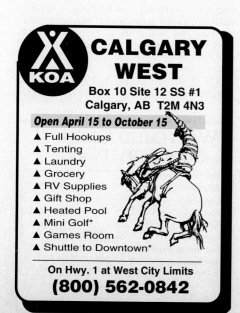

destination for Red Deer residents, with swimming beach and marina. Sylvan Lake Provincial Park has picnicking and swimming. Private campgrounds and waterslide nearby. ▲

CB 302.5 (486.8 km) E 80.2 (129.1 km) Access road east to community of BLACK-FALDS (pop. 1,500). Tourist services and accommodations.

CB 309.1 (497.4 km) E 73.1 (117.6 km) Junction with Highway 12. Exit east for LACOMBE (pop. 6,000); all visitor facilities. Camping at Michener Park; 21 sites. Site of the Federal Agricultural Research Station;

Working oil pump near Edmonton, "Oil Capital of Canada." (© David Creith/Sahtu)

Devonian Way Bypass

This bypass route circles the southwest edge of Edmonton, connecting Highway 2 and Highway 16 via Secondary Highway 19 (Devonian Way) and Highway 60. **Distance from Highway 2 and Devonian Way junction (J) is shown.**

J 0 Junction with Highway 19, Devonian Way, at Milepost CB 372. Follow Devonian Way west.

J 0.4 (0.7 km) Rest area to south.

J 2.1 (3.4 km) Capital Raceway to south, Amerlea Meadows equestrian facility to north.

J 5.2 (8.3 km) Rabbit Hill Ski area to west.

J 8.2 (13.2 km) Junction with Highway 60 (Edmonton truck bypass). Turn north on Highway 60 for Devon and Yellowhead Highway; turn south at intersection and drive 0.6 mile/1 km for Leduc No. 1 well historic site. A 174-foot/53-m derrick marks the site at which oil was struck on February 13, 1947, making Edmonton the "Oil Capital of Canada." Visitors may climb to the drilling floor to view drilling equipment and tools.

J 9.2 (14.8 km) Dump station.

J 10.2 (16.4 km) Turn east on Athabasca Avenue for downtown DEVON; all visitor services. Camping at Devon Lions Club Campground, 180 sites on North Saskatchewan River; follow signs for Patrick O'Brien Memorial Park. The campground is adjacent to Devon Golf & Country Club. ▲

Devon Lions Club Campground. See display ad this section. ▲

J 10.6 (17 km) Bridge over North Saskatchewan River.

J 13.8 (22.2 km) University of Alberta Devonian Botanic Garden; alpine garden, 5-acre Kurimoto Japanese Garden, and other special collections gardens set in natural landscape. Live Exotic Butterfly Showhouse with 30 species of butterflies. Open daily, 10 A.M. to 7 P.M. in summer, shorter hours rest of year. Fee charged.

J 16.9 (27.2 km) Junction with Secondary Highway 627; turn east for Edmonton.

J 22.7 (36.6 km) Junction with Yellowhead Highway 16; turn to **Milepost E 10**.

Return to Milepost E 10 or CB 372 East Access Route

open to the public weekdays, 8 A.M. to 4:30 P.M.

Exit west on Highway 12 for Aspen Beach Provincial Park at Gull Lake (6 miles/10 km); camping, swimming. ▲

CB 325 (524.7 km) E 56.2 (90.4 km) Junction with Highway 53 east to PONOKA (pop. 5,000); all visitor facilities. Camping at Ponoka Stampede Trailer Park, May to October. Ponoka's Stampede is held June 29 to July 3 at Stampede Park. ▲

CB 340.7 (548.3 km) E 41.5 (66.8 km) Northbound-only access to Wetaskiwin rest area with picnic tables and information centre (open May to September); restrooms, gas service and groceries.

CB 345.3 (555.7 km) E 36.9 (59.4 km) Junction of Highway 13 east to Wetaskiwin, site of the Reynolds–Alberta Museum and Aviation Hall of Fame.

CB 356 (572.9 km) E 26.2 (42.2 km) Turnout to east with litter barrels and pay phone.

CB 366 (589 km) E 16.2 (26.1 km) Exit to LEDUC (pop. 12,500); all visitor facilities. Founded and named for the Leduc oil field. The Leduc well was drilled on Feb. 13, 1947, before an invited asssembly of businesspeople, government officials and reporters. It was the 134th try for Imperial Oil after drilling 133 dry wells, and it was wildly successful. The 200-million barrel Leduc oil field was the first in a series of post-war oil and natural gas finds that changed the economy of Alberta.

CB 372 (598.6 km) E 10.2 (16.4 km) Junction with Highway 19 west and Edmonton Bypass route (see DEVONIAN WAY BYPASS log this section). Access to Leduc No. 1 well historic site.

NOTE: Northbound motorists wishing to avoid heavy traffic through Edmonton may exit west on Highway 19 (Devonian Way) for Devon Bypass route. Drive 8.2 miles/13.2 km west on Highway 19, then 14.5 miles/23.3 km north on Highway 60 to junction with Yellowhead Highway 16, 10 miles/16 km west of Edmonton (see **Milepost E 10** *this section).*

Highway 2 northbound becomes Calgary Trail. Access to Edmonton International Airport.

CB 377.9 (608.2 km) E 4.3 (6.9 km) Stoplight at Ellerslie (grain elevator). Access to golf course and private campground; follow Ellerslie west to 127th and turn south to 41st Avenue SW.

Whitemud Creek Golf & RV Park. See display ad this section. ▲

CB 382.2 (615 km) E 0 Junction with Whitemud Drive. Turn east for Highway 16 East, turn west for Highway 16 West (see YELLOWHEAD HIGHWAY 16 section). Continue north for Edmonton city centre (description follows).

Whitemud Drive west continues as Highway 2, crossing the North Saskatchewan River, then turns north to become 170 Street. Access to West Edmonton Mall on 170 Street.

Edmonton

E 0 DC 367 (590.6 km) Capital of Alberta, 1,853 miles/2982 km from Fairbanks, AK. **Population:** 627,000; area 875,000. **Elevation:** 2,182 feet/668m. **Emergency Services:** Phone 911 for all emergency services. **Hospitals:** Grey Nun's, 34th Avenue and 66th Street; Misericordia, 16940 87th Ave.; Royal Alexandra, 10240 Kingsway Ave.; University, 84th Avenue and 112th Street.

Visitor Information: Edmonton Tourism operates visitor information centres downtown and on Highway 2 south. Or write Edmonton Tourism, Dept. MI 97, 9797 Jasper Ave. #104, Edmonton, AB T5J 1N9; phone (403) 496-8400 or 1-800-463-4667 for information.

Private Aircraft: Edmonton International Airport 14 miles/22.5 km southwest and Edmonton Municipal north side of downtown. See Canadian Flight Supplement.

The North Saskatchewan River winds through the centre of Edmonton, its banks lined with public parks. Edmonton Colisium is home to the Edmonton Oilers NHL hockey team. The Edmonton Trappers baseball team play at Telus Field. Major attractions include the Edmonton Space & Science Centre; Muttart Conservatory; Alberta Legislature Building; the Provincial Museum of Alberta, with its Aboriginal Peoples Gallery; and Fort Edmonton Park, Canada's largest living history park.

Fort Edmonton Park features more than 60 period buildings on 158 acres. Costumed interpreters bring history to life on 1885 Street, 1905 Street, 1920 Street and in the Hudson's Bay Co. fort (1846). The original fort was established in 1795 as part of the westward expansion of the fur trade, and by 1846 its main function was to prepare the pemmican and build the York boats necessary to make the journey to York Factory on

the Hudson Bay to bring out furs and return with trade goods each summer.

Activities and attractions at the park include a steam train ride, stagecoach and streetcar rides; blacksmithing and ropemaking demonstrations; retail shops and food outlets. Open 10 A.M. daily, May to September; special events year-round. Contact Fort Edmonton Park, Box 2359, Edmonton, AB T5J 2R7; phone (403) 496-8787.

Also on the list of major attractions for visitors to Edmonton is the world's largest shopping mall—West Edmonton Mall. The mall features some 800 stores and services, a waterpark, ice arena, aquariums, aviaries and some 90 eating establishments. Located on 87 Avenue at 170 Street, the shopping mall is open 7 days a week.

Known as Canada's festival city, Edmonton hosts a number of events throughout the year. These events include: Northern Alberta Children's Festival (May 20–24, 1997); Jazz City International Festival (June 27–July 6, 1997); Street Performers Festival (July 11–20, 1997); Klondike Days (July 17–26, 1997); Heritage Festival (Aug. 2–4, 1997); Edmonton Folk Music Festival (Aug. 7–10, 1997); and Fringe Theatre Event

(Aug. 15–24, 1997).

There are 80 hotels and motels in Edmonton and some 2,000 restaurants. Within the Edmonton vicinity there are sev-

EDMONTON ADVERTISERS

Comfort Inn ....Ph. (403) 484-4415
Fort Edmonton Park ....Ph. (403) 496-8787
Rainbow Campground .....Ph. (403) 434-5531

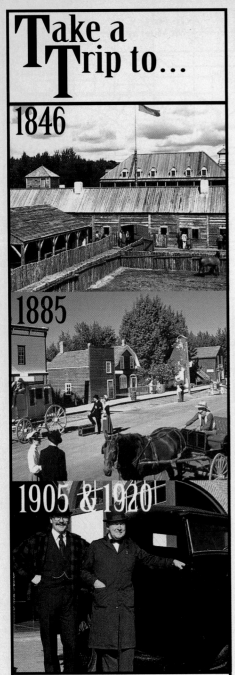

Take a Trip to...

1846

1885

1905 & 1920

Travel through Time . . .

It's living history at its best! Join the costumed characters and experience life the old-fashioned way. Over seventy homes and businesses in four time eras, 1846, 1885, 1905 and 1920. Shop or browse your way through history in our six retail stores or enjoy the hospitality of years past at our food outlets. All you can ride steam train and street cars are included in the price of admission.

OPEN MAY 18 TO SEPTEMBER 1, 1997.

Fort Edmonton Park

Edmonton, Alberta

Call (403) 496-8787

---

eral campgrounds. Rainbow Campground has 85 sites, hookups, dump station, laundry facilities and showers; from Highway 2 drive west 2 miles/3.2 km on Whitemud Drive to 119 Street and 45 Avenue. Located off Highway 2 south (Calgary Trail), west of Ellerslie Road via 127th to 41st Avenue SW, is Whitemud Creek Golf & RV Park. Just west of the city limits off Highway 16 West there is Glowing Embers Travel Centre, at the Devon Overpass, with 273 sites and all facilities. ▲

East Access Route Log

(continued)

HIGHWAY 16 WEST

This section of the log shows distance from Edmonton (E) followed by distance from Dawson Creek (DC).

E 0 DC 367 (590.6 km) Downtown Edmonton. Take Jasper Avenue westbound (becomes 16A then Yellowhead 16 at city limits).

E 10 (16 km) **DC 357** (574.5 km) **Junction** of Highways 16 West and 60 (Devon Overpass); access to private campground. ▲

Glowing Embers Travel Centre. See display ad this section.

NOTE: Southbound travelers may bypass Edmonton by taking Highway 60 south, then Highway 19 east to Highway 2 (see DEVONIAN WAY BYPASS log on page 28).

E 18 (29 km) **DC 349** (561.6 km) **SPRUCE GROVE** (pop. 13,076). All visitor facilities including motels, restaurants, gas and service stations, grocery stores, farmer's market, shopping malls and all emergency services. Recreational facilities include a golf course, swimming pool, skating and curling rinks, parks, and extensive walking and cycling trails. The chamber of commerce tourist information booth, located on Highway 16, is open year-round; phone (403) 962-2561.

E 24 (38.7 km) **DC 345** (555.2 km) **STONY PLAIN** (pop. 7,405). All visitor facilities including hotels, restaurants, supermarkets, shopping mall and gas stations with major repair service; RCMP and hospital; outdoor swimming pool, tennis courts and 18-hole golf course. The Multicultural Heritage Centre here has historical archives, a craft shop and home-cooked meals. Other attractions include 16 outdoor murals; Oppertshauser Art Gallery; the Andrew Wolf Winery; and the Pioneer Museum at Exhibition Park. Visitor information centre at Rotary Park rest area. Camping at Lions RV Park and Campground; 26 sites. ▲

Bears and Bedtime Mfg. features handmade, collectable teddy bears made of highest quality synthetic and mohair furs. All bears have moveable heads and limbs. Also available are: bear making supplies, teddy bear books, cards, Cherished Teddies and other gift items. Hours: Monday–Saturday 10 A.M.–6 P.M. 1-800-461-BEAR(2327). See ad in the YELLOWHEAD HIGHWAY section. [ADVERTISEMENT]

E 25.6 (41.2 km) **DC 341.4** (549.4 km) Edmonton Beach turnoff to south; campground. ▲

E 26.1 (42 km) **DC 340.9** (548.6 km) Hubbles Lake turnoff to north.

E 27.2 (43.8 km) **DC 339.8** (546.8 km) Restaurant, gas station and store to north.

E 27.7 (44.6 km) **DC 339.3** (546 km) Andrew Wolf Wine Cellars; visitors welcome.

E 28 (45 km) **DC 334** (545.6 km) Multicultural Heritage Centre, a regional museum, with restaurant and crafts shop. Open daily.

E 31 (49.9 km) **DC 336** (540.7 km) **Junction** of Yellowhead Highway 16 and Highway 43. Turn north onto Highway 43. (If you are continuing west on Yellowhead Highway 16 for Prince George or Prince

---

Rupert, BC, turn to **Milepost E 25** in the YELLOWHEAD HIGHWAY section.)

HIGHWAY 43

E 36.9 (59.4 km) **DC 330.1** (531.2 km) **Junction** of Highways 43 and 33 (Grizzly Trail). Continue on Highway 43.

E 37.3 (60 km) **DC 329.7** (530.6 km) Turnout to east with litter barrel and historical information sign about construction of the Alaska Highway.

E 37.9 (61 km) **DC 329.1** (529.6 km) **Gunn General Store & Campground**. See display ad this section. ▲

E 38.7 (62.3 km) **DC 328.3** (528.3 km) Gas station to east.

E 39.2 (63.1 km) **DC 327.8** (527.5 km) Highway 633 west to Alberta Beach Recreation Area on Lac Ste. Anne. Facilities include a municipal campground (open May 15 to Sept. 15) with 115 sites. ▲

E 41.6 (66.9 km) **DC 325.4** (523.7 km) ONOWAY (pop. 671) has a medical clinic, dentist and veterinary clinic. Other services include gas, propane, banks and bank machine, grocery stores, laundromat, restaurants, motel, car wash, post office, pharmacy, RV park with hookups and dump station. Information booth and Elks campground with 8 sites. ▲

E 45.4 (73.2 km) **DC 321.5** (517.4 km) Alberta government campground with dump station, water, toilets and stoves. ▲

E 45.9 (73.9 km) **DC 321.1** (516.7 km) Restaurant and gas station.

E 48 (77.2 km) **DC 318.9** (513.2 km) **Lessard Lake** county campground; water, stoves, boat launch, fishing for pike and perch. Golf course to west. ⚓▲

E 63.7 (102.5 km) **DC 303.3** (488.1 km) Gas station.

E 72 (115.8 km) **DC 295** (474.8 km) SANGUDO (pop. 405) is on a 0.3-mile/0.4-km side road. Restaurants, motel and hotel accommodations; gas station with garage open 7 days a week; grocery, clothing and liquor stores; antique shop; banks, post office, pharmacy, laundromat and car wash. Oval race car track with racing in summer; shale baseball diamonds; elk farm tours. A public campground with 14 sites, showers and flush toilets, is located at the sportsground. ▲

E 74.4 (119.7 km) **DC 292.6** (470.9 km) Pembina River bridge.

E 75.4 (121.3 km) **DC 291.6** (469.3 km) Gas station and restaurant to south.

E 79.5 (128 km) **DC 287.5** (462.7 km) Second longest wooden railway trestle in the world crosses highway and Paddle River. The C.N.R. Rochfort Bridge trestle is 2,414 feet/736m long and was originally built in 1914.

E 80.6 (129.7 km) **DC 286.4** (460.9 km) ROCHFORT BRIDGE. Trading post (open daily, year-round) with gas, convenience store, gift shop, restaurant and Lac St. Anne Pioneer Museum. Camping. ▲

Rochfort Bridge Trading Post—A fun stop. Fresh bread and pies baked from scratch: rhubarb, saskatoon berries, sour-cream and raisin pies, and more. Home-style meals. Licensed. Verandah. One of the largest all-Canadian gift stores. Distinctive items, including rare First Nations art: birch bark biting, fish scale art and moose tufting. Par 3 golf course with rentals. And you can photograph our cute donkeys. [ADVERTISEMENT]

E 83.1 (133.7 km) **DC 283.9** (456.1 km) Paved turnouts with litter barrels both sides of highway.

E 85 (136.8 km) **DC 282** (453.8 km) MAYERTHORPE (pop. 1,615). One mile/1.6 km from the highway on a paved access road. Hotel, motel, restaurant, grocery store, gas stations with repair service, car wash, hospital, laundromat, post office, RCMP and banks. A public campground with 30 sites (no hookups, pit toilets) and 9-hole golf course are located 1 mile/1.6 km south of town. Airstrip located 2 miles/3.2 km southwest of town; no services. (Most northbound air travelers use Whitecourt airport, which has fuel.) ▲

E 87 (140 km) **DC 280** (450.6 km) Gas station and restaurant at junction with Highway 658 north to Goose Lake.

E 109 (175.4 km) **DC 258** (415.2 km) Lions Club Campground; 74 sites, flush toilets, showers, water, tables and firepits. Fee charged. ▲

Whitecourt

E 111.8 (179.9 km) **DC 255.2** (410.7 km). Located two hours from Edmonton. **Population:** 7,100. **Emergency Services: Police**, phone (403) 778-5454. **Fire Department**, phone (403) 778-2311. **Hospital** located on Hilltop, phone (403) 778-2285. Ambulance service available.

WHITECOURT ADVERTISERS

CJ's Liquor ....Mountain Shopping Strip
Ernie O's Restaurant ....Ph. (403) 778-4844
Fas Gas & am pm................................Hwy. 43
Guest house, The..............Ph. (403) 778-4844
McDonald's ....Hwy. 43
Renford Inn.......................Ph. (403) 778-3133
Sagitawah Tourist Park.....Ph. (403) 778-3734
Tags Food & Gas/A&W ....3711 Highway St.
Whitecourt Lions Club
   Campground................................Hwy. 43

Visitor Information: Tourist information booth on Highway 43 west at the traffic lights. The helpful staff will assist with travel plans and directions to Whitecourt sights and activities. The booth is fully stocked with pamphlets and brochures. Open daily, 9 A.M. to 6 P.M., May 1 to Sept. 1; weekdays only, 9 A.M. to 5 P.M., September through April. Free dump station and freshwater fill-up adjacent tourist booth. Information is also available from the Chamber of Commerce, P.O. Box 1011, Whitecourt, AB T7S 1N9; phone (403) 778-5363, fax 778-2351.

Elevation: 2,567 feet/782m. **Radio:** 1400 CJYR-AM, 107.5 SKUA-FM. **Television:** 10 channels. **Newspaper:** *Whitecourt Star* (weekly); *Whitecourt Advertiser* (biweekly).

Private Aircraft: Airport 4 miles/6.4 km south on Highway 32; elev. 2,567 feet/782m; length 5,800 feet/1,768m; paved; fuel 80, 100, jet (24-hour, self-serve). Aircraft maintenance, 24-hour flight service station, all-weather facility.

Transportation: Air—Local charter air service available; helicopter and fixed-wing aircraft. **Bus**—Greyhound service to Edmonton,

Roadside sign near Whitecourt warns motorists to watch for moose.
(Roger Pickenpaugh)

Grande Prairie, Peace River and points north.

Located at the junction of Highways 43 and 32, Whitecourt dubs itself the "Gateway to the Alaska Highway and the fabulous North." Established as a small trading, trapping and forestry centre, Whitecourt became an important stop for Alaska Highway travelers when a 106-mile section of Highway 43 connecting Whitecourt and Valleyview was completed in October 1955. This new route was 72 miles shorter than the old Edmonton to Dawson Creek route via Slave Lake.

Several major forest industries operating in and around Whitecourt offer tours. Visitors may observe state-of-the-art technologies at sawmills, medium-density fiberboard production and pulp plants. Check with the tourist information booth or chamber of commerce for tour times.

The Eric S. Huestis Demonstration Forest, northwest of town on Highway 32 (see **Milepost E 117.1**), has 4.3 miles/7 km of self-guided trails with interpretive sites and information signs describing forest management techniques and the forest life-cycle; phone (403) 778-7165.

Recreational activities include an excellent 18-hole public golf course and fishing in area creeks, rivers and lakes (boat rentals at Carson–Pegasus Provincial Park). Swimming, inline skating, tennis, gold panning, walking trails, beach volleyball and river boating are also enjoyed in summer. In the fall, big game hunting is very popular. During the winter there is ice fishing, snowmobiling and cross-country skiing on area trails, downhill skiing at a local facility, skating and curling, bowling and swimming at the indoor pool.

There are 14 hotels/motels, a bed and breakfast, 23 restaurants, 14 gas stations, several laundromats, 2 malls, 6 liquor stores and 5 banks. Most services are located on the highway or 2 blocks north in the downtown business district. Some gas stations and restaurants are open 24 hours.

This full-service community also supports a library and 7 churches. The Legion, located in the business district, is open year-round.

Service clubs (Lions, Kinsmen) and community organizations (Masons, Knights of Columbus) welcome visitors.

A popular wilderness area nearby is Carson–Pegasus Provincial Park, located 14.6 miles/23.5 km west and north of town on Highway 32 (paved). The park has 182 campsites, electrical hookups, dump station, boat launch, boat rentals, concession, convenience store, hot showers and laundry facilities. Powered sites and showers are open year-round. There are 2 lakes at the park: **McLeod (Carson) Lake**, stocked with rainbow trout, has a speed limit of 12 kmph for boaters; **Little McLeod (Pegasus) Lake** has northern pike and whitefish, electric motors and canoes only. Eagle River Outfitting (phone 403/778-3251), located 7 miles/11.3 km south of town via Highway 32, offers camping and wilderness activities. ⬥▲

East Access Route Log

(continued)

E 111.9 (180.1 km) DC 255.1 (410.5 km) Beaver Creek bridge.

CAUTION: The highway between Whitecourt and Valleyview is known locally as "Moose Row" and "Moose Alley." Several moose-vehicle accidents occur yearly. Northbound travelers, watch for moose on road, especially at dusk and at night.

E 112.4 (180.9 km) DC 254.6 (409.7 km) McLeod River.

E 112.6 (181.2 km) DC 254.4 (409.4 km) Railroad crossing.

E 112.7 (181.4 km) DC 254.3 (409.2 km) **Junction** with Highway 32 South (paved). Access to Eagle River Outfitting, 7 miles/11.3 km south; camping, wilderness activities. Highway 32 leads 42 miles/68 km to Yellowhead Highway 16 (see **Milepost E 97.5** in the YELLOWHEAD HIGHWAY section). ▲

E 112.9 (181.7 km) DC 254.1 (408.9 km) Gas stations both sides of highway.

E 113.4 (182.5 km) DC 253.6 (408.1 km) Turnoff to north for Sagitawah Tourist Park (RV camping) and Riverboat Park, both at the confluence of the McLeod and Athabasca rivers. Riverboat Park has a boat launch, picnic area and toilets. ▲

E 113.6 (182.8 km) DC 253.4 (407.8 km) Athabasca River bridge.

E 115.6 (186 km) DC 251.4 (404.6 km) Vehicle inspection station to north.

E 117.1 (188.4 km) DC 249.9 (402.2 km) **Junction** with Highway 32 North (paved). Access to Eric S. Huestis Demonstration Forest (self-guided trails) and Carson–Pegasus Provincial Park. The provincial park, 9.3 miles/15 km north, has 182 campsites, electrical hookups, group camping area, tables, flush toilets, showers, water, dump station, firewood, store, laundromat and playground. (Powered sites and showers open year-round.) Boat launch, boat rentals and rainbow trout fishing are available. ⬥▲

E 117.6 (189.2 km) DC 249.4 (401.4 km) Alberta Newsprint Co. to south.

E 122 (196.3 km) DC 245 (394.3 km) Turnout with litter barrel.

E 122.5 (197.1 km) DC 244.5 (393.5 km) Chickadee Creek government campground; 7 sites, pit toilets, water, tables and firepits. ▲

E 124.3 (200 km) DC 242.7 (390.6 km) Chickadee Creek.

E 131.8 (212.1 km) DC 235.2 (378.5 km) Turnouts with litter barrels both sides of highway.

E 140.5 (226.1 km) DC 226.5 (364.5 km) Two Creeks government campground; 8 campsites, pit toilets, water, picnic tables and firepits. ▲

E 142.5 (229.3 km) DC 224.5 (361.3 km) Turnout with litter barrel to south.

E 143 (230.1 km) DC 224 (360.5 km) Turnout with litter barrel to north.

E 152 (244.6 km) DC 215 (346 km) Iosegun Creek government campground; 12 sites, pit toilets, water, tables and firepits.

E 159 (255.9 km) DC 208 (334.7 km) Fox Creek airport.

Fox Creek

E 162 (260.7 km) DC 205 (329.9 km) **Population:** 2,259. **Elevation:** 2,800 feet/853m. **Emergency Services:** RCMP, phone (403) 622-3740. **Ambulance**, phone (403) 622-3000. **Hospital**, phone (403) 622-3545. **Visitor Information:** Tourist Information Centre at the Rig Earth Resource Park, open in summer; gift shop and coffee area; phone (403) 622-2000. Off-season contact the Town Office at (403) 622-3896 for information.

Private Aircraft: Fox Creek airport, 3 miles/4.8 km south on Highway 43; elev. 2,840 feet/866m; length, 2,950 feet/899m; paved; no fuel. Unattended.

All visitor facilities including a hotel, 3 motels and gas stations with repair service. Grocery store open daily until midnight. Convenience stores, pharmacy, laundromat, liquor stores, restaurants, banks and bank machines.

Recreation facilities include a 9-hole golf course with grass greens and driving range; outdoor swimming pool; tennis courts; and ice arena with 4 sheet curling rink.

A popular winter activity is snowmobiling. Snowmobile enthusiasts can ride for miles on the "Golden Triangle" that links the communities of Swan Hills, Whitecourt and Fox Creek.

Municipal campground with 17 sites, full hookups, showers and dump station ▲

Fox Creek is in the centre of oil and gas exploration and production. (A Jomax 4, 150-foot/46m drilling rig is on display at Rig Earth Resource Park.) North America's largest known natural gas field is here. The forestry industry is also prominent.

Fox Creek is also a popular outdoor recreation area, with plenty of hunting and fishing in summer. Two local lakes popular with residents and visitors are **Iosegun** and **Smoke lakes**, which are located within 10 miles/16 km on either side of the townsite on good gravel road. Camping, boat launch and fishing for northern pike, perch and pickerel are favorites for this area. ◄▲

East Access Route Log

(continued)

E 167 (268.7 km) **DC 200** (321.9 km) Turnout with litter barrel.

E 169.5 (272.8 km) **DC 197.5** (317.8 km) Turnouts with litter barrels both sides of highway.

E 172 (276.8 km) **DC 195** (313.8 km) Pines government campground; 25 sites, shelter, firewood, pump water, tables and pit toilets. ▲

E 182.1 (293 km) **DC 184.9** (297.6 km) Turnout with litter barrel.

E 186.4 (300 km) **DC 180.6** (290.6 km) **Sands Wilderness Campground & R.V. Park.** 24-hour security campground. Power and unserviced sites, tenting area. Spacious pull-throughs with power. Water fill-up and dump station. Laundromat, showers. Concession; hot and cold snacks. Horseshoe pits and mini-golf. Children's playground. Free firewood. Guests have said, "One of the nicest campgrounds in Canada." Outdoor adventures—trail rides and raft trips. Your host—"Wild Bill" Sands, Box 511, Valleyview, AB T0H 3N0. Phone (403) 524-2207, fax (403) 524-3288. [ADVERTISEMENT] ▲

E 192 (309 km) **DC 175** (281.6 km) **LITTLE SMOKY** (pop. about 50). Motel, RV park, tea house, gift shop, pay phone, propane, grocery store, service station and post office. ▲

Little Smoky Motel & Campground. See display ad this section. ▲

E 192.2 (309.3 km) **DC 174.8** (281.3 km) Little Smoky River bridge.

E 193.5 (311.4 km) **DC 173.5** (279.2 km) Waskahigan (House) River bridge at confluence with Smoky River. Government campground with 24 sites, pit toilets, water, tables and firepits. ▲

E 197 (317 km) **DC 170** (273.6 km) Turnout.

E 206.7 (332.6 km) **DC 160.3** (258 km) Turnout with litter barrel.

E 208.5 (335.5 km) **DC 158.5** (255.1 km)

Peace pipeline storage tanks.

E 210.8 (339.2 km) **DC 156.2** (251.4 km) Valleyview Riverside golf course.

E 213.2 (343.1 km) **DC 153.8** (247.5 km) Valleyview tourist information centre (phone 403/524-2410); pay phone, postal service, souvenirs, picnic tables, flush toilets. Open daily in summer, 8 A.M. to 8 P.M.

E 213.4 (343.4 km) **DC 153.6** (247.2 km) Valleyview airport to west.

Private Aircraft: Valleyview airport; elev. 2,434 feet/742m; length, 3,300 feet/1,006m; paved; no fuel. Unattended.

CAUTION: The highway between Valleyview and Whitecourt is known locally as "Moose Row" and "Moose Alley." Several moose-vehicle accidents occur yearly. Southbound travelers, watch for moose on road, especially at dusk and at night.

Valleyview

E 214.1 (344.4 km) **DC 152.9** (246.1 km) **Junction of Highways 43 and 34,** approximately 4 hours drive time from Edmonton. **Population:** 1,855. **Emergency Services: RCMP,** phone (403) 524-3343. **Fire Department,** phone (403) 524-3211. **Ambulance,** phone (403) 524-3916. **Hospital,** Valleyview General, 45 beds, phone (403) 524-3356.

Visitor Information: Major tourist information centre and rest stop located 0.9 mile/1.5 km south of Valleyview on Highway 43. Open daily, 8 A.M. to 8 P.M. from May through Labour Day weekend; phone (403) 524-2410, fax (403) 524-2727, e-mail valvadm@vvw-TEQ.Net. Postal service, souvenirs and refreshments, as well as regional travel and community events and services information. For information on small business opportunities, contact the Valleyview Regional Economic Development Board office at (403)524-3942.

Elevation: 2,400 feet/732m. **Newspaper:** *Valley Views* (weekly). **Transportation:** Air–Airport 0.7 mile/1.1 km south (see Milepost E 213.4). **Bus**–Greyhound.

Valleyview, known as the "Portal to the Peace Country" of northwestern Alberta, is located at the junction of Highways 43 and 34. From Valleyview, Highway 34 leads west to Grande Prairie and Dawson Creek. Highway 43 continues north to Peace River. From Peace River, travelers may follow the Mackenzie Highway to Northwest Territories (see the MACKENZIE ROUTE section for details).

Highway 43 also connects with Highway 2 east to Athabasca, the Slave Lake route from Edmonton used by Alaska Highway travelers until 1955, when Highway 43 was completed to Whitecourt.

Originally called Red Willow Creek when it was homesteaded in 1916, Valleyview boomed with the discovery of oil and gas in the 1950s, and services grew along with the population. Today, Valleyview's economy has diversified to include the oil and gas industry, forestry, tourism, agriculture and government services. Farming consists mainly of grain, oilseed, beef cattle and forage production.

The community has a full range of services including banks, automatic teller machines, post office, a library, several churches and a veterinary clinic.

All visitor facilities available, including 5 motels and hotels, several restaurants, gas stations (many with major repair service, propane and diesel), laundromat, grocery, liquor store, clothing and hardware stores, a bakery, gift shops and a golf course. Some gas stations and restaurants open 24 hours a day.

The area boasts many lakes and streams, abundant wildlife, and lush vegetaton, including berries. Summer travelers can take advantage of the long summer days here by attending local rodeos, fairs and festivals; playing a round of golf on one of the local golf courses; visiting one of the provincial parks along Sturgeon Lake; taking a dip in the outdoor swimming pool in town; or exploring the wilderness by all-terrain vehicle, horse, canoe or hiking trail.

Horizon Motel, Restaurant & Gift Shop. At the Horizon, we have built our business on loyalty and customer satisfaction. An Alberta Best property, clean, well-appointed rooms, several nonsmoking and deluxe family suites available, reasonable rates. Our Westside Cafe, "where to turn when you simply must have a good meal… ," tastefully decorated, featuring Western and Chinese menu. Open daily 6 A.M. to 10 P.M. Tour buses welcome. Quality souvenirs and gifts. Bank rate of exchange paid on U.S. funds. We take pride in our service; stop in and experience for yourself! Phone (403) 524-3904. Fax (403) 524-4223. [ADVERTISEMENT] ▲

Lion's Den Campground, west end of town, has 19 sites with hookups, tables, showers and toilets. Full-service private campground (Sherk's RV Park) with 56 sites, close to town. ▲

East Access Route Log
(continued)

E 216 (347.6 km) DC 151 (243 km) Highway 43 continues north 86 miles/138.4 km to **PEACE RIVER** (pop. 6,690). Highway 43 **junctions** with the Mackenzie Highway 12

Grande Prairie

To Edmonton

Highway 2 Bypass

Rec-Plex
Visitor Information Centre
Rotary Campsite
Reservoir
Regional College
To Dawson Creek
Richmond Ave.
Museum
Centennial Park
Provincial Building & Courthouse
Hospital
N.A.R.
Bear Creek
Wapiti Road
To Grande Cache
To Campground and Golf

Microwave towers to east.

E 259.5 (417.6 km) **DC 107.5** (173 km) Smoky River bridge and government campground; 30 sites, shelter, firepits, firewood, tables, pit toilets, water pump and boat launch. ▲

E 262 (421.6km) **DC 105** (169 km) **West Smoky RV Campsites.** You will find us on the west side of Smoky River. (New–1996) Pull-through sites, power, fresh water, washrooms, showers, laundromat, dumping station, picnic tables, fire pits, free wood, mini-golf, horseshoes and play area. 5 minutes from food store, gas, restaurant. 20 minutes from Grande Prairie major shopping and services. Owners Cliff and Berniece Sydbo. Phone/fax (403) 538-3024. [ADVERTISEMENT] ▲

E 264 (424.9 km) **DC 103** (165.7 km) **BEZANSON.** Post office, gas station with diesel, cafe, liquor store, grocery, general store, propane.

E 269 (432.9 km) **DC 98** (157.7 km) Kleskun Hills Park to north 3 miles/5 km. The park features an ancient sea bottom with fossils of dinosaurs and marine life.

E 270.6 (435.5 km) **DC 96.4** (155.1 km) Turnout to north with historical sign about the Kleskun Hills.

E 283.5 (456.2 km) **DC 83.5** (134.4 km) Weigh scales to north.

E 283.8 (456.7 km) **DC 83.2** (133.9 km) Railroad crossing.

E 284 (457 km) **DC 83** (133.6 km) Junction, Highways 34 and 2. Westbound travelers turn south for Grande Prairie and Highway 2 to Dawson Creek (log follows). Turn north on Highway 2 for Sexsmith (8.5 miles/13.7 km), site of the Sexsmith Blacksmith Shop, and Grimshaw (105 miles/169 km), Mile 0 of the Mackenzie Highway to Northwest Territories (see MACKENZIE ROUTE section). ▲

ALBERTA HIGHWAY 2

From its junction with Highway 34, Highway 2 leads south into Grande Prairie (description follows). To reach Grande Prairie city centre, keep straight ahead on Highway 2 (Clairmont Road) as it becomes 100th Street and follow it downtown. To skirt the downtown area, take the Highway 2 Bypass. Highway 2 becomes 100th Avenue (Richmond Avenue) on the west side of Grande Prairie.

NOTE: Bighorn Highway 40 (paved) connects Grande Prairie with Grande Cache and Yellowhead Highway 16. To reach the Bighorn Highway, follow Wapiti Road (108th Street) south from Highway 2 on the west side of Grande Prairie. See BIGHORN HIGHWAY log page 37.

Grande Prairie

E 288 (463.5 km) **DC 79** (127.1 km). Located at **junction** of Highways 2 and 34. **Population:** 31,000. **Emergency Services:** RCMP, phone (403) 538-5700. **Fire Department,** phone (403) 532-2100. **Ambulance,** phone (403) 532-9511. **Hospital,** Queen Elizabeth, 10409 98th St., phone (403) 538-7100.

Visitor Information: Chamber of Commerce office at 10011 103rd Ave.; open weekdays 8:30 A.M. to 4:30 P.M. Visitor service center located off Highway 2 Bypass on 106th Street at Bear Creek Reservoir, open 9 A.M. to 9 P.M. in July and August, shorter hours in June.

Private Aircraft: Airport 3 miles/4.8 km west; elev. 2,195 feet/669m; length 6,500

miles/19 km west of Peace River. See the MACKENZIE ROUTE section for a description of Peace River and the log of the Mackenzie Highway to Northwest Territories.

Highway 34 begins westbound from Valleyview; continue west on Highway 34.

ALBERTA HIGHWAY 34

E 222.6 (358.2 km) **DC 144.4** (232.4 km) 24-hour convenience store and gas.

E 224.7 (361.6 km) **DC 142.3** (229 km) Access north to **Sturgeon Lake**; fishing and camping. Williamson Provincial Park (1.2 miles/2 km) has 60 campsites, boat launch, showers and dump station. Sturgeon Lake Campground has 102 sites, some hookups, tables, showers, laundry, dump station and store. Fishing for perch, pickerel, northern pike and whitefish. ◂▲

E 227 (365.3 km) **DC 140** (225.3 km) **CALAIS** (pop. about 550); post office and grocery store.

E 230 (370.1 km) **DC 137** (220.5 km) Private campground and marina on **Sturgeon Lake**; fishing, boat rentals. ◂▲

Cosy Cove Campground & Marina. See display ad this section.

E 232 (373.3 km) **DC 135** (217.3 km) Sturgeon Heights. Turnoff for Youngs Point Provincial Park, 6 miles/10 km northeast; 97 campsites (some with electrical hookups), firewood, showers, playground, hiking trails, dump station, boat launch, fish cleaning station, beach, fishing in **Sturgeon Lake.** ◂▲

E 235 (378.2 km) **DC 132** (212.4 km) Turnouts both sides of highway; historic marker.

E 240 (386.2 km) **DC 127** (204.4 km) **CROOKED CREEK** (pop. 10); gas station, grocery, post office and pay phone.

E 246 (395.9 km) **DC 121** (194.7 km) **DeBOLT,** a small farming community north of highway with a general store and district museum. Garage with gas on highway.

E 253.8 (408.7 km) **DC 113.2** (181.9 km) Junction. Forestry Trunk Road leads 632 miles/1017 km south, intersecting Yellowhead Highway 16 and Trans-Canada Highway 1, to Highway 3.

E 255.2 (410.7 km) **DC 111.8** (179.9 km)

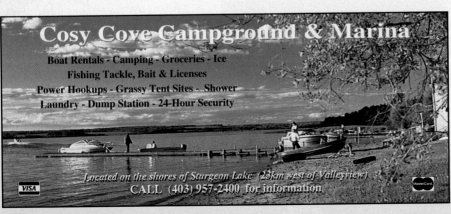

feet/1,981m; paved; fuel 80, 100, jet. 24-hour flight service station.

Elevation: 2,198 feet/670m. **Transportation: Air**—Scheduled air service to Vancouver, BC, Edmonton, Calgary, and points north. **Bus**—Greyhound.

Grande Prairie was first incorporated as a village in 1914, as a town in 1919, and as a city in 1958, by which time its population had reached nearly 8,000.

With a strong and diverse economy based on agriculture (cereal grains, fescue, honey, livestock), forestry (a bleached kraft pulp mill, sawmill and oriented strand board plant), and oil and gas, Grande Prairie is a regional centre for much of northwestern Alberta and northeastern British Columbia. The trumpeter swan is the symbol of Grande Prairie and is featured throughout the city.

A variety of shopping is available at 2 major malls, several strip malls and a well-developed downtown area. Visitor facilities include several restaurants, hotels, motels, and bed and breakfasts. Recreation facilities include 2 swimming pools, 3 18-hole golf courses, a par 3 golf course, ball diamonds, amusement park, tennis courts, public library, a public art gallery and 3 private galleries. Churches representing almost every denomination are located in Grande Prairie. There are several public schools and a regional college.

(Continues on page 39)

GRANDE PRAIRIE ADVERTISERS

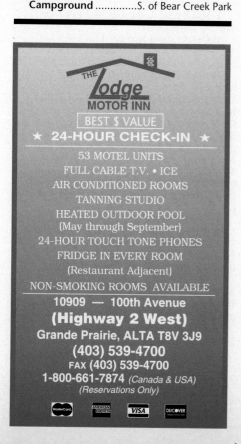

Bighorn Highway 40 Log

This 207-mile/333.2-km paved highway, completely paved in 1996, connects Yellowhead Highway 16 and Highway 2, and the communities of Hinton, Grande Cache and Grande Prairie.

Distance from Yellowhead Highway 16 junction (Y) is followed by the distance from Grande Prairie (GP).

Y 0 GP 207 (333.2 km) **Junction** of Highways 16 and 40. (See **Milepost E 177** in the YELLOWHEAD HIGHWAY 16 section.) Log follows Highway 40 northbound.

Y 2.1 (3.4 km) **GP 204.9** (329.8 km) Community of **ENTRANCE** (pop. 79) to west.

Y 3 (4.8 km) **GP 204** (328.4 km) Athabasca River bridge.

Y 3.7 (5.9 km) **GP 203.3** (327.3 km) Access road to west leads 10 miles/16 km to the community of **BRULE** (pop. 161), which has a guest ranch with trail riding, fishing and cross-country skiing in winter. ◄━

Y 8.5 (13.6 km) **GP 198.5** (319.6 km) Access road leads west 4 miles/7 km to Athabasca Lookout Nordic Centre; cross-country and biathlon skiing, hiking trails and day lodge.

Y 8.9 (14.3 km) **GP 198.1** (318.9 km) Turnout to east with litter barrels and information sign about William A. Switzer Provincial Park.

Y 9.1 (14.7 km) **GP 197.9** (318.5 km) Entering William A. Switzer Provincial Park northbound.

Y 9.8 (15.8 km) **GP 197.2** (317.4 km) Access road leads east to Jarvis Lake day-use area; pump water, public phone, beach and boat launch.

Y 12.8 (20.5 km) **GP 194.2** (312.7 km) Kelley's Bathtub day-use area to west; hiking trail, public phone, swimming.

Y 15.2 (24.5 km) **GP 191.8** (308.7 km) Winter Creek.

Y 15.3 (24.7 km) **GP 191.7** (308.5 km) Side road to east leads 1.2 miles/2 km to Cache Lake and 2.4 miles/4 km to Graveyard Lake. Cache Lake campground has 14 sites, sewer hookups, water pump, picnic tables, shelter, children's playground, camping fee $7.50. Graveyard campground has 16 sites, sewer hookups, water available at Cache Lake campground, camping fee $7.50. ▲

Y 16.8 (27 km) **GP 190.3** (306.2 km) Access road to east leads to **Gregg Lake** day-use area and campground; 164 sites, sewer hookups, tap water, picnic tables, shelter, children's playground, fish-cleaning stand, beach, hiking trails, public phone. Camping fee $13. ◄━▲

Y 17.6 (28.4 km) **GP 189.4** (304.8 km) Turnout to west with litter barrels and information sign about William A. Switzer Provincial Park for southbound travelers.

Y 22.9 (36.9 km) **GP 184.1** (296.3 km) Wildhay River bridge.

Y 25.6 (41.2 km) **GP 181.4** (292 km) Side road to west leads 20 miles/32 km to Rock Lake campground on Rock Lake; 96 sites, sewer hookups, water pump, picnic

tables, shelter, hiking trails, boat launch, camping fee $7.50. ▲

Y 28.9 (46.5 km) **GP 178.1** (286.7 km) Entering Grande Cache ranger district northbound.

Y 30.6 (49.3 km) **GP 176.4** (283.9 km) Fred Creek.

Y 36.3 (58.5 km) **GP 170.7** (274.7 km) Pinto Creek.

Y 40.5 (65.2 km) **GP 166.5** (268 km) Bridge over the Little Berland River.

Y 43.2 (69.6 km) **GP 163.8** (263.6 km) Fox Creek.

Y 47.4 (76.3 km) **GP 159.6** (256.9 km) Small airstrip to east.

Y 48.4 (77.9 km) **GP 158.6** (255.3 km) Bridge over the Big Berland River. Big Berland River government campground at north end of bridge to west has 12 sites, sewer hookups, water pump, picnic tables, shelter, camping fee $7.50. ▲

Y 52.9 (85.2 km) **GP 154.1** (248 km) Hendrickson Creek.

Y 56.4 (90.7 km) **GP 150.6** (242.5 km) Access road to east leads 1.8 miles/3 km to Hucklebury Tower.

Y 57.4 (92.3 km) **GP 149.6** (240.9 km) Shand Creek.

Y 61.3 (98.6 km) **GP 145.7** (234.6 km) Burleigh Creek.

Y 65.2 (105 km) **GP 141.8** (228.2 km) Pierre Grey's Lakes government campground to east; 83 sites, sewer hookups, pump water, picnic tables, shelter, fireplaces, firewood, hiking trails, boat launch, camping fee $7.50. ▲

Y 66.1 (106.4 km) **GP 140.9** (226.8 km) Entering **MUSKEG RIVER** (pop. 22) northbound; pay phone.

Y 66.7 (107.3 km) **GP 140.3** (225.9 km) Highway maintenance station to north.

Y 67 (107.8 km) **GP 140** (225.4 km) Lone Teepee Creek.

Y 67.9 (109.3 km) **GP 139.1** (223.9 km) **Junction** with Highway 734 (Forestry Trunk Road, gravel) which leads north 116 miles/187 km to Highway 34. There are no services along the highway.

Y 69.4 (111.7 km) **GP 137.6** (221.5 km) Turnout to south.

Y 70 (112.6 km) **GP 137** (220.6 km) Veronique River bridge.

Y 72.3 (116.4 km) **GP 134.7** (216.8 km) Findley Creek.

Y 74.1 (119.3 km) **GP 132.9** (213.9 km) Muskeg River bridge.

Y 74.9 (120.6 km) **GP 132.1** (212.6 km) Mason Creek day-use area; picnic facilities and hiking trail to the Muskeg River.

Y 75.1 (120.8 km) **GP 131.9** (212.3 km) Mason Creek.

Y 75.7 (121.8 km) **GP 131.3** (211.4 km) Grande Cache airport to south.

Y 80.8 (130.1 km) **GP 126.2** (203.1 km) Susa Creek.

Y 82 (132 km) **GP 125** (201.2 ▸

Bighorn Highway 40 Log (continued)

Washa Creek.

Y 84.1 (135.3 km) GP 122.9 (197.9 km) Carconte Creek.

Y 84.5 (136 km) GP 122.5 (197.2 km) Grande Cache Lake to south; picnic area, swimming, boat launch.

Y 85.3 (137.3 km) GP 121.7 (195.9 km) Allen Creek.

Y 86.7 (139.5 km) GP 120.3 (193.7 km) **Victor Lake** to south; canoeing and fishing.

Y 88.1 (141.7 km) GP 118.9 (191.5 km) Entering Grande Cache northbound. Visitor information centre to east.

Grande Cache

Y 88.2 (142 km) GP 118.8 (191.2 km) Located 116 miles/188 km south of Grande Prairie. **Population:** 3,842. **Emergency services:** RCMP, phone (403) 827-2222. **Hospital**, phone (403) 827-3701. **Ambulance**, phone (403) 827-3600. **Fire department**, phone (403) 827-3600. **Visitor information:** Tourist information centre is located on 100th Street (Highway 40) at the south entrance into town, open 8:30 A.M. to 9 P.M. July 1 through Labour Day.

Elevation: 4,200 feet/1,280m. **Private Aircraft:** Grande Cache airport, 12 miles/19 km east on Highway 40; elev. 4,117 feet/1,255m; length 5,000 feet/1,524m; asphalt; no fuel available.

Grande Cache was established in 1969 in conjunction with resource development by McIntyre Porcupine Coal Ltd. In 1980 a sawmill was constructed by British Columbia Forest Products Ltd. and in 1984 a medium security correctional centre was built.

Historically, the location was used as a staging area for fur trappers and Natives prior to their departure to trap lines in the valleys and mountain ranges now known as Willmore Provincial Park. Upon their return, they stored large caches of furs while waiting for transportation opportunities to trading posts.

Today Grande Cache, nestled on the leeward side of the Rocky Mountains, is a picturesque and vibrant community. Visitor facilities include 2 hotels, 4 motels, 2 banks, restaurants, laundromats, service stations with repair facilities, car washes and a library. Shopping facilities include several small shopping centres, 2 supermarkets, a bakery, sporting goods store and department store.

Recreational facilities include a recreation centre which houses a curling rink, swimming pool, skating rink, fitness rooms and saunas. Grande Cache Golf and Country Club, located in the northeast part of town, has 9 holes, grass greens, club house, pro shop, food and beverages, and banquet facilities.

Camping at Marv Moore municipal campground on the south side of the highway, at the north end of town just past the golf course. There are 55 sites, all hookups, showers, flush toilets, public phone, children's playground. Camping fee from $8. ▲

Big Horn Highway Log

(continued)

Y 88.7 (142.7 km) GP 118.3 (190.5 km) Highway 40 descends northbound to the Smoky River.

Y 91.3 (146.9 km) GP 115.7 (186.3 km) Blue Bridge provincial campground to south has 22 sites, sewer hookups, no water, shelters, firewood, firepits, tables, pit toilets, boat launch. Camping fee $7.50. Trail access to Willmore Wilderness Park. ▲

Y 91.5 (147.2 km) GP 115.5 (186 km) **Smoky River** bridge, fishing for arctic grayling, Dolly Varden and whitefish. ◄

Y 92.3 (148.6 km) GP 114.7 (184.6 km) Turnoff to south for Willmore Wilderness Park and Hell's Gate campground (4 miles/6.4 km south) with 10 sites, sewer hookups, horse holding areas, camping fee $5.50. ▲

Y 95.1 (153.4 km) GP 111.7 (179.8 km) Grande Cache gun range to east. Northbound, the highway parallels the Northern Alberta Resource Railroad and the Smoky River.

Y 100.8 (162.2 km) GP 106.2 (171 km) Turnout to east overlooks Smoky River Coal Ltd. and H.R. Milner Generating Station.

Y 104.8 (168.7 km) GP 102.2 (164.5 km) Entering Grande Prairie Forest northbound, entering Edson Forest southbound.

Y 106.7 (171.7 km) GP 100.3 (161.5 km) Turnoff to east for Sheep Creek day-use area; shaded picnic tables, water pump, firepits, firewood, litter barrels, outhouses and gravel parking areas. Boat launch on the Smoky River.

Y 107.1 (172.4 km) GP 99.9 (160.8 km) Sheep Creek. Sheep Creek campground to east; 9 sites, sewer hookups, water pump, camping fee $5.50. ▲

Y 108.4 (174.5 km) GP 98.6 (158.7 km) Entering Game Country Tourist Zone northbound, Evergreen Tourist Zone southbound.

Y 110.1 (177.2 km) GP 96.9 (156 km) Wayandie Road. Highway ascends steep hill northbound, some sections of 7 percent grade.

Y 115.9 (186.5 km) GP 91.1 (146.7 km) Small turnout to east.

Y 125.1 (201.3 km) GP 81.9 (131.9 km) Southview recreation area to east; gravel parking area, shaded picnic tables, litter barrels, outhouses, highbush cranberries in season.

Y 128.5 (206.8 km) GP 78.5 (126.4 km) *CAUTION: logging trucks next 36 miles/60 km northbound.*

Y 130.4 (209.8 km) GP 76.6 (123.4 km) 16th base line sign marks north–south hunting boundary.

Y 142 (228.6 km) GP 65 (104.6 km) Distance marker indicates Grande Prairie 62 miles/100 km.

Y 145.6 (234.3 km) GP 61.4 (98.9 km) Kakwa River bridge.

Y 145.9 (234.8 km) GP 61.1 (98.4 km) Turnoff for **Kakwa River** campground and day-use area; 14 sites, sewer hookups, picnic tables, firewood, firepits, water pump, litter barrels, outhouses, gravel parking area. Camping fee $5.50. Fishing for arctic grayling. ◄▲

Y 155.2 (249.7 km) GP 51.8 (83.5 km) Side road to west leads 7 miles/11 km to Unocal oil field office.

Y 159.1 (256.1 km) GP 47.9 (77.1 km) Access road to east leads 3.6 miles/6 km to **Musreau Lake** campground and day-use area. There are 50 picnic sites, 69 campsites, sewer hookups, picnic tables, firewood, firepits, waterpump, litter barrels, outhouses, equestrian trails, boat launch and fishing. ◄▲

Y 161.8 (260.4 km) GP 45.2 (72.8 km) Sheep Creek.

Y 164.3 (264.4 km) GP 42.7 (68.8 km) Cutbank River bridge. River access at north end of bridge. Historic sites and museum sign.

Y 165.6 (266.5 km) GP 41.4 (66.7 km) Elk Creek.

Y 165.8 (266.8 km) GP 41.2 (66.4 km) *CAUTION: Logging trucks next 36 miles/60 km southbound.*

Y 172.2 (277.1 km) GP 34.8 (56.1 km) Distance marker indicates Grande Prairie 31 miles/50 km.

Y 179.5 (288.9 km) GP 27.5 (44.3 km) Canfor Road leads east to Gold Creek Gas Plant and Highway 734.

Y 180.9 (291.1 km) GP 26.1 (42.1 km) Big Mountain Creek.

Y 182.8 (294.1 km) GP 24.2 (39.1 km) Bald Mountain Creek.

Y 189.4 (304.5 km) GP 17.6 (28.5 km) Access road leads west 0.1 mile/0.2 km to picnic area and 7 miles/11 km to Grovedale.

Y 191.1 (307.5 km) GP 15.9 (25.7 km) Bent Pipe Creek.

Y 199.7 (321.3 km) GP 7.3 (11.8 km) **Junction** with Highway 666 which leads southwest to O'Brien Provincial Park and day-use area; water pump, firewood, playground, hiking trails. Also access to Nitehawk ski resort, which has a 460-foot/140-m rise, 3 runs, ski lifts and food service. Highway 666 continues from this junction 5 miles/8 km to Grovedale. ▲

Y 199.8 (321.5 km) GP 7.2 (11.6 km) Wapiti River bridge.

Y 200.1 (322 km) GP 6.9 (11.1 km) Entering Grovedale ranger district southbound.

Y 201.6 (324.4 km) GP 5.4 (8.7 km) Access road leads east 15 miles/25 km to the Dunes golf and winter club; 18 holes, grass greens, driving range, pro shop.

Y 207 (333.2 km) GP 0 **Junction** of Highways 40 and 2 at Grande Prairie.

Return to Milepost E 284 East Access Route

(Continued from page 37)

Area attractions include Muskoseepi Park, which follows the Bear Creek corridor. The park includes 9 miles/15 km of paved walking and biking trails, a bird sanctuary at Crystal Lake, picnic areas, swimming pool, lawn bowling, mini-golf, a stocked pool, playground and canoe, paddleboat and bike rentals. Visitor services are available in the Pavilion. Nearby is the Grande Prairie Museum & Pioneer Village and the Regional College, a unique circular facility designed by Douglas Cardinal. Several of the downtown buildings have murals by local artists.

Weyerhaeuser offers tours of their pulp mill and sawmill in summer; phone (403) 539-8213 for details.

The area has prime hunting for both migratory birds and big game. Area lakes are the nesting sites of the trumpeter swan. Hiking, camping and fishing are popular outdoor activities.

Annual events include the Stompede the first weekend in June, several smaller rodeos, Canada Games, Highland games, pari-mutuel racing during July, the County Fair, Heritage Day and the Dinosaur Festival. Contact the visitor information center for more information.

Two campsites within the city limits offer showers and full hookups. Rotary Park public campground is located off the Highway 2 Bypass at the northwest edge of town near the college. Bear Creek Campground is located at the south end on 100 Avenue. ▲

Grande Prairie Museum. Dinosaurs once roamed the Grande Prairie area long before aboriginal tribes arrived some 8,000 years ago. Explorers, trappers and fur traders came, to be followed by missionaries and pioneer families. Grande Prairie Museum presents these fascinating stories and much, much more. Check the Internet or phone (403) 532-5482. [ADVERTISEMENT]

Wee Links Golf & Campground. Campground, Pitch & Putt Golf Course (grass greens) and driving range at a secluded setting within Grande Prairie city limits. Clean washrooms, hot coin showers, pay phone, water and power at sites, firepits, snacks, hiking/biking trails. 68 Avenue and 100 Street. VISA and MasterCard. Reservations (403) 538-4501. [ADVERTISEMENT] ▲

East Access Route Log
(continued)
HIGHWAY 2 WEST
E 298 (479.6 km) DC 69 (111 km) Saskatoon Island Provincial Park is 1.9 miles/3 km north on park road; 96 campsites, dump station, boat launch, swimming, playground; Saskatoon berry picking in July; game preserve for trumpeter swans.

E 299 (481.2 km) DC 68 (109.4 km) WEMBLEY (pop. 1,424) has a hotel (banking service and liquor store at hotel), post office, 2 grocery stores, gas stop, car wash and restaurants. Picnicking and camping at Sunset Lake Park in town. Camping May 1 to Oct. 15 at Pipestone Creek County Park, 9 miles/14.5 km south; 99 sites, showers, flush toilets, dump station, boat launch, firewood, fishing, playground, fossil display and an 18-hole golf course with grass greens nearby. ◆▲

Beaverlodge

E 311 (500.5 km) DC 56 (90.1 km) **Population:** 1,808. **Elevation:** 2,419 feet/737m. **Emergency Services:** RCMP, phone 911. **Ambulance,** phone 911. **Hospital,** Beaverlodge Municipal Hospital, phone (403) 354-2136.

Visitor Information: Located in the restored Lower Beaver Lodge School at Pioneer Campsite on the north side of Highway 2 at the west end of town.

Private Aircraft: DeWit Airpark 2 miles/3.2 km south; elev. 2,289 feet/1,698m; length 3,000 feet/914m; paved; no fuel.

Beaverlodge is a service centre for the area with a provincial courthouse, RCMP, hospital, medical and dental clinic. There are 9 churches, schools, a swimming pool and tennis courts.

Visitor services include 3 motels, 8 restaurants and gas stations. There are supermarkets, banks, a drugstore, car wash and sporting goods store. Beaverlodge Area Cultural Centre, at the south end of town, features local arts and crafts as well as a tea room. South Peace Centennial Museum is west of town (see **Milepost E 312**). Camping is available at the municipal Pioneer Campsite (19 sites, showers, dump station, electrical hookups, tourist information). The Beaverlodge Airpark, 2 miles/3.2 km south of town, is becoming a popular stopover on the flying route to Alaska. ▲

Beaverlodge is the gateway to Monkman Pass and Kinuseo Falls. Beaverlodge is also home to Canada's most northerly Agricultural Research Station (open to the public), and serves as regional centre for grain trans-

Walking trails in Muskoseepi Park near the Grande Prairie Museum. (Earl L. Brown, staff)

portation, seed cleaning and seed production. Cereal grains, such as wheat, barley and oats, are the main crops in the area. The PRT Alberta Inc. reforestation nursery here, visible from the highway as you enter town, grows about 8 million seedlings a year. Tours are available; phone (403) 354-2288.

Town of Beaverlodge. See display ad this section.

East Access Route Log
(continued)

E 312 (502.1 km) **DC 55** (88.5 km) South Peace Centennial Museum to east, open daily in summer; phone (403) 354-8869. Well worth a stop, the museum features vintage vehicles and working steam-powered farm equipment from the early 1900s. Open 10 A.M. to 8 P.M., mid-May through mid-October. The annual Pioneer Day celebration, held here the third Sunday in July, attracts several thousand visitors.

E 312.4 (502.7 km) **DC 54.6** (87.9 km) Turnoff for Driftwood Ranch Wildlife Haven, 14.3 miles/23 km west, a private collection of exotic and endangered animals. Opens May 1 for season; phone (403) 356-3769 for more information.

E 314.3 (505.8 km) **DC 52.6** (84.8 km) Golf course. This joint project of Hythe and Beaverlodge residents has a clubhouse that was once an NAR station. The 9-hole par 35 course has grass greens. Visitors are welcome; rentals available.

E 320 (515 km) **DC 47** (75.6 km) **HYTHE** (pop. 681) is an agricultural service community and processing center for fruit and berry crops, especially saskatoon berries. Canola is also a major crop. The town has a motel, a bed and breakfast, restaurant, laundromat, gas station, tire repair, car wash, outdoor covered heated swimming pool, complete shopping facilities and a hospital. Municipal campground in town with 17 sites, showers, dump station and playground. The information centre is housed in the Tags Food and Gas store. Inquire locally for directions to Riverside Bison Ranch. An old 1910 tack shop, staffed by volunteers in summer, is located between the highway and railroad tracks. ▲

E 329 (529.4 km) **DC 38** (61.1 km) Junction with Highway 59 east to Sexsmith.

E 337 (542.3 km) **DC 30** (48.3 km) **DEMMITT,** an older settlement, site of a sawmill (worth a visit), postal service, cafe and gas.

E 340 (547.2 km) **DC 27** (43.4 km) Railway crossing.

E 341 (548.8 km) **DC 26** (41.8 km) Public campground to east; 15 sites, shelter, firewood, tables, pit toilets, pump water and playground. ▲

E 341.3 (549.2 km) **DC 25.7** (41.3 km) Vehicle inspection station to west.

E 342 (550.4 km) **DC 25** (40.2 km) Gas, diesel and convenience store.

E 343.3 (552.5 km) **DC 23.7** (38.1 km) Alberta–British Columbia border. Turnout with litter barrels and pay phone.

TIME ZONE CHANGE: Alberta is on Mountain time; most of British Columbia is on Pacific time.

E 345.1 (555.4 km) **DC 21.9** (35.2 km) **Junction** with Heritage Highway 52 (gravel surface) which leads 18.5 miles/30 km south to **One Island Lake** Provincial Park (30 campsites, fee charged, rainbow and brook trout fishing) and 92 miles/148 km southwest from Highway 2 to Tumbler Ridge townsite, built in conjunction with the North East Coal development. Monkman Provincial Park, site of spectacular Kinuseo Falls, lies south of Tumbler Ridge. A campground with viewing platform of falls is accessible via a 25-mile/40-km road from Tumbler Ridge. Heritage Highway loops north 59.5 miles/96 km from Tumbler Ridge to join Highway 97 just west of Dawson Creek (see **Milepost PG 237.7** in the WEST ACCESS ROUTE section).

E 345.7 (556.3 km) **DC 21.3** (34.3 km) Tupper Creek bridge.

E 347 (558.5 km) **DC 20** (32.1 km) Swan Lake Provincial Park, with 41 campsites, picnic area, playground and boat launch, is 1.2 miles/2 km north of the tiny hamlet of **TUPPER,** which has a general store. ▲

E 347.9 (559.9 km) **DC 19.1** (30.7 km) Sudeten Provincial Park day-use area; 8 picnic tables. Plaque tells of immigration to this valley of displaced residents of Sudetenland in 1938–39.

E 348.9 (561.5 km) **DC 18.1** (29.1 km) Tate Creek bridge.

E 349.7 (562.7 km) **DC 17.3** (27.8 km) Side road west to community of Tomslake.

E 356.3 (573.4 km) **DC 10.7** (17.2 km) Turnout to east with litter barrel.

E 358 (576.1 km) **DC 9** (14.5 km) Historic sign tells of Pouce Coupe Prairie.

E 359.4 (578.4 km) **DC 7.6** (12.2 km) Railway crossing.

E 360 (579.3 km) **DC 7** (11.2 km) Weigh scales to east.

E 360.4 (580 km) **DC 6.6** (10.6 km) Bissett Creek bridge. Regional park located at south end of bridge.

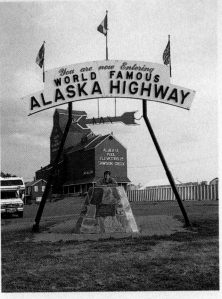

Alaska Highway cairn is a favorite photo stop on the way into Dawson Creek. (© Chris Sharp)

E 361 (581 km) **DC 6** (9.6 km) **POUCE COUPE** (pop. 832; elev. 2,118 feet/646m). **Visitor Information:** Tourist Bureau Office located in Pouce Coupe Museum, 5006 49th Ave. (1 block south of Highway 2). Open 8 A.M. to 5 P.M., May 15 to Sept. 15. Phone (403) 786-5555.

The Pouce Coupe area was first settled in 1898 by a French Canadian, who set up a trading post in 1908. The Edson Trail, completed in 1911, brought in the main influx of settlers from Edmonton in 1912. Historical artifacts are displayed at the Pouce Coupe Museum, located in the old NAR railroad station.

The village has a motel, hotel, restaurant, post office, gas station, dump station, car wash and food store. Camping at Regional Park, open May to September; hookups. ▲

The Pouce Coupe Museum. See display ad this section.

E 364.5 (586.6 km) **DC 2.5** (4 km) Dawson Creek airport.

E 367 (590.6 km) **DC 0 DAWSON CREEK,** the beginning of the Alaska Highway. For details turn to the ALASKA HIGHWAY section.

Alaska Highway via
WEST ACCESS ROUTE

Connects: Seattle, WA, to Dawson Creek, BC   **Length:** 817 miles
Road Surface: Paved   **Season:** Open all year
Highest Summit: Pine Pass 3,068 feet
Major Attractions: Fraser River Canyon/Hell's Gate, Barkerville

(See maps, pages 42–43)

	Cache Creek	Dawson Creek	Prince George	Seattle
Cache Creek		527	277	290
Dawson Creek	527		250	817
Prince George	277	250		567
Seattle	290	817	567	

Early morning light colours the fertile Fraser River valley near Chilliwack. (© David Creith/Sahtu)

The West Access Route links Interstate 5, Trans-Canada Highway 1 and BC Highway 97 to form the most direct route to Dawson Creek, BC, for West Coast motorists. This has been the major western route to the start of the Alaska Highway since 1952, when the John Hart Highway connecting Prince George and Dawson Creek was completed.

The West Access Route junctions with Yellowhead Highway 16 at Prince George. This east–west highway connects with the Alaska State Ferry System and BC Ferries at Prince Rupert, and with the East Access Route to the Alaska Highway at Edmonton. Turn to the YELLOWHEAD HIGHWAY 16 section for a complete log of that route.

INTERSTATE HIGHWAY 5
The West Access Route begins in the city of **SEATTLE, WA** (pop. 493,846), the Alaska gateway city since the Klondike Gold Rush days, when it became the major staging and departure point for most of the gold seekers. Seattle was also southern terminus of the Alaska Marine Highway System until 1989, when the Alaska state ferries moved to the Fairhaven Terminal at Bellingham, WA (I-5, Exit 250). Seattle–Tacoma International Air-port is the departure point for jet flights to Alaska. The air terminal is located 10 miles/16 km south of city center via Inter-state 5 (Exit 154).

Like most interstate routes in the United States, I-5 has physical mileposts along its route and corresponding numbered exits. Exit numbers and physical mileposts reflect distance from Mile 0 at the OR–WA border. I-5 in Oregon and Washington is logged in *Northwest Mileposts®*, available from Vernon Publications Inc.; phone 1-800-726-4707.

From Seattle, drive 92 miles north on I-5 to Bellingham and turn off onto Highway 539 north (Exit 256), which goes north 12 miles to Highway 546, which will take you another 13 miles to Highway 9 and Sumas, WA, at the U.S.–Canada border (customs open 24 hours a day). Then follow BC High-way 11 a short distance north from the Huntingdon, BC, border crossing to Abbots-ford. This route is a scenic drive through rural Whatcom County via 2-lane highways. *The MILEPOST®* log begins on Trans-Canada Highway 1 near Abbotsford.

Travelers may also continue on I-5 to the international border at Blaine (22 miles/ 35.4 km beyond Exit 256), the more direct route if you are bound for Vancouver, BC.

From Seattle to Abbotsford via Sumas it is 120 miles. From Abbotsford to Cache Creek, it is 170 miles; from Cache Creek to Prince George, 277 miles; and from Prince George to Dawson Creek it is 250 miles.

West Access Route Log

TRANS-CANADA HIGHWAY 1
The West Access Route log is divided into 3 sections: Abbotsford to Cache Creek; Cache Creek to Prince George; and Prince George to Dawson Creek.
This section of the log shows distance from Abbotsford (A) followed by dis-tance from Cache Creek (CC).

A 0 CC 170 (273.6 km) Exit 92. **Junction** of Trans-Canada Highway 1 and Highway 11 south to the international border crossing at Sumas–Huntingdon. Highway 11 north to **ABBOTSFORD** (pop. 60,400), all visitor ser-vices. Abbotsford is the "Raspberry Capital of Canada" and is the home of the Abbots-ford International Airshow in August.

Highway 11 north crosses the bridge over the Fraser River to Mission, and connects with Highway 7 to Harrison Hot Springs. This 2-lane highway traverses the rural farm-land on the north side of the Fraser River, rejoining Trans-Canada Highway 1 at Hope (see HIGHWAY 7 log on page 44).

A 1.9 (3 km) **CC 168.1** (270.5 km) Exit 95 to Whatcom Road and westbound exit to Sumas River rest area. Access to Sumas Mountain Provincial Park; hiking.

A 5.3 (8.5 km) **CC 164.7** (265.1 km) Exit 99 to Sumas River rest area (eastbound only); tables, toilet, pay phones.

A 8.8 (14.2 km) **CC 161.2** (259.4 km) Exit 104 to small farming community of Yarrow and road to Cultus Lake. The Lower Fraser Valley is prime agricultural land.

CAUTION: Watch for farm vehicles crossing freeway.

A 15 (24.1 km) **CC 155** (249.4 km) Exit 116 to Lickman Road; access south to Visitor Inforcentre, open daily in summer, and Cot-tonwood Meadows RV park. Chilliwack Antique Powerland museum located behind the infocentre. ▲

WEST ACCESS ROUTE Seattle, WA, to Lac La Hache, BC

(map continues next page)

Scale

| 0 | | 20 | Miles |
| 0 | 20 | | Kilometres |

Key to mileage boxes

miles/kilometres
miles/kilometres
from:

A- Abbotsford
CC- Cache Creek
PG- Prince George

Map Location

Principal Route

Paved ▬▬▬ Unpaved ▬ ▬ ▬

Other Roads

Paved ▬▬▬ Unpaved ▬ ▬ ▬

Ferry Routes •••••• **Hiking Trails** ┄┄┄

❋ Refer to Log for Visitor Facilities

? Visitor Information ☒ Fishing

▲ Campground ✈ Airport ✈ Airstrip

Key to Advertiser Services
C -Camping
D -Dump Station
d -Diesel
G -Gas (reg., unld.)
I -Ice
L -Lodging
M-Meals
P -Propane
R -Car Repair (major)
r -Car Repair (minor)
S -Store (grocery)
T -Telephone (pay)

PG-189/304km
CC-88/142km

● Lac La Hache

CC-85/136.8km Big Country KOA CDILST
CC-78.2/125.8km 108 Resort

❋ 100 Mile House

Cariboo Highway

70 Mile House

CC-25.5/41km Gold Trail RV Park CDT
Parkies Clothing
and Variety Store
Pioneer Service &
Towing Rr
Round-Up Motel L

Clinton

Cariboo Wagon Road

Pavilion Lake

Lillooet

CC-19.9/32km Lakeview Campsite & RV Park CD

CC-7/11.3km Hat Creek Ranch
CC-2.5/4km Cache Creek Campground CDIMST
CC-1.2/2km Horsting's Farm Market

❋ Cache Creek

Ashcroft

PG-277/446km
CC-0
A-170/274km

A-164.3/264.4km
Ashcroft Manor &
Tea House

Logan Lake

A-141.2/227.2km Acacia Grove CL
Log Cabin Pub M
The Steel Head Inn
A-139.1/223.9km Number One Fruit Stand
A-137/220.5km Big Horn, B.C. CGIMrT

Spences Bridge

Lytton

A-117.8/189.6km
Lytton Chamber
of Commerce
Totem Motel

A-101/162.5km
Blue Lake Resort CDLM

North Bend
Boston Bar

A-94/151.3km
Canyon Alpine RV Park &
Campground C

A-88/141.6km Anderson Creek Campground CD

Hell's Gate

A-83.6/134.5km Hell's Gate Airtram

Yale

A-72.1/116km Colonial Inn CLT

A-47/75.6km Wild Rose Good Sampark CDIST
A-17/27.4km Comfort Inn Ricky's Restaurant
A-15/24.1km Cottonwood Meadows RV Country Club C

Harrison Hot Springs

Coquihalla Highway

CC-120/193km
A-50/80km

Princeton

To Osoyoos

Vancouver

⑦

Mission

Abbotsford

Chilliwack

Hope

A-26.5/42.5km
Bridal Falls Camperland
Minter Gardens M

PG-447/719km
CC-170/274km
A-0

Alaska State Ferry
(see MARINE ACCESS
ROUTES section)

Vancouver Island

⑨⑨

Blaine

⑤⑥⑤

Sumas

Ferndale

⑤③⑨

Bellingham

Manning Provincial Park

BRITISH COLUMBIA

CANADA
UNITED STATES

WASHINGTON

▲ Mount Baker
10,778 ft./3,285m

Victoria

To Okanogan

Mount Vernon

North Cascades Highway

②⓪

CASCADE MOUNTAINS

⑤

Everett

②

To Wenatchee

Seattle

To Ellensburg

⑤ ⑨⓪

COAST MOUNTAINS

Garibaldi Provincial Park

Golden Ears Provincial Park

Strait of Georgia

Strait of Juan de Fuca

Puget Sound

LILLOOET

RANGE

Fraser River

Lillooet Lake

Lillooet River

Harrison Lake

Thompson River

Nicola R.

Wells Gray Provincial Park

Thompson River

To Tete Juane Cache

Lac La Hache

Canim Lake

Mahood Lake

Horse Lake

Bridge Lake

②④

Little Fort

⑤

Green Lake

Bonaparte R.

Bonaparte Lake

⑨⑦

Loon Lake

①②

Kamloops Lake

Kamloops

South Thompson River

To Salmon Arm

To Osoyoos

⑤ ⑤A

Coquihalla Highway

Merritt

⑤

⑧

N

W   E

S

③

WEST ACCESS ROUTE *Lac La Hache, BC, to Dawson Creek, BC*

To Wonowon
(see ALASKA HIGHWAY section)

BRITISH COLUMBIA | ALBERTA

Williston Lake 🎣

Peace River

Hudson's Hope Loop Road
(see HUDSON'S HOPE LOOP section)

Fort St. John

29

River

97

Hudson's Hope

Boucher L.

DC-0
PG-250/402km
CC-527/848km

DC-62/100km
PG-188/302km

Big Lake

Moberly L.

Dawson Creek ❄?⛺✛

49 → **To RYCROFT**

East Pine

❄⛺ Chetwynd

Groundbirch

J-0

2

PG-144.3/232.2km Silver Sands
Lodge CGLMrS

Pine River

PG-183.7/295.6km Wildmare
Grove Campsite CDT

29

Heritage Highway

97 LeMoray

Azouzetta L.

🎣⛺✛ **Mackenzie**

Pine Pass
3,068 ft./935m

Murray R.

To GRANDE PRAIRIE
(see EAST ACCESS ROUTE section)

J-18/29km Alexander Mackenzie Hotel and Mall LM
District of Mackenzie CDdGILMPRrST

39

Bullmoose Creek

J-55.9/90km
District of
Tumbler
Ridge

DC-155/249km
PG-95/153km

Pack River

Misinchinka River
PG-95.2/153.2km
Mackenzie Junction
Cafe CDdGILMPST

⛺ **Tumbler Ridge**

Tudyah Lake 🎣⛺

McLeod R.

McLeod Lake
Fort McLeod
PG-71.8/115.5km Whiskers
Bay Resort CILM

J-56/90km

McLeod's Lake

⛺ **Bear Lake**

PG-44.8/72.1km Grizzly Inn
Restaurant, Motel
& RV Park CDdGILMST

Carp Lake 🎣

Crooked River

Tacheeda Lakes

Parsnip R.

ROCKY MOUNTAINS

Map Location

Scale
0 ____ 20 Miles
0 ____ 20 Kilometres

Key to mileage boxes
miles/kilometres
miles/kilometres from:
CC- Cache Creek
PG- Prince George
DC- Dawson Creek
J- Junction

Davie Lake ⛺

John Hart Highway

Salmon River

🎣 *Summit L.*

97

N
W ✦ E
S

PG-26.9/43.3km Historic Huble Homestead

DC-250/402km
PG-0
CC-277/446km

PG-14.7/23.6km Salmon Valley Resort CDST

PG-6.4/10.3km Hartway RV Park CDIT

PG-1.5/2.4km Hart Highway Mohawk DdGIMPST
McQuik Lube & Oil dGIMPS

To Prince Rupert
(see YELLOWHEAD
HIGHWAY 16 section)

❄?⛺
🎣✛ **Prince George**

16

Nechako River

Tabor L.

16

Cluculz L.

Bednesti L.

Purden Lake

Principal Route
Paved / Unpaved
Other Roads
Paved / Unpaved
Ferry Routes / **Hiking Trails**

❄ Refer to Log for Visitor Facilities
? Visitor Information   🎣 Fishing
⛺ Campground   ✛ Airport ✛ Airstrip

Key to Advertiser Services
C -Camping
D -Dump Station
d -Diesel
G -Gas (reg., unld.)
I -Ice
L -Lodging
M -Meals
P -Propane
R -Car Repair (major)
r -Car Repair (minor)
S -Store (grocery)
T -Telephone (pay)

CC-274/440.9km Sintich Trailer Park CDT
CC-273/439.3km Southpark RV Park

Fraser River

To Tete Jaune Cache
(see YELLOWHEAD HIGHWAY 16 section)

BRITISH COLUMBIA
ALBERTA

CC-268.3/431.8km Bee Lazee RV Park CDIST

CC-264.9/426.5km Prince George Fallow Deer Farm

CC-258.3/415.7km Great Canadian Park C

97

CARIBOO MOUNTAINS

COLUMBIA MOUNTAINS

⛺ **Hixon**

CC-241/387.8km Canyon Creek Campground CD
Hixon Fireplace Inn M

J-50/80.5km Becker's Lodge Ltd. CLM

Cariboo Highway

J-46.7/75.2km The
Wells Hotel

Bowron Lake

Fraser River

⛺

J-16.7/26.9km
Cottonwood
Historic Site

Wells

⛺ **Bowron Lake
Provincial Park**

⛺ **Cottonwood**

26

Barkerville ❄

*Cottonwood
Dragon L.*

*R. Jack of
Clubs Lake*

J-51/82km

Glaciated Area

PG-74/119km
CC-203/327km
J-0

❄?🎣 **Quesnel**

CC-197.5/317.8km
Valhalla Motel &
Family Restaurant LM

CC-196/315.4km Robert's
Roost Campsite CDIT

CC-194.7/313.3km
A Little Bit Country

CC-193.2/310.9km Mary's Gifts

Quesnel R.

🎣 **Likely**

🎣 *Quesnel
Lake*

**Wells Gray
Provincial Park**

CC-179.9/289.6km Cariboo Place Campsite CDIT

Fraser River

**McLeese
Lake**

⛺ 🎣

CC-166/267km The Castle
CC-164/263.9km Cariboo Wood Shop

McLeese L.

⛺ 🎣 *Horsefly
Lake*

Horsefly

FRASER PLATEAU

⛺ **Soda Creek**

CC-136.4/219.5km
Wildwood RV Park C

Hendrix Lake

CC-141.8/228.2km Whispering Willows
Outpost Campground and Store CDS

PG-149/240km
CC-128/206km

❄? **Williams Lake**

⛺ **150 Mile House**

CC-96/154.5km Crystal Springs Campsite (Historical) Resort Ltd. CDILST
CC-93.4/150.3km Kokanee Bay Motel and Campground CDILST
CC-93.3/150.1km Clancys' dGMP
CC-92/148.1km Fir Crest Resort CDILEST

To Bella Coola ← **20**

Williams Lake

97

Eagle Creek

⛺ **Lac La Hache**

Canim L.

Mahood L.

PG-189/304km
CC-88/142km

⛺ 🎣 *Lac La Hache*

(map continues previous page)

INTERIOR PLATEAU

Highway 7 Log

An older route than Trans-Canada Highway 1, Highway 7 connects Vancouver and Hope via the north bank of the Fraser River. This log follows Highway 11 to its junction with Highway 7 at Mission, then Highway 7 to Hope via Harrison Hot Springs. This route is a scenic—and slower—alternative to Trans-Canada Highway 1.

Distance is measured from junction (J) of Trans-Canada Highway 1 and Highway 11 at Abbotsford.

J 0 Junction of Highways 1 and 11 at Abbotsford (Exit 92). Follow signs for Highway 11 North. This is a 2-lane road, with passing lanes, through a scenic valley of agricultural lands.

J 5.5 (8.9 km) Matsqui Trail Regional Park; 6 miles/10 km of Fraser River dikes for walking.

J 6.8 (10.9 km) Fraser River bridge.

J 7.4 (11.9 km) Exit to **MISSION** (pop. 31,000), named for a Roman Catholic mission built in 1861. Facilities include 2 motels, bed and breakfasts, restaurants and gas stations. The major attraction here is the Westminster Abbey, a Benedictine seminary completed in 1982 and known for its view and stained glass. The ruins of the original mission and school are located in Fraser River Heritage Park.

Follow signs northeast to Highway 7.

J 8.5 (13.7 km) **Junction** with Highway 7; follow signs east for Agassiz and Harrison Hot Springs.

9.1 (14.7 km) Access to Fraser River Heritage Park, site of the ruins of St. Mary's Mission and Indian school, a day-use area with good views of the Fraser River valley and Mount Baker. Norma Kenney House on park grounds has a gift shop and food service.

J 9.4 (15.1 km) Visitor Infocentre; parking, restrooms.

J 10.9 (17.5 km) Turnoff for Nielson Regional Park and Hatzic Lake; picnic tables, swimming.

J 11 (17.7 km) Hatzic Rock, an important spiritual and habitation site for the people of the Stolo nation; open 8 A.M. to dusk.

J 11.1 (17.8 km) Hatzic Lake turnoff. Watch for fruit and vegetable stands in summer.

J 13 (20.9 km) Inch Creek Fish Hatchery turnoff.

J 13.2 (21.3 km) Dewdney; general store, post office and grocery.

J 13.4 (21.6 km) Nicomen Slough bridge.

J 20 (32.2 km) Deroche; general store and gas.

J 25.5 (41.1 km) Squaqum Park; picnicking.

J 25.7 (41.6 km) Harrison Bay ("Sasquatch country"); store, camping, gas.

J 26.5 (42.7 km) Harrison Mills (unincorporated).

J 27.4 (44.1 km) Morris Valley Road north to Hemlock Valley ski area and Chehalis River Hatchery.

J 27.7 (44.6 km) Gas station to north.

J 28 (45 km) Swing bridge over Harrison River.

J 29 (46.6 km) Kennedy Road. Turn south for Kilby General Store and Farm, a BC Heritage site, and Kilby Provincial Historic Park; picnicking and a fully stocked 1928 general store museum (open daily in summer).

J 31.9 (51.3 km) Brio Springs; stop for spring water.

J 32.4 (52.1 km) Stop-of-interest plaque about Fraser River Delta.

Begin 11 percent downgrade eastbound; 3 lanes.

J 35.2 (56.6 km) Gas station.

J 37.2 (59.8 km) **Junction** with Highway 9 south to Agassiz. Turnoff to north for **HARRISON HOT SPRINGS** (pop. 700), 4 miles/6.4 km. Known as the "Spa of Canada," this resort town on the shore of Harrison Lake has 2 hot mineral springs. Harrison public hot pool is open daily. Motels, restaurants and other services available. Boat tours of the lake depart from the Harrison Hotel. Beach, good windsurfing and other water sports. Camping, picnicking and hiking at Sasquatch Provincial Park north of town. ▲

There are several private campgrounds on Highway 7 north to Harrison Hot Springs.

J 44.6 (71.8 km) Turnout to south overlooking Fraser River valley.

J 46 (74 km) Johnson Slough. Rest area to north.

J 48.3 (77.7 km) Ruby Creek bridge.

J 55.7 (89.7 km) **Junction** with Trans-Canada Highway 1 north of Hope (see **Milepost A 51.5** this section).

**Return to Milepost A 0 or A 51.5
West Access Route**

Cottonwood Meadows RV Country Club. Exit 116. Highly rated and recommended by Good Sam, Woodalls, Tourism B.C. New, secure, clean, well-maintained, full service park. Easy access, electronic gates, well lit and well managed. Lazy stream, full hooks, cable TV, wide level sites, paved roadways. Nicest washrooms, laundromat, clubhouse, Jacuzzi, pay phone. Near U.S. border crossing, shopping centers, golf courses. Pets on leash only. Open end of March to early November. VISA, MasterCard. 44280 Luckakuck Way, Chilliwack, BC V2R 4A7. Telephone (604) 824-PARK (7275). ▲
[ADVERTISEMENT]

A 16.8 (27.1 km) **CC 153.2** (246.5 km) Highway 119B to Chilliwack Airport.

A 17 (27.4 km) **CC 153** (246.2 km) Exit 119 north to Chilliwack (all services, description follows) and south to Sardis (all services) and Cultus Lake Provincial Park.

Cultus Lake Provincial Park has 300 campsites; water, flush and pit toilets, showers, firewood, water, boat launch, swimming, fishing, canoeing, kayaking, and hiking and walking trails. Cultus Lake resort area also offers water slides, go-carts and other activities. ☛▲

CHILLIWACK (pop. 63,000) has motels, restaurants, shopping malls, banks, gas stations, RV parks and other services. There is a library, 2 movie theatres and an arts centre. The Canadian Military Engineers Museum is located off Vedder Road. Recreational attractions include golf and the popular Cultus Lake area with water park, boat rentals, horseback riding and camping. ▲

Comfort Inn. See display ad this section.

Ricky's Restaurant. See display ad this section.

A 18 (29 km) **CC 152** (244.6 km) Exit 123 Prest Road north to Rosedale, south to Ryder Lake.

A 23.2 (37.4 km) **CC 146.8** (236.2 km) Exit 129 for Annis Road and RV park. ▲

A 26.5 (42.5 km) **CC 143.5** (230.9 km) Exit 135 to Highway 9 east to Harrison Springs and alternate route Highway 7 to Hope and Vancouver (see HIGHWAY 7 log this section). Westbound exit for Bridal Veil Falls. Also exit here for access to Minter Gardens, which rivals Victoria's famous Butchart Gardens for beauty. The 27 acres of floral displays feature 11 themed gardens, topiary figures and a rare collection of Chinese Penjing Rock Bonsai. Opens 9 A.M. daily, April through October. Entertainment is scheduled Sundays and holidays, weather

---

permitting.

Exit north for Cheam Lake Wetlands Regional Park. Once mined for its marl deposits, Cheam Lake is now a wildlife habitat; interpretive trails, good bird watching.

Minter Gardens. See display ad this section.

Bridal Falls Camperland. If you are heading to Alaska using the western route, spending a day or two in the beautiful Bridal Falls area is a must. Camperland is a full-facility, 5-star RV resort featuring a huge heated pool, hot tubs, clubhouse, licensed restaurant and large sites (50-amp) that will accommodate the largest RVs. Within 1 mile are numerous tourist attractions, restaurants, museums, golf. Call (604) 794-7361, mention *The MILEPOST®* when reserving. Another campground owned by the same company is the Cedars RV Resort, in Ferndale, Washington, just minutes south of the U.S./Canadian border on Interstate 5. The Cedars is also a full-facility RV resort featuring a new Olympic-sized pool, lots of pull-throughs and easy access off I-5 just north of Bellingham. Call (360) 384-2622.
[ADVERTISEMENT] ▲

A **27.3** (43.9 km) CC **142.7** (229.6 km) Exit 138 to Popkum Road. Eastbound access to Bridal Veil Falls Provincial Park to south; picnicking, trail to base of falls. Also access to small community of Popkum and various roadside attractions, including water slide, Sandstone Gallery rock and gem museum, and prehistoric-themed amusement park. Food, gas and lodging.

A **34.5** (55.5 km) CC **135.5** (218.1 km) Exit 146 Herrling Island, a cottonwood tree farm (no access or services), visible from highway.

A **40.5** (65.2 km) CC **129.5** (208.4 km) Exit 153 to Laidlaw (no services) and access to Jones (Wahleach) Lake. Although F.H. Barber Provincial Park is noted here on BC provincial park maps, travelers should be aware that the park is totally undeveloped and has no access and no facilities.

A **42.5** (68.4 km) CC **127.5** (205.2 km) Truck weigh scales; public phone.

A **44.7** (71.9 km) CC **125.3** (201.6 km) Exit 160 to Hunter Creek rest area; tables,

toilet and pay phone. Hunter Creek Visitor Infocentre operates here daily, 9 A.M. to 5 P.M., mid-May to Labour Day weekend.

A **45.5** (73.2 km) CC **124.5** (200.4 km) Exit 165 to Flood/Hope Road. Access to RV parks and Hope airport. Vancouver Soaring Association is located at Hope Airport and offers glider rides on summer weekends; phone (604) 521-5501 for cost and schedule. Also access this exit to Silver Skagit Road (see **Milepost A 48.5**). ▲

A **47** (75.6 km) CC **123** (197.9 km) **Wild Rose Good Sampark**. On Highway 1 east (from Vancouver) 4.8 km (3 miles) west of Hope; take Flood–Hope Road exit 165. On Highway 1 west (from Hope) take Flood–Hope Road exit 168. Full hookups, 15–30 amps, tenting, level grassy sites in parklike setting, 60-foot pull-throughs, free cable TV, free hot showers, laundry, playground, clubroom, horseshoes, firepits, picnic tables, a limited store. Ice, wood, pay phone, sani-station, near restaurant. Senior citizen discount, weekly rates, MasterCard, VISA. Small pets. Cancellation policy—two days. Open April 1 to Oct. 1. Phone (604) 869-9842, fax 869-3171. Toll-free reservations in Canada and U.S.A. Phone 1-800-463-7999.
[ADVERTISEMENT] ▲

A **48.5** (78.1 km) CC **121.5** (195.5 km) Exit 168 to Silverhope Creek. Access to RV park. Also access to Silver Skagit Road which leads south 37 miles/60 km through the Skagit Valley past Silver Lake Provincial Park and Skagit Valley Provincial Park. ▲

A **48.7** (78.4 km) CC **121.3** (195.2 km) Silver Creek, Flood–Hope Road exit.

A **50** (80.5 km) CC **120** (193.1 km) **Junction** of Trans-Canada Highway 1, Highway 3

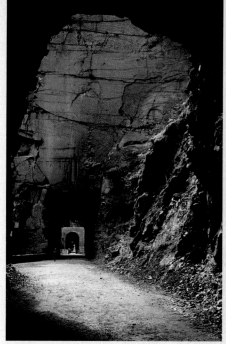

View through Othello Quintette Tunnels at Hope. (Liz Bryan)

(Crowsnest Highway) and Highway 5 (Coquihalla Highway). Use Exit 170 northbound for Trans-Canada Highway 1 to Hope.

Hope

A **50.2** (80.8 km) CC **119.8** (192.8 km) **Population**: 7,118. **Elevation**: 140 feet/43m. **Emergency Services**: RCMP, Fire Department, Ambulance, phone 911. **Hospital**, 1275 7th Ave., phone (604) 869-5656. **Visitor Information**: Visitor InfoCentre and museum building, corner of Hudson Bay Street and Water Avenue, on the right northbound as you enter town. Open daily 8 A.M. to 8 P.M. in July and August, 9 A.M. to 5 P.M. in May, June and September; weekdays only, 10 A.M. to 4 P.M., rest of the year.

Hope is on a bend of the Fraser River where it flows through a picturesque gap in the forested Coast Mountains near Mount Hope (elev. 6,000 feet/1,289m). It is a popular tourist stop with complete services. About 30 motels and resorts are in Hope or just outside town on Trans-Canada Highway 1 and on Highway 3. Other facilities include auto body shops, service stations, department stores, restaurants and grocery stores.

Hope is rapidly becoming known for its collection of locally crafted chain saw carvings. There are approximately 25 of these large wooden carvings throughout the downtown area. Ask at the Visitor InfoCentre for directions to see all the carvings.

The major attraction in the Hope area is the Coquihalla Canyon Provincial Recreation Area, the focus of which is the Othello Quintette Tunnels. The 5 rock tunnels which cut through the tortuous canyon were

part of the Kettle Valley Railway. This stretch of railway has been restored as a walking trail through the tunnels and across bridges. The tunnels are accessible from downtown Hope via Kawkawa Lake Road and Othello Road, about a 10-minute drive.

Other Hope attractions include the Rainbow Junction Community Art Centre, the Japanese Friendship Garden, miles of mountain biking and hiking trails, and many summer festivals.

The Coquihalla Highway, completed in 1987, connects Hope with the Trans-Canada Highway just west of Kamloops, a distance of 118 miles/190 km. This is a 4-lane divided highway; toll charged.

There are private campgrounds on all roads into town. The town campground on Kawkawa Lake Road has 31 RV sites, 81 tent sites, coin showers and sani-station. ▲

West Access Route Log
(continued)

A 50.7 (81.6 km) **CC 119.3** (191.9 km) Bridge over Fraser River. Turnout at north end, access to pedestrian bridge across the Fraser.

A 51.5 (82.8 km) **CC 118.5** (190.7 km) **Junction** with Highway 7, which leads west to Harrison Hot Springs and Vancouver. See side road log on page 44.

A 53.1 (85.5 km) **CC 116.9** (188.1 km) Rest area (westbound access only) with picnic tables to west by Lake of the Woods.

A 60.8 (97.8 km) **CC 109.2** (175.7 km) Easy-to-miss turnoff (watch for sign 400m before turn) for Emory Creek Provincial Park east of highway; 34 level gravel sites in trees, water, fire rings, picnic tables, firewood, flush and pit toilets, and litter barrels. Camping fee April to October. Hiking and walking trails. Gold panning and fishing in **Fraser River.** ◄▲

Very much in evidence between Hope and Cache Creek are the tracks of the Canadian National and Canadian Pacific railways. Construction of the CPR—Canada's first transcontinental railway—played a significant role in the history of the Fraser and Thompson river valleys. Begun in 1880, the CPR line between Kamloops and Port Moody was contracted to Andrew Onderdonk.

A 64.8 (104.3 km) **CC 105.2** (169.3 km) YALE (pop. 500; elev. 250 feet/76m). **Emergency Services: Police, Fire Department, Ambulance**, phone 911. **Visitor Information:** In the museum, phone (604) 863-2324. Visitor facilities include motels, stores, gas stations and restaurants.

Yale was the head of navigation for the Lower Fraser River and the beginning of the overland gold rush trail to British Columbia's goldfields. The Anglican Church of Saint John the Divine here was built for the miners in 1859 and is the oldest church still on its original foundation in mainland British Columbia. Next to the church is Yale Museum and a bronze plaque honouring Chinese construction workers who helped build the Canadian Pacific Railway. Walking around town, look for the several plaques relating Yale's history. Daily guided walking tours of historic Yale are offered in summer; fee charged, includes admission to museum and church. Phone (604) 863-2428 for more information.

A 65.6 (105.5 km) **CC 104.5** (168.2 km) Entering Fraser Canyon northbound. The Fraser River and canyon were named for Simon Fraser (1776–1862), the first white man to descend the river in 1808. This is the

Favorite spot for photos of Fraser River railway bridges is at Milepost A 113.6.
(Judy Parkin, staff)

dry forest region of British Columbia, and it can be a hot drive in summer. The scenic Fraser Canyon travelers drive through today was a formidable obstacle for railroad engineers in 1881.

A 66 (106.2 km) **CC 104** (167.4 km) Yale Tunnel, first of several northbound through the Fraser Canyon.

A 67.3 (108.3 km) **CC 102.7** (165.2 km) Turnout to east with plaque about the Cariboo Waggon Road, which connected Yale with the Cariboo goldfields near Barkerville. Built between 1861 and 1863 by the Royal Engineers, it replaced an earlier route to the goldfields—also called the Cariboo Waggon Road—which started from Lillooet.

A 68.4 (110.1 km) **CC 101.6** (163.5 km) Saddle Rock Tunnel. This 480-foot-/146-m-long tunnel was constructed from 1957–58.

A 72.1 (116 km) **CC 97.9** (157.5 km) **Colonial Inn.** In scenic Fraser Canyon. Cabin-style sleeping and kitchen units with showers and satellite TV. Pay phones. Picnic area with barbecues. Mountain views. Campground with full hookups and showers. For reservations call (604) 863-2277 or write RR #1, Yale, BC V0K 2S0. Stop and smell the flowers. [ADVERTISEMENT] ▲

A 72.3 (116.3 km) **CC 97.7** (157.2 km) Sailor Bar Tunnel, nearly 984 feet/300m long. There were dozens of bar claims along the Fraser River in the 1850s bearing colourful names such as Sailor Bar.

A 76.5 (123.1 km) **CC 93.5** (150.5 km) Spuzzum (unincorporated), gas station and food.

A 77.1 (124.1 km) **CC 92.9** (149.5 km) Stop of interest at south end of Alexandra Bridge, built in 1962, the second largest fixed arch span in the world at more than 1,640 feet/500m in length.

A 77.5 (124.8 km) **CC 92.5** (148.9 km) Alexandra Bridge Provincial Park, picnic areas and interpretive displays on both sides of highway. Hiking trail down to the old Alexandra Bridge, still intact. This suspension bridge was built in 1926, replacing the original built in 1863.

A 77.8 (125.2 km) **CC 92.2** (148.4 km) Historic Alexandra Lodge (closed), is the last surviving original roadhouse on the Cariboo Waggon Road.

A 79.5 (128 km) **CC 90.5** (145.6 km) Alexandra Tunnel.

A 80.5 (129.5 km) **CC 89.5** (144 km) Rest area by Copper Creek to east.

A 82.6 (133 km) **CC 87.4** (140.7 km) Hells Gate Tunnel (328 feet/100m long).

A 83.3 (134 km) **CC 86.7** (139.5 km) Ferrabee Tunnel (328 feet/100m long).

A 83.6 (134.5 km) **CC 86.4** (139 km) Hells Gate, the narrowest point on the Fraser River and a popular attraction. (Northbound traffic park at lot immediately south of attraction on east side of road; southbound traffic park on west side of road at attraction.) Two 25-passenger airtrams take visitors some 500 feet down across the river to a restaurant and shop complex. Footbridge across river to view fishways where some 2 million salmon pass through each year. A display details the life cycle of the salmon, the construction of the International Fishways and the history of Hells Gate. Trams operate daily, April through October. There is also a steep trail down to the fishways; strenuous hike.

Hells Gate was well named. It was by far the most difficult terrain for construction of both the highway and the railway. To haul supplies for the railway upstream of Hells Gate, Andrew Onderdonk built the stern-wheel steamer *Skuzzy*. The *Skuzzy* made its way upstream through Hells Gate in 1882, hauled by ropes attached to the canyon walls by bolts.

Hell's Gate Airtram. See display ad this section.

A 83.8 (134.9 km) **CC 86.2** (138.7 km) Hells Gate turnaround for travelers who miss the Hells Gate parking lot.

A 85.7 (137.9 km) **CC 84.3** (135.7 km) China Bar Tunnel, built in 1960. It is almost 2,300 feet/700m long, one of the longest tunnels in North America. Point of interest sign at south end about Simon Fraser.

A 88 (141.6 km) **CC 82** (132 km) **Anderson Creek Campground.** Quiet, secluded, some riverfront locations. Try fishing or view the rafters. Easy turn around at bottom of hill. Pull-throughs, shaded parking, washrooms and free hot showers. 30-amp service, sani-station, reasonable rates. In season, help yourself to fresh fruit off the old orchard trees. Phone (604) 867-9125. [ADVERTISEMENT] ▲

A 91 (146.5 km) **CC 79** (127.1 km) **BOSTON BAR** (pop. 885; elev. 400 feet/ 122m). **Emergency Services: Police, Fire Department, Ambulance,** phone 911. Services include gas stations, cafes, grocery stores, motels and private RV parks. Site of the J.S. Jones Timber Mill; tours may be available in summer, phone (604) 867-9214 for information. Boston Bar was the southern landing for the steamer *Skuzzy,* which plied the Fraser River between here and Lytton during construction of the CPR.

North Bend, located across the river from Boston Bar, is a former railway community with a picturesque old station and round-house. Old cable cage from the aerial car ferry that once served North Bend is on display at the CN station in Boston Bar

North Bend is the access point for the Nahutlatzin Valley. River rafting trips are available on the Nahutlatzin River.

Airtrams offer a dramatic view of the Fraser River at Hells Gate. (Courtesy of Hell's Gate Airtram)

A 94 (151.3 km) **CC 76** (122.3 km) **Canyon Alpine RV Park & Campground.** Still the best-kept secret in the Fraser Canyon, but quickly being discovered and described as "...one of the nicest parks on the Alaskan route." Secure RV parking and tenting 3 miles north of Boston Bar. 31 level, pull-through sites, fully serviced with 30 amp, water, sewer and cable TV. Easy access and turnarounds for rigs over 35 feet. 14-foot entrance gate clearance. Away from traffic noise and railroads. Clean washrooms. Hot showers. Shaded sites. Fire rings. Free firewood. 50 yards south of restaurant, store, laundromat and telephones. Pets on leash welcome. 10 minutes from world famous Hell's Gate Airtram. Open April 15 to Oct. 15. 50490 Trans-Canada Highway. Toll free 1-800-644-PARK. Your friendly hosts, Martha and Fred Jost. [ADVERTISEMENT] ▲

A 101 (162.5 km) **CC 69** (111 km) Turnoff for Blue Lake Lodge and Blue Lake Resort, 0.6 mile/1 km gravel road (first 0.3 mile/0.5 km steep and winding).

Blue Lake Resort. 1 km off highway on quiet, family oriented, private trout lake. Wooded RV/tent sites, power, water, some sewer, pull-throughs, pet area, sani-dump. Log lodge with accommodation. Non-smoking bedrooms. Continental breakfast included. Full-menu service, gourmet dinners. Licensed premises. Outdoor patio with hot tub. Service, pampering and serenity is our specialty. On the same property are rustic wilderness cabins (need bedding), kitchenettes, central washrooms, laundry, free showers. Swimming in crystal clear lake. Boat and canoe rentals. Hiking and trout fishing, abundant wildlife. Security gate closed 10 P.M.–7 A.M. Your hosts Hal and Karen Geddes. Phone (250) 867-9624 or fax (250) 867-9246. [ADVERTISEMENT] ▲

A 112.8 (181.5 km) **CC 57.2** (92.1 km) Viewpoint to west overlooking the Fraser River.

A 113.6 (182.9 km) **CC 56.4** (90.7 km) Canadian National and Canadian Pacific railways cross over the Fraser River here;

a favorite spot for photos. Gravel turnout to east.

A 114.6 (184.5 km) **CC 55.4** (89.2 km) Skupper rest area (northbound only); toilets, tables, litter barrels.

A 117.8 (189.6 km) **CC 52.2** (84 km) Junction with Highway 12 to Lillooet. Turn west here for community of Lytton (description follows).

LYTTON (pop. 400; elev. 561 feet/171m). **Emergency Services:** RCMP, phone (250) 455-2225. **Fire Department**, phone (250) 455-2333. **Ambulance**, phone 1 (250) 374-5937. **Hospital**, St. Bartholomew's, phone (250) 455-2221. **Visitor Information:** Visitor Infocentre, 400 Fraser St., phone (250) 455-2523. Located at the confluence of the Thompson and Fraser rivers, Lytton acts as headquarters for river raft trips. All visitor facilities are available. Sand bars at Lytton yielded much gold, and river frontage has been set aside for recreational gold panning. Lytton has recorded the highest temperature in British Columbia, 111°F/44°C.

Lytton. Rafting capital of British Columbia in the scenic Fraser Canyon. Public pool at Infocentre. Whitewater rafting on the Thompson River with raft rides through Hells Gate on the Fraser during August and September. Hike the Stein and Botannie valleys. Trail rides available. Enjoy Native and gold rush history in the Fraser Canyon and gold rush country. Natural attractions include the "Jelly Roll," a rare geological formation. Arrange for sawmill and woods tours. At the confluence of the Thompson and Fraser rivers. Pan for gold at water's edge. Visitor Infocentre at 400 Fraser St., phone (250) 455-2523. [ADVERTISEMENT]

Totem Motel. Old-fashioned charm and hospitality. 12 cottage-style units and 3 rooms in lodge. Air-conditioned. Kitchens, cable TV. Some queen-sized beds. Garden overlooking the Fraser River. Reasonable rates. Some nonsmoking rooms. Clean. No pets. Cor and Sylvia Vandenbos. Phone (250) 455-2321. Fax (250) 455-6696. P.O. Box 580, Lytton, BC V0K 1Z0. [ADVERTISEMENT]

A 121.2 (195.2 km) **CC 48.8** (78.4 km) Rafting centre. Watch for rafters in the river during the summer months.

A 122.8 (197.6 km) **CC 47.2** (76 km) Skihist Provincial Park to east; 58 campsites on east side of highway with water, flush and pit toilets, firewood and dump station. Picnic area on west side of highway (good place to watch the trains go by); wheelchair-accessible restrooms. &▲

A 134.7 (216.8 km) **CC 35.3** (56.8 km) Goldpan Provincial Park to west alongside river; 14 campsites, picnic area, water, firewood, canoeing, kayaking, fishing. ⬅▲

A 136 (218.9 km) **CC 34** (54.7 km) In summer, watch for fruit stands selling locally grown produce along the highway. Watch for bighorn sheep on the hillsides in the fall.

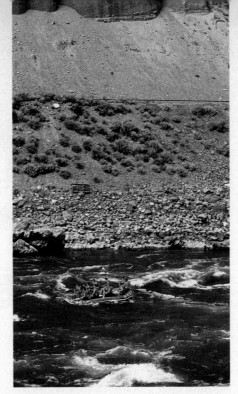

River rafters float down the Thompson River. (Judy Parkin, staff)

A 137 (220.5 km) **CC 33** (53.1 km) **Big Horn, BC.** Bring your binoculars! Depending on month and season, you may see eagles, osprey, bears, deer or big horn sheep on our mountain face. Large viewing windows in our cafe. Enjoy our extra-deep-dish pies, custom burgers. Vegetarian dishes available. We also sell fishing tackle, fresh fruit (June–September), local rocks and minerals, fireworks, souvenirs. Trading post. Fuel. 24-hour towing BCAA. Tire shop. Dry overnight parking. Family operated. Box 98, Spences Bridge, BC V0K 2L0. (250) 458-2333. [ADVERTISEMENT] ▲

A 139.1 (223.9 km) **CC 30.9** (49.7 km) **Number One Fruit Stand.** Fresh fruit and produce in season. Free fruit samples for customers. Succulent hot buttered corn from June–October. Sweet, yellow-fleshed watermelon. Syrups and jams from local fruit. Local honey. Soft drinks. Snacks. Fair U.S. exchange. Proposed for 1997: open year-round with convenience items. (250) 458-2493. [ADVERTISEMENT]

A 140 (225.3 km) **CC 30** (48.3 km) Junction with Highway 8 to Merritt and south access to Spences Bridge. Plaque here about the great landslide of 1905.

A 141.2 (227.2 km) **CC 28.8** (46.3 km)

North access to SPENCES BRIDGE (pop. 300; elev. 760 feet/231m) located at the confluence of the Thompson and Nicola rivers. Services include lodging, camping, restaurant, pub and grocery with tackle and fishing licenses. A record 30-lb., 5-oz. steelhead was caught in the Thompson River in 1984. Look for an osprey nest atop the hydroelectric pole on the east side of the river.

Acacia Grove. One block off Highway 1. RV park, cabins with kitchen units, tenting. Serene river valley setting overlooking the Thompson River, famous for steelhead, salmon, rainbow trout fishing and rafting. Visit with the mountain sheep August to May. Horseback riding, cycling arranged. Pull-throughs, full service, laundromat, free hot showers, flush toilets, groceries and gift shop. Gazebo and barbecue area will accommodate large groups. Open year-round. Your hosts Ed and Gayleen Streifel. Phone/fax (250) 458-2227. Box 69, Spences Bridge, BC V0K 2L0. [ADVERTISEMENT] ▲

Log Cabin Pub. You will appreciate this unique log structure. The logs were specially selected and prepared locally. Some spanning 50 feet. It features an assortment of antique guns and stuffed animals. The pub offers spirits, beverages and a light menu. Beer and coolers to go. April–December, Sunday–Thursday 11 A.M.–12:30 A.M., Friday–Saturday 11 A.M.–1:30 A.M. (250) 458-2215. [ADVERTISEMENT]

Steelhead Inn. A beautiful country inn on the scenic Thompson River offering old-fashioned bed and breakfast. Comfortable lodging and fine dining in BC's oldest operating hotel. Recently renovated, the inn provides the traveler with a pleasant and relaxing atmosphere. There are 12 lovely rooms, some with private bath and some with shared bath. The licensed dining room offers superb food and has a fabulous view overlooking the river with either patio or indoor seating. Stop by—you'll be glad you did. 1-888-458-2398. [ADVERTISEMENT]

A 153.4 (246.9 km) **CC 16.6** (26.7 km) Viewpoint overlooking Thompson River with plaque about the Canadian Northern Pacific (now the Canadian National Railway), Canada's third transcontinental railway, completed in 1915.

A 158.4 (255 km) **CC 11.6** (18.7 km) Red Hill rest area to east; tables, toilets, litter barrels, pay phone.

A 164.3 (264.4 km) **CC 5.7** (9.2 km) Stop of interest sign to east describes Ashcroft Manor, a roadhouse on the Cariboo Waggon Road. Summer temperatures in this dry and desertlike region typically reach the high 80s and 90s (26°C to 32°C).

Ashcroft Manor & Tea House. See display ad this section.

Fields under black plastic mesh tarps—which may be seen as the highway descends northbound—are ginseng, an Asian medicinal root crop. The world supply of North American ginseng, which takes 4 years to mature, is grown in the southern Cariboo.

A 164.5 (264.7 km) **CC 5.5** (8.9 km) Junction with road to ASHCROFT, a small village on the Thompson River with full tourist facilities just east of the highway. Historic Ashcroft supplanted Yale as gateway to the Cariboo with the arrival of the Canadian Pacific Railway in 1885. There are a number of original buildings with distinctive architectural details. Ashcroft Museum houses a fine collection of artifacts tracing the history of the region. Logan Lake, east of Ashcroft, is the site of the second largest open-pit copper mine in North America (tours available).

Also **junction** with Highway 97C to Logan Lake and Merritt.

A 168.2 (270.7 km) **CC 1.8** (2.9 km) Second turnoff northbound for Ashcroft and road to Logan Lake.

Cache Creek

A 170 (273.6 km) **PG 277** (445.8 km) Located at the junction of Trans-Canada Highway 1 and Highway 97. **Population:** 1,200. **Elevation:** 1,508 feet/ 460m. **Emergency Services:** RCMP, phone (250) 453-2216. **Ambulance**, phone 1-250-374-5937. **Hospital**, phone (250) 453-5306.

Visitor Information: Write Box 460, Cache Creek, BC V0K 1H0; fax (250) 457-9669.

Cache Creek has ample facilities for the traveler (most located on or just off the main highways), including motels, restaurants, service stations and grocery store. Private campgrounds are available east of Cache Creek on Trans-Canada Highway 1 (across from the golf course) and just north of town on Highway 97.

A post office and bus depot are on Todd Road. Nearby, Cariboo Jade Shoppe offers free stone-cutting demonstrations in summer. On display out front is a 2,850-lb. jade boulder. Public park and swimming pool on the Bonaparte River, east off Highway 97 at the north edge of town.

CACHE CREEK ADVERTISERS

Bonaparte Motel ....Ph. (250) 457-9693
Brookside Campsite ....1 km E. of jct.
Cache Creek
    Campground ....4 km N. on Hwy. 97
Cariboo Jade & Gift
    Shoppe ....Ph. (250) 457-9566
Desert Motel.....................Ph. (250) 457-6226
Tumbleweed Motel ....Ph. 1-800-667-1501
Wander-Inn
    Restaurant ....Ph. (250) 457-6511

The settlement grew up around the confluence of the creek and the Bonaparte River. The Hudson's Bay Co. opened a store here, and Cache Creek became a major supply point on the Cariboo Waggon Road. Today, hay and cattle ranching, ginseng farming, mining, logging and tourism support the community. Area soils are dry but fertile. Residents claim that with irrigation, nearly anything can be grown here.

From the junction, Highway 97 leads north 277 miles/445.8 km to Prince George. Kamloops is 52 miles/83.7 km east via Trans-Canada Highway 1. Traveling north from Cache Creek the highway generally follows the historic route to the Cariboo goldfields.

Brookside Campsite. 1 km east of Cache Creek on Highway 1, full (30 amp) and partial hookups, pull-throughs, tent sites, super clean heated wash and laundry rooms, free showers, sani-stations, store, playground, nature path, heated pool, golf course adjacent, pets on leash, pay phones. VISA, MasterCard, C.P. two days. Good Sam. Box 737, Cache Creek, BC V0K 1H0. Phone (250) 457-6633. [ADVERTISEMENT] ♿▲

Cariboo Jade & Gift Shoppe. Jade has been prized for over 7,000 years, and has at times been more valued than gold. Even today, it is reputed to bring its possessor good health and fortune. Nephrite jade, British Columbia's provincial gem stone, is very tough (4 times harder than marble) and difficult to work; but the finished piece always reveals unforgettable beauty. The Cariboo Jade & Gift Shoppe has the largest selection of BC jade in Canada; some items are crafted on-premise. Its 30-year reputation has been built on the variety, quantity and quality of hand-picked semi-precious stone gift items from around the world. Stop by to see the 2,850-lb. jade boulder standing out front, and find out why so many visitors rave about this shop. At the junction in centre of Cache Creek. [ADVERTISEMENT]

West Access Route Log

(continued)
BC HIGHWAY 97/CARIBOO HIGHWAY
From Cache Creek, continue north on BC Highway 97 for Dawson Creek. Kilometreposts on this section of highway are located on the east side of the highway facing west, so that they may be seen by traffic traveling in either direction. Highway 97 between Cache Creek and Prince George is called the Cariboo Highway, and the region is locally referred to as "Super, Natural Cariboo Country." Contact the Cariboo Tourist Assoc., P.O. Box 4900, Williams Lake, BC V2G 2VB; phone toll free 1-800-663-5885.
This section of the log shows distance from Cache Creek (CC) followed by distance from Prince George (PG).

CC 0 PG 277 (445.8 km) Cache Creek, **junction** of Trans-Canada Highway 1 and Highway 97.
CC 1.2 (2 km) **PG 275.8** (443.8 km) **Horsting's Farm Market.** See display ad this section.
CC 2.5 (4 km) **PG 274.5** (441.8 km) **Cache Creek Campground**, 3 km north of Cache Creek on Highway 97 north. Full hookups, pull-throughs and tenting, sanistation, store, country kitchen restaurant,

laundromat, coin showers, heated washrooms. Outdoor pool and whirlpool (no charge). 18-hole mini-golf, horseshoes, seasonal river swimming and fishing. P.O. Box 127, Cache Creek, BC V0K 1H0. For reservations, phone (250) 457-6414. [ADVERTISEMENT] ▲

CC 7 (11.3 km) **PG 270** (434.5 km) **Junction** with Highway 99 west to Lillooet (46.5 miles/75 km) and Vancouver (209 miles/336.5 km) via Whistler and Blackcombe ski areas. (Formerly Highway 12, this route was designated as part of Highway 99 when the logging road between Lillooet and Pemberton was paved, making it possible to drive to the Cariboo from Vancouver via Squamish. Highway 99, promoted as the "Sea to Sky Highway," is logged in *Northwest Mileposts®*, available from Vernon Publications Inc.; phone 1-800-726-4707.)

Drive 0.4 mile/0.7 km west on Highway 99 for Hat Creek Heritage Ranch, a restored Cariboo Trail roadhouse and farm with reconstructed barn, working blacksmith shop, wagon and trail rides, and tours. Open daily 10 A.M. to 6 P.M., mid-May to mid-October Phone 1-800-782-0922 for current information.

Hat Creek Ranch at Milepost CC 7 is a good example of a Cariboo trail roadhouse and farm. (© Carmen Scott)

Hat Creek Ranch. See display ad this section.

Marble Canyon Provincial Park, 17.5 miles/28 km west on Highway 99, has 34 campsites, picnicking, swimming and hiking trails. ▲

CC 10 (16 km) **PG 267** (430 km) Gravel turnout with plaque about the BX stagecoaches that once served Barkerville. Formally known as the BC Express Company, the BX served the Cariboo for 50 years.

CC 13.6 (21.9 km) **PG 263.4** (423.9 km) Paved road leads east to **Loon Lake**, rainbow fishing, boat launch. Camping at Loon Lake Provincial Park (16 miles/26 km); 14 sites, water, pit toilets, firewood. ◄▲

CC 16.6 (26.7 km) **PG 260.4** (419.1 km) Carguile rest area.

CC 19.9 (32 km) **PG 257.1** (413.7 km) **Lakeview Campsite & RV Park.** See display ad this section. ▲

CC 25 (40.2 km) **PG 252** (405.5 km) **Junction** with Pavilion Mountain Road west to Pavilion via Kelly Lake. Camping at Downing Provincial Park (11 miles/18 km);

25 sites, swimming, fishing. ◄▲

CC 25.5 (41 km) **PG 251.5** (404.7 km) **CLINTON** (pop. 900, area 4,000; elev. 2,911 feet/887m). **Visitor Information:** Available at various local businesses; look for signs. All visitor facilities are available, including 3 motels, campground, gas stations, 24-hour towing and stores. Originally the site of 47 Mile Roadhouse, a gold-rush settlement on the Cariboo Waggon Road from Lillooet, today Clinton is called the "guest Ranch Capital of British Columbia." The museum, housed in a building of local, handmade red brick that once served as a courthouse, has fine displays of pioneer tools and items from the gold rush days, and a scale model of the Clinton Hotel. Clinton pioneer cemetery just north of town. Clinton boasts the oldest continuously held event in the province, the Clinton Ball (in May the weekend following Victoria Day), an annual event since 1868.

Clinton has its own sign forest. Visitors may sign a wooden slab (donated by the local sawmill) and add it to the sign forest.

Round-up Motel. See display ad this section.

Gold Trail RV Park. Fully serviced sites, 30-amp power. Pull-throughs. Immaculate. Washrooms with flush toilets, handicap-equipped. Free hot showers for guests. On highway in town; easy walking to all amenities. Well-lit level sites. Grassed and landscaped. Sani-station. 1640 Cariboo Highway North, Clinton, BC V0K 1K0. (250) 459-2519. [ADVERTISEMENT]

Parkies Clothing and Variety Store. The largest selection of moccasins in the Cariboo. Deli and freshly-made submarine sandwich, pizza counter. Colour laser copies and fax service. Fishing tackle. Fishing and hunting licenses. Souvenirs. Large assortment of wildlife T-shirts, sweatshirts and western hats. Video rentals. Historical books and *The MILEPOST®* for sale. The friendly place where the flags are flying. VISA and MasterCard accepted. Box 538, Clinton, BC V0K 1K0. Phone/fax (250) 459-2535. [ADVERTISEMENT]

Pioneer Service and Towing. 24-hour towing service for all RVs, fifth wheels, trailers and motorcycles. Contract towing for BCAA/CAA/AAA. Complete major and minor repairs during regular shop hours: oil, lube, tire sales and repairs, brakes, tune-ups, air conditioning. In Clinton 311 Smith Avenue. (250) 459-2253. [ADVERTISEMENT]

CC 31 (49.9 km) **PG 246** (395.9 km) Dirt and gravel road leads 21 miles/34 km west to **Big Bar Lake** Provincial Park; 33 campsites, water, pit toilets, firewood, swimming, fishing and boat launch. 🐟▲

Clinton Lookout and Big Bar rest area to east just north of turnoff; toilets, tables, litter barrels.

CC 35 (56.3 km) **PG 242** (389.5 km) Loop road leads east 3 miles/5 km to Painted Chasm geological site and Chasm Provincial Park picnic area. This 1-mile/1.6-km-long bedrock box canyon was cut by glacial meltwaters.

CC 45 (72.4 km) **PG 232** (373.4 km) **70 MILE HOUSE** (unincorporated), originally a stage stop named for its distance from Lillooet, Mile 0. General store, post office, restaurant, motel, gas station with diesel and bus depot.

North Bonaparte Road leads east 7.5 miles/12 km to Green Lake Provincial Park; 121 campsites, water, toilets, firewood, dump station, swimming and boat launch. Rainbow and kokanee fishing at **Green Lake**. Paved road leads north to Watch Lake, east to Bonaparte Lake, and northeast to join Highway 24 at Bridge Lake. 🐟▲

CC 58.8 (94.7 km) **PG 218.2** (351.1 km) **83 MILE HOUSE;** restaurant, gas, propane, store, public phone. Turnoff for Green Lake.

CC 66 (106.2 km) **PG 211** (339.6 km) **Junction** with Highway 24 East to Lone Butte Bridge Lake and Little Fort (60 miles/96.5 km) on Yellowhead Highway 5. Highway 24 provides access to numerous fishing lakes and resorts, including **Bridge Lake** Provincial Park (31 miles/50 km east) with 20 campsites. 🐟▲

100 Mile House

CC 72 (115.9 km) **PG 205** (329.9 km) **Population:** 1,900. **Elevation:** 3,050 feet/930m. **Emergency Services: Police,** phone (250) 395-2456. **Ambulance,** phone 1-250-374-5937. **Hospital,** phone (250) 395-2202. **Visitor Information:** At the log cabin by 100 Mile House Marsh (a bird sanctuary at the south edge of town); phone (250) 395-5353, fax 395-4085. Look for the 39-foot-/12-m-long skis! Or contact the Cariboo Tourist Assoc.,

100 MILE HOUSE ADVERTISERS

Loon Complex, The ....755 Alder Ave.
99 Mile Motel ....Ph. (250) 395-2255
100 Mile Motel &
  RV Park ....Ph. (250) 395-2234

P.O. Box 4900, Williams Lake, BC V2G 2VB; phone toll free 1-800-663-5885.

This large, bustling town was once a stop for fur traders and later a post house on the Cariboo Waggon Road to the goldfields. In 1930, the Marquess of Exeter established the 15,000-acre Bridge Creek Ranch here. Today, 100 Mile House is the site of 2 lumber mills, and an extensive log home building industry.

Visitor services include restaurants, motels, a campground, gas stations with repair service, stores, a post office, 2 golf courses, a government liquor store, 2 supermarkets and banks. Shopping malls and the downtown area are located east of the highway. Centennial Park in town has picnic sites and walking trails.

100 Mile House is a popular destination for snowmobiling and cross-country skiing in winter. It is also the jumping-off point for fishermen headed for Canim Lake and Mahood Lake in Wells Gray Provincial Park. (Well-known for its spectacular waterfalls, including 460-foot/140-m Helmcken Falls, 4th largest in Canada, Wells Gray main entrance is from Yellowhead Highway 5 at Clearwater. Yellowhead Highway 5 is logged in *Northwest Mileposts®*, available from Vernon Publications Inc.; phone 1-800-726-4707.)

Horse Lake Road leads east from 100 Mile House to **Horse Lake** (kokanee) and other fishing lakes of the high plateau. 🐟

99 Mile Motel. Air-conditioned sleeping and housekeeping units. Fridges in all units, housekeeping units with microwave ovens. DD touchtone phones, remote control cable TV, super channel and TSN, courtesy in-room coffee and tea. Carports, winter plug-ins, freezer available for guests, bowling, legion; supermarket and cross-country ski trails. Senior citizens discount, commercial rates, partially wheelchair accessible, small dogs only. Highway 97, 100 Mile House, BC V0K 2E0. (250) 395-2255 (call collect). [ADVERTISEMENT] ♿

100 Mile Motel and RV Park. 310 Highway 97. Centrally located. Ground level sleeping and housekeeping units. DD phones, cable TV. RV park and campground, quiet setting, pull-throughs with 30-amp service, showers, flush toilets, cable TV (mid-April to end of October), close to all amenities. Your hosts Mark and Teresa Livingston. 100 Mile House, BC. Phone (250) 395-2234. [ADVERTISEMENT] ▲

The Loon Complex. Major and minor automotive and RV repairs provided by qualified, conscientious mechanics. Oversized pressure wash bays where you do the washing, or we can do it for you. Special detail bay for shampooing, hand waxing and inte-

rior cleaning. Car rentals. 755 Alder Ave., adjacent to Highway 97 on south side of town. (250) 395-3394. [ADVERTISEMENT]

West Access Route Log
(continued)

CC 74 (119 km) **PG 203** (326.7 km) **Junction** with road east to **Ruth, Canim** and **Mahood** lakes. Resorts and fishing at all lakes. Camping at Canim Beach Provincial Park (27 miles/43 km); 16 sites, water, pit toilets, swimming. Access to Canim Falls. 🐟▲

CC 78.2 (125.8 km) **PG 198.8** (319.9 km) **108 Mile Ranch,** a recreational community built in the 1970s, was once a cattle ranch. Motel and golf course.

108 Resort. See display ad this section.

CC 80.5 (129.5 km) **PG 196.5** (316.2 km) Rest area to west beside 108 Mile Lake. Alongside is 108 Heritage Site with some of the original log buildings from 108 Mile Ranch, and others relocated from 105 Mile. Guided tours; open May to early September.

CC 85 (136.8 km) **PG 192** (309 km) **Big Country KOA.** Located on 60 acres of rolling ranchland 3 miles south of Lac La Hache. Heated swimming pool, free showers, store, gift shop, laundromat, games room. Extra-long shady pull-throughs; shaded grassy tent sites; camping cabin. Full hookup facilities, sani-dump, phone. Pets welcome. VISA,

MasterCard. (250) 396-4181. Box 68, Lac La Hache, BC V0K 1T0. [ADVERTISEMENT]　　▲

CC 88 (141.6 km) **PG 189** (304.2 km) **LAC LA HACHE** (pop. 400; elev. 2,749 feet/838m), unincorporated. Motels, stores, gas stations and a museum. The community holds a fishing derby in July and a winter carnival in mid-February. Lac La Hache is French for "Ax Lake." There are many stories of how the lake got its name, but Molly Forbes, local historian, says it was named by a French–Canadian *coureur de bois* (voyageur) "because of a small ax he found on its shores."

Lac La Hache, lake char, rainbow and kokanee; good fishing summer and winter (great ice fishing).

CC 92 (148.1 km) **PG 185** (297.7 km) **Fir Crest Resort** (Good Sam). Quiet parklike setting just two minutes from Highway 97, but away from traffic noise. Full hookups including pull-throughs, camping and cabins on the lakeshore. Sandy beach, swimming, games room, groceries, sani-dump, laundromat. Full marina with boat, motor, canoe and tackle rentals. Show this ad for a 10 percent discount. Phone (250) 396-7337. [ADVERTISEMENT]　　▲

CC 93.3 (150.1 km) **PG 183.7** (295.6 km) **Clancys'** restaurant, truck stop (full-serve gas, diesel, propane), convenience store and gifts. Open 7 A.M.–12 A.M. 2 acres, paved parking, air-conditioned, licensed with home cooking and homemade desserts. Very easy access to pumps for any length of vehicle. American exchange. Clancys', located Mile 122, Highway 97 at Kokanee Bay. [ADVERTISEMENT]

CC 93.4 (150.3 km) **PG 183.6** (295.4 km) **Kokanee Bay Motel and Campground.** Relaxation at its finest right on the lakeshore. Fish for kokanee and char or take a refreshing dip. We have a modern, comfortable motel, cabins. Full trailer hookups, grassy tenting area, hot showers, laundromat. Aquabike, boat and canoe rentals. Fishing tackle and ice. Phone (250) 396-7345. Fax (250) 396-4990. [ADVERTISEMENT]　　▲

CC 96 (154.5 km) **PG 181** (291.3 km)

Crystal Springs Campsite (Historical) Resort Ltd. Visit the Cariboo's best. We honour Good Sam, AAA and are a Good Neighbor Park. 8 miles north of Lac La Hache. Parklike setting on lakeshore. Showers, flush toilets, laundromat, full (20- and 30-amp pull-throughs) and partial hookups, boat rentals. New chalets, winterized. Groceries, tackle, camping supplies, handicrafts. Games room, playground, picnic shelter. Pets on leash. Public beach and boat launch adjacent, fishing. Your hosts, Doug and Lorraine Whitesell. Phone (250) 396-4497. [ADVERTISEMENT]　　&▲

CC 96 (154.5 km) **PG 181** (291.3 km) **Lac La Hache** Provincial Park; 83 campsites, lakeshore picnic area, water, flush and pit toilets, firewood, dump station, boat launch, swimming, hiking trail and fishing. Camping on east side of highway, picnicking and boat launch on west side of highway.　　◆▲

CC 97 (156.1 km) **PG 180** (289.7 km) San Jose River parallels highway to west. Canadian artist A.Y. Jackson painted in this valley.

CC 104.4 (168 km) **PG 172.6** (277.7 km) Stop of interest sign commemorating the miners, traders and adventurers who came this way to the Cariboo goldfields in the 1860s.

CC 116.6 (187.6 km) **PG 160.4** (258.1 km) 148 Mile Ducks Unlimited conservation area. This is an important waterfowl breeding area in Canada and offers good bird watching for bald eagles, osprey, great horned owls, American kestrels and pileated woodpeckers.

CC 118.5 (190.7 km) **PG 158.5** (255.1 km) **150 MILE HOUSE**, so named because it was 150 miles from Lillooet on the old Cariboo Waggon Road. The post office, which serves about 1,200 people in the area, was established in 1871. Hotel, restaurant, pub, gas station with repair service and a store open daily. Hunting and fishing licenses available at the store.

CC 119.1 (191.7 km) **PG 157.9** (254.1 km) **Junction** with road to **Quesnel** and

Horsefly lakes. Horsefly Lake Provincial Park (40 miles/65 km) has 22 campsites. Fishing for rainbow and lake trout.　　◆▲

Williams Lake

CC 128 (206 km) **PG 149** (239.8 km) Located at the junction of Highway 97 and Highway 20 to Bella Coola. **Population:** 36,737. **Elevation:** 1,922 feet/586m. **Emergency Services: Police,** phone (250) 392-6211. **Hospital,** phone (250) 392-4411. **Ambulance,** (250) 392-5402.

Visitor Information: Visitor Infocentre located on east side of highway just south of the junction of Highways 97 and 20, open year-round; phone (250) 392-5025, fax (250) 392-4214. Write 1148 S. Broadway, Williams Lake, BC V2G 1A2. Or contact the Cariboo Tourism Association, P.O. Box 4900, Williams Lake, BC V2G 2V8; phone toll free 1-800-663-5885.

The administrative and transportation hub of the Cariboo–Chilcotin region, Williams Lake has complete services, including hotels/motels, restaurants, an 18-hole golf course and par-3 golf course, a twin sheet arena and pool complex. Highway 97 northbound bypasses the business and shopping districts of downtown Williams Lake, which are situated to the west of the highway. Motels, gas stations and fast-food restaurants are located on frontage roads paralleling Highway 97 on the south side of town.

A museum featuring the ranching and rodeo history of the region is located downtown at the corner of 4th Avenue and Borland; open year-round.

The airport, 7 miles/11 km north of town on Highway 97, is served by daily flights to Vancouver and other interior communities.

Located on the shore of the lake of the same name, it was named for Shuswap Indian Chief Willyum. The town grew rapidly with the advent of the Pacific Great Eastern Railway (now B.C. Railway) in 1919, to become a major cattle marketing and shipping centre for the Cariboo–Chilcotin. Today the city has the largest and most active cattleyards in the province. Lumber and mining for copper-molybdenum are the mainstays of the economy.

The famous Williams Lake Stampede, British Columbia's premier rodeo, is held here annually on the July 1 holiday. The 4-day event draws contestants from all over Canada and the United States. The rodeo grounds are located in the city.

At the north end of Williams Lake is Scout Island Nature Center. This island is reached by a causeway, with boardwalks providing access to the marshes. A nature house is open May to August.

Highway 20 travels west from Williams Lake 282 miles/454 km to Bella Coola, giving access to the Chilcotin country's excellent fishing, Tweedsmuir Provincial Park, and the remote central coast. The highway is paved for the first 200.4 miles/334 km. Well-maintained gravel for 73.8 miles/123 km. At Heckman Pass (elev. 5,000 feet/1,524m), 218.5 miles/352 km west of Williams Lake, the highway descends a section of narrow, switchbacked road with an 18 percent grade for 5.4 miles/9 km. Beyond "the hill," the road is paved to Bella Coola. Highway 20, the Chilcotin Highway, is logged in *Northwest Mileposts®* (Vernon Publications Inc.; phone 1-800-726-4707).

West Access Route Log

(continued)

CC 136.4 (219.5 km) PG 140.6 (226.3 km) Wildwood Road; gas station, store, access to private campground.   ▲

Wildwood RV Park. See display ad this section.   ▲

C 141.3 (227.3 km) PG 135.7 (218.4 km) Turnout with litter barrel.

CC 141.8 (228.2 km) PG 135.2 (217.6 km) Whispering Willows Outpost Campground and Store. RV pull-throughs, sani-dump. Power and water hookups, free hot showers, flush toilets. Level spacious treed area for camping. Safe firepits, wood available. Teepee for rent. Play area. Confectionary store. Pets and horse trailers welcome, corrals available. Deep Creek runs by Whispering Willows Campground, RR 4, Site 12, Comp. 46, Williams Lake, BC V2G 4M8. (250) 989-0359. [ADVERTISEMENT]   ▲

CC 145.3 (233.9 km) PG 131.7 (211.9 km) Turnout with litter barrel.

CC 147.8 (237.9 km) PG 129.2 (207.9 km) Replica of a turn-of-the-century roadhouse (current status of services unknown) at junction with side road which leads west 2.5 miles/4.5km to the tiny settlement of

SODA CREEK. The original wagon road to the goldfields ended here and miners went the rest of the way to Quesnel by river steamboats. Soda Creek became an important transfer point for men and supplies until the railway went through in 1920. Soda Creek was so named because the creek bed is carbonate of lime and the water bubbles like soda water.

CC 155 (249.4 km) PG 122 (196.4 km) McLEESE LAKE, small community with gas stations, cafe, post office, store, pub, private campground and motel on McLeese Lake. The lake was named for a Fraser River steamboat skipper. McLeese Lake, rainbow to 2 lbs., troll using a flasher, worms or flatfish lure.   🐟▲

Junction with road to Beaver Lake and on to Likely. Historic Quesnelle Forks, a heritage site with a Forestry campsite, is located near Likely. Travelers may continue north from Likely to Barkerville and rejoin Highway 97 at Quesnel.

CC 155.5 (250.2 km) PG 121.5 (195.5 km) Rest area to west overlooking McLeese Lake.

CC 160 (257.5 km) PG 117 (188.3 km) Turnout with litter barrel to west with plaque about Fraser River paddle-wheelers.

CC 164 (263.9 km) PG 113 (181.8 km) Cariboo Wood Shop. Specializing in Canadiana gifts, custom wood working on premises, hand-carved faces, unique custom wood boxes. Pottery, wheat weaving, souvenirs, toys and puzzles. Music tapes and CDs. Fresh fudge, 24 varieties; ask about our seasonal special! Easy access drive-through loop for RVs. Open 7 days a week 9:30 A.M.–5:30 P.M. Groups welcome. Phone (250) 747-8397. [ADVERTISEMENT]

CC 166 (267 km) PG 111 (178.6 km) Glass sculpture museum and rock shop. the Castle. See display ad this section.

CC 166.5 (267.9 km) PG 110.5 (177.8 km) Marguerite rest area. View upriver to Marguerite reaction cable ferry across the Fraser River. Ferry crossing takes 10 minutes, operates 7 A.M. to 6:45 P.M.; 2 cars and 10 passengers, no charge.

CC 168.5 (271.2 km) PG 108.5 (174.6 km) Basalt columns to east create a formation known as the Devil's Palisades. Cliff swallows nest in the columns.

CC 169.8 (273.2 km) PG 107.2 (172.5 km) Stone cairn commemorates Fort Alexandria, the last North West Co. fur-trading post established west of the Rockies, built in 1821. The actual site of the fort is across the river. Cairn also marks the approximate farthest point reached by Alexander Mackenzie in his descent of the Fraser in 1793.

CC 179.9 (289.6 km) PG 97.1 (156.2 km) Cariboo Place Campsite. We have the Cariboo in the palm of our hands. Beautiful natural park setting. A convenient and delightful stop, just off Highway 97. Pull-through bays for large units, tenters welcome. Exceptionally clean showers and washrooms. Laundromat. Picnic tables and firepits. Sani-dump station. Electrical hookups. Drinking water. Pets welcome

but must be leashed. Rates $13–$14 plus tax. Electrical extra. Open 24 hours. [ADVERTISEMENT].   ▲

CC 180 (289.7 km) PG 97 (156.1 km) Australian rest area to west with toilets, tables and litter barrels. Private campground to east.   ▲

CC 188.5 (303.4 km) PG 88.5 (142.4 km) Kersley (unincorporated), gas and food.

CC 188.6 (303.6 km) PG 88.4 (142.3 km) Restaurant, gas and private campground. ▲

CC 193.2 (310.9 km) PG 83.8 (134.9 km) Mary's Gifts, located 100 yards east of Highway 97 on Dragon Lake Road. Exciting wonderland of Canadian handcrafted gifts. Moccasins, gold and pewter jewellery, gourmet products, pottery and framed prints. Official Bradford Exchange dealer. Canadian souvenirs. Open daily 9 A.M. to 5 P.M. Easy RV access. Mail orders. Box 32, Dragon Lake Road, RR 1, Quesnel, BC V2J 3H5. Phone (250) 747-2993. [ADVERTISEMENT]

CC 194.7 (313.3 km) PG 82.3 (132.4 km) A Little Bit Country. Come in and choose from our hand-picked assortment of antiques and collectables, including Depression glass, china, hand tools, antique furniture and farmhouse collectables. Enjoy a trip down memory lane. P.O. Box 73, Jasper Rd., Quesnel, BC V2J 4P2. (250) 747-3919. On Highway 97; access on Jasper Road. [ADVERTISEMENT]

CC 196 (315.4 km) PG 81 (130.4 km) South end of loop road east to Dragon Lake, a small, shallow lake popular with Quesnel families. Camping and fishing for rainbow.   🐟▲

CC 196 (315.4 km) PG 81 (130.4 km) Robert's Roost Campsite located 6 km south of Quesnel and 2 km east of Highway 97 in a parklike setting on beautiful Dragon Lake. Grass sites, both partial and fully serviced. 15- and 30-amp service. Sani-dump, fishing, boat rental, swimming, horseshoes, playground, coin-operated showers, flush toilets and laundromat. Can accommodate any length unit. Limited accommodation. Approved by Tourism BC. Hosts: Bob and Vivian Wurm, 3121 Gook Road, Quesnel, BC V2J 4K7. Phone (250) 747-2015. [ADVERTISEMENT]   ▲

CC 197.5 (317.8 km) PG 79.5 (127.9 km) Valhalla Motel & Family Restaurant. Quietly situated at the top of Dragon Hill 3 km south of Quesnel. All rooms have air conditioning, individual electric heat, colour televisions, direct dial telephones, queen beds, refrigerators. Nonsmoking rooms available. Complete family dining facilities. Complimentary coffee. Guest laundry. Winter plug-ins. Close to fairgrounds, recreation centre, racing oval, shopping centre. Senior discount. Pets welcome. Major credit cards.

2010 Valhalla Rd., Quesnel, BC V2J 4C1. (250) 747-1111. [ADVERTISEMENT]

Quesnel

CC 203 (326.7 km) PG 74 (119.1 km). Located at the confluence of the Fraser and Quesnel rivers. **Population: 10,000. Elevation: 1,789 feet/545m. Emergency Services:** Emergency only, phone 911. **RCMP,** phone (250) 992-9211. **Ambulance,** phone (250) 992-3211. **Hospital,** phone (250) 992-2181.

Visitor Information: Located on the west side of the highway just north of Quesnel River bridge, in LeBourdais Park. Open year-round. Write Quesnel Visitor Infocentre, Stn. A, 703 Carson Ave., Quesnel, BC V2J 2B6; phone (250) 992-8716, or toll free 1-800-992-4922. For information on the Cariboo Tourist Region, contact the Cariboo Tourist Assoc., P.O. Box 4900 Williams Lake, BC V2G 2VB; phone toll free 1-800-663-5885.

Quesnel (kwe NEL) began as a supply town for the miners in the gold rush of the 1860s. The city was named for fur trader Jules Maurice Quesnel, a member of Simon Fraser's 1808 expedition and later a political figure in Quebec. Today, forestry is the dominant economic force in Quesnel, with 2 pulp mills, a plywood plant, and 5 sawmills and planer mills. Check with the Visitor Infocentre about tours.

Accommodations include 3 hotels, 15 motels, 5 bed and breakfasts and 8 campgrounds. There are gas stations (with diesel and propane), 2 shopping malls and 45 restaurants offering everything from fast food to fine dining. Golf and a recreation

centre with pool are available.

Visitors can take a walking tour of the city along the Riverfront Park trail system. The 3.1-mile/5-km north Quesnel trail starts at Ceal Tingley Park at the confluence of the Fraser and Quesnel rivers. The west Quesnel trail is a 2.7-mile/4.3-km walk through a residential area. Trail information is available at the Visitor Infocentre.

Local attractions include the Quesnel Museum and Archives, located adjacent the Visitor Infocentre, which boasts the largest collection of Chinese artifacts west of Ottawa.

There are some interesting hoodoo formations and scenic canyon views at Pinnacles Provincial Park, 5 miles/8 km west of Highway 97; picnicking. It is a 1.1-mile/1.8-km walk round-trip from the parking area to the pinnacle viewpoints.

Quesnel offers gold panning tours, guided hiking tours and Voyager canoe trips on the Fraser River. Boat tours are also available on other area rivers. Contact the Visitor Infocentre for more information.

A worthwhile side trip is Highway 26, which intersects Highway 97 at **Milepost CC 206.** This 51-mile/82-km paved highway leads to Barkerville Provincial Historic Park, a reconstructed and restored Cariboo gold rush town. (See HIGHWAY 26 side road log page 56.) Gold Pan City Stage Lines offers charter and scheduled tours of Barkerville and surrounding area from Quesnel.

Billy Barker Days, a 4-day event held the third full weekend in July, commemorates the discovery of gold at Barkerville in 1862. Held in conjunction with the Quesnel Rodeo, Billy Barker Days is the third largest outdoor family festival in the province. For more information, write Box 4441, Quesnel, BC V2J 3J4. The Barlow Creek Music Festival takes place on Highway 26 the weekend after Billy Barker Days.

West Access Route Log
(continued)

CC 206 (331.5 km) **PG 71** (114.3 km) Quesnel airport. **Junction** with Highway 26 to Barkerville and Bowron Lake. See HIGHWAY 26 side road log on page 56.

CC 210 (338 km) **PG 67** (107.8 km) **Ten Mile Lake** Provincial Park; 142 campsites, flush toilets, picnic area, boat launch, good swimming beach, nature trails, dump station. Self-guided trail to beaver colony, good bird watching (pileated woodpeckers, warblers, snowy owls). Good fishing for rainbow to 3 lbs. ◀

10 Mile Lake Provincial Park—Clean, friendly park one paved kilometer from Highway 97. Quiet, treed sites with table and firepit. Some pull-throughs available. Coin operated hot showers. Security gates closed 11 P.M.–7 A.M. 30 kms of hiking and maintained mountain bike trails. Playground. Ask about our park naturalist program. Only one hour to Barkerville. [ADVERTISEMENT] ▲

CC 214.2 (344.7 km) **PG 62.8** (101.1 km) Cottonwood River bridge. Turnout with litter barrels and stop-of-interest sign at south end of bridge describing railway bridge seen upriver.

CC 218.7 (352 km) **PG 58.3** (93.8 km) Hush Lake rest area to west; toilets, tables, litter barrels.

CC 226 (363.7 km) **PG 51** (82 km) **Cinema 2nd Hand.** General store, groceries. Movie rentals, souvenirs. Local artwork, circle drive. 9 A.M.–9 P.M. every day. Free

Cottonwood House on Highway 26 east of Quesnel. (Judy Parkin, staff)

camping, picnic tables, firepits and wood, toilet, some long pull-throughs, some shady sites, hiking trail, phone. Welcome to friendly Cinema, BC. Vic and Theresa Olson, RR 1 Box 1, Site 10, Hixon, BC V0K 1S0. (250) 998-4774. [ADVERTISEMENT] ▲

CC 229.6 (369.5 km) **PG 47.4** (76.3 km) Strathnaver (unincorporated), no services.

CC 241 (387.8 km) **PG 36** (58 km) HIXON (pop. 1,500) has a post office, 2 motels, gas stations, grocery stores, 2 restaurants (1 with licensed premises), a pub and private campground. Hixon is the Cariboo's most northerly community. Extensive placer mining took place here in the early 1900s. Southbound motorists watch for roadside display about points of interest in the Cariboo region located just north of Hixon. ▲

Canyon Creek Campground (CAA). Very long pull-through sites (100 feet) with 30 amps and water. Full hookups. Tent spaces in the trees with firepits. Modern

restroom, hot showers, laundromat, sani-station. Grocery stores, restaurant and pub within easy walking distance. Nature trail by the creek. Swimming hole and fishing pools (in season). Pets welcome. Joe and Melanie welcome you (250) 998-4384. Box 390, Hixon, BC V0K 1S0. [ADVERTISEMENT] ▲

Hixon Fireplace Inn. Excellent cuisine. Food preparation on the premises. Soups and chowders. In-season specialties. Try our delicious pies. Easy RV access, ample parking. Monday to Saturday 7 A.M. to 8 P.M., Sunday noon to 8 P.M. Your hosts Dave and Fran Krieger. Most major credit cards, Interac. Wir spechen Deutch. (250) 998-4518. [ADVERTISEMENT]

(Continues on page 58)

Highway 26 Log

This 51-mile/82-km paved road leads to Barkerville Historic Town in the historic Cariboo gold fields (active mining under way). Gas available in Wells.

Distance from Highway 97 junction (J) is shown.

J 0 Junction with Highway 97 at **Milepost CC 206**. Visitor Infocentre on southeast side of junction.

J 0.8 (1.3 km) Barlow Creek residential area; grocery, food and fuel. Eastbound, Highway 26 accesses local roads. Watch for deer.

J 13 (21 km) Rest area and interpretive trails to south. Wooden rail "snake" and wire fences with wooden top rail allow deer and moose to safely jump them, while penning domestic livestock.

J 15.2 (24.5 km) Cottonwood River bridge. The river is named for the black cottonwood trees growing alongside it.

J 16.7 (26.9 km) Cottonwood House Historic Site, a restored and furnished log roadhouse built in 1864. Gift shop, coffee

shop, picnicking and guided tours by costumed docents. Open May to September.

Cottonwood House Historic Site. "Original Buildings." Step back in time and visit the general store. Take a wagon ride on the original Cariboo Wagon Road in our "Democrat Surrey." Experience the 1800s at one of the oldest remaining roadhouses. Sit down to homemade soup and sandwiches. Fresh bakery fare made in our own bakery. Try some "bannock" made in our wood stove. Overnight parking for self-contained RVs at reasonable rates. Admission $2 adult, $4 family. Groups welcome. Open 8 A.M. to 5 P.M. (250) 992-3997. Just 20 minutes on the Barkerville Highway. [ADVERTISEMENT]

J 20.1 (32.4 km) Swift River Forest Road leads 0.2 mile/0.3 km to Lightning Creek Forest Service recreation site (first turn on left); free camping, 14-day limit. CAUTION: Active logging road, drive with headlights on. ▲

J 21.4 (34.5 km) Lover's Leap viewpoint and Mexican Hill Summit, one of the steepest grades on the original Cariboo Waggon Road, to the south.

J 27.1 (43.6 km) Historical stop of interest marker for Charles Morgan Blessing's grave. Blessing, from Ohio, was murdered on his way to Barkerville in 1866. His killer, John Barry, was caught when he gave Blessing's keepsake gold nugget stickpin, in the shape of a skull, to a Barkerville dance-hall girl. John Barry was the only white man hanged in the Cariboo during the gold rush.

J 37.3 (60.1 km) Stanley Road and Boulder Gold Mines (active claim). Stanley Road is a 1.9-mile/3-km loop road that

Barkerville historic town dates back to the Cariboo gold rush. (© Carmen Scott)

leads past the gold-rush ghost towns of Stanley and VanWinkle, the old Lightning Hotel, and gold rush-era gravesites. A worthwhile sidetrip.

J 38.6 (62.2 km) Stanley (Loop) Road, Chisholm Creek. Remnants of Stanley townsite and cemetery dating back to 1800's. The authentic Stanley Trail leads from the townsite through the remnants of Van Winkle, ending at the Richfield Courthouse in Barkerville.

J 40.2 (64.7 km) Devil's Canyon paved turnout to south. This was the highest point on the Cariboo Waggon Road.

J 42.9 (69 km) Slough Creek, site of much hydraulic mining activity after Joe Shaw discovered gold here in 1870.

J 44.9 (72.2 km) Paved turnout to litter

WELLS ADVERTISERS

Hubs Motel ....Ph. (250) 994-3313
Northwood Family
   Restaurant ....Ph. (250) 994-3325
St. George's Gallery.....Ph. (250) 994-3492
Sunshine Cottage ....Ph. (250) 994-3342
Wells Hotel, The ....Ph. 1-800-860-2299
Wells Service Station ...Ph. (250) 994-3224
White Cap Motor Inn &
   RV Park ....Ph. 1-800-377-2028

barrel to south. **Jack o' Clubs Lake**; fishing for rainbows, lake trout and Dolly Varden.

J 45.2 (72.7 km) Rest area on peninsula to south with picnic tables, pit toilets and boat launch.

J 45.7 (73.6 km) Paved turnout with litter barrels to south.

J 46.1 (74.2 km) Lakeshore turnout with area information sign.

J 46.7 (75.2 km) **WELLS** (pop. 300, elevation 4,200 feet/1280m) offers all visitor facilities, including motels, restaurants, liquor outlet, groceries, gas, fishing and hunting licenses, 24-hour towing and mechanics, art schools, laundromat and full-service RV park The closest banking facilities are in Quesnel. Wells dates to the 1930s when the Cariboo Gold Quartz Mine, promoted and developed by Fred Wells, brought hundreds of workers to this valley. The mine closed in 1967, but the town has continued as a service centre and attraction for tourists. There are numerous art galleries and gift shops, some housed in refurbished buildings from the 1930s. Guided and self-guided tours of the town are available. A museum with displays of local mining history is open daily from June to September.

Recreation in the area is centered around some 30 miles/50 km of marked trails leading into alpine country. Summer activities include hiking historical trails, mountain biking (rentals available), gold panning, llama trekking and fishing. In winter, trails are groomed for skiing, snowmobiling and dogsledding.

The local Legion hosts horseshoes and bocci tournaments, has a pub and offers potluck suppers throughout the year. Winter events include: Yamafest in November; Rondezvous 97 and the Gold Rush Dogsled races in January; Snowarama in February; and the Great Canadian Hillclimb in March.

The Wells Hotel. Minutes from Barkervill/Bowron, enjoy simple elegance at this newly restored heritage country inn. Treat yourself in the hotel's Pooley Street Cafe: hot cinnamon buns, delicious soups, housemade pastas, fresh salads and more. Sip a cappucino or fine wine. Relax in our fireplace lounge with hardwood floors and library. Soak blissfully in the outdoor hot tub. 17 cozy, simple rooms include memorable breakfasts. Walk to galleries, museum, gift shops. Entering Wells from Quesnel: first left on Pooley Street, 100 yards, the bright yellow building. Easy RV parking. VISA/MasterCard/AMEX. 1-800-860-2299. [ADVERTISEMENT]

J 49.6 (79.8 km) Barkerville Provincial Park Forest Rose Campground to north. Lowhee Campground to south; 170 campsites, picnic areas and dump stations. ▲

J 50 (80.5 km) Gravel road leads north 18 miles/29 km to **Bowron Lakes** Provincial Park, noted for its interconnecting chain of lakes and the resulting 72-mile/116-km canoe circuit which takes from 7 to 10 days to complete. Visitor information available at registration centre next to main parking lot where

canoeists must register and pay circuit fees. Reservations recommended in July and August (required for 7 or more people); phone (250) 992-3111.

Airfield at junction with 2,500-foot/762-m paved runway, elev. 4,180 feet/1,274m.

There are 2 private lodges at the north end of the lake with restaurants, camping (at Becker's Lodge), a general store and canoe rentals. Provincial park campground has 25 sites, water, pit toilets, firewood and a boat launch. Swimming, fishing, canoeing, kayaking and hiking. ◄▲

Becker's Lodge. Overlooking Bowron Lake and the snowcapped Cariboo Mountains from our beautifully restored lodge restaurant, open for breakfast, lunch and dinner. We also offer cabins, chalets and bungalows, campsites with firepits and picnic tables. Hot showers, flush toilets, coin laundry. Licensed canoe outfitter for the Bowron Lake Wilderness Park. Canoe/kayak day-rentals. Store. Reservations: 1-800-808-4761. Local calls: (250) 992-8864. [ADVERTISEMENT] ▲

J 50.1 (80.7 km) Entrance to Barkerville; admission charged. Admisssion fees in 1996 for a 2-day pass were: Adults, $5.50; youth and seniors, $3.25; children, $1; and families, $10.75.

J 50.3 (81.7 km) Former site of Cameronton, named for John A. "Cariboo" Cameron who found gold in this area. Also in this area is Williams Creek, the richest gold-producing creek during the gold rush.

J 50.9 (81.9 km) Turnoff on 1.8-mile/2.9-km side road for gold rush cemetery and Government Hill Campground (0.2 mile/0.4 km), New Barkerville (0.4 mile/0.7 km) and Grubstake Store (0.7 mile/1.1 km). ▲

J 51 (82.1 km) **BARKERVILLE**, a provincial historic town; open year-round, phone (604) 994-3332. Visitor information at Reception Centre.

Barkerville was named for miner Billy Barker, who struck gold on Williams Creek. The resulting gold rush in 1862 created Barkerville. Virtually a ghost town when the provincial government began restoration in 1958, today Barkerville's buildings and boardwalks are faithful restorations or reconstructions from the town's heyday. Visitors can pan for gold, shop at the old-time general store, watch a blacksmith at work, or take in a show at the Theatre Royal. Restaurants and food service available. It is best to visit between June 1 and Labour Day, when the Theatre

Royal offers performances and all exhibits are open.

The Theatre Royal is extremely popular with visitors. The half-hour spring show plays daily (except Saturdays) from 12:45 to 1:15 P.M. between May 11 and June 14, 1997. Regular season begins June 15, 1997, with 1800s-style musical dramas playing daily (except Fridays) at 1 and 4 P.M. Regular season shows continue until Labour Day. Between June 28 and Aug. 31 there is also an 8 P.M. show on Saturdays and Sundays that is fashioned after a 1930s-style radio variety show. Admission is charged at all shows.

History comes alive at Barkerville thanks to interpreters and street performers who represent actual citizens of the town in 1870, discuss "current" events with visitors, conduct tours and stage daily dramas throughout the summer.

Beyond Main Street, the Cariboo Waggon Road leads on (for pedestrians only) to Richfield, 1 mile/1.6 km, to the courthouse of "Hanging" Judge Begbie.

**Return to Milepost CC 206
West Access Route**

BARKERVILLE ADVERTISERS

Prince George is British Columbia's third largest city. (Eero Sorila)

(Continued from page 55)

CC 247.6 (398.5 km) PG 29.4 (47.3 km) Woodpecker rest area to west; toilets, tables, litter barrels.

CC 257.7 (414.7 km) PG 19.3 (31 km) Stoner (unincorporated), no services.

CC 258.3 (415.7 km) PG 18.7 (30.1 km) **Great Canadian Park.** See display ad this section. ▲

CC 261.8 (421.3 km) PG 15.2 (24.5 km) Red Rock (unincorporated); ice; gas station with diesel; pay phone.

CC 264.9 (426.3 km) PG 12.1 (19.5 km) **Prince George Fallow Deer Farm.** Specializing in farm raised venison. Fresh, frozen, no preservatives, 100 percent venison. Available in various cuts in addition to delicious low-fat venison burgers, smokies and jerky. Serving fresh-cooked venison or beef burgers, ice cream and cold drinks. Informational deer tour wagon ride. Fee charged. Gift store featuring fine local crafts. Open May–September 9 A.M.–8 P.M. Groups welcome. (250) 330-4340. [ADVERTISEMENT]

CC 268.3 (431.8 km) PG 8.7 (14 km) **Bee Lazee RV Park, Campground & Honey Farm.** See display ad this section. ▲

CC 270.6 (435.5 km) PG 6.4 (10.3 km) Junction with bypass road to Yellowhead 16 East. Keep left for Prince George; continue straight ahead for Jasper and Edmonton. If you are headed east on Yellowhead Highway 16 for Jasper or Edmonton, turn to **Milepost E 450** in the YELLOWHEAD HIGHWAY 16 section and read the log back to front.

CC 273 (439.3 km) PG 4 (6.4 km) **Southpark RV Park.** See display ad this section. ▲

CC 273.4 (440 km) PG 3.6 (5.8 km) Access to Prince George airport to east.

CC 274 (440.9 km) PG 3 (4.8 km) **Sintich Trailer Park.** See display ad this section. ▲

CC 275.2 (442.8 km) PG 1.8 (2.8 km) Bridge over the Fraser River. Turn right at north end of bridge then left at stop sign for city centre via Queensway. This is the easiest access for Fort George Park; follow Queensway to 20th Avenue and turn east.

Continue straight ahead for Highway 16 entrance to city.

CC 276 (444.1 km) PG 1 (1.6 km) **Junction** of Highway 97 with Yellowhead 16 West. Description of Prince George follows. If you are headed west on Yellowhead Highway 16 for Prince Rupert, turn to **Milepost PG 0** in the YELLOWHEAD HIGHWAY 16 section. Prince Rupert is port of call for Alaska state ferries and BC Ferries (see MARINE ACCESS ROUTES section for details).

Prince George

CC 277 (445.8 km) **Population:** 75,000, area 160,000. **Emergency Services:** RCMP, phone (250) 562-3371, emergency only, phone 911. **Fire Department,** phone 911. **Ambulance,** 24-hour service, phone 911. **Poison Control Centre,** phone (250) 565-2442. **Hospital,** Prince George Regional, phone (250) 565-2000; emergency, phone (250) 565-2444.

Visitor Information: Tourism Prince George, Dept. MP, 1198 Victoria St., phone (250) 562-3700 or fax 563-3584, or toll free

1-800-668-7646. Open year-round, 8:30 A.M. to 5 P.M. weekdays September to June, daily in July and August. Visitor centre, junction Yellowhead 16 and Highway 97; open daily mid-May to Labour Day, 9 A.M. to 8 P.M., phone (250) 563-5493.

Elevation: 1,868 feet/569m. **Climate:** The inland location is tempered by the protection of mountains. The average annual frost-free period is 85 days, with 1,793 hours of bright sunshine. Dry in summer; chinooks off and on during winter which, accompanied by a western flow of air, break up the cold weather. Summer temperatures average 72°F/22°C with lows to 46°F/8°C. **Radio:** CKPG 550, CJCI 620, BC-FM 94.3, CBC-FM 91.5, C-101 FM. **Television:** 36 channels via cable. **Newspaper:** *The Citizen* (daily except Sunday); *Prince George This Week* (Sunday); *Free Press* (Sunday).

Prince George is located at the confluence of the Nechako and Fraser rivers, near the geographical centre of British Columbia. It is the fourth largest city in British Columbia. Hub of the trade and travel routes of the province, Prince George is located at the junction of Yellowhead Highway 16—linking Prince Rupert on the west coast with the Interior of Canada—and Highway 97, which runs south to Vancouver and north to Dawson Creek.

In the early 1800s, Simon Fraser of the North West Trading Co. erected a post here which he named Fort George in honour of the reigning English monarch. In 1906, survey parties for the transcontinental Grand Trunk Pacific Railway (later Canadian National Railways) passed through the area, and with the building of the railroad a great land boom took place. The city was incorporated in 1915 under the name Prince George. Old Fort George is now a park and

PRINCE GEORGE ADVERTISERS

picnic spot and the site of Fort George Museum.

Prince George is primarily an industrial centre, fairly dependent on the lumber industry, with 3 pulp mills, sawmills, planers, dry kilns, a plywood plant and 2 chemical plants to serve the pulp mills. Oil refining, mining and heavy construction are other major area industries. The Prince George Forest Region is the largest in the province.

Prince George is the focal point of the central Interior for financial and professional services, equipment and wholesale firms, machine shops and many services for the timber industry. Canada's newest university opened here in the fall of 1994. The campus of the University of Northern British Columbia is located at the top of Cranbrook Hill.

Agriculture in central British Columbia is basically a forage-livestock business, for which the climate and soils are well suited. Dairying and beef are the major livestock enterprises, with minor production in sheep and poultry.

ACCOMMODATIONS/VISITOR SERVICES

Prince George offers 5 hotels, 17 motels, 9 RV parks, and more than 2 dozen bed and breakfasts. Most accommodations are within easy reach of the business district. There are more than 80 restaurants in the city. Most stores are open 7 days a week. The usual hours of operation are: Sunday, noon to 5 P.M.; Saturday and Monday through Wednesday, 9:30 A.M. to 6 P.M.; Thursday and Friday, 9:30 A.M. to 9 P.M.

Cozy Corner Bed & Breakfast. A warm welcome greets you, relaxing hot tub, 2 guest rooms with TV/VCR. Room 1 has king, 2 twin beds, sitting area. Room 2 has queen bed, TV/VCR. Both have private bathrooms. Full breakfast. Reservations: Linda Malcolm, 7131 Harvard Crescent, Prince George, BC V2N 2V6. Phone (250) 964-7550, fax (250) 964-9056, e-mail: malcolm@pgonline.com.
[ADVERTISEMENT]

TRANSPORTATION

Air: Prince George airport is southeast of the city, serviced by Canadian Airlines International, Air BC and Central Mountain Air.

Limousine service to and from the airport.

Railroad: VIA Rail connects Prince George with Prince Rupert and Jasper, AB. Passenger service south to Vancouver via British Columbia Railway 3 days a week.

Bus: Greyhound. City bus service by Prince George Transit & Charter Ltd.

ATTRACTIONS

City View: Follow Connaught Drive to the viewpoint at Connaught Hill Park for a panoramic view of the city.

City Landmarks: Centennial Fountain at the corner of 7th Avenue and Dominion Street depicts the early history of Prince George in mosaic tile. A cairn at Fort George Park commemorates Sir Alexander Mackenzie.

Fort George Park is the largest park in Prince George and a good stop for travelers with its playgrounds, picnic tables, barbecue facilities and museum. The Fort George Railway operates on weekends and holidays at the park from a railway building patterned after the original Grand Trunk Pacific stations.

Fraser Fort George Regional Museum. Located in Fort George Park at 333 20th Avenue, the museum includes an explorations gallery focusing on the region's natural history and environment. A history hall provides an overview of the area's developmental history and includes an interactive multimedia film display. Open daily in summer, 10 A.M. to 5 P.M. Wheelchair accessible. Admission fee charged. For more information phone (250)562-1612.

Giscome Portage Regional Park, next to the scenic Fraser River, includes the Huble Homestead, which dates from 1912. These

original and reconstructed buildings are surrounded by grazing land and forest. Picnic tables and snackbar. Guided interpretive tours during peak season; admission free. Located north of Prince George on Highway 97; turn east off the highway at **Milepost PG 26.9** and drive 3.7 miles/ 6 km.

Cottonwood Island Park, located on the Nechako River (see city map), has picnic facilities and extensive nature trails.

Central B.C. Railway and Forestry Museum features a dozen original railway buildings, including 2 stations. Among the 50 pieces of rolling stock are 5 locomotives, a 1903 snow plow, a 1913 100-ton steam wrecking crane and a 90-foot 100-ton turntable. Items from 8 past and present railway companies are displayed. There is also a small collection of forestry, mining and agricultural machinery. Located at 850 River Road next to Cottonwood Island Nature Park. Open May to September 6 days a week from 9:30 A.M. to 5 P.M. For more information phone (250)563-7351.

Golf Courses. Aspen Grove Golf Club is 9 miles/14.5 km south of the city; Yellowhead Grove Golf Club, Pine Valley Golf Club, and Prince George Golf and Curling Club are on Yellowhead Highway 16 West.

Swimming. Four Seasons Swimming Pool at the corner of 7th Avenue and Dominion Street has a pool, water slide, diving tank and fitness centre. Open to the public afternoons and evenings.

Rockhounding. The hills and river valleys in the area provide abundant caches of Omineca agate and Schmoos. For more information, contact Prince George Rock and Gem Club, phone (250) 562-4526; or Spruce City Rock and Gem Club, phone (250) 562-1013.

Tennis Courts. A total of 20 courts currently available to the public at 3 places: 20th Avenue near the entrance to Fort George Park; at Massey Drive in Carrie Jane

Gray Park; and on Ospika Boulevard in the Lakewood Secondary School complex.

Industrial Tours are available from mid-May through August by contacting Tourism Prince George at (250) 562-3700. Tours, which are on weekdays only, include Northwood Pulp and Timber, and North Central Plywoods. Tours of Prince George Pulp and Intercon Pulp are available on request.

Tours of the Pacific Western Brewery are available; reservations required. Phone (250) 562-2424 or 1-800-663-8002, Monday through Friday.

Special Events: Elks May Day celebration; Prince George Regional Forest Exhibition in May (even years); Folkfest on July 1, Canada Day; Prince George Live, Sunday through Thursday during July and August; International Food Festival in August; Annual Sandblast Skiing in August; Prince George Airshow in August; Prince George Exhibition in July; Oktoberfest in October; and the winter Mardi Gras Festival in mid-February. Details on these and other events are available from Tourism Prince George; phone (250) 562-3700.

Side Trips: Prince George is the starting point for some of the finest holiday country in the province. There are numerous lakes and resorts nearby, among them: Bednesti Lake, 30 miles/48 km west of Prince George; Cluculz Lake, 44 miles/71 km west; Purden Lake, 42 miles/68 km east; and Tabor Lake, 6 miles/10 km east.

AREA FISHING: Highways 16 and 97 are the ideal routes for the sportsman, with year-round fishing and easy access to lakes and rivers. Hunters and fishermen stop over in Prince George as the jumping-off place for some of North America's finest big game hunting and fishing. For more information contact Fish & Wildlife at (250) 565-6145, or Tourism Prince George, phone (250) 562-3700.

West Access Route Log
(continued)
BC HIGHWAY 97/HART HIGHWAY
The John Hart Highway, completed in 1952, was named for the former B.C. premier who sponsored its construction. The highway is a 2-lane paved highway with both straight stretches and winding stretches.
This section of the log shows distance from Prince George (PG) followed by distance from Dawson Creek (DC).

PG 0 DC 250 (402.3 km) John Hart Bridge over the Nechako River. The 4-lane highway extends 6.5 miles/10.5 km northbound through the commercial and residential suburbs of Prince George.
PG 1.5 (2.4 km) DC 248.5 (399.9 km) Truck weigh scales. 24-hour gas station with diesel and propane; lube and oil service.

Hart Highway Mohawk. See display ad on page 62.
McQuik Lube & Oil. See display ad this section.
PG 2.5 (4 km) DC 247.5 (398.3 km) RV service centre.
PG 6.4 (10.3 km) DC 243.6 (392 km) **Hartway RV Park.** Shaded, fully-serviced sites. Pull-throughs. Free hot showers, laun

dromat, 30-amp, cable TV. Groceries nearby. Phone. On-site antique and gift shop. On south Kelly Road adjacent to highway. Access at stop light (Handlen Road Junction); south of RV park. 7729 South Kelly Rd., Prince George, BC V2K 3H5. (250) 962-8848. [ADVERTISEMENT] ▲
PG 6.5 (10.5 km) DC 243.5 (391.9 km)

Free guided tours are offered at historic Huble Homestead, Milepost PG 26.9.
(Judy Parkin, staff)

Two-lane highway (with passing lanes) begins abruptly northbound.

PG 14.6 (23.5 km) **DC 235.4** (378.8 km) Salmon River bridge. Litter barrel and river access to west at north end of bridge.

PG 14.7 (23.6 km) **DC 235.3** (378.7 km) **Salmon Valley Resort** campgrounds, RV park and convenience store, on over 20

acres along the scenic Salmon River. All facilities are wheelchair accessible including showers. 50 treed sites, 8 pull-throughs, all with fire rings, tables, laundry. Limited water and power 15–30 amp. Swimming and camping on the Salmon that's second to none. Fair fishing for rainbows, grayling and spring salmon. "Home of the Happy Camper." Phone (250) 971-2212. Fax (250) 971-2229. [ADVERTISEMENT]   ♿▲

PG 16.4 (26.4 km) **DC 233.6** (375.9 km) Highway overpass crosses railroad tracks.

PG 22 (35.4 km) **DC 228** (366.9 km) Gravel turnouts both sides of highway.

PG 26.5 (42.6 km) **DC 223.5** (359.7 km) Paved turnout to east with litter barrels and point of interest sign about Crooked River Forest Recreation Area.

PG 26.9 (43.3 km) **DC 223.1** (359 km) Access west 3.7 miles/6 km to Giscome Portage regional park via Mitchell Road. Site of historic Huble Homestead; guided tours, picnicking. Free admission.

Historic Huble Homestead. Relax and visit a historic Northern BC settlement. Scenic location next to the mighty Fraser River. Original, furnished log buildings. Includes the Huble's house—the oldest home in the region. Farm animals. Numerous picnic tables. Guided interpretive tours. Free admission. Just 6 km east of Highway 97. Phone (250) 960-4400. [ADVERTISEMENT]

PG 28.2 (45.4 km) **DC 221.8** (356.9 km) Turnoff to west for **Summit Lake**, a resort area popular with Prince George residents; lake char and rainbow fishing spring and fall.   ⟋

PG 29.3 (47.2 km) **DC 220.7** (355.2 km) Westcoast Energy compressor station.

PG 30.7 (49.4 km) **DC 219.3** (352.9 km) Second turnoff to west for Summit Lake.

PG 36.6 (58.9 km) **DC 213.4** (343.4 km) Cottonwood Creek.

PG 38.8 (62.4 km) **DC 211.2** (339.9 km) Paved turnout with litter barrel.

PG 40.6 (65.3 km) **DC 209.4** (337 km) Railroad crossing.

PG 42 (67.6 km) **DC 208** (334.7 km) Slow down for sharp turn across railroad tracks.

PG 43.9 (70.6 km) **DC 206.1** (331.7 km) Turnoff to west for Crooked River Provincial Park; 90 campsites, picnic area, flush toilets, tables, firepits, dump station. Camping fee charged. Also horseshoe pits, volleyball, playground, trails, swimming and paddleboat rentals. Powerboats prohibited. Picnic shelter with wood stove. **Crooked River** and area lakes have fair fishing for rainbow, Dolly Varden, grayling and whitefish.   ⟋▲

Highway 97 follows the Crooked River north to McLeod Lake.

PG 44.8 (72.1 km) **DC 205.2** (330.1 km) **BEAR LAKE** (unincorporated). Population

A yearling black bear photographed near the highway. (© J. Peery)

300; gas, diesel, propane, grocery, restaurant, motel, RV park, gift shop, post office and ambulance station. Highway maintenance camp. ▲

The 2 lumber mills in town are the main industry of the area, employing approximately two-thirds of the community. Information on area fishing, hiking, hunting and swimming may be obtained from the Bear Lake Community Commision; phone (250) 972-4488, or write general delivery, Bear Lake, BC V0J 3G0.

Grizzly Inn, Restaurant, Motel & RV Park. See display ad this section. ▲

PG 50.7 (81.6 km) **DC 199.3** (320.7 km) Angusmac Creek.

PG 54.2 (87.2 km) **DC 195.8** (315.1 km) Tumbler Ridge branch line British Columbia Railway connects Tumbler Ridge with the B.C. Railway and Canadian National Railway, allowing for shipments of coal from Tumbler Ridge to Ridley Island near Prince Rupert.

PG 55.6 (89.5 km) **DC 194.4** (312.8 km) Large gravel turnout with litter barrel to west.

PG 56.1 (90.3 km) **DC 193.9** (312 km) Large gravel turnout with litter barrel to west.

PG 57 (91.7 km) **DC 193** (310.6 km) Large gravel turnout with litter barrel to west.

PG 60.8 (97.8 km) **DC 189.2** (304.5 km) Turnout with litter barrel to east.

PG 62.4 (100.4 km) **DC 187.6** (301.9 km) Large gravel turnout with litter barrel to east.

PG 65.2 (104.9 km) **DC 184.8** (297.4 km) Lomas Creek.

PG 67.9 (109.3 km) **DC 182.1** (293 km) Large, double-ended, paved rest area to west

beside small lake; litter barrels, picnic tables and pit toilets.

PG 68.8 (110.7 km) **DC 181.2** (291.6 km) 42 Mile Creek.

PG 71.8 (115.5 km) **DC 178.2** (286.8 km) **Whiskers Bay Resort** has beautiful lakeside camping spots on a quiet bay, some with electricity and water. Hot showers. Cabins with showers, fridges and cooking facilities. Fishing is right off our dock or in the many surrounding lakes. Sunsets are sensational and hummingbirds are bountiful. The cafe offers breakfast, lunch, wonderful burgers, homemade pies, soups, the best coffee on the highway and real northern hospitality. Come visit us! [ADVERTISEMENT] ▲

PG 76.6 (123.3 km) **DC 173.4** (279.1 km) First view northbound of McLeod Lake and view of Whisker's Point.

PG 77.7 (125 km) **DC 172.3** (277.3 km) Turnoff to west for Whisker's Point Provincial Park on McLeod Lake. This is an exceptionally nice campground with a paved loop road, 69 level gravel sites, a dump station, tap water, flush toilets, boat ramp, fire rings, firewood and picnic tables. Also horseshoe pits, volleyball, playground and picnic shelter. Camping fee charged. Boat launch, swimming, sandy beach and fishing. ←♦▲

McLeod Lake has fair fishing for rainbow, lake char and Dolly Varden, spring and fall, trolling is best. ←♦

PG 81.4 (131 km) **DC 168.6** (271.3 km) Lodge (closed).

PG 84 (135.2 km) **DC 166** (267.1 km) Food, gas, camping and lodging. ▲

PG 84.5 (136 km) **DC 165.5** (266.3 km) **FORT McLEOD** (unincorporated) has a gas station, grocery, motel and cafe. A monument here commemorates the founding of

Fort McLeod, oldest permanent settlement west of the Rockies and north of San Francisco. Founded in 1805 by Simon Fraser as a trading post for the North West Trading Co., the post was named by Fraser for Archie McLeod.

PG 84.7 (136.3 km) **DC 165.3** (266 km) **McLEOD LAKE** (unincorporated), post office, store, lodging and liquor store.

PG 85 (136.8 km) **DC 165** (265.5 km) Turnoff for Carp Lake Provincial Park, 20 miles/32 km west via a gravel road; 105 campsites on Carp and War lakes, limited island camping, picnic tables, firepits, boat launch, fishing and swimming. Also tap water, dump station, horseshoe pits, playground and picnic shelter with wood stove. Ten-minute walk to scenic War Falls. Camping fee charged. Park access road follows the McLeod River to Carp Lake. ←▲

Carp Lake, rainbow June through September; special restrictions in effect, check current posted information. **McLeod River**, rainbow from July, fly-fishing only. ←

PG 85.6 (137.8 km) **DC 164.4** (264.6 km) Paved turnout with litter barrel to west.

PG 87.6 (141 km) **DC 162.4** (261.4 km) Westcoast Energy compressor station and McLeod Lake school.

PG 89.8 (144.5 km) **DC 160.2** (257.8 km) Turnoff to west for Tudyah Lake Provincial Park; 36 campsites, picnic tables, fire rings, firewood, pit toilets, drinking water. Also swimming, boat ramp, fishing. Camping fee charged. ▲

Tudyah Lake, shore access, rainbow, Dolly Varden and some grayling in summer and late fall. **Pack River** (flows into Tudyah Lake), fishing for: grayling (catch-and-release only), June 1 to July 1; rainbow, June 10 to November; large Dolly Varden, Sept. 15 to Oct. 10, spinning. ←

PG 89.9 (144.7 km) **DC 160.1** (257.6 km) Bear Creek bridge.

PG 93.9 (151.1 km) **DC 156.1** (251.2 km) Gas, food and lodging (open year-round).

PG 94.7 (152.4 km) **DC 155.3** (249.9 km) Parsnip River bridge. This is the Rocky Mountain Trench, marking the western boundary of the Rocky Mountains. Northbound motorists begin gradual climb through the Misinchinka then Hart ranges of the Rocky Mountains.

Parsnip River, good fishing for grayling and Dolly Varden, some rainbow, best from August to October; a boat is necessary. ←

PG 95.2 (153.2 km) **DC 154.8** (249.1 km) Junction with Highway 39 (paved), which leads 18 miles/29 km to the community of Mackenzie (description follows). Food, gas, lodging, camping and tourist information at junction. Signed trailheads along Highway 39 are part of the Mackenzie Demonstration

Forest. There are 8 self-guiding trails in the demonstration forest, each focusing on an aspect of forest management. Interpretive signs are posted along each trail.

Mackenzie Junction Cafe. See display ad on page 63. ▲

Mackenzie

J 18 (29 km) Located 18 miles/29 km northwest of the John Hart Highway 97 via Highway 39. **Population:** 5,796. **Emergency Services:** Emergency only, phone 911. **RCMP,** phone (250) 997-3288. **Hospital,** 12 beds. **Ambulance,** phone 911.

Visitor Information: Visitor/tourist information booth in the railway caboose located at the junction of Highways 97 and 39. Or write the Chamber of Commerce, Box 880, Mackenzie, BC V0J 2C0; (250) 997-5459.

Elevation: 2,300 feet/701m. **Radio:** CKMK 1240, CKPG 1240; CBC-FM 990. **Television:** Channels 3, 13 and cable.

A large, modern, planned community, Mackenzie was built in 1965. The city was named after Alexander Mackenzie, early explorer. It lies at the south end of Williston Lake, the largest manmade reservoir on the continent. Construction of the new town in what had been just wilderness was sparked by the Peace River Dam project and the need to attract skilled employees for industrial growth. Mackenzie was incorporated in May 1966 under "instant town" legislation; the first residents moved here in July 1966. Industry here includes mining and forestry, with 4 sawmills, a paper mill and 2 pulp mills. Inquire about mill tours at the Infocentre.

On display in Mackenzie is the "world's largest tree crusher." The 56-foot-long electrically powered Le Tourneau G175 tree crusher was used in clearing land at the Peace River Power Project in the mid-1960s.

Attractions include swimming, waterskiing, fishing and boating at Morfee Lake, a 10-minute walk from town. There are boat launches on both Morfee Lake and Williston Lake reservoir. Good view of Mackenzie and Williston Lake reservoir from the top of Morfee Mountain (elev. 5,961 feet/1,817m); check with Infocentre for directions. There are self-guided hiking trails at John Dahl Regional Park, located behind the recreation centre.

The Mackenzie and District Museum, located at the Ernie Bodin Community Centre, offers exhibits on early settlers, area wildlife and lakes, and the birth of the town; phone (250) 997-3021.

Mackenzie has all visitor facilities, including motels, restaurants, shopping malls, gas stations, swimming pool, tennis courts, 9-hole golf course and other recreation facilities. There is also a paved 5,000-foot/1,524-m airstrip.

There is a municipal RV park with 20 sites, flush toilets, showers and sani-dump. Fee only for electrical hookups. Fishing for rainbow, Dolly Varden, arctic char and grayling in Williston Lake. ⊷▲

Alexander Mackenzie Hotel & Mall. See display ad this section.

District of Mackenzie. See display ad this section.

West Access Route Log
(continued)

PG 95.2 (153.2 km) DC 154.8 (249.1 km) Junction with Highway 39 to Mackenzie; food, gas, lodging and tourist booth.

PG 95.5 (153.7 km) DC 154.5 (248.6 km) Highway crosses railroad tracks.

PG 98.9 (158.2 km) DC 151.1 (243.2 km) Gravel turnout with litter barrel to east.

PG 106 (170.6 km) DC 144 (231.7 km) Turnout with litter barrel to east.

PG 108.4 (174.4 km) DC 141.6 (227.9 km) Highway maintenance yard.

PG 108.5 (174.6 km) DC 141.5 (227.7 km) Bridge over Honeymoon Creek.

NOTE: Watch for road construction next 14 miles/22.4 km northbound in 1997.

PG 109.6 (176.4 km) DC 140.4 (225.9 km) Powerlines crossing highway carry electricity south from hydro dams in the Hudson Hope area. (See HUDSON'S HOPE LOOP section.)

PG 110.5 (177.8 km) DC 139.5 (224.5 km) Slow down for sharp curve across railroad tracks.

PG 112.3 (180.7 km) DC 137.7 (221.6 km) Bridge over Rolston Creek; dirt turnout by small falls to west.

PG 115.3 (185.6 km) DC 134.7 (216.8 km) Bijoux Falls Provincial Park; pleasant picnic area adjacent falls on west side of highway. This day-use area has paved parking for 50 cars, pit toilets and picnic tables. Good photo opportunity.

Misinchinka River, southeast of the highway; fishing for grayling, whitefish and Dolly Varden. ➤

PG 116.3 (187.2 km) DC 133.7 (215.2 km) Highway crosses under railroad.

PG 119.3 (191.8 km) DC 130.8 (210.5 km) Crossing Pine Pass (elev. 3,068 feet/935m), the highest point on the John Hart-Peace River Highway. Beautiful view of the Rockies to the northeast. Good highway over pass; steep grade southbound.

PG 119.4 (192.2 km) DC 130.6 (210.2 km) Turnoff to Powder King Ski Village. Skiing November to late April; chalet with ski shop, cafeteria, restaurant and lounge, hostel-style hotel. This area receives an annual average snowfall of 495 inches. Campground at Powder King Ski Village, open in summer. ▲

PG 121.4 (195.4 km) DC 128.6 (207 km) Viewpoint to east with point of interest sign about Pine Pass and view of Azouzetta Lake. Pit toilet and litter barrels.

PG 122.4 (197 km) DC 127.6 (205.3 km) Pine Valley Park, open year-round; cafe, lodge, campground on Azouzetta Lake. Very scenic spot. Spectacular hiking on Murray Mountain Trail; inquire at lodge for details. A scuba diving school operates at Azouzetta Lake in summer. Fishing for rainbow (stocked lake) to 1¹/₂ lbs., flies or lures, July to October. Boat launch. ➤▲

NOTE: Watch for road construction next 14 miles/22.4 km southbound in 1997.

PG 125.5 (202 km) DC 124.5 (200.3 km) Microwave station and receiving dish to west.

PG 125.7 (202.3 km) DC 124.3 (200 km) Westcoast Energy compressor station.

PG 128.7 (207.1 km) DC 121.3 (195.2 km) Power lines cross highway.

PG 131.1 (211 km) DC 118.9 (191.3 km) Turnout with litter barrel.

PG 140.6 (226.3 km) DC 109.4 (176.1 km) Bridge over Link Creek.

PG 141.4 (227.5 km) DC 108.6 (174.8 km) Gravel turnout with litter barrels.

PG 142.3 (229 km) DC 107.7 (173.3 km) Bridge over West Pine River.

PG 142.8 (229.8 km) DC 107.2 (172.5 km) Bridge over West Pine River.

PG 143 (230.1 km) DC 107 (172.2 km) Paved rest area with litter barrels and pit toilets beside Pine River.

PG 143.4 (230.8 km) DC 106.6 (171.6 km) Bridge over West Pine River, B.C. Railway overpass.

PG 144.3 (232.2 km) DC 105.7 (170.1 km) Food, gas, towing, lodging and camping; autotel 784-9443. ▲

Silver Sands Lodge. See display ad this section. ▲

PG 146.1 (235.1 km) DC 103.9 (167.2 km) Cairns Creek.

PG 146.9 (236.4 km) DC 103.1 (165.9 km) Gravel access road to Pine River to south.

PG 148.2 (238.5 km) DC 101.8 (163.8 km) LeMoray (unincorporated). Lodge to north of highway was closed in 1996, current status unknown. Highway maintenance camp.

PG 148.3 (238.7 km) DC 101.7 (163.7 km) Gravel turnout to south.

PG 148.8 (239.5 km) DC 101.2 (162.9 km) Lillico Creek.

PG 149.7 (240.9 km) DC 100.3 (161.4 km) Marten Creek.

PG 150.4 (242 km) DC 99.6 (160.3 km) Big Boulder Creek.

PG 156.2 (251.4 km) DC 93.8 (151 km) Fisher Creek.

PG 156.9 (252.5 km) DC 93.1 (149.8 km) Large gravel turnout with litter barrel to south beside Pine River.

PG 159.9 (257.3 km) DC 90.1 (145 km) Crassier Creek.

PG 161.7 (260.2 km) DC 88.3 (142.1 km) Westcoast Energy compressor station.

PG 163.6 (263.3 km) DC 86.4 (139 km) Pine Valley rest areas, both sides of highway, with picnic tables and pit toilets. View of Pine River to south.

PG 169.5 (272.8 km) DC 80.5 (129.5 km) Turnout with picnic tables, pit toilets and litter barrel to south overlooking the beautiful Pine River valley.

PG 172.4 (277.4 km) DC 77.6 (124.9 km) Westcoast Energy (natural gas), Pine River plant. View of the Rocky Mountain foothills to the south and west.

PG 177.4 (285.5 km) DC 72.6 (116.8 km) Turnout with litter barrel.

PG 181.9 (292.7 km) DC 68.1 (109.6 km) Bissett Creek.

PG 183.6 (295.5 km) DC 66.4 (106.9 km) Turnout with litter barrels at Wildmare Creek.

PG 183.7 (295.6 km) DC 66.3 (106.7 km) Wildmare Grove Campsite. 50 sites. 32 long pull-throughs, back-ins, with full hookups, firepits and picnic tables. Tent sites. Quiet, beautifully treed with easy access to and from the highway. Hot showers, flush toilets, sani-station and pay phone. 3 miles west of Chetwynd on Highway 97. Phone (250) 788-2747. Box 42, Chetwynd, BC V0C 1J0. [ADVERTISEMENT] ▲

PG 184.1 (296.3 km) DC 65.9 (106 km) Truck stop; gas, diesel, food and lodging.

Chetwynd

PG 187.6 (301.9 km) DC 62.4 (100.4 km) Located on Highway 97 at the junction with Highway 29 north to the Alaska Highway via Hudson's Hope, and south to Tumbler Ridge. Population: 3,000, area 8,000. Emergency Services: RCMP, phone (250) 788-9221. Hospital, Poison Control Centre and Ambulance, phone (250) 788-3522. Fire Department, phone (250) 788-2345.

Visitor Information: Chamber of Commerce, open 9 A.M. to 5 P.M. July 1 to Labour Day weekend; open 9 A.M. to 4 P.M. rest of year. Write Box 1000, Chetwynd V0C 1J0, or phone (250) 788-3345 or 788-3655; fax 788-7843. Chetwynd Infocentre is located on the North Access Road adjacent to Highway 97 in town by the traffic lights, welcome to

CHETWYND ADVERTISERS

Chetwynd sign and bear sculpture.

Elevation: 2,017 feet/615m. **Radio:** CFGP 105, CISN-FM 103.9, CJDC 890, CKNL 560, CBC 1170, CFMI-FM 102. **Television:** 7 channels (includes CBC, BCTV, ABC, CBS and NBC) plus pay cable.

The town was formerly known as Little Prairie and is a division point on the British Columbia Railway. The name was changed to honour the late British Columbia Minister of Railways Ralph Chetwynd, who was instrumental in the northward extension of the province-owned railway. In recent years, Chetwynd's collection of chainsaw sculptures has earned it the title, "Chain Saw Sculpture Capital of the World." The Infocentre has a map showing locations of the 2 dozen sculptures in town.

Chetwynd lies at the northern end of one of the largest known coal deposits on earth. Access from Chetwynd south to Tumbler Ridge and the resource development known as the North East Coal is via Highway 29 south, a 56-mile/90-km paved road (see

Chainsaw sculpture of bears welcomes visitors to Chetwynd. *(Earl L. Brown, staff)*

HIGHWAY 29 SOUTH side road log this section). Forestry, mining, natural gas processing, ranching and farming are the main industries in Chetwynd. Louisiana Pacific has a modern nonpolluting pulp mill here. Free guided tours are available of Canadian Forest Products (250/788-2231) and Chetwynd Forest Industries (250/788-2686) soft wood sawmills.

Chetwynd is a fast-growing community with several large motels, fast-food outlets, restaurants, banks and 2 bank machines, post office, 2 laundromats, gas stations, supermarkets, art gallery and 2 9-hole golf courses. Good traveler's stop with easy access to all services. (Heavy commercial and industrial traffic often fill up local motels and campgrounds; reserve ahead.) Chetwynd & District Leisure Pool has a wave machine, whirlpool, sauna and weight room; open daily 6 A.M. to 10 P.M., visitors welcome.

The Little Prairie Heritage Museum, located on Highway 97 at the west end of town, features the region's pioneer days; inquire at infocentre for directions. The museum is open from the first Tuesday in July to the last Saturday in August.

Chetwynd has established a 30-mile/50-km scenic trail system for hiking and mountain biking. Contact the Visitor Infocentre for more details.

Municipal campground in town with 20 sites and dump station; fee charged. There's also a dump station at the 51st Avenue car/truck wash. There are private RV parks in town and on Highway 97. Moberly Lake Provincial Park is 12 miles/19.3 km north of Chetwynd via Highway 29 north (see **Milepost PG 187.9**) and 1.9 miles/3 km west via a gravel road. The park has 109 campsites, beach, picnic area, playground, nature trail, boat launch and a private marina next door with boat rental and concession. There's good swimming at huge Moberly Lake on a warm summer day. Worth the drive. ▲

Westwind RV Park. Chetwynd's newest and most modern. On Highway 97 North towards Dawson Creek. 50 large pull-through sites with full hookups. New restrooms, showers and laundry facility with handicap access. RV wash, Sani-station. All sites have 30-amp service and lawn. On town water and sewer. Picnic area, fire pits, playground, free hot showers, public phone and cable available. Walking distance to leisure pool. Owner lives on site for supervision and security. Your hosts David and Laurie Gayse. Phone (250) 788-2199, fax (250) 788-2086. [ADVERTISEMENT]　&▲

West Access Route Log

(continued)

PG 187.8 (302.2 km) **DC 62.2** (100.1 km) Highway crosses railroad tracks.

PG 187.9 (302.4 km) **DC 62.1** (99.9 km) Junction with Highway 29 north, which leads 12 miles/19.3 km to Moberly Lake, 36.5 miles/58.7 km to Peace River Provincial Recreation Area and Peace Canyon dam, and 40.4 miles/64.9 km to community of Hudson's Hope and access to W.A.C. Bennett Dam; Highway 29 north connects with the

SHORT CUT COMING FROM ALASKA

Alaska Highway 53.7 miles/86.4 km north of Dawson Creek. (See HUDSON'S HOPE LOOP section for details.)

Highway climbs next 12 miles/19 km for Dawson Creek-bound motorists.

PG 189.4 (304.8 km) **DC 60.6** (97.5 km) Junction with Highway 29 (paved) south to Gwillim Lake and Tumbler Ridge (see HIGHWAY 29 SOUTH side road log on page 68). Tumbler Ridge is also accessible from **Milepost PG 237.7** via the Heritage Highway.

District of Tumbler Ridge. See display ad this section.

PG 199.3 (320.7 km) **DC 50.7** (81.6 km) Gravel turnouts with litter barrels both sides of highway.

PG 201.2 (323.8 km) **DC 48.8** (78.5 km)

Slow down for sharp curve across railroad tracks.

PG 204.3 (328.8km) **DC 45.7** (73.5km) Access to Louisianna Pacific Pulp Mill to north.

PG 205.6 (330.9 km) **DC 44.4** (71.5 km) Turnout with litter barrel and a commanding view of the East Pine River valley to the south.

PG 206.5 (332.3 km) **DC 43.5** (70 km) Sharp curves approximately next 2 miles/3.2 km as highway descends toward Dawson Creek. View of Table Mountain.

PG 207.9 (334.6 km) **DC 42.1** (67.7 km) Highway crosses under railroad.

PG 208.1 (334.9 km) **DC 41.9** (67.4 km) Sharp turn to south at west end of bridge for

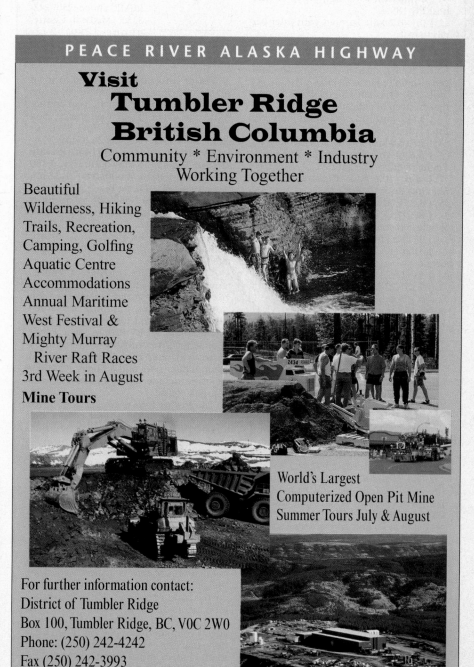

PEACE RIVER ALASKA HIGHWAY

Visit
Tumbler Ridge British Columbia

Community * Environment * Industry
Working Together

Beautiful
Wilderness, Hiking
Trails, Recreation,
Camping, Golfing
Aquatic Centre
Accommodations
Annual Maritime
West Festival &
Mighty Murray
River Raft Races
3rd Week in August

Mine Tours

World's Largest
Computerized Open Pit Mine
Summer Tours July & August

For further information contact:
District of Tumbler Ridge
Box 100, Tumbler Ridge, BC, V0C 2W0
Phone: (250) 242-4242
Fax (250) 242-3993
Visitor Info Centre: (250) 242-4702
email: tr-econ@pris.bc.ca.

SUPER, NATURAL BRITISH COLUMBIA®

Highway 29 South Log

Highway 29 South is a paved road that leads 55.9 miles/90 km from **Milepost PG 189.4** to the community of Tumbler Ridge. Travelers may return to Highway 97 via Highway 29, or via the Heritage Highway, a paved road that leads 59.5 miles/95 km from Tumbler Ridge to junction with Highway 97 at **Milepost PG 237.7**.

Distance from Highway 97 junction (J) is shown.

J 0 Junction with Highway 97 at **Milepost PG 189.4.**

J 0.1 (0.2 km) Turnout with litter barrels to east.

Highway 29 climbs next 2.3 miles/3.7 km southbound.

J 1.9 (3.1 km) Distance marker indicates Tumbler Ridge 88 km.

J 2.8 (4.5 km) Sign: Trucks check brakes, steep hill ahead.

J 3 (4.8 km) Large gravel turnouts with litter barrels both sides of highway.

J 5.5 (8.8 km) Twidwell Bend bridge.

J 5.6 (9 km) Access road east to Long Prairie (8 miles/12.9 km).

J 6.6 (10.6 km) Highway parallels Sukunka River to west.

J 8.2 (13.2 km) Zonnebeke Creek.

J 8.5 (13.7 km) Natural Springs Resort; 9-hole golf course.

J 9 (14.5 km) Kilometrepost 15.

J 10.6 (17 km) Bridge over Dickebush Creek.

J 11 (17.7 km) Sanctuary River.

J 13.7 (22 km) **Junction** with Sukunka Forest Road, which leads west 11 miles/17.7 km to Sukunka Falls. *NOTE: Radio-controlled road, travellers must monitor channel 151.325 MHz.*

J 13.8 (22.2 km) Highway climbs next 3 miles/4.8 km southbound.

J 16.7 (26.9 km) Turnouts with litter barrels both sides of highway.

J 21.6 (34.8 km) Turnout with litter barrels to east.

J 26.9 (43.3 km) Turnouts with litter barrels both sides of highway.

J 28.4 (45.7 km) Paved road leads east 1.2 miles/1.9 km to **Gwillim Lake** Provincial Park (gate closed 11 P.M. to 7 A.M.); 49 campsites, picnic tables, firewood and firepits. Day-use area and boat launch. Fishing for lake trout, grayling and pike. Camping fee $7 to $12.   ◄▬◄▲

J 40.8 (65.6 km) Access road leads west 9 miles/14.5 km to Bullmoose Mountain and mine. Mine tours may be available; phone (250) 242-5221 for current information.

J 41.1 (66.1 km) Turnout to east.

J 41.5 (66.8 km) Bridge over Bullmoose Flats River.

J 46.1 (74.2 km) Turnout with litter barrels to east. Phillips Way Summit, elev. 3,695 feet/1,126m.

J 51.4 (82.7 km) Bullmoose Creek bridge.

J 52.6 (84.3 km) Wolverine River bridge.

J 54.1 (87 km) Murray River bridge.

J 54.8 (88.2 km) Flatbed Creek bridge.

J 54.9 (88.3 km) Flatbed Creek Campground; 28 sites, hookups, water, flush toilets, showers, dump station, picnic tables and playground. Camping fee $10.   ▲

J 55.9 (90 km) Turnoff for community of Tumbler Ridge (description follows).

Tumbler Ridge

Located 116.5 miles/ 187.5 km southwest of Dawson Creek via Highways 97 and 29. **Population:** 3,800. **Emergency Services: RCMP,** phone (250) 242-5252. **Medical Centre,** phone (250) 242-5271. **Ambulance,** phone 1-800-461-9911. **Fire Department,** phone (250) 242-5555.

Visitor Information: Located in town at Southgate Road and Front Street, across from the hospital. Open year-round. Write the Chamber of Commerce, Box 606, Tumbler Ridge, BC V0C 2W0, or phone (250) 242-4702, fax 242-5159.

Elevation: 3,000 feet/914m. **Private Aircraft:** 9 miles/15 km south; elev. 3,150 feet/960m, length 4,000 feet/ 1,218m; asphalt; fuel 80, 100, Jet B.

Tumbler Ridge was built in conjunction with development of the North East Coal resource. Construction of the townsite began in 1981. It is British Columbia's newest community, incorporated June 1, 1984.

Visitor facilities include a motel, restaurants, retail and grocery outlets, service stations with major repairs, car wash and a laundromat. Camping at Flatbed Creek Campground just outside of town and at Monkman RV Park in town. Recreational facilities include a community centre with arena, curling rink, weight room, indoor pool and a library. Outdoor facilities include tennis courts and a 9-hole golf course.   ▲

The Visitor Infocentre provides a free slide presentation on Tumbler Ridge history and development. The Grizzly Valley Days Maritime West Festival, held Aug. 19–25, 1997, includes a parade, cod barrel race, Mr. Grizzly Valley contest, craft fair and other activities.

Major attraction in the area is Monkman Provincial Park, site of spectacular 225-foot/69-m Kinuseo (keh-NEW-see-oh or Keh-NEW-soh) Falls. The falls and a 42-site campground are accessible from Tumbler Ridge via a 37-mile/60-km dirt road (watch for trucks) south from town. Viewing platform of falls is a short walk from the campground. For more information on the park, contact BC Parks in Fort St. John, phone (250) 787-3407.   ▲

The Quintette Mine is the World's largest computerized open pit mine. Coal mine tours are available at Quintette Mine south of town and at Bullmoose Mine (see **Milepost J 40.7** on Highway 29); inquire locally.

District of Tumbler Ridge. See display ad on page 67.

Return to Milepost PG 189.4 West Access Route

East Pine Provincial Park (0.5 mile on gravel road); picnicking and boat launch on Pine River. Turnout with litter barrel at park entrance.

From East Pine Provincial Park, canoeists may make a 2-day canoe trip down the Pine River to the Peace River; take-out at Taylor Landing Provincial Park (at **Milepost DC 34** on the Alaska Highway).

PG 208.2 (335.1 km) **DC 41.8** (67.3 km) Bridge across East Pine River. Railroad also crosses river here.

PG 208.3 (335.2 km) **DC 41.7** (67.1 km) Turnout with litter barrel to south.

PG 209.8 (337.6 km) **DC 40.2** (64.7 km) East Pine (unincorporated) has a store, gas station and distinctive treehouse.

PG 211.7 (340.7 km) **DC 38.3** (61.6 km) Turnout with litter barrel to north.

PG 221.5 (356.5 km) **DC 28.5** (45.9 km) Turnouts with litter barrels both sides of highway.

PG 222 (357.3 km) **DC 28** (45 km) Groundbirch (unincorporated); store, liquor outlet, gas, propane, diesel, post office and camping.   ▲

PG 230.7 (371.3 km) **DC 19.3** (31.1 km) Progress (unincorporated), highway maintenance yard, cairn and pay phone.

PG 234.4 (377.2 km) **DC 15.6** (25.1 km) Turnout with litter barrels to north.

PG 237.7 (382.5 km) **DC 12.3** (19.8 km) **Junction** with Heritage Highway, which leads 59.5 miles/96 km (paved) south to the community of Tumbler Ridge and access roads to the North East Coal Development. (Tumbler Ridge is also accessible via Highway 29 south from Chetwynd. See side road log this section.)

From Tumbler Ridge, the Heritage Highway continues 92 miles/148 km east and north to connect with Highway 2 southeast of Dawson Creek. Inquire locally about road conditions.

PG 238 (383 km) **DC 12** (19.3 km) Kiskatinaw River bridge.

PG 240.7 (387.4 km) **DC 9.3** (15 km) Arras (unincorporated), cafe and gas station.

PG 247.9 (398.9 km) **DC 2.1** (3.4 km) Small turnout with litter barrel and point of interest sign to south.

PG 248 (399.1 km) **DC 2** (3.2 km) Private RV Park.   ▲

PG 249.9 (402.2 km) **DC 0.1** (0.2 km) Entering Dawson Creek. Private campground on south side of highway; Rotary Lake Park and camping on north side of highway.   ▲

PG 250 (402.3 km) **DC 0 Junction** of the Hart Highway and Alaska Highway; turn right for downtown Dawson Creek, Mile Zero of the Alaska Highway. See the description of Dawson Creek in the ALASKA HIGHWAY section.

HUDSON'S HOPE LOOP

Connects: Chetwynd, BC, to Alaska Hwy.   **Length:** 87 miles
Road Surface: Paved   **Season:** Open all year
Steepest Grade: 10 percent
Major Attraction: W.A.C. Bennett Dam

(See map, page 70)

	Alaska Hwy	Chetwynd	Hudson's Hope
Alaska Hwy		87	47
Chetwynd	87		40
Hudson's Hope	47	40	

View of scenic farmland along the Peace River from turnout on Highway 29.
(Earl L. Brown, staff)

The Hudson's Hope Loop links the John Hart Highway (Highway 97) with the Alaska Highway (also Highway 97). This 86.9-mile/139.8-km paved loop road provides year-round access to the town of Hudson's Hope, W.A.C. Bennett Dam, Peace Canyon Dam and Moberly Lake. As a shortcut bypassing Dawson Creek, the Hudson's Hope Loop saves 28.9 miles/46.5 km. Highway 29 is a good, scenic 2-lane road but is steep and winding in places.

A popular side trip with Alaska Highway travelers today, and an alternate access route to the Alaska Highway, Highway 29 was only a 53-mile/85.3-km side road to the Hudson Hope Coal Mines in the 1950s. In the 1960s, with construction of the W.A.C. Bennett Dam under way, Alaska Highway travelers drove the side road to see the Peace River dam site. The highway was completed to Chetwynd in 1968.

Hudson's Hope Loop Log

Distance from Chetwynd (C) is followed by distance from Alaska Highway junction (AH).

C 0 AH 86.9 (139.8 km) **Junction** of Highways 29 and 97 at Chetwynd (see **Milepost PG 187.6** in the WEST ACCESS ROUTE section for description of Chetwynd).

C 0.5 (0.8 km) **AH 86.4** (139 km) Truck weigh scales to west. Highway climbs next 4.3 miles/7 km westbound.

C 2.3 (3.7 km) **AH 84.6** (136.1 km) Jackfish Road to east.

C 5 (8 km) **AH 81.9** (131.8 km) Turnout with litter barrel to west.

C 12 (19.3 km) **AH 74.9** (120.5 km) Gravel access road leads 2 miles/3.2 km west to **Moberly Lake** Provincial Park on south shore; 109 campsites, swimming, waterskiing, picnicking, drinking water, dump station, boat launch, $9.50 camping fee. This beautiful 9-mile-/14.5-km-long lake drains at its east end into Moberly River, which in turn runs into the Peace River. Fishing for lake trout, Dolly Varden and whitefish. ⇌▲

Moberly Lake Marina & Resort. See display ad this section.

C 12.2 (19.6 km) **AH 74.7** (120.2 km) Moberly River bridge; parking area with litter barrel at south end.

C 15.9 (25.6 km) **AH 71** (114.3 km) Highway cairn is memorial to John Moberly, fur trader and explorer who first landed here in 1865.

C 16.4 (26.4 km) **AH 70.5** (113.5 km) Spencer Tuck Regional Park; picnic tables, swimming, fishing and boat launch. ⇌

C 17.4 (28 km) **AH 69.5** (111.8 km)

Harv's Resort, on the north shore of beautiful Moberly Lake. Treed picnic sites, large grass picnic field, cabins, campsites, 40 full-service 30-amp hookups. Swimming, fishing, pay phone, laundromat and showers. Store, restaurant. Gas, oils, propane, hunting and fishing licenses. Boat rental and dock. Boat launch and golf course nearby. Your hosts, Harve and Darlene Evans. Open till 10 P.M. daily. Phone (250) 788-9145. [ADVERTISEMENT] ▲

C 18.3 (29.5 km) **AH 68.6** (110.4 km) **MOBERLY LAKE.** Post office, cafe, store and pay phone.

C 18.5 (29.8 km) **AH 68.4** (110.1 km) Moberly Lake and District Golf Club, 0.7 mile/1.1 km from highway; 9 holes, grass greens, rentals, clubhouse, licensed lounge. Open May to September.

C 25.4 (40.9 km) **AH 61.5** (99 km) Cameron Lake camping area; tables, water, toilets, firewood, playground, horseshoe pits, boat launch (no motorboats) and swimming. Camping fee by donation. ▲

C 30.7 (49.4 km) **AH 56.2** (90.4 km) Gravel turnout with litter barrel to east. Highway descends northbound to Hudson's Hope.

C 35.9 (57.8 km) **AH 51** (82.1 km) Suspension bridge over Peace River; paved turnouts at both ends of bridge with concrete totem pole sculptures. View of Peace Canyon Dam.

C 36.5 (58.7 km) **AH 50.4** (81.1 km) Turnoff to west for Dinosaur Lake Campground and B.C. Hydro Peace Canyon Dam.

HUDSON'S HOPE LOOP *Chetwynd, BC, to Milepost DC 53.7 Alaska Highway*

The dam's visitor centre, 0.6 mile/1 km on paved access road, is open from 8 A.M. to 4 P.M. daily from late May through Labour Day; Monday through Friday the rest of the year (closed holidays). Self-guided tour includes a full-scale model of duck-billed dinosaurs (hadrosaurs), a tableau portraying Alexander Mackenzie's discovery of the Peace River canyon and a section on local

pioneering. A pictorial display traces the construction of the Peace Canyon Dam. You may view the dam spillway from the visitor centre. Get permission before walking across top of dam. Phone (250) 783-9943 for a guided tour (groups of 8 or more).

Dinosaur Lake Campground, on Dinosaur Lake, has 30 campsites with firepits, water, toilets and tables. Boat launch and

swimming area. Camping fee by donation.▲

C 38.3 (61.6 km) AH 48.6 (78.2 km) Alwin Holland Memorial Park (0.5 mile/ 0.8 km east of highway) is named for the first teacher in Hudson's Hope, who willed his property, known locally as The Glen, to be used as a public park. There are 17 campsites, picnic grounds, barbecues and water. Camping fee by donation. ▲

C 38.9 (62.6 km) AH 48 (77.2 km) Welcome to Hudson's Hope sign.

C 39 (62.8 km) AH 47.9 (77.1 km) King Gething Park; small campground with 15 grassy sites, picnic tables, cookhouse, flush toilets, showers and dump station east side of highway. Camping fee by donation. ▲

Hudson's Hope

C 40.4 (65 km) AH 46.5 (74.8 km) Population: 1,050. Emergency Services: RCMP, phone (250) 783-5241. Fire Department, phone (250) 783-5700. Ambulance, phone 112-562-7241. Medical Clinic, phone (250) 783-9991.

Visitor Information: A log building

HUDSON'S HOPE ADVERTISERS

B.C. Hydro ....Ph. (250) 783-5211 or 9943
District of
Hudson's Hope ....Ph. (250) 783-9901
Hudson's Hope
Museum ....Across from Info Centre
Marg's Mini Mart ....Adjacent to Tempo Gas

houses the tourist information booth at Beattie Park, across from the museum and St. Peter's Anglican United Church. Open daily mid-May to the end of August, hours are 10 A.M. to 7 P.M. Phone (250) 783-9154 or write Box 330, Hudson's Hope, BC V0C 1V0. (Off-season, phone the district office at 250/783-9901.)

Elevation: 1,707 feet/520m. **Climate:** Summer temperatures range from 60°F/16°C to 90°F/32°C, with an average of 135 frost-free days annually. **Radio:** CBC, CKNL 560, CJDC 870. **Television:** Channels 2, 5, 8, 11 and cable.

Private Aircraft: Hudson's Hope airstrip, 3.7 miles/6 km west; elev. 2,200 feet/671m; length 5,200 feet/1,585m; asphalt.

Hudson's Hope is the third oldest permanently settled community in British Columbia. The site was first visited in 1793 by Alexander Mackenzie. In 1805 a Hudson's Bay trading post was established here by Simon Fraser. In 1916, after the fur-trading days were over, a major influx of settlers arrived in the area. It was the head of navigation for steamboats on the lower Peace River until 1936, the year of the last scheduled steamboat run. Area coal mines supplied Alaska Highway maintenance camps during the 1940s.

Modern development of Hudson's Hope was spurred by construction of the Peace Power project in the 1960s. Today the area's principal claim to fame is the 600-foot-/183-m-high W.A.C. Bennett Dam at the upper end of the Peace River canyon, 15 miles/24.1 km west of Hudson's Hope. The 100-million-ton dam is one of the largest earth-fill structures in the world and Williston Lake, behind it, is the largest body of fresh water in British Columbia. The dam provides about 20 percent of British Columbia's hydroelectricity. Tours of the Gordon M. Shrum generating station are available daily from mid-May to the end of September, weekdays only the remainder of the year (closed holidays). Phone (250) 783-5211 for information. Tours are available each hour on the half hour from 9:30 A.M. to 4:30 P.M. Self-guided tours are available at the Peace Canyon Dam.

Also of interest is the Hudson's Hope Museum on Highway 29 in town. The museum has a fine collection of artifacts and dinosaur fossils from the Peace District. It offers hands-on paleontology and dinosaur activities, and is well worth a visit. Souvenir shop in the museum. The active congregation of the log-constructed St. Peter's Anglican United Church (next to the museum) welcomes visitors to look inside.

Several hiking trails have been developed in the area. Descriptions and a map are available at the Hudson's Hope tourist information booth.

Visitor services in Hudson's Hope include a motel, hotel, 2 bed and breakfasts, 3 restaurants, 2 service stations, a laundromat, supermarket, bakery, and convenience and hardware stores. There are also a bank, post office, fitness centre, liquor store, community hall, library, swimming pool, tennis courts, and numerous parks and playgrounds. Sightseeing and flightseeing tours are available locally. The main business district is along Highway 29 and adjoining streets. The RCMP office is at the corner of 100th Street and 100th Avenue.

Marg's Mini Mart. Be sure to drop in when in Hudson's Hope. We've got something for everyone. Coffee, groceries, snacks, ice cream and ice. Video rentals and souvenirs. Fishing tackle and live bait; fishing and hunting licenses. Open daily until 10 P.M., (next to Tempo Gas). We look forward to meeting you! (250) 783-5257. [ADVERTISEMENT]

Hudson's Hope Loop Log

(continued)

C 41.2 (66.3 km) **AH 45.7** (73.5 km) Turnout to north with Hudson's Hope visitor map.

CAUTION: Watch for deer between here and the Alaska Highway, especially at dusk and at night.

C 44 (70.8 km) **AH 42.9** (69 km) Lynx Creek bridge.

C 48.3 (77.7 km) **AH 38.6** (62.1 km) Pay phone, north side of road.

C 48.4 (77.9 km) **AH 38.5** (62 km) Turnout to north for view of the Peace River.

C 50.9 (81.9 km) **AH 36** (57.9 km) Farrell Creek bridge and picnic site.

C 56.6 (91.1 km) **AH 30.3** (48.8 km) Pull-through turnout with litter barrels. View of Peace River valley.

C 57.1 (91.9 km) **AH 29.8** (48 km) Turnout to south with litter barrels and view of Peace River valley.

C 59.3 (95.4 km) **AH 27.6** (44.4 km) Turnout to south with litter barrels.

C 64.7 (104.1 km) **AH 22.2** (35.7 km) Halfway River.

C 67.2 (108.1 km) **AH 19.7** (31.7 km) Rest area to south with point of interest sign, litter barrel and toilet. A slide occurred here on May 26, 1973, involving an estimated 10 million to 15 million cubic yards of overburden. Slide debris completely blocked the river channel for some 12 hours, backing up the river an estimated 24 feet/7.3m above normal level.

C 68.4 (110.1 km) **AH 18.5** (29.8 km) Milepost 19.

C 71.1 (114.4 km) **AH 15.8** (25.4 km) Turnout to north.

C 71.4 (114.9 km) **AH 15.5** (24.9 km) Milepost 16.

C 73.5 (118.3 km) **AH 13.4** (21.6 km) Beaver dam to north.

C 74.2 (119.4 km) **AH 12.7** (20.4 km) **Pine Ridge Campground.** A relaxing owner-operated campground, halfway between Fort St. John and Hudson's Hope. 100 spacious sites, some with power. Showers, washer and dryer, spring water and confectionery. Cooking shelter, firepits and firewood, horseshoe pits, ping pong, ball diamonds, child-proof fence. Very reasonable rates. Gates open 7 A.M.–10 P.M. (Pets on a leash please.) Your hosts, the Bentley's, (250) 262-3229 mid-May to mid-September. [ADVERTISEMENT]

C 74.6 (120.1 km) **AH 12.3** (19.8 km) Cache Creek 1-lane bridge. Turnout to north at east end of bridge for picnic area with litter barrels.

C 76.6 (123.3 km) **AH 10.3** (16.6 km) Turnout with litter barrel to north overlooking Bear Flat in the Peace River valley. Highway begins climb eastbound. *CAUTION: Switchbacks.*

C 78.1 (125.7 km) **AH 8.8** (14.2 km) Highest point on Highway 29 (2,750 feet/838m) overlooking Peace River Plateau. Highway descends on a 10 percent grade westbound. *CAUTION: Switchbacks.*

C 86.9 (139.8 km) **AH 0 Junction** with the Alaska Highway, 6.7 miles/10.8 km north of Fort St. John (see **Milepost DC 53.7** in the ALASKA HIGHWAY section). Truck stop at junction with gas, diesel, propane, tire repair, restaurant and convenience store.

CAUTION: Watch for deer on the highway between here and Hudson's Hope, especially at dusk and at night.

1

Connects: Dawson Creek, BC, to Fairbanks, AK   **Length:** 1,488 miles
Road Surface: Paved   **Season:** Open all year
Highest Summit: Summit Lake 4,250 feet
Major Attractions: Muncho Lake, Liard Hotsprings, Watson Lake
Signforest, SS *Klondike*, Kluane Lake, Trans-Alaska Pipeline Crossing

(See maps, pages 73–77)

	Dawson Cr.	Delta Jct.	Fairbanks	Ft. Nelson	Haines Jct.	Tok	Watson Lk.	Whitehorse
Dawson Cr.		1390	1488	283	985	1282	613	895
Delta Jct.	1390		98	1107	405	108	777	495
Fairbanks	1488	98		1205	593	206	875	593
Ft. Nelson	283	1107	1205		702	999	330	612
Haines Jct.	985	405	593	702		297	372	90
Tok	1282	108	206	999	297		669	387
Watson Lk.	613	777	875	330	372	669		282
Whitehorse	895	495	593	612	90	387	282	

Looking south down the Alaska Highway near Whitehorse, YT, at White Mountain. (Earl L. Brown, staff)

The Alaska Highway stretches in a northwesterly direction from Mile 0 at Dawson Creek, BC, through Yukon Territory to Mile 1520 at Fairbanks, AK. Actual driving distance is 1,488 miles/2,394.6 km. Although the Alaska Highway does not compare with highways in the Lower 48, it is no longer a wilderness road but rather a road through the wilderness. The Alaska Highway is driven by thousands of people each year in all sorts of vehicles. The highway is open and maintained year-round.

For more information, contact Peace River Alaska Highway Tourist Assoc., P.O. Box 6850M, Fort St. John, BC V1J 4J3; phone toll free 1-888-785-2544 or (250) 785-2544, fax 785-4424.

Road Conditions

All of the Alaska Highway between Dawson Creek, BC, and Fairbanks, AK, is asphalt-surfaced. Repaving and highway improvement continue. Surfacing of the Alaska Highway ranges from poor to excellent.

There are still some stretches of poor surfacing with many chuckholes, gravel breaks (sections of gravel ranging from a few feet to several miles), hardtop with loose gravel, deteriorated shoulders and bumps. On the northern portion of the highway—in Yukon Territory and on into Alaska—watch for frost heaves. This rippling effect in the pavement is caused by the freezing and thawing of the ground. Drive slowly in sections of frost heaves to avoid breaking an axle or trailer hitch.

Surfacing on much of the highway is fair, with older patched pavement and a minimum of gravel breaks and chuckholes. There are also sections of excellent surfacing where highway maintenance crews have recently upgraded the road.

Loose gravel patches are common on the Alaska Highway and are often signed. *CAUTION: Slow down for loose gravel! Excessive speeds can lead to loss of control of your vehicle.*

Travelers should keep in mind that road conditions are subject to change! Weather and traffic may cause deterioration of newer pavement, while construction may improve older sections. Always be alert for bumps and holes in the road and for abrupt changes in highway surfacing. There are stretches of narrow, winding road without shoulders. Also watch for soft shoulders.

Always watch for construction crews along the Alaska Highway. Extensive road construction may require a detour or travelers may be delayed while waiting for a pilot car to guide them through the construction. Motorists may encounter rough driving at construction areas, and muddy roadway if there are heavy rains while the roadbed is torn up.

For current road conditions from Dawson Creek to the BC–YT border, phone the Peace River Alaska Highway Tourist Assoc. in Fort St. John at (250) 785-2544, or the Dawson Creek Visitor Infocentre at (250) 782-9595. The BC Ministry of Highways provides a recorded message on road conditions on the Alaska Highway in BC; phone (250) 774-7447. For recorded message on current road conditions on the Alaska Highway and other highways in Yukon Territory, phone (403) 667-8215 for daily road report.

Detailed weather information for the Canadian portion of the Alaska Highway is available from Atmospheric Environment Service of Environment Canada. For 24-hour recorded weather information between Dawson Creek and Sikanni Chief, phone (250) 784-2244 or (250) 785-7669; for detailed weather information, phone the weather office at (250) 785-4304 between 6:15 A.M. and 4:45 P.M.; or for weather broadcasts, tune to 580 AM. Between Sikanni Chief and the BC–YT border, phone (250) 774-6461 for 24-hour recorded message; for detailed weather information phone (250) 774-2302 between 3 A.M. and 6:15 P.M.; or tune your radio to 590 AM for weather broadcasts. Between the BC–YT border and the YT–AK border, phone (403) 668-6061 for 24-hour recorded message; for detailed weather information phone (403) 667-8464 (24 hours a day); or tune your radio to CBC Yukon (570 AM) for weather broadcasts. Regional weather forecasts are also supplied to local visitor information centres, local hotels and motels, and lodges along the highway.

Road conditions along the Alaska Highway may be summarized as follows. Good pavement first 300 miles/483 km (through Fort Nelson) with recent resurfacing improving some sections. Watch for surface changes and continued construction in some areas. Between Fort Nelson and the (continues on page 78)

ALASKA HIGHWAY Dawson Creek, BC, to Milepost DC 409

To Fort Simpson, NWT
(see LIARD HIGHWAY section)

Kotcho Lake

Trout River

Toad River

Fort Nelson River

Kledo Creek

Raspberry Creek

Muncho Lake Provincial Park

**F-1079/1736km
DC-409/655km**

Toad River (Historical Mile 422)
DC-407.5/652km The Poplars Campground CDGLMPrST
DC-404.6/647.4km Toad River Lodge CDdGILMPrT

McDonald R.

(map continues next page)

DC-333/532.5km
Steamboat CdGlMrT

77

**F-1205/1939km
DC-283/454km**

Fort Nelson (Historical Mile 300)

DC-277.9/447.2km Husky 5th Wheel Truck Stop and RV Park CDdGIMPRrST

Summit (Historical Mile 392)

Steamboat (Historical Mile 351)

DC-278.4/448km Trapper's Den

Clarke Lake

Andy Bailey L.

DC-357.5/571.5km
Tetsa River Guest Ranch and
Campground CDGLrS

97

Prophet River

Jackfish Creek

Fort Nelson River

Summit Lakk

Tetsa R.

Racing R.

**F-1115/1794km
DC-373/597km**

Stone Mountain Provincial Park

Muskwa River

Fontas River

ROCKY MOUNTAINS

Prophet River (Historical Mile 233)
DC-227/364.7km Prophet River Services CdGLMPrT

Bougie Creek

Prophet River

Minaker R.

River

Trutch Mountain Bypass

Buckinghorse R.

Sikanni Chief

DC-173.4/278.5km Buckinghorse River Lodge CdGILMT

Mason Creek

Sikanni Chief (Historical Mile 162)
DC-159.4/256.5km Sikanni River RV Park CDGILPST

Beatton River

DC-144.5/232.5km Mae's Kitchen and Ed's Garage dGLMRrT

DC-140.4/225.9km Pink Mountain Campsite & RV Park CDdGILPST
Pink Mountain Motor Inn CDdGILMPST

Pink Mountain (Historical Mile 143)

Cypress Creek

97

**F-1348/2169km
DC-140/226km**

**F-1387/2232km
DC-101/162km**

DC-101.5/163.3km 102 Husky CDdGLMT

Wonowon (Historical Mile 101)

DC-101/161.7km Blueberry Esso & Motel dGILMPST
Hall's Food and Gas dGILMPT

River

DC-71.1/115.4km The Shepherd's Inn CGILMPT

Halfway River

Charlie Lake

**F-1441/2319km
DC-47/76km**

DC-53.7/86.4km Mile 54 Shell Truck Stop dGIMPrST

DC-51.5/82.9km Ron's RV Park CDT

DC-50.6/81.4km Charlie Lake General Store dGIST
Paradise Lane Bed & Breakfast L
Rotary RV Park CDT

Charlie Lake

Fort St. John

DC-41.3/66.5km
The Honey Place

Hudson's Hope Loop
(see HUDSON'S HOPE LOOP section)

29

Peace River

DC-43.7/70.3km Sourdough
Pete's RV Park & Troy's
Amusement Park CDST

Taylor

DC-35/56.3km Redwood
Esso and Taylor
Lodge dGILPST

Peace R.

97

Williston Lake

W.A.C. Bennett Dam

Hudson's Hope

DC-9.5/15.3km Farmington Fairways
& Campground CDIT

29

DC-3.4/5.5km
The Trading Post

Pine R.

Dawson Creek

Moberly Lake

Chetwynd

97

**F-1488/2395km
DC-0**

To Prince George
(see WEST ACCESS ROUTE section)

Pine River

John Hart Highway

Murray River

To Grande Prairie
(see EAST ACCESS ROUTE section)

Kiskatinaw River

BRITISH COLUMBIA
ALBERTA

Map Location

Scale
0   20 Miles
0   20 Kilometres

Key to mileage boxes
miles/kilometres
miles/kilometres
from:

F-Fairbanks
DC-Dawson Creek

Principal Route
Paved   Unpaved
Other Roads
Paved   Unpaved
Ferry Routes   **Hiking Trails**

Refer to Log for Visitor Facilities

Visitor Information   Fishing

Campground   Airport   Airstrip

Key to Advertiser Services
C -Camping
D -Dump Station
d -Diesel
G -Gas (reg., unld.)
I -Ice
L -Lodging
M -Meals
P -Propane
R -Car Repair (major)
r -Car Repair (minor)
S -Store (grocery)
T -Telephone (pay)

ALASKA HIGHWAY *Milepost DC 409 to Teslin, YT*

(map continues previous page)

F-1079/1736km
DC-409/698km

Muncho Lake
(Historical Mile 456)

F-1051/1692km
DC-436/698km

ROCKY MOUNTAINS

Muncho Lake Provincial Park

DC-443.7/710.3km J & H Wilderness Resort CDdGILMT
DC-443.6/710.1km Muncho Lake Lodge CDGILMT
DC-477.9km Northern Rockies/Highland Glen Lodge CDdGLMT
DC-442.2/707.9km Trout & Toad River Raft Adventures

DC-477.1/763.8km Liard River Lodge CDGILMrT

Liard River
(Historical Mile 496)

DC-477.8/764.9km Trapper Ray's
Liard Hotsprings Lodge CdGILMPrT

97

Liard River

Smith River

F-964/1551km
DC-524/839km

Fireside (Historical Mile 543)

Hillgren Lakes

Coal River

Contact Cr.

Irons Creek

Highland River

Contact Creek (Historical Mile 635)

DC-570/912.9km Contact Creek Lodge dGIMPT

DC-575.9/922km Iron Creek Lodge CDdGILMrT

DC-610.5/1017.7km Campground Services CDdGIIPrST

Kechika River

F-875/1408km
DC-613/1021km

Watson Lake (Historical Mile 635)

Lower Post (Historical Mile 620)

DC-619.6/1032km Green Valley RV Park CDIST

4

(Historical Watson Mile 642)
Upper Liard Village

DC-626.2/1043km Junction 37 Services CDdGILMPrT

37

To Ross River
(see CAMPBELL HIGHWAY section)

To Cassiar
(see CASSIAR HIGHWAY section)

Dease River

Frances River

Simpson Lake

Sambo Lake

DC-627/1043.9km Alaska Highway's Best Coffee Stop M
The Northern Beaver Post M

DC-687.2/1143.8km Rancheria Hotel-Motel CdGILMrT

DC-710/1180.9km Swift River Lodge dGILMrT

Albert Cr.

Little Rancheria River

River

Rancheria

1

DC-698.4/1161.6km Walker's Continental Divide CGILMT

Swift River (Historical Mile 733)

MOUNTAINS

Wolf Lake

CASSIAR

Morley R.

Smart R.

Seagull Cr.

Morley L.

Screw Cr.

Swift River

Swan L.

Swift Lake

Nisutlin Lake

Liard River

DC-752.9/1252km Morley River Lodge CDdGILMT

DC-769.6/1282.5km Dawson Peaks Northern Resort CDILM

Nisutlin Bay

Morley Bay

Gladys Hall L.

F-712/1145km
DC-776/1294km

Teslin (Historical Mile 804)

F-737/1185km
DC-752/1249km

1

Deadman Cr.

Flat Cr.

(map continues next page)

Nisutlin River

Scale
| 0 | 20 Miles |
| 0 | 20 Kilometres |

Key to mileage boxes
miles/kilometres
miles/kilometres from:

F-Fairbanks **DC**-Dawson Creek

Map Location

Key to Advertiser Services
C -Camping
D -Dump Station
d -Diesel
G -Gas (reg., unld.)
I -Ice
L -Lodging
M -Meals
P -Propane
R -Car Repair (major)
r -Car Repair (minor)
S -Store (grocery)
T -Telephone (pay)

Principal Route
Paved
Unpaved

Other Roads
Paved
Unpaved

Ferry Routes **Hiking Trails**

Refer to Log for Visitor Facilities
Visitor Information
Campground   Airport   Airstrip
Fishing

YUKON TERRITORY
BRITISH COLUMBIA

N E
W S

ALASKA HIGHWAY   Teslin, YT, to Milepost DC 1136

To Ross River
(see CANOL ROAD section)

Nisutlin River

BIG SALMON RANGES

Teslin River

Quiet Lake

6

(map continues previous page)

Teslin
(Historical Mile 804)

Johnson's Crossing
DC-808.9/1392.5km Johnson's Crossing
Campground Services CDdGIST

DC-836.8/1346km Johnson's Crossing
Deadman Cr. Little Teslin L. Lone Tree Cr.

Jake's Corner
(Historical Mile 866)
DC-784.3/1306.7km Mukluk
Annie's Salmon Bake CDLM
DC-776.3/1294km Yukon
Motel CDdGILMPrT

Jake's Corner Inc. Teslin
dGILMPT

Squanga L. Squanga

F-712/1145km
DC-776/1294km

To Atlin
(see ATLIN ROAD section)

Atlin Lake

Surprise Lake

Hall L.
Gladys L.
Flat Cr.

7

Tagish L.

Tutshi Lake

Little Atlin L.

F-593/955km
DC-895/1487km

(Historical Mile 918)
Whitehorse ☒ ?
DC-884/1470.2km Hi-Country RV Park CDIPST
DC-882.6/1468km Philmar RV Service and Supply RrT
DC-881/1465.5km Pioneer RV Park CDdGIPT
DC-873.5/1453.3km Sourdough Country
Campsite CDIT

M'Clintock River

DC-874.4/1455km
Carcross Corner Services dGMPST
Yukon Rock Shop

DC-850/1413.5km
Lakeview Resort &
Marina CDILMT

Carcross

Tagish
Tagish Road
(see TAGISH ROAD section)

8

White Pass & Yukon Route

2

To Skagway
(see KLONDIKE HIGHWAY section)

Lake Bennett

YUKON TERRITORY
BRITISH COLUMBIA

Laberge Lake

Lake

Fox Lake

2

To Dawson City
(see KLONDIKE LOOP section)

Yukon River

1

Fish Cr. Wolf Cr.

DC-888.6/1477.5km
Kopper King DdGILMST

DC-882.9/1468.5km Mountain
Ridge Motel & RV Park CL

F-614/988km
DC-874/1455km

Takhini River

Mendenhall R.
Stony Cr.

F-545/876km
DC-944/1568km

Champagne
(Historical Mile 974.6)

DC-964.6/1602.2km
Otter Falls Cutoff CdGIST

Taye L.
Cracker Cr.

Kusawa Lake

Sixmile Lake

Dezadeash Lake

F-503/809km
DC-985/1635km

Sixmile L.

Kathleen Lake

Mush Lake

Bates Lake

3

To Haines
(see HAINES
HIGHWAY section)

Aishihik

Aishihik
Lake

West Aishihik River

Sekulmun Lake

Kluane Museum of Natural History T

DC-1084.6/1797.2km Kluane Wilderness
Village CDdGILMPRrT
DC-1062/1759.8km Dalan Campground CD
DC-1061.6/1759.2km Burllbilly Hill
DC-1061.5/1759km Burwash Landing Resort
& RV Park CDdGILMT

Burwash Landing
(Historical Mile 1093)
DC-1035.3/1717km Cottonwood RV
Park & Campground CDIS
DC-1034.9/1693km Kluane Bed and Breakfast L
DC-1023.7/1698.5km Trans North Helicopters
DC-1020.3/1645.9km Mackintosh
Lodge CDGILMrT

Kluane Lake

Destruction Bay
(Historical Mile 1083)

Soldier's Summit

Boutillier Summit
3,293 ft./1,003m

Bear Creek Summit
3,294 ft./1,004m

DC-991.6/1645.9km Mackintosh
Lodge CDGILMrT

DC-1051.7/1743.3km Sehja Services & RV Park CDdGILMST
DC-1051.5/1743km Talbot Arm Motel CDdGILMPST

DC-1061.3/1758.7km
Duke River Trading Co. CDItST

F-437/703km
DC-1052/1743km

▲ Mount Steele
16,644 ft./5,073m

▲ Mount Luciana
17,147 ft./5,226m

Haines
Junction
(Historical Mile 1016)

Marshall Cr.

Pine L.

Kloo L.

Sulphur River

Jarvis Cr.

Slims R.

Christmas Cr.

Kaskawulsh R.

Dezadeash R.

Kathleen L.

Alsek River

ST. ELIAS MOUNTAINS
Glaciated Area

Kluane National Park

▲ Mount Logan
19,520 ft./5,950m

▲ Mount Vancouver
15,840 ft./4,828m

▲ Mount Hubbard
15,015 ft./4,577m

DAWSON RANGE

Tincup Lake

Pickhandle Lake

Koidern R.

Donjek River

Kluane R.

White R.

F-352/567km
DC-1136/1883km

(map continues next page)

DC-1135/1880km White River Motor Inn CDdGILMrT
DC-1113.8/1844.8km Pine Valley Motel & Cafe CdGLMrT

Scale
0 20 Miles
0 20 Kilometres

Key to mileage boxes
miles/kilometres
miles/kilometres from:

F-Fairbanks
DC-Dawson Creek

Map Location

Principal Route
Paved
Unpaved
Other Roads
Paved
Unpaved
Ferry Routes Hiking Trails
☒ Refer to Log for Visitor Facilities
? Visitor Information ⦿ Fishing
▲ Campground + Airport ✈ Airstrip

Key to Advertiser Services
C–Camping
D–Dump Station
d–Diesel
G–Gas (reg., unld.)
L–Lodging
M–Meals
P–Propane
R –Car Repair (major)
r –Car Repair (minor)
S –Store (grocery)
T–Telephone (pay)

ALASKA HIGHWAY Milepost DC 1136 to Milepost DC 1378

DAWSON RANGE

YUKON TERRITORY

CANADA

UNITED STATES

ALASKA

Snag ○

Beaver Creek ▲ (Mile 1202)

F-320/514km
DC-1169/1935km

F-298/480km
DC-1190/1969km
Refer to log for
explanation of mileage

F-352/567km
DC-1136/1883km

(map continues previous page)

DC-1226/1973km Scottie Creek Services CDdGST
DC-1225.5/1972.2km Border City Lodge CDdGILM

Port Alcan
(Mile 1222)

F-298/480km
DC-1222/1966km
Refer to log for
explanation of mileage

DC-1168.5/1934.5km
Beaver Creek Motor Inn CdGLMT
Westmark Inn

NUTZOTIN MOUNTAINS

Scottie Creek

Island Lake

Mirror Creek

Nabesna River

Tetlin National Wildlife Refuge

Wrangell-Saint Elias National Park and Preserve

Chisana River

Chisana River

DC-1264/2034.2km Naabia Niign Campground & Athabascan Indian Crafts CDGIST
Northway Airport Lodge & Motel dGILMPT
DC-1263/2032.5km Wrangell View Service Center CDdGILMPRT
DC-1253.6/2017.4km Frontier Surplus

Northway Junction

Gardiner

Deadman Lake

Chisana River

Yarger Lake

F-256/412km
DC-1264/2034km

H ← Northway

Midway Lake

Tanana River

Beaver Cr.

Tetlin Junction

F-218/356km
DC-1302/2095km

To Chicken
(see TAYLOR HIGHWAY section)

F-206/331km
DC-1314/2115km

DC-1313.9/2114.5km
Tok Machie & Welding/Tok
Northern Exposures r
Rod's Automotive r
DC-1312.9/2100.6km
DC-1312.7/2112.5km Wayfarer's Motel L

DC-1313.1/2113.1km
Tok Gateway Salmon
Bake & RV Park CDMT
DC-1313.2/2113.3km
Willard's Full Service Repair R
DC-1313.3/2113.5km Bull Shooter
Sporting Goods & RV Park, The Cl
Eska Trading Post
Northstar CDdGIMT
Village Texaco Foodmart dGIPST
Young's Motel & Fast Eddy's Restaurant LMT

Tetlin Lake

DC-1313.4/2113.6km
Tok RV Village CDIT

MENTASTA MOUNTAINS

MENTASTA MOUNTAINS

Tok

DC-1317/2119.4km
Mukluk Land
DC-1315.7/2117.3km Rita's
Campground RV Park and
Cheryl's Old Fashion Bed &
Breakfast CDILT
DC-1315/2116.2km Tundra
Lodge and RV Park CDIT
DC-1314.8/2103.6km Northern
Energy Corp. DdGPr

To Anchorage
(see GLENN HIGHWAY section)

Tanacross

Mansfield Lake

Moon Lake

Yerrick Cr.

Tanana River

Sheep Cr.

ALASKA RANGE

Robertson River

West Fork

Glaciated Area

▲ Dot Lake

DC-1361.3/2190.2km Dot Lake Lodge CDdGIMPST

F-142/229km
DC-1378/2218km

(map continues next page)

Chief Cr.
Bear Creek
Berry Creek
Sears Cr.
River Dry Cr.
Johnson River

Scale

Miles	
0	10
Kilometres	
0	10

Key to mileage boxes

miles/kilometres
from:
miles/kilometres

F- Fairbanks
DC- Dawson Creek

Key to Advertiser Services
C –Camping
D –Dump Station
d –Diesel
G –Gas (reg., unld.)
I –Ice
L –Lodging
M –Meals
P –Propane
R –Car Repair (major)
r –Car Repair (minor)
S –Store (grocery)
T –Telephone (pay)

Principal Route
Paved
Unpaved
Other Roads
Paved
Unpaved
Ferry Routes
Hiking Trails
Refer to Log for Visitor Facilities
Visitor Information
Campground
Fishing
Airport
Airstrip

Map Location

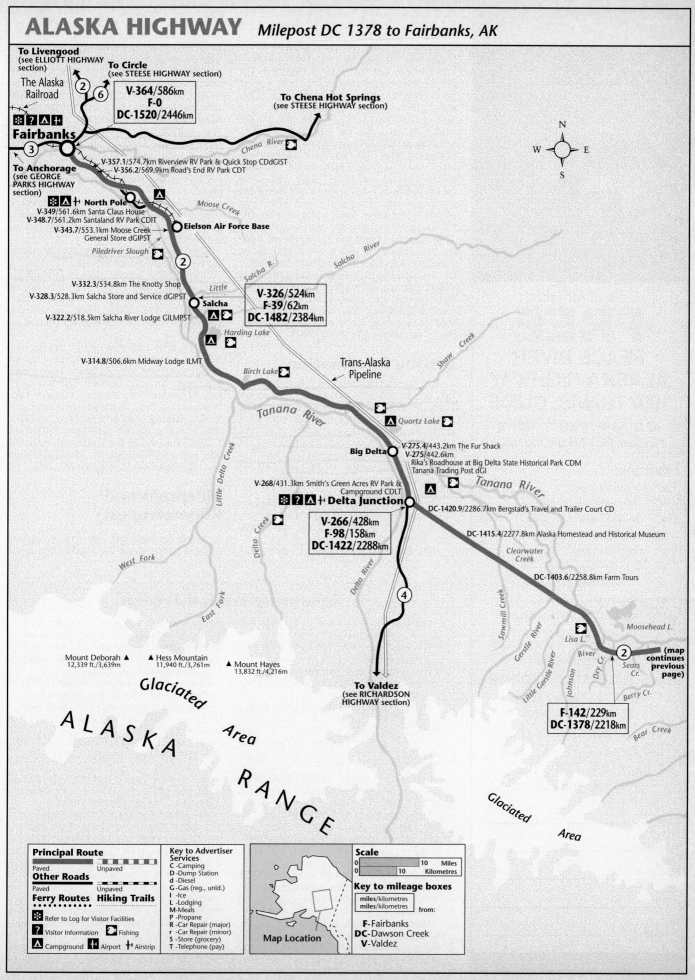

ALASKA HIGHWAY
Milepost DC 1378 to Fairbanks, AK

To Livengood
(see ELLIOTT HIGHWAY section)

To Circle
(see STEESE HIGHWAY section)

V-364/586km
F-0
DC-1520/2446km

To Chena Hot Springs
(see STEESE HIGHWAY section)

The Alaska Railroad

Fairbanks

Chena River

To Anchorage
(see GEORGE PARKS HIGHWAY section)

V-357.1/574.7km Riverview RV Park & Quick Stop CDdGIST
V-356.2/569.9km Road's End RV Park CDT

Moose Creek

North Pole
V-349/561.6km Santa Claus House
V-348.7/561.2km Santaland RV Park CDIT
V-343.7/553.1km Moose Creek General Store dGIPST

Eielson Air Force Base

Piledriver Slough

Salcha R.

Salcha River

V-332.3/534.8km The Knotty Shop
V-328.3/528.3km Salcha Store and Service dGIPST
V-322.2/518.5km Salcha River Lodge GILMPST

Little

Salcha

V-326/524km
F-39/62km
DC-1482/2384km

Harding Lake

V-314.8/506.6km Midway Lodge ILMT

Birch Lake

Trans-Alaska Pipeline

Shaw Creek

Tanana River

Little Delta Creek

Quartz Lake

V-275.4/443.2km The Fur Shack
V-275/442.6km
Rika's Roadhouse at Big Delta State Historical Park CDM
Tanana Trading Post dGI

Big Delta

Tanana River

V-268/431.3km Smith's Green Acres RV Park & Campground CDLT

Delta Junction

V-266/428km
F-98/158km
DC-1422/2288km

DC-1420.9/2286.7km Bergstad's Travel and Trailer Court CD

DC-1415.4/2277.8km Alaska Homestead and Historical Museum

Clearwater Creek

Delta Creek

West Fork

Delta River

East Fork

DC-1403.6/2258.8km Farm Tours

Sowmill Creek

Gerstle River

Little Gerstle River

Johnson River

Dry Cr.

Lisa L.

Moosehead L.

(4)

Mount Deborah ▲
12,339 ft./3,639m

▲ Hess Mountain
11,940 ft./3,761m

▲ Mount Hayes
13,832 ft./4,216m

Sears Cr.

(map continues previous page)

Berry Cr.

F-142/229km
DC-1378/2218km

Bear Creek

To Valdez
(see RICHARDSON HIGHWAY section)

Glaciated Area

ALASKA

RANGE

Glaciated Area

Principal Route
Paved ▬▬▬ Unpaved ▬ ▬ ▬
Other Roads
Paved ___ Unpaved _ _ _
Ferry Routes •••• **Hiking Trails**

❄ Refer to Log for Visitor Facilities
❓ Visitor Information ⊠ Fishing
⛺ Campground ✈ Airport ✦ Airstrip

Key to Advertiser Services
C -Camping
D -Dump Station
d -Diesel
G -Gas (reg., unld.)
I -Ice
L -Lodging
M -Meals
P -Propane
R -Car Repair (major)
r -Car Repair (minor)
S -Store (grocery)
T -Telephone (pay)

Map Location

Scale
0 ___ 10 Miles
0 ___ 10 Kilometres

Key to mileage boxes
miles/kilometres
miles/kilometres
from:
F-Fairbanks
DC-Dawson Creek
V-Valdez

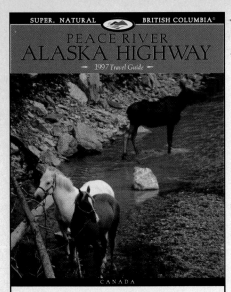
BC–YT border, the Alaska Highway crosses the Rocky Mountains, so be prepared for narrow, winding road and some rough spots in surfacing due to deterioration from weather and traffic. Also watch for construction projects on this stretch. Between the BC–YT border and Haines Junction, expect fair to excellent road with a few rough spots and sections of narrow, winding road. From Haines Junction to the YT–AK border, the road is in fair condition with some narrow, winding sections without shoulders. Between Historical Mile 1118 (Kluane Wilderness Village) and Beaver Creek there is both improved road and rough road, with some gravel patches and winding road; watch for continued road construction in 1997. The highway between Beaver Creek and the YT–AK border was under reconstruction in 1996, and has been much improved, however, continue to watch for rough spots, gravel surface and road construction in 1997. On the Alaska portion of the Alaska Highway, expect fair to good surfacing, but watch for frost heaves and narrow sections of road without shoulders. Also watch for continued road construction on the highway between the YT–AK border and Tok in 1997.

Driving Information

The Alaska Highway is a 2-lane highway that winds and rolls across the wilderness. There are sections of road with no centerline and stretches of narrow highway with little or no shoulder. The best advice is to take your time; drive with your headlights on at all times; keep to the right on hills and corners; watch for wildlife on the road; and—as you would on any highway anywhere else—drive defensively.

There are relatively few steep grades on the Alaska Highway. The highest summit on the highway is at Summit Lake, elev. 4,250 feet/1,295m.

Dust and mud are generally only a prob-

lem in construction areas. There are many sections of hardtop with loose gravel and gravel breaks along the highway. Flying gravel—which may damage headlights, radiators, gas tanks, windshields and paint—is still a problem. Side roads and access roads to campgrounds and other destinations are generally not paved. Gravel road is treated with calcium chloride to keep the dust down. This substance corrodes paint and metal; Wash your vehicle as soon as possible. In heavy rains, calcium chloride and mud combine to make a very slippery road surface; drive carefully! Keep in mind that many highways in the Yukon and some highways in Alaska are gravel.

Travelers with trailers should be especially cautious in areas of frost heaving. This corrugated road surface can be especially hard on trailer hitches.

Gas, food and lodging are found along the Alaska Highway on an average of every 20 to 50 miles. (The longest stretch without services is about 100 miles.) Not all businesses are open year-round, nor are most services available 24 hours a day. There are dozens of government and private campgrounds along the highway.

Remember that you will be driving in 2 different countries that use 2 different currencies: For the best rate, exchange your money at a bank. There are banks in Dawson Creek, Fort St. John, Fort Nelson, Watson Lake, Whitehorse, Tok, Delta Junction and Fairbanks. Haines Junction has banking service at the general store. See GENERAL INFORMATION in the back of the book for more details on Customs Requirements, Driving Information, Holidays and Money/Credit Cards.

Mileposts and Kilometreposts

Mileposts were first put up at communities and lodges along the Alaska Highway in

Emergency Medical Services

Milepost DC 0 Dawson Creek to **DC 47** Fort St. John. Dawson Creek ambulance (250) 782-2211; RCMP (250) 782-5211.

Milepost DC 47 Fort St. John to **DC 222.3** Bougie Creek bridge. Fort St. John ambulance (250) 785-2079; RCMP (250) 785-6617.

Milepost DC 222.3 Bougie Creek bridge to **DC 373.3** Summit Lake Lodge. Fort Nelson ambulance (250) 774-2344, hospital (250) 774-6916; RCMP (250) 774-2777.

Milepost DC 373.3 Summit Lake Lodge to **DC 605.1** BC–YT border. Toad River ambulance (250) 232-5351; Fort Nelson RCMP (250) 774-2777.

Milepost DC 605.1 BC–YT border to **DC 710** Swift River. *NOTE: Yukon area code will change to (867) in October 1997.* Watson Lake ambulance (403) 536-4444; RCMP (403) 536-5555 or (403) 667-5555.

Milepost DC 710 Swift River to **DC 821** Squanga Lake. Teslin ambulance (403) 390-4444 or (403) 667-3333; RCMP (403) 390-5555 or (403) 667-5555.

Milepost DC 821 Squanga Lake to **DC 936.8** Mendenhall River bridge. Whitehorse ambulance (403) 667-3333; RCMP (403) 667-5555.

Milepost DC 936.8 Mendenhall River bridge to **DC 1023.7** Kluane Lake Lodge. Haines Junction ambulance (403) 634-4444 or (403) 667-3333; RCMP (403) 634-5555 or (403) 667-5555.

Milepost DC 1023.7 Kluane Lake Lodge to **DC 1122.7** Longs Creek. Destruction Bay ambulance (403) 841-3333 or 1-403-667-3333; RCMP (403) 634-5555 or (403) 667-5555.

Milepost DC 1122.7 Longs Creek to **DC 1189.8** YT–AK border. *NOTE: Yukon area code will change to (867) in October 1997.* Beaver Creek RCMP (403) 862-5555 or (403) 667-5555; Ambulance (403) 862-3333 or (403) 667-3333.

Milepost DC 1221.8 YT–AK border to **DC 1314.2** Tok. Northway EMS (907) 778-2211. Port Alcan Rescue Team (Alaska Customs) (907) 774-2252.

Milepost DC 1314.2 Tok to **DC 1361.3** Dot Lake. Tok ambulance (907) 883-2300 or 911.

Milepost DC 1361.3 to **DC 1422** Delta Junction. Delta Rescue Squad phone 911 or (907) 895-4600; Alaska State Troopers (907) 895-4800.

Milepost DC 1422 Delta Junction to **DC 1520** Fairbanks. Dial 911.

the 1940s to help motorists know where they were in this vast wilderness. Today, those original mileposts remain a tradition with communities and businesses on the highway and are still used as mailing addresses and reference points, although the figures no longer accurately reflect driving distance.

When Canada switched to the metric system in the mid-1970s, the mileposts were replaced by kilometreposts. These posts are located on the right-hand side of the highway (Alaska-bound). Kilometreposts, consisting of reflective white numerals on green signs, are up along the British Columbia portion of the Alaska Highway every 3 miles/5 km. In Yukon Territory, white posts with black numerals are up along the highway every 1.2 miles/2 km. There are stretches of straightened and improved highway where kilometreposts are missing.

The kilometerage of the British Columbia portion of the Alaska Highway was recalibrated by the government in the fall of 1990, with kilometreposts corrected to reflect current driving distances. As of our press time, kilometreposts along the Yukon Territory portion of the Alaska Highway still reflected the metric equivalent of the historical mileposts. Thus, at the BC–YT border (**Historical Mile 627**) the kilometerage from Dawson Creek is given as 967.6 km on the BC side and 1009 km on the YT side.

The MILEPOST® log of the Alaska Highway gives distance from Dawson Creek to the AK–YT border as actual driving distance in miles from Dawson Creek followed by kilometre distance based on the kilometreposts. Use our mileage figure from Dawson Creek to figure correct distance between points on the Alaska Highway in Canada. Use our kilometre figure from Dawson Creek to pinpoint location in reference to physical kilometreposts on the Alaska Highway in Canada. On the Alaska portion of the highway, mileposts are based on historical miles, so distance from Dawson Creek in the log is given according to the mileposts up along the road. This figure is followed by the metric equivalent in kilometres.

NOTE: Due to road reconstruction, many kilometreposts have been removed.

Traditional milepost figures in Canada are indicated in the text as **Historical Mile**. Where the governments of British Columbia, Yukon and Alaska have installed commemorative mileposts, the text reads **Historic Milepost**. Restored in 1992 to commemorate the 50th anniversary of the construction of the Alaska Highway, many of these historic markers are accompanied by signs and interpretive panels. These mileposts reflect the original or traditional mileage and do not reflect actual driving distance.

A Brief History of the Alaska Highway

Construction of the Alaska Highway officially began on March 9, 1942, and ended eight months and 12 days later on Oct. 25, 1942. But an overland link between Alaska and the Lower 48 had been studied as early as 1930 under President Herbert Hoover's authorization. It was not until the bombing of Pearl Harbor in December 1941 that construction of the highway was deemed a military necessity. Alaska was considered vulnerable to a Japanese invasion. On Feb. 6, 1942, approval for the Alaska Highway was

Dawson Creek is surrounded by rolling farmland. (Earl L. Brown, staff)

given by the Chief of Staff, U.S. Army. On Feb. 11, President Roosevelt authorized construction of the pioneer road.

The general route of the highway, determined by the War Department, was along a line of existing airfields from Edmonton, AB, to Fairbanks, AK. This chain of airfields was known as the Northwest Staging Route, and was used to ferry more than 8,000 war planes from Great Falls, MT, to Ladd Air Force Base in Fairbanks, AK, as part of the Russian–American Lend Lease Program. The planes were flown from Fairbanks to Nome, then on to Russia.

In March 1942, rights-of-way through Canada were secured by formal agreement between the 2 countries. The Americans agreed to pay for construction and turn over the Canadian portion of the highway to the Canadian government after the war ended. Canada furnished the right-of-way, and waived import duties, sales taxes, income taxes and immigration regulations, and provided construction materials along the route.

A massive mobilization of men and equipment began. Regiments of the U.S. Army Corps of Engineers were moved north to work on the highway. By June, more than 10,000 American troops had poured into the Canadian North. The Public Roads Administration tackled the task of organizing civilian engineers and equipment. Trucks, road-building equipment, office furniture, food, tents and other supplies all had to be located and then shipped north.

Road work began in April, with crews working out of the 2 largest construction camps, Whitehorse and Fort St. John. The highway followed existing winter roads, old Indian trails, rivers and, on occasion, "sight" engineering.

For the soldiers and civilian workers, it was a hard life. Working 7 days a week, they endured mosquitoes and black flies in summer, and below zero temperatures in winter. Weeks would pass with no communication between headquarters and field par-

ties. According to one senior officer with the Public Roads Administration, "Equipment was always a critical problem. There never was enough."

In June 1942, the Japanese invaded Attu and Kiska islands in the Aleutians, adding a new sense of urgency to completion of the road. Crews working from east and west connected at Contact Creek on Sept. 25. By October, it was possible for vehicles to travel the entire length of the highway. The official opening of the Alaska Highway was a ribbon-cutting ceremony held Nov. 20, 1942, on Soldier's Summit at Kluane Lake. (A rededication ceremony was held Nov. 20, 1992, as part of the 50th anniversary celebration of the Alaska Highway.) The Alaska Highway was named an International Historical Engineering Landmark in 1996.

Dawson Creek

Milepost 0 of the Alaska Highway. **Population:** 12,000, area 66,500. **Emergency Services:** RCMP, phone (250) 782-5211. **Fire Department**, phone (250) 782-5000. **Ambulance**, phone (250) 782-2211. **Hospital and Poison Centre**, Dawson Creek and District Hospital, 11000 13th St., phone (250) 782-8501.

Visitor Information: At NAR (Northern Alberta Railway) Park on Alaska Avenue at 10th Street (one block west of the traffic circle), in the building behind the railway car. Open year-round, 8 A.M. to 7 P.M. daily in summer, 10 A.M. to 4 P.M. Tuesday through Saturday in winter. Phone (250) 782-9595. Trained visitor information counsellors can answer questions about weather and road conditions, local events and attractions. Plenty of public parking in front of the refurbished grain elevator that houses the Dawson Creek Art Gallery and Museum.

Elevation: 2,186 feet/666m. **Climate:** Average temperature in January is 0°F/-18°C; in July it is 60°F/15°C. The average annual snowfall is 72 inches with the average depth of snow in midwinter at 19.7 inches. Frost-free days total 97, with the first frost of the year occurring about the first week of September. **Radio:** CJDC 890. **Television:** 13 channels via cable including pay TV. **Newspapers:** *Peace River Block News* (daily); *The Mirror* (weekly).

Private Aircraft: Dawson Creek airport, 2 miles/3.2 km southeast; elev. 2,148 feet/655m; length 5,000 feet/1,524m; asphalt; fuel 100, jet. Floatplane base parallels runway.

Dawson Creek lies 367 miles/591 km northwest of Edmonton, AB, and 250 miles/402 km northeast of Prince George, BC.

Dawson Creek (like Dawson City in the Yukon Territory) was named for George

Mercer Dawson of the Geological Survey of Canada, whose geodetic surveys of this region in 1879 helped lead to its development as an agricultural settlement. The open level townsite is surrounded by rolling farmland, part of the government-designated Peace River Block.

The Peace River Block consists of 3.5 million acres of arable land in northeastern British Columbia, which the province gave to the Dominion Government in 1883 in return for financial aid toward construction of the Canadian Pacific Railway. (While a route through the Peace River country was surveyed by CPR in 1878, the railroad was eventually routed west from Calgary through Kicking Horse Pass.) The Peace River Block was held in reserve by the Dominion Government until 1912, when some of the land was opened for homesteading. The federal government restored the Peace River Block to the province of British Columbia in 1930.

Today, agriculture is an important part of this area's economy. The fields of bright yellow flowers (in season) in the area are canola, a hybrid of rapeseed that was developed as a low cholesterol oil seed. Raw seed is processed in Alberta and Japan. The Peace River region also produces most of the province's cereal grain, along with fodder, cattle and dairy cattle. Other industries include the production of honey, hogs, eggs and poultry. Some potato and vegetable farming is also done here.

On the British Columbia Railway line and the western terminus of the Northern Alberta Railway (now Canadian National Railway), Dawson Creek is also the hub of

Dawson Creek

DAWSON CREEK ADVERTISERS

Alahart RV Park..................Ph. (250) 782-4702
Alaska Hotel Cafe & Dew Drop
    Inn Pub ....55 paces south of Mile 0 Post
Bed & Breakfast Inn
    Margaree ....Ph. (250) 782-4319
Boston Pizza............................1525 Alaska Ave.
Dawson Creek Art Gallery ....NAR Park
Dawson Creek Coin
    Laundry Ltd.........5 blocks S. of traffic circle
Dawson Creek Tourist
    Information Bureau.....Ph. (250) 782-9595
Farmington Fairways &
    Campground.........Ph. (250) 843-7774
Handy Crafters Corner
    Co-op............................Ph. (250) 782-6470
Joy Propane ....4805 S. Access Rd.
King Koin Laundromat..................Across from
    BC Government Bldg.
Lodge Motor Inn, The ......Ph. (250) 782-4837
Mile 0 RV Park & Campsite.....Adjacent Walter
    Wright Pioneer Village
Northern Lights RV Park Ltd.........1 mile from
    Alaska Hwy. Jct. on Hwy. 97 S.
Northwinds Lodge ....1 block E. Co-op Mall
Organic Farms Bakery.......Ph. (250) 782-6533
Peace Villa Motel...................1641 Alaska Ave.
Red Roof
    Bed & Breakfast..........Ph. (250) 786-5581
TLC Car Wash.................Across from Northern
    Lights College
Trail Inn, The ....Ph. (250) 782-8595
Treasure House Imports ....10109 10th St.
Tubby's RV Park......................1913 Hart Hwy.
United Spring &
    Brake Ltd........Directly behind McDonald's
Voyageur Motor Inn.........Ph. (250) 782-1020

four major highways: the John Hart Highway (Highway 97 South) to Prince George; the Alaska Highway (Highway 97 North); Highway 2, which leads east to Grande Prairie, AB; and Highway 49, which leads east to Spirit River and Donnelly.

The Northern Alberta Railway reached Dawson Creek in 1931. As a railhead, Dawson Creek was an important funnel for supplies and equipment during construction of the Alaska Highway in 1942. Some 600 carloads arrived by rail within a period of five weeks in preparation for the construction program, according to a report by the Public Roads Administration in 1942. A "rutted provincial road" linked Dawson Creek with Fort St. John, affording the only approach to the southern base of operations. Field headquarters were established at Fort St. John and Whitehorse. Meanwhile, men and machines continued to arrive at Dawson Creek. By May of 1942, 4,720 carloads of equipment had arrived by rail at Dawson Creek for dispersement to troops and civilian engineers to the north.

With the completion of the Alaska Highway in 1942 (and opening to the public in 1948) and the John Hart Highway in 1952, Dawson Creek expanded both as a distribution centre and tourist destination. Dawson Creek was incorporated as a city in 1958.

The development of oil and natural gas exploration in northeastern British Columbia, and related industries such as pipeline construction and oil storage, has contributed to the economic expansion of Dawson Creek. The city is also one of the major supply centres for the massive resource development

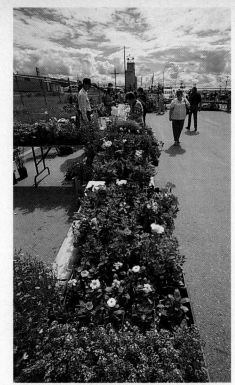

Flowers on sale at Saturday farmer's market at the grain elevator.
(Earl L. Brown, staff)

known as North East Coal, southwest of Dawson Creek. Access to the coal development and the town of Tumbler Ridge is via the Heritage Highway, which branches off the John Hart Highway just west of Dawson Creek and also branches off Highway 2 southeast of the city. Highway 29 extends south from Chetwynd to Tumbler Ridge.

Provincial government offices and social services for the South Peace region are located in Dawson Creek. The city has a modern 100-bed hospital, a public library and a college (Northern Lights). There are also an indoor swimming pool, 2 skating arenas, a curling rink, bowling alley, golf course, art gallery, museum, tennis and racquetball courts. There are numerous churches in Dawson Creek (check at the Visitor Info-centre for location and hours of worship).

ACCOMMODATIONS/VISITOR SERVICES

There are 14 hotels/motels, several bed and breakfasts, and dozens of restaurants. Department stores, banks, grocery, an organic bakery, drug and hardware stores, and many specialty shops are located both downtown and in the 2 shopping centres, Co-op Mall and Dawson Mall. Visitors will also find laundromats, car washes, gas stations and automotive repair shops. The liquor store is adjacent the NAR Visitor Infocentre on Alaska Avenue.

There are 4 campgrounds in Dawson Creek, 2 located on either side of the Hart Highway at its junction with the Alaska Highway and 2 located on Alaska Avenue. There is a private campground on the Hart Highway, 2 miles/3.2 km west from the Alaska Highway junction. There are also campgrounds (both private and provincial) north of Dawson Creek on the Alaska Highway. ▲

The Alaska Hotel Cafe & Dew Drop Inn Pub combines the spirit of Northern Adventure with Old World charm. *Where to Eat in Canada*, which lists the 500 top restaurants, suggests, "It is a good idea to start out on the Alaska Highway with a good meal under your belt, and there's no better place than the Alaska Cafe." The cafe also holds membership in World Famous Restaurants International. The pub features live entertainment nightly, a hot spot in town. The building, having 15 "rooms with charm," provides a perfect backdrop for the Kux-Kardos collection of antiques and works of art (tours available). At the Alaska, our philosophy is Deluxe Evolutionary ... "Always changing for the better." Phone (250) 782-7998 to reserve. Pets welcome. Located 55 paces south of the mile "0" post. A definite must to experience. [ADVERTISEMENT]

Northern Lights RV Park welcomes you! Enjoy peaceful surroundings just 1.5 miles from Dawson Creek. Spacious, level pull-throughs with your own lawn and picnic table. Check out our souvenir shop or try fly fishing in our trout pond. Come to see the attractions in our area? Day trips to the WAC Bennett Dam, Kinuseo Falls and the Kiskatinaw Bridge all offer gorgeous scenery and abundant wildlife. Or, just sit back and relax while we pamper you and your rig to prepare you for your Alaska Highway Adventure! Your hosts—the Bates Family. Phone (250) 782-9433. [ADVERTISEMENT]

Organic Farms Bakery. Using grain crops from our family farm, 100 percent certified organic stoneground flour. Specializing in German-style rye, spelt and whole wheat breads, buns, pretzels, croissants and pastries. Flours and spelt pastas. Taste the difference! 1425–97 Ave., Dawson Creek (look for our colourful bakery), just off Alaska Ave.

Phone (250) 782-6533. [ADVERTISEMENT]

TRANSPORTATION

Air: Scheduled service from Dawson Creek airport to Prince George, Vancouver, Edmonton, Grande Prairie and Calgary via Air BC. The airport is located 2 miles/3.2 km south of the Alaska Avenue traffic circle via 8th Street/Highway 2; there is a small terminal at the airport. There is also a floatplane base.

Railroad: Canadian National Railroad and British Columbia Railway provide freight

service only. B.C. Railway provides passenger service from Vancouver to Prince George.

Bus: Greyhound service to Prince George and Vancouver, BC; Edmonton, AB; and Whitehorse, YT. Dawson Creek also has a city bus transit system.

ATTRACTIONS

NAR Park, on Alaska Avenue at 10th Street (near the traffic circle), is the site of the Visitor Infocentre, which is housed in a restored railway station; phone (250) 782-9595. The Visitor Infocentre offers a self-guided historical walking tour with descriptions of Dawson Creek in the early 1940s during construction of the Alaska Highway.

Also at the station is the Dawson Creek Station Museum, operated by the South Peace Historical Society, which contains pioneer artifacts and wildlife displays. Be sure to leave enough time to view the hour-long video about the building of the Alaska Highway. Souvenirs and restrooms at the museum.

In front of the station is a 1903 railway car, called "The Blue Goose Caboose," serving snacks and ice cream. Adjacent to the station is a huge wooden grain elevator, which has been refurbished; its annex now houses an art gallery. Good display of Alaska Highway construction photos; restroom, gift shop. The last of Dawson Creek's old elevators, it was bought and moved to its present location through the efforts of community organizations. Every Saturday in summer there is an outdoor farmer's market featuring flowers, produce, baked goods and crafts for sale.

Inquire at the Visitor Infocentre for the location of Bear Mountain Community Forest. This Ministry of Forests recreation area features interpretive trails on the flora and fauna of the area. It is located 6 miles/10 km south of the city.

Recreational facilities in Dawson Creek include a bowling alley, miniature golf, indoor pool, 2 ice arenas, curling rink, 18-hole golf course, tennis courts and an outdoor pool at Rotary Lake Park.

Walter Wright Pioneer Village and Mile 0 Rotary Park. The entrance to the village is highlighted by Gardens North, consisting of 9 separate gardens, including a memorial rose garden. Bring a camera to capture the amazing variety of perennials and annuals that grow in the North. The pioneer village contains an impressive collection of local pioneer buildings, including: a teahouse; antiques and collectibles shop; and a general store. Souvenirs and Gardens North seeds are available. Admission is $1. Food service available at the Mile 1 Cafe.

PEACE RIVER ALASKA HIGHWAY

DAWSON CREEK

DAWSON
CREEK

FT ST. JOHN   48
FORT NELSON   300
WHITEHORSE   918
FAIRBANKS   1523

MILE
"0"

ALASKA HIWAY

For further information contact
Dawson Creek Visitor Information Bureau
Department MP
900 Alaska Avenue
Dawson Creek, BC V1G 4T6

Tel (250) 782-9595
Fax (250) 782-9538

SUPER, NATURAL   BRITISH COLUMBIA®

Adjacent to the village is the Sudeten Memorial Hall. "A Mile Zero Welcome," a presentation about Dawson Creek, then and now, by Marilyn Croutch, is held either in Sudeten Hall or the old Dawson School in summer; phone (250) 782-7144. Check with the Visitor Infocentre for details on entertainment offerings. Also located here is Rotary Lake, an outdoor man-made swimming facility; restrooms and picnic areas are found throughout Rotary Park.

Special Events. Mile Zero Celebration Days held in May. July 1st festivities take place at Sudenten Hall. The Fall Fair and Stampede in August features the largest amateur rodeo in North America.

Tumbler Ridge Side Trip. To reach Tumbler Ridge, drive west from Dawson Creek 12 miles/20 km on Highway 97 to junction with the Heritage Highway (see **Milepost PG 237.7** in the WEST ACCESS ROUTE section), or drive west 60.6 miles/97.5 km to junction with Highway 29 South (see **Milepost PG 189.4** in the WEST ACCESS ROUTE section). Heritage Highway 52 (paved) leads south 59.5 miles/96 km to the community of Tumbler Ridge. Highway 29 South is a paved maintained road all the way to Tumbler Ridge. Tumbler Ridge is the townsite for Quintette Coal Limited's large-scale surface mines, and also serves workers of the Bullmoose Mine. Tours of Quintette and Bullmoose mines are available; inquire at the Visitor Infocentre in Tumbler Ridge. The huge coal processing plant and overhead conveyor are visible from the road. Monkman Provincial Park, site of spectacular

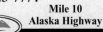

225-foot/69-m Kinuseo (Keh-NEW-see-oh) Falls, lies south of Tumbler Ridge. Contact BC Parks in Fort St. John (phone 250/787-3407) or Tumbler Ridge Infocentre (250/242-4702) for more information.

At Tumbler Ridge, motorists have a choice: return to Highway 97 via Highway 52; return to Highway 97 via Highway 29 South to Chetwynd; or continue on the Heritage Highway loop, 76 miles/123 km via all-gravel road and 16 miles/25 km via paved road, to Highway 2 southeast of Dawson Creek. (Highway 29 South offers the best road surface.) There are no services on the Heritage Highway except at Tumbler Ridge, which has a motel, campgrounds, restaurants, a bank and shopping. On gravel stretches of the road, watch for poor road conditions in wet weather.

Alaska Highway Log

BC HIGHWAY 97
Distance* from Dawson Creek (DC) is followed by distance from Fairbanks (F). Original mileposts are indicated in the text as Historical Mile.
*Mileages from Dawson Creek are based on actual driving distance. Kilometres from Dawson Creek are based on physical kilometreposts. Read Mileposts and Kilometreposts in the introduction on page 78 for an explanation of how this highway is logged.

DC 0 F 1488 (2394.6 km) **Mile 0** marker of the Alaska Highway on 10th Street in downtown Dawson Creek.

Northbound: Good pavement approximately next 284 miles/457 km (through Fort Nelson). Watch for road construction and surface changes from Pink Mountain north.

DC 1.2 (1.9 km) **F 1486.8** (2392.7 km) **Junction** of the Alaska Highway and John Hart Highway.

Prince George-bound travelers turn to the end of the WEST ACCESS ROUTE section and read log back to front. Alaska-bound travelers continue with this log.

DC 1.5 (2.4 km) **F 1486.5** (2392.2 km) Mile 0 Rotary Park, Walter Wright Pioneer Village and Mile 0 Campground to west. ▲

DC 1.7 (2.7 km) **F 1486.3** (2391.9 km) **Historic Milepost 2.** Sign about Cantel Repeater Station. Cantel telephone–teletype lines stretched from Alberta to Fairbanks, AK, making it one of the world's longest open wire toll circuits at the time.

DC 2 (3.2 km) **F 1486** (2391.4 km) Recreation centre and golf course to west. Louisiana Pacific waferboard plant to east.

DC 2.7 (4.3 km) **F 1485.3** (2390.3 km) Truck scales and public phone to east. Truck stop to west; gas, cafe.

DC 2.9 (4.7 km) **F 1485.1** (2390 km) Northern Alberta Railway (NAR) tracks.

DC 3.3 (5.3 km) **F 1484.7** (2389.3 km) Turnout with litter barrel to east. **Historic Milepost 3**; historic sign marks Curan & Briggs Ltd. Construction Camp, U.S. Army Traffic Control Centre.

DC 3.4 (5.5 km) **F 1484.6** (2389.2 km) **Historical Mile 3. The Trading Post** to east. See display ad this section.

DC 9.5 (15.3 km) **F 1478.5** (2379.3 km) Golf course, driving range and RV park. ▲

Farmington Fairways and Campground. 9-hole par-36 golf course, grass greens, treed fairways. Driving range, licensed clubhouse, rentals available. 28-site

View from jet boat of Peace River crossing, south of Taylor. (Earl L. Brown, staff)

shaded campground, firepits, tables, pit toilets and sani-station. RV park with 23 pull-through hookups. Camp under the trees and golf at your leisure. (250) 843-7774. (VISA and MasterCard.) Enjoy super, natural scenic adventure. [ADVERTISEMENT] ▲

DC 11.2 (18 km) **F 1476.8** (2376.6 km) Turnout with litter barrels to west.

DC 11.5 (18.5 km) **F 1476.5** (2376.1 km) Turnout with litter barrels to east.

DC 13.1 (21.1 km) **F 1474.9** (2373.5 km) **Historic Milepost 13** "Start of Storms Contracting Co. Ltd. contract."

DC 14.8 (24 km) **F 1473.2** (2370.8 km) Farmington (unincorporated).

DC 15.8 (25.4 km) **F 1472.2** (2369.2 km) Farmington store to west; gas, groceries, phone.

DC 17.3 (27.8 km) **F 1470.7** (2366.8 km) Exit east for loop road to Kiskatinaw Provincial Park. Follow good 2-lane paved road (old Alaska Highway) 2.5 miles/4 km for Kiskatinaw Provincial Park. This interesting side road gives travelers the opportunity to drive the original old Alaska Highway and to cross the historic curved wooden Kiskatinaw River bridge. Sign at bridge notes that this 531-foot-/162-m-long structure is the only original timber bridge built along the Alaska Highway that is still in use today. The

provincial park has 28 campsites, drinking water, firewood, picnic tables, fire rings, outhouses and garbage containers. Camping fee $7 to $12. ▲

DC 17.5 (28.2 km) **F 1470.5** (2366.5 km) Distance marker indicates Fort St. John 29 miles/47 km.

DC 19.4 (31.2 km) **F 1468.6** (2363.4 km) Large turnout to east.

DC 19.8 (31.9 km) **F 1468.2** (2362.8 km) Highway descends northbound to Kiskatinaw River.

DC 20.9 (33.6 km) **F 1467.1** (2361 km)

Kiskatinaw River bridge. *CAUTION: Strong crosswinds on bridge.* Turnout with litter barrel and picnic tables to east at north end of bridge. View of unique bridge support.

DC 21.6 (34.5 km) **F 1466.4** (2359 km) Loop road to Kiskatinaw Provincial Park and Kiskatinaw River bridge (see **Milepost DC 17.3**).

DC 25.4 (41 km) **F 1462.6** (2353.8 km) NorthwesTel microwave tower to east. Alaska Highway travelers will be seeing many of these towers as they drive north.

The Northwest Communications System was constructed by the U.S. Army in 1942–43. This land line was replaced in 1963 with the construction of 42 microwave relay stations by Canadian National Telecommunications (Cantel, now NorthwesTel) between Grande Prairie, AB, and the YT–AK border.

DC 30.5 (49.1 km) **F 1457.5** (2345.5 km) Turnout to east with litter barrels. Turnout to west with litter barrels, pit toilet and historical marker about explorer Alexander Mackenzie.

Highway begins steep winding descent northbound to the Peace River bridge. *CAUTION: Trucks check your brakes.* Good views to northeast of Peace River valley and industrial community of Taylor. Some wide gravel shoulder next 4 miles/6.4 km for northbound traffic to pull off.

DC 32.1 (51.6 km) **F 1455.9** (2343 km) Large turnout with litter barrels. Viewpoint with information panel.

DC 33.8 (54.4 km) **F 1454.2** (2340.2 km) Pingle Creek.

DC 34 (54.7 km) **F 1454** (2339.9 km) Access to Taylor Landing Provincial Park; boat launch, parking and fishing. Jet boat outfitter. Also access to Peace Island Regional Park, 0.5 mile/0.8 km west of the highway, situated on an island in the **Peace River** connected to the south shore by a causeway. Peace Island has 35 shaded campsites with gravel pads, firewood, fire rings, picnic tables, picnic shelter, toilets, potable water, playground and horseshoe pits. There are also 4 large picnic areas and a tenting area. Camping fee. Open Memorial Day to Labour Day. Nature trail, good bird watching and good fishing in clear water. Boaters should use caution on the Peace River since both parks are downstream from the W.A.C. Bennett and Peace Canyon dams and water levels may fluctuate rapidly.　◄◆▲

DC 34.4 (55.4 km) **F 1453.6** (2339.3 km) Peace River bridge. Gas pipeline bridge visible to east.

Bridging the Peace was one of the first goals of Alaska Highway engineers in 1942. Traffic moving north from Dawson Creek was limited by the Peace River crossing, where 2 ferries with a capacity of 10 trucks per hour were operating in May. Three different pile trestles were constructed across the Peace River, only to be washed out by high water. Work on the permanent 2,130-foot suspension bridge began in December 1942 and was completed in July 1943. One of 2 suspension bridges on the Alaska Highway, the Peace River bridge collapsed in 1957 after erosion undermined the north anchor block of the bridge. The cantilever and truss-type bridge that crosses the Peace River today was completed in 1960.

DC 35 (56.3 km) **F 1453** (2338.3 km) **Historic Milepost 35 at TAYLOR** (pop. 821; elev. 1,804 feet/550m), located on the north bank of the Peace River. **Visitor Information:** On left northbound (10114–100 St.); phone (250) 789-9015. Inquire here about industrial tours of Canadian Forest Products, Fiberco Pulpmill and Greenhouse Complex. Taylor is an industrial community clustered around a Westcoast Energy Inc. gas-processing plant and large sawmill. Established in 1955 with the discovery and development of a natural gas field in the area, Taylor is the site of a pulp mill and plants that handle sulfur processing, gas compressing, high-octane aviation gas production and other byproducts of natural gas. The Westcoast Energy natural gas pipeline reaches from here to Vancouver, BC, with a branch to western Washington.

The fertile Taylor Flats area has several market gardens and roadside stands in summer. A hotel, motels, cafes, grocery store, private RV park, gas station and post office are located here. Free municipal dump station and potable water located behind the North Taylor Inn. This year Taylor will host the 25th Anniversary of the Class A World Gold Panning Championship on Aug. 2–3, 1997. Recreation facilities include a championship 18-hole golf course, a motorcross track and a recreation complex with swimming pool, curling rink and district ice centre for skating (open year-round). ▲

Redwood Esso and Taylor Lodge. See display ad this section.

DC 36.3 (58.4 km) **F 1451.7** (2336.2 km) Railroad tracks.

DC 40 (64.5 km) **F 1448** (2330.3 km) **Historical Mile 41.** Post office; private campground. ▲

DC 40.3 (64.9 km) **F 1447.7** (2329.8 km) Exit east for Fort St. John airport.

DC 40.4 (65 km) **F 1447.6** (2329.6 km) B.C. Railway overhead tracks.

DC 40.9 (65.8 km) **F 1447.1** (2328.8 km) **Historic Milepost 42** "Access Road to Fort St. John Airport."

DC 41.3 (66.5 km) **F 1446.7** (2328.2 km) **Historical Mile 42.3. The Honey Place** to west. See display ad this section.

DC 43.7 (70.3 km) **F 1444.3** (2324.3 km) Miniature golf, driving range and RV park. ▲

Sourdough Pete's RV Park & Troy's Amusement Park. See display ad this section. ▲

DC 44.6 (71.7 km) **F 1443.4** (2322.9 km) Access to Fort St. John via 86th Street. Private RV park. ▲

DC 45.7 (73.5 km) **F 1442.3** (2321.1 km) **Historic Milepost 47,** Fort St. John/"Camp Alcan" sign. In 1942 Fort St. John "exploded." What had been home to 200 became a temporary base for more than 6,000.

DC 45.8 (73.7 km) **F 1442.2** (2320.9 km) South access to Fort St. John via 100th Street. Exit east for Visitor Infocentre and downtown Fort St. John.

DC 47 (75.6 km) **F 1441** (2319 km) **Historical Mile 48.** North access to Fort St. John via 100th Avenue to downtown. Truck stop with 24-hour gas and food.

Fort St. John

Fort St. John

DC 47 (75.6 km) **F 1441** (2319 km) Located approximately 236 miles/ 380 km south of Fort Nelson. **Population:** 15,500; area 40,000. **Emergency Services:** RCMP, phone (250) 787-8100. **Fire Department,** phone (250) 785-2323. **Ambulance,** phone (250) 785-2079. **Hospital,** on 100th Avenue and 96th Street, phone (250) 785-6611.

Visitor Information: Visitor Infocentre located behind the 150-foot oil derrick in the museum, 9323 100th St. (Fort St. John, BC V1J 4N4); phone (250) 785-3033. Open year-round: 8 A.M. to 8 P.M. in summer, 8:30 A.M. to 5 P.M. the rest of the year. Visitors may also contact the Ministry of Environment & Parks, Parks and Outdoor Recreation Division, regarding wilderness hiking opportunities along the Alaska Highway. The Ministry is located at 10003–110 Ave., Room 250, Fort St. John, BC V1J 6M7;

phone (250) 787-3407.

Elevation: 2,275 feet/693m. **Radio**: CKNL 560. **Television**: Cable. **Newspaper**: *Alaska Highway News* (daily), *The Northerner* (weekly).

Private Aircraft: Fort St. John airport, 3.8 miles/6.1 km east; elev. 2,280 feet/695m;

length 6,900 feet/2,103m and 6,700 feet/2,042m; asphalt; fuel 80, 100. Charlie Lake airstrip, 6.7 miles/10.8 km northwest; elev. 2,680 feet/817m; length 1,800 feet/549m; gravel; fuel 80, 100.

Visitor services are located just off the Alaska Highway and in the city centre, a few blocks north of the highway. Fort St. John is a large modern city with all services available.

Fort St. John is set in the low, rolling hills of the Peace River Valley. The original Fort St. John was established in 1806 on the muddy banks of the Peace River, about 10 miles south of the present townsite, as a trading post for the Sikanni and Beaver Indians. The earlier Rocky Mountain Fort site, near the mouth of the Moberly River, dates from 1794. (Fort St. John celebrated its 200th birthday in 1994.) A granite monument, located on Mackenzie Street (100th Street) in Fort St. John's Centennial Park, is inscribed to Sir Alexander Mackenzie, who camped here on his journey west to the Pacific Ocean in 1793. Mackenzie was looking for trade routes for the North West fur company. He reached Bella Coola on July 22, 1793.

In 1942, Fort St. John became field headquarters for U.S. Army troops and civilian engineers working on construction of the Alaska Highway in the eastern sector. It was the largest camp, along with Whitehorse (headquarters for the western sector), of the dozen or so construction camps along the highway. Much of the field housing, road building equipment and even office supplies were scrounged from old Civilian Conservation Corps camps and the Work Projects Administration.

As reported by Theodore A. Huntley of the Public Roads Administration, "A narrow winter road from Fort St. John to Fort Nelson, 256 miles north, provided the only access to the forest itself. From Fort St. John north and west for almost 1,500 miles the wilderness was broken only by dog and pack trails or short stretches of winter road, serviceable only until made impassable by the spring thaw. Within 6 months the first vehicle to travel overland to Alaska would roll into Fairbanks. Thus was a highway born."

The Alaska Highway was opened to the traveling public in 1948, attracting vacationers and homesteaders. An immense natural oil and gas field discovered in 1955 made Fort St. John the oil capital of British Columbia. Land of the New Totems, referring to the many oil rigs, became the slogan for the region.

An extension of the Pacific Great Eastern Railway, now called British Columbia Railway, from Prince George in 1958 (continued to Fort Nelson in 1971), gave Fort St. John a link with the rail yards and docks at North Vancouver.

Today, Fort St. John is the hot spot in North America for natural gas, but it also depends on other industries, including forestry and agriculture. Farms in the North Peace region raise grain and livestock, such as sheep and cattle. Bison are also raised locally. The fields of clover and alfalfa have also attracted bees, and honey is produced for both local markets and export.

TRANSPORTATION

Air: Canadian Regional Airlines and Central Mountain Air to Fort Nelson, Whitehorse, Vancouver, Grande Prairie, Edmonton and Prince George. **Bus:** Coachways service to Prince George, Vancouver, Edmonton and Whitehorse; depot at 10355 101st Ave., phone (250) 785-6695.

ACCOMMODATIONS/VISITOR SERVICES

Numerous major motels, hotels, bed and breakfasts, restaurants, fast-food outlets and full-service gas stations are located on the Alaska Highway and in town. Other services include supermarkets, laundromats, several banks (automatic teller machines at Totem Mall and downtown at Charter Banks), a car wash and shops. The Totem Mall is located on the Alaska Highway. Indoor leisure pool, with waterslide, wave pool and children's play area at North Peace Recreation Centre; phone (250) 785-6148 for schedule. The North Peace Cultural Centre has a library, a 413-seat theatre, a gallery/gift shop and cafe. Open 6 days a week, 9 A.M. to 3 P.M.

Fort St. John RV Park, located at the east end of Centennial Park behind the visitor centre and museum, has 35 sites, showers, a laundry, dump station and hookups; senior citizen rates. Fresh water fill-up and dump station located at the northwest corner of 86th Street and the Alaska Highway. Also camping north of the city at Beatton and Charlie Lake provincial parks, and at private and Rotary campgrounds at Charlie Lake. ▲

ATTRACTIONS

Centennial Park, located on 100th Street, has a museum, the Visitor Infocentre and an RV park. The Fort St. John–North Peace Museum houses more than 6,000 artifacts from the region, including items from Finch's Store (the first store in Fort St. John), an 1806 Fort St. John post, a trapper's cabin and early-day schoolroom. The museum gift shop offers a good selection of local and Northwest books. Inquire at the Visitor Infocentre about local hiking trails, fishing, boat tours, trail rides and the lily farm. The tourist centre and museum are open 8 A.M.

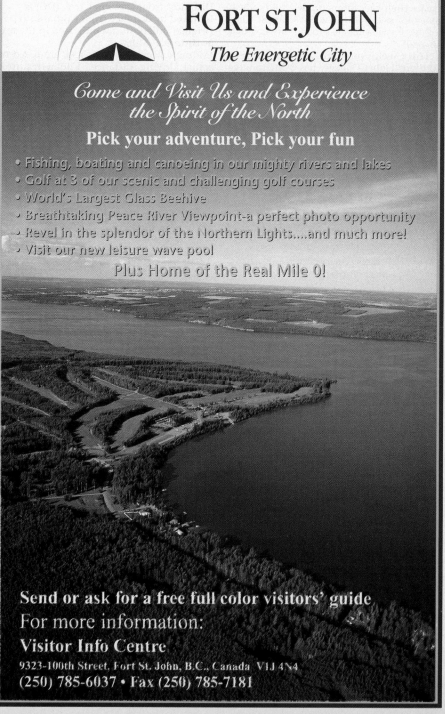

to 8 P.M. daily in summer.

Directly in front of the Visitor Infocentre is a 150-foot oil derrick, presented to the North Peace Historical Society and the people of Fort St. John. Check with the North Peace Museum at (250) 787-0430 about summer entertainment at the derrick.

Play golf. Fort St. John's only in-town golf course is Links Golf Course, just off the Bypass Road at 86 Street; 9 holes, pro shop and lounge. Phone (250) 785-9995. The Lakepoint Golf Course, on Golf Course Road at Charlie Lake, is rated one of the nicest courses in British Columbia. Open 8 A.M. to 9 P.M. daily; 18 holes, pro shop, lounge and restaurant. Phone (250) 785-5566.

Industry and agriculture of the area are showcased for the public at various places. Check with the Infocentre for directions and details. Canada Forest Products offers tours of their mills, phone (250) 785-8906 for details. The Honey Place, just south of town on the Alaska Highway, offers guided tours, fresh honey for sale, and the world's Largest Glass Beehive for viewing year-round; phone (250) 785-4808.

Fish Creek Community Forest, adjacent Northern Lights College, has 3 interpretive trails to view forest management activities and learn more about the forest. Cross-coun-

try ski trails in winter. From the Alaska Highway follow 100th Street north 1.2 miles/2 km to parking area at college.

W.A.C. Bennett Dam is a major attraction in the area. For an interesting side trip, drive north from Fort St. John on the Alaska Highway to **Milepost DC 53.7** and take Highway 29 west 46.5 miles/74.8 km to Hudson's Hope. Highway 29 follows the original Canadian government telegraph trail of 1918. Hudson's Hope, formerly a pioneer community established in 1805 by explorer Simon Fraser, grew with construction of the W.A.C. Bennett Dam, which is located 13.5 miles/21.7 km west of town. B.C. Hydro's Peace Canyon dam is located approximately 4 miles/6.4 km south of Hudson's Hope. Turn to the HUDSON'S HOPE LOOP section for more information.

Alaska Highway Log

(continued)

Distance* from Dawson Creek (DC) is followed by distance from Fairbanks (F). Original mileposts are indicated in the text as Historical Mile.

*Mileages from Dawson Creek are based on actual driving distance. Kilometres from Dawson Creek are based on physical kilometreposts. Please read Mileposts and Kilometreposts in the introduction for an explanation of how this highway is logged.

DC 45.8 (73.7 km) F 1442.2 (2320.9 km) South access to Fort St. John via 100th Street.

DC 47 (75.6 km) F 1441 (2319 km) Mile 48. North access to Fort St. John via 100th Avenue.

DC 48.6 (78.2 km) F 1439.4 (2316.4 km) Historic Milepost 49 commemorates "Camp Alcan."

DC 49.5 (79.6 km) F 1438.5 (2315 km) Exit for Beatton Provincial Park, 5 miles/8 km east via paved road; 37 campsites, picnic shelter, wood stove, horseshoe pits, volleyball net, playground, baseball field, sandy beach, swimming and boat launch. Camping fee $7 to $12. Fishing for northern pike, walleye (July best) and yellow perch in **Charlie Lake.** ◄▲

DC 50.6 (81.4 km) F 1437.4 (2313.2 km) CHARLIE LAKE (unincorporated), gas, diesel and propane, grocery, pub, post office, bed and breakfast, private RV parks and Ministry of Energy, Mines and Petroleum. Access to lakeshore east side of highway; boat launch, no parking. At one time during construction of the Alaska Highway, Charlie Lake was designated Mile 0, as there was already a road between the railhead at Dawson Creek and Fort St. John, the eastern sector headquarters for troops and engineers.

Charlie Lake General Store. See display ad this section.

Paradise Lane Bed & Breakfast. See display ad this section.

Rotary R.V. Park. See display ad this section. &▲

DC 51.2 (82.4 km) F 1436.8 (2312.2 km) Historic Milepost 52. Charlie Lake Mile 0 Army Tote Road. Site of a major distribution camp for workers and supplies heading north. 12 American soldiers also drowned here in 1942 while crossing the lake aboard pontoon barges.

DC 51.5 (82.9 km) F 1436.5 (2311.7 km) Ron's R.V. Park. Historical Mile 52. Treed sites with complete RV hookups, shaded lawned tenting areas, picnic tables, firepits, firewood provided. Walking trails, playground, flush toilets, hot showers, laundromat, pay phone, ice. Shaded full-hookup pull-throughs, good drinking water. Large

Visitor centre at W.A.C. Bennett Dam, west on Highway 29. (Earl L. Brown, staff)

boat launching facilities nearby. Boat rentals. Quiet location away from hectic city confusion. Post office, golf course, fishing licenses, Red Barn Pub nearby. Charlie Lake, world famous for walleye and northern pike fishing. Phone (250) 787-1569. [ADVERTISEMENT] ▲

DC 52 (83.7 km) F 1436 (2311 km) Exit east on Charlie Lake Road for lakeshore picnicking.

DC 53.6 (86.3 km) F 1434.4 (2308.4 km) Truck weigh scales east side of highway.

DC 53.7 (86.4 km) F 1434.3 (2308.2 km) **Junction** with Highway 29 and truck stop with restaurant, gas and diesel (open year-round). Highway 29 leads west 47 miles/75.6 km to Hudson's Hope and the W.A.C. Bennett Dam, then south to connect with the Hart Highway at Chetwynd (see HUDSON'S HOPE LOOP section).

Mile 54 Shell Truck Stop. See display ad this section.

Turn east for Charlie Lake Provincial Park, just off highway; paved loop road (with speed bumps) leads through campground. There are 58 shaded sites, picnic tables, kitchen shelter with wood stove, firepits, firewood, outhouses, dump station, water and garbage. Level gravel sites, some will accommodate 2 large RVs. Camping fee $7 to $12. Playfield, playground, horseshoe pits, volleyball net and a 1.2-mile/2-km hiking trail down to lake. Watch for wildflowers. Because of the wide variety of plants here, including some that may not be seen elsewhere along the Alaska Highway, Verna E. Pratt's *Wildflowers Along the Alaska Highway* includes a special list of species for this park. Fishing in **Charlie Lake** for walleye, northern pike and yellow perch. Access to the lake for vehicles and boats is from the Alaska Highway just east of the park entrance. Boat launch and picnic area at lake. ⤙▲

DC 63.6 (102 km) F 1424.4 (2292.3 km) Microwave tower to east.

DC 65.4 (105 km) F 1422.6 (2289.4 km) Turnout with litter barrel to west.

DC 71.7 (115.4 km) F 1416.3 (2279.3 km) **Historical Mile 72**. Food, gas, camping, lodging and crafts store. ▲

The Shepherd's Inn. We specialize in making folks at home, offering regular and breakfast specials, complete lunch and dinner menu. Low-fat buffalo burgers. Our specialties: homemade soups, home-baked sweet rolls, cinnamon rolls, blueberry and

bran muffins, bread, biscuits and trappers bannock. Delicious desserts, rhubarb-strawberry, Dutch apple and chocolate dream pie, cherry and strawberry cheesecake. Hard ice cream. Specialty coffees: Norwegian Mint, Swiss Almond. Herb teas. Refreshing fruit drinks from local fruits: blueberry and raspberry coolers. Caravaners and bus tours ... a convenient and delightful stop on your Alaska Highway adventure! You may reserve your stop–break with us. Full RV hookups, motel service 24 hours. Quality Husky products. Your "Husky Buck" is a great traveling idea. Phone (250) 827-3676. An oasis on the Alcan at Mile 72. [ADVERTISEMENT] ▲

DC 72.8 (117.1 km) F 1415.2 (2277.5 km) **Historic Milepost 73** commemorates Beatton

River Flight Strip, 1 of 4 gravel airstrips built for American military aircraft during WWII. Road to Prespetu and Buick Creek.

DC 79.1 (127.3 km) F 1408.9 (2267.3 km) **Historical Mile 80** paved rest area to west with litter barrels, picnic tables, water and flush toilets. Information panel on Alaska Highway parks.

DC 91.4 (147.1 km) F 1396.6 (2247.5 km) **Historical Mile 92**. Westcoast Energy compressor station to west.

DC 94.6 (152.2 km) F 1393.4 (2242.4 km) Oil pump east of highway behind trees.

DC 101 (161.7 km) F 1387 (2232.1 km) **Historic Milepost 101**. WONOWON (pop. 150), unincorporated, has 3 gas stations (gas, diesel, propane), 3 restaurants, 2 motels, camping, a food store, pub and post office. Formerly known as Blueberry, Wonowon was the site of an official traffic control gate during WWII. Wonowon Horse Club holds an annual race meet and gymkhana at the track beside the highway, where the community club holds its annual snowmobile rally in February. ▲

The historic sign and interpretive panel here commemorate Blueberry Control Station, "site of the Blueberry Control Gate, a 24-hour military checkpoint operated by U.S. Army personnel through the war years."

The Alaska Highway follows the Blueberry and Prophet river drainages north to Fort Nelson. The Blueberry River, not visible from the highway, lies a few miles east of Wonowon.

Blueberry Esso & Motel. See display ad this section.

Hall's Food & Gas. See display ad this section. ▲

DC **101.5** (163.3 km) F **1386.5** (2231.3 km) Food, diesel, gas, camping and lodging to east; open year-round.

102 Husky. See display ad this section. ▲

DC **103.5** (166.5 km) **1384.5** (2228.1 km) Historic Milepost **104** marks start of

Adolphson, Huseth, Layer & Welch contract during Alaska Highway construction.

DC **114** (183.2 km) F **1374** (2211.2 km) Paved turnout with litter barrel to east.

DC **124.3** (200 km) F **1363.7** (2194.6 km) The Cut (highway goes through a small rock cut). Relatively few rock cuts were necessary during construction of the Alaska Highway in 1942–43. However, rock excavation was often made outside of the roadway to obtain gravel fill for the new roadbed.

DC **135.3** (217.7 km) F **1352.7** (2176.9 km) Gravel turnout to east.

CAUTION: Northbound travelers watch for moose next 15 miles/24 km, especially at dusk and at night. ▲

DC **140.4** (225.9 km) F **1347.6** (2168.7 km) Historical Mile **143,** PINK MOUNTAIN (pop. 99, area 300; elev. 3,600 feet/1,097m). Post office, grocery, motels, restaurant, campgrounds, gas stations (gas, diesel, propane) with minor repair service. Bus depot at Pink Mountain Motor Inn east side of highway. Pink Mountain is home to Darryl Mills, Canadian champion bullrider.

Pink Mountain Campsite & R.V. Park, on the left northbound. Take it easy folks, you've arrived at one of the nicest campgrounds on the highway ... coffee's always on. Unleaded Tempo gas, diesel, metered propane for RVs and auto. Post office, general store, liquor store, fishing and hunting licenses. Souvenirs—you'll like our prices. Shaded campsites, picnic tables, firepits and firewood. Tents and RVs welcome. Full hookups, power hookups, water and sani-

dump. Pull-throughs. Something for everyone. Cabins starting at $20 (weekly rates

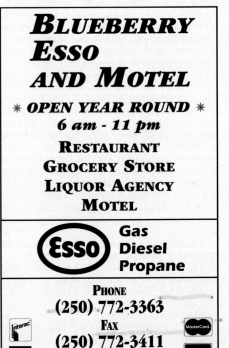

available), reservations recommended. Laundromat and clean showers. Open year-round. VISA and MasterCard. Phone and fax (250) 774-1033. Your hosts, Ron and Pat.

Pink Mountain Motor Inn. Mile 143, a welcome stopping point for all travelers. 34 rooms, gift shop, and licensed restaurant with pies and pastries and home-cooked meals. The perfect lunch break stop for bus tours. For RVs, electric hookups, gravel sites. Treed camping and picnic tables. Water, hot showers, laundromat. Dump station. Caravans welcome, reservations recommended. Full line of Esso products. Fax (250) 774-1071. Phone (250) 772-3234. We hope you're enjoying your Alaska Highway Adventure!

DC 144.1 (231.9 km) **F 1343.9** (2162.7 km) **Historical Mile 147.** Sportsman Inn to east.

DC 144.5 (232.5 km) **F 1343.5** (2162.1 km) **Historical Mile 147.** Restaurant and vehicle repair (towing service).

Mae's Kitchen and Ed's Garage to east. See display ad this section.

DC 144.7 (232.9 km) **F 1343.3** (2161.8 km) **Historic Milepost 148** commemorates Suicide Hill, one of the most treacherous hills on the original highway noted for its ominous greeting: "Prepare to meet thy maker." Beatton River bridge. The Beatton River was named for Frank Beatton, a Hudson's Bay Co. employee. The Beatton River flows east and then south into the Peace River system.

DC 146 (234 km) **F 1342** (2159.7 km) **Private Aircraft:** Sikanni Chief flight strip to east; elev. 3,258 feet/993m; length, 6,000 feet/1,829m; current status unknown. Well-known local pilot Jimmy "Midnight" Anderson used the Sikanni Chief airstrip.

DC 150.3 (241.9 km) **F 1337.7** (2152.8 km) *CAUTION: Southbound travelers watch for moose next 15 miles/24 km, especially at dusk and at night.*

DC 155.6 (250.4 km) **F 1332.4** (2144.2 km) Large double-ended, gravel turnout with litter barrels. *CAUTION: Slow down! Watch for loose gravel.*

DC 156.6 (252 km) **F 1331.4** (2142.6 km) Sikanni Hill. *CAUTION: Slow down for hill.*

DC 159.2 (256.2 km) **F 1328.8** (2138.4 km) Sikanni Chief River bridge (elev. 2,662 feet/811m). To the west you may see steel

View of Pink Mountain valley from Mile 143 Alaska Highway. *(Earl L. Brown, staff)*

St. Paul's church at Milepost DC 226.5.
(Earl L. Brown, staff)

stanchions, all that remains of the historic wooden Sikanni bridge, which was destroyed by arson July 10, 1992. The original timber truss bridge built across the Sikanni Chief River in the spring of 1943 was the first permanent structure completed on the Alaska Highway. Highway construction crews rerouted much of the pioneer road built in 1942 and replaced temporary bridges with permanent structures in 1943. The Sikanni Chief River flows east and then north into the Fort Nelson River, which flows into the Liard River and on to the Mackenzie River, which empties into the Arctic Ocean. Check at the lodge for information on Sikanni River Falls (see **Milepost DC 168.5**).

Sikanni Chief River, fair fishing at mouth of tributaries in summer for pike; grayling to 2¹/₂ lbs.; whitefish to 2 lbs.

DC 159.4 (256.5 km) F 1328.6 (2138.1 km) **Historical Mile 162. SIKANNI CHIEF.** Food, gas, lodging and camping.

Sikanni River RV Park. This riverside RV park offers a beautiful, natural setting for your enjoyment, with easy access to well graveled, long sites. Its reputation for both cleanliness and beauty has made it a popular destination. Make it a must on your list. Reservations recommended. Resident owners. Clean, safe, secure. Recommended as a fueling stop in "Alaska Highway—An Insiders Guide" for 6 years. Located at the bottom of Sikanni River Hill. Phone (250) 774-1028. [ADVERTISEMENT] ▲

DC 160 (257.5 km) F 1328 (2137.2 km) "Drunken forest" on hillside to west is shallow-rooted black spruce trees growing in unstable clay-based soil that is subject to slide activity in wet weather.

DC 160.4 (258.1 km) F 1327.6 (2136.5 km) Section of the old Alaska Highway is visible to east; no access.

DC 168.5 (271.2 km) F 1319.5 (2123.5 km) Gravel road west to Sikanni River Falls. This private road is signed "Travel at own risk." Drive in 10.5 miles/16.9 km to parking area with picnic tables at B.C. Forest Service trailhead; 10-minute hike in on well-marked trail to view falls. Gravel access road has some steep hills and a single-lane bridge. *CAUTION: Do not travel in wet weather. Not recommended for vehicles with trailers.*

IMPORTANT: Watch for moose on highway northbound to **Milepost DC 200**, *especially at dusk. Drive carefully!*

DC 172.5 (277.6 km) F 1315.5 (2117 km) Polka Dot Creek.

DC 173.1 (278.6 km) F 1314.9 (2116 km) Buckinghorse River bridge; access to river at north end of bridge.

DC 173.2 (278.7 km) F 1314.8 (2115.9 km) **Historical Mile 175.** Inn with gas and camping to east at north end of bridge. Also turnoff east for Buckinghorse River Provincial Park. Follow the narrow gravel road past the gravel pit 0.7 mile/1.1 km along river to camping and picnic area. Camping fee $7 to $12. The park has 30 picnic tables, side-by-side camper parking, firewood, fire rings, water pump, outhouses and garbage containers. Fishing for grayling in **Buckinghorse River**. Swimming in downstream pools. ▲

DC 173.4 (279 km) F 1314.6 (2115.6 km) **Historical Mile 175. Buckinghorse River Lodge**, on left northbound. Motel, cafe with home cooking, hard ice cream and ice cream novelties. Bed and breakfast available. Service station, large parking area, free camping. Look forward to our friendly atmosphere. Picnic tables and beautiful scenery. A great spot to take a break for fishing or walking. Phone (250) 773-6468. ▲

[ADVERTISEMENT]

DC 176 (283.2 km) F 1312 (2111.4 km) South end of 27-mile/43-km Trutch Mountain bypass. Completed in 1987, this section of road rerouted the Alaska Highway around Trutch Mountain, eliminating the steep, winding climb up to Trutch Summit (and the views). Named for Joseph W. Trutch, civil engineer and first governor of British Columbia, Trutch Mountain was the second highest summit on the Alaska Highway with an elevation of 4,134 feet/1,260m. The new roadbed cuts a wide swath through the flat Minaker River valley. The river, not visible to motorists, is west of the highway; it was named for local trapper George Minaker. Trutch Mountain is to the east of the highway. Motorists can see part of the old highway on Trutch Mountain.

DC 182.8 (294.2 km) F 1305.2 (2100.4 km) Large gravel turnout with litter barrel to west.

DC 199.1 (320 km) F 1288.9 (2074.2 km) Large gravel turnout with litter barrels.

DC 202.5 (325.5 km) F 1285.5 (2068.8 km) Turnout with litter barrels at north end of Trutch Mountain bypass (see **Milepost DC 176**).

CAUTION: Southbound travelers watch for moose on highway, especially at dusk, to Sikanni Chief. Drive carefully!

DC 204.2 (328 km) F 1283.8 (2066 km) **Beaver Creek**; fishing for grayling to 2¹/₂ lbs.

DC 217.2 (349.3 km) F 1270.8 (2045.1 km) Turnoff to west for Prophet River Provincial Park, 0.4 mile/0.6 km via gravel road. Side-by-side camper parking (36 sites), picnic tables, firewood, fire rings, water pump, outhouses and garbage containers. Camping fee $7 to $12. The park access road crosses an airstrip (originally an emergency airstrip on the Northwest Air Staging Route) and part of the old Alaska Highway (the Alcan). This provincial park is also the first stop on the self-guided Forest Ecology Tours (Ecotours) established by the Fort Nelson Forest District. A pamphlet, available from their office in Fort Nelson (phone 250/774-3936), describes the forests at various sites along the Alaska Highway. This Ecotour stop is noted for its trembling aspen stands and mature white spruce. ▲

The Alaska Highway roughly parallels the Prophet River from here north to the Muskwa River south of Fort Nelson.

Private Aircraft: Prophet River emergency airstrip; elev. 1,954 feet/596m; length 6,000 feet/1,829m; gravel.

DC 218.2 (350.7 km) F 1269.8 (2043.5 km) View of Prophet River to west.

DC 222.3 (357.2 km) F 1265.7 (2036.9 km) Bougie Creek bridge; turnout with litter barrel beside creek at south end of bridge. At this Ecotour stop, note the typical climax white spruce stand and trees of a variety of ages.

CAUTION: Watch for rough road approaching Bougie Creek bridge from either direction.

DC 224.8 (360.6 km) F 1263.2 (2032.8 km) Microwave tower to east.

DC 226.2 (363.4 km) F 1261.8 (2030.6 km) Prophet River Indian Reserve to east.

DC 226.5 (363.9 km) F 1261.5 (2030.1 km) St. Paul's Roman Catholic Church to east.

DC 227 (364.7 km) F 1261 (2029.3 km) **Historical Mile 233. PROPHET RIVER**, gas, diesel, propane, food, camping and lodging. Prophet River Services is on the left northbound; Prophet River Inn on right. Southbound travelers note: Next service 68 miles/109 km. ▲

Prophet River Services. See display ad this section. ▲

DC 227.6 (366.3 km) F 1260.4 (2028.4 km) **Historic Milepost 234**, Adsett Creek Highway Realignment. This major rerouting eliminated 132 curves on the stretch of highway that originally ran between Miles 234 and 275. Turnout with litter barrels.

DC 227.7 (366.4 km) F 1260.3 (2028.2 km) Adsett Creek.

DC 230.7 (371.3 km) F 1257.3 (2023.3 km) Natural gas pipeline crosses beneath highway.

DC 232.9 (374.8 km) F 1255.1 (2019.8 km) Turnout to west with litter barrels.

DC 235.5 (378.4 km) F 1252.5 (2015.6 km) Mesalike topography to the east is Mount Yakatchie.

DC 241.5 (388 km) F 1246.5 (2006 km) Parker Creek.

DC 245.9 (395.7 km) F 1242.1 (1998.9 km) Gravel turnout with litter barrels.

DC 261.1 (420.2 km) F 1226.9 (1974.4 km) Turnout with litter barrels to east.

DC 264.6 (425.2 km) F 1223.4 (1968.8 km) Jackfish Creek bridge. Ecotour stop; note the variety of trembling aspen stands and the white spruce seedlings under them.

DC 265.5 (426.5 km) F 1222.5 (1967.4 km) Turnoff to east for Andy Bailey Lake Provincial Park (day use only) via 6.8-mile/11-km dirt and gravel access road. (Large RVs and trailers note: only turn-around space on access road is approximately halfway in.) The park is located on **Andy Bailey Lake** (formerly Jackfish Lake); picnic tables, fire rings, firewood, water, outhouses, garbage containers, boat launch (no powerboats), swimming and fair fishing for northern pike. Bring insect repellent! 🐟

DC 270.8 (435.1 km) F 1217.2 (1958.8 km) Gas pipeline crosses highway overhead.

DC 271 (435.4 km) F 1217 (1958.5 km) Westcoast Energy gas processing plant to east. Petrosul (sulfur processing) to west.

DC 272.4 (437.6 km) F 1215.6 (1956.3 km) Access to downhill skiing to east.

DC 276.2 (443.8 km) F 1211.8 (1950 km) Rodeo grounds to west. The rodeo is held in August.

DC 276.7 (444.6 km) F 1211.3 (1949.3 km) Railroad tracks. Microwave tower.

DC 277.5 (446.2 km) F 1210.5 (1948 km) Muskwa Heights (unincorporated), an industrial area with rail yard, plywood plant, sawmill and bulk fuel outlet. More than 7,000 carloads of logs were shipped from here in 1995.

DC 277.9 (447.2 km) F 1210.1 (1947.4 km) Truck stop with gas, restaurant and RV campground. ▲

Husky 5th Wheel Truck Stop and RV Park. See display ad this section. ▲

DC 278.1 (447.5 km) F 1209.9 (1947.1 km) Truck scales to west. Turnoff for Chopstick manufacturing plant. This plant produces 6 million pairs of chopsticks a day. Tours by appointment only.

DC 278.4 (448 km) F 1209.6 (1946.6 km) **Trapper's Den.** Historic Mile 293. Owned and operated by a local trapping family. Moose horns, diamond willow, Northern novelties, books, artwork. Fur hats, headbands, earmuffs. Birchbark baskets, moosehair tuftings. Mukluks, moccasins, mits and gloves. Professionally tanned furs. See our "Muskwa River Pearls." Photographers

welcome. Located ½ mile north of Husky 5th Wheel RV Park on the Alaska Highway. VISA, MasterCard. Mail orders. Open 10 A.M. to 6 P.M. daily or phone for appointment. John, Cindy and Mandy Wells. Box 1164, Fort Nelson, BC V0C 1R0. (250) 774-3400. Recommended. [ADVERTISEMENT]

DC 279 (448.6 km) F 1209 (1945.6 km) Site of oriented strand board plant processing aspen and balsam poplar. This 400,000-square-foot building is the largest industrial building of its kind in the province.

DC 281 (451.4 km) F 1207 (1942.4 km) **Muskwa River** bridge, lowest point on the Alaska Highway (elev. 1,000 feet/305m). The Muskwa River flows to the Fort Nelson River. Fair fishing at the mouth of tributaries for northern pike; some goldeye. The Fort Nelson River is too muddy for fishing. The Muskwa River valley exhibits typical river-bottom balsam poplar and white spruce stands, according to the Fort Nelson Forest District's Forest Ecology Tours pamphlet. 🐟

The Alaska Highway swings west at Fort Nelson above the Muskwa River, winding southwest then northwest through the Canadian Rockies.

DC 283 (454.3 km) F 1205 (1939.2 km) Entering Fort Nelson northbound. Fort Nelson's central business district extends along the highway from the private campground at the east end of the city to the private campground at the west end. Businesses and services are located both north and south of the highway.

Fort Nelson

DC 283 (454.3 km) F 1205 (1939.2 km) **Historical Mile 300. Population:** 5,000; area 6,500. **Emergency Services:** RCMP, phone (250) 774-2777. **Fire Department,** phone (250) 774-2222. **Hospital,** 35 beds, phone (250) 774-6916. **Ambulance,** phone (250) 774-2344. Medical, dental and optometric clinics. Visiting veterinarians and chiropractors.

Visitor Information: Located in the Recreation Centre at the west end of town, open 8 A.M. to 8 P.M. Inquire here about local attractions, industrial tours and information about the Liard Highway. Fort Nelson Heritage Museum across the highway from the Infocentre. Contact the Town of Fort Nelson by writing Bag Service 399, Fort Nelson, BC V0C 1R0; phone (250) 774-6400 (seasonal) or (250) 774-2541 (all year).

Elevation: 1,383 feet/422m. **Climate:** Winters are cold with short days. Summers are hot and the days are long. In mid-June (summer solstice), twilight continues throughout the night. The average number

of frost-free days annually is 116. Last frost occurs about May 11, and the first frost Sept. 21. Average annual precipitation of 16.3 inches. **Radio:** CFNL 590, CBC 1610. **Television:** Channels 8 and cable. **Newspaper:** *Fort Nelson News* (weekly).

Transportation: Air—Scheduled service to Edmonton, Calgary and Grande Prairie, and to Prince George and Vancouver via

Canadian Regional Airlines. Charter service available. **Bus**—Greyhound service. **Railroad**—B.C. Railway (freight service only).

Private Aircraft: Fort Nelson airport, 3.8 air miles/6.1 km east northeast; elev. 1,253 feet/382m; length 6,400 feet/1,950m; asphalt; fuel 80, 100, Jet B. Gordon Field, 4 miles/6.4 km west; elev. 1,625 feet/495m approximately; length 2,000 feet/610m; turf; fuel 80.

Fort Nelson is located in the lee of the Rocky Mountains, surrounded by the Muskwa, Nelson and Prophet rivers. The area is heavily forested with white spruce, poplar and aspen. Geographically, the town is located about 59° north latitude and 122° west longitude.

Flowing east and north, the Muskwa, Prophet and Sikanni Chief rivers converge to form the Fort Nelson River, which flows into the Liard River, then on to the Mackenzie River, which empties into the Arctic Ocean. Rivers provided the only means of transportation in both summer and winter in this isolated region until 1922, when the Godsell Trail opened, connecting Fort Nelson with Fort St. John. The Alaska Highway linked Fort Nelson with the Outside in 1942.

In the spring, the Muskwa River frequently floods the low country around Fort Nelson and can rise more than 20 feet/6m. At an elevation of 1,000 feet/305m, the Muskwa (which means "bear") is the lowest point on the Alaska Highway. There was a danger of the Muskwa River bridge washing out every June during spring runoff until

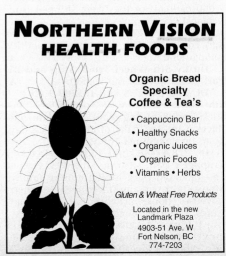

1970, when a higher bridge—with piers arranged to prevent log jams—was built.

Fort Nelson's existence was originally based on the fur trade. In the 1920s, trapping was the main business in this isolated pioneer community populated with less than 200 Indians and a few white men. Trappers still harvest beaver, wolverine, weasel, wolf, fox, lynx, mink, muskrat and marten. Other area wildlife includes black bear, which are plentiful, some deer, caribou and a few grizzly bears. Moose remains an important food source for the Indians.

Fort Nelson aboriginal people are mostly Slave (slay-vee), who arrived here about 1775 from the Great Slave Lake area and speak an Athabascan dialect.

Fort Nelson was first established in 1805 by the North West Fur Trading Co. The post, believed to have been located about 80 miles/129 km south of Nelson Forks, was named for Lord Horatio Nelson, the English admiral who won the Battle of Trafalgar.

A second Fort Nelson was later located south of the first fort, but was destroyed by fire in 1813 after Indians massacred its 8 residents. A third Fort Nelson was established in 1865 on the Nelson River's west bank (1 mile from the present Fort Nelson airport) by W. Cornwallis King, a Hudson's Bay Co. clerk. This trading post was built to keep out the free traders who were filtering in from the Mackenzie River and Fort St. John areas. The free traders' higher fur prices were a

Aerial view of Fort Nelson, at Historical Mile 300 on the Alaska Highway. *(Earl L. Brown, staff)*

FORT NELSON ADVERTISERS

Ardendale
 Bed & Breakfast...........Ph. (250) 774-2433
Best Western
 Woodlands Inn ....Ph. (250) 774-6669
Bluebell Inn, The..............Ph. 1-800-663-5267
Coachouse Inn ....Ph. (250) 774-3911
Dan's Neighborhood Pub.........S. end of town
Dixie Lee ....Ph. (250) 774-6226
Fabric Fun........................New Landmark Plaza
Fort Nelson Bed &
 Breakfast.....................Ph. (250) 774-6050
Fort Nelson Heritage
 Museum ....Across from Travel Infocentre
Fort Nelson Hotel ....Ph. (250) 774-6971
Fort Nelson
 Service Centre ....Ph. (250) 774-7950
Home On The Hill
 Bed & Breakfast...........Ph. (250) 774-3000
KaCee's Koin Kleaners ..Next to IGA Foodstore
Mary's Place......................Ph. (250) 774-7900
Mini-Price Inn ....Ph. (250) 774-2136
Northern Husky..............................Downtown
Northern Lights Deli.........Ph. (250) 774-3311
Northern Vision Health
 Foods.............................New Landmark Plaza
Pioneer Motel ....Ph. (250) 774-6459
Poplar Hills Golf &
 Country Club ....Ph. (250) 774-3862
Provincial Motel................Ph. (250) 774-6901
Red Rose Convenience Store ...S. end of town
Scooby's Snuggle-Up
 Bed & Breakfast...........Ph. (250) 774-2613
Spiritfire Family
 Books 'n Things ....Ph. (250) 774-4870
Sukhi's Coin-Op
 Laundromat.................Ph. (250) 774-7786
Tirecraft ....Ph. (250) 774-6372
Town of Fort Nelson........Ph. (250) 774-2541
Westend R.V. Campground
 and Mini-Golf ....Ph. (250) 774-2340

threat to the Hudson's Bay Co., which in 1821 had absorbed the rival North West Fur Trading Co. and gained a monopoly on the fur trade in Canada.

This Hudson's Bay Co. trading post was destroyed by a flood in 1890 and a fourth Fort Nelson was established on higher ground upstream and across the river, which is now known as Old Fort Nelson. The present town of Fort Nelson is the fifth site.

Fort Nelson saw its first mail service in 1936. Scheduled air service to Fort Nelson—by ski- and floatplane—also was begun in the 1930s by Yukon Southern Air (which was later absorbed by CPAir, now Canadian Airlines International and Canadian Regional Airlines). The Canadian government began construction of an airport in 1941 as part of the Northwest Air Staging Route, and this was followed by perhaps the biggest boom to Fort Nelson—the construction of the Alaska Highway in 1942. About 2,000 soldiers were bivouacked in Fort Nelson, which they referred to as Zero, as it was the beginning of a road to Whitehorse and another road to Fort Simpson. Later Dawson Creek became Mile 0 and Fort Nelson Mile 300.

Fort Nelson expanded in the 1940s and 1950s as people came here to work for the government or to start their own small businesses: trucking, barging, aviation, construction, garages, stores, cafes, motels and sawmills. It is surprising to consider that as recently as the 1950s, Fort Nelson was still a pioneer community without power, phones, running water, refrigerators or doctors. Interesting recollections of Fort Nelson's early days may be found in Gerri Young's book *The Fort Nelson Story*; available at the museum.

Fort Nelson was an unorganized territory until 1957 when it was declared an Improvement District. Fort Nelson took on village status in 1971 and town status in 1987.

Forestry is a major industry here with a veneer plant, plywood plant, oriented strand board plant and sawmill complex. Chopsticks are manufactured at a local plant for export to Asian markets. Check with the Infocentre about scheduled industrial tours.

Forestry products are shipped south by truck and rail. Fort Nelson became a railhead in 1971 with the completion of a 250-mile extension of the Pacific Great Eastern Railway (now British Columbia Railway) from Fort St. John.

Agriculture is under development here with the recent establishment of the 55,000-acre McConachie Creek agricultural subdivision.

Northeastern British Columbia is the only sedimentary area in the province currently producing oil and gas. Oil seeps in the Fort Nelson area were noted by early residents. Major gas discoveries were made in the 1960s when the Clarke Lake, Yoyo/Kotcho, Beaver River and Pointed Mountain gas reserves were developed. The Westcoast Energy natural gas processing plant at Fort Nelson, the largest in North America, was constructed in 1964. This plant purifies the gas before sending it south through the 800-mile-long pipeline that connects the Fort

Fort Nelson Heritage Museum displays pioneer artifacts, Alaska Highway history and area wildlife. (Earl L. Brown, staff)

Nelson area with the British Columbia lower mainland. Sulfur, a byproduct of natural gas processing, is processed in a recovery plant and shipped to outside markets in pellet form.

ACCOMMODATIONS/VISITOR SERVICES

Fort Nelson has 10 hotels/motels, 3 bed and breakfasts, several gas stations and restaurants, a pub, fast food, deli and health food outlets; laundromat; bookstore; an auto

supply store, department stores and other services, most located north and south just off the Alaska Highway. The post office and liquor store are on Airport Drive. There are 2 banks, both with bank machines, on the business frontage road north of the highway. Fresh water fill-up and free municipal dump station adjacent the blue chalet near the museum. Inquire at the Infocentre for location of local churches and their hours of worship.

Ardendale Bed & Breakfast. Welcome to our large log home overlooking a beautiful view of the mountains. Very comfortable rooms, one with en suite and two with private bath. Spa, cable TV. Evening snack available and an excellent breakfast of your choice. Beautiful draft horses and cart horse. Our hobby farm is close to the golf course and cross-country skiing. Laundry facilities. Smoking outdoors on deck. Phone (250) 774-2433, fax (250) 774-2436. VISA. 7635 Old Alaska Highway. Frank and Gail Parker, Box 427, Fort Nelson, BC V0C 1R0. [ADVERTISEMENT]

Fort Nelson Bed & Breakfast. (Nonsmoking). For your convenience and privacy, our B&B is a self-contained unit on one side of our duplex. En suite bathrooms. Home-style breakfast. Laundry facilities. Cable TV. "Come and be spoiled." Your hosts, Doug and Renee. Box 58, Fort Nelson, BC V0C 1R0. (250) 774-6050. VISA. Open year-round. (Member—Northern Network of B&B's.) [ADVERTISEMENT]

"Spiritfire" Family Books 'n' Things. Our cozy bookstore carries a good range of northern, historical, wildlife and travel titles ... Fishing, hunting and gold mining. Crafting, biographies and autobiographies, nice selection of Christian books, videos, music and giftware. Family-oriented books and lots more. Browsers welcome. 101 Nicmac Building—directly behind bus depot. (250) 774-4870. [ADVERTISEMENT]

Fort Nelson has 3 campgrounds: one is located at the north (or west) end of town near the museum; one is at the south (or east) end of town; and one is at Muskwa Heights area south of Fort Nelson. ▲

Westend R.V. Campground and Mini-Golf welcome you to Fort Nelson! Located in town, next to the museum, only a few short minutes walk from restaurants, banking, bingo, local stores and the free welcome visitors program. Over 130 sites, lots of shade and grass, gravelled sites with full hookups and pull-throughs. Grassy tenting areas with cooking shelter and a playground. Caravans

welcomed, covered meeting place, handicap facilities, free car wash and firewood. Drinking water, coin-op hot showers and laundry. Pay phones. Confectionary, ice, souvenirs, Indian crafts and tanned furs. Open April 1 –Oct. 31. Your hosts, Chris and Sandra Brown, invite you to take a look at their beautiful wild animal displays. Nearby, Wolverine Sportsplex with 5-pin bowling alley, par T golf, racquetball, squash court and weight room. Licensed restaurant and lounge area. Bingo hall. We hope you enjoy our northern hospitality. Phone (250) 774-2340. [ADVERTISEMENT] &▲

ATTRACTIONS

Fort Nelson offers travelers a free "Welcome Visitor Program" on summer evenings (Monday through Thursday in 1996) at 6:45 P.M. at the Phoenix Theatre. These interesting and entertaining presentations are put on by local residents and range from slide shows to talks on items of local interest. Check with the Visitor Infocentre or

Canada is on the metric system; see the conversion chart in GENERAL INFORMATION.

at the Town Square for details.

The Fort Nelson Heritage Museum, across the highway from the Travel Infocentre, has excellent displays of pioneer artifacts, Alaska Highway history, wildlife (including a white moose), a spruce bark canoe, and souvenirs and books for sale. Outside the museum is the new (1996) Chadwick Ram, a bronze sculpture by Rick Taylor. The statue commemorates the world record stone sheep taken in the Muskwa Valley area in 1936. This nonprofit museum charges a modest admission fee. Native crafts are displayed at the Fort Nelson–Liard Native Friendship Centre, located on 49th Avenue.

The recreation centre, across from the museum, has tennis courts; hockey and curling arena for winter sports. There is also a sportsplex with bowling alley. Swimming pool, swirl pool, sauna and gym located in the Aqua Centre on Simpson Trail. For golfers, the Poplar Hills Golf and Country Club just north of town on the Old Alaska Highway, has grass greens; open daily.

A community demonstration forest is open to the public. There is a forest trail (0.6 mile/1 km, half-hour walk), a silviculture trail (1.9 miles/3 km, 45-minute walk) and a Native trail. Located off the Simpson Trail via Mountainview Drive; check at the Infocentre for trail guide.

Fort Nelson hosts a number of annual benefits, dances, tournaments and exhibits. Check locally for details and dates on all events. Summer events include a rodeo in August. Winter events include a big cash prize curling bon spiel in February, Trapper's Rendezvous in March and the Canadian Open Sled Dog Races in December (with local racers from the well-known Streeper Kennels). Eddy Streeper is a two-time World Champion (Anchorage) and also an Open North American Champion (Fairbanks) sled dog racer. Streeper Kennels is located on Radar Road.

Alaska Highway Log

(continued)

Distance* from Dawson Creek (DC) is followed by distance from Fairbanks (F). Original mileposts are indicated in the text as Historical Mile.

*Mileages from Dawson Creek are based on actual driving distance. Kilometres from Dawson Creek are based on physical kilometreposts. Please read Mileposts and Kilometreposts in the introduction for an explanation of how this highway is logged.

DC 284 (456.4 km) F 1204 (1937.6 km)

Historic Milepost 300, historic sign and interpretive panel at west end of Fort Nelson. Visitor information in the Recreation Centre north side of highway, log museum south side of highway. Private campground adjacent museum. ▲

Northbound: Watch for sections of rough, narrow, winding road and breaks in surfacing between Fort Nelson and the BC–YT border (approximately next 321 miles/516.5 km).

Southbound: Good pavement, wider road, next 284 miles/457 km (to Dawson Creek).

DC 284.5 (457.5 km) F 1203.5 (1936.8 km) Fort Nelson Forest District Office to north provides a pamphlet of self-guided Forest Ecology Tours on the Alaska and Liard highways; phone (604) 774-3936.

DC 284.7 (458.2 km) F 1203.3 (1936.5 km) **Junction** with south end of Old Alaska Highway (Mile 301–308). The Muskwa Valley bypass between Mile 301 and 308 opened in 1992.

DC 287.9 (462.6 km) F 1200.1 (1931.3 km) Access to Poplar Hills Golf and Country Club, located on Old Alaska Highway; 9-hole golf course, driving range, grass greens, clubhouse (licensed), golf club rentals. Open 8 A.M. to dusk, May to October.

DC 291 (467.6 km) F 1197 (1926.3 km) Parker Lake Road. **Junction** with north end of Old Alaska Highway (Mile 308–301).

DC 292 (469.9 km) F 1196 (1924.7 km) Private airstrip alongside highway; status unknown.

DC 301 (483.5 km) F 1187 (1910.2 km) **Junction** with Liard Highway (BC Highway 77) north to Fort Liard, Fort Simpson and other Northwest Territories destinations. See LIARD HIGHWAY section and the MACKENZIE ROUTE section for details.

DC 304.1 (489.4 km) F 1183.9 (1905.3 km) **Historic Milepost 320**. Sign marks start of Reese & Olson contract during construction of the Alaska Highway.

DC 308.2 (495.3 km) F 1179.8 (1898.7 km) Raspberry Creek. Turnout with litter barrels to south.

DC 316.6 (506.2 km) F 1171.4 (1885.1 km) Turnout with litter barrel to south.

DC 318.4 (509.1 km) F 1169.6 (1882.2 km) Kledo Creek bridge.

DC 318.7 (509.5 km) F 1169.3 (1881.8 km) Kledo Creek wayside rest area to north (unmaintained).

DC 322.7 (516 km) F 1165.3 (1875.3 km) Steamboat Creek bridge. Highway begins climb northbound up Steamboat Mountain; some 10 percent grades.

DC 329 (526.1 km) F 1159 (1865.2 km) Pull-through turnout with litter barrel to south.

DC 333 (532.5 km) F 1155 (1858.7 km) **Historic Milepost 351. STEAMBOAT** (unincorporated), lodge with food, gas, diesel and camping to south; open year-round. Historical sign marks start of Curran & Briggs Ltd. contract during construction of the Alaska Highway. ▲

Steamboat at **Historical Mile 351**. Cafe with fresh baked bread, pies and pastry. Husky gas, diesel and oil products. Level pull-throughs, RV parking with a view. Public phone. Picnic area (pets on a leash, please). Ice, souvenirs and handicrafts. Your hosts, Willa and Ken MacRae and family. Open year-round. Phone (250) 774-3388. ▲

[ADVERTISEMENT]

DC 333.7 (533.5 km) F 1154.3 (1857.6 km) Winding road ascends Steamboat Mountain westbound. Views of the Muskwa River valley and Rocky Mountains to the southwest from summit of 3,500-foot/ 1,067-m Steamboat Mountain, named because of its resemblance to a steamship. *Caution: Narrow road; watch for sharp curves and rough spots.*

DC 334.3 (534.5 km) **F 1153.7** (1856.6 km) Turnout with view and litter barrel to south.

DC 336.7 (538.5 km) **F 1151.3** (1852.8 km) Turnout to south with litter barrels and pit toilets. Highway descends for westbound travelers.

DC 339.1 (542.5 km) **F 1148.9** (1848.9 km) Drinking water to north. *CAUTION: Hairpin curve!*

DC 342.8 (548 km) **F 1145.2** (1843 km) View of Indian Head Mountain, a high crag resembling the classic Indian profile.

DC 343.4 (549 km) **F 1144.6** (1842 km) Turnout with litter barrel, outhouse and point of interest sign to south.

IMPORTANT: DO NOT FEED BEARS!

DC 345 (551.5 km) **F 1143** (1839.4 km) Scenic Teetering Rock viewpoint with litter barrel and outhouses to north. Teetering Rock is in the distance on the horizon. Fort Nelson Forest District (phone 250/774-3936) has developed a 7.6-mile-/12.3-km-long trail to Teetering Rock; steep climbs. Stay on well-marked trails, keep pets on leash; it is easy to get lost in this country.

DC 346.4 (553.9 km) **F 1141.6** (1837.2 km) Mill Creek, which flows into the Tetsa River. The highway follows the Tetsa River westbound. The Tetsa heads near Summit Lake in the northern Canadian Rockies.

Tetsa River, good fishing for grayling to 4 lbs., average 1¹/₂ lbs., flies or spin cast with lures; Dolly Varden to 7 lbs., average 3 lbs., spin cast or black gnat, coachman, Red Devils, flies; whitefish, small but plentiful, use flies or eggs, summer. ●◄

DC 346.5 (554 km) **F 1141.5** (1837 km) Turnoff to south for Tetsa River Provincial Park, 1.2 miles/1.9 km via gravel road. Grass tenting area, 25 level gravel sites in trees, picnic tables, fire rings, firewood, outhouses, water and garbage containers. Camping fee $7 to $12. ▲

DC 351 (561.2 km) **F 1137** (1829.8 km) *CAUTION: Slow down, dangerous curve!*

DC 357.5 (571.5 km) **F 1130.5** (1819.3 km) **Historical Mile 375.** Gas, store, cabins and private campground. Trail rides by reservation; phone (604) 774-1005. ▲

Tetsa River Guest Ranch & Campground. A favourite stopping spot along the highway. Fresh bread and baking daily. Treed and open camping sites, some pull-throughs, water and power hookups, dump station. Showers, store. Rustic log cabins with kitchenettes. Bed and breakfast. Great fishing! Licenses and local information. Guided fishing trips. Local arts and handiwork. Experience Rocky Mountain wilderness by horseback. (Reservations recommended.) (250) 774-1005. [ADVERTISEMENT] ▲

DC 358.6 (573.3 km) **F 1129.4** (1817.5 km) Highway follows Tetsa River westbound. Turnouts next 0.2 mile/0.3 km south to river.

DC 360.2 (575.9 km) **F 1127.8** (1815 km) Turnout with litter barrel, picnic site. Ecotour stop: Note the aspen-dominated slopes on the north side of the Tetsa River, and the white spruce on the south side.

DC 364.4 (582.6 km) **F 1123.6** (1808.2 km) Gravel turnout to south.

DC 365.6 (584.6 km) **F 1122.4** (1806.3 km) Tetsa River bridge No. 1, clearance 17 feet/5.2m.

DC 366 (585.4 km) **F 1122** (1805.6 km)

A landmark on the Alaska Highway is Indian Head Mountain. This view is from Milepost DC 342.8. *(Earl L. Brown, staff)*

Pull-through turnout with litter barrel to north.

DC 367.3 (587.3 km) **F 1120.7** (1803.5 km) Tetsa River bridge No. 2.

The high bare peaks of the central Canadian Rockies are visible ahead westbound.

DC 371.5 (594.2 km) **F 1116.5** (1796.8 km) South boundary of Stone Mountain Provincial Park. Stone sheep are indigenous to the mountains of northern British Columbia and southern Yukon Territory. They are darker and somewhat slighter than the bighorn sheep found in the Rocky Mountains. Dall or white sheep are found in the mountains of Yukon, Alaska and Northwest Territories.

CAUTION: Northbound, watch for caribou and stone sheep along the highway. DO NOT FEED WILDLIFE. DO NOT STOP VEHICLES ON THE HIGHWAY TO TAKE PHOTOS; use shoulders or turnouts.

DC 372.7 (596 km) **F 1115.3** (1794.9 km) Pull-through turnout with litter barrel to north.

DC 373.3 (597 km) **F 1114.7** (1793.9 km) **Historical Mile 392. SUMMIT LAKE** (unincorporated), lodge with gas, diesel, propane, cafe, camping and lodging. The peak behind Summit Lake is Mount St. George (elev. 7,419 feet/2,261m) in the Stone Mountain range. The Summit area is known for dramatic and sudden weather changes. ▲

DC 373.5 (597.4 km) **F 1114.5** (1793.5 km) Rough gravel side road leads 1.5 miles/ 2.5 km to Flower Springs Lake trailhead, 4.3 miles/7 km to microwave tower viewpoint. Not suitable for motorhomes, trailers or low clearance vehicles.

DC 373.6 (597.6 km) **F 1114.4** (1793.4 km) Gravel turnout and Summit Lake provincial campground to south at east end of Summit Lake. **Historic Milepost 392** sign and interpretive panel mark the highest summit on the Alaska Highway, elev. 4,250 feet/1,295m. A very beautiful area of bare rocky peaks (which can be snow-covered anytime of the year). The provincial campground has 28 level gravel sites; picnic tables; water and garbage containers; information shelter; boat launch. Camping fee $7 to $12. Hiking trails to Flower Springs Lake and Summit Peak. Fair fishing for lake trout, whitefish and rainbows in **Summit Lake.** ●◄▲

DC 375.6 (600.8 km) **F 1112.4** (1790.2 km) Turnout to north.

DC 375.9 (601.3 km) **F 1112.1** (1789.7 km) Picnic site to south with tables and litter barrel on Rocky Crest Lake.

DC 376 (601.5 km) **F 1112** (1789.5 km) Erosion pillars north of highway (0.6-mile/ 1-km hike north); watch for caribou. Northbound, the highway winds through a rocky limestone gorge, before descending into the wide and picturesque MacDonald River valley. Turnouts next 2.5 miles/4 km northbound with views of the valley. Watch for Stone sheep along rock cut.

DC 378.2 (605.1) **F 1109.8** (1786 km)

Baba Canyon to north.

DC **378.6** (605.7 km) F **1109.4** (1785.4 km) **Historical Mile 397.** Rocky Mountain Lodge to south; gas, lodging, store and camping. ▲

DC **379.7** (607.4 km) F **1108.3** (1783.6 km) Turnout to south.

DC **380.7** (609 km) F **1107.3** (1782 km) North boundary of Stone Mountain Provincial Park. *CAUTION: Southbound, watch for wildlife alongside and on the road. DO NOT FEED WILDLIFE.*

DC **381.2** (611.2 km) F **1106.8** (1781.2 km) Highway winds along above the wide rocky valley of MacDonald Creek. MacDonald Creek and river were named for Charlie McDonald, a Cree Indian credited with helping Alaska Highway survey crews locate the best route for the pioneer road.

DC **382.2** (612.8 km) F **1105.8** (1779.5 km) Trail access via abandoned Churchill Mines Road (4-wheel drive only beyond river) to Wokkpash Recreation Area, located 12 miles/20 km south of the highway, which adjoins the southwest boundary of Stone Mountain Provincial Park. This remote area features extensive hoodoos (erosion pillars) in Wokkpash Gorge, and the scenic Forlorn Gorge and Stepped Lakes. Contact the Parks District Office in Fort St. John before venturing into this area; phone (250) 787-3407.

DC **383.3** (614.6 km) F **1104.7** (1777.8 km) 113 Creek. The creek was named during construction of the Alaska Highway for its distance from Mile 0 at Fort Nelson. While Dawson Creek was to become Mile 0 on the completed pioneer road, clearing crews began their work at Fort Nelson, since a rough winter road already existed between Dawson Creek and Fort Nelson. Stone Range to the northeast and Muskwa Ranges of the Rocky Mountains to the west.

DC **384.2** (615.4 km) F **1103.8** (1776.3 km) 115 Creek provincial campground to southwest, adjacent highway; double-ended entrance. Side-by-side camper parking (8 sites), water, garbage containers, picnic tables. Camping fee $7 to $12. Access to the riverbank of 115 Creek and **MacDonald Creek.** Beaver dams nearby. Fishing for grayling and Dolly Varden. ◂▲

DC **385.4** (616.6 km) F **1102.6** (1774.4 km) 115 Creek bridge. Turnout to south at east end of bridge with tables and litter barrels. Like 113 Creek, 115 Creek was named during construction of the pioneer road for its distance from Fort Nelson, Mile 0 for clearing crews.

DC **390.5** (624.8 km) F **1097.5** (1766.2 km) **Historical Mile 408.** MacDonald River Services (was closed in 1996; current status unknown).

DC **392.5** (627.8 km) F **1095.5** (1763 km)

Watch for stone sheep and other wildlife along the highway. (Earl L. Brown, staff)

MacDonald River bridge, clearance 17 feet/5.2m. Highway winds through narrow valley.

MacDonald River, fair fishing from May to July for Dolly Varden and grayling. ◂

DC **394.8** (631.8 km) F **1093.2** (1759.3 km) Turnout with litter barrel to east.

DC **396.1** (633.8 km) F **1091.9** (1757.2 km) Folding rock formations on mountain face to west. The Racing River forms the boundary between the Sentinel Range and the Stone Range, both of which are composed of folded and sedimentary rock.

DC **399.1** (638.6 km) F **1088.9** (1752.4 km) Stringer Creek.

DC **400.7** (641.1 km) F **1087.3** (1749.8 km) Racing River bridge, clearance 17 feet/5.2m. River access to north at east end of bridge. Ecotour stop: Note the open south-facing slopes on the north side of the river that are used as winter range by stone sheep, elk and deer. Periodic controlled burns encourage the growth of forage grasses and shrubs, and also allow chinook winds to clear snow from grazing grounds in winter.

Racing River, grayling to 16 inches; Dolly Varden to 2 lbs., use flies, July through September. ◂

DC **404.6** (647.4 km) F **1083.4** (1743.5 km) **Historical Mile 422.** TOAD RIVER (unincorporated), situated in a picturesque valley. Highway maintenance camp, school and private residences on north side of highway. Toad River Lodge on south side of highway with cafe, gas, tire repair, propane, camping and lodging. Ambulance service. Toad River Lodge is open year-round. The lodge is known for its collection of hats, which numbers more than 4,000. Also, inquire at the lodge about good wildlife viewing locations nearby. ▲

Toad River Lodge. See display ad this section. ▲

Private Aircraft: Emergency gravel airstrip; elev. 2,400 feet/732m; length 2,300 feet/701m. Unattended; no fuel.

DC 405.5 (648.8 km) F 1082.5 (1742.1 km) Turnout to south with **Historic Milepost 422.** Sign and interpretive panel commemorate Toad River/Camp 138 Jupp Construction.

DC 406.3 (650.1 km) F 1081.7 (1740.8 km) Turnout with litter barrels to north.

DC 407.5 (652 km) F 1080.5 (1738.8 km) **Historical Mile 426.** Food, gas, propane, tire repair, cabins and camping south side of highway. Inquire here about local hiking trails. ▲

The Poplars Campground. See display ad this section. ▲

DC 409.2 (654.6 km) F 1078.8 (1736.1 km) South boundary of Muncho Lake Provincial Park.

DC 410.6 (656.8 km) F 1077.4 (1733.9 km) Turnout with information panel on area geology. Impressive rock folding formation on mountain face, known as Folded Mountain.

DC 411 (657.4 km) F 1077 (1733.2 km) Beautiful turquoise-coloured Toad River to north. The highway now follows the Toad River westbound.

Toad River, grayling to 16 inches; Dolly Varden to 10 lbs., use flies, July through September. ⇷

DC 415.5 (664.7 km) F 1072.5 (1726 km) 150 Creek bridge. Creek access to south at east end of bridge.

DC 417.6 (668.2 km) F 1070.4 (1722.6 km) Centennial Falls to south.

DC 419.8 (671.7 km) F 1068.2 (1719 km) **Toad River** bridge. Turnout with litter barrel to south at west end of bridge; fishing. ⇷

DC 422.6 (676.2 km) F 1065.4 (1714.5 km) Watch for moose in pond to north; morning or evening best.

DC 423 (676.8 km) F 1065 (1713.9 km) Double-ended turnout with litter barrel to north. Excellent wildlife viewing area; watch for Stone sheep, caribou, bear and moose.

CAUTION: Watch for Stone sheep along the highway (or standing in the middle of the highway). DO NOT FEED WILDLIFE. Do not stop vehicles on the highway to take photos; use shoulders or turnouts.

DC 423.1 (677 km) F 1064.9 (1713.7 km) The highway swings north for Alaska-bound travelers. Highway climbs next 6 miles/9.7 km northbound. For Dawson Creek-bound travelers, the highway follows an easterly direction.

DC 424.1 (678.7 km) F 1063.9 (1712.1 km) **Historic Milepost 443** at Peterson Creek No. 1 bridge. The creek was named for local trapper Pete Peterson, who helped Alaska Highway construction crews select a route through this area. Historic sign marks start of Campbell Construction Co. Ltd. contract during construction of the Alaska Highway.

DC 424.3 (679 km) F 1063.7 (1711.8 km) The Village; gas, snacks and camping. ▲

DC 429.5 (688.9 km) F 1058.5 (1703.4 km) Viewpoint to east with information shelter and litter barrels. Information panel on geology of "Sawtooth Mountains."

DC 436.5 (698.5 km) F 1051.5 (1692.2 km) **Historic Milepost 456.** Entering MUNCHO LAKE (pop. 24; elev. 2,700 feet/823m). Muncho Lake businesses extend from here north along the east shore of Muncho Lake to approximately Milepost DC 443.7. Businesses in Muncho Lake include 4 lodges, gas stations with towing and repair, restaurants, cafes and campgrounds. The post office is located at Double G Service; open year-round. ▲

Photo of Muncho Lake taken from the viewpoint at Milepost DC 444.9. *(Earl L. Brown, staff)*

A historic sign and interpretive panel mark Muncho Lake/Refueling Stop, Checkpoint during Alaska Highway construction. The road around the lake was a particular challenge. Workers had to cut their way through the lake's rocky banks. Horses were used to haul away the rock. The Muncho Lake area offers hiking in the summer and cross-country skiing in the winter. Narrated boat tours of Muncho Lake are available in summer; check with Double G Service. This highly recommended tour highlights the history and geography of the area. Boat rentals are available from J&H Wilderness Resort and Highland Glen Lodge. Flightseeing and fly-in fishing service available from Liard Air at Highland Glen Lodge. An annual lake trout derby is held in June; inquire locally for dates.

CAUTION: Watch for Stone sheep and caribou on the highway north of here. Please DO NOT FEED WILDLIFE. Please do not stop on the highway to take photos; use shoulders or turnouts.

DC 436.9 (699.2 km) F 1051.1 (1691.5 km) Gravel airstrip to west; length 1,200 feet/366m. View of Muncho Lake ahead northbound. The highway along Muncho Lake required considerable rock excavation by the Army in 1942. The original route went along the top of the cliffs, which proved par-

ticularly hazardous. (Portions of this hair-raising road can be seen high above the lake.) The Army relocated the road by benching into the cliffs a few feet above lake level.

Muncho Lake, known for its beautiful deep green and blue waters, is 7 miles/11 km in length, and 1 mile/1.6 km in width; elevation of the lake is 2,680 feet/817m. The colours are attributed to copper oxide leaching into the lake. Deepest point has been reported to be 730 feet/223m, although recent government tests have not located any point deeper than 400 feet/122m. The lake drains the Sentinel Range to the east and the Terminal Range to the west, feeding the raging Trout River in its 1,000-foot/305-m drop to the mighty Liard River. The mountains surrounding the lake are approximately 7,000 feet/2,134m high.

Muncho Lake, fishing for Dolly Varden; some grayling; whitefish to 12 inches; lake trout (record to 50 lbs.), use spoons, spinners, diving plug or weighted spoons, June and July best. The lake trout quota is 3 trout per person; minimum size 15¾ inches. Make sure you have a current British Columbia fishing license and a copy of the current regulations. Also rainbow trout. ⇷

DC 437.7 (700.5 km) F 1050.3 (1690.2 km) Strawberry Flats Campground, Muncho Lake Provincial Park; 15 sites on rocky

lakeshore, picnic tables, outhouses, garbage containers. Camping fee $7 to $12. ▲
CAUTION: Watch for bears in area.
DC 442.2 (707.9 km) F 1045.8 (1683 km) Historical Mile 462. Northern Rockies/ Highland Glen Lodge (open year-round) with lodging, restaurant, gas and camping west side of highway. Flying service for sightseeing and fly-in fishing. ▲

Northern Rockies/Highland Glen Lodge, Mile 462, Muncho Lake, BC. Toll-free reservation line: 1-800-663-5269. Phone (250) 776-3481, fax (250) 776-3482. New hotel, lakeshore chalets and motel rooms. The newest and largest log building in BC. Featuring a 45-foot-high fireplace in open-ceiling dining room. Restaurant with European-trained chef and bakery. Lakeshore RV park, children's playground. Fly-in fishing trips into the Arctic and Pacific watersheds for: arctic grayling, Dolly Varden, rainbow trout, lake trout, northern pike and walleye. Air taxi service, glacier and Muncho Lake local sightseeing flights. [ADVERTISEMENT] ▲

Trout and Toad River Raft Adventures invites you to take a break from driving and view our mountains and wildlife at the pace of a river. In Muncho Lake Provincial Park, we offer raft trips for just about everyone. Children and seniors are welcome! The upper Trout and Toad rivers offer scenic floats. The lower Trout River offers an exciting whitewater ride to its confluence with

the Liard River, just minutes from the Liard Hot Springs. Join our B.C. certified raft guides and choose from half- or full-day trips. All equipment supplied. For information and reservations call 1-800-663-5209 June–August; (403) 637-3843 in the off-season or stop by our trip center at Mile 462 next to The Northern Rockies Lodge on Muncho Lake, Jewel of the Northern Rockies! VISA. [ADVERTISEMENT]

DC 442.9 (709 km) F 1045.1 (1681.9 km) Turnoff to west for MacDonald campground, Muncho Lake Provincial Park; 15 level gravel sites, firewood, picnic tables, outhouses, boat launch, information shelter, pump water, on Muncho Lake. Camping fee $7 to $12. *CAUTION: Watch for bears in area.* ▲
DC 443.6 (710.1 km) F 1044.4 (1680.8 km) Historical Mile 463. Muncho Lake Lodge; gas, propane, food, camping and lodging. ▲

Muncho Lake Lodge. See display ad this section. ▲

DC 443.7 (710.3 km) F 1044.3 (1680.6 km) Historical Mile 463.1. J&H Wilderness Resort; food, gas, store, boat rentals, tackle, lodging and camping available. Muncho Lake businesses extend south to Milepost DC 436.5. ▲

J&H Wilderness Resort. See display ad this section. ▲

DC 444.9 (712.2 km) F 1043.1 (1678.7 km) Muncho Lake viewpoint to west with information panel, large parking area, picnic tables, litter barrels and outhouses. View of Peterson Mountain at south end of lake.

NOTE: Watch for Stone sheep on highway next 10 miles/16 km northbound.

DC 453.3 (725.6 km) F 1034.7 (1665.1 km) Turnout with litter barrel to east.

NOTE: Watch for Stone sheep on highway next 10 miles/16 km southbound.

DC 454 (726.7 km) F 1034 (1664 km) Mineral lick; watch for Stone sheep. There is a trailhead 0.2 mile/0.3 km off the highway; a 5- to 10-minute loop hike takes you to viewpoints overlooking the Trout River valley and the steep mineral-laden banks frequented by sheep, goats, caribou and elk. Good photo opportunities, early morning best. CAUTION: Steep banks, slippery when wet. Bring insect repellent.

DC 455.5 (729.2 km) F 1032.5 (1661.6 km) Turnout with litter barrel and message board to west.

DC 457.7 (732.7 km) F 1030.3 (1658.1 km) Trout River bridge. The Trout River drains into the Liard River. The highway follows the Trout River north for several miles.

Trout River, grayling to 18 inches; whitefish to 12 inches, flies, spinners, May, June and August best.

DC 458.9 (734.6 km) F 1029.1 (1656.1 km) Gravel turnout to east.

DC 460.7 (737.4 km) F 1027.3 (1653.2 km) Prochniak Creek bridge. The creek was named for a member of Company A, 648th Engineers Topographic Battalion, during construction of the Alaska Highway. North boundary of Muncho Lake Provincial Park.

DC 463.3 (741.6 km) F 1024.7 (1649 km) Watch for curves next 0.6 mile/1 km northbound.

DC 465.6 (745.3 km) F 1022.4 (1645.3 km) Turnout with litter barrel to east.

DC 466.3 (746.3 km) F 1021.7 (1644.2 km) CAUTION: Dangerous curves next 3 miles/5 km northbound.

DC 468.9 (749.5 km) F 1019.1 (1640 km) Pull-through turnout with litter barrel to east. This Ecotour stop shows the extent of the 1959 fire that swept across the valley bottom. Lodgepole pine, trembling aspen and paper birch are the dominant species re-establishing this area.

DC 471 (754.1 km) F 1017 (1636.7 km) First glimpse of the mighty Liard River for northbound travelers. Named by French-Canadian voyageurs for the poplar ("liard") that line the banks of the lower river. The Alaska Highway parallels the Liard River from here north to Watson Lake. The river offered engineers a natural line to follow during routing and construction of the Alaska Highway in 1942.

DC 472.2 (756 km) F 1015.8 (1634.7 km) Washout Creek.

DC 474.3 (759.5 km) F 1013.7 (1631.3 km) Turnout with litter barrel to west.

DC 476.7 (763 km) F 1011.3 (1627.5 km) Lower Liard River bridge. This is the only suspension bridge on the Alaska Highway.

The 1,143-foot suspension bridge was built by the American Bridge Co. and McNamara Construction Co. of Toronto in 1943.

The Liard River flows eastward toward the Fort Nelson River and parallels the Alaska Highway from the Lower Liard River bridge to the BC–YT border. The scenic Grand Canyon of the Liard is to the east and not visible from the highway. Good fishing for Dolly Varden, grayling, northern pike and whitefish.

DC 477.1 (763.8 km) F 1010.9 (1626.8 km) Historical Mile 496. LIARD RIVER (unincorporated), lodge with gas, store,

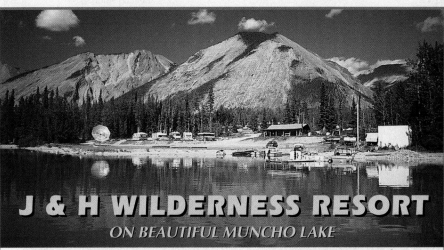

pay phone, food, camping and lodging to west; open year-round. ▲

Liard River Lodge. See display ad this section.

DC 477.7 (764.7 km) F 1010.3 (1625.9 km) **Historic Milepost 496.** Turnoff to north for Liard River Hotsprings Provincial Park, long a favorite stop for Alaska Highway travelers. The park has become so popular in recent years that the campground fills up very early each day in summer. Overflow day-parking area across highway from park entrance. The park is open year-round. This well-developed provincial park has 53 large, shaded, level gravel sites (some will accommodate 2 RVs), picnic tables, picnic shelter, water, garbage containers, firewood, fire rings, playground and heated restrooms at the hot springs with wheelchair accessible toilet. Camping fees to $15.50. Pay phone at park entrance. ♿▲

A boardwalk leads to the pools, crossing a wetlands environment that supports more than 250 boreal forest plants, including 14 orchid species and 14 plants that survive at this latitude because of the hot springs. Also watch for moose feeding in the pools. There are 2 hot springs pools with water temperatures ranging from 108˚ to 126˚F/42˚ to 52˚C. Nearest is the Alpha pool with a children's wading area. Beyond the Alpha pool is Beta pool, which is larger and deeper. Both have changing rooms. Beta pool is about a 0.4-mile/0.6-km walk. Plenty of parking at trailhead.

Excellent interpretive programs and

Liard River Hotsprings is a favorite stop for highway travelers. (Earl L. Brown, staff)

nature walks in summer; check schedule posted at park entrance and at information shelter near trailhead. Emergency phone at park headquarters. *CAUTION: BEWARE OF BEARS!*

DC 477.8 (764.9 km) F 1010.2 (1625.7 km) **Historical Mile 497.** Liard Hotsprings Lodge (open year-round) with food, gas, lodging and camping. Fishing, sightseeing charter trips and jetboat tours available. ⛵▲

Trapper Ray's Liard Hotsprings Lodge. See display ad this section. ▲

DC 482.8 (772.9 km) F 1005.2 (1617.7 km) Teeter Creek. A footpath leads upstream; 10-minute walk to falls. Grayling fishing.

DC 485.4 (777 km) F 1002.6 (1613.5 km) Small turnout overlooking the Liard River.

DC 489 (783.6 km) F 999 (1607.7 km) **Private Aircraft:** Liard River airstrip; elev. 1,400 feet/427m; length 4,000 feet/1,219m; gravel.

NOTE: Northbound travelers watch for road construction between Kilometreposts 787 and 823 in 1997. Also watch for sections of rough surface, gravel breaks and loose gravel next 118.5 miles/190.7 km (to BC–YT border).

DC 495 (792.3 km) F 993 (1598 km) **Historic Milepost 514. Smith River** bridge, clearance 17 feet/5.2m. Access to Smith River Falls via 1.6-mile/2.6-km gravel road; not recommended for large RVs or trailers or in wet weather. There is a hiking trail down to 2-tiered Smith River Falls from the parking area. Grayling fishing. ⛵

The historic sign here commemorates Smith River Airport Road. The old airstrip, part of the Northwest Staging Route, is located in a burned-over area about 25 miles/40 km from the highway (accessible by 4-wheel drive only).

DC 509.4 (815.6 km) **F 978.6** (1574.9 km) Large turnout with litter barrel to east.

DC 513.9 (822.8 km) **F 974.1** (1567.6 km) **Historical Mile 533. COAL RIVER,** lodge with gas, diesel, food, camping and lodging. ▲

DC 514.2 (823.2 km) **F 973.8** (1567.1 km) **Historical Mile 533.2.** Coal River bridge. The Coal River flows into the Liard River south of the bridge.

DC 519.5 (831.4 km) **F 968.5** (1558.6 km) Sharp easy-to-miss turnoff to west for undeveloped "do-it-yourself campsite" (watch for sign). Small gravel parking area with outhouse, litter barrels, and beautiful view of the Liard River (not visible from the highway). Although signed "Whirlpool Canyon," this scenic stretch of the Liard River has been identified by one astute reader as Mountain Portage Rapids, with Whirlpool Canyon being located farther downriver. ▲

DC 524.2 (839.2 km) **F 963.8** (1551 km) **Historical Mile 543. FIRESIDE** (unincorporated). Highway maintenance camp and truck stop with services. Sign reads: *Please keep pets in vehicles.* This community was partially destroyed by fire in the summer of 1982. Evidence of the fire can be seen from south of Fireside north to Lower Post. The 1982 burn, known as the Eg fire, was the second largest fire in British Columbia history, destroying more than 400,000 acres.

DC 524.7 (840 km) **F 963.3** (1550.2 km) Good view of Liard River and Cranberry Rapids to west.

DC 527.7 (845 km) **F 960.3** (1545.4 km) *IMPORTANT:* Rerouting of the Alaska High-way was under way in 1996 for the next 12.7 miles/20.4 km. The new highway will bypass the dangerous curves in the LeQuil Creek area and shorten the road by approximately 2 miles/3.2 km. In 1997, watch for continued road construction, soft spots and gravel surfacing on new highway section.

DC 530 (848.7 km) **F 958** (1541.7 km) Gravel turnout with litter barrels to south.

DC 540.4 (865.3 km) **F 947.6** (1525 km) North end of rerouting of Alaska Highway (see **Milepost DC 527.7**).

DC 545.9 (874.2 km) **F 942.1** (1516.1 km) Turnout with litter barrel to west overlooking the Liard River.

DC 550.9 (882.2 km) **F 937.1** (1508 km) **Historical Mile 570.** Allen's Lookout; very large pull-through turnout with picnic tables, outhouse and litter barrel to west overlooking the Liard River. Goat Mountain to west. Legend has it that a band of outlaws took advantage of this sweeping view of the Liard River to attack and rob riverboats. ▲

DC 555 (888.8 km) **F 933** (1501.5 km) Good berry picking in July among roadside raspberry bushes; watch for bears.

DC 556 (890.4 km) **F 932** (1499.9 km) Highway swings west for Alaska-bound travelers.

DC 562.5 (900.8 km) **F 925.5** (1489.4 km) Large gravel turnout with litter barrel.

DC 567.9 (909.4 km) **F 920.1** (1480.7 km) **Historic Milepost 588.** Contact Creek bridge. Turnout to south at east end of bridge with tables, toilets, litter barrels and information shelter. Contact Creek was named by soldiers of the 36th Regiment from the south and the 340th Regiment from the north who met here Sept. 24, 1942, completing the southern sector of the Alaska Highway. Historic sign and interpretive panel.

DC 568.3 (910.2 km) **F 919.7** (1480.1 km) First of 7 crossings of the BC–YT border. Large gravel turnout to north with point of interest sign about the Yukon Territory. "The Yukon Territory takes its name from the Indian word *Youcon,* meaning 'big river.' It was first explored in the 1840s by the Hudson's Bay Co., which established several trading posts. The territory, which was then considered a district of the Northwest Territories, remained largely untouched until the Klondike Gold Rush, when thousands of people flooded into the country and communities sprang up almost overnight. This sudden expansion led to the official formation of the Yukon Territory on June 13, 1898."

DC 570 (912.9 km) **F 918** (1477.3 km) **Historical Mile 590. CONTACT CREEK,** lodge open year-round; food, gas, diesel, car repair, towing, car wash and pay phone. **Contact Creek Lodge.** See display ad this section.

DC 573.9 (918.9 km) **F 914.1** (1471.1 km) Irons Creek bridge. Turnout with litter barrel to south at east end of bridge. According to the folks at Iron Creek Lodge, Irons Creek was named during construction of the Alaska Highway for the trucks that stopped here to put on tire irons (chains) in order to make it up the hill.

DC 575.9 (922 km) **F 912.1** (1467.8 km) **Historical Mile 596.** Iron Creek Lodge; food, gas, diesel, dump station, lodging and camping. Private stocked lake at campground. ➤◄▲ **Iron Creek Lodge.** See display ad this section. ▲

DC 582 (931.8 km) **F 906** (1458 km) NorthwesTel microwave tower.

DC 585 (937 km) **F 903** (1453.2 km) **Hyland River** bridge; good fishing for rainbow, Dolly Varden and grayling. 🐟

NOTE: Watch for logging trucks northbound to Watson Lake.

DC 585.3 (937.2 km) **F 902.7** (1452.7 km) **Historical Mile 605.9.** Hyland River bridge. The Hyland River is a tributary of the Liard River. The river was named for Frank Hyland, an early-day trader at Telegraph Creek on the Stikine River. Hyland operated trading posts throughout northern British Columbia, competing successfully with the Hudson's Bay Co., and at one time printing his own currency.

DC 598.7 (957.5 km) **F 889.3** (1431.2 km) Access to **LOWER POST** (unincorporated), at **Historical Mile 620**, via short gravel road; cafe and store. A B.C. Forest Service field office is located here. This British Columbia settlement is a historic Hudson's Bay Co. trading post and the site of an Indian village. The Liard and Dease rivers meet near here. The Dease River, named for Peter Warren Dease, a fur trader for the Hudson's Bay Co., heads in Dease Lake to the southwest on the Cassiar Highway.

DC 605.1 (967.6 km) **F 882.9** (1420.8 km) **Historic Milepost 627** marks official BC–YT border; Welcome to the Yukon sign. Monitor CB Channel 9 for police. The Alaska Highway (Yukon Highway 1) dips back into British Columbia several times before making its final crossing into the Yukon Territory near Morley Lake (**Milepost DC 751.5**).

NOTE: Kilometreposts on the Yukon Terri-tory portion of the highway reflect historical mileposts. Kilometreposts on the British Columbia portion of the highway reflect actual driving distance. There is approximately a 40-kilometre difference at the BC–YT border between these measurements.

Northbound: Good paved highway with wide shoulders next 380 miles/611.5 km to Haines Junction, with the exception of some short sections of narrow road and occasional gravel breaks.

Southbound: Watch for rough, narrow, winding road and breaks in surfacing between border and Fort Nelson (approximately 321 miles/516.6 km).

DC 606.9 (1011.9 km) **F 881.1** (1418 km) Lucky Lake picnic area to south; ball diamond and 1.2-mile/2-km hiking trail to Liard River Canyon (watch for signs), observation platform with information panels at river. **Lucky Lake** is a popular local swimming hole for Watson Lake residents, who installed a water slide here. Relatively shallow, the lake warms up quickly in summer, making it one of the few area lakes where swimming is possible. Stocked with rainbow trout. 🐟

According to R. Coutts in *Yukon Places & Names*, Lucky Lake was named by American Army Engineer troops working on construction of the Alaska Highway in 1942: "A young woman set up a tent business and clients there referred to transactions as 'a change of luck.'"

DC 609.2 (1015.5 km) **F 878.8** (1414.3 km) Paved drive-through rest area with litter barrel and outhouses to north.

DC 610.4 (1017.5 km) **F 877.6** (1412.3 km) Weigh station.

DC 610.5 (1017.7 km) **F 877.5** (1412.2 km) **Mile 632.5. Campground Services** at Mile 632.5 is the largest and best equipped RV park in Watson Lake, the gateway to the

Yukon. The park features full or partial hookups and pull-throughs, tent sites, playground, firepits and a screened kitchen.

Coin-op showers, laundry and car wash. Good Sam Park. A food market stocks groceries, "chester fried" chicken, convenience items, movie rentals, fishing tackle, licenses and ice. Gasoline and diesel and ICG propane are available at the self-serve pumps. A licensed mechanic is available for repairs, alignments, tire changes, etc. Agents for Western Union money transfers. Open for business year-round, serving the traveler's needs for over 25 years! Phone (403) 536-7448. [ADVERTISEMENT] ▲

Watson Lake

DC 612.9 (1021 km) **F 875.1** (1408.3 km). **Historic Milepost 635.** "Gateway to the Yukon," located 329 miles/529 km from Fort Nelson, 274 miles/441 km from Whitehorse. **Population:** 1,749. **Emergency Services:** RCMP, phone (403) 536-5555 (if no answer call toll-free 1-403-667-5555). **Fire Department**, phone (403) 536-2222. **Ambulance**, phone (403) 536-4444. **Hospital**, phone (403) 536-4444.

Visitor Information: Located in the Alaska Highway Interpretive Centre behind the Signpost Forest, north of the Alaska Highway; access to the centre is from the Campbell Highway. Phone (403) 536-7469. The town of Watson Lake provides a toll-free number (Lower 48 only) for information on local attractions; phone 1-800-663-5248.

Elevation: 2,265 feet/690m. **Climate:** Average temperature in January is -15°F/-26°C, in July 57°F/14°C. Record high temperature 93°F/34°C in June 1950, record low -74°F/-59°C in January 1947. Annual snowfall is 90.6 inches. Driest month is April, wettest month is September. Average date of last spring frost is June 2; average date of first fall frost is Sept. 14. **Radio:** CBC 990, CKYN-FM 96.1 (Visitor Radio CKYN is broadcast from the visitor information centre from mid-May to mid-September). **Television:** Channel 8 and cable.

Private Aircraft: Watson Lake airport, 8 miles/12.9 km north of Campbell Highway; elev. 2,262 feet/689m; length 5,500 feet/1,676m and 3,530 feet/1,076m; asphalt; fuel 100, jet. Heliport and floatplane bases also located here. The Watson Lake airport terminal building was built in 1942. The log structure has been designated a Heritage Building.

In the late 1800s, Watson Lake was known as Fish Lake. The lake was later renamed Watson, for Frank Watson of Yorkshire, England. He gave up on the gold rush in 1898 to settle here on its shores with his Indian wife. Today, Watson Lake is an important service stop on the Alaska and Campbell highways (Campbell Highway travelers, fill your gas tanks here!); a communication and distribution centre for the southern Yukon; a base for trappers, hunters and fishermen; and a supply point for area mining and mineral exploration.

Watson Lake businesses are located along either side of the Alaska Highway. The lake itself is not visible from the Alaska Highway. Access to the lake, airport, hospital and Mount Maichen ski hill is via the Campbell Highway (locally referred to as Airport Road). The ski area is about 4 miles/6.4 km out the Campbell Highway from town.

Watson Lake was an important point during construction of the Alaska Highway in 1942. The airport, built in 1941, was one of the major refueling stops along the Northwest Staging Route, the system of airfields through Canada to ferry supplies to Alaska and later lend-lease aircraft to Russia. Of the nearly 8,000 aircraft ferried through Canada, 2,618 were Bell P–39 Airacobras. A full-scale replica of the P–39 Airacobra is displayed at the Alaska Highway Interpretive Centre by the Signpost Forest.

The Alaska Highway helped bring both people and commerce to this once isolated settlement. A post office opened here in July 1942. The economy of Watson Lake is based on services and also the forest products industry. White spruce and lodgepole pine are the two principal trees of the Yukon and provide a forest industry for the territory. White spruce grows straight and fast wherever adequate water is available, and it will grow to extreme old age without showing decay. The lodgepole pine developed from

Aerial view of Watson Lake. Wye Lake Park may be seen on the right. (Earl L. Brown, staff)

WATSON LAKE ADVERTISERS

Belvedere Motor Hotel.....Ph. (403) 536-7712
Big Horn Hotel ....Ph. (403) 536-2020
Campground Services ....E. edge of town
Cedar Lodge Motel...........Ph. (403) 536-7406
Claim Jumper's Inn B&B ...Ph. (403) 536-7021
Downtown R.V. Park ....Ph. (403) 536-2646
Gateway Motor Inn ....Ph. (403) 536-7744
Green Valley Trailer
    Park ....Kmpost 1032 Alaska Hwy.
Grunow Motors ....Ph. (403) 536-2272
Hougen's Department
    Store ....Alaska Hwy.
Jer-Cal Holdings Ltd.......................Downtown
Napa Auto Parts ....Ph. (403) 536-2521
O'Neill Repairs........1 blk. S. of Signpost Forest
Totem Oil ....Ph. 1-800-661-0550
Town of Watson Lake ....Ph. (403) 536-7778
Watson Lake Hotel......Next to Signpost Forest
Watson Lake Rodeo..........Ph. (403) 536-2272

WE PROVIDE MANY OF THE YUKON'S MOST WELCOME SIGHTS.

Chevron

Even though the Yukon is one of the prettiest places on earth, sometimes nothing looks as good as a Chevron station.

You can always count on us for quality fuel, great service, and plenty of locations to help you along your way.

NORTH 60° PETRO

the northern pine and can withstand extreme cold, grow at high elevations and take full advantage of the almost 24-hour summer sunlight of a short growing season.

ACCOMMODATIONS/VISITOR SERVICES

There are several hotels/motels, a bed and breakfast, restaurants and gas stations with unleaded, diesel and propane, automotive and tire repair. Dump stations available at local campgrounds and service stations. There are department, variety, grocery and hardware stores. The complex on the north side of the highway that contained the post office, fire hall, government liquor store and library burned down in 1996. The location of these facilities was unknown at presstime. The RCMP office is east of town centre on the Alaska Highway. There is 1 bank in Watson Lake, Canadian Imperial Bank of Commerce; it is open Monday through Thursday from 10 A.M. to 3 P.M., Friday 10 A.M. to 6 P.M., closed holidays. Automatic teller machine available 24 hours. Check at the Visitor Information Centre for locations of local churches. Dennis Ball Memorial Swimming Pool is open weekdays in summer. (The pool staff operates the Lucky Lake waterslide on weekends in summer from 1–4 P.M.)

Belvedere Motor Hotel, located in the centre of town, is Watson Lake's newest and finest hotel. It offers such luxuries as Jacuzzi tubs in the rooms, waterbeds, and cable TV, and all at competitive prices. Dining is excellent, whether you decide to try the superb dining room menu, or the coffee shop menu. Phone (403) 536-7712, fax (403) 536-7563. [ADVERTISEMENT]

Big Horn Hotel. New in 1993. 29 beautiful rooms. Centrally located on the Alaska Highway in downtown Watson Lake, YT. Our rooms are quiet, spacious, clean and they boast queen-size beds and complimentary coffee. You get quality at a reasonable price. Available to you are king-size motionless waterbeds, Jacuzzi rooms, kitchenette suites. We know you'll enjoy staying with us. Book ahead. Phone (403) 536-2020, fax (403) 536-2021. [ADVERTISEMENT]

Claim Jumper's Inn. Built in 1948, the two-story, log Claim Jumper's Inn is the oldest house in Watson Lake. Extensively restored, this historic home is now a unique B&B and eatery. We offer clean, cozy rooms, with shared or private bath, at the most rea-

sonable rates in the Yukon. Our public dining room features: all-you-can-eat sourdough pancake and bannock breakfasts; light lunches; Yukon afternoon tea; wild game and salmon BBQs; and our Innkeeper's Dinner. We invite all travelers to join us for our nightly campfire with music, story-telling and Robert Service recitals by Gascan Larry. Bring an instrument and join the fun! With a little luck you may sample our homemade mead, and blueberry and rhubarb wines as we plan to bring the Yukon's first cottage winery into production. Phone/fax (403) 536-7021. See display ad. [ADVERTISEMENT]

Watson Lake Hotel. The historic Watson Lake Hotel. We're right in the heart of Watson Lake's historical Signpost Forest. Enjoy northern hospitality at its finest. Ample parking on our 6 acres of property. Quiet outside modern units (renovated May 1993), boardwalk gift shops and espresso bar. Senior, government, military and corporate discounts. Present this editorial for your 5-cent coffee in Watson's Daytime Grill.

(See our display ad.) Phone (403) 536-7781. [ADVERTISEMENT]

The turnoff for Watson Lake Yukon government campground is 2.4 miles/3.9 km west of the Signpost Forest via the Alaska Highway; see description at **Milepost DC 615.3.** There is a private campground at **Milepost DC 619.6,** 4.3 miles/6.9 km past the turnoff for the government campground; a private campground 2.4 miles/3.9 km east of the Signpost Forest on the Alaska Highway (see **Milepost DC 610.5**); and an RV park located downtown. ▲

Downtown R.V. Park, situated in the centre of town. 71 full-hookup stalls, 19 with pull-through parking; showers; laundromat. Free truck/trailer, motorhome wash with overnight stay. Easy walking distance to stores, garages, hotels, restaurants, liquor store, banking, churches, information centre and the world-famous Signpost Forest. Just across the street from Wye Lake Park. Excellent hiking trails. Phone (403) 536-2646 in summer, 536-2224 in winter. [ADVERTISEMENT] ▲

TRANSPORTATION

Air: Scheduled service to Whitehorse via Alkan Air; to Prince George, Vancouver, Victoria, Smithers and Dease Lake via Central Mountain Air. Helicopter charters available from Frontier Helicopters and Trans North Helicopters.

Bus: Scheduled service to Edmonton and Whitehorse via Coachways.

Taxi and **Car Rental:** Available.

ATTRACTIONS

The **Alaska Highway Interpretive Centre,** operated by Tourism Yukon, is well

---

Watson Lake's famous Signpost Forest numbers well over 31,000 signs. (Earl L. Brown, staff)

worth a visit. Located behind the Signpost Forest, north of the Alaska Highway. Excellent slide presentation and displays, including photographs taken in the mid-1940s showing the construction of the Alaska Highway in this area, and a brief Alaska Highway video. Full-scale reproduction of a P–39 Airacobra fighter plane on display just outside the centre. The centre is open daily, May to mid-September. Free admission. Phone (403) 536-7469.

Northern Lights Centre. The only planetarium in North America featuring the myth and science of the northern lights. Using advanced video and laser technology, the new (1997) centre offers 2 different presentations on the aurora borealis. Afternoon and evening showings daily from May to September. Admission charged. Located across from the Signpost Forest.

The Watson Lake Signpost Forest, seen at the north end of town at the junction of the Alaska and Robert Campbell highways, was started by Carl K. Lindley of Danville, IL, a U.S. Army soldier in Company D, 341st Engineers, working on the construction of the Alaska Highway in 1942. Travelers are still adding signs to the collection, which numbers well over 31,000. Visitors are encouraged to add a sign to the Signpost Forest. **Historic Milepost 635** is located at the Signpost Forest.

Special Events. The 3rd annual Watson Lake Rodeo (NRA-approved) will be held at Lucky Lake July 5–6, 1997. A parade, 8 main events and junior events will be featured.

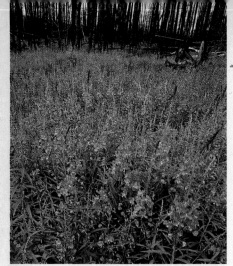

Fireweed, Yukon's territorial flower, grows back quickly in burn areas. (© David Creith/Sahtu)

Wye Lake Park offers a picnic area and boardwalk trails for viewing birds. There is also a bandshell, kitchen shelter and handicap-accessible restrooms. The lake attracts both migrating birds (spring and fall) and resident species, such as nesting grebes. Native plants and flowers are identified by plaques. The development of this park was initiated by a local citizens group. &

St. John the Baptist Anglican Church has a memorial stained-glass window designed by Yukon artist Kathy Spalding. Titled "Our Land of Plenty," the window features a scene just north of Watson Lake

off the Campbell Highway.

Drive the Campbell Highway. This good gravel road offers an excellent wilderness highway experience. Motorists can travel the entire 373 miles/600 km of the Campbell Highway, stopping at Ross River and Faro en route, to junction with the Klondike Highway at Carmacks. Or drive north 52 miles/83 km from Watson Lake to Simpson Lake for picnicking, fishing and camping. (See CAMPBELL HIGHWAY section for details.)

Play golf at Upper Liard, 6 miles/9.6 km north of Watson Lake on the Alaska Highway. The 9-hole, par-35 course has grass greens and is open daily May through September. Phone (403) 536-2477.

Explore the area. Take time to fish, canoe a lake, take a wilderness trek or sightsee by helicopter. Outfitters in the area offer guided fishing trips to area lakes. Trips can be arranged by the day or by the week. Check with the visitor information centre.

AREA FISHING: Watson Lake has grayling, trout and pike. **McKinnon Lake** (walk-in only), 20 miles/32 km west of Watson Lake, pike 5 to 10 lbs. **Tooally Lake,** string of lakes 14 miles/23 km long, 90 air miles/145 km east, lake trout 8 to 10 lbs.; pike 5 to 10 lbs.; grayling 1 to 3 lbs. **Stewart Lake,** 45 air miles/72 km north northeast; lake trout, grayling. ><(((°>

Alaska Highway Log

(continued)
YUKON HIGHWAY 1
Distance* from Dawson Creek (DC) is followed by distance from Fairbanks (F). Original mileposts are indicated in the

text as Historical Mile.

*Mileages from Dawson Creek are based on actual driving distance. Kilometres from Dawson Creek are based on physical kilometreposts. Please read Mileposts and Kilometreposts on page 78.

DC 612.9 (1021 km) **F 875.1** (1408.3 km) Watson Lake Signpost Forest at the **junction** of the Campbell Highway (Yukon Route 4) and Alaska Highway. The Campbell Highway leads north to Ross River and Faro (see CAMPBELL HIGHWAY section), to junction with the Klondike Highway to Dawson City. Campbell Highway travelers should fill gas tanks in Watson Lake. The first 6 miles/9.7 km of the Campbell Highway is known locally as Airport Road; turn here for access to visitor information (in the Alaska Highway Interpretive Centre), airport, hospital and ski hill.

DC 615.3 (1025 km) **F 872.7** (1404.4 km) Turnoff to north for Watson Lake Recreation Park. Drive in approximately 2 miles/3 km for Watson Lake Yukon government campground; 55 gravel sites, most level, some pull-through, drinking water, kitchen shelters, outhouses, firepits, firewood and litter barrels. Camping fee $8. ▲

There is a separate group camping area and also a day-use area (boat launch, swimming, picnicking at Watson Lake). Follow signs at fork in access road. Trails connect all areas.

DC 618.5 (1030 km) **F 869.5** (1399.3 km) Watch for livestock.

DC 619.6 (1032 km) **F 868.4** (1397.5 km) **Green Valley R.V. Park.** Phone (403) 536-2276. Just 7 miles west of Watson Lake, quiet greenbelt area along Liard River. Friendly service, clean facilities. Pay phone. Serviced and unserviced sites, dump station, grassy tent sites, riverside camping, firepits, car wash, laundry, showers, grocery, coffee, pastries, ice, souvenirs, free gold panning, game room, fishing licenses and tackle. Fish for grayling and dollies. Pick wild strawberries and raspberries in season. Cold beer and off sales. Bikers welcome. Your hosts: Ralph and Marion Bjorkman. [ADVERTISEMENT] ▲

DC 620 (1032.4 km) **F 868** (1396.9 km) Upper Liard River bridge. The Liard River heads in the St. Cyr Range in southcentral Yukon Territory and flows southeast into British Columbia, then turns east and north to join the Mackenzie River at Fort Simpson, NWT.

Liard River, grayling, lake trout, whitefish and northern pike.

DC 620.2 (1032.7 km) **F 867.8** (1396.5 km) **Historical Mile 642. UPPER LIARD VILLAGE,** site of Our Lady of the Yukon Church. Gas, food, lodging and camping. ▲

DC 620.3 (1033 km) **F 867.7** (1396.4 km) Greenway's Greens golf course to south with 9 holes, par 35, grass greens, open daily in summer.

DC 620.8 (1033.7 km) **F 867.2** (1395.6 km) Albert Creek bridge. Turnout with litter barrel to north at east end of bridge. A sign near here marks the first tree planting project in the Yukon. Approximately 200,000 white spruce seedlings were planted in the Albert Creek area in 1993.

DC 626.2 (1043 km) **F 861.8** (1386.9 km) **Historic Milepost 649. Junction** with the Cassiar Highway, which leads south to Yellowhead Highway 16 (see CASSIAR HIGHWAY section). Services here include towing, gas, store with souvenirs, propane, car repair, car wash, laundromat, cafe, camping and lodging.

Junction 37 Services. See display ad this section.

DC 627 (1043.9 km) **F 861** (1385.6 km) **Alaska Highway's Best Coffee Stop.** See display ad this section.

The Northern Beaver Post. Historical Mile 649.9. As with trading posts of the past, The Northern Beaver Post is an essential stop for any traveler. Here you will find unique, quality items which are often as useful as they are decorative. In the friendly atmosphere of the Post, discover a fine selection of Native crafts, jewellery, gold, jade, authentic Eskimo carvings, furs, woolens, northern art, tufting, sweatshirts and tees, cards, gifts and more. Show us this editorial and receive 10 percent off your purchase of a Beaver Post T-shirt or sweat shirt. Open 7 A.M. to 10 P.M. 7 days a week, May through October. Caravans and bus tours welcome. Free overnight RV parking. Don't miss the famous Elvis Presly Mile 649er BBQ ribs available at our Elvis Presly dinner show. Reservations requested. Celebrate the newly released album. Don't miss "Alaska Highway's Best Coffee Stop" next door—fresh home baking. VISA, MasterCard, Discover. Shipping and mail order available. Phone (403) 536-2307, fax (403) 536-7667. [ADVERTISEMENT]

DC 627.3 (1044.5 km) **F 860.7** (1385.1 km) Large gravel turnout and rest area with litter barrels and pit toilets.

DC 630 (1050.8 km) **F 858** (1380.8 km) Several hundred rock messages are spelled out along the highway here. The rock messages were started in summer 1990 by a Fort Nelson swim team.

DC 633 (1055.6 km) **F 855** (1375.9 km) Gravel turnout to north. *NOTE: Watch for road construction northbound between Kilometreposts 1056 and 1062 in 1997.*

DC 637.8 (1063.3 km) **F 850.2** (1368.2 km) Microwave tower access road.

DC 639.8 (1066.5 km) **F 848.2** (1365 km) Hill and sharp curve.

DC 647.2 (1078.5 km) **F 840.8** (1353.1 km) Turnout with litter barrel on Little Rancheria Creek to north.

DC 647.4 (1079 km) **F 840.6** (1352.8 km) Little Rancheria Creek bridge. Northbound winter travelers put on chains here.

DC 650.6 (1084 km) **F 837.4** (1347.6 km) Highway descends westbound to Big Creek.

DC 651.1 (1084.8 km) **F 836.9** (1346.8

km) Big Creek bridge, clearance 17.7 feet/ 5.4m. Turnout at east end of bridge.

DC 651.2 (1085 km) **F 836.8** (1346.7 km) Turnoff to north for Big Creek Yukon government day-use area, adjacent highway on Big Creek; gravel loop road, outhouses, firewood, kitchen shelter, litter barrels, picnic tables, drinking water.

DC 652.5 (1087.3 km) **F 835.5** (1344.6 km) Sign reads: "Northbound winter travelers chains may be removed."

NOTE: Watch for road construction northbound between kilometreposts 1089 and 1102 in 1997.

DC 658.4 (1096.7 km) **F 829.6** (1335.1 km) Pull-through turnout south side of highway.

DC 662.3 (1102.9 km) **F 825.7** (1328.8 km) NorthwesTel microwave tower road to north.

NOTE: Recent highway reconstruction and straightening in this area has resulted in the dis-

placement of many kilometreposts.

DC 664.1 (1105.8 km) **F 823.9** (1325.9 km) Double-ended turnout to north to Lower Rancheria River.

DC 664.3 (1106.2 km) **F 823.7** (1325.6 km) Bridge over Lower Rancheria River. For northbound travelers, the highway closely follows the Rancheria River west from here to the Swift River. Northern bush pilot Les Cook was credited with helping find the best route for the Alaska Highway between Watson Lake and Whitehorse. Cook's Rancheria River route saved engineers hundreds of miles of highway construction.

Rancheria River, fishing for Dolly Varden and grayling.

DC 665.1 (1110.4 km) **F 822.9** (1324.3 km) Scenic viewpoint.

DC 667.2 (1113.7 km) **F 820.8** (1320.9 km) Turnout to south.

DC 667.6 (1114.3 km) **F 820.4** (1320.2 km) Large double-ended turnout with litter

barrel to south.

DC 671.9 (1118.7 km) **F 816.1** (1313.3 km) Spencer Creek.

DC 673.4 (1121 km) **F 814.6** (1310.9 km) Improved highway and view of Cassiar Mountains westbound.

DC 677 (1126.9 km) **F 811** (1305.1 km) Turnout with litter barrel to south overlooking the Rancheria River. Trail down to river.

According to R.C. Coutts, author of *Yukon: Places & Names*, the Rancheria River was named by Cassiar miners working Sayyea Creek in 1875, site of a minor gold rush at the time. Rancheria is an old Californian or Mexican miners' term from the Spanish, meaning a native village or settlement. It is pronounced Ran-che-RI-ah.

DC 678.5 (1129.3 km) **F 809.5** (1302.7 km) George's Gorge, culvert.

DC 683.2 (1137 km) **F 804.8** (1295.2 km) NorthwesTel microwave tower to south.

DC 684 (1138.4 km) **F 804** (1293.9 km) Turnout with litter barrel overlooking Rancheria River. *CAUTION: Watch for livestock on or near highway in this area.*

DC 687.2 (1143.8 km) **F 800.8** (1288.7 km) **Historic Milepost 710.** Rancheria Hotel–Motel to south; gas, food, camping and lodging. Open year-round. Historic sign and interpretive panel on highway lodges. ▲

Rancheria Hotel–Motel. See display ad this section. ▲

DC 687.4 (1143.9 km) **F 800.6** (1288.4 km) Turnoff to south for private campground (formerly Rancheria Yukon government campground) adjacent highway overlooking Rancheria River. The Rancheria is a tributary of the Liard River. ▲

DC 689.2 (1146.6 km) **F 798.8** (1285.5 km) Canyon Creek.

DC 690 (1148 km) **F 798** (1284.2 km) Highway follows the Rancheria River. This stretch of highway was reconstructed in 1995.

DC 692.5 (1152 km) **F 795.5** (1280.2 km) Young Creek.

DC 694.2 (1155 km) **F 793.8** (1277.5 km) **Historical Mile 717.5.** Abandoned building.

DC 695.2 (1156.5 km) **F 792.8** (1275.8 km) Rancheria Falls recreation site has a good gravel and boardwalk trail to the falls; easy 10-minute walk. Large parking area with toilets and litter barrels at trailhead.

DC 697.4 (1160 km) **F 790.6** (1272.3 km) Beautiful view of the Cassiar Mountains.

DC 698.4 (1161.6 km) **F 789.6** (1270.7 km) **Historical Mile 721.** Walker's Continental Divide; gas, food, camping and lodging. ▲

Walker's Continental Divide. Fresh baking daily, mouthwatering cinnamon rolls, rhubarb pie, muffins, tarts and donuts. Breakfast served all day—try our sourdough pancakes. Gift shop, hard ice cream. Motel with clean, comfortable, cozy rooms. Proposed for 1997—full service RV park with laundromat, showers and trailer dump. Clean washrooms. Hospitality spoken here, free of charge. [ADVERTISEMENT] ▲

DC 698.7 (1162 km) F 789.3 (1270.2 km) Upper Rancheria River bridge, clearance 17.7 feet/5.4m. For northbound travelers, the highway leaves the Rancheria River.

DC 699.1 (1162.8 km) F 788.9 (1269.6 km) Large gravel turnout to north with point of interest signs, outhouses and litter barrels. This marks the Continental Divide, the water divide between rivers that drain into the Arctic Ocean via the Mackenzie River system and those that drain into the Pacific Ocean via the Yukon River system. All rivers crossed by the Alaska Highway between here and Fairbanks, AK, drain into the Yukon River system.

DC 699.6 (1163.3 km) F 788.4 (1268.8 km) Historic Milepost 722. Pine Lake airstrip to north (status unknown).

DC 702.2 (1168 km) F 785.8 (1264.6 km) Swift River bridge. For northbound travelers, the highway now follows the Swift River west to the Morley River.

DC 706.2 (1174.5 km) F 781.8 (1258.2 km) Steep hill for westbound travelers.

DC 709.7 (1180 km) F 778.3 (1252.5 km) Seagull Creek.

DC 710 (1180.9 km) F 778 (1252 km) Historic Milepost 733, SWIFT RIVER. Lodge with food, gas, lodging, car repair, pay phone and highway maintenance camp. Open year-round.

Swift River Lodge. Friendly haven in a beautiful mountain valley. Tasty cooking with a plentiful supply of coffee. Mouth-watering homemade pies and pastries fresh daily. Wrecker service, welding and repairs. Reasonable rates. Gas and diesel at some of the best prices on the highway. Clean restrooms; gifts; and public phone. [ADVERTISEMENT]

DC 710.5 (1181.5 km) F 777.5 (1251.2 km) Historical Mile 733.5. The highway re-enters British Columbia for approximately 42 miles/68 km northbound.

DC 712.7 (1185 km) F 775.3 (1247.7 km) Partridge Creek.

DC 716 (1190.3 km) F 772 (1242.4 km) Gravel turnout with litter barrels.

DC 718.5 (1194.2 km) F 769.5 (1238.3 km) Screw Creek.

DC 719.6 (1196 km) F 768.4 (1236.6 km) Historical Mile 743. Turnout with litter barrel to south on Swan Lake. Fishing for trout and whitefish. The pyramid-shaped mountain to south is Simpson Peak. ◄

DC 724.2 (1203.7 km) F 763.8 (1229.2 km) Pull-through turnout to south.

DC 727.9 (1209.5 km) F 760.1 (1223.2 km) Logjam Creek.

DC 735.8 (1222.5 km) F 752.2 (1210.5 km) Smart River bridge. The Smart River flows south into the Cassiar Mountains in British Columbia. The river was originally called Smarch, after the Indian family of that name who lived and trapped in this area. The Smarch family currently includes well-known carver Keith Smarch.

DC 741.4 (1231.7 km) F 746.6 (1201.5 km) Microwave tower access road to north.

DC 744.1 (1236 km) F 743.9 (1197.2 km) Upper Hazel Creek. *HALFWAY*

DC 745.2 (1238 km) F 742.8 (1195.4 km) Lower Hazel Creek.

DC 746.9 (1240.7 km) F 741.1 (1192.6 km) Turnouts both sides of highway; litter barrel at south turnout.

DC 749 (1245 km) F 739 (1189.3 km) Andrew Creek.

DC 751.5 (1249.2 km) F 736.5 (1185.2 km) Morley Lake to north. The Alaska Highway re-enters the Yukon Territory northbound. This is the last of 7 crossings of the YT–BC border.

DC 752 (1250 km) F 736 (1184.4 km) Sharp turnoff to north for Morley River Yukon government day-use area; large gravel parking area, picnic tables, kitchen shelter, water, litter barrels and outhouses. Fishing. ◄

DC 752.3 (1251 km) F 735.7 (1184 km) Morley River bridge; turnout with litter barrel to north at east end of bridge. Morley River flows into the southeast corner of Teslin Lake. The river, lake and Morley Bay (on Teslin Lake) were named for W. Morley Ogilvie, assistant to Arthur St. Cyr on the 1897 survey of the Telegraph Creek–Teslin Lake route.

Morley Bay and River, good fishing near mouth of river for northern pike 6 to 8 lbs., best June to August, use small Red Devils; grayling 3 to 5 lbs., in May and August, use small spinner; lake trout 6 to 8 lbs., June to August, use large spoon.

DC 752.9 (1252 km) F 735.1 (1183 km) Historic Milepost 777.7. Morley River Lodge, food, gas, diesel, towing, tires, camping and lodging. Open year-round. ▲

Morley River Lodge. See display ad this section. ▲

DC 754.8 (1256 km) **F 733.2** (1179.9 km) *CAUTION: Watch for livestock on highway.*

DC 757.9 (1261 km) **F 730.1** (1174.9 km) Small marker to south (no turnout) reads: "In memory of Max Richardson 39163467, Corporal Co. F 340th Eng. Army of the United States; born Oct. 10, 1918, died Oct. 17, 1942. Faith is the victory."

DC 761.5 (1267.9 km) **F 726.5** (1169.1 km) Strawberry Creek.

DC 764.1 (1273.7 km) **F 723.9** (1165 km) Hayes Creek.

DC 769.6 (1282.5 km) **F 718.4** (1156.1 km) **Historical Mile 797.** Food, lodging and camping. ▲

Dawson Peaks Northern Resort. Slow down folks! No need to drive any farther. Fishing's good, coffee's on, camping is easy and the rhubarb pie can't be beat. Couple that with our renowned Yukon hospitality and you'll have one of the best experiences on your trip. We're looking forward to seeing you this summer. [ADVERTISEMENT] ▲

DC 776 (1292 km) **F 712** (1145.8 km) Nisutlin Bay (Nisutlin River) bridge, longest water span on the Alaska Highway at 1,917 feet/584m. The Nisutlin River flows into Teslin Lake here. Good view northbound of the village of Teslin and Teslin Lake. Teslin Lake straddles the BC–YT border; it is 86 miles/138 km long, averages 2 miles/3.2 km across, and has an average depth of 194 feet/59m. The name is taken from the Indian name for the lake—Teslintoo ("long, narrow water").

Turnout with litter barrel and point of interest sign at south end of bridge, east side of highway.

Historic Milepost 804 at the north end of the bridge, west side of the highway; historic sign and interpretive panel, parking area, marina and day-use area with picnic tables and boat ramp. Turn west on side road here for access to Teslin village (description follows).

DC 776.3 (1294 km) **F 711.7** (1145.3 km) Entering Teslin **(Historic Milepost 804)** at north end of bridge. Gas, food, camping and lodging along highway.

Yukon Motel, just right (northbound) on the north side of Nisutlin Bridge. An excellent stop for a fresh lake trout dinner (or full menu), accompanied by good and friendly service topped off with a piece of fantastic rhubarb and strawberry pie (lots of fresh baking). Soft ice cream. Recently renovated. Three satellite TV channels. Open year-round, summer hours 6–11. New lakeshore RV park (mosquito control area), 70 sites, full and partial hookups. "Good Sam Park"—washhouse rated TL 9.5. A real home away from home on the shore of beautiful Nisutlin Bay. Phone (403) 390-2575. [ADVERTISEMENT] ▲

Teslin

Located at **Historic Milepost 804,** 111 miles/179 km southeast of Whitehorse, 163 miles/263 km northwest of Watson Lake. **Population:** 465. **Emergency Services: RCMP,** phone (403) 390-5555 (if no answer call toll free 1-403-667-5555). **Fire Department,** phone (403) 390-2222. **Nurse,** phone (403) 390-4444.

Elevation: 2,239 feet/682.4m. **Climate:** Average temperature in January, -7°F/-22°C, in July 57°F/14°C. Annual snowfall 66.2

inches/168.2 cm. Driest month April, wettest month July. Average date of last spring frost is June 19; first fall frost Aug. 19. **Radio:** CBC 940; CHONFM 90.5; CKRW 98.7. **Television:** Channel 13.

The village of Teslin, situated on a point of land at the confluence of the Nisutlin River and Teslin Lake, began as a trading post in 1903. Today the community consists of a trading post, Catholic church, health centre and post office. There is a 3-sheet regulation curling rink and a skating rink.

Teslin has one of the largest Native populations in Yukon Territory and much of the community's livelihood revolves around traditional hunting, trapping and fishing. In addition, some Tlingit residents are involved in the development of Native woodworking crafts (canoes, snowshoes and sleds); traditional sewn art and craft items (moccasins, mitts, moose hair tufting, gun cases); and the tanning of moose hides.

George Johnston Museum, renovated in 1991, is located on the left side of the highway heading north. The museum, run by the Teslin Historical Museum Society, is open daily, 9 A.M. to 7 P.M. in summer; minimal admission fee, wheelchair accessible. (Get your Yukon Gold Explorer's Passport stamped at the museum.) The museum displays items from gold rush days and the pioneer mode of living, Indian artifacts and many items of Tlingit culture. A Tlingit Indian, George Johnston (1884–1972) was an innovative individual, known for his trapping as well as his photography. With his camera he captured the life of the inland

Tlingit people of Teslin and Atlin between 1910 and 1940. Johnston also brought the first car to Teslin, a 1928 Chevrolet. Since the Alaska Highway had not been built yet, George built a 3-mile road for his "Teslin taxi." In winter, he put chains on the car and drove it on frozen Teslin Lake. The '28 Chevy has been restored and is now on permanent display at the museum. For more information, write the Teslin Historical Museum Society, Box 146, Teslin, YT Y0A 1B0; phone (403) 390-2550, or fax 390-2828. &

Teslin is located west of the Alaska Highway, accessible via a short side road from the north end of Nisutlin Bay bridge. Nisutlin Trading Post in the village has groceries and general merchandise. Gas, diesel and propane, car repair, gift shop, restaurants and motels are found along the Alaska Highway. There is 1 bank, located in the Tlingit Band office building; open Monday, Wednesday, Thursday and Friday, 11 A.M to 2 P.M., in summer. The Teslin area has an air charter service, boat rentals and houseboat tours.

Nisutlin Trading Post, on short loop road, left northbound in Teslin Village. A pioneer store established in 1928, and located on the shore of Nisutlin Bay, an "arm" of Teslin Lake. This store handles a complete line of groceries, general merchandise including clothing, hardware, fishing tackle and licenses. Open all year 9 A.M. to 5:30 P.M. Closed Sunday. Founded by the late R. McCleery, Teslin pioneer, the trading post is now operated by Mr. and Mrs. Bob Hassard. Phone 390-2521, fax 390-2103. [ADVERTISEMENT]

Teslin Lake, excellent fishing for trout, grayling, pike and whitefish. King salmon in

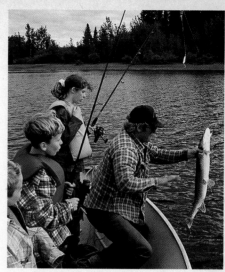

Landing a pike at Teslin Lake.
(Earl L. Brown, staff)

August. Guides and boats available at Nisutlin Bay Marina. ✦

Alaska Highway Log
(continued)

Distance* from Dawson Creek (DC) is followed by distance from Fairbanks (F). Original mileposts are indicated in the text as Historical Mile.

*Mileages from Dawson Creek are based on actual driving distance. Kilometres from Dawson Creek are based on physical kilometreposts. Please read Mileposts and Kilo-

---

TESLIN ADVERTISERS

George Johnston
 Museum ....Ph. (403) 390-2550
Nisutlin Trading Post ....Ph. (403) 390-2521
Village of Teslin ....Ph. (403) 390-2530
Yukon Motel ....Ph. (403) 390-2575

metreposts in the introduction for an explanation of how this highway is logged.

DC 777 (1295 km) F 711 (1144.2 km) **Historic Milepost 805. Private Aircraft:** Teslin airstrip to east; elev. 2,313 feet/705m; length 5,500 feet/1,676m; gravel; fuel 100, jet. Runway may be unusable during spring breakup.

DC 779.1 (1298.5 km) F 708.9 (1140.8 km) **Historical Mile 807.** Halsteads'; current status of services unknown.

DC 779.5 (1299 km) F 708.5 (1140.2 km) Fox Creek.

DC 784.3 (1306.7 km) F 703.7 (1132.5 km) **Historical Mile 812.** Mukluk Annie's; food, lodging and camping. ▲

Mukluk Annie's Salmon Bake. See display ad this section. ▲

DC 785.2 (1308 km) F 702.8 (1131 km)

Historical Mile 813. Teslin Lake Yukon government campground to west; 27 sites (some level) in trees on **Teslin Lake**, water pump, litter barrels, kitchen shelter, firewood, firepits, picnic tables. Camping fee $8. Fishing. Boat launch 0.3 mile/0.5 km north of campground. ◄▲

DC 785.3 (1308.2 km) F 702.7 (1130.8 km) Tenmile Creek.

DC 788.9 (1314 km) F 699.1 (1125 km) Lone Tree Creek.

DC 794.6 (1323 km) F 693.4 (1115.9 km) Deadman's Creek.

DC 800.8 (1333.3 km) F 687.2 (1105.9 km) Robertson Creek.

DC 801.6 (1334.4 km) F 686.4 (1104.6 km) **Historic Milepost 829.** Brooks' Brook. According to R.C. Coutts in *Yukon: Places & Names*, this stream was named by black

Army engineers who completed this section of road in 1942, for their company officer, Lieutenant Brooks.

DC 808.2 (1345 km) F 679.8 (1094 km) **Junction** with the Canol Road (Yukon Highway 6) which leads northeast to the Campbell Highway. (See the CANOL ROAD section for details.) Historic sign and interpretive panel about the Canol Project.

The Canol (Canadian Oil) Road was built in 1942–44 to provide access to oil fields at Norman Wells, NWT. Conceived by the U.S. War Dept., the $134 million project was abandoned soon after the war ended in 1945. Canol truck "graveyard" nearby.

DC 808.6 (1345.6 km) F 679.4 (1093.3 km) Teslin River bridge, third longest water span on the highway (1,770 feet/539m), was constructed with a very high clearance above the river to permit steamers of the British Yukon Navigation Co. to pass under it en route from Whitehorse to Teslin. River steamers ceased operation on the Teslin River in 1942. Before the construction of the Alaska Highway, all freight and supplies for Teslin traveled this water route from Whitehorse.

DC 808.9 (1346 km) F 679.1 (1092.9 km) **Historic Milepost 836. JOHNSON'S CROSSING** to east at north end of bridge; store, food and camping. One of the original lodges on the Alaska Highway, the history of Johnson's Crossing is related in Ellen Davignon's *The Cinnamon Mine*. Access to Teslin River; boat launch, no camping on riverbank. ▲

Johnson's Crossing Campground Services. Located across the Teslin River bridge, home of the "world famous cinnamon buns," including a small store with a full array of mouth-watering baked goods, souvenirs and groceries. Full-service RV campground facilities include treed pull-throughs, complete laundry and washhouse facilities, Chevron gasoline products, cold beer and ice, and great fishing. Treat yourselves to the historically scenic Km 1347 (Mile 836) Alaska Highway, Yukon Y1A 9Z0. (403) 390-2607. [ADVERTISEMENT] ▲

Teslin River, excellent grayling fishing from spring to late fall, 10 to 15 inches, use spinner or red-and-white spoons for spinning or black gnat for fly-fishing. King salmon in August.

Canoeists report that the Teslin River is

wide and slow, but with gravel, rocks and weeds. Adequate camping sites on numerous sand bars; boil drinking water. Abundant wildlife—muskrat, porcupine, moose, eagles and wolves—also bugs and rain. Watch for bear. The Teslin enters the Yukon River at Hootalinqua, an old steamboat landing and supply point (under restoration). Roaring Bull rapids: choppy water. Pull out at Carmacks. Inquire locally about river conditions before setting out.

DC 809.1 (1346.5 km) **F 678.9** (1092.5 km) Access road east to the Teslin River. The Big Salmon Range, also to the east, parallels the Teslin. For Alaska-bound travelers, the highway now swings west.

DC 812.8 (1352.5 km) **F 675.2** (1086.6 km) Little Teslin Lake on south side of highway.

DC 819.8 (1364 km) **F 668.2** (1075.3 km) In mid-June, the roadside is a profusion of purple Jacob's ladder and yellow dandelions.

DC 820.3 (1364.8 km) **F 667.7** (1074.5 km) Seaforth Creek bridge.

DC 820.4 (1365 km) **F 667.6** (1074.4 km) Large turnout to south; picnic area.

DC 820.6 (1365.3 km) **F 667.4** (1074 km) Squanga Lake to northwest. Named Squanga by Indians for a type of whitefish of the same name found in the lake. Watch for **Historic Milepost 843**, with historic sign about Squanga Lake flightstrip. Look for the eagle's nest in the old observation tower.

DC 821 (1366 km) **F 667** (1073.4 km) Turnoff to northwest to **Squanga Lake** Yukon government campground: 13 sites, kitchen shelter, drinking water. Small boat launch. Fishing for northern pike, grayling, whitefish, rainbow and burbot. ◄▲

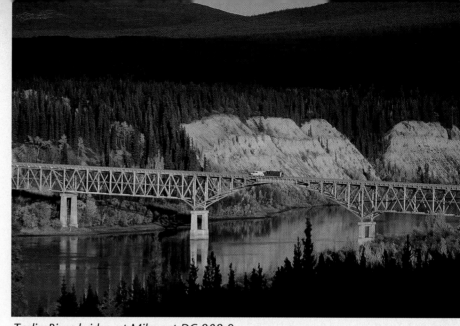

Teslin River bridge at Milepost DC 808.9. (© Beth Davidow)

DC 827.5 (1376.8 km) **F 660.5** (1062.9 km) White Mountain, to the southeast, was named by William Ogilvie during his 1887 survey, for Thomas White, then Minister of the Interior. The Yukon government introduced mountain goats to this area in 1981.

DC 836.8 (1392.5 km) **F 651.2** (1048 km) **Historic Milepost 866. Junction**, commonly known as **JAKE'S CORNER; gas, food and lodging**. There's also a large collection on the premises of artifacts from the Canol Project, Alaska Highway construction, and the gold rush. The Alaska Highway junctions here with Yukon Highway 7 south to Atlin, a very scenic spot that is well worth a side trip (see ATLIN ROAD section). This turnoff also provides access to Yukon Highway 8 to Carcross and Klondike Highway 2 to Skagway, AK. (Klondike Highway 2 junctions with the Alaska Highway at **Milepost DC 874.4**.) Yukon Highway 8 is a scenic alternative to driving the Carcross–Alaska Highway por-

ON WAY BACK!!

Travel the Carcross and Tagish Loop

STOP

Don't miss the opportunity to drive the Original Alaska Highway. The alternate route to Whitehorse, the Carcross/Tagish loop, offers fantastic scenery and is the original Alaska Highway route which follows the GOLD RUSH TRAIL OF 1898! A short side trip from Carcross allows you to preview Alaska at Skagway. **Strike it rich by entering our free draw for 1 troy ounce of Gold!!**

Mention the Milepost and enter the free gold draw at any of the participating businesses. No purchase necessary. Draw date September 30th, 1997.

tion of Klondike Highway 2 (see TAGISH ROAD and KLONDIKE HIGHWAY 2 sections for details).

Jake's Corner Inc. See display ad this section.

There are 2 versions of how Jake's Corner got its name. In 1942, the U.S. Army Corps of Engineers set up a construction camp here to build this section of the Alcan Highway and the Tagish Road cutoff to Carcross for the Canol pipeline. (The highway south to Atlin, BC, was not constructed until 1949–50.) The camp was under the command of Captain Jacobson, thus Jake's Corner. However, another version that predates the Alcan construction is that Jake's Corner was named for Jake Jackson, a Teslin Indian who camped in this area on his way to Carcross. Roman "Jake" Chaykowsky (1900–1995) operated Jake's Corner Service here for many years. It was known locally as The Crystal Palace, after the first lodge Chaykowsky had owned at Judas Creek, just up the road.

DC 843.2 (1402.7 km) **F 644.8** (1037.7 km) Judas Creek bridge.

DC 850 (1413.5 km) **F 638** (1026.7 km) Turnoff to west for Lakeview Resort on Marsh Lake; camping, lodging, restau-

rant, boat rentals and boat launch. ▲

Marsh Lake, excellent fishing for grayling and northern pike.

Lakeview Resort & Marina, a spectacular setting on the shore of Marsh Lake, just 2 km off the Alaska Highway. Restaurant and lounge with panoramic view of lake and mountains. Motel rooms, cabins, convenience store, ice and liquor off-sales. RV park, partial and full hookups, camping, laundromat, showers, marina and boat rentals. Budget friendly rates. Km 1414, Alaska Highway, Yukon. Mailing address— P.O. Box 4759, Whitehorse, YT Y1A 4N6. Phone (403) 399-4567, fax (403) 399-4747. [ADVERTISEMENT] ▲

DC 851.6 (1416 km) **F 636.4** (1024.1 km) Several access roads along here which lead to summer cottages. Marsh Lake is a popular recreation area for Whitehorse residents.

DC 852.7 (1417.8 km) **F 635.3** (1022.4 km) Good view of Marsh Lake to west. The highway parallels this beautiful lake for several miles. Marsh Lake (elev. 2,152 feet/ 656m) is part of the Yukon River system. It is approximately 20 miles/32 km long and was named in 1883 by Lt. Frederick Schwatka, U.S. Army, for Yale professor Othniel Charles Marsh.

DC 854.4 (1421 km) **F 633.6** (1019.6 km) **Historic Milepost 883**, Marsh Lake Camp historic sign. Boat ramp turnoff to west.

DC 854.8 (1421.2 km) **F 633.2** (1019 km) Caribou Road leads northwest to Airplane Lake; hiking trail, good skiing and snowmachining in winter. This road was bulldozed

out to get men and equipment into a small lake where an airplane had made an emergency landing.

DC 859.9 (1432 km) **F 628.1** (1010.8 km) **Historical Mile 890.** Turnoff to west for Marsh Lake Yukon government campground via 0.4-mile/0.6-km gravel loop road: 47 sites, most level, some pull-through; outhouses, firewood, firepits, litter barrels, picnic tables, kitchen shelter, water pump. Camping fee $8. ▲

For group camping and day-use area, follow signs near campground entrance. Day-use area includes sandy beach, change house, picnic area, playground, kitchen shelter and boat launch.

DC 861.1 (1433.9 km) **F 626.9** (1008.9 km) **M'Clintock River**, named by Lieutenant Schwatka for Arctic explorer Sir Francis M'Clintock. This river flows into the north end of Marsh Lake. Boat ramp turnoff to west at north end of bridge. M'Clintock River is narrow, winding and silty with thick brush along shoreline. However, it is a good river for boat trips, especially in late fall.

DC 864.3 (1437 km) **F 623.7** (1003.2 km) Bridge over Kettley's Canyon.

DC 867.3 (1441.8 km) **F 620.7** (998.9 km) **Historic Milepost 897.** Yukon River bridge. Turnout to north for day-use area and boat launch on **Yukon River** at Marsh Lake bridge near Northern Canada Power Commission (NCPC) control gate. Point of interest sign and litter barrels. From here (elev. 2,150 feet/645m) the Yukon River flows 1,980 miles/3,186 km to the Bering Sea. Good fishing for grayling, jackfish and some trout. ⤙

DC 873.5 (1453.3 km) **F 614.5** (988.9 km) **Historical Mile 904.** Sourdough Country Campsite to east. ▲

Sourdough Country Campsite. See display ad this section. ▲

DC 874.4 (1455 km) **F 613.6** (987.5 km) **Historical Mile 905. Junction** with Klondike Highway 2 (Carcross Road) which leads south to Carcross and Skagway. (See KLONDIKE HIGHWAY 2 section.) Restaurant, convenience store, gas, diesel, propane, car repair and rock shop here.

Carcross Corner Services. See display ad this section.

Yukon Rock Shop. See display ad this section.

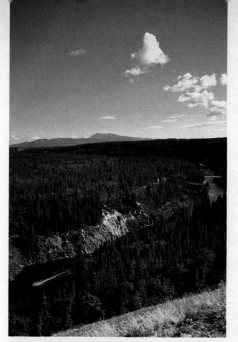

Boat trips up scenic Miles Canyon are available from Whitehorse. (Earl L. Brown, staff)

DC 874.6 (1455.3 km) **F 613.4** (987.1 km) Whitehorse city limits. Incorporated June 1, 1950, Whitehorse expanded in 1974 from its original 2.7 square miles/6.9 square kilometres to 162 square miles/421 square kilometres.

DC 875.6 (1456.9 km) **F 612.4** (985.5 km) Kara Speedway to west.

DC 875.9 (1457.4 km) **F 612.1** (985 km) Cowley Creek.

DC 876.8 (1459 km) **F 611.2** (983.6 km) **Historical Mile 906.** Wolf Creek Yukon government campground to east. An 0.8-mile/1.3-km gravel loop road leads through this campground: 49 sites, most level, some pull-through; kitchen shelters, water pumps, picnic tables, firepits, firewood, outhouses, litter barrels, playground. Wolf Creek self-guiding trail; varied and abundant plant life, views of and access to Yukon River. Camping fee $8. Fishing in **Wolf Creek** for grayling. ◄▲

DC 879.4 (1463 km) **F 608.6** (979.4 km) Highway crosses abandoned railroad tracks of the White Pass & Yukon Route (WP&YR) narrow-gauge railroad. Construction of the WP&YR began in May 1898 at the height of the Klondike Gold Rush. Completion of the railway in 1900 linked the port of Skagway, AK, with Whitehorse, YT, providing passenger and freight service for thousands of gold seekers. The WP&YR ceased operation in 1982, but started limited service again in 1988 between Skagway and Fraser. See the WHITE PASS & YUKON ROUTE section for more information and current schedule.

DC 879.6 (1463.3 km) **F 608.4** (979.1 km) Point of interest sign about 135th meridian to east; small turnout. Gas station.

DC 879.8 (1463.7 km) **F 608.2** (978.8

km) **Historic Milepost 910.** Historic sign reads: "McCrae originated in 1900 as a flag stop on the newly-constructed White Pass & Yukon Railway. During WWII, this area served as a major service and supply depot, a major construction camp and a recreation centre." McCrae truck stop to east.

DC 880.4 (1464.5 km) **F 607.6** (977.8 km) Turnoff to west for Whitehorse Copper Mines (closed). Road to east leads to Yukon River.

DC 881 (1465.5 km) **F 607** (976.8 km) **Historic Milepost 911.** Site of Utah Construction Co. Camp. Pioneer RV Park, store and self-serve gas to east. ▲

Pioneer R.V. Park. See display ad this section. ▲

DC 881.3 (1466 km) **F 606.7** (976.4 km) White Pass & Yukon Route's Utah siding to east. This was also the site of an Army camp where thousands of soldiers were stationed during construction of the Alaska Highway.

DC 881.7 (1466.6 km) **F 606.3** (975.7 km) Sharp turnoff to east (watch for camera viewpoint sign) to see Miles Canyon. Drive down side road 0.3 mile/0.5 km to fork. The right fork leads to Miles Canyon parking lot. From the parking area it is a short walk to the Miles Canyon bridge; good photo spot. Cross bridge for easy hiking trails overlooking Yukon River. A 1.1-mile/1.7-km hiking trail from the bridge leads to the historic site of CANYON CITY, a gold rush settlement that existed from 1897 to 1900 as a portage point around Miles Canyon and Whitehorse Rapids. Two tramways, each several miles long, transported goods along the east and west sides of the river. Completion of the White Pass & Yukon Route in 1900 made the trams obsolete, and the settlement was abandoned. Canyon City is currently undergoing archaeological excavation. Interepreter on site weekdays in July and part of August. No restrooms or litter barrels available at site; plan accordingly.

The left fork on this side road leads to

Schwatka Lake Road, which follows the lake and intersects the South Access Road into Whitehorse. Turnouts along road overlook Miles Canyon.

DC 881.9 (1466.9 km) **F 606.1** (975.4 km) Riding stable with daily trail rides in summer.

DC 882.6 (1468 km) **F 605.4** (974.3 km) **Historical Mile 912.** RV service and supply.

Philmar RV Service and Supply. See display ad this section.

DC 882.9 (1468.5 km) **F 605.1** (973.8 km) **Mountain Ridge Motel & RV Park.** See display ad this section. ▲

DC 883.2 (1468.9 km) **F 604.8** (973.3 km) **Historical Mile 913.** Gas, diesel and mini-mart.

DC 883.7 (1469.7 km) **F 604.3** (972.5 km) Turnout to east with litter barrel, outhouses and information sign.

DC 884 (1470.2 km) **F 604** (972 km) **Hi-Country R.V. Park.** Good Sam. New facilities to serve the traveler. Large wooded sites, electric and water hookups, dump station, hot showers. Picnic tables and firepits, gift shop with wildlife display. Propane.

Whitehorse Vicinity

To Dawson City

To Fairbanks

MacPherson

Alaska Highway

Crestview

Yukon River

Porter Creek Mall

Wann Rd.

Porter Creek

Mountain View Golf Course

Fish Lake Road

Range Road

Takhini

Yukon College, Yukon Archives, Yukon Arts Centre

Kopper King

Marwell

Long Lake Road

Valleyview

McIntyre

Two Mile Hill

Granger

Hillcrest

Downtown (See detailed map this section)

Grey Mountain Nature Trail

Transportation Museum

Yukon Beringia Interpretive Centre

Riverdale

Airport

Dam and Fish Ladder

Schwatka Lake

Yukon Gardens

South Access Road

Chadburn Lake Road

Alaska Highway

Miles Canyon

Yukon River

White Pass & Yukon Route

To Dawson Creek

MacRae

Floatplane base on Schwatka Lake. The lake was formed by damming the Yukon River. *(Earl L. Brown, staff)*

Conveniently located on the highway at the south access to Whitehorse, next to beautiful Yukon Gardens. Mile 913.4 Alaska Highway. P.O. Box 6081, Whitehorse, YT Y1A 5L7; phone (403) 667-7445. [ADVERTISEMENT] ▲

DC 884 (1470.2 km) **F 604** (972 km). First exit northbound for Whitehorse. Exit east for Robert Service Way (also known as

South Access Road) to Whitehorse via 4th Avenue and 2nd Avenue. At the turnoff is Yukon Gardens botanical exhibit. At Mile 1.4/2.3 km on this access road is the side road to Miles Canyon and Schwatka Lake; at Mile 1.6/2.6 km is Robert Service Campground (tent camping only) with a picnic area for day use; at Mile 2.6/4.2 km is the SS *Klondike* National Historic Site, turn left for downtown Whitehorse. ▲

NOTE: Watch for construction and detours on Robert Service Way (South Access Road) in 1997.

DC 884.5 (1471.1 km) **F 603.5** (971.2 km) Government weigh scale and vehicle inspection station to west.

DC 885.7 (1472.9 km) **F 602.3** (969.3 km) Site of the new (1997) Yukon Beringia Interpretive Centre. The Centre displays Ice Age artifacts, including a cast of the largest woolly mammoth skeleton ever recovered.

DC 885.8 (1473.1 km) **F 602.2** (969.1 km) Yukon Transportation Museum features exhibits on all forms of transportation in the North (see Attractions in the WHITEHORSE section for more details). A mural on the front of the museum depicts the methods of transportation used in construction of the Alaska Highway in 1942. The 16-by-60-foot/5-by-8-m mural was painted by members of the Yukon Art Society. Open mid-May to mid-September. Admission fee. (Get your Yukon Gold Explorer's Passport stamped here.)

Cairns in front of the museum commemorate 18 years of service on the Alaska Highway (1946–64) by the Corps of Royal Canadian Engineers. Near this site, the U.S. Army officially handed over the Alaska Highway to the Canadian Army on April 1, 1946.

DC 886.2 (1473.8 km) **F 601.8** (968.5 km) Turnoff to east for Whitehorse International Airport. Built for and used by both U.S. and Canadian forces during WWII. Watch for the DC–3 weathervane (see Attractions in the WHITEHORSE section for details).

DC 887.4 (1475.6 km) **F 600.6** (966.5 km) Second (and last) exit northbound for Whitehorse. North access road to Whitehorse (exit east) is via Two-Mile Hill and 4th Avenue. Access to private RV park. At Mile 1.2/1.9 km on this access road is Qwanlin Mall.

Alaska Highway log continues on page 145. Description of Whitehorse follows.

Whitehorse

Historic Milepost 918. Located on the upper reaches of the Yukon River in Canada's subarctic at latitude 61°N. Whitehorse is 100 miles/160 km from Haines Junction; 109 miles/175 km from Skagway, AK; 250 miles/241 km from Haines, AK; and 396 miles/637 km from Tok, AK. **Population:** 22,911. **Emergency Services:** RCMP, Fire Department, Ambulance, Hospital, phone 911.

Visitor Information: Tourism Yukon's

Visitor Reception Centre is located in the centre of Whitehorse, next to the Yukon Territorial Government Building, on 2nd Avenue. This exciting new (1996) building houses a multi-image slide presentation on Yukon national parks and historical sites, and a large display area that includes Whitehorse and surrounding attractions. Visitor guides and touch-screen terminals are available. Obtain daily, updated information on accommodations, weather and road conditions, or use the touch-screen terminals to print out information on attractions, restaurants or events in Whitehorse. The centre is open mid-May to mid-September; phone (403) 667-2915. Or contact Tourism Yukon, Box 2703, Whitehorse, YT Y1A 2C6; phone (403) 667-5340; fax (403) 667-3546; Internet www.parallel.ca/Yukon.

The city of Whitehorse offers year-round visitor information through their Tourism Coordinator; phone (403) 668-8687.

Through the year 2000, Whitehorse is celebrating many gold rush anniversaries and their Anniversary Coordinator can be reached at (403) 668-8665. Phone either of these numbers for information or write: Toursim Coordinator, City of Whitehorse, 2121 Second Avenue, Whitehorse, YT Y1A 1C2. Access up-to-date information on events, accommodations and attractions on the City of Whitehorse Internet web page at www.City.Whitehorse.YK.ca.

Whitehorse Visitor Radio, CKYN "Yukon

WHITEHORSE ADVERTISERS

A Taste of '98 Yukon River
  Tours ....Ph. (403) 633-4767
Airline Inn Hotel ....Across from airport
Alaska Direct
  Busline, Inc. ....Ph. (403) 668-4833
Alkan Air ....Ph.(403) 668-2107
Anne Doyles Art
  Studio ....Corner 2nd & Lambert
Bonanza Inn ....Ph. (403) 668-4545
Broke BookWorms, The ....210B Ogilvie St.
Budget Car and
  Truck Rental ....Ph. (403) 667-6200
Canada Campers ....Ph. 1-800-461-7368
Casey's Bed & Breakfast ....Ph. (403) 668-7481
City of Whitehorse............Ph. (403) 668-8665
C.J. Trail Rides & D Bar Diamond
  Children's Farm..........Ph. (403) 393-1400
Coffee • Tea & Spice ....Qwanlin Mall
Dairy Queen.......................2nd Ave. at Elliott
Edgewater Hotel, The .....Ph. (403) 667-2572
Fireweed R.V. Services ....Ph. (403) 668-5046
Four Seasons
  Bed & Breakfast ....Ph. (403) 667-2161
4th Ave Petro-Canada......Ph.(403) 667-4003
Frantic Follies ......Westmark Whitehorse Hotel
Gold Rush Inn (Best Western)......411 Main St.
Happy Daze R.V. Center...Ph. (403) 667-7069
Hawkins House Bed &
  Breakfast ....Ph. (403) 668-7638
Heart's Content B&B.......Ph. (403) 667-4972
Hi-Country R.V. Park......Mile 913.4 Alaska Hwy.
High Country Inn ....Ph. 1-800-554-4471
Klondike Recreational
  Rentals Ltd. ....Ph. (403) 668-2200
Klondike Rib &
  Salmon BBQ ....Ph. (403) 667-7554
Learning to Fly Fly Shop.......Ph. (403) 668-FLYS
Listers Rentals Ltd. ....Ph. (403) 668-2776
MacKenzie's RV Park......Km 1484 Alaska Hwy.
Mac's Fireweed Books ....203 Main St.
Midnight Sun Gallery & Gifts.....205C Main St.
Murdoch's ....207 Main St.
Norcan Car and
  Truck Rentals..............Ph. (403) 668-2137

North West Company
  Trading Post, The.........Next to bus depot
Pizza Hut ....Ph. (403) 667-6766
Pot O' Gold ....4th Ave. & Wood
Qwanlin Mall, The.............4th Ave. & Ogilvie
Regina Hotel............................102 Wood St.
Roadhouse Inn ....Ph. (403) 667-2594
Sky High Wilderness
  Ranches ....Ph. (403) 667-4321
Special Discoveries. ....Ph. (403) 667-6765
SS *Klondike* National
  Historic Site.................Beside Yukon River
Stop In Family Hotel........Ph. (403) 668-5558
Stratford Motel ....Ph. (403) 667-4243
Takhini Hot Springs ....Takhini Hot Springs Rd.
Tamarack Welding &
  The Spring Shop......Mile 922 Alaska Hwy.
Three Beans
  Natural Foods.............Ph. (403) 668-4908
Totem Oil......................Ph. 1-800-661-0550
Town & Mountain
  Hotel, The ....Ph. (403) 668-7644
Trail of '98 RV Park..........Ph. (403) 668-3768
Trails North Car & Truck
  Stop Ltd. ....Mile 922 Alaska Hwy.
Up North Bed &
  Breakfast ....Ph. (403) 667-7905
Westmark Klondike Inn......Ph. 1-800-544-0970
Westmark Whitehorse....Ph. 1-800-544-0970
Whitehorse Chamber of
  Commerce ....Ph. (403) 667-7545
Whitehorse Performance
  Centre ....4th Ave. at Jarvis
Whitehorse Shell ....Mile 913 Alaska Hwy.
White Pass & Yukon
  Route ....Ph. (403) 668-RAIL
Yukon Inn, The.........................4220 4th Ave.
Yukon Native
  Products ....Across from McDonalds
Yukon Radiator....................108 Industrial Rd.
Yukon Tire Centre Ltd. ......107 Industrial Rd.
Yukon Transportation
  Museum ....Ph. (403) 668-4792

ALASKA HIGHWAY • Whitehorse

Whitehorse Welcomes You During the Year of Transportation

Whitehorse celebrates Canada Day (July 1) with a parade. (© Beth Davidow)

Gold" 96.1 FM, broadcasts current events as well as heritage and Gold Rush anniversary event information. Tune in at the City Limits for approximately 30 minutes of driving and listening before reaching the downtown Visitor Reception Centre.

SS *Klondike* greets the visitor arriving in Whitehorse from the South. This site, operated by Parks Canada, has a visitor centre with helpful information for tourists.

Elevation: 2,305 feet/703m. **Climate:** Wide variations are the theme here with no two winters alike. The lowest recorded temperature is -62°F/-52°C and the warmest 94°F/35°C. Mean temperature for month of January is -6°F/-21°C and for July 57°F/14°C. Annual precipitation is 10.3 inches, equal parts snow and rain. On June 21 Whitehorse enjoys 19 hours, 11 minutes of daylight and on Dec. 21 only 5 hours, 37 minutes. **Radio:** CFWH 570, CBC network with repeaters throughout territory; CBC Montreal; CKRW 610, local; CKYN-FM 96.1, summer visitor information station, "Yukon Gold," broadcasts mid-May to mid-September; CHON-FM 98.1. **Television:** CBC–TV live, colour via ANIK satellite, Canadian network; WHTV, NADR (First Nation issues), local cable; CanCom stations via satellite, many channels. **Newspapers:** *Whitehorse Star* (weekdays); *Yukon News* (twice-weekly).

Private Aircraft: Whitehorse International Airport, 3 runways; has approach over city and an abrupt escarpment; elev. 2,305 feet/703m; main runway length 7,200 feet/2,195m; surfaced; fuel 80, 100, jet fuel available. Customs clearance available.

Floatplane base on Schwatka Lake above Whitehorse Dam (take the South Access Road from Alaska Highway and turn on road by the railroad tracks).

DESCRIPTION

Whitehorse has been the capital of Yukon Territory since 1953, and serves as the centre for transportation, communications and supplies for Yukon Territory and the Northwest Territories.

The downtown business section of Whitehorse lies on the west bank of the Yukon River. The Riverdale subdivision is on the east side. The low mountains rising behind Riverdale are dominated by Canyon Mountain, known locally as Grey Mountain. Wolf Creek, Hillcrest and Granger subdivisions lie south of the city; McIntyre subdivision is to the west; and Porter Creek, Takhini and Crestview subdivisions are north of the city. The Takhini area is the location of the Yukon College campus.

Downtown Whitehorse is flat and marked at its western limit by a rising escarpment dominated by the Whitehorse International Airport. Originally a woodcutter's lot, the airstrip was first cleared in 1920 to accommodate 4 U.S. Army planes on a test flight from New York to Nome. Access to the city is by Two-Mile Hill from the north and by Robert Service Way (South Access Road) from the south; both connect with the Alaska Highway.

In 1974, the city limits of Whitehorse were expanded from the original 2.7 square miles/6.9 square kilometres to 162 square miles/421 square kilometres making Whitehorse at one time the largest metropolitan area in Canada. More than two-thirds of the population of Yukon Territory live in the city. Whitehorse is the hub of a network of about 2,664 miles/4,287 km of all-weather roads serving Yukon Territory.

HISTORY, ECONOMY

When the White Pass & Yukon Route railway was completed in July 1900, connecting Skagway with the Yukon River, Whitehorse came into being as the northern terminus. Here the famed river steamers connected the railhead to Dawson City, and some of these boats made the trip all the way to St. Michael, a small outfitting point on Alaska's Bering Sea coast.

Klondike stampeders landed at Whitehorse to dry out and repack their supplies after running the famous Whitehorse Rapids. (The name Whitehorse was in common use by the late 1800s; it is believed that the first miners in the area thought that the foaming rapids resembled white horses' manes and so named the river rapids.) The rapids are no longer visible since construction of the Yukon Energy Corporation's hydroelectric dam on the river. This dam created man-made Schwatka Lake, named in honour of U.S. Army Lt. Frederick Schwatka, who named many of the points along the Yukon River during his 1883 exploration of the region.

The gold rush brought stampeders and the railroad. The community grew as a transportation centre and trans-shipment point for freight from the Skagway–Whitehorse railroad and the stern-wheelers plying the Yukon River to Dawson City. The river was the only highway until WWII, when military expediency built the Alaska Highway in 1942.

Whitehorse was headquarters for the western sector during construction of the Alaska Highway. Fort St. John was headquarters for the eastern sector. Both were the largest construction camps along the highway.

The first survey parties of U.S. Army engineers reached Whitehorse in April of 1942. By the end of August, they had constructed a pioneer road from Whitehorse west to White River, largely by following an existing winter trail between Whitehorse and Kluane Lake. November brought the final breakthrough on the western end of the highway, marking completion of the pioneer road.

During the height of the construction of the Alaska Highway, thousands of American military and civilian workers were employed in the Canadian North. It was the second boom period for Whitehorse.

There was an economic lull following the war, but the new highway was then opened to civilian travel, encouraging new development. Mineral exploration and the development of new mines had a profound effect on the economy of the region, as did the steady growth of tourism. The Whitehorse Copper Mine, located a few miles south of the city in the historic Whitehorse copper belt, is now closed. The Grum Mine site north of Faro produced lead, silver and zinc concentrates for Cyprus–Anvil (1969–1982) and Curragh Resources (1986–1992). It was reopened in 1994 by Anvil Range Mining Corp. (mine tours available). Gold mining activity has been taking place southwest of Whitehorse in the last few years. Stop by the Yukon Chamber of Mines office on Main Street for information on mining and rockhounding in Yukon Territory. The Chamber of Mines log building also houses a mineral display.

Because of its accessibility, Whitehorse became capital of the Yukon Territory (replacing Dawson City in that role) on March 31, 1953.

Bridges built along the highway to Dawson City, after Whitehorse became capital of the territory, were too low to accommodate the old river steamers, and by 1955 all steamers had been beached. After her last run in 1960, the SS *Keno* was berthed on the riverbank in Dawson City where she became a national historic site in 1962. The SS *Klondike* was moved through the streets of Whitehorse in 1966 to its final resting place as a riverboat museum beside the Robert Campbell bridge.

ACCOMMODATIONS/VISITOR SERVICES

Whitehorse offers 22 hotels and motels for a total of about 840 rooms. Several hotels include conference facilities; most have cocktail lounges, licensed dining rooms and taverns. Rates range from $60 to $150 for a double room with bath. Bed-and-breakfast accommodations are also available.

The city has 31 restaurants downtown and in surrounding residential subdivisions that serve meals ranging from French cuisine to fast food; 14 have liquor licenses.

Whitehorse has a downtown shopping district stretching 6 blocks along Main Street. The Qwanlin Mall at 4th Avenue and Ogilvie has a supermarket and a variety of shops. The Yukon Centre Mall on 2nd Avenue has a liquor store. The Riverdale Mall is located on the east side of the river in the Riverdale subdivision. Another shopping mall is located in the Porter Creek subdivision north of the city on the Alaska Highway.

In addition to numerous supermarkets, garages and service stations, there are churches, movie houses, beauty salons and a covered swimming pool. Whitehorse also has several banks with automatic teller machines. (Many businesses in Whitehorse participate in the Fair Exchange Program, which guarantees an exchange rate within 4 percent of the bank rate set once a week on Mondays. Participating businesses display the Fair Exchange logo.)

NOTE: There is no central post office in Whitehorse. Postal services are available in Qwanlin Mall at Coffee • Tea & Spice; The Hougen Centre on Main Street (lower floor below Shoppers Drugs); and in Riverdale and Porter Creek subdivisions. Stamps are available at several locations. General delivery pickup at corner of 3rd Avenue and Wood Street.

Specialty stores include gold nugget and ivory shops where distinctive jewelry is manufactured, and Indian craft shops specializing in moose hide jackets, parkas, vests, moccasins, slippers, mukluks and gauntlets. Inuit and Indian handicrafts from Canada's Arctic regions are featured in some stores.

Whitehorse Chamber of Commerce businesses welcome you to Whitehorse! Our Chamber of Commerce members invite you to peruse our joint full-page color ad for great savings! Advertisers on this page are offering you, our visitor, great discounts on their product or services. Write or stop by the Chamber for your free discount coupon book. [ADVERTISEMENT]

Hawkins House Bed & Breakfast. Enjoy the Yukon's most luxurious accommodations in our Victorian home in downtown Whitehorse. Turn-of-the-century charm includes a grand foyer, guest parlor, high ceilings, balconies, hardwood floors, and historical and cultural themes. Rooms feature private bath, telephone, cable TV and VCR, bar sink and fridge, quality beds, soundproofing and a great view of the downtown and surrounding mountains. Jacuzzis® and claw foot tub available. Enjoy a 5-minute walk to Main Street shops and restaurants. Non-smoking. Open year-round. Français, Deutsch. Phone (403) 668-7638, fax (403) 668-7632, or write 303 Hawkins St., Whitehorse, YT, Canada Y1A 1X5. [ADVERTISEMENT]

High Country Inn. During your stay in Whitehorse, relax and enjoy real northern hospitality at the High Country Inn. We offer 100 rooms with a wide choice of comfortable, affordable lodging. Select from economical single rooms to deluxe suites, complete with kitchen. Treat yourself to breakfast in the "Great North Pancake House," or dine outdoors and enjoy cocktails on the patio of our famous "Yukon Mining Co." We are located downtown with great views, elevators, guest laundry, exercise room, and the nicest lobby and lounge in Whitehorse. Just good old-fashioned quality at surprisingly affordable prices. AAA approved (3 stars), Senior discounts. (Reservations recommended) Phone 1-800-554-4471 or (403) 667-4471, fax (403) 667-6457. E-mail: highcinn@yknet.yk.ca — Web site: http://tourYukon.com/HCHOME/HTM (see our display advertisement). [ADVERTISEMENT]

Klondike Rib & Salmon BBQ. Located in 2 of the oldest buildings in Whitehorse at Second and Steele, across from the Frantic Follies and Westmark Hotel. A delicious salmon BBQ, and Texas BBQ ribs, English-style fish and chips, and specialty northern food like bison burgers, caribou, musk-ox and fresh bannock. Just some of the mouth-watering fare served in a unique historic Klondike Airways Building with historical exhibits as part of the fascinating decor. (403) 667-7554. [ADVERTISEMENT]

There is a private RV park on Two-Mile Hill and on 2nd Avenue downtown. Tent camping only is available at Robert Service Park on Robert Service Way (South Access Road). There are 4 private campgrounds south of downtown Whitehorse on the Alaska Highway (see **Mileposts DC 873.5, 881, 882.9** and **883.7** in the highway log), and 1 private campground 6 miles/9.6 km north of the city on the highway (see **Milepost DC 891.9**). Wolf Creek Yukon government campground is 7 miles/11 km south of Whitehorse on the Alaska Highway. A private campground and Yukon government campground are located at Marsh Lake.

Welcome to the Yukon!

Yukon residents depend on Totem Oil every day for the finest fuel, diesel, automobile repair and convenience store items. Visitors traveling to the Yukon will discover the same level of service and quality throughout the Yukon Territory. Our 22 Totem Oil service stations will help energize your northern adventure.

Call 1-800-661-0550

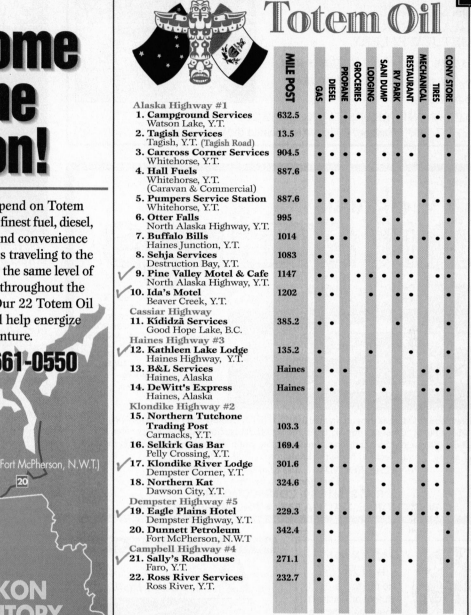

Totem Oil

	MILE POST	GAS	DIESEL	PROPANE	GROCERIES	LODGING	SANI DUMP	RV PARK	RESTAURANT	MECHANICAL	TIRES	CONV STORE
Alaska Highway #1												
1. **Campground Services** Watson Lake, Y.T.	632.5	●	●	●								●
2. **Tagish Services** Tagish, Y.T. (Tagish Road)	13.5	●	●								●	●
3. **Carcross Corner Services** Whitehorse, Y.T.	904.5	●	●	●	●			●	●			●
4. **Hall Fuels** Whitehorse, Y.T. (Caravan & Commercial)	887.6	●	●	●						●	●	
5. **Pumpers Service Station** Whitehorse, Y.T.	887.6	●	●	●	●					●	●	●
6. **Otter Falls** North Alaska Highway, Y.T.	995	●	●		●	●			●			●
7. **Buffalo Bills** Haines Junction, Y.T.	1014	●	●					●			●	●
8. **Sehja Services** Destruction Bay, Y.T.	1083	●	●							●	●	●
✓ 9. **Pine Valley Motel & Cafe** North Alaska Highway, Y.T.	1147	●	●		●	●			●		●	●
✓ 10. **Ida's Motel** Beaver Creek, Y.T.	1202	●	●			●						●
Cassiar Highway												
11. **Kídidzà Services** Good Hope Lake, B.C.	385.2	●	●									
Haines Highway #3												
✓ 12. **Kathleen Lake Lodge** Haines Highway, Y.T.	135.2	●				●			●			
13. **B&L Services** Haines, Alaska	Haines	●	●							●	●	●
14. **DeWitt's Express** Haines, Alaska	Haines							●			●	●
Klondike Highway #2												
15. **Northern Tutchone Trading Post** Carmacks, Y.T.	103.3	●	●	●	●					●	●	●
16. **Selkirk Gas Bar** Pelly Crossing, Y.T.	169.4	●	●	●				●				
✓ 17. **Klondike River Lodge** Dempster Corner, Y.T.	301.6	●	●	●	●	●		●	●	●	●	●
18. **Northern Kat** Dawson City, Y.T.	324.6	●	●								●	●
Dempster Highway #5												
✓ 19. **Eagle Plains Hotel** Dempster Highway, Y.T.	229.3	●	●		●	●		●	●	●	●	●
20. **Dunnett Petroleum** Fort McPherson, N.W.T	342.4	●	●									
Campbell Highway #4												
✓ 21. **Sally's Roadhouse** Faro, Y.T.	271.1	●	●			●	●		●			
22. **Ross River Services** Ross River, Y.T.	232.7	●	●		●							

Totem Oil
FROM THE WESTERN PIONEER FAMILY OF SERVICE COMPANIES.

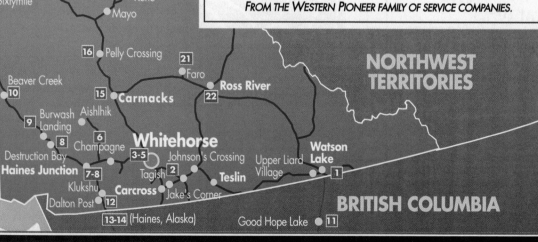

Old Crow

(Fort McPherson, N.W.T.)

20

19

YUKON TERRITORY

ALASKA

Dawson City — 18 / 17

Elsa
Keno
Mayo
Sixtymile

16 Pelly Crossing

21 Faro

22 Ross River

15 Carmacks

Beaver Creek — 10

Burwash Landing — 9
Aishlhik
8
6 Champagne
Destruction Bay
Haines Junction — 7-8

Whitehorse
3-5
Johnson's Crossing
2
Tagish
Teslin
Klukshu
12 Carcross
Jake's Corner
Dalton Post

Upper Liard Village
Watson Lake
1

NORTHWEST TERRITORIES

BRITISH COLUMBIA

13-14 (Haines, Alaska)
Good Hope Lake ● 11

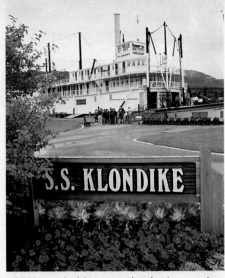

This grand old stern-wheeler is a major attraction in Whitehorse. (Earl L. Brown, staff)

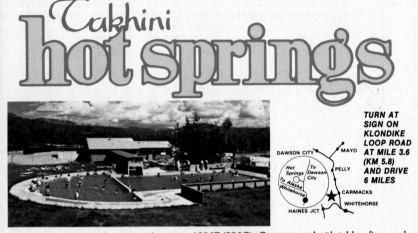
Takhini Hot Springs on the Klondike Loop is also a popular camping spot (1/2-hour drive from Whitehorse). ▲

IMPORTANT: RV caravans should contact private campground operators well in advance of arrival regarding camping arrangements. At our press time, there was no designated RV parking in downtown Whitehorse.

TRANSPORTATION

Air: Service by Canadian Airlines International and Alkan Air daily to major cities and Yukon communities. Air North to Dawson City, Old Crow, Jueau and Fairbanks, AK. (Air North offers a 21-day Klondike Explorer's Pass between Juneau, Old Crow, Fairbanks, Whitehorse and Dawson City). Royal Airlines and N.W.T. Air offer summer service with connections to major Canadian and U.S. cities. Whitehorse International Airport is reach from the Alaska Highway.

Seaplane dock on Schwatka Lake just above the Whitehorse Dam (take South Access Road, renamed the Robert Service Way in 1996, from Alaska Highway and turn right on road by the railroad tracks to reach the base). Flightseeing tours available.

Trans North Air offers helicopter sightseeing tours from the airport.

Bus: Greyhound service to Watson Lake, Dawson Creek, Prince George and other points in southern Canada. Norline serves Mayo and Dawson City. Alaska–Yukon

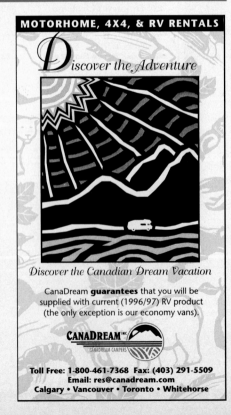

Motorcoaches serves Skagway and Haines, phone 1-800-288-1305 or contact office at 4th Avenue Residence. North West Stage Lines to Haines Junction, Beaver Creek, Faro, Carmacks and Ross River. Alaska Direct Busline to Skagway, Dawson City, Anchorage and Fairbanks; phone (403) 668-4833.

Whitehorse Transit offers downtown and rural service. Planned for 1997, an attractions bus that picks up at hotels, motels, campgrounds and attractions; round-trip service with off/on privileges.

Railroad: Arrangements for WhitePass & Yukon Route rail trips may be made by phoning WP&YR in Whitehorse at (403) 668-RAIL, or contacting local travel agencies (see WHITE PASS & YUKON ROUTE section).

Taxi: 5 taxi companies operate in Whitehorse.

Car, Truck, Motorhome and Camper Rentals: Several local and national agencies are located in Whitehorse.

ATTRACTIONS

The **SS** *Klondike* **National Historic Site** is hard to miss. This grand old stern-wheeler sits beside the Yukon River near the Robert Campbell bridge. After carrying cargo and passengers between Whitehorse and Dawson City from 1937 until the 1950s, the SS *Klondike* went into permanent retirement on the bank of the Yukon River, donated to the people of Canada by the White Pass & Yukon Route. Refurbished by Parks Canada, the stern-wheeler is open to the public. Built by British Yukon Navigation Co., the SS *Klondike* is 210 feet/64m long and 41.9 feet/12.5m wide. Visitor information centre, gift shop and public parking at the site. A film on the history of riverboats is shown continuously in a tent theatre adjacent the boat. Tours of the stern-wheeler leave on the half hour. The 20-minute film is shown prior to each tour. Admission fee charged. Large groups are advised to book tours in advance. Contact Canadian Identity, 300 Main St., Room 105, Whitehorse, YT Y1A 2B5; phone (403) 667-3970, fax (403) 668-3769. The SS *Klondike* visitor centre and stern-wheeler are open from mid-May to mid-September.

Live Shows. Frantic Follies, a very popular vaudeville stage show, is held nightly June through mid-September, at the Westmark Whitehorse Hotel. 1997 marks the

Whitehorse became capital of Yukon Territory on March 31, 1953.

28th season for this 1½-hour show which features a chorus line, rousing music and hilarious skits from Robert W. Service ballads. Visitors are advised to get tickets in advance; available at the box office in the Westmark or phone (403) 668-2042.

The Canteen Show is a light-hearted revue of 1940s Whitehorse and the construction of the Alaska Highway. Inquire locally for location and times.

Special Events. Whitehorse has a full schedule of events throughout 1997. Spring visitors can attend the Rotary Music Festival (April 13–14); the Celebration of Swans (trumpeter and tundra) returning to M'Clintock Bay (April 13–20); the Square Dance Jamboree (May 23–25); and the Society of Yukon Artists of Native Ancestry Festival (May 30–31). The Footsteps in Time exhibition will be at the Yukon Arts Centre Gallery from May 22 throughout the summer.

Also in summer is the National Aboriginal Day Festivities, June 21. Canada Day kicks off July, with a parade and celebrations at Rotary Peace Park. Then on July 10, Whitehorse welcomes the "Ton of Gold" arriving from Dawson City on its way to Seattle, WA. (This gold rush centennial event commemorates the arrival of the first shipment of gold from the Klondike to Seattle.) The Ton of Gold–Ton of Fun Festival takes place at Rotary Park July 11–12. The Yukon Sourdough Rendezvous Gold Rush Bathtub Race marks Discovery Day Weekend, Aug. 16, at Rotary Park. Agricultural exhibits take over the park on Aug. 23–24, when the Klondyke Harvest Fair is under way.

Take a hike with the Yukon Conservation Society (YCS). Every summer the society offers free guided nature walks, ranging in difficulty from easy to strenuous, from July to late August. Trips are 1 to 6 hours in length and informative guides explain the local flora, fauna, geology and history along the trails. The YCS conducts interpretive walks at Canyon City (see **Milepost DC 881.7**) during the summer on a regular basis, including evenings and weekends. For a schedule of hikes, contact the Yukon Conservation Society, at 302 Hawkins St.; phone (403) 668-5678.

World's largest weathervane. Located in front of the Whitehorse International Airport is the world's largest weathervane—a Douglas DC-3. This vintage plane (registration number CF–CPY) flew for several Yukon airlines from 1946 until 1970, when it blew an engine during takeoff. The plane was restored by Joe Muff with the help of the Yukon Flying Club and the Whitehorse community. It is now owned and managed by the Yukon Transportation Museum. The restored plane was mounted on a rotating pedestal in 1981 and now acts as a weathervane, pointing its nose into the wind.

The Yukon Transportation Museum, located on the Alaska Highway adjacent to the Whitehorse Airport (see **Milepost DC 885.8**), features exhibits on all forms of transportation in the North. Displays inside include the full-size replica of the *Queen of the Yukon* Ryan monoplane, sister ship to Lindbergh's *Spirit of St. Louis;* railway rolling stock; Alaska Highway vintage vehicles, dogsleds and stagecoaches. Also featured are the Chilkoot Trail, the Canol Highway and bush pilots of the North. The museum includes video theatres and a gift shop. Plenty of parking. Admission charged. Open daily, 9 A.M. to 6 P.M., mid-May to mid-September. Write P.O. Box 5867, Whitehorse, YT Y1A 5L6 or phone (403) 668-4792, fax 633-5547.

Historical walking tours of Whitehorse are conducted by the Yukon Historical & Museums Association. Tour guides wear period costumes for these walks that take in the city's heritage buildings. Meet at the Donnenworth House, 3126 3rd Ave.; phone 667-4704. Fee charged. There are tours Monday through Saturday from June to the end of August. For self-guided tours, *A Walking Tour of Yukon's Capital* or *Exploring Old*

Whitehorse are available from local stores or from the Yukon Historical & Museums Assoc., Box 4357, Whitehorse, YT Y1A 3T5.

MacBride Museum, on 1st Avenue between Steele and Wood streets, showcases Yukon's cultural and natural history in 4 indoor galleries and outdoor displays. The Museum Shop features books, local arts and crafts and northern souvenirs. Admission charged. Open daily late-May to Labour Day. Phone (403) 667-2709, fax 633-6607 or write Box 4037, Whitehorse, YT Y1A 3S9.

Yukon Arts Centre on Range Road hosts a variety of special events. (Earl L. Brown, staff)

Old Log Church Museum, 1 block off Main on Elliott at 3rd. Built in 1900 by Rev. R.J. Bowen for the Church of England, this recently restored log church and rectory have been declared the first territorial historic sites in the Yukon. The museum, located in the log church, displays relics of pioneer northern missions. Open to the public June to September; admission fee. Anglican (Episcopal) services are held Sundays at 10:30 A.M.

Yukon Government Building, 2nd Avenue and Hawkins, open 9 A.M. to 5 P.M. Administrative and Legislative headquarters of Yukon Territory, the building contains some notable artworks. On the main floor mall is an acrylic resin mural, 120 feet/37m long, which portrays the historical evolution of the Yukon. The 24 panels, each measuring 4 by 5 feet/1.2 by 1.5m, highlight events such as the arrival of Sir John Franklin at Herschel Island in 1825, the Klondike Gold Rush, and the coming of the automobile. The mural was created by Vancouver, BC, artist David MacLagen.

In the Legislative Chamber, an 18-by-12-foot/5-by-4m tapestry is an abstraction of the fireweed plant, Yukon's floral emblem. The Yukon Women's Tapestry, 5 panels each 7-by-13-feet/2-by-4m, hangs in the legislative library lounge. The wool panels portray the role of women in the development of the territory, depicting the 5 seasons of the North; spring, summer, autumn, winter and "survival," the cold gray season between winter and spring and fall and winter. Begun by the Whitehorse Branch of the Canadian Federation of Business and Professional Women in 1976 to mark International Women's Year, the wall hangings were stitched by some 2,500 Yukoners.

Yukon Gardens, located at the junction of the Alaska Highway and Robert Service Way (South Access Road), is the only formal northern botanical garden. The 22-acre site features more than 100,000 wild and domestic flowers; vegetables, herbs and fruits; scenic pathways and floral displays; a children's "Old MacDonald's farm"; gift shop; and fresh produce in summer. Open daily in summer. Admission charged.

C.J. Trail Rides and D Bar Diamond Children's Farm. Enjoy picturesque horseback rides through boreal forests and alpine meadows on our 1700-acre ranch. Guided 1-hour, 2-hour and 4-hour trails. (Overnight excursions available by advance booking.) Good wildlife and bird viewing opportunities, spectacular views of the Yukon River

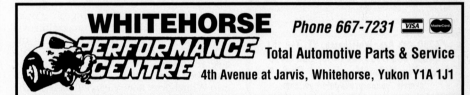
1897 - 1997

Discover Whitehorse – Transportation Hub of the Yukon
1997 - Celebrating The Year of Transportation & Transportation Routes

In 1897, stampeders and their guides navigated Miles Canyon and the White Horse rapids on their search for Klondike Gold.

One hundred years later, we welcome a new generation of stampeders to help us celebrate our transportation heritage. Modern day Whitehorse is built on transportation from the mighty sternwheelers that plied the Yukon River to the White Pass & Yukon Route Railway and to the creation of the Alaska Highway. Many exciting events and attractions are planned all year round to pay tribute to these and other modes of transportation.

Stake Your Claim at the Ton of Gold - Ton of Fun Festival!
July 10-13 Rotary Peace Park.

You will be taken back to the days of sternwheelers steaming and stampeders racing at this festival which celebrates the Year of Transportation and the Centennial Reenactment of the Ton of Gold voyage.

In July 1897, sixty-eight "Klondike Millionaires" arrived in Seattle, Washington from Dawson City on board the S.S. Portland with a Ton of Gold. With the arrival of the rich miners, news of the Gold Strike flashed around the world.

On July 10th, put on your Klondike attire and join the fun in welcoming the descendants of the "Klondike Millionaires" and their gold to Whitehorse (BBQ, entertainment & gold display). On July 11th (noon), help us send off these modern day "argonauts" in a parade of antique vehicles.

The festival continues from July 11-13 with a variety of exciting activities, themed to celebrate our gold rush and transportation history, including a transportation mini-theme park for kids; displays; artwork; crafts; entertainment including music, storytelling (transportation tales), drama; a film

festival and much more. There will also be events happening at other venues around the city such as the Transportation Museum.

Call the City's Anniversaries Office at 668-8665 for more information about this event and others throughout the summer.

We are proud to be the Yukon's major transportation hub and your host during the Year of Transportation.

For more information contact:
Anniversaries Coordinator
(MP-97) City of Whitehorse
2121 Second Avenue, Whitehorse
Yukon Y1A 1C2
Ph: (403) 668-8665
Fax: (403) 668-8664

Ask about the 1997 Whitehorse Calendar of Events & Attractions

Valley. Day rates and group discounts. Your host, Jim Dillabough, (403) 393-1400. Or write Box 4465, Whitehorse, Yukon Y1A 2R6. [ADVERTISEMENT]

A Taste of '98 Yukon River Tours. The best 3-hour river tour in the Yukon. Experience gold rush history first hand, and discover the abundant wildlife of the Whitehorse area on our motorized steel pontoon river crafts. Our tours, as well as our unique craft, were designed to enhance your Yukon experience and the thrill of discovery. Just $36 per person (group rates available). Daily at 2 P.M. and 7 P.M. Phone (403) 633-4767. [ADVERTISEMENT]

Whitehorse Rapids Fishway. The fish ladder was built in 1959 to provide access for chinook (king) salmon and other species above the Yukon Energy Corporation hydroelectric dam. Displays installed and viewing area improved in 1992. Located at the end of Nisutlin Drive in the Riverdale suburb. Open daily, 9 A.M. to 5 P.M. from May 25 to July 1, 8 A.M. to 10 P.M. from July to September. Interpretive displays and viewing decks.

Mountain View Public Golf Course, located in Porter Creek subdivision on the Yukon River, is accessible via the Porter Creek exit off the Alaska Highway or from Range Road; 18 holes, grass greens; green fees. Midnight Sun Golf Tournament June 21, 1997.

Picnic in a park. Picnicking on a small island in the Yukon River, accessible via footbridge from 2nd Avenue, north of the railroad tracks. Picnic facilities are also available at Robert Service Campground, located on Robert Service Way (South Access Road) into Whitehorse. Rotary Peace Park is central to downtown and a popular picnic spot.

Whitehorse Public Library, part of the Yukon Government Building on 2nd Avenue, has a room with art displays and books about the Yukon and the gold rush. It features a large double stone and copper fireplace, comfortable chairs, tables and helpful staff. Open noon to 9 P.M. weekdays, 10 A.M.

to 6 P.M. Saturday, 1 to 9 P.M. Sunday and closed holidays. Phone (403) 667-5239

Yukon Archives is located adjacent Yukon College at Yukon Place. The archives was established in 1972 to acquire, preserve and make available the documented history of the Yukon. The holdings, dating from 1845, include government records, private manuscripts, corporate records, photographs, maps, newspapers (most are on microfilm), sound recordings, university theses, books, pamphlets and periodicals. Visitors are welcome. Phone (403) 667-5321 for hours, or write Box 2703, Whitehorse, YT Y1A 2C6, for more information.

Boat Tours. Yukon River tours are offered by A Taste of '98 Yukon River Tours. The 3-hour tours depart from near the old WP&YR train depot in downtown Whitehorse. The MV *Youcon Kat,* docked across from the MacBride Museum, offers 2 1/2-hour trips down the Yukon. Tours of scenic Miles Canyon, aboard the MV *Schwatka,* depart from the dock on Schwatka Lake. Miles Canyon is accessible by road: take Schwatka Lake Road off Robert Service Way (South Access Road) into Whitehorse, or turn off the Alaska Highway (see **Milepost DC 881.7**); follow signs.

Day trips from Whitehorse. Marsh Lake, 24 miles/39 km south of Whitehorse on the Alaska Highway, and Takhini Hot Springs, 17 miles/27 km north of town via the Alaska and Klondike highways, are within easy driving distance of Whitehorse. The Yukon Government Marsh Lake Recreation Site, at Army Beach on Marsh Lake, a scenic 30-minute drive from city centre, offers an excellent day-use area and campgound. In the winter, trails originating from this recreation site are used for cross-country skiing and snowmobiling. In spring, this is a popular swan migration viewing area. "Swan Haven" viewing site is equipped with binoculars. Lakeview Resort at Marsh Lake offers boat rentals. Takhini Hot Springs offers swimming, horseback riding and camping.   ▲

Longer trips (which you may want to extend to an overnight) are to Atlin, about 2 1/2 hours by car, and Skagway, 3 hours by car. Skagway is an old gold rush town and shouldn't be missed during the Klondike Gold Rush Centennial. It is a port of call for both the Alaska state ferries and cruise ships. Skagway is also home to the famed White Pass & Yukon Route Railway, said to be the most scenic railway in the world as it climbs through beautiful mountain terrain to White Pass summit. Book ahead for the trip. Complete your Skagway visit with a trip to Dyea, a short drive from downtown, to see the start of the Chilkoot Trail and a gold rush graveyard. Atlin, which also dates from 1898, is known for its spectacular scenery. Visitors heading for Skagway should call ahead for accommodations if they expect to overnight. You may make a circle tour, driving down to Skagway then turning off onto the Tagish Road on your way back and continuing on to Atlin via the Atlin Road.

Rockhounding and Mining. A wide variety of minerals can be found in the Whitehorse area. Sources of information for rock hounds and gold panners include the Yukon Rock Shop, at the junction of the Alaska Highway and Klondike Highway 2 (Carcross Road), which has mineral samples, gold pans and nuggets; the Yukon Chamber of Mines on Main Street, which has mineral displays and information on rockhounding and mining in the Yukon; and Murdoch's gem shop on Main Street, which displays gold nugget jewellery and gold rush artifacts and photos.

The following rockhounding location is suggested by Fred Dorward of the Whitehorse Gem & Mineral Club (26 Sunset Dr. N., Whitehorse, YT Y1A 4M8). Drive north on the Alaska Highway to the Fish Lake Road turnoff (**Milepost DC 889.4**), located 2 miles/3.2 km from the north entrance to Whitehorse. About 0.5 mile/0.8 km in on Fish Lake Road, park and walk across McIntyre Creek to the old Copper King mine workings. Excellent but small specimens of brown garnet, also serpentine. *IMPORTANT: Rock hounds should exercise extreme caution when exploring. Do not enter old mine workings. Please respect No Trespassing signs.*

Canoe, Raft or Boat to Dawson City. Canoe rentals by the day, week or month, and guide services are available in Whitehorse. From the Yukon River's outlet at Marsh Lake south of Whitehorse to the Alaska border it is 530 river miles/853 km; from Whitehorse to Dawson City it is 410 river miles/660 km. There is a boat launch at Rotary Peace Park, behind the Yukon Government Bldg. You may also launch at Deep Creek Campground on Lake Laberge. Contact Up North Canoe Rentals, phone (403) 667-7905.

NOTE: Before leaving on any river or other wilderness trip, for your own protection, report your plans and itinerary to the RCMP. Be guided by the advice in government publications regarding travel on the Yukon's rivers and lakes. Do not attempt the Five Finger Rapids on the Yukon

River without qualified advice.

For more information on wilderness travel, contact Tourism Yukon office, located between 2nd and 3rd on Hawkins; phone (403) 667-5340. Hikers planning to do the Chilkoot Trail should check with Parks Canada, in the Federal Building at 4th and Main; phone (403) 668-2116. A Chilkoot Trail fee is proposed for 1997.

Mount McIntyre Recreation Centre, 0.9 mile/1.5 km west of the Alaska Highway (see **Milepost DC 887.6**), has 70 kilometres of groomed cross-country ski trails (open for hiking, running and mountain biking in summer). Contact Whitehorse Cross-Country Ski Club, P.O. Box 4639, Whitehorse, YT Y1A 3Y7.

Sportsmen can obtain complete information on fishing and hunting in the Whitehorse area by writing Tourism Yukon, Box 2703, Whitehorse, YT Y1A 2C6. They will provide lists of guides and advise what licenses are required.

AREA FISHING: Fish for rainbow and coho salmon in the following lakes: **Hidden, Scout, Long, Jackson** and **McLean.** Inquire locally for directions. Nearby fly-in fishing lakes are accessible by charter plane; see advertisements in this section. **Yukon River,** fish for grayling below the dam and bridge. Fishing below the dam prohibited in August during the salmon run. ➥

Alaska Highway Log
(continued from page 129)
Distance* from Dawson Creek (DC) is followed by distance from Fairbanks (F). Original mileposts are indicated in the text as Historical Mile.
*Mileages from Dawson Creek are based on actual driving distance. Kilometres from Dawson Creek are based on physical kilometreposts. Please read Mileposts and Kilometreposts in the introduction for an explanation of how this highway is logged.

DC 887.4 (1475.6 km) **F 600.6** (966.5 km) First exit southbound for Whitehorse. North access road to Whitehorse (exit east) is via Two-Mile Hill and 4th Avenue.

DC 887.6 (1476 km) **F 600.4** (966.2 km) Turnoff to west on Hamilton Boulevard for Mount McIntyre Recreation Centre (0.9 mile/1.5 km); 70 kilometres of cross-country ski trails (summer hiking and biking), chalet for indoor waxing, curling and bonspiels. Truck weigh scales west side of highway.

DC 888.6 (1477.5 km) **F 599.4** (964.6 km) **Historical Mile 918.3.** Turnoff for

Kopper King restaurant, motel, grocery, gas and diesel.

Kopper King. See display ad this section.
DC 889.3 (1478.6 km) **F 598.7** (963.5 km) McIntyre Creek.

DC 889.4 (1478.8 km) **F 598.6** (963.3 km) Fish Lake Road to west. Located only 9.3 miles/15 km from Whitehorse, Fish Lake and adjacent Bonneville Lakes were the site of a Kwanlin Dun First Nations archaeology project documenting the long history of habitation in this area.

DC 890.1 (1479.9 km) **F 597.9** (962.2 km) Rabbit's Foot Canyon.

DC 890.5 (1480.6 km) **F 597.5** (961.6 km) Turnoff to Porter Creek to east.

DC 891 (1481.4 km) **F 597** (960.8 km) Porter Creek grocery.

DC 891.3 (1482 km) **F 596.7** (960.3 km) **Historical Mile 921,** laundromat, gas and other businesses.

DC 891.5 (1482.3 km) **F 596.5** (959.9 km) Clyde Wann Road and Porter Creek subdivision, a residential suburb of Whitehorse. Access to Range Road and Mountain View Golf Course (18 holes).

DC 891.6 (1482.4 km) **F 596.4** (959.8 km) **Historical Mile 922.** Trails North Car & Truck Stop, and Tamarack Welding and Spring Shop are located here.

DC 891.8 (1482.5 km) **F 596.2** (959.5 km) MacDonald Road to north; auto repair.

DC 891.9 (1484 km) **F 596.1** (959.3 km) **Historical Mile 922.5.** Access to MacKenzie's RV Park. Azure Road. ▲

DC 894.3 (1486.4 km) **F 593.7** (955.4 km) Turnoff east to Cousins dirt airstrip.

DC 894.5 (1486.7 km) **F 593.5** (955.1 km) Rest area to west with litter barrels, outhouses, information sign and pay phone.

DC 894.8 (1487.2 km) **F 593.2** (954.6 km) **Junction** with Klondike Highway 2 to Dawson City (see KLONDIKE LOOP section). Turn off on Klondike Highway 2 for Takhini Hot Springs (swimming, camping), 3.8 miles/6.1 km north. ▲

For Alaska-bound travelers, the highway

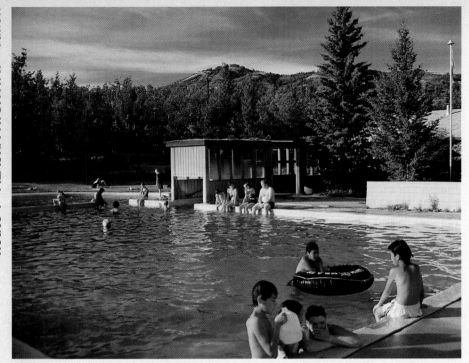

Swimming at Takhini Hot Springs, located 10 miles/16 km from the Alaska Highway on the Klondike Loop. (Earl L. Brown, staff)

now swings west.

DC 895.5 (1488.3 km) **F 592.5** (953.5 km) Turnoff to south for Haeckel Hill. Not recommended for hiking as this area is used for target practice.

DC 899.1 (1495.4 km) **F 588.9** (947.7 km) Turnoff for 3-mile/4.8-km loop drive on old section of Alaska Highway. Access to stocked lake. ◄━━►

DC 901.6 (1499.3 km) **F 586.4** (943.7 km) Turnoff to north to sled dog track.

DC 905.4 (1507.1 km) **F 582.6** (937.6 km) **Historic Milepost 937.** Camera viewpoint turnout to north with point of interest sign about the old Dawson Trail. There were at least 50 stopping places along the old Dawson Trail winter stagecoach route between Whitehorse and Dawson City, and from 1 to 3 roadhouses at each stop. At this point, the stagecoach route crossed the Takhini River. This route was discontinued in 1950 when the Mayo–Dawson Road (now Klondike Highway 2) was constructed.

DC 908.7 (1512.4 km) **F 579.3** (932.3 km) Private farm and windmill; good example of Yukon agriculture. Facilities for overnighting large livestock.

DC 914.7 (1525 km) **F 573.3** (922.6 km) Takhini River bridge. According to R. Coutts in *Yukon: Places & Names,* the name Takhini derives from the Tagish Indian *tahk,* meaning mosquito, and *heena,* meaning river.

DC 922.7 (1535 km) **F 565.3** (909.7 km) Watch for horses and other livestock grazing on open range near highway.

DC 924.5 (1538.4 km) **F 563.5** (906.4 km) Stoney Creek.

DC 924.7 (1538.7 km) **F 563.3** (906.5 km) View of Mount Bratnober.

DC 926 (1540.8 km) **F 562** (904.4 km) Turnout to south with litter barrels and information panels on Takhini River valley, Kusawa Lake, and the changing landscape and wildlife of the area. Point of interest sign about 1958 burns; more than 1.5 million acres/629,058 hectares of Yukon forest lands were burned in 1958. Campfires were responsible for most of these fires.

DC 927.3 (1542.9 km) **F 560.7** (902.3 km) Turnoff to south for viewpoint (1.9 miles/3 km) and Kusawa Lake Yukon government campground (15 miles/24 km). Access road to campground is a narrow, winding gravel road, very slippery when wet; not recommended for long trailers or heavily loaded vehicles. ▲

Day-use area with sandy beach, boat dock, kitchen shelter and drinking water;

boat launch 0.6 mile/1 km south. Campground at north end of lake has 48 sites, kitchen shelter, firepits and drinking water. Camping fee $8.

Kusawa Lake (formerly Arkell Lake), located in the Coast Mountains, is 45 miles/72 km long and averages 2 miles/3.2 km wide, with a shoreline perimeter of 125 miles/200 km. An access road to the lake was first constructed by the U.S. Army in 1945 to obtain bridge timbers for Alaska Highway construction.

Kusawa Lake, lake trout to 20 lbs., good to excellent; also grayling and pike. ━►

DC 936.8 (1558 km) **F 551.2** (887 km) Mendenhall River bridge. A tributary of the Takhini River, the Mendenhall River—like the Mendenhall Glacier outside Juneau, AK—was named for Thomas Corwin Mendenhall (1841–1924), superintendent of the U.S. Coast & Geodetic Survey.

DC 939.5 (1562.3 km) **F 548.5** (882.7 km) View of 3 prominent mountains northbound (from left to right): Mount Kelvin; center mountain unnamed; and Mount Bratnober.

DC 942.2 (1565.5 km) **F 545.8** (878.4 km) Native traditional camp interpretive site; fee charged, open May to October.

DC 942.8 (1567.6 km) **F 545.2** (877.4 km) NorthwesTel microwave tower to south.

DC 943.5 (1568.5 km) **F 544.5** (876.3 km) **Historic Milepost 974.** Historic sign and interpretive panel about **CHAMPAGNE.** Originally a camping spot on the Dalton Trail to Dawson City, established by Jack Dalton in the late 1800s. In 1902, Harlow "Shorty" Chambers built a roadhouse and trading post here, and it became a supply centre for first the Bullion Creek rush and later the Burwash Creek gold rush in 1904. The origin of the name is uncertain, although one account is that Dalton's men—after successfully negotiating a herd of cattle through the first part of the trail—celebrated here with a bottle of French champagne. Today, it is home to members of the Champagne–Aishihik Indian Band. There is an Indian cemetery on right westbound, just past the log cabin homes; a sign there reads: "This cemetery is not a tourist attraction. Please respect our privacy as we respect yours."

For northbound travelers, the Alaska Highway parallels the Dezadeash River (out of view to the south) from here west to Haines Junction. The Dezadeash Range is to the south and the Ruby Range to the north.

DC 944.4 (1570 km) **F 543.6** (874.8 km) Gravel turnout with litter barrel.

DC 955.8 (1588 km) **F 532.2** (856.5 km) First glimpse northbound of Kluane Range.

DC 957 (1590 km) **F 531** (854.5 km) **Historic Milepost 987.** Cracker Creek. Former roadhouse site on old stagecoach trail. Watch for "Old Man Mountain" on right northbound (the rocky crags look like a face, particularly in evening light).

DC 964.6 (1602.2 km) **F 523.4** (842.3 km) **Historical Mile 995.** Otter Falls Cutoff, junction with Aishihik Road. Gas station, store and camping to south, Aishihik Road turnoff to north. ▲

Otter Falls Cutoff. See display ad this section. ▲

Aishihik Road leads 84 miles/135 km north to the old Indian village of Aishihik (AYSH-ee-ak, means high place). Northern Canada Power Commission built a 32-megawatt dam at the foot of Aishihik Lake in 1976 to supply power principally to the mining industry. Flow hours for the Otter Falls hydro project are given at the start of Aishihik Road. This is a narrow, gravel road, maintained for summer travel only to the government campground. Aishihik Road is not recommended for large RVs and trailers.

There is a day-use recreation site at Otter Falls, 18.6 miles/30 km distance; picnic shelter, tables, outhouses and boat ramp.

The Yukon government Aishihik Lake Campground is located at the south end of Aishihik Lake, approximately 26 miles/41.8 km distance; 13 sites, drinking water, picnic tables, firepits, kitchen shelter, boat launch and playground. Camping fee $8. ▲

Aishihik Lake, fishing for lake trout and grayling. As with most large Yukon lakes, ice is not out until late June. Low water levels may make boat launching difficult. *WARNING: Winds can come up suddenly on this lake.* **Pole Cat Lake**, just before the Aishihik weather station; fishing for pike. ✦

CAUTION: Bears in area. Other wildlife includes eagles, moose and caribou.

DC 965.6 (1603.8 km) **F 522.4** (840.7 km) **Historic Milepost 996.** Turnoff to north at east end of Aishihik River bridge (watch for camera viewpoint sign) to see Canyon Creek bridge. The original bridge was built about 1920 by the Jacquot brothers to move freight and passengers across the Aishihik River to Silver City on Kluane Lake, and from there by boat to Burwash Landing. The bridge was reconstructed in 1942 by Army Corps of Engineers during construction of the Alaska Highway. It was rebuilt again in 1987.

DC 965.7 (1604 km) **F 522.3** (840.5 km) Aishihik River bridge.

DC 966.3 (1605 km) **F 521.7** (839.6 km) View of impressive Kluane Range ice fields straight ahead northbound between Kilometreposts 1604 and 1616.

DC 974.9 (1619 km) **F 513.1** (825.7 km) Turnout to south on Marshall Creek.

DC 977.1 (1622.4 km) **F 510.9** (822.2 km) Double-ended turnout to north. The rugged snowcapped peaks of the Kluane Icefield Ranges and the outer portion of the St. Elias Mountains are visible to the west, straight ahead northbound.

The Kluane National Park Icefield Ranges are Canada's highest and the world's largest nonpolar alpine ice field, forming the interior wilderness of the park. In clear weather, Mount Kennedy and Mount Hubbard, 2 peaks that are twice as high as the front ranges seen before you, are visible from here.

DC 979.3 (1626 km) **F 508.7** (818.6 km) Between Kilometreposts 1626 and 1628, look for the NorthwesTel microwave repeater station on top of Paint Mountain. The station was installed with the aid of helicopters and supplied by the tramline carried by high towers, which is also visible from here.

DC 980.8 (1628.4 km) **F 507.2** (816.2 km) Turnoff to north for Yukon government Pine Lake recreation park and campground. Day-use area has sandy beach, boat launch and dock, group firepits, drinking water and 7 tent sites near beach. The Pine Lake Regatta, held here in mid-July, is the "biggest beach party in the Yukon." The campground, adjacent **Pine Lake** with a view of the St. Elias Mountains, has 33 sites, outhouses, firewood, litter barrels, kitchen shelter, playground and drinking water. Camping fee $8. Fishing is good for lake trout, northern pike and grayling. ✦▲

DC 980.9 (1628.5 km) **F 507.1** (816.1 km) Access road to floatplane dock.

DC 982.2 (1630.8 km) **F 505.8** (814 km) Turnoff to north for Haines Junction airport. Flightseeing tours of glaciers, fly-in fishing and air charters available; fixed-wing aircraft or helicopters. **Private Aircraft:** Haines Junction airstrip; elev. 2,150 feet/655m; length 5,000 feet/1,524m; gravel. Fuel sales (100L) from Sifton Air.

Highway swings to south for last few miles into Haines Junction, offering a panoramic, close-up view of the Auriol Range straight ahead.

DC 984.8 (1635 km) **F 503.2** (809.8 km) Northbound travelers turn right (southbound travelers turn left) on Kluane Street for Kluane National Park Visitor Centre.

DC 985 (1635.3 km) **F 503** (809.5 km) **Historic Milepost 1016**, junction of Alaska Highway and Haines Highway (Haines Road).

IMPORTANT: THIS JUNCTION CAN BE CONFUSING; CHOOSE YOUR ROUTE CAREFULLY! Fairbanks- and Anchorage-bound travelers TURN RIGHT at this junction for continuation of Alaska Highway (Yukon Highway 1); highway log follows description of Haines Junction, YT. Continue straight ahead (south) on the Haines Highway (Yukon Highway 3) for port of Haines, AK; see HAINES HIGHWAY section. (Haines-bound motorists note: It is a good idea to fill up with gas in Haines Junction. Gas is available en route only at Kathleen Lake Lodge.)

Haines Junction

DC 985 (1635.3 km) **F 503** (809.5 km) **Historic Milepost 1016**, at the **junction** of the Alaska Highway (Yukon Highway 1) and the Haines Highway (Yukon Highway 3, also known as the Haines Road). Driving distance to Whitehorse, 100 miles/161 km; YT–AK border, 205 miles/330 km; Tok, 296 miles/476 km; and Haines, 150.5 miles/242 km. **Population:** 811. **Elevation:** 1,956 feet/

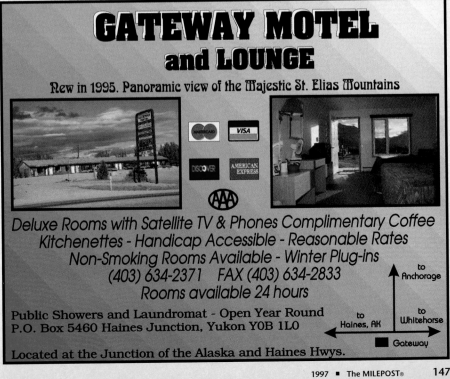

596m. **Emergency Services: RCMP,** phone (403) 634-5555.or (403) 667-5555 **Fire Department,** phone (403) 634-2222. **Nursing Centre,** phone (403) 634-4444. **Radio:** 106.1 FM.

Visitor Information: At the Kluane National Park and Yukon government visitor information centre, 0.2 mile/0.3 km east of the junction just off the Alaska Highway. Phone (403) 634-2345. Interpretive exhibits, displays and an outstanding multi-image slide presentation are featured. The centre is open 8 A.M. to 8 P.M. daily from May to September, Monday through Friday the rest of the year.

Haines Junction was established in 1942 during construction of the Alaska Highway. The first buildings here were Army barracks for the U.S. Army Corps of Engineers. The engineers were to build a new branch road connecting the Alaska Highway with the port of Haines on Lynn Canal. The branch road—today's Haines Highway—was completed in 1943.

The Our Lady of the Way Catholic mission in Haines Junction was built in 1954, using parts from an old Army hut left from highway construction days. The octagonal log St. Christopher's Anglican Church was built in 1987, replacing a 1955 structure built from an old garage used in the pipeline project.

Haines Junction is still an important stop for travelers on the Alaska and Haines highways. Services are located along both highways, and clustered around Village Square at the junction, where a 24-foot monument depicts area wildlife.

Haines Junction offers an excellent range of accommodations. Visitor services include motels, 5 bed and breakfasts, restaurants, gas stations, garage services, groceries, souvenirs and a bakery that last summer hosted a popular "coffee house" on Monday nights, with an open mike for traveling musicians. There is a full-facility indoor heated swimming pool with showers available; open daily from May to late-August, fee charged. Also here

HAINES JUNCTION ADVERTISERS

are a RCMP office, Lands and Forest District Office and health centre. The post office and bank are located in Madley's General Store. (Banking service weekday afternoons; extended hours on Fridays.) The Commissioner James Smith Administration Building, at Kilometre 255.6 Haines Road, 0.2 mile/0.3 km south from the Alaska Highway junction, contains the government liquor store and public library. The airport is located on the Alaska Highway just east of town (see **Milepost DC 982.2**).

Haines Junction is on the eastern boundary of Kluane National Park Reserve. Admin-

Welcome to the North Country!

Popular photo subject in Haines Junction is the wildlife monument in the village square. (Earl L. Brown, staff)

Haines Junction, Yukon

"Gateway to Kluane"

Haines Junction is the ideal base for year round adventure travel for all ages in and around Kluane National Park and Tatshenshini-Alsek Provincial Park. You can go glacier flightseeing, river rafting, mountain biking, horseback riding, hiking, fishing and hunting! Join us for these special events in 1997:

June 6-7   Alsek Music Festival
Music Under The Mountains with North of 60 talent!   (403) 634-2520

End of June   Kluane National Park Interpretive Programs Begin
Join knowledgeable interpreters for park events. Fees apply. (403) 634-7207

Saturday, June 21   Kluane to Chilkat International Bike Relay
Form a team and cycle one of the most scenic routes in the world! Last year 800 people did!   (403) 634-2293

Tuesday, July 1   Canada Day
Celebrate Canada's 130th Birthday Haines Junction style!   (403) 634-2293

Late July   Pine Lake Regatta & Softball Tournament
There's fun for all at the Yukon's biggest beach party!   403-634-2352

For more information about **Haines Junction** *and* **Kluane Country**, *contact the Village of Haines Junction Box 5339, Haines Junction, YT Y0B 1L0 403-634-2293 or Fax 403-634-2008*

istration offices and the visitor centre for the park are located north of town along with the park warden and general works station. Kluane (pronounced kloo-WA-nee) National Park Reserve encompasses extensive ice fields, mountains and wilderness. There is one campground, Kathleen Lake, located 16 miles/27 km south of town on the Haines Highway. There are numerous hiking trails of varying degrees of difficulty; check with the park visitor centre or see Vivien Lougheed's *Kluane Park Hiking Guide* (1992).

Flightseeing the park by fixed-wing aircraft or helicopter from Haines Junction is a popular way to see Kluane's scenery; check with charter services at the airport.

The park was first suggested in 1942, and in 1943 land was set aside and designated the Kluane Game Sanctuary. A formal park region was established in 1972 and the national park boundaries were official in 1976. In 1980, Kluane National Park Reserve, along with Wrangell–St. Elias National Park in Alaska, became a joint UNESCO World Heritage Site. Kluane has become a world-class wilderness destination among outdoor recreation enthusiasts. Hikers note: There is mandatory registration (fee charged) for overnight trips into the park. Hikers may also check at the park office for current information on bear sightings.

For more information on Kluane

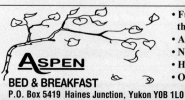

National Park Reserve, stop by the excellent visitor centre and see the exhibits and the award-winning multi-image slide presentation (shown on the hour and half hour). Also check at the visitor centre for a schedule of guided hikes, walks and campfire talks; these interpretive programs are available daily from the third week in June through August. Fees are charged for interpretive events. Contact Kluane National Park at Box 5495, Haines Junction, YT Y0B 1L0, or phone (403) 634-7209, fax (403) 634-7208.

Haines Junction is also headquarters for the new Tatshenshini–Alsek Wilderness

Park. Created in 1993, the park protects the magnificent Tatshenshini and Alsek rivers area in Canada, where the 2 rivers join and flow (as the Alsek) to the Gulf of Alaska at Dry Bay. Known to riverrunners as "the Tat," the Tatshenshini is famous for its whitewater rafting, stunning scenery and wildlife. Due to a dramatic increase in river traffic in recent years, permits are required from the park agencies (the National Park Service in Alaska and B.C. Parks in Canada). Locally, Kluane Park Adventure Center (403/634-

2313) offers rafting trips to the Tatshenshini. Contact Access Kluane Tours and Information at (403) 634-2816. For more information about the park, contact Tatshenshini–Alsek Wilderness Park, Box 5495, Haines Junction, YT Y0B 1L0; phone (403) 634-7209, fax (403) 634-7208.

Picnicking available at day-use area on the Dezadeash River, located at the west edge of town on the Haines Highway, which also has a wheelchair-accessible trail. Other outdoor recreation available locally includes guided fishing and boating (canoe and boat rentals available).

RV camping available at several campgrounds in and near town. Dump stations and water are also available at local service station and campgrounds. Yukon government campground located 4.2 miles/6.7 km east of junction on the Alaska Highway at Pine Lake. ▲

Special events in Haines Junction include the Alsek Music Festival held June 6–7, 1997, and the Pine Lake Regatta in July (see **Milepost DC 980.8**). Also remember that July 1st is Canada Day (the anniversary of Canada's confederation) and is celebrated with parades and flags.

Bicycling offers several events, including the Trail of '42 Road Race (May 31, 1997) and the Kluane to Chilkat International Bike Relay (June 21, 1997), which attracted 850 cyclists last year. *IMPORTANT: Watch for cyclists on the Alaska and Haines highways during these events.*

Cabins. Rustic log cabin rentals (available year-round) in the scenic Alsek Valley along Bear Creek. Ideal wooded location for a relaxing get away from it all—access to hiking trails … or just take it easy. For information or reservations—call Joe and Anne Zeindler. (403) 634-2454. Box 2116, Haines Junction, YT Y0B 1L0. [ADVERTISEMENT]

Alaska Highway Log

(continued)

Distance* from Dawson Creek (DC) is followed by distance from Fairbanks (F). Original mileposts are indicated in the text as Historical Mile.

*Mileages from Dawson Creek are based on actual driving distance. Kilometres from Dawson Creek are based on physical kilometreposts. Please read Mileposts and Kilometreposts in the introduction for an explanation of how this highway is logged.

DC 985 (1635.3 km) F 503 (809.5 km) Junction of the Alaska Highway (Yukon Highway 1) and the Haines Highway (Yukon Highway 3). Markers indicate distance to Destruction Bay 67 miles/108 km, Beaver Creek 186 miles/299 km.

Northbound: From Haines Junction to the YT–AK border, the Alaska Highway is in fair to good condition but narrow, often without shoulders. Watch for frost heaves north from Destruction Bay to Beaver Creek.

Southbound: Good paved highway with wide shoulders next 380 miles/611.5 km (from here to Watson Lake) with the exception of some short sections of narrow road and occasional gravel breaks. *NOTE: This junction can be confusing; choose your route carefully!* Whitehorse-bound travelers TURN LEFT at junction for continuation of Alaska Highway (Yukon Highway 1); highway log follows description of Haines Junction. TURN RIGHT for the Haines Highway (Yukon Highway 3) to the port of Haines, AK; see HAINES HIGHWAY section for log. (Haines-bound motorists note: Between Haines Junction, YT, and Haines, AK, a distance of 151.6 miles/246 km, gas is available only at Kathleen Lake Lodge, summers only, and 33 Mile Roadhouse.)

DC 985.3 (1635.9 km) F 502.7 (809 km) Kluane RV Kampground; RV and tent camping, gas, diesel, dump station, pay phone. ▲

DC 985.8 (1636.5 km) F 502.2 (808.2 km) Historical Mile 1017. Alcan Fuels; gas, diesel, propane, auto repair and towing. Open daily, year-round.

DC 985.9 (1636.7 km) F 502.1 (808 km) Stardust Motel and RV Park. ▲

DC 986.6 (1637.8 km) F 501.4 (806.9 km) Highway follows the Kluane Ranges which are to the west. Livestock open range in this area: Watch for horses and cattle!

DC 987.8 (1639.8 km) F 500.2 (805 km) Historical Mile 1019. Kluane National Park warden headquarters. (Visitor information in Haines Junction at the visitor centre.)

DC 988.3 (1640.6 km) F 499.7 (804.1 km) Rest area to west with pit toilets.

DC 991.4 (1645.6 km) F 496.6 (799.1 km) Photo stop on right northbound. A short hike uphill leads to lookout and information sign about ancient lakes in the area.

Highway climbs next 9 miles/14.5 km northbound to Bear Creek Summit.

DC 991.6 (1645.9 km) F 496.4 (798.9 km) Historic Milepost 1022, Mackintosh Trading Post historic sign. Lodge to east; food, gas, lodging and camping. Helicopter flightseeing service across from lodge. Trailhead to west for Alsek Pass trail; 18 miles/29 km long, suitable for shorter day hikes, mountain bikes permitted. ▲

Mackintosh Lodge offers something for everyone, from our delicious homemade meals and fresh baking from "Gramma's Kitchen" to our comfy rooms with handmade quilts. A favorite stopping spot for Alaskan travelers. Across from the lodge, the

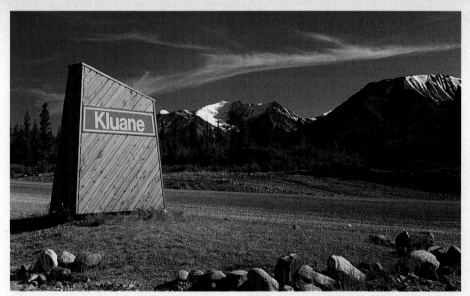

Kluane National Park sign on the Alaska Highway north of Haines Junction.
(Earl L. Brown, staff)

Alsek Trail leads to Kluane National Park, a world heritage site. "Majestic mountains make for Mackintosh miracles." [ADVERTISEMENT]

DC 1000.1 (1660 km) **F 487.9** (785.2 km) Bear Creek Summit (elev. 3,294 feet/ 1,004m), highest point on the Alaska Highway between Whitehorse and Fairbanks.

Glimpse of Kloo Lake to north of highway between Kilometreposts 1660 and 1662.

DC 1003.5 (1665.4 km) **F 484.5** (779.7 km) Jarvis Creek.

DC 1003.6 (1665.6 km) **F 484.4** (779.5 km) **Historic Milepost 1035.** Turnout to west next to Jarvis Creek. Pretty spot for a picnic. Trail rides may be available here with Ruby Range Trail Rides.

Jarvis Creek, grayling 8 to 16 inches, good all summer; Dolly Varden 8 to 10 inches, best in early summer.

DC 1013.6 (1682 km) **F 474.4** (763.5 km) Beautiful view to west of the snow-covered Kluane Ranges. For northbound travelers, the Alaska Highway parallels the Kluane Ranges from Haines Junction to Koidern, presenting a nearly unbroken chain of 7,000- to 8,000-foot/2,134- to 2,438-m summits interrupted only by a few large valleys cut by glacier-fed rivers and streams. West of the Kluane Ranges is the Duke Depression (not visible from the highway), a narrow trough separating the Kluane Ranges from the St. Elias Mountains. Major peaks in the St. Elias (not visible from the highway) are: Mount Logan, Canada's highest peak, at 19,545 feet/5,959m (recalculated in 1992 from 19,520 feet by a scientific expedition); Mount St. Elias, 18,008 feet/5,489m; Mount Lucania, 17,147 feet/5,226m; King Peak, 16,971 feet/5,173m; Mount Wood, Mount Vancouver, Mount Hubbard and Mount Steele, all over 15,000 feet/4,572m. Mount Steele (16,664 feet/5,079m) was named for Superintendent Sam Steele of the North West Mounted Police. As commanding officer of the NWMP in the Yukon in 1898, Steele established permanent detachments at the summits of the White and Chilkoot passes to ensure not only that gold stampeders obeyed Canadian laws, but also had sufficient supplies to carry them through to the gold fields.

DC 1016.5 (1686.7 km) **F 471.5** (758.8 km) Turnout to west with view of Kluane Ranges.

DC 1017.2 (1687.8 km) **F 470.8** (757.7 km) Christmas Creek.

DC 1019.8 (1692 km) **F 468.2** (753.5 km) First glimpse of Kluane Lake for northbound travelers at Boutillier Summit (elev. 3,293 feet/1,003m), second highest point on the highway between Whitehorse and Fairbanks.

DC 1020 (1692.5 km) **F 468** (753.2 km) Turnout to east with information plaques on area history and geography.

DC 1020.3 (1693 km) **F 467.7** (752.7 km) **Historic Milepost 1053.** Historic sign and interpretive panel at turnoff for Silver City. Access to a bed and breakfast. Follow dirt and gravel road east 3.1 miles/5 km to ruins of Silver City. This old trading post, with roadhouse and North West Mounted Police barracks, was on the wagon road from Whitehorse to the placer goldfields of Kluane Lake (1904–24). Good photo opportunities.

Kluane Bed and Breakfast. Just 3 miles off the highway at historical Silver City on the shore of Kluane Lake. Private, heated, A-frame cabins with mountain view, cooking and shower facilities, full family-style breakfast. Your hosts—The Sias Family, a sixth generation Yukon family. Contact mobile operator, 2M 3924, Destruction Bay channel. Reservations recommended. C/o Box 5459, Haines Junction, YT Y0B 1L0. [ADVERTISEMENT]

DC 1020.9 (1694 km) **F 467.1** (751.7 km) Silver Creek.

DC 1022.5 (1696.5 km) **F 465.5** (749.1 km) Turnoff to east for Kluane Lake Research Station; station and airstrip are 0.9 mile/1.4 km via a straight gravel road. This research station is sponsored by the Arctic Institute of North America, University of Calgary.

Highway follows west shore of Kluane Lake next 39 miles/63 km northbound to Burwash Landing.

DC 1023.7 (1698.5 km) **F 464.3** (747.2 km) **Historical Mile 1056.** Kluane Camp commemorative plaque. Kluane Lake Lodge (closed). Trans North helicopter base operates here, offering flightseeing trips in summer. These highly recommended flightseeing trips offer spectacular views of the Slims River Valley and Kaskawulsh Glacier.

Trans North Helicopters. See display ad this section.

Spectacular view of Kaskawulsh Glacier from the air. (Earl L. Brown, staff)

DC 1026.8 (1703.4 km) **F 461.2** (742.2 km) Slim's River East trail turnoff (2-mile/3.3-km access road, not recommended for motorhomes); parking at trailhead. This 12.4-mile/20-km trail is rated "easy" by the *Kluane Hiking Guide.*

DC 1027.8 (1705 km) **F 460.2** (740.6 km) Slim's River bridge (clearance 17.7 feet/5.4m). Slim's River, which flows into Kluane Lake, was named for a packhorse that drowned here during the 1903 Kluane gold rush. Sheep Mountain is directly ahead for northbound travelers. The highway winds along Kluane Lake: Drive carefully!

DC 1028.8 (1706.6 km) **F 459.2** (739 km)

Sheep Mountain visitor information centre. Excellent interpretive programs, laser disc information videos, parking and outhouses are available. Open mid-May to mid-September. Hours are 9 A.M. to 5 P.M. June through August, 9:30 A.M. to 5 P.M. in May and September. Stop here for information on Kluane National Park's flora and fauna. A viewing telescope is set up to look for sheep on Sheep Mountain. This is the sheep's winter range; best chance to see them is late August and September, good chance in late May to early June.

DC 1029 (1706.9 km) **F 459** (738.7 km) Slim's River West trail; trailhead adjacent

visitor information centre.

The small white cross on the side of Sheep Mountain marks the grave of Alexander Clark Fisher, a prospector who came into this area about 1906.

DC 1030.7 (1709.5 km) **F 457.3** (735.9 km) **Historic Milepost 1061.** Soldier's Summit. The Alaska Canada Military Highway was officially opened with a ribbon-cutting ceremony here on blizzardy Nov. 20, 1942. A rededication ceremony was held Nov. 20, 1992, commemorating the 50th anniversary of the highway. A trail leads up to the original dedication site from the parking area.

Several turnouts overlooking Kluane Lake next mile northbound. This beautiful lake is the largest in Yukon Territory, covering approximately 154 square miles/400 square km. The Ruby Range lies on the east side of the lake. Boat rentals are available at Destruction Bay and Burwash Landing.

Kluane Lake, excellent fishing for lake trout, northern pike and grayling. ◄━

DC 1031.9 (1711.7 km) **F 456.1** (734 km) The Bayshore (current status unknown).

DC 1034.5 (1715.8 km) **F 453.5** (729.8 km) Williscroft Creek.

DC 1034.9 (1717 km) **F 453.1** (729.2 km) **Historical Mile 1067.** Cottonwood campground to east. ▲

Cottonwood RV Park and Campground. See display ad this section. ▲

DC 1039.7 (1724.7 km) **F 448.3** (721.4 km) Congdon Creek trailhead to west; 16-mile/26-km hike to Sheep Mountain.

DC 1039.9 (1725 km) **F 448.1** (721.1 km) **Historical Mile 1072.** Turnoff to east for Congdon Creek Yukon government campground on Kluane Lake. Drive in 0.4 mile/0.6 km via gravel loop road; tenting area, 77 level sites (some pull-through), outhouses, kitchen shelters, water pump, firewood, firepits, picnic tables, sandy beach, interpretive talks, playground, boat launch. Camping fee $8. ▲

DC 1040.4 (1725.6 km) **F 447.6** (720.3 km) Congdon Creek. According to R. Coutts, *Yukon: Places & Names,* Congdon Creek is believed to have been named by a miner after Frederick Tennyson Congdon. A lawyer from Nova Scotia, Congdon came to the Yukon in 1898 and held various political posts until 1911.

DC 1046.9 (1735.3 km) **F 441.1** (709.9 km) Nines Creek. Turnout to east.

DC 1047.3 (1736.2 km) **F 440.7** (709.2 km) Mines Creek.

DC 1048.9 (1739 km) **F 439.1** (706.6 km) Bock's Brook.

DC 1051.5 (1743 km) **F 436.5** (702.5 km) **Historic Milepost 1083. DESTRUCTION BAY** (pop. less than 100). **Emergency Services: Health clinic,** phone (403) 841-4444; **Ambulance,** phone (403) 841-3333; **Fire Department,** phone (403) 841-2221. Located on the shore of Kluane Lake, Destruction Bay is one of several towns that grew out of the building of the Alaska Highway. It earned its name when a storm destroyed buildings and materials here. Destruction Bay was one of the many relay stations spaced at 100-mile intervals to give truck drivers a break and a chance to repair their vehicles. Historic sign adjacent historic milepost. A highway maintenance camp is located here. Destruction Bay has camping, boat launch, boat rentals and guided fishing tours. A fishing derby is held first weekend in July. Food, gas, camping and lodging available at the Talbot Arm (open year-

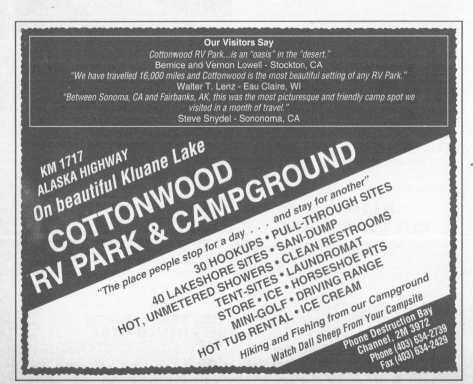

round) and Sehja Services. Glacier flightseeing trips available.

Talbot Arm Motel in Destruction Bay at historic Mile 1083 Alaska Highway has been offering Yukon visitors a modern, clean and friendly stop since 1967. Built and managed by the Van der Veen family, Talbot Arm has been setting the standard for rural lodges. In 1988 we were recognized by our peers for our efforts by winning the Sourdough Award from Tourism Industry Association and Customers Service Award from Chevron. Recently we have added 2 attractions to our list of services: Ruby Range Airways Ltd. is headquartered at Talbot Arm and is offering glacier flights in Kluane National Park and surrounding area. Enjoy a scenic flight over the largest non-polar icefield in the world and Canada's most majestic peaks in a Cessna 182P piloted by Neil Hardy. Talbot Arm Fishing Tours are also arranged at the lodge. Our 3 available guides have over 50 years total experience hunting the huge Kluane Lake trout. A day in a boat on our crystal clear waters in the best scenery in the

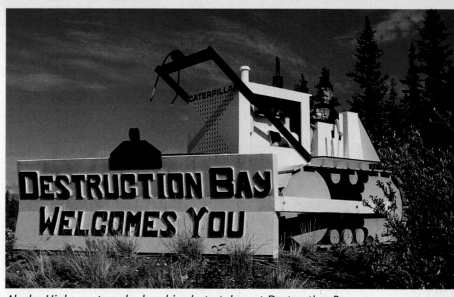

Alaska Highway traveler has his photo taken at Destruction Bay. (Earl L. Brown, staff)

TALBOT ARM MOTEL

Rebuilt in 1987 and Ready to Serve All Alaska highway Travellers Year-Round
WITH

- **32 MODERN SPACIOUS CLEAN ROOMS**
  Complimented with Satellite TV and Laundromat
- **90-SEAT CAFETERIA**
  Good Food Already Prepared for Tour Groups and Others
- **FULL SERVE DINING ROOM**
  Friendly, Efficient Waitered Service for Families, Truckers, and Small Groups

• **INTIMATE LOUNGE** Relaxing . . . Drinks also served in the Dining Room

- **CHEVRON SERVICE STATION**
  Gasoline, Diesel, Oils and Other Automotive Necessities including Towing, Tire repair, Propane, etc.
- **GENERAL STORE**
  Local and Canadian-made Souvenirs, T-Shirts, Sunglasses, Fresh, Frozen and Canned Goods, Cigarettes, *Film*, Toiletries and Some Drug Store Remedies.
- **CAMPER and MOTORHOMES • RV PARK**
  Propane, Dump Station, Electric Hookups, Drinking Water, Store Showers, laundromat, Large clean Restrooms • ICE

• GLACIER AIR TOURS • GUIDED FISHING TRIPS • BOAT RENTALS

—FOR RESERVATIONS—CALL: (403) 841-4461
WRITE: Box M, Destruction Bay, Yukon, Y0B 1H0

 DEDICATED SERVICE TO TRAVELLERS SINCE 1967
Garry and Sheree Van der Veen, Your Hosts

Yukon won't soon be forgotten. [ADVERTISEMENT]

DC 1051.7 (1743.3 km) **F 436.3** (702.1 km) **Sehja Services & RV Park.** Historical mile "1083"—original equipment site of camp 1083 and the first full service lodge on the Alcan Highway. Beautifully nestled against the St. Elias mountains overlooking Kluane (clue-ah-knee) Lake. Reasonable rates, clean facilities, home cooking with 5 star service. Guided fishing charters available. Your host, Loren Maluorno. Phone (403) 841-4807. [ADVERTISEMENT] ▲

DC 1051.9 (1743.6 km) **F 436.1** (701.8 km) Rest area with litter barrels and toilet.

DC 1055.1 (1748.8 km) **F 432.9** (696.7 km) Lewes Creek.

DC 1058.3 (1753.9 km) **F 429.7** (691.5 km) Halfbreed (Copper Joe) Creek trailhead.

DC 1061.3 (1758.7 km) **F 426.7** (686.7 km) Store, post office and general auto repairs.

Duke River Trading Co. See display ad this section.

DC 1061.5 (1759 km) **F 426.5** (686.4 km) **Historic Milepost 1093.** Turnoff to east for **BURWASH LANDING,** (pop. 110) a village with post office, community hall, church, museum and lodge, 24-hour gas, food, camping and lodging on Kluane Lake. Boat rentals and Kluane Lake fishing trips available. Helicopter flightseeing trips of Kluane National Park are also available out of Burwash Landing.

Burwash Landing was settled in 1904 by the Jacquot brothers, Louis and Eugene, as a supply centre for local miners. The log mission here, Our Lady of the Holy Rosary, was built in 1944. The historic sign here reads: "After months of rough camp life, American soldiers were surprised and delighted when they reached this prosperous little settlement which seemed like an oasis in the wilderness. Burwash also became the home of Father Eusebe Morisset, an Oblate Missionary, who served as an auxiliary chaplain

World's largest gold pan is next to Kluane Museum in Burwash Landing.
(© Beth Davidow)

with the American Army."

Burwash Landing is also known for its black spruce burl bowls. Burls start as an irritation or infection in the spruce. The tree sends extra sap as healant, which creates a growth or burl. After the tree dies, the burl is cut out and smoothed into a bowl. Check out Burlbilly Hill for more information.

The highly recommended Kluane Museum of Natural History is located on the east side of the highway at the turnoff; open 9 A.M. to 9 P.M. in summer; phone (403) 841-5561. The museum features a video room with Northern interest videos; wildlife, minerals and other natural history exhibits; and has a souvenir shop displaying locally made handicrafts. Admission is charged. Yukon Gold Explorer's Passports are stamped here. Next to the museum is the world's largest gold pan, measuring 28 feet/8m high.

Burwash Landing Resort & RV Park. See display ad this section. ▲

Kluane Museum of Natural History. See display ad this section.

DC 1061.6 (1759.2 km) **F 426.4** (686.2 km) **Burlbilly Hill.** The most unique stop at Mile 1093 is "Burlbilly Hill," 200 feet north of the museum. The visitor will see rows of "burly logs" on the hill. Another surprise is a small woodshop with its variety of finely finished burl products, "burl bowls" and "diamond willow canes." Come and watch Obie and Dubie at work. Wir sprechen deutsch!

[ADVERTISEMENT]

DC 1062 (1759.8 km) **F 426** (685.5 km) **Dalan Campground.** Turn off north, to Dalan Campground, 1 km off the Alaska Highway on the shores of beautiful Kluane Lake, "largest lake in the Yukon." Owned and operated by Kluane First Nation, this campground offers 25 individual private campsites, RVs welcome! Firewood, water pump, picnic tables, firepits and dump station are available. New for 1997 in Burwash—community recreation centre with library, weight room, kitchen and hall rental. Laudromat and showers adjacent. For additional information, call (403) 841-4274.

[ADVERTISEMENT] ▲

DC 1062.7 (1761 km) **F 425.3** (684.4 km) **Historic Milepost 1094. Private Aircraft:** Burwash Yukon government airstrip to north; elev. 2,643 feet/806m; length 6,000 feet/1,829m; gravel, no fuel.

DC 1067 (1768.8 km) **F 421** (677.5 km) Duke River bridge (clearance 17.7 feet/5.4m). The Duke River flows into Kluane Lake; named for George Duke, an early prospector.

DC 1071.9 (1776.5 km) **F 416.1** (669.6 km) Turnout to north. Burwash Creek, named for Lachlin Taylor Burwash, a mining recorder at Silver City in 1903.

DC 1076.7 (1784.1 km) **F 411.3** (661.9 km) Sakiw Creek.

DC 1077.3 (1785.1 km) **F 410.4** (660.5 km) Rest area with information panels and observation platform overlooking Kluane River.

DC 1078.5 (1787 km) **F 409.5** (659 km) Buildings to west belong to Hudson Bay Mining and Smelting Co.'s Wellgreen Nickel Mines, named for Wellington Bridgeman Green, the prospector who discovered the mineral showing in 1952. During the mine's operation, from May 1972 to July 1973, three shiploads of concentrates (averaging 13,000 tons each) were trucked to Haines, AK. The material proved to be too insufficient to be economical. No facilities or services.

DC 1079.4 (1788.5 km) **F 408.6** (657.6 km) Quill Creek.

DC 1080.9 (1791 km) **F 407.1** (655.1 km) Glacier Creek. Kluane River to east of highway.

DC 1083.5 (1795.5 km) **F 404.5** (651 km) Historic Milepost 1117. Turnout. Sign commemorates 1st Lt. Roland Small, of the 18th Engineers Regiment, who died in a jeep acci-

Sunset on beautiful Kluane Lake. (Earl L. Brown, staff)

dent near this site during construction of the Alaska Highway in 1942. Short road to Kluane River; no turnaround.

DC 1084.6 (1797.2 km) **F 403.4** (649.2 km) **Historical Mile 1118.** Kluane Wilderness Village; gas, restaurant, camping and lodging. Open year-round. Viewing platform of: Mount Kennedy, Mount Logan and Mount Lucania. Halfway mark between Whitehorse and Tok.   ▲

Kluane Wilderness Village offers all amenities to modern day travelers. 24-hour service station. Full-menu restaurant, "Scully's Saloon" and comfortable accommodation. Our Good Sam R.V. Park (with Satellite TV) is the ideal resting location between Whitehorse and Tok, nestled in the beautiful Kluane Mountains. See our display ad for more. Phone/fax (403) 841-4141.

[ADVERTISEMENT]

DC 1086.6 (1799.5 km) **F 401.4** (646 km) Swede Johnson Creek. Turnout to east.

DC 1087.4 (1801.7 km) *NOTE: Watch for some sections of rough road northbound next 104 miles/168 km. Some gravel patches, some winding sections. Drive carefully, especially vehicles with trailers. Road surface can be particularly hard on trailer hitches. Various road construction projects may be under way. Suggested maximum speed limit 45 mph/70 kmph to the Alaska border.*

DC 1091.3 (1808 km) **F 396.7** (638.4 km) Buildings to east are a dormant pump station once used to pressure up fuel being transferred from Haines to Fairbanks.

DC 1095 (1814 km) **F 393** (632.4 km) NorthwesTel microwave tower visible ahead northbound.

DC 1095.4 (1814.6 km) **F 392.6** (631.8 km) Abandoned Mountain View Lodge. View of Donjek River Valley.

Alaska Highway workers faced one of their toughest construction jobs during completion of the Alaska Highway in 1943 from the Donjek River to the Alaska border. Swampy ground underlain by permafrost, numerous creeks, lakes and rivers, plus a thick insulating ground cover made this section particularly difficult for road builders.

DC 1096.3 (1816 km) **F 391.7** (630.4 km) Turnout to west with view of Donjek River Valley and the Icefield Ranges of the St. Elias Mountains. Interpretive display.

DC 1099.7 (1819.5 km) **F 388.3** (624.9 km) **Historic Milepost 1130.** Turnout with interpretive panel on the Donjek River bridge. Sign reads: "Glacial rivers, like the Donjek, posed a unique problem for the builders of the Alaska Highway. These braided mountain streams would flood after a heavy rainfall or rapid glacial melt, altering the waters' course and often leaving bridges crossing dry ground."

DC 1100 (1820 km) **F 388** (624.4 km) Donjek River bridge (clearance 17.4 feet/5.3m). Access to river at north end of bridge on west side of highway. This wide silty river is a major tributary of the White River. According to R. Coutts, *Yukon: Places & Names*, the Donjek is believed to have been named by Charles Willard Hayes in 1891 from the Indian word for a peavine that grows in the area.

DC 1113.5 (1844.4 km) **F 374.5** (602.7 km) **Edith Creek** bridge, turnout to west.

Try your hand at gold panning here, "colours" have been found. Grayling fishing, June through September.

DC 1113.8 (1844.8 km) **F 374.2** (602.2 km) **Historical Mile 1147. Pine Valley Motel and Cafe.** Thanks to all our customers for your patronage from your hosts Carmen and Dave. Don't let the construction get you down, drop in for a relaxing break. We have Totem Oil unleaded and diesel available (seniors gas discount). Tire repairs, towing available, minor repairs and welding. RV park and campground, pull-throughs, water and power hookups, hot showers included, picnic tables. Gold panning and good fishing at Edith Creek. Motel units, cabins with colour TV. Newly renovated licensed cafe with full menu and bakery, featuring hearty soups, homemade bread, pies and pastries, fresh daily. Ice cream parlour. Enjoy a scenic view of the mountains while our friendly morning cook prepares you up a mean breakfast, or sink your teeth into some of Carmen's wonderful sweet rolls. Take-out for cold beer, wine and spirits. Pay phone, cubed ice, fishing license and tackle, souvenirs. Book exchange available. Harleys welcome. Free cup of coffee in the morning to get you going with your overnight stay. MasterCard, Discover and VISA. Interac direct payment available. Bon jour et bon vacances! Phone/fax (403) 862-7407. [ADVERTISEMENT] ▲

DC 1118.3 (1852.2 km) **F 369.7** (595 km) Koidern River bridge No. 1.

NOTE: Watch for road construction between Kilometreposts 1852 and 1872 in 1997.

DC 1118.8 (1853 km) **F 369.2** (594.2 km) **Historical Mile 1152.** Lake Creek Yukon government campground just west of highway; 30 large level sites (6 pull-through), water pump, litter barrels, firewood, firepits, picnic tables, kitchen shelter and outhouses. Camping fee $8. ▲

DC 1122.7 (1859.5 km) **F 365.3** (587.9 km) **Historical Mile 1156.** Longs Creek.

DC 1125 (1863.5 km) **F 363** (584.2 km)

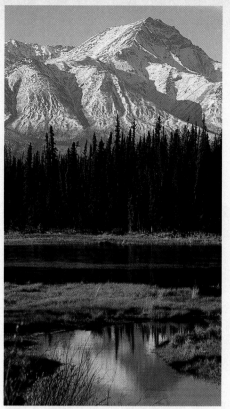

Kluane mountains reflected in a creek along the Alaska Highway. (© Beth Davidow)

Turnout to east with litter barrel.

DC 1125.7 (1864.7 km) **F 362.3** (583 km) **Pickhandle Lake** to west, good fishing from boat for northern pike all summer; also grayling, whitefish and lingcod. ✦

DC 1128 (1868.4 km) **F 360** (579.3 km) Aptly named Reflection Lake to west mirrors the Kluane Ranges. The highway parallels this range between Koidern and Haines Junction.

DC 1130.6 (1872.6 km) **F 357.4** (575.2 km) **Historical Mile 1164.** Lodge. There are 2 "lodges" at Koidern; continue north past Koidern River bridge No. 2 for Bear Flats Lodge at Koidern.

DC 1130.7 (1872.8 km) **F 357.3** (575 km) Koidern River bridge No. 2.

DC 1133.7 (1877.6 km) **F 354.3** (570.2 km) **Historic Milepost 1167.** Bear Flats Lodge (current status unknown).

DC 1135 (1880 km) **F 353** (568 km) **Historical Mile 1169.** White River Motor Inn; food, gas, lodging and camping. Open year-round. ▲

White River Motor Inn. See display ad this section. ▲

DC 1135.6 (1881 km) **F 352.4** (567.1 km) White River bridge, clearance 17.1 feet/5.2m. The White River, a major tributary of the Yukon River, was named by Hudson's Bay Co. explorer Robert Campbell for its white colour, caused by the volcanic ash in the water. *This river is considered very dangerous; not recommended for boating.*

CAUTION: Slow down for sharp turn in road at north end of bridge.

DC 1141.5 (1890.5 km) **F 346.5** (557.6 km) **Moose Lake** to west, grayling to 18 inches, use dry flies and small spinners, midsummer. Boat needed for lake. ✦

DC 1144.3 (1895 km) **F 343.7** (553.1 km) Sanpete Creek, named by an early prospector after Sanpete County in Utah.

DC 1147.5 (1900.3 km) **F 340.5** (548 km) Dry Creek No. 1. Turnout to east.

DC 1150.3 (1904.5 km) **F 337.7** (543.5 km) **Historical Mile 1184.** Dry Creek No. 2. Historical marker to west about the Chrisna gold rush.

DC 1155 (1911.8 km) **F 333** (535.9 km) Small Lake to east.

DC 1155.2 (1913 km) **F 332.8** (535.6 km) **Historical Mile 1188.** Turnoff for Snag Junction Yukon government campground, 0.4 mile/0.6 km in on gravel loop road. There are 15 tent and vehicle sites (some level), a kitchen shelter, outhouses, picnic tables, firewood, firepits and litter barrels. Camping fee $8. Small-boat launch. Swimming in

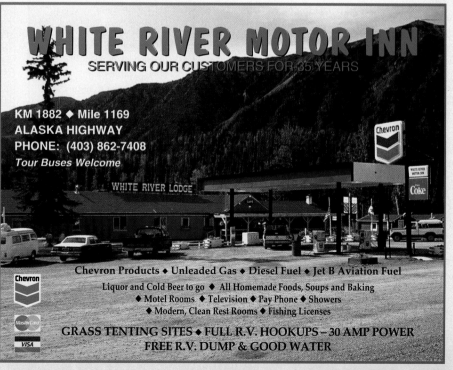

Small Lake. A dirt road (status unknown) connects the Alaska Highway here with the abandoned airfield and Indian village at Snag to the northeast. ▲

DC 1162.1 (1924.5 km) F 325.9 (524.5 km) Inger Creek.

DC 1165.7 (1930 km) F 322.3 (518.7 km) View of Nutzotin Mountains to northwest, Kluane Ranges to southwest. On a clear day you should be able to see the snow-clad Wrangell Mountains in the distance to the west.

DC 1167.2 (1932.4 km) F 320.8 (516.3 km) Beaver Creek plank bridge, clearance 17.1 feet/5.2m.

Beaver Creek

DC 1168.5 (1934.5 km) F 319.5 (514.2 km) Historic Milepost 1202. Driving distance to Haines Junction, 184 miles/295 km; to Tok, 113 miles/182 km; to Haines, 334 miles/537.5 km. Population: 143. Emergency Services: RCMP, phone (403) 862-5555. Ambulance, phone (403) 862-3333. Visitor Information: Yukon government visitor information centre, open daily late May through mid-September. Phone (403) 862-7321. The visi-

Snowshoe hare are abundant in the North. (© Craig Brandt)

tor centre has a book of dried Yukon wildflowers for those interested in the flora of the territory. Get your Yukon Gold Explorer's Passport stamped here.

Site of the old Canadian customs station. Local residents were pleased to see customs relocated north of town in 1983, having long endured the flashing lights and screaming sirens set off whenever a tourist forgot to stop.

Beaver Creek is 1 of 2 sites where Alaska Highway construction crews working from opposite directions connected the highway. In October 1942, Alaska Highway construction operations were being rushed to conclusion as winter set in. Eastern and western sector construction crews (the 97th and 18th Engineers) pushed through to meet at a junction on Beaver Creek on Oct. 28., thus making it possible for the first time for vehicles to travel the entire length of the highway. East–west crews had connected at Contact Creek on Sept. 24, 1942.

Motels, gas stations with repair service, a post office and licensed restaurants are located here. Beaver Creek is also an overnight stop for bus travelers. Private RV park with hookups, hot showers, store, laundry and dump station. ▲

The interesting looking church here is Our Lady of Grace mission. Built in 1961, it is 1 of 3 Catholic missions on the north Alaska Highway (the others are in Burwash Landing and Haines Junction). Services from the last Sunday of May to first Sunday of September. There is a public swimming pool beside the community club. Check with the information centre about the live stage show at the Westmark Inn, evenings in summer; admission charged.

Beaver Creek Motor Inn. See display ad this section. ▲

Westmark Inn. See display ad this section.

Alaska Highway Log
(continued)

Distance* from Dawson Creek (DC) is followed by distance from Fairbanks (F). Original mileposts are indicated in the text as Historical Mile.

*Mileages from Dawson Creek are based on actual driving distance. Kilometres from Dawson Creek are based on physical kilometreposts. Please read Mileposts and Kilometreposts in the introduction for an explanation of how this highway is logged.

DC 1169.7 (1936.3 km) F 318.3 (512.2 km) Rest area to west with litter barrels, picnic tables and outhouses.

DC 1170.3 (1937.3 km) F 317.7 (511.3 km) **Private Aircraft:** Beaver Creek airstrip; elev. 2,129 feet/649m; length 3,740 feet/1,140m; gravel; no fuel. Airport of entry for Canada customs.

DC 1170.5 (1937.6 km) F 317.5 (511 km) Beaver Creek Canada customs station; phone (403) 862-7230. Open 24 hours a day year-round. All traffic entering Canada must stop here for clearance. (See Customs Requirements in the GENERAL INFORMATION section.)

NOTE: Narrow winding road northbound from here to border (next 19.4 miles/31.2 km). Road reconstruction has improved this stretch of highway over past years.

DC 1175.4 (1945.5 km) F 312.6 (503.1 km) Snag Creek plank bridge.

DC 1176.3 (1946.9 km) F 311.7 (501.6 km) Mirror Creek.

DC 1178.3 (1952 km) F 309.7 (498.4 km) Lake to east, turnout to west.

DC 1186 (1963 km) F 302 (486 km) Little Scottie Creek.

DC 1189.5 (1967.5 km) F 298.5 (480.4 km) Historic Milepost 1221. Turnout with plaque and other markers at Canada–U.S.

international border. Litter barrels. From the viewing decks, note the narrow clearing marking the border. This is part of the 20-foot-/6-m-wide swath cut by surveyors from 1904 to 1920 along the 141st meridian (from Demarcation Point on the Arctic Ocean south 600 miles/966 km to Mount St. Elias in the Wrangell Mountains) to mark the Alaska–Canada border. This swath continues south to mark the boundary between southeastern Alaska and Canada. Portions of the swath are cleared periodically by the International Boundary Commission.

TIME ZONE CHANGE: Alaska observes Alaska time; Yukon Territory observes Pacific time. See Time Zones in the GENERAL INFORMATION section for details.

DC 1189.8 (1968 km) F 298.2 (479.9 km) **Historical Mile 1221.8.** U.S. customs border station.

IMPORTANT: *The MILEPOST® log now switches to physical mileposts for north-bound travelers.* For southbound travelers, the log is based on actual driving distance. The Alaska Highway is approximately 32 miles/51 km shorter than the traditional figure of 1,221.8 miles between Dawson Creek and the YT–AK border. Please read the information on Mileposts and Kilometreposts in the introduction to the Alaska Highway.

Northbound: Fair to good pavement to Fairbanks. Watch for frost heaves, potholes and pavement breaks next 40 miles/64 km. NOTE: *Watch for road construction northbound to Tok.*

Southbound: Narrow, winding road to Haines Junction. Improved highway to Beaver Creek, fair to good pavement to Haines Junction. Watch for frost heaves, rough spots, gravel breaks and road construction.

ALASKA ROUTE 2
Distance* from Dawson Creek (DC) is followed by distance from Fairbanks (F).
*Mileages from Dawson Creek and Fairbanks are based on physical mileposts in Alaska. Kilometres given are the metric equivalents of these mileages.

DC 1221.8 (1966.3 km) F 298.2 (479.9 km) Port Alcan U.S. Customs and Immigration Service border station, open 24 hours a day year-round; pay phone (credit card and collect calls only) and restrooms. All traffic entering Alaska must stop for clearance. Phone (907) 774-2242; emergencies, (907) 774-2252. Read through the GENERAL INFORMATION section for details on alcoholic beverages, holidays, customs requirements, fishing regulations, driving and other aspects of travel in Alaska and Canada.

Border Branch U.S. post office is located here (ZIP 99764); ask for directions at the custom office.

DC 1222.5 (1967.4 km) F 297.5 (478.8 km) Tetlin National Wildlife Refuge boundary sign to west.

DC 1223.4 (1968.9 km) F 296.6 (477.3 km) Scotty Creek bridge.

DC 1224.6 (1970.7 km) F 295.4 (475.4 km) Double-ended gravel turnout to southwest at Highway Lake with USF&WS interpretive sign on wetlands. Beaver lodges southwest side of highway.

DC 1225.4 (1972 km) F 294.6 (474.1 km) USF&WS Desper Creek parking area and canoe launch.

DC 1225.5 (1972.2 km) F 294.5 (473.9 km) **Border City Lodge.** See display ad this section.   ▲

DC 1226 (1973 km) F 294 (473.1 km) **Scottie Creek Services.** See display ad this section.

DC 1227.8 (1975.9 km) F 292.2 (470.2 km) Large double-ended paved parking area to southwest with USF&WS interpretive sign on migratory birds and area geography. View to south of lakes in Chisana (SHOE-sanna)

River valley along Scotty Creek and west to the Wrangell Mountains. The Chisana gold rush took place in 1913. A mining camp was established on Cross Creek near the Chisana River, 38 miles southeast of Nabesna in the Wrangell Mountains. The settlement's population peaked at 148 in 1920.

DC 1229 (1977.8 km) **F 291** (468.3 km) USF&WS log cabin visitor center to south. Viewing deck and outdoor displays on wildlife and other subjects. Indoor wildlife displays and mounts. Deckside nature talks given daily. Restrooms (wheelchair accessible). Open 7 A.M. to 7 P.M. Memorial Day to Labor Day. Current highway conditions and fishing information posted on bulletin board. ⅄

CAUTION: Watch for frost heaves, patches and potholes northbound and southbound.

DC 1230.9 (1980.9 km) **F 289.1** (465.3 km) View of Island Lake.

DC 1233.3 (1984.7 km) **F 286.7** (461.4 km) Large paved double-ended parking area to northeast on old alignment. Watch for bears.

DC 1237 (1990.7 km) **F 283** (455.4 km) Trail to **Hidden Lake** (1 mile/1.6 km); rainbow fishing. USF&WS interpretive signs on rainbow trout and black spruce bogs. ✦

DC 1240 (1995.5 km) **F 280** (450.6 km) Turnout to west; no easy turnaround. Access to **Willow Lake** for fishing. ✦

DC 1240.3 (1996 km) **F 279.7** (450.1 km) Vertical culverts on either side of highway are an experiment to keep ground from thawing and thus prevent frost heaves.

DC 1243.6 (2001.3 km) **F 276.4** (444.8 km) Paved turnout. Scenic viewpoint to south on loop road has USF&WS interpretive signs on fire management and the effects of forest fires on the natural history of area.

DC 1246.6 (2006.1 km) **F 273.4** (440 km) **Historic Milepost 1248. Gardiner Creek** bridge; parking to west at south end of bridge. Grayling fishing.

DC 1247.6 (2007.8 km) **F 272.4** (438.4 km) Paved double-ended viewpoint to east.

DC 1249.3 (2010.5 km) **F 270.7** (435.6 km) **Historic Milepost 1254. Deadman Lake** USF&WS campground, 1.2 miles/1.9 km in on dirt road. Turnout at highway junction with campground access road. The campground has 18 sites on long loop road, firepits, toilets, picnic tables, no drinking water, boat ramp, interpretive signs, information board and self-guided nature trail. Wheelchair accessible. Scenic spot. Swimming and fishing. Northern pike average 2 feet, but skinny (local residents call them "snakes"); use wobbling lures or spinners. ⅄✦▲

DC 1250.1 (2011.8 km) **F 269.9** (434.3 km) Rest area to west. Double-ended paved parking area, 4 picnic tables, concrete fireplaces, toilets, no water.

DC 1252.2 (2015.2 km) **F 267.8** (431 km) Double-ended gravel turnout to southwest with USF&WS interpretive sign on solar basins (warm ponds and shallow marshes).

DC 1253 (2016.5 km) **F 267** (429.7 km) Views of lakes and muskeg in Chisana River valley.

DC 1253.6 (2017.4 km) **F 266.4** (428.7 km) **Frontier Surplus.** Military surplus goods. Clothing, sleeping bags, extreme cold weather "bunny boots," military tents, ammunition, tanned furs. Alaska T-shirts and caps. Local crafts, shed moose and caribou antlers. Antler products, belt buckles, bolo ties, hat racks, handmade ulus. "Moosquitoes," diamond willow lamps and canes, finished or unfinished. Used Alaska license plates, cold pop.

Log cache at the USF&WS visitor center at Milepost DC 1229. (© Corinne Smith/RKI)

Open late every day. Motorhome and RV loop. Phone (907) 778-2274. [ADVERTISEMENT]

DC 1256.3 (2021.7 km) **F 263.7** (424.4 km) Northway state highway maintenance-camp; no services.

DC 1256.7 (2022.5 km) **F 263.3** (423.7 km) Lakeview USF&WS campground on beautiful Yarger Lake; 8 sites, tables, toilets, firepits, firewood, no drinking water.

Wheelchair accessible. Interpretive signs. *NOTE: No turnaround space. Not recommended for trailers, 5th wheelers or large RVs. (Large vehicles use Deadman Lake Campground at Milepost DC 1249.3.)* ⅄▲

This is a good place to view ducks and loons. Look for the St. Elias Range to the south, Wrangell Mountains to the southwest and Mentasta Mountains to the west.

Roadside wildflowers include sweet pea, pale yellow Indian paintbrush, yarrow and Labrador tea.

DC 1260.2 (2028 km) **F 259.8** (418.1 km) 1260 Inn roadhouse (closed in 1996, current status unknown).

DC 1263 (2032.5 km) **F 257** (413.6 km) **Wrangell View Service Center.** See display ad this section. ▲

DC **1263.5** (2033.4 km) F **256.5** (412.8 km) Chisana River parallels the highway to the southwest. This is the land of a thousand ponds, most unnamed. Good trapping country. In early June, travelers may note numerous cottony white seeds blowing in the wind; these seeds are from a species of willow.

DC **1264** (2034.2 km) F **256** (412 km) Northway Junction. Campground, gas, laundromat, store, and Native arts and crafts shop located at junction. An Alaska State Trooper is also stationed here. ▲

Naabia Niign Campground & Athabascan Indian Crafts. See display ad this section. ▲

A 7-mile/11.3-km side road leads south across the Chisana River bridge to the community of Northway (description follows). A boat launch at Chisana River bridge is one of 3 boat access points to Tetlin National Wildlife Refuge.

Northway

Located 7 miles/11.3 km south of the Alaska Highway via a side road. **Population:** 364 (area). **Emergency Services: Alaska State Troopers,** phone (907) 778-2245. **EMS,** phone (907) 778-2211. **Fire Department, Clinic.**

Elevation: 1,710 feet/521m. **Climate:** Mean monthly temperature in July, 58.5°F/15°C. In January, -21°F/-30°C. Record high 91°F/33°C in June 1969; record low -72°F/-58°C in January 1952.

Private Aircraft: Northway airport, adjacent south; elev. 1,716 feet/523m; length 5,147 feet/1,569m; asphalt; fuel 100LL, Jet B, MOGAS; customs available.

Northway has a community hall, post office and modern school. FAA station and customs office are at the airport. Visitor services include motels, liquor store, propane, gas stations and air taxi service.

Historically occupied by Athabascan Indians, Northway was named to honor the village chief who adopted the name of a riverboat captain in the early 1900s. (Chief Walter Northway died in 1993. He was thought to be 117 years old.) The rich Athabascan traditions of dancing, crafts, and hunting and trapping continue today in Northway Village. Local Athabascan handicrafts available for purchase include birchbark baskets, beadwork accessories, and moose hide and fur items such as moccasins, mukluks, mittens and hats.

Northway's airport was built in the 1940s as part of the Northwest Staging Route. This cooperative project of the United States and Canada was a chain of air bases from Edmonton, AB, through Whitehorse, YT, to Fairbanks. This chain of air bases helped build up and supply Alaska defense during WWII and also was used during construction of the Alcan and the Canol project. Lend-lease aircraft bound for Russia were flown up this route to Ladd Field (now Fort Wainwright) in Fairbanks. Northway is still an important port of entry for air traffic to Alaska, and a busy one.

Northway is located within Tetlin National Wildlife Refuge. Established in 1980, the 730,000-acre refuge stretches south from the Alaska Highway and west from the Canadian border. The major physical features include rolling hills, hundreds of small lakes and 2 glacial rivers (the Nabesna and Chisana) which combine to form the Tanana River. The refuge has a very high density of nesting waterfowl. Annual duck production in favorable years exceeds 50,000. Among the larger birds using the refuge are trumpeter swans, sandhill cranes, Pacific and common loons, osprey, bald eagles and ptarmigan. Other wildlife includes moose, black and grizzly bear, wolf, coyote, beaver, red fox, lynx and caribou. Activities allowed on the refuge include wildlife observation, hunting, fishing, camping, hiking and trapping. Check with refuge personnel at the USF&WS office in Tok prior to your visit for more detailed information. Write Refuge Manager, Tetlin National Wildlife Refuge, Box 779, Tok, AK 99780; or phone (907) 883-5312. Information on the refuge is also available at the USF&WS visitor center at **Milepost DC 1229** on the Alaska Highway.

Confluence of Moose Creek and Chisana River, about 0.8 mile/1.3 km downstream from Chisana River bridge on Northway Road, south side of river, northern pike to 15 lbs., use red-and-white spoon, spring or fall. **Chisana River**, downstream from bridge, lingcod (burbot) to 8 lbs., use chunks of liver or meat, spring. **Nabesna Slough**, south end of runway, grayling to 3 lbs., use spinner or gold flies, late May. ☞

Northway Airport Lodge & Motel. See display ad this section.

Alaska Highway Log

(continued)

DC 1267.4 (2039.6 km) **F 252.6** (406.5 km) Wonderful view of the Tanana River at Beaver Slide.

DC 1268.1 (2040.8 km) **F 251.9** (405.4 km) Beaver Creek bridge. The tea-colored water flowing in the creek is the result of tannins absorbed by the water as it flows through muskeg. This phenomenon may be observed in other Northern creeks.

DC 1269 (2042.2 km) **F 251** (403.9 km) Historic Milepost 1271. Scenic viewpoint. Double-ended gravel turnout to west has a litter barrel and USF&WS interpretive sign about the Tanana River, largest tributary of the Yukon River.

DC 1272.7 (2048.2 km) **F 247.3** (398 km) Scenic viewpoint. Double-ended paved turnout to west with USF&WS interpretive sign on pond ecology and mosquitoes.

To the northwest the Tanana River flows near the highway; beyond, the Kalukna River snakes its way through plain and marshland. Mentasta Mountains are visible to the southwest.

DC 1273.9 (2050.1 km) **F 246.1** (396 km) Paved parking area with litter barrel to west by Tanana River.

In June, wild sweet peas create thick borders along the highway. This is rolling country, with aspen, birch, cottonwood, willow and white spruce.

DC 1275.5 (2052.7 km) **F 244.5** (393.5 km) Slide area next 0.3 mile/0.5 km northbound.

DC 1279 (2058.3 km) **F 241** (387.8 km) Highway cuts through sand dune stabilized by aspen and spruce trees.

DC 1281 (2061.5 km) **F 239** (384.6 km) Rough road, pavement cracks.

DC 1284.6 (2067.3 km) **F 235.4** (378.8 km) Large double-ended paved turnout to east.

DC 1285.7 (2069.1 km) **F 234.3** (377.1 km) Granite intrusion in older metamorphosed rock is exposed by road cut.

DC 1289 (2074.4 km) **F 231** (371.7 km) First view northbound of 3.4-mile-/5.5-km-long Midway Lake.

DC 1289.4 (2075 km) **F 230.6** (371.1 km) Historic Milepost 1292. Turnout uphill on east side of highway with litter barrels, view of Midway Lake and the Wrangell Mountains. USF&WS interpretive signs on Wrangell–St. Elias National Park and Native peoples.

NOTE: Difficult access for large vehicles and trailers, easier access from southbound lane.

DC 1290 (2076 km) **F 230** (370.1 km) Beautiful view of Midway Lake southbound.

DC 1291 (2077.6 km) **F 229** (368.5 km) Watch for frost heaves.

DC 1292.4 (2079.8 km) **F 227.6** (366.3 km) Paved turnout west side.

DC 1293.7 (2081.9 km) **F 226.3** (364.2 km) Paved turnout west side.

DC 1294.3 (2082.9 km) **F 225.7** (363.2 km) Bad pavement break.

DC 1301.7 (2094.8 km) **F 218.3** (351.3 km) Historic Milepost 1306. **Tetlin Junction**, Alaska Highway and Taylor Highway (Alaska Route 5) junction. 40 Mile Roadhouse; status of services unknown. The Taylor Highway (gravel, open summer only) heads northeast via Jack Wade Junction to Eagle (see TAYLOR HIGHWAY section) and to Yukon Highway 9 (Top of the World Highway) to Dawson City. (See KLONDIKE LOOP section for log of Yukon Highway 9 and description of Dawson City.)

NOTE: If you are traveling to Dawson City, keep in mind that both the Canada and U.S. customs stations are closed at night; you CANNOT cross the border unless customs stations are open. Customs hours in summer have been 8 A.M. to 9 P.M. Alaska time, 9 A.M. to 10 P.M. Pacific time on the Canadian side. Extended hours were in effect on a trial basis in 1996. Travelers are advised to check for current times at the Tok Visitor Center.

DC 1302.7 (2096.4 km) **F 217.3** (349.7 km) Scenic viewpoint at paved turnout to southwest.

DC 1303.4 (2097.5 km) **F 216.6** (348.6 km) Tanana River bridge. Informal parking area and boat launch to east at north end of bridge. Tanana (TAN-uh-naw), an Indian name, was first reported by the Western Union Telegraph Expedition of 1886.

Scenery along the Alaska Highway between the border and Tok. (Ruth von Spalding)

According to William Henry Dall, chief scientist of the expedition, the name means "mountain river." The Tanana is the largest tributary in Alaska of the Yukon River. From here the highway parallels the Tanana to Fairbanks. The Alaska Range looms in the distance.

DC 1304.6 (2099.5 km) **F 215.4** (346.6 km) Evidence of 1990 burn from here north to Tok. The Tok River fire occurred in July of 1990 and burned 97,352 acres. The fire closed the Alaska and Glenn highways at times and threatened the town of Tok.

DC 1306.6 (2102.7 km) **F 213.4** (343.4 km) Road east to lake.

DC 1308.5 (2105.7 km) **F 211.5** (340.4 km) Weigh station and turnoff to U.S. Coast Guard loran-C station and signal towers.

This loran (long range navigation) station is 1 of 7 in Alaska. A series of four 700-foot/213-m towers suspends a multi-element wire antenna used to transmit navigation signals. These signals may be used by air, land and sea navigators as an aid in determining their position. This station is located here as necessary for good geometry with 2 Gulf of Alaska loran transmitting stations.

DC 1308.8 (2106.3 km) **F 211.2** (339.9 km) Paved turnout to west.

DC 1309.2 (2106.9 km) **F 210.8** (339.2 km) Tok River State Recreation Site; 25 campsites, overflow parking, tables, firepits, toilets (wheelchair accessible), litter barrels, nature trail, boat launch and pay phone. Check bulletin board for schedule of interpretive programs. Camping fee $10/night or annual pass. *CAUTION: Swift water.* &▲

Annual passes good for unlimited camping at all Alaska state parks within a calendar year are available for $75 for Alaska residents and $200 for nonresidents. Annual daily parking pass is $25, annual boat launch pass is $50. Super Pass (camping, boat launch and parking) is available to Alaska residents only for $135. Passes may be purchased at the Alaska Public Lands Information Center in Tok.

DC 1309.4 (2107.2 km) **F 210.6** (338.9 km) Tok River bridge.

DC 1312.7 (2112.5 km) **F 207.3** (333.6 km) Tok community limits. Mountain views ahead northbound.

Wayfarer's Motel. See display ad this section.

DC 1312.8 (2112.7 km) **F 207.2** (333.4 km) Tok Dog Mushers Assoc. track and

buildings. Paved bike trail from Tok ends here.

DC 1312.9 (2112.8 km) **F 207.1** (333.3 km) **Rod's Automotive**. All automotive work. RVs, light trucks and towing. Estimates given first. Come in and have some coffee with us. Open Monday–Saturday 8 A.M.–6 P.M. Phone (907) 883-2886. [ADVERTISEMENT]

DC 1313 (2113 km) **F 207** (333.1 km) Airstrip. See Private Aircraft information in Tok section. Entering Tok (northbound), description follows. Tok is located at the junction of the Alaska Highway and Tok Cutoff (Glenn Highway). Anchorage-bound travelers turn west on the Tok Cutoff (see the TOK CUTOFF/GLENN HIGHWAY section). Fairbanks-bound travelers continue north on the Alaska Highway.

Southbound travelers: Driving distance from Tok to Beaver Creek is 113 miles/ 182 km; Haines Junction 296 miles/476 km; Haines (departure point for Alaska state ferries) 446.5 miles/718.5 km; and Whitehorse 396 miles/637 km.

DC 1313.1 (2113.1 km) **F 206.9** (332.9 km) **Tok Gateway Salmon Bake and RV Park**. Vacationers should not miss Tok's Gateway Salmon Bake, featuring outdoor flame-grilled Alaska king salmon, halibut,

ribs and reindeer sausage. Buffalo burgers. Chowder. Good food, friendly people; casual dining at its best. Open 11 A.M. to 9 P.M., except Sunday 4 to 9 P.M. Free shuttle bus service from local hotels and RV parks. Wooded RV and tent sites with tables, clean restrooms, dump station and water. Free dry camping with dinner. Phone (907) 883-5555. [ADVERTISEMENT] ▲

DC 1313.2 (2113.3 km) **F 206.8** (332.8 km) **Willard's Full Service Repair**. See display ad this section.

DC 1313.3 (2113.5 km) **F 206.7** (332.6 km) **Eska Trading Post**, on the left northbound. Home of frozen yogurt and premium quality hand-dipped Alaskan ice cream. Along with our audio books for sale and book swap, check out our video and Nintendo rentals, popcorn, candy, pop and "hex" tanning unit. [ADVERTISEMENT]

DC 1313.3 (2113.5 km) **F 206.7** (332.6 km) **Village Texaco Foodmart**. Filtered unleaded and premium gas and diesel. Lubricants and propane. Automatic teller machine, laundromat, phone cards, pay phones and clean restrooms. Deli chicken, burritos, mojos, snacks, pop, ice, milk shakes, ice cream and espresso. RV supplies. Alaskan souvenirs. Across highway from Tok RV Village. See display ad this section. [ADVERTISEMENT]

DC 1313.3 (2113.5 km) **F 206.7** (332.6 km) **Northstar**. See display ad this section. ▲

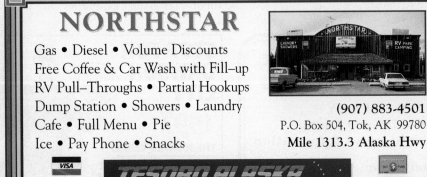

DC 1313.3 (2113.5 km) F 206.7 (332.6 km) **Young's Motel** and **Fast Eddy's Restaurant.** A touch of Alaskana in a modern setting. Affordable, clean and spacious. We cater to the independent highway traveler. Open year-round with all the

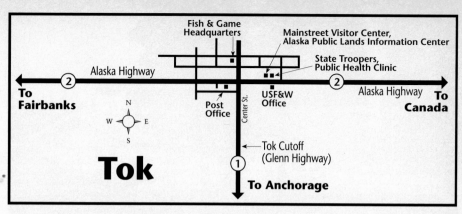

amenities: telephones, private baths, satellite TV, ample parking. Nonsmoking rooms available. Check in at Fast Eddy's full-service restaurant, open 6 A.M. to midnight. Reserve early! P.O. Box 482, Tok, AK 99780. (907) 883-4411; fax (907) 883-5023. [ADVERTISEMENT]

DC 1313.3 (2113.5 km) F 206.7 (332.6 km) **The Bull Shooter Sporting Goods & RV Park**, Tok, Alaska. Fishing and hunting licenses. Sporting goods. Large selection of fishing gear and tackle. Camping supplies. Guns and ammo. Plan to stay at the Bull Shooter's nice, quiet RV park. 30 spaces, 24 pull-throughs. Full or partial hookups, 30-amp electric, dump station, good drinking water. Non-metered showers, restrooms, ice and phone. We accept VISA and MasterCard. Welcome to Alaska! We are on the left as you come into Tok. P.O. Box 553, Tok, AK 99780. Reservations accepted. Call (907)

883-5625. See display ad in Tok section. [ADVERTISEMENT] ▲

DC 1313.4 (2113.6 km) F 206.6 (332.5 km) **Tok RV Village.** Alaska's finest. Good Sam or KOA cards honored. Convenient pull-through spaces with 30-amp power. Full and partial hookups, clean restrooms and showers, dump station, laundry, vehicle wash, picnic tables, public phones. Gift shop. RV supplies, ice. MasterCard, VISA and Discover. Located across highway from Village Texaco Foodmart. Restaurants, liquor store, night club, hardware store, oil change and lube service nearby. See display ad in Tok section. [ADVERTISEMENT] ▲

DC 1313.9 (2114.5 km) F 206.1 (331.7 km) **Tok Machine & Welding/Tok Northern Exposures 1-Hour Photo.** Your one stop in Tok for RV repair needs. Machine shop and certified welder; oil change; lubrication; (907) 883-5670. Get your film developed

next door and have your "olde tyme" portrait taken. Film, batteries, albums, frames, gifts; (907) 883-5424. On your left northbound. See display ad. [ADVERTISEMENT]

DC 1314.1 (2114.8 km) F 205.9 (331.3 km) Tok Civic Center; Alaska Public Lands Information Center and Tok Mainstreet Visitor Center.

Tok

DC 1314.2 (2115 km) F 205.8 (331.2 km) At the junction of the Alaska Highway and Tok Cutoff (Glenn Highway) between the Tanana River to the north and the Alaska Range to the southwest. **Population: 1,405. Emergency Services: Alaska State Troopers,** phone (907) 883-5111. **Fire Department,**

Stop in at the Tok Mainstreet Visitor Center for local and state information.
(Ruth von Spalding)

phone (907) 883-2333. **Community Clinic,** across from the fire hall on the Tok Cutoff, phone (907) 883-5855 during business hours. **Ambulance,** phone (907) 883-2300 or 911. EMT squad and air medivac available. **Public Health Clinic,** next to the Alaska State Troopers at **Milepost 1314.1,** phone (907) 883-4101.

Visitor Information: The Tok Mainstreet Visitor Center, operated by the Tok Cham-

ber of Commerce, is located in the Tok Civic Center at the junction of the Alaska Highway and Tok Cutoff. This huge log building is a center for local and state information, trip planning, art exhibits and shows. The state-operated Alaska Public Lands Information Center here sells Alaska State Park

annual passes and books Alaska Marine Highway reservations; phone (907) 883-5667. The center offers free coffee, public telephones and restrooms, a message board and gift shop. It is open daily 7 A.M. to 9 P.M., May 1 to Oct. 1. Write Box 389, Tok, AK 99780; phone (907) 883-5775 or 883-5887.

The U.S. Fish & Wildlife Service office is located at **Milepost DC 1314.1** next to the grocery store, directly across the highway from the State Troopers. Visitors are welcome. Stop in for information regarding Tetlin National Wildlife Refuge. Office hours are 8 A.M. to noon and 1 to 4:30 P.M., weekdays. Write Box 155, Tok, AK 99780, or phone (907) 883-5312.

Elevation: 1,635 feet/498m. **Climate:** Mean monthly temperature in January, -19°F/-29°C; in July 59°F/14°C. Record low was -71°F/-57°C in January 1965; record high, 96°F/36°C in June 1969. **Radio:** FM stations are 90.5, 91.1 (KUAC-FM, University of Alaska Fairbanks) and 101.5. **Television:** Satellite channel 13. **Newspaper:** *Mukluk News* (twice monthly).

Private Aircraft: Tok Junction, 1 mile/1.6 km east; elev. 1,630 feet/497m; length 2,510 feet/765m; asphalt; fuel 100 LL; unattended. Tok airstrip, 2 miles/3.2 km south; elev. 1,670 feet/509m; length 1,690 feet/515m; gravel; no fuel, unattended. Tok NR 2 airstrip across the highway to the west of Tok airstrip, is private.

Tok had its beginnings as a construction camp on the Alcan Highway in 1942. Highway engineer C.G. Polk was sent to Fairbanks in May of 1942 to take charge of Alaskan construction, and start work on the road between Tok Junction and Big Delta. Work was also under way on the Gulkana–Slana–Tok Junction road (now the Tok Cutoff on the Glenn Highway to Anchorage). But on June 7, 1942, a Japanese task force invaded Attu and Kiska islands in the Aleutians, and the Alcan took priority over the Slana cutoff.

The name Tok (rhymes with poke) was long believed to be derived from Tokyo Camp, patriotically shortened during WWII to Tok. There exist at least three other versions of how Tok got its name. According to local author Donna Blasor-Bernhardt in *Tok,*

TOK ALASKA

Good Sampark

Village TEXACO

TOK RV VILLAGE

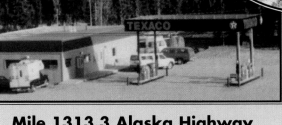

Mile 1313.3 Alaska Highway
P.O. Box 739
Tok, Alaska 99780
Phone (907) 883-4660

Foodmart
Laundromat
Deli
Alaskan Souvenirs
Clean Restrooms
Gas • Diesel • Propane
ATM Machine • Phone Cards

Mile 1313.4 Alaska Highway
P.O. Box 739 • Tok, Alaska 99780
(907) 883-5877 • Fax (907) 883-5878
1-800-478-5878
Toll Free in Alaska   Reservations Accepted

95 Sites • Full & Partial Hookups
Pull Thrus • Tent Sites • 30-Amp. Power
Dump Station • Vehicle Wash Facility
Gift Shop • Hunting & Fishing Licenses
Clean Restrooms & Showers • Laundry
RV Supplies • Good Sam or KOA Discounts

We thank all of you wonderful customers who
help to make our business such a great success.

The Jernigan Family

Come visit the
TOK RV VILLAGE GIFT SHOP

*A small gift shop
full of surprises*

T-shirts • Sweatshirts
Hats • Videos
Postcards • Jewelry
Alaskan Made Crafts

Quality Gifts
at Reasonable Prices

COMCHEK TCHEK NTS CCIS CCC

the Real Story (1996), Tok was named for a young husky pup during construction of the Alaska Highway in 1942.

Because Tok is the major overland point of entry to Alaska, it is primarily a trade and service center for all types of transportation, especially for summer travelers coming up the Alaska Highway. A stopover here is a good opportunity to meet other travelers and swap experiences. Tok is the only town in Alaska that the highway traveler must pass through twice—once when arriving in the state and again on leaving the state. The governor proclaimed Tok "Mainstreet Alaska" in 1991. Townspeople are proud of this designation and work hard to make visi-

tors happy and to represent their community and state.

Tok's central business district is at the junction of the Alaska Highway and Tok Cutoff (Glenn Highway). From the junction, homes and businesses spread out along both highways on flat terrain dotted with densely timbered stands of black spruce.

Tok has 13 churches, a public library, an elementary school, a 4-year accredited high school and a University of Alaska extension program. Local clubs include the Lions, Disabled American Veterans, Veterans of Foreign Wars and Chamber of Commerce

ACCOMMODATIONS/VISITOR SERVICE

There are 8 hotels/motels, a variety of restaurants and several gas stations in town, as well as bed and breakfasts in Tok, just north of Tok Junction along the Alaska Highway and south on the Glenn Highway (Tok Cutoff). Grocery, hardware and sporting goods stores, bakery, beauty shop, gift shops, liquor stores, auto repair and auto parts stores, wrecker service, laundromats and a post office are also available. The bank is located across the highway from the Public Lands Information Center. There is an automatic teller machine at Village Texaco.

The willow ptarmigan, Alaska's state bird, turns white in winter. (© Beth Davidow)

Tok AYH youth hostel is located on Pringle Road, 0.8 mile/1.3 km south of **Milepost DC 1322.6**; phone (907) 883-3745.

There are several private RV parks in Tok. Nearby state campgrounds include: Tok River State Recreation Site at **Milepost DC 1309.2** and Moon Lake State Recreation Site at **Milepost DC 1331.9** Alaska Highway; and Eagle Trail State Recreation Site at **Milepost GJ 109.3** Tok Cutoff (Glenn Highway) 16 miles/25 km west. ▲

A WinterCabin Bed & Breakfast. New log cabins with sun porch. Quiet surroundings on original site of the world famous "Tent In Tok." Owned and operated by author/Poet Laureate Donna Blasor-Bernhardt. Share the atmosphere various media personalities (including Charles Kuralt's TV crew) have found so inviting. Ample parking, picinic tables, continental-plus breakfast. Shared bathouse, oversize bathtub. Nonsmoking. (907) 883-5655. See display ad. [ADVERTISEMENT]

Golden Bear Motel. Quiet location, 62 deluxe units, RV park with wooded pull-through sites, heated bathhouse, laundry; fine restaurant. Open 6 A.M. to 11 P.M. Our gift shop carries an extensive selection of Alaskana, jewelry, T-shirts and souvenirs. The friendly atmosphere you came to Alaska to find! See display ad this section. [ADVERTISEMENT] ▲

Golden Dreams Bed and Breakfast will begin your Alaskan adventure. Awaiting you are personalized photo albums depicting 20 years of gold mining, dog mushing and trapping adventures. Our hot breakfast, served on fine china and crystal, will leave our guests feeling pampered and loved. Group and senior discounts. Warm hospitality with your comfort our priority. Leave with a genuine gold flake! Hebrews 13:2. Smoke and alcohol-free. (907) 883-5659 or 1-800-880-5659; Box 106, Tok, AK 99780. 3.5 miles west of Tok. [ADVERTISEMENT]

Sourdough Campground's Pancake Breakfast, served 7–11 A.M. (June, July, August). Genuine "Sourdough!" Full and

partial RV hookups. Dry campsites. Showers included. Guaranteed clean restrooms. High-pressure car wash. Open-air museum with gold rush memorabilia. Free evening video program. Located 1.7 miles from the junction toward Anchorage on Tok Cutoff (Glenn Highway). See display ad this section. [ADVERTISEMENT] ▲

Snowshoe Motel. 24 units with private baths. Excellent accommodations for fami-

lies or 2 couples traveling together. In-room phones, satellite TV. Free continental breakfast served summers only. Our guests are invited to enjoy panoramic mountain views and sunsets from our Midnight Sun Room. We provide barbecue facilities and a place to make your own cocktails. 1-800-478-4511 or (907) 883-4511. [ADVERTISEMENT]

The Stage Stop, bed and breakfast for people and horses. Private cabin and 3 large

Dog mushing is Alaska's state sport and a popular winter pastime in Tok.
(© Barbara Willard)

rooms with king and queen beds, one with private bath, plus full breakfast. Quiet location Mile 1.7 Tok Cutoff highway. New barn and corrals for horses. Reasonable rates from $35. Open all year. Mary Underwood, Box 69, Tok, AK 99780. Phone (907) 883-5338. In Alaska, 1-800-478-5369. [ADVERTISEMENT]

Tok Lodge, located on Glenn Highway, 1 block from junction. Alcan Room serves buses, leaving full-service restaurant open for car traffic. 36 new motel rooms. Common comments are: "nicest rooms on the highway" and "best meal since leaving home." Locally owned by Pam and Bud Johnson for 22 years. Mini-Mart and liquor store located on premises. See display ad this section. [ADVERTISEMENT]

Tundra Lodge & RV Park. Spacious, tree-shaded camping sites. Full and partial hookups; 20-, 30-, 50-amp power. Tent sites. Pull-throughs. Clean restrooms and showers included in price. Picnic tables, fire rings and wood. Dump station. Laundromat. Vehicle wash. Pay phone. Ice. Cocktail

Paved Bike Paths   Nature Trails   Fishing   Evening Sled Dog Demos

Bird Watching   Pan for Gold   Flight-Seeing   Ribs BBQing

Tok Chamber of Commerce
Welcomes You To Alaska

PARTIAL MEMBERSHIP SPONSORS

MAINSTREET VISITOR CENTER

Trip planning, travel information. Wildlife displays, gifts, open 7am to 8pm daily. Friendly, helpful staff.

(907) 883-5775

TOK NORTHERN EXPOSURES

1 hour photo, cameras, film, batteries, Alaska photo albums, other gifts.

(907) 883-5424

TOK MACHINE SHOP & WELDING

Certified Welder
Repairs

(907) 883-5670

BURNT PAW

Free dog team show, 7:30pm, except Sun., next to Post Office. Log gift shop w/ sod roof. Box 7, Tok

(907) 883-4121

CABINS OUTBACK B&B

@ Burnt Paw, nightly rentals log cabins; rustic outside, all conveniences inside. Summer. Box 7, Tok

(907) 883-4121

GRIZZLY AUTO. SERVICE CENTER

Welding, towing, tires, engines, Specialist in R.V. repair. 1 Mile Tok Cut-off
WELCOME GOOD SAM

(907) 883-5514

NORTH STAR

Mi. 1313.3 Alaska Highway Gas, diesel, propane, car wash, showers, laundromat, cafe.

LOOSE MOOSE ESPRESSO CAFE

Lunch specials, mostly vegetarian
Espresso • Bulk coffee • Quiche Soups • Cheesecake • Pies
On the Alaska Hwy. next to bakery

(907) 883-5282

A WINTERCABIN B&B

Alaskan experience the easy way! Log cabins with sun porch. Separate bath house. Quiet Continental breakfast.

(907) 883-5655

CLEFT OF THE ROCK B&B

Cabins, rooms, full breakfast

(907) 883-4219 or (907) 883-5963

FAX Alaska only 1-800-478-5646
http://www.akpub.com/akbbrv/cleft.html

ALASKA BIKING ADVENTURES

See the Alaska wilderness most miss. Guided wilderness bike trips/bike rental, group rates. Reservations required.

(907) 883-4219,
FAX (907) 883-5963

JACK WADE GOLD CO.

Mining Museum-Antique display. Alaska gold nugget jewelry made in-store. Year-round, 7am-7pm.

(907) 883-5887
1 block south on Tok Cut-off

RITA'S CAMPGROUND/RV PARK

Cheryls Old Fashion B&B. Alaska Hwy. Mi. 1315.7, Alaska Pioneers

(907) 883-4342
"A relaxing Alaska atmosphere"

ALL ALASKA GIFTS & CRAFTS

Quality T-shirts, jewelry, Native crafts, Eskimo dolls, Jorgensen Bros. Wildlife displays. You'll like our prices.
At main intersection in Tok.

TOK LODGE

Historical lodge w/10 rooms & 38 new motel units. Gift shop, cocktail lounge w/ patio dining. Cafe specializes in home cooking featuring prime rib, salmon, halibut & daily lunch specials, sourdough breakfasts. Open year-round.

Reservations
1-800-478-3007

P.O. Box 135 CM, Tok, Ak. 99780

TOK LIQUOR MINI-MART

Full line of beverages, ice, snacks, grocery items. 2 blocks south on Tok Cut-off

SOURDOUGH CAMPGROUND

Full hook-ups, wooded sites, Sourdough breafast daily 7am-llam.

(907) 883-5543
1 1/2 Mi. on Tok Cut-off

TOK SAVEWAY

Open 24 hrs. year-round
Tesoro gas, groceries, motel one block south on Tok Cut-off.

(907) 883-5389

SNOWSHOE GIFTS

Souvenirs, fine art, carvings, prints, jewelry, Alaska made gifts. Adjacent to SnowShoe Motel.

(907) 883-4181

SNOWSHOE MOTEL

24 Modern units w/satellite color TV, phones. Year-round. Summer: FREE continental breakfast, new BBQ area.

Reservations:
(907) 883-4511
Ak./YT: 1-800-478-4511
FAX: (907) 883-4512

P.O. Box 559, Tok, AK 99780
Hosts: Paul & Geneva Smith
Candy & Dannie Troupe

YOUNG'S CHEVRON

Volume Discounts, Foodmart Gas, diesel, propane, fast lube, full auto service center. Tire sales/service & RV wash. Alcan Espresso. At the Junction.

YOUNG'S CAFE

Breakfast ALL DAY!
Sourdough hotcakes, full menu, homemade pies & goodies, daily lunch specials. At the Junction in Tok.

TUNDRA LODGE & RV PARK

78 Large shaded sites, 30-50 Amp. service Tent sites, RV wash, laundromat, cocktail lounge.

(907) 883-7875
FAX 883-7876

40 MILE AIR FLIGHTSEEING TOURS

Scenic/photo., glaciers, wildlife, mountains, historic Native village. Fish./Hunt. charters.

(907) 883-5191

GATEWAY SALMON BAKE

Salmon, Halibut, Buffalo, Ribs. Free camping w/dinner purchase. Alaska's Finest Food. Free Shuttle.

(907) 883-5555

lounge and meeting room. See display ad Mile 1315 Alaska Highway. [ADVERTISEMENT] ▲

TRANSPORTATION

Air: Charter air service available; inquire at Tok state airstrip (Milepost DC 1313). Charter flightseeing and fly-in fishing trips available. Scheduled passenger and freight service between Tok, Delta Junction and Fairbanks 4 days a week via 40-Mile Air.

Bus: See Bus Lines in the GENERAL INFORMATION section for scheduled service to other communities.

ATTRACTIONS

Tok Civic Center. Located at the junction of the Tok Cutoff and the Alaska Highway, this 7,000-square-foot building houses the Tok Mainstreet Visitor Center, the Alaska Public Lands Information Center and the Tok Community Library. Huge natural spruce logs support an open-beamed, cathedral ceiling. Large picture windows frame the Alaska Range. Displays include: the gold rush; rock, gems and fossils; Alaskan wildlife; waterfowl; and Alaska Highway memorabilia. The Alaska Public Lands Information Center offers videos on Alaska destinations and trip-planning services. Alaska Marine Highway reservations may be booked here. Restrooms, pay phone and message board.

Local Events: There is a variety of things to do in Tok, thanks to local individuals, businesses and clubs. Local campgrounds offer slide shows, movies, gold panning, a salmon bake, miniature golf and sourdough pancake breakfasts. Sled dog demonstrations are given at Burnt Paw gift shop and at the Westmark.

Other local events include bingo games and softball games at the local field. Visitors are welcome at the senior citizens center. The Tok triathlon (12 miles of biking, 10 of canoeing and 5 of jogging) and Tok Trot are both held annually. Tok's Fourth of July celebration is a major event, complete with a parade, picnic and games. Check at the Mainstreet Visitor Center for more information on these local events.

Bike Trail: A wide paved bike trail extends southeast from Tok on the Alaska Highway as far east as the Dog Mushers Assoc. track, and as far west as Tanacross Junction; approximate length is 13.2 miles/21.2 km. You may also bike out the Tok Cutoff past Sourdough Campground. Travelers may park their vehicles in and around Tok and find a bike trail nearby leading into or out of Tok.

"GLENN HIGHWAY 1 BLOCK FROM JUNCTION"

Native Crafts: Tok is a trade center for the Athabascan Native villages of Tanacross, Northway, Tetlin, Mentasta, Dot Lake and Eagle. Several of the Native women make birch baskets, beaded moccasins, boots and beaded necklaces. Examples of Native work may be seen at the Native-operated gift shop at Northway junction and at several gift shops and other outlets in Tok.

The state of Alaska has a crafts identification program which identifies authentic Native and Alaskan handicrafts. This symbol is of a polar bear.

Birch baskets were once used in the Native camps and villages. Traditionally they had folded corners, which held water, and were even used for cooking by dropping heated stones into the liquid in the baskets. The baskets are made by peeling the bark from the birch trees, usually in the early summer months. The bark is easiest to work with when moist and pliable. It is cut into shape and sewn together with strips of spruce root dug out of the ground and split. If the root is too dry it is soaked until it is manageable. Holes are put in the birch bark with a punch or screwdriver, and the spruce root is laced in and out. Native women dye the spruce root with food coloring, watercolors or berry juice. A few Natives also make birch canoes and birch baby carriers.

Many of the moccasins and mukluks for sale in Tok are made with moose hide that has the "Native tan." This means moose hide tanned by the Native. First the excess fat and meat is scraped off the hide, then it is soaked in a soap solution (some use a mixture of brains and ashes). After soaking, all the moisture is taken out by constant scraping with a dull knife or scraper. The hide is then scraped again and rubbed together to soften it. Next it is often smoke-cured in rotted spruce wood smoke. The tanning process takes from a few days to a week.

Beading can be a slow and tedious process. Most women say if they work steadily all day they can put the beading on one moccasin, but usually they do their beadwork

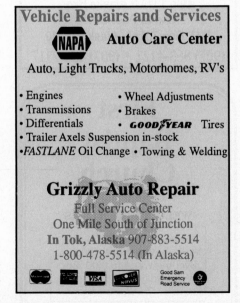
Please mention *The MILEPOST®* to our advertisers!

over a period of several days, alternating it with other activities.

Snowshoe Fine Arts and Gifts invites you to come browse and shop in our gift store. See our gallery of art prints, figurines, Alaska Native-made carvings, masks, dolls, birch and grass baskets, and beadwork. Jewelry made of natural Alaska gemstones, ivory

and gold nugget. Lots of caps, T-shirts and sweatshirts. Souvenir items and Alaska-made products. Phone (907) 883-4181. [ADVERTISEMENT]

Sled Dog Breeding and Training: Dog mushing is Alaska's official state sport, and Tok has become known as the "Sled Dog Capital of Alaska," with at least 1 out of every 3 people in town involved in some way with raising dogs. Kennels range in size from 100 dogs to a single family pet. Visitors who come to Tok seeking either a pet or a racing sled dog will probably find what they are looking for here.

The Siberian husky is the most popular sled dog and oftentimes has distinctive blue eyes. The Alaskan malamute is much larger than the Siberian and is used for hauling heavy loads at a slower pace. Both breeds are AKC recognized. The Alaskan husky (or husky) is a catchall term for any of the arctic breeds or northern types of dogs and is usu-

Fully-packed motorcycles from Maine parked outside a Tok cafe. (Ruth von Spalding)

ally a cross. Sled dogs may be any registered breed or crossbreed, since mushers look for conformation, attitude and speed when putting together a working team rather than pedigrees. Common strains in racing dogs have included Irish setter, Labrador and wolf, among others.

Sled Dog Trails and Races: Tok boasts a well-known and long-established dog mushing trail, which draws many world-class and recreational mushers. The 20.5-mile/33-km trail begins at the rustic log Tok Dog Mushers Assoc. building at **Milepost DC 1312.8** on the Alaska Highway. The trail is a favorite with spectators because it affords many miles of viewing from along the Alaska Highway.

Racing begins in late November and extends through the end of March. Junior mushers include 1-, 2-, 3- and 5-dog classes; junior adult mushers include 5- and 8-dog classes. Open (unlimited) classes can run as many as 16 dogs.

The biggest race of the season in Tok is

the Race of Champions, held in late March, which also has the largest entry of any sprint race in Alaska. Begun in 1954 as a bet between 2 roadhouse proprietors, today the Race of Champions includes over 100 teams in 3 classes competing for prize money and trophies. It is considered to be the third leg of sled dog racing's "triple crown," following the Fur Rendezvous in Anchorage and the Fairbanks North American Championship.

Visitors are also welcome to attend the Tok Native Assoc.'s potlatch, held the same weekend as the race, in the Tok school gym.

AREA FISHING: Fly-in fishing to area lakes for northern pike, grayling and lake trout; inquire at Tok state airstrip. There are 43 lakes in the Delta–Tok area that are stocked by the Alaska Dept. of Fish and Game. Lakes are stocked primarily with rainbow trout; other stocked species include arctic grayling, lake trout, arctic char and king salmon. Most of these lakes are located close to the road system, but there are walk-in lakes available as well. Most easily accessible are **North Twin, South Twin** and **Mark lakes.** There is a trailhead 0.5 mile/0.8 km east of the Gerstle River bridge for **Big Donna Lake** (3.5-mile/5.6-km hike) and **Little Donna Lake** (4.5 miles/7.2 km). **Quartz Lake,** north of Delta Junction, is a popular spot for rainbow trout and silver salmon. Consult ADF&G offices in Tok or Delta Junction for other locations.

Alaska Highway Log
(continued)

DC 1314.8 (2115.9 km) F 205.2 (330.2 km) **Northern Energy Corp.** See display ad this section.

DC 1315 (2116.2 km) F 205 (329.9 km) **Tundra Lodge and RV Park.** See display ad this section. ▲

DC 1315.7 (2117.3 km) F 204.3 (328.8 km) **Rita's Campground RV Park & Cheryl's Old Fashion Bed & Breakfast Cabin.** See display ad this section. ▲

DC 1316.6 (2118.8 km) F 203.4 (327.3 km) Scoby Road, Sundog Trail. Access to bed and breakfasts.

DC 1317 (2119.4 km) F 203 (326.7 km) **Mukluk Land.** See display ad this section.

DC 1322.6 (2128.5 km) F 197.4 (317.7 km) Pringle Road. Tok youth hostel, housed in a wall tent, is located 0.8 mile/1.3 km south; 10 beds, tent space available.

DC 1324.6 (2131.7 km) F 195.4 (314.5 km) Tanacross fireguard station.

DC 1324.7 (2131.8 km) F 195.3 (314.3 km) Gravel access road to Tanacross airstrip. (See also **Milepost DC 1325.7**)

DC 1325.6 (2133.3 km) F 194.4 (312.8 km) **Historic Milepost 1328.**

DC 1325.7 (2133.4 km) F 194.3 (312.7 km) **Tanacross Junction.** End of paved bike trail from Tok and access to Tanacross.

Drive in 1.2 miles/1.9 km on gravel road to junction, turn left for village of **TANACROSS** (pop. 106), home of the once numerous branch of the Tanah, or Tinneh, Indians. This village of colorful modern houses is built on a short 0.7-mile/1.1-km loop road. Turn right at junction and drive 0.2 mile/0.3 km for access road to airstrip, or 0.3 mile/0.5 km to reach Tanana River and view across river of the white church steeple in the old village of Tanacross which burned down in 1979. Road eventually dead ends in residential area.

Private Aircraft: Tanacross airstrip; elev. 1,549 feet/472m; 2 runways, length 5,000 feet/1,524m and 5,100 feet/1,554m; asphalt; unattended.

DC 1327.4 (2136.2 km) F 192.6 (310 km) Parking area at lake to north.

DC 1330.1 (2140.5 km) F 189.9 (305.6 km) Paved turnout with litter container to east. View of Alaska Range to the west.

DC 1330.7 (2141.5 km) F 189.3 (304.6 km) Paved turnout to east.

DC 1331.9 (2143.5 km) F 188.1 (302.7 km) Moon Lake State Recreation Site, 0.2 mile/0.3 km north off highway; 15 campsites, toilets, tables, water, firepits, swimming (watch for floatplanes). Camping fee $10/night or annual pass. ▲

DC 1333.6 (2146.2 km) F 186.4 (300 km) **Historic Milepost 1339.** Yerrick Creek bridge.

DC 1335 (2148.4 km) F 185 (297.7 km) Watch for moose.

DC 1338.2 (2153.5 km) F 181.8 (292.6 km) Highway crosses Cathedral Creeks 3 times between here and **Milepost DC 1339.**

DC 1342.2 (2160 km) F 177.8 (286.1 km) Sheep Creek culvert.

DC 1344.5 (2163.8 km) F 175.5 (282.4 km) **Historic Milepost 1352.** Double-ended paved parking area to east. Interpretive panel on the "father of the international highway," Donald MacDonald. Alaska Range to the south. Good photo stop.

DC 1347.2 (2168 km) F 172.8 (278 km) **Forest Lake** trailhead; 6 mile/9.6 km ATV trail (not easy access) to lake stocked with rainbow trout.

DC 1347.3 (2168.2 km) F 172.7 (277.9 km) Entering Game Management Unit 20D northbound, Unit 12 southbound.

DC 1347.5 (2168.5 km) F 172.5 (277.6 km) Robertson River bridge. The river was named by Lt. Henry T. Allen for a member of his 1885 expedition.

DC 1348 (2169.3 km) F 172 (276.8 km) Bad frost heaves.

DC 1348.1 (2169.5 km) F 171.9 (276.6 km) Side road west to parking lot at old Haines pipeline right-of-way. Hike in 0.3

mile/0.5 km for **Robertson No. 2 Lake;** rainbow fishing. ⊷

DC 1348.8 (2170.6 km) F 171.2 (275.5 km) *CAUTION*: Very bad frost heaves.

DC 1350.5 (2173.3 km) F 169.5 (272.8 km) Double-ended paved turnout to west. Rough road next mile northbound.

DC 1353.7 (2178.5 km) F 166.3 (267.6 km) Jan Lake Road. Drive in 0.5 mile/0.8 km to parking area with boat launch and toilets. No overnight camping, carry out garbage. **Jan Lake** is stocked with rainbow; use spinners, flies, or salmon eggs with bobber. Dot Lake Native Corp. land, limited public access. ⊷

DC 1357.3 (2184.4 km) F 162.7 (261.8 km) Bear Creek bridge. Paved turnout to west.

DC 1358.7 (2186.6 km) F 161.3 (259.6 km) Chief Creek bridge. Paved turnout to west at north end of bridge.

DC 1361.3 (2190.2 km) F 158.7 (255.4 km) **DOT LAKE** (pop. 70). Lodge with gas, groceries, restaurant, car wash, motel, camping and post office (closed Sunday). Headquarters for the Dot Lake (Athabascan) Indian Corp. Homesteaded in the 1940s, a school was established here in 1952. Dot Lake's historic chapel was built in 1949. ▲

Dot Lake Lodge. See display ad this section. ▲

Camper at Moon Lake state recreation site, Milepost DC 1331.9. (© Susan Cole Kelly)

DC 1361.6 (2191 km) F 158.4 (254.9 km) **Historic Milepost 1368.** Gravel turnout by lake to east. Rough narrow road northbound. Wild blue irises bloom in roadside ditches in June.

DC 1370.2 (2205.1 km) F 149.8 (241.1 km) Double-ended paved parking area to east.

DC 1370.5 (2205.4 km) F 149.5 (240.6 km) **Historic Milepost 1376.** Alaska Highway interpretive panel on "the Crooked Road."

DC 1371.5 (2207.2 km) F 148.5 (239 km) Berry Creek bridge. Parking area to west.

DC 1374.2 (2211.5 km) F 145.8 (234.6 km) Sears Creek bridge. Parking area to west.

DC 1376 (2214.4 km) F 144 (231.7 km) Entering Tok Management Area, Tanana State Forest southbound.

DC 1378 (2217.6 km) F 142 (228.5 km) Bridge over Dry Creek. Evidence of forest fire next mile northbound.

DC 1379 (2219.2 km) F 141 (226.9 km) Double-ended paved turnout with mountain views to west.

DC 1380.5 (2221.6 km) F 139.5 (224.5 km) Johnson River bridge. A tributary of the Tanana River, the Johnson River was named by Lt. Henry T. Allen in 1887 for Peder Johnson, a Swedish miner and member of his party.

DC 1381.1 (2222.6 km) F 138.9 (223.5 km) Paved turnout to west. Access road to **Lisa Lake** (stocked).

DC 1383.9 (2227.1 km) F 136.1 (219 km) **Craig Lake** access west side of highway via 0.5-mile/0.8-km trail; rainbow trout fishing. ◂━

DC 1385 (2228.9 km) F 135 (217.3 km) Double-ended gravel turnout. Tanana River access.

*CAUTION: Watch for major road construction between **Mileposts DC 1386 and 1398** in 1997 and 1998.*

DC 1388.4 (2234.4 km) F 131.6 (211.8 km) Little Gerstle River bridge (to be replaced in 1997 and 1998).

DC 1391.9 (2240 km) F 128.1 (206.2 km) Trailhead to **Big Donna Lake**, 3.5 miles/5.6 km, and **Little Donna Lake**, 4.5 miles/7.2 km; stocked with rainbow. ◂━

DC 1392.3 (2240.6 km) F 127.7 (205.5 km) Cummings Road through Delta barley project. *CAUTION: Watch for buffalo (bison) on highway between here and Delta Junction.*

On the southwest side of the Alaska Highway approaching Delta Junction is the Bison Sanctuary. This range provides the bison herd with autumn and winter grazing on over 3,000 acres of grassland. It was developed to reduce agricultural crop depredation by bison.

DC 1392.7 (2241.3 km) F 127.3 (204.9 km) Gerstle River Black Veterans Recognition bridge. The river was named for Lewis Gerstle, president of the Alaska Commercial Co., by Lt. Henry T. Allen, whose 1885 expedition explored the Copper, Tanana and Koyukuk river regions for the U.S. Army Dept. of the Columbia.

Rest area on north side of bridge, overnight RV parking and camping permitted; toilets, tables and firepits. ▲

DC 1395.5 (2245.8 km) 124.5 (200.4

km) Evidence of 1994 forest fire southwest side of highway next 32 miles/4.8 km northbound.

DC 1398 (2249.8 km) F 122 (196.5 km) Watch for bison next 15 miles/24 km northbound.

CAUTION: Watch for major road construction next 12 miles/19 km southbound in 1997 and 1998.

DC 1401.2 (2255 km) F 118.8 (191.2 km) Double-ended gravel turnout.

DC 1403.6 (2258.8 km) F 116.4 (187.3 km) Sawmill Creek Road to northeast. This rough gravel road goes through the heart of the Delta barley fields. A sign just off the highway explains the barley project. Visiting farmers are welcome to talk with local farmers along the road, except during planting (May) and harvesting (August or September) when they are too busy. Commercial farm tours available.

Farm Tours. See display ad this section.

DC 1403.9 (2259.3 km) F 116.1 (186.8 km) Sawmill Creek bridge.

DC 1408 (2265.9 km) F 112 (180.2 km) Access to University of Alaska Agricultural and Forestry Experiment Station. Major research at this facility concentrates on agricultural cropping, fertilization and tillage management.

DC 1410 (2269.1 km) F 110 (177 km) Access road north to Delta barley project.

DC 1411 (2270.7 km) F 109 (175.4 km) Look for wild irises in roadside ditches in June.

DC 1411.7 (2271.8 km) F 108.3 (174.3 km) Double-ended gravel turnout. Scenic view of Alaska Range to south.

DC 1413.3 (2274.4 km) F 106.7 (171.7 km) Grain storage facility.

DC 1414.9 (2277 km) F 105.1 (169.1 km) Clearwater Road leads north past farmlands to Clearwater State Recreation Site campground and junctions with Remington Road. Stay on pavement leading to Jack Warren Road, which goes west to the Richardson Highway at **Milepost DC 1424.3 (V 268.3).** Good opportunity to see area agriculture; see Delta Vicinity map this section.

To reach the state campground, follow Clearwater Road 5.2 miles/8.4 km north to junction with Remington Road; turn right and drive 2.8 miles/4.5 km east for Clearwater state campground, situated on the bank of Clearwater Creek.

There are 15 campsites, toilets, tables, firepits, water and boat ramp. Camping fee $8/night or annual pass. ▲

Delta–Clearwater River (local reference; stream is actually Clearwater Creek, which flows northwest to the Tanana River), boat needed for best fishing; beautiful spring-fed stream; grayling and whitefish; silver salmon spawn here in October. **Goodpaster River,** accessible by boat via Delta–Clearwater and Tanana rivers; excellent grayling fishing. ◂━

DC 1415.4 (2277.8 km) F 104.6 (168.3 km) Dorshorst Road; access to homestead farm and private museum, open to public June 1 to Sept. 15, admission charged.

Alaska Homestead & Historical Museum. See display ad this section.

DC 1420.7 (2286.3 km) F 99.3 (159.8 km) Alaska State Troopers.

DC 1420.9 (2286.7 km) F 99.1 (159.5 km) **Bergstad's Travel and Trailer Court.** See display ad this section. ▲

Delta Junction

DC 1422 (2288.4 km) F 98 (157.7 km) V 266 (428.1 km). Located at the junction of the Alaska and Richardson highways. **Population:** 736. **Emergency Services:** Emergencies only phone 911. **Alaska State Troopers,** in the Jarvis Office Center at **Milepost DC 1420.7,** phone (907) 895-4800. **Fire Department** and **Ambulance Service,** emergency only phone 911. **Clinics.** Two doctors and 2 dentists in private practice at Family Medical Center.

Visitor Information: Visitor Center junction of Alaska and Richardson highways, open daily 8 A.M. to 7:30 P.M., May to mid-September; phone (907) 895-9941 or (907) 895-5069. The visitor center has a garden with local grains, flowers and vegetables, and a pay phone. Highway information, phone (907) 451-2207. Dept. of Fish and Game at north edge of town, **Milepost DC 1422.8;** phone (907) 895-4632.

City Hall and the Delta Junction Library, located at **Milepost V 266.5,** are also good sources of information. City Hall, open 2 P.M. to 5 P.M. weekdays, has a pay phone, public restrooms and can give local directions. The library has a free paperback book

DELTA JUNCTION ADVERTISERS

✔**Alaska 7 Motel** .....Mile 270.3 Richardson Hwy.
Bed & Breakfast at the
    Home of Alys ....Ph. (907) 895-4128
Buffalo Center Auto
    Parts..............................Ph. (907) 895-4251
Delta Chamber of
    Commerce ....Ph. (907) 895-5068
Delta Laundry and Thrift
    Store ....Mile 267.5 Richardson Hwy.
Diehl's Delights .....In Diehl's Shopping Center
Diehl's Shopping
    Center ....0.5 mile N. of visitor center
Granite View Sports &
    Gifts.....................Across from visitor center
Interior Texaco ....Ph. (907) 895-4067
Jack's Liquor &
    Convenience Store ......Ph. (907) 895-1051
Jack's Tesoro Service.........Ph. (907) 895-1052
✔**Kelly's Country Inn**
    Motel ....Ph. (907) 895-4667
Nissel Tree B&B ....Ph. (907) 895-4441
OK Fuel Company ....Across from post office
Peggy's Alaskan Cabbage Patch
    Bed & Breakfast...........Ph. (907) 895-4200
Pizza Bella Family
    Restaurant ....Across from visitor center
Smith's Green Acres RV Park &
    Campground ....Ph. 1-800-895-4369
Tanana Bed and
    Breakfast......................Ph. (907) 388-5500

Delta
Junction
Vicinity

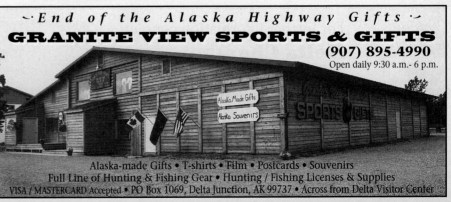

End of the ALASKA HIGHWAY . . .
Delta Junction, Alaska

End of the Alaska Highway certificates available, $1

photo courtesy Sheryl L. Mills

ANNUAL EVENTS:
- ☛ Delta Deep Freeze Classic
- ☛ Festival of Lights – February
- ☛ Memorial Day Buffalo Wallow Square Dance Jamboree
- ☛ July 4th Buffalo Barbecue
- ☛ Deltana Fair, last weekend in July
- ☛ Summer Mud Bog Races

ACTIVITIES:
- ➤➤ Delta Agricultural Project
- ➤➤ Farmers Market
- ➤➤ Pipeline Pump Station Tours
- ➤➤ Historical Sites

photo courtesy Nanci Ruthschild-Kennedy

- ➤➤ Fine dining, Motels and Bed & Breakfasts
- ➤➤ Great fishing, hunting in season
- ➤➤ Hiking throughout the season
- ➤➤ Quartz Lake: fishing, hiking, camping, picnics
- ➤➤ Four state campgrounds
- ➤➤ Several private RV parks with full hookups
- ➤➤ Largest free-roaming bison herd in Alaska

Alaska's Friendly Frontier

For further information contact:

Delta Chamber of Commerce

PO Box 987MP
Delta Junction, AK 99737

(907) 895-5068 (year 'round)
(907) 895-5069 (summer only)
(907) 895-5141 (Fax)

photo courtesy Mike Kingston

and magazine exchange, Anchorage newspaper, public fax and copier service. The library, open Wednesdays and Saturdays, also offers free Alaska video programs to any traveler waiting for vehicle repairs in Delta (ask at the circulation desk).

Elevation: 1,180 feet/360m. **Climate:** Mean monthly temperature in January, -15°F/-26°C; in July 58°F/14°C. Record low was -66°F/-54°C in January 1989; record high was 88°F/31°C in August 1990. Mean monthly precipitation in July, 2.57 inches/6.5cm. **Radio:** KUAC-FM 91.7 broadcasts from University of Alaska Fairbanks; Fort Greely broadcasts on 90.5 FM and 93.5 FM. **Television:** Three channels from Fairbanks.

Private Aircraft: Delta Junction airstrip, 1 mile/1.6 km north; elev. 1,150 feet/350m; length 2,400 feet/731m; gravel. Allen Army Airfield, 3 miles/4.8 km south; elev. 1,277 feet/389m; 3 asphalt-surfaced runways available, length to 7,500 feet/2,286m; fuel J4; joint-use military/civil airport (prior permission required).

Delta Junction is at the actual end of the Alaska Highway. From here, the Richardson Highway leads to Fairbanks. (*The MILEPOST®* logs this stretch of highway as a continuation of the Alaska Highway.) Have your picture taken with the monument in front of the visitor center that marks the highway's end. The chamber of commerce visitor center also has free brochures describing area businesses and attractions, and displays of Alaska wildflowers, mounted animals and furs to touch. Travelers may also purchase certificates here, certifying that they have reached the end of the Alaska Highway.

Delta Junction is also the first view of the

View of the Alaska Range across the braided Delta River at Delta Junction.
(Jerrianne Lowther, staff)

trans-Alaska pipeline for travelers coming up the Alaska Highway from Canada. A good spot to see and photograph the pipeline is at **Milepost V 275.4**, 9.5 miles/15.3 km north of town, where the pipeline crosses the Tanana River. Pump station No. 9, accessible from **Milepost V 258.3** Richardson Highway, offers tours daily from June to August; stop by or phone (907) 869-3270. There is

also an interesting display of pipe used in 3 Alaska pipeline projects outside the visitor center in Delta Junction.

Named after the nearby Delta River, Delta Junction began as a construction camp on the Richardson Highway in 1919. (It was first known as Buffalo Center because of the American bison that were transplanted here in the 1920s.)

The Richardson Highway, connecting Valdez at tidewater with Fairbanks in the Interior, predates the Alaska Highway by 20 years. The Richardson was already a wagon road in 1910, and was updated to automobile standards in the 1920s by the Alaska Road Commission (ARC).

Since the late 1970s, the state has encouraged development of the agricultural industry in the Delta area. They have conducted local land disposal programs involving more than 112,000 acres. These programs generated 37 farms averaging 2,310 acres and 169 small farms averaging 161 acres.

In 1996, nearly 40,000 acres were in some form of agricultural use (including production of barley, oats, wheat, forage, pasture, grass seed, canola, potatoes, field peas, forage brassicas) and conservation use. Barley is the major feed grain grown in Delta. It is an excellent energy feed for cattle, hogs and sheep. Production acreages are determined by the anticipated in-state demand for barley.

Delta barley is stored on farms or in a local co-op elevator, sold on the open market or used to feed livestock. Small-scale farming of vegetables, 3 commercial potato farms, 5 active dairies, a dairy processing center, 6 beef producers, 2 beef feedlots, 3 swine producers, 3 bison ranches and 4 commercial greenhouses all contribute to Delta Junction's agriculture.

ACCOMMODATIONS/VISITOR SERVICES

Delta Junction has 2 motels, several bed and breakfasts, restaurants, gas stations, a laundromat and dry cleaners, a coin-operated car wash, a shopping center, post office, bank with automated banking machine and other businesses. There are several churches. Delta Community Park, on Kimball Street one block off the highway, has softball and soccer fields.

Delta international hostel north of town: turn at **Milepost V 271.7** (Tanana Loop Road), drive 1 mile/1.6 km and turn right on Tanana Loop Extension then left on a gravel road named Main Street, USA (follow signs). Sleeping bags are required. Fee: $7 per night. Hostel open Memorial Day through Labor Day; phone (907) 895-5074.

There are private RV parks just south and just north of town. Two public campgrounds are located nearby: Delta state campground at **Milepost V 267.1**, and Clearwater state campground on Remington Road (see **Milepost DC 1414.9 and V 268.3**). ▲

Alaska 7 Motel, 16 large, clean, comfortable rooms with full bath and showers. Color TV and courtesy coffee in each room. Kitchenettes and phone available. Comfort at a comfortable price. Open year-round. Major credit cards accepted. Milepost 270.3 Richardson–Alaska Highway. Phone (907) 895-4848. See display ad this section. [ADVERTISEMENT]

Tanana Bed and Breakfast. Wilderness adventure begins with scenic boat ride down Tanana River. En route you may see bald eagles soaring overhead or moose grazing on the bank. You'll know you've left civilization when you disembark onto pristine land covered with wildflowers, berries and towering spruce. Blue-ribbon grayling fishing at your back door in rambling, wilderness stream. Alaskan sourdough pancake, reindeer sausage breakfast prepared by your park ranger host. Open May through September. See display ad. [ADVERTISEMENT]

TRANSPORTATION

Air: Scheduled service via 40-Mile Air from Tok to Fairbanks; Delta stop on request. Local air service available. **Bus:** See Bus Lines in the GENERAL INFORMATION section for scheduled service to other communities.

ATTRACTIONS

Buffalo Herd. American bison were transplanted into the Delta Junction area in the 1920s. Because the bison have become costly pests to many farmers in the Delta area, the 90,000-acre Delta Bison Sanctuary was created south of the Alaska Highway in 1980. However, keeping the bison on their refuge and out of the barley fields is a continuing problem. Summer visitors who wish to look at the bison are advised to visit the viewpoint at **Milepost V 241.3** on the Richardson Highway; use binoculars. The herd contained 482 bison in 1992 when the last census was taken by the ADF&G.

Special Events: Delta Junction celebrates a traditional Fourth of July with a Buffalo Barbecue. Buffalo Wallow, a 4-day square dance festival hosted by Buffalo Squares, is held every Memorial Day weekend. The Buffalo Squares also sponsors a campout and dance at Delta state campground the second Saturday in July.

The Deltana Fair is held the last weekend in July. The fair includes a barbecue, Lions' pancake breakfast, local handicrafts, horse show, livestock display and show, games, concessions, contests and a parade. A highlight of the fair is the Great Alaska Outhouse Race, held on Sunday, in which 4 pushers and 1 sitter compete for the coveted "Golden Throne" award.

A Festival of Lights is held each February in Delta Junction. This special event, designed to break up the monotony of long winter nights, features a parade of lights where the local citizenry builds and decorates floats with lights. There are also dog races, fireworks, square dancing, ice sculpting and more. It was -40°F/-40°C for the 1994 festival—an evening to remember, according to residents!

Area Museums. Alaska Homestead & Historical Museum, located approximately 6 miles/9.6 km east of town at **Milepost DC 1415.4** Alaska Highway, offers guided tours of an authentic Alaska homestead farm. There's also a large collection of historical farming equipment. Open June 1 to Sept. 15, daily 10 A.M. to 7 P.M.

North of town about 8 miles/12.9 km at **Milepost V 275** Richardson–Alaska Highway

is Rika's Roadhouse at Big Delta State Historical Park. This restored roadhouse was built in 1910. Open daily in summer.

The Sullivan Roadhouse, relocated across from the visitor center, was originally built in 1906. Open daily in summer as a walk-through museum.

Tour the agriculture of the area by driving Sawmill Creek Road (turn off at **Milepost DC 1403.6** Alaska Highway) and Clearwater Road (see **Milepost DC 1414.9**). Sawmill Creek Road goes through the heart of the grain-producing Delta Ag Project. Local farmers welcome visiting farmers' questions in between planting and harvesting. Commercial farm tours are available at the Hollenback farm on Sawmill Creek Road. Along Clearwater and Remington roads you may view the older farms, which produce forage crops and livestock. Tanana Loop Road (**Milepost V 271.7**), Tanana Loop Extension and Mill–Tan Road also go past many farms. The visitor information center in downtown Delta Junction can answer many questions on local agriculture.

AREA FISHING: Delta–Clearwater River, grayling and whitefish; silver salmon spawn here in October. Access via Clearwater Road or Jack Warren Road (see Delta Vicinity map). (Although USGS topographic maps show this tributary of the Tanana River as Clearwater Creek, local residents refer to the stream as the Delta–Clearwater River.) **Goodpaster River,** accessible by boat via Delta–Clearwater and Tanana rivers; excellent grayling fishing.

There are 43 lakes in the Delta–Tok area that are stocked by the Alaska Dept. of Fish and Game. Lakes are stocked primarily with rainbow trout, and also with arctic grayling, lake trout, arctic char and king salmon. Most of these lakes are located close to the road system, but there are walk-in lakes available as well. **Quartz Lake,** at **Milepost V 277.7** north of Delta Junction, one of the most popular fishing lakes in the Delta area, is also the largest and most easily accessed of area lakes; angler success is excellent. Consult ADF&G offices in Delta or Tok for other locations. ◄

Richardson–Alaska Highway Log

Although logged here as a natural extension of the Alaska Highway, the highway between Delta Junction and Fairbanks is designated as part of the Richardson Highway, with existing mileposts showing distance from Valdez.

Distance from Valdez (V) is followed by distance from Dawson Creek (DC) and distance from Fairbanks (F).

V 266 (428 km) **DC 1422** (2288.5 km) **F 98** (157.7 km) Delta Junction visitor information center sits at the junction of the Alaska and Richardson highways. Turn south for Valdez (see RICHARDSON HIGHWAY section). Continue north for Fairbanks.

V 266.3 (428.6 km) **DC 1422.3** (2289 km) **F 97.7** (157.2 km) Delta Junction post office.

V 266.4 (428.7 km) **DC 1422.4** (2289.1 km) **F 97.6** (157.1 km) City Park Carwash.

V 266.5 (428.9 km) **DC 1422.5** (2289.2 km) **F 97.5** (156.9 km) Delta Junction library and city hall. Library hours are 11 A.M. to

6 P.M. Monday through Thursday and 11 A.M. to 4 P.M. Friday and Saturday; free paperback book and magazine exchange, Alaska videos, public fax and copier service. City Hall is open 9 A.M. to 5 P.M. weekdays; pay phone and public restrooms.

V 266.8 (429.4 km) **DC 1422.8** (2289.7 km) **F 97.2** (156.4 km) Alaska Dept. of Fish and Game office.

V 267 (429.7 km) **DC 1423** (2290 km) **F 97** (156.1 km) BLM airstrip; current status unknown.

V 267.1 (429.8 km) **DC 1423.1** (2290.2 km) **F 96.9** (155.9 km) Delta state campground to east; 24 sites, water, tables, shelter with covered tables, toilets, $8 nightly fee or annual pass. Large turnout at campground entrance. Turnout on west side of highway on bank of the Delta River offers excellent views of the Alaska Range. ▲

V 267.2 (430 km) **DC 1423.2** (2290.4 km) **F 96.8** (155.7 km) Alaska Division of Forestry office.

V 267.3 (430.2 km) **DC 1423.3** (2290.5 km) **F 96.7** (155.6 km) Medical clinic.

V 267.5 (430.5 km) **DC 1423.5** (2290.9 km) **F 96.5** (155.3 km) Laundromat with showers, thrift store.

V 268 (431.3 km) **DC 1424** (2291.6 km) **F 96** (154.5 km) **Smith's Green Acres RV Park & Campground.** Avoid the rush and the crowds, stay with us. One of Alaska's finest RV parks. 9.5 Good Sam rating. From a guest: "One of the best we've seen in Alaska." Great trout and grayling fishing nearby. See display ad in Delta Junction section. [ADVERTISEMENT] ▲

V 268.3 (431.7 km) **DC 1424.3** (2292.1 km) **F 95.7** (154 km) **Junction** with Jack Warren Road (see Delta Vicinity map this section). Turn here for access to Clearwater state campground (10.5 miles/16.9 km). Clearwater campground has toilets, tables, water and boat launch; pleasant campsites on bank of river. Camping fee $8/night or annual pass. ▲

Driving this loop is a good opportunity to see local homesteads. Note that mileposts on these paved side roads run backward from Mile 13 at this junction to Mile 0 at the junction of Clearwater Road and the Alaska Highway.

V 270.3 (435 km) **DC 1426.3** (2295.3 km) **F 93.7** (150.8 km) Alaska 7 Motel.

V 271.7 (437.2 km) **DC 1427.7** (2297.6 km) **F 92.3** (148.5 km) Tanana Loop Road. Turn here for Delta Junction youth hostel. To make a loop drive through farmlands, follow Tanana Loop Road approximately 1 mile/1.6 km, turn right on Tanana Loop Extension, which connects with Jack Warren Road. Turn west on Jack Warren Road to return to highway.

V 272.1 (437.9 km) **DC 1428** (2298 km) **F 92** (148 km) Fire station.

V 275 (442.6 km) **DC 1431** (2303.9 km) **F 89** (143.2 km) **The Tanana Trading Post.** See display ad this section.

V 275 (442.6 km) **DC 1431** (2303.9 km) **F 89** (143.2 km) **Rika's Roadhouse at Big Delta State Historical Park.** Turn northeast at Rika's Road for Rika's Roadhouse and Landing on the banks of the Tanana River. Tour buses welcome. Parking areas with restrooms at both park entrances. The newly renovated Rika's Roadhouse offers worldwide postal service and gift shop specializing in fox furs, gold, diamond willow and interlocking wood puzzles. Visit the barn, Signal Corp station, sod-roofed museum and other historic structures. Live farm animals. Guides are available to walk with you through the history of this important crossroads on the Valdez–Fairbanks trail.

Meals served 9 A.M. to 5 P.M. in our Packhouse Restaurant, home of the Alaska Baking Co. Try our famous bear claws and homemade muffins. The Packhouse Restaurant also offers homemade soups, fresh salads and sandwiches. Guests love our homemade pies: strawberry–rhubarb, blueberry, apple, pecan and chocolate truffle. Overnight RV parking and dump station. After the dust of the highway, the green gardens of the 10-acre park are a welcome haven. Brochure available. P.O. Box 1229, Delta Junction, AK 99737. Phone (907) 895-4201 or 895-4938 anytime. Free admission. Handicapped access. See display ad this section. [ADVERTISEMENT] ♿▲

Rika's Roadhouse was built in 1910 by John Hajdukovich. In 1923, Hajdukovich sold it to Rika Wallen, a Swedish immigrant who had managed the roadhouse since 1917. Rika ran the roadhouse into the late 1940s and lived there until her death in 1969. Big Delta State Historical Park campground; camping fee $8/vehicle, dump station ($3). ▲

V 275.4 (443.2 km) **DC 1431.4** (2303.6 km) **F 88.6** (142.6 km) Big Delta Bridge across the Tanana River; spectacular view of pipeline suspended across river. Slow down for parking area at south end of bridge with litter barrels and interpretive sign about pipeline.

From here to Fairbanks there are views of the Tanana River and the Alaska Range to the south. Farming community of BIG DELTA (pop. 400); gas, store, 2 bars, a church, Kenner Sawmill and Tanana River boat landing.

The Fur Shack. See display ad this section.

V 277.7 (446.9 km) **DC 1433.7** (2307.2 km) **F 86.3** (138.9 km) Turnoff to east for Quartz Lake Recreation Area. Drive in 2.5 miles/4 km on gravel road to intersection: turn left for Lost Lake, continue straight ahead for Quartz Lake (another 0.3 mile/ 0.5 km). Lost Lake, 0.2 mile/0.3 km from intersection, has 8 campsites with picnic tables, toilet, and a large parking area with tables and litter barrels. A shallow, picturesque lake with no fish. Quartz Lake has more developed campsites on good loop road, firepits, water, tables, toilet and 2 boat launches. Boat launch fee $3 or annual boat launch pass. Camping fees at both campgrounds: $8/night or annual pass. A trail connects Lost Lake and Quartz Lake camping areas. ▲

Private cabins are scattered along the northern and eastern shorelines of Quartz Lake. About half the land along the lake is undeveloped and there is no road access beyond the campground. The lake covers 1,500 acres, more than 80 percent of which is less than 15 feet/5m deep. Maximum depth is 40 feet/12m. Aquatic vegetation covers most of the lake surface, hampering swimmers and waterskiers. Boat and motor rentals available from Black Spruce Lodge. **Quartz Lake** offers excellent fishing for stocked rainbow to 18 inches, silver salmon to 13 inches and Arctic char; use spinners, plugs and artificial flies. Ice fishing in winter. For more information phone the ADF&G office in Delta at (907) 895-4632.

V 277.9 (447.2 km) **DC 1433.9** (2307.5

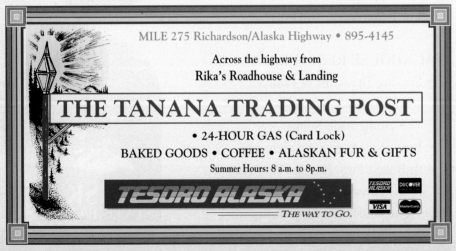

km) **F 86.1** (138.6 km) Former U.S. Army petroleum station, now closed. Pay phone beside highway.

V 278.2 (447.7 km) **DC 1434.2** (2308 km) **F 85.8** (138.1 km) South end of long double-ended turnout to west. Several of these long turnouts northbound are old sections of the Alaska Highway.

V 280.3 (451.1 km) **DC 1436.3** (2311.4 km) **F 83.7** (134.7 km) Gravel turnout to east.

V 282 (453.8 km) **DC 1438** (2314.2 km) **F 82** (132 km) Watch for frost cracking.

V 284 (457 km) **DC 1440** (2317.4 km) **F 80** (128.7 km) Watch for moose.

V 286.6 (461.2 km) **DC 1442.6** (2321.6 km) **F 77.4** (124.6 km) Shaw Creek bridge; boat launch and snack shop. Excellent wildflower displays of sweet peas blooming in June.

V 286.7 (461.4 km) **DC 1442.7** (2321.7 km) **F 77.3** (124.4 km) **Shaw Creek** road. Good to excellent early spring and fall grayling fishing; subject to closure (check locally). Good view northbound of Tanana River which parallels the highway. Fireweed, pale oxytrope, sweet peas bloom along roadside.

V 287.2 (462.2 km) **DC 1443.2** (2322.5 km) **F 76.8** (123.6 km) Turnout and road to slough to east. Birch trees are thick along this stretch of highway.

V 288 (463.5 km) **DC 1444** (2323.8 km) **F 76** (122.3 km) Panoramic view to the south with vistas of 3 great peaks of the Alaska Range: Mount Hayes, elev. 13,832 feet/4,216m, almost due south; Hess Mountain, elev. 11,940 feet/3,639m, to the west (right) of Mount Hayes; and Mount Deborah, elev. 12,339 feet/3,761m, to the west (right) of Hess Mountain. Mount Hayes is named for Charles Hayes, an early member of the U.S. Geological Survey. Mount Deborah was named in 1907 by the famous Alaskan Judge Wickersham for his wife.

V 289.8 (466.4 km) **DC 1445.8** (2326.7 km) **F 74.2** (119.4 km) Paved double-ended turnout to east.

V 291.8 (469.6 km) **DC 1447.8** (2329.9 km) **F 72.2** (116.2 km) Northbound truck lane begins.

V 292.8 (471.2 km) **DC 1448.8** (2331.5 km) **F 71.2** (114.6 km) Truck lane ends. View of Tanana River valley.

V 294 (473.1 km) **DC 1450** (2333.5 km) **F 70** (112.7 km) Paved double-ended turnout.

V 294.2 (473.5 km) **DC 1450.2** (2333.8 km) **F 69.8** (112.3 km) Southbound truck lane begins.

V 294.9 (474.6 km) **DC 1450.9** (2334.9 km) **F 69.1** (111.2 km) Game Management Unit boundary between 20B and 20D. Entering Fairbanks North Star borough northbound.

V 295 (474.7 km) **DC 1451** (2335.1 km) **F 69** (111 km) Site of the original old Richardson Roadhouse, which burned down in December 1982.

V 295.4 (475.4 km) **DC 1451.4** (2335.7 km) **F 68.6** (110.4 km) Banner Creek bridge; historic placer gold stream.

V 296.4 (477 km) **DC 1452.4** (2337.3 km) **F 67.6** (108.8 km) Paved turnout to west; view of Alaska Range and Tanana River to south.

V 297.7 (479.1 km) **DC 1453.7** (2339.4 km) **F 66.3** (106.7 km) Large gravel parking area to west below highway; good scenic viewpoint. Paved access road to Tanana River.

V 298.2 (479.9 km) **DC 1454.2** (2340.2 km) **F 65.8** (105.9 km) Scenic viewpoint; paved double-ended turnout to west. Watch for frost heaves and dips.

V 301.7 (485.5 km) **DC 1457.7** (2345.9 km) **F 62.3** (100.3 km) South end of long double-ended turnout to west.

V 304.3 (489.7 km) **DC 1460.3** (2350 km) **F 59.7** (96.1 km) Small paved turnout to east.

V 305.2 (491.2 km) **DC 1461.2** (2351.5 km) **F 58.8** (94.6 km) Birch Lake Road to east; access to military recreation area (restricted).

V 306 (492.4 km) **DC 1462** (2352.8 km) **F 58** (93.3 km) Large parking area to east overlooking **Birch Lake**; unimproved gravel boat launch and beach; fish from shore in spring, from boat in summer, for rainbow and silver salmon. Many Fairbanks residents have summer homes at Birch Lake.

V 306.1 (492.6 km) **DC 1462.1** (2352.9 km) **F 57.9** (93.2 km) Turnoff to west for **Lost Lake**. Drive in 0.7 mile/1.1 km on dirt road; silver salmon fishing. ◄►

V 307.2 (494.3 km) **DC 1463.2** (2354.7 km) **F 56.8** (91.4 km) Birch Lake highway maintenance station.

V 308.4 (496.3 km) **DC 1464.4** (2356.6 km) **F 55.6** (89.5 km) South end of long double-ended turnout to east.

V 310 (498.9 km) **DC 1466** (2359.2 km) **F 54** (86.9 km) Double-ended paved parking area to west.

V 313 (503.7 km) **DC 1469** (2364 km) **F 51** (82.1 km) Paved double-ended turnout to west. Access to **Silver Fox Pond**; stocked with arctic char. ◄►

V 314.8 (506.6 km) **DC 1470.8** (2366.9 km) **F 49.2** (79.2 km) **Midway Lodge** is open 7 A.M. to 11 P.M. daily. Bar open till ? Breakfast anytime, famous homemade chili,

royal ½-pound hamburgers, fresh pies. Clean rooms starting at $35. Showers. Gifts. We are a family-oriented stop on the Alaska Highway and welcome your visit. 11191 Richardson Highway, Salcha, AK 99714. Phone (907) 488-2939. [ADVERTISEMENT]

V 317.9 (511.6 km) **DC 1473.9** (2371.9 km) **F 45.4** (73.1 km) Double-ended gravel turnout to west.

V 319.3 (513.8 km) **DC 1475.3** (2374.2 km) **F 44.7** (71.9 km) Access road leads east to Harding Lake summer homes.

V 319.8 (514.7 km) **DC 1475.8** (2375 km) **F 44.2** (71.1 km) Second access road northbound leads east to Harding Lake summer homes. Access to **Little Harding Lake**, king salmon fishing. ◄►

V 321.5 (517.4 km) **DC 1477.5** (2377.8 km) **F 42.5** (68.4 km) **Harding Lake** State Recreation Area turnoff; drive east 1.5 miles/2.4 km on paved road to campground. Park headquarters, drinking water fill-up and dump station ($3 charge) at campground entrance. Picnic grounds on lakeshore, swimming, boat ramp ($5 launch fee or annual boat launch pass), ball fields and about 80 campsites. Camping fee $8/night or annual pass. Fishing for lake trout, arctic char, burbot, northern pike and salmon. Lake is reported to be "hard to fish." Worth the drive! *Bring your insect repellent. You may need it!* ◄►▲

V 322.2 (518.5 km) **DC 1478.2** (2378.9 km) **F 41.8** (67.3 km) Salcha post office and

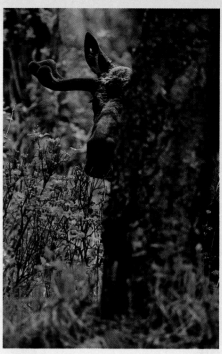

lodge with food, gas and camping.

Salcha River Lodge. See display ad this section.

V 323.1 (520 km) **DC 1479.1** (2380.3 km) **F 40.9** (65.8 km) **Salcha River** State Recreation Site; large parking area with 75 sites, boat ramp ($3 launch fee or annual boat launch pass), picnic area, toilets and water. Camping fee $8/night per vehicle or annual pass. Fishing for king and chum salmon, grayling, sheefish, northern pike and burbot. ◄►▲

V 323.4 (520.4 km) **DC 1479.4** (2380.4 km) **F 40.6** (65.3 km) Salcha River bridge.

V 324 (521.4 km) **DC 1480** (2381.7 km) **F 40** (64.4 km) Clear Creek bridge.

V 324.6 (522.4 km) **DC 1480.6** (2382.7 km) **F 39.4** (63.4 km) Double-ended gravel turnout to east.

V 324.8 (522.7 km) **DC 1480.8** (2383 km) **F 39.2** (63.1 km) Munsons Slough bridge.

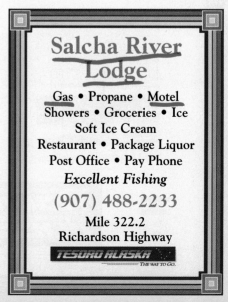

V 325.5 (523.8 km) **DC 1481.5** (2384.2 km) **F 38.5** (62 km) The community of **SALCHA** (pop. 354) stretches along the highway in both directions. The elementary school is located here. The post office (ZIP 99714) is at **Milepost V 322.2.**

V 326.4 (525.3 km) **DC 1482.4** (2385.6 km) **F 37.6** (60.5 km) Salcha Baptist log church to west.

V 327 (526.2 km) **DC 1483** (2386.6 km) **F 37** (59.5 km) Picturesque log home to west.

V 327.7 (527.4 km) **DC 1483.7** (2387.7 km) **F 36.3** (58.4 km) Little Salcha River bridge.

V 328.3 (528.3 km) **DC 1484.3** (2388.7 km) **F 35.7** (57.4 km) Salcha Store and Service. See display ad this section.

V 330.4 (531.7 km) **DC 1486.4** (2392.1 km) **F 33.6** (54.1 km) Johnson Road. Access to Pump Station 8.

V 331.7 (533.8 km) **DC 1487.7** (2394.2 km) **F 32.3** (52 km) Salcha Fairgrounds.

V 332.2 (534.6 km) **DC 1488.2** (2395 km) **F 31.8** (51.2 km) Access east to **31-Mile Pond**; stocked with arctic char. ⬥

V 332.3 (534.8 km) **DC 1488.3** (2395.1 km) **F 31.7** (51 km) **The Knotty Shop.** Stop and be impressed by a truly unique Alaskan gift shop and wildlife museum. Jim and Paula have attempted to maintain a genuine Alaskan flavor—from the unusual burl construction to the Alaskan wildlife displayed in a natural setting to the handcrafted Alaskan gifts. Don't miss the opportunity to stop and browse. See display ad this section. Show us *The MILEPOST®* advertisement for a free small ice cream cone. [ADVERTISEMENT]

V 334.5 (538.3 km) **DC 1490.5** (2398.7 km) **F 29.5** (47.5 km) Public dumpster at gravel pit.

V 334.7 (538.6 km) **DC 1490.7** (2399 km) **F 29.3** (47.2 km) South boundary of Eielson AFB. Watch for various military aircraft taking off and landing to the east. Aircraft include Air Force F-16s, F-15s, KC-135s, C-130s, C-141s, OA-10s, Navy A-6s, F-14s and others.

V 335.1 (539.3 km) **DC 1491.1** (2399.6 km) **F 28.9** (46.5 km) Access east to **28-Mile Pond**; stocked with rainbow and silver salmon. ⬥

V 340.7 (548.3 km) **DC 1496.7** (2408.6 km) **F 23.3** (37.5 km) Divided highway begins for northbound traffic. *CAUTION: Watch for heavy traffic southbound turning east into the base, 7–8 A.M. and merging northbound traffic, 3:45–5:30 P.M., weekdays.*

V 341 (548.8 km) **DC 1497** (2409.1 km) **F 23** (37 km) Entrance to **EIELSON AIR FORCE BASE**, constructed in 1943 and named for Carl Ben Eielson, a famous Alaskan bush pilot. A weekly tour is offered for groups of 10 or more. Phone the Public Affairs office at (907) 377-1410 for reservations and more information.

V 343.7 (553.1 km) **DC 1499.7** (2413.5 km) **F 20.3** (32.7 km) Moose Creek Road and general store; diesel, gas, propane.

Moose Creek General Store. See display ad this section.

Piledriver Slough parallels the highway from here north, flowing into the Tanana River. It is stocked with rainbow trout. Check with general store for access and fishing information. **Bathing Beauty Pond**, stocked with rainbow, arctic char and grayling, is accessible via Eielson Farm Road off Moose Creek Road.

V 344.7 (554.7 km) **DC 1500.7** (2415 km) **F 19.3** (31.1 km) Moose Creek bridge.

V 345.5 (556 km) **DC 1501.5** (2416.4 km) **F 18.5** (29.8 km) *CAUTION: Highway crosses Alaska Railroad tracks.*

V 346 (556.8 km) **DC 1502** (2417.2 km) **F 17.9** (28.8 km) Chena Flood Channel bridge. Upstream dam is part of flood control project initiated after the Chena River left its banks and flooded Fairbanks in 1967.

Alaska Highway 7 miles/11.3 km outside of Fairbanks at **Milepost V 357.1.**

North Pole

V 349.5 (562.3 km) DC 1505.5 (2422.8 km) F 14.5 (23.3 km) West of the Alaska Highway. **Population:** 1,456. **Emergency Services:** Emergencies only phone 911. **Police**, phone (907) 488-6902. **Alaska State Troopers,** phone (907) 452-2114. **Fire Department,** phone (907) 488-2232.

Visitor Information: At **Milepost V 348.7.** Open 8 A.M. to 7 P.M. daily, Memorial Day to mid-September.

Elevation: 500 feet/152m. **Radio:** KJNP-AM 1170, KJNP-FM 100.3; also Fairbanks stations.

Private Aircraft: Bradley Sky Ranch, 0.9 mile/1.4 km northwest; elev. 483 feet/147m; length 4,100 feet/1,250m; gravel; fuel 100.

North Pole has most visitor facilities including restaurants, a motel, bed and breakfasts, campgrounds, laundromats, car wash, grocery and gas stops, gift stores, library, churches, a public park, pharmacy and supermarket. The post office is on Santa Claus Lane.

North Pole has an annual Winter Carnival with sled dog races, carnival games, food booths and other activities. There's a big summer festival weekend celebration, held July 5–7, 1996, with carnival rides, food booths, arts and crafts booths, and a parade.

In 1944 Bon V. Davis homesteaded this area. Dahl and Gaske Development Co.

V 346.7 (558 km) DC 1502.7 (2418.4 km) F 17.3 (27.8 km) Laurance Road. Turn right northbound for Chena Lakes Recreation Area (follow signs, 2.2 miles/3.5 km to entrance). Constructed by the Army Corps of Engineers and run by Fairbanks North Star Borough, the recreation area has 80 campsites, 92 picnic sites (some with handicap access), pump water, volleyball courts and a 250-acre lake with swimming beach. **Chena Lake** is stocked with silver salmon, arctic char, grayling and rainbow trout. Nonmotorized boats may be rented from a concessionaire. The **Chena River** flows through part of the recreation area and offers good grayling fishing and also northern pike, whitefish and burbot. Hiking and self-guiding nature trails. Open year-round. Fee charged Memorial Day to Labor Day; day use $3 per vehicle, camping $6 per day. ◄▲

V 347.1 (558.6 km) DC 1503.1 (2419 km) F 16.9 (27.2 km) Newby Road.

V 347.7 (559.6 km) DC 1503.7 (2419.9 km) F 16.3 (26.2 km) Exit west for St. Nicholas Drive, east for Dawson Road.

V 348.7 (561.2 km) DC 1504.7 (2421.5 km) F 15.3 (24.6 km) North Pole Visitor Information Center; open 8 A.M. to 7 P.M. daily, Memorial Day to mid-September. Turn right on Mission Road for radio station KJNP, turn left northbound for 5th Avenue businesses, RV park and Santa Claus House.

Santaland RV Park. Good Sampark. Center of North Pole, next to Santa Claus House, home of Dancer and Prancer, North Pole's resident reindeer. City water, full service pull-throughs, car wash. Free private showers, laundry, pay phones. Handicapped accessible. Tour sales and reservations. Daily shuttle bus to Fairbanks points of interest. See display ad, or call 1-888-488-9123 or (907) 488-9123. [ADVERTISEMENT] &▲

V 349 (561.6 km) DC 1505 (2422 km) F 15 (24.1 km) Santa Claus House. In 1949, Con Miller began wearing a Santa Claus suit on business trips throughout the territory, bringing the spirit of St. Nicholas to hundreds of children for the first time. Here the Miller family continues this tradition. Ask about Santa's Christmas letter. Mail your cards and letters here for authentic North Pole postmark. Enjoy the unique gift shop and exhibits. Summer hours: 8 A.M.–8 P.M. daily, Memorial Day through Labor Day. Ride the Snowy River Railroad daily except Sunday, summers only. Visit with Santa Claus summers and Christmas season only. Santa's reindeer, Dancer and Prancer, live on the grounds all summer long. Santa Claus

House winter hours: 10 A.M.–6 P.M. (closed January and February for Santa's annual vacation). See display ad this section. [ADVERTISEMENT]

V 349.5 (562.3 km) DC 1505.5 (2422.8 km) F 14.5 (23.3 km) North Pole and North Pole Plaza to the left northbound via Santa Claus Lane; Badger Road to the right. Truck stop with diesel, 2 small shopping malls, motel and other businesses are located on Badger Road. Santa Claus Lane has several businesses along it, and connects with 5th Avenue, which loops back to the highway at **Milepost V 348.6.** Badger Road is a loop road leading 12 miles/19.3 km along Badger Slough and providing access to a RV park, salmon bake, convenience store with gas, and several bed and breakfasts. It re-enters the

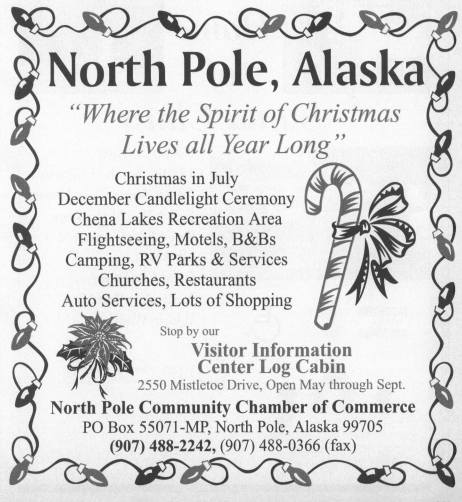

SANTALAND RV
PARK & CAMPGROUND

Good Sampark

125 St. Nicholas Drive
P.O. Box 55317
North Pole, AK 99705
907-488-9123 or
Toll Free 1-888-488-9123

Home of Santa Claus

- Country Setting
- 15 Min. South of Fairbanks
- Next to Santa Claus House
- Full & Partial Hook ups
- Very Clean Unmetered Showers
- Great City Water
- North Pole Post Mark
- Vehicle Wash

VISA **MasterCard**

TOUR SALES AND RESERVATIONS

bought the Davis homestead, subdivided it and named it North Pole, hoping to attract a toy manufacturer who could advertise products as being made in North Pole.

North Pole is the home of many Fairbanks commuters. It has an oil refinery that produces heating fuel, jet fuel and other products. Eielson and Wainwright military bases are nearby.

Radio station KJNP, operated by Calvary's Northern Lights Mission, broadcasts music and religious programs on 1170 AM and 100.3 FM. They also operate television station KJNP Channel 4. Visitors are welcome between 8 A.M. and 10 P.M.; tours may be arranged. KJNP is located on Mission Road about 0.6 mile/1 km northeast of the Alaska Highway. The missionary project includes a dozen hand-hewn, sod-roofed homes and other buildings constructed of spruce logs.

NORTH POLE ADVERTISERS

Beaver Lake Resort
  Motel ....Ph. (907) 488-9600
Bo's Logos..............................North Pole Plaza
Elf's Den, The.................Next to visitor center
Jolly Acres Motel...................3068 Badger Rd.
KJNP...Mission Rd.
North Pole Chamber
  of Commerce...............Ph. (907) 488-2242
North Pole Coffee Roasting
  Company ....220 Parkway
Santa Claus House..................St. Nicholas Dr.
Santaland RV Park &
  Campground......................St. Nicholas Dr.

AM 1170 **KJNP** **FM 100.3**
RADIO AM 50,000 W FM 25,000 W

BOX 56359 NORTH POLE

All are welcome . . .
Log Cabins • Sod Roofs
The True Alaskan Motif
. . . to our community

Channel 4 • TV

Bibles For Others

ALASKA 99705-1359

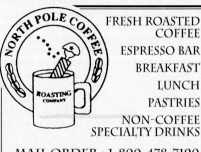

FRESH ROASTED COFFEE
ESPRESSO BAR
BREAKFAST
LUNCH
PASTRIES
NON-COFFEE SPECIALTY DRINKS

MAIL ORDER · 1-800-478-7190
220 PARKWAY 488-7190
P.O. BOX 56960
NORTH POLE, AK 99705
Stock your motorhome with Santa's blend or fresh roasted coffee beans ground to order.
SEE LOG AD AT MILE 349.5

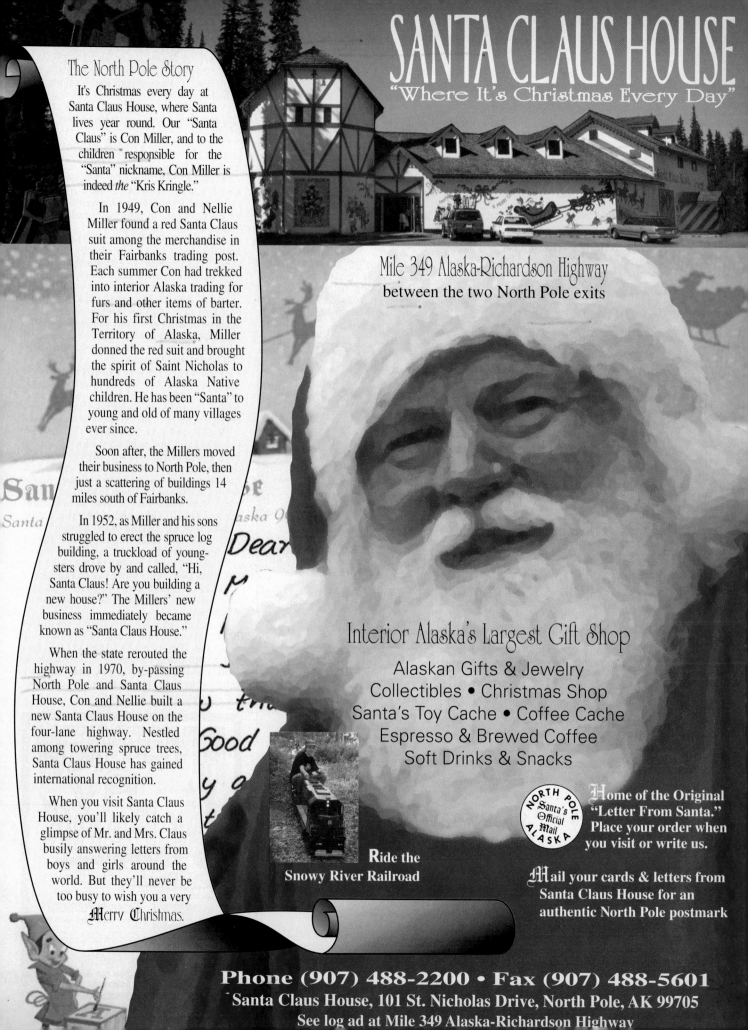

SANTA CLAUS HOUSE
"Where It's Christmas Every Day"

The North Pole Story

It's Christmas every day at Santa Claus House, where Santa lives year round. Our "Santa Claus" is Con Miller, and to the children responsible for the "Santa" nickname, Con Miller is indeed *the* "Kris Kringle."

In 1949, Con and Nellie Miller found a red Santa Claus suit among the merchandise in their Fairbanks trading post. Each summer Con had trekked into interior Alaska trading for furs and other items of barter. For his first Christmas in the Territory of Alaska, Miller donned the red suit and brought the spirit of Saint Nicholas to hundreds of Alaska Native children. He has been "Santa" to young and old of many villages ever since.

Soon after, the Millers moved their business to North Pole, then just a scattering of buildings 14 miles south of Fairbanks.

In 1952, as Miller and his sons struggled to erect the spruce log building, a truckload of youngsters drove by and called, "Hi, Santa Claus! Are you building a new house?" The Millers' new business immediately became known as "Santa Claus House."

When the state rerouted the highway in 1970, by-passing North Pole and Santa Claus House, Con and Nellie built a new Santa Claus House on the four-lane highway. Nestled among towering spruce trees, Santa Claus House has gained international recognition.

When you visit Santa Claus House, you'll likely catch a glimpse of Mr. and Mrs. Claus busily answering letters from boys and girls around the world. But they'll never be too busy to wish you a very **Merry Christmas**.

Mile 349 Alaska-Richardson Highway
between the two North Pole exits

Interior Alaska's Largest Gift Shop

Alaskan Gifts & Jewelry
Collectibles • Christmas Shop
Santa's Toy Cache • Coffee Cache
Espresso & Brewed Coffee
Soft Drinks & Snacks

Ride the
Snowy River Railroad

Home of the Original "Letter From Santa." Place your order when you visit or write us.

Mail your cards & letters from Santa Claus House for an authentic North Pole postmark

NORTH POLE
Santa's
Official
Mail
ALASKA

Phone (907) 488-2200 • Fax (907) 488-5601
Santa Claus House, 101 St. Nicholas Drive, North Pole, AK 99705
See log ad at Mile 349 Alaska-Richardson Highway

Full-service campgrounds at Santaland RV Park downtown, Road's End RV Park at **Milepost V 356.2** and Riverview RV Park at **Milepost V 357.1** Alaska–Richardson Highway. North Pole Public Park, on 5th Avenue, has tent sites in the trees along a narrow dirt road; no camping fee. Dump station available at North Pole Plaza. ▲

North Pole Coffee Roasting Company offers gourmet coffee beans from around the world roasted right here in North Pole. Coffee shop, espresso bar, pastries, breakfast, lunches. Gifts and T-shirts. Mail order. From exit, turn south on Santa Claus Lane. We're at 220 Parkway, on your right, just beyond North Pole Plaza Mall. (907) 488-7190. See display ad, North Pole section. [ADVERTISEMENT]

Richardson–Alaska Highway Log

(continued)

V 350.2 (563.6 km) **DC 1506.2** (2423.9 km) **F 13.8** (22.2 km) Peridot Street.

V 350.6 (564.2 km) **DC 1506.6** (2424.6 km) **F 13.4** (21.6 km) *CAUTION: Highway crosses Alaska Railroad tracks.*

V 351 (564.9 km) **DC 1507** (2425.3 km) **F 13** (20.9 km) Twelvemile Village exit. Greenhouse with floral displays.

V 354.4 (570.3 km) **DC 1510.4** (2430.7 km) **F 9.6** (15.4 km) Old Richardson Highway exit.

V 356.2 (573.2 km) **DC 1512.2** (2433.6 km) **F 7.8** (12.6 km) **Road's End RV Park.** Just 6.5 miles south of Fairbanks on the Richardson–Alaska Highway. Halfway between North Pole and Fairbanks. Full and partial hookups, tent camping, showers, laundry, pay phone, good water. Easy access. Reasonable rates. Weekly and monthly rates available. VISA/MasterCard accepted. Cash discounts given. (907) 488-0295. [ADVERTISEMENT] ▲

V 357.1 (574.7 km) **DC 1513.1** (2435 km) **F 6.9** (11.1 km) Badger Road. This loop road connects with the Alaska Highway again at North Pole. Motel, RV park, salmon bake, bed and breakfasts, and other businesses are located on Badger Road.

Riverview RV Park. See display ad this section.

V 357.6 (575.5 km) **DC 1513.6** (2435.8 km) **F 6.4** (10.3 km) Weigh stations both sides of highway.

V 358.6 (577.1 km) **DC 1514.6** (2437.4 km) **F 5.4** (8.7 km) Entrance to Fort Wainwright.

V 359.2 (578.1 km) **DC 1515.2** (2438.4 km) **F 4.8** (7.7 km) *CAUTION: Highway crosses Alaska Railroad tracks.*

V 359.6 (578.7 km) **DC 1515.6** (2439.1 km) **F 4.4** (7.1 km) West truck route (Old Richardson Highway) exit for westbound traffic only. Access to motels, restaurants and Cushman Street business area.

V 360.6 (580.3 km) **DC 1516.6** (2440.7 km) **F 3.4** (5.5 km) Denali Park/Parks Highway (Alaska Route 3) exit northbound to bypass Fairbanks via the Robert J. Mitchell expressway. Hospital this exit.

V 361 (581 km) **DC 1517** (2441.4 km) **F 3** (4.8 km) Exit via 30th Avenue to Big Bend business area for east- and westbound traffic. Access to motels, restaurants, Old Richardson Highway, Van Horn Road, Cushman Street and downtown Fairbanks.

V 361.3 (581.4 km) **DC 1517.3** (2441.8 km) **F 2.7** (4.3 km) 30th Avenue overpass; exits both sides of highway. A heart-shaped picture created from plantings of yellow flowers represents the Golden Heart of Fairbanks.

V 363 (584.2 km) **DC 1519** (2444.6 km) **F 1** (1.6 km) Turn right on Gaffney Road for Fort Wainwright; left on Airport Way for downtown Fairbanks, University of Alaska, Alaskaland and George Parks Highway (Alaska Route 3). Follow city center signs to downtown Fairbanks and visitor information center. Go straight ahead on the Steese Expressway for Gavora Mall, Bentley Mall, Fox, Steese and Elliott highways, and Chena Hot Springs Road.

V 363.3 (584.7 km) **DC 1519.3** (2445 km) **F 0.7** (1.1 km) 10th Avenue exit to Fairbanks.

V 363.6 (585.1 km) **DC 1519.6** (2445.6 km) **F 0.4** (0.6 km) Steese Expressway crosses Chena River.

V 363.9 (585.6 km) **DC 1519.9** (2446 km) **F 0.1** (0.2 km) 3rd Street exit. Gavora Mall.

V 364 (585.8 km) **DC 1520** (2446.2 km) **F 0 FAIRBANKS.** College Road exit route to University of Alaska, Bentley Mall and city center (turn left). For details see FAIRBANKS section, beginning on page 405.

The summer maximum of daylight hours in Fairbanks is 21 hours and 49 minutes.

LIARD HIGHWAY 77 7

Connects: Alaska Hwy. to Mackenzie Hwy.   **Length:** 244 miles
Road Surface: Gravel   **Season:** Open all year
Steepest Grade: 10 percent
Major Attraction: Nahanni National Park

(See map, page 198)

	Fort Liard	Fort Nelson	Fort Simpson
Fort Liard		126	176
Fort Nelson	126		302
Fort Simpson	176	302	

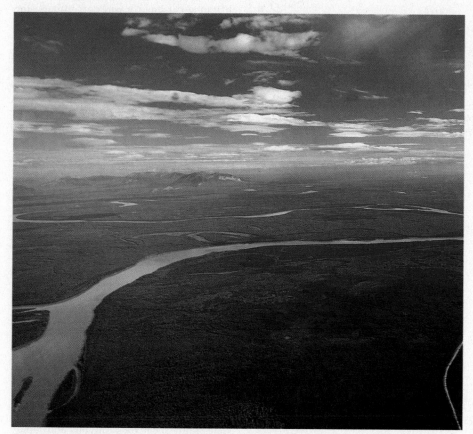

View of Liard River and Liard Highway on a flightseeing trip out of Fort Liard.
(Earl L. Brown, staff)

The Liard Highway, also called the Liard Trail or "Moose Highway" (after the road sign logo), is named for the Liard River Valley through which it runs for most of its length. The Liard Highway begins about 17 miles/27 km north of Fort Nelson on the Alaska Highway and leads northeast through British Columbia and Northwest Territories for 244.4 miles/393.4 km to junction with the Mackenzie Highway (NWT Highway 1).

The Liard is a relatively straight 2-lane gravel road through boreal forest and muskeg. In French, Liard means "black poplar," and this wilderness highway (officially opened in June 1984) is a corridor through a forest of white and black spruce, trembling aspen and balsam poplar.

The road can be dusty when dry and very muddy when wet. Poor road conditions (potholes, lack of grading) were reported on the BC portion of the Liard Highway in 1996. The NWT portion of the highway is well-maintained. Travelers may check current road conditions on the BC section of the highway (first 85 miles/136.8 km of the road) by inquiring at the Visitor Infocentre in Fort Nelson, BC. Travel information for the Northwest Territories is available from Northwest Territories Tourism; phone toll free weekdays 1-800-661-0788. Food, gas and lodging are available at Fort Liard. Gas and accommodations are also available at the Mackenzie Highway junction. It is a good idea to fill up in Fort Nelson.

Although the Northwest Territories portion of the Liard Highway parallels the Liard River, there is little access to the river. Travelers may enhance their trip by visiting Blackstone Territorial Park and exploring Nahanni National Park by air charter out of Fort Liard, Fort Simpson or Fort Nelson. Blackstone Territorial Park is accessible by road. Along the highway, travelers may walk the cut lines, drive to abandoned construction camps, swim in the borrow pits and bird watch at the barge landings. Remember to bring along lots of insect repellent!

Fishing the highway streams is only fair, but watch for wildlife such as moose, black bear, wood bison and grouse.

Liard Highway Log

Physical kilometreposts are up on the British Columbia portion of the highway about every 5 kilometres, starting with km 0 at the Alaska Highway junction and ending at the BC–NWT border. Kilometreposts are up about every 2 kilometres on the Northwest Territories portion of the highway, starting with Km 0 at the BC–NWT border and ending at the junction with the Mackenzie Highway.
Distance from the junction with the Alaska Highway (A) is followed by distance from the Mackenzie Highway junction (M).

A 0 M 244.4 (393.4 km) **Junction** with the Alaska Highway.

A 6.2 (10.1 km) **M 238.2** (383.3 km) Beaver Creek.

A 6.4 (10.3 km) **M 238** (383.1 km) Short side road east to Beaver Lake recreation site; 2 picnic tables, litter barrels, pit toilets, firewood, turnaround space. Short hike downhill through brush to floating dock; limited lake access.

A 14.3 (23.1 km) **M 230.1** (370.3 km) Stanolind Creek. Beaver dams to west.

A 15.6 (25.2 km) **M 228.8** (368.2 km) Gravel pit to west.

A 17.5 (28.2 km) **M 226.9** (365.2 km) Pond to west and cut line through trees shows Cat access in summer, ice road in winter.

A 21.1 (34 km) **M 223.3** (359.4 km) Westcoast Transmission Pipeline crossing. Pipeline transports natural gas from Pointed Mountain near Fort Liard to the company's gas plant on the Alaska Highway just south of Fort Nelson.

A 23.9 (38.4 km) **M 220.5** (355 km) Gravel pit to west.

A 24.2 (38.9 km) **M 220.2** (354.5 km) Road begins descent northbound to Fort Nelson River.

A 26.4 (42.5 km) **M 218** (350.9 km) Fort Nelson River bridge, single lane, reduce speed. The Nelson bridge is the longest Acrow bridge in the world at 1,410 feet/430m. It is 14 feet/4m wide, with a span of 230 feet/70m from pier to pier. The Acrow bridge, formerly called the Bailey bridge after its designer Sir Donald Bailey, is designed of interchangeable steel panels coupled with pins for rapid construction.

A 26.6 (42.9 km) **M 217.8** (350.5 km) Turnout at north end of bridge with pit

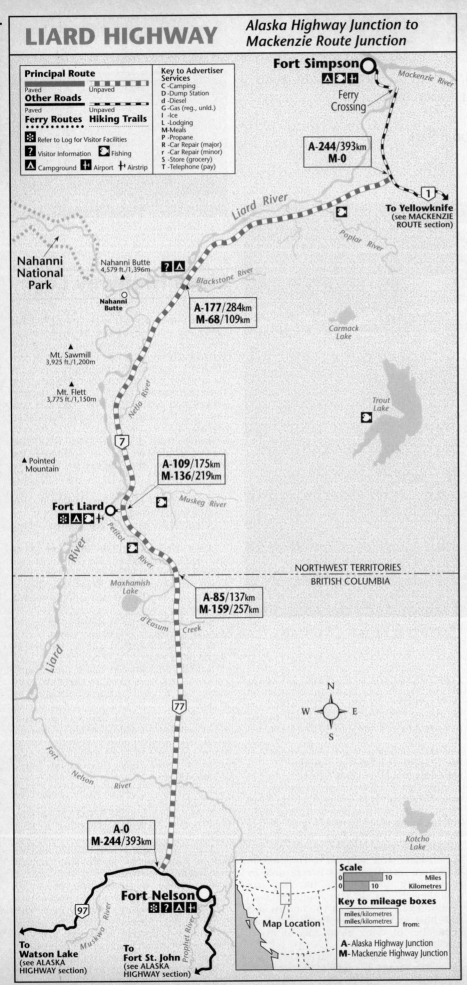

LIARD HIGHWAY

Alaska Highway Junction to Mackenzie Route Junction

Principal Route
Paved
Other Roads
Paved   Unpaved
Ferry Routes   **Hiking Trails**

Key to Advertiser Services
C -Camping
D -Dump Station
d -Diesel
G -Gas (reg., unld.)
I -Ice
L -Lodging
M -Meals
P -Propane
R -Car Repair (major)
r -Car Repair (minor)
S -Store (grocery)
T -Telephone (pay)

Refer to Log for Visitor Facilities
Visitor Information   Fishing
Campground   Airport   Airstrip

Fort Simpson

Mackenzie River

Ferry Crossing

A-244/393km
M-0

Liard River

To Yellowknife
(see MACKENZIE ROUTE section)

Poplar River

Nahanni National Park

Nahanni Butte
4,579 ft./1,396m

Blackstone River

A-177/284km
M-68/109km

Carmack Lake

Nahanni Butte

Mt. Sawmill
3,925 ft./1,200m

Mt. Flett
3,775 ft./1,150m

Netla River

Trout Lake

Pointed Mountain

A-109/175km
M-136/219km

Fort Liard

Muskeg River

Petitot River

Liard River

Maxhamish Lake

NORTHWEST TERRITORIES
BRITISH COLUMBIA

A-85/137km
M-159/257km

d'Easum Creek

Liard River

77

Fort Nelson River

Kotcho Lake

A-0
M-244/393km

Fort Nelson

97

Muskwa River

Prophet River

To Watson Lake
(see ALASKA HIGHWAY section)

To Fort St. John
(see ALASKA HIGHWAY section)

N
W   E
S

Scale
0   10   Miles
0   10   Kilometres

Key to mileage boxes
miles/kilometres
miles/kilometres
from:

Map Location

A- Alaska Highway Junction
M- Mackenzie Highway Junction

---

toilet, table and garbage container.

A 39.7 (63.9 km) **M 204.7** (329.5 km) **Tsinhia Creek**, grayling run for about 2 weeks in spring.

A 43.4 (69.8 km) **M 201** (323.5 km) Trapper's cabin to east.

A 51.8 (83.3 km) **M 192.6** (310.1 km) Side road leads west 1.9 miles/3 km to Tsinhia Lake and dead-ends in soft sandy track. A recreation site is planned at Tsinhia Lake.

A 59.2 (95.3 km) **M 185.2** (298.1 km) There are several winter roads in this area used by the forest, oil and gas industries. To most summer travelers these roads look like long cut lines or corridors through the Bush.

The Liard Highway replaced the old Fort Simpson winter road that joined Fort Nelson and Fort Simpson. The original Simpson Trail was first blazed in November 1942 by Alaska Highway engineers, including the 648th, Company A detachment.

A 69.4 (111.7 km) **M 175** (281.7 km) Bridge over d'Easum Creek. Good bird-watching area.

A 71.4 (115 km) **M 173** (278.4 km) Access to Maxhamish Lake via 8-mile/13-km winter road accessible in summer by all-terrain vehicles only. A recreation site is planned for Maxhamish Lake.

A 74 (119.1 km) **M 170.4** (274.3 km) Wide unnamed creek flows into Emile Creek to east. Good bird-watching area, beaver pond.

A 75.4 (121.4 km) **M 169** (272 km) Highway emerges from trees northbound; view west of Mount Martin (elev. 4,460 feet/1,360m) and the Kotaneelee Range.

A 80.6 (129.7 km) **M 163.8** (263.7 km) View northwest of mountain ranges in Northwest Territories.

A 81.2 (130.7 km) **M 163.2** (262.6 km) Highway begins descent (7 percent grade) northbound to Petitot River.

A 82.8 (133.2 km) **M 161.6** (260.2 km) Petitot River bridge. The **Petitot River** is reputed to have the warmest swimming water in British Columbia (70°F/21°C). A 9-hour canoe trip to Fort Liard is possible from here (some sheer rock canyons and rapids en route). Good bird-watching area. Also freshwater clams, pike and pickerel; short grayling run in spring.

The Petitot River was named for Father Petitot, an Oblate missionary who came to this area from France in the 1860s.

The Petitot River bridge was the site of the official opening of the Liard Highway on June 23, 1984. The ceremony was marked by an unusual ribbon-cutting: A 1926 Model T Ford, carrying dignitaries, was driven through the ribbon (which stretched for about 20 feet before snapping) while a guard of kilted pipers from Yellowknife played. The Model T, driven by Marl Brown of Fort Nelson, had been across this route in March 1975 just weeks after the bush road had been punched through by Cats and seismic equipment. This earlier trip, in which Mr. Brown was accompanied by Mickey Hempler, took 44 hours from Fort Nelson to Fort Simpson.

A 84.1 (135.4 km) **M 160.3** (258 km) Crest of Petitot River hill (10 percent grade).

A 85 (136.8 km) **M 159.4** (256.6 km) BC–NWT border. TIME ZONE CHANGE: British Columbia observes Pacific time, Northwest Territories observes Mountain time.

Northwest Territories restricts liquor

cal location. Several luxuriant local gardens. The Liard River here is approximately 1,500 feet/450m wide, fairly swift and subject to occasional flooding. **Radio** and **Television:** CBC radio (microwave), a Native language station from Yellowknife and a community radio station; 4 channels plus CBC Television (Anik), TVNC and private satellite receivers. Canadian Aerodrome Radio Station (CARS) operates Monday through Friday 8 A.M. to 7 P.M. .

Private Aircraft: Fort Liard airstrip; elev. 700 feet/213m; length 2,950 feet/899m; gravel; fuel 100/130 (obtain from Deh Cho Air Ltd.).

Transportation: Air—Charter service year-round via Deh Cho Air. **Barge**—Nonscheduled barge service in summer. Scheduled and charter taxi service available.

This small, well-laid-out settlement of traditional log homes and new modern

Quill decorated birch-bark baskets on display in Fort Liard. (© Lyn Hancock)

importation as follows: 1 40-oz. hard liquor, 1 40-oz. wine or 1 dozen bottles of beer per person. *NOTE: Area codes in the Northwest Territories are scheduled to change from (403) to (867) in October of 1997.*

A 85.2 (137.1 km) **M 159.2** (256.2 km) Turnout to east with litter barrels.

A 107 (172.2 km) **M 137.4** (221.1 km) Vehicle inspection station and weigh scales to east.

A 108.6 (174.8 km) **M 135.8** (218.5 km) **Junction** with side road that leads 4 miles/6.4 km to Fort Liard (description follows). Gas and diesel available in Fort Liard. Tourist information is available at the Acho Craft Shop; phone (403) 770-4161; fax (403) 770-4160. Current status of proposed tourist centre here unknown.

Views from road into Fort Liard across the Liard River of Mount Coty (elev. 2,715 feet/830m) and Pointed Mountain (elev. 4,610 feet/1,405m) at the southern tip of the Liard Range.

Fort Liard

Located on the south bank of the Liard River near its confluence with the Petitot River (known locally as Black River because of its colour), about 50 miles/80 km south of Nahanni Butte. **Population:** 428. **Emergency Services:** RCMP, phone (403) 770-4221. **Fire Depart-**

ment, phone (403) 770-2222. **Nursing Station,** phone (403) 770-4301.

Elevation: 700 feet/213m. **Climate:** There is no permafrost here. Good soil and water, a long summer season with long hours of daylight, and comparatively mild climate considering Fort Liard's geographi-

FORT LIARD ADVERTISERS

Acho Dene Native Crafts Ph. (403) 770-4161
Deh Cho Air Ltd. ....Ph. (403) 770-4103
Hamlet of Fort Liard ....Ph. (403) 770-4104
Liard Valley General Store
 & Motel Ltd.................Ph. (403) 770-4441

Open log shelter at Hay Lake campground in Fort Liard. (© Lyn Hancock)

housing is located among tall poplar, spruce and birch trees on the south bank of the Liard River. The residents live a comparatively traditional life of hunting, trapping, fishing and making handicrafts, although there are more people taking jobs in construction and highway maintenance. Fort Liard residents are well known for the high quality of their birch-bark baskets and porcupine quill workmanship.

Recreation and sightseeing in the area include swimming and fishing (for pike, pickerel, goldeye and spring grayling; at the confluence of the Liard and Petitot rivers; air charter or canoe trip to Trout Lake, Bovie Lake, Fisherman's Lake, 300-foot/91-m-high Virginia Falls in Nahanni National Park, Tlogotsho Plateau, or scenic Liard and Kotaneelee mountain ranges. Good viewing for Dall sheep, grizzly bear and caribou. Canoe rentals available from Deh Cho Air Ltd. The traditional Dene settlement of **TROUT LAKE** (pop. 60) is also accessible by air from Fort Liard.

The North West Co. established a trading post near here at the confluence of the Liard and Petitot rivers called Riviere aux Liards in 1805. The post was abandoned after the massacre of more than a dozen residents by Indians. It was re-established in 1820, then taken over by the Hudson's Bay Co. in 1821 when the 2 companies merged. The well-known geologist Charles Camsell was born at Fort Liard in 1876.

Facilities here include a motel with 12 rooms, 6 with kitchenettes (reservations suggested), 2 general stores, playground, outdoor rink, craft shop (open 1–5 P.M. weekdays, extended hours in summer), snack bar, restaurant, the modern Acho Dene School and a Roman Catholic mission. There is no bank in Fort Liard. Gas, diesel and propane fuel available.

Community-run Hay Lake Campground located just off the access road into Fort Liard; campsites, picnic tables, toilets and floating dock. Campground road may be slippery when wet. ▲

Liard Highway Log
(continued)

A 113.3 (182.4 km) M 131.1 (211 km) **Muskeg River** bridge; turnout at north end. Gravel bars on the river make a good rest area. Trapper's cabin on left. Fishing for pike, pickerel and freshwater clams. The Muskeg River is the local swimming hole for Fort Liard residents. ◄

A 124.9 (201 km) M 119.5 (192.4 km) Rabbit Creek bridge. Highway now runs close to the Liard River with good views of Liard Range to the west and northwest for the next 13 miles/21 km northbound.

A 128 (206 km) M 116.4 (187.4 km) Kilometrepost 70.

A 131.1 (211 km) M 113.3 (182.4 km) Good view of Mount Flett (elev. 3,775 feet/1,150m) ahead northbound.

A 136.7 (220 km) M 107.7 (173.4 km) Access to Liard River (15-minute hike) via Paramount Mine winter road, an abandoned exploration road across the Liard River into the Liard Range.

A 146.9 (236.4 km) M 97.5 (157 km) Short road west to locally named Whissel Landing on the Liard River, where road construction materials were brought in by barge during construction of the Liard Highway.

A 147.3 (237 km) M 97.1 (156.4 km) Road widens for an emergency airstrip.

A 157.8 (253.9 km) M 86.6 (139.5 km) Netla River bridge. The Netla River Delta is an important waterfowl breeding habitat, and Indian fishing and hunting area.

A 163.7 (263.4 km) M 80.7 (130 km) Road widens for an emergency airstrip.

A 165.9 (267 km) M 78.5 (126.4 km) Turnoff to west for winter ice road that leads 13.8 miles/22.3 km to the Dene settlement of **NAHANNI BUTTE** (pop. 87), at the confluence of the South Nahanni and Liard rivers. Summer access by boat or floatplane.

A 171.8 (276.5 km) M 72.6 (116.8 km) Creek Bridge, once called Scotty's Creek after an old trapper who had a cabin upstream. There are many such cabins in this area that once belonged (and still do) to prospectors and trappers, but they are not visible to the motorist. Stands of white spruce, white birch and balsam poplar along highway.

A 176.3 (283.7 km) M 68.1 (109.7 km) Bridge over Upper Blackstone River. Picnic day-use area on riverbank with tables, firewood, firepits and garbage containers.

A 176.6 (284.2 km) M 67.8 (109.2 km) Blackstone River bridge.

A 179.1 (288.3 km) M 65.3 (105.1 km) Entrance to Blackstone Territorial Park; 19 campsites with tables and firepits; firewood, water and garbage containers, boat dock and restroom. The boat launch is usable only in high water early in the season; use boat launch at Cadillac Landing, **Milepost A 182.9**, during low water. The visitor information building, built with local logs, is located on the bank of the Liard River with superb views of Nahanni Butte (elev. 4,579 feet/1,396m). The centre is open mid-May to mid-September. ▲

A 180.9 (291.2 km) M 63.5 (102.2 km) Entrance to Lindberg Landing, the homestead of Liard River pioneers Edwin and Sue Lindberg. The Lindbergs offer a bed and breakfast; rustic accommodations, bring your own sleeping bag. By appointment only. Contact Mobile Telephone JR36644 Arrowhead Channel, or write Sue and Edwin Lindberg, Box 28, Fort Simpson, NWT XOE ONO.

Blackstone Aviation operates floatplane flightseeing trips of Nahanni National Park from here. (See description of Nahanni National Park under Fort Simpson attractions in the MACKENZIE ROUTE section.)

A 182.9 (294.3 km) M 61.5 (99.1 km) Barge landing once used to service Cadillac Mine and bring in construction materials. Access to river via 0.6-mile/0.9-km road (muddy when wet).

A 192.8 (310.3 km) M 51.6 (83.1 km) Road widens for emergency airstrip.

A 197.8 (318.4 km) M 46.6 (75 km) Kilometrepost 180.

A 211.3 (340.1 km) M 33.1 (53.3 km) Bridge over Birch River.

A 216.7 (348.8 km) M 27.7 (44.6 km) Kilometrepost 210.

A 222.8 (358.5 km) M 21.6 (34.9 km) Good grayling and pike fishing in **Poplar River** culverts. ◄

A 223 (358.8 km) M 21.4 (34.6 km) Dirt road on left northbound leads 4 miles/6.4 km to Liard River; 4-wheel drive recommended. Wide beach, good spot for viewing wildlife.

A 228.1 (367.1 km) M 16.3 (26.3 km) Microwave tower to east. Vegetation changes northbound to muskeg with black spruce, tamarack and jackpine.

A 235.6 (379.2 km) M 8.8 (14.2 km) Kilometrepost 240.

A 244.2 (393 km) M 0.2 (0.4 km) Road maintenance camp.

A 244.4 (393.4 km) M 0 **Junction** with the Mackenzie Highway (NWT 1). "Checkpoint": 24-hour gas, diesel, propane; licensed restaurant and 4-room motel. Phone (403) 695-2953. Turn right (south) for Hay River and Yellowknife; turn left (north) for Fort Simpson. See **Milepost G 550.6** on the Mackenzie Highway in the MACKENZIE ROUTE section for log.

Connects: Grimshaw, AB to Western NWT   **Length:** 1,231 miles
Road Surface: 47% paved, 53% gravel   **Season:** Open all year
Major Attractions: Nahanni National Park;
Wood Buffalo National Park

(See maps, pages 202–203)

	Ft. Resolution	Ft. Simpson	Ft. Smith	Valleyview	Yellowknife
Ft. Resolution		358	185	560	391
Ft. Simpson	358		431	692	393
Ft. Smith	185	431		633	464
Valleyview	560	692	633		725
Yellowknife	391	393	464	725	

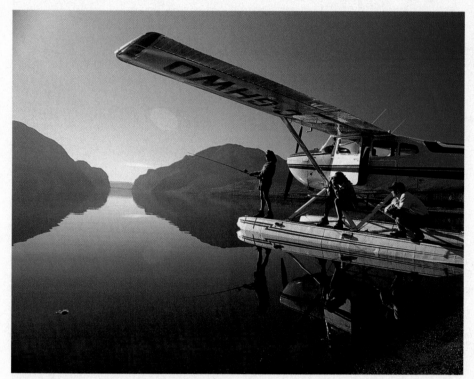

Fly-in fishing on Little Doctor Lake, 65 air miles west of Fort Simpson. (©Lyn Hancock)

Named for explorer Alexander Mackenzie, who in 1779 navigated Great Slave Lake and sailed to the mouth of the Mackenzie River seeking a trade route for the Hudson's Bay Co., the Mackenzie Route is an adventure for modern explorers. It is not a trip for the impulsive. While there are accommodations, gas stations and other services in cities and settlements along the highways, long distances require that motorists plan in advance.

The Mackenzie Route covers the following highways: Alberta Highway 35 and NWT Highway 1 to Fort Simpson (Mackenzie Highway) and the extension to Wrigley; Highway 2 to Hay River; Highway 3 to Yellowknife; Highway 4 (Ingraham Trail); Highway 5 to Fort Smith; and Highway 6 to Fort Resolution. NWT Highway 7, the Liard Highway, connecting the Mackenzie Highway with the Alaska Highway north of Fort Nelson, is covered in the LIARD HIGHWAY section. The Dempster Highway (NWT Highway 8) to Inuvik is covered in the DEMPSTER HIGHWAY section.

Allow at least 2 weeks to travel the entire route. For general information on travel in the Northwest Territories, phone Northwest Territories Tourism toll free at 1-800-661-0788 during business hours on weekdays.

Northwest Territories highways are both paved and gravel. Asphalt chip seal surfacing is under way on the remaining gravel portions of Highways 1 (Mackenzie Highway) and 3 (Yellowknife Highway). Gravel road is treated with calcium chloride to control the dust; wash your vehicle when possible. For road conditions phone 1-800-661-0750.

In summer, the Northwest Territories government provides free ferry service for cars and passengers across the Mackenzie River to Fort Providence, across the Liard River to Fort Simpson and across the Mackenzie River to Wrigley. In winter, traffic crosses on the ice. For current ferry information call (403) 873-7799 in Yellowknife, or 1-800-661-0751.

The Mackenzie Highway begins at Grimshaw, AB. There are several routes to Grimshaw to choose from (see map). *The MILEPOST®* logs the Valleyview–Peace River route to the Mackenzie Highway via Highways 43 and 2.

Log of the Valleyview–Peace River Route to the Mackenzie Highway

Distance from Valleyview (V) is followed by distance from Mackenzie Highway (MH).

ALBERTA HIGHWAY 43

V 0 MH 101.1 (162.7 km) **Junction** of Highways 34 and 43. Follow Highway 43 north.

V 0.6 (1 km) **MH 100.5** (161.6 km) Turnoff to west for downtown Valleyview (see description of Valleyview in the EAST ACCESS ROUTE section).

V 2.2 (3.5 km) **MH 98.9** (159.3 km) **Junction** with Secondary Road 669 which leads east 20 miles/32 km to Sunset House Community Campground on Snipe Lake; 20 sites, firewood, playground, boat launch, camping fee. ▲

V 4 (6.4 km) **MH 97.1** (156.3 km) Sturgeon Creek.

V 18 (29 km) **MH 83.1** (133.7 km) East Dollar Lake to west.

V 23.1 (37.2 km) **MH 78** (125.6 km) Entering Midnight Twilight Tourist Zone northbound, entering Game Country Tourist Zone southbound.

V 25.1 (40.4 km) **MH 76** (122.3 km) **Junction** with Secondary Road 676 to Whitmud Creek, 14 miles/22 km west.

V 28.3 (45.6 km) **MH 72.8** (117.3 km) Entering Grande Prairie Forest southbound.

V 29.1 (46.8 km) **MH 72** (115.8 km) Little Smokey River bridge. Little Smokey River provincial recreation area to west on south bank of river; 12 sites, shelters, picnic tables, camping fee. ▲

V 30.3 (48.8 km) **MH 70.8** (114 km) **Junction** with Highway 2A east, a spur road which leads 17 miles/27 km to junction with Highway 2.

V 31.3 (50.4 km) **MH 69.8** (112.3 km) Turnout with litter barrels to east.

V 32.4 (52.1 km) **MH 68.7** (110.6 km) Entering Peace River Forest northbound.

V 36.4 (58.6 km) **MH 64.7** (104.2 km) Community of **GUY** (pop. 57) to east; pay phone. Access road leads west 7 miles/11 km to Five Star Golf Course; 9 holes, grass greens, pro shop.

V 40.5 (65.2 km) **MH 60.6** (97.5 km) **Junction** with Secondary Road 679 to Highway 2 and Winigami Lake Provincial Park (19 miles/30.5 km east).

V 48.7 (78.4 km) **MH 52.4** (84.4 km) **Donnelly Corners, junction** of Highways 2 and 49. **DONNELLY** (pop. 450) has a hotel, restaurants, stores, service stations with repair facilities and a library. Historic site 3 miles/5 km south of town features a fully operational 1904 Case Steam Engine. High-

MACKENZIE ROUTE *Valleyview, AB, to Steen River, AB*

(map continues next page)

Wood Buffalo National Park

Pine Lake

Steen River

FS-324/521km
G-267/429km

Zama

Meander River

35

FS-417/671km
G-174/280km
J-0

Habay

Chateh

58

58

High Level

Fort Vermilion

Jean D'or Prairie

J-49/78km

Rainbow Lake

G-173.6/279.3km MacKenzie Crossroads Museum & Visitors Centre T

La Crete

697 Ferry Crossing

88

J-85/136km

Paddle Prairie

Keg River

To Slave Lake

FS-502/807km
G-89/143km

Twin Lakes

ALBERTA

BRITISH COLUMBIA

Peace River

Hotchkiss

Manning

FS-590/950km
G-0

35

Dixonville

V-101/163km
MH-0

To Fort St. John

64

Grimshaw
Fairview

V-88/142.3km Travellers Motor Hotel LMT

Peace River

To Fort Vermilion

To Fort St. John
(see ALASKA HIGHWAY section)

2

Ferry

Heart River

744

88

To Fort McMurray

Dunvegan

49

Rycroft

Wanham

Girouxville

Donnelly

To Prince George
(see WEST ACCESS ROUTE section)

Dawson Creek

Woking

McLennan

Winagami Lake

Lesser Slave Lake

63

2

49

2

2A

Slave Lake

Northern Woods & Waters Route

Athabasca River

Sexsmith

2

Smoky River

43

High Prairie

2

33

To Lac La Biche

55

Grande Prairie

34

Valleyview

V-0
MH-101/163km

33

44

43

32

33

Grizzly Trail

Map Location

Scale
0   20 Miles
0   20 Kilometres

Key to mileage boxes
miles/kilometres
miles/kilometres from:
FS-Fort Simpson
G-Grimshaw **J**-Junction
MH-Mackenzie Hwy.
V-Valleyview

Whitecourt

Westlock

32

43

Chip Lake

Lac Saint Anne

River

16

Edmonton

16 To Saskatoon

To Jasper
(see YELLOWHEAD HIGHWAY 16 section)

McLeod River

Wabamun Lake

North Saskatchewan

2

To Calgary
(see EAST ACCESS ROUTE section)

Principal Route
Paved _____
Unpaved ▪▪▪▪▪▪

Other Roads
Paved _____
Unpaved ▪ ▪ ▪ ▪

Ferry Routes   ## Hiking Trails
▪▪▪▪▪▪▪▪▪▪

✳ Refer to Log for Visitor Facilities
❓ Visitor Information   ▣ Fishing
⛺ Campground   ✈ Airport   ✛ Airstrip

Key to Advertiser Services
C -Camping
D -Dump Station
d -Diesel
G -Gas (reg., unld.)
I -Ice
L -Lodging
M -Meals
P -Propane
R -Car Repair (major)
r -Car Repair (minor)
S -Store (grocery)
T -Telephone (pay)

MACKENZIE ROUTE Steen River, AB, to Yellowknife, NWT

way 43 ends northbound. Continue on Highway 2 North.

ALBERTA HIGHWAY 2

V 61 (98.1 km) **MH 40.1** (64.5 km) Access leads west 7 miles/11 km to JEAN COTE (pop. 65), and 18 miles/28 km to Rainbow Trout Park and Campground; 55 sites, hookups, picnic tables, shelter, firewood, playground, rental cabins, mini-golf, horseshoe pits. Camping fee $9.   ▲

V 66.1 (106.5 km) **MH 35** (56.3 km) Entering Land of the Mighty Peace Tourist Zone northbound, Midnight Twilight Tourist Zone southbound.

V 67.2 (108.1 km) **MH 33.9** (54.6 km) Access road leads east 5.5 miles/9 km to Reno.

V 70.7 (113.8 km) **MH 30.4** (49 km) Nampa visitor centre and museum to west. NAMPA (pop. 500) was founded in 1917 when the East Dunvegan and BC Railway Company built a line through the area. Visitor facilities include a hotel, motel, restaurants, grocery and retail stores, service stations with repair facilities and a library. Recreational facilities include a curling rink, ball diamonds and tennis courts. Heart River Golf Club, 5 miles/8 km northeast, has 9 holes. Camping at Mill Brown Memorial Park.   ▲

V 71.3 (114.7 km) **MH 29.8** (48 km) Junction with Secondary Road 683 which leads west 6 miles/10 km to Secondary Road 744 to Marie Reine.

V 72.1 (116 km) **MH 29** (46.6 km) Heart River bridge.

V 73.4 (118.1 km) **MH 27.7** (44.6 km) South Harmon Road east to Harmon Valley Fairgrounds (14 miles/23 km).

V 73.5 (118.3 km) **MH 27.6** (44.4 km) Access road leads east 3 miles/5 km to Harmon Valley Golf Course.

V 75.3 (121.2 km) **MH 25.8** (41.6 km) Grain storage equipment on both sides of highway.

V 79.6 (128.1 km) **MH 21.5** (34.6 km) North Harmon Valley Road east to Harmon Valley Fairgrounds (12 miles/20 km).

V 84.3 (135.7 km) **MH 16.8** (27 km) Junction with Secondary Road 688 (Three Creeks Road) which leads east 5 miles/8 km

to ST. ISIDORE (pop. 180); gas station, pay phone and library.

V 85 (136.8 km) **MH 16.1** (25.9 km) Highway begins descent northbound into Peace River Valley.

V 87.6 (141 km) **MH 13.5** (21.7 km) Turnout to east with information sign about Peace River.

Peace River

V 88.4 (142.3 km) **MH 12.7** (20.5 km). Located on the banks of the Peace River, 15 miles/24 km northeast of Grimshaw (Mile 0 of the Mackenzie Highway). **Population:** 6,700. **Emergency Services: RCMP**, phone (403) 624-6611. **Hospital**, phone (403) 624-7500. **Ambulance** and **Fire Department**, phone (403) 624-3911.

Visitor Information: Tourist Information located in the NAR station at the first right after the railway trestle at the east entrance to downtown; phone (403) 624-2044. Open mid-May to mid-September, 9 A.M. to 9 P.M. The Mighty Peace Tourist Association, at the north end of Main Street in the restored railway station, also has information on northern Alberta destinations; phone (403) 624-4042.

Elevation: 1,066 feet/325m. **Private Aircraft:** Peace River airport, 7 miles/11.2 km west; elev. 1,873 feet/571m; length 5,000 feet/1,524m; asphalt; fuel 80, 100, Jet B.

An important transportation centre on the Peace River, the town of Peace River was incorporated in 1919, 3 years after the railroad reached Peace River Crossing. Today, Peace River is a centre for government services in the region. Area industry includes Peace River Pulp, Shell Canada and farming.

Visitor facilities include 3 hotels, a motel and many restaurants. Camping at Lions Club Campground on the west side of the river; 85 sites, hookups, restrooms, dump station and laundry.   ▲

There are 9 campgrounds along the Peace River. For details, contact the Peace Valley Conservation, Recreation and Tourism Soci-

Twelve-Foot Davis statue in Peace River.
(Earl L. Brown, staff)

ety, phone (403) 835-2616 or fax 835-3131.

The Centennial Museum (on the south side of town along the river) houses archives and exhibits on Sir Alexander Mackenzie, the fur trade and local history. Historical re-enactments in summer. Open 9 A.M. to 5 P.M. Monday to Wednesday, noon to 8 P.M. Thursday to Saturday. (May 1 to Aug. 31); 9 A.M. to 5 P.M. weekdays Sept. 1 to April 31. Rail transportation exhibit at restored NAR railway station. Museum phone (403) 624-4261.

Visitors can take the Historic Mackenzie Moose Walking Trail by following the moose tracks from the Centennial Museum to

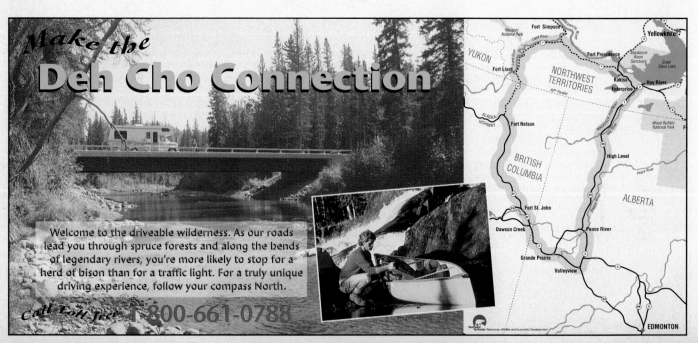

various points of interest around town. The tour includes the statue of Twelve-Foot Davis, a gold miner who struck it rich on a 12-foot strip of land between 2 larger claims in the Cariboo gold fields. He invested his $15,000 in gold in a string of trading posts along the Peace. He is buried on Grouard Hill overlooking the Peace River Valley.

Travellers Motor Hotel. 144 units, air conditioned, colour TV satellite service, courtesy in-room coffee, plug-ins, complimentary passes to golf course, indoor swimming pool, fitness centre. Courtesy airport limo, restaurant, dining room, pub, banquet and meeting room facilities. All major credit cards accepted. Senior citizen discount, commercial rates. 9510–100 St., Box 7290, Peace River, AB T8S 1S9. 1-800-661-3227. Phone (403) 624-3621, fax (403) 624-4855.
[ADVERTISEMENT]

Log of Valleyview–Peace River Route
(continued)

V 89.2 (143.5 km) MH 11.9 (19.1 km) Peace River bridge.

V 90 (144.8 km) MH 11.1 (17.9 km) Junction with Secondary Road 684 which leads southwest 15 miles/24 km to Secondary Road 740 and the Shaftsbury Ferry Crossing of the Peace River.

V 90.8 (146.1 km) MH 10.3 (16.5 km) Junction with Secondary Road 743 which leads north 10 miles/16 km to Secondary Road 686 to the Mackenzie Highway. Access to Peace View golf course, 2.5 miles/4 km north; 9 holes, sand greens, pro shop.

V 91.6 (147.4 km) MH 9.5 (15.3 km) Turnout to south with information sign about Peace River.

V 94.7 (152.4 km) MH 6.4 (10.3 km) Peace River airport to south.

V 96 (154.5 km) MH 5.1 (8.2 km) **Roma Junction, junction** with Highway 2A to Grimshaw (7 miles/12 km southwest).

V 97.1 (156.3 km) MH 4 (6.5 km) Access road leads 1.2 miles/2 km to Mighty Peace golf course; 18 holes, licensed dining room, pro shop, camping.

V 99.1 (159.5 km) MH 2 (3.2 km) Access road leads south 0.6 mile/1 km to Wilderness Park; picnic tables, outhouses, hiking trails.

V 101.1 (162.7 km) MH 0 Junction with Highway 35 (Mackenzie Highway).

Mackenzie Highway Log

ALBERTA HIGHWAY 35
Distance from Grimshaw (G) is followed by distance from Fort Simpson (FS).

Grimshaw

G 0 FS 590.4 (950.2 km) Mile 0 of the Mackenzie Highway. **Population:** 2,812. **Emergency Services:** RCMP, phone (403) 332-4666. **Hospital** and **Ambulance**, phone (403) 332-1155. **Fire Department**, phone (403) 332-4430. **Visitor Information:** In the NAR railway car located adjacent the centennial monument marking Mile 0 of the Mackenzie Highway.

Named for pioneer doctor M.E. Grim-

shaw, who established a practice at Peace River Crossing in 1914, Grimshaw developed as a community centre for area farmers and as a shipping point with the arrival of the railroad in 1921. Scheduled air service from Edmonton and High Level to Peace River airport, 8 miles/12.8 km east.

Grimshaw became a town in February 1953. Local resources are wheat and grains, livestock, gravel, lumber, gas and oil.

Grimshaw has 1 motel, 2 hotels, 6 service stations, 2 car washes, a laundromat and all other visitor facilities. RV dump station and drinking water located south of the Mile 0 marker and 2 blocks east. Camping just north of town (see **Milepost G 1.9**). There are also an outdoor swimming pool, tennis courts, golf course and seasonal market garden located here.

Mackenzie Highway Log
(continued)

G 0.2 (0.4 km) FS 590.2 (949.8 km) **Private Aircraft:** Airstrip to west; elev. 2,050 feet/625m; length, 3,000 feet/914m; turf; fuel 80, 100.

G 1.9 (3 km) FS 588.5 (947.2 km) Grimshaw provincial campsite and Queen Elizabeth Provincial Park to west. Grimshaw campsite has 20 sites, picnic shelter, firepits, firewood, tables, outhouses, water pump and no camping fee. Queen Elizabeth park (located 3 miles/5 km west) on Lac Cardinal has 56 campsites, picnic shelter, firewood, firepits, toilets, playground and swimming. ▲

G 2.8 (4.6 km) FS 587.6 (945.6 km) Junction of Highways 35 and 2 East.

G 3.4 (5.5 km) FS 587 (944.7 km) Sign about construction of the Mackenzie Highway.

G 4.1 (6.6 km) FS 586.3 (943.6 km) Turnout to east with litter barrels.

G 5 (8 km) FS 585.4 (942.1 km) Junction with Chinook Valley Road to east.

G 6.9 (11.1 km) FS 583.5 (939.1 km) Truck scales to west.

G 7.8 (12.5 km) FS 582.6 (937.6 km) Bear Creek Drive and Bear Creek golf course to west; 9 holes, sand greens, clubhouse.

G 8.6 (13.8 km) FS 581.8 (936.3 km) Junction with Secondary Road 737 (Warrensville) to west.

G 12.3 (19.8 km) FS 578.1 (930.3 km) Road widens to 4 lanes northbound.

G 12.6 (20.3 km) FS 577.8 (929.8 km) Junction with Secondary Road 686 to east.

G 13 (20.9 km) FS 577.4 (929.2 km) Road narrows to 2 lanes northbound.

G 19 (30.6 km) FS 571.4 (919.5 km) Entering Manning Ranger District northbound.

G 20.8 (33.5 km) FS 569.6 (916.7 km) Chinook Valley to east; cafe, pay phone and 24-hour gas station with tire repair.

G 21 (33.8 km) FS 569.4 (916.3 km) Chinook Valley Road to east.

G 23 (37 km) FS 567.4 (913.1 km) Whitemud River.

G 25.1 (40.4 km) FS 565.3 (909.8 km) **DIXONVILLE** (pop. 200) has a post office, gas station, souvenir shop, museum, store and cafe. Sulphur Lake provincial campground is located 34 miles/55 km west via Highway 689 (the first 14 miles/22.5 km are paved, the remainder is gravel to the camp-

ground).

G 26.9 (43.3 km) FS 563.5 (906.8 km) Sulphur Lake Road leads west to junction with Highway 689 from Dixonville.

G 38.4 (61.8 km) FS 552 (888.4 km) **Junction** with Secondary Road 690 east to Deadwood (6.8 miles/11 km). There is a private exotic bird farm located 2 miles/3.2 km east then 1 mile/1.6 km south. The Bradshaws have geese, peacocks, turkeys, pheasants and other birds; visitors welcome.

G 44.4 (71.5 km) FS 546 (878.7 km) Buchanan Creek.

G 46.8 (75.4 km) FS 543.6 (874.8 km) Community of **NORTH STAR** (pop. 52) to east.

Manning

G 50.6 (81.4 km) FS 539.8 (868.8 km) Located on the Notikewin River at the junction of Highways 35 and 691. **Population:** 1,260. **Emergency Services:** RCMP, phone (403) 836-3007. **Hospital** and **Ambulance**, phone (403) 836-3391. **Fire Department**, phone (403) 836-3000.

Visitor Information: In the information centre. There is a playground adjacent the centre and a dump station across the street.

Named for an Alberta premier, Manning was established in 1947. The railway from Roma, AB, to Pine Point, NWT, reached Manning in September 1962. Today, Manning is a service centre and jumping-off point for hunters and fishers.

Manning has 5 restaurants, 3 hotel/motels, a pharmacy, food market, golf course, swimming pool and ice rink. Attractions here include the Battle River Pioneer Museum, located on the grounds of the Battle River Agricultural Society, 0.6 mile/1 km east via Highway 691. The museum, which features tools and machinery from the pioneer days, is open daily 1–5 P.M., from June 1 to mid-September. A small ski hill is located 12.5 miles/20 km northeast of town via Highways 691 and 741; 1 T-lift and 3 runs.

Turn east at the information centre for Manning municipal campground; 14 sites on the banks of the Notikewin River, fireplaces, tables, water and flush toilets. ▲

NOTE: Last sizable community with all facilities for the next 123 miles/198 km northbound.

Mackenzie Highway Log
(continued)

G 50.7 (81.6 km) FS 539.7 (868.5 km) Downtown Manning; bridge over the Notikewin River.

G 52.9 (85.1 km) FS 537.5 (865.1 km) **Private Aircraft:** Manning airstrip to west; elev. 1,611 feet/491m; length 5,577 feet/1,700m; asphalt; fuel 100/130, Jet B.

G 53.2 (85.6 km) FS 537.2 (864.5 km) Hotel, restaurant and service station to west.

G 54.6 (87.8 km) FS 535.8 (862.4 km) Community of Notikewin to west.

G 60.6 (97.6 km) FS 529.8 (852.6 km) Hotchkiss River bridge.

G 60.8 (97.8 km) FS 529.6 (852.4 km) Hotchkiss Provincial Park to east; 10 sites, picnic shelter, tables, firepits, fishing, outhouses and water pump. No camping fee. ⬤▲

G 61.3 (98.6 km) FS 529.1 (851.6 km) Community of **HOTCHKISS** to east, golf

Highway 58 East Log

Distance is measured from junction with the Mackenzie Highway (J).

J 0 **Junction** with Mackenzie Highway at High Level.

J 0.2 (0.4 km) High Level Lions Club Campground to south; 33 sites, no camping fee, picnic shelter, stoves, firewood, tables, toilets, water pump. ▲

J 0.4 (0.6 km) High Level rodeo grounds to north.

J 1.5 (2.5 km) Bushe River bridge.

J 2.4 (3.8 km) Small grocery and gas pumps to north.

J 15.3 (24.7 km) Turnoff to south for Machesis Lake Campground, 16 miles/27 km via gravel road; 21 sites, picnic shelter, firepits, firewood, tables, toilets, water. Fishing for rainbows in **Machesis Lake.** ⬤▲

J 20.3 (32.7 km) Turn south for Eleske Shrine (5 miles/8 km), Child Lake Reserve Native church and burial grounds. The Eleske Shrine, on the banks of the Boyer River, was built in 1950 and dedicated to St. Bernadette in hopes that the grotto would cure a tuberculosis epidemic in the community.

J 22.3 (35.9 km) Entering Fort Vermilion Ranger District eastbound.

J 27 (43.5 km) Turnout with litter barrels to north.

J 28 (45 km) Ponton River bridge.

J 35.4 (57 km) **Junction** of Highways 58 and 88. From this junction, Highway 58 turns to gravel road and continues 37 miles/59 km east to junction with a 5-mile/8-km side road to Jean D'or Prairie (no services). Highway 88 (renumbered and renamed the Bicentennial Highway to commemorate the 200th anniversary of Fort Vermilion in 1988) leads south to Fort Vermilion (log follows), then continues 255 miles/410 km to Slave Lake. Highway 88 is paved to Fort Vermilion; the 150-mile/242-km section to Red Earth Creek is gravel; the remaining 105 miles/168 km to Slave Lake are paved. There are no services along the road south of Fort Vermilion, and travel is not recommended on the gravel portion in wet weather.

HIGHWAY 88

J 40 (64.3 km) Boyer River bridge.

J 42.6 (68.5 km) Side road leads west 8.5 miles/14 km to Rocky Lane.

J 43.1 (69.3 km) Historical sign about Fort Vermilion and access to Fort Vermilion provincial campground (0.1 mile/0.2 km east); 16 sites, picnic shelter, fireplace, firewood, tables, toilets, water, no camping fee. ▲

J 43.4 (69.8 km) Fort Vermilion Bridge over the Peace River.

J 45.2 (72.7 km) **Junction** with Secondary Road 697 which leads south to Le Crete (21.5 miles/34.6 km) and rejoins the Mackenzie Highway at **Milepost G 136.2** (75.3 miles/121.2 km from here).

J 48 (77.2 km) **Junction** with Highway 88 south to Red Earth and Slave Lake (255miles/410 km). Continue straight ahead for Fort Vermilion (description follows).

J 48.5 (78 km) **FORT VERMILION** (pop. 850), located on the Peace River. **Emergency Services: RCMP,** phone (403) 927-3258. **Hospital,** St. Theresa phone (403) 927-3761. A trading post was established near here by the North West Co. in 1786. By 1831, the Hudson's Bay Co. had established a prosperous trading enterprise at Fort Vermilion. The area's farming potential gained attention when Fort Vermilion's wheat took top prize at the 1893 Chicago World's Fair. Transportation to the community was by riverboat until the Mackenzie Highway was built in the 1950s. The Peace River bridge was completed in 1974.

Visitor facilities include a hotel, motel, 3 restaurants, service stations, bank, laundromat and liquor store. The airport is located just east of town. Attractions include historic homes and buildings dating back to the mid-1800s. Pick up a walking tour brochure from the visitor centre; phone (403) 927-3216.

**Return to Milepost G 174
Mackenzie Highway**

---

course to west. Hotchkiss has a post office, service station, pay phone, coffee bar, grocery, and fuel and propane available. Condy Meadow golf course; 9 holes, grass greens, pro shop.

G 63.3 (101.8 km) FS 527.1 (848.3 km) Large lumber plant to west.

G 66.9 (107.6 km) FS 523.5 (842.6 km) Meikle River bridge.

G 71.2 (114.6 km) FS 519.2 (835.5 km) Turnout with litter barrel to west.

G 74.3 (119.5 km) FS 516.1 (830.7 km) **Junction** with Highway 692 and access to Notikewin Provincial Park (18.6 miles/30 km) on the Notikewin and Peace rivers. Highway 692 is fairly straight with pavement for the first 8 miles/13 km followed by good gravel surface to the park, although the road narrows and the surfacing may be muddy in wet weather as you approach the park. Just past the entrance to the park is the Top of Hill trailer drop-off site; 10 campsites with tables, toilets, water pump and garbage container. The park road then winds down the hill for 1.4 miles/2.2 km (not recommended for trailers, slippery when wet) to the riverside campground and day-use area; 19 campsites on the **Notikewin River** and 6 picnic sites on the **Peace River;** facilities include tables, water pump, pit toilets, garbage containers, firepits, boat launch and fishing. *CAUTION: Bears in area.* ⬤▲

G 88.4 (142.3 km) FS 502 (807.9 km) Twin Lakes Lodge to east; gas, food, lodging, pay phone and fishing supplies.

G 88.9 (143 km) FS 501.5 (807.2 km) Twin Lakes Campground to west; 30 shaded sites, picnic shelter, fireplaces, firewood, tables, outhouses, water; beach, boat launch (no gas motors). No camping fee. **Twin Lakes** is stocked with rainbow; good fishing June to September. ⬤▲

G 95.8 (154.1 km) FS 494.6 (796.1 km) Turnout to west.

G 102.9 (165.6 km) FS 487.5 (784.6 km) Kemp Creek.

G 111.2 (179 km) FS 479.2 (771.2 km) **Junction** with Highway 695 East which leads 24 miles/38 km to community of **CARCAJOU** (pop. 50). Access to Keg River airstrip 0.4 mile/0.6 km east. **Private Aircraft:** Keg River airstrip; elev. 1,350 feet/410m; approximate length 2,700 feet/832m; turf; emergency only.

G 112.3 (180.8 km) FS 478.1 (769.4 km) Keg River bridge. The community of **KEG RIVER** (area pop. 400) just north of the bridge has a gas station, post office, grocery, cafe, motel, pay phone and airstrip.

G 115.6 (186 km) FS 474.8 (764 km) **Junction** with Secondary Road 695 West. This paved road leads 9 miles/14.5 km to Keg River Post.

G 124 (199.6 km) FS 466.4 (750.6 km) Boyer River bridge.

G 129.5 (208.4 km) FS 460.9 (741.8 km) **PADDLE PRAIRIE** (pop. 164) has a gas station, grocery store and cafe. Paddle Prairie is a Metis settlement. The Metis culture, a combination of French and Amerindian, played a key role in the fur trade and development of northwestern Canada.

G 134.2 (216 km) FS 456.2 (734.2 km) Turnout to west with litter barrels.

G 135.1 (217.4 km) FS 455.3 (732.7 km) Boyer River Campground to east; 8 sites, tables, firewood, firepits, picnic shelter, toilets and water pump. ▲

G 136.2 (219.2 km) FS 454.2 (731 km) **Junction** with Secondary Road 697, which leads northeast 75 miles/121 km to junction with Highway 88 near Fort Vermilion (see description of Fort Vermilion in the HIGHWAY 58 EAST side road log this page). This is a 2-lane, mostly paved road with a ferry crossing of the Peace River at Tompkin's Landing, 11 miles/18 km east from here. The ferry operates 24 hours a day, except in heavy fog, and carries 6 cars or 4 trucks. Highway 697 provides access to **BUFFALO HEAD PRAIRIE** (pop. 453), 43.6 miles/70.2 km east, which has a small store and gas. Also access to **LA CRETE** (pop. 902), 53.8 miles/86.6 km east and north, Canada's most northerly agricultural community. La Crete has a motel, 3 restaurants, service stations with repair facilities, car wash, grocery, hardware and retail stores, a laundromat and bank. Recreation facilities include a golf course and a sports complex with hockey, curling and bowling.

G 141 (226.9 km) FS 449.4 (723.2 km) Entering High Level Ranger District northbound.

G 146.3 (235.4 km) FS 444.1 (714.7 km) Chuckegg Creek.

G 153.5 (247 km) FS 436.9 (703.2 km) Turnout with litter barrel to west. Watch for waterfowl in small lakes along highway.

G 161.2 (259.4 km) FS 429.2 (690.7 km) Bede Creek.

G 161.9 (260.5 km) FS 428.5 (689.6 km) Parma Creek.

G 165.5 (266.3 km) FS 424.9 (683.9 km)

Melito Creek.

G 170.6 (274.6 km) **FS 419.8** (675.6 km) Turnout with litter barrel to west.

G 171.9 (276.7 km) **FS 418.5** (673.5 km) Private campground with hot showers and electrical hookups. ▲

G 173.3 (278.9 km) **FS 417.1** (671.3 km) **Junction** with Highway 58 West, which leads 84.5 miles/136 km to Rainbow Lake. See side road log of HIGHWAY 58 WEST on page 208.

High Level

G 173.6 (279.3 km) **FS 416.8** (670.9 km) Located at the junction of Highways 35 and 58. **Population:** 3,004. **Emergency Services: RCMP,** phone (403) 926-2226. **Hospital,** 25 beds, 6 doctors, phone (403) 926-3791. **Ambulance,** phone (403) 926-2545. **Fire Department,** phone (403) 926-3141.

Visitor Information: The visitors centre and Mackenzie Crossroads Museum are located at the south end of town. Open year-round. Summer hours 9 A.M. to 9 P.M. daily. Includes displays, souvenirs and rest area. RV dump at Shell station. **Radio:** 530 AM, 89.9, 104.1-FM.

Begun as a small settlement on the Mackenzie Highway after WWII, High Level grew with the oil boom of the 1960s and completion of the railroad to Pine Point. High Level has a strong agricultural economy and boasts the most northerly grain elevators in Canada. The community is also supported by a sawmill complex and serves as a transportation centre for the northwestern Peace River region. There is scheduled air service to Edmonton daily.

Visitor facilities include a hotel, 6 motels, restaurants and service stations with major repair. There are also an ice arena and curling rink, golf course, swimming pool, playgrounds, banks, schools and churches. Recreation includes hunting (moose, caribou, deer) and fishing for northern pike, perch, walleye, whitefish, goldeye and grayling.

There is a private campground at the south edge of town. A campground operated by the local Lions Club is located just east of town on Highway 58. ▲

Mackenzie Crossroads Museum and Visitors Centre is a must-see. Open year-round, the centre features tourist information, museum, interpretive centre and outdoor rest area. Displays include the "Northern Trading Post," farming, trapping and an outstanding collection of historical photographs. Souvenir items for sale. Summer hours 9 A.M.–9 P.M. 7 days/week. Phone (403) 926-4811, fax (403) 926-3044.

Mackenzie Highway Log

(continued)

G 173.6 (279.3 km) **FS 416.8** (670.9 km) Downtown High Level.

G 174 (280 km) **FS 416.4** (670.2 km) **Junction** with Highway 58 East to Jean D'or Prairie and Highway 88 to Fort Vermilion. See side road log of HIGHWAY 58 EAST on opposite page.

G 176.2 (283.5 km) **FS 414.2** (666.7 km) High Level golf and country club to east. Open daily, May 1 to first snow, until midnight. Clubhouse, grass greens and 9 holes.

G 181.1 (291.5 km) **FS 409.3** (658.7 km)

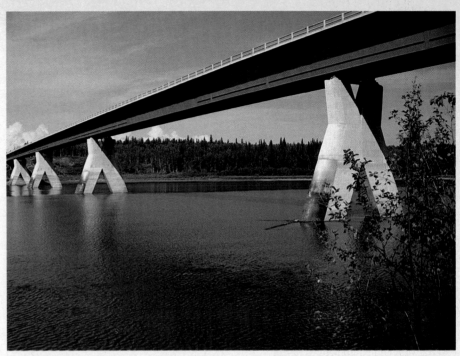

Fort Vermilion bridge across the Peace River on Highway 88 east of High Level.
(Earl L. Brown, staff)

Private Aircraft: High Level airport; elev. 1,110 feet/338m; length 5,000 feet/1,524m; asphalt; fuel 80, 100, Jet B. Floatplane base at Footner Lake, 0.6 mile/1 km west.

G 193.4 (311.2 km) **FS 397** (639 km) Turnoff to west for Hutch Lake Recreation Area; parking, 8 picnic sites with tables and firepits, toilets. Short path leads down to lake. Bring mosquito repellent.

G 196 (315.5 km) **FS 394.4** (634.7 km) Hutch Lake provincial campground, 2.9 miles/4.6 km west; 12 sites, firepits, firewood, tables, toilets. Beach and boat launch on Hutch Lake. Hiking trails. Good spot for bird watchers. Camping fee $7.50. ▲

G 196.8 (316.7 km) **FS 393.6** (633.5 km) Turnouts with litter barrels both sides of highway.

G 207.3 (333.6 km) **FS 383.1** (616.6 km) Wooden railway bridge to east.

G 219.3 (352.9 km) **FS 371.1** (597.3 km) **MEANDER RIVER** (pop. 340) has a post office, gas, grocery store and confectionary with pay phone. *NOTE: Last gas northbound until Enterprise at Milepost G 345.8, 126.5 miles/203.6 km from here.*

G 221.5 (356.4 km) **FS 368.9** (593.7 km) Mission Creek.

G 223.8 (360.1 km) **FS 366.6** (590.1 km) The Mackenzie Highway crosses the Hay River here and follows it north into Northwest Territories.

G 227.5 (366.2 km) **FS 362.9** (584 km) Railway bridge over Hay River to east. Construction of the Great Slave Lake Railway (now part of Canadian National Railway's Peace River Division) was one of the largest railway construction projects since the boom of the first transcontinental railway lines in the late 1800s and early 1900s in Canada. The line extends 377 miles/607 km from Roma Junction near Peace River, AB, to Hay River, NWT, on the shore of Great Slave Lake. (A 54-mile/87-km branch line extended the line to the now-defunct lead–zinc mine at Pine Point, NWT.) Opened for traffic in 1964, the line carries mining

shipments south and supplies north to Hay River.

G 228.1 (367.1 km) **FS 362.3** (583.1 km) Gravel road leads west 39 miles/63 km to ZAMA (pop. 200), an oil field community. Drilling and related operations take place at Zama in winter. Zama is the southern terminal of the interprovincial pipeline, carrying Norman Wells crude to Edmonton refineries.

G 231.5 (372.5 km) **FS 358.9** (577.6 km) Slavey Creek.

G 241.2 (388.2 km) **FS 349.3** (562 km) Rough patch in pavement. Watch for frost heaves north to NWT border.

G 243.5 (391.9 km) **FS 346.9** (558.3 km) Paved turnout with litter barrels to west.

G 250.2 (402.6 km) **FS 340.2** (547.5 km) Lutose Creek.

G 263.3 (423.7 km) **FS 327.1** (526.5 km) Steen River bridge.

G 266.7 (429.2 km) **FS 323.7** (521 km) **STEEN RIVER** (pop. 25) to east; no services.

G 266.9 (429.5 km) **FS 323.5** (520.7 km) Steen River Forestry Tanker Base to west. Grass airstrip.

G 268.1 (431.5 km) **FS 322.3** (518.7 km) Sams' Creek.

G 270.1 (434.7 km) **FS 320.3** (515.4 km) Jackpot Creek.

G 276.2 (444.5 km) **FS 314.2** (505.6 km) Bannock Creek.

G 283.3 (455.9 km) **FS 307.1** (494.2 km) Indian Cabins Creek.

G 284 (457 km) **FS 306.4** (493.2 km) **INDIAN CABINS** (pop. 10); no services, historic log church. The old Indian cabins that gave this settlement its name are gone, but nearby is an Indian cemetery with spirit houses.

G 285.3 (459.1 km) **FS 305.1** (491 km) Delphin Creek.

G 293.7 (472.7 km) **FS 296.7** (477.5 km) 60th parallel. Border between Alberta and Northwest Territories. The Mackenzie Highway now changes from Alberta Highway 35 to NWT Highway 1.

Highway 58 West Log

Distance is measured from junction with the Mackenzie Highway (J).

J 0 Junction with Mackenzie Highway at High Level.

J 6.1 (9.8 km) High Level Sporting Assoc. and Gun Club to north.

J 27.2 (43.8 km) Paved turnout with litter barrels to south.

J 31.2 (50.2 km) Entering Rainbow Lake Ranger District westbound.

J 44.2 (71.1 km) Bridge over Chinchaga River.

J 46.3 (74.5 km) Large turnout and gravel stockpiles to south.

J 50 (80.5 km) Bridge over East Sousa Creek.

J 56.5 (90.9 km) Bridge over West Sousa Creek.

J 56.9 (91.6 km) **Junction** with secondary road north to communities of Chateh, Habay and Zama.

J 59.7 (96.1 km) North Canadian Oils Ltd. wells and equipment to north.

J 60.7 (97.7 km) Oil pumping station to north.

J 63.3 (101.8 km) Paved turnout with litter barrel to north.

J 65.3 (105.1 km) Power station to north.

J 70.3 (113.1 km) Side road leads north to the Zama Tower.

J 70.7 (113.8 km) Esso Resources Canada oil production plant to north.

J 71.5 (115 km) Rainbow Lake Field

Office to north.

J 76.8 (123.6 km) Side road leads north to Rainbow Lake gas plant.

J 80.5 (129.5 km) Oil station to south. Side road leads south to Rainbow Processing Plant.

J 82.5 (132.8 km) Turnout with picnic table to south.

J 84.5 (136 km) **RAINBOW LAKE** (pop. 1,146). **Emergency Services: RCMP**, phone (403) 321-3753. **Nursing Station**, phone (403) 356-3646. **Fire Department**, phone (403) 956-3934. **Radio:** 103.7-FM.

Private Aircraft: Rainbow Lake airport 0.8 mile/1.3 km west, 0.5 mile/0.8 km south on Frontage Road; elev. 1,100 feet/335m; length 4,550 feet/1,390m; asphalt; fuel 80, 100, Jet B.

A service community for oil and natural gas development in the region. The first oil well was brought in by Banff Oil and Gas in 1965 at the Rainbow field. (The Zama field was discovered in 1967.)

Visitor facilities include a hotel, motel with licensed restaurant, 3 gas stations and a bank. The community also supports a school, 3 churches, 2 car washes, a grocery store, gift shop, laundromat and a 9-hole golf course. Rainbow Lake Campground is located 14 miles/24 km south of town via a secondary road.

Return to Milepost G 173.3 Mackenzie Highway

NWT HIGHWAY 1

Highway 1 begins its own series of kilometre markers, starting with Kilometre 0 at the border, which appear about every 2 kilometres.

Distance from Grimshaw (G) is followed by distance from Fort Simpson (FS) and distance from the AB–NWT border (B).

G 293.7 (472.7 km) **FS 296.7** (477.5 km) **B 0** AB–NWT border, 60th Parallel. A government visitor information centre here has brochures, maps, fishing licenses, camping permits, a dump station and emergency radiophone. Dene (Indian) arts and crafts are on display. Also check here on road and ferry conditions before proceeding. The visitor centre is open May 15 to Sept. 15 from 8 A.M. to 10 P.M.

60th Parallel Campground and picnic area adjacent visitor centre. Facilities include 12 campsites, 5 picnic sites, kitchen shelter and drinking water. The park overlooks the Hay River and canoeists may launch here. Information on canoeing the river can be obtained at the visitors centre. ▲

Driving distances from the border to destinations in Northwest Territories are as follows (see individual highway logs this section for details): Hay River 76 miles/122 km; Fort Simpson 297 miles/478 km; Wrigley 430 miles/694 km; Fort Providence 140 miles/225 km; Yellowknife 330 miles/531 km; Fort Smith 238 miles/383 km.

G 295.5 (475.6 km) **FS 294.9** (474.6 km) **B 1.8** (2.9 km) Reindeer Creek.

G 318.5 (512.6 km) **FS 271.9** (437.6 km)

B 24.8 (39.9 km) Grumbler Rapids, just off highway, is audible during low water periods in late summer.

G 319.1 (513.5 km) **FS 271.3** (436.6 km) **B 25.4** (40.8 km) Swede Creek.

G 319.8 (514.6 km) **FS 270.6** (435.5 km) **B 26.1** (42 km) Large turnout and gravel stockpile to west.

G 334.2 (537.8 km) **FS 256.2** (412.4 km) **B 40.5** (65.1 km) Mink Creek.

G 335.5 (539.9 km) **FS 254.9** (410.2 km) **B 41.8** (67.3 km) Large turnout and gravel stockpile to west.

G 338.8 (545.3 km) **FS 251.6** (404.9 km) **B 45.1** (72.6 km) Twin Falls Gorge Territorial Park; Alexandra Falls picnic area to east. Paved parking area and gravel walkway to falls viewpoint, overlooking the Hay River, which plunges 109 feet/33m to form Alexandra Falls. Excellent photo opportunities; easy hike down to top of falls. A walking trail connects with Louise Falls.

G 340.3 (547.6 km) **FS 250.1** (402.6 km) **B 46.6** (74.9 km) Turnoff to east for Louise Falls picnic area and campground, now part of Twin Falls Gorge Territorial Park; 18 campsites, 6 picnic sites, kitchen shelters, tables, toilets, firepits, firewood, water. Hiking trails to viewpoint overlooking 3-tiered Louise Falls, which drops 50 feet/15m. (It is not advisable to walk down to the water.) Hike along bluff 3 miles/5 km for Alexandra Falls. ▲

G 341.9 (550.2 km) **FS 248.5** (400 km) **B 48.2** (77.5 km) Escarpment Creek picnic area; tables, shelter, toilets, firepits, garbage container, water pump. Spectacular series of

waterfalls downstream.

G 342.1 (550.5 km) **FS 248.3** (399.7 km) **B 48.4** (77.8 km) Highway crosses Escarpment Creek.

G 345.4 (555.9 km) **FS 245** (394.3 km) **B 51.7** (83.2 km) Truck weigh scales to east, service station to west. Entering Enterprise northbound.

G 345.8 (556.5 km) **FS 244.6** (393.7 km) **B 52.1** (83.8 km) **Junction** of Highway 1 and Highway 2. Highway 2 leads 23.6 miles/38 km from here to **HAY RIVER** (pop. 2,891), the hub for transportation on Great Slave Lake and a major service centre with all visitor facilities (see HAY RIVER HIGHWAY log on page 211 for details on Hay River). Continue on Highway 1 for Enterprise (description follows) and Fort Simpson.

ENTERPRISE (pop. 56), a highway community with food, grocery store, gas, diesel and lodging. Pay phone. It is a good idea to fill up gas tanks here. View of Hay River Gorge just east of the highway.

NOTE: *Last gas southbound until Meander River at* **Milepost G 219.3**, *126.5 miles/203.6 km from here.*

G 369.3 (594.3 km) **FS 221.1** (355.8 km) **B 75.6** (121.6 km) Turnout to north with view of McNally Creek Falls.

Highway crosses McNally Creek northbound.

G 370.5 (596.2 km) **FS 219.9** (353.9 km) **B 76.8** (123.6 km) Large paved turnout to north with litter barrels and scenic view.

G 374.7 (603 km) **FS 215.7** (347.2 km) **B 81** (130.3 km) Easy-to-miss Hart Lake Fire Tower access road turnoff leads 0.5 mile/0.8 km to picnic area and forest fire lookout tower. Panoramic view over more than 100 square miles/259 square km of forest to Great Slave Lake and Mackenzie River. Path to ancient coral reef. CAUTION: *Keep the fly repellent handy and stay away from the edge of escarpment.*

G 378.9 (609.8 km) **FS 211.5** (340.4 km) **B 85.2** (137.1 km) Crooked Creek.

G 379.4 (610.5 km) **FS 211** (339.7 km) **B 85.7** (137.8 km) Trapper's cabin to north.

G 385.6 (620.5 km) **FS 204.8** (329.6 km) **B 91.9** (147.9 km) Side road to highway maintenance camp.

G 391.7 (630.3 km) **FS 198.7** (319.9 km) **B 98** (157.6 km) Turnout with litter barrels.

G 398.2 (640.8 km) **FS 192.2** (309.3 km) **B 104.5** (168.2 km) Highway maintenance camp and stockpiles to north.

G 398.7 (641.7 km) **FS 191.7** (308.5 km) **B 105** (169 km) Access road leads south 4.5 miles/7.2 km to Lady Evelyn Falls where the Kakisa River drops 49 feet/15m over an escarpment. Staircase down to viewing platform. Hiking trail to base of falls; swimming and wading. Ample parking, interpretive display, territorial campground with 10 tent sites, 18 RV sites and 5 picnic sites; tables, firepits, firewood, garbage containers, water pump, kitchen shelters. At end of road, 4 miles/6.4 km past campground, is Slavey Indian village and **Kakisa Lake**; fair fishing for walleye, pike and grayling. ➤◄▲

G 399.6 (643.1 km) **FS 190.8** (307.1 km) **B 105.9** (170.4 km) Kakisa River bridge.

G 399.8 (643.4 km) **FS 190.6** (306.8 km) **B 106.1** (170.7 km) Kakisa River bridge picnic area with 10 sites, tables, fireplaces and firewood. Hiking trails along river lead upstream to Lady Evelyn Falls. Fair fishing in **Kakisa River** for grayling. ➤◄

G 410.5 (660.6 km) **FS 179.9** (289.5 km) **B 116.8** (187.9 km) Turnout with litter barrels, log cabin, outhouse, picnic tables

Traditional embroidered mukluks on display in Fort Simpson. (© Lyn Hancock)

and map display on Highways 1 and 3.

G 410.9 (661.2 km) **FS 179.5** (289 km) **B 117.2** (188.5 km) **Junction** of Highway 1 and Highway 3. Highway 3 (paved and gravel) leads 212.5 miles/342 km north to Yellowknife, capital of Northwest Territories (see YELLOWKNIFE HIGHWAY log on page 211). Highway 1 (gravel) leads west 179.5 miles/289 km to Fort Simpson. Continue with this log for Fort Simpson.

G 411.1 (661.6 km) **FS 179.3** (288.5 km) **B 117.4** (188.9 km) Pavement ends, gravel begins, westbound.

G 438.4 (705.5 km) **FS 152** (244.7 km) **B 144.7** (232.8 km) Emergency survival cabin and turnout with litter barrels and outhouse to south.

G 450.5 (725 km) **FS 139.9** (225.1 km) **B 158.6** (255.3 km) Turnout to north with parking and scenic view.

G 466.2 (750.3 km) **FS 124.2** (199.9 km) **B 172.5** (277.6 km) Bouvier River.

G 467.2 (751.9 km) **FS 123.2** (198.3 km) **B 173.5** (279.2 km) Emergency survival cabin and turnout with litter barrels to south.

G 471.9 (759.5 km) **FS 118.5** (190.7 km) **B 180.1** (289.8 km) Turnout to north.

G 473.9 (762.6 km) **FS 116.5** (187.6 km) **B 180.2** (289.9 km) Wallace Creek. Scenic canyon to north.

G 477 (767.6 km) **FS 113.4** (182.6 km) **B 183.3** (294.9 km) Highway maintenance camp to south.

G 477.6 (768.6 km) **FS 112.8** (181.6 km) **B 183.9** (295.9 km) Redknife River.

G 488.7 (786.4 km) **FS 101.7** (163.8 km) **B 195** (313.7 km) Morrissey Creek.

G 491.7 (791.8 km) **FS 98.7** (158.8 km) **B 199.8** (321.6 km) Winter ice road leads south 78 miles/126 km to **TROUT LAKE** (pop. 66), a Dene settlement.

G 494.1 (795.3 km) **FS 96.3** (155 km) **B 202** (325.1 km) Trout River bridge.

G 495 (796.3 km) **FS 95.4** (153.5 km) **B 202.8** (326.4 km) Turnout to south with litter barrels.

G 495.7 (797.8 km) **FS 94.7** (152.4 km) **B 202** (325 km) Whittaker Falls (Sambaa Deh) Territorial Park, overlooking the **Trout River.** There are 3 picnic sites, 8 campsites, tables, litter barrels, showers, kitchen shelter, firepits and firewood. Walk along the river to view large deposits of shale and limestone. Grayling fishing, use dry flies in deep pools. Hike to Coral Falls. ➤▲

G 498.1 (801.6 km) **FS 92.3** (148.5 km) **B 206.1** (331.7 km) Emergency survival cabin and turnout with litter barrels to north.

G 523.7 (842.8 km) **FS 66.7** (107.3 km) **B 229.9** (370 km) **Ekali Lake** access; pike and pickerel fishing. 🐟

G 527.4 (848.7 km) **FS 63** (101.4 km) **B 233.6** (376 km) Winter ice road leads 17 miles/27 km to **JEAN MARIE RIVER** (pop. 67), a traditional Slavey community known for its hand-crafted moose hide clothing decorated with moose tufting, porcupine quilling and embroidery. Accessible in summer by plane or boat from Fort Simpson. This winter road is being upgraded to all-weather standards and is scheduled for completion in 1997.

G 530.5 (853.7 km) **FS 59.9** (96.5 km) **B 236.8** (381 km) Emergency survival cabin and turnout to north with outhouse and litter barrels.

G 534.8 (860.7 km) **FS 55.6** (89.5 km) **B 241.1** (388 km) I.P.L. pipeline camp and pump station to north. Highway crosses pipeline.

G 536.3 (863 km) **FS 54.1** (87 km) **B 242.6** (390.4 km) Microwave tower to south.

G 550.4 (885.8 km) **FS 40** (64.4 km) **B 256.7** (413.1 km) Jean Marie Creek bridge.

G 550.5 (885.9 km) **FS 39.9** (64.3 km) **B 256.8** (413.2 km) "Checkpoint"; 24-hour gas, diesel, propane, licensed restaurant and accommodations. Phone (403) 695-2953. Open year-round.

G 550.6 (886.1 km) **FS 39.8** (64.1 km) **B 256.9** (413.4 km) **Junction** with the Liard Highway (NWT Highway 7), which leads south to Fort Liard and junctions with the Alaska Highway near Fort Nelson. See LIARD HIGHWAY section for details.

G 552 (888.4 km) **FS 38.4** (61.8 km) **B 258.3** (415.7 km) Turnout to east.

G 563.7 (907.1 km) **FS 26.7** (43.1 km) **B 270** (434.4 km) Emergency survival cabin and turnout with litter barrels and outhouse to west.

G 577.8 (929.8 km) **FS 12.6** (20.4 km) **B 284.1** (457.1 km) Highway crests hill; view of Liard River ahead. Ferry landing 3,280 feet/1,000m.

G 578.2 (930.5 km) **FS 12.2** (19.7 km) **B 284.5** (457.8 km) Liard River Campground to accommodate travelers who miss the last ferry at night, has 5 sites, tables, firepits, water, outhouse and garbage container. ▲

G 578.5 (930.9 km) **FS 11.9** (19.3 km) **B 284.8** (458.2 km) Free government-operated Liard River ferry operates daily May through October from 8 A.M. to 11:40 P.M., 7 days a week. Crossing time is 6 minutes. Capacity is 8 cars or 2 trucks, with a maximum total weight of 130,000 lbs./59,090 kg. An ice bridge opens for light vehicles in late November and heavier vehicles as ice thickens. *NOTE: No crossing possible during breakup (about mid-April to mid-May) and freezeup (mid-October to mid-November.).* For ferry information phone (403) 873-7799, or

1-800-661-0751.

G 580.7 (934.6 km) **FS 9.7** (15.6 km) **B 287** (461.9 km) Fort Simpson airport. See Private Aircraft information in Fort Simpson.

G 588.1 (946.4 km) **FS 2.3** (3.8 km) **B 294.4** (473.7 km) **Junction** with Fort Simpson access road which leads 2.3 miles/3.8 km to Fort Simpson (description follows). The extension of NWT Highway 1 to Wrigley was completed in 1994; see WRIGLEY EXTENSION log following Fort Simpson description.

G 589.7 (949 km) **FS 0.7** (1.2 km) **B 296** (476.3 km) Causeway to Fort Simpson Island.

G 590.1 (949.6 km) **FS 0.3** (0.6 km) **B 296.4** (476.9 km) Turnoff for village campground. ▲

Fort Simpson

G 590.4 (950.2 km) **FS 0** **B 296.7** (477.5 km) Located on an island at the confluence of the Mackenzie and Liard rivers. **Population:** 1,450. **Emergency Services: RCMP,** phone (403) 695-3111. **Hospital** (12 beds), for medical emergency phone (403) 695-2291. **Fire Department** (volunteer), phone (403) 695-2222.

Visitor Information: Village office operates a visitor booth June through August. The visitor information centre is open until 8 P.M., 7 days a week in summer; closed Sundays in winter. Nahanni National Park information centre on Main Street has a photo

Fort Simpson is an important transportation centre on the Mackenzie River.
(© Lyn Hancock)

exhibit and films. The centre is open 8:30 A.M. to 5 P.M., 7 days a week in July and August, weekdays the rest of the year.

Television: Channels 2, 4, 6, 7, 9, 11. **Transportation:** Scheduled service to Yellowknife via Buffalo Airways and Yellowknife and Whitehorse, YT via First Air. Fixed wing and helicopter charters available. **Rental cars**–Available. **Taxi service**–Available.

Private Aircraft: Fort Simpson airport; elev. 554 feet/169m; length 6,000 feet/1,829m; asphalt; fuel 100, Jet B. Fort Simpson Island; elev. 405 feet/123m; length 3,000 feet/914m; gravel; fuel 100, Jet B.

Fort Simpson is a full-service community. There is a motel with kitchenettes, 2 bed and breakfasts and a hotel; dining at the hotel (licensed premises) and 2 restaurants in town; gas stations with repair service (unleaded, diesel and propane available); 2 grocery stores, department store, hardware store, a bank, laundromat, post office, crafts shop and sports shop. Small engine repair shop and mechanics available. Fort Simpson has grade schools, churches (Anglican, Catholic and Pentecostal), the Stanley Isaiah Senior Citizen's Centre, and various territorial and federal offices. Recreational facilities include an arena, curling rink, gym, ball diamond, tennis, small indoor pool, golf course and a boat launch at government wharf. A number of community activities are held at the Papal Site, a large field with a cross, log tepee and stone monument commemorating Pope John Paul II's visit here in 1987.

Public campground at edge of town in wooded area has 30 campsites and 4 picnic sites. ▲

Fort Simpson is the oldest continuously occupied site on the Mackenzie River, dating from 1804 when the North West Co. established its Fort of the Forks. There is a historical marker on the bank of the Mackenzie. The Hudson's Bay Co. began its post here in 1821. At that time the fort was renamed after Sir George Simpson, one of the first governors of the combined North West Co. and Hudson's Bay Co. Fort Simpson served as the Mackenzie District headquarters for the Hudson's Bay Co. fur-trading operation. Its key location on the Mackenzie River also made Fort Simpson an important transportation centre. Anglican and Catholic missions were established here in 1858 and 1894.

Fort Simpson continues to be an important centre for the Northwest Territories water transport system. Visitors may walk along the high banks of the Mackenzie River and watch the boat traffic and floatplanes. According to resident Lyn Hancock, one of the easiest places to get down to the water is by Alfred Faille's cabin on Mackenzie Drive. Faille was a well-known Fort Simpson pioneer and prospector.

For visitors, Fort Simpson has Slavey crafts, such as birch-bark baskets and beadwork. Fort Simpson is also the jumping-off point for jet boat trips on the North Nahanni River; Mackenzie River traffic; and fly-in trips to Nahanni National Park.

The 4,766-square-km **NAHANNI NATIONAL PARK**, listed as a unique geological area on the UNESCO world heritage site list, is accessible only by nonpowered boat or aircraft. Located southwest of Fort Simpson near the Yukon border, day-trip flightseeing tours of the park may be arranged in Fort Simpson, Fort Liard and Yellowknife, and from Fort Nelson, BC, and Watson Lake, YT. Highlights include the spectacular Virginia Falls (300 feet/90m, twice as high as Niagara Falls). One of the most popular attractions in the park is running the South Nahanni River or its tributary, the Flat River. The South Nahanni River route stretches about 186 miles/300 km from Rabbitkettle Lake to the eastern park boundary. Rabbitkettle Hot Springs, a major feature on the upper section of the river, is reached by trail (restricted access, hikers must be guided by park staff). Near the east park boundary is Kraus Hot Springs, on the remains of the old Kraus homestead. The Flat River route stretches 80 miles/128 km from Seaplane Lake to the confluence with the South Nahanni. Charter air service for canoe drop-offs is available in Fort Simpson.

In order to evenly distribute visitor use and maintain ecological integrity within Nahanni National Park Reserve, the park has implemented a mandatory reservation system for overnight use. Twelve guided and 12 non-guided visitors are allowed in the park each day. The maximum length of stay at Virginia Falls is 2 nights. Reservations may be made by telephone or fax. User fees are charged. The seasonal overnight-use fee is $100, payable by VISA or MasterCard at the time a reservation is made. (Seasonal user fees are transferable to any national park in Northwest Territories.) A day-use fee of $10 per person is charged to those visitors flying into Virginia Falls for a day trip. Reservations are not required for day trips. Contact Nahanni National Park Reserve, Box 348, Fort Simpson, NT X0E 0N0; phone (403) 695-2310, fax 695-2446.

AREA FISHING: Willow, Dogface and **Trout lakes** accessible by air. Good fishing for trout and grayling. Inquire locally. ⤙

The Maroda Motel. See display ad this section.

Mackenzie Highway Log
(continued)
WRIGLEY EXTENSION
Improved to all-weather road standards, this former trail to Wrigley officially opened in 1994 as part of Highway 1 (although it's still referred to locally as the "road to Wrigley"). Slippery when wet. Use caution approaching all bridges. Driving time is approximately 3 hours between Fort Simpson and Wrigley. Allow at least 2 hours from Wrigley to the Camsell ferry crossing.
Distance from Fort Simpson (FS) is followed by distance from Wrigley (W).

FS 0 W 137 (220.5 km) **Junction** with Fort Simpson access road.

FS 9.5 (15.3 km) **W 127.5** (205.2 km) Single-lane bridge over Martin River. *CAUTION: Slow down for steep descent to bridge.*

FS 17.9 (28.8 km) **W 119.1** (191.7 km) Creek crossing. *CAUTION: Slow down, steep drop-offs and no guardrails.*

FS 33.4 (53.7 km) **W 103.6** (166.7 km) Single-lane bridge over Shale Creek.

FS 34 (54.7 km) **W 103** (165.8 km) Turnout to east.

FS 46.6 (75 km) **W 90.4** (145.5 km) Ferry crossing of the Mackenzie River at Camsell Bend (Ndulee Crossing). Ferry operates daily, 9 to 11 A.M. and 2 to 8 P.M. Capacity is 6 cars or 4 trucks. NOTE: There are no overnight facilities for anyone missing the ferry. Ferry does not operate in fog. Be prepared to wait.

FS 71 (114.3 km) **W 66** (106.2 km) Mackenzie Mountains come into view to the west, northbound.

FS 73.5 (118.3 km) **W 63.5** (102.2 km) Highway maintenance camp to east.

FS 94.2 (151.6 km) **W 42.8** (68.9 km) Willowlake River bridge, longest bridge in the Northwest Territories.

FS 95.2 (153.2 km) **W 41.8** (67.3 km) Highway climbs steep hill northbound.

FS 97.7 (157.2 km) **W 39.3** (63.2 km) Turnout to west at top of hill with litter barrels and scenic view of the Mackenzie River.

FS 110.9 (178.5 km) **W 26.1** (42 km) Single-lane wooden bridge over the "River Between Two Mountains."

FS 112.6 (181.2 km) **W 24.4** (39.3 km) Scenic view of the Mackenzie River to west.

FS 121.5 (195.5 km) **W 15.5** (25.1 km) Wrigley interprovincial pipeline pump station and radio tower to east.

FS 128.9 (207.4 km) **W 8.1** (13 km) Single-lane bridge over Smith's Creek.

FS 131.1 (211 km) **W 5.9** (9.5 km) Highway maintenance camp to west.

FS 132.2 (212.7 km) **W 4.8** (7.7 km) **Junction** with winter ice road to east which leads north to Fort Norman, Norman Wells, Fort Franklin and Fort Good Hope. Winter road mileages are as follows: Wrigley to Fort Norman, 148 miles/238 km; Fort Norman to Norman Wells, 50 miles/80 km; Norman Wells to Fort Good Hope, 91 miles/147 km; Norman Wells to Franklin, 68 miles/110 km.

FS 132.9 (213.9 km) **W 4.1** (6.6 km) Turnoff to west for Wrigley airport. **Private Aircraft:** Wrigley airport, 4 miles/7 km south of town; elev. 493 feet/142m; length 3,500 feet/1,148m; gravel; fuel 80.

FS 136.8 (220.1 km) **W 0.2** (0.4 km) Airport Lake, Wrigley community campground; 12 sites, firepits and washrooms. Suitable for RVs; located on high dry ground in mostly birch and white spruce trees. ▲

FS 137 (220.5 km) **W 0 WRIGLEY** (pop. 200; 90 percent Dene ancestry). **Emergency Services:** RCMP, station manned intermittently. **Nursing Station**, with full-time nurse, phone (403) 587-3441.

Visitor Information: Visitor Information Centre manned by knowledgeable young people, open daily in summer; local crafts.

The Hudson's Bay Co. built a trading post here in 1870 called Fort Wrigley. The fort was abandoned in 1910 due to disease and famine, and the inhabitants moved down river. Although a church and school were built at that site in 1957, the community decided to move to higher ground in 1965. 15 homes were built at the "new" townsite of present-day Wrigley. The church, school and other buildings were moved from the old townsite by boat. Wrigley is the home of the Pehdzeh Ki First Nation.

Visitor facilities here include the Petanea Hotel and restaurant; co-op store and craft shop; Ed's Mobile Mechanical Service; a convenience store; and a government gas station operating 9 A.M. to 6 P.M. weekdays and 1 to 6 P.M. weekends. There is also a community-built, walk-in campground with washrooms and fireplaces along the bank of the Mackenzie River, with picturesque, bug-free views of the Mackenzie Mountains. ▲

Hay River Highway Log

NWT HIGHWAY 2
Highway 2 is paved from Enterprise to Hay River; watch for rough spots in the surfacing. Kilometreposts along the highway reflect distance from Enterprise.
Distance from Enterprise (E) is followed by distance from Hay River (H).

E 0 H 23.6 (38 km) **Junction** of Highways 1 and 2.

E 8.7 (14 km) **H 14.9** (24 km) Private campground 0.7 mile/1.1 km east. Market garden in season. ▲
Paradise Garden Campground. See display ad this section.

E 11.6 (18.6 km) **H 12** (19.4 km) Sawmill Road to east.

E 16 (25.7 km) **H 7.6** (12.3 km) Gravel road leads east 0.6 mile/1 km to Hay River golf course; large log clubhouse, driving range, 9 holes (par 36), artificial greens. Site

of the NWT Open every second year in late August.

E 20 (32.3 km) **H 3.6** (5.7 km) **Junction** with Highway 5 to Fort Smith (see Fort Smith Highway Log this section).

E 22.4 (36 km) **H 1.2** (2 km) Chamber of Commerce Welcome to Hay River sign. Parking area to east.

Hay River

E 23.6 (38 km) **H 0** Located on the south shore of Great Slave Lake at the mouth of the Hay River, on both the mainland and Vale Island. **Population:** 3,800 **Emergency Services:** Police, phone (403) 874-6555. **Fire Department**, phone (403) 874-2222. **Hospital**, phone (403) 874-6512.

Visitor Information: Visitor information centre, just east of the highway, is housed in a 2-story brown structure. The centre is open daily, late May to early September; 9 A.M. to 9 P.M.. There is a dump station located here. Write the Chamber of Commerce at Box 4291, Hay River, NT X0E 0R0; phone (403) 874-2565.

Radio: CKHR-FM 107.3, 93.7, 100.1-FM. **Television:** Channels 2 through 13 via satellite. **Newspaper:** *The Hub* (weekly). **Transportation: Air**–Canadian Regional Airline, First Air, Landa Aviation, Carter Air and Buffalo Airways. **Bus**–Coachways. **Rental cars**–Available.

Private Aircraft: Hay River airport; elev. 543 feet/165m; length 6,000 feet/1,830m, paved; 4,000 feet/1,219m, gravel; fuel 100, Jet B.

Hay River was established in 1868 with the building of a Hudson's Bay Co. post. Today's economy combines transportation, communications, commercial fishing and service industries.

The community is the transfer point from highway and rail to barges on Great Slave Lake bound for arctic and subarctic communities. Hay River harbour is also home port of the Mackenzie River barge fleet that plies the river in summer.

The airstrip was built in 1942 on Vale Island by the U.S. Army Corps of Engineers. Vale Island was the townsite until floods in 1951 and 1963 forced evacuation of the population to the mainland townsite, where most of the community is now concentrated. Vale Island, referred to as "Old Town," is bounded by Great Slave Lake and the west and east channels of the Hay River.

The town boasts the tallest building in the Northwest Territories—a 17-story apartment high-rise that can be seen for miles around— and a purple high school designed by Douglas Cardinal. Hay River also has Paradise Gardens,

the largest market-gardening operation in Northwest Territories, and Perron's Funny Farm, one of the few livestock producers in the territories.

There are 10 restaurants, gas stations with unleaded gas, propane and repair service, and grocery stores. Reservations are a must at the town's 5 hotels/motels; lodgings may be heavily booked in the busy summer season. There is also a bed and breakfast.

Other facilities include 2 banks, a laundromat, and a variety of gift and arts and crafts shops.

Hay River has schools, churches, a civic centre with a swimming pool (1 of only 2 year-round swimming pools in Northwest Territories), curling sheets, hockey arena and dance hall. Northwest Territories Centennial Library headquarters is located here. There is a public boat launch at Porritt Landing on Vale Island.

There is a public campground, Hay River Centennial Park, on Vale Island (follow the signs; it is about 6 miles/10 km past the information centre). There are 21 sites (4 with electrical hookups), showers, firewood and firepits, picnic area, playground and horseshoe pit. Camping fee is $15 per night. Open mid-May to mid-September. ▲

Great sportfishing area with fly-in fishing camps (check with the chamber of commerce). Boat rentals on nearby **Great Slave Lake**, where northern pike up to 40 lbs. are not unusual. Inconnu (sheefish), pickerel and grayling also found here. ⊸

Yellowknife Highway Log

NWT HIGHWAY 3
Distance from the junction of Highways 1 and 3 (J) is followed by distance from Yellowknife (Y).

J 0 Y 212.5 (342 km) **Junction** of Highways 1 and 3. Turn right northbound for Fort Providence, Rae–Edzo and Yellowknife.

The first 84.8 miles/136.5 km of Highway 3 are paved. There are 2 stretches of gravel— one 18 miles/29 km, the other 56.2 miles/ 90.4 km—with the remainder of the highway paved. Plans call for continued paving of this highway.

J 4.8 (7.7 km) **Y 207.7** (334.3 km) Chikilee Creek.

J 4.9 (7.9 km) **Y 207.6** (334.1 km) Wolf Skull Creek.

J 9.1 (14.7 km) **Y 203.4** (327.3 km) Dory Point maintenance camp to west.

J 10.6 (17 km) **Y 201.9** (324.9 km) Turnoff for winter ice crossing to east.

J 13.2 (21.2 km) **Y 199.3** (320.8 km) Dory Point picnic area to east with 5 sites and kitchen shelter, no drinking water; overlooking Mackenzie River with view of passing riverboats.

J 13.9 (22.4 km) **Y 198.6** (319.6 km) Campground with hookups, service station with regular, unleaded and diesel, and restaurant. ▲

J 14.5 (23.3 km) **Y 198** (318.6 km) Dory Point marine access camp to west.

J 15.1 (24.3 km) **Y 197.4** (317.7 km) Free government-operated Mackenzie River ferry operates daily May through October or November from 6 A.M. to midnight. Crossing time is 8 minutes. Capacity is 10 cars or 4 trucks, with a maximum total weight of 220,000 lbs./100,000 kg. An ice bridge opens for light vehicles in December and heavier vehicles as ice thickens. *NOTE: No crossing possible during breakup (about April to mid-May).* Ice breaking procedures now keep the channel open for the ferry during freezeup while an ice bridge is being constructed. For ferry information phone (403) 873-7799 or 1-800-661-0751.

J 15.9 (25.6 km) **Y 196.6** (316.4 km) Sign indicates Mackenzie Wood Bison Sanctuary. The wood bison are not often seen along the highway; however, sandhill cranes, squirrels, spruce grouse and ptarmigan may be seen in season.

J 19.4 (31.2 km) **Y 193.1** (310.8 km) Motel, restaurant and service station with unleaded, diesel and propane. Pay phone.

J 19.6 (31.6 km) **Y 192.9** (310.4 km) **Junction** with access road which leads 2.8 miles/4.5 km west to Fort Providence (description follows). Gas station with unleaded, diesel, propane, restaurant and tire repair. There is an airstrip located 0.4 mile/0.6 km west on the access road. *NOTE: It is a good idea to fill gas tanks here if you are bound for Yellowknife. Next gas available is in Rae–Edzo.*

Big River Service Centre. See display ad this section.

Fort Providence territorial campground is located 0.7 mile/1.1 km west of the highway on the access road; 30 sites, tables, firewood, kitchen shelter, garbage container, pump water and dump station. Situated on the banks of the Mackenzie River. Rental boats, boat launch and fishing nearby. ▲

Entering Mackenzie Bison Sanctuary northbound.

Fort Providence

Located on the Mackenzie River, 2.8 miles/4.5 km northwest of Highway 3. **Population:** 688. **Emergency Services: Police,** phone (403) 699-3291. **Fire Department,** phone (403) 699-4222. **Nursing station,** phone (403) 699-4311.

Elevation: 550 feet/168m. **Radio:** 1230. **Television:** Channels 6 and 13 (CBC). **Transportation: Air**–Air Providence and

charter service. **Bus**–Coachways.

Private Aircraft: Fort Providence airstrip; elev. 530 feet/162m; length 3,000 feet/915m; gravel; fuel emergency only.

Facilities include 2 motels, 2 restaurants, gas stations with minor repair service, grocery and general stores.

A Roman Catholic mission was established here in 1861. Although noted for its early agricultural endeavors, Fort Providence is traditionally a trapping community. Three historical markers in the community commemorate the roles of the church and explorer Alexander Mackenzie in settling the area.

Unique and popular with northern collectors is the moose hair embroidery found in local gift shops. Local craftswomen are also noted for their porcupine quill work. Along with seeing the crafts, visitors may cruise the Mackenzie River. Spectacular photo opportunities here for sunsets on the Mackenzie.

Good to excellent fishing in **Mackenzie River;** guides and cabins available, also boats and air charter trips. Northern pike to 30 lbs., May 30 to September, use large Red Devils; grayling and pickerel from 1 to 6 lbs., June to September., use anything (small Red Devils will do). ◄

Yellowknife Highway Log

(continued)

J 26.4 (42.5 km) **Y 186.1** (299.5 km) Side road west to highway maintenance camp and stockpiles.

J 27.5 (44.3 km) **Y 185** (297.7 km) Bluefish Creek.

J 37 (59.5 km) **Y 175.5** (282.4 km) Large turnout to east at sand and gravel stockpiles.

J 38.7 (62.3 km) **Y 173.8** (279.7 km) Small gravel turnout to east.

J 42.3 (68.1 km) **Y 170.2** (273.9 km) Turnout to east with litter barrels and sign about Mackenzie Bison Sanctuary.

J 51.7 (83.2 km) **Y 160.8** (258.8 km) Turnout to west.

J 59.2 (95.3 km) **Y 153.3** (246.7 km) Telecommunications building to east.

J 75.6 (121.6 km) **Y 136.9** (220.4 km) Chan Lake picnic area to east with kitchen shelter, tables, firepits and firewood. No drinking water. Watch for waterfowl.

J 76.1 (122.5 km) **Y 136.4** (219.5 km) Turnout with litter barrels to east.

J 84 (136 km) **Y 127.7** (205.5 km) Pavement ends, gravel begins, northbound.

J 100 (160.9 km) **Y 112.5** (181.1 km) Turnout with litter barrels, outhouse and highway map sign to east. Watch for buffalo.

J 102.8 (165.4 km) **Y 109.7** (176.5 km) Gravel ends, pavement begins, northbound.

J 104.4 (168 km) **Y 108.1** (174 km) Telecommunications building to east.

J 124.7 (200.7 km) **Y 87.8** (141.3 km) Entering Yellowknife District northbound.

J 129.7 (208.8 km) **Y 82.8** (133.2 km) Turnout with litter barrels to east. Northbound travelers may notice the trees are getting shorter as you move farther north.

J 140.2 (225.7 km) **Y 72.3** (116.3 km) Turnout to east. Highway descends northbound to Mosquito Creek.

J 141.2 (227.3 km) **Y 71.3** (114.7 km) Highway crosses **Mosquito Creek.** Fishing for pickerel and whitefish, May and June. ◄

J 144.2 (232 km) **Y 68.3** (110 km) North Arm Territorial Park on the shores of Great Slave Lake. Picnic area with kitchen shelter, tables, toilets, firewood and firepits. Low-

bush cranberries and other berries in area. *Beware of bears.*

J 148.3 (238.6 km) **Y 64.2** (103.3 km) **Junction** with winter ice road north to communities of Lac La Marte and Rae Lakes.

J 148.5 (239 km) **Y 64** (103 km) **Junction** with access road west to community of Edzo (see description at **Milepost J 152.2**).

J 148.8 (239.5 km) **Y 63.7** (102.5 km) Picnic area to west. Pickerel fishing in **West Channel** in spring. ◄

J 149.3 (240.2 km) **Y 63.2** (101.8 km) West Channel.

J 151.5 (243.8 km) **Y 61** (98.2 km) Bridge over **Frank Channel,** which extends from the head of the North Arm of Great Slave Lake to the Indian village of Rae. Watch for turnoff to Rabesca's Bear Healing Rock; lodging, mud baths, boating and fishing for whitefish. ◄

J 152.2 (245 km) **Y 60.3** (97 km) **Junction** with road which leads west 7 miles/11.2 km to community of Rae (description follows).

RAE–EDZO (pop. about 2,000). **Emergency Services: RCMP,** in Rae, phone 392-6181. **Nursing station** in Edzo, phone 371-3551. **Radio:** 105.9-FM. The 2 hamlets of Rae and Edzo contain the territories' largest Dene (Indian) community. The Rae area, where most of the community resides, is an old Indian hunting spot and the site of 2 early trading posts. The Edzo site was developed in 1965 by the government to provide schools and an adequate sanitation system. Rae has grocery stores, a post office, Native crafts shop, 2 hotels, food service and gas stations with regular, unleaded and diesel. Pay phones are located at the community sports centre and at the cafe.

J 152.3 (245.1 km) **Y 60.2** (96.9 km) Pavement ends, gravel begins, eastbound.

J 159.8 (257.2 km) **Y 52.7** (84.8 km) Stagg River bridge. After crossing the North Arm of Great Slave Lake, the highway swings southeast toward Yellowknife. Winding road to Yellowknife, good opportunities to see waterfowl in the many small lakes.

J 160.4 (258.1 km) **Y 52.1** (83.9 km) Turnout with litter barrels to south.

J 189.2 (304.5 km) **Y 23.3** (37.5 km) Turnout with litter barrels to north.

J 189.5 (304.9 km) **Y 23** (37.1 km) Boundary Creek.

J 203.8 (328 km) **Y 8.7** (14 km) Yellowknife city limits.

J 208.5 (335.5 km) **Y 4** (6.5 km) Gravel ends, pavement begins.

J 208.7 (335.8 km) **Y 3.8** (6.2 km) Yellowknife Golf Club to north; 9 holes, sand greens, pro shop, licensed clubhouse. Built on the Canadian Shield, the course is mostly sand and bedrock. Each player gets a small piece of carpet to take along on the round as their own portable turf. Site of the June 21 Midnight Tournament. Some modified rules have been adopted by this Far North golf course, among them: "No penalty assessed when ball carried off by raven."

J 209.8 (337.7 km) **Y 2.7** (4.3 km) Yellowknife airport to south.

J 210 (338 km) **Y 2.5** (4 km) Fred Henne Territorial Park on Long Lake. Attractive public campground with 82 sites, water, firewood, firepits, picnic area, boat launch, snack bar, showers and pay phone. Daily and seasonal rates available; open from mid-May to mid-September. Sandy beach and swimming in Long Lake. Interpretive trail. ▲

J 210.5 (338.7 km) **Y 2** (3.3 km) Old Airport Road access to Yellowknife. Just past the

To Airport and Highway 3

To Airport

To Ingrahm Trail (Highway 4)

Legislative Assembly

Old Airport Road

Frame Lake

Niven Lake

Prince of Wales Northern Heritage Centre

Pedestrian causeway

Visitor Centre

Back Bay

City Hall

RCMP

Courthouse

Scotia Mall

49 Ave.

YK Centre

Floatplane base

Hospital

Kam Lake

Wiley Road

Morrison Drive

Latham Island

To Kam Lake Industrial Subdivision

Franklin Ave.

50A Ave.

Post Office

50 Ave.

44 St.

Ingrahm Drive

Pilot's Monument

Forest Drive

Ave.

51 Ave.

56 St. 55 St. 54 St. 53 St. 52 St. 51 St. 50 St. 49 St. 48 St. 47 St.

Floatplane base

Cruise boats

51a

Draw Ave.

Yellowknife Bay

Jolliffe Island

Con Road

54 Ave.

Rat Lake

Great Slave Lake

To Con Mines

Yellowknife

turnoff is the Welcome to Yellowknife sign and the hard-to-miss Wardair Bristol freighter to the south. A historical plaque commemorates the Bristol freighter, which was the first wheel-equipped aircraft to land at the North Pole. Picnic sites nearby.

J 211.4 (340.2 km) **Y 1.1** (1.8 km) Stock Lake to south.

J 211.7 (340.7 km) **Y 0.8** (1.3 km) **Junction** of Highway 3 and Highway 4 (Ingraham Trail); see log this section.

Yellowknife

J 212.5 (342 km) **Y 0** On the north shore of Great Slave Lake, approximately 940 miles/1513 km from Edmonton, AB. **Population:** 17,500. **Emergency Services: RCMP,** phone (403) 920-8311. **Fire Department** and **Ambulance,** phone (403) 873-3434 or 873-2222. **Hospital,** Stanton Yellowknife, phone (403) 920-4111.

Visitor Information: Northern Frontier Regional Visitors Centre, showcasing the culture and crafts of the area, is located at 4807 49th St. Reservation desk for booking tours. Open daily year-round; summer hours 8 A.M. to 8 P.M. Phone (403) 873-4262. Information also available from Northwest Territories Tourism, P.O. Box 1320, Yellowknife, NT X1A 2L9. Phone 1-800-661-0788 or (403) 873-7200. Or write the Chamber of Commerce, No. 6, 4807 49th St. (MP), Yellowknife, NWT X1A 3T5; phone (403) 920-4944.

Radio: 1240, 1340, 101.1-FM. **Television:** Channel 8; 15 cable channels. **Newspapers:** *News/North* (weekly); *Yellowknifer* (twice weekly).

Private Aircraft: Yellowknife airport; elev. 674 feet/205m; length 7,500 feet/ 2,286m; asphalt; fuel 100/130, Jet B. Floatplane bases located at East Bay and West Bay of Latham Island.

Yellowknife, capital of Northwest Territories and considered the only "city" in Northwest Territories, is a relatively new community. White settlers arrived in the 1930s with the discovery of gold in the area and radium at Great Bear Lake.

Cominco poured its first gold brick in 1938. WWII intervened and gold mining was halted until Giant Yellowknife Mines began milling May 12, 1948. It was not until 1960 that the road was completed connecting the city with the provinces. Yellowknife became capital of the Northwest Territories in 1967.

The most recent mining boom in Yellowknife was the discovery of diamonds north of Yellowknife at Lac de Gras in 1992. The find set off a rush of claim stakers. An estimated 150 companies have staked claims in an area stretching from north of Yellowknife to the Arctic coast, and east from the North Arm of Great Slave Lake to Hudson Bay.

For 2 to 6 weeks each spring, vehicle traffic to Yellowknife is cut off during breakup on the Mackenzie River crossing near Fort Providence. All fresh meat, produce and urgent supplies must be airlifted during this period, resulting in higher prices.

Yellowknife has continued to develop as a mining, transportation and government administrative centre for the territories.

ACCOMMODATIONS/VISITOR SERVICES

Acommodations at 3 hotels, 3 motels, 14 bed and breakfasts, and the YWCA (co-ed). There are 47 restaurants, 7 dining lounges (no minors), 18 cocktail lounges and several shopping malls. Northern handicraft shops for fur parkas and other Native crafts are a specialty here, and there are shops specializing in Northern art.

TRANSPORTATION

Air: Scheduled air service to Edmonton via NWT Airways and Canadian Airlines International; Winnipeg via NWT Airways. Carriers serving Yellowknife and Arctic communities are NWT Airways, Canadian Airlines International, Ptarmigan Airways, Simpson Air, Air Providence and First Air. Charter service available. **Bus:** Greyhound from Edmonton with connections at Enterprise. **Rentals:** Several major car rental agencies; boat and canoe rentals.

ATTRACTIONS

Northern Frontier Regional Visitors Centre. (MP5) No. 4, 4807 49th St., Yellowknife, Northwest Territories X1A 3T5. Featuring interpretive displays, exhibits and a bush plane elevator ride. Information on things to see and do. A tour reservation desk operates during the summer. Open year-round, 7 days a week (8 A.M. to 6 P.M. summer hours). Phone (403) 873-4262, fax 873-3654.

Prince of Wales Northern Heritage Centre. Opened in 1979, this large museum complex was built to collect, preserve, document, exhibit, study and interpret the North's natural and cultural history. For visitors there are a variety of temporary exhibits ranging from Inuit stone sculpture to historical photographs, and permanent exhibits in the galleries. The orientation gallery gives general background on the Northwest Territories; the south gallery tells the story of the land, and the Dene and Inuit people; the north gallery shows the arrival of the Euro–Canadians. The centre is located on Frame Lake, accessible via 48th Street or by way of a pedestrian causeway behind City Hall.

Tours. There are a variety of local tours offered. Public tours of the Legislative Assembly are available by calling the Coordinator of Public Information at (403) 669-2230. Visitors may take a 2- or 3-hour tour of the city or a 2-hour cruise on Great Slave Lake. Local tour operators also offer tours out Ingraham Trail (NWT Highway 4).

Explore Yellowknife. Walk along the popular Frame Lake Trail with its views of Yellowknife's skyline, including the Armed Forces Northern Headquarters and Legislative Assembly buildings. The trail is a favorite with dog walkers, bicyclists, birdwatchers and commuters. Drive or walk down the hill and around the "Rock" where the original town sprang up on Yellowknife

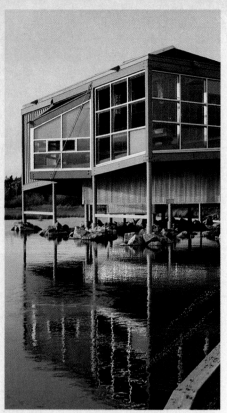

Distinctive Yellowknife visitor centre on Frame Lake. (© Lyn Hancock)

Bay and where there are now barges, fishing boats and a large floatplane base; climb steps to the cairn on top of the rock, a tribute to early-day bush pilots who opened up this country in the 1930s and 1940s. The log Wildcat Cafe at the bottom of the rock is open May to September. Drive out to Old Town on Latham Island to see some of the creative solutions builders have found to the problem of building on solid rock.

The Yellowknife Bookcellar. See display ad this section.

Ingraham Trail Log

NWT HIGHWAY 4
NWT Highway 4 begins in Yellowknife and extends 44 miles/71 km along an almost continuous chain of lakes and streams, ending at Tibbett Lake. In winter, this highway is used as part of the 380-mile/612-km ice road to Lupin gold mine. The winter road also serves Lac de Gras, heart of the diamond rush.
Distance from Yellowknife (Y) is followed by distance from Tibbett Lake (T).

Y 0 T 44.1 (70.9 km) **Junction** of Highways 3 and 4.
Y 1.9 (3.1 km) **T 42.2** (67.9 km) Giant Yellowknife Mines main office. The mine has been operating since 1947.
Y 3.1 (5 km) **T 41** (66 km) Side road leads north 3 miles/5 km to Vee Lake.
Y 4.7 (7.5 km) **T 39.4** (63.4 km) Single-lane bridge across the **Yellowknife River.** Historical sign at north end of bridge about the Ingraham Trail. Picnic area with tables and boat launch. Good fishing for northern pike, lake trout and grayling.

Y 6.1 (9.8 km) **T 38** (61.2 km) Turnoff to south by 2 transmission towers for 7-mile/11-km road to Detah Indian village; no services.
Y 11.9 (19.2 km) **T 32.2** (51.7 km) **Prosperous Lake** picnic area and boat launch to north. Fishing for northern pike, whitefish and lake trout.
Y 14.9 (24 km) **T 29.2** (46.9 km) **Madeline Lake.** Boat launch to north. Fishing for northern pike, whitefish, cisco and yellow perch.
Y 16.4 (26.4 km) **T 27.7** (44.5 km) **Pontoon Lake** picnic area and boat launch to south. Fishing for northern pike, whitefish, cisco and suckers.
Y 17.5 (28.2 km) **T 26.6** (42.7 km) Side road leads north 1 mile/1.6 km to Prelude Lake territorial campground with 45 campsites, 20 picnic sites, boat launch and swimming. Prelude Wildlife Trail is a 1½- hour walk. The trail has 15 interpretive stations showing the adaptations and relationships of wildlife in the North. Boat rentals, cabins and a restaurant located here. ▲

Fishing in **Prelude Lake** for lake trout, grayling, whitefish, cisco, burbot, suckers and northern pike.

Good views of Prelude Lake from the highway next 10 miles/16 km eastbound.
Y 28.6 (46 km) **T 15.5** (24.9 km) Powder Point on Prelude Lake to north; parking area. Boat launch for canoeists doing the route into Hidden Lake Territorial Park, Lower Cameron River, or 4-day trip to Yellowknife River bridge.
Y 30.1 (48.4 km) **T 14** (22.5 km) Cameron River Falls trailhead to north; parking. This 0.6-mile/1-km trail leads to cliffs overlooking Cameron River Falls.
Y 35.4 (57 km) **T 8.7** (13.9 km) Bailey bridge across Cameron River; parking area, picnicking, canoeing, hiking and swimming.
Y 37.9 (61 km) **T 6.2** (9.9 km) **Reid Lake** territorial campground with 50 campsites, 10 picnic sites, kitchen shelter, swimming, hiking trail, boat launch and fishing. Canoe launch point for Upper Cameron River and Jennejohn Lake routes. *CAUTION: Watch for bears.* ▲
Y 44.1 (70.9 km) **T 0** Tibbett Lake. End of road. Launch point for Pensive Lakes canoe route (advanced canoeists only).

Fort Smith Highway Log

NWT HIGHWAY 5
Distance from Highway 2 junction (J) followed by distance from Fort Smith (FT).

J 0 FT 166 (267.2 km) Highway 5 begins its own series of markers giving distances in kilometres.
J 1.3 (2.2 km) **FT 164.7** (265 km) Railroad and auto bridge crosses Hay River.
J 1.5 (2.5 km) **FT 164.5** (264.7 km) Access road leads north 3.7 miles/5.9 km to Hay River reserve.
The first 37.7 miles/60.8 km of Highway 5 are paved. Watch for construction and rough spots in surfacing. There are no services or gas available until Fort Smith.
J 5.4 (8.8 km) **FT 160.6** (258.4 km) Highway crosses Sandy Creek.
J 11 (17.7 km) **FT 155** (249.5 km) Highway maintenance yard to south.
J 17.3 (27.9 km) **FT 148.7** (239.3 km)

Birch Creek bridge.
J 23.7 (38.2 km) **FT 142.3** (229 km) Highway crosses Twin Creek.
J 30.3 (48.8 km) **FT 135.7** (218.4 km) Good gravel road leads 1 mile/1.6 km north to **Polar Lake.** Lake is stocked with rainbow; no motorboats allowed. Good bird watching. ►
J 33.8 (54.4 km) **FT 132.2** (212.7 km) Buffalo River bridge.
J 34.1 (55 km) **FT 131.9** (212.2 km) Turnout to north with litter barrel and map.
J 37.3 (60 km) **FT 128.7** (207.1 km) **Junction** with Highway 6 east to Pine Point and Fort Resolution (see log this section). Highway 5 turns south for Fort Smith (continue with this log). Highway maintenance camp.
J 54 (87 km) **FT 112** (180.2 km) Turnoff for **Sandy Lake,** 8 miles/13 km south; swimming, sandy beach, fishing for northern pike. ►
J 54.2 (87.2 km) **FT 111.8** (180 km) Pavement ends, gravel begins, southbound.
J 59.6 (96 km) **FT 106.4** (171.2 km) Entrance to Wood Buffalo National Park. Established in 1922 to protect Canada's only remaining herd of wood bison, **WOOD BUFFALO NATIONAL PARK** (a UNESCO world heritage site) is a vast wilderness area of 44,800 square kilometres with the greater portion located in the northeast corner of Alberta. Park headquarters and Visitor Reception Centre are located in Fort Smith and Fort Chipewyan; excellent audio-video presentations, exhibits and visitor information are available. Or write Wood Buffalo National Park, Box 750, Fort Smith, NT X0E 0P0; or phone (403) 872-7900 Fort Smith or (403) 697-3662 Fort Chipewyan.

The wood bison, a slightly larger and darker northern relative of the Plains bison, numbered about 1,500 in the area, representing the largest free-roaming herd in Canada at the time the park was established. Soon after this more than 6,600 Plains bison were moved from southern Alberta to the park. Today's herd of about 3,500 bison is considered to be mostly hybrids.

Also found within the park are many species of waterfowl and the world's only remaining natural nesting grounds of the endangered whooping crane.

The park is open year-round. Check the schedule of events at the park office.
J 63.8 (102.7 km) **FT 102.2** (164.4 km) Paralleling most of the highway to Fort Smith are hydro transmission power lines carrying power to Fort Smith, Pine Point and Fort Resolution that is generated at the Taltson Dam in the Canadian Shield north of the Slave River.

Much of the flora along this stretch of highway is new growth following the devastating forest fires of 1981. *NOTE: To report a forest fire, call the operator toll free and ask for Zenith 5555.*
J 66 (106.2 km) **FT 100** (160.9 km) Picnic area with tables to north at Angus Fire Tower. The sinkhole seen here is an example of karst topography. Sinkholes are formed when the roofs of caves (formed by underground water dissolving bedrock) collapse.

Buffalo wallow beside highway from here to approximately **Milepost J 98.9.**
J 74 (119.2 km) **FT 92** (148 km) Highway crosses Nyarling River, which runs underground beneath the dry creekbed.
J 74.2 (119.4 km) **FT 91.8** (147.7 km) Turnout to south with litter barrel.
J 98.9 (159.2 km) **FT 67.1** (108 km) Highway maintenance building to north.

J 110.8 (178.4 km) **FT 55.2** (88.8 km) Highway crosses Sass River. Shallow lakes from here south to Preble Creek provide nesting areas for whooping cranes.

J 116.2 (187 km) **FT 49.8** (80.1 km) Highway crosses Preble Creek.

J 121.2 (195 km) **FT 44.8** (72.1 km) Wetlands pull off with litter barrel and interpretive signs.

J 130.5 (210 km) **FT 35.5** (57.1 km) The highway leaves and reenters Wood Buffalo National Park several times southbound.

J 131 (211 km) **FT 34.9** (56.1 km) Little Buffalo River bridge. Camping and picnic area. ▲

J 142.5 (229.4 km) **FT 23.5** (37.8 km) Turnoff for Parsons Lake Road (narrow gravel) which leads south 8 miles/13 km to Salt Plains overlook. Interpretive exhibit and viewing telescope. Springs at the edge of a high escarpment bring salt to the surface and spread it across the huge flat plain; only plants adapted to high salinity can grow here. Fine view of a unique environment. Gravel parking area with tables, firepits and toilets at overlook; hiking trail down to Salt Plains (bring boots). *CAUTION: Parsons Lake Road beyond the overlook may be impassable in wet weather.*

J 144.7 (232.8 km) **FT 21.4** (34.4 km) Turnout to south and gravel stockpile.

J 147.3 (237 km) **FT 18.7** (30.1 km) Pavement begins eastbound into Fort Smith.

J 147.9 (238 km) **FT 18.1** (29.1 km) Salt River bridge.

J 151.6 (244 km) **FT 14.4** (23.2 km) Thebacha (Salt River) private campground and picnic area 10 miles/16 km north via good gravel road. Located on the **Salt River**; 8 sites, toilets, parking, small-boat launch (cruise down to Slave River), and fishing for pike, walleye, inconnu and goldeye. ◆▲

J 163.4 (263 km) **FT 2.6** (4.2 km) Turnoff to north for Fort Smith airport and Queen Elizabeth Park campground with 19 campsites, 15 picnic sites, water, kitchen shelter, showers and dump station. Short hike from campground to bluff overlooking Rapids of the Drowned on the Slave River; look for pelicans feeding here. ▲

Fort Smith

J 166 (267.2 km) **FT 0** **Population:** 2,460. **Emergency Services: RCMP,** phone (403) 872-2107. **Fire Department,** phone (403) 872-6111. **Health Centre,** phone (403) 872-2713. **Visitor Information:** Chamber of commerce information centre in Conibear Park, open June to September. For general information on the area, contact the Economic Development and Tourism Office, Box 390, Fort Smith, NT X0E 0P0.

Climate: Mean high temperature in July 75°F/24°C; mean low 48°F/9°C. **Radio:** 860, 101.9-FM. **Television:** Channels 12 (local) and 5 (CBC) plus 15 cable channels. **Newspaper:** *Slave River Journal.*

Transportation: Air—Canadian Regional Airlines provides scheduled service; there are also 3 charter air services. **Bus**—Available. **Rental cars**—Available.

Private Aircraft: Fort Smith airport; elev. 666 feet/203m; length, 6,000 feet/1,829m; asphalt; fuel 80, 100.

Fort Smith began as a trading post at a favorite campsite of the portagers traveling the 1,600-mile/2575-km water passage from

Watch for pelicans feeding in the Slave River rapids. (© Lyn Hancock)

Fort McMurray to the Arctic Ocean. The 4 sets of rapids, named (south to north) Cassette, Pelican, Mountain and the Rapids of the Drowned, separate the Northwest Territories from Alberta. In 1874 Hudson's Bay Co. established a permanent post, and the Roman Catholic mission was transferred here in 1876. By 1911 the settlement had become a major trading post for the area.

There are a 2 hotels, a motel, 2 groceries, a takeout outlet, 3 bars, 3 convenience stores, and gas stations with unleaded gas and repair service.

Wood Buffalo National Park headquarters is located in the Federal Building on McDougal Road, which also houses the post office. The multi-image presentation here is highly recommended. Exhibit area and trip planning assistance available at the visitor reception area. You can drive from Fort Smith to Peace Point via an all-weather gravel road. There are several hiking trails off the road, a picnic area at the Salt River, and a 36-site campground at Pine Lake, 38 miles/61 km south of Fort Smith. There is also a good opportunity for seeing bison on the road between Pine Lake and Peace Point. Contact the park office, phone (403) 872-7900.

Other attractions in Fort Smith include Northern Life Museum, which features a comprehensive view of the area's Native culture and life of the white settlers since the mid-19th century.

Fort Resolution Highway Log

NWT HIGHWAY 6
Distance from junction with Highway 5 (J) is followed by distance from Fort Resolution (FR).

J 0 **FR 55.9** (90 km) **Junction** of Highways 5 and 6. The first 14.7 miles/23.7 km of the highway is paved; the rest is gravel to Fort Resolution. Narrow shoulders.

J 13.2 (21.3 km) **FR 42.7** (68.7 km) Main access road north to **PINE POINT**; no services. A mining town, Pine Point was built in the 1960s by Cominco Ltd. The open-pit lead–zinc mine shut down in 1987. Once a

community of almost 2,000 residents, most people moved out in 1988, and houses and structures have been moved or destroyed. The Great Slave Lake Railway (now CNR) was constructed in 1961 from Roma, AB, to Pine Point to transport the lead–zinc ore to market.

J 14.6 (23.6 km) **FR 41.3** (66.4 km) Secondary access road to Pine Point.

J 14.7 (23.7 km) **FR 41.2** (66.3 km) Pavement ends, gravel begins, eastbound. Dust-free zone to Fort Resolution.

J 15.8 (25.5 km) **FR 40.1** (64.5 km) Pine Point airport to north, microwave and satellite dish to south.

J 24.6 (39.6 km) **FR 31.3** (50.3 km) Tailing piles from open-pit mining to south.

J 32.3 (52 km) **FR 23.6** (38 km) Turnoff to north for Dawson Landing viewpoint on Great Slave Lake, accessible via a 25-mile/40-km bush road (not recommended in wet weather).

J 36.5 (58.8 km) **FR 19.4** (31.2 km) Turnout to north with litter barrel.

J 37.8 (60.8 km) **FR 18.1** (29.1 km) Glimpse of Great Slave Lake to north.

J 41.4 (66.7 km) **FR 14.5** (23.3 km) Bridge over **Little Buffalo River.** Good fishing for northern pike and walleye. ◆

J 42.4 (68.3 km) **FR 13.5** (21.7 km) Access road to Little Buffalo River Indian village.

J 54.5 (87.7 km) **FR 1.4** (2.2 km) Campground to west; 5 gravel sites, outhouses, tables and firepits. ▲

J 55.9 (90 km) **FR 0 FORT RESOLUTION** (pop. 447), located on the south shore of Great Slave Lake on Resolution Bay. **Emergency Services: RCMP,** phone (403) 394-4111. This historic community grew up around a Hudson's Bay Co. post established in 1786, and was named Fort Resolution in 1821 when the Hudson's Bay Co. and North West Co. united. Missionaries settled in the area in 1852, establishing a school and hospital to serve the largely Chipewyan population. Walking tours through the village may be arranged. The road connecting Fort Resolution with Pine Point was built in the 1960s.

Today's economy is based on trapping, and a logging and sawmill operation. There are a small motel, 2 general stores, a gas station with minor repair service, a post office and cafe. Meals are also available at the community hall.

YELLOWHEAD HIGHWAY 16

Connects: Edmonton, AB, to Prince Rupert, BC **Length:** 906 miles
Road Surface: Paved   **Season:** Open all year
Highest Summit: Obed Summit, 3,819 feet
Major Attractions: Jasper National Park, Mt. Robson, Fort St. James
(See maps, pages 217-219)

	Edmonton	Jasper	Prince George	Prince Rupert	Terrace
Edmonton		216	450	906	816
Jasper	216		234	690	600
Prince George	450	234		456	366
Prince Rupert	906	690	456		90
Terrace	816	600	366	90	

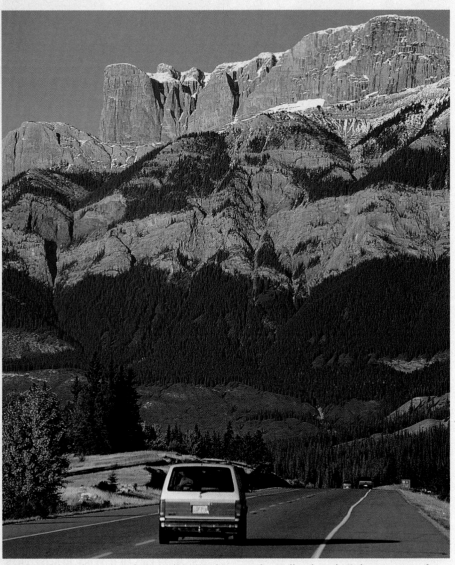

Approaching the rugged Canadian Rockies on the Yellowhead Highway east of Jasper. (© Beth Davidow)

Yellowhead Highway 16 Log

The Yellowhead Highway log is divided into 2 sections: Edmonton to Prince George, and Prince George to Prince Rupert. Kilometre-posts on Yellowhead reflect distances within highway maintenance districts; *The MILE-POST®* periodically notes these physical posts as reference points.
This section of the log shows distance from Edmonton (E) followed by distance from Prince George (PG).

E 0 PG 450 (724.2 km) **EDMONTON** city limit. See page 29 in the EAST ACCESS ROUTE section for description of city.

E 4 (6.4 km) **PG 446** (717.8 km) **Junction** of Highways 16 West and 60 (Devon Overpass); access to Glowing Embers Travel Centre campground with 273 sites. ▲

E 12 (19.3 km) **PG 438** (704.9 km) **SPRUCE GROVE** (pop. 13,076). All visitor facilities including motels, restaurants, gas and service stations, grocery stores, farmer's market, shopping malls and all emergency services. Recreational facilities include a golf course, swimming pool, 2 ice skating rinks, a curling rink, and extensive walking and cycling trails. The chamber of commerce tourist information booth, located on Highway 16, is open year-round; phone (403) 962-2561.

E 18.1 (29.1 km) **PG 431.9** (695.1 km) **STONY PLAIN** (pop. 7,800). All visitor facilities including hotels, restaurants, super-

Yellowhead Highway 16 is a paved trans-Canada highway extending from Winnipeg, MB, through Saskatchewan, Alberta, and British Columbia to the coastal city of Prince Rupert. (The highway connecting Masset and Queen Charlotte on Graham Island has also been designated as part of Yellowhead Highway 16.) *The MILEPOST®* logs Yellowhead Highway 16 from Edmonton, AB, to Prince Rupert, BC, a distance of 906 miles/1,458 km.

Yellowhead Highway 16 terminates at Prince Rupert, BC, where you may connect with the Alaska Marine Highway System to southeastern Alaska cities, and the British Columbia ferry system to Port Hardy on Vancouver Island and Skidegate in the Queen Charlotte Islands (see MARINE ACCESS ROUTES section).

This is a major east–west route, providing access to a number of attractions in Alberta and British Columbia. Yellowhead Highway 16 is also a very scenic highway, passing through mountains, forest and farmland. Visitor services are readily available in towns along the way, and campsites may be found in towns and along the highway at both private and provincial park campgrounds. (It is unsafe and illegal to overnight in rest areas.)

YELLOWHEAD HIGHWAY 16
Edmonton, AB, to Prince George, BC

PG-450/724km
E-0
Edmonton
To Saskatoon

To Calgary
(see EAST ACCESS ROUTE section)

Spruce Grove
Stony Plain
E-18.1/29.1km
Bears & Bedtime Mfg. Inc.
Stony Plain Highway Inn LM
E-22/35.4km The
Multicultural Heritage Centre M

Athabasca River

Grizzly Trail

33

To Slave Lake

Lac Saint Anne

Falls

Isle Lakes

Wabamun Lake

North Saskatchewan River

43

Whitecourt

Wildwood

Entwistle

Carisford

Chip L.

Mackay

Nojack

Pembina River

Carrot Creek

Niton Junction

16

Edson

E-114.9/185km Ernie O's Restaurant M
The Guest House L

Marlboro

Obed

Sundance Cr.

McLeod River

Hinton

Pocahontas
Talbot Lake

PG-234/377km
E-216/348km

Jasper
National
Park

Icefields
Parkway

To Lake Louise

ALBERTA

Columbia Icefield

BRITISH COLUMBIA

Banff
National
Park

Yoho
National
Park

Kootenay National Park

Columbia River

Columbia Icefield

Glaciated Area

Columbia River

To Grande Prairie
(see EAST ACCESS ROUTE section)

To Dawson Creek
(see EAST ACCESS ROUTE section)

Athabasca R.

Bighorn Highway

40

Grande Cache

ROCKY MOUNTAINS

ALBERTA
BRITISH COLUMBIA

Willmore
Wilderness
Park

Mount Robson
12,972 ft/3,954m

Tete Jaune
Lodge CtM

E-279.6/450.1km

Jasper

93

Jasper L.

Luceme L.

Yellowhead
Pass
3,760 ft/1,146m

Yellowhead Pass

Kinbasket Lake

Athabasca R.

Glaciated Area

Glaciated Area

5

To Kamloops

North Thompson River

Mount Robson Provincial Park

Tete Jaune Cache

PG-168/270km
E-282/454km

Wells Gray
Provincial
Park

COLUMBIA MOUNTAINS

Fraser River

Goat R.

E-409.5/659.1km
Purden Lake and Ski Resorts CdGLMPT

E-318.8/513.1km McBride Chevron DGPS
North Country Lodge
E-317.4/510.8km Beaverview Campsite CDIT
E-309.5/498.2km Deer Meadows Golf Course & Campground C

McBride

Slim Cr.

Bowron River

CARIBOO MOUNTAINS

PR-456/734km
PG-0
E-450/724km

Purden Lake

Tabor Lake

To Dawson Creek
(see WEST ACCESS ROUTE section)

97

Prince George
(see WEST ACCESS ROUTE section)

16

(map continues
next page)

97

To Williams Lake
(see WEST ACCESS ROUTE section)

Scale
miles/kilometres
0   20   Miles
0   20   Kilometres

Key to mileage boxes
miles/kilometres
from:
E-Edmonton
PG-Prince George
PR-Prince Rupert

Key to Advertiser Services
C -Camping
D -Dump Station
d -Diesel
G -Gas (reg., unld.)
I -Ice
L -Lodging
M -Meals
P -Propane
R -Car Repair (major)
r -Car Repair (minor)
S -Store (grocery)
T -Telephone (pay)

♠ Refer to Log for Visitor Facilities
? Visitor Information
▲ Campground ✈ Airport + Airstrip

Map Location

Principal Route
Paved
Unpaved

Other Roads
Paved
Unpaved Hiking Trails

Ferry Routes ••••••••

YELLOWHEAD HIGHWAY 16 *Prince George, BC, to Topley, BC*

Scale

Miles
Kilometres

Key to mileage boxes

miles/kilometres
miles/kilometres
from:

E-Edmonton
PG-Prince George
PR-Prince Rupert
J-Junction

Key to Advertiser Services

C -Camping
D -Dump Station
d -Diesel
G -Gas (reg., unld.)
I -Ice
L -Lodging
M -Meals
P -Propane
R -Car Repair (major)
r -Car Repair (minor)
S -Store (grocery)
T -Telephone (pay)

Principal Route
Paved
Unpaved

Other Roads
Paved
Unpaved

Ferry Routes
Hiking Trails

⊠ Refer to Log for Visitor Facilities
? Visitor Information
▲ Campground   ✈ Airport   ✦ Fishing

Map Location

OMINECA MOUNTAINS

CARIBOO MOUNTAINS

INTERIOR PLATEAU

To Dawson Creek
(see WEST ACCESS ROUTE section)

To Williams Lake
(see WEST ACCESS ROUTE section)

97

PR-456/734km
PG-0
E-450/724km

Prince George

PG-14.9/24km North
Country Arts & Crafts

Purden Lake

Bowron River

Fraser River

Tabor Lake

Bednesti Lake

Cluculz Lake

Nechako River

Chuckwagon Cafe M
Siesta Motel L

PG-60.5/97.4km Dave's RV Park CDT

PR-396/637km
PG-61/97km
Vanderhoof

PG-58.7/94.5km Nulki Lake RV Park CDT

PG-39.5/63.6km Brookside Resort CDGIPST

Kenney Dam Road

27

Fort St. James

To Manson Creek

Nescoslie River

Stuart River

Pinchi Lake

Tezzeron Lake

Stuart Lake

Tachie

Tachie River

Trembleur Lake

Fraser L.

Tachick Lake

PG-89.2/143.5km Piper's Glen RV Resort CD

Fort Fraser

PG-91.7/147.6km Orange Valley Motel RV Park and Campground CDILT

PR-359/577km
PG-98/157km

Fraser Lake

Stellako R.

Endako

PG-100/160.9km Glenannan Tourist Area CLM

Nechako River

Knewstubb Lake

Kenney Dam

Cheslatta Lake

Natalkuz Lake

Taltapin Lake

Uncha Lake

Takysie Lake

Ferry

Tchesinkut Lake

Burns Lake

PR-315/506km
PG-141/227km

PG-137.3/221km Burns Lake KOA CDILST

35

Francois Lake Road

Francois Lake

Ootsa Lake

Tweedsmuir Provincial Park

PG-146/235km Babine Lake Resort CLMS

Pinkut Lake

?

PG-140.9/226.8km Sandy's RV and Camping Resort CDILST

Burns Lake

Decker Lake

Rose Lake

Babine Lake

Granisle

Topley Landing

Topley

PR-280/451km
PG-175/282km

(map continues next page)

N
E
W
S

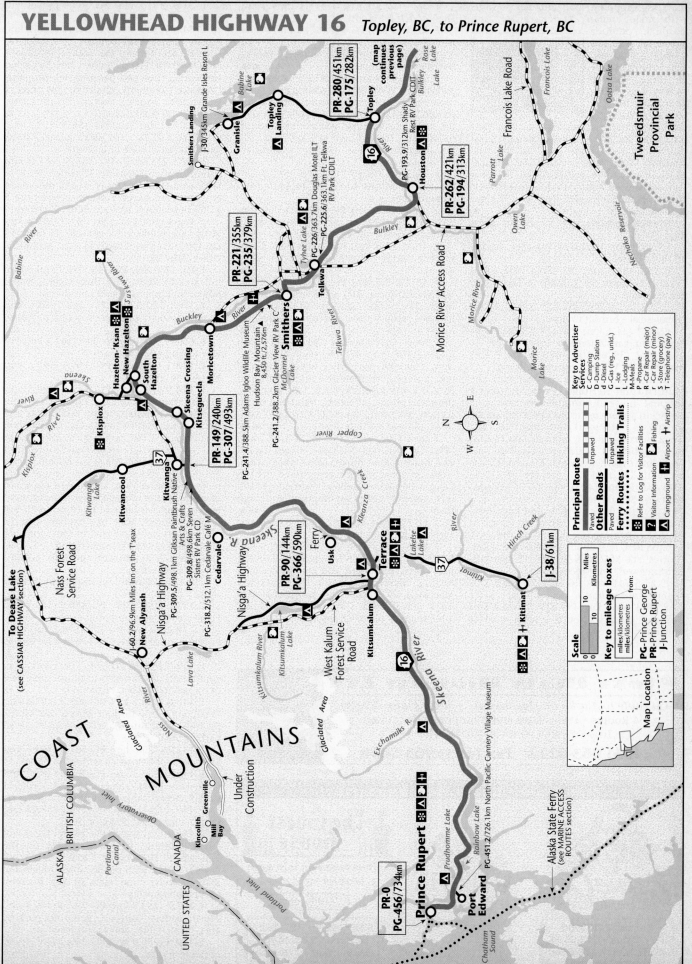

YELLOWHEAD HIGHWAY 16 · *Topley, BC, to Prince Rupert, BC*

PR-280/451km
PG-175/282km
Topley (map continues previous page)

PG-193.9/312km Shady Rest RV Park CDIT

16

PG-225.6/363.1km Ft. Telkwa RV Park CDILT
PG-226/363.7km Douglas Motel ILT

PR-262/421km
PG-194/313km
Houston

PR-221/355km
PG-235/379km

Tyhee Lake

Smithers

Telkwa

PG-241.2/388.2km Glacier View RV Park C
PG-241.4/388.5km Adams Igloo Wildlife Museum
Hudson Bay Mountain 8,450 ft./2,576m

Moricetown

Hazelton · 'Ksan
New Hazelton
South Hazelton

Kispiox

Skeena Crossing
Kitseguecla

PR-149/240km
PG-307/493km

PG-309.5/498.1km Gitksan Paintbrush Native Arts & Crafts
PG-309.8/498.6km Seven Sisters RV Park CD
PG-318.2/512.1km Cedarvale Café M

Kitwancool

Kitwanga

37

Cedarvale

To Dease Lake (see CASSIAR HIGHWAY section)

J-60.2/96.9km Miles Inn on the T'seax

New Aiyansh

Nisga'a Highway

PR-90/144km
PG-366/590km

Ferry
Usk

Terrace

37

J-38/61km

Kitsumkalum

16

Kitimat

West Kalum Forest Service Road

Nass Forest Service Road

COAST MOUNTAINS

Greenville
Kincolith
Mill Bay

Under Construction

PR-0
PG-456/734km
Prince Rupert

Port Edward

PG-451.2/726.1km North Pacific Cannery Village Museum

Alaska State Ferry (see MARINE ACCESS ROUTES section)

Tweedsmuir Provincial Park

Francois Lake Road

Morice River Access Road

Key to Advertiser Services
C - Camping
D - Dump Station
d - Diesel
G - Gas (reg., unld.)
I - Ice
L - Lodging
M - Meals
P - Propane
R - Car Repair (major)
r - Car Repair (minor)
S - Store (grocery)
T - Telephone (pay)

Principal Route
Paved — Unpaved
Other Roads
Paved ···· Unpaved
Ferry Routes — **Hiking Trails**

⛺ Refer to Log for Visitor Facilities
? Visitor Information
🎣 Fishing
✈ Airport — ✈ Airstrip
△ Campground

Scale
Miles
Kilometres

Key to mileage boxes
miles/kilometres from:
miles/kilometres
PG-Prince George
PR-Prince Rupert
J-Junction

Map Location

markets, shopping mall and gas stations with major repair service; RCMP and hospital; outdoor swimming pool and 18-hole golf course. The Multicultural Heritage Centre nearby (see Milepost E 22) has historical archives, a

craft shop and home-cooked meals. Other attractions include 16 outdoor murals; a teahouse; Oppertshauser Art Gallery; the Andrew Wolf Winery; and the Pioneer Museum at Exhibition Park. Visitor information centres at Rotary Park and rest area. Camping at Lions RV Park and Campground; 26 sites. ▲

Bears & Bedtime Mfg. See display ad on page 216.

Stony Plain Highway Inn. See display ad this section.

E 19.6 (31.5 km) PG 430.4 (692.7 km) Turnoff to south for Edmonton Beach and campground. ▲

E 20.1 (32.3 km) PG 429.9 (691.9 km) Hubbles Lake turnoff to north.

E 21.2 (34.1 km) PG 428.8 (690.1 km) Restaurant, gas station and store to north.

E 21.7 (35 km) PG 428.3 (689.2 km) Andrew Wolf Winery; visitors welcome.

E 22 (35.4 km) PG 428 (688.8 km) **The Multicultural Heritage Centre.** Features a regional museum, unique restaurant, a public art gallery featuring Canadian artists, as well as both local and imported craft shops. Award-winning grounds and historically significant buildings complete this rewarding experience. Open Monday to Saturday 10 A.M. to 4 P.M., Sunday 10 A.M. to 6:30 P.M. Phone (403) 963-2777. Address: 5411 – 51 St. [ADVERTISEMENT]

E 25 (40.2 km) PG 425 (684 km) **Junction** with Highway 43. Turn north for access to Alaska Highway (see page 30 in the EAST ACCESS ROUTE section) and Northwest Territories (see MACKENZIE ROUTE section). Continue west for Prince George.

E 25.5 (41 km) PG 424.5 (683.2 km) Hubbles Lake to north.

E 30.3 (48.8 km) PG 419.7 (675.4 km) Gas and groceries south side of road at junction.

E 30.9 (49.8 km) PG 419.1 (674.4 km) Sign: Watch for moose.

E 33 (53.1 km) PG 417 (671.1 km) **Wabamun Lake** Provincial Park, 1 mile/1.6 km south on access road; 288 campsites, fishing, boating and swimming. ➥▲

E 34.7 (55.9 km) PG 415.3 (668.3 km) Village of **WABAMUN** with gas, convenience store, car wash, laundromat, dump station, hotel and post office. Park with shelter, tables, litter barrels, washroom and flush toilets. Also located here is Trans Alta Utilities generating station, which generates electricity from coal.

E 38.5 (61.9 km) PG 411.5 (662.3 km) Emergency phone to south. Propane, fuel and groceries.

E 42.5 (68.4 km) PG 407.5 (655.8 km) **FALLIS** (pop. 190); no services. Strip mining of coal on north side of highway.

E 46.2 (74.4 km) PG 403.8 (649.8 km) Private campground/RV park, open year-round. ▲

E 48.7 (78.3 km) PG 401.3 (645.9 km) **GAINFORD** (pop. 205). Cafe, hotel and post office. Free public campground at west end of town with 8 sites, firewood, tables, pit toilets and water. ▲

E 56.6 (91.1 km) PG 393.4 (633.1 km) **ENTWISTLE** (pop. 477). Restaurants, gas station, 2 motels, post office, swimming pool and grocery store. **Pembina River** Provincial Park, 1.9 miles/3.1 km north; 129 campsites, firewood, tables, pit toilets, water and dump station. Camping fee $11. Fishing, swimming, playground and phone. ➥▲

E 66.2 (106.5 km) PG 383.8 (617.7 km) **WILDWOOD** (pop. 375), the "Bingo Capital of Canada." Post office, hotel, gas station, restaurants and shops. Campground at **Chip Lake** with 14 sites, tables, firewood, pit toilets, water, fishing, swimming and boat launch. ➥▲

E 68.7 (110.6 km) PG 381.3 (613.6 km) View of Chip Lake to north.

E 81.5 (131.1 km) PG 368.5 (593.1 km) **NOJACK** and **MACKAY** (pop. 250). Grocery, post office, restaurant and gas station with towing, diesel and major repair service. Mackay is 1.9 miles/3.1 km north of Nojack on a gravel road. Campgrounds 1 mile/1.6 km and 3 miles/4.8 km west of town on Highway 16. ▲

E 81.6 (131.4 km) PG 368.4 (592.8 km) Emergency phone.

E 84.6 (136.1 km) PG 365.4 (588.1 km) Private campground to north. ▲

E 89.5 (144 km) PG 360.5 (580.2 km) **NITON JUNCTION.** Hamlet has 2 gas stations with tires and parts, diesel, propane, car wash, pay phone, groceries, post office, 2 restaurants, lounge, motel. Private campground with full hookups. ▲

E 93.7 (150.8 km) PG 356.3 (573.4 km) **CARROT CREEK**, post office, grocery store, gas station, car wash and phone.

E 97.5 (157 km) PG 352.5 (567.2 km) **Junction** with Highway 32 which leads to Whitecourt and Highway 43, 42 miles/67.6 km north on paved road. (See **Milepost E 112.7** in the EAST ACCESS ROUTE section.)

E 102.1 (164.4 km) PG 347.9 (559.8 km) Wolf Lake public campground, 33 miles/53 km south on gravel road; 14 sites, pit toilets, tables, litter barrels. ▲

E 105 (169 km) PG 345 (555.2 km) Edson rest area to south with flush toilets, water, tables, shelter, phone and sani-dump.

E 106 (170.6 km) PG 344 (553.6 km) Rosevear Road; eastbound access to Edson rest area.

E 110 (177.1 km) PG 340 (547.1 km) Private campground to south. ▲

E 113.1 (182 km) PG 336.9 (542.2 km) McLeod River bridge.

E 114.9 (185 km) PG 335.1 (539.2 km) **EDSON** (pop. 7,323). Large highway community with 14 motels, many restaurants and gas stations; 18-hole golf course, indoor pool; hospital and RCMP post. Tourist information to south; turn left west bound onto 55th Street. There is camping at Lions Club Campground east of town (42 sites), and at Willmore Recreation Park, 3.7 miles/6 km south of town on the McLeod River. Campground resort, 5 miles/8 km east of Edson, with full hookups; open May to October. Edson's economy is based on coal mining, forestry, oil, natural gas and manufacturing.

Ernie O's Restaurant and Pub. See display ad this section.

The Guest House. See display ad this section.

E 123.2 (198.3 km) PG 326.8 (525.9 km) Food, gas, lodging and phone.

E 128 (206 km) PG 322 (518.2 km) Government campground to north adjacent to highway. ▲

E 133 (214 km) PG 317 (510.2 km) Small community of Marlboro to north. First view of Canadian Rockies westbound.

E 140.8 (226.6 km) PG 309.2 (497.6 km) Westbound-only turnout with picnic tables, pit toilets and litter barrels; generous, paved parking area.

E 142.7 (229.6 km) PG 307.3 (494.6 km) Eastbound-only turnout with litter barrels.

E 148.1 (238.3 km) PG 301.9 (485.9 km) Obed Lake public campground to north; 13 sites, firewood, tables, pit toilets and water. ▲

E 150.3 (241.9 km) PG 299.7 (482.3 km) **OBED.** Phone, gas and groceries.

E 156.4 (251.8 km) PG 293.6 (472.4 km) Obed Summit, highest elevation on the Yellowhead Highway at 3,819 feet/1,164m. Paved turnout with picnic tables, toilets and litter barrels; good view of the Rockies, weather permitting.

E 157.7 (253.9 km) PG 292.3 (470.3 km) Treed roadside turnout; generous parking area, picnic tables, toilets and litter barrels.

E 160.8 (258.8 km) PG 289.2 (465.4 km) Motel to south.

E 166.7 (268.3 km) PG 283.3 (455.9 km)

HINTON (pop. 8,537). All visitor facilities including hotels and motels, golf course, hospital, dentist, RCMP and recreation complex with indoor pool. Campground with 50 sites, hookups and dump station. Site of St. Regis (Alberta) Ltd. pulp mill; tours of mill complex may be arranged. ▲

E 171 (275.3 km) **PG 279** (448.9 km) South **junction** with Highway 40.

E 172.2 (277.1 km) **PG 277.8** (447.1 km) **Junction** with Bighorn Highway 40, which leads north 90 miles/145 km (paved) to Grande Cache then another 117 miles/188 km (gravel) to Grande Prairie. See BIG HORN HIGHWAY log on page 37. William A. Switzer Provincial Park 16.8 miles/27 km north; camping, picnicking, fishing. ▲

E 176.8 (284.5 km) **PG 273.2** (439.7 km) Maskuta Creek picnic area with tables, shelter, toilets and litter barrels.

E 177.8 (286.2 km) **PG 272.2** (438 km) Weigh scales and pay phone.

E 179 (288.1 km) **PG 271** (436.1 km) Public campground 3.1 miles/5 km north. ▲

E 181.5 (292.2 km) **PG 268.5** (432 km) Private campground, pay phone. ▲

E 182.4 (293.6 km) **PG 267.6** (430.6 km) Point of interest sign about Athabasca River to north.

E 182.9 (294.4 km) **PG 267.1** (429.8 km) Resort with lodging to north.

E 184.2 (296.5 km) **PG 265.8** (427.7 km) East entrance to Jasper National Park; public phones. Park fees charged on a per-person basis and must be paid by all visitors using facilities in Rocky Mountain national parks.

Highway 16 has restricted speed zones where wildlife sightings are frequent. Drive carefully and watch out for moose, elk, white-tailed and mule deer, mountain goats, bighorn sheep, and black and grizzly bears. *NOTE: It is illegal to feed, touch, disturb or hunt wildlife in the national park. All plants and natural objects are also protected and may not be removed or destroyed.*

E 185.6 (298.8 km) **PG 264.4** (425.4 km) Fiddle River bridge.

E 187.6 (302 km) **PG 262.4** (422.2 km) Weather permitting, layering in mountains is quite apparent. It is speculated that the Rockies were once part of a sea bed that was lifted from the water and folded. The visible layers are sedimentary deposits laid on the bottom of the sea.

E 189 (304.2 km) **PG 261** (420 km) **POCAHONTAS.** Grocery, motel, cafe and gas station with minor repair service. **Junction** with Miette Hot Springs Road, which leads 0.6 mile/1 km south to Park Service campground (140 sites) and 11 miles/17.7 km south to Miette Hot Springs and resort. There are 2 thermal pools; towels and bathing suits for rent; admission fee. Beautiful setting, look for mountain goats. ▲

E 192 (309 km) **PG 258** (415.2 km) Turnout with cairn to south. Mineral lick here is frequented by goats and sheep. Watch for wildlife, especially at dawn and dusk. Many turnouts next 25 miles/40 km westbound.

E 193 (310.6 km) **PG 257** (413.6 km) First Rocky River bridge westbound.

E 194.3 (312.7 km) **PG 255.7** (411.5 km) Second Rocky River bridge westbound.

E 203 (326.7 km) **PG 247** (397.5 km) Two bridges spanning the Athabasca River. Watch for elk and stone sheep.

E 205.1 (330.1 km) **PG 244.9** (394.1 km) Snaring River bridge.

E 206.7 (332.7 km) **PG 243.3** (391.5 km) Jasper airfield to south.

E 208.1 (335 km) **PG 241.9** (389.2 km) Snaring overflow camping south. ▲

E 208.4 (335.4 km) **PG 241.6** (388.8 km) Snaring rest area to south.

E 208.8 (336 km) **PG 241.2** (388.2 km) Palisades picnic area.

E 212.9 (342.6 km) **PG 237.1** (381.6 km) Access road to Jasper Park Lodge, Maligne Lake and park office. The area is home to a large population of harlequin ducks, endangered elsewhere.

E 215.8 (347.3 km) **PG 234.2** (376.9 km) **Junction** with Highway 93A. Lodging and restaurant to south.

E 216.6 (348.6 km) **PG 233.4** (375.6 km) Access to Jasper and **junction** with Highway 93, the scenic Icefields Parkway, south to Banff past Columbia Icefield.

Many residents in this area maintain hummingbird feeders. The 2 species of hummingbirds found in the Canadian Rockies are the Rufous and the Calliope.

Jasper is also in elk territory. Elk can be dangerous during calving (May through June) and mating (August through October), so stay back at least 40 paces.

NOTE: No fuel next 62.5 miles/100.6 km westbound.

E 217.1 (349.5 km) **PG 232.9** (374.7 km) Miette River.

E 222.2 (357.6 km) **PG 227.8** (366.6 km) Paved turnout to north with outhouses, litter barrels and interpretive sign about Yellowhead Pass. Many turnouts next 25 miles/40 km eastbound.

E 223.2 (359.3 km) **PG 226.8** (364.9 km) Meadow Creek.

E 223.4 (359.5 km) **PG 226.6** (364.7 km) Trailhead for Virl Lake, Dorothy Lake and Christine Lake.

E 226.1 (363.9 km) **PG 223.9** (360.3 km) Clairvaux Creek.

E 229.4 (369.3 km) **PG 220.6** (354.9 km) West entrance to Jasper National Park; park fee must be paid by all visitors using facilities in Rocky Mountain national parks.

E 231.6 (372.7 km) **PG 218.4** (351.5 km)

Yellowhead Pass (elev. 3,760 feet/1,146m), Alberta–British Columbia border. Named for an Iroquois trapper and guide who worked for the Hudson's Bay Co. in the early 1800s. His light-colored hair earned him the name Tete Jaune ("yellow head") from the French voyageurs.

East entrance to Mount Robson Provincial Park. Portal Lake picnic area with tables, toilets, information board and hiking trail.

TIME ZONE CHANGE: Alberta observes Mountain standard time. Most of British Columbia observes Pacific standard time. Both observe daylight saving time. See Time Zones in the GENERAL INFORMATION section for details.

E 232.8 (374.7 km) **PG 217.2** (349.5 km) Kilometrepost 75. Kilometreposts on Yellowhead Highway 16 reflect distances within highway maintenance districts; *The MILEPOST®* periodically notes these physical posts as reference points.

E 235.8 (379.6 km) **PG 214.2** (344.6 km) Rockingham Creek.

E 236.2 (380.1 km) **PG 213.8** (344.1 km) **Yellowhead Lake**; picnic tables, viewpoint, boat launch and fishing. 🐟

E 238 (383 km) **PG 212** (341.2 km) Lucerne Campground; 32 sites, picnic tables, drinking water, firewood and swimming; camping fee charged. ▲

E 239.3 (385.2 km) **PG 210.7** (339 km) Fraser Crossing rest area to south; litter barrels and toilets.

E 239.4 (385.3 km) **PG 210.6** (338.9 km) Fraser River bridge No. 1.

E 242.4 (390.1 km) **PG 207.6** (334.1 km) Fraser River bridge No. 2.

E 245.2 (394.6 km) **PG 204.8** (329.6 km) Kilometrepost 55.

E 246.2 (396.2 km) **PG 203.8** (328 km) Grant Brook Creek.

E 249 (400.8 km) **PG 201** (323.4 km) Moose Creek bridge.

E 251.1 (404.2 km) **PG 198.9** (320 km) Turnout at east end of Moose Lake; information kiosk, tables, litter barrels, toilet and

Watch for elk and other wildlife along Yellowhead Highway 16. (© Marlene Ford/Sahtu)

Overlook at Berg Lake, accessible by trail from Milepost E 268.8. (© Marlene Ford/Sahtu)

boat launch.

E 255.5 (411.2 km) PG 194.5 (313 km) Turnout with litter barrels.

E 257.5 (414.4 km) PG 192.5 (309.8 km) Kilometrepost 35.

E 263.7 (424.4 km) PG 186.3 (299.8 km) Paved turnout with litter barrels.

E 268 (431.3 km) PG 182 (292.9 km) Overlander Falls rest area to south; pit toilets and litter barrels. Hiking trail to Overlander Falls, about 30 minutes round-trip.

E 268.8 (432.7 km) PG 181.2 (291.4 km) Viewpoint of Mount Robson (elev. 12,972 feet/3,954m), highest peak in the Canadian Rockies, and Visitor Infocentre. Parking, picnic tables, restrooms, litter barrels, gas and restaurant. Berg Lake trailhead; hike-in campgrounds. Private campground north of highway. Robson Meadows government campground south of highway with 125 sites, dump station, showers, pay phone, interpretive programs, tables, firewood, flush toilets, water and horseshoe pits; group camping; camping fee charged. ▲

E 269.4 (433.6 km) PG 180.6 (290.6 km) Robson River government campground to north with 19 sites (some wheelchair-accessible), tables, firewood, pit toilets, showers, water and horseshoe pits; camping fee charged. ♿▲

E 269.8 (434.3 km) PG 180.2 (289.9 km) Kilometrepost 15.

E 269.9 (434.4 km) PG 180.1 (289.8 km) Robson River bridge. Look for Indian paint-

brush June through August. The bracts are orange-red while the petals are green.

E 270.3 (435.1 km) PG 179.7 (289.1 km) West entrance to Mount Robson Provincial Park. Turnout with litter barrels and statue.

E 270.5 (435.3 km) PG 179.5 (288.9 km) Gravel turnout to south.

E 271.4 (436.8 km) PG 178.6 (287.4 km) Swift Current Creek.

E 274.4 (441.7 km) PG 175.6 (282.5 km) Mount Terry Fox Provincial Park picnic area with tables, restrooms and viewing telescope. The information board here points out the location of Mount Terry Fox in the Selwyn Range of the Rocky Mountains. The peak was named in 1981 to honour cancer victim Terry Fox, who, before his death from the disease, raised some $25 million for cancer research during his attempt to run across Canada.

E 276.3 (444.7 km) PG 173.7 (280.5 km) Gravel turnout to north with Yellowhead Highway information sign.

E 276.4 (444.9 km) PG 173.6 (280.3 km) Rearguard Falls Provincial Park picnic area. Easy half-hour round-trip to falls viewpoint. Upper limit of 800-mile/1,300-km migration of Pacific salmon; look for chinook in late summer.

E 277.8 (447.1 km) PG 172.2 (277.1 km) Gravel turnout to south overlooking Fraser River.

E 278.2 (447.8 km) PG 171.8 (276.4 km) Weigh scales.

E 278.7 (448.6 km) PG 171.3 (275.6 km) Tete Jaune Cache rest area with tables, litter barrels and toilets.

E 279 (449.1 km) PG 171 (275.1 km) Junction with Yellowhead Highway 5 to the small community of TETE JAUNE CACHE (0.5 mile/0.8 km south of junction) and Kamloops (208 miles/335 km south), British Columbia's fourth largest settlement. Food, gas and lodging just west of the junction. Yellowhead Highway 5 opened in 1969. A year earlier, construction of the section of the highway east from Prince George to Tete Jaune Cache had connected Highway 16

with a rough road east to Jasper National Park. The final link in Northern Trans-provincial Highway 16 (now Yellowhead Highway 16)—between Prince George and Edmonton—officially opened in 1969.

E 279.1 (449.2 km) PG 170.9 (275 km) Turnoff for gas, general store and deli, camping and lodging.

NOTE: No fuel eastbound next 62.5 miles/100.6 km.

E 279.6 (450.1 km) PG 170.4 (274.1 km) Private lodging, restaurants.

E 283.1 (455.7 km) PG 166.9 (268.5 km) Spittal Creek Interpretive Forest; hiking trails, tables, litter barrels and toilets. Kilometrepost 140.

E 288.2 (463.8 km) PG 161.8 (260.4 km) Private resort. Lodging, restaurant.

E 289.1 (465.3 km) PG 160.9 (258.9 km) Small River rest area by stream with tables, toilets and litter barrels.

E 293.6 (472.5 km) PG 156.4 (251.7 km) Horsey Creek.

E 295.4 (475.5 km) PG 154.6 (248.7 km) Kilometrepost 120.

E 300 (482.9 km) PG 150 (241.3 km) Turnoff to south for settlement of Dunster; gas and general store.

E 303.8 (489 km) PG 146.2 (235.2 km) Holiday Creek rest area with toilets, picnic tables, litter barrel and hiking trails.

E 304.3 (489.7 km) PG 145.7 (234.5 km) Baker Creek rest area with tables, litter barrels and toilets.

E 308.5 (496.6 km) PG 141.5 (227.6 km) Kilometrepost 100.

E 308.9 (497.2 km) PG 141.1 (227 km) Nevin Creek.

E 312 (502.1 km) PG 138 (222.1 km) Turnouts at both ends of Holmes River bridge.

E 317.4 (510.8 km) PG 132.6 (213.4 km) **Beaverview Campsite.** See display ad this section. ▲

E 317.9 (511.6 km) PG 132.1 (212.6 km) Fraser River bridge. A forest fire swept through the Robson Valley in 1912. As you look at the sides of the mountain to the north of the highway, it is possible to distinguish the new growth which has taken place in the last 81 years.

E 318.2 (512.1 km) PG 131.8 (212.1 km) Turnout to north with litter barrels.

E 318.8 (513.1 km) PG 131.2 (211.1 km) McBRIDE (pop. 700; elev. 2,369 feet/722.1m), located in the Robson Valley by the Fraser River. The Park Ranges of the Rocky Mountains are to the northeast and the Cariboo Mountains are to the southeast. A road leads to Teare Mountain lookout for a spectacular view of countryside. The village of McBride was established in 1913 as a divisional point on the railroad and was named for Richard

McBride, then premier of British Columbia. Forest products are a major industry here today.

Visitor Information: Visitor Infocentre located in railcar on south side of Highway 16. Look for the carved grizzly bear family in front. When the Infocentre isn't open, try the McBride Village Office. Located beside the railcar in the same parking lot, it is open 9 A.M. to 5 P.M.

McBride has all visitor facilities, including 5 hotels/motels, 2 bed and breakfasts, 2 supermarkets, 2 convenience/video stores, clothing stores, restaurants, pharmacy, hospital and gas stations. A library, museum and neighborhood pub are 1.9 miles/3 km from town. There is a private campground just east of town. Dump station located at the gas station. ▲

While in McBride, watch wood ducks, scoters, teals and more at the Horseshoe Lake Bird Watch. In late summer, see the salmon run in the Holmes River. In winter, go cross-country skiing on developed trails and snowmobiling in the backcountry. Helicopter service available for fly-in skiing and hiking.

McBride Chevron. See display ad this section.

North Country Lodge. See display ad this section.

NOTE: Next gas westbound is 90.7 miles/146 km from here (Purden Lake).

E 321.9 (518.1 km) **PG 128.1** (206.1 km) Dore River bridge.

E 326.7 (525.8 km) **PG 123.3** (198.4 km) Macintosh Creek.

E 328.8 (529.2 km) **PG 121.2** (195 km) Clyde Creek.

E 333.1 (536.2 km) **PG 116.9** (188 km) Kilometrepost 60.

E 336.9 (542.3 km) **PG 113.1** (181.9 km) West Twin Creek bridge.

E 343.6 (553.1 km) **PG 106.4** (171.1 km) Goat River bridge. Paved rest area to north with tables, toilets and litter barrels.

E 346.7 (558 km) **PG 103.3** (166.2 km) Little LaSalle Recreation Area and BC Forest Service site. Small lake, small wharf, toilet.

E 351.2 (565.2 km) **PG 98.8** (159 km) Snowshoe Creek.

E 351.8 (566.2 km) **PG 98.2** (158 km) Kilometrepost 30.

E 354.9 (571.2 km) **PG 95.1** (153 km) Catfish Creek.

E 360.7 (580.6 km) **PG 89.3** (143.6 km) Ptarmigan Creek bridge.

E 363.8 (585.6 km) **PG 86.2** (138.6 km) Turnout with litter barrels to north.

E 369.2 (594.1 km) **PG 80.8** (130.1 km) Dome Creek.

E 371.5 (597.9 km) **PG 78.5** (126.3 km) Food, phone.

E 373.3 (600.8 km) **PG 76.7** (123.4 km) Slim Creek paved rest area to south with information kiosk, tables, playground, litter barrels and wheelchair-accessible toilets. Watch for bears. ♿

E 373.4 (601 km) **PG 76.6** (123.2 km) Ministry of Highways camp.

E 374.1 (602.1 km) **PG 75.9** (122.1 km) Slim Creek bridge.

E 382.5 (615.6 km) **PG 67.5** (108.6 km) Kilometrepost 100.

E 385.6 (620.7 km) **PG 64.4** (103.5 km) Driscol Creek.

E 386.4 (621.9 km) **PG 63.6** (102.3 km) Forests in this area have been destroyed by the hemlock looper, an insect which has killed or damaged over 45.9 million cubic feet/1.3 million cubic metres of wood in British Columbia.

E 387.6 (623.9 km) **PG 62.4** (100.3 km) Gravel turnout with litter barrel to north.

E 388.9 (626 km) **PG 61.1** (98.2 km) Lunate Creek.

E 391.8 (630.6 km) **PG 58.2** (93.6 km) Grizzly hiking trail to south.

E 392 (630.9 km) **PG 58** (93.3 km) Hungary Creek. Watch for Ministry of Forests signs indicating the year in which a logged area was replanted. Wildflowers include fireweed, mid-July through August.

E 394.8 (635.4 km) **PG 55.2** (88.8 km) Kilometrepost 80.

E 395.8 (637 km) **PG 54.2** (87.2 km) Sugarbowl Creek.

E 400.5 (644.6 km) **PG 49.5** (79.6 km) Paved turnout with litter barrel to north.

E 407 (655.1 km) **PG 43** (69.1 km) Kilometrepost 60.

E 408.2 (657 km) **PG 41.8** (67.2 km) Kenneth Creek.

E 408.4 (657.4 km) **PG 41.6** (66.8 km) Purden Mountain ski resort.

E 409.5 (659.1 km) **PG 40.5** (65.1 km) Purden Lake resort with gas, phone, lodging and camping. ▲

Purden Lake and Ski Resorts. Campground with lakefront camping; hookups. Cabin rentals, boat rentals, boat launch. Good rainbow trout fishing. Cafe, gas station (propane, diesel, unleaded). Cafe and gas open 7 A.M. to 8 P.M. Ski area with 23 runs, 2 double chairs, T-bar, day lodge, ski rentals, ski school, cafeteria. P.O. Box 1239, Prince George, BC V2L 4V3. (250) 565-7777.
[ADVERTISEMENT] ▲

NOTE: Next gas eastbound is 90.7 miles/146 km from here (McBride).

E 411.2 (661.9 km) **PG 38.8** (62.3 km) **Purden Lake** Provincial Park, 1.9 miles/3 km from highway; 78 campsites, 48 picnic sites, tables, water, dump station, firewood, playground and horseshoe pits. This recreation area offers a sandy beach, change houses, swimming, walking trails, waterskiing and boat launch. Good rainbow fishing to 4 lbs., trolling. Camping fee charged. ◣▲

E 412.6 (664.1 km) **PG 37.4** (60.1 km) Bowron River bridge. Paved rest area to north beside river, on west side of bridge; toilets, tables and litter barrels. Entrance on curve; use care.

E 420.7 (677.1 km) **PG 29.3** (47.1 km) Kilometrepost 40.

E 421 (677.6 km) **PG 29** (46.6 km) Vama Vama Creek.

E 424 (682.4 km) **PG 26** (41.8 km) Wansa Creek.

E 427.1 (687.4 km) **PG 22.9** (36.8 km) Willow River bridge. Rest area at west end of bridge beside river; tables, litter barrels, toilets and nature trail. The 1.2-mile-/1.9-km-long Willow River Forest Interpretation Trail is an easy 45-minute walk.

E 429.5 (691.3 km) **PG 20.5** (32.9 km) Bowes Creek.

Moose along Yellowhead Highway 16.
(© David Creith/Sahtu)

E 429.7 (691.6 km) **PG 20.3** (32.6 km) Turnout to north with litter barrels and information board on 1961 forest fire and moose habitat. Circle trail to moose observation site.

E 433 (697 km) **PG 17** (27.2 km) Kilometrepost 20.

E 435.2 (700.5 km) **PG 14.8** (23.7 km) Tabor Mountain ski hill.

E 435.4 (700.8 km) **PG 14.6** (23.4 km) Gravel turnout to north with litter barrels.

E 437.6 (704.3 km) **PG 12.4** (19.9 km) Access to **Tabor Lake**; good fishing for rainbow in spring. ◣▲

E 444.8 (715.9 km) **PG 5.2** (8.3 km) **Junction,** Highway 16B with Highway 97 south bypass. See page 58 in the WEST ACCESS ROUTE for log of Highway 97 South.

E 450 (724.2 km) **PG 0 PRINCE**

GEORGE (see description on pages 58-61). **Junction** with Highway 97 north to Dawson Creek and the beginning of the Alaska Highway.

Turn to page 61 in the WEST ACCESS ROUTE section for the log of Highway 97 North. Continue west on Yellowhead Highway 16 for Prince Rupert (log follows).

Yellowhead Highway 16 Log

(continued)
This section of the log shows distance from Prince George (PG) followed by distance from Prince Rupert (PR).

PG 0 PR 456 (733.8 km) Junction of Highways 16 and 97 (Central Avenue/Cariboo Highway) in Prince George. From Prince George to Prince Rupert, Highway 16 is a 2-lane highway with 3-lane passing stretches. Fairly straight, with no high summits, the highway follows the valleys of the Nechako, Bulkley and Skeena rivers, paralleling the Canadian National Railway route. There are few services between towns.

PG 1.4 (2.3 km) PR 454.6 (731.6 km) Junction with Domano Blvd.; access to bed and breakfast.

PG 3 (4.8 km) PR 453 (729 km) Blue Spruce RV Park and Campground to north. ▲

PG 4.8 (7.7 km) PR 451.2 (726.1 km) West Lake Provincial Park 8 miles/12.9 km south; day-use area with picnic shelter, swimming, fishing and boat launch. ◣

PG 14.9 (24 km) PR 441.1 (709.9 km) North Country Arts & Crafts. See display ad this section.

PG 32.1 (51.7 km) PR 423.9 (682.2 km) Rest area to north with picnic tables, toilets and litter barrels.

PG 38 (61.2 km) PR 418 (672.7 km)

Access to lakeside resort and fishing at **Cluculz Lake** (not visible from highway). Rainbow to 3³/₄ lbs. by trolling, use snell hook and worms; kokanee to 1¹/₂ lbs., troll with snell hook and worms, in spring; char to 57 lbs., use large flatfish, spoons, plugs and weights, early spring and late fall; whitefish to 5 lbs., year-round. Very good fishing in spring; ice goes out about the first week of May. Good ice fishing December to March. In September kokanee are at their peak. *Lake gets rough when windy.* ◣▲

PG 39.1 (62.9 km) PR 416.9 (670.9 km) Cluculz rest area to south with flush toilets (summer only), picnic tables and litter barrels.

PG 39.5 (63.6 km) PR 416.5 (670.3 km) Brookside Resort. Stay in a quiet pine forest next to Cluculz Creek. Serviced and unserviced sites. 50- and 30-amp spacious, shaded,

level pull-throughs. Tent and camper sites with tables. Picnic shelters with barbecue pits. Renovated, clean washrooms. Sanidump, laundromat, convenience store, snack bar, driving range. Free hot showers for registered guests. Ice. Propane. Telephone. Proposed: gasoline and boat gas. VISA and MasterCard. RR # 1, Site 16, Comp. 75, Vanderhoof, BC V0J 3A0. Phone 1-888-441-0035. [ADVERTISEMENT] ▲

PG 58.7 (94.5 km) PR 397.3 (639.4 km) Dave's RV Park. See display ad this section. ▲

Vanderhoof

PG 60.5 (97.4 km) PR 395.5 (636.5 km). Population: 4,025; area 12,000. **Emergency Services: Police,** phone (250) 567-2222. **Fire Department,** phone (250) 567-2345. **Ambulance,** phone 112-562-7241. **Hospital,** St. John's, Northside District, phone (250) 567-2211.

Visitor Information: Visitor Infocentre downtown on Burrard Avenue, 1 block off Highway 16. Write Vanderhoof & District Chamber of Commerce, Box 126-MP, Vanderhoof, BC V0J 3A0; phone (250) 567-2124.

Elevation: 2,086 feet/636m. **Radio:** CJCI 620, CFPR-FM 96.7, CKPG 550, CIVH 1340, CIRX-FM 95.9. **Television:** Channels 2, 4, 5,

6, 8. **Newspapers:** *Omineca Express–Bugle* (weekly). **Transportation: Air**—Vanderhoof airport, 2 miles/3.2 km from intersection of Highways 16 and 27; 5,000-foot/1,524-m paved runway. Seaplane landings on Nechako River at corner of View Street and Boundary Avenue. **Railroad**—VIA Rail, station at 2222 Church Ave. **Bus**—Greyhound.

Vanderhoof is the geographical centre of British Columbia. The city was named for Chicago publisher Herbert Vanderhoof, who founded the village in 1914 when he was associated with the Grand Trunk Development Co. Today, Vanderhoof is the supply and distribution centre for a large agricultural, lumbering and mining area.

The community's history is preserved at Vanderhoof Heritage Village Museum, just off Highway 16. Relocated pioneer structures furnished with period artifacts recall the early days of the Nechako Valley.

Located on the Nechako River, Vanderhoof is a stopping place in April and September for thousands of migrating waterfowl. The river flats upstream of the bridge are a bird sanctuary. Pelicans have been spotted feeding at Tachick Lake south of town.

There are 7 hotels and motels and 19 restaurants in the town. All shopping facilities and several gas stations. Dump station at Dave's RV Park and Riverside Campground. Municipal campground is on Burrard Avenue close to downtown; second municipal campground west of town on Highway 16. An 18-hole golf course is located 1.9 miles/3.1 km north of town. ▲

Area attractions include Fort St. James (see description page 225), Tachick Lake and Kenney Dam. Follow the gravel road southwest from Vanderhoof 60 miles/97 km to Kenney Dam. At the time of its construction in 1951, it was North America's largest earth-filled dam. Near the dam site are Cheslatta Falls and Nechako River canyon (good area for rockhounding). Beautiful Tachick Lake (18 miles/29 km south) has a modern log fishing resort and a lodge which serves European food. Also access to Sai' Kuz Park on Nulki Lake, with annual fishing derby, Native dancers, Native crafts, gambling and more (phone 250/567-4916); see fishing information following. Kenney Dam Road turnoff is at the Kwik-Save gas station on Highway 16.

Nulki Lake, 10 miles/16 km west on Kenney Dam Road, rainbow to 6 or 7 lbs., average 2 lbs., use worms, year-round. **Tachick Lake,** 18 miles/29 km south on Kenney Dam Road, rainbow 2 to 7 lbs. year-round, largest fish in the area were taken from this lake; several small lakes in the area abound with rainbow and kokanee. Fishing charters available at Vanderhoof airport. ◣

Muk Tuk's Chuckwagon Cafe. See display ad this section.

Siesta Motel. See display ad this section.

Fort St. James

Fort St. James

Located 37 miles/59.5 km north of Vanderhoof on Highway 27. **Population:** 1,983. **Emergency Services: Police,** phone (250) 996-8269. **Ambulance:** phone 1-562-7241. **Elevation:** 2,208 feet/673m. **Radio:** CKPG 550, CJCI 1480; CBC-FM 107.0.

Fort St. James is the home of **FORT ST. JAMES NATIONAL HISTORIC SITE.** Established in 1806 by Simon Fraser as a fur trading post for the Northwest Co., Fort St. James served throughout the 19th century as headquarters for the Hudson's Bay Co.'s New Caledonia fur trade district. The fur warehouse, fish cache, men's house, officers' dwelling and trade shop have been restored in 1896-style and are open to the public. Check with the Visitor Infocentre regarding program information.

From mid-May through September, visitors may experience "living history." Staff members, dressed in period costumes, play out historic scenarios, demonstrate old-time skills and provide interesting facts about fur trade history. Hours are 9 A.M. to 5 P.M. daily. For the remainder of the year, the site is closed. Admission fee.

The historic site and village are located on Stuart Lake. Named for John Stuart, the man who succeeded Simon Fraser as head of the New Caledonia district, the 59-mile-/95-km-long lake is the southernmost in a 3-lake chain which provides hundreds of miles of boating and fishing. Fort St. James also boasts the Nation Lakes, a chain of 4 lakes (Tsayta, Indata, Tchentlo and Chuchi) connected by the Nation River.

Attractions include the Our Lady of Good Hope Catholic Church and the Chief Kwah burial site. The recently renovated church is one of the oldest in British Columbia. Open for summer evening services only, check schedule. Chief Kwah was one of the first Carrier Indian chiefs to confront early white explorers. His burial site is located on the Nak'azdli Indian Reserve at the mouth of the Stuart River. At Cottonwood Park on the shore of Lake Stuart, look for a model of a Junkers airplane, which depicts the Fort's major role in early bush flying in Northern British Columbia.

Fort St. James has a hotel, 2 lodges, resort, 4 motels, 2 bed and breakfasts, 3 private campgrounds, and a number of surrounding lodges and settlements, such as Tachie, Manson Creek and Germansen Landing in the Omineca Mountains. Other services in Fort St. James include 3 gas stations, 4 dump stations, a government marina, 2 private marinas and several restaurants. The district also has a theatre and 2 shopping centres. Picnicking and swimming at Cottonwood Park on Stuart Lake. A 9-hole golf

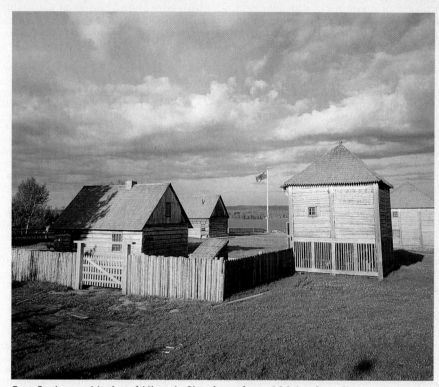

Fort St. James National Historic Site dates from 1806, when Simon Fraser established a fur trading post for the Northwest Co. (Eero Sorila)

course overlooks Stuart Lake; rentals available. Murray Ridge ski area, a 20-minute drive from town, has 21 downhill ski runs and 18.5 miles/30 km of cross-country ski trails.

Stuart River Campgrounds. Treed sites, tenting to full hookups, showers and laundry, firepits and firewood, pay phone. Playgrounds, horseshoe pits; marina with launching ramp and moorage space. Great fishing! River and lake charters, fishing licenses and tackle. Your hosts, George and Heather Malbeuf, Box 306, Fort St. James, BC V0J 1P0. (250) 996-8690. [ADVERTISEMENT] ▲

Camping is also available at **Paarens Beach** Provincial Park, located 6.8 miles/10.9 km off Highway 27 on Sowchea Bay Road; 36 campsites, picnic shelter, picnic tables, toilets, water, firepits, boat launch and swimming;

camping fee. Sowchea Bay Recreation Area, located 10.6 miles/17.1 km off Highway 27 on Sowchea Bay Road, has 30 campsites, camping fee, picnic tables, toilets, water, firepits boat launch and swimming. ▲

Good fishing in **Stuart Lake** for rainbow and char (to trophy size), kokanee and Dolly Varden. ◢

Return to Milepost PG 60.5 or PG 64.7 Yellowhead Highway 16

FORT ST. JAMES ADVERTISERS

Fort St. James Chamber
   of Commerce ......Ph. (250) 996-7023
Stuart River
   Campground ......Ph. (250) 996-8690

Heading for the ferries in Prince Rupert? See the MARINE ACCESS ROUTES section for schedules and fares.

Yellowhead Highway 16 Log
(continued)

PG 60.5 (97.4 km) **PR 395.5** (636.5 km) First **junction** westbound with Highway 27, which extends north from Vanderhoof several hundred miles. The 37 miles/60 km to Fort St. James are fully paved; see page 225.

PG 61.1 (98.3 km) **PR 394.9** (635.5 km) Vanderhoof Municipal Campground, pleasantly situated on a creek. ▲

PG 64.7 (104.1 km) **PR 391.3** (629.7 km) Second **junction** westbound with Highway 27 (see description at **Milepost PG 60.5**). This route skirts Vanderhoof. Truck weigh scales to north.

PG 73.7 (118.6 km) **PR 382.3** (615.2 km) Sawmill to south.

PG 83.8 (134.9 km) **PR 372.2** (599 km) Turnout to south with view of Nechako River. The Grand Trunk Pacific Railway was completed near this site in 1914. The railroad (later the Canadian National) linked Prince Rupert, a deep-water port, with interior British Columbia. Entering Lakes District. This high country has over 300 freshwater lakes.

PG 84.3 (135.7 km) **PR 371.7** (598.2 km) **FORT FRASER** (pop. 600). **Radio:** CBC-FM 102.9. Small community with food, gas, propane, lodging and first-aid station. Gas station with hot showers, convenience store and restaurant. Named for Simon Fraser, who established a trading post here in 1806. Now a supply centre for surrounding farms and sawmills. The last spike of the Grand Trunk Railway was driven here on April 7, 1914.

PG 85.1 (137 km) **PR 370.9** (596.9 km) Nechako River bridge. Turnout to south with parking, litter barrels and access to **Nechako River;** fishing for rainbow and Dolly Varden, June to fall. At the east end of Fraser Lake, the Nautley River—less than a mile long—drains into the Nechako River. ◄━

PG 87 (140 km) **PR 369** (593.8 km) Beaumont Provincial Park, on beautiful **Fraser Lake,** north side of highway; site of original Fort Fraser. Boat launch, swimming, hiking, fishing, 49 campsites, picnic tables, firewood, flush toilets, water, playground, horseshoe pits, dump station. Fishing for rainbow and lake trout, burbot, sturgeon and Dolly Varden. ◄━▲

PG 89.2 (143.5 km) **PR 366.8** (590.3 km) **Pipers Glen RV Resort.** See display ad this section. ▲

PG 90.7 (146 km) **PR 365.3** (587.9 km) Dry William Lake rest area to south with picnic tables, toilets and litter barrels.

PG 91.7 (147.6 km) **PR 364.3** (586.3 km) **Orange Valley Motel, RV Park and Campground.** Easy access featuring level sites, large pull-throughs, electricity, water, some with sewer. Free showers, flush toilets, sanidump, treed shaded sites with picnic tables. Firepits, firewood; freezer space available. Quiet relaxed setting. Pay phone, hiking trails, beaver dam. Phone (250) 699-6350. ▲
[ADVERTISEMENT]

PG 93.8 (151 km) **PR 362.2** (582.9 km) Fraser Lake sawmill to north.

PG 95.5 (153.7 km) **PR 360.5** (580.2 km) Rest area to north. Trail to Fraser Lake.

PG 97.5 (156.9 km) **PR 358.5** (576.9 km) **FRASER LAKE** (pop. 1,400; elev. 2,580 feet/ 786m). **Visitor Information:** Visitor Infocentre and museum in log building at east edge of town. **Radio:** CJCI 1450. Small community with all facilities. Created by Endako Mines Ltd. in 1964 on an older townsite; named after the explorer Simon Fraser. Endako Mines Ltd. began operating in 1965 and was Canada's largest molybdenum mine until production slowed in 1982. Mining resumed in 1986. Mine tours are available on Wednesdays; check with the Visitor Infocentre for reservations. Also located here is Fraser Lake Sawmills, the town's largest employer.

PG 100 (160.9 km) **PR 356** (572.9 km) **Junction** with main access road south to scenic Francois Lake; also accessible via roads from Burns Lake to Houston. Francois Lake Road (chip seal surfacing) leads south 7 miles/11 km to the east end of Francois Lake (where the Stellako River flows from the lake) and back to Highway 16 at Endako. (It does not link up to the Francois Lake Ferry, south of Burns Lake.) Molyhills golf course and several resorts with camping, cabins and boats are located on this scenic rural road along the lake through the Glenannan area. ▲

Glenannan Tourist Area. See display ad this section.

Francois Lake, good fishing for rainbow to 5 lbs., May to October; kokanee to $^3/_4$ lb., use flashers, willow leaf, flashers with worms, flatfish or spinners, August and September; char to 30 lbs., use large flatfish or spoon, June and July. **Stellako River** is considered one of British Columbia's better fly-fishing streams with rainbow over 2 lbs., all summer; whitefish averaging 1 lb., year-round. ◄━

PG 100.1 (161.1 km) **PR 355.9** (572.7 km) Bridge over Stellako River. Highway passes through the Stellako Indian Reserve.

PG 105.9 (170.4 km) **PR 350.1** (563.4 km) **ENDAKO.** A small highway community with grocery (closed Sunday), post office, pub and gas station with minor repair service. Turnoff for molybdenum mine just east of town. Several private campgrounds are located along Francois Lake Road to the south in the Glenannan area. ▲

PG 107 (172.2 km) **PR 349** (561.6 km) Endako River bridge.

PG 110.5 (177.8 km) **PR 345.5** (556 km) Savory rest area to north beside Watskin Creek.

PG 113.3 (182.3 km) **PR 342.7** (551.5 km) Ross Creek.

PG 122.1 (196.5 km) **PR 333.9** (537.3 km) Paved turnout to south.

PG 126.1 (202.9 km) **PR 329.9** (530.9 km) Babine Forest Products sawmill to south.

PG 133.7 (215.2 km) **PR 322.3** (518.7 km) Rest area to south with toilet, tables, litter barrels and Tintagel Cairn point of interest.

PG 137.3 (221 km) **PR 318.7** (512.9 km) **Burns Lake K.O.A.,** a day's drive from Prince Rupert ferry. Cabins, tenting to full hookups, store, heated showers, laundromat, game room, playground. Mini-golf, lake swimming. Open May 1 to Sept. 30. Pay phone. Your host, Ed Brown, Box 491, Burns Lake, BC V0J 1E0. Phone (250) 692-3105, 1-800-562-0905.
[ADVERTISEMENT] ▲

PG 139.9 (225.1 km) **PR 316.1** (508.7 km) Welcome to Burns Lake sign.

PG 140.9 (226.8 km) **PR 315.1** (507.1 km) **Junction** with scenic Highway 35 (paved) south to **Tchesinkut, Francois, Takysie** and **Ootsa** lakes; lodging, camping and fishing. Another of the Yellowhead's popular fishing areas with a variety of family-owned camping and cabin resorts. ◄━▲

Sandy's RV and Camping Resort. Over 50 full service, easy access sites along the shores of Francois Lake. Hot showers, laundromat, boat rentals, launch, marina, cabins and more. Enjoy northern hospitality only 18 paved miles south of Burns Lake on Highway 35 located on a true fishing lake. Rainbow, kokanee and lake trout. May 15–Oct. 1. Phone/fax (250) 695-6321. Box 42, Burns Lake, BC V0J 1E0. [ADVERTISEMENT] ▲

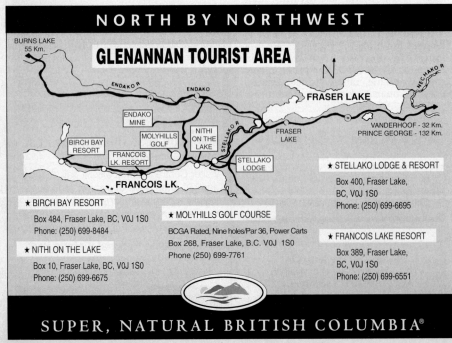

NORTH BY NORTHWEST

GLENANNAN TOURIST AREA

BURNS LAKE 55 Km.

ENDAKO R
ENDAKO
ENDAKO MINE
MOLYHILLS GOLF
BIRCH BAY RESORT
FRANCOIS LK. RESORT
NITHI ON THE LAKE
STELLAKO R
FRASER LAKE
STELLAKO LODGE
FRANCOIS LK.

NECHAKO R
FRASER LAKE
VANDERHOOF - 32 Km.
PRINCE GEORGE - 132 Km.

★ STELLAKO LODGE & RESORT
Box 400, Fraser Lake, BC, V0J 1S0
Phone: (250) 699-6695

★ BIRCH BAY RESORT
Box 484, Fraser Lake, BC, V0J 1S0
Phone: (250) 699-8484

★ MOLYHILLS GOLF COURSE
BCGA Rated, Nine holes/Par 36, Power Carts
Box 268, Fraser Lake, B.C. V0J 1S0
Phone (250) 699-7761

★ FRANCOIS LAKE RESORT
Box 389, Fraser Lake, BC, V0J 1S0
Phone: (250) 699-6551

★ NITHI ON THE LAKE
Box 10, Fraser Lake, BC, V0J 1S0
Phone: (250) 699-6675

SUPER, NATURAL BRITISH COLUMBIA®

Burns Lake

PG 141.3 (227.4 km) PR 314.7 (506.4 km) **Population:** 2,500; area 10,000. **Visitor Information:** Government Visitor Infocentre along Highway 16 on the west side of the village. The Infocentre also houses a museum, art gallery and the Chamber of Commerce.

Elevation: 2,320 feet/707m. **Radio:** CFLD 730, CJFW-FM 92.9, CBC-FM 99.1. Transportation: Greyhound Bus, VIA Rail.

Burns Lake began about 1911 as a construction camp for the Grand Trunk Pacific Railway. Forestry is the economic mainstay of the area today, with ranching and tourism also important.

Located in the heart of the Lakes District, Burns Lake boasts "3,000 miles of fishing." Species include rainbow trout, char and salmon. Small family-owned fishing resorts offering lodging and camping are tucked along these lakes, offering quality vacation experiences.

Burns Lake is also the gateway to Tweedsmuir Provincial Park, 50 miles/80 km south. This huge wilderness park is accessible by boat, trail and air.

Rock hounds can visit Eagle Creek opal deposits, a short drive south of Burns Lake (not recommended for motorhomes). It is about an hour's hike to the opal beds from the parking lot.

There are 4 gas stations, a dump station on Railway Avenue, 5 hotels/motels, 5 bed and breakfasts, 14 restaurants, several gift shops—many of which feature local crafts and artists—and 3 shopping malls.

The Burns Lake Municipal Park, also called Radley Beach, is located next to the civic centre and offers a pleasant setting for a picnic. On the north shore of the lake, the park has picnic tables, a small pier, a municipal campground and swimming area. ▲

Travelers can also visit Nourse Creek Falls, take a self-guided forest tour or go hiking.

From Burns Lake, Highway 35 (paved) extends south 18 miles/29 km past Tchesinkut Lake to Francois Lake ferry landing. A free 36-car ferry departs from the south shore on the hour, from the north shore on the half-hour. From the south shore of Francois Lake, Highway 35 continues to Takysie Lake and Ootsa Lake, with access to a number of other fishing lakes. There are several resorts along Highway 35 offering camping and lodging. Gas stations, stores and food service are also available. ⊷▲

Yellowhead Highway 16 Log
(continued)

PG 146 (235 km) PR 310 (498.9 km) Side road leads north to Babine Lake, the longest natural lake in the province. One of British Columbia's most important salmon producing lakes, Babine Lake drains into the Skeena River. Excellent fishing for char and trout in summer. At Mile 15/24.1 km on this road is Ethel F. Wilson Provincial Park on Pinkut Lake; 10 campsites, fishing, swimming, drinking water, toilets, firewood, picnic tables, boat launch. Tours of nearby Pinkut Fish Hatchery available. Look for pictographs on cliffs across from hatchery. Pendleton Bay Provincial Park on Babine Lake, open May to October, offers 20 campsites, picnic tables, fishing, swimming and boat launch. Resorts with cabins and camping on Babine Lake. ⊷▲

Babine Lake Resort, 48 km from Burns Lake. British Columbia's largest natural body of water. Good fishing. Photographer's dream. Self-contained cabins, power, water hookups, showers, tenting, boats, smokehouses, store, licensed dining by reservation only. Ausserdem sprechen wir deutsch. Accepting VISA. Bill and Traude Hoff welcome you. Box 528, Burns Lake. (250) 964-4692 or 1-600-700-1026. [ADVERTISEMENT] ▲

PG 150 (241.4 km) PR 306 (492.4 km) Small community of DECKER LAKE.

Decker Lake, good char and trout fishing; fly-fishing in Endako River, which joins Decker and Burns lakes. ⊷

PG 153.3 (246.7 km) PR 302.7 (487.1 km) Palling rest area with picnic tables, toilets and litter barrels.

PG 157.1 (252.8 km) PR 298.9 (481 km) Baker Lake airstrip to south is used by firefighting tankers. Weather station. Emergency telephone.

PG 160.2 (257.8 km) PR 295.8 (476 km) Rose Lake to south.

PG 165.2 (265.9 km) PR 290.8 (468 km) Broman Lake, rainbow and char to 4 lbs., use white-winged flies, spring and summer. ⊷

PG 169.1 (272.1 km) PR 286.9 (461.7 km) Six Mile Summit (elev. 4,669 feet/1,423m) to west. China Nose Mountain, with steep west-facing cliff, is visible to the south.

PG 175.5 (282.4 km) PR 280.5 (451.4 km) TOPLEY (pop. 300). Grocery, post office, cafe, motel and gas station. Turn north here for Babine Lake Recreation Area. This paved side road leads north to Topley Landing and Granisle on Babine Lake (descriptions follow). From its junction with the highway at Topley, mileages are as follows: Mile 23.6/38 km, private lodge; Mile 24.4/39.3 km, turnoff to village of Topley Landing; Mile 28.8/46.3 km, Fulton River spawning channel; Mile 28/45.1 km, Red Bluff Provincial Park with 43 campsites, picnicking and day-use facilities, boat launch, drinking water, toilets, firewood, swimming, fishing and hiking; Mile 30.6/49 km, Lions Beach Park with 16 campsites, picnicking and day-use facilities, boat launch, dock, toilets, firewood, swimming and fishing; Mile 31.4/50.5 km, Granisle; Mile 33.4/53.8 km, begin 16-mile/25.7-km gravel road to Smithers Landing Road, which connects Smithers Landing and Smithers. *CAUTION: Watch for moose along road.* ⊷▲

TOPLEY LANDING has several resorts and an unmaintained provincial park. It is also the home of the restored, historic Church of Angels; open June through

Fulton River teems with spawning sockeye salmon. (Judy Parkin, staff)

September. This rustic log church has a collage of angels, a museum and gift shop.

The government-operated Fulton River spawning channel has 2 major spawning channels on the river that connect Fulton Lake and Babine Lake. Babine Lake, which flows into the Skeena River, is one of the largest freshwater habitats for sockeye salmon. The salmon enhancement project at Fulton River produces about 95 million sockeye fry annually. The sockeye run takes place in August and September. Tours may be available at hatchery office.

GRANISLE (pop. 600) was established in 1965 as a company town for the Granisle Copper Mine. In 1972, Noranda Bell Mines Copper Division went into operation. Granisle Copper was closed in 1982 and the Noranda mine was closed in 1992. During mining excavations, a mammoth skeleton was unearthed. The fossilized remains were donated to the Museum of Civilization in Ottawa–Hull. Granisle has become a retirement community and remains a resort area for fishing, boating, waterskiing and camping on Babine Lake. Facilities at Granisle include a convenience store, liquor outlet, hotel with licensed restaurant, resort condominiums, post office, museum, boat rentals, marina and tackle shop. Dump station, showers, laundromat and fresh water available at the Visitor Infocentre. ▲

Grande Isles Resort. See display ad on page 227.

Babine Lake, rainbow 6 to 8 lbs.; lake trout to 40 lbs., use spoons, flashers and red-and-white spoons, May through November. When fishing early in the year, use a short troll. ⌁

PG 175.8 (282.9 km) PR 280.2 (450.9 km) Rest area to south with view of coastal mountains.

PG 193.9 (312 km) PR 262.1 (421.8 km) **Shady Rest RV Park.** See display ad this section. ▲

Houston

PG 194.3 (312.7 km) PR 261.7 (421.2 km) **Population:** 3,960. **Emergency Services: Police,** phone (250) 845-2204. **Ambulance,** phone 112-562-7241. **Visitor Information:** Visitor Infocentre in log building on Highway 16 across from the mall; open year-round. Write Houston Visitor Infocentre, Box 396, Houston, BC V0J 1Z0, or phone (250) 845-7640.

Elevation: 1,949 feet/594m. **Radio:** CFBV 1450, CFPR-FM 102.1, CJFW-FM 105.5. **Transportation:** Greyhound bus, VIA Rail.

Established in the early 1900s, Houston was a tie-cutting centre during construction of the Grand Trunk Pacific Railway in 1912. It was named for Prince Rupert newspaperman John Houston, the former mayor of Nelson, BC. Logging continued to support the local economy with the rapid growth of mills and planer mills in the 1940s and 1950s. Houston was incorporated as a village in 1957.

The Equity Silver Mine began production in 1980. Production ceased in January 1994 and equipment was dismantled.

Today, the main industry in Houston is forest products. The 2 large sawmills here, Houston Forest Products and Northwood Pulp and Timber, offer forestry-awareness tours. The Chamber of Commerce and Visitor Infocentre arrange tours of the sawmills and also offer a day-long tour through the area's forests to provide a first-hand look at the forest industry.

Hunting, canoeing, cross-country skiing and especially sportfishing are major attractions here with the Bulkley River, nearby Morice River and several lakes. Look for the World's Largest Fly Fishing Rod on display at the Visitor Infocentre. The 60-foot-long anodized aluminum fly rod was designed by a local avid fly fisherman and built by local volunteers. (The 21-inch fly is a fluorescent "Skykomish Sunrise.")

Houston has all visitor facilities, including motels, campgrounds, restaurants, gas stations, a shopping centre and golf courses. ▲

Pleasant Valley Motel. 52 newly renovated rooms with good beds. Some non-smoking and kitchenette units. Handicap access. Cable TV. Public telephone. Guest laundromat. Full-service restaurant, well-known for homestyle cooking and generous portions. For reservations call collect (250) 845-2246, fax (250) 845-3065. 3030 Highway 16, Houston, BC V0J 1Z0. [ADVERTISEMENT] ♿

Yellowhead Highway 16 Log
(continued)

PG 197.4 (317.7 km) PR 258.6 (416.2 km) **Junction** with the Morice River access road which extends 52 miles/84 km south to Morice Lake. Approximately 20 miles/32 km along the Morice River Road you can turn east on a gravel road which leads past Owen Lake and Nadina River Road to Francois Lake. From Francois Lake ferry landing Highway 35 leads north to Burns Lake.

The 2 famous salmon and steelhead streams, **Morice** and **Bulkley,** unite near Houston, and it is possible to fish scores of pools all along the Morice River. *NOTE: Special requirements apply to fishing these streams; check with Fish and Game office.* ⌁

PG 198.5 (319.4 km) PR 257.5 (414.4 km) Bulkley River bridge; picnic spot with tables, litter barrel and toilets.

PG 202.5 (325.9 km) PR 253.5 (408 km) View of Morice River valley eastbound. Westbound travelers are in the Bulkley River valley.

PG 205.3 (330.4 km) PR 250.7 (403.5

HOUSTON ADVERTISERS

Houston and District Chamber
   of Commerce ....Ph. (250) 845-7640
Houston Motor Inn...........Ph. (250) 845-7112
Pleasant Valley Motel.......Ph. (250) 845-2246

km) Hungry Hill Summit (elev. 2,769 feet/844m). To the north are the snow-capped peaks of the Babine Mountains, to the west is the Hudson Bay Range.

PG 222.8 (358.6 km) PR 233.2 (375.3 km) Bulkley View paved rest area with picnic tables, toilets and litter barrels.

PG 225.6 (363.1 km) PR 230.4 (370.8 km) Ft. Telkwa R.V. Park. See display ad this section. ▲

PG 226 (363.7 km) PR 230 (370.1 km) TELKWA (pop. 959). A pleasant village at the confluence of the Telkwa and Bulkley rivers (you can fish from Riverside Street or the riverbanks). Visitor Inøfocentre at the village office and museum. Facilities include a grocery, post office and a gas station with auto repair. Lodging at Douglas Motel, dining at 3 restaurants. A unique shop found here is Horsfield Leather, which specializes in handmade fishing rod cases, leather water bottles and other leather goods. Fishing and hunting information, licenses and supplies available at the general store. Kinsmen Barbecue is held over Labour Day weekend; games, contests and demolition derby. Eddy Park, on the western edge of town beside the Bulkley River, is a good spot for picnicking (look for the wishing well). St. Stephen's Anglican Church was built in 1911 and the bell and English gate added in 1921. Other Heritage buildings date back to 1908.

Douglas Motel beside beautiful Bulkley River. Riverview units, suites, log cabin with fireplace in relaxing resort atmosphere. Hot pool, sauna complex, kitchens, cablevision, queen beds, electric heat, summer ceiling fans, picnic area, firepit, barbecues, horseshoe pitch, summer outdoor sports equipment. Salmon and steelhead fishing. Walking distance to stores, restaurants and lake. VISA and MasterCard. Douglas Family, (250) 846-5679. [ADVERTISEMENT]

PG 226.5 (364.5 km) PR 229.5 (369.3 km) Turnoff to north for Tyhee Lake Provincial Park; 55 campsites, 20 picnic tables, dump station, hiking trails, fishing, swimming, boat launch. Seaplane base at lake; charter fly-in fishing. ✦▲

Also turnoff here on the Telkwa High Road, which intersects with Babine Lake access road (gravel), which leads 46 miles/74 km north to Smithers Landing on Babine Lake and 56 miles/90 km to Granisle.

Tyhee Lake, rainbow and lake trout to 2 lbs., June through August; Kamloops trout to 2 lbs. Babine River, steelhead to 40 lbs., late fall. Telkwa River, spring and coho salmon to 24 lbs., summer to fall. ✦

PG 231.5 (372.6 km) PR 224.5 (361.3 km) Second turnoff westbound for Babine Lake.

PG 232.8 (374.6 km) PR 223.2 (359.2 km) Riverside Recreation Centre; golf, restaurant and campground. ▲

PG 233.1 (375.1 km) PR 222.9 (358.7 km) Turnoff to north on gravel road for Driftwood Canyon Provincial Park; picnic area and toilets. Fossil beds in shale outcroppings along creekbank. This gravel side road continues north to Smithers Landing.

PG 233.7 (376.1 km) PR 222.3 (357.7 km) Bridge over Bulkley River.

Smithers

PG 235.4 (378.8 km) PR 220.6 (355 km). Population: 5,000; area 30,000. Emergency Services: Police, phone (250) 847-3233. Hospital and Poison Centre, 3950 8th Ave., phone (250) 847-2611. Ambulance, phone 1-562-7241. Visitor Information: Visitor Infocentre at the intersection of Highway 16 and Main Street, east side of highway, in the railcar adjacent to the museum; open daily June through August. The Chamber of Commerce, located above the museum in the Central Park Building, provides information year-round.

Elevation: 1,621 feet/494m. Climate:

SMITHERS ADVERTISERS

Aspen Motor Inn ....Ph. (250) 847-4551
Capri Motor Inn................Ph. (250) 847-4226
Riverside Recreation
  Centre.........................Ph. (250) 847-3229
Smitty's Family
  Restaurant ....Ph. (250) 847-3357
Wash The Works..............Ph. (250) 847-4177

Relatively warmer and drier than mountainous areas to the west, average temperature in July is 58°F/14°C, in January 14°F/-10°C; annual precipitation, 13 inches. Radio: CFBV 1230, CFPR-FM 97.5. Television: Channels 5, 13 and cable. Newspaper: Interior News (weekly).

Transportation: Air—Scheduled service to Vancouver and Terrace via Canadian Airlines International. Daily flights to Prince George, Terrace and Burns Lake via Central Mountain Air. Railroad—VIA Rail. Bus—Greyhound. Car Rentals—Available.

Sitting amidst rugged mountains, the alpine flavour of the town has been enhanced by Swiss-style storefronts that have been added to many of the buildings. Reconstructed in 1979, Main Street offers many shops and restaurants. Incorporated as a village in 1921, Smithers officially became

Lake Kathlyn, just west of Smithers, does not permit power boats. (Eero Sorila)

a town in Canada's centennial year, 1967. The original site was chosen in 1913 by construction crews working on the Grand Trunk Pacific Railway (the town was named for one-time chairman of the railway A.W. Smithers). Today it is a distribution and supply centre for farms, mills and mines in the area.

Smithers is the largest town in the Bulkley Valley and the site of Hudson Bay Mountain, a popular ski area (skiing from November to mid-April).

Smithers has several motels, gas stations, restaurants, laundromat/car wash and good shopping. Government liquor store located on Queen Street at Broadway Avenue. There are 2 18-hole golf courses, both with rentals and clubhouses.

There is a municipal campground with security and firewood (no hookups) at Riverside Park on the Bulkley River; turn north at the museum across from Main Street and drive up the hill about a mile and watch for sign. There are private campgrounds located east and west of town; see highway log. A dump station is located beside the railcar Infocentre on the corner of Highway 16 and Main Street. ▲

Special events include the Bulkley Valley Fall Fair, held on the last weekend in August each year, one of the largest agricultural exhibitions in the province. The Midsummer Music Festival, June 21–22, 1997, features local, regional and national artists.

Smithers offers a number of scenic drives.

Hudson Bay Mountain (elev. 8,700 feet/2,652m) is a 14-mile/23-km drive from Highway 16; the plateau above timberline at the ski area is a good spot for summer hikes. In the winter months, Smithers boasts one of the largest ski hills in northern British Columbia. A 6,000-foot/1,829-m triple chair and 2 T-bars climb the 1,750-foot/533-m vertical, offering skiers 18 different runs.

Fossil hunters should drive to Driftwood Canyon Provincial Park; turn off Highway 16 just east of the Bulkley River bridge (travelers are advised to stop first at the Visitor Infocentre in town for a map and directions). A display at the park illustrates the fossils, such as metasequoia, a type of redwood which occurs in the shale formation.

Adams Igloo Wildlife Museum, just west of town on Highway 16, has an excellent display of mammals found in British Columbia.

A beautiful spot not to be missed is Twin Falls and Glacier Gulch. Take the 4-mile-/6.4-km-long gravel road (steep in places) from Highway 16 on the western edge of town.

A 2.2-mile-/3.5-km-long interpretive nature trail with native wildlife and plant species is 10 miles/16 km west of Smithers on the Hudson Bay Mountain Ski Hill road in Smithers Community Forest. This trail can also be used in winter for cross-country skiing, and connects to other cross-country ski trails. Detailed maps of the area showing all hiking trails are available at the infocentre.

An extensive list of lake and river fishing spots in the area, with information on boat launches and boat rentals, is available from the Smithers District Chamber of Commerce, Box 2379, Smithers, BC V0J 2N0; phone (250) 847-9854; or ask at the Visitor Infocentre. ◄

Moose, mule deer, grizzly and black bears, mountain goats and caribou are found in the area, and guides and outfitters are available locally. All species of grouse can be hunted in the Bulkley Valley during the fall. Information is available from the Fish and Wildlife Branch office in Smithers.

Yellowhead Highway 16 Log
(continued)

PG 237.8 (382.7 km) **PR 218.2** (351.1 km) Paved access road to Lake Kathlyn. There is a municipal park with small beach and boat launch located here. Powerboats not permitted. Closed to waterfowl hunting. Side road continues 4 miles/6.4 km (gravel) to Twin Falls and Glacier Gulch.

PG 238.9 (384.5 km) **PR 217.1** (349.4 km) Road to north leads to Smithers airport.

PG 241.2 (388.2 km) **PR 214.8** (345.7 km) **Glacier View RV Park.** Wake up to a panoramic view of the Hudson Bay Glacier. Eight level gravel sites with 15-/30-amp service and water hookups. Dry pull-throughs up to 55 feet. Pit toilets. Walking distance to Wildlife Museum. Easy access. Reservations: RR 1, S 9 C 31, Smithers, BC V0J 2N0, (250) 847-3961. [ADVERTISEMENT] ▲

PG 241.4 (388.5 km) **PR 214.6** (345.4 km) **Adams Igloo Wildlife Museum.** The finest collection of big game animals, fur-bearers and birds native to British Columbia. Mounted life-size and displayed in their natural habitat. The inside mural, painted by leading wildlife artist Tom Sander, gives a 3-dimensional impression for realism. Stop at the White Dome, 6 miles west of Smithers beside one of the highway's most beautiful viewpoints. Fur rugs and souvenirs for sale. Ted Moon, Curator. [ADVERTISEMENT]

PG 241.5 (388.6 km) **PR 214.5** (345.2 km) Hudson Bay rest area to west with picnic tables, toilets and litter barrels. Beautiful view of Hudson Bay Mountain.

PG 249.5 (401.5 km) **PR 206.5** (332.3 km) Trout Creek bridge. Store with groceries, post office and phone; fishing licenses available.

PG 255.5 (411.2 km) **PR 200.5** (322.7 km) Turnout to north with picnic tables and view of Bulkley River and Moricetown Canyon; good photo stop.

PG 255.7 (411.5 km) **PR 200.3** (322.3 km) Short side road on the north side of the highway leads to Moricetown Canyon and Falls on the Bulkley River and Moricetown campground. For centuries a famous Indian fishing spot, Indians may still be seen here gaffing, jigging and netting salmon in July and August. A worthwhile stop. ▲

PG 257.9 (415 km) PR 198.1 (318.8 km) MORICETOWN (pop. 680; elev. 1,341 feet/409m). **Radio:** CBC-FM 96.5. Moricetown has a gas station with minor repair service and diesel fuel. There is a handicraft store. A campground is located in Moricetown Canyon (turnoff at **Milepost PG 255.7**). Moricetown is an Indian reserve and village, the oldest settlement in the Bulkley Valley. Traditionally, the Native people (Wet'su-wet'en) took advantage of the narrow canyon to trap salmon. The centuries-old Indian settlement ('Kyah Wiget) is now named after Father A.G. Morice, a Roman Catholic missionary. Born in France, Father Morice came to British Columbia in 1880 and worked with the Indians of northern British Columbia from 1885 to 1904. He achieved world recognition for his writings in anthropology, ethnology and history.

PG 271.5 (436.9 km) PR 184.5 (296.9 km) Turnoff to north for Forest Service campsite (7.5 miles/12.1 km) with pit toilets, tables and litter barrels. Fishing in **Suskwa River**; coho salmon to 10 lbs., use tee-spinners in July; steelhead to 20 lbs., use Kitamat #32 and soft bobbers in late fall. ◄▲

PG 276.5 (445 km) PR 179.5 (288.9 km) Turnoff to north for **Ross Lake** Provincial Park; 25 picnic sites, boat launch (no powerboats), swimming. Fishing for rainbow to 4 lbs. ◄

PG 278.5 (448.2 km) PR 177.5 (285.7 km) Turnout with litter barrel and Hazelton area map.

PG 278.8 (448.7 km) PR 177.2 (285.2 km) Entering New Hazelton (see description following), the first of 3 communities westbound sharing the name Hazelton; the others are Hazelton and South Hazelton.

PG 279 (449 km) PR 177 (284.8 km) Junction of Highway 16 with Highway 62 to Hazelton, 'Ksan and Kispiox (descriptions follow). The turnoff for Highway 62 is located just west of the railway overpass in New Hazelton, as you leave the community westbound on Highway 16. The easy-to-miss turn is on the north side (right for westbound travelers) of Highway 16 between the overpass and the Visitor Infocentre at the base of the hill.

New Hazelton

PG 279 (449 km) PR 177 (284.8 km) Junction of Highway 16 and Highway 62 to Hazelton, 'Ksan and Kispiox. **Population:** area 1,300. **Emergency Services: Police,** phone (250) 842-5244. **Visitor Information:** Visitor Infocentre in 2-story log building at the junction. Look for the 3 statues representing the gold rush

HAZELTON AREA ADVERTISERS

Hazeltons' Deli, The ....Ph. (250) 842-5622
Hazeltons Travel Info Centre ....Hwy. 16
Kispiox River Resort &
   Campground ....Ph. (250) 842-6182
'Ksan Campground..........Ph. (250) 842-5297
Robber's Roost Lodge .....Ph. (250) 842-6916
Sportsman
   Kispiox Lodge ....Ph. 1-888-547-7469
28 Inn................................Ph. (250) 842-6006

Hazelton/Kitwanga Area

packer Cataline, the Northwest miner, and the Upper Skeena logger. Museum located in Infocentre.

Elevation: 1,150 feet/351m. **Radio:** CBC 1170. **Transportation:** VIA Rail. Greyhound bus.

This small highway community has gas stations, major auto repair, restaurants, cafes, post office, general store, a hotel and a motel. Laundromat, propane, sporting goods, and hunting and fishing licenses available in town. Mount Rocher Deboule,

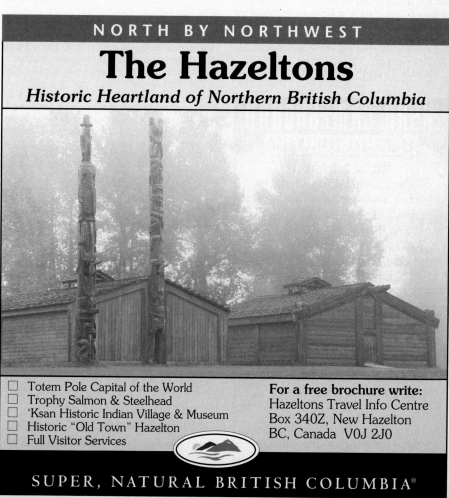

NORTH BY NORTHWEST

The Hazeltons
Historic Heartland of Northern British Columbia

☐ Totem Pole Capital of the World
☐ Trophy Salmon & Steelhead
☐ 'Ksan Historic Indian Village & Museum
☐ Historic "Old Town" Hazelton
☐ Full Visitor Services

For a free brochure write:
Hazeltons Travel Info Centre
Box 340Z, New Hazelton
BC, Canada V0J 2J0

SUPER, NATURAL BRITISH COLUMBIA®

elev. 8,000 feet/2,438m, towers behind the town.

Attractions here include historic Hazelton, the Indian village of 'Ksan and sportfishing the Bulkley and Kispiox rivers. Descriptions follow.

HAZELTON. Situated at the confluence of the Skeena and Bulkley rivers, Hazelton grew up at "The Forks" as a trans-shipping point at the head of navigation on the Skeena and a wintering place for miners and prospectors from the rigorous Interior. Thomas Hankin established a Hudson's Bay Co. trading post here in 1868. The name Hazelton comes from the numerous hazelnut bushes growing on the flats.

Cataline, famous pioneer packer and traveler, is buried near here in an unmarked grave at Pioneer Cemetery. Jean Caux (his real name) was a Basque who, from 1852 to 1912, with loaded mules plodding 12 miles/ 19 km a day, supplied mining and construction camps from Yale and Ashcroft northward through Hazelton, where he often wintered. His mule trails became roads; his exploits are legends.

For some years, before the arrival of the railroad and highways, supplies for trading posts at Bear and Babine lakes and the Omineca goldfields moved by riverboat from the coast to Hazelton and from there over trails to the backcountry. Some of the Yukon gold rushers passed through Hazelton on their way to the Klondike, pack trains having made the trip from Hazelton to Telegraph Creek over the old Telegraph Trail as early as 1874.

This community has reconstructed much of what the town was like in the 1890s. Look for the antique machinery downtown. The history of the Hazelton area can be traced by car on the Hand of History tour. Pick up a brochure from the Visitor Infocentre showing the location of the 19 historic sites on the driving tour.

'KSAN INDIAN VILLAGE Museum, a

Mount Rocher Deboule dominates the landscape in the Hazeltons. (Judy Parkin, staff)

replica Gitksan Indian village, is 4.5 miles/7.2 km from Highway 16. It was constructed at the junction of the Bulkley and Skeena rivers by the 'Ksan Assoc. with the assistance of the governments of Canada and British Columbia. There are 6 communal houses, totem poles and dugout canoes. At the Carving House of All Times, master carvers produce Native arts and crafts which can be purchased in the Today House of the Arts.

For a nominal charge from May to September, you can join a guided tour of the communal houses. Performances of traditional dancing and singing are presented every Friday evening during July and August in the Wolf House.

A well-maintained full-service trailer park and campground on the banks of the Skeena and Bulkley rivers is operated by the Gitanmaax Indian Band from the Gitanmaax Reserve. ▲

KISPIOX (pop. 825) Indian village and 3 fishing resorts are 20 miles/32 km north on a good paved road at the confluence of the

Skeena and Kispiox rivers. Kispiox is noted for its stand of totems. There is a market garden (fresh vegetables) located approximately 7 miles/11 km north on the Kispiox Road (about 2 miles/ 3.2 km before the Kispiox totem poles). Camping, cabins and fishing at lodges and campgrounds in the valley. Valley residents host the Kispiox Rodeo the first weekend of June. This excellent event has run annually since 1952. ◄▲

Kispiox River Resort & Campground. Beautiful location on banks of Kispiox River in peaceful valley setting. Excellent fishing throughout the year including spring salmon, cutthroat and rainbow trout, Dolly Varden and steelhead. Campground. Housekeeping cabins. Showers. Laundry. Tenters welcome. Fishing licenses. Guides. Tackle. 26 miles from Highway 16. Kispiox Valley Road. RR 1, Hazelton, BC V0J 1Y0. (250) 842-6182. [ADVERTISEMENT] ▲

Sportsman Kispiox Lodge. Attractive river setting. Deluxe cabins and rooms. Complete dining and lounge facilities with homecooked meals. Wilderness trail rides, hiking, historical, wildlife and natural history tours, whitewater rafting, canoeing and scenic river tours. Unlimited angling opportunities. Our specialty: workshops, retreats and seminars. Kispiox Valley Road, R.R. 1, Box 2, Site M, Hazelton, BC V0J 1Y0. 1-888-547-7469; fax (250) 842-6458. [ADVERTISEMENT]

Bulkley River, Dolly Varden to 5 lbs.;

spring salmon, mid-July to mid-August; coho salmon 4 to 12 lbs., Aug. 15 through September, flies, spoons and spinners; steelhead to 20 lbs., July through November, flies, Kitamats, weighted spoons and soft bobbers. **Kispiox River** is famous for its trophy-sized steelhead. Check on regulations and obtain a fishing license before your arrival. Fishing is done with single-hook only, with catch-release for steelhead between Aug. 15 and Sept. 30. Season is July 1 to Nov. 30 for salmon, trout and steelhead. Excellent fly-fishing waters: spring salmon, July to early August; coho salmon, late August to early September; steelhead from September until freezeup. Sizable Dolly Vardens and cutthroat. Steelhead average 20 lbs., with some catches over 30 lbs.

Yellowhead Highway 16 Log
(continued)

PG 281.4 (452.9 km) **PR 174.6** (281 km) Turnoff to north for 2-mile/3.2-km loop road through small community of **SOUTH HAZELTON**; restaurant, general store, gas station with minor repair, lodging.

PG 285 (458.7 km) **PR 171** (275.2 km) **Seeley Lake** Provincial Park; 20 campsites, drinking water, pit toilets, firewood, sani-dump, day-use area with picnic tables, swimming, fishing.

PG 294.7 (474.3 km) **PR 161.3** (259.6 km) Skeena Crossing. Historic Canadian National Railways bridge (see plaque at Kitseguecla).

PG 295.9 (476.2 km) **PR 160.1** (257.6 km) **KITSEGUECLA**, Indian village. Totem poles throughout village are classic examples, still in original locations. Historical plaque about Skeena Crossing.

PG 306.6 (493.4 km) **PR 149.4** (240.4 km) Gas station and cafe at **junction** with Cassiar Highway (BC Highway 37). Bridge across Skeena River to Kitwanga and Cassiar Highway to Stewart, Hyder, AK, and Alaska Highway. This is the principal access to the Cassiar Highway. Alternate access via Nass Road at **Milepost PG 369.3**. See CASSIAR HIGHWAY section.

Highway passes Seven Sisters peaks; the highest is 9,140 feet/2,786m.

PG 309.5 (498.1 km) **PR 146.5** (235.8 km) **Gitksan Paintbrush Native Arts & Crafts.** Silver and gold jewelry: rings, earrings, bracelets. Limited edition prints and originals. Smoked moosehide moccasins, beaded leatherwork. Wood carvings, cedar baskets. Clothing and souvenirs. Quality merchandise, most from local artists. Excellent prices. Easy access. Summer hours 9 A.M.–7 P.M. P.O. Box 97, Kitwanga, BC V0J 2A0. Phone or fax (250) 849-5085. [ADVERTISEMENT]

PG 309.8 (498.6 km) **PR 146.2** (235.3 km) **Seven Sisters RV Park and Campground.** Outstanding value. Beautiful park-like setting. Many treed sites. Fresh water, sani-dump, picnic tables at every site, flush toilets, shower, firepits with free firewood, all for $9. Excellent salmon fishing close by. Tenters and cyclists welcome. (250) 849-5489 for reservations. Box 338, Kitwanga, BC V0J 2A0. [ADVERTISEMENT]

PG 312.4 (502.7 km) **PR 143.6** (231.1 km) Boulder Creek rest area; parking for large vehicles; toilets, litter barrels and picnic tables.

PG 316.5 (509.3 km) **PR 139.5** (224.5 km) Gravel turnout to north with litter barrel.

PG 318.2 (512.1 km) **PR 137.8** (221.8 km) CEDARVALE, cafe. Loop road through

The peaks of the Seven Sisters are visible on a clear day from turnout at Milepost PG 316.5. (Judy Parkin, staff)

rural setting. Historical plaque about Holy City.

Cedarvale Café. Known for quality food and friendly, efficient service. Specializing in homemade burgers, pies, shakes and fries, with delicious daily specials. Relaxing atmosphere, camping spots and picnic tables. Tour buses welcome. Summer hours: Monday–Friday 7 A.M.–10 P.M., Saturday and Sunday 8 A.M.–8 P.M. Winters hours: Monday–Friday 9 A.M.–9 P.M., Saturday and Sunday 10 A.M.–8 P.M. (250) 849-5539. [ADVERTISEMENT]

PG 322.9 (519.6 km) **PR 133.1** (214.2 km) Gravel turnout to north on Skeena River.

PG 324.8 (522.7 km) **PR 131.2** (211.1 km) Turnout with historical plaque about Skeena riverboats. Watch for bears fishing the river for salmon in late July and early August.

PG 329.3 (529.9 km) **PR 126.7** (203.9 km) Gravel turnout to north with litter barrel.

PG 335.8 (540.4 km) **PR 120.2** (193.4 km) Watch for fallen rock on this stretch of highway.

PG 345.2 (555.5 km) **PR 110.8** (178.3 km) Rest area on river with water pump, picnic tables, toilets and litter barrels. Historical plaque about Skeena River steamboats.

PG 345.5 (556 km) **PR 110.5** (177.8 km) Skeena Cellulose private bridge across Skeena River to access tree farms on north side.

PG 352.6 (567.4 km) **PR 103.4** (166.4 km) Tiny chapel to south serves small community of **USK**; the village is reached via the reaction ferry seen to north. The nondenominational chapel is a replica of the pioneer church that stood in Usk until 1936, when the Skeena River flooded, sweeping away the village and the church. The only item from the church to survive was the Bible, which was found floating atop a small pine table.

PG 354.9 (571.1 km) **PR 101.1** (162.7 km) Side road leads 0.5 mile/0.8 km south to **Kleanza Creek** Provincial Park; 21 campsites, 25 picnic sites, fishing, drinking water, toilets, firewood, wheelchair access. Short trail to remains from Cassiar Hydraulic Mining Co. gold-sluicing operations here (1911–14).

PG 360.7 (580.5 km) **PR 95.3** (153.4 km) Gas and lodging. **Copper (Zymoetz) River**, can be fished from Highway 16 or follow local maps. Coho salmon to 10 lbs., use teespinners in July; steelhead to 20 lbs., check locally for season and restrictions.

PG 362.4 (583.2 km) **PR 93.6** (150.6 km) Turnout to north with tourist information sign and area map.

PG 365.1 (587.6 km) **PR 90.9** (146.3 km) Four-way stop; east access to Terrace and **junction** with Highway 37 south to Kitimat. For access to downtown Terrace, turn north here and continue over 1-lane bridge. For west access to Terrace and continuation of Yellowhead Highway 16 westbound, go straight at intersection. Turn off for Kitimat, 37 miles/60 km south via Highway 37.

Kitimat is a major port and home to several industries. (See log of HIGHWAY 37 SOUTH on page 234.)

PG 365.6 (588.4 km) **PR 90.4** (145.5 km) Bridge over **Skeena River**. Ferry Island municipal campground; 68 sites, some electrical hookups. Covered picnic shelters, barbecues, walking trails and a fishing bar are also available.

Westbound, highway crosses railway overpass.

PG 366.2 (589.3 km) **PR 89.8** (144.5 km) Terrace Chamber of Commerce Visitor Infocentre.

PG 366.3 (589.5 km) **PR 89.7** (144.4 km) Stoplight; west access to Terrace. Turn north at intersection for downtown (description of Terrace begins on page 235).

Continue through intersection on Highway 16 westbound for Prince Rupert, *(Continues on page 235)*

Highway 37 South Log

Fishermen line the banks of the Kitimat River for steelhead and salmon. (Staff)

Distance is measured from the junction with Yellowhead Highway 16 (J).

J 0.9 (1.4 km) Krumm Road. Turn east for golf course.

J 3.1 (5 km) Terrace–Kitimat airport access road.

J 7.9 (12.7 km) Lakelse Lake Provincial Park parking area and trail to Gruchy's Beach.

J 8.7 (14 km) Lakelse Lake Provincial Park parking areas and picnic area; tables, toilets, showers, changehouses and beach. Park headquarters located here.

J 10.6 (17.1 km) Waterlily Bay; food, lodging, boat launch.

J 11.4 (18.3 km) Lakelse Lake Provincial Park Furlong Bay campground and picnic area; 156 vehicle and tent campsites, nature trails, swimming, sandy beach, flush toilets, showers, dump station, boat launch, drinking water, wheelchair access, firewood and interpretive programs. ♿▲

13.8 (22.2 km) Onion Lake hiking and ski trails to west.

J 20.6 (33.2 km) Access to Kitimat River.

J 27.4 (44.1 km) Kitimat Airpark landing strip for small planes.

J 34.8 (56 km) Hirsch Creek Park to west; picnic area, camping, fishing and hiking. ◄▲

J 35 (56.3 km) Hirsch Creek bridge.

J 35.8 (57.6 km) Kitimat Travel Infocentre to east.

J 36.2 (58.3 km) Minette Bay Road leads east to MK Bay Marina.

J 36.6 (58.9 km) Viewpoint of Douglas Channel and city map. Picnic tables, garden.

Kitimat

J 37.6 (60.5 km) Located at the head of Douglas Channel. **Population:** 12,000. **Emergency Services: RCMP**, phone (250) 632-7111. **Fire Department**, phone (250) 639-9111. **Ambulance**, phone (250) 632-5433. **Hospital**, phone (250) 632-2121. **Radio:** CKTK 1230; CBC-FM 101.1, CJFW-FM 103.1. **Newspaper:** *The News Advertiser* (weekly); *Northern Sentinel* (weekly).

This community was planned and built in the early 1950s when the B.C. government attracted Alcan (Aluminum Co. of Canada) to establish a smelter here. Today, Kitimat is a major port and home to several industries. Free tours are available (primarily in summer, reservations recommended) at Alcan, (250) 639-8259; Eurocan Pulp and Paper, (250) 639-3597; Methanex Corp., (250) 639-9292; and Kitimat fish hatchery, (250) 639-9616. Tour Mike's Wildlife Museum to see over 100 mounts; admission fee; (250) 632-7083.

Kitimat's location at the head of Douglas Channel makes it a popular boating, fishing and scuba diving destination. There are several charter operators.

Kitimat has all visitor facilities, including a modern shopping mall, restaurants and motels; library, theatre, swimming pool and gym; and an 18-hole golf course. Many scenic hiking trails are available. A free guide to area day hikes is available at the Visitor Infocentre. The Centennial Museum is located at city centre. Information on local Native art, canoe trips and heli-adventures available at the Chamber of Commerce, Box 214 (M), Kitimat, BC V8C 2G7; phone 1-800-664-6554 or

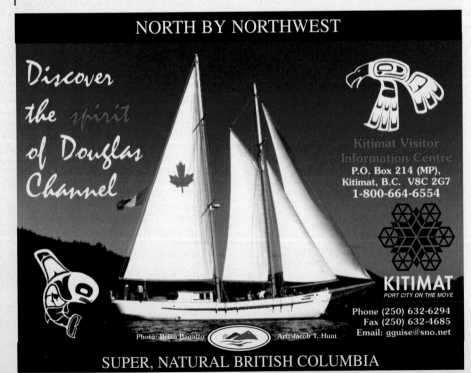

KITIMAT ADVERTISERS

Alcan Smelters and
  Chemicals Ltd. ....Ph. (250) 639-8259
Kitimat Chamber
  of Commerce ....Ph. (250) 632-6294
MK Bay Marina ....Ph. (250) 632-6401

(250) 632-6294; fax (250) 632-4685.

There is camping at Radley Park in town; electrical hookups, showers, fishing, toilets, playground and dump station. (Radley Park—on the other side of the river—is also the site of a 165-foot/50-m Sitka spruce, largest of its kind in the province.) There is also camping at Hirsch Creek Park on the edge of town and private campgrounds. ◄▲

Local fishermen line the banks of the **Kitimat River** in May for the steelhead run. Chinook salmon run in June and July. Coho run from August into September. ◄

Kitimat also offers many winter activities, including cross-country skiing and indoor ice rinks. Downhill skiing at nearby Terrace and Smithers.

Return to Milepost PG 365.1
Yellowhead Highway 16

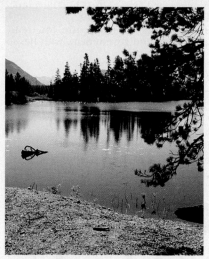

Onion Lake at Milepost J 13.8 on Highway 37 South. (Judy Parkin, staff)

(Continued from page 233)
eastbound for Prince George.
CAUTION: No gas or services available between Terrace and Prince Rupert.

Terrace

Located on the Skeena River. City centre is located north of Highway 16: Exit at overpass (**PG 366.3**) or at Highway 37 junction (**PG 365.1**). **Population:** 12,000; area 20,000. **Emergency Services:** Police, fire and ambulance located at intersection of Eby Street and Highway 16. **Police**, phone (250) 635-4911. **Fire Department**, phone (250) 638-8121. **Ambulance**, phone (250) 638-1102. **Hospital**, phone (250) 635-2211.

Visitor Information: Visitor Infocentre located in the chamber of commerce log building at **Milepost PG 366.2**. Open daily in summer, 9 A.M. to 8 P.M.; weekdays in winter, 8:30 A.M. to 4:30 P.M. Write 4511 Keith Ave, Terrace, BC V8G 1K1; phone (250) 635-2063. Information also available from Municipal Hall, #5-3215 Eby St.; open weekdays, phone (250) 635-6311.

Elevation: 220 feet/67m. **Climate:** Average summer temperature is 69°F/21°C; yearly rainfall 36 inches, snowfall 71.5 inches. **Radio:** CFTK 590; CFPR-FM 95.3, CJFW-FM 103.9. **Television:** 8 channels (cable). **Newspapers:** *Terrace Standard* (weekly) *Terrace Times* (weekly).

Terrace has become an important service stop for motorists heading up the Cassiar Highway to the Alaska Highway. It is the last large retail-commercial centre for travelers

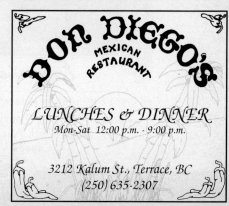

until they reach the similar-sized community of Whitehorse, YT.

Tom Thornhill, the first white settler, found an Indian village just east of the present location of Terrace in 1892. When stern-wheelers were plying the Skeena, the first farmer in the area, George Little, gave land to the community that became a port of call and post office in 1905. Originally it was known as Little Town, and later was named Terrace because of the natural terraces cut by the river. The village site was laid out in 1910 and the Grand Trunk Pacific Railway reached Terrace in 1914. The municipality was incorporated in 1927.

Terrace is a regional centre for trade, entertainment and government, with ties to the forestry industry.

ACCOMMODATIONS/VISITOR SERVICES

There are 17 motels/hotels, 20 restaurants and 2 shopping centres. The government liquor store is at 3250 Eby St. There are 4 laundromats. The community has a library and art gallery, indoor swimming pool, tennis courts and a golf course.

Public campgrounds are located at Ferry Island, turn off at Skeena River bridge (**Milepost PG 365.6**); Kleanza Creek, 10 miles/16.1 km east of Terrace; and Lakelse Lake, 11.7 miles/18.8 km south. There are 4 private campgrounds, one on the Skeena River, one at the east edge of the city (follow signs at junction of Highways 16 and 37), and 2 affiliated with motels on the west side of Terrace. Fisherman's Park, on the east side of the Kalum River, provides picnic facilities. ▲

TRANSPORTATION

Air: Canadian Airlines International, Air BC and Central Mountain Air from Terrace-Kitimat airport on Highway 37 South.

Railroad: VIA Rail, 4531 Railway Ave.

Bus: Farwest Bus Lines, Greyhound and Seaport Limousine with connection between Terrace and Stewart/Hyder.

Car Rentals: Available.

Example of log building technique at Heritage Park. (Judy Parkin, staff)

ATTRACTIONS

Heritage Park is a collection of original log buildings from this region. Chosen to represent both the different aspects of pioneer life, as well as different log building techniques, the structures include a trapper's cabin, miner's cabin and lineman's cabin. The 9 structures also house artifacts from the period. Managed by the Terrace Regional Museum Society; guided tours available in summer, admission charged.

Lakelse Lake Provincial Park at Furlong Bay, 11.4 miles/18.3 km south of Highway 16 on Highway 37, offers campsites and day-use facilities,, boat launch, sandy beaches, swimming, nature trails and interpretive programs. ▲

Hiking trails in the Terrace area range from easy to moderate. Terrace Mountain Nature Trail is a 3.2-mile/5.1-km uphill hike which offers good views of the area; it begins at Halliwell and Anderson streets. Check with the Visitor Infocentre for details on other area trails.

Special events in Terrace include the Skeena Valley Fall Fair, Labour Day weekend; River Boat Days, B.C. Day weekend; and the Terrace Trade Show in May.

Nisga'a Memorial Lava Bed Provincial Park. The lava beds are 42 miles/67 km north of Terrace via the Nisga'a Highway (see NISGA'A HIGHWAY/NASS ROAD log on page 238). Limited picnic spots; limited camping; interesting hikes. Canada's youngest volcano last erupted approximately 300 years ago, burying 2 Indian villages. &

Sportfishing. Fish on the banks of the province's second largest river, the **Skeena.** Terrace is ideally situated for sportfishing, with easy access to the **Copper, Kalum, Kitimat** and **Lakelse rivers.** Cutthroat, Dolly Varden and rainbow are found in all lakes and streams; salmon (king and coho) from May to late autumn. Kings average 40 to 70 lbs.; coho 14 to 20 lbs. Check locally for season and restrictions on steelhead. Information and fishing licenses are available from B.C. Government Access Centre, 3220 Eby St., Terrace (phone 250/638-6515), and at most sporting goods stores. 🐟

Yellowhead Highway 16 Log
(continued)

PG 366.3 (589.5 km) **PR 89.7** (144.4 km) Stoplight; west access to Terrace. Turn north at intersection for downtown. Continue through intersection eastbound for Prince George, westbound for Prince Rupert.

PG 366.5 (589.8 km) **PR 89.5** (144 km) **Junction** with Nisga'a Highway (Kalum Lake Road) to New Aiyansh. See NISGA'A HIGHWAY/NASS ROAD log page 238.

PG 367.9 (592.1 km) **PR 88.1** (141.8 km) Access road to boat launch (fee charged) on the Kitsumkalum River downstream from Highway 16 bridge; RV parking.

Leaving Terrace, Highway 16 is in good condition westbound although the few straightaways are interrupted by some amazing 70-degree zigzags as the highway crosses the railroad tracks. The highway along the Skeena River is spectacular, with waterfalls cascading down the steep rock faces.

PG 369.3 (594.3 km) **PR 86.7** (139.5 km) KITSUMKALUM. Grocery store and House of Sim-oi-Ghets craft center. This Native enterprise on reserve land handles only authentic arts and crafts such as totem poles, leather goods and local carvings.

This is also the **junction** with West Kalum Forest Service Road, which leads north 15 miles/24 km to Kitsumkalum Provincial Park with 20 campsites. This narrow gravel logging road joins the Nisga'a Highway, which turns into another forest service road, Nass Road, that joins the Cassiar Highway. (Nisga'a Highway, also known as Kalum Lake Road from Terrace, is paved to the junction with Nass Road; see NISGA'A HIGHWAY/NASS ROAD log this section.) ▲

Beyond the Nass Road junction, the Nisga'a Highway is a narrow gravel and pavement road used by logging trucks. The Cassiar Highway junctions with the Yellowhead Highway at Kitwanga, **Milepost PG 306.6**; see the CASSIAR HIGHWAY section.

PG 373 (600.3 km) **PR 83** (133.6 km)

Shames Mountain Ski Area.

PG 380.2 (611.9 km) **PR 75.8** (122 km) Paved turnout with litter barrels to south alongside the Skeena River; watch for fishermen during salmon season.

PG 387.2 (623.1 km) **PR 68.8** (110.7 km) Rest area on left westbound with picnic tables, toilets and water pump.

PG 393.1 (632.6 km) **PR 62.9** (101.2 km) *CAUTION! Highway turns sharply across railroad tracks.*

PG 395.2 (636 km) **PR 60.8** (97.8 km) *CAUTION: Carwash Rock overhangs highway. Water cascades down mountain and onto highway during heavy rains.*

PG 395.5 (636.5 km) **PR 60.5** (97.4 km) Sharp curves and falling rocks approximately next mile westbound.

PG 397.2 (639.2 km) **PR 58.8** (94.6 km) *CAUTION: Slow down for sharp curve and steep grade.*

PG 400.6 (644.7 km) **PR 55.4** (89.2 km) **Exchamsiks River** Provincial Park; 20 campsites and 20 picnic sites among old-growth Sitka spruce. Open May to October, camping fee, water and pit toilets. Good salmon fishing in Exchamsiks River. Access to Gitnadoix River canoeing area across Skeena River. ►◄▲

PG 401.1 (645.5 km) **PR 54.9** (88.4 km) Very pleasant rest area north side of road at west end of bridge; boat launch on Exchamsiks River. Toilets, tables and litter barrels.

PG 402.4 (647.6 km) **PR 53.6** (86.3 km) Conspicuous example of Sitka spruce on north side of highway. Aboriginal people ate its inner bark fresh or dried in cakes, served with berries. As you travel west, the vegetation becomes increasingly influenced by the maritime climate.

PG 406 (653.4 km) **PR 50** (80.5 km) Kasiks River; boat launch.

PG 416.4 (670.1 km) **PR 39.6** (63.7 km) Kwinitsa River bridge and boat launch. No public moorage.

PG 421.1 (677.7 km) **PR 34.9** (56.2 km) Telegraph Point rest area to south on bank of Skeena River; paved turnout with outhouses, picnic tables, litter barrels and water pump. Watch for seals and sea lions in spring and during salmon season.

PG 427.8 (688.5 km) **PR 28.2** (45.4 km) Basalt Creek rest area to south with picnic tables.

PG 431.8 (695 km) **PR 27.5** (44.3 km) Khyex River bridge. Remains of old sawmill visible at west end of bridge to south.

PG 432.5 (696 km) **PR 23.5** (37.8 km) Turnout to south.

PG 435 (700 km) **PR 21** (33.8 km) Watch for pictograph, visible from the road for eastbound traffic only, possibly a boundary marker for Chief Legaic over 150 years ago. It was rediscovered in the early 1950s by Dan Lippett of Prince Rupert.

PG 435.5 (700.9 km) **PR 20.5** (33 km) Scenic viewpoint to south with litter barrels and historical plaque about Skeena River. Highway leaves Skeena River westbound. Abandoned townsite of Port Essington visible on opposite side of river.

PG 437.2 (703.6 km) **PR 18.8** (30.2 km) Green River Forest Service road.

PG 440.5 (708.9 km) **PR 15.5** (24.9 km) Rainbow Summit, elev. 528 feet/161m.

PG 442.8 (712.6 km) **PR 13.2** (21.2 km) Side road south to Rainbow Lake Reservoir; boat launch. The reservoir water is used by the pulp mill on Watson Island.

PG 445.4 (716.8 km) **PR 10.6** (17.1 km) **Prudhomme Lake** Provincial Park; 24 campsites, well water, toilets, firewood, fishing,

Nisga'a Highway/Nass Road Log

The Nisga'a Highway/Nass Forest Service Road junctions with Yellowhead Highway 16 west of Terrace at **Milepost PG 366.5** and travels north to the join the Cassiar Highway at **Milepost J 44.9**. Total driving distance is 98.6 miles/158.7 km and the first 39.3 miles/63.2 km are paved; the remainder is gravel. Services along this route are limited. Grading on the gravel sections often turns up sharp rocks, especially in the lava sections, and travelers are advised to carry a spare tire. Portions of the road are narrow and winding, and there are many 1-lane bridges. Fuel is available at New Aiyansh, which is the major settlement on this route. Limited campsites are available.

There is active logging in the area and travelers share the route with logging and local traffic. Motorists are advised to exercise caution and drive with headlights on. Between New Aiyansh and the Cassiar Highway, there are a number of Y-intersections and, in most instances, the route is signed; however, if in doubt, follow the road which parallels the hydro lines.

Yellow kilometre markers begin at **Milepost J 58.5** and continue to the Cassiar Highway. These markers are used by loggers when reporting their road positions and marker '0' is at the Ginlulak log dump near Greenville. During winter, depending on logging activity, the eastern portion of the road may not be maintained (plowed).

Distance is measured from junction (J) with Yellowhead Highway 16.

J 0 Junction with Yellowhead Highway 16 at **Milepost PG 366.5.**

J 7 (11.2 km) Finlay Lake to west.

J 13.7 (22 km) Kitsumkalum River to west.

J 17.4 (28 km) View of Kitsumkalum Lake to west.

J 19.8 (31.9 km) Paved turnout to west overlooking Kitsumkalum Lake.

J 23 (37 km) Rosswood settlement at the head of the lake, named for Annie Ross, who homesteaded here with her 4 children at the turn of the century.

J 25.8 (41.5 km) Rosswood General Store; groceries, fishing tackle (open year-round).

J 30.4 (48.9 km) Entering Skeena Cellulose Tree Farm License #1. Twenty-five year tree farm licenses are issued by the Crown and define the terms of timber harvest, including taxation, reforestation and long-term planning requirements.

J 31.4 (50.5 km) One-lane bridge crosses Cedar River.

J 37 (59.6 km) Sand Lake, marshy area to south. Watch for wildlife.

J 39.3 (63.2 km) Pavement ends, gravel begins, northbound.

J 39.5 (63.6 km) Gainor Lake west.

J 42.2 (67.9 km) Southern park boundary for Nisga'a Memorial Lava Bed Park. Lava Lake to west. Narrow winding road next 6.2 miles/10 km northbound. *Note: Removal of lava prohibited; stay on designated trails and roads.*

The flow is thought to be the most recent volcanic eruption in Canada (approximately 300 years ago). It covers an area approximately 6.3 miles/10 km long and 1.8 miles/3 km wide and was created by a volcano less than 361 feet/100m high. The eruption produced little ash or cinder, but large quantities of basalt. The eruption destroyed 2 villages and killed more than 2,000 people.

The flow entered the Tseax Valley, filling it to depths of more than 98 feet/30m, and blocking the upper section of the valley. Waters from the surrounding drainage filled the valley to form the 180 foot-/55m-deep Lava Lake, which in turn drains into the permeable lava flow and reappears approximately 1.2 miles/2 km downstream as the Tseax River and Vetter Creek.

J 46 (74.1 km) Access to Lava Lake on west side of road.

J 48.3 (77.8 km) North end of Lava Lake. Sil Tax picnic site; toilets, litter barrels, tables, park information. No overnight camping.

J 48.7 (78.4 km) Lava flow to east. Interpretive sign, trail (0.6 mile/1 km) and photo viewpoint.

J 50.1 (80.6 km) One-lane wooden bridge.

J 54.7 (88 km) Beaupre Falls trail (10 minutes round trip).

J 56.2 (90.5 km) Vetter Falls viewpoint and "phantom fish." Near Vetter Falls the Tseax River divides; the western channel flows into the Nass River. The eastern channel flows over Vetter Falls to join Vetter Creek. Just east of the Vetter Falls campsite, the runoff sinks into channels below the lava. Often, steelhead spawning in the Tseax River return to the ocean; occasionally the fish take the eastern channel and go over the falls, becoming trapped in this section of the river. They starve and become "snake-like" in appearance. Locals refer to them as "phantom fish."

J 58.5 (94.1 km) **Junction** with road to Gitwinksihlkw (Canyon City) and Greenville. Information sign. Turn east (right). Road presently ends at Greenville. Vetter Falls campsite to northwest; tables, fire rings, and toilets. Water from creek; recommend boiling. ▲

Nisga'a Enterprises operates a fishing lodge at Nass Harbour with good fishing and ocean kayaking. ⟋

J 59.6 (95.9 km) Northern boundary for Nisga'a Memorial Lava Bed Park; information, toilets, viewpoint. Turnout by creek to south. One-lane wooden bridge.

J 60.1 (96.7 km) RCMP station to north.

J 60.2 (96.9 km) Village of **NEW AIYANSH** to south is the major settlement on the Nisga'a Highway. Repairs, gas, grocery and convenience stores, community hall with Native design, a school, post office, first aid, fire and police stations, post office and gift shop are available. Area bed and breakfast and lodge operators offer meals and accommodation. Limited campsites are available. ▲

Miles Inn on The T'Seax. See display ad this section.

J 67.7 (109 km) Northbound: Highway becomes Nass Forest Service Road at Y-intersection. Keep left for Nass Camp/Bill-Nor Tillicum Lodge (all visitor services), keep right for Cassiar Highway.

J 71.3 (114.7 km) BC Forest Recreation Site on Dragon Lake. A medium, semi-open, user-maintained site with good water and broad access; mixed forest; boat launch. ▲

J 73.7 (118.6 km) Y-intersection: Keep to right for Cassiar Highway, left for Alice Arm/Kitsault. Follow hydro lines.

J 80.5 (129.5 km) One-lane wooden bridge with turnouts at each end. Leaving Skeena Tree Fall License #1 northbound.

J 94.8 (152.5 km) Y-intersection: Follow yellow kilometreposts on right side of road for Cassiar Highway.

J 98.6 (158.7 km) **Junction** with Cassiar Highway 37 (see Cassiar Highway section).

Return to Milepost PG 366.5 Yellowhead Highway or J 46.8 Cassiar Highway

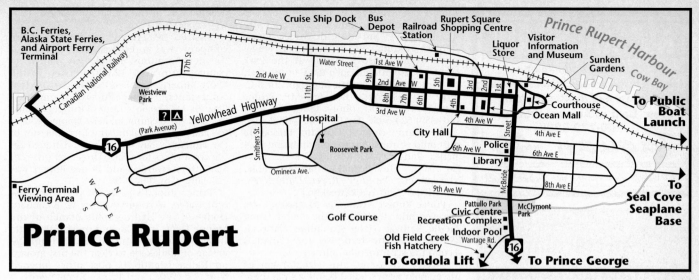

Prince Rupert

camping fee.

PG 446.3 (718.2 km) PR 9.7 (15.6 km) Turnoff for Diana Lake Provincial Park, 1.5 miles/2.4 km south via single-lane gravel road (use turnouts). Day-use facility. Very pleasant grassy picnic area on lakeshore with 50 picnic tables, kitchen shelter, firewood, grills, wheelchair access, outhouses, water pump and garbage cans. Parking for 229 vehicles. The only freshwater swimming beach in the Prince Rupert area. Fish viewing at Diana Creek on the way into the lake; 2 hiking trails.

PG 451.2 (726.1 km) PR 4.8 (7.7 km) Junction. Turnoff for **PORT EDWARD**, pulp mill and historic cannery. The North Pacific Cannery Village and Fishing Museum at Port Edward is open daily in summer. Built in 1889, this is the oldest cannery village on the north coast. Phone (250) 628-3538 for more information.

North Pacific Cannery Village Museum. See display ad this section.

PG 451.3 (726.3 km) PR 4.7 (7.6 km) Galloway Rapids. Bridge crossing to Prince Rupert, on Kaien Island.

PG 451.5 (726.6 km) PR 4.5 (7.2 km) Galloway Rapids rest area to south with litter barrels, picnic tables and visitor information sign. View of Watson Island pulp mill.

PG 453 (729 km) PR 3 (4.8 km) Ridley Island access road. Ridley Island is the site of terminals used for the transfer of coal and grain from—respectively, the North East Coal resource near Dawson Creek and Canada's prairies—to ships.

PG 453.4 (729.7 km) PR 2.6 (4.2 km) Oliver Lake rest area to south just off highway; picnic tables, grills, firewood. Point of interest sign about bogs.

PG 453.7 (730.2 km) PR 2.2 (3.6 km) Shoe Tree or Tree of Lost Soles to east. Tongue-in-cheek local attraction which has grown over years. Worn-out footwear is hung from trees in this local shrine to shoes.

PG 454.1 (730.8 km) PR 1.9 (3.1 km) Mount Oldfield and Butze Rapids hiking trails.

PG 455.4 (732.9 km) PR 0.6 (1 km) Turnoff to north for viewpoint of Butze Rapids, a series of reversing rapids. The action of the tidal waters creates quantities of foam as the waters flow through the rapids. It is from these "foaming waters" that the island takes its Indian name *Kaien*.

PG 456 (733.8 km) PR 0 Prince Rupert industrial park on the outskirts of Prince Rupert. Continue straight ahead 3 miles/4.8 km for the Visitor Infocentre in downtown Prince Rupert. Yellowhead Highway 16 becomes McBride Street as you enter the city centre.

CAUTION: No gas or services available eastbound between Prince Rupert and Terrace.

Prince Rupert

Located on Kaien Island near the mouth of the Skeena River, 90 miles/145 km by air or water south of Ketchikan, AK. **Population:** 17,500; area 25,000. **Emergency Services:** Phone 911 for **Police**, **Ambulance** and **Fire Department.** RCMP, 6th Avenue and McBride Street, non-emergency phone (250) 624-2136. **Hospital**, Prince Rupert Regional, phone (250) 624-2171.

Visitor Information: Visitor Infocentre at 1st Avenue and McBride Street. Open daily in summer, 9 A.M. to 9 P.M. Travel information is also available at the Park Avenue Campground; open daily in summer, 9 A.M. to 9 P.M., and until midnight for B.C. Ferry arrivals. Write Box 669-MP, Prince Rupert, BC V8J 3S1, phone (800) 667-1994 and (250) 624-5637, fax (250) 627-8009.

Elevation: Sea level. **Climate:** Temperate with mild winters. Annual precipitation 95.4 inches. **Radio:** CHTK 560, CBC 860; CJFW-FM 101.9. **Television:** 12 channels, cable. **Newspaper:** *The Prince Rupert Daily News, Prince Rupert This Week* (weekly).

Prince Rupert, "Gateway to Alaska," was surveyed prior to 1905 by the Grand Trunk Pacific Railway (later Canadian National Railways) as the terminus for Canada's second transcontinental railroad.

Twelve thousand miles/19,300 km of survey lines were studied before a final route along the Skeena River was chosen. Some 833 miles/1,340 km had to be blasted from solid rock, 50 men drowned and costs rose to $105,000 a mile (the final cost of $300 million was comparable to Panama Canal construction) before the last spike was driven near Fraser Lake on April 7, 1914. Financial problems continued to plague the company, forcing it to amalgamate to

PRINCE RUPERT ADVERTISERS

become part of the Canadian National Railways system in 1923.

Charles M. Hays, president of the company, was an enthusiastic promoter of the new terminus, which was named by competition from 12,000 entries. While "Port Rupert" had been submitted by two contestants, "Prince Rupert" (from Miss Eleanor M. Macdonald of Winnipeg) called to mind the dashing soldier–explorer, cousin to Charles II of England and first governor of the Hudson's Bay Co., who had traded on the coast rivers for years. Three first prizes of $250 were awarded and Prince Rupert was officially named in 1906.

Prince Rupert's proposed port and adjacent waters were surveyed by G. Blanchard Dodge of the Hydrographic branch of the Marine Dept. in 1906, and in May the little steamer *Constance* carried settlers from the village of Metlakatla to clear the first ground on Kaien Island. Its post office opened Nov. 23, 1906, and Prince Rupert, with a tent-town population of 200, began an association with communities on the Queen Charlotte Islands, with Stewart served by Union steamships and Canadian Pacific Railways boats, and with Hazelton 200 miles/322 km up the Skeena River on which the stern-wheelers of the Grand Trunk Pacific and the Hudson's Bay Co. traveled.

Incorporated as a city March 10, 1910, Prince Rupert attracted settlers responding to the enthusiasm of Hays, with his dreams of a population of 50,000 and world markets supplied by his railroad. Both the city and the railway suffered a great loss with the death of Charles M. Hays when the *Titanic* went down in April 1912. Even so, work went ahead on the Grand Trunk Pacific. Two years later the first train arrived at Prince Rupert, linking the western port with the rest of Canada. Since then, the city has progressed through 2 world wars and economic ups and downs to its present period of growth and expansion, not only as a busy port but as a visitor centre.

During WWII, more than a million tons of freight and 73,000 people, both military and civilian, passed through Prince Rupert on their way to military operations in Alaska and the South Pacific.

Construction of the pulp operations on Watson Island in 1951 greatly increased the economic and industrial potential of the

View from Mount Hays of Prince Rupert harbour. (Virginia Kimmett)

facilities on Ridley Island. Other industries include fishing and fish processing, and the manufacture of forest products.

Prince Rupert is underlaid by muskeg (a deep bog common to Northwest Canada and Alaska) over solid rock, which makes for a difficult foundation to build on. Many sites are economically unfeasible for development as they would require pilings 70 feet/21m or more into the muskeg to provide a firm foundation. Some of the older buildings have sagged slightly as a result of unstable foundations.

ACCOMMODATIONS/VISITOR SERVICES

More than a dozen hotels and motels accommodate the influx of ferry passengers each summer. Many restaurants feature fresh local seafood in season.

Modern supermarkets, shopping centres and a hospital are available. Government liquor store is at the corner of 2nd Avenue and Highway 16. There are 5 main banks, the Civic Centre Recreation Complex, 18-hole golf course, racquet centre, bowling alley, a swimming pool and tennis courts.

Park Avenue Campground on Highway 16 in the city has 87 campsites with hookups, unserviced sites, restrooms with hot showers, coin-operated laundry facilities, children's play area and picnic shelters. There are 24 campsites at Prudhomme Lake Provincial Park, 12.5 miles/20.1 km east on Highway 16. A private RV park on McBride Street offers camper and trailer parking. ▲

TRANSPORTATION

Air: Harbour Air and Inland Air Charter to outlying villages and Queen Charlotte Islands; Canadian Airlines International daily jet service to Terrace and Vancouver; Taquan Air daily floatplane service in summer to Ketchikan, AK; and Air BC to Vancouver with connecting flights to Victoria (weekly air services in winter).

area. The operations include a pulp mill and a kraft mill.

With the start of the Alaska State Ferry System in 1963, and the British Columbia Ferry System in 1966, Prince Rupert's place as an important visitor centre and terminal point for highway, rail and marine transportation was assured.

Prince Rupert is the second major deep-sea port on Canada's west coast, exporting grain, pulp, lumber and other resources to Europe and Asia. Prince Rupert has also become a major coal and grain port with

Prince Rupert airport is located on Digby Island, which is connected by city-operated ferry to Prince Rupert. There is a small terminal at the airport. The airport ferry leaves from the Fairview dock, next to the Alaska state ferry dock; fare is charged for the 20-minute ride. Check with the Canadian Airlines International office at the downtown Rupert Mall (office is open for passenger check-in only when planes are arriving or departing). Air BC check-in at corner of 6th Street and 1st Avenue West. Bus service to airport from airline check-in areas.

There is a seaplane base at Seal Cove with airline and helicopter charter services.

Ferries: British Columbia Ferry System, Fairview dock, phone (250) 624-9627, provides automobile and passenger service from Prince Rupert to Port Hardy, and between Prince Rupert and Skidegate in the Queen Charlotte Islands. For details, see MARINE ACCESS ROUTES section.

Alaska Marine Highway System, Fairview dock, phone (250) 627-1744 or 1-800-642-0066, provides automobile and passenger service to southeastern Alaska. See MARINE ACCESS ROUTES section.

NOTE: Vehicle storage is available; inquire at the Information Centre.

Car Rentals: Tilden, phone (250) 624-5318, and Budget, phone (250) 627-7400.

Taxi: Available. Prince Rupert taxi cabs are powered by LNG (liquefied natural gas); phone (250) 624-2185.

Railroad: VIA Rail, in British Columbia, phone 1-800-561-8630 (from Manitoba west to British Columbia) or 1-800-561-3949 (from the United States).

Bus: Greyhound, phone (250) 624-5090. Farwest Bus Lines, phone (250) 624-6400. Charter sightseeing tours available.

ATTRACTIONS

Take a Tour. Tour the city's historic and scenic points of interest. Maps are available at the Visitor Infocentre. Scattered throughout the city are 18 large cedar totem poles, each with its own story. Most are reproductions by Native craftsmen of the original Tsimshian (SHIM shian) poles from the mainland and the Haida (HI duh) carvings from the Queen Charlotte Islands. The originals are now in the British Columbia Provincial Museum in Victoria. Several totem poles may be seen at Service Park, near 3rd Avenue W. and Fulton.

Check with the Museum of Northern British Columbia (1st and McBride) about tours of area archaeological sites. Included is a stop at "Old" Metlakatla in Prince Rupert harbour ("new" Metlakatla is located on Annette Island near Ketchikan, AK; see METLAKATLA section.)

Cannery Tour. North Pacific Cannery Village Museum at Port Edward (turn off Highway 16 at **Milepost PG 451.2**). Built in 1889, this restored heritage site has dozens of displays on this once-major regional industry. A live performance highlights the history of the cannery. Open daily in summer, closed Mondays and Tuesdays October through April; admission charged. Phone (250) 628-3538.

Archaeology Tours. Prince Rupert's inner harbour shelters more than 150 archaeological sites dating back 5,000 years. This fascinating harbour tour visits these sites and offers full descriptions of early inhabitants. The tour stops at the historic First Nations village of Metlakatla and at Dodge Cove. Guided by knowledgeable museum staff you'll travel in an enclosed ferry with ample window seating. Regular departures. Reserve with Museum of Northern British Columbia, Box 669, Prince Rupert, BC V8J 3S1. Phone (250) 624-3207. [ADVERTISEMENT]

Watch the Seaplanes. From McBride Street, head north on 6th Avenue E. (watch for signs to seaplane base); drive a few miles to Solly's Pub, then turn right to Seal Cove seaplane base. Visitors can spend a fascinating hour here watching seaplanes loading, taking off and landing. Helicopter and seaplane tours of the area are available at Seal Cove.

Visit the Queen Charlotte Islands. Ferry service is available between Prince Rupert and Skidegate on Graham Island, largest of the 150 islands and islets that form the Queen Charlotte Islands. Located west of Prince Rupert—a 6- to 8-hour ferry ride—Graham Island's paved road system connects Skidegate with Masset, the largest town in the Queen Charlottes. Scheduled flights from Prince Rupert to Sandspit and Masset are available. Island attractions include wild beaches, Haida culture, flora and fauna. Read THE QUEEN CHARLOTTES on opposite page for more information.

Kwinitsa Station Railway Museum. Built in 1911, Kwinitsa Station was one of nearly 400 identical stations along the Grand Trunk Pacific Railway line. In 1985 the station was moved to the Prince Rupert waterfront. Restored rooms, exhibits and videos tell the story of early Prince Rupert and the role the railroad played in the city's development. Open daily in summer; contact the Museum of British Columbia for more information.

Museum of Northern British Columbia/Art Gallery displays an outstanding collection of artifacts depicting the settlement history of British Columbia's north coast. Traveling art collections are displayed in the gallery, and works by local artists are available for purchase. Centrally located at 1st Avenue and McBride Street, marked by several tall totem poles. Summer hours 9 A.M. to 8 P.M. Monday through Saturday; winter hours 10 A.M. to 5 P.M. Monday through Saturday. Phone (250) 624-3207. *In 1997, the museum will move across the street to 100 First Avenue East.*

"Photographs and Memories" is a well done multimedia production on Prince Rupert's history. The exhibit's location for 1997 was undetermined at press time. Contact the infocentre for details.

Performing Arts Centre offers both professional and amateur theatre, with productions for children, and classical and contemporary plays presented. The 700-seat facility may be toured in summer; phone

(250) 627-8888.

Special Events. Seafest is a 4-day celebration, held the second weekend in June, which includes a parade and water-jousting competition. Indian Culture Days, a 2-day event held during Seafest, features Native food, traditional dance, and arts and crafts. The All Native Basketball Tournament, held in February, is the largest event of its kind in Canada.

The Civic Centre Recreation Complex located on McBride Street (Highway 16) welcomes visitors. Activities include fitness gym, squash, basketball and volleyball. Supervised children's activities during summer. Ice skating and roller skating rinks also located at the centre. Phone (250) 624-6707 for more information.

Swim at Diana Lake. This provincial park, about 13 miles/21 km from downtown on Highway 16, offers the only freshwater swimming in the Prince Rupert area. Picnic tables, kitchen shelter, parking and beach.

Swim at Earl Mah Aquatic Centre, located next to the Civic Centre Recreation Complex. There is an indoor swimming pool, tot pool, weight room, saunas, showers, whirlpool, slides and diving boards. Access for persons with disabilities. Phone (250) 627-7946. An admission fee is charged.

Golf Course includes 18-hole course, resident pro, equipment rental, clubhouse and restaurant. Entrance on 9th Avenue W.

Go Fishing. Numerous freshwater fishing areas are available near Prince Rupert. For information on bait, locations, regulations and licensing, contact local sporting goods stores or the Visitor Infocentre. This area abounds in all species of salmon, steelhead, crab and shrimp. Public boat launch facility is located at Rushbrook Public Floats at the north end of the waterfront. Public floats are also available at Fairview, past the Alaska state ferry terminal near the breakwater.

Harbour Tours and Fishing Charters are available. For information, contact the Prince Rupert Infocentre at 1-800-667-1994.

The Queen Charlottes

Also called Haida Gwaii (a Haida expression meaning "islands of the people"), the Queen Charlotte Islands are situated 50 miles/80 km off the west coast of British Columbia. To get the most from a trip to the Queen Charlottes, some fairly extensive planning is required. But for those who make the effort, and also enjoy a more rustic experience, the results can be very satisfying.

There are 150 islands in the Queen Charlottes archipelago. The 2 largest islands are Graham and Moresby. Most of the Charlottes 6,000 residents live on Graham. Tourism to the Charlottes began with the introduction of ferry service in 1980.

The climate is moderated by the Japanese current. Summers are predictably dry and sunny, with temperatures averaging 64° F/17° C. Winters are wet and often mild, averaging 40° F/4° C. The annual precipitation is 53.4 inches/1356 mm, and since the islands lie in one of the windiest regions of Canada, there is usually a coastal breeze. Visitors should take note that the weather can change very rapidly and is given to extremes.

The islands are sometimes referred to as the Canadian Galapagos because of the unique adaptations that have evolved in some species. Portions of the islands seem to have remained ice-free during glaciation, and it is speculated that some of today's flora and fauna may have existed continuously for the last 100,000 years.

The Golden Spruce is one of the most famous and easier-to-reach natural attractions, 4 miles/6 km south of Port Clements on Graham Island. The 300-year-old golden-needled tree stands 165 feet/49.5m high. A rare mutation, this excellent specimen is one of only a few such trees known to exist.

Also of particular interest are the wild beaches. Naikoon Provincial Park, encompassing the northeast corner of Graham Island, conserves sandy beach and dunes from Tlell to the northern tip of the island.

Haida culture is a major attraction in the Charlottes. Although nature has reclaimed old villages depopulated by smallpox in the 19th century, the Haida culture continues to thrive: new poles and canoes are carved, and long house architecture is adapted to today's needs. Argillite sculpture, silver and gold jewellery, prints and weavings of contemporary Haida artists are found in shops and studios.

The Queen Charlotte Island Museum at Skidegate, rated as a '"must see" attraction, has exhibits on Haida culture, natural history and island geology. The logging museum at Port Clements describes the modern settlement history.

Many visitors elect wilderness drives and camping. There are approximately 90 miles/145 km of paved highway on Graham and Moresby islands, and hundreds of miles of unpaved logging roads. Private logging roads provide recreational access to wilderness areas, like Rennell Sound on the rugged west coast on Graham Island. Visitors should check with logging companies to find out what haul roads are active, to pick up maps, and to receive briefing on logging road etiquette before setting out.

Gwaii Haanas ("place of wonder") National Park Reserve/Haida Heritage Site encompasses the lower half of Moresby Island and surrounding islands. It offers a diversity of landscapes and natural features. Special protected areas include the Haida village sites at Skedans, Tanu and Ninstints on Sgan Gwaii (Anthony Island), a UNESCO World Heritage Site. Travel in this remote and rugged area is not for the inexperienced. There are no roads to or in the park and no developed facilities. Reservations and registration are required. Contact Parks Canada at P.O. Box 37, Queen Charlotte, BC, V0T 1S0; phone (250) 559-8818; e-mail: gwaiicomm@? island.net.ca. Tour companies registered to operate in the area offer a range of services. User fees are proposed for 1997.

Accommodations, restaurants, groceries, fuel and repair services are available in Masset, Queen Charlotte, Port Clements and Sandspit. Limited services in smaller communities. Most island businesses are owner-operated, and business hours vary; plan accordingly. The number of hotel/motel rooms is limited, but bed and breakfasts are a good alternative. There are bank machines and medical facilities in both Masset and Queen Charlotte.

Camping is available at Agate Beach in Naikoon Park; in Masset; at Misty Meadows in Tlell; in Queen Charlotte at Rennell Sound; and at Gray Bay, Mosquito Lake and Moresby Camp on Moresby. Hookups are available in Masset, Queen Charlotte and Sandspit.

The B.C. Ferry Corporation provides year-round sailings between Prince Rupert and Skidegate on Graham Island. Travelers are strongly urged to make advance reservations. The crossing time is approximately 6 hours.

To reach Moresby Island, there is scheduled service between Skidegate and Alliford Bay aboard the car-carrying MV *Kwuna* ferry. The crossing takes 20 minutes. A paved 6.8-mile/11 km road connects Aliford Bay and Sandspit.

Canadian Airlines International offers jet service between Vancouver and Sandspit on Moresby Island. From Prince Rupert, Harbour Air provides scheduled service to Masset, Sandspit and Queen Charlotte. Shuttle service between Queen Charlotte and the airport at Sandspit.

Budget and Tilden car rentals and taxi service are available in Masset and Queen Charlotte on Graham Island and Sandspit on Moresby. There is no scheduled public transit between island communities.

For more information on travel in the Queen Charlottes, contact Visitor Infocentre, P.O. Box 819, Queen Charlotte, BC V0T 1S0, phone (250) 559-8316, fax (250) 559-8952. Or visit the Sandspit Visitor Infocentre at Sandspit airport, open mid-May to September.

CASSIAR HIGHWAY

Connects: Yellowhead Hwy. 16 to Alaska Hwy. **Length:** 446 miles
Road Surface: 80% paved, 20% gravel **Season:** Open all year
Highest Summit: Gnat Pass 4,072 feet
Major Attractions: Bear and Salmon glaciers, Stikine River

(See map, page 245)

	Alaska Hwy.	Dease Lake	Iskut	Stewart/Hyder	Yellowhead Hwy.	Watson Lake
Alaska Hwy.		145	196	390	446	14
Dease Lake	145		51	245	301	159
Iskut	196	51		194	250	210
Stewart/Hyder	390	245	194		136	404
Yellowhead Hwy.	446	301	250	136		460
Watson Lake	14	159	210	404	460	

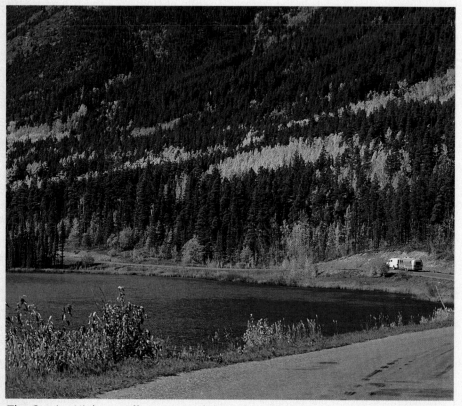

The Cassiar Highway offers outstanding and varied scenery. (© Beth Davidow)

log for distances between services. Be sure your vehicle is mechanically sound with good tires. It is a good idea to carry a spare tire and extra fuel, especially in the off-season. In case of emergency, motorists are advised to flag down trucks to radio for help. It is unlawful to camp overnight in turnouts and rest areas unless otherwise posted. Camp at private campgrounds or in provincial park campgrounds.

NOTE: *According to the Ministry of Highways, litter barrels on the Cassiar Highway are often moved to areas which are being used more frequently. Litter barrels may not be in the same location from season to season. The MILEPOST® log indicates their location as of summer 1996.*

For a recorded message on road conditions on the Cassiar Highway, in Canada phone 1-900-451-4997 (75 cents per minute charged). Current road conditions are also available by phoning the Highways Maintenance Contractor at (250) 771-3000 (if no answer, contact the District Highways office at 250/771-4511).

The Cassiar Highway junctions with Yellowhead Highway 16 at the Skeena River bridge (**Milepost PG 306.6** in the YELLOWHEAD HIGHWAY 16 section) and travels north to the Stewart, BC–Hyder, AK, access road, Telegraph Creek access road and Dease Lake, ending at the Alaska Highway 13.3 miles/21.4 km west of Watson Lake, YT (See **Milepost DC 626.2** in the ALASKA HIGHWAY section). Total driving distance is 446.1 miles/718 km. Travelers driving between Prince George and the junction of the Alaska and Cassiar highways will save 123.5 miles/198.7 km by taking the Cassiar Highway. (Yellowhead–Cassiar route is 752.7 miles/1,211.4 km; Alaska Highway route is 876.2 miles/1,410.1 km.) The Cassiar is a rougher road with fewer facilities than the Alaska Highway, but the Cassiar Highway offers a most enjoyable adventure drive with outstanding and varied scenery.

Completed in 1972, much of the Cassiar has been leveled, straightened and brought up to all-weather standards. The highway is paved from **Milepost J 0** to Meziadin junction. From Meziadin junction to the Alaska Highway, the highway is surfaced (pavement or seal coat) with the exception of 4 short gravel sections totaling 80.9 miles/130.2 km. Ongoing highway improvement projects under way in summer. On gravel stretches watch for washboard and potholes. Gravel road may be dusty in dry weather and muddy in wet weather. Seal coat is subject to deterioration from weather and traffic. A few bridges are still single lane. Watch for potholes at bridge ends and slippery bridge decks. There are several 8 percent grades. Drive with your headlights on. The Cassiar Highway is the route of commercial truckers headed north of 60°.

Watch for logging trucks on the lower Cassiar Highway and freight trucks anywhere on the highway. *WARNING: Exercise extreme caution when passing or being passed by these trucks; reduce speed and allow trucks adequate clearance.*

Increasingly popular with motorists in recent years, both because of its savings in travel time and its diverse scenery, the Cassiar also provides access to Hyder and Stewart. These communities are described in detail in this section beginning on page 248.

Food, gas and lodging are available along the Cassiar Highway, but check the highway

Cassiar Highway Log

BC HIGHWAY 37
Kilometreposts are along the Cassiar Highway every 5 km. Because the posts do not always accurately reflect driving distance, mileages from the Yellowhead Highway 16 junction are based on actual driving distance while kilometres are based on physical kilometreposts as they occurred in summer 1996.
Distance from junction with the Yellowhead Highway (J) is followed by distance from Alaska Highway (AH).

J 0 AH 446.1 (718 km) **Junction** with Yellowhead Highway 16 (see **Milepost PG 306.6** in the YELLOWHEAD HIGHWAY 16 section). Gas station. Bridge across Skeena River from Yellowhead Highway 16 to start of Cassiar Highway.

J 0.2 (0.4 km) **AH 445.9** (717.6 km) Turn east on side road to view totem poles of **GITWANGAK**. The Native reserve of Gitwangak was renamed after sharing the name Kitwanga with the adjacent white settlement. Gitwangak has some of the finest authentic

CASSIAR HIGHWAY
Yellowhead Highway Junction to Alaska Highway Junction

Map Location

Scale
0   20   Miles
0   20   Kilometres

Key to mileage boxes
miles/kilometres
miles/kilometres
from:
J-Junction
AH-Alaska Highway
M-Meziadin Lake Junction
D-Dease Lake Junction

To Ross River
(see CAMPBELL HIGHWAY section)

To Teslin
(see ALASKA HIGHWAY section)

Watson Lake

YUKON TERRITORY
BRITISH COLUMBIA

To Fort Nelson
(see ALASKA HIGHWAY section)

AH-0
J-446/718km

J-446.1/723.7km Junction 37 Services CDdGILMPrT

Baking Powder Creek

AH-74/118km
J-372/600km

Boya Lake

Centreville
Cassiar

Good Hope Lake
Good Hope Lake

J-371.3/602.2km Jade City
J-371.1/601.9km Grizzly Gas Bar & Den dGIMS

McDame Post

Vines L.

Cotton Lake

J-352.8/572.4km Moose Meadows Resort CLS

Cottonwood R.
Pine Tree Lake

Joe Irwin Lake
Beady Creek

Dease Lake

Tasto Creek

AH-145/234km
D-0
J-301/484km

Dease Lake

J-257.7/418.1km Forty Mile Flats CDdGLMr
J-256/415.4km Trappers Souvenirs
J-255.2/414.1km Bear Paw Ranch Wilderness Resort L
J-251.8/408.3km Mountain Shadow RV Park & Campground CDLT

D-70/113km

Telegraph Creek

AH-196/315km
J-250/403km

D-70.1/112.8km Stikine RiverSong Cafe, Lodge and
General Store GLMST
Stikine RiverSong Boat Tours

Glenora

Morchuea L.

Iskut

Kluachon L.

J-250.2/405.75km Kluachon Centre GST
J-248.3/402.5km Tenajon Motel & Cafe LMT
J-248.2/402.3km Red Goat Lodge CLT

Eddontenajon
Lake

Mount Edziza ▲
9,143 ft./2,787m   Tatogga L.

J-240.7/390.2km Harbour Air Ltd.
Tatogga Lake Resort CDdGrT

Kinaskan L.

Natadesleen
Lake

Mount Edziza
Provincial Park

Spatsizi
Wilderness
Provincial
Park

SKEENA MOUNTAINS

Thomas Creek
Devil Creek

Bob
Quinn L.

Ningunsaw R.

Iskut River   Snowbank
Creek

J-153.6/248.8km Bell II
Crossing, Ltd
CDdGILMPrT

BRITISH COLUMBIA
ALASKA

Wrangell

AH-350/563km
M-0
J-96/155km

Bowser Lake

Mount Bell-Irving
5,148 ft./1,569m

◄ J-96.2/156.4km Club Mez Corner Store IS
Meziadin Junction Services DdGIMPrST

Alaska State Ferry
(see MARINE ACCESS ROUTES section)

Premier

Salmon River   **Bear**
Glacier

Meziadin L.

Meziadin
R.

J-85.7/138.9km Meziadin General Store/Van Dyke
Camp Services Ltd. DdGIPST

Hyder

Prince of
Wales
Island

Stewart

M-41/66km

AH-399/643km
J-47/75km

Nass Forest
Service Road

Ketchikan

Alice Arm

New Aiyansh

Kitwanga
L.

J-2.6/4.2km Kitwanga Auto Service dGPr
J-2.5/4km Cassiar RV Park

Kitwancool

Dragon
L.

Hazelton
New Hazelton

Nass

Kitwanga

South Hazelton

Kitseguecla

Lava Lake

Nisga'a
Highway

AH-446/718km
J-0

To Prince George
(see YELLOWHEAD
HIGHWAY 16 section)

West Kalum
Forest Service
Road

Kitsumkalum Lake

UNITED STATES
CANADA

Prince Rupert

Dixon Entrance

Terrace

To Kitimat
(see YELLOWHEAD HIGHWAY 16 section)

CASSIAR
MOUNTAINS

COAST
MOUNTAINS
Glaciated
Area

Albert Cr.
Cormier Cr.

Watson
Lake

Blue River

French Cr.

Dease River

Liard River

Tahltan R.
Tuya R.
Tanzilla River
Stikine R.

Stikine River

Bell-Irving R.

Nass River

Skeena R.

Skeena

Portland Inlet
Portland Canal
Observatory Inlet

Key to Advertiser
Services
C -Camping
D -Dump Station
d -Diesel
G -Gas (reg., unld.)
I -Ice
L -Lodging
M -Meals
P -Propane
R -Car Repair (major)
r -Car Repair (minor)
S -Store (grocery)
T -Telephone (pay)

Principal Route
Paved   Unpaved
Other Roads
Paved   Unpaved
Ferry Routes   **Hiking Trails**

Refer to Log for Visitor Facilities
Visitor Information   Fishing
Campground   Airport   Airstrip

totem poles in the area. Also here is St. Paul's Anglican Church (the original old bell tower standing beside the church dates back to 1893) and one of the last existing Grand Trunk Pacific railway stations.

J 2.5 (4 km) **AH 443.6** (714 km) Kitwanga post office, a private RV park, and a bed and breakfast. ▲

Cassiar RV Park. See display ad this section.

J 2.6 (4.2 km) **AH 443.5** (713.8 km) South end of 1.6-mile/2.5-km loop access road which leads to **KITWANGA** (pop. 1,200). **Radio:** CBC 630 AM. **Emergency Services:** Ambulance. The business area of Kitwanga has a visitor information booth (open June to August, local crafts for sale), gas station, car wash, a general store and small restaurant. There is a free public campground. (Donations for campground upkeep gratefully accepted at the Kitwanga Tempo service station.) ▲

Kitwanga is at the crossroads of the old upper Skeena "grease trail" trade. The "grease" was eulachon (candlefish) oil, which was a trading staple among tribes of the Coast and Interior. The grease trails are believed to have extended north to the Bering Sea.

A paved turnout with litter barrel and sign on the Kitwanga access road mark Kitwanga Fort National Historic Site, where a wooden fortress and palisade once crowned the large rounded hill here. Seven interpretive panels along the trail up Battle Hill explain the history of the site. Kitwanga Fort was the first major western Canadian Native site commemorated by Parks Canada.

Kitwanga Auto Service. See display ad this section.

J 4 (6.5 km) **AH 442.1** (711.5 km) North end of 1.6-mile/2.6-km loop access road (Kitwanga North Road) to Kitwanga; see description preceding milepost.

J 4.1 (6.6 km) **AH 442** (711.4 km) **Junction** with alternate access route (signed Hazelton–Kitwanga Road) from Hazelton to the Cassiar Highway via the north side of the Skeena River.

J 5 (8 km) **AH 441.1** (710 km) The mountain chain of Seven Sisters is visible to southwest (weather permitting) next 4 miles/6.4 km northbound.

J 12.5 (20.2 km) **AH 433.6** (697.9 km) Turnout with litter barrels to west.

J 12.6 (20.3 km) **AH 433.5** (697.7 km) Highway follows Kitwanga River and former grease trail route.

J 13 (21 km) **AH 433.1** (697.1 km) South access to **KITWANCOOL**, a small Indian village with many fine old totems, some recently restored. Guided tours of the totem poles may be available; inquire at the Visitor Infocentre. A Native craft shop in the village sells local art. The village of Kitwancool was originally called Gitanyow, meaning place of many people, but was renamed Kitwancool, meaning place of reduced number, after many of its inhabitants were killed in raids.

J 16.1 (26.1 km) **AH 430** (692.1 km) North access to Kitwancool.

J 18.8 (30.4 km) **AH 427.3** (687.8 km) Bridge over Moonlit Creek.

J 18.9 (30.7 km) **AH 427.2** (687.5 km) Rest area north of creek, east of road, with tables, toilets and litter barrels. Road west is the old highway and access to **Kitwanga Lake.** Fishing, camping and boat launch spots on lake. Old highway may be in poor condition; drive carefully. It rejoins the main highway at Mile 24.1. Access to the lake is strictly from the old highway. ◄▲

J 19.9 (32.2 km) **AH 426.2** (686 km) Access to Kitwanga Lake.

J 21.3 (34.5 km) **AH 424.8** (683.7 km) Good views of Kitwanga Lake to west; old highway visible, below west, winding along lakeshore.

J 26.1 (42.2 km) **AH 420** (676 km) Kitwancool Forest Road to west.

J 38.8 (62.9 km) **AH 407.3** (655.5 km)

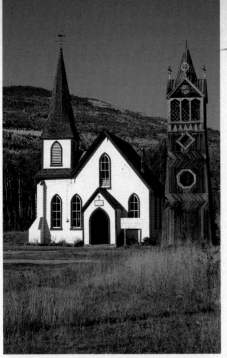

Anglican church and old bell tower in Gitwangak, Milepost J 0.2. (© Carmen Scott)

Cranberry River bridge No. 1. A favorite salmon stream in summer; consult fishing regulations.

J 46.5 (75.3 km) **AH 399.6** (643.2 km) Paved turnout to west.

J 46.8 (75.9 km) **AH 399.3** (642.6 km) **Junction** with the Nass Forest Service Road to **NEW AIYANSH** (38.4 miles/61.8 km) and Terrace. *NOTE: This intersection is easy to miss.* See NISGA'A HIGHWAY/NASS ROAD log on page 238. A B.C. Forest Service campsite is 27 miles/44 km west at Dragon Lake; room for 10 to 12 vehicles, cartop boat launch. Bed and breakfast at New Aiyansh.

J 47.1 (76.3 km) **AH 399** (642.2 km) Cranberry River bridge No. 2. Turnout with toilets, tables and litter barrels.

J 53.1 (86 km) **AH 393** (632.6 km) BC Hydro power line crosses and parallels highway. Completed in 1990, this line links Stewart to the BC Hydro power grid. Previously, Stewart's power was generated by diesel fuel.

Entering Kalum Forest District northbound. Watch for signs telling dates of logging activity, and observe patterns of regrowth.

J 58.6 (94.9 km) **AH 387.5** (623.7 km) Kelly Lake rest area at north end of lake on west side of highway, with tables, toilet and litter barrels. First view northbound of Nass River.

J 64.1 (103.8 km) **AH 382** (614.9 km) Paved turnout.

J 65.6 (106.4 km) **AH 380.5** (612.4 km) View of Nass River to west. The Nass River is one of the province's prime producers of sockeye salmon.

J 66.4 (107.7 km) **AH 379.7** (611.1 km) Views northbound (weather permitting) of the Coast Mountains to the west. Cambrian ice field to west.

J 70.1 (113.6 km) **AH 376** (605.2 km) Paved turnout with litter barrel to west.

J 78.7 (127.4 km) **AH 367.4** (591.3 km) Paved turnout with litter barrel.

J 85 (137.8 km) **AH 361.1** (581.2 km) Paved turnout with litter barrels to west.

J 85.7 (138.9 km) **AH 360.4** (580.1 km)

Elsworth logging camp and Van Dyke camp services; open to public; fuel, groceries, dump station, hunting and fishing licenses, emergency phone. Private airstrip.

Meziadin Lake General Store. See display ad this section.

J 87.9 (142.4 km) **AH 358.2** (576.6 km) *CAUTION: 1-lane bridge over Nass River.* Paved rest area with picnic tables, toilets and litter barrel to east at south end of bridge. A plaque at the north end commemorates bridge opening in 1972 that joined roads to form Highway 37. The gorge is almost 400 feet/122m wide; main span of bridge is 186 feet/57m. Bridge decking is 130 feet/40m above the riverbed.

J 89.4 (145 km) **AH 356.7** (574.1 km) Tintina Logging Road.

J 93.1 (151 km) **AH 353** (568.1 km) Tintina Creek. Along with Hanna Creek, this stream produces 40 percent of the sockeye salmon spawning in the Meziadin Lake watershed.

J 94.3 (152.8 km) **AH 351.8** (566.3 km) Large gravel turnout to west with litter barrels.

J 94.4 (153 km) **AH 351.7** (566 km) Bridge over Hanna Creek South. Sockeye salmon spawn here in autumn and can be observed from creek banks and bridge deck. It is illegal to fish for or harass these fish. *CAUTION: Watch for bears.*

J 95.6 (155.3 km) **AH 350.5** (564.2 km) **Meziadin Lake** Provincial Park; 46 campsites (many on lake), drinking water, toilets, wheelchair access, swimming, firewood, bear-proof garbage containers, boat launch. The lake has a significant fish population, including rainbow trout, mountain whitefish and Dolly Varden. Fishing is especially good at the mouths of small streams draining into Meziadin Lake.

Four species of salmon spawn in the lake. This is one of only 3 lakes in the province where salmon spawn in the bays and inlets of a lake. *CAUTION: Watch for bears. The hills around the lake are prime bear habitat.*

J 96.2 (156.4 km) **AH 349.9** (563.1 km) **Meziadin Lake Junction** (Mezy-AD-in); Cassiar Highway junctions with the access road to Stewart, BC, and Hyder, AK. Fuel, propane, minor car repair, food, laundry, RV parking and dump station. See page 248 for log of STEWART, BC–HYDER, AK, ACCESS ROAD. *NOTE: This junction can be confusing. Choose your route carefully.*

Club Mez Corner Store. See display ad this section. ▲

Meziadin Junction Services. See display ad this section. ▲

J 97.5 (158.5 km) **AH 348.6** (561.1 km) Travelers will notice large areas of clear-cut along the southern half of the Cassiar Highway. Bark beetle infestation necessitated the harvest of timber along this particular stretch of highway. After logging, it was reforested.

J 100.8 (164.8 km) **AH 345.3** (555.8 km)
(Continues on page 252)

Stewart, BC–Hyder, AK, Access Road Log

HIGHWAY 37A
Distance is measured from Meziadin Lake Junction (M).

M 0 Junction with Cassiar Highway at **Milepost J 96.2.** Visitor information cabin, status unconfirmed at press time.

M 2.8 (4.6 km) Highway maintenance yard.

M 7.7 (12.4 km) Surprise Creek bridge.

M 10.1 (16.3 km) Turnout to north with view of hanging glaciers.

M 10.4 (16.7 km) Turnout to south with view of hanging glaciers.

M 11.5 (18.5 km) Windy Point bridge.

M 12.5 (20.1 km) Cornice Creek bridge.

M 13.5 (21.7 km) Strohn Creek bridge.

M 14.4 (23.2 km) Rest area with litter barrels, view of Bear Glacier.

M 15.4 (24.8 km) Turnouts along lake into which Bear Glacier calves its icebergs. Watch for falling rock from slopes above road in spring. Morning light is best for photographing spectacular Bear Glacier. At one time the glacier reached this side of the valley; the old highway can be seen hundreds of feet above the present road.

M 17.5 (28.8 km) Cullen River bridge.

M 19.8 (31.9 km) Huge delta of accumulated avalanche snow. Little shoulder; no stopping.

M 21 (33.8 km) Argyle Creek.

M 22.4 (36.1 km) Narrow, steep-walled Bear River canyon. Watch for rocks on road.

M 23.9 (38.5 km) Turnout with litter barrel to north.

M 24.3 (39.1 km) Bear River bridge.

M 28.9 (46.5 km) Turnout with litter barrel to south.

M 29.4 (47.4 km) Bitter Creek bridge.

M 31.8 (51.2 km) Wards Pass cemetery. The straight stretch of road along here is the former railbed from Stewart.

M 36.1 (58.1 km) Bear River bridge and welcome portal to Stewart.

M 37.8 (60.8 km) Highway joins main street of Stewart (description follows).

M 40.1 (64.4 km) U.S.–Canada border. Hyder (description follows).

TIME ZONE CHANGE: Stewart observes Pacific time, Hyder observes Alaska time. See Time Zones in the GENERAL INFORMATION section.

Stewart, BC–Hyder, AK

Stewart is at the head of Portland Canal on the AK–BC border. **Hyder** is 2.3 miles/3.7 km beyond Stewart. **Population: Stewart** about 1,000; **Hyder** 85. **Emergency Services:** In Stewart, **RCMP**, phone (250) 636-2233. EMS personnel and Medivac helicopter in Hyder. **Fire Department**, phone (250) 636-2345. **Hospital** and **Ambulance**, Stewart Health Care Facility (3 beds), phone (250) 636-2221.

Visitor Information: Stewart Visitor Infocentre (Box 306, Stewart, BC V0T 1W0), located in Chamber of Commerce/Infocentre Building on 5th Avenue; phone (250) 636-9224 or fax (250) 636-2199. Limited off-season hours. Hyder Information Center and Museum is located on the right as you drive into Hyder.

Elevation: Sea level. **Climate:** Maritime, with warm winters and cool rainy summers. Summer temperatures range from 41°F/5°C to 57°F/14°C; winter temperatures range from 25°F/-4°C to 43°F/6°C. Average temperature in January is 27°F/-3°C; in July, 67°F/19°C. Reported record high 89°F/32°C, record low -18°F/-28°C. Slightly less summer rain than other Northwest communities, but heavy snowfall in winter. **Radio:** CFPR 1450, CJFW-FM 92.9, CFMI-FM 101. **Television:** Cable, 15 channels.

Private Aircraft: Stewart airport, on 5th Street; elev. 10 feet/3m; length 3,900 feet/1,189m; asphalt; fuel 80, 100.

Stewart and Hyder are on a spur of the Cassiar Highway, at the head of Portland Canal, a narrow saltwater fjord approximately 90 miles/145 km long. The fjord forms a natural boundary between Alaska and Canada. Stewart has a deep harbour and boasts of being Canada's most northerly ice-free port.

Prior to the coming of the white man, Nass River Indians knew the head of Portland Canal as *Skam-A-Kounst*, mean-

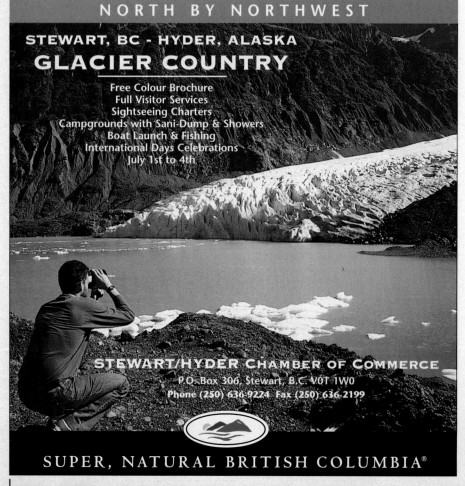
STEWART ADVERTISERS

Bear River Trailer Court Ltd.........Hwy. 37A
Bitter Creek Cafe and
   Marmot Bay Trading ....5th Ave.
Brothers' Bakery & Deli ....5th Ave.
King Edward Motel/
   Hotel ....5th & Columbia
Seaport Limousine ....Ph. (250) 636-2622
Stewart Lions Campground &
   RV Park ....Ph. (250) 636-2537
Stewart Tourist
   Information ....Ph. (250) 636-9224

ing safe place, probably referring to the place as a retreat from the harassment of the coastal Haidas. The Nass came here annually to hunt birds and pick berries. Little evidence of their presence remains.

In 1896, Captain D.D. Gaillard (after whom the Gaillard Cut in the Panama Canal was later named) explored Portland Canal for the U.S. Army Corps of Engineers. Two years after Gaillard's visit, the first prospectors and settlers arrived. Among them was D.J. Raine, for whom a creek and mountain in the area were named. The Stewart brothers arrived in 1902 and in 1905 Robert M. Stewart, the first postmaster, named the town Stewart. Hyder was first called Portland City. It was then renamed Hyder, after Canadian mining engineer Frederick B. Hyder, when the U.S. Postal Authority told residents there were already too many cities named Portland.

Gold and silver mining dominated the early economy. Hyder boomed with the discovery of rich silver veins in the upper Salmon River basin in 1917–18. Hundreds of pilings, which supported structures during this boom period, are visible on the tidal flats at Hyder.

Hyder became an access and supply point for the mines, while Stewart served as the centre for Canadian mining activity. Mining ceased in 1956, with the exception of the Granduc copper mine, which operated until 1984. Currently, Westmin Resources Ltd. operates a gold and silver mine. Today the economy is driven by forestry, mining and tourism.

ACCOMMODATIONS/VISITOR SERVICES
Stewart: 3 hotels/motels, 3 restaurants, 1 grocery store, 2 churches, service

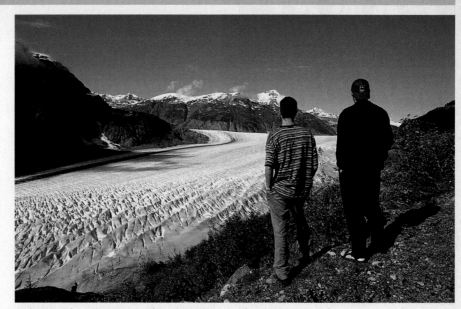

Salmon Glacier is a popular attraction in the Stewart–Hyder area. (© Beth Davidow)

stations, dry cleaners, laundromat, pharmacy, post office, a bank (open 10 A.M. to 3 P.M. Monday through Thursday, Friday until 6 P.M.), liquor store and other shops. Camping at 2 campgrounds/RV parks with washrooms, showers and hookups. ▲

Hyder: 2 groceries, 3 gift shops, a post office, 3 cafes, a Baptist church, 2 motels and 2 bars. Boat launch at salt water, tenting area and RV park with TV reception. Visitor infocentre and museum. Laundromat, public restroom and showers. There is no bank in Hyder. There are no automatic teller machines in Stewart/Hyder.

St. Paul's Orthodox Church. "World's smallest cathedral." Come visit our little chapel by the sea in historic Hyder, Alaska.

Stewart, BC–Hyder, AK, Access

All faiths welcome. Phone (250) 636-2708 for schedule of services. Bus tours and caravans welcome. Services daily. The Orthodox Church is the oldest Christian church in the world. Divine liturgy 10 A.M. Sunday. [ADVERTISEMENT]

Canal Trading Post. "Downtown Hyder's leading gift store." Smoked salmon. Gold nuggets. Totem poles. Rare jewelry. Ice cream. Candy. Cold drinks. T-shirts. Postcards. Sweat shirts. Diamonds. Furs. Emeralds. Native carvings. Soapstone. Ulu knives. U.S. mail drop. Fishing licenses. Alaska state ferry information. Captain Terry's RV wash. Free maps to bear viewing area! Canadian funds at par. Open 7 days. 10 A.M. to 10 P.M. (250) 636-2708. MasterCard. VISA, Amex. [ADVERTISEMENT]

Captain Terry's Junk O Rama. Exotic junk. Free maps to bear viewing area. Sporting goods. Bait. Crab traps. Fishing tackle. Black powder guns. Knives. Antiques. Collectibles. Smoked salmon. Buy–sell–trade. Come visit our friendly, courteous staff. Downtown Hyder. Next door to St. Paul's Orthodox Church. (250) 636-9060. MasterCard, VISA, Amex. Proposed for 1997. [ADVERTISEMENT]

Captain Terry's RV Wash. Tired of the mud? We'll get 'em clean. Best rates. Best service. We'll wash the wilderness out of your RV. Caravans our specialty. Phone (250) 636-2708. The dirtier, the better. We're located right next to the world famous Canal Trading Post in downtown Hyder, Alaska. MasterCard, VISA, Amex. [ADVERTISEMENT]

TRANSPORTATION

Air: Taquan Air scheduled service from Hyder to Ketchikan. **Bus:** Limousine service to Terrace with connections to Greyhound and airlines. **Ferry:** Service between Ketchikan and Hyder. See the Alaska state ferry schedules (Southern Panhandle) in the MARINE ACCESS ROUTES section. *IMPORTANT: Check ferry departure times carefully!*

ATTRACTIONS

Historic Buildings: In Stewart, the former fire hall at 6th and Columbia streets built in 1910, which now houses the Historical Society Museum; the Empress Hotel (now occupied by a hardware store) on 4th Street; and St. Mark's Church (built in 1910) on 9th Street at Columbia. On the border at Eagle Point is the stone storehouse built by Captain D.D. Gaillard of the U.S. Army Corps of Engineers in 1896. This is the oldest masonry building in Alaska. Originally 4 of these buildings were built to hold exploration supplies. This one was subsequently used as a cobbler shop and jail. Storehouses Nos. 3 and 4 are included on the (U.S.) National Register of Historic Places.

Stewart Historical Society Museum, in the fire hall, has a wildlife exhibit on the main floor and an exhibit of historical items on the top floor. Included is a display on movies filmed here: "Bear Island" (1978), John Carpenter's "The Thing" (1981), and "The Ice Man" (1982).

Hyder's night life is well-known, and has helped Hyder earn the reputation and town motto of "The Friendliest Little Ghost Town in Alaska."

Recreation in Stewart includes winter sports at the indoor skating rink; an outdoor tennis court; ball parks; hiking trails; and a self-guided historical walking tour.

Sightseeing tours of the area take in active and abandoned mine sites, such as Granduc, and glaciers, including the spectacular Salmon Glacier. Other sights include nearby Fish Creek and Summit Lake at the toe of Salmon Glacier. Once a year, usually in August, the ice dam holding back Summit Lake breaks, and the force of the meltwater results in a spectacular flooding of the Salmon River valley at Hyder. Chum and pink salmon are seen in their spawning colors in Fish Creek during August; they ascend the streams and rivers in great numbers to spawn. Visitors may photograph feeding bald eagles and black bears which are drawn to the streams by the salmon.

Visit the old mines. A 30-mile-/48-km-long road leads to movie locations and former mine sites. *CAUTION: The road is narrow and winding.* Access to Premier Mine, Big Missouri Mine and Salmon Glacier. Inquire at the Stewart Infocentre for more information.

International Days. Fourth of July begins July 1 as Stewart and Hyder celebrate Canada Day and Independence Day. Parade and fireworks.

Charter trips by small boat on Portland Canal and vicinity available for sightseeing and fishing. Flightseeing air tours available.

AREA FISHING: Portland Canal, salmon to 50 lbs., use herring, spring and late fall; coho to 12 lbs. in fall, fly-fishing. *(NOTE: Alaska or British Columbia fishing license required, depending on whether you fish U.S. or Canadian waters in Portland Canal.)* **Fish Creek,** up the Salmon River road from Hyder, Dolly Varden 2 to 3 lbs., use salmon eggs and lures, best in summer. Fish Creek is a fall spawning ground for some of the world's largest chum salmon; it is illegal to kill chum in fresh water in British Columbia. It is legal to harvest chum from both salt and fresh water in Alaska.

Return to Milepost J 96.2 on the Cassiar Highway

(Continued from page 247)

Hanna Creek North river and bridge. Gravel turnout at north end of bridge on west side of road with litter barrel.

J 104.1 (169.2km) **AH 342** (550.5 km) Large paved turnout to west with litter barrels.

J 109.8 (178.5 km) **AH 336.3** (541.3 km) Pavement ends, gravel begins northbound.

NOTE: There was considerable construction northbound to the Bell–Irving River bridge in 1996. Driving distance over this stretch may vary from log due to detours. Project is scheduled for completion in summer 1998.

J 116 (189.2 km) **AH 330.1** (531.3 km) Bell I rest area at north end of Bell–Irving bridge; picnic tables, pit toilets, litter barrels.

J 118.2 (192.2 km) **AH 327.9** (527.7 km) Spruce Creek bridge.

J 122.8 (198.9 km) **AH 323.3** (520.3 km) Bell–Irving River parallels highway.

J 125.1 (202.5 km) **AH 321** (516.7 km) Cousins Creek.

J 126.7 (205.2 km) **AH 319.4** (514.1 km) Ritchie Creek bridge, wooden-decked, slippery when wet.

J 130.4 (211.2 km) **AH 315.7** (508.1 km) Taft Creek bridge, wooden-decked, slippery when wet.

J 136.1 (220.4 km) **AH 310** (499 km) Deltaic Creek.

J 141.5 (229.2 km) **AH 304.6** (490.3 km) Glacier Creek.

J 142 (230 km) **AH 304.1** (489.5 km) Seal coat begins, gravel ends northbound.

J 143.6 (232.7 km) **AH 302.5** (486.8 km) Skowill Creek.

J 145.1 (235 km) **AH 301** (484.5 km) Large gravel turnout with litter barrels.

J 148.1 (239.8 km) **AH 298** (479.7 km) Oweegee Creek.

J 152.1 (246.2 km) **AH 294** (473.2 km) Provincial rest area by **Hodder Lake**; information kiosk, tables, litter barrels, pit toilets, cartop boat launch. Fly or troll for small rainbows. ◄

J 153.6 (248.8 km) **AH 292.5** (470.7 km) Food, gas, diesel, propane, pay phone and lodging.

Bell II Crossing Ltd. See display ad this section. ▲

J 153.8 (249.3 km) **AH 292.3** (470.5 km) Second crossing northbound of Bell–Irving River.

J 156.8 (254.2 km) **AH 289.3** (465.6 km) Large gravel turnout with litter barrel.

J 159.2 (258.1 km) **AH 286.9** (461.7 km) Snowbank Creek.

J 161.2 (261.1 km) **AH 284.9** (458.6 km) Avalanche area: No stopping in winter or spring. Avalanche chutes are visible on slopes to west in summer. Highway serves as emergency airstrip. Watch for aircraft landing or taking off; keep to side of road!

J 161.6 (261.8 km) **AH 284.5** (457.9 km) Redflat Creek.

J 164.1 (266 km) **AH 282** (453.8 km) Revision Creek.

J 165.1 (267.6 km) **AH 281** (452.2 km) Fan Creek.

J 167.3 (271 km) **AH 278.8** (448.7 km) Avalanche area. No stopping.

J 168.7 (273.2 km) **AH 277.4** (446.5 km) Turnout with litter barrels to east overlooking large moose pasture, beaver ponds.

J 169.6 (274.9 km) **AH 276.5** (445 km)

Spawning sockeye salmon in Hanna Creek. (Judy Parkin, staff)

Ningunsaw Pass (elev. 1,530 feet/466m). Nass–Stikine water divide; turnout with litter barrels to west beside **Ningunsaw River**. Mountain whitefish and Dolly Varden. The highway parallels the Ningunsaw northbound. Watch for fallen rock on road through the canyon. The Ningunsaw is a tributary of the Stikine watershed. ◄

J 169.9 (275.4 km) **AH 276.2** (444.5 km) Beaverpond Creek.

J 170.3 (276 km) **AH 275.8** (443.9 km) Liz Creek.

J 172.7 (279.9 km) **AH 273.4** (440 km) Alger Creek. The massive piles of logs and debris in this creek are from a 1989 avalanche. Avalanche chutes visible to west.

J 173 (280.3 km) **AH 273.1** (439.5 km) Large gravel turnout to east with litter barrel.

J 174.8 (283.2 km) **AH 271.3** (436.7 km) Gamma Creek.

J 175.6 (284.5 km) **AH 270.5** (435.4 km) Bend Creek.

J 176.9 (286.9 km) **AH 269.2** (433.2 km) Ogilvie Creek.

J 177.8 (288.2 km) **AH 268.3** (431.9 km) Point of interest sign about Yukon Telegraph line. The 1,900-mile/3,057-km Dominion Telegraph line linked Dawson City with Vancouver. Built from 1899–1901, the line was a route for prospectors and trappers headed to Atlin, BC; it was replaced by radio in the 1930s.

J 178 (288.6 km) **AH 268.1** (431.5 km) Echo Lake. Flooded telegraph cabins are visible in the lake below. Good view of Coast Mountains to west. Spectacular cliffs seen to the east are part of the Skeena Mountains (Bowser Basin).

J 181 (293.7 km) **AH 265.1** (426.6 km) Bob Quinn Forest Service Road, under construction as the Iskut Mining Road, will provide year-round access to goldfields west of the Ningunsaw River. The road will follow the Iskut River Valley toward the Stikine River, with a side branch to Eskay Creek gold deposit.

J 181.5 (294.4 km) **AH 264.6** (425.9 km) **Little Bob Quinn Lake**, rainbow and Dolly Varden, summer and fall. Access to Bob Quinn Lake at **Milepost J 183.3**. ◄

J 182.2 (295.3 km) **AH 263.9** (424.7 km) Bob Quinn flight airstrip. This is a staging site for supplies headed for the Stikine/Iskut goldfields. Paved rest area with litter barrels, picnic tables and toilet.

J 183.3 (297 km) **AH 262.8** (423 km) Bob Quinn highway maintenance camp; helicopter base. Emergency assistance. Access to Bob Quinn Lake; toilet, picnic table, cartop boat launch.

J 187 (303.1 km) **AH 259.1** (417 km) Gravel turnout with litter barrels on both sides of road.

J 188.3 (305.2 km) **AH 257.8** (415 km) Old kilometrepost 150, which reflects distance from Meziadin Junction.

J 190.2 (308.4 km) **AH 255.9** (411.8 km) Devil Creek Canyon bridge.

J 191.1 (309.7 km) **AH 255** (410.5 km) Gravel turnout with litter barrel to west.

J 191.6 (310.7 km) **AH 254.5** (409.6 km) Devil Creek Forest Service Road.

J 193.6 (313.9 km) **AH 252.5** (406.4 km) Thomas Creek.

Highway passes through Iskut burn, where fire destroyed 78,000 acres in 1958. This is also British Columbia's largest huckleberry patch.

Northbound, the vegetation begins to change to northern boreal white and black spruce. This zone has cold, long winters and low forest productivity. Look for trembling aspen and lodgepole pine.

Southbound, the vegetation changes to become part of the interior cedar–hemlock zone. Cool wet winters and long dry summers produce a variety of tree species including western hemlock and red cedar, hybrid white spruce and subalpine fir.

J 196.3 (318.1 km) **AH 249.8** (402 km) Large gravel turnout with litter barrel to west.

J 197.3 (319.6 km) **AH 248.8** (400.5 km) Slate Creek.

J 198.4 (321.74 km) **AH 247.7** (398.6 km) Gravel turnout with litter barrels to east.

J 199 (321 km) **AH 247.1** (397.7 km) Brake–check pullout.

J 199.7 (323.7 km) **AH 246.4** (396.6 km) Durham Creek.

J 203.7 (330.2 km) **AH 242.4** (390.1 km) Gravel begins, seal coat ends northbound.

J 204 (330.6 km) **AH 242.1** (389.7 km) Gravel turnout with litter barrels to west.

J 205.1 (332.4 km) **AH 241** (387.9 km) Single-lane bridge crosses Burrage River, northbound traffic yields. Note the rock pinnacle upstream to east.

J 205.5 (333 km) **AH 240.6** (387.2 km) Iskut River to west.

J 206.8 (335 km) **AH 239.3** (385.2 km) Gravel turnout to west.

J 207.8 (336.6 km) **AH 238.3** (383.6 km) Emergency airstrip crosses road; no stopping, watch for aircraft.

J 213 (345.4 km) **AH 233.1** (375.1 km) Rest area by Eastman Creek; picnic tables, outhouses, litter barrels, and information sign with map and list of services in Iskut Lakes Recreation Area. The creek was named for George Eastman (of Eastman Kodak fame), who hunted big game in this area before the highway was built.

J 216 (350.2 km) **AH 230.1** (370.3 km) Slow down for 1-lane bridge across Rescue Creek, northbound traffic yields.

J 217.7 (352.9 km) **AH 228.4** (367.6 km) Slow down for 1-lane bridge over Willow Creek, northbound traffic yields.

J 218.3 (353.9 km) **AH 227.8** (366.6 km) Willow Creek Forest Service Road.

J 219.9 (356.6 km) **AH 226.2** (364 km) Gravel turnout with litter barrels to east.

J 220.6 (357.7 km) **AH 225.5** (362.9 km) Natadesleen Lake trailhead to west; toilets and litter barrel. Hike 0.6 mile/1 km west to lake.

J 222.6 (360.9 km) **AH 223.5** (359.7 km) Gravel turnout to west.

J 223.9 (362.9 km) **AH 222.2** (357.7 km) Snapper Creek.

J 225.1 (365 km) **AH 221** (355.7 km) Entrance to Kinaskan campground with 50 sites, outhouses, firewood, picnic and day-use area, wheelchair access, swimming, 2 hiking trails, drinking water and boat launch on **Kinaskan Lake**; rainbow fishing, July and August. Start of 15-mile/24.1-km hiking trail to Mowdade Lake in Mount Edziza Provincial Park.

J 225.2 (365.2 km) **AH 220.9** (355.5 km) Seal coat begins, gravel ends northbound.

J 230.1 (373.1 km) **AH 216** (347.6 km) Turnout with litter barrel and view of Kinaskan Lake to west.

J 231.1 (374.6 km) **AH 215** (346.1 km) Small lake to east.

J 233.1 (377.9 km) **AH 213** (342.8 km) Gravel turnout with litter barrels to east.

J 233.4 (378.4 km) **AH 212.7** (342.3 km) Todagin Creek 1-lane bridge, northbound traffic yields.

J 239.4 (388.1 km) **AH 206.7** (332.7 km)

Floatplanes provide access to wilderness areas for hikers and canoeists. (Judy Parkin, staff)

Gravel turnout to west.

J 240.7 (390.2 km) **AH 205.4** (330.6 km) **Harbour Air Ltd.** See display ad this section.

Tatogga Lake Resort. See display ad this section. ▲

J 240.8 (390.3 km) **AH 205.3** (330.5 km) Jackman Creek.

J 241.3 (391.1 km) **AH 204.8** (329.7 km) Coyote Creek.

J 241.9 (392.1 km) **AH 204.2** (328.7 km) Ealue Lake (EE-lu-eh) turnoff. Small B.C. Forest Service recreation area, 7.5 miles/12 km off highway on gravel access road. Rustic sites, picnic tables, rock fire rings (bring own firewood), user-maintained, no fee. ▲

J 244.5 (396.4 km) **AH 201.6** (324.5 km) Turnout with litter barrel.

J 244.6 (396.6 km) **AH 201.5** (324.3 km) Spatsizi trailhead to east. Turnout with litter

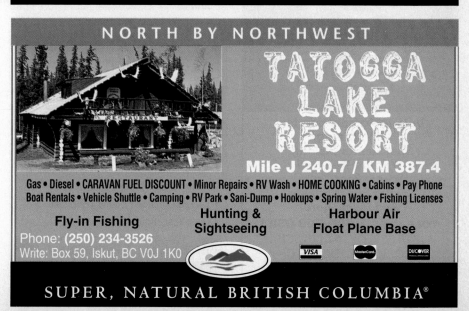

barrel beside **Eddontenajon Lake** (Ed-don-TEN-ajon). It is unlawful to camp overnight at turnouts. People drink from the lake; be careful not to contaminate it. Use dump stations. Breakup in late May; freezeup early November. Rainbow fishing July and August.

J 248.2 (402.3 km) **AH 197.9** (318.6 km) **Red Goat Lodge.** The complete wilderness resort offering first-class lakeshore camping for RVs and tenters, a bed and breakfast with unparalleled reputation. Crushed gravel RV sites are landscaped to the same exacting standards of B.C. Parks, with TV, deluxe hot showers, washrooms, laundry, phone. Canoe rentals, guided canoe tours, instruction. Fishing is excellent from shore, boat launch. Choose Red Goat for real quality. AAA approved and undoubtedly the best facility on Highway 37. May to September. Tony and Doreen Shaw, Iskut, BC. Phone and fax (250) 234-3261. [ADVERTISEMENT] ▲

Wildflowers carpet a hillside near Iskut. (Eero Sorila)

J 248.3 (402.5 km) **AH 197.8** (318.4 km) **Tenajon Motel & Cafe.** See display ad this section.

J 250 (405.4 km) **AH 196.1** (315.6 km) B.C. Hydro generating plant, supplies power for Iskut area.

J 250.2 (405.7 km) **AH 195.9** (315.3 km) **ISKUT** (pop. 300). Small Tahltan Indian community with post office, grocery store, public phone, motel and gas station. Quality beaded moccasins available locally. Camping and cabins available at local lodges and guest ranches. Horse trips, canoe rentals and river rafting may be available; inquire at local lodges and resorts. Clinic open 1–3 P.M., 5 days a week. ▲

Kluachon Centre. See display ad this section.

Private Aircraft: Eddontenajon airstrip, 0.6 mile/1 km north of Iskut; elev. 3,100 feet/945m; length 3,000 feet/914m; gravel; fuel available at Trans-Provincial Airlines

base south on Eddontenajon Lake.

J 251.8 (408.3 km) **AH 194.3** (312.7 km) **Mountain Shadow.** 50 miles south of Dease Lake. A quiet, secluded, park-like setting with spectacular mountain vistas and lake views. Set away from highway noise and traffic for a restful stop over or extended stay. Short nature walk for exclusive access to Kluachon Lake with excellent fishing. Wilderness trails, bird and wildlife viewing. A unique, private and breathtaking wilderness setting. [ADVERTISEMENT] ▲

J 255.2 (414.1 km) **AH 190.9** (307.2 km) **Bear Paw Ranch Wilderness Resort.** Experience our deluxe Alpine Hotel. Fine dining in our spectacular "View Dining Room." Hot tub, lounge, souvenir/gift shop, guided wilderness tours. If it's relaxation or wilderness adventure, if it's family fun or a romantic getaway, if it's "sourdough frontier excitement" or luxury stress release that you're after—the Bear Paw Supplies. VISA,

MasterCard. [ADVERTISEMENT] ▲

J 256 (415.4 km) **AH 190.1** (306 km) **Trapper's Souvenirs.** See display ad this section.

J 257.7 (418.1 km) **AH 188.4** (303.3 km) **Forty Mile Flats.** See display ad this section. ▲

J 260.6 (423 km) **AH 185.5** (298.5 km) Turnout with litter barrels to west. From here the dormant volcano of Mount Edziza (elev. 9,143 feet/2,787m) and its adjunct cinder cone can be seen to the southwest. The park, not accessible by road, is a rugged wilderness with a glacier, cinder cones, craters and lava flows. Panoramic view of Skeena and Cassiar mountains for next several miles northbound. Information signs.

J 261.8 (424.9 km) **AH 184.3** (296.6 km) Turnoff to Morchuea Lake B.C. Forest Service campsite. Rustic, some tables, rock fire rings (bring firewood), no fee. ▲

J 263.3 (427.3 km) **AH 182.8** (294.2 km) Gravel begins, seal coat ends, northbound.

J 264 (428.4 km) **AH 182.1** (293.1 km) Entering Stikine River Recreation Area.

J 266.3 (432.1 km) **AH 179.8** (289.4 km) Steep grade. Winding road next 1.2 miles/2 km northbound.

J 267.2 (433.6 km) **AH 178.9** (287.9 km) Hairpin turn: Keep to right. Highway descends to Stikine River in switchbacks.

J 269 (436.6 km) **AH 177.1** (285 km) Turnout with litter barrels and toilets to south. Tourist map and services directory for area located here.

J 269.5 (437.3 km) **AH 176.6** (284.3 km) Stikine River bridge.

J 271.3 (440.2 km) **AH 174.8** (281.4 km) Turnout to east with litter barrel.

J 273.4 (443.6 km) **AH 172.7** (278 km) Leaving Stikine River Recreation Area northbound.

J 274.1 (444.8 km) **AH 172** (276.8 km) Seal coat begins, gravel ends, northbound.

J 277.3 (450 km) **AH 168.8** (271.6 km)

Turnout on Upper Gnat Lake; tables, toilets, litter barrels. Long scar across Gnat Pass valley to east is grading preparation for B.C. Railway's proposed Dease Lake extension from Prince George. Construction was halted in 1977. Grade is visible for several miles northbound.

J 279 (452.7 km) **AH 167.1** (268.9 km) Large gravel turnout with litter barrel to east at Tees Creek.

J 282 (457.6 km) **AH 164.1** (264.1 km) Gravel turnout with litter barrel to east.

J 283.9 (460.7 km) **AH 162.2** (261.1 km) Gravel turnout to east.

J 284.2 (461.3 km) **AH 161.9** (260.5 km) Upper Gnat Rest Area.

J 284.5 (461.7 km) **AH 161.6** (260.1 km) Wilderness trail rides.

J 285.8 (463.8 km) **AH 160.3** (258 km) Turnout overlooking **Lower Gnat Lake**, abundant rainbow. ◄

J 287.9 (467.1 km) **AH 158.2** (254.7 km) Turnout with litter barrel.

J 290.6 (467.7 km) **AH 155.5** (250.2 km) Gnat Pass Summit, elev. 4,072 feet/1,241m.

J 291.7 (473.3 km) **AH 154.4** (248.5 km) Steep grade, 8 percent downhill.

J 295.2 (479.1 km) **AH 150.9** (242.8 km) **Tanzilla River** bridge. Pleasant rest area with picnic tables and outhouses at north end of bridge beside river. Fishing for grayling to 16 inches, June and July; use flies. ◄

J 296.5 (481.2 km) **AH 149.6** (240.7 km) Dalby Creek.

J 298.4 (484.1 km) **AH 147.7** (237.8 km) Turnout with litter barrel to west.

J 300.2 (487.1 km) **AH 145.9** (234.9 km) Divide (elev. 2,690 feet/820m) between Pacific and Arctic ocean watersheds.

J 300.9 (488.3 km) **AH 145.2** (233.7 km) **Junction** with Telegraph Creek Road and access to Dease Lake (description follows). See TELEGRAPH CREEK ROAD log on page 256.

Stikine River canyon near Dease Lake.
(Judy Parkin, staff)

Dease Lake

Located just west of the Cassiar Highway. **Emergency Services:** RCMP detachment. **Private Aircraft:** Dease Lake airstrip, 1.5 miles/2.4 km south; elev. 2,600 feet/792m; length 6,000 feet/1,829m; asphalt; fuel JP4, 100. **Visitor Information:** Write Dease Lake and Tahltan District Chamber of Commerce, *(Continues on page 257)*

Telegraph Creek Road Log

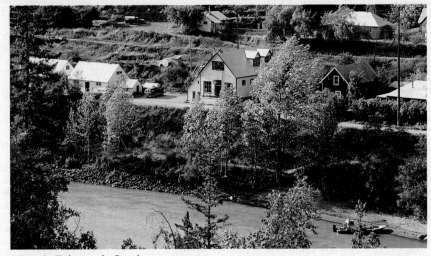

Historic Telegraph Creek. (© Gary Fiegehen)

Built in 1922, this was the first road in the Cassiar area of northern British Columbia. The scenery is remarkable and the town of Telegraph Creek is a picture from the turn of the century. Many of the original buildings remain from the gold rush days.

CAUTION: Telegraph Creek Road has some steep narrow sections and several sets of steep switchbacks; it is not recommended for trailers or large RVs. Car and camper drivers who are familiar with mountain driving should have no difficulty, although some motorists consider it a challenging drive even for the experienced. DRIVE CAREFULLY! Use caution when road is wet or icy. Very slippery when wet. Watch for rocks and mud. There are no visitor facilities en route. Allow a minimum of 2 hours driving time with good conditions. Check road conditions at highway maintenance camp or RCMP office in Dease Lake before starting the 70.1 miles/112.8 km to Telegraph Creek. Phone the Stikine RiverSong Cafe (250) 235-3196 for weather and road conditions. **Distance from Dease Lake junction (D) on the Cassiar Highway is shown.**

D 0 Dease Lake junction, Milepost J 300.9 Cassiar Highway.

D 0.9 (1.4 km) **Junction** with road to Dease Lake. Turn left for Telegraph Creek.

D 1.4 (2.3 km) Entrance to airport.

D 3.1 (5 km) Pavement ends, gravel begins westbound.

D 5 (8 km) Entering Tanzilla Plateau.

D 7.2 (11.6 km) Tatsho Creek (Eightmile).

D 15.9 (25.6 km) 16 Mile Creek.

D 17.1 (27.5 km) Augustchilde Creek, 1-lane bridge.

D 18.8 (30.3 km) 19 Mile Creek.

D 20.2 (32.5 km) 22 Mile Creek. Turnout with litter barrels south.

D 22.4 (36 km) Tanzilla River to south.

D 35.7 (57.5 km) Cariboo Meadows. Entering old burn area for 12 miles/19.3 km.

D 36.7 (59.1 km) Entering Stikine River Recreation Area. Tuya River valley view-point to north; turnout with litter barrels. Short walk uphill for good views and photographs.

D 37.7 (60.6 km) Approximate halfway point to Telegraph Creek from Dease Lake. Turnout with litter barrels to north. Excellent view of Mount Edziza on clear days.

D 45.5 (73.2 km) Begin 18 percent grade as road descends canyon; steep and narrow with switchbacks.

D 46 (74.1 km) Turnout with litter barrels to south.

D 47.2 (76 km) Tuya River bridge.

D 47.7 (76.8 km) End of burn area.

D 49 (78.9 km) Road makes Y–intersection. Old road to left; keep right for newer section.

D 50.4 (81.1 km) Old road rejoins newly constructed section.

D 50.8 (81.7 km) Golden Bear Mine access road. Private.

D 51.1 (82.2 km) Twenty percent downhill grade for approximately 0.6 mile/1 km. Day's Ranch on left.

D 54.2 (87.3 km) Rest area with table, toilet and litter barrel; overlooks river gorge.

D 55.7 (89.7 km) Road runs through lava beds, on narrow promontory about 150 feet/51m wide, dropping 400 feet/122m on each side to Tahltan and Stikine rivers. Sudden 180-degree right turn begins steep descent to Tahltan River and Indian fishing camps. Excellent views of the Grand Canyon of the Stikine and Tahltan Canyon can be seen by walking a short distance across lava beds to promontory point. Best views of the river canyon are by flightseeing trip. The Stikine River canyon is only 8 feet/2.4 m wide at its narrowest point.

D 56.1 (90.3 km) Sudden 180-degree turn begins 18 percent downhill grade to Tahltan River.

D 56.5 (90.9 km) Tahltan River bridge. Turnout with litter barrel south, on north side of bridge. Traditional communal Indian smokehouses adjacent to road at bridge. Smokehouse on north side of bridge is operated by a commercial fisherman; fresh and smoked salmon sold. There is a commercial inland fishery on the Stikine River, one of only a few such licensed operations in Canada.

D 57.5 (92.6 km) Start of very narrow road on ledge rising steeply up the wall of the Stikine Canyon for 3 miles/4.8 km, rising to 400 feet/122m above the river.

D 60 (96.6 km) Ninemile Creek.

D 60.1 (96.7 km) Old Tahltan Indian community above road. Private property: No trespassing! Former home of Tahltan bear dogs. The Tahltan bear dog, believed to be extinct, was only about a foot high and weighed about 15 pounds. Short-haired, with oversize ears and shaving-brush tail, the breed was recognized by the Canadian Kennel Club. First seen by explorer Samuel Black in 1824, the dogs were used to hunt bears.

D 61.8 (99.5 km) Eightmile Creek bridge. Spectacular falls into canyon on left below. Opposite the gravel pit at the top of the hill there is a trailhead and parking on the west side of the creek.

D 63.1 (101.5 km) Turnout. Good photos of Stikine Canyon to east.

D 69.1 (111.2 km) Indian community. Road follows steep winding descent into old town, crossing a deep narrow canyon via a short bridge. Excellent picture spot 0.2 mile/0.3 km from bridge. Glenora Road junction on right.

D 70.1 (112.8 km) TELEGRAPH CREEK (pop. 300; elev. 1,100 feet/335m). Former head of navigation on the Stikine and once a telegraph communication terminal. During the gold rush, an estimated 5,000 stampeders set off from Telegraph Creek to attempt the Stikine–Teslin Trail to the gold-fields in Atlin and the Klondike.

There are a cafe, lodge, general store, post office, and a public school and nursing station here. Gas, minor auto and tire repair are available. Stikine River trips and charter flights are available. Anglican church services held weekly; Roman Catholic services held every-other week.

Residents make their living fishing commercially for salmon, doing local construction work and guiding visitors on hunting, fishing and river trips. Telegraph Creek is becoming a jumping-off point for wilderness hikers headed for Mount Edziza Provincial Park.

The scenic view along the main street bordering the river has scarcely changed since gold rush days. The 1898 Hudson's Bay Co. post, which now houses the River-Song Cafe, is a recognized Heritage Building. Historic St. Aidan's Church (Anglican) and several other buildings pre-dating 1930 are also located here.

A 12-mile/19.3-km road continues west to Glenora, site of attempted railroad route to the Yukon and limit of larger riverboat navigation. There are 2 primitive B.C. Forest Service campsites on the road to Glenora. Several spur roads lead to the Stikine River and to Native fish camps. ▲

RiverSong Lodge & Cafe. Awaken to the restful song of the Stikine River. Located on the banks of the great river, the RiverSong offers restful accommodation in a renovated, historic (1898) Hudson's Bay Post, great food including fresh home-baked bread and pies, sockeye salmon, comfortable rooms plus gifts, groceries and gas. Rooms include shared bath, sitting room and kitchen. Continental breakfasts available June 1 through Labour Day. Reservations recommended. (250) 235-3196 or message/fax (250) 235-3194. [ADVERTISEMENT]

Stikine RiverSong Boat Tours. Tour the historic Stikine River route to the Klondike from the covered comfort of our enclosed riverboat. You are guaranteed to find the scenery spectacular as you motor/float down the great river. Pass through the Coast Mountains, glacier country and Stikine LaConte Wilderness Area to the Pacific Ocean at Wrangell, Alaska. One hour, 1/2 day, day trips and overnight camping trips. Information and reservations: (250) 235-3196 or message/fax (250) 235-3194. [ADVERTISEMENT]

**Return to Milepost J 300.9
Cassiar Highway**

Box 338, Dease Lake, BC V0C 1L0. Phone (250) 771-3900.

Dease Lake has motels, gas stations (with regular, unleaded, diesel, propane and minor repairs), food stores, restaurant, a post office, hardware/sporting goods, highway maintenance centre and government offices. Charter flights and regular air service to Terrace and Smithers with interprovincial connections. Information kiosks at south entrance to town. ▲

A Hudson's Bay Co. post was established by Robert Campbell at Dease Lake in 1838, but abandoned a year later. The lake was named in 1834 by John McLeod of the Hudson's Bay Co. for Chief Factor Peter Warren Dease. Laketon, on the west side of the lake (see Milepost J 327.7), was a centre for boat building during the Cassiar gold rush of 1872–80. In 1874, William Moore, following an old Indian trail, cut a trail from Telegraph Creek on the Stikine River to the gold rush settlement on Dease Lake. This trail became Telegraph Creek Road, which was used in 1941 to haul supplies for Alaska Highway construction and Watson Lake Airport to Dease Lake. The supplies were then ferried down the Dease River.

Today, Dease Lake is a government centre and supply point for the district. The community has dubbed itself the "jade capital of the world." Jade is available locally. It is a popular point from which to fly-in, hike-in, or pack-in by horse to Mount Edziza and Spatsizi wilderness parks.

Trapper's Den Gift Shoppe. Quality Canadian and British Columbian gift items ranging from local jade to Native moccasins

and cottage crafts. Come visit the "Trapper" in his "den." Very reasonable jade prices. VISA/MasterCard accepted. Located around the corner from the grocery store, just 200 feet off Highway 37. Box 70, Dease Lake, BC V0C 1L0. (250) 771-3224. [ADVERTISEMENT]

Cassiar Highway Log
(continued)

J 300.9 (488.3 km) AH 145.2 (233.7 km) **Dease Lake Junction.** Junction with access road to Dease Lake and Telegraph Creek Road (see log opposite page).

J 301.7 (489.6 km) AH 144.4 (232.4 km) Hotel Creek.

J 308.8 (501.3 km) AH 137.3 (220.9 km) Turnout with litter barrel to west.

J 309.6 (502.5 km) AH 136.5 (219.7 km) Serpentine Creek.

J 309.8 (502.9 km) AH 136.3 (219.3 km) Seal coat ends northbound, gravel begins and extends 16.4 miles/26.4 km. Seal coat southbound extends 35.7 miles/57.5 km.

J 313.5 (508.7 km) AH 132.6 (213.5 km) Gravel turnout to west with litter barrel.

J 314.1 (509.8 km) AH 132 (212.4 km) Good views of Dease Lake, limited access to lake shore.

J 315.7 (512.3 km) AH 130.4 (209.9 km) Gravel turnout to west.

J 316.3 (513.3 km) AH 129.8 (208.9 km) Halfmoon Creek.

J 318.8 (517.4 km) AH 127.3 (204.9 km) Rabid Grizzly rest area with picnic tables, travel information signs, litter barrels and outhouses. View of Dease Lake.

J 322.1 (522.8 km) AH 124 (199.5 km) Gravel turnout to west.

J 324.2 (526.1 km) AH 121.9 (196.2 km) Black Creek.

J 326.2 (529.4 km) AH 119.9 (192.9 km) Pavement begins northbound and extends to end of highway at Alaska Highway junction; watch for resurfacing project. Pavement ends southbound; gravel begins and extends 16.4 miles/26.4 km.

J 326.3 (529.5 km) AH 119.8 (192.8 km) Sawmill Point Recreation Site to west; side road leads to **Dease Lake** for fishing. Lake trout to 30 lbs., use spoons, plugs, spinners, June to October, deep trolling in summer, spin casting in fall. 🐟

J 327.2 (531.2 km) AH 118.9 (191.4 km) Dorothy Creek.

J 327.7 (532 km) AH 118.4 (190.5 km) The site of the ghost town Laketon lies across the lake at the mouth of Dease Creek. Laketon was the administrative centre for the district during the Cassiar gold rush (1872–80). Boat building was a major activity along the lake during the gold rush years, with miners heading up various creeks and

---

Pine Tree Lake offers good fishing.
(Judy Parkin, staff)

rivers off the lake in search of gold. Today's miners ford the lake when the water is low to reach claims on the northwest side.

J 330.2 (535.9 km) **AH 115.9** (186.5 km) Beady Creek. Entering the Cassiar Mountains northbound.

J 333.5 (541.1 km) **AH 112.6** (181.3 km) Turnout to west with litter barrels.

J 333.8 (541.7 km) **AH 112.3** (180.7 km) Turnout with litter barrel to west. **Dease River** parallels the highway. Grayling to 17 inches; Dolly Varden and lake trout to 15 lbs.; northern pike 8 to 10 lbs., May through September. 🐟

Marshy areas to west; good moose pasture. Watch for wildlife, especially at dawn and dusk.

J 334.4 (542.7 km) **AH 111.7** (179.7 km) Packer Tom Creek, named for a well-known Indian who lived in this area.

J 336.1 (545.4 km) **AH 110** (177 km) Elbow Lake.

J 342 (554.7 km) **AH 104.1** (167.5 km) Pyramid Creek.

J 342.4 (555.6 km) **AH 103.7** (166.9 km) Dease River 2-lane concrete bridge.

J 343.9 (558 km) **AH 102.2** (164.5 km) Beale Creek.

J 348.7 (561.1 km) **AH 97.4** (156.7 km) Road widens. Generous paved pullout to east overlooking Pine Tree Lake.

J 350.9 (563.4 km) **AH 95.2** (153.2 km) Turnout beside **Pine Tree Lake.** Good grayling and lake char fishing. 🐟

J 351 (569.5 km) **AH 95.1** (153.1 km) Burn area. An abandoned campfire started the fire in July 1982.

J 352.8 (572.4 km) **AH 93.3** (150.2 km) **Moose Meadows,** (formerly Mighty Moe's, under new management)—Ideal for nature lovers. Tranquil setting on Cotton Lake and Dease River. Enjoy the scenery and the evening cry of the loons. Potential wildlife may include beaver, moose, mountain goats and a variety of birds. Dry sites. Hot showers. Pit toilets. Some extra-long pull-throughs. Group sites. Cabin. Boat launch. Canoe rentals and shuttles for river trips from 6 to 180 miles. Emergency phone. Reasonable rates. Box 299, Dease Lake, BC V0C 1L0. Radio phone (250) N416219. Chicken Neck Channel. Voice call Whitehorse operator. [ADVERTISEMENT] ▲

J 353.7 (573.9 km) **AH 92.4** (148.7 km) Gravel turnout with litter barrels to east. Views of Needlenose Mountain southbound.

J 357.9 (580.9 km) **AH 88.2** (141.9 km) **Cottonwood River** bridge; rest area 0.4 mile/0.6 km west on old highway on south side of river. Fishing for grayling and whitefish. Early summer runs of Dolly Varden. 🐟

J 358.7 (582 km) **AH 87.4** (140.7 km) Cottonwood River rest area No. 2 is 0.5 mile/0.8 km west on old highway on north side of river.

J 363.6 (589.8 km) **AH 82.5** (132.8 km) Turnout to west beside **Simmons Lake;** information kiosk, picnic tables, picnic shelter, toilets, small beach and dock. Fishing for lake trout. 🐟

J 365.3 (592.7 km) **AH 80.8** (130 km) Road runs on causeway between Twin Lakes.

J 365.8 (593.5 km) **AH 80.3** (129.2 km) **Vines Lake,** named for bush pilot Lionel Vines; fishing for lake trout. 🐟

J 366.9 (595.3 km) **AH 79.2** (127.4 km) Limestone Creek.

J 367.3 (595.9 km) **AH 78.8** (126.8 km) Lang Lake and creek. Needlepoint Mountain visible straight ahead southbound.

J 369.8 (599.9 km) **AH 76.3** (122.8 km) Cusak gold mine visible on slopes to east. Gold mined on the far side of the mountain is processed in the mill here.

J 370.1 (600.3 km) **AH 76** (122.3 km) Side road east leads to McDame Lake.

J 370.9 (601.6 km) **AH 75.2** (121 km) Trout Line Creek.

J 371.1 (601.9 km) **AH 75** (120.7 km) JADE CITY (pop. 12), named for the jade deposits found to the east of the highway community. The huge jade boulders that visitors can see being cut here are from the Princess Jade Mine, 82 miles/132 km east, one of the largest jade claims in the world.

Grizzly Gas Bar & Den. See display ad this section.

J 371.3 (602.2 km) **AH 74.8** (120.4 km) Jade store and RV park. ▲

Jade City. World famous jade capital. Extensive selection of raw jade, jade jewellery and carvings crafted from local Cassiar and Princess jade. Best jade and jewellery prices in the North. Rock hounds will appreciate the extensive selection of raw Canadian gemstones and jewellery. Ask about our RV park discount. See display ad this section. Jesus is Lord. [ADVERTISEMENT]

J 372.5 (604.1 km) **AH 73.6** (118.5 km) **Cassiar junction.** Cassiar Road to west leads

9.7 miles/15.6 km to the former Cassiar townsite and Cassiar Asbestos Mine. Continue straight ahead for Alaska Highway.

CASSIAR (pop. 25) was the company town of Cassiar Mining Corp. Much of the world's high-grade chrysotile asbestos came from Cassiar. The mine closed in March 1992, and the site is closed to visitors. It is now the site of a B.C. Chrysotile Corp. reclamation project. No services available.

J 372.7 (604.4 km) **AH 73.4** (118.2 km) Snow Creek.

J 372.8 (605.6 km) **AH 73.3** (117.9 km) Gravel turnout with litter barrel to east.

J 373.5 (606.1 km) **AH 72.6** (116.8 km) Deep Creek.

J 377.4 (612.2 km) **AH 68.7** (110.6 km) No. 3 North Fork Creek.

J 378.4 (613.9 km) **AH 67.7** (108.9 km) No. 2 North Fork Creek.

J 381 (618 km) **AH 65.1** (104.7 km) Historic plaque about Cassiar gold.

CENTREVILLE (pop. 2; elev. 2,600 feet/ 792m), a former gold rush town of 3,000. The only evidence of Centreville along the highway today is the town name painted on an old piece of mining equipment parked on the east side of the road. Centreville was founded and named by miners for its central location between Sylvester's Landing (later McDame Post) at the junction of McDame Creek with the Dease River, and Quartzrock Creek, the upstream limit of pay gravel on McDame Creek. A miner named Alfred Freeman washed out the biggest all-gold (no quartz) nugget ever found in British Columbia on a claim near Centreville in 1877; it weighed 72 ounces. Active mining in area.

J 381.1 (618.2 km) **AH 65** (104.6 km) No. 1 North Fork Creek.

J 385.2 (625 km) **AH 60.9** (98 km) **GOOD HOPE LAKE** (pop. 100), Indian village with limited services; fuel may be available.

Turn east on Bush Road and drive 9 miles/14.5 km for **McDAME POST**, an early Hudson's Bay post, at the **confluence of Dease River and McDame Creek**. Good fishing and hunting here. 🐟

J 386.9 (627.7 km) **AH 59.2** (95.3 km) Turnout to east alongside Aeroplane Lake.

J 387.7 (629 km) **AH 58.4** (94 km) Dry Creek.

J 389.5 (631.9 km) **AH 56.6** (91.1 km) Mud Lake to east.

J 393.6 (638.5 km) **AH 52.5** (84.5 km) Turnout with litter barrels at entrance to **Boya Lake** Provincial Park. The park is 1.6 miles/2.6 km east of highway; 45 campsites, picnic area on lakeshore, boat launch, toilets, wheelchair access, walking trails, drinking water, firewood and swimming. Fishing for lake char, whitefish and burbot. Attendant on duty during summer. ♿🐟▲

J 393.7 (638.6 km) **AH 52.4** (84.4 km) Turnout. Horseranch Range may be seen on the eastern horizon northbound. These mountains date back to the Cambrian period, or earlier, and are the oldest in northern British Columbia. According to the Canadian Geological Survey, this area contains numerous permatites with crystals of tourmaline, garnet, feldspar, quartz and beryl. Road crosses Baking Powder Creek and then follows Dease River.

J 397.9 (645.4 km) **AH 48.2** (77.6 km) Camp Creek.

J 399.4 (648 km) **AH 46.7** (75.1 km) Beaver Dam Creek.

J 400.3 (649.4 km) **AH 45.8** (73.7 km)

Blue Lakes, Milepost J 429.7, offers picnic tables and fishing. (© Beth Davidow)

Beaver Dam rest area with visitor information sign to west.

J 400.6 (649.8 km) **AH 45.5** (73.3 km) Leaving Cassiar Mountains, entering Yukon Plateau, northbound.

J 402.5 (652.9 km) **AH 43.6** (70.2 km) Baking Powder Creek.

J 410.9 (666.5km) **AH 35.2** (56.7 km) Gravel access road to French Creek B.C. Forest Service campsite 0.6 miles/1 km from highway. Rustic. Tables, rock fire ring (bring firewood), small boat launch into Dease River, no fee. ▲

J 411.2 (667 km) **AH 34.9** (56.1 km) French Creek 2-lane concrete bridge.

J 417.5 (677.2 km) **AH 28.6** (46.1 km) Twentyeight Mile Creek. Cassiar Mountains rise to south.

J 420.2 (681.8 km) **AH 25.9** (41.6 km) Wheeler Lake to west.

J 422.9 (686.1 km) **AH 23.2** (37.3 km) Blue River Forest Service Road to east.

J 426.3 (691.5 km) **AH 19.8** (31.9 km) Blue River 2-lane concrete bridge.

J 429.7 (697.1 km) **AH 16.4** (26.4 km) Turnout at **Blue Lakes**; litter barrels, picnic tables and fishing for pike and grayling. 🐟

J 431.5 (700 km) **AH 14.6** (23.5 km) Mud Hill Creek.

J 436 (707.4 km) **AH 10.1** (16.2 km) Old Faddy Forest Service Road.

J 440.1 (714 km) **AH 6** (9.6 km) Turnout with litter barrels beside Cormier Creek.

J 441.3 (718.5 km) **AH 4.8** (7.7 km) High Lake to east.

J 444 (720.3 km) **AH 2.1** (3.4 km) Turnout to west at BC–YT border, 60th parallel. Information sign. Yukon Territory's flag consists of 3 vertical panels of colour: blue, representing the rivers and lakes; green symbolizing forests; and white

signifying snow. The Yukon coat of arms appears on the central panel, framed by 2 stems of fireweed, the territory's floral emblem. The flag was chosen from a design competition sponsored in 1967. Yukon Territory was made a district of Northwest Territories in 1895 and became a separate territory in June 1898, at the height of the Klondike Gold Rush. *NOTE: Drive with headlights on at all times in Yukon Territory.*

J 445.3 (722.5 km) **AH 0.8** (1.2 km) **Albert Creek**. Good grayling fishing. Yukon Territory fishing license required. 🐟

J 446.1 (723.7 km) **AH 0** Junction of Cassiar Highway with Alaska Highway. Gas, store, campground and RV park, cafe, souvenirs, laundromat, camp-style motel, saloon, propane, towing and car repair at junction. Turn left for Whitehorse, right for Watson Lake, 13.6 miles/21.9 km southeast. Watson Lake is the nearest major community. ▲

Junction 37 Services. See display ad this section.

Turn to **Milepost DC 626.2** in the ALASKA HIGHWAY section (page 118) for log of Alaska Highway from this junction.

KLONDIKE LOOP 2 9

Connects: Alaska Hwy. to Taylor Hwy.   **Length:** 406 miles
Road Surface: 80% paved, 20% gravel
Season: Hwy. 2 open all year, Hwy. 9 closed in winter
Major Attraction: Dawson City

(See maps, pages 261-262)

	Alaska Hwy. Jct.	Carmacks	Dawson City	Taylor Hwy Jct.	Whitehorse
Alaska Hwy Jct.		103	327	406	10
Carmacks	103		225	303	113
Dawson City	327	225		79	337
Taylor Hwy Jct.	406	303	79		416
Whitehorse	10	113	337	416	

Summer sunset on the Yukon River was photographed at 1 A.M. from an overlook above Dawson City. (© Michael DeYoung)

The "Klondike Loop" refers to the 327-mile/527-km-long stretch of Yukon Highway 2 (the North Klondike Highway, also sometimes called the "Mayo Road"), from its junction with the Alaska Highway north of Whitehorse to Dawson City; the 79-mile/127-km Top of the World Highway (Yukon Highway 9); and the 96 miles/154 kms of the Taylor Highway (Alaska Route 5) that connect with the Alaska Highway near Tok. The North Klondike Highway and Top of the World Highway are logged in this section. The Taylor Highway is logged in the TAYLOR HIGHWAY section following.

Alaska-bound motorists turn off the Alaska Highway north of Whitehorse (**Milepost DC 894.8**); follow the Klondike Highway to Dawson City; ferry from there across the Yukon River; drive west via the Top of the World Highway into Alaska; then take the Taylor Highway south back to the Alaska Highway near Tok (**Milepost DC 1301.7**). Total driving distance is 501 miles/806 km. (Driving distance from Whitehorse to Tok via the Alaska Highway is approximately 396 miles/637 km.)

All of the Klondike Highway between the Alaska Highway junction and Dawson City is asphalt-surfaced. Beware of Yukon Alaska Transport trucks, each carrying up to 50 tons of lead–zinc concentrates, operating between Faro on the Campbell Highway and the port of Skagway on the south Klondike Highway. The trucks are 8½ feet wide and 85 feet long. *Drive with your headlights on at all times.*

Watch for road construction on the Top of the World Highway (Yukon Highway 9). This is a gravel road with some hills. A truly scenic route, but slippery in wet weather with some steep grades and winding sections. The first 19 miles/30 km of the Top of the World Highway is scheduled for gravel surfacing in 1997, between Kilometreposts 0 and 30 on the Canadian side. Check with the Dawson City Visitor Centre for current road and weather conditions; phone (403) 993-5566. The Taylor Highway (Alaska Route 5) is a narrow, gravel road with some steep, winding sections and washboard (see the TAYLOR HIGHWAY section). Both the Taylor and Top of the World highways are not maintained from mid-October to April

and the arrival of snow effectively closes the roads for winter. Yukon Highway 2 is open year-round.

Travelers should be aware that the Top of the World Highway (reached by ferry from Dawson City) may not open until late spring. In heavy traffic, there may be a wait of 3 hours or longer for the ferry. Customs stations are open in summer only, 12 hours a day: most likely 9 A.M. to 9 P.M. (Pacific time). There are no restrooms, services or currency exchanges available at the border.

The highway between Skagway and the Alaska Highway, sometimes referred to as the South Klondike, is also designated Klondike Highway 2 (see KLONDIKE HIGHWAY 2 section for log of that road).

Kilometreposts along the highway to Dawson City reflect distance from Skagway. Our log's driving distances were measured in miles from the junction of the Alaska Highway to Dawson City by our field editor. These mileages were converted into kilometres with the exception of the kilometre distance following Skagway (**S**). That figure reflects the physical location of the kilometrepost and is not necessarily an accurate conversion of the mileage figure.

The route from Whitehorse to Dawson City began as a trail, used first by Natives, trappers and prospectors, and then by stampeders during the Klondike Gold Rush of 1897–98. Steamships also provided passenger service between Whitehorse and Dawson City. A road was built connecting the Alaska Highway with the United Keno Hill Mine at Mayo in 1950. By 1955, the Mayo Road had been upgraded for automobile traffic and extended to Dawson City. In 1960, the last of 3 steel bridges, crossing the Yukon, Pelly and Stewart rivers, was completed. The only ferry crossing remaining is the Yukon River crossing at Dawson City. Mayo Road (Yukon Highway 11) from Stewart Crossing to Mayo, Elsa and Keno was redesignated the Silver Trail in 1985 (see SILVER TRAIL section for road log).

Emergency Medical Services: On Yukon Highway 2 from **Milepost J 0** to **J 55.6** (Whitehorse to Braeburn Lodge), phone Whitehorse Ambulance toll free 1-667-3333 or RCMP 1-667-3333. From **Milepost J 55.6** to **J 169.4** (Braeburn Lodge to Pelly Crossing), phone Carmacks Medical Emergency (403) 863-4444 or RCMP (403) 863-5555. From **Milepost J 169.4** to **J 242.9** (Pelly Crossing to McQuesten River Lodge), phone

KLONDIKE LOOP *Milepost J 0 to Milepost J 296*

(map continues next page)

Klondike River

OGILVIE MOUNTAINS

Elsa

Keno

J-296/476km
D-31/50km
S-415/669km

Flat Creek

Clear Creek

Halfway Lakes

Duncan Creek

Minto Lake

Mayo Lake

McQuesten River

Minto Cr.

Janet Lake

Moose Creek

Stewart River

J-229.1/368.7km
Moose Creek
Lodge LM

Mayo

Silver Trail
(see SILVER TRAIL section)

River

Ethel Lake

J-214/345km
D-113/182km
S-334/538km

Stewart
Crossing

J-213.9/344.2km Stewart Crossing Chevron dGPrST

Stewart

Crooked Creek

Willow Creek

J-169/273km
D-158/254km
S-289/465km

J-169.4/272.6km Selkirk Gas Bar & Grocery CDdGIST

Fort Selkirk

Pelly Crossing

Yukon

Von Wilczek Lakes

Pelly

Tatlmain Lake

River

DAWSON

River

Minto

J-148/238.2km Minto Resorts Ltd. RV Park CDI
Pristine River Runs

RANGE

Tatchun Lake

Drury Lake

Tatchun River

To Ross River
(see CAMPBELL
HIGHWAY section)

Frenchman Lake

Little Salmon Lake

N
W   E
S

Carmacks

Little Salmon River

Yukon

J-103/165km
D-225/361km
S-222/357km

River

Twin Lakes

▲ Conglomerate Mountain
3,362 ft./1,025m

J-55.6/89.5km Braeburn Lodge Ltd. CdGLMr

Braeburn Lake

Nordenskiold

Little Fox Lake

Fox Lake

Lake Laberge

Testlin River

J-29.8/48km Cranberry Point Bed & Breakfast CL

Fox Creek

J-20.4/32.8km Mom's Bakery and
Kimberly's Place ILMST

Takhini Hot Springs

To Haines Junction
(see ALASKA HIGHWAY section)

J-0
D-327/527km
S-119/192km

Takhini River

Yukon

To Jake's Corner
(see ALASKA HIGHWAY section)

Whitehorse

Scale
0   10   Miles
0   10   Kilometres

Key to mileage boxes
miles/kilometres
miles/kilometres
from:

Map Location

J- Junction
D- Dawson City
S- Skagway

Principal Route
Paved   Unpaved
Other Roads
Paved   Unpaved
Ferry Routes   Hiking Trails

Refer to Log for Visitor Facilities
Visitor Information   Fishing
Campground   Airport   Airstrip

Key to Advertiser Services
C -Camping
D -Dump Station
d -Diesel
G -Gas (reg., unld.)
I -Ice
L -Lodging
M -Meals
P -Propane
R -Car Repair (major)
r -Car Repair (minor)
S -Store (grocery)
T -Telephone (pay)

KLONDIKE LOOP
Milepost J 296 to Tetlin Junction, Alaska Highway (includes Taylor Highway)

Klondike Loop Log

Mayo Medical Emergency (403) 996-4444 or RCMP (403) 996-5555. From **Milepost J 242.9** to **J 327.2** and on Yukon Highway 9 from **Milepost D 0** to **D 66.1** (McQuesten River Lodge to Dawson City to Alaska border), phone Dawson City Medical Emergency (403) 993-4444 or RCMP (403) 993-5555. From **Milepost D 66.1** to **D 78.8** (Alaska border to Taylor Highway), phone Tok Area EMS at 911 or (907) 883-5111.

NOTE: Yukon Territory area code is scheduled to change from (403) to (867) in October 1997.

Klondike Loop Log

YUKON HIGHWAY 2
This section of the log shows distance from junction with the Alaska Highway (J) followed by distance from Dawson City (D) and distance from Skagway (S). Physical kilometreposts show distance from Skagway.

J 0 D 327.2 (526.6 km) **S 119.2** (191.8 km) **Junction** with the Alaska Highway (Milepost DC 894.8).

J 0.6 (1 km) **D 326.6** (525.6 km) **S 119.8** (192.8 km) Road west leads to McPherson subdivision.

J 1 (1.6 km) **D 326.2** (525 km) **S 120.2** (193.4 km) Ranches, farms and livestock next 20 miles/32 km northbound.

J 2.3 (3.7 km) **D 324.9** (522.9 km) **S 121.5** (195.5 km) Takhini River bridge. The Takhini flows into the Yukon River.

J 3.8 (6.1 km) **D 323.4** (520.4 km) **S 123** (197.9 km) Takhini Hot Springs Road. Drive west 6 miles/9.7 km via paved road for Takhini Hot Springs; bed and breakfasts, camping, cafe, trail rides, ski trails in winter. The source of the springs maintains a constant 117°F/47°C temperature and flows at 86 gallons a minute. The hot springs pool averages 100°F/38°C year-round. The water contains no sulfur. The chief minerals present are calcium, magnesium and iron. ▲

Trappers and Indians used these springs around the turn of the century, arriving by way of the Takhini River or the old Dawson Trail. During construction of the Alaska Highway in the early 1940s, the U.S. Army maintained greenhouses in the area and reported remarkable growth regardless of the season.

J 6.7 (10.8 km) **D 320.5** (515.8 km) **S 125.9** (202.6 km) Start odometer test section next 5 km northbound.

J 7 (11.3 km) **D 320.2** (515.3 km) **S 126.2** (203.1 km) Whitehorse rodeo grounds to west. Yukon Rodeo scheduled for July 11–12, 1997.

J 9.4 (15.1 km) **D 317.8** (511.4 km) **S 128.6** (207 km) Sawmill to west.

J 10.7 (17.2 km) **D 316.5** (509.3 km) **S 129.9** (209 km) Shallow Bay Road. Access to Northern Splendor Reindeer Farm. This reindeer farm is 0.8 mile/1.3 km east. The farm is open to visitors in summer from 7 A.M. to 6 P.M.; there is an admission charge. Pull-through drive for big rigs.

J 12.7 (20.4 km) **D 314.5** (506.1 km) **S 131.9** (212.2 km) Horse Creek Road leads east to Lower Laberge Indian village and lakeshore cottages. **Horse Creek**; good grayling fishing from road. ◄►

J 15.1 (24.3 km) **D 312.1** (502.3 km) **S 134.3** (216.1 km) Access to bed and breakfast, 0.9 miles/1.5 km west.

J 15.8 (25.4 km) **D 311.4** (501.1 km) **S 135** (217.2 km) Microwave site near road.

J 16.8 (27 km) **D 310.4** (499.5 km) **S 136** (219.1 km) Large turnout to west.

J 17.4 (28 km) **D 309.8** (498.6 km) **S 136.6** (220 km) Lake Laberge to east. The Yukon River widens to form this 40-mile-/64-km-long lake. Lake Laberge was made famous by Robert W. Service with the lines: "The Northern Lights have seen queer sights. But the queerest they ever did see, was that night on the marge of Lake Lebarge I cremated Sam McGee," (from his poem "The Cremation of Sam McGee").

J 18.2 (29.3 km) **D 309** (497.3 km) **S 137.4** (221.1 km) Gravel pit turnout to east.

J 20.3 (32.7 km) **D 306.9** (493.9 km) **S 139.5** (224.5 km) Deep Creek.

J 20.4 (32.8 km) **D 306.8** (493.7 km) **S 139.6** (224.6 km) Turnoff for Lake Laberge Yukon government campground. On the campground road are a bed and breakfast, small store, bakery, canoe rentals, emergency phone and message post. The campground is situated 1.8 miles/2.9 km east on Lake Laberge next to Deep Creek (see description following).

Mom's Bakery & Kimberly's Place. Mom's Bakery, home of sourdough bread, pancakes, giant cinnamon buns, pastries. Relax on the patio amidst a northern garden. Fishing licenses, ice, telephone. Yukon host Tracie Harris, Box 4177, White-

horse, Yukon Y1A 3S9. Phone 2M4554, Whitehorse YJ Channel. At Kimberly's Place, snuggle down for the night in the Trapper's Cabin Bed & Breakfast, or visit the Country Cupboard Store for espresso and ice cream.
[ADVERTISEMENT]

Lake Laberge Yukon government campground has 22 RV sites, $8 camping fee, resident campground host, group camping area, kitchen shelter, water, boat launch, and fishing for lake trout, grayling and northern pike. Interpretive panels located lakeside at the campground highlight the 30-mile Heritage River. *CAUTION: Storms can blow up quickly and without warning on Lake Laberge, as on other northern lakes. Canoes and small craft stay to the west side of the lake, where the shoreline offers safe refuges. The east side of the lake is lined with high rocky bluffs, and there are few places to pull out. Small craft should not navigate the middle of the lake.* ⚓▲

J 20.9 (33.6 km) **D 306.3** (492.9 km) **S 140.1** (225.5 km) View of Lake Laberge for southbound travelers.

J 21.2 (34.1 km) **D 306** (492.4 km) **S 140.4** (225.9 km) Northbound the highway enters the Miners Range, plateau country of the Yukon, an immense wilderness of forested dome-shaped mountains and high ridges, dotted with lakes and traversed by tributaries of the Yukon River. To the west, Pilot Mountain in the Miners Range (elev. 6,739 feet/2,054m) is visible.

J 22.8 (36.7 km) **D 304.4** (489.9 km) **S 142** (228.5 km) **Fox Creek**; grayling, excellent in June and July. ⚓

J 23.5 (37.8 km) **D 303.7** (488.7 km) **S 142.7** (229.8 km) Marker shows distance to Dawson City 486 km.

J 26.9 (43.3 km) **D 300.3** (483.3 km) **S 146.1** (235.1 km) Gravel pit turnout to east.

J 28.8 (46.3 km) **D 298.4** (480.2 km) **S 148** (238.2 km) Highway now follows the east shoreline of Fox Lake northbound.

J 29.4 (47.3 km) **D 297.8** (479.2 km) **S 148.6** (239.1 km) Turnout to west on Fox Lake. Historic sign here reads: "In 1883, U.S. Army Lt. Frederick Schwatka completed a survey of the entire length of the Yukon River. One of many geographical features that he named was Fox Lake, which he called Richthofen Lake, after geographer Freiherr Von Richthofen. Known locally as Fox Lake, the name was adopted in 1957. The Miners Range to the west was named by geologist/explorer George Mercer Dawson in 1887 'for the miners met by us along the river.'"

J 29.8 (48 km) **D 297.4** (478.6 km) **S 149** (239.8 km) **Cranberry Point Bed & Breakfast.** Open year-round. Wonderful northern wilderness experience, right on beautiful Fox Lake. Woodstove cooking, full breakfast, other meals arranged! Comfortable guestroom and cabin. Limited dry camping. Reservations recommended: radio phone Whitehorse mobile operator, JJ3-9257 Fox Lake Channel. Km 240 Klondike Hwy., Site 15, #91, Whitehorse, Yukon Y1A 5W8.
[ADVERTISEMENT]

J 34.8 (56 km) **D 292.4** (470.6 km) **S 154** (247.8 km) Turnoff west for **Fox Lake** Yukon government campground; 30 RV and 3 tent-only sites, $8 camping fee, kitchen shelter, drinking water and boat launch. Good fishing for lake trout and burbot from the shore at the campground; excellent grayling year-round. ⚓▲

J 35.2 (56.6 km) **D 292** (469.9 km) **S 154.4** (248.5 km) Turnout with view of

Watch for ore trucks along the Klondike Highway. (Earl L. Brown, staff)

Fox Lake. Good photo spot.

J 39.8 (64.1 km) **D 287.4** (462.5 km) **S 159** (255.8 km) North end of Fox Lake.

J 42 (67.6 km) **D 285.2** (459 km) **S 161.2** (259.4 km) **Little Fox Lake** to west; lake trout 3 to 8 lbs., fish the islands. ⚓

J 43.8 (70.5 km) **D 283.4** (456.1 km) **S 163** (262.1 km) Double-ended turnout with litter barrel to west beside Little Fox Lake. Small boat launch.

J 49.5 (79.7 km) **D 277.7** (446.9 km) **S 168.7** (271.5 km) Large turnout to west.

J 50.1 (80.6 km) **D 277.1** (445.9 km) **S 169.3** (272.4 km) First glimpse of Braeburn Lake for northbound travelers.

J 52.5 (84.5 km) **D 274.7** (442.1 km) **S 171.7** (276.3 km) Gravel pit turnout to east. *CAUTION: Watch for elk along highway.*

J 55.6 (89.5 km) **D 271.6** (437.1 km) **S 174.8** (281.5 km) Braeburn Lodge to west; food, gas, lodging and minor car repairs. One Braeburn Lodge cinnamon bun will feed 4 people. The lodge is also home of the 200-mile/320-km "Cinnamon Bun" Dog Sled Race, held the first weekend in February.

Braeburn Lodge. See display ad this section.

Private Aircraft: Braeburn airstrip to east, dubbed Cinnamon Bun Strip; elev. 2,350 feet/716m; length 3,000 feet/914m; dirt strip; wind sock.

J 55.8 (89.8 km) **D 271.4** (436.8 km) **S 175.1** (281.8 km) Side road to Braeburn Lake.

J 66.3 (106.7 km) **D 260.9** (419.9 km) **S 185.5** (298.5 km) Photo stop; pull-through turnout on east side of highway with information sign about Conglomerate Mountain (elev. 3,361 feet/1,024m). Sign reads: "The Laberge Series was formed at the leading edge of volcanic mud flows some 185 million years ago (Early Jurassic). These flows solidified into sheets several kilometres long and about 1 km wide and 100m thick. This particular series of sheets stretches from Atlin, BC, to north of Carmacks, a distance of about 350 km. Other conglomerates of this series form Five Finger Rapids."

Rock hounds can find pieces of conglomerate in almost any borrow pit along this stretch of highway.

J 71.6 (115.2 km) **D 255.6** (411.3 km) **S 190.8** (307 km) Turnouts on both sides of highway between Twin Lakes. These 2 small lakes, 1 on either side of the road, are known for their beauty and colour.

J 72.3 (116.4 km) **D 254.9** (410.2 km) **S 191.5** (308.2 km) Turnoff to west for **Twin Lakes** Yukon government campground; 18 sites, $8 camping fee, drinking water, boat launch. Lake is stocked. Enjoyable fishing for lake trout, grayling and pike. Good swimming for the *hardy!* ◄▲

J 81.4 (131 km) **D 245.8** (395.6 km) **S 200.6** (323 km) Large turnout with litter barrel to east at remains of Montague House, a typical early-day roadhouse which offered lodging and meals on the stagecoach route between Whitehorse and Dawson City. A total of 52 stopping places along this route were listed in the Jan. 16, 1901, edition of the *Whitehorse Star* under "On the Winter Trail between White Horse and Dawson Good Accommodations for Travellers." Montague House was listed at Mile 99. Good photo stop.

J 87.4 (140.7 km) **D 239.8** (385.9 km) **S 206.6** (332.5 km) Small lake to west.

J 93.7 (150.8 km) **D 233.5** (375.8 km) **S 212.9** (343.9 km) Side road to east, information sign about agate deposits.

J 100.1 (161.1 km) **D 227.1** (365.5 km) **S 219.3** (352.9 km) Carmacks town limits.

J 101.3 (163 km) **D 225.9** (363.5 km) **S 220.5** (354.8 km) **Nordenskiold River** to west was named by Lt. Frederick Schwatka, U.S. Army, for Swedish arctic explorer Erik Nordenskiold. Good grayling and pike fishing all summer. This river, which parallels the highway for several miles, flows into the Yukon River at Carmacks.

J 101.5 (163.3 km) **D 225.7** (363.2 km) **S 220.7** (355.2 km) Pull-through rest area to east with large mural of *Moment at Tantalus Butte.* Litter barrels and outhouses.

Carmacks

J 102.7 (165.3 km) **D 224.5** (361.3 km) **S 221.9** (357.1 km). Located on the banks of the Yukon River, Carmacks is the only highway crossing of the Yukon River between Whitehorse and Dawson City. **Population:** 489. **Emergency Services: RCMP,** phone (403) 863-5555. **Fire Department,** phone (403) 863-2222. **Nurse,** phone (403) 863-4444. **Ambulance,** phone (403) 863-444. **Forest Fire Control,** (403) 863-5271.

Private Aircraft: Carmacks airstrip; elev. 1,770 feet/539m; length 5,200 feet/1,585m; gravel; no fuel.

Carmacks was once an important stop for Yukon River steamers traveling between Dawson City and Whitehorse, and it continues as a supply point today for modern river travelers. Carmacks has survived—while other river ports have not—as a service centre for highway traffic and mining interests. Carmacks was also a major stopping point on the old Whitehorse to Dawson Trail.

Carmacks was named for George Carmack, who established a trading post here in the 1890s. Carmack had come North in 1885, hoping to strike it rich. He spent the next 10 years prospecting without success. In 1896, when the trading post went bankrupt, Carmack moved his family to Fortymile, where he could fish to eat and cut timber to sell. That summer, Carmack's remarkable persistence paid off—he unearthed a 5-dollar pan of coarse gold, during a time when a 10-cent pan was considered a good find. That same winter, he extracted more than a ton of gold from the creek, which he renamed Bonanza Creek, and its tributary, Eldorado. When word of Carmack's discovery reached the outside world the following spring, it set off the Klondike Gold Rush.

Traveler facilities include a hotel, motel, bed and breakfast, the village-operated Tantalus Campground on the bank of the Yukon River; restaurant, gas bar, general store (with groceries, bakery and hardware) and laundromat at Hotel Carmacks; post office and bank (both with limited hours), general store, gas bar and dump station at Northern Tutchone Trading Post. The trading post also has some Native crafts for sale. There are also churches, a school, swimming pool, service centre, cafe and a community library. A 1.2-mile/2-km interpretive boardwalk makes it possible to enjoy a stroll along the Yukon River; beautiful view of countryside and Tantalus Butte, gazebo and park at end of trail. Wheelchair accessible. ▲♿

The Northern Tutchone First Nations Interpretive Centre, under construction in 1997, will feature archaeological displays of Native life in a series of indoor and outdoor exhibits.

Carmacks is also an excellent area for rock hounds. There are 5 agate trails in the area, which can double as good, short hiking trails.

Check locally for boat tours to Five Finger and Rink rapids and Fort Selkirk. Fort Selkirk was an important trading post and subsequent RCMP post (see **Milepost J 148.6**). Helicopter service and local canoe and hiking tours available. Abundant fishing in area rivers and lakes: salmon, grayling, northern pike, lake and rainbow trout, whitefish and ling cod. ◄

Northern Tutchone Interpretive

Centre, located along the Klondike Highway just north of the bridge in Carmacks, Yukon (an oasis on your northern excursion). The indoor and outdoor exhibits and displays give you a glimpse into one of the oldest cultures in North America. Make sure you view the world's only reconstruction of a traditional mammoth snare! [ADVERTISEMENT]

Klondike Loop Log
(continued)

J 103.2 (166.1 km) D 224 (360.5 km) S 222.4 (357.9 km) Yukon River bridge. Turnout and parking area at south end of bridge; 2.3-mile-/3.7-km-long trail to Coal Mine Lake.

J 103.3 (166.2 km) D 223.9 (360.3 km) S 222.5 (358.1 km) Northern Tutchone Trading Post with store, gas and diesel, vehicle repair and post office at north end of Yukon River bridge. Fishing tackle and licenses available.

J 104.4 (168 km) D 222.8 (358.6 km) S 223.6 (359.8 km) **Junction** with Campbell Highway (Yukon Highway 4), also known as Watson Lake–Carmacks Road, which leads east and south to Faro, Ross River and Watson Lake. See CAMPBELL HIGHWAY section.

J 105.1 (169.1 km) D 222.1 (357.4 km) S 224.3 (361 km) Side road east to Tantalus Butte Coal Mine; the coal was used in Cyprus Anvil Mine's mill near Faro for drying concentrates. The butte was named by Lt. Frederick Schwatka because it is seen many times before it is actually reached.

J 105.4 (169.6 km) D 221.8 (356.9 km) S 224.6 (361.4 km) Turnout to west with litter barrels, information sign, view of Yukon River Valley.

J 108 (173.8 km) D 219.2 (352.8 km) S 227.2 (365.3 km) Side road west to agate site for rock hounds.

J 110 (177 km) D 217.2 (349.5 km) S 229.2 (368.8 km) Small lake to west.

J 117.5 (189.1 km) D 209.7 (337.5 km) S 236.7 (378.5 km) Pull-through rest area to west with toilets, litter barrels and viewing platform for Five Finger Rapids. Information sign here reads: "Five Finger Rapids named by early miners for the 5 channels, or fingers, formed by the rock pillars. They are a navigational hazard. The safest passage is through the nearest, or east, passage." Stairs (219 steps) lead down to a closer view of the rapids.

J 118.9 (191.3 km) D 208.3 (335.2 km) S 238.1 (380.6 km) Tatchun Creek. Side road to Five Finger Rapids boat-tour operator.

J 119 (191.5 km) D 208.2 (335.1 km) S 238.2 (380.8 km) First turnoff (northbound) to east for **Tatchun Creek** Yukon government campground; 12 sites, $8 camping fee, kitchen shelter and drinking water. Good fishing for grayling, June through September; salmon, July through August. ⚓◀▲

J 119.1 (191.7 km) D 208.1 (334.9 km) S 238.3 (380.9 km) Second turnoff (northbound) east for Tatchun Creek Yukon government campground.

J 119.6 (192.5 km) D 207.6 (334.1 km) S 238.8 (381.8 km) Side road leads east to **Tatchun Lake.** Follow side road 4.3 miles/6.9 km east to boat launch and pit toilets. Continue past boat launch 1.1 miles/1.8 km for Tatchun Lake Yukon government campground with 20 sites, $8 camping fee, pit toilets, firewood, litter barrels and picnic tables. Fishing for northern pike, best in spring or fall. ⚓◀▲

This maintained side road continues east

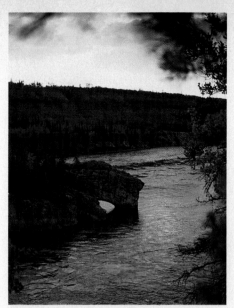
View of one of the channels of Five Finger Rapids, Milepost J 117.5. (Earl L. Brown, staff)

past Tatchun Lake to Frenchman Lake, then loops south to the Campbell Highway, approximately 25 miles/40 km distance. The main access to Frenchman Lake is from the Campbell Highway.

J 121.8 (196 km) D 205.4 (330.6 km) S 241 (388 km) Tatchun Hill.

J 126.6 (203.7 km) D 200.6 (322.8 km) S 245.8 (395.8 km) Large turnout overlooking Yukon River.

J 126.9 (204.2 km) D 200.3 (322.3 km) S 246.1 (396.3 km) Highway descends hill, northbound. Watch for falling rocks.

J 132 (212.4 km) D 195.2 (314.1 km) S 251.2 (404.5 km) McGregor Creek.

J 135 (217.3 km) D 192.2 (309.3 km) S 254.2 (409.4 km) Northbound, first evidence of the huge forest fires of 1995. The fires started on June 12, one burning on either side of the Yukon River. The fires were finally extinguished at the end of July, after they had consumed 325,000 acres of forest.

J 136.6 (219.8 km) D 190.6 (306.7 km) S 255.8 (411.9 km) Good representation of White River ash layer for approximately one mile northbound. About 1,250 years ago a layer of white volcanic ash coated a third of the southern Yukon, or some 125,000 square miles/323,725 square km, and it is easily visible along many roadcuts. This distinct line conveniently provides a division used by archaeologists for dating artifacts: Materials found below this major stratigraphic marker

are considered to have been deposited before A.D. 700, while those found above the ash layer are postdated A.D. 700. The small amount of data available does not support volcanic activity in the White River area during the same period. One theory is that the ash could have spewn forth from a single violent volcanic eruption. The source may be buried under the Klutlan Glacier in the St. Elias Mountains in eastern Alaska.

J 144 (231.7 km) D 183.2 (294.8 km) S 263.2 (423.8 km) McCabe Creek.

J 148 (238.2 km) D 179.2 (288.4 km) S 267.2 (430.4 km) Private RV park and boat tours. Trees along this portion of highway were burned in a 1995 forest fire. Amazingly, the businesses in the immediate surrounding area were spared.

Pristine River Runs. See display ad this section.

Minto Resorts Ltd. R.V. Park. 1,400-foot Yukon River frontage. Halfway between Whitehorse and Dawson City on the Old Stage Road, Minto was once a steamboat landing and trading post. 27 sites, wide easy access, picnic tables, firepits, souvenirs, fishing licenses, ice, snacks, pop. Coin-op showers and laundry, clean restrooms, dump station and water. Bus tour buffet, reservation only. Caravans welcome. Wildlife viewing opportunities. Try fishing the river. Owned and operated by Yukoners. Come and visit us! See display ad this section. [ADVERTISEMENT] ▲

J 148.6 (239.1 km) D 178.6 (287.4 km) S 267.8 (431.4 km) Minto Road, a short loop road, leads west to location of the former riverboat landing and trading post of **MINTO**. Minto Landing Yukon government campground (closed in 1996, current status unknown) is located 1.2 miles/1.9 km west on the grassy banks of the Yukon River. Large flat grassy area may be used for parking. Check with Pristine River Runs about river tours to Sheep Mountain and Fort Selkirk leaving daily from Minto Resorts.

FORT SELKIRK, 25 river miles/40 km from here, was established by Robert Campbell in 1848 for the Hudson's Bay Co. In 1852, the fort was destroyed by Chilkat Indians, who had dominated the fur trade of central Yukon—trading here with the Northern Tutchone people (Selkirk First Nation), who used the area as a seasonal home and

St. Andrew's Anglican Church, built in 1931, is the most elaborate building at Fort Selkirk. Fort Selkirk, on the Yukon River, is accessible by boat. (Earl L. Brown, staff)

exchanged furs for the Chilkats' coastal goods—until the arrival of the Hudson's Bay Co. The site was occupied sporadically by traders, missionaries and the RCMP until the 1950s. About 40 buildings—dating from 1892 to 1940—still stand in good repair. A river trip to Fort Selkirk lets travelers see the fort virtually unchanged since the turn of the century. A highly recommended side trip, if time permits. Government preservation and interpretation staff are available on site.

Private Aircraft: Minto airstrip; elev. 1,550 feet/472m; length 5,000 feet/1,524m; gravel.

J 160.3 (258 km) D 166.9 (268.6 km) S 279.5 (450.5 km) Side road east to Von Wilczek Lakes.

J 162.8 (262 km) D 164.4 (264.6 km) S 282 (454.5 km) Northern limits of damage from 1995 fires.

J 163.4 (263 km) D 163.8 (263.6 km) S 282.6 (455.5 km) Rock Island Lake to east.

J 164.2 (264.2 km) D 163 (262.3 km) S 283.4 (456.8 km) Turnout. Small lake to west.

J 168.7 (271.5 km) D 158.5 (255.1 km) S 287.9 (464 km) Road west to garbage dump.

J 169.4 (272.6 km) D 157.8 (253.9 km) S 288.6 (465 km) Side road to PELLY CROSSING (pop. about 290). RCMP, phone (403) 537-5555. There are a nursing station, post office, general store with phone, camp-

ground, and gas station with unleaded, diesel, tire repair and dump station, 24-hour pump access with VISA card. Banking is available at the Band office. ▲

This Selkirk Indian community attracted residents from Minto when the highway to Dawson City was built. School, mission and sawmill located near the big bridge. The local economy is based on hunting, trapping, fishing and guiding. The Selkirk Indian Band has erected signs near the bridge on the history and culture of the Selkirk people.

The Selkirk Heritage Centre (under construction in 1997) is located adjacent to the Selkirk Gas Bar. The centre will offer a self-guided tour of First Nation heritage.

Selkirk Gas Bar. See display ad this section.

J 169.7 (273.1 km) D 157.5 (253.5 km) S 288.9 (465.5 km) Pelly River bridge.

J 170.4 (274.2 km) D 156.8 (252.3 km) S 289.6 (467 km) Turnout with litter barrel to east. View of Pelly Crossing and river valley. A historical marker here honours the Canadian Centennial (1867–1967). The Pelly River was named in 1840 by explorer Robert Campbell for Sir John Henry Pelly, governor of the Hudson's Bay Co. The Pelly heads near the Northwest Territories border and flows approximately 375 miles/603 km to the Yukon River.

J 171.5 (276 km) D 155.7 (250.6 km) S 290.7 (468.6 km) Private Aircraft: Airstrip to east; elev. 1,870 feet/570m; length 3,000 feet/914m; gravel. No services.

J 179.6 (289 km) D 147.6 (237.5 km) S 298.8 (481.7 km) Pull-through turnout to east.

J 180.9 (291.1 km) D 146.3 (235.4 km) S 300.1 (483.8 km) Small lake to west.

J 183.8 (295.8 km) D 143.4 (230.8 km) S 303 (488.6 km) Large turnout to west. Bridge over Willow Creek.

J 185.5 (298.5 km) D 141.7 (228 km) S 304.7 (491.3 km) Side road west to Jackfish Lake.

J 195.6 (314.8 km) D 131.6 (211.8 km) S 314.8 (506.6 km) Access road west to Wrong Lake (stocked); fishing. ⊶

J 197.4 (317.7 km) D 129.8 (208.9 km) S 316.6 (511 km) Turnout with litter barrel to west. Winding descent begins for northbound traffic.

J 203.6 (327.7 km) D 123.6 (198.9 km) S 322.8 (521 km) Pull-through turnout to east.

J 205.9 (331.4 km) D 121.3 (195.2 km) S 325.1 (524.6 km) Crooked Creek; pike; grayling, use flies, summer best. ⊶

J 207.2 (333.4 km) D 120 (193.1 km) S 326.4 (526.7 km) Pull-through turnout with litter barrel to east at turnoff for Ethel Lake Yukon government campground. Drive in 16.6 miles/26.7 km on narrow and winding side road (not recommended for large RVs) for campground; 14 sites, boat launch, fishing. Camping fee $8. ⊶▲

J 213.8 (344.1 km) D 113.4 (182.5 km) S 333 (537.3 km) Stewart Crossing government maintenance camp to east.

J 213.9 (344.2 km) D 113.3 (182.3 km) S 333.1 (537.5 km) Stewart Crossing Lodge (camping, food), private RV park and campground, and gas station with towing, tires and minor repair, east side of highway. Turnout with information sign west side of highway; Silver Trail information booth (unmanned) contains information on the Silver Trail, or listen to a 5-minute message on the radio at 93.3 FM. ▲

In 1886 **STEWART CROSSING** was the site of a trading post established by Arthur Harper, Alfred Mayo and Jack McQuesten to support gold mining in the area. Later a roadhouse was built here as part of the Whitehorse to Dawson overland stage route. Stewart Crossing also functioned as a fuel stop for the riverboats and during the 1930s was a transfer point for the silver ore barges from Mayo.

Harper, Mayo and McQuesten are 3 prominent names in Yukon history. Harper, an Irish immigrant, was one of the first white men to prospect in the Yukon, although he never struck it rich. He died in 1898 in Arizona. (His son, Walter Harper, was on the first complete ascent of Mount McKinley in 1913. Walter died in 1918 in the SS *Princess Sophia* disaster off Juneau.)

Mayo, a native of Maine, explored, prospected and traded in the Yukon until his death in 1924.

McQuesten, like Harper, worked his way north from the California goldfields. Often referred to as the "Father of the Yukon" and a founding member of the Yukon order of Pioneers, Jack Leroy Napoleon McQuesten ended his trading and prospecting days in 1898 when he moved to California. He died in 1909 while in Seattle for the Alaska–Yukon–Pacific Exposition.

Stewart Crossing Chevron. See display ad this section.

J 214.3 (344.9 km) **D 112.9** (181.7 km) **S 333.5** (538 km) Stewart River bridge. The Stewart River flows into the Yukon River upstream from Dawson City.

J 214.4 (345 km) **D 112.8** (181.5 km) **S 333.6** (538.2 km) **Silver Trail (Stewart Crossing) Junction** at north end of Stewart River bridge. Marker shows distance to Dawson 182 km. The Silver Trail Information Centre is located in the restored Binet House in Mayo; phone (403) 996-2926 in summer. The Silver Trail (Yukon Highway 11) leads northeast to Mayo, Elsa and Keno; see SILVER TRAIL section.

Yukon Gold Explorer's Passports are stamped at the Keno City Mining Museum and the Binet House in Mayo, 2 of 14 passport stamp locations.

J 214.8 (345.7 km) **D 112.4** (180.9 km) **S 334** (538.8 km) View to west of Stewart River and mountains as highway climbs northbound.

J 220.8 (355.3 km) **D 106.4** (171.2 km) **S 340** (545.1 km) Dry Creek.

J 224.4 (361.1 km) **D 102.8** (165.4 km) **S 343.6** (556.2 km) Access to Stewart River to west. Historical information sign about Stewart River. A major tributary of the Yukon River, the Stewart River was named for James G. Stewart, who discovered it in 1849. Stewart was assistant to Robert Campbell of the Hudson's Bay Co.

J 229.1 (368.7 km) **D 98.1** (157.9 km)

S 348.3 (561.9 km) **Moose Creek Lodge**. A must for Yukon travelers! An authentic trapper's cabin featuring a large selection of Northern books, souvenirs and crafts. In our cozy cafe, enjoy a hearty sourdough pancake breakfast, our scrumptious cinnamon buns, homebaked sourdough bread. Hearty homemade soups, delicious belt-bustin' sandwiches and burgers, mouthwatering homebaked pies. Try our Triple Berry Crumble or Chocolate Heaven ice cream dessert. Meet Max the Mosquito and Murray the Moose! Smokehouse. Cozy rustic economical log cabins. For reservations, phone (403) 667-1324; fax (403) 996-2139; or write Bag 1, Mayo, YT Y0B 1M0. Moose Creek is also serving group tours in their beautiful open-air gazebo, reservations a must. VISA and MasterCard. Your hosts, the Lefler family.
[ADVERTISEMENT]

J 229.2 (368.9 km) **D 98** (157.7 km) **S 348.4** (562 km) Moose Creek bridge.

J 229.5 (369.3 km) **D 97.7** (157.2 km) **S 348.7** (562.4 km) Turnout to west at turnoff for Moose Creek Yukon government campground adjacent to **Moose Creek** and Stewart River; good picnic spot. There are 30 RV sites, 6 tent-only sites, kitchen shelter, playground and playfield. Camping fee $8. Short trail to Stewart River. Good fishing for grayling, 1 to 1¹/₄ lbs.

J 242.7 (390.6 km) **D 84.5** (136 km) **S 361.9** (583.7 km) McQuesten River, a tributary of the Stewart River, named for Jack (Leroy Napoleon) McQuesten.

J 242.9 (390.9 km) **D 84.3** (135.7 km) **S 362.1** (584 km) McQuesten, a lodge with cafe, cabins and RV sites. Site of Old McQuesten River Lodge to east. ▲

J 247.5 (398.3 km) **D 79.7** (128.3 km) **S 366.7** (590.1 km) Partridge Creek Farm.

Organic vegetables in season.

J 249.3 (401.2 km) **D 77.9** (125.4 km) **S 368.5** (594 km) **Private Aircraft:** McQuesten airstrip 1.2 miles/1.9 km west; elev. 1,500 feet/457m; length 5,000 feet/1,524m; gravel and turf. No services.

J 251.3 (404.4 km) **D 75.9** (122.1 km) **S 370.5** (596.5 km) Clear Creek, access via side road west.

J 260.4 (419.1 km) **D 66.8** (107.5 km) **S 379.6** (612 km) Barlow Lake, access via 0.6-mile-/1-km-long side road west.

J 263.7 (424.4 km) **D 63.5** (102.2 km) **S 382.9** (617.2 km) Beaver Dam Creek.

J 266 (428.1 km) **D 61.2** (98.5 km) **S 385.2** (621 km) Willow Creek.

J 268.5 (432.1 km) **D 58.7** (94.5 km) **S 387.7** (625 km) Flat Hill.

J 268.8 (432.6 km) **D 58.4** (94 km) **S 388** (625.5 km) Gravel Lake to east.

J 272.1 (437.9 km) **D 55.1** (88.7 km) **S 391.3** (630.8 km) Meadow Creek.

J 272.5 (438.5 km) **D 54.7** (88 km) **S 391.7** (631.4 km) Rest area with litter barrel to south.

J 276.5 (445 km) **D 50.7** (81.6 km) **S 395.7** (637.9 km) French Creek.

J 279.7 (450.1 km) **D 47.5** (76.4 km) **S 398.9** (643.1 km) Stone Boat Creek.

J 288.9 (464.9 km) **D 38.3** (61.6 km) **S 408.1** (657.9 km) Rest area.

J 289.3 (465.6 km) **D 37.9** (61 km) **S 408.5** (658.5 km) Geologic point of interest turnout, with information sign, to east overlooking Tintina Trench. This geologic feature, which extends hundreds of miles across Yukon and Alaska, provides visible proof of plate tectonics.

J 295.1 (474.9 km) **D 32.1** (51.7 km) **S 414.3** (667.8 km) Flat Creek.

J 295.9 (476.2 km) **D 31.3** (50.4 km)

S 415.1 (669 km) Klondike River to east.

J 297.6 (478.9 km) **D 29.6** (47.6 km) **S 416.8** (671.9 km) Large turnout to east with historic sign about Klondike River and information sign on Dempster Highway.

J 298 (479.6 km) **D 29.2** (47 km) **S 417.2** (672.5 km) Watch for livestock.

J 301.6 (485.4 km) **D 25.6** (41.2 km) **S 420.8** (678.5 km) **Dempster Corner, junction** of Klondike Highway and the Dempster Highway (Yukon Highway 5). Klondike River Lodge east side of highway just north of the junction; open year-round, food, lodging, camping, gas, diesel and propane. The Dempster Highway leads northeast to Inuvik, NWT. See DEMPSTER HIGHWAY section for log of that road. (Details on the Dempster are also available from the Western Arctic Information Centre in Dawson City.) ▲

Klondike River Lodge. See display ad this section.

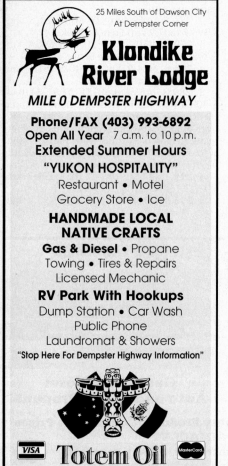

J 307.3 (494.5 km) **D 19.9** (32 km) **S 426.5** (687.4 km) Goring Creek.

J 308.4 (496.3 km) **D 18.8** (30.3 km) **S 427.6** (689.2 km) Turnout to north with access to the Klondike River.

J 315.2 (507.3 km) **D 12** (19.3 km) **S 434.4** (700 km) Turnoff to north for Klondike River Yukon government campground, located on Rock Creek near the Klondike River; 38 sites, kitchen shelter, drinking water, playground. Camping fee $8. ▲

J 315.7 (508.1 km) **D 11.5** (18.5 km) **S 434.9** (700.8 km) Dawson City airport to south. **Private Aircraft:** Runway 02-20; elev. 1,211 feet/369m; length 5,000 feet/1,524m; gravel; fuel 80 (in drums at Dawson City), 100, JP4. Flightseeing trips and air charters available.

J 317.1 (510.3 km) **D 10.1** (16.3 km) **S 436.3** (703.4 km) Hunker Creek Road to south. Access to Goldbottom Mining Tours, 9 miles/15km south, a family-run placer mine offering tours and gold panning; fee charged. **Goldbottom Mining Tours and Gold Panning.** See display ad this section.

J 318.4 (512.4 km) **D 8.8** (14.2 km) **S 437.6** (705.4 km) Turnout to south with point of interest sign about Hunker Creek. Albert Hunker staked the first claim on Hunker Creek Sept. 11, 1896. George Carmack made the big discovery on Bonanza Creek on Aug. 17, 1896. Hunker Creek is 16 miles/26 km long, of which 13 miles/21 km was dredged between 1906 and 1966.

J 318.9 (513.2 km) **D 8.3** (13.4 km) **S 438.1** (706.1 km) Bear Creek Road.

J 319.6 (514.3 km) **D 7.6** (12.2 km)

S 438.8 (707.2 km) Turnout with historic sign about the Yukon Ditch and tailings to north. To the south is Bear Creek historical site, operated by Parks Canada. Open 9:30 A.M. to 5 P.M. daily in summer, with scheduled tours. Admission: adults $2.25, children 12 and under free. This 62-acre compound of the Yukon Consolidated Gold Corp. features complete blacksmith and machinery shops and Gold Room.

J 323.3 (520.3 km) **D 3.9** (6.3 km) **S 442.5** (712 km) Callison industrial area; charter helicopter service, mini-storage, bulk fuel plant and heavy equipment repairs.

J 324.5 (522.2 km) **D 2.7** (4.3 km) **S 443.7** (714 km) Bonanza Creek Road to Discovery Claim and historic Dredge No. 4, largest wooden hull dredge in North America. Restoration of the dredge is under way. Interpretive centre on site; tours 9 A.M. to 5 P.M. daily June through August. Admission: adults $2.25, children 12 and under free. Bonanza Creek Road is maintained for 10 miles/16.1 km. Commercial RV park and gold panning at junction. ▲

GuggieVille. Good Sam. This clean, attractive campground is built on dredge tailings at the former site of the Guggenheim's mining camp. 72 RV sites with water and electricity, 28 unserviced sites,

public showers ($2 each). Car wash, dump station and laundromat are available. A mining display is open to the public free of charge. Gold panning discount for those staying at GuggieVille. Phone (403) 993-5008. Fax (403) 993-5006. Winter phone/fax (250) 558-3334. [ADVERTISEMENT] ▲

J 324.7 (522.5 km) **D 2.5** (4 km) **S 443.9** (715.3 km) Campground, gas station and store.

Dawson City R.V. Park & Campground and **Bonanza Shell.** See display ad this section. ▲

J 324.8 (522.7 km) **D 2.4** (3.9 km) **S 444** (715.5 km) Klondike River bridge.

J 325.3 (523.5 km) **D 1.9** (3.1 km) **S 444.5** (716.4 km) Large turnout with information sign and map.

J 325.8 (524.3 km) **D 1.4** (2.3 km) **S 445** (717.2 km) Dome Road to north leads 5.7 miles/9.2 km to Dome Mountain (elev. 2,911 feet/887m), which offers views of Dawson City, the Yukon and Klondike rivers, Bonanza Creek and the Ogilvie Mountains.

J 325.9 (524.5 km) **D 1.3** (2.1 km) **S 445.1** (717.4 km) Trans North Helicopter base on left northbound; Klondike goldfield tours. Rock face on right northbound is known locally as Crocus Bluff; short, interpretive foot trail leads to viewpoint overlooking Klondike River and Dawson City.

J 326.1 (524.8 km) **D 1.1** (1.8 km) **S 445.3** (717.7 km) Fifth Avenue. Turnout with sign about the Klondike River to south: "With headwaters in the Ogilvie Mountains, the Klondike River and its tributaries gave birth to the world's greatest gold rush—the Klondike Gold Rush of '98."

J 327.2 (526.6 km) **D 0** **S 446.4** (719.5 km) Dawson City, ferry at Yukon River. *Description of Dawson City follows. Log of Klondike Loop continues on page 279.*

Dawson City

J 327.2 (526.6 km) **D 0 S** 446.4 (719.5 km) Located 165 miles/266 km south of the Arctic Circle on the Yukon River at its junction with the Klondike River. **Population:** 2,019. **Emergency Services: RCMP,** 1st Avenue S., phone (403) 993-5555. **Fire Department,** phone (403) 993-2222. **Nursing station,** phone (403) 993-4444. **Ambulance,** phone (403) 993-4444.

Visitor Information: Visitor Reception Centre, operated by Tourism Yukon and Parks Canada, at Front and King streets, is housed in a replica of the 1897 Alaska Commercial Co. store. Yukon information and a Dawson City street map are available. Video disks on a variety of subjects, particularly Dawson attractions and history. Walking tours are part of the daily schedule. Get your Yukon Gold Explorer's Passport stamped here and at the Dawson City Museum. Open daily, 8 A.M. to 8 P.M. mid-May to mid-September, phone (403) 993-5566, fax 993-6449. Dawson City has lots to do and see. If you want to take it all in, plan for 3 days to cover most of the attractions.

The Dempster Highway and Northwest Territories Information Centre is located in the B.Y.N. (British Yukon Navigation) Building on Front Street, across from the Yukon visitor centre; open 9 A.M. to 9 P.M., June to September. Information on Northwest Territories and the Dempster Highway. Phone (403) 993-6167, fax 993-6334.

Discovery Day celebrations take place August 15 to 18 in 1997.

Elevation: 1,050 feet/320m. **Climate:** There are 20.9 hours of daylight June 21, 3.8 hours of daylight on Dec. 21. Mean high in July, 72°F/22.2°C. Mean low in January, -30.5°F/-34.7°C. First fall frost end of August, last spring frost end of May. Annual snowfall 59.8 inches. **Radio:** CBC 560; CFYT-FM 106,

Historic Dredge No. 4 is located on Bonanza Creek Road. (Earl L. Brown, staff)

CKYN-FM 96.1 (summer visitor station). **Television:** CBC Anik Channel 7 and 14 other channels via cable. **Newspaper:** *Klondike Sun* (semi-monthly).

Private Aircraft: Dawson City airport located 11.5 miles/18.5 km southeast (see **Milepost J 315.7**). Customs available.

Historically, Dawson City dates from the discovery of gold on a Klondike River tributary (Rabbit Creek, renamed Bonanza Creek) in 1896. Previously, the site had been a Native fish camp. There were several hundred prospectors in the Fortymile area before the big strike, and most of them swarmed over the Klondike creeks, staking claims long before stampeders began trickling into the

country the following year. See *Dawson City's Heyday* on page 277 for a look at the community during the gold rush years.

Dawson City was Yukon's first capital, when the Yukon became a separate territory in 1898. But by 1953, Whitehorse—on the railway and the highway, and with a large airport—was so much the hub of activity that the federal government moved the capital from Dawson City, along with 800 civil servants, and years of tradition and pride. Some recompense was offered in the form of a road linking Whitehorse with the mining at Mayo and Dawson City. With its completion, White Pass trucks replaced White Pass *(Continues on page 276)*

DAWSON CITY ADVERTISERS

"THE ENTERTAINMENT CAPITAL OF THE YUKON"

DAWSON CITY

Diamond Tooth Gerties
Canada's Only Northern Casino

Discover the delights of Diamond Tooth Gerties, Canada's oldest and most unique gambling hall. Many have struck it rich in this turn of the century casino that, unlike other Canadian casinos, combines live entertainment, beverage and food service with slot machines, blackjack tables, roulette wheels and more. Meet Diamond Tooth Gertie and cheer her Can Can girls in one of three nightly shows.

Outstanding Tours & Exhibits
Take a step back in time!

Thrill to the excitement of the Klondike's wildest boom town. Rich, "living" history around every corner. Gold nugget jewelry, native crafts, superb shopping and unusual gifts. Gold panning excursions and informative guided tours. Centennial Events and Festivals. National historic treasures and a museum without equal. Whatever your pleasure, please remember... you will need a week to see it all!

Gaslight Follies
At the Palace Grand Theatre

A high energy, musical comedy performed in one of the most magnificent theatres ever built! The Gaslight Follies is a professional show that is original and written to reflect the lavish and exciting times of the gold rush era. There's no show or theatre like the Palace Grand anywhere in the North. It's a must see! Theatre tours daily.

Klondike
VISITORS ASSOCIATION

DON'T MISS WHAT TRAVELLERS CALL...
"The best part of our northern vacation... it takes a week to see it all!"

Send for your Dawson City Information Package today!
P.O.Box 389M, Dawson City, Yukon, Canada Y0B 1G0
Tel: (403) 993-5575   Fax: (403) 993-6415
e mail: KVA@Dawson.net

ACCOMMODATIONS

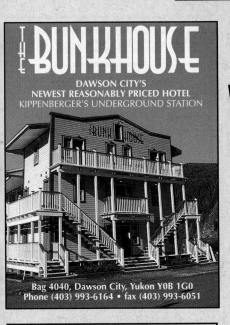

THE BUNKHOUSE

DAWSON CITY'S
NEWEST REASONABLY PRICED HOTEL
KIPPENBERGER'S UNDERGROUND STATION

Bag 4040, Dawson City, Yukon Y0B 1G0
Phone (403) 993-6164 • fax (403) 993-6051

For Accommodation
Information, Contact
The Visitors Reception Centre
(403) 993-5566

"DAWSON CITY" BED & BREAKFAST

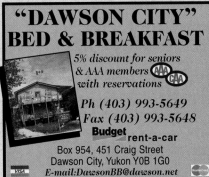

5% discount for seniors
& AAA members
with reservations

Ph (403) 993-5649
Fax (403) 993-5648

Budget rent-a-car

Box 954, 451 Craig Street
Dawson City, Yukon Y0B 1G0
E-mail:DawsonBB@dawson.net

FIFTH AVE 700

5th AVENUE BED & BREAKFAST

Friendly and Comfortable!
Next to the Museum
Box 722, Dawson City, Yukon Y0B 1G0
Ph/Fax (403)993-5941/email:5thAve@dawson.net

KLONDIKE KATE'S CABINS & RESTAURANT

Clean, Affordable
Accommodation,
Full Service Restaurant
3rd Ave. and King St.

P.O. Box 417,
Dawson City,
Yukon Y0B1G0
Phone (403) 993-6527
Fax: (403) 993-6044

Dawson City, Yukon

White Ram Manor Bed & Breakfast

Look for the PINK HOUSE at 7th & Harper

- **Sun Decks**
- **Hot Tub**
- **BBQ**
- **Picnic Area**
- **Canoe Rentals**

John & Gail Hendley
Ph: (403) 993-5772 • Fax: 993-6509
Box 302, Dawson City, Yukon Y0B 1G0

GOLD GOLD GOLD GOLD GOLD GOLD GOLD GOLD GOLD GOLD

GuggieVille

CLEAN AND QUIET CAMPGROUND
ON FAMOUS BONANZA CREEK

*3 Minutes From City Centre
on Bonanza Road*

★ HOOKUPS
★ GOLD PANNING
★ GIFT SHOP
★ SHOWERS
★ CAR WASH
★ LAUNDROMAT

Box 311, Dawson City, Yukon Territory Y0B 1G0
(403) 993-5008 or Winter Ph/Fax (250) 558-3334

GOLD GOLD GOLD GOLD GOLD GOLD GOLD GOLD GOLD

GOLD RUSH CAMPGROUND RV PARK

*Full facilities
Downtown location!*
5th Ave & York St. Dawson City
Phone: (403) 993-5247

ATTRACTIONS

When in town visit the . . .

DAWSON CITY MUSEUM

*Open 10 a.m. - 6 p.m.
Victoria Day - Labour Day*

KINGS OF THE KLONDIKE GALLERY
City Life Gallery - Visible Storage
Movies - Demonstrations
"Meet a Klondike Character"
Gift Shop
Resource Library
Historic Train Collection

Located on 5th Avenue in the Old Territorial Administration Building
Ph: (403) 993-5291 • FAX: (403) 993-5839 • email: can-dcm@unmedia.ca
dcmuseum@yknet.yk.ca • P.O. Box 303, Dawson City, Yukon Y0B 1G0

Smoked Salmon Barbeque

*For reservations:
FRONT STREET BIRCH CABIN
Box 859, Dawson City, Yukon Y0B 1G0
Ph: (403) 993-5482*

Yukon River Cruise

ATTRACTIONS

The George Black ferries vehicles across the Yukon River. (Earl L. Brown, staff)

(Continued from page 270)
river steamers.

New government buildings were built in Dawson, including a fire hall. In 1962 the federal government reconstructed the Palace Grand Theatre for a gold rush festival that featured the Broadway musical, *Foxy*, with Bert Lahr. A museum was established in the Administration Building and tours and entertainments were begun.

Dawson City was declared a national historic site in the early 1960s. Parks Canada is currently involved with 35 properties in Dawson City. Many buildings have been restored, some reconstructed and others stabilized. Parks Canada offers an interpretive program each summer for visitors to this historic city.

Dawson City is hosting a "Decade of Centennials" to 2002. Highlights include the Klondike Gold Rush Centennial and the completion of the White Pass and Yukon Route Railway. For further information on events, contact the Klondike Centennial Society, Bag 1996, Dawson City, YT Y0B 1G0.

ACCOMMODATIONS/VISITOR SERVICES

Accustomed to a summer influx of visitors, Dawson has modern hotels and motels (rates average $75 and up) and several bed and breakfasts. The community has a bank, automatic teller machine, restaurants, 5 laundromats (4 with showers), 2 grocery stores (with bakeries), general stores, souvenir shops, churches, art galleries, post office, government offices, government liquor store, information centre, hostel, swimming pool and plenty of entertainment. Many Dawson City merchants abide by the Fair Exchange Policy, offering travelers an exchange rate within 4 percent of the banks'. Dawson City's hotels and motels fill up early, especially at times of special events. Reservations are a must from June through August.

Bear Creek Bed & Bannock. First Nation family offers "a touch of culture." This 4 bedroom, full facility guest house is separate from the main home. We offer a continental breakfast with fresh bannock. Elder and family discounts in a quiet, natural setting 10 minutes from town. Handicap accessible. Reservations recommended. Open June 1, 1997. (403) 993-6765 or (403) 993-5605. [ADVERTISEMENT]

5th Avenue Bed and Breakfast. Located adjacent to the museum overlooking Victory Gardens. A modern home with a historic finish, serving a hearty, healthy, all-you-can-eat breakfast. We guarantee comfort, cleanliness and courteous service along with the most convenient location in town. VISA. Call or write Larry and Pat Vezina, Box 722, Dawson City, YT Y0B 1G0. Phone (403) 993-5941. [ADVERTISEMENT]

Klondike Kate's Cabins and Restaurant. We offer you charming, clean and affordable accommodations with private bath. Located near all major attractions. Enjoy the friendly atmosphere of our restaurant, set in a 1904 historic building. Dine inside or on our outdoor patio. We serve ethnic foods, espresso coffees and feature a $3.99 breakfast special. Box 417, Dawson City, YT Y0B 1G0. Phone (403) 993-6527. Fax (403) 993-6044. [ADVERTISEMENT]

There are 2 Yukon government (YTG) campgrounds in the Dawson area. Yukon River YTG campground is across the Yukon River (by ferry) from town, adjacent to the west-side ferry approach (see **Milepost D 0.2** on Top of the World Highway log, following Dawson City section). Klondike River YTG campground is southeast of town near the airport (see **Milepost J 315.2**). Private RV parks in the Dawson area include Gold Rush Campground, downtown at 5th and York; GuggieVille, east of town at **Milepost J 324.5**; and Dawson City R.V. Park and Campground at **Milepost J 324.7**. ▲

TRANSPORTATION

Air: Dawson City airport is 11.5 miles/18.5 km southeast of the city. Alkan Air provides scheduled service to Inuvik, NWT, Old Crow, Mayo and Whitehorse. Air North connects Dawson City with Whitehorse (daily service in summer); with Old Crow and Juneau (3 times weekly in summer); and Fairbanks (4 times weekly in summer). Charter and flightseeing tours available from Bonanza Aviation. Helicopter tours from Trans North Air and Fireweed.

Ferry: The Yukon government operates a free 24-hour ferry, the *George Black*, across the Yukon River from about the third week in May to mid-October (depending upon breakup and freezeup); ferry departs Dawson City on demand. The ferry carries vehicles and passengers across to the public campground and is the only connection to the Top of the World Highway (Yukon Highway 9). Be prepared to wait 3 hours or more during peak traffic periods (2 hours is quite common).

Bus: Service between Whitehorse and Dawson City by Norline coaches; 3 times weekly June through September. Service between Inuvik, NWT, and Dawson City by Gold City; 2 times weekly. Service from Whitehorse via Dawson City to Tok, AK, by Alaska Direct Buslines; weekly. Check with agent at Gas Shack or Gold City Tours for more information.

DAWSON CITY'S HEYDAY

Following the historic discovery of gold on Bonanza Creek in August of 1896, Dawson City grew out of a marshy swamp near the confluence of the Yukon and Klondike rivers. In 2 years it became the largest city in Canada west of Winnipeg, with a population that fluctuated between 30,000 and 40,000 people—not as large as Seattle, but much larger than Victoria.

Its founder was Joe Ladue, a former prospector-turned-outfitter, who was on the scene early. He knew from experience that merchants in gold camps prospered more than miners. He had a sawmill at the mining camp of Sixtymile and, while miners staked their claims, Ladue staked out a townsite instead.

Anticipating the coming building boom, Ladue rafted his sawmill to the new townsite, which he had already named Dawson City, in honour of George M. Dawson, a government geologist who helped survey the boundary between Alaska and Northwest Territories.

"I commenced erecting the first house in that region on Sept. 1, 1896," Ladue wrote later. "Within 6 months from that date there were over 500 houses erected, which included stores, supply stations, hotels, restaurants, saloons and residences."

Fortune smiled on Ladue. Everyone bought his lumber. He owned 160 acres, the government owned 22 acres, and his home doubled as Dawson's first saloon. He sold the first lots at prices ranging from $5 to $25 to $300. Town lots later fetched as much as $40,000 each.

Dawson's reputation as a booming, bawdy frontier town was largely the result of over-zealous writers. The rush was a phenomenon that they all hyped and exploited to sell their newspapers, guide books and magazines as gold fever swept the continent and abroad. Rags-to-riches stories of miners were popular subjects. Dawson had plenty of dance halls, saloons and brothels. It had tons of gold, vats of whisky, and gamblers and 'scarlet women' caught up in a riotous swirl of social activity with an international cast. Some reports contained accurate facts and descriptions while others were embellished, exaggerated or contained complete falsehoods.

To many early writers, Dawson City was a great curiosity. It was a "boomtown in a bog." It had miners who wore filthy clothes caked with mud, and miners who were also filthy rich. In contrast, some dance-hall girls wore $1,500 gowns imported from Paris. More fortunes were won and lost in the gambling halls of Dawson than in the goldfields.

Some of its residents dined on champagne, oysters and caviar for breakfast, while others existed on stale bread, lard and tea. While many ate beans 3 times a day, many more went hungry. Society matrons held lavish tea parties and served canapés on Limoges china, while the poor and indigent perished in nearby hospitals from scurvy, typhoid and dysentery. There were plenty of doctors in Dawson, but at $200 a visit, few people consulted them.

Dawson could have been a wide-open town where "anything goes," but it also had the North West Mounted Police. The reality is that the period of chaos lasted only for a few months in 1898. Constables of the North West Mounted Police, who earned $1.25 a day, worked long and hard to maintain law and order through the rush. Dance-hall girls and prostitutes also worked long and hard, and they earned ten times more money.

In its early years, fire was the greatest threat to the town. Dawson was made of wood and canvas, and it was built in a hurry. Its buildings, cabins and tents were heated with primitive wood stoves, and they were lit by candles and coal oil lamps.

The town was only a year old when its first major fire occurred on Thanksgiving Day, Nov. 25, 1897. The temperature was -58°C when a blaze broke out in the M & N saloon after a dance-hall girl threw a burning lamp at a rival. The blaze destroyed 2 saloons and the Opera House.

The second fire occurred on Oct. 14, 1898. Ironically, it was started by the same dance-hall girl, who had left a candle burning on a block of wood. Flames consumed 2 hotels, the post office and most of Front Street. In all, 26 buildings were destroyed.

But the worst inferno erupted in April 1899, when the entire business district was destroyed. After fire wiped out the business district again on Jan. 10, 1900, the situation finally got better, as more buildings were made of galvanized iron and tin, and fire fighting equipment improved.

Prior to the heyday of 1898, a community of cabins and tents had begun to take shape. Reactions of newcomers varied, but their first impressions were the same: Dawson City's name was a misnomer. They expected a city, but found only a camp.

After the river ice went out in May of 1898, the first small boats appeared in early June. The trickle became an armada as they arrived by the hundreds. In the weeks that followed, the hundreds became thousands as riverboats arrived on the scene, all loaded down with supplies and equipment.

As people poured into Dawson, their boats were crowded 3 to 6 deep along 2 miles of waterfront. Tents congested the riverbank and spread up the hillside behind the town.

By summer more than 20 saloons were operating, which prompted the American consul to quip that they were the only businesses that could afford the astronomical rents and real estate prices. Part of their success was due to their armies of "percentage women" who encouraged patrons to buy over-priced liquor, for which they received a percentage of the house receipts. Unfortunately, it also encouraged drunkenness and gave some women opportunities to commit theft and fraud.

Newspapers were among the first companies to establish themselves. Other small businesses included butchers, bakers, grocers, clothiers, tobacconists, blacksmiths, brothels and gambling halls.

It was inevitable that the new arrivals became disillusioned when they learned that the gold-bearing creeks had all been staked. Speculators had claimed the rest. Many had come expecting to find nuggets on the ground. They had spent everything and exhausted themselves getting there.

When they looked for work, the surplus of labourers had driven wages down, while the demand for food and clothing had sent prices soaring. A meal that cost 15 cents in Seattle was $2.50 in Dawson. Five dollars usually bought a meal of beans, stewed apples, bread and coffee. Hundreds began selling their outfits in a 24-hour bazaar along the waterfront, to pay for their passage home.

By the summer of 1898 the carnival atmosphere gave way to the raw reality of heat, mosquitoes, mud, filth, stench and disease. Horses got stuck in the muck of the street, and wagons sank up to their axles. Pedestrians waded knee-deep through what writer T.C. Down described as "this festering mass of putrid muskeg." Typhoid broke out in July and was rampant through the summer. The town's 2 small hospitals were filled to capacity.

On June 13, 1898, the federal government created a separate Yukon Territory. Commissioner William Ogilvie headed the new territorial council and the cleanup of Dawson City began. A fire department was organized; a city engineer was appointed to construct drainage ditches; and regulations were made for garbage disposal and drinking water. Squatters and their debris were evicted from the waterfront and action began on public works, nuisances, hospitals, burials, and the licensing of theatres and other businesses. Handguns were made illegal in Dawson.

Environmental laws, however, hadn't been invented yet. In the spring of 1899, when the river ice was due to go out, government officials ordered the town's garbage piled out on the ice. At breakup the Yukon River swallowed what it could, and delivered the rest downstream.

Just when order was being created out of all the turmoil, a major gold discovery was made in Nome, AK, and an exodus began. News had filtered into Dawson during the winter of 1898, prompting hundreds of gold-seekers to head out along the frozen river. Many more waited until the opening of navigation, and the first steamboats of 1899 left Dawson crammed full of passengers.

As the Klondike Gold Rush subsided, the drain continued throughout the following 2 decades. A solid core of permanent residents refused to leave. They stayed on to supervise the town's continued, if sporadic, development. That same core exists here today, with a year-round population of about 2,000 people. To them, Dawson may be a city with a past, but its future still looks bright.

(Excerpted from an article by Ken Spotswood, courtesy of Yukon Anniversaries Commission.)

The SS Keno was the last steamer to run the Yukon River. (Eero Sorila)

Taxi: Airport taxi service available from downtown hotels. Scheduled and charter limo service available from Gold City Tours.

Rental Car: Car and truck rentals at Norcan, located in the Northern Superior Bldg.

Boat: Service to Eagle, AK, on the *Yukon Queen*. Canoe rentals available from Dawson Trading Post and at the hostel across the river.

ATTRACTIONS

Take a Walking Tour. Town-core tours leave the Visitor Reception Centre 2 times daily in summer. The Fort Herchmer Northwest Mounted Police walking tour starts outside the restored Commissioner's Residence on Front Street. This handsome building was once the residence of Hon. George Black, M.P., Speaker of the House of Commons, and his famous wife, Martha Louise, who walked to Dawson City via the Trail of '98 and stayed to become the First Lady of the Yukon. Pierre Berton's boyhood home has also been restored. Berton is the author of *Klondike Lost*, an account of the Klondike Gold Rush. Pick up a schedule of daily events at the Visitor Reception Centre.

Take a Bus Tour. Motorcoach and van tours of Klondike creeks, goldfields and Dawson City are available; inquire at Gold City Tours (ask about step-on guide service, too). For a panoramic view of Dawson City, the Klondike River, Bonanza Creek and Yukon River, take the bus or drive the 5 miles/8 km to the top of Dome Mountain (elev. 2,911 feet/887m).

Take a River Tour: Yukon River Cruises offers tours aboard the miniature stern-wheeler launch *Yukon Lou* leaving the dock behind Birch Cabin booking office near SS *Keno* at 1 P.M. daily in summer, and traveling to Pleasure Island and the stern-wheeler graveyard. Cruise takes 1¹/₂ hours. Fishwheel Charter offers guided 2-hour river tours 4 times a day; tickets at the Trading Post. Westours (Grayline Yukon) operates the *Yukon Queen* on the Yukon River between Dawson City and Eagle, AK; check with the Grayline Yukon office about tickets. One-way and round-trip passage is sold on a space-available basis. The trip takes 4 hours downstream to Eagle, and 6 hours back to Dawson.

Cruise the Yukon River. Cruise from Dawson City down the famous Yukon River to Eagle, Alaska aboard the MV *Yukon Queen*. Retrace the old sternwheeler route of this historic gold rush area as you cruise past abandoned settlements among the forested hills. A hearty prospector's meal is included. Daily departures. Roundtrip fare is $135 U.S. per person. Prices subject to change. Call (403) 993-5599. [ADVERTISEMENT]

Pleasure Island Restaurant. Don't miss the riverboat cruise on the MV *Yukon Lou* (refurbished 1996). See the old stern-wheeler shipyard, historic Native village of Moosehide and stop in at Pleasure Island for an all-you-can-eat smoked salmon barbecue. Dinner includes garden fresh salad and slow-baked potatoes, topped off by homemade chocolate cake. Steak available on request. This is a "must" when in Dawson City. For reservations phone (403) 993-5482 or (907) 468-4460 (September–May). Group rates. [ADVERTISEMENT]

Visit the Palace Grand Theatre. This magnificently reconstructed theatre, now a national historic site, is home to the "Gaslight Follies," a turn-of-the-century entertainment. Performances nightly except Tuesday, from late May to early September. Arizona Charlie Meadows opened the Palace Grand in 1899, and today's visitors, sitting in the curtained boxes around the balcony, will succumb to the charm of this beautiful theatre. Tours of the building are conducted once daily by Parks Canada, June through September. Films and presentations daily in summer.

Gambling. Klondike Visitors Assoc. (a nonprofit community organization) operates Diamond Tooth Gertie's Gambling Hall, open May to September. There are Klondike gambling tables (specially licensed in Yukon), 56 "Vegas-style" slot machines, bar service and floor shows nightly. You may have a soft drink if you prefer, and still see the cancan girls present their floor show. Persons under 19 not admitted. Gertie's

hosts Yukon Talent Night in August.

Visit the Dawson City Museum. Housed in the renovated Territorial Administration Building on 5th Avenue, the museum is open daily from 10 A.M. to 6 P.M., mid-May through early September; by appointment year-round. Featured are the Kings of the Klondike and City Life Galleries, hourly audiovisual and dramatic presentations, and the museum's collection of narrow-gauge locomotives, including a Vauclain-type Baldwin engine, the last one in existence in Canada. Weekly lecture series during summer; check for schedule. The films "City of Gold" and "The Yukoner" are shown daily. A selection of silent film serials, news and documentary reels from 1903 to 1929 is shown in the gallery. Also take part in the "Meet a Klondike Character" show and explore the "Klondike Gold" CD Rom.

The museum has a gift shop, wheelchair ramp, resource library, genealogy service and an extensive photography collection. A nominal admission fee is charged. For more information write the museum at Box 303, Dawson City, YT Y0B 1G0; phone (403) 993-5291, fax 993-5839. &

Art's Gallery offers limited edition and original works by Northern artists, and specializes in Yukon-made crafts; pottery, baskets, moosehair tuftings. Featuring soapstone carvings and unique creations from Canada's Arctic. Mastodon, antler, silver jewellery, and a wide selection of Klondike and illustrated children's books also offered, with post and art cards too! We ship everywhere! Third Ave. across from Old Post Office. (403) 993-6967. [ADVERTISEMENT]

Peabody's Photo Parlour. Capture summer memories with a unique Klondike photo in 1900s costurmes. Same-day film processing (ask about our 1-hour service), film and camera supplies. Northern artwork, a great selection of postcards, Yukon souvenirs. VISA, MasterCard. Located on Front Street between Princess and Queen streets. Phone (403) 993-5209. [ADVERTISEMENT]

SS *Keno* National Historic Site. The SS *Keno* was the last steamer to run the Yukon River when she sailed from Whitehorse in 1960 to her present berth on the riverbank next to the bank. Although she is closed to the public, an interpretive display is set up beside the site.

Historic Harrington's Store, 3rd Avenue and Princess Street, houses a photographic exhibit entitled "Dawson As They Saw It." Open daily.

Visit Robert Service's Cabin. Highly recommended. On the hillside on 8th Avenue, the author–bank clerk's cabin has been restored by Parks Canada. Stories and poetry recitals (by actor Tom Byrne) are offered daily in summer at 10 A.M. and 3 P.M. Photos are welcomed, but no videotaping. Audio and video cassettes may be purchased at Robert Service's Cabin or at downtown retail outlets. Visitors come from every part of the world to sign the guest book on the rickety desk where Service wrote his famous poems, including "The Shooting of Dan McGrew" and "The Cremation of Sam McGee." Open 9 A.M. to noon and 1–5 P.M. daily. Admission: adults $6, children $3.

Visit the Historic Post Office, where you may buy stamps; all first-class mail sent from here receives the old hand-cancellation stamp. Open daily.

Fire Fighters Museum, located at the fire hall at 5th Avenue and King Street, is open Monday through Saturday, 12:30 to 5:30 P.M.

Visit the Jack London Interpretive Centre: Along 8th Avenue and past Service's home is Jack London's cabin, built from half of the logs saved from the original cabin in the Bush where the writer stayed on his way to the Klondike. Also at the site are a cache for perishables and a museum with photos and memorabilia. Interpretation daily at 1 P.M. No admission charged. Dick North, author of *Cabin Fever–the Story of Jack London in Alaska and Yukon*, is curator and consultant at the cabin. 1997 marks the 100th anniversary of Jack London's arrival in the area. The Jack London Festival, held Sept. 17–21, 1997, will commemorate this event.

Special Events. Dawson City hosts a number of unique and unusual celebrations during the year. The Commissioner's Ball is held June 7, 1997. This gala event, commemorating Yukon becoming a territory in 1898, features turn-of-the-century fashion. The Yukon Gold Panning Championship is held July 1 each year in Dawson City. Then on July 19, 1997, it's the Canadian Airlines International Dome Race, which attracts over 200 runners each year from all over the world. The 4.6-mile/7.4-km course rises a total elevation of 1,850 feet/564m.

The 18th Annual Dawson City Music Festival, July 18–20, 1997, features entertainers and artists from Canada and the United States, free workshops, dances and dinners. Tickets and information from the Music Festival Assoc., Box 456, Dawson City, YT Y0B 1G0. Phone (403) 993-5584.

If you are near Dawson Aug. 15–18, 1997, be sure to join the Discovery Festival fun when Yukon Order of Pioneers stages its annual parade. This event is a Yukon holiday commemorating the Klondike gold discovery of Aug. 17, 1896.

The Great Klondike International Outhouse Race, held the Sunday of Labour Day weekend (Aug. 31, 1997), is a race of outhouses (on wheels) over a 1.9 mile/3-km course through the streets of Dawson City; before the race, all contestants must recite original limericks.

Other Dawson City summer events include the International Gold Show, May 16–17, 1997; the Klondike Country Jamboree, Aug. 16–17, 1997; Gertie's International Dart Tournament, Sept. 5–7, 1997; and the Yukon Talent Night, Sept. 26, 1997.

Wintertime festivities include the Yukon Quest Dog Sled Race, Feb. 14–16, 1997; the Centennial Ball, Feb. 15, 1997; Trek Over the Top, Feb. 27 to March 2, 1997; Snowmobile Excursion, March 6–9, 1997; and Thawdi Gras, March 21–23, 1997.

See the Midnight Sun: If you are in Dawson City on June 21, be sure to make it to the top of the Dome by midnight, when the sun barely dips behind the 6,000-foot/1,829-m Ogilvie Mountains to the north—the picture of a lifetime. There's quite a local celebration on the Dome on June 21, so for those who don't like crowds, a visit before or after summer solstice will also afford fine views and photos. Turnoff for Dome Mountain is at **Milepost J 325.8**; it's about a 5-mile/8-km drive.

Pan for Gold: The chief attraction for most visitors is panning for gold. There are several mining operations set up to permit you to actually pan for your own "colours" under friendly guidance. Take Bonanza Creek Road from **Milepost J 324.5** up famous Bonanza Creek, past Dredge No. 4, Discovery Claim and miles of gravel tailings worked over 2 and 3 times in the continuing

search for gold. The Klondike Visitors Assoc. sponsors a public panning area at No. 6 above Discovery, 13 miles/21 km from Dawson City on Bonanza Creek Road. Check with the Visitor Reception Centre for more information.

Klondike Nugget & Ivory Shop features a unique display of gold nuggets from the Klondike creeks. The purity of natural gold can range from 61 percent to 96 percent ... You can see the differences for yourself in our display located on Front and Queen streets. Don't miss the 9-foot mammoth tusk also on exhibit! (403) 993-5432. [ADVERTISEMENT]

Bear Creek Camp, (see **Milepost J 319.6** on the Klondike Highway), was operated by Yukon Consolidated Gold Corp. until 1966. Tours are conducted by Parks Canada interpreters; check with the Visitor Reception Centre for current tour schedule. The compound features the Gold Room, where the gold was melted and poured into bricks, complete blacksmith and machinery shops, and other well-preserved structures. Open 9:30 A.M. to 5 P.M. from mid-June to late August. Admission: adults $3, children 12 and under free.

Hike the historic Ridge Road. Originally built in 1899 to move mining supplies along Bonanza Creek, the Ridge Road was abandoned by 1902. The road was restored in 1996 into a 20-mile/32-km historic hiking trail. Travel time is 1½ to 2 days by foot (or 4–6 hours by mountain bike) and includes interpretive signs and building remnants along the route. There are 2 tent campgrounds on the trail, at Mile 6.8/11 km and Mile 13.1/21 km, with firepits and running water.

Klondike Loop Log

(continued)

YUKON HIGHWAY 9

The Top of the World Highway (Yukon Highway 9) connects Dawson City with the Taylor Highway (Alaska Route 5). A free ferry carries passengers and vehicles from Dawson

City across the Yukon River to the beginning of the Top of the World Highway. NOTE: The ferry wait in heavy traffic may be 3 hours or longer. The Alaska Highway is 174.5 miles/280.8 km from here; Eagle, AK, is 143.4 miles/230.8 km from here. Allow plenty of time for this drive; average speed for this road is 25 to 40 mph/40 to 64 kmph. DRIVE WITH YOUR HEADLIGHTS ON! Yukon Highway 9 and the Taylor Highway (Alaska Route 5) in Alaska are not maintained from mid-October to April and the arrival of snow effectively closes the roads for winter.

CAUTION: Road conditions on some sections of the Alaska portion of this road were rough in 1996. The Top of the World Highway is also scheduled for gravel surfacing in 1997 between Kilometreposts 0 and 30 on the Canadian side (Mile 0 to 19). Check with the Dawson City Visitor Reception Centre for current road and weather conditions; phone (403) 993-5566.

IMPORTANT: U.S. and Canada customs are open from about May 15 to Sept. 15. In summer 1996, customs was open 7 days a week, 9 A.M. to 9 P.M. (Pacific time) on the Canadian side; 8 A.M. to 9 P.M. (Alaska time.) on the U.S. side. Check with the RCMP or Visitor Reception Centre in Dawson City to make certain the border crossing at **Milepost D 66.1** *will be open. Serious fines are levied for crossing the border without clearing customs! There are no restrooms, services or currency exchanges available at the border.*

This section of the log shows distance from Dawson City (D) followed by distance from junction with the Taylor Highway (T) at Jack Wade Junction. Physical kilometreposts show distance from Dawson City.

D 0 T 78.8 (126.8 km) **DAWSON CITY.** Free ferry crosses the Yukon River daily in summer.

D 0.2 (0.3 km) **T 78.6** (126.5 km) **Yukon River** government campground on river-

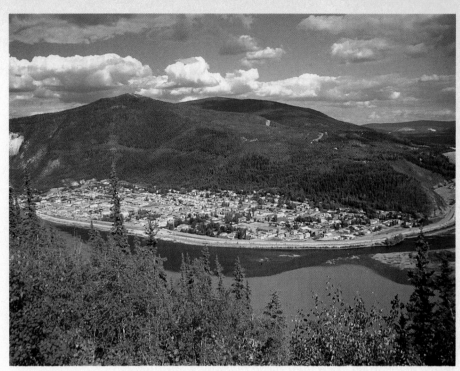

View of Dawson City from the Top of the World Highway. (Earl L. Brown, staff)

A "top of the world" view from Yukon Highway 9. (© Harry M. Walker)

bank opposite Dawson City; 74 RV sites, 24 tent-only sites, 2 kitchen shelters, playground and drinking water. Camping fee $8. Within walking distance of stern-wheeler graveyard. Put in and takeout spot for Yukon River travelers. ▲

D 2.7 (4.4 km) **T 76.1** (122.5 km) Access to 9-hole golf course via 3.2-mile/5.1-km gravel road; rentals.

D 2.9 (4.6 km) **T 75.9** (122.1 km) Turnout for viewpoint overlooking Dawson City and the Yukon and Klondike rivers.

D 3.2 (5 km) **T 75.6** (121.7 km) Turnout with good view of Yukon River and river valley farms.

D 8.7 (14 km) **T 70.1** (112.8 km) Interpretive displays about the Fortymile caribou herd.

D 9 (12.4 km) **T 69.8** (112.3 km) Rest area with pit toilets, picnic tables, litter barrels and information sign about Top of the World Highway (also has ferry information for travelers to Dawson City).

D 11 (15.6 km) **T 67.8** (109.1 km) "Top of the world" view as highway climbs above tree line.

D 16.4 (26.2 km) **T 62.4** (100.4 km) Snow fence along highway next 8 miles/13 km westbound.

D 18.4 (29.4 km) **T 60.4** (97.2 km) Large turnout on left.

D 29.2 (47 km) **T 49.6** (79.8 km) Evidence of 1989 burn.

D 32.1 (51.2 km) **T 46.7** (75.2 km) First outcropping (westbound) of Castle Rock. Turnout to south with panoramic view of countryside.

D 33.1 (52.8 km) **T 45.7** (73.5 km) Distance marker shows customs 52 km, Dawson City 53 km.

D 35.2 (56 km) **T 43.6** (70.2 km) Main outcropping of Castle Rock; lesser formations are also found along this stretch. Centuries of erosion have created these formations. Turnout on left westbound.

D 37.4 (59 km) **T 41.4** (66.6 km) Unmaintained road leads 25 miles/40 km to the former settlement of Clinton Creek, which served the Cassiar Asbestos Mine from 1967–79. There are no facilities or services available there. Distance marker shows U.S. border 43 km.

The confluence of the Yukon and Fortymile rivers is 3 miles/4.8 km below the former townsite of Clinton Creek. Clinton Creek bridge is an access point on the Fortymile River National Wild and Scenic River system, managed by the Bureau of Land Management. The Fortymile River offers intermediate and advanced canoeists over 100 miles/160 km of challenging water.

Yukon River, near Clinton Creek, grayling to 3 lbs. in April; chum salmon to 12 lbs. in August; king salmon to 40 lbs., July and August. **Fortymile River**, near Clinton Creek, grayling to 3 lbs. during spring breakup and fall freezeup; inconnu (sheefish) to 10 lbs. in July and August. ◄

D 54 (85.6 km) **T 24.8** (39.9 km) Old sod-roofed cabin on right westbound, originally a supply and stopping place for the McCormick Transportation Co.

D 54.3 (86.1 km) **T 24.5** (39.4 km) Road forks left westbound to old mine workings at Sixtymile, which have been reactivated by Cogasa Mining Co. Keep to right for Alaska. The road winds above timberline for many miles. The lack of fuel for warmth and shelter made this a perilous trip for the early sourdoughs.

D 64.1 (101.9 km) **T 14.7** (23.7 km) Large gravel turnout. Information sign about Top of the World Highway viewpoint.

D 65.2 (103.7 km) **T 13.6** (21.9 km) Pull-through rest area with toilet and litter barrels; good viewpoint. Just across the highway, short hike to cairn, excellent viewpoint. Highest point on Top of the World Highway (elev. 4,515 feet/1,376 m).

D 66.1 (105.1 km) **T 12.7** (20.4 km) U.S.–Canada border (elev. 4,127 feet/1,258m). Customs only; no public facilities available.

Canada Customs and Immigration Little Gold Creek office is open 9 A.M. to 9 P.M. (Pacific time) from about May 15 to Sept. 15. All traffic entering Canada must stop here. The U.S. border station Poker Creek office, just past the Canadian station, is open 8 A.M. to 9 P.M. (Alaska time) from about May 15 to Sept. 15. All traffic entering the United States must stop here. Both stations are closed in winter. A short hike up the hill behind U.S. border station provides good viewpoint. *NOTE: Customs hours of operation subject to change.*

TIME ZONE CHANGE: Alaska observes Alaska time; Yukon Territory observes Pacific time. See Time Zones in GENERAL INFORMATION section for details.

D 67.1 (108 km) **T 11.7** (18.8 km) Double-ended turnout to north with viewing platform to see mountains; toilet, litter barrel, aluminum can recycling bin.

D 69.2 (111.4 km) **T 9.6** (15.4 km) **BOUNDARY.** Boundary Lodge was one of the first roadhouses in Alaska; food, gas, lodging, diesel, tire repair, emergency phone.

Boundary Inc. See display ad this section.

Watch your gas supply. Between here and Tetlin Junction on the Alaska Highway, gas is available again only at Chicken, **Milepost TJ 66.5.** From here to Eagle, gas may be available at O'Brien Creek Lodge, **Milepost TJ 125.4.** Gas is available in Eagle.

Private Aircraft: Boundary airstrip; elev. 2,940 feet/896m; length 2,100 feet/640m; earth and gravel; fuel 80; unattended.

D 78 (125.6 km) **T 0.8** (1.3 km) Viewpoint.

D 78.8 (126.9 km) **T 0 Jack Wade Junction, Milepost TJ 95.7** on the Taylor Highway. The Taylor Highway (Alaska Route 5), also known as the Eagle Road or Eagle Cutoff, leads north 64.6 miles/104 km to Eagle, AK, or south 95.7 miles/154 km to Tetlin Junction, just east of Tok, on the Alaska Highway. *CAUTION: The Taylor Highway is a narrow, winding, mountain road. Drive carefully!*

NOTE: Eagle-bound and Alaska Highway-bound travelers turn to **Milepost TJ 95.7** *on page 284 in the TAYLOR HIGHWAY section to continue log. Eagle-bound travelers continue with log forward from* **Milepost TJ 95.7.** *Alaska Highway-bound travelers read log backward from* **Milepost TJ 95.7.**

TAYLOR HIGHWAY ⑤

Connects: Alaska Hwy. (Tetlin Jct.) to Eagle, AK   **Length:** 160 miles
Road Surface: Gravel   **Season:** Closed in winter
Steepest Grade: 9 percent
Major Attraction: Fort Egbert

(See map, page 262)

	Chicken	Dawson City	Eagle	Tok
Chicken		109	94	78
Dawson City	109		144	187
Eagle	94	144		172
Tok	78	187	172	

Jack Wade No. 1 gold dredge at Milepost TJ 86 on the Taylor Highway.
(Earl L. Brown, staff)

The 160.3-mile/258-km Taylor Highway (Alaska Route 5) begins at Tetlin Junction on the Alaska Highway and ends at the small town of Eagle on the Yukon River. This is a beautiful "top of the world" drive, and Eagle is well worth a visit. Construction of the Taylor Highway began in 1946, and was completed to Eagle in late 1953, providing access to the historic Fortymile Mining District.

The Taylor Highway is a narrow, winding, dusty mountain road with many steep hills and some hairpin curves. Allow plenty of time to drive its length. The road surface is gravel, with sporadic soft spots during breakup or after heavy rains. Road surface ranges from very poor to good depending on maintenance. The first 23 miles/36.8 km were reconstructed in 1996, providing improved road conditions from Tetlin Junction to Chicken. Shoulders are narrow and may be unstable. Large RVs and trailers especially should use caution in driving this road. Watch for large tanker trucks, some with double trailers, hauling fuel between Tetlin Junction and Boundary. (Your best defense is to pull over and stop, if possible.) The Taylor Highway is not maintained from mid-October to April, and the arrival of

snow effectively closes the road for winter.

The Taylor is the shortest route to Dawson City, YT, from Alaska. Drive 95.7 miles/154 km north on the Taylor Highway to Jack Wade Junction, and turn east on the Top of the World Highway (Yukon Highway 9) for Dawson City. (See end of KLONDIKE LOOP section for log of Yukon Highway 9.)

Dawson City-bound travelers keep in mind that gas is available only at Chicken and at Boundary Lodge. Also, the U.S. and Canadian customs offices at the border are open from about mid-May to mid-September. Probable customs hours for summer 1997 are 9 A.M. to 9 P.M. Alaska time on the Canadian side. Extended customs hours were in effect in 1996 on an experimental basis. Check for current hours at the Tok visitors center. There are no restrooms, services or currency exchanges available at the border.

IMPORTANT: You cannot cross the border unless the customs office for the country you are entering is open. Severe fines are levied for crossing without clearing customs. Officials at Canadian customs are concerned about child abductions. If you are traveling with children, remember to bring identification for them. (See the GENERAL INFORMATION section for

specific customs restrictions.)

NOTE: All gold-bearing ground in area is claimed. Do not pan in streams.

The highway also provides river runners with access to the Fortymile River National Wild and Scenic River system. A brochure on access points and float times is available from the Bureau of Land Management, 1150 University Ave., Fairbanks, AK 99709-3844; phone (907) 474-2350.

The Forymile Mining District is home range for the Fortymile caribou herd. Once a massive herd of 500,000 animals, the herd is now stable at about 23,000 caribou. The herd moves east across the highway in late fall for the winter, and returns again in spring for calving. During the summer, small bands of caribou can sometimes be seen in the high country above timberline. The Fortymile Caibou Planning Team, a group of Alaskan and Yukon residents, was created to develop a strategy for restoring the caribou herd and other area wildlife. State, federal and territorial agencies sponsored the effort and provide logistical support. In support of this effort, an art contest was held in Tok for local area artists. The winning entries appear on interpretive displays located at the turnout at **Milepost TJ 22.1**. Information on the plan is available in Tok at the Alaska Dept. of Fish and Game office and in Dawson at the Fish and Wildlife Branch of Yukon Renewable Resources.

Emergency medical services: Between Tetlin Junction and O'Brien Creek bridge at **Milepost TJ 113.2**, phone the Tok Area EMS at 911 or (907) 883-5111. Between O'Brien Creek bridge and Eagle, phone the Eagle EMS at (907) 547-2300 or (907) 547-2211. Use CB channel 21.

Taylor Highway Log

Distance from Tetlin Junction (TJ) is followed by distance from Eagle (E).

TJ 0 E 160.3 (258 km) Tetlin Junction. Junction with the Alaska Highway at **Milepost DC 1301.7**. 40 Mile Roadhouse; current status of services unknown.

Begin 9 miles/14.5 km of winding road up out of the Tanana River valley. Highway traverses stabilized sand dunes first 5 miles/8 km.

TJ 4.5 (7.2 km) E 155.8 (250.7 km) Gravel turnout to east. A 0.7-mile/1.1-km trail leads to **Four Mile Lake**; rainbow trout

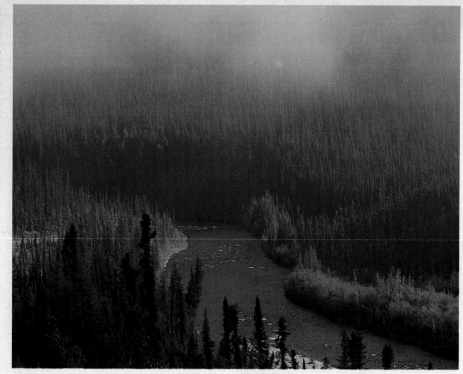

Morning mist on the Fortymile River. (© Michael DeYoung)

and sheefish.

TJ 5.4 (8.7 km) **E 154.9** (249.3 km) Evidence of 1990 forest fire known as the Porcupine burn.

TJ 5.9 (9.5 km) **E 154.4** (248.5 km) Entering Tok Management Area, Tanana Valley State Forest, northbound.

TJ 6 (9.7 km) **E 154.3** (248.3 km) Double-ended turnout to east, easy for trailers.

Wildflowers along the highway include arnica, chiming bells, wild roses and Labrador tea. As the name suggests, Labrador tea leaves (and flowers) may be steeped in boiling water to make tea. However, according to Janice Scofield, author of *Discovering Wild Plants*, Labrador tea contains a narcotic toxin that can cause ill effects if used too frequently or in high concentrations.

NOTE: Winding road northbound. Watch for ruts and soft spots and for loose gravel on curves.

TJ 9.4 (15.1 km) **E 150.9** (242.8 km) Entering Game Management Unit 20E northbound; entering GMU 12 southbound. Road begins gradual climb of Mount Fairplay for northbound travelers.

TJ 10 (16 km) **E 150.3** (240.5 km) Double-ended turnout to east.

TJ 12.1 (19.5 km) **E 148.2** (238.5 km) Entering Tok Management Area, Tanana State Forest, southbound.

TJ 14.6 (23.5 km) **E 145.7** (234.5 km) Small turnout to west. Blueberries in season.

TJ 16 (25.7 km) **E 144.3** (232.2 km) Parking at one of Mount Fairplay's several summits.

TJ 18.9 (30.2 km) **E 141.4** (226.2 km) Double-ended turnout to west.

TJ 21.2 (34.1 km) **E 139.1** (223.9 km) Long descent northbound.

TJ 22.1 (35.4 km) **E 138.2** (221.1 km) Fortymile Caribou Herd interpretive displays by local artists.

TJ 22.4 (35.8 km) **E 137.9** (220.6 km) Double-ended turnout to east.

TJ 23 (37 km) **E 137.3** (221 km) Scenic views, Alaska Range to west.

TJ 27 (43.5 km) **E 133.3** (214.5 km) Small turnout to west.

TJ 28.3 (45.5 km) **E 132** (212.4 km) Turnout with view to west.

TJ 32.8 (52.8 km) **E 127.5** (205.2 km) Turnout to west.

TJ 34.4 (55.4 km) **E 125.9** (202.6 km) Double-ended turnout with view to west. Nine-percent downgrade northbound.

TJ 35.1 (56.5 km) **E 125.2** (201.5 km) Entering Fortymile Mining District northbound. The second-oldest mining district in Alaska, gold was first discovered here in 1886. Claims were filed in both Canada and Alaska due to boundary uncertainties.

Double-ended turnout to east near summit of Mount Fairplay (elev. 5,541 feet/1,689m). Interpretive sign, viewing platform, litter barrels, aluminum recycling, toilet, wheelchair accessible. ♿

Highway descends a 9-percent grade northbound. Southbound, the road descends for the next 25 miles/40 km from Mount Fairplay's summit, winding through heavily forested terrain. Panoramic views of the Fortymile River forks' valleys. Views of the Alaska Range to the southwest.

TJ 39.1 (62.9 km) **E 121.2** (195 km) Large turnout to west, no easy turnaround.

TJ 41 (65.6 km) **E 119.3** (190.9 km) Watch for soft shoulders.

TJ 43 (69.2 km) **E 117.3** (188.8 km) Logging Cabin Creek bridge (abrupt edge on bridge); small turnout to west at south end of bridge. Side road to creek. This is the south end of the Fortymile River National Wild and Scenic River system managed by BLM.

TJ 49 (78.9 km) **E 111.3** (179.1 km) Loop roads through BLM West Fork Recreation Site; 25 sites (7 pull-through sites), tables, firepits, no water, covered tables, toilets, dumpsters. Access point of Fortymile River canoe trail. Improved campground. ▲

TJ 49.3 (79.3 km) **E 111** (178.6 km) Bridge over West Fork of the Dennison Fork of the Fortymile River. Access point for Fortymile River National Wild and Scenic River system.

TJ 50.5 (81.3 km) **E 109.8** (176.7 km) Taylor Creek bridge. Watch for potholes and rough road at bridge approaches (abrupt edge on bridge). All-terrain vehicle trail to Taylor and Kechumstuk mountains; heavily used in hunting season.

TJ 57 (91.7 km) **E 103.3** (166.2 km) Scenic viewpoint turnout to east, no easy turnaround.

TJ 58.9 (94.8 km) **E 101.4** (163.2 km) Scenic viewpoint turnout to east.

TJ 62.5 (100.6 km) **E 97.8** (157.4 km) Turnout to west. Drive-in, no easy turnaround.

TJ 63.2 (101.7 km) **E 97.1** (156.3 km) View of Chicken.

TJ 63.3 (101.9 km) **E 97** (156.1 km) Turnout to west. Drive-in, no easy turnaround.

TJ 63.7 (102.5 km) **E 96.6** (155.5 km) Steep descent northbound to Mosquito Fork.

TJ 64.1 (103.2 km) **E 96.2** (154.8 km) Well-traveled road leads to private buildings, not into Chicken.

TJ 64.3 (103.5 km) **E 96** (154.5 km) Bridge over Mosquito Fork of the Fortymile River; day-use area with table, toilet and litter barrel at north end of bridge. The Mosquito Fork is a favorite access point for the Fortymile National Wild and Scenic River system, according to the BLM.

TJ 66 (106.2 km) **E 94.3** (151.8 km) Entering **CHICKEN** (pop. 37), northbound. *(NOTE: Driving distance between **Mileposts TJ 66** and **67** is 0.7 mile.)* This is the newer commercial settlement of Chicken. The original mining camp (abandoned, private property) is north of Chicken Creek (see **Milepost TJ 67**). Chicken is a common name in the North for ptarmigan. One story has it that the early miners wanted to name their camp ptarmigan, but were unable to spell it and settled for Chicken. Access point for the Fortymile River canoe trail is below Chicken airstrip.

Fuel is available in Chicken. Gas is also available at O'Brien Creek Lodge, en route to Eagle, **Milepost TJ 125.4**; in Boundary, en route to Canada (Top of the World Highway, **Milepost D 69.2**); or in Tok.

TJ 66.3 (106.7 km) **E 94** (151.3 km) Chicken post office (ZIP code 99732) located on hill beside the road. The late Ann Purdy lived in this area. The book *Tisha* is based on her experiences as a young schoolteacher in the Alaska Bush.

TJ 66.4 (106.9 km) **E 93.9** (151.1 km) Airport Road. Access to Chicken airstrip and "downtown" Chicken. Combination grocery store, restaurant, bar and gas station located here.

Private Aircraft: Chicken airstrip, adjacent southwest; elev. 1,640 feet/500m; length 2,500 feet/762m; gravel; maintained year-round.

The Chicken Creek Salmon Bake uses only wild Alaska–Yukon king salmon. Besides salmon, we also feature halibut, barbeque chicken, buffalo and reindeer burgers, our famous potato salad and salmon chowder. All are offered daily from 4 P.M. to 8 P.M. Another good reason to visit Beautiful Downtown Chicken, Alaska! [ADVERTISEMENT]

Chicken Mercantile Emporium, Chicken Creek Cafe, Saloon and Gas. Unfortunately, as too often happens, the main road bypasses the most interesting part

Beautiful Downtown Chicken Alaska

CHICKEN CREEK
CAFE

GREAT HOMEMADE FOOD!

Hamburgers - Pies
Pastries and Cinnamon Buns

Chicken Mercantile Emporium

World Famous Chicken T-Shirts
Chicken Souvenirs, Local Gold

Tisha Books

CHICKEN CREEK
SALMON BAKE

Wild Yukon King Salmon
Halibut

HISTORIC OLD CHICKEN

TOURS MEET AT CHICKEN CAFE DAILY

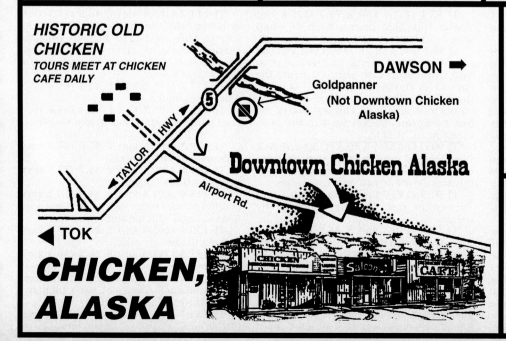

DAWSON ➡

Goldpanner
(Not Downtown Chicken Alaska)

Downtown Chicken Alaska

Airport Rd.

TAYLOR HWY

◄ TOK

CHICKEN, ALASKA

CHICKEN GAS

Always the Lowest Priced Gas, and Friendliest Service in CHICKEN

Propane   Diesel

REMEMBER!

To find **_REAL_** Downtown Chicken Alaska you have to Turn Off the Taylor Hwy.

View of Boundary on the Top of the World Highway, which junctions with the Taylor Highway at Milepost TJ 95.7. (Earl L. Brown, staff)

of Chicken. If it's modern facilities you are looking for, original Chicken is not for you. The Chicken Creek Saloon and Cafe are some of the last remnants of the old frontier Alaska. It is a trading post where local miners (some straight out of Jack London) trade gold for supplies and drink. Tisha's schoolhouse and other historic buildings may be seen on the walking tour of old Chicken, meeting daily at the Chicken Creek Cafe at 1 P.M. It's also possible to purchase an autographed copy of *Tisha* at the Chicken Mercantile Emporium. Hunting and fishing licenses are for sale at the Emporium. A wealth of gifts abound in the Chicken Mercantile Emporium, and the cafe is famous throughout Alaska for its excellent food, homemade pies, pastries and cinnamon buns. For a bird's-eye view of this spectacular country and fantastic photo opportunities, check out the local flightseeing service. Chicken Creek Saloon, Cafe and Mercantile Emporium are a rare treat for those with the courage to stray just a few hundred yards from the beaten path. Major credit cards accepted. Note: The Goldpanner, located on the main road, is not the same as "Beautiful Downtown Chicken, Alaska." [ADVERTISEMENT]

TJ 66.6 (107.2 km) **E 93.7** (150.8 km) Chicken Creek bridge.

TJ 67 (107.8 km) **E 93.3** (150.1 km) View of abandoned old townsite of Chicken. The road in is blocked off, and the dozen or so old buildings are owned by a mining company. Private property, do not trespass. Guided walking tours available; inquire at Chicken Creek Cafe. Look upstream (northwest) on Chicken Creek to see the old gold dredge, which was shut down in the 1960s.

TJ 68.2 (109.8 km) **E 92.1** (148.2 km) BLM Chicken field station; information and emergency communications. Trailhead for Mosquito Fork Dredge trail (3 miles/4.8 km round-trip). *NOTE: Watch for potholes and soft spots.*

TJ 68.9 (110.9 km) **E 91.4** (147.1 km) Lost Chicken Creek. Site of Lost Chicken Hill Mine, established in 1895. Mining was under way in this area several years before the Klondike Gold Rush of 1897–98. The first major placer gold strike was in 1886 at Franklin Gulch, a tributary of the Fortymile. Hydraulic mining operations in the creek.

TJ 70 (112.7 km) **E 90.3** (145.3 km) Turnouts at gravel pits on both sides of road.

TJ 71.7 (115.4 km) **E 88.6** (142.6 km) Steep descent northbound as road switchbacks down to South Fork. Watch for June wildflowers: pink wild roses, blue lupine, chiming bells and white Labrador tea.

TJ 74.4 (119.7 km) **E 85.9** (138.2 km) South Fork River access road.

TJ 74.5 (119.9 km) **E 85.8** (138.1 km) South Fork DOT/PF state highway maintenance station.

TJ 75.3 (121.2 km) **E 85** (136.8 km) South Fork bridge. Day-use area with toilet and litter barrels at south end of bridge, west side of road. Access point for the Fortymile River National Wild and Scenic River system. The muddy, bumpy road leading into the brush is used by miners.

TJ 76.8 (123.6 km) **E 83.5** (134.4 km) Turnout to west. View of oxbow lakes in South Fork valley.

TJ 78.5 (126.3 km) **E 81.8** (131.6 km) Views of Fortymile River valley northbound to **Milepost TJ 82.**

TJ 78.8 (126.8 km) **E 81.5** (131.2 km) Steep descent northbound.

TJ 81.9 (131.8 km) **E 78.4** (126.2 km) Walker Fork bridge.

TJ 82.1 (132.1 km) **E 78.2** (125.8 km) Walker Fork BLM campground; 16 camp sites, 2 picnic sites with covered tables. ▲

TJ 86.1 (138.6 km) **E 74.2** (119.4 km) Old Jack Wade No. 1 dredge in creek next to road. Turnout to east. This is actually the Butte Creek Dredge, installed in 1934 below the mouth of Butte Creek and eventually moved to Wade Creek. This was one of the first bucketline dredges used in the area, according to the BLM.

TJ 90 (144.8 km) **E 70.3** (113.1 km) Jack Wade, an old mining camp that operated until 1940. Active mining is under way in this area. *Do not trespass on mining claims.*

TJ 91.9 (147.9 km) **E 68.4** (110.1 km) Turnout to east. Primitive campsite by stream.

TJ 93.5 (150.5 km) **E 66.8** (107.5 km) *Slow down for hairpin curve.* Road climbs northbound. Road width varies from here to Eagle. *NOTE: Large vehicles use turnouts when meeting oncoming vehicles.*

TJ 95.7 (154 km) **E 64.6** (104 km) **Jack Wade Junction.** Continue north on the Taylor Highway for Eagle. Turn east for Boundary Lodge and the Alaska–Canada border. Dawson City is 78.8 miles/126.8 km

east via the Top of the World Highway. The Top of the World Highway (Yukon Highway 9) is a winding gravel road with some steep grades. Slippery in wet weather, closed by snow. Drive carefully.

Dawson City-bound travelers turn to the end of the KLONDIKE LOOP section (page 280) and read the Top of the World Highway log back to front. Eagle-bound travelers continue with this log.

TJ 96 (154.5 km) **E 64.3** (103.5 km) Turnout. Lupine and chiming bells bloom in June. View to the north-northeast of Canada's Ogilvie Mountains in the distance.

TJ 99.5 (160.1 km) **E 60.8** (97.8 km) Road winds around the summit of Steele Creek Dome (elev. 4,015 feet/1,224m) visible directly above the road to the east. *CAUTION: Road is slippery when wet.*

TJ 99.6 (160.3 km) **E 60.7** (97.7 km) *CAUTION: Slow down for hairpin curve.*

TJ 105.5 (169.8 km) **E 54.8** (88.2 km) Scenic viewpoint to east. The road descends next 7 miles/11.3 km northbound to the valley of the Fortymile River, so named because its mouth was 40 miles below Fort Reliance, an old trading post near the confluence of the Yukon and Klondike rivers. Along the road are abandoned cabins, tailings and dredges.

TJ 109.2 (175.7 km) **E 51.1** (82.2 km) *CAUTION: Slow down for hairpin curve!*

TJ 109.7 (176.5 km) **E 50.6** (81.4 km) *CAUTION: Steep, narrow, winding road northbound. Slow down!* Frequent small turnouts and breathtaking views to north and west. Watch for arctic poppies and lupine along the highway in June.

TJ 112.6 (181.2 km) **E 47.7** (76.8 km) Fortymile River bridge; parking area at south end of bridge, toilet, canoe launch, trash cans. No camping. Active mining in area. Nearly vertical beds of white marble can be seen on the northeast side of the river. Access to the Fortymile River National Wild and Scenic River system.

TJ 112.8 (181.5 km) **E 47.5** (76.4 km) Private home and mining camp.

TJ 113.1 (182 km) **E 47.2** (76 km) O'Brien Creek DOT/PF highway maintenance camp located here.

TJ 113.2 (182.2 km) **E 47.1** (75.8 km) O'Brien Creek bridge. Access to creek.

TJ 114.2 (183.8 km) **E 46.8** (75.3 km) Winding road northbound with rock slide areas to **Milepost TJ 116**; highway parallels O'Brien Creek to Liberty Fork; several turnouts. *CAUTION: Watch for small aircraft using road as runway.*

TJ 117.2 (188.6 km) **E 43.1** (69.4 km) Alder Creek bridge.

TJ 118.2 (190.2 km) **E 42.1** (67.8 km) Road narrows northbound: Watch for falling rock next 1.5 miles/2.4 km northbound.

TJ 119.7 (192.6 km) **E 40.6** (65.3 km) Slide area, watch for rocks.

TJ 124.6 (200.5 km) **E 35.7** (57.5 km) Columbia Creek bridge.

TJ 125.4 (201.8 km) **E 34.9** (56.2 km) O'Brien Creek Lodge; gas. Nearest gas stations in Eagle, Chicken and Boundary.

TJ 130.5 (208.8 km) **E 29.8** (47.7 km) Turnout to east.

TJ 131.5 (211.6 km) **E 28.8** (46.3 km) King Solomon Creek bridge. Highway follows King Solomon Creek next 0.5 mile/0.8 km northbound. (The creek has a tributary named Queen of Sheba.)

TJ 135.7 (218.4 km) **E 24.6** (39.6 km) *CAUTION: Slow down for hairpin curve.*

TJ 135.8 (218.5 km) **E 24.5** (39.4 km)

Sunset on the Yukon River at Eagle. (Jerrianne Lowther, staff)

Eagle

Population: 146. **Emergency Services:** Eagle EMS (907) 547-2300 or (907) 547-2211; use CB channel 21; Eagle health clinic. **Visitor Information:** Contact the Eagle Historical Society and Museums (Box 23, Eagle, 99738; phone 907/547-2325; fax 907/547-2232) for information on area tours, museums and events.

The National Park Service office, headquarters for Yukon–Charley Rivers National Preserve, is located on the banks of the Yukon River at the base of Fort Egbert. Reference library available to the public. Office hours are 8 A.M. to 5 P.M. weekdays. The National Park Service Visitor Center offers

North Fork Solomon Creek bridge.

TJ 141 (226.9 km) **E 19.3** (31.1 km) Glacier Mountain management area; walk-in hunting only. Top of the world views to west.

TJ 143.2 (230.5 km) **E 17.1** (27.5 km) Turnout on summit. Top of the world views. Road begins winding descent northbound to Yukon River.

TJ 148 (236.8 km) **E 12.3** (19.7 km) Two small turnouts.

TJ 149.1 (239.9 km) **E 11.2** (18 km) Bridge over Discovery Fork. Turnout to east by creek.

TJ 150.7 (242.5 km) **E 9.6** (15.4 km) Old cabin by creek to west is a local landmark. Private property.

TJ 151.8 (244.3 km) **E 8.5** (13.7 km) American Creek bridge No. 1. Outcroppings of asbestos, greenish or gray with white, and serpentine along creekbank. Doyon Ltd. claims ownership of surface and mineral estates on these lands; do not trespass.

TJ 152.5 (245.4 km) **E 7.8** (12.6 km) Bridge No. 2 over American Creek.

TJ 153.2 (246.5 km) **E 7.1** (11.4 km) Small turnout. Springwater piped to road.

TJ 153.6 (247.2 km) **E 6.7** (10.8 km) Small turnout. Springwater piped to road.

TJ 159.3 (256.4 km) **E 1** (1.6 km) Gas station.

TJ 159.7 (257 km) **E 0.6** (1 km) Historical sign about the settlement of Eagle.

TJ 160.3 (258 km) **E 0** Fourth Avenue, Eagle (description follows). Eagle school to east. Side road to west leads 1 mile/1.6 km to Fort Egbert mule barn, officers' quarters and parade ground. The U.S. Army established Fort Egbert in 1899, then abandoned it in 1911. From here a road leads 0.8 mile/1.3 km to Eagle Campground; 13 sites. ▲

maps and books for sale. Also a video on the preserve is shown on request. Informal talks and interpretive programs available. Visitor center hours are 8 A.M. to 5 P.M. daily in summer (Memorial Day weekend through Labor Day weekend). Check at the visitor center for information on the Yukon River, Yukon–Charley Rivers National Preserve and other parklands in Alaska. (Write them at Box 167, Eagle 99738, or phone 907/547-2233.)

Elevation: 820 feet/250m. **Climate:** Mean monthly temperature in July 59°F/15°C; in January -13°F/-25°C. Record low -71°F/-57°C in January 1952; record high 95°F/35°C in July 1925. July also has the greatest mean number of days (21) with temperatures above 70°F/21°C. Mean precipitation in July, 1.94 inches; in December, 10.1 inches. Record snow depth 42 inches in April 1948.

Transportation: By road via the Taylor Highway (closed by snow October to April); air taxi, scheduled air service; dog team and snow machine in winter. Eagle is also accessible via the Yukon River. U.S. customs available at post office for persons entering Alaska via the Yukon River or by air.

Private Aircraft: Eagle airstrip, 2 miles/3.2 km east; elev. 880 feet/268m; length 3,500 feet/1,067m; gravel; unattended.

This small community was once the supply and transportation center for miners working the upper Yukon and its tributaries. Francois Mercier established his Belle Isle trading post here in 1874. With the establishment of Fort Egbert in 1889, Eagle became the military center for the upper Yukon. By 1898, Eagle's population was 1,700. Gold strikes in Fairbanks and Nome lured away many, and by 1910, the population had dwindled to 178.

In the center of town stands a windmill and wellhouse (hand-dug in 1903); the well still provides water for over half the town's population. There are gas stations, restaurants, gift shops, museum store, post office, showers, laundromat, hardware store and mechanic shop with tire repair. Groceries and sundries are available. Fax service is available at both stores. Overnight accommodations at the motel, rental cabins and bed and breakfasts. RV parking with hookups is available or stay at Eagle BLM campground just outside town (turn left on 4th Avenue

and left again along airstrip at Fort Egbert). Eagle Village, an Athabascan settlement, is 3 miles/4.8 km from Eagle. ▲

Eagle, perched on the south bank of the Yukon River below Eagle Bluff (elev. 1000 feet/305m), remains relatively untouched. Locals still practice traditional subsistence activities—fishing with nets, gathering berries, gardening and handcrafting necessities—and many of the town's original cabins, over 100 years old, are used today.

In celebration of the Klondike Gold Rush Centennial, Eagle is hosting its own centennial festivities. June 21–24, 1997, travel by river from Dawson City, YT, to Eagle in a flotillas; with contests, games and activities along the way. Visit Eagle's tent city June 24–29, 1997, to see what life was like in 1897. To find out more about these events and others, contact the Eagle Historical Society and Museums; phone (907) 547-2325, fax (907) 547-2232.

Eagle also boasts the largest museum system in the state. Walking tours, offered by the Eagle Historical Society and Museums, include the Wickersham Courthouse, Waterfront Customs House and the Mule Barn, Water Wagon Shed and NCO quarters at Fort Egbert. Tours are guided by long-time Eagle residents and begin at 9 A.M. daily (from the courtroom upstairs in the courthouse), Memorial Day through Labor Day; cost is $5, members of Eagle Historical Society and Museums and children under 12 free (annual society membership: $10 individual, $15 family). Special tours may be arranged. Books, maps and gifts available at the museum store in the courthouse. For more information, contact the Eagle Historical Society and Museums (Box 23, Eagle 99738; phone 907/547-2325; fax 907/547-2232). Fort Egbert, renovated and restored by the Bureau of Land Management, has an interpretive exhibit and a photo display showing the stages of reconstruction. Videos of the Eagle area are shown every Monday at 7 P.M. in the public library. Lectures, slide presentations and other features are conducted every Thursday at 7 P.M (June 15 through Labor Day).

Historically an important riverboat landing, Eagle is still a popular jumping-off point for Yukon River travelers. Most popular is a summer float trip from Eagle downriver through the **YUKON–CHARLEY RIVERS NATIONAL PRESERVE** to Circle. Length of the Eagle–Circle trip is 154 river miles/248 km, with most trips averaging 5 to 10 days. Float trips may also be made from Dawson City, YT, to Circle (252 miles/406 km, 7 to 10 days) with a halfway stop at Eagle. Boaters also often float the Fortymile to the Yukon River, then continue to the boat landing at Eagle to take out. Commercial boat trips are also available. Westours (Gray Line Yukon) operates the *Yukon Queen* daily boat service between Eagle and Dawson City, YT. Breakup on the Yukon is in May; freezeup in October. For details on weather, clothing, gear and precautions, contact the National Park Service, Box 167, Eagle 99738; phone (907) 547-2233.

Eagle Canoe Rentals. Canoe rentals on the Yukon River between Dawson City, Yukon Territory; Eagle City, Alaska; and Circle City. Brochures available, or call for details. From April to October: Dawson City River Hostel, Dieter Reinmuth, Box 32, Dawson City, YT Y0B 1G0, (403) 993-6823; or Eagle Canoe Rentals, Mike Sager, Box 4, Eagle, AK 99738; (907) 547-2203. [ADVERTISEMENT]

National Park Service headquarters in Eagle. (Jerrianne Lowther, staff)

GLENN HIGHWAY/TOK CUTOFF ① ④

Connects: Tok to Anchorage, AK   **Length:** 328 miles
Road Surface: Paved   **Season:** Open all year
Highest Summit: Eureka Summit 3,322 feet
Major Attractions: Matanuska Glacier, Palmer State Fair

(See maps, pages 288–289)

	Anchorage	Glennallen	Palmer	Tok	Valdez
Anchorage		189	42	328	304
Glennallen	189		147	139	115
Palmer	42	147		286	262
Tok	328	139	286		254
Valdez	304	115	262	254	

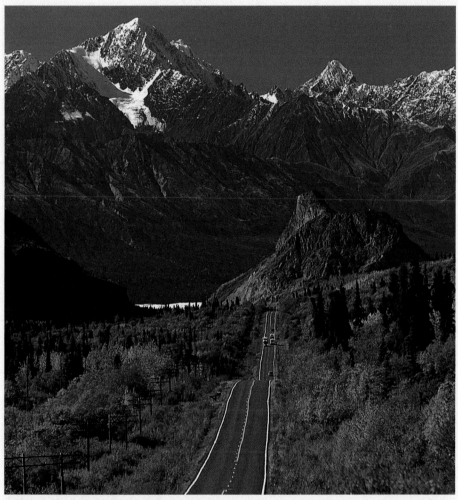

Approaching Lion Head (Glacier Point) and Matanuska Glacier, westbound on the Glenn Highway at Milepost A 114.3. (© Michael DeYoung)

or (907) 883-5111. Between Duffy's and Gakona Junction, phone the Copper River EMS at Glennallen at (907) 822-3203 or 911. From Gakona Junction to Anchorage phone 911. CB channel 9 between **Milepost A 30.8** and Anchorage.

Tok Cutoff Log

ALASKA ROUTE 1
Physical mileposts read from **Milepost 125** at Tok to **Milepost 0** at Gakona Junction, the north junction with the Richardson Highway.
Distance from Gakona Junction (GJ) is followed by distance from Anchorage (A) and distance from Tok (T).

GJ 125 (201.2 km) **A 328** (527.8 km) **T 0** Tok (see description beginning on page 167 in the ALASKA HIGHWAY section).
    GJ 124.2 (199.9 km) **A 327.2** (526.6 km) **T 0.8** (1.3 km) Tok Community Center.
    GJ 124.1 (199.7 km) **A 327.1** (526.4 km) **T 0.9** (1.4 km) Tok Community Clinic, Tok Fire Station.
    GJ 124 (199.6 km) **A 327** (526.2 km) **T 1** (1.6 km) Dept. of Natural Resources.
    GJ 123.9 (199.4 km) **A 326.9** (526.1 km) **T 1.1** (1.8 km) Dept. of Transportation and Public Facilities, Tok Station.
    GJ 123.7 (199.1 km) **A 326.7** (525.8 km) **T 1.3** (2.1 km) Borealis Avenue.
    GJ 123.3 (198.4 km) **A 326.3** (525.1 km) **T 1.7** (2.7 km) **Hayner's Trading Post.** Alaskan handmade jewelry and gifts, beads and supplies, greeting and note cards. Sporting goods and black powder supplies. Custom leather work and repairs. Free coffee and tea. Open year-round. Summer hours 10 A.M. to 8 P.M. Rocky and Sue Hayner, owners. (907) 883-5536. See display ad in Tok in the ALASKA HIGHWAY section.
[ADVERTISEMENT]
    GJ 122.8 (197.6 km) **A 325.8** (524.3 km) **T 2.2** (3.5 km) **Sourdough Campground's Pancake Breakfast** served 7–11 A.M. June, July, August. Genuine "Sourdoughs." Full and partial RV hookups. Dry campsites. Showers included. Guaranteed clean restrooms. High-pressure car wash. Free evening video program. Located 1.7 miles from the junction toward Anchorage on Tok Cutoff (Glenn Highway). See display ad in

The Glenn Highway/Tok Cutoff (Alaska Route 1) is the principal access route from the Alaska Highway west to Anchorage, a distance of 328 miles/527.8 km. This route includes the 125-mile/201-km Tok Cutoff, between Tok and the Richardson Highway junction; a 14-mile/22.5-km link via the Richardson Highway; and the 189-mile/304-km Glenn Highway, between the Richardson Highway and Anchorage.

It is a full day's drive between Tok and Anchorage on this paved all-weather highway. There is some spectacular scenery along the Glenn Highway with mountain peaks to the north and south. Road conditions are generally good. The highway between Tok and Glennallen has some very narrow sections with no shoulders. There is also winding road without shoulders from about Tahneta Pass to Palmer. Watch for frost heaves and pavement breaks along the entire highway. Watch for road construction between **Milepost A 109 and A 188** in 1997. Slow down at signs saying Bump— they mean it!

Four side roads are logged in this section: the Nabesna Road to the old Nabesna Mine, which also provides access to Wrangell–St. Elias National Park and Preserve; Lake Louise Road to Lake Louise Recreation Area; the Hatcher Pass Road, connecting the Glenn and George Parks highways to Independence Mine State Historical Park; and the Old Glenn Highway, an alternate route between Palmer and Anchorage.

Emergency medical services: Between Tok and Duffy's Roadhouse at **Milepost GJ 63**, phone the Alaska State Troopers at 911

GLENN HIGHWAY *Tok Cutoff (GJ-125 to GJ-0) to Milepost A 160*

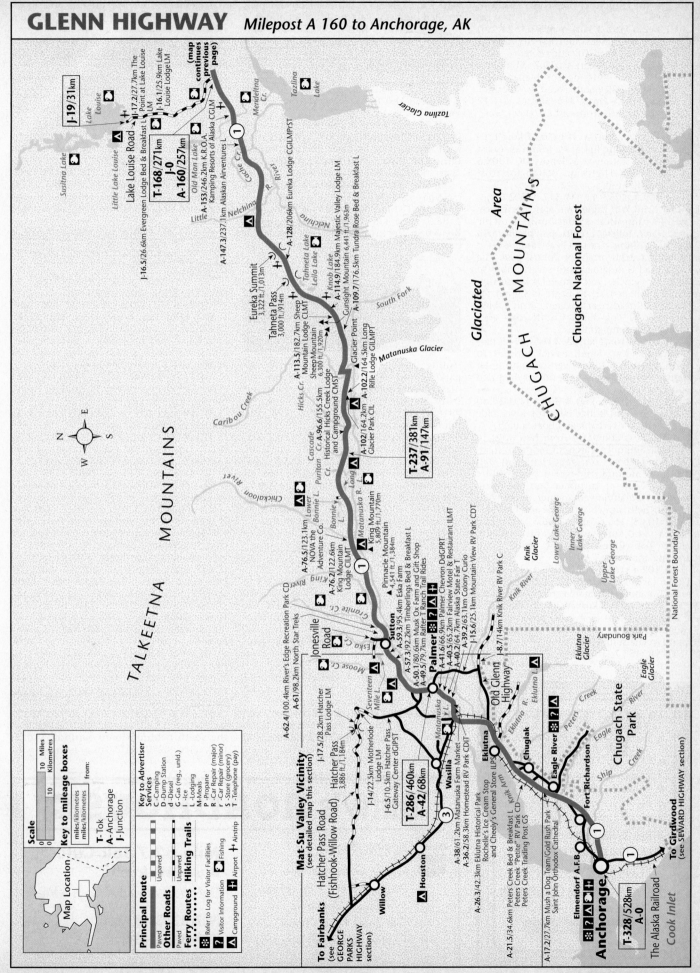

GLENN HIGHWAY Milepost A 160 to Anchorage, AK

J-19/31km

(map continues previous page)

J-17.2/27.7km The Point at Lake Louise LM
J-16.1/25.9km Lake Louise Lodge LM

Lake Louise Road

J-16.5/26.6km Evergreen Lodge Bed & Breakfast L
J-0
T-168/271km
A-160/257km

A-153/246.2km K.R.O.A. Kamping Resorts of Alaska CGLM
A-147.3/237.1km Alaskan Alrventures L
A-128/206km Eureka Lodge CGILMPST
A-114.9/184.9km Majestic Valley Lodge LM
A-109.7/176.5km Tundra Rose Bed & Breakfast L

Eureka Summit
3,322 ft./1,013m

Tahneta Pass
3,000 ft./914m

A-113.5/182.7km Sheep Mountain Lodge CLMT
SheepMountain 6,300 ft./1,920m
A-102.2/164.5km Long Rifle Lodge GILMPT
Glacier Point
A-96.6/155.5km Historical Hicks Creek Lodge and Campground CMST
A-102/164.2km Glacier Park CIL

T-237/381km
A-91/147km

A-76.5/123.1km Lower NOVA the Adventure Co.
A-76.2/122.6km King Mountain Lodge CILMT
King Mountain Lodge CILMT
King Mountain 5,809 ft./1,384m

A-62.4/100.4km River's Edge Recreation Park CD
A-61/98.2km North Star Treks

A-59.3/95.4km Eska Farm
Pinnacle Mountain 4,541 ft./1,384m

A-57.3/92.2km Timberlings Bed & Breakfast L
A-50.1/80.6km Musk Ox Farm and Gift Shop
A-49.5/79.7km Rafter T Ranch Trail Rides

A-41.6/66.9km Palmer Chevron DdGPRT
A-40.5/65.2km Fairview Motel & Restaurant ILMT
A-40.2/64.7km Alaska State Fair T
A-39.2/63.1km Colony Curio
A-38/61.2km Matanuska Farm Market
A-36.2/58.3km Homestead RV Park CDIT

A-26.3/42.3km Eklutna Historical Park
Rochelle's Ice Cream Stop and Cheely's General Store ILPS

A-21.5/34.6km Peters Creek Bed & Breakfast L
Peters Creek "Petite" RV Park CD
Peters Creek Trading Post GS

A-17.2/27.7km Mush a Dog Team/Gold Rush Park
Saint John Orthodox Cathedral

I-15.6/25.1km Mountain View RV Park CDT
I-8.7/14km Knik River RV Park C

Sutton
Jonesville Road
Chickaloon River
Caribou Creek

TALKEETNA MOUNTAINS

CHUGACH MOUNTAINS

Glaciated Area

Chugach National Forest

Tazlina Glacier
Matanuska Glacier
Knik Glacier
Eklutna Glacier
Eagle Glacier

Chugach State Park

Susitna Lake
Little Lake Louise
Lake Louise
Little Susitna Lake
Old Man Lake
Mendeltna Cr.
Tazlina Lake
Tahneta Lake
Leila Lake
Knob Lake

Nelchina River
Little Nelchina R.
Coyte Cr.
South Fork
Hicks Cr.
Cascade Cr.
Puritan Cr.
Bonnie L.
Lower Bonnie L.
Long Lake
Matanuska R.
King River
Granite Cr.
Moose Cr.
Seventeenmile L.
Eska Cr.
Knik River
Eklutna R.
Peters Creek
Eagle River
Ship Creek

Lower Lake George
Inner Lake George
Upper Lake George

National Forest Boundary
Park Boundary

Old Glenn Highway

Palmer
Eklutna
Chugiak
Eagle River
Fort Richardson
Elmendorf A.F.B.
Anchorage
Wasilla
Houston
Willow

T-286/460km
A-42/68km

T-328/528km
A-0

Mat-Su Valley Vicinity
(see detailed map this section)

Hatcher Pass Road
(Fishhook-Willow Road)

Hatcher Pass
3,886 ft./1,184m

J-17.5/28.2km Hatcher Pass Lodge LM
J-14/22.5km Motherlode Lodge LM
Gateway Center dGIPST
J-6.5/10.5km Hatcher Pass
Gateway Center dGIPST

To Fairbanks
(see GEORGE PARKS HIGHWAY section)

To Girdwood
(see SEWARD HIGHWAY section)

The Alaska Railroad
Cook Inlet

Map Location

Scale
10 Miles
10 Kilometres

Key to mileage boxes
miles/kilometres from:
T - Tok
A - Anchorage
J - Junction

Principal Route
Paved
Unpaved
Other Roads
Paved
Unpaved
Ferry Routes
Hiking Trails

▲ Refer to Log for Visitor Facilities
? Visitor Information
▲ Campground ✈ Airport + Airstrip

Key to Advertiser Services
C - Camping
D - Dump Station
d - Diesel
G - Gas (reg., unld.)
I - Ice
L - Lodging
M - Meals
P - Propane
R - Car Repair (major)
r - Car Repair (minor)
S - Store (grocery)
T - Telephone (pay)

N E W S (compass)

Tok in the ALASKA HIGHWAY section.

▲

GJ 122.6 (197.3 km) A 325.6 (524 km) T 2.4 (3.9 km) Bayless and Roberts Airport. Paved bike trail from Tok ends here.

GJ 116.7 (187.8 km) A 319.7 (514.5 km) T 8.3 (13.4 km) Entering Tok Management Area, Tanana Valley State Forest, westbound.

GJ 113 (181.9 km) A 316 (508.5 km) T 12 (19.3 km) Beautiful mountain views westbound.

GJ 110 (177 km) A 313 (503.7 km) T 15 (24.1 km) Flashing lights are from U.S. Coast Guard loran station at **Milepost DC 1308.5** on the Alaska Highway. Watch for frost heaves westbound.

GJ 109.3 (175.9 km) A 312.3 (502.6 km) T 15.7 (25.3 km) Eagle Trail State Recreation Site; 40 campsites, 15-day limit, 4 picnic sites, water, toilets, firepits, pay phone, rain shelter, hiking trail, Clearwater Creek. Camping fee $10/night or annual pass. The access road is designed with several loops to aid larger vehicles. A 0.9-mile/1.4-km section of the pioneer trail to Eagle is signed for hikers; trailhead near covered picnic tables. The historic Tok–Slana Cutoff road goes through this campground. ▲

GJ 104.5 (168.2 km) A 307.5 (494.9 km) T 20.5 (33 km) Small paved turnout to north. **Little Tok River** overflow runs under highway in culvert; fishing for grayling and Dolly Varden. ◀━

GJ 104.1 (167.5 km) A 307.1 (494.2 km) T 20.9 (33.6 km) Bridge over Tok River, side road north to riverbank and boat launch.

Wildlife is abundant from here west to Mentasta Summit. Watch for moose in roadside ponds, bears on gravel bars and Dall sheep on mountainsides. For best wildlife viewing, stop at turnouts and use good binoculars. Wildflowers include sweet peas, chiming bells, arnica, oxytrope and lupine.

GJ 103.5 (166.6 km) A 306.5 (493.3 km) T 21.5 (34.6 km) Paved turnout to north. **Little Tok River** overflow; fishing for grayling and Dolly Varden. ◀━

GJ 102.4 (164.8 km) A 305.4 (491.5 km) T 22.6 (36.4 km) Entering Tok Management Area, Tanana Valley State Forest, eastbound.

GJ 99.3 (159.8 km) A 302.3 (486.5 km) T 25.7 (41.4 km) Rest area; paved double-ended turnout to north. Cranberries may be found in late summer.

GJ 98 (157.7 km) A 301 (484.4 km) T 27

(43.5 km) Bridge over Little Tok River, which parallels highway. Parking at end of bridge.

GJ 97.7 (157.2 km) A 300.7 (483.9 km) T 27.3 (43.9 km) *CAUTION: Watch for sections of narrow highway (no shoulders), bumps, dips and pavement breaks and frost heaves next 20 miles/32.2 km westbound.*

GJ 95.2 (153.2 km) A 298.2 (479.9 km) T 29.8 (48 km) Rest area; paved turnout to south.

GJ 91 (146.4 km) A 294 (473.1 km) T 34 (54.7 km) Gravel turnout to north. Side road with bridge (weight limit 20 tons) across **Little Tok River;** good fishing for grayling, 12 to 14 inches, use small spinner. ◀━

GJ 90 (144.8 km) A 293 (471.5 km) T 35 (56.3 km) Small paved turnout to south.

GJ 89.8 (144.5 km) A 292.8 (471.2 km) T 35.2 (56.6 km) **Mineral Lakes Bed & Breakfast.** Cabins on lake with sourdough breakfast. Open year-round. Northern pike

fishing trips, boating, walking trails, RV parking and gift shop. Come relax—an Alaskan rural getaway. Your hosts, Gary and Patty Stender. HC72, Box 830, Tok, AK 99780-9410. Phone (907) 883-5498. Fall hunters welcome. [ADVERTISEMENT]

GJ 89.5 (144 km) A 292.5 (470.7 km) T 35.5 (57.1 km) **Mineral Lakes.** These are sloughs of the Little Tok River and provide both moose habitat and a breeding place for waterfowl. Good fishing for northern pike and grayling. ◀━

GJ 89 (143.2 km) A 292 (469.9 km) T 36 (57.9 km) Small paved turnout to south.

GJ 86.7 (139.5 km) A 289.7 (466.2 km) T 38.3 (61.6 km) Good place to spot moose.

GJ 85.7 (137.9 km) A 288.7 (464.6 km) T 39.3 (63.2 km) Turnout to north.

GJ 83.2 (133.9 km) A 286.2 (460.6 km) T 41.8 (67.3 km) Bridge over Bartell Creek. Just beyond is the divide between the drainage of the Tanana River, tributary of the Yukon River system flowing into the Bering Sea, and the Copper River system, emptying into the North Pacific near Cordova.

GJ 81 (130.4 km) A 284 (457 km) T 44 (70.8 km) Access road to **MENTASTA LAKE** (pop. 72), a Native village.

GJ 79.4 (127.8 km) A 282.4 (454.5 km) T 45.6 (73.4 km) Mentasta Summit (elev. 2,434 feet/742m). Watch for Dall sheep on mountainsides. Boundary between Game

Management Units 12 and 13C and Sport-fish Management Units 8 and 2. Mountain views westbound.

GJ 78.1 (125.7 km) A 281.1 (452.4 km) T 46.9 (75.5 km) **Mentasta Lodge.** See display ad this section.

GJ 78 (125.5 km) A 281 (452.2 km) T 47 (75.6 km) View for westbound traffic of snow-covered Mount Sanford (elev. 16,237 feet/4,949m).

GJ 77.9 (125.4 km) A 280.9 (452.1 km) T 47.1 (75.8 km) Paved turnout to north by Slana Slough; salmon spawning area in August. Watch for beavers.

GJ 76.3 (122.8 km) A 279.3 (449.5 km) T 48.7 (78.4 km) Bridge over Mabel Creek. Mastodon flowers (marsh fleabane) in late July; very large (to 4 feet) with showy seed heads.

CAUTION: Watch for sections of narrow highway (no shoulders), bumps, dips, pavement breaks and frost heaves next 20 miles/32.2 km eastbound.

GJ 76 (122.3 km) A 279 (449 km) T 49 (78.8 km) Bridge over Slana Slough.

GJ 75.6 (121.7 km) A 278.6 (448.3 km) T 49.4 (79.5 km) Bridge over Slana River. Rest area to south with large paved parking area, toilets and picnic tables along the river. This river flows from its source glaciers some 55 miles/88.5 km to the Copper River.

GJ 74 (119.1 km) A 277 (445.8 km) T 51 (82.1 km) Large paved turnout to south overlooking Slana River.

GJ 69 (111 km) A 272 (437.7 km) T 56 (90.1 km) Turnout to north.

GJ 68 (109.4 km) A 271 (436.1 km) T 57 (91.7 km) Carlson Creek bridge. Paved turnout to south at west end of bridge.

GJ 65.5 (105.4 km) A 268.5 (432.1 km) T 59.5 (95.8 km) Paved turnout to south; viewpoint.

GJ 64.2 (103.3 km) A 267.2 (430 km) T 60.8 (97.8 km) Bridge over **Porcupine Creek** State Recreation Site 0.2 mile/0.3 km from highway; 12 forested campsites on loop road, 15-day limit, $10 nightly fee (concessionaire-operated, annual state park pass not accepted), drinking water, firepits, toilets, picnic tables and fishing (wood and charcoal available from concessionaire at Hart D Ranch, Mile 0.7 Nabesna Road). Low-bush cranberries in fall. *CAUTION: Watch for bears.* ◀▲

GJ 63 (101.4 km) A 266 (428 km) T 62 (99.8 km) Scenic viewpoint with view of Wrangell Mountains. The dominant peak to the southwest is Mount Sanford, a dormant volcano; the pinnacles of Capital Mountain can be seen against its lower slopes. Mount Jarvis (elev. 13,421 feet/4,091m) is visible to the south behind Mount Sanford; Tanada Peak (elev. 9,240 feet/2,816m) is more to the south. (Tanada Peak is sometimes mistaken for Noyes Mountain.)

Walk up the gravel hill to view Noyes Mountain (elev. 8,147 feet/2,483m), named for U.S. Army Brig. Gen. John Rutherford Noyes, a one-time commissioner of roads in the territory of Alaska. Appointed adjutant general of the Alaska National Guard in 1953, he died in 1956 from injuries and frostbite after his plane crashed near Nome.

GJ 62.7 (100.9 km) A 265.7 (427.6 km) T 62.3 (100.3 km) Duffy's Roadhouse. See display ad this section.

Private Aircraft: Duffy's Tavern airstrip; elev. 2,420 feet/737m; length 1,800 feet/548m; gravel; unmaintained.

GJ 61 (98.2 km) A 264 (424.9 km) T 64 (103 km) Midway Service. See display ad this section.

GJ 60.8 (97.8 km) A 263.8 (424.6 km) T 64.2 (103.3 km) Bridge over Ahtell Creek; grayling. Parking area to north at east end of bridge. This stream drains a mountain area of igneous rock, where several gold and silver-lead claims are located.

GJ 59.8 (96.2 km) A 262.8 (422.9 km) T 65.2 (104.9 km) Junction with Nabesna Road. See NABESNA ROAD log page 292.

GJ 59.7 (96.1 km) A 262.7 (422.8 km) T 65.3 (105.1 km) View of Tanada Peak, Mount Sanford, Mount Blackburn and Mount Drum to the south and southwest. The Mentasta Mountains are to the east.

GJ 57 (91.7 km) A 260 (418.4 km) T 68 (109.4 km) Scenic viewpoint overlooking Cobb Lakes.

GJ 55.2 (88.8 km) A 258.2 (415.5 km) T 69.8 (112.3 km) Tanada Peak viewpoint; gravel turnout to south.

GJ 53 (85.3 km) A 256 (412 km) T 72 (115.9 km) Grizzly Lake. Watch for horses on road.

Grizzly Lake Ranch Bed & Breakfast. See display ad this section. ▲

GJ 44.6 (71.8 km) A 247.6 (398.5 km) T 80.4 (129.4 km) Turnout to north. Eagle Trail access (not marked).

GJ 43.8 (70.5 km) A 246.8 (397.1 km) T 81.2 (130.6 km) Bridge over Indian River. This is a salmon spawning stream, usually late-June through July. Picnic site to south at west end of bridge with tables, 2 firepits, toilets.

GJ 43.4 (69.8 km) A 246.4 (396.5 km) T 81.6 (131.3 km) Double-ended gravel turnout to south.

GJ 41.2 (66.3 km) A 244.2 (393 km) T 83.8 (134.8 km) Long, double-ended turnout overlooking pond.

GJ 40.1 (64.5 km) A 243.1 (391.2 km) T 84.9 (136.6 km) Small paved turnout to south. Fish Creek BLM trailhead.

GJ 39 (62.8 km) A 242 (389.5 km) T 86 (138.4 km) Views of the Copper River valley and Wrangell Mountains. Looking south, peak on left is Mount Sanford and on right is Mount Drum (elev. 12,010 feet/3,661m).

Look for cotton grass and mastodon flowers in late July and August.

CAUTION: Rough road next 2 miles/3.2 km eastbound.

GJ 38.7 (62.2 km) A 241.7 (389 km) T 86.3 (138.8 km) Paved turnout to north. Mankoman Lake trail.

GJ 35.5 (57.1 km) A 238.5 (383.8 km) T 89.5 (144 km) Chistochina River Bridge No. 2. Mount Sanford is first large mountain to the southeast, then Mount Drum.

GJ 35.4 (57 km) A 238.4 (383.7 km) T 89.6 (144.2 km) Chistochina River Bridge No. 1; parking at west end. Chistochina

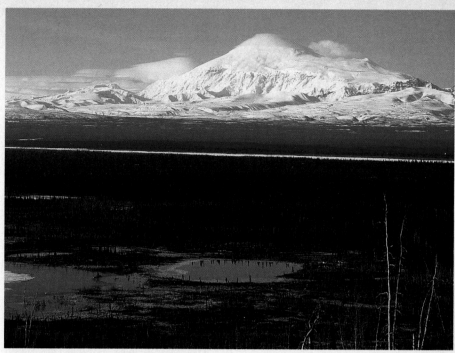

Mount Sanford, seen from Milepost GJ 39, is distinguished from nearby Mount Drum by its more rounded top. (© Beth Davidow)

River trailhead. This river heads in the Chistochina Glacier on Mount Kimball (elev. 10,300 feet/3,139m). Chistochina is thought to mean marmot creek.

GJ 34.7 (55.8 km) A 237.7 (382.5 km) T 90.3 (145.3 km) Posty's Sinona Creek Trading Post (current status unknown).

GJ 34.6 (55.7 km) A 237.6 (382.4 km) T 90.4 (145.5 km) Bridge over Sinona Creek. Sinona is said to mean place of the many burls, and there are indeed many burls on area spruce trees.

GJ 34.4 (55.4 km) A 237.4 (382 km)

T 90.6 (145.8 km) Sinona Creek RV Campground. See display ad this section. ▲

(Continues on page 293)

Nabesna Road Log

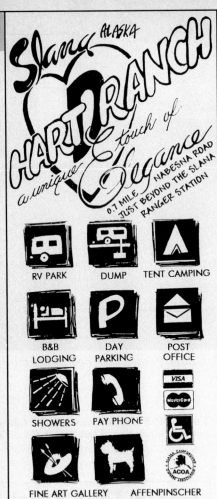

The Nabesna Road leads 45 miles/72.4 km southeast from **Milepost GJ 59.8** Glenn Highway (Tok Cutoff) to the old mining community of Nabesna. This side trip can be enjoyable for campers; there are no formal public campgrounds but there are plenty of beautiful spots to camp and a private campground at Mile 0.7/1.1 km. The area also offers good fishing. Horses are permitted on all trails. Off-road vehicles must have permits from the National Park Service. The Nabesna Road provides access to the northwest corner of Wrangell–St. Elias National Park and Preserve. The National Park Service ranger station at Slana has information on current Nabesna Road conditions and on backcountry travel in the park. (The Wrangell–St. Elias National Park visitor center is near Copper Center on the old Richardson Highway.)

The first 4 miles/6.4 km of road is chip seal surface, the remainder is gravel. Beyond **Milepost J 28.6** the road becomes rough and crosses several creeks which may be difficult to ford. The state-maintained road ends at Mile 42; vehicles are not recommended beyond this point.
Distance is measured from the junction with the Glenn Highway (J).

J 0.1 (0.2 km) Slana highway maintenance station.

J 0.2 (0.3 km) Slana NPS ranger station; information on road conditions and on Wrangell–St. Elias National Park and Preserve. Open 8 A.M. to 5 P.M. daily, June 1 through September. USGS maps and natural history books for sale. Phone (907) 882-5238. For more information contact: Superintendent, Wrangell–St. Elias National Park and Preserve, P.O. Box 439, Copper Center, AK 99573; phone (907) 822-5234.

J 0.7 (1.1 km) Slana post office and Hart D Ranch complex. The picturesque ranch is the home and studio of sculptor Mary Frances DeHart. The ranch offers RV and tent camping, an art gallery, bed and breakfast accommodations, pay phone and dog kennels (DeHart raises Affenpinscscher dogs).

Hart D Ranch. See display ad this section.

J 1 (1.6 km) SLANA (pop. 39), once an Indian village on the north bank of the Slana River, now refers to this general area. Besides the Indian settlement, Slana boasted a popular roadhouse, now a private home. Slana elementary school is located here.

J 1.5 (2.4 km) Slana River Bridge; undeveloped camping area. Boundary between Game Management Units 11 and 13C.

J 2 (3.2 km) BLM homestead area next 2 miles/3.2 km southbound. Blueberries in the fall; grouse are seen in this area.

J 3.9 (6.2 km) Entering Wrangell–St. Elias National Park and Preserve. The Glenn Highway follows the northern boundary of the preserve between Slana and Gakona Junction; Nabesna Road provides access to the northwest corner of the park.

J 4 (6.4 km) Turnouts. Hard surface ends, gravel begins, southbound.

J 7 (11.3 km) Road crosses **Rufus Creek** culvert. Dolly Varden to 8 inches, June to October. Watch out for bears, especially during berry season.

J 8.9 (14.3 km) Rough turnout.

J 11 (17.7 km) Suslota Lake trailhead No. 1 to north.

J 11.4 (18.3 km) Gravel pit, room to park or camp.

J 12.2 (19.6 km) Road crosses Caribou Creek culvert.

J 12.5 (20.1 km) Turnout to southeast; Copper Lake trailhead.

J 13.1 (21.1 km) Suslota Lake trailhead No. 2 to north.

J 15 (24.1 km) Turnout.

J 15.4 (24.8 km) Beautiful views of Mount Sanford and Tanada Peak in the Wrangell Mountains, across the great plain of the Copper River.

J 16 (25.7 km) Turnout to northeast.

J 16.6 (26.7 km) Turnout to southwest.

J 16.9 (27.2 km) Turnout by large lake which reflects Mount Sanford.

J 18 (29 km) Pond to northeast. The highly mineralized Mentasta Mountains are visible to the north. This is sparsely timbered high country.

J 18.8 (30.3 km) Caribou Creek culvert.

J 19.3 (31.1 km) Turnout at gravel pit to northwest. Look for poppies, lupine, arnica and chiming bells in season.

J 19.7 (31.7 km) Hiking trail to north.

J 21.2 (34.1 km) Turnout at gravel pit to northwest.

J 21.8 (35.1 km) Rock Creek culvert.

J 22.3 (35.9 km) Rock Lake; turnouts both sides of road.

J 22.9 (36.8 km) Long Lake.

J 23.4 (37.7 km) Turnout. Floatplane landing.

J 24.4 (39.3 km) Turnout to southwest with view of Wrangell Mountains. Tanada Lake trail.

J 25.2 (40.6 km) Boundary between Sportfish Areas C and K, and Game Management Areas 11 and 12.

J 25.5 (41 km) Lodge. Glimpse of Tanada Lake beneath Tanada Peak to the south.

Silvertip Lodge & Air Service. See display ad this section.

J 25.9 (41.7 km) Little Jack Creek.

J 26.1 (42 km) Access road to private campground and floatplane service at Jack Lake; no turnaround. ▲

J 27 (43.5 km) Turnouts to north and south.

J 28.2 (45.4 km) Turnouts at Twin Lakes; primitive campsite, good place to observe waterfowl. Wildflowers in June include Lapland rosebay, lupine and 8-petalled mountain avens.

AREA FISHING: Twin Lakes, grayling 10 to 18 inches, mid-May to October, flies or small spinner; also burbot. **Copper Lake** (fly in from Long Lake or Jack Lake), lake trout 10 to 12 lbs., mid-June to September, use red-and-white spoon; kokanee 10 to 12 inches, mid-June to July, use small spinner; grayling 12 to 20 inches, July through September; also burbot. **Long** and **Jack lakes,** grayling fishing. **Tanada Lake** (fly in from Long Lake or Jack Lake), grayling and lake trout. ✦

J 28.6 (46 km) **Sportsmen's Paradise Lodge** is located 28.6 miles from the Glenn Highway on the Nabesna Gold

Mine Road. Miles of magnificent views on this old road to the former Nabesna Gold Mine. Free camper parking, sandwiches, bar, air taxi service, fishing, boating, hunting. A side trip not to miss. Fly-in fishing to Copper Lake, boats, motors, light-housekeeping cabins available. Dick and Lucille Frederick, your hosts. Phone (907) 822-5288 (radiophone). [ADVERTISEMENT] ▲

J 28.6 (46 km) The road deteriorates beyond this point and you may have to ford several creeks. Inquire at lodge here or Slana Ranger Station about road conditions.

J 29.6 (47.6 km) Trail Creek crosses road; no culvert but road has gravel base here. Easy to drive through creek, especially in fall. Overnight hikers may hike up Lost Creek and return via Trail Creek.

J 31.4 (50.5 km) Road crosses Lost Creek, a very wide expanse of water in spring and may remain difficult to cross well into summer. Loose gravel makes it easy to get stuck in creek if you spin your wheels. Scout it out first. If you hesitate once in the creek, wheels may dig in. The road crosses several more creeks beyond here; these may also be difficult to ford.

J 31.6 (50.9 km) Boyden Creek (may have to ford after rain or during spring melt).

J 32.4 (52.1 km) Chalk Creek culvert.

J 33 (53.1 km) Big Grayling Lake hiking trail. Horses allowed.

J 34.1 (54.9 km) Radiator Creek culvert.

J 35 (56.3 km) Creek (must ford).

J 36 (57.9 km) Jack Creek Bridge.

J 36.1 (58.1 km) Informal campsites with picnic tables (1 north, 2 south). The road crosses 5 creeks the next 4.3 miles/6.9 km southbound. Watch for loose gravel in creekbeds.

J 41 (66 km) A marked trail, approximately 5 miles/8 km long, leads to Nabesna River and old Reeves Field airstrip, once used to fly gold out and supplies in to mining camps. Devil's Mountain is to the left of the trail. The trail on the river also leads to the old Indian village of Khiltat.

J 41.4 (66.6 km) Skookum Creek in culvert.

J 42 (67.6 km) Devil's Mountain Lodge (private property). State-maintained road ends. Hiking only recommended beyond this point. Bed and breakfast, trail rides, flightseeing and showers available.

End of the Road B&B. See display ad this section.

K-AIR, St. Elias Alpine Guides. Enjoy stunning flights over the Nabesna Glacier up towards Mount Blackburn. Or get dropped off within sweeping views of the Wrangell Mountains and glaciers for a guided day hike or backpacking trip with an experienced alpine guide. Call (907) 277-6867 for guided trips; (907) 822-5312 for flying. [ADVERTISEMENT]

J 45 (72.4 km) **NABESNA** (area pop. less than 25; elev. 3,000 feet/914m). No facilities. This region has copper reserves, as well as gold in the streams and rivers, silver, molybdenum and iron ore deposits. Tailings deposits here are currently closed to the public. Nabesna gold mine is located here. Area residents subsist on caribou, Dall sheep, moose, bear, fish and small game. Fire fighting and trapping also provide some income. Big game hunting is popular in this area; registered guides and several outfitters have headquarters along Nabesna Road.

Return to Milepost GJ 59.8 Glenn Highway (Tok Cutoff)

Yellow, daisy-like arnica blooms in June in dry, gravelly areas. (Jerrianne Lowther, staff)

(Continued from page 291)

GJ 34.1 (54.9 km) **A 237.1** (381.6 km) **T 90.9** (146.3 km) Chistochina ball fields.

GJ 32.9 (52.9 km) **A 235.9** (379.6 km) **T 92.1** (148.2 km) Road access to Native village of **CHISTOCHINA** (pop. 43).

Private Aircraft: Barnhart airstrip, 3 miles/4.8 km north; elev. 1,930 feet/588m; length 2,500 feet/762m; earth; unattended. Chistochina airstrip, adjacent southwest; elev. 1,850 feet/564m; length 2,000 feet/ 610m; turf and gravel.

GJ 32.8 (52.8 km) **A 235.8** (379.5 km) **T 92.2** (148.4 km) Chistochina Lodge.

GJ 30.1 (48.4 km) **A 233.1** (375.1 km) **T 94.9** (152.7 km) Paved turnout to south.

CAUTION: Road narrows eastbound; no shoulders. Watch for frost heaves.

GJ 28.1 (45.2 km) **A 231.1** (371.9 km) **T 96.9** (155.9 km) Double-ended paved parking area to south with a marker on the Alaska Road Commission. The ARC was established in 1905, the same year the first automobile arrived in Alaska at Skagway. The ARC operated for 51 years, building roads, airfields, trails and other transportation facilities. It was replaced by the Bureau of Public Roads (referred to by some Alaskans at the time as the Bureau of Parallel Ruts) in 1956. In 1960 the Bureau of Public Roads was replaced by the Dept. of Public Works.

GJ 24 (38.6 km) **A 227** (365.3 km) **T 101** (162.5 km) Large rest area to south with paved double-ended parking area, toilets, picnic tables and firepits on grass under trees; paths lead to Copper River. Mount Sanford is to the southeast, Mount Drum to the south.

GJ 20.9 (33.6 km) **A 223.9** (360.3 km) **T 104.1** (167.5 km) Turnout to Buster Gene trailhead to south.

GJ 17.8 (28.6 km) **A 220.8** (355.3 km) **T 107.2** (172.5 km) **Tulsona Creek** bridge. Good grayling fishing.

GJ 11.6 (18.7 km) **A 214.6** (345.4 km) **T 113.4** (182.5 km) Yellow pond lily (*Nuphar polysepalum*) in ponds along highway.

GJ 9.4 (15.1 km) **A 212.4** (341.8 km) **T 115.6** (186 km) Paved turnout to north by lake. Fox Lake BLM trailhead.

GJ 8.8 (14.2 km) **A 211.8** (340.8 km) **T 116.2** (187 km) Paved turnout to north. BLM trailhead.

GJ 6.3 (10.1 km) **A 209.3** (336.8 km) **T 118.7** (191 km) Paved turnout to southeast.

GJ 4.7 (7.6 km) **A 207.7** (334.3 km) **T 120.3** (193.6 km) **The River Wrangellers.** See display ad this section.

GJ 4.2 (6.8 km) **A 207.2** (333.4 km) **T 120.8** (194.4 km) **Gakona, AK. R.V. Wilderness Campsite.** See display ad this section.

GJ 3 (4.8 km) **A 206** (331.5 km) **T 122** (196.3 km) **Riverview Bed & Breakfast.** See display ad this section.

GJ 2.7 (4.3 km) **A 205.7** (331 km) **T 122.3** (196.8 km) **GAKONA** (area pop. 200). The village of Gakona lies between the Gakona and Copper rivers. (Gakona is

Athabascan for "rabbit".) Originally Gakona was a Native wood and fish camp, and fish wheels are still common. The post office is located on the highway here.

GJ 2 (3.2 km) **A 205** (330 km) **T 123** (198 km) Gakona Lodge, entered on the National Register of Historic Places in 1977. Originally one of several roadhouses providing essential food and lodging for travelers, it opened in 1905 and was first called Doyle's Ranch. The original carriage house is now a restaurant.

Gakona Lodge & Trading Post and **The Carriage House Dining Room.** See display ad this section.

GJ 1.8 (2.9 km) **A 204.8** (329.6 km) **T 123.2** (198.3 km) Bridge over Gakona River. Entering Game Management Unit 13B westbound and 13C eastbound. The highway climbs a short hill and joins the Richardson Highway 1.8 miles/2.9 km from this bridge. From the hill there is a fine view of the many channels where the Gakona and Copper rivers join.

GJ 1 (1.6 km) **A 204** (328.3 km) **T 124** (200 km) Rest area to south has paved turnout overlooking the valley of the Gakona and Copper rivers; picnic tables and litter barrels. View of Mount Drum and Mount Sanford. Good photo stop.

GJ 0 A 203 (326.7 km) **T 125** (201.2 km) **Gakona Junction.** Lodge. Junction of Tok Cutoff (Alaska Route 1) with the Richardson Highway (Alaska Route 4); the 2 roads share a common alignment for the next 14 miles/22.5 km westbound.

Turn north here for Delta Junction via the Richardson Highway (see **Milepost V 128.6** in the RICHARDSON HIGHWAY section). Turn south for Anchorage or Valdez. *NOTE: This junction can be confusing. Choose your route carefully.*

Gakona Junction Village. See display ad this section.

Richardson Highway Log

ALASKA ROUTE 4
Physical mileposts for the next 14 miles/22.5 km southbound give distance from Valdez. **Distance from Anchorage (A) is followed by distance from Tok (T) and distance from Valdez (V).**

A 203 (326.7 km) **T 125** (201.2 km) **V 128.6** (207 km) **Junction** of the Tok Cutoff with the Richardson Highway at Gakona Junction. Watch for frost heaves between here and **Milepost V 124.**

A 201 (323.5 km) **T 127** (204.4 km) **V 126.9** (204.2 km) Access road to **GULKANA** (pop. 100) on the bank of the Gulkana River. Camping is permitted along the river by the bridge. Grayling fishing and good king and sockeye salmon fishing (June and July) in the **Gulkana River.** Most of the Gulkana River frontage in this area is owned by Gulkana village and managed by Ahtna, Inc. Ahtna lands are closed to the public for hunting, fishing and trapping. ⚓▲

A 200.9 (323.3 km) **T 127.1** (204.5 km) **V 126.8** (204 km) Gulkana River Bridge. Entering Game Management Unit 13B eastbound, 13A westbound.

A 200.3 (322.3 km) **T 127.7** (205.5 km) **V 126.2** (203.1 km) Inn.

A 200.1 (322 km) **T 127.9** (205.8 km) **V 126** (202.8 km) Paved double-ended turnout to north.

A 197.3 (317.5 km) **T 130.7** (210.3 km) **V 123.2** (198.3 km) Large paved turnout to south.

A 192.1 (309.1 km) **T 135.9** (218.7 km) **V 118.1** (190 km) **Private Aircraft:** Gulkana airstrip; elev. 1,578 feet/481m; length 5,000 feet/1,524m; asphalt; fuel 100. Flying service located here.

A 192 (309 km) **T 136** (218.9 km) **V 118** (189.9 km) Dry Creek State Recreation Site; 58 campsites, 15-day limit, $10 nightly fee or annual pass, 4 picnic sites, toilets, picnic shelter. *Bring mosquito repellent!* ▲

A 189.5 (305 km) **T 138.5** (222.9 km) **V 115.5** (185.9 km) **Glennallen Quick Stop Truck Stop.** Stop for friendly family service, gas, diesel, convenience store with ice, pop, snacks, postcards, ice cream, specialty items, pay phone and free coffee. Truck, caravan, senior citizen discounts. Several interesting items on display, including an authentic Native Alaskan fish wheel. Full-service restaurant adjacent. See display ad this section. [ADVERTISEMENT]

A 189.5 (305 km) **T 138.5** (222.9 km) **V 115.5** (185.9 km) **Rendezvous Cafe.** See display ad this section.

A 189 (304.2 km) **T 139** (223.7 km) **V 115** (185.1 km) **Junction** of the Richardson Highway (Alaska Route 4) with the Glenn Highway (Alaska Route 1). Turn south here on the Richardson Highway for Valdez (see **Milepost V 115** in the RICHARDSON HIGHWAY section). Continue west on the Glenn Highway for Anchorage. *NOTE: This junction can be confusing. Choose your route carefully. See map page 294.*

Greater Copper Valley Chamber of Commerce Visitor Information center, convenience store with automatic teller machine and gas station. Alaska State Troopers, Dept. of Motor Vehicles, Fish and Wildlife Protection and courthouse located on east side of highway.

Greater Copper Valley Chamber of Commerce Visitor Center in log cabin; open 8 A.M. to 7 P.M. daily in summer. There's also a convenience grocery and a gas station (with diesel) at junction.

Greater Copper Valley Chamber of Commerce. See display ad this section.

The Hub of Alaska and Hub Maxi-Mart. See display ad this section.

Glenn Highway Log

ALASKA ROUTE 1
Physical mileposts between Glennallen and Anchorage show distance from Anchorage. **Distance from Anchorage (A) is followed by distance from Tok (T).**

A **188.7** (303.7 km) T **139.3** (224.2 km) **Northern Nights Campground and "No Frills" RV Park.** See display ad this section. ▲

A **188.3** (303 km) T **139.7** (224.8 km) Trans–Alaska pipeline passes under the highway.

A **187.8** (302.2 km) T **140.2** (225.6 km) **The Hitchin' Post.** The little place with the big reputation. Known for our great fries, KC-style BBQ ribs on Saturday nights and our big breakfasts. Enjoy the picnic tables, eat indoors or stop at our drive-through. Located across from the car wash and RV park. See display ad. [ADVERTISEMENT]

A **187.5** (301.7 km) T **140.5** (226.1 km) **Tastee–Freez.** This popular spot features an excellent menu of fast food, including breakfast, with some of the lowest prices on the highway. We satisfy appetites of all sizes, from a quick taco to double cheeseburgers, cooked fresh and fast. Our comfortable dining room displays a selection of the finest original drawings and handmade gifts. Plan to stop! See display ad in Glennallen section. [ADVERTISEMENT]

A **187.2** (301.3 km) T **140.8** (226.6 km) National Bank of Alaska; 24-hour automatic teller machine. Post office a block north of highway. Description of Glennallen follows.

Glennallen

A 187 (300.9 km) **T 141** (226.9 km) Near the south junction of Glenn and Richardson highways. **Population:** 928. **Emergency Services: Alaska State Troopers, Milepost A 189**, phone (907) 822-3263. **Fire Department**, phone 911. **Ambulance**, Copper River EMS, phone (907) 822-3203 or 911. **Clinic, Milepost A 186.6**, phone (907) 822-3203. **Road Conditions**, phone (907) 822-5511.

Visitor Information: The Greater Copper Valley Chamber of Commerce Visitor Center is located in the log cabin at the junction of the Glenn and Richardson highways. **Milepost A 189**; open 8 A.M. to 7 P.M. daily in summer, phone (907) 822-5555. The Alaska Dept. of Fish and Game office is located at **Milepost A 186.2** on the Glenn Highway, open weekdays 8 A.M. to 5 P.M.; phone (907) 822-3309.

Elevation: 1,460 feet/445m. **Climate:** Mean monthly temperature in January -10°F/-23°C; in July, 56°F/13°C. Record low was -61°F/-52°C in January 1975; record high, 90°F/32°C in June 1969. Mean precipitation in July, 1.53 inches/3.9cm. Mean precipitation (snow/sleet) in December, 11.4 inches/29cm. **Radio:** KCAM 790, KOOL 107.1, KUAC-FM 92.1. **Television:** KYUK (Bethel) and Wrangell Mountain TV Club via satellite; Public Broadcasting System.

Private Aircraft: Gulkana airstrip, 4.3 miles/6.9 km northeast of Glennallen at

Milepost A 192.1; elev. 1,578 feet/481m; length 5,000 feet/1,524m; asphalt; fuel 100. Parking with tie downs. Mechanic available.

The name Glennallen is derived from the combined last names of Capt. Edwin F. Glenn and Lt. Henry T. Allen, both leaders in the early exploration of the Copper River region.

Glennallen lies at the western edge of the huge Wrangell–St. Elias National Park and Preserve. It is a gateway to the Wrangell Mountains and the service center for the Copper River basin. Glennallen is also a fly-in base for several guides and outfitters.

Four prominent peaks of the majestic Wrangell Mountains are to the east; from left they are Mounts Sanford, Drum, Wrangell and Blackburn. The best views are on crisp winter days at sunset. The rest of the countryside is relatively flat.

The main business district is 1.5 miles/ 2.4 km west of the south junction of the Glenn and Richardson highways. There are also several businesses located at the south junction. About two-thirds of the area's residents are employed by trade/service firms; the balance hold various government positions. Offices for the Bureau of Land Management, the Alaska State Troopers and Dept. of Fish and Game are located here. There are several small farms in the area. There is a substantial Native population in the area and the Native-owned Ahtna Corp. has its headquarters near Glennallen on the Richardson Highway.

Also headquartered here is KCAM radio, which broadcasts on station 790. KCAM broadcasts area road condition reports daily and also airs the popular "Caribou Clatter," which will broadcast personal messages. Radio messages are still a popular form of communication in Alaska and a necessary one in the Bush. Similar radio programs throughout the state are KJNP's "Trapline Chatter"; KYAK's "Bush Pipeline"; KHAR's "Northwinds"; and KIAK's "Pipeline of the North."

ACCOMMODATIONS/VISITOR SERVICES

Because of its strategic location, most traveler services are available. During summer months reservations are advised for visitor accommodations. Glennallen has several lodges and motels and a variety of restaurants. Auto parts, groceries, gifts, clothing, propane, sporting goods and other supplies are available at local stores. Services include a bank and automatic teller machine, a dentist, several churches, a chiropractic center, a laundromat, gas stations and major auto repair.

New Caribou Hotel, Gift Shop and Restaurant. The New Caribou Hotel in downtown Glennallen, on the edge of the largest national park in America, was completed fall of 1990. This 55-unit modern facility features custom built furniture, state-of-the-art color coordinated Alaskan decor, 6 rooms with 2-person whirlpool baths, 2-bedroom, fully furnished suites with kitchens and cooking facilities. Alaskan art, handicap facilities, conference rooms, phones and fax lines, satellite TV. Large full menu restaurant with banquet room, unique Alaskan gift shop (a must stop in your travels). All major credit cards accepted. Tour buses welcome. Airport transportation. Ask us for travel and visitor information. Open year-round. Phone (907) 822-3302. Toll free in Alaska phone (800) 478-3302, fax (907) 822-3711.
[ADVERTISEMENT]

There are private campgrounds west of town on the Glenn Highway (see **Milepost A 183.6, A 173** and **A 170.5**) and east of town at **Milepost A 188.7**. There are 2 private RV parks in Glennallen and at **Milepost V 110.5** Richardson Highway (4.5 m/7.2 km south of the junction). Northeast of Glennallen 5 miles/8 km is Dry Creek state campground (see **Milepost A 192**). ▲

TRANSPORTATION

Bus: Scheduled service between Anchorage and Whitehorse via Glennallen. Bus service between Glennallen and McCarthy via Copper Center and Chitina in summer.

ATTRACTIONS

Fourth of July weekend is a major event in Glennallen. Activities include the Ahtna Arts and Crafts Fair, a music festival, raft race, parade and salmon bake.

Recreational opportunities in the Glennallen area include hunting, river running, bird watching and fishing. According to the ADF&G, approximately 50 lakes in the Glennallen area are stocked with grayling, rainbow trout and coho salmon. A complete list of lakes, locations and species is available at the Copper River Valley Visitor Center at **Milepost A 189**, or from the ADF&G office at **Milepost A 186.2**. Locally, there is good grayling fishing in **Moose Creek; Tulsona Creek** to the east at **Milepost GJ 17.5**; west on the Glenn Highway at **Tolsona Creek, Milepost A 173**; and **Mendeltna Creek, Milepost A 152.8**. **Lake Louise**, approximately 27 miles/43 km west and 19 miles/30.5 km north from Glennallen, offers excellent grayling and lake trout fishing.

Many fly-in lakes are located in the Copper River basin and Chugach Mountains near Glennallen. **Crosswind Lake**, large lake trout, whitefish and grayling, early June to early July. **Deep Lake**, all summer for lake trout to 30 inches. **High Lake**, lake trout to 22 inches, June and early July with small spoons; some rainbow, fly-fishing; cabin, boats and motors rental. **Tebay Lakes**, excellent rainbow fishing, 12 to 15 inches, all summer, small spinners; cabin, boats and motors rental. **Jans Lake**, 12- to 14-inch silver salmon, June, spinners; also rainbow. **Hanagita Lake**, excellent grayling fishing all summer; also lake trout and steelhead in September. **Minnesota Lake**, lake trout to 30 inches, all summer; boat only, no cabins. ✦

Glenn Highway Log

(continued)

A **186.6** (300.3 km) T **141.4** (227.6 km) Cross Road Medical Center clinic. Alaska Bible College, the state's only accredited resident 4-year bible college, is located behind the clinic.

A **186.4** (300 km) T **141.6** (227.9 km) Bureau of Land Management district office; phone (907) 822-3217.

A **186.2** (299.7 km) T **141.8** (228.2 km) Alaska State Dept. of Fish and Game; phone (907) 822-3309.

A **186.1** (299.5 km) T **141.9** (228.4 km) Copper Valley library.

The Territory of Alaska became the 49th state on Jan. 3, 1959.

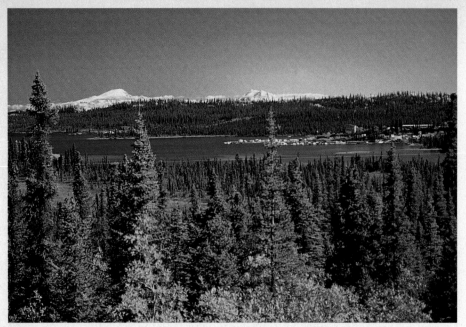

Lake Louise recreation area is located 19 miles/31 km north from Milepost A 159.8. *(Shelley Metcalf)*

A **186** (299.3 km) T **142** (228.5 km) **Moose Creek** culvert; good grayling fishing in spring.

A **183.6** (295.5 km) T **144.4** (232.4 km) **Brown Bear Rhodehouse.** Because of the excellent food, reasonable prices and Alaskan hospitality, this famous old lodge is a favorite eating and gathering place for local people and travelers alike. If eating in the Glennallen area, we recommend stopping here, and if coming from south it is well worth the extra few minutes wait. Superb steaks and seafood are the specialties, along with broasted chicken and the widest sandwich selection in the area. Your hosts, Doug and Cindy Rhodes, have managed to take one of the largest grizzly brown bear photograph collections anywhere. So, if not dining, you will enjoy just stopping and looking at the many photographs that cover the walls or listening to a few bear tales in the lounge. This is the only place in the area that with one stop you have a campground, camping cabins, motel, restaurant and bar. This is also the only place on the highway to get a bucket of golden brown broasted chicken to go. Phone (907) 822-3663.
[ADVERTISEMENT]   ▲

A **183** (294.5 km) T **145** (233.3 km) *CAUTION: Watch for frost heaves.*

A **182.2** (293.2 km) T **145.8** (234.6 km) **Basin Liquors, Paper Shack Office Supply.** Liquor store opens 8 A.M., 7 days a week, 365 days a year. Liquor, snacks, ice, cigarettes. We

invite you to take a break; walk around in one of the most beautiful yards on the Glenn Highway, longtime home of pioneer resident "Gramma Ole" Hanson. [ADVERTISEMENT]

A **176.6** (284.2 km) T **151.4** (243.6 km) Paved turnout to south with interpretive sign about the Wrangell Mountains and view east across the Copper River valley to Mount Drum. Northeast of Mount Drum is Mount Sanford and southeast is Mount Wrangell (elev. 14,163 feet/4,317m), a semi-active volcano. Mount Wrangell last erupted in 1912 when lava flowed to its base and ash

fell as far west as this point.

Wildflowers growing along the roadside include lupine, cinquefoil, oxytrope, Jacob's ladder and sweet pea.

A **174.7** (281.1 km) T **153.3** (246.7 km) Double-ended paved turnout to south.

A **173** (278.4 km) T **155** (249.4 km) **Tolsona Wilderness Campground & RV Park.** AAA approved, Good Sam Park. This

beautiful campground, located three-quarter mile north of the highway, is surrounded on 3 sides by untouched wilderness. Each shady campsite is situated beside sparkling Tolsona Creek and is complete with table, litter barrel and fireplace. It is a full-service campground with tent sites, restrooms, dump station, coin-op showers, laundromat, water and electric hookups for RVs. While there, browse through their collection of neat old stuff from the turn of the century. These relics from Grandma's kitchen and Grandpa's workshop in a logging or sawmill camp will bring back memories of a simpler time. See how many items you can identify. Public phone. Open from May 20 through Sept. 10. $12 to $18 per night. Phone (907) 822-3865. [ADVERTISEMENT]   ♿▲

Tolsona Creek, grayling to 16 inches, use mosquito flies in still, clear pools behind obstructions, June, July and August. Best fishing 1.5 miles/2.4 km upstream from highway. **Tolsona** and **Moose lakes**, rainbow trout, burbot, grayling to 16 inches, all summer; good ice fishing for burbot in winter; boats, food and lodging.   ✦

A **170.5** (274.4 km) T **157.5** (253.5 km) **Tolsona Lake**, grayling to 16 inches, burbot, rainbow. **Crosswind Lake**, 18 miles/29 km north by floatplane, excellent fishing for lake trout, grayling and whitefish.   ✦

Tolsona Lake Resort. See display ad this section.   ▲

A **169.3** (272.3 km) T **158.7** (255.4 km) **Mae West Lake** trail. Paved double-ended turnout to south. The long narrow lake, fed by Little Woods Creek, is a little less than 1 mile/1.6 km away. Grayling fishing.   ✦

CAUTION: Watch for frost heaves and rough pavement several miles westbound.

A **168** (270.4 km) T **160** (257.5 km) Soup Lake to north. Trumpeter swans can sometimes be seen in lakes and ponds along this section of highway. In June and July look for wildflowers such as sweet pea, fireweed, lupine, cinquefoil, oxytrope, Jacob's ladder and milk-vetch.

A **166.1** (267.3 km) T **161.9** (260.5 km) Atlasta House, a local landmark, was named by the homesteader who was happy to have a real house at last.

A **166** (267.2 km) T **162** (260.7 km) Tolsona Mountain (elev. 2,974 feet/906m), a prominent ridge just north of highway, is a landmark for miles in both directions. This area is popular with berry-pickers in late summer and early fall. Varieties of wild berries include blueberries, lowbush cranberries and raspberries.

A **165.9** (267 km) T **162.1** (260.9 km) Paved double-ended turnout to south and 2-mile/3.2-km hiking trail to **Lost Cabin Lake**;
(Continues on page 302)

Lake Louise Road Log

This scenic gravel road leads north 19.3 miles/31 km from **Milepost A 159.8** Glenn Highway to Lake Louise Recreation Area. It is open year-round. Lake Louise is known for its lake trout fishing; ice fishing in winter. Excellent cross-country skiing. Many turnouts and parking areas along the road; views of Tazlina Glacier and Lake; berry picking for wild strawberries and blueberries (July and August), and cranberries (September).

Distance is measured from the junction with the Glenn Highway (J).

J 0.2 (0.3 km) **Junction Lake** to east; grayling fishing.

J 1.1 (1.8 km) Turnout with view of Tazlina Glacier and Crater Lake.

J 1.2 (1.9 km) Double-ended turnout to west. Just north is the road west to **Crater Lake.** There are a number of small lakes along the road with good fishing for grayling.

J 5.2 (8.4 km) **Old Road Lake and Round Lake** trails to east; rainbow fishing.

J 6 (9.7 km) **Mendeltna Creek** trail to west (0.5 mile/0.8 km); grayling fishing.

J 7 (11.2 km) **Forgotten Lake** trail to east (0.1 mile/0.2 km); grayling fishing.

J 9.4 (15.1 km) Beautiful pothole lakes. First view of Lake Louise northbound.

J 11 (17.7 km) Good view on clear days of the Alaska Range and Susitna River valley.

J 11.5 (18.5 km) Road west to **Caribou Lake;** grayling fishing. Turnout to east by Elbow Lake.

J 14 (22.5 km) Boundary of Matanuska–Susitna Borough.

J 15.5 (24.9 km) Gas station, public dumpster.

J 16 (25.7 km) **North and South Jan's Lakes** trails to north (0.4 mile/0.6 km); fishing.

J 16.1 (25.9 km) **Lake Louise Lodge.** See display ad this section.

J 16.5 (26.6 km) **Evergreen Lodge Bed & Breakfast.** See display ad this section.

J 16.8 (27 km) **Conner Lake,** rainbow and grayling fishing.

J 17.2 (27.7 km) Side road to lodge and Lake Louise State Recreation Area's Army Point and Lake Louise campgrounds; 52 campsites on 2 loop roads, firepits, toilets (handicap accessible), covered picnic tables at lakeshore and a boat launch. Well water. Camping fee $10/night or annual pass. Swimming in Lake Louise. Winter ski trail access.

J 17.2 (27.7 km) **The Point Lodge at Lake Louise.** See display ad this section.

J 17.6 (28.3 km) Turnout to west. Winter ski trail access.

J 18.8 (30.3 km) Airport road to west. **Private Aircraft:** Lake Louise airstrip; elev. 2,450 feet/747m; length 2,000 feet/610m; gravel. Seaplane base adjacent.

J 19.3 (31 km) Road ends at Lake Louise rest area; picnic tables, fireplaces, toilets, parking, boat launch.

Lake Louise, excellent grayling and lake trout fishing; lake trout 20 to 30 lbs., average 10 lbs., good year-round, best spring through July, then again in late September; early season use herring or whitefish bait, cast from boat; later (warmer water) troll with #16 red-and-white spoon, silver Alaskan plug or large silver flatfish; grayling 10 to 12 inches, casting flies or small spinners, June, July and August; in winter jig for lake trout.

Susitna Lake can be reached by boat across Lake Louise; burbot, excellent lake trout and grayling fishing. Both lakes can be rough; underpowered boats not recommended. **Dinty Lake,** access by boat across Lake Louise; grayling and lake trout fishing.

Return to Milepost A 159.8 Glenn Highway

Secluded lakes dot the countryside along the Glenn Highway. Many offer fly-in fishing opportunities. *(© Barbara Willard)*

(Continued from page 300)
grayling fishing.

A 162.3 (261.2 km) **T 165.7** (266.7 km) Paved turnout to south. Wildflowers include Jacob's ladder, tundra rose, paintbrush, yarrow, dwarf fireweed and lupine.

A 162 (260.7 km) **T 166** (267.1 km) **Tex Smith Lake** to north; stocked with rainbow.

A 161 (259 km) **T 167** (268.7 km) *CAU-TION: Bad frost heaves next 0.4 mile/0.6 km eastbound.*

A 159.8 (257.2 km) **T 168.2** (270.7 km) **Junction** with 19.3-mile/31-km Lake Louise Road (gravel) to Lake Louise Recreation Area. See LAKE LOUISE ROAD log on page 301 for details.

A 159.6 (256.8 km) **T 168.4** (271 km) **Little Junction Lake** trailhead, 0.3-mile/0.4-km hike south; grayling.

A 157 (252.6 km) **T 171** (275.2 km) *CAUTION: Watch for bumps in pavement and frost heaves westbound to Milepost A 135.*

A 156.9 (252.5 km) **T 171.1** (275.3 km) Trails to south to **DJ Lake** 0.5 mile/0.8 km (rainbow fishing) and **Sucker Lake** 4 miles/6.4 km (grayling and burbot).

A 156.4 (251.7 km) **T 171.6** (276.1 km) Views of Tazlina Glacier in the distance, eastbound as the highway crests hills. The glacier feeds into 20-mile/32-km-long Tazlina Lake at its foot.

A 156.3 (251.5 km) **T 171.7** (276.3 km) **Buffalo Lake**; stocked with rainbow.

A 156.2 (251.4 km) **T 171.8** (276.5 km) Tazlina Glacier Lodge.

A 156 (251 km) **T 172** (276.8 km) **Private Aircraft:** Tazlina airstrip; elev. 2,450 feet/747m; length 1,200 feet/366m; gravel; unattended.

A 155.8 (250.7 km) **T 172.2** (277.2 km) **Arizona Lake** to south; fishing for grayling.

A 155.6 (250.4 km) **T 172.4** (277.4 km) Paved turnout to south.

A 155.2 (249.8 km) **T 172.8** (278.1 km) **Gergie Lake** 1.3 mile/2.1 km to south; fishing for grayling and rainbow.

A 153 (246.2 km) **T 175** (281.6 km) **K.R.O.A. Kamping Resorts of Alaska** on the Little Mendeltna, a natural spring-fed stream. Excellent fishing for grayling, whitefish and others. Many lakes nearby. Fishing, hunting guides available. Gateway to Tazlina Lake and Glacier. Ski, hiking, snow machine trails. Modern hookups. Pull-throughs. Laundromat. Hot showers. Can handle any size caravan. Rustic cabins. Brick-oven fresh dough pizza. Homemade cinnamon rolls. Museum of Alaska's Drunken Forest, a large collection of unusual and artistic natural designs of trees. Minerals. Artifacts of Alaska's drunken forest. Free. [ADVERTISEMENT] ▲

A 152.8 (245.9 km) **T 175.2** (282 km) Mendeltna Creek bridge.

AREA FISHING: Mendeltna Creek, good fishing north to Old Man Lake; watch for bears. (The Mendeltna Creek drainage is closed to the taking of salmon.) Excellent fishing for grayling to $17^1/2$ inches and whitefish to 16 inches, May to November, use spinners and flies. Walk or boat away from the bridge.

A 152.7 (245.7 km) **T 175.3** (282.1 km) Paved double-ended rest area to north with picnic tables, dumpster and toilets. Rough road.

A 150 (241.4 km) **T 178** (286.4 km) Eastbound view of Mount Sanford and Mount Drum straight ahead.

A 149 (239.8 km) **T 179** (288.1 km) **Ryan Lake**; fishing for grayling and rainbow.

A 147.3 (237.1 km) **T 180.7** (290.8 km) **Alaskan Airventures.** See display ad this section.

A 147.3 (237.1 km) **T 180.7** (290.8 km) **Cache Creek** culvert. Grayling in late May and June. Trail leading from parking area to lake, approximately 0.5 mile/0.8 km. Small picnic area on east side of highway. Steep approach.

A 147 (236.6 km) **T 181** (291.3 km) *CAUTION: Very bad frost heaves next 0.7 mile/1.1 km westbound.*

A 144.9 (233.2 km) **T 183.1** (294.7 km) Lottie Sparks (Nelchina) Elementary School.

A 141.2 (227.2 km) **T 186.8** (300.6 km) Nelchina state highway maintenance station. Slide Mountain trailhead located behind station.

A 137.6 (221.4 km) **T 190.4** (306.4 km)

Little Nelchina State Recreation Site 0.3 mile/0.5 km from highway; 11 campsites, 15-day limit, no camping fee, no drinking water, tables, firepits, toilet, boat launch. Watch for moose and bear. ▲

A 137.5 (221.3 km) T 190.5 (306.6 km) Little Nelchina River bridge.

A 137 (220.5 km) T 191 (307.4 km) Boundary of Matanuska–Susitna Borough.

A 135.7 (218.4 km) T 192.3 (309.5 km) Small paved turnout. Highway widens eastbound. Truck lane next 2.3 miles/3.7 km westbound.

A 134.8 (216.9 km) T 193.2 (310.9 km) Watch for livestock on highway.

A 133 (214 km) T 195 (313.8 km) Paved trunout to north.

A 132.1 (212.6 km) T 195.9 (315.2 km) Caribou crossing. Gravel turnout to north. View of Mount Sanford eastbound. Caribou and moose seen in this area in winter. (The Nelchina caribou herd travels through here October through November.)

A 131 (210.8 km) T 197 (317 km) View west to the notch of Gunsight Mountain. From here to Eureka Summit there are views of the Wrangell and Chugach mountains.

A 130.3 (209.7 km) T 197.7 (318.2 km) Old Man Creek trailhead parking to north. Old Man Creek 2 miles/3 km; Crooked Creek 9 miles/14.5 km; Nelchina Town 14.5 miles/ 23 km. Established trails west from here to Palmer are part of the Chickaloon–Knik–Nelchina trail system.

A 129.3 (208.1 km) T 198.7 (319.8 km) Eureka Summit (elev. 3,322 feet/1,013m). Highest point on the Glenn Highway, near timberline, with unobstructed views south toward the Chugach Mountains. The Nelchina Glacier winds downward through a cleft in the mountains. To the northwest are the peaks of the Talkeetnas, and to the west the highway descends through river valleys which separate these 2 mountain ranges. This is the divide of 3 big river systems: Susitna, Matanuska and Copper.

A 128.9 (207.4 km) T 199.1 (320 km) Snow poles along roadside guide snowplows in winter.

A 128 (206 km) T 200 (321.9 km) Site of the first lodge on the Glenn Highway, the Eureka Roadhouse, which was opened in 1937 by Paul Waverly and has operated continuously ever since. The original log building is next to Eureka Lodge.

Eureka Lodge. See display ad this section.

Private Aircraft: Skelton airstrip; elev. 3,289 feet/1,002m; length 2,400 feet/732m; gravel; fuel mogas; unattended.

A 127 (204.4 km) T 201 (323.4 km) Gravel turnout to south.

A 126.4 (203.4 km) T 201.6 (324.4 km) Watch closely for turnout to Belanger Creek–Nelchina River trailhead parking to south. Eureka Creek 1.5 miles/2.4 km; Goober Lake 8 miles/13 km; Nelchina River 9 miles/14.5 km.

A 125 (201.2 km) T 203 (326.7 km) Gunsight Mountain (elev. 6,441 feet/1,963m) is visible to the west for the next few miles to those approaching from Glennallen. The notch or "gunsight" is plain if one looks closely. Eastbound views of snow-covered Mount Sanford (weather permitting), Mount Drum, Mount Wrangell and Mount Blackburn.

A 123.3 (198.4 km) T 204.7 (329.4 km) Belanger Pass trailhead: Belanger Pass 3 miles/5 km; Alfred Creek 6.5 miles/10.5 km; Albert Creek 8 miles/13 km.

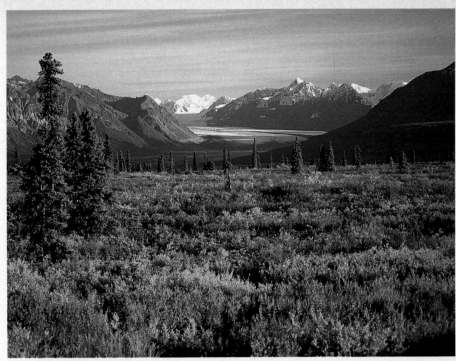

Nelchina Glacier seen from Eureka Summit, Milepost A 129.3. *(Jerrianne Lowther, staff)*

A 123.1 (198.1 km) T 204.9 (329.8 km) Old Tahneta Inn (closed).

Private Aircraft: Tahneta Pass airstrip; elev. 2,960 feet/902m; length 1,100 feet/ 335m; gravel/dirt. Floatplanes land on Tahneta Lake.

A 122.9 (197.8 km) T 205.1 (330 km) Gunsight Mountain Lodge (current status unknown).

A 122 (196.3 km) T 206 (333.5 km) Tahneta Pass (elev. 3,000 feet/914m). Double-ended paved turnout to north. Leila Lake trailhead (unsigned) on old alignment to north; grayling 8 to 14 inches abundant through summer, best fishing June and July. Burbot, success spotty for 12 to 18 inches in fall and winter. 🐟

A 120.8 (194.4 km) T 207.2 (333.4 km) Boundary of Sportfish Management Area 2 and Sheep Mountain Closed Area.

A 120.3 (193.6 km) T 207.7 (334.3 km) View eastbound overlooks Tahneta Pass. The largest lake is Leila Lake; in the distance is Tahneta Lake. Drive carefully along the southern part of Tahneta Pass.

NOTE: Watch for road construction westbound to Milepost A 109 in 1997–98.

A 118.6 (190.9 km) T 209.4 (337 km) Double-ended gravel turnout to south.

A 118.5 (190.7 km) T 209.5 (337.1 km) FAA road south to communication towers.

A 118.3 (190.4 km) T 209.7 (337.5 km) Large gravel turnout to south.

A 117.8 (189.5 km) T 210.2 (338.2 km) Turnout with viewpoint. Looking southeast of the highway, a tip of a glacier can be seen coming down South Fork Canyon. Knob Lake and the "knob" (elev. 3,000 feet/914m) can be seen to the northeast.

A 117.6 (189.3 km) T 210.4 (338.6 km) Squaw Creek trailhead: Squaw Creek 3.5 miles/5.6 km; Caribou Creek 9.5 miles/ 15 km; Alfred Creek 13 miles/21 km; Sheep Creek 15 miles/24 km.

A 115 (185 km) T 213 (342.8 km) Between Mileposts A 115 and 116 there are 3 turnouts with views of mineralized Sheep Mountain and Matanuska Glacier area.

A 114.9 (184.9 km) T 213.1 (342.9 km) Majestic Valley Lodge combines the rustic charm of a quaint mountain lodge with modern conveniences to cater to the indi-

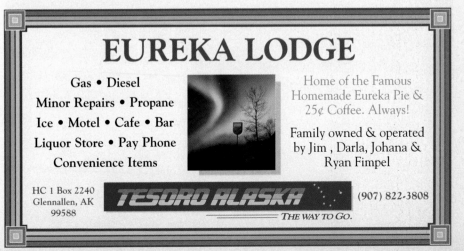

vidual 4 seasons of the year. Enjoy hiking treks, viewing Dall sheep and other wildlife in the Gunsight Reserve, blueberry picking, glacier walks, cross-country skiing and snow-mobiling. Gourmet meals, wood-stove sauna and an imposing view top off a relaxing day in the mountains. Cozy rooms include private baths, quilted coverings and use of the large viewing lounge. We offer trans-portation for groups to and from the lodge. Phone (907) 746-2930. See display ad.

[ADVERTISEMENT]

A 114.5 (184.3 km) **T 213.5** (343.6 km) In season, on slopes adjacent the highway and along old creek beds back from the road, are many kinds of flowers, including lupine, Labrador tea, bluebells, fireweed, chiming bells and large patches of forget-me-nots, Alaska's state flower.

A 114.3 (183.9 km) **T 213.7** (343.9 km) For Anchorage-bound travelers a vista of incomparable beauty as the road descends in a long straightaway toward Glacier Point, also known as the Lion Head, an oddly formed rocky dome.

A 114 (183.5 km) **T 214** (344.4 km) Winding road, long stretches without shoul-ders, watch for rocks and frost heaves west-bound between here and Palmer.

A 113.5 (182.7 km) **T 214.5** (345.2 km) **Sheep Mountain Lodge.** Our charming log lodge, established in 1946, has been serving travelers for half a century. We're famous for our wholesome homemade food, fresh baked breads, pastries and desserts. Our comfortable guest cabins, all with private bathrooms, boast spectacular mountain views. We also have RV hookups, full bar,

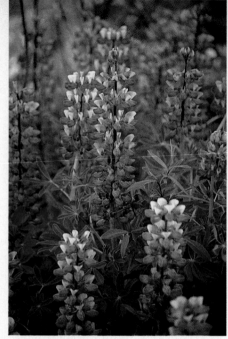

Nootka lupine and arctic lupine are found in Alaska. Both species are poisonous. *(© Susan Cole Kelly)*

liquor store and Alaskan gifts. You can watch Dall Sheep through our telescope and relax in the hot tub or sauna after a day of traveling or hiking. HC03 Box 8490, Palmer, AK 99645. Phone (907) 745-5121; fax (907) 745-5120. See display ad this section.

[ADVERTISEMENT]

Private Aircraft: Sheep Mountain air-strip; elev. 2,750 feet/838m; length 2,300 feet/701m; gravel/dirt; unattended.

A 113.5 (182.7 km) **T 214.5** (345.2 km) As the highway descends westbound into the valley of the Matanuska River, there is a view of the great glacier which is the main headwater source and gives the water its milky color.

A 113 (181.9 km) **T 215** (346 km) Gravel turnout to Sheep Mountain airstrip.

A 112.5 (181.1 km) **T 215.5** (346.8 km) View to north of Sheep Mountain (elev. 6,300 feet/1,920m) for 11 miles/17.7 km between Tahneta Pass and Caribou Creek. Sheep are often seen high up these slopes. The area surrounding Sheep Mountain is closed to the taking of mountain sheep.

A 112 (180.2 km) T 216 (347.6 km) Gravel turnout by creek. View westbound of Lion Head and first view of Matanuska Glacier.

A 111 (178.6 km) T 217 (349.2 km) Sharp curves and falling rocks for the next mile westbound.

A 110.3 (177.5 km) T 217.7 (350.3 km) Watch for mountain sheep.

A 109.7 (176.5 km) T 218.3 (351.3 km) Paved turnout to south. Access to bed and breakfast.

Tundra Rose Bed & Breakfast. See display ad this section.

A 109.5 (176.2 km) T 218.5 (351.6 km) Paved turnout to south.

A 109 ((175.4 km) T 219 (352.4 km) NOTE: Watch for road construction eastbound to Milepost A 118 in 1997–98.

A 108.4 (174.4 km) T 219.6 (353.4 km) Large gravel turnout to south.

A 107.8 (173.5 km) T 220.2 (354.4 km) Turnout with view of Glacier Point (Lion Head) and Matanuska Glacier. Exceptional picture stop.

A 107.1 (172.4 km) T 220.9 (355.5 km) Large gravel turnouts to south, viewpoint.

A 106.8 (171.9 km) T 221.2 (356 km) Caribou Creek Bridge and Caribou Creek trailhead. Hiking distances: Squaw Creek 9 miles/14.5 km; Alfred Creek 13 miles/21 km; Sheep Creek 15 miles/24 km; and Squaw Creek trailhead 18.5 miles/30 km. Caribou Creek trail zigzags up the mountainside between the highway and the creek, and leads back behind Sheep Mountain. A pleasant hike for good walkers.

Highway makes a steep descent (from both directions) down to Caribou Creek. The banks of this stream provide good rockhounding, particularly after mountain storms. There are turnouts on both sides of the highway here. Fortress Ridge (elev. 5,000 feet/1,524m) above the highway to the north. Sheep Mountain reserve boundary.

A 106 (170.6 km) T 222 (357.3 km) Large gravel turnout overlooking Caribou Creek canyon. Steep descent eastbound.

A 105.8 (170.3 km) T 222.2 (357.6 km) Road (closed to public) to FAA station on flank of Glacier Point. Mountain sheep occasionally are seen on the upper slopes.

A 105.5 (169.8 km) T 222.5 (358.1 km) Gravel turnout to south.

A 105.3 (169.4 km) T 222.7 (358.4 km) Turnout with views of Matanuska Glacier and the FAA station on Glacier Point.

A 104.1 (167.5 km) T 223.9 (360.3 km) Access to Glacier View School, which overlooks Matanuska Glacier.

A 104 (167.4 km) T 224 (360.5 km) From here to Milepost A 98 several kinds of wild orchids and other wildflowers may be found along the trails into the roadside brush.

A 102.8 (165.4 km) T 225.2 (362.4 km) Paved turnout to south with view of Matanuska Glacier.

A 102.2 (164.5 km) T 225.8 (363.4 km) Long Rifle Lodge. Welcome to Alaska's most fabulous dining view of the Matanuska Glacier. We offer a complete breakfast, lunch and dinner menu, specializing in home-cooked meals. Twenty-five wildlife mounts make our lodge a "must see" for all ages. Numerous hiking, cross-country skiing and snowmobile trails surround the area. In addition, we have motel rooms, gasoline, 24-hour wrecker service, laundry, showers, gift shop and a full-service lounge. Phone

Hikers follow a ridge in the Sheep Mountain area. (© Michael DeYoung)

1-800-770-5151. See display ad this section.

A 102 (164.2 km) T 226 (363.7 km) Access to foot of Matanuska Glacier via Glacier Park Resort. Admission fee charged.

Glacier Park. We would like to invite you to experience the Matanuska Glacier, at Glacier Park of Alaska. A 540-acre private resort located at the terminus of the Matanuska Glacier, in the heart of the

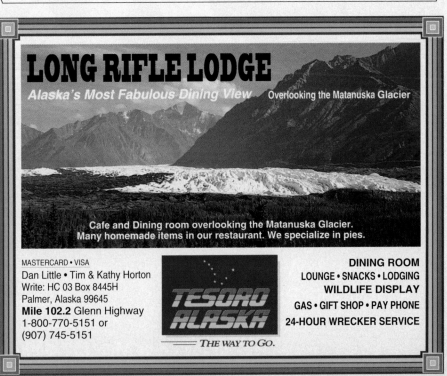

Chugach Mountains. This is a great addition to your vacation. We offer glacier tours, hiking, backcountry adventures, recreation camping, tent camping, gift shop, rooms, laundry, showers, liquor store, film, snack foods, picnic area, snow machining, cross-country skiing. Flightseeing with Glacier Air. Motorcoaches and tours welcome. Open all year. Access at Milepost 102 Glenn Highway. HC03 Box 8449, Palmer, AK 99645. Phone (907) 745-2534. See display ad. [ADVERTISEMENT] ▲

A 101.7 (163.7 km) T 226.3 (364.2 km) Paved turnout with good view of Matanuska Glacier, which heads in the Chugach Mountains and trends northwest 27 miles/43.5 km. Some 18,000 years ago the glacier reached all the way to the Palmer area. The glacier's average width is 2 miles/3.2 km; at its terminus it is 4 miles/6.4 km wide. The glacier has remained fairly stable the past 400 years. At the glacier terminus meltwater drains into a stream which flows into the Matanuska River.

A 101 (162.5 km) T 227 (365.3 km) Matanuska Glacier State Recreation Site; 12 campsites on loop drive, 15-day limit, $10, nightly fee or annual pass, handicap accessible, water and toilets. Excellent views of the glacier from hiking trails along the bluff. (Use caution when walking near edge of bluff.) Wildflowers here in late July include fireweed, yarrow and sweet peas. &▲

A 100.8 (162.2 km) T 227.2 (365.6 km) Large gravel turnout to south.

A 99.2 (159.6 km) T 228.8 (368.2 km) Gravel turnout to south, with viewpoint. Pinochle–Hicks Creek trail. Winding road with steep grades westbound.

A 97 (156 km) T 231 (371.7 km) Gravel turnout to north.

A 96.6 (155.5 km) T 231.4 (372.4 km) Private campground, lodge and store. Hicks Creek was named by Captain Glenn in 1898 for H.H. Hicks, the guide of his expedition. Ridges back from here, right side Anchorage-bound, are good rockhound areas. Anthracite Ridge has jasper, rosy-banded agate, petrified wood and rock crystal. Difficult to reach on foot.

Historical Hicks Creek Lodge and Campground. Creekside camping, camp store, pay phone. Quaint log cafe with charming frontier decor. We are known for our homemade soups and chili. Enjoy great Alaskan hospitality. Owner-operators Bob and Noreen Mills live on premises. Open year-round. (907) 745-0597. P.O. Box 2769, Palmer, AK 99645. [ADVERTISEMENT] ▲

A 96.4 (155.1 km) T 231.6 (372.7 km) Small gravel turnout to south.

A 94.9 (152.7 km) T 233.1 (375.1 km) Victory Road. Slide area. Look for lupine and wild sweet pea.

A 93.4 (150.3 km) T 234.6 (377.5 km) Cascade state highway maintenance camp.

A 93 (149.7 km) T 235 (378.2 km) Gravel turnouts both sides of highway. Views of Amulet Peak and Monument Glacier and Valley.

A 91.3 (146.9 km) T 236.7 (380.9 km) Cascade Creek culvert.

A 91 (146.4 km) T 237 (381.4 km) First view eastbound of Matanuska Glacier.

A 90.6 (145.8 km) T 237.4 (382 km) Paved turnout to south.

A 90.1 (145 km) T 237.9 (382.9 km) Turnout to south.

Long Lake is a favorite fishing spot for Anchorage residents. (© Susan Cole Kelly)

A 89 (143.2 km) T 239 (384.6 km) Purinton Creek trailhead. Bridge over Purinton Creek. Good blueberry patches in season if you can beat the bears to them. The stream heads on Anthracite Ridge and flows into the Matanuska River. Westbound, watch for coal seams along the highway.

A 87.8 (141.3 km) T 240.2 (386.5 km) Two small gravel turnouts to south.

A 87.6 (141 km) T 240.4 (386.9 km) Large gravel turnout above Weiner Lake.

A 87.4 (140.6 km) T 240.6 (387.2 km) **Weiner Lake** access; fishing for rainbow and grayling. 🐟

A 87.3 (140.5 km) T 240.7 (387.4 km) Turnout. Highway descends eastbound.

A 86.8 (139.7 km) T 241.2 (388.2 km) Slide area: Watch for falling rock.

A 86.5 (139.2 km) T 241.5 (388.6 km) Good gravel turnout overlooking Long Lake to south.

A 85.3 (137.3 km) T 242.7 (390.6 km) **Long Lake**, in a narrow canyon below the highway, is a favorite fishing spot for Anchorage residents. Fair for grayling to 18 inches, spring through fall; fish deeper as the water warms in summer. Good ice fishing in winter for burbot, average 12 inches. Long Lake State Recreation Site has 9 campsites, 15-day limit, no camping fee, no water, tables, firepits and toilets. Wildflowers include roses, sweet pea, paintbrush and lupine. Long upgrade begins eastbound. 🔵▲

A 84.6 (136.1 km) T 243.4 (391.7 km) There are several gravel turnouts westbound.

A 84.3 (135.7 km) T 243.7 (392.2 km) Large double-ended turnout. View of Matanuska River and unnamed mountains.

A 84.1 (135.3 km) T 243.9 (392.5 km) Large double-ended gravel turnout.

CAUTION: Watch for road equipment in slide areas next 4 miles/6.4 km eastbound.

A 83.2 (133.9 km) T 244.8 (394 km) Narrow gravel road to Ravine and Lower Bonnie lakes. (Side road not signed.) Drive in 0.8 mile/1.3 km on side road to reach **Ravine Lake**; fishing from shore for rainbow. **Lower Bonnie Lake** is a 2-mile/3.2-km drive from the highway; Bonnie Lake State Recreation Site has 8 campsites, 15-day limit, no camping fee, no water, toilets and boat launch. Fishing for grayling and rainbow. Steep and winding road beyond Ravine Lake is not recommended for large vehicles or trailers;

during rainy season this side road is not recommended for any vehicle. 🔵▲

A 82 (132 km) T 246 (395.9 km) Pyramid-shaped King Mountain is to the right (westbound) of the milepost as you look across the canyon. Several small gravel turnouts westbound. Highway ascends steeply eastbound.

A 80.8 (130 km) T 247.2 (397.8 km) Entering Matanuska Valley Moose Range westbound. Large gravel turnout to south.

A 79.5 (127.9 km) T 248.5 (399.9 km) Views of King Mountain (elev. 5,809 feet/1,770m).

A 79.1 (127.3 km) T 248.9 (400.6 km) Gravel turnout to south.

A 78.2 (125.8 km) T 249.8 (402 km) Gravel turnout with view of King Mountain and Matanuska River.

A 77.7 (125 km) T 250.3 (402.8 km) Chickaloon River bridge. Gravel turnout. Boundary between Game Management Units 13 and 14. The old Chickaloon Road winds upstream. Travelers have reported seeing no trespassing and private property signs a short distance up this road, indicating Native land claims along the road and river. Inquire locally about public access to the Chickaloon River via this side road before driving in.

A 77.5 (124.7 km) T 250.5 (403.1 km) Gravel turnout to south. Steep ascent eastbound. Highway parallels Matanuska River.

A 76.5 (123.1 km) T 251.5 (404.7 km) **CHICKALOON** (pop. 145); general store, gas station and river rafting office.

NOVA the Adventure Co. Since 1975. Scenic family float here in Chickaloon or join us on Lionshead, the most popular whitewater trip in Alaska—where the converging Matanuska Glacier produces several miles of class IV whitewater excitement, and a lunch

stop across the river provides a chance to hike on the moraine for a fantastic overview of the glacier. Several trips daily, including our Mid-Night-Sun-Run, mid-summer only. Suitable for first-timers, minimum age 12. All river gear provided. Check-in at main office here or rendezvous at Hicks Creek, Mile 96. Call 1-800-746-5753 for information and reservations. [ADVERTISEMENT]

A 76.2 (122.6 km) T 251.8 (405.2 km) King Mountain Lodge, established 1947, oldest continuously operated lodge on the Glenn Highway, with its own resident ghost. Authentic Alaskan atmosphere in the plank-floor bar ("Chickaloon Performing Arts Center") dates from coalmining days. Stay in a real miner's cabin or camp free along the Matanuska River. All cooking from scratch. Famous sausage gravy, musk ox or buffalo burgers. Home of the King Mountain Burger, the most bodacious burger of all. ▲ [ADVERTISEMENT]

A 76.1 (122.5 km) T 251.9 (405.4 km) King Mountain State Recreation Site. Pleasant campground on the banks of the Matanuska River with 22 campsites, 2 picnic sites, fireplaces, picnic tables, water, toilets. Camping fee $10/night or annual pass; 15-day limit. King Mountain to the southeast. ▲

CAUTION: Watch for road equipment in slide areas westbound to Milepost A 60.

A 73 (117.5 km) T 255 (410.4 km) Ida Lake/Fish Lake subdivision. Chickaloon River loop road.

A 72.3 (116.4 km) T 255.7 (411.5 km) Ida Lake is visible to the west through trees.

A 71.2 (114.6 km) T 256.8 (413.3 km) End slide area. Beaver pond to north.

A 71 (114.4 km) T 257 (413.6 km) Turnouts to south by Matanuska River.

A 70.6 (113.6 km) T 257.4 (414.2 km) Access to Matanuska River to south.

A 69.7 (112.2 km) T 258.3 (415.7 km) Chickaloon post office (ZIP code 99674) in office of private campground with RV hookups. ▲

A 68.6 (110.4 km) T 259.4 (417.5 km) Slide areas. Highway winds along bank of the Matanuska River. Several gravel turnouts; watch for soft shoulders along highway.

A 68 (109.4 km) T 260 (418.4 km) Pinnacle Mountain (elev. 4,541 feet/1384m) rises directly southeast of the highway—easy to identify by its unusual top. Cottonwoods and aspen along the highway. Talkeetna Mountains to the north.

A 66.8 (107.5 km) T 261.2 (420 km) Large turnout by lake.

A 66.5 (107 km) T 261.5 (420.8 km) King River bridge. Turnouts both sides of road.

AREA FISHING: King River (Milepost A 66.5), trout, early summer best, use eggs. **Granite Creek** (Milepost A 62.4), small Dolly Varden and trout, spring or early summer, use flies or single eggs. **Seventeen-mile Lake** (Milepost A 57.9 or 60.9), small grayling, early spring, use flies or spinners;

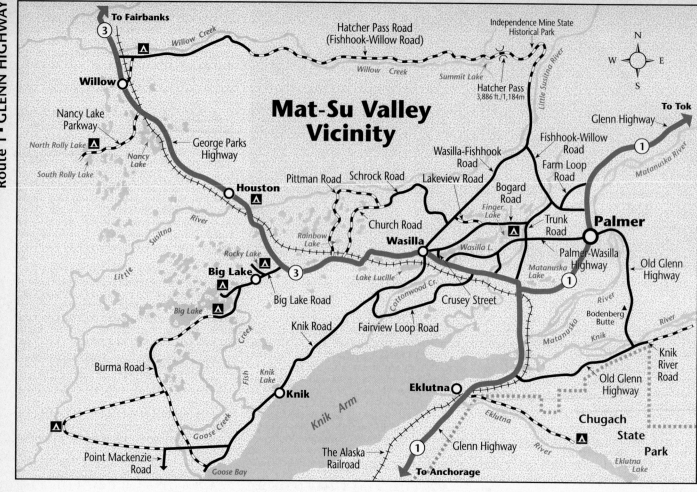

Mat-Su Valley Vicinity

trout, early spring, use eggs. **Eska Creek** (Milepost A 60.8), small Dolly Varden, spring, use flies or single eggs; silver salmon, August or September, use eggs. **Moose Creek** (Milepost A 54.6), trout and Dolly Varden, summer, use eggs.

A 66.4 (106.8 km) T 261.6 (421 km) King River trailhead (no sign in 1996); King River Crossing 5 miles/8 km.

A 62.7 (100.9 km) T 265.3 (426.9 km) Large gravel turnout with interpretive sign to south along Matanuska River. Dwarf fireweed and sweet pea in June.

A 62.4 (100.4 km) T 265.6 (427.4 km) Granite Creek bridge and access to private campground. ▲

River's Edge Recreation Park. Nestled between 2 mountain ranges on the banks of a clear-water creek, our campground offers secluded campsites with picnic tables and fire pits for tents and RVs. We have fresh well water, restrooms, private hot showers with dressing room, dump station and a few electrical hookups. Spawning king salmon, nesting bald eagles, wildflowers and berries. Site reservations accepted (907) 746-2267. Open mid-May to mid-September. [ADVERTISEMENT]

A 62.2 (100.1 km) T 265.8 (427.7 km) Sutton post office. Sign in at their guest book.

A 61.6 (99.1 km) T 267.6 (430.6 km) Alpine Historical Park, an open-air museum. featuring the concrete ruins of the Sutton Coal Washery (1920–22). Access via Elementary School Road. The museum is still under development. Donations accepted.

A 61 (98.2 km) T 267 (429.7 km) SUTTON (pop. 340) was established as a railroad siding about 1918 for the once-flourishing coal industry and is now a small highway community. Sutton has a fire department, general store, post office and gas station. Fossilized shells and leaves can be found in this area 1.7 miles/2.7 km up the Jonesville Road. Inquire locally for directions.

North Star Treks. Guided mountain hikes to Eska Falls. Day hike with panoramic views, wildflowers, meadows, alpine terrain, cascading waterfalls between Granite and Eska Mountain. Reservations recommended 24 hours in advance. Reasonable rates. Life-long residents of the area. More hikes, adventure tours and cross-country ski treks available. Call (907) 745-3144. [ADVERTISEMENT]

A 60.9 (98 km) T 267.1 (429.8 km) Jonesville Road. Access to Coyote Lake Recreation Area (3 miles/4.8 km); day-use area with pavilion, covered picnic tables, toilets, fireplaces, trails and swimming. Also access to Seventeenmile Lake (for recommended access see **Milepost A 57.9**). Drive north 1.7 miles/2.7 km to end of pavement; continue straight ahead for residential area and old Jonesville and Eska coal mines; turn left where pavement ends for Seventeenmile Lake. From the turnoff on Jonesville Road it is 3.1 miles/5 km via a rough dirt road (may be muddy) to **Seventeenmile Lake**; undeveloped parking area on lakeshore, boat launch, good grayling fishing. Inquire at local businesses about road conditions. ◄▲

A 60.8 (97.8 km) T 267.2 (430 km) Eska Creek bridge.

A 60.7 (97.7 km) T 267.3 (430.2 km) Paved double-ended turnout to south; pavement break.

A 60 (96.6 km) T 268 (431.3 km) Long, winding descent eastbound.

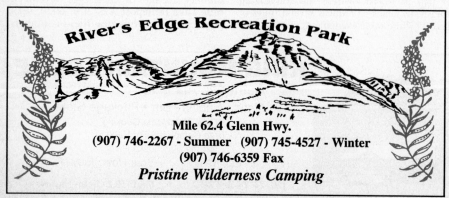

CAUTION: Watch for road equipment in slide areas eastbound to Milepost A 76.

A 59.3 (95.4 km) **T 268.7** (432.4 km) **Eska Farm.** Fresh, locally-grown vegetables and berries in season. We grow Alaska's best tomatoes. Locally made crafts and gifts. Visit our farm market gardens and greenhouses. Our picnic area makes a perfect lunch stop. Take a short nature walk to a scenic view point with a beautiful view of the Matanuska River and the Chugach Mountains. Owned and operated by long-time Alaskans. Easy access for RVs. See display ad this section.
[ADVERTISEMENT]

A 58.6 (94.3 km) **T 269.4** (433.5 km) Small gravel turnout to south. View of Matanuska River.

A 57.9 (93.2 km) **T 270.1** (434.7 km) 58 Mile Road. Access to Palmer Correctional Center. Alternate access (see also **A 60.9**) to Seventeenmile Lake. Drive north 0.5 mile/ 0.8 km; turn right and drive 1.7 miles/ 2.7 km; turn left, drive 0.3 mile/0.5 km; turn right, drive 0.2 mile/0.3 km; turn right again and drive 0.2 mile/0.3 km to lake. Undeveloped camping on lakeshore.

A 57.3 (92.2 km) **T 270.7** (435.6 km) **Timberlings Bed and Breakfast.** An incredible treasure among B&Bs. Log house on 150

acres of wooded hills with panoramic mountain views. Fantastic breakfast, artist hosts, exotic birds, friendly dogs. In-room TV, VCR. One guest room, shared bath. Call ahead: (907) 745-4445. Buz and Alma Blum, P.O. Box 732, Palmer, AK 99645.
[ADVERTISEMENT]

A 56.7 (91.2 km) **T 271.3** (436.6 km) Entering Matanuska Valley Moose Range eastbound.

A 54.6 (87.9 km) **T 273.4** (440 km) Bridge over Moose Creek. Highway ascends steeply from creek in both directions. Look for fossils in the road bank on the west side of the highway.

A 54 (86.9 km) **T 274** (440.9 km) Truck lane starts westbound.

ESKA FARM

Farm-Fresh Vegetables & Berries in Season
Local Crafts & Gifts
Gardens & Greenhouses
Picnic Area ▪ Nature Walk
Scenic View Point
Easy Access for RVs

See log ad at Mile 59.3 Glenn Highway

Irrigating farmland in the Mat–Su Valley. (© Barbara Willlard)

A 53.6 (86.3 km) **T 274.4** (441.6 km) Truck lane ends westbound.

A 53 (85.3 km) **T 275** (442.6 km) Side road to Buffalo Coal Mine. Access to Wishbone Lake 4-wheel-drive trail. Wild rose, geranium and chiming bells bloom along this section of highway.

A 52.3 (84.2 km) **T 275.7** (443.7 km) Soapstone Road. Wild geraniums in June.

A 51.2 (82.4 km) **T 276.8** (445.5 km) Fire station.

A 50.9 (81.9 km) **T 277.1** (445.9 km) Farm Loop Road, a 3-mile/4.8-km loop road connecting with Fishhook–Willow Road.

A 50.1 (80.6 km) **T 277.9** (447.2 km) Turn here for the Musk Ox Farm.

Musk Ox Farm and Gift Shop. The world's only domestic musk-oxen farm. The animals are combed for the precious qiviut,

which is then hand-knit by Eskimos in isolated villages, aiding the Arctic economy. During the farm tours in the summer, you can see these shaggy ice age survivors romping in beautiful pastures with Pioneer Peak as a backdrop. Open May to September. Phone (907) 745-4151. P.O. Box 587,

Palmer, AK 99645. [ADVERTISEMENT]

A 49.5 (79.7 km) **T 278.5** (448.2 km) **Junction** with Hatcher Pass (Fishhook–Willow) Road which leads west and north over Hatcher Pass to connect with the George Parks Highway at **Milepost A 71.2** north of Willow. Trail rides at Mile 5.2. See HATCHER PASS ROAD log page 310.

Rafter T Ranch Trail Rides. See display ad this section.

A 49 (78.9 km) **T 279** (449 km) Entering Palmer, which extends to **Milepost A 41.** Actual driving distance between **Milepost 49** and **42** is 1 mile/1.6 km. Just beyond here the highway emerges on a hill overlooking the Matanuska Valley, a view of the farms and homes of one of Alaska's agricultural areas, and the business center of Palmer.

A 42.1 (67.8 km) **T 285.9** (460.1 km) Arctic Avenue leads east through Palmer to the Old Glenn Highway, a scenic alternate

(Continues on page 311)

Hatcher Pass Road Log

The 49-mile-/79-km-long Hatcher Pass (Fishhook–Willow) Road leads north and west from **Milepost A 49.5** on the Glenn Highway to **Milepost A 71.2** on the George Parks Highway, providing access to Independence Mine State Historical Park (see Mat–Su Valley Vicinity map on page 308). It is a mostly gravel road, not recommended for large RVs or trailers beyond **Milepost J 14**. The road usually does not open until late June or early July and snow may close the pass in September. The road stays open to the historical park and to Hatcher Pass Lodge in winter, a popular winter sports area for snowmobiling and cross-country skiing. **Distance from junction with the Glenn Highway (J) is followed by distance from junction with the George Parks Highway (GP).**

J 0 GP 49.1 (79 km) **Junction** with the Glenn Highway at **Milepost A 49.5**. Fishhook–Willow Road heads west through farm country.

J 1.4 (2.3 km) **GP 47.7** (76.8 km) **Junction** with Farm Loop Road.

J 2.4 (3.9 km) **GP 46.7** (75.2 km) **Junction** with Trunk Road.

J 6.5 (10.5 km) **GP 42.5** (68.4 km) **Hatcher Pass Gateway Center.** See dis-

Visitors explore Independence Mine State Historical Park. (© Susan Cole Kelly)

play ad this section.

J 6.8 (10.9 km) **GP 42.3** (68.1 km) **Junction** with Wasilla–Fishhook Road.

J 7.2 (11.6 km) **GP 41.9** (67.4 km)

Edgerton Parks Road to Wasilla.

J 8.1 (13 km) **GP 41** (66 km) Hatcher Pass Management Area boundary.

J 8.5 (13.7 km) **GP 40.6** (65.3 km) Little Susitna River bridge. Pavement ends, gravel begins, northbound. Road parallels river; turnouts westbound.

J 9 (14.5 km) **GP 40.1** (64.5 km) Entering Hatcher Pass public-use area westbound. No flower picking or plant removal without a permit.

J 14 (22.5 km) **GP 35.1** (56.5 km) Side road to lodges and access to mine and trails. Trailhead parking for Gold Mint and Arkose Ridge trails.

Motherlode Lodge. See display ad on page 312.

Hatcher Pass Road begins climb to Hatcher Pass via a series of switchbacks. There are several turnouts the next 2.4 miles/3.9 km westbound.

J 14.6 (23.5 km) **GP 34.5** (55.5 km) Archangel Valley Road to Mabel and Fern mines and Reed Lakes. Road crosses private property (do not trespass). Winter trails (snowmobiles prohibited east of Archangel Road). Reed Lakes Trail access.

J 16.4 (26.4 km) **GP 32.7** (52.6 km) Parking lot to east, snowmobile trail to west.

J 17.3 (27.8 km) **GP 31.8** (51.2 km) Gold Cord Road provides year-round access to lodge and Independence Mine State Historical Park (1.5 miles/2.4 km). The 271-acre **INDEPENDENCE MINE STATE HISTORICAL PARK** includes several buildings and old mining machinery. Park visitor center is housed in the red-roofed building, which was built in 1939 to house the mine manager. The visitor center and assay office are open 11 A.M. to 7 P.M. daily from June through Labor Day; weekends the rest of the year. (Hours and days may vary.) Guided tours of the bunkhouse, mess hall and warehouse are given from June to Labor Day (weather permitting) for a nominal fee; phone visitor center at (907) 745-2827 or phone 745-3975 in Palmer for current information. Groups of 20 or more call ahead for tours. Office hours and tour times may vary, but visitors are always welcome to explore on their own.

Alaska Pacific Consolidated Mine Co., one of the largest gold producers in the Willow Creek mining district, operated here from 1938 through 1941. The Gold Cord Mine buildings (private property) are visible on the hill above and to the north of Independence Mine.

Recreational gold panning is permitted in the park. Some pans are available for loan at the visitor center.

Snowmobiling is prohibited in the park.

J 17.5 (28.2 km) **GP 31.6** (50.8 km) **Hatcher Pass Lodge.** See display ad this section.

J 18.7 (30.1 km) **GP 30.4** (48.9 km) Entering Summit Lake State Recreation Site; no ground fires permitted.

J 18.9 (30.4 km) **GP 30.1** (48.4 km) Hatcher Pass Summit (elev. 3,886 feet/ 1,184m). Several turnouts westbound.

J 19.2 (30.9 km) **GP 29.8** (48 km) Summit Lake, headwaters of Willow Creek. Summit Lake State Recreation Site under development. The road follows Willow Creek from here to the George Parks Highway.

J 20.4 (32.8 km) **GP 28.6** (46 km) Upper Willow Creek Valley Road to mine.

J 23.8 (38.3 km) **GP 25.3** (40.7 km) Craigie Creek Road (very rough) leads to mine sites. Remains of historic Lucky Shot and War Baby mines on hillside are visible on hillside ahead westbound.

J 24.3 (39.1 km) **GP 24.8** (39.9 km) Beaver lodges and dams.

J 25.6 (41.2 km) **GP 23.5** (37.8 km) View of Beaver Ponds to west; mine site visible to south below road. Road begins descent westbound into Little Willow Creek valley; numerous turnouts.

J 30.3 (48.8 km) **GP 18.7** (30.1 km) Leaving Hatcher Pass public-use area westbound.

J 34.2 (55 km) **GP 14.9** (24 km) Little Willow Creek bridge; large parking area.

J 38.9 (62.6 km) **GP 10.2** (16.4 km) Gravel ends, pavement begins, westbound.

J 47.9 (77.1 km) **GP 1.2** (1.9 km) Willow Creek State Recreation Area Deception Creek Campground; 7 campsites, 15-day limit, $10 nightly fee per vehicle or annual pass, covered picnic tables, water, toilets (wheelchair accessible). ♿▲

J 48 (77.2 km) **GP 1.1** (1.8 km) Deception Creek Bridge.

J 48.2 (77.5 km) **GP 0.9** (1.4 km) Deception Creek picnic area. Back road into Willow from here.

J 48.5 (78.1 km) **GP 0.6** (1 km) Road crosses Alaska Railroad tracks.

J 49.1 (79 km) **GP 0 Junction** with George Parks Highway at **Milepost A 71.2.** (Turn to the GEORGE PARKS HIGHWAY section.)

Return to Milepost A 49.5 Glenn Highway or Milepost A 71.2 George Parks Highway

Palmer

(Continued from page 309) route to Anchorage that rejoins the highway at **Milepost A 29.6.**

Highlights along the old Glenn Highway include the original Matanuska Colony Farms, U-pick vegetable farms, campgrounds and salmon-spawning viewing areas. See OLD GLENN HIGHWAY log on page 314 (Anchorage-bound travelers read log back to front). Access to Palmer High School west at this junction.

Palmer

A 42 (67.6 km) **T 286** (460.3 km) In the Matanuska Valley northeast of Anchorage. The city extends from about **Milepost A 49** to **A 41,** an actual driving distance of 2.1 miles/3.4 km. **Population: 4,100. Emergency Services:** Phone 911. **Alaska State Troop**ers, phone (907) 745-2131. **City Police,** phone (907) 745-4811. **Fire Department** and **Ambulance,** phone (907) 745-3271. **Valley Hospital,** 515 E. Dahlia, phone (907) 745-4813.

Visitor Information: Visitor center in log cabin across the railroad tracks on South Valley Way at East Fireweed Avenue. Pick up a brochure and map of downtown Palmer's historic buildings. Open daily 8 A.M. to 7 P.M. May to Sept. 15; weekdays 9 A.M. to 4 P.M. mid-September to May. Pay phone. Small museum in basement; Alaskan-made gifts may be for sale on main floor. Mailing address: Chamber of Commerce, P.O. Box 45, Palmer, AK 99645. Matanuska Valley Agricultural Showcase adjacent visitor center features flower and vegetable gardens.

Excellent local library, located at 655 S. Valley Way; open Monday through Saturday. Paperback and magazine exchange. Wheelchair accessible. ♿

Elevation: 240 feet/74m. **Climate:** Tem-

Palmer visitor center showcases Matanuska Valley flowers and vegetables.
(© Barbara Willard)

peratures range from 4° to 21°F/-16° to -6°C in January and December, with a mean monthly snowfall of 8 to 10 inches. Record low was -40°F/-40°C in January 1975. Temperatures range from 44° to 68°F/7° to 20°C in June and July, with a mean monthly precipitation of 2 inches. Record high was 89°F/32°C in June 1969. Mean annual rainfall is 15.5 inches, with 50.7 inches of snow.
Radio: Anchorage stations; KMBQ (Wasilla).
Television: Anchorage channels and cable.
Newspaper: *The Frontiersman* (twice weekly).
  Private Aircraft: Palmer Municipal Air-

port, adjacent southeast; elev. 232 feet/71m; length 6,000 feet/1,829m; asphalt; fuel 100LL, Jet A1, B. Butte Municipal, 6 miles/9.7 km southeast; elev. 64 feet/19m; length 1,800 feet/549m; gravel; unattended. Seaplane base on Finger Lake.

Palmer is a commercial center for the Matanuska and Susitna valleys (collectively referred to as the Mat-Su valleys). The town was established about 1916 as a railway station on the Matanuska branch of the Alaska Railroad.

In 1935, Palmer became the site of one of

the most unusual experiments in American history: the Matanuska Valley Colony. The Federal Emergency Relief Administration, one of the many New Deal relief agencies created during Franklin Roosevelt's first year in office, planned an agricultural colony in Alaska to utilize the great agricultural potential in the Matanuska–Susitna valleys, and to get some American farm families—struck by first the dust bowl, then the Great Depression—off the dole. Social workers picked 203 families, mostly from the northern counties of Michigan, Wisconsin and Minnesota, to join the colony, because it was thought that the many hardy farmers of Scandinavian descent in those 3 states would have a natural advantage over other ethnic groups. The colonists arrived in Palmer in the early summer of 1935, and though the failure rate was high, many of their descendants still live in the Matanuska Valley. Palmer gradually became the unofficial capital of the Matanuska Valley, acting as headquarters for a farmers cooperative marketing organization and as the business and social center for the state's most productive farming region.

Palmer is Alaska's only community that developed primarily from an agricultural economy. (Real estate now takes a close second to agriculture.) The growing season averages 80 to 110 days a year, with long hours of sunshine. The University of Alaska Fairbanks has an Agricultural and Forestry Experiment Station Office and a district Cooperative Extension Service Office here. The university also operates its Matanuska Research Farm, located on Trunk Road off the George Parks Highway, about a 7-mile/11.3-km drive from Palmer. The university farm conducts research in agronomy, horticulture, soil science and animal science.

PALMER ADVERTISERS

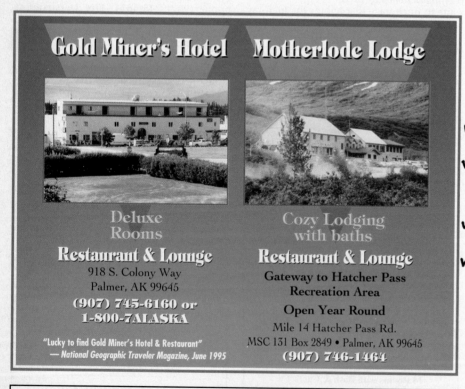

The community has a hospital, the Mat–Su College (University of Alaska), a library, banks, the Mat–Su Borough offices, borough school district, and several other state and federal agency offices. Palmer has churches representing most denominations. The United Protestant Church in Palmer, the "church of a thousand logs," dates from Matanuska Colony days and is one of the oldest churches in Alaska still holding services. It is included in the National Register of Historic Places.

ACCOMMODATIONS/VISITOR SERVICES

Palmer has all visitor facilities including 3 hotels, 2 motels, bed and breakfasts, gas stations, grocery stores, laundromat, auto repair and parts, and shopping. The Matanuska Valley region has several lake resorts offering boat rentals, golf, fly-in fishing, hunting and horseback riding.

There is a private RV park on Smith Road off the Old Glenn Highway. There are also private campgrounds on the Glenn Highway a few miles west of Palmer. The Mat–Su Borough operates Matanuska River Park, located 1.1 miles/1.8 km south of town at Mile 17.5 Old Glenn Highway; 80 campsites for tents or RVs, picnic area, water, dump station (fee charged), firewood for sale, flush toilets, hot showers, camping fee. **Finger Lake** State Recreation Site, about 6 miles/9.7 km northwest of Palmer just off Bogard Road, has 69 campsites, 7-day limit, toilets, water, trails, boating and fishing. Camping fee $10/night. To reach Finger Lake, take Palmer–Wasilla Highway north 4 miles/6.4 km from **Milepost A 41.8** to Trunk Road, then follow Trunk Road to Bogard Road. 🛶▲

Blueberry Cottage Gifts, Collectibles, Children's Gifts. Mile 3.2 Palmer/Wasilla Highway (Midtown Business Park), in the Big Blue Colonial House. Fun shop—children's gift area. Yankee candles, Boyd's full-line dealer, Lang stationery and cards, local artisans. Relax and browse in our potpourri-free shop. Open Monday–Saturday. Phone (907) 746-2939. [ADVERTISEMENT]

Farm Country Bed & Breakfast. Clean, comfortable, quiet atmosphere 2 miles from Palmer. Country-style home or bed and breakfast cabin. Plenty of room to accommodate 9–12 people. Mountain and glacier views. Farm animals to view. Cable TV, courtesy shuttle. Local tours available. Dining, flightseeing, golfing nearby. Tour and lodging packages available for groups. Major credit cards accepted. If you have a little country in ya, you'll love our hospitality. Open year-round. Reservations suggested. Phone (907) 745-1234 or (907) 746-0243; fax (907) 745-1234. P.O. Box 876922, Wasilla, AK 99687. [ADVERTISEMENT]

Mountain View RV Park offers breathtaking views of the Matanuska mountains.

Watch wildlife from your door. Full hookups, hot showers included. New bathrooms and laundromat, dump station. Good

Sam Park. Half-day scenic airboat tours on Knik River. Call (907) 745-5747 for reservations. Mail forwarding. Write P.O. Box 2521, Palmer, AK 99745. From Mile A 42.1 Glenn Highway (Arctic), follow Old Glenn Highway 2.8 miles. Turn east on Smith Road, drive 0.6 mile, turn right (0.3 mile). We're 3.7 miles from the Glenn Highway. See display ad this section. [ADVERTISEMENT] 🛶▲

Niebrugge Studio. Award-winning Alaskan artist Gail Niebrugge's private working studio—visit by appointment to purchase original paintings of Alaska landscape and wildlife. Gail's limited editions are available in major galleries and gift shops throughout Alaska. Call (907) 746-3256 for

directions and to schedule your appointment. [ADVERTISEMENT]

TRANSPORTATION

Air: No scheduled service, but the local airport has a number of charter operators.
Bus: Charter service only.

ATTRACTIONS

Go Swimming: The 25m swimming pool is open to the public 6 days a week (closed Sundays)—$4 for adults and showers are available. The pool is located at Palmer High School; phone (907) 745-5091.

Get Acquainted: Stop at the visitor information center, a log building just off the

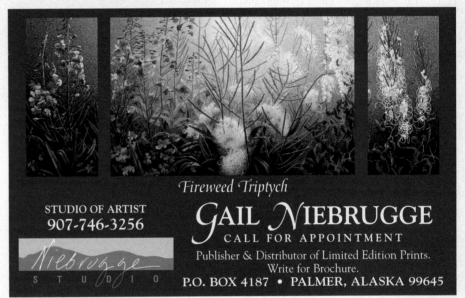

Fireweed Triptych

STUDIO OF ARTIST
907-746-3256

Niebrugge STUDIO

GAIL NIEBRUGGE
CALL FOR APPOINTMENT

Publisher & Distributor of Limited Edition Prints.
Write for Brochure.
P.O. BOX 4187 • PALMER, ALASKA 99645

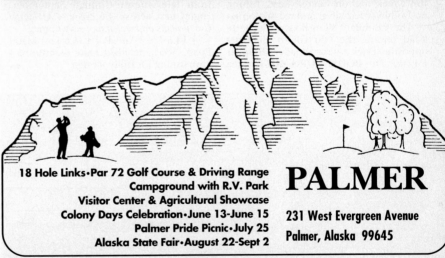

18 Hole Links•Par 72 Golf Course & Driving Range
Campground with R.V. Park
Visitor Center & Agricultural Showcase
Colony Days Celebration•June 13-June 15
Palmer Pride Picnic•July 25
Alaska State Fair•August 22-Sept 2

PALMER

231 West Evergreen Avenue
Palmer, Alaska 99645

Musk Ox Farm

- Mile 50.1 Glenn Hwy, Palmer
- A scenic Matanuska Valley farm
- Learn about the history of this unique animal on the guided tour
- Gift Shop featuring hand knit qiviut items

Open daily 10am-6pm, May-Sept.

Phone 907-745-4151
PO Box 587, Palmer, AK 99645

Old Glenn Highway (Palmer Alternate) Log

This 18.6-mile/29.9-km paved road is a scenic alternate route between Palmer and Anchorage, exiting the Glenn Highway at **Milepost A 29.6** and rejoining the Glenn Highway at **Milepost A 42.1**. The Old Glenn Highway goes through the heart of the original Matanuska Colony agricultural lands.

Distance from south junction with the Glenn Highway (J) is followed by distance from Palmer (P).

J 0 P 18.6 (29.9 km) Exit from Glenn Highway at **Milepost A 29.6.**

J 6.1 (9.8 km) **P 12.3** (19.8 km) Goat Creek Bridge.

J 7.2 (11.6 km) **P 11.4** (18.3 km) View of Bodenburg Butte across Knik River.

J 8.7 (14 km) **P 9.9** (15.9 km) **Junction** with Knik River Road, a gravel side road which leads to a RV park and a view of Knik Glacier. Pioneer Ridge/Knik River trailhead 3.6 miles/5.8 km from bridge. Knik River Road dead ends 11.4 miles/18.3 km from here.

Knik River RV Park. See display ad this section. ▲

J 8.8 (14.2 km) **P 9.8** (15.8 km) Knik River bridge; parking at east end of bridge.

J 11.4 (18.3 km) **P 7.2** (11.6 km) Butte branch U.S. post office. Pioneer Peak dominates the skyline southbound.

J 11.5 (18.5 km) **P 7.1** (11.4 km) South junction with Bodenburg Butte Loop Road which leads west (see description following), and **junction** with Plumley Road to east. Plumley Road provides access to **Jim Creek** trail off Caudill Road; fishing for Dolly Varden, silver and red salmon.🐟

The 5.8-mile/9.3-km Bodenburg Butte Road rejoins the Old Glenn Highway opposite Dack Acres Road (**Milepost J 12.6**). The **BODENBURG BUTTE** area

Pioneer Peak looms above an old barn. (© Loren Taft, Alaskan Images)

(pop. 1,232) has original Matanuska Colony farms and a commercial reindeer farm (visitors welcome, fee charged).

J 12.6 (20.3 km) **P 6** (9.7 km) **Junction** with Dack Acres Road, north end of Bodenburg Butte Loop Road (see **Milepost J 11.5**).

J 13.3 (21.4 km) **P 5.3** (8.5 km) Turnout to west. Bodenburg Creek parallels highway next 0.7 mile/1.1 km northbound; red and pink salmon spawn here from late August through September. Eagles nest across the creek. *CAUTION: Use turnouts and watch for heavy traffic.*

J 14.5 (23.3 km) **P 4.1** (6.6 km) Maud Road. Access to **Mud Lake** (4 miles/6.4 km); fishing for Dolly Varden.🐟

J 15.6 (25.1 km) **P 3** (4.8 km) **Junction** with Smith Road. Access to private campground. Trail rides may be available at a nearby ranch.

Mountain View RV Park. See display ad this section. ▲

J 16.1 (25.9 km) **P 2.5** (4 km) Clark-Wolverine Road; access to Lazy Mountain recreation area hiking trails. Drive in 0.7 mile/1.1 km; turn right on Huntly Road at T; drive 1 mile/1.6 km on gravel road and take right fork to recreation area and overlook. Picnic tables, toilets, berry picking.

J 16.8 (27 km) **P 1.8** (2.9 km) Matanuska River bridge. Access to river. *CAUTION: Watch for bridge construction in 1997.*

J 17.5 (28.2 km) **P 1.1** (1.8 km) Matanuska River Park; 51 campsites, picnic area, some pull-through sites, water, fireplaces, dump station, flush toilets, hot showers. Camping, shower and dump station fees charged. ▲

J 17.7 (28.5 km) Palmer airport.

J 18.6 (29.9 km) **P 0 Junction** of Old Glenn Highway (Arctic Avenue) at Palmer, **Milepost A 42.1** Glenn Highway.

Return to Milepost A 42.1 or A 29.6 Glenn Highway

"main drag" (across the railroad tracks at the intersection of East Fireweed Avenue and South Valley Way). The center includes a museum, artifacts, a gift shop and agricultural showcase garden.

Visit the Musk Ox Farm. Located east of Palmer on the Glenn Highway at **Milepost 50.1,** the Musk Ox Farm is the only place in the world these exotic animals are raised domestically. Hunted to near extinction in Alaska in 1865, the species was reintroduced in the 1930s. The farm is open May to September; admission is charged.

Visit a Reindeer Farm, located 8.1 miles/ 11.5 km south of Palmer via the Old Glenn Highway to Bodenburg Loop Road. This commercial reindeer farm is open daily in summer; admission is charged.

Play Golf. Palmer links golf course has 18 holes (par 72, USGA rated), rental carts and clubs, driving range and clubhouse. Phone (907) 745-4653.

Enjoy Water Sports. Fishing, boating, waterskiing and other water sports are popular in summer at Finger Lake west of Palmer. Kepler–Bradley Lakes State Recreation Area on Matanuska Lake has canoe rentals; turn off the Glenn Highway at **Milepost A 36.4.**

The Alaska State Fair, an 11-day annual event ending on Labor Day (Aug. 22 to Sept. 1, 1997), has agricultural exhibits from farms throughout Alaska. There are also food booths, games and rides. This is a very popular event, and fairgoers from Anchorage can tie up traffic. But it's worth the drive just to see the huge vegetables. Phone (907) 745-4827.

Other Special Events. The Palmer Pride Picnic takes place July 25, 1997. Colony Days Celebration is June 13–15, 1997.

Visit Scenic Hatcher Pass: A 6- to 8-hour drive from **Milepost A 49.5** near Palmer that climbs through the beautiful Hatcher Pass Recreation Area and connects with the George Parks Highway at **Milepost A 71.2.** Access to Independence Mine State Historical Park. See HATCHER PASS ROAD this section.

See the Matanuska Glacier: Drive 50 miles/80 km east on the Glenn Highway from Palmer to visit this spectacular 27-mile/43.5-km-long glacier, one of the few you can drive to and explore on foot. Access to the foot of the glacier is through a private campground at **Milepost A 102;** admission charged. If you're not interested in getting close, there are several vantage points along the highway and from trails at Matanuska Glacier Campground, **Milepost A 101.**

Glenn Highway Log
(continued)

A 41.8 (67.3 km) **T 286.2** (460.6 km) Junction with Palmer–Wasilla Highway. Gas station and shopping mall. West Evergreen Avenue access to downtown Palmer.

Carrs Pioneer Square shopping mall, located at this junction, is the site of a bronze sculpture by Jacques and Mary Regat dedicated to the Matanuska Valley pioneers.

Palmer–Wasilla Highway (see log on page 368 in the GEORGE PARKS HIGHWAY section) leads northwest 10 miles/16 km to the George Parks Highway. It provides access to a car wash, several other businesses, Mat–Su College, Finger Lake State Recreation Site (via Trunk and Bogard roads) and Wolf Lake State Recreation Site. At Mile 1.9 on the Palmer–Wasilla Highway is the Crevasse Moraine trailhead; parking, picnic tables, fireplaces and access to 5 loop hiking trails.

A 41.6 (66.9 km) **T 286.4** (460.9 km) Palmer Chevron. See display ad this section.

A 41.2 (66.3 km) **T 286.8** (461.5 km) First access road to Palmer business district for eastbound travelers.

A 40.5 (65.2 km) **T 287.5** (462.7 km) Fairview Motel & Restaurant. See display ad this section.

A 40.2 (64.7 km) **T 287.8** (463.2 km) Main entrance to fairgrounds (site of Alaska State Fair) and Herman Field (home of the Mat–Su Miners baseball team). Alaska State Fair is held the end of August to Labor Day (Aug. 22 to Sept. 1, 1997).

Alaska State Fair. See display ad this section.

A 39.2 (63.1 km) **T 288.8** (464.8 km) Outer Springer Loop. Gift shop. Short, steep trail to **Meiers Lake;** grayling fishing.

Colony Curio. A unique Alaskan gift shop with something for everyone. Our shop carries a broad selection of made-in-Alaska products, with a large variety of

Native and local crafts. Located next to the gift shop are 2 Matanuska colony homes, on the original Meiers' homestead. See authentic farm equipment, a true Alaskan garden and our 10-foot carved bear. Stop in for the friendly atmosphere you came to Alaska to find. See display ad this section. [ADVERTISEMENT]

A 38 (61.2 km) **T 290** (466.7 km) **Matanuska Farm Market.** See display ad this section.

A 37.4 (60.2 km) **T 290.6** (467.7 km) Kepler Drive; access to private campground and lake. ▲

A 37.2 (59.9 km) **T 290.8** (468 km) **Echo Lake** turnout; parking and trail to lake. Fishing for landlocked salmon and rainbow. ⬥

A 37 (59.5 km) **T 291** (468.3 km) Echo Lake Road.

A 36.4 (58.6 km) **T 291.6** (469.3 km) Kepler–Bradley Lakes State Recreation Area on Matanuska Lake; day-use area with water, toilets, parking, picnic tables, canoe rentals, fishing and hiking. Wheelchair-accessible trail to lake. The lakes are **Matanuska Lake, Canoe Lake, Irene Lake** and **Long Lake.** ♿

A 36.2 (58.3 km) **T 291.8** (469.6 km) **The Homestead RV Park.** Beautiful, wooded setting overlooking the scenic Matanuska Valley. Good Sam, AAA, 64 sites, pull-throughs to 70 feet, tent sites. Very clean restrooms and showers. Electric and water hookups; dump station; also, on-site portable dumping. Laundry. Picnic tables, pay phone. Enclosed pavillion and Matanuska Amphitheatre, home of the musical narrative "Cream Puff Pioneers." Area tours, evening entertainment. Square dancing Thursday nights. Walking and jogging trails, trout fishing nearby. Handicap access. Commuting distance to Anchorage. Caravans welcome. Phone (907) 745-6005. Toll free in Alaska 1-800-478-3570. See display ad this section. [ADVERTISEMENT] ♿▲

A 35.3 (56.8 km) **T 292.7** (471.1 km) CAUTION: Traffic signal at busy junction of the Glenn Highway and George Parks Highway (Alaska Route 3), which form a common highway into Anchorage. If headed for Fairbanks or Mount McKinley turn north on the George Parks Highway. See **Milepost A 35** GEORGE PARKS HIGHWAY section for details.

A 34.9 (56.2 km) **T 293.1** (471.7 km) CAUTION: Highway crosses the Alaska Railroad tracks.

A 34 (54.7 km) T 294 (473.1 km) Paved double-ended turnout west side of highway. Rabbit Slough.

A 32.4 (52.1 km) T 295.6 (475.7 km) Palmer Hay Flats state game refuge. According to the ADF&G, this is the most heavily utilized waterfowl hunting area in Alaska. Access to the refuge is via Fairview Loop Road off the George Parks Highway.

A 31.5 (50.7 km) T 296.5 (477.2 km) Bridge over the Matanuska River, which is fed by the Matanuska Glacier.

A 30.8 (49.6 km) T 297.5 (478.8 km) There are 2 Knik River bridges. Exits to parking areas below highway between the bridges. The Knik River comes down from the Knik Glacier to the east and splits into several branches as it approaches Knik Arm. Game Management Unit 14C boundary. Also boundary of Matanuska–Susitna Borough.

Moose winter in this area, and the cows and calves may be seen early in the morning and in the evening as late as early July. In winter, watch for moose on the road between here and Anchorage.

A 29.6 (47.6 km) T 298.4 (480.2 km) Exit to the Old Glenn Highway (Palmer Alternate). See OLD GLENN HIGHWAY log on page 314.

A 27.3 (43.9 km) T 300.7 (483.9 km) The highway crosses a swampy area known locally as Eklutna Flats. These flats are a protected wildflower area (picking flowers is strictly prohibited). Look for wild iris, shooting star, chocolate lily and wild rose in early June.

A 26.8 (43.1 km) T 301.2 (484.7 km) Highway crosses Alaska Railroad via overpass.

A 26.3 (42.3 km) T 301.7 (485.5 km) Eklutna overpass, exits both sides of highway. Access to Eklutna Road (description follows), the village of Eklutna and also access to Thunderbird Falls (see **Milepost A 25.3**) for Anchorage-bound travelers. West of the highway is the Indian village of **EKLUTNA** (pop. 25), site of Eklutna Historical Park, which preserves the heritage and traditions of the Athabascan Alaska Natives. Attractions include the historic St. Nicholas Russian Orthodox Church and a hand-built Siberian prayer chapel. Admission fee charged. Open daily mid-May to mid-September. The bright little grave houses or spirit houses in the cemetery are painted in the family's traditional colors.

Eklutna Historical Park. See display ad this section.

Eklutna Road leads east 10 miles/16.1 km to Eklutna Lake Recreation Area in Chugach State Park. General store at Mile 9. The recreation area has a campground, picnic area and hiking trails. The campground has 50 sites, drinking water, pit toilets and a 15-day limit. Camping fee $10/night or annual pass. The 32-unit picnic area is located at the trailhead parking lot, which will accommodate 80 cars and has a boat launch for hand-carried boats. Three trails branch off the trailhead: Twin Peaks, Lakeside and Bold Ridge. The Lakeside trail skirts Eklutna Lake and gives access to Eklutna Glacier (12.7 miles/20.4 km). **Eklutna Lake** is the largest lake in Chugach State Park, measuring approximately 7 miles long by a mile wide. Fed by Eklutna Glacier, it offers fair fishing for Dolly Varden. *CAUTION: After-*

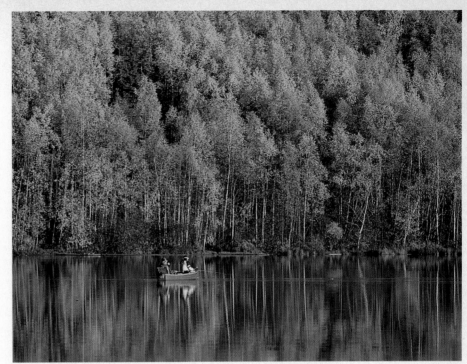

Aptly named Mirror Lake reflects fall colors. (© Harry Walker Photo)

noon winds can make the lake dangerous for boaters. Interpretive displays on wildlife and a telescope for viewing Dall sheep, eagles and other wildlife are located at the trailhead. ◄▲

Rochelle's Ice Cream Stop and Cheely's General Store. Best milkshakes, old fashioned banana splits, espresso, fishing licenses, ice, groceries, picnic supplies, propane, Eklutna Lake posters, and mountain bikes for rent. Cabins for rent—located within Chugach State Park wildlife viewing area. Shower and laundry available. Phone (907) 688-6201, fax (907) 688-6150. In Alaska 1-800-764-6201. [ADVERTISEMENT]

A 25.7 (41.3 km) T 302.3 (486.5 km) Highway crosses Eklutna River.

A 25.3 (40.7 km) T 302.7 (487.1 km) Thunderbird Falls exit (northbound traffic only) and northbound access to Eklutna Road (see **Milepost A 26.3** for description). Drive about 0.3 mile/0.5 km to parking area. Thunderbird Falls is about 1 mile/1.6 km from the highway. The scenic trail to the falls winds through private property on a 25-foot right-of-way and follows a hillside down to Thunderbird Creek. The falls are just upstream. *CAUTION: Do not climb the steep cliffs overhanging the falls!*

A 24.5 (39.4 km) T 303.5 (488.4 km) Southbound exit to Edmonds Lake residential area and Mirror Lake picnic wayside. The shallow, 73-acre **Mirror Lake** is located at the foot of Mount Eklutna; rainbow. ▲🐟

A 23.6 (38 km) T 304.4 (489.9 km) Access to Mirror Lake picnic wayside for northbound traffic only.

A 23 (37 km) T 305 (490.8 km) North Peters Creek overpass, exits both sides of highway.

A 21.5 (34.6 km) T 306.5 (493.3 km) South Peters Creek underpass, exits both sides of highway. Access to Peters Creek and portion of the Old Glenn Highway, which parallels the newer highway south to Eagle River, and provides access to a number of local services. PETERS CREEK services

include gas stations, grocery, car wash, body repair shop and restaurant.

Peters Creek Bed & Breakfast. Located on the north shore of Peters Creek only

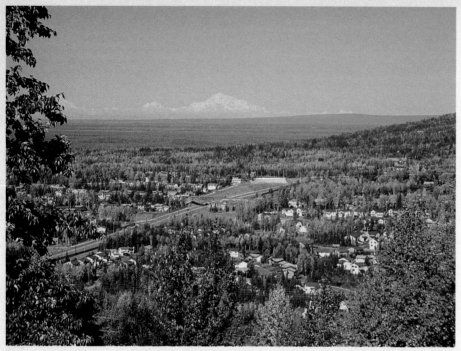

View of Eagle River, with Mount McKinley in the distance, from Hiland Road.
(© Barbara Willard)

peaceful break from your travels. Visit this unique, geodesic-dome cathedral, with birch ceiling and beautiful icons. Discover how this church connects to the early church and how Christianity came to Alaska 200 years ago. Bookstore. Monastery Drive off Old Glenn. (907) 696-2002. [ADVERTISEMENT]

A 15.3 (24.6 km) **T 312.7** (503.2 km) Exits for Fire Lake residential area, Old Glenn Highway and Eagle River.

A 13.4 (21.6 km) **T 314.6** (506.3 km) Eagle River overpass. Exit east for community of Eagle River (all visitor services), the North Anchorage Visitor Information Center and Eagle River Road to Chugach State Park Nature Center (a highly recommended stop); descriptions follow.

Eagle River

A 13.4 (21.6 km) **T 314.6** (506.3 km) **Population:** Area 18,040. **Emergency Services: Clinic,** phone (907) 694-2807. **Visitor Information:** The Anchorage Convention and Visitors Bureau North Anchorage Visitor Information Center is located in the Parkgate Building, along with the Southcentral Alaska Museum of Natural History, in downtown Eagle River. Stop by for information on Anchorage events, parking maps and brochures, or phone (907) 696-4636. For information on Eagle River, contact the Chugiak–Eagle River Chamber of Commerce, P.O. Box 770353, Eagle River, AK 99577; phone (907) 694-4702. You can also visit the Chamber office at 11401 Old Glenn Highway, Ste. 110A, in the Eagle River Shopping Center.

The Chugiak–Eagle River area was homesteaded after WWII when the new Glenn Highway opened this rural area northeast of Anchorage. Today, the Eagle River community offers a full range of businesses, most located near or on Business Boulevard and the Old Glenn Highway east off the Glenn Highway. There are motels, restaurants, supermarkets, laundromat, post office, gas stations and shopping center. Eagle River also has 30 churches, 9 public schools, a library and recreation center.

0.8 mile, from exit. Handicap accessible; open year-round. Rooms have private baths, cable TV, VCR, refrigerator, full Alaskan breakfast. Lovely new home, wooded setting, smoke-free environment, major credit cards accepted. Phone 1-800-405-3465, (907) 688-3465, fax (907) 688-3466. [ADVERTISEMENT]

Peters Creek "Petite" RV Park. See display ad this section. ▲

Peters Creek Trading Post. See display ad this section.

A 21.2 (34.1 km) **T 306.8** (493.7 km) Peters Creek bridge.

A 20.9 (33.6 km) **T 306.9** (493.9 km) North Birchwood Loop Road underpass, exits both sides of highway; turn east for community of **CHUGIAK** and for portion of Old Glenn Highway, which leads south to Eagle River and north to Peters Creek. There are many services and attractions in the Peters Creek–Chugiak–Eagle River area.

A 20.4 (32.8 km) **T 307.6** (495 km) Exit for North Birchwood Loop Road, Chugiak post office, senior center and services.

A 17.2 (27.7 km) **T 310.8** (500.2 km) South Birchwood Loop Road underpass, exits both sides of highway. Access to St. John Orthodox Cathedral, sled dog demonstrations, Chugiak High School and Old Glenn Highway.

Mush A Dog Team/Gold Rush Park. Year-round—a must see! Experience Alaska's living history—sled dog rides, gold panning, antiques at Pioneer Village on creek. Open daily, closed Sunday. Turn at South Birchwood exit. Drive ³/₄ mile past High School. Signs on left. Phone (907) 688-1391. [ADVERTISEMENT]

Saint John Orthodox Cathedral. Take a

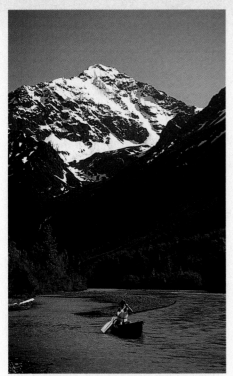

Canoes can put in at Mile 7.5 Eagle River Road. (© Michael DeYoung)

Attractions in Eagle River include artist Jon Van Zyle's studio and the Southcentral Alaska Museum of Natural History. The museum features 20 exhibits on Cook Inlet, dioramas of local ecosystems, and a duck-billed dinosaur skeleton. Located across from McDonald's at the corner of Easy

EAGLE RIVER ADVERTISERS

Eagle River/Chugiak Vicinity

To Wasilla
Eklutna

Knik Arm

Peters Creek

A 23.6

A 23

A 21.5

A 20.9

Glenn Highway

N. Birchwood Lp.

Beach Lake

Hardson Reservation

Chugiak Elementary School

Chugiak

S. Birchwood Loop

Birchwood Elementary School

Old Glenn Highway

Psalm Lake

Chugiak High School

A 17.2

S. Birchwood Loop

Monastery Dr.

Clunie Lake

Lower Fire Lake

Upper Fire Lake

Chugach State Park

Glenn Highway

A 17.2

N. Eagle River Access Road

N. Eagle River Loop

Business Blvd.

A 13.4

Eagle River

Eagle River Road

VFW Road

S. Eagle River Loop

A 11.6

Eagle River Bypass Rd.

Hiland Dr.

Eagle River

To Anchorage

Old Glenn Highway

Eklutna Village Road

Eklutna Rd.

The Alaska Railroad

Edmonds Lake

Mirror Lake

Peters Creek

Thunderbird Cr.

Little Peters Creek

Street and Old Glenn Highway; phone (907) 694-0819 for hours. Boondock Sporting Goods store on Eagle River Loop Road has an antique gun display and also rents fishing tackle.

From downtown Eagle River, follow scenic Eagle River Road (paved) 12.7 miles/20.4 km to reach the Chugach State Park Nature Center. Beautiful views of the Chugach Mountains from the center's veranda; telescopes are set up for viewing Dall sheep and other wildlife. The center has a pay phone and restrooms, and is the trailhead for the Old Iditarod–Crow Pass trail. There are also short hiking trails from the center and guided hikes and naturalist programs. The center is staffed part time; hours vary in summer and winter. Phone (907) 694-2108 for current information.

Kayaks, rafts and canoes can put in at Mile 7.5 Eagle River Road at the **North Fork Eagle River** access/day-use area with paved parking, toilets, fishing for rainbow trout, Dolly Varden and a limited king salmon fishery, along with cross-country skiing and snow machining in winter. The Eagle River offers class II, III and IV float trips. Check with rangers at Chugach State Park for information on river conditions.

Eagle River Car Wash and Duck Pond. Facilities available for washing cars, campers, trucks, boats and travel homes. Vacuums available. A duck pond on the premises is open to the public and features cedar viewing decks for observing some of the natural wild Alaskan waterfowl in their natural habitat. Mile 15.5 Old Glenn Highway. Turn off at North Eagle River access for car wash. See display ad this section.
[ADVERTISEMENT]

Glenn Highway Log
(continued)

A 12.8 (20.6 km) **T 315.2** (507.3 km) Eagle River Bridge.

A 11.6 (18.7 km) **T 316.4** (509.2 km) Hiland Road exit. Access to Alaska State Forest Nursery and Eagle River Campground in Chugach State Park. The nursery welcomes visitors; phone (907) 694-5880 for tours.

Eagle River Campground, 1.4 miles/2.3 km from the highway, has 58 campsites, walk-in tent camping, a 4-day camping limit, picnic shelter (may be reserved in advance), dump station, pay phones, flush toilets and drinking water. Camping fee $15/night. Day-use fee $3. Canoe/kayak staging area. This is one of the most popular campgrounds in the state. Phone the state park office at (907) 345-5014 for information. ▲

A 10.6 (17.1 km) **T 317.4** (510.8 km) Truck weigh stations on both sides of highway. Pay phones.

The last 9 miles/14.5 km of the Glenn Highway has been designated the Veterans' Memorial Parkway.

A 7.5 (12.1 km) **T 320.5** (515.8 km) Southbound exit to **FORT RICHARDSON** and Arctic Valley road. *CAUTION: Watch for moose.*

A 6.1 (9.8 km) **T 321.9** (518 km) Northbound exit to Fort Richardson and Arctic Valley Road. Road to Arctic Valley Ski Area is steep and winding but offers spectacular views of Anchorage and Cook Inlet. It is approximately 7.5 miles/12 km to the ski area. Alpine wildflowers in spring, good berry picking in late summer. Not recommended for large vehicles.

A 6 (9.7 km) **T 322** (518.2 km) Ship Creek.

A 4.4 (7.1 km) **T 323.6** (520.8 km) Muldoon Road overpass. (Exit here to connect with Seward Highway via Muldoon and Tudor roads bypass.) U.S. Air Force Hospital and Bartlett High School to the north, Muldoon Road to the south. Exit south on Muldoon for Centennial Park municipal campground. To reach the campground, go south on Muldoon to first left (Boundary); go about 100 yards then make a second left; continue about quarter-mile to campground entrance. There is a bicycle trail from Muldoon Road to Mirror Lake, **Milepost A 23.6.** ▲

A 3 (4.8 km) **T 325** (523 km) Boniface Parkway; access to businesses. Russian Jack Springs city campground is located south of the Glenn Highway on Boniface Parkway just north of DeBarr. Turn north for Elmendorf AFB. ▲

A 1.8 (2.9 km) **T 326.2** (525 km) Bragaw Street.

A 0.7 (1.1 km) **T 327.3** (526.7 km) Reeve Boulevard; access to **ELMENDORF AFB.**

A 0.3 (0.5 km) **T 327.7** (527.4 km) Concrete Street. Access to Elmendorf AFB.

A 0 T 328 (527.9 km) The Glenn Highway ends at Medfra Street. Continue straight ahead on 5th Avenue (one way westbound) to downtown Anchorage. Turn left at Gambell Street (one way southbound) for the Seward Highway and Kenai Peninsula. See ANCHORAGE section following for description of city.

ANCHORAGE

(See maps, pages 322 and 324)

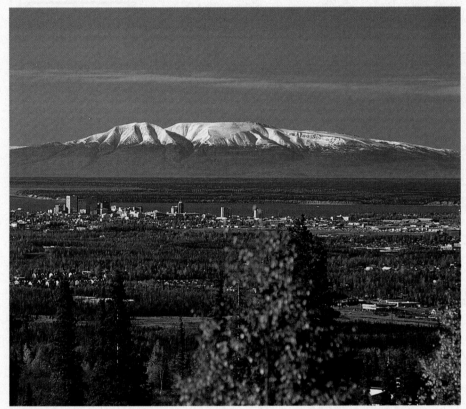

View of Anchorage with Mount Susitna, the "sleeping lady," in background.
(© Barbara Willard)

Located on the upper shores of Cook Inlet, at 61° north latitude and 150° west longitude, Anchorage is in the heart of Alaska's southcentral gulf coast. The townsite is on a low-lying alluvial plain bordered by mountains, dense forests of spruce, birch and aspen, and water. Cook Inlet's Turnagain Arm and Knik Arm define the broad peninsula on which the city lies. Anchorage is situated 358 miles/576 km south of Fairbanks via the George Parks Highway; 304 miles/489 km from Valdez, southern terminus of the trans-Alaska pipeline, via the Glenn and Richardson highways; 2,459 driving miles/3,957 km via the West Access Route, Alaska Highway and Glenn Highway/Tok Cutoff, 1,644 nautical miles/2,646 km, and 3 hours flying time from Seattle. Anchorage has been called the "Air Crossroads of the World." In terms of nonstop air mileages, Anchorage is the following distance from each of these cities: Amsterdam, 4,475/7,202 km; Chicago, 2,839/4,569 km; Copenhagen, 4,313/6,941 km; Hamburg, 4,430/7,129 km; Honolulu, 2,780/4,474 km; London, 4,487/7,221 km; Paris, 4,683/7,536 km; San Francisco, 2,015/3,243 km; Seattle, 1,445/2,325 km; Tokyo, 3,460/5,568 km.

Population: Anchorage Municipality 257,780. **Emergency Services: Police, Fire Department, Ambulance** and **Search & Rescue**, phone 911, CB Channel 9. **Police**, phone (907) 786-8500. **Alaska State Troopers**, phone (907) 269-5511. **Hospitals:** Alaska Regional Hospital, phone (907) 276-1131; Alaska Native Medical Center, phone (907) 279-6661; Providence, Alaska Medical Center, phone (907) 562-2211; Elmendorf Air Force Base emergency room, phone (907) 552-5555. **Dental Emergencies**, phone (907) 279-9144 (24-hour service). **Emergency Management**, phone (907) 267-4904. **Suicide Intervention**, phone (907) 563-3200 (24-hour service). **Rape & Assault**, phone (907) 276-7273. **Battered Women**, phone (907) 272-0100. **Pet Emergency**, phone (907) 274-5636. **Poison Control**, phone (907) 261-3193. **Road Conditions**, statewide, phone 1-800-478-7675 or (907) 273-6037.

Visitor Information: Log Cabin Visitor Information Center, operated by the Anchorage Convention and Visitors Bureau, is at 4th Avenue and F Street; open daily, year-round. Hours are 7:30 A.M. to 7 P.M. June through August; 8 A.M. to 6 P.M. in May and September; and 9 A.M. to 4 P.M. the remainder of the year. The cabin offers a wide assortment of free brochures and maps. Write 524 W. 4th Ave., Anchorage 99501; phone (907) 274-3531; Internet, http://www.alaska.net/~acvb.; e-mail at acvb@alaska.net. The bureau also operates a year-round visitor information phone with a recorded message of the day's special events and attractions, including films, plays, sports events and gallery openings, and it produces several publications including 2 visitor guides, a restaurant directory, a fall/winter discount book and a monthly calendar of events; phone (907) 276-3200. Additional visitor information centers are open daily at Anchorage International Airport, one on the lower level for passengers arriving on domestic flights; another in the customs-secured area of the international concourse; and a third in the lobby of the international terminal. The North Anchorage Visitor Information Center is located in the Parkgate Building, just off the Glenn Highway at 11723 Old Glenn Highway. The Anchorage Convention and Visitors Bureau offers information on community events, phone (907) 276-4118.

The Alaska Public Lands Information Center, 605 W. 4th, in the historic Federal Building, has extensive displays and information on outdoor recreation lands in Alaska; phone (907) 271-2737. (See detailed description under Attractions, this section.)

Elevation: 38 to 120 feet/16 to 37m, with terrain nearly flat throughout the bowl area.

Climate: Anchorage has a climate closely resembling that of the Rocky Mountains area. Shielded from excess Pacific moisture by the Kenai Mountains to the south, the city has an annual average of only 15.9 inches of precipitation. Winter snowfall averages about 70 inches per year, with snow on the ground typically from October to April. Anchorage is in a transition zone, between the moderating influence of the Pacific Ocean and the extreme temperatures found in interior Alaska. The average temperature in January (coldest month) is 15°F/-9°C; in July (warmest month), 58°F/14°C. A record 40 days of 70°F/21°C temperatures or higher was set in 1936, according to the National Weather Service. Record high was 85°F/29°C in June of 1969. Record low was -34°F/-37°C in January 1975. The growing season in the area is 100 to 120 days and typically extends from late May to early September. Anchorage has a daily maximum of 19 hours, 21 minutes of daylight in summer, and 5 hours, 28 minutes in winter. Prevailing wind direction is north.

Radio: KENI 550, KHAR 590, KYAK 650, KBYR 700, KFQD 750, KLEF 98.1, KFFR 1020, KKSD 1080, KRUA-FM 88.1, KATB-FM 89.3, KSKA-FM 91.1, KJMM-FM 94.5, KEAG-FM 97.3, KYMG-FM 98.9, KBFX-FM 100.5, KGOT-FM 101.3, KKRD-FM 102.1, KMXS-FM 103.1, KBRJ-FM 104.1, KNIK-FM 105.3,

(Continues on page 326)

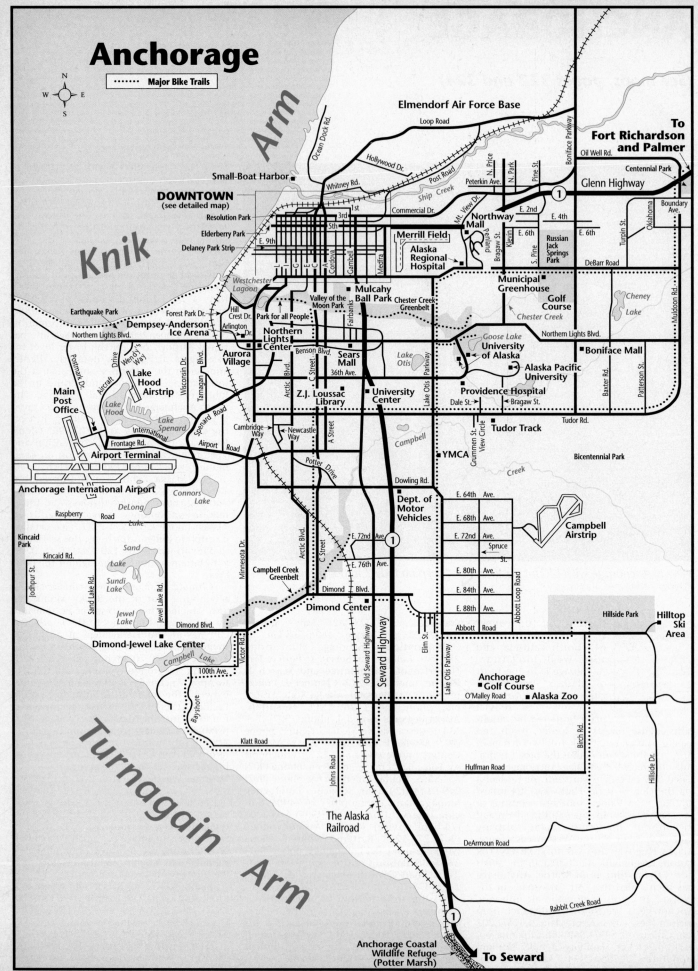

Anchorage

········· Major Bike Trails

Knik Arm

Turnagain Arm

Elmendorf Air Force Base

Loop Road

To Fort Richardson and Palmer

Centennial Park

Glenn Highway

Hollywood Dr.

Oil Well Rd.

Ocean Dock Rd.

Small-Boat Harbor

Whitney Rd.

Post Road

Ship Creek

Peterkin Ave.

N. Price

N. Park

Pine St.

Boniface Parkway

Oklahoma

Boundary Ave.

DOWNTOWN
(see detailed map)

Commercial Dr.

Mt. View Dr.

Northway Mall

E. 2nd

E. 4th

Turpin St.

Resolution Park

1st

3rd

5th

E. 6th

E. 6th

Klevin

S. Pine

Elderberry Park

E. 9th

Merrill Field

Bragaw St.

Ingra

DeBarr Road

Delaney Park Strip

Cordova

Campbell

Medfra

Alaska Regional Hospital

Russian Jack Springs Park

Westchester Lagoon

Municipal Greenhouse

Golf Course

Cheney Lake

Earthquake Park

Forest Park Dr.

Valley of the Moon Park

Mulcahy Ball Park

Chester Creek Greenbelt

Chester Creek

Muldoon Rd.

Dempsey-Anderson Ice Arena

Hill Crest Dr.

Park for all People

Fairbanks

Northern Lights Blvd.

Northern Lights Blvd.

Arlington Dr.

Northern Lights Center

Benson Blvd.

Goose Lake

University of Alaska

Boniface Mall

Postmark Dr.

Wendy's Way

Aurora Village

Sears Mall

36th Ave.

Lake Otis

Alaska Pacific University

Wisconsin Dr.

Turnagain Blvd.

Arctic Blvd.

C Street

Lake Otis Parkway

Baxter Rd.

Patterson St.

Main Post Office

Aircraft Drive

Lake Hood Airstrip

Lake Hood

Spenard Road

Z.J. Loussac Library

University Center

Providence Hospital

Dale St.

Bragaw St.

Lake Spenard

Cambridge Way

Newcastle Way

A Street

Grummen St.

View Circle

Tudor Track

Tudor Rd.

Frontage Rd.

International Airport Road

Potter Drive

Campbell

Airport Terminal

Campbell Creek

YMCA

Bicentennial Park

Anchorage International Airport

Connors Lake

Dowling Rd.

DeLong Lake

Dept. of Motor Vehicles

E. 64th Ave.

Campbell Airstrip

Raspberry Road

E. 68th Ave.

Kincaid Park

Sand Lake

E. 72nd Ave.

E. 72nd Ave.

Spruce St.

Kincaid Rd.

Sundi Lake

E. 76th Ave.

E. 80th Ave.

Jodhpur St.

Sand Lake Rd.

Jewel Lake Rd.

Minnesota Dr.

Arctic Blvd.

C Street

Dimond Blvd.

E. 84th Ave.

Abbott Loop Road

Hillside Park

Hilltop Ski Area

Jewel Lake

Campbell Creek Greenbelt

E. 88th Ave.

Dimond Blvd.

Dimond Center

Abbott Road

Dimond-Jewel Lake Center

Victor Rd.

Campbell Lake

Old Seward Highway

Seward Highway

Elim St.

Anchorage Golf Course

Lake Otis Parkway

100th Ave.

Bayshore

O'Malley Road

Alaska Zoo

Birch Rd.

Klatt Road

Huffman Road

Hillside Dr.

Johns Road

The Alaska Railroad

DeArmoun Road

Rabbit Creek Road

Anchorage Coastal Wildlife Refuge (Potter Marsh)

To Seward

Downtown Anchorage

Whitney Rd. • Ship Creek • Post Road
Ship Creek Salmon Viewing Platform
Warehouse Ave.
Alaska Railroad Depot
Alaska Native Medical Center
W. 1st • E. 1st • E. 1st
W. 2nd • E. 2nd
W. 3rd • E. 3rd
The Alaska • Christensen
Oscar Anderson House • Resolution Park
W. 4th • Old Federal Bldg. • Sunshine Mall • Post Office Mall • Pioneer Schoolhouse • E. 4th • Mile 0 Glenn Highway
Elderberry Park
State Court Bldg. • Log Cabin Visitor Center • Old City Hall • Convention Center • W. 5th • A Street • E. 5th
Visual Arts Center • 5th Ave. Mall • Center for the Performing Arts • W. 6th • E. 6th
Bus Accommodation Center • City • Police Fire • Anchorage Museum of History and Art • W. 7th • E. 7th
Hostel • Hall • Federal Bldg. • City Cemetery • W. 8th • E. 8th
W. 9th • E. 9th • Gambell St. • Ingra St. • Medfra St.
Delaney Park Strip • Neighborhood Health Center
W. 10th • Barrow St. • Cordova St. • Denali St. • Eagle St. • Fairbanks St. • E. 10th
W. 11th • E. 11th • Hyder St. • Ingra St. • Juneau St. • Karluk St. • Latouche St. • Medfra St. • Nelchina St. • Orca St.
W. 12th • E. 12th
W. 13th • I Street • H Street • G Street • F Street • E Street • D Street • C Street • B Street • A Street • E. 13th
P Street • O Street • N Street • M Street • Inlet Pl. • K Street • W. 14th • E. 14th
W. 15th • E. 15th
Virginia Ct. • L Street • Coffey Ln. • W. 16th • W. 15th Ter. • Avenues West • Avenues East • E. 15th Ter. • George M. Sullivan Sports Arena • Mile 0 Seward Highway • Tyonek Dr. • McHugh Ln.
E. 16th • E. 16th Ter.
Mulcahy Ball Park • Ben Boeke Arena
Knik Arm

$22

The movement of Portage Glacier is measured in inches per day. Our cruise is measured in gasps per hour.

Never before has something that moves so slow inspired reactions so large. Gray Line of Alaska's Portage Glacier cruise takes you aboard the mv Ptarmigan for a comfortable one–hour cruise to within 300 yards of this massive active glacier. Narrated by a representative from the US Forest Service, this tour gives you an up-close view of one of the most spectacular glaciers in all of Alaska.

Departures: Daily, May 19–Sept 15 at 10:30 am, 12:00 pm, 1:30 pm, 3:00 pm, and 4:30 pm.
Later departures may be available during the season.
Please contact Portage Glacier Cruises at (907) 783–2983.

Gray Line of Alaska
A DIVISION OF HOLLAND AMERICA LINE-WESTOUR

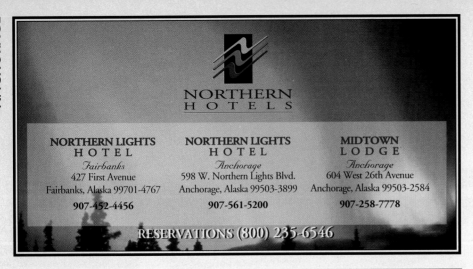

Summer maximum of daylight hours in Anchorage is 19 hours and 21 minutes.

(Continued from page 321)
KWHL-FM 106.5, KASH-FM 107.5. **Television:** KTUU (NBC), Channel 2; KTBY (Fox), Channel 4; KYES (independent), Channel 5; KAKM (PBS), Channel 7; KTVA (CBS), Channel 11; KIMO (ABC), Channel 13; and UHF channels. Pay cable television is also available. **Newspapers:** *Anchorage Daily News* (daily); *Alaska Journal of Commerce, Anchorage Press* (weekly); *Chugiak-Eagle River Star* (semi-weekly).

Private Aircraft: Anchorage airports provide facilities and services to accommodate all types of aircraft. Consult the *Alaska Supplement,* the *Anchorage VFR Terminal Area Chart* and *Terminal Alaska Book* for the following airports: Anchorage International, Merrill Field, Campbell airstrip, and Lake Hood seaplane and strip.

HISTORY AND ECONOMY

In 1914 Congress authorized the building of a railroad linking an ocean port with the

ANCHORAGE ADVERTISERS

interior river shipping routes. The anchorage at the mouth of Ship Creek was chosen as the construction camp and headquarters for the Alaskan Engineering Commission. By the summer of 1915 the camp's population, housed mainly in tents, had grown to about 2,000.

The name Anchorage (earlier names included Woodrow, Ship Creek, Ship Creek Landing and Knik Anchorage) was chosen by the federal government when the first post office opened in May 1915. A few months later the bluff south of the creek was cleared and surveyed, and 655 lots, on 347 acres, were auctioned off by the General Land Office for $148,000. The intersection of 4th Avenue and C Street was regarded as the center of the business district, and by late summer about 100 wooden structures had been built. Anchorage continued to prosper and was incorporated in 1920.

Anchorage's growth has been in spurts, propelled by: (1) construction of the Alaska Railroad and the transfer of its headquarters from Seward to Anchorage in 1917; (2) colonization of the Matanuska Valley, a farming region 45 miles/72 km to the north, in 1935; (3) construction of Fort Richardson and Elmendorf Field in 1940; (4) oil discoveries between 1957 and 1961 in Cook Inlet; and (5) the development of North Slope oil fields

and the construction of the trans-Alaska pipeline—all since 1968.

The earthquake of March 27, 1964, which caused millions of dollars in damage, resulted in a flurry of new construction. Government relief funds (in the form of Small Business

Administration loans) were offered to those who wished to rebuild. Most did, and a distinctly new Anchorage began to emerge.

In the 1970s and 1980s, Anchorage underwent a population and construction boom tied to oil production. Oil companies located their headquarters in Anchorage. ARCO completed its 21-story office tower in 1983. The decline in oil prices in recent years has brought about a slower economy than was enjoyed in those "boom" years. Today, Anchorage is a center of commerce and distribution for the rest of Alaska.

DESCRIPTION

Anchorage is a sprawling city, bordered on the east by the stunningly beautiful Chugach Mountain Range and on the west by Knik Arm of Cook Inlet. On a clear day, you can catch a tantalizing glimpse of Mount McKinley, 135 miles/217 km to the north.

Many new buildings dot the Anchorage skyline. Millions of dollars were allocated by the legislature for Project 80s, the largest construction program in Anchorage's history. Perhaps best known is the Alaska Center for the Performing Arts, located at the corner of 5th Avenue and F Street. Construction costs on the center grew from an original estimate of $22 million to more than $70 million. Visitors may notice the fences on the center's roof: these had to be added to prevent snow from sliding off the steep pitch of the roof and onto pedestrians below. Other completed projects include the George M. Sullivan Sports Arena, William A. Egan Civic and Convention Center, Z.J. Loussac Public Library, and a major expansion and renovation of the Anchorage Museum of History and Art.

With its curious mixture of the old frontier and the jet age, Anchorage is truly a unique place. In profile, the town has:

• About 80 schools, including special education and alternative public programs and a number of privately operated schools, also the University of Alaska, Alaska Pacific University and Alaska Business College.

• More than 200 churches and temples.

• Z.J. Loussac Public Library, plus 4 branch libraries, National Bank of Alaska Heritage Library Museum, Dept. of the Interior's Alaska Resource Library, the Oil Spill Public Information Center, Alaska State Library Services for the Blind and the University of Alaska Library.

• Municipal bus service and 7 taxi services.

• In the arts—Dance: Alaska Center for Performing Arts; Alaska Dance Theatre; Anchorage Concert Assoc.; Anchorage Opera; Ballet Alaska. Music: Alaska Airlines Autumn Classics; Anchorage Concert Chorus; Anchorage Community Concert Band; Anchorage Concert Assoc.; Anchorage Children's Choir; Anchorage Symphony Orchestra; Anchorage Festival of Music; Sweet Adelines (Cheechako and Sourdough chapters); University of Alaska Anchorage Singers; Young People's Concerts. Theater: Out North Theater Company; Alaska Junior Theater; Alaska Theatre of Youth; Anchorage Community Theatre; Alaska Stage Company; Valley Performing Arts; UAA Theatre; Alaska Festival Theatre; Cyrano's Off Center Playhouse. Art: About 20 art galleries.

• An award–winning trail system, including 75 miles of summer hiking trails, 120 miles of paved bike trails and 105 miles of maintained ski trails.

ACCOMMODATIONS/VISITOR SERVICES

There are more than 70 motels and hotels in the Anchorage area with prices for a double room ranging from $50 to $70 and up. Reservations are a must. Bed-and-breakfast accommodations are also available in more than 100 private residences.

Hostelling International–Anchorage is located at 700 H St., 1 block from the People Mover Transit Center in downtown Anchorage. The hostel is open 7:30 A.M. to noon and 5 P.M. to midnight, June through September; 8:30 A.M. to noon and 5 P.M. to 11 P.M., October through May. Cost for members is $15 per night, nonmembers $18. American Youth Hostel cards available at the hostel or by mail. The hostel has dormitory rooms with bunkbeds, kitchen facilities, common rooms, laundry room and TV room. For information or to make reservations no less than 1 day in advance with VISA or MasterCard, phone (907) 276-3635, or write for reservations (prepayment required): 700 H St., Anchorage 99501.

Spenard Hostel International is a non-affiliated hostel located on the bus line at 2845 W. 42nd Place. Cost is $12–$15 per night. For more information or to make reservations, phone (907) 248-5036. E-mail: spnrdhstl@alaskalife.net.

Restaurants number more than 600, with many major fast-food chains, formal dining rooms and specialty establishments including Italian, Japanese, Korean, Chinese (Cantonese and Mandarin), Mexican, Polynesian, Greek, German, Sicilian, Thai, soul food, seafood, smorgasbord and vegetarian.

Arctic Fox Bed & Breakfast Inn. 326 E. 2nd Ct., Anchorage, AK 99501. Phone (907) 272-4818, fax (907) 272-4819. Quiet, convenient, downtown location with beautiful inlet view. Tastefully decorated rooms and

Home.
Coming & Going.

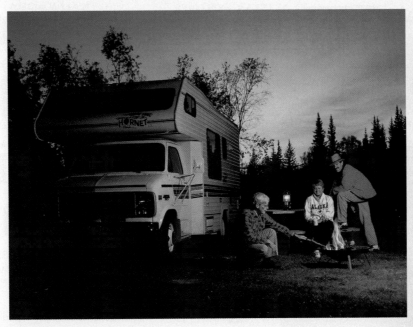

MotorHOME is where the heart is.
So put your heart into exploring Alaska at your OWN pace. Relax. View breath-taking scenery, sights & wildlife from your mobile living room.

Remember, only ABC Motorhomes offers you the convenient "ONE WAY—EITHER WAY" advantage...featuring Alaska from Anywhere USA!

ABC MOTORHOME & CAR RENTALS

ABC MOTORHOMES
2360 Commercial Dr.
Anchorage, Alaska 99501

toll free: 800-421-7456
phone: 907-279-2000
fax : 907-243-6363

ABC Rental Bonuses

- **Convenient airport locations**
- *Unlimited mileage!*
- **Housekeeping/Linen package**
- **No cleaning charges**
- **Complete orientation**
- **Full coverage insurance**
- **24-hour customer assistance**
- **Alaska's largest fleet**
- **Experience since 1961**
- *"ONE WAY"* advantages!

Pickup/Drop-off locations: Anchorage, Skagway, Seattle (WA), ElkharT (IN), Phoenix (AZ).

1•800•421•7456

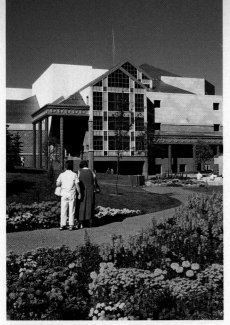

Performing Arts Center in Anchorage Town Square. (© Loren Taft)

corporate suites with moderate summer rates, low winter rates. Near all major downtown hotels, restaurants, museum, bike trail, train station and Ship Creek (salmon fishing). Laundry facilities, private baths, TV and phone in rooms. [ADVERTISEMENT]

Caribou Inn. 501 L Street, Anchorage, AK 99501. Clean, comfortable rooms in an excellent downtown Anchorage location. Shared or private bath, some with kitchenettes. Daily or weekly rates, major credit cards accepted. Free shuttle to airport and train station. (907) 272-0444 or fax (907) 274-4828. E-mail: caribou@alaska.net. [ADVERTISEMENT]

Glacier Way Bed & Breakfast. 2051 Glacier St., Anchorage, Alaska. Five luxurious rooms, hilltop setting, quiet, close to town. Stay includes: Jacuzzi, Habitat, pool, table tennis at no extra charge. Back yard accesses 180 miles of bike trails, ski trails. $65 single, $75 doubles and special rates for off season. Call (907) 337-5201, (907) 277-7148 or Wayne at (907) 279-1994. [ADVERTISEMENT]

"K" Street Bed & Breakfast. Downtown, 2 blocks to coastal trail, market, dining and bus line. Near airport, railroad and shopping. Healthy breakfast, gourmet coffee, teas. Private or shared bath with sitting areas. Secure area, ample parking, smoke-free. Hostess 21-year resident. Fully licensed. Phone/fax (907) 279-1443. 1443 "K" Street, Anchorage, AK 99501. [ADVERTISEMENT]

North Country Castle Bed & Breakfast. Luxuriate in our spacious, sunny, warm Victorian home! Relax on any of 4 decks with sparkling mountain and Cook Inlet views. Explore moose trails on our forested acreage or amble down our country road to nearby hiking paths. Only minutes from major Anchorage attractions and the wilds of Alaska. Bounteous breakfasts. Year-round. Credit cards accepted. P.O. Box 111876, Anchorage, AK 99511. (907) 345-7296. [ADVERTISEMENT]

Park View Bed & Breakfast, 1320 West 10th Avenue, Anchorage, AK 99501, (907) 276-6649. Alaskana decorated home, located in quiet downtown, on the park setting with mountain and inlet water views. Walking distance to coastal trail, museum, shops and attractions. Deluxe continental breakfast. 10 minutes to airport. Smoke-free. Open year-round. [ADVERTISEMENT]

Puffin Inn. Experience comfortable, qual-

ity accommodations and exceptional service at reasonable rates. Our friendly Alaskan hospitality includes complimentary coffee, muffin and daily newspaper. Located near Lake Hood floatplane airport with courtesy airport shuttle, nonsmoking rooms, cable TV and freezer space for your hunting and fishing needs. Handicap accessible. 4400 Spenard Rd., Anchorage, AK 99517. Phone (907) 243-4044. Fax (907) 248-6853. (800) 4PU-FFIN. &

Puffin Place Studios & Suites. Relax and

MERRILL FIELD

HOSPITALITY AND CONVENIENCE

INN

420 SITKA STREET • ANCHORAGE, AK 99501

(907) 276-4547 • FAX (907) 276-5064

1-800-898-4547

- 2 RESTAURANTS ON PREMESIS
- KITCHENETTES AVAILABLE
- QUEEN & KING BEDS
- FREE CONTINENTAL BREAKFAST
- FREE AIRPORT SHUTTLE
- COIN-OP LAUNDRY
- HONEYMOON SUITE WITH LARGE JACUZZI

ALL ROOMS HAVE HAIRDRYERS, CABLE TV & HBO, REFRIGERATORS AND MICROWAVE OVENS

enjoy 1 of our 38 attractively furnished studios and 1-bedroom suites featuring fully equipped kitchens with microwaves. Within walking distance of restaurants, shopping and Tony Knowles Coastal Trail, our amenities include: courtesy airport shuttle, nonsmoking rooms, laundry facility, freezer space, cable TV. Weekly and monthly rates offered October–May. 1058 W. 27th, Anchorage, AK 99503, (907) 279-1058. Fax (907) 257-9595. (800) 71-PLACE. [ADVERTISEMENT]

Snowshoe Inn Bed & Breakfast. 826 K Street, Anchorage, AK 99501. Phone (907) 258-7669. Fax (907) 258-7463. Convenient downtown location, private lodging, smoke-free environment, quiet, beautifully decorated rooms/suites with private and shared bath, TV and phone in each room. Amenities: laundry, freezer space, free parking. Open year-round. [ADVERTISEMENT]

Susie's Lake View Bed & Breakfast. Enjoy the quiet setting overlooking scenic Campbell Lake. Unwind with a leisure tour of our quaint garden setting. The large deck areas offer comfortable privacy for an individual or big enough for a family barbecue. Start or end your day with a steamy hot tub—available 24 hours a day and located where it should be … outside. Continental or traditional breakfast. Business travelers welcome. Located only 11 minutes from the airport. VISA and MasterCard accepted. 9256 Campbell Terrace, Anchorage, AK 99515. Phone (907) 243-4624. [ADVERTISEMENT]

The Teddy Bear House Bed & Breakfast. Experience a traditional home stay in our uniquely decorated home in a quiet south Anchorage neighborhood, 15 minutes from

ROYAL SUITE LODGE

2 locations to serve you better!

Downtown
Royal Suite Annex
441 E. 15th Ave., Anch., AK 99501
Near downtown & Sullivan Arena

Midtown
Royal Suite Lodge
3811 Minnesota Dr., Anch., AK 99503
Near Airport

For Reservations call 1-800-282-3114

THE ROYAL SUITE ANNEX
(a division of the Royal Suite Lodge)

Excellent Location • Apartment Style Units • Full Kitchen • Non-Smoking Suites Available
Cable TV with HBO • Newly Remodeled • Free Airport Shuttle • Free Local Phone

Heidi's BED & BREAKFAST
Privacy and Affordability with an Alaskan Touch
CENTRALLY LOCATED
Private Two Bedroom Apartment
ATTACHED TO OUR HOME
- Off-Street Parking
- Eat-In Kitchen
- Private Phone & TV
- 5 Min. to Airport
- Easy Access to City Bus & Downtown
Complimentary Continental Breakfast
3904 Lois Drive • Anchorage, AK 99517
(907) 563-8517

LAKESHORE MOTOR INN

IF YOU STAY ANYWHERE ELSE YOU'LL PAY TOO MUCH! *We Guarantee It!*

- Free Airport Shuttle
- Family Suites with Kitchens
- Cable TV/HBO, Phones, Laundry
- Fish Freezers • Non Smoking Rooms
- Visa • MC • Diner's Club

NEW ROOMS Too!

For Reservations & References Call:
1-800-770-3000 or (907) 248-3485
3009 Lakeshore Drive • Anchorage, Alaska

Parkwood Inn

Formerly known as the Bonanza Lodge
ANCHORAGE RESERVATIONS: 1-800-478-3590
Spacious Studio Suites • Kitchens in Every Room
Government & Senior Discounts • Near Shopping Centre & Theaters
4455 Juneau St., Anchorage, AK 99503 • (907) 563-3590

airport and downtown. Close to Anchorage Zoo and shopping. Twin or queen beds. Private and shared bath. Continental or traditional breakfast. Large deck for your relaxation. Open year-round. No smoking. P.O. Box 190265, Anchorage, AK 99519; (907) 344-3111. [ADVERTISEMENT]

12th & L Bed and Breakfast. Downtown Anchorage. Private baths, cable TV. Free phone and laundry. Convenient, casual, comfortable, congenial and clean. Flexible check in/check out. Low winter rates. Informative brochure. (907) 276-1225. Fax (907) 276-1224. Web address http://www.custom-cpu.com/commercial/twelfth/ [ADVERTISEMENT]

Anchorage has 2 public campgrounds: Centennial Park, open from May through September, and Lions Camper Park, open July and part of August on an as-needed basis. Fees are $13 for non-Alaskans and $11 for Alaska residents. To reach Centennial Park, take the Muldoon Road exit south off the Glenn Highway, take the first left onto Boundary, take the next left and follow the signs. Lions Camper Park is located at 5800 Boniface Parkway, half a mile south of

Log cabin visitor center on 4th Avenue is open year-round. (© Susan Cole Kelly)

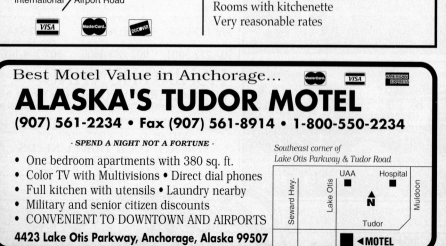
the Glenn Highway. Centennial, recommended for large RVs, has 90 RV sites and 40 tent sites. Lions has 50 tent sites. Both feature barracks-type showers, flush toilets, water and dump stations and no hookups. Between May and September, phone (907) 333-9711 for details on either park. In the off-season, phone (907) 343-6397.

Chugach State Park has campgrounds located near Anchorage at Bird Creek (Seward Highway), and at Eagle River and Eklutna Lake (Glenn Highway). Anchorage also has several private campgrounds. ▲

Anchorage RV Park. Join us for the opening season of Anchorage's newest and finest RV park. 195 full-hookup spaces, beautiful main lodge with laundry, restrooms and showers, camp store and community room, paved streets. Easy access off Glenn Highway, next to bike trails. Alaska Native owned and operated. Season: mid-May through September. To make reservations call 1-800-400-7275, (907) 338-7275, 7300 Oilwell Rd., Anchorage, AK 99504. [ADVERTISEMENT]

Highlander Camper Park. 42 full hookup spaces, free showers, clean restrooms. Located across from the Sears Mall. A quiet location within walking distance of grocery

store, beauty salons, bank, restaurants and more. 2704 Fairbanks Street, Anchorage, AK 99503. Reservations (907) 277-2407. [ADVERTISEMENT] ▲

TRANSPORTATION

Air: More than a dozen international and domestic air carriers and numerous intrastate airlines serve Anchorage International Airport, located 6.5 miles/10.5 km from downtown. Limousine service to and from major downtown hotels is available.

Ferry: There is no ferry service to Anchorage. The nearest port is Whittier on Prince William Sound, served by Alaska state ferry from Cordova and Valdez. Whittier is accessible by train from either Anchorage or Portage on the Seward Highway. See the Southwestern Ferry Schedules in the MARINE ACCESS ROUTES section for details.

Cruise Ships: See Cruise Ships in the MARINE ACCESS ROUTES section for ships making Anchorage a port of call.

Railroad: The Alaska Railroad offers daily passenger service in summer from Anchorage to Seward and to Fairbanks via Denali National Park (Mount McKinley). In addition, a shuttle train for both foot passengers and vehicles operates daily between Portage and Whittier, connecting with the Alaska Marine Highway to Valdez and Cordova. Winter service is reduced. *NOTE: Rail transportation is NOT available between Anchorage and Portage.*

See the ALASKA RAILROAD section for passenger schedules. For more information, write the railroad at Passenger Services Dept., Box 107500, Anchorage 99510-7500; phone

1-800-544-0552 or (907) 265-2494, fax 265-2323.

The Alaska Railroad depot is located on 1st Avenue, within easy walking distance of downtown.

Bus: Local service via People Mover, which serves most of the Anchorage bowl from Peters Creek to Oceanview. Fares are $1 for adults, 50¢ for youth 5 to 18, 25¢ for senior citizens and disabled citizens with transit identification. Monthly passes are sold at the Transit Center (6th Avenue and H Street), the Dimond Transit Center and municipal libraries. Day passes are also available for $2.50 at the Transit Center, Dimond Transit Center and 7–11 stores. For bus route information, phone the Rideline at (907) 343-6543.

Taxi: There are 7 taxi companies.

Car and Camper Rentals: There are more than 2 dozen car rental agencies located at the airport and downtown. There are also several RV rental agencies (see advertisements this section).

RV Parking: The Anchorage Parking Authority offers a lot with spaces for oversized vehicles (motorcoaches, campers, large trucks) at 3rd Avenue, north of the Holiday Inn, between A and C streets. Parking is $5 per space, per day. For more information, phone (907) 276-PARK or (800) 770-ACAR.

Highway: Anchorage can be reached via the Glenn Highway and the Seward Highway. See GLENN HIGHWAY and SEWARD HIGHWAY sections for details.

ATTRACTIONS

Get Acquainted: Stop by the Log Cabin Visitor Information Center at 4th Avenue and F Street, open 7:30 A.M. to 7 P.M. June through August; 8 A.M. to 6 P.M. in May and September; and 9 A.M. to 4 P.M. the remainder of the year; phone (907) 274-3531. Free visitor guidebooks.

Take a Historic Walking Tour: Start at the Log Cabin Visitor Information Center at 4th Avenue and F Street. The Anchorage Convention and Visitors Bureau's *Anchorage Visitors Guide* suggests an excellent downtown walking tour.

Take a Tour: Several tour operators offer local and area sightseeing tours. These range from a 1-hour narrated trolley tour of Anchorage to full-day tours of area attractions such as Portage Glacier and Alyeska Resort. Two-day or longer excursions by motorcoach, rail, ferry and air to nearby attractions such as Prince William Sound or remote areas are also available. Inquire at your hotel, see ads this section, or contact a travel agent.

Anchorage City Trolley Tours. It's fun. It's 1-hour. It's only $10. A lively, informative, 1-hour sightseeing tour of Alaska's largest city. Located at the historic Fourth

Avenue Theatre between F and G streets. Departs hourly. 9 A.M.–6 P.M. 630 West 4th Avenue #1, Anchorage, Alaska 99501. (907) 257-5603. [ADVERTISEMENT]

The Alaska Public Lands Information Center, located in the historic Federal Build-

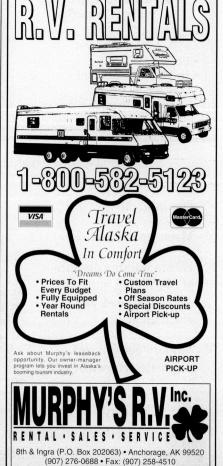

ing on 4th Avenue and F Street, offers a wide variety of information on all of Alaska's state and federal parks, forests and wildlife refuges. Displays, video programs and computers permit self-help trip-planning. Expert staff provide additional assistance and supply maps, brochures and other aids. Federal passports (Golden Age, Eagle and Access) and state park passes are available. Reservations may be made here (in person or by mail only) for Kenai Fjords National Park cabins and for U.S. Forest Service cabins throughout the state. The center is open year-round. Summer hours are 10 A.M. to 5:30 P.M. daily; open in winter 10 A.M. to 5:30 P.M. Monday through Friday, closed weekends and holidays. Phone (907) 271-2737 or write the center at 605 W. 4th Ave., Suite 105, Anchorage 99501, for more information.

The Anchorage Museum of History and Art, located at 121 W. 7th Ave., is a must stop. One of the most visited attractions in Anchorage, the museum features permanent displays of Alaska's cultural heritage and artifacts from its history. The 15,000-square-foot/1,400-square-meter Alaska Gallery on the second floor is the museum's showcase, presenting Alaska Native cultures—Aleut, Eskimo and Indian—and displays about the Russians, New England whalers, also gold rush, WWII, statehood and Alaska today. Displays include full-scale dwellings and detailed miniature dioramas. The gallery contains some 300 photographs, more than 1,000 artifacts, 33 maps, and specially made ship and aircraft models. The main floor of the museum consists of 6 connecting galleries displaying Alaska art, such as works by Sydney Laurence. Also on the 1st floor are a Children's Gallery and 3 temporary exhibition galleries. The museum has a reference library and archives, a free film series and public tours (daily in summer), the Museum Shop and a cafe in the atrium. Admission is $5 for adults, $4.50 for seniors, under 18 free. Open 9 A.M. to 6 P.M. daily, May 9 to Sept. 21; 10 A.M. to 6 P.M. Tuesday through Saturday, and 1–5 P.M. Sunday, in winter (closed Monday and holidays). Phone (907) 343-6173 for recorded

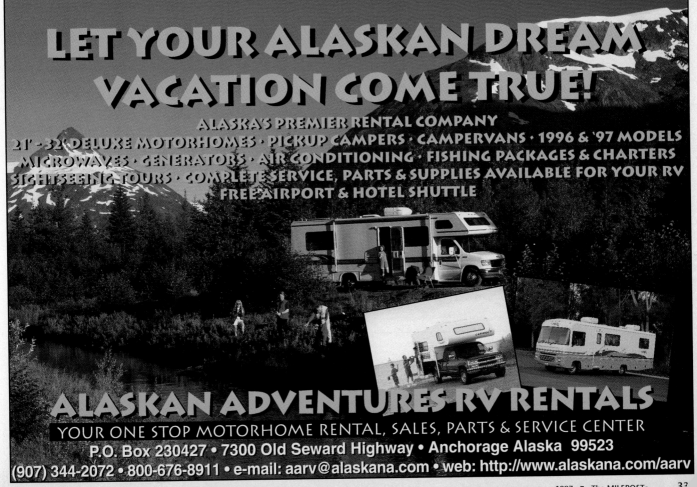

information about special shows, or (907) 343-4326 during business hours.

Visit the Oscar Anderson House Museum, one of the city's first wood-frame houses. Built in 1915, it was home to Oscar Anderson, a Swedish immigrant and early Anchorage pioneer and businessman. Now on the National Register of Historic Places, it has been beautifully restored and is well worth a visit. Located in the north corner of Elderberry Park, at the west end of 5th Avenue, 420 M St. Open mid-May to mid-September for guided tours. Hours are 11 A.M. to 4 P.M., Tuesday through Saturday. Swedish Christmas tour, first 2 weekends in December. Adults, $3; seniors over 65, $2; children 5 to 12, $1. Group tours may be arranged year-round by appointment. Phone (907) 274-2336; fax (907) 274-3600.

Tracy Anna Bader Design Studio/ Denali Wear. "Original Art to Wear Outdoors.™" Visit this contemporary Alaskan artist, working in her colorful storefront studio, creating exclusive coats, novelty jackets, vests, blankets and accessories. Custom orders a specialty. For hours phone/fax (907) ART-WEAR (278-9327). Look for the beautiful flower box downtown at 416 G Street. [ADVERTISEMENT]

The Knitting Frenzy Store. Best source for yarn, fiber, books, patterns, supplies for use in knitting, weaving, spinning, crochet and tatting. Largest Alaskan inventory. Choose a project for the road! Open Monday through Saturday 10–6. Day phone (907) 563-2717. In Alaska, 1-800-478-8322. 4240 Old Seward Hwy. #18, corner of Old Seward and Tudor. [ADVERTISEMENT]

Discover Alaska in our motorhomes!

The ideal way to see Alaska – at your own pace!

- Comfortable, convenient, clean self-contained units
- 20' - 27' motorhomes
- Sleeps up to 8 people
- Housekeeping and fishing packages available
- Free airport pickup in Anchorage
- Free linens

MAKE RESERVATIONS EARLY!

(907) 562-7051
(800) 421-3456
FAX (907) 562-7053

Clippership Motorhome Rentals

5401 Old Seward Highway
Anchorage, Alaska 99518

Laura Wright Alaskan Parkys. Known worldwide for beautiful Eskimo-style summer and winter parkas. Off the rack or custom-made. Started by Laura Wright in Fairbanks in 1947 and continuing the tradition is granddaughter Sheila Ezelle. Purchase "Wearable Alaskan Art" for the whole family at 343 W. 5th Ave., Anchorage, AK 99501. Phone (907) 274-4215. Bank cards welcome. Mail and phone orders accepted. We airmail worldwide. [ADVERTISEMENT]

Oomingmak, Musk Ox Producers' Co-operative, is a Native owned co-operative specializing in knitted masterpieces. Using Qiviut, the soft and rare fiber from the arctic Musk Oxen, our 250 Native Alaskan knitters create hats and scarves in a variety of traditional patterns from their culture. Since 1969, this co-operative organization has provided the opportunity for Native women to earn a supplementary income while still pursuing their subsistence lifestyle. For over 25 years, the exquisite items the co-op members make on their knitting needles have been worn with pride and enjoyment by satisfied customers from around the world. We invite you to visit us in downtown Anchorage at the little brown house with the Musk Ox mural on the corner of 6th and H streets. (907) 272-9225, 604 H Street, Anchorage, AK 99501. [ADVERTISEMENT]

Exercise Your Imagination: Visit the Imaginarium, 737 W. 5th Ave., Suite 140 (across from the Westmark Hotel), a hands-on science discovery center offering unique insights into the wonders of nature, science and technology. Open daily year-round Monday through Saturday 10 A.M. to 6 P.M.,

RV SERVICE CENTER
"Largest In Interior Alaska"

- Factory Trained Technicians
- Parts & Accessory Showroom
- Rental Cars
- Servicing All Makes & Models
- Complete Body Shop
- Quick Service "While You Wait"

JOHNSON RV SERVICE CENTER
562-1750 • Tudor & Old Seward • Anchorage

FAIRBANKS RV SERVICE CENTER
249 Alta Way • 907-452-4279 • Fairbanks

SIX ROBBLEES' INC.

- Trailer Suspensions
- Custom Installation and Repair Shop
- Trailer Hitches
- Tires & Wheels
- Much More. . . .

201 East Dimond
(Kings Row Mall)
907-344-7497

3000 Commercial Drive
907-276-5171

DEAN'S
AUTOMOTIVE & RV SERVICE CENTER
FEATURING THE LATEST EQUIPMENT

276-5731
1131 E. 7TH AVE., ANCHORAGE

OPEN MON - FRI 8-6 SAT 8-5

- Electric tune-ups
- Starters
- Shocks
- Brakes
- Alternators

- Engines
- Electrical
- Automatic Transmissions
- Auto Air Conditioning
- Wheel Alignment

CERTIFIED I/M STATION

Firestone
DEALER

10% Senior Discount

Sunday noon to 5 P.M., closed major holidays. Adults, $5; seniors, $4; children 2 to 12, $4. Wheelchair accessible. Phone (907) 276-3179.

Tour a Campus: Two colleges are located in Anchorage: the University of Alaska Anchorage at 3211 Providence Dr. and Alaska Pacific (formerly Alaska Methodist) University at 4101 University Dr.

Alaska Pacific University was dedicated June 29, 1959, the same year that Alaska became the 49th state. Now the state's largest private 4-year university, APU's first students were enrolled in the fall of 1960. The university offers liberal arts-based educational programs for all ages, including an annual Elderhostel. The APU campus is located on 270 forested acres, featuring the 3-tiered Atwood Fountain, Waldron Carillon Bell Tower and the Jim Mahaffey Trail System for skiers, runners, hikers and mountain bikers. Phone (907) 561-1266 or 1-800-252-7528 for tours or information about university programs or access the university on the Internet at http:// www.alaska.net/~apu.

The University of Alaska Anchorage is 1 of 3 regional institutions in the state's university system (the others are in Fairbanks and Southest Alaska). For information on tours of the UA campus in Anchorage, phone (907) 786-1529.

Go to the Zoo: The Alaska Zoo is located on 25 acres of wooded land and displays more than 85 species of Alaskan wildlife, including glacier bears, polar bears, brown and black bears, reindeer, moose, Dall sheep, otters, wolves, foxes, Bactrian camels, musk-oxen and wolverines. Be sure to stop in at the gift shop, located on your right as you enter. The zoo is open 9 A.M. to 6 P.M. daily from May 1 to Oct. 1; 10 A.M. to 5 P.M. the remainder of the year. Drive south from the downtown area on the Seward Highway to **Milepost S 120.8.** Take O'Malley exit, turn left on O'Malley Road and proceed 2 miles/ 3.2 km to the zoo, which will be on your left. Admission $6 for adults, $5 for seniors, $4 for students 13 to 18, and $3 for children 3 to 12. Free admission for children under 3. Handicap parking, wheelchair accessible. Phone (907) 346-3242 for details.

See Alaskan Wildlife: Fort Richardson Alaskan Fish and Wildlife Center, located in Building 600 on Fort Richardson Military Reservation, has a display of approximately 250 mounts and trophies of Alaskan sport fish, birds and mammals, including a world-record Dall sheep. Open year-round, free admission. Phone (907) 384-0431 for hours. Elmendorf Air Force Base Wildlife Museum is open year-round from 10 A.M. to 2 P.M. weekdays, and 1 P.M. to 5 P.M. weekends. Displays include more than 200 native Alaskan species from big game to small birds and fish. Wheelchair access but not to restroom. Enter the base from the intersection of Boniface Parkway and the Glenn Highway. Ask guards for directions to Building 4-803. Phone (907) 552-2282 for details.

See an Old Schoolhouse: The Pioneer Schoolhouse at 3rd Avenue and Eagle Street is a 2-story memorial to the late Ben Crawford, an Anchorage banker. It was the first school in Anchorage. The interior is not open to the public.

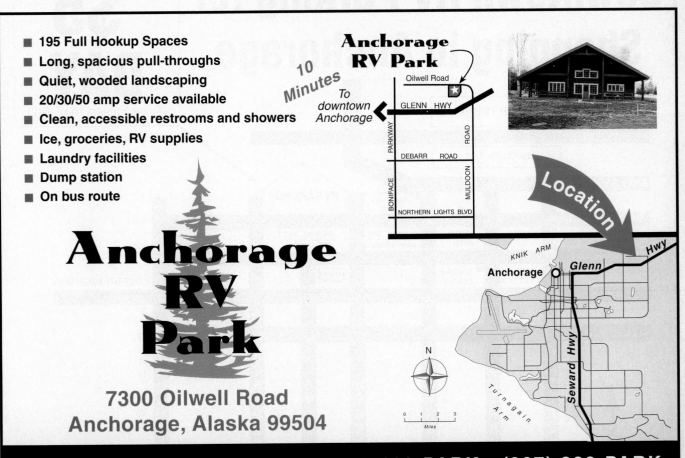

RV / AUTO PARKING

in

Downtown Anchorage !

For a quick trip through Alaska's largest city use this map to locate your convenient parking place for only $5.00 per day.

Anchorage Parking Authority (907) 276-PARK

Downtown RV Parking for Shopping in Anchorage

*$5 DAY

(Rates subject to review)

*Other location rates vary.

RAILROAD TERMINAL

1ST AVENUE

PARKING LOT

2ND AVENUE

PARKING LOT

RV PARKING !

3RD AVENUE

HILTON HOTEL

PARKING LOT
POST OFFICE

PARKING LOT
HOLIDAY INN

4TH AVENUE

VISITOR'S CENTER

PARKING GARAGE

5TH AVENUE

GLENN HIGHWAY

6TH AVENUE

PARKING GARAGE

G STREET

F STREET

E STREET

C STREET

B STREET

A STREET

GAMBEL

SEWARD HWY

N

Visit the Library, City Hall, Federal Building, Post Office: The city hall offices are at 6th Avenue and G Street. The Z.J. Loussac Public Library is located at 36th Avenue and Denali Street. The Federal Building, located at 7th Avenue and C Street, is one of the largest and most modern office buildings in Anchorage. The lobby features a multimedia collection of artwork, and the cafeteria is open to the public. In downtown Anchorage, the U.S. Post Office is located on the lower level of the Post Office Mall at 4th Avenue and D Street. The main post office, located near the airport, offers all services, 24 hours a day. Smaller postal stations are located throughout the city.

"Whaling Wall": Stop by D Street between 5th and 6th avenues for a sight of the 400-foot long, 5-story airbrushed mural of beluga whales, bowhead whales and seals by artist Wyland covering the west wall of J.C. Penney.

Visit Wolf Song of Alaska, at the corner of 6th Avenue and C Street in downtown Anchorage. Features over 4,000 square feet of educational exhibits and displays, focusing on the wolf's natural history, its historical relation to humans, and its role as a major symbol in human folklore, art and religion. Also in the education center are wildlife dioramas, wolf photography and art, and a gift shop that includes educational books, tapes and videos. Open daily in summer; hours vary in winter. Parking is available on the street and at garages at 6th Avenue and E Street, or 5th Avenue and C Street. RV parking is available 3 blocks north of the center at 3rd Avenue and C Street. For more information about "experiencing the wolf," phone (907) 274-WOLF or (907) 346-3073.

4th Avenue Theatre. Built in 1947 by Alaska millionaire "Cap" Lathrop, this Anchorage landmark has been refurbished and now operates as a gift shop, cafe, museum exhibit and live entertainment center. Much of the original art-deco design has been preserved and the trademarks of the theater have been restored, including the ceiling lights marking the Big Dipper and the bas-relief gold leaf murals. There is no admission fee to the theater. General admission is charged for the entertainment. The 4th Avenue Theatre is located a half block from the visitor center. For more information phone (907) 257-5650.

Visit the Saturday Market. Located at the Lower Bowl parking lot, corner of Third and E Street, this open-air market is held Saturdays from Memorial Day weekend to Labor Day weekend. Hours are approximately 10 A.M. to 6 P.M. (subject to change). There is no admission fee. The market features Alaska products, fresh produce, fish, arts and crafts, antiques, food and entertainment. There are also garage-sale and used-car-sale areas. For more information, contact the Anchorage Parking Authority at (907) 276-7275 or the Downtown Anchorage Assoc. at (907) 276-5015.

Visit the Port of Anchorage: The Anchorage waterfront, with its huge cargo cranes off-loading supplies from container ships, makes an interesting stop, especially in winter when ice floes drift eerily past the dock on the fast-moving tide. Visitors may watch activity on the dock from a viewing platform on the 3rd floor of the port office building. To get there, drive north from the downtown area on A Street, take the Port off-ramp and follow Ocean Dock Road to the office about 1.5 miles/2.4 km from downtown. A good viewpoint of the port for downtown walkers is at the northeast corner of 3rd Avenue and Christensen Drive.

Heritage Library Museum, in the National Bank of Alaska, Northern Lights Boulevard and C Street, has an excellent collection of historical artifacts, Native tools,

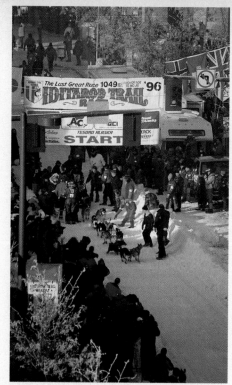

Start of the Iditarod Trail Sled Dog Race. (© James D. Ronan)

clothing and weapons, paintings by Alaskan artists and a research library. Free admission. Open weekdays noon to 5 P.M. between Memorial Day and Labor Day, noon to 4 P.M. at other times of the year. Phone (907) 265-2834.

Charter a Plane: Dozens of air taxi operators are based in Anchorage. Fixed-wheel (skis in winter) planes or floatplanes may be chartered for flightseeing trips to Mount McKinley and Prince William Sound, for fly-in hunting and fishing or just for transportation. Scheduled flightseeing trips by helicopter are also available.

Watch Small Planes: Drive out to Merrill Field, Lake Hood or Lake Spenard for an afternoon of plane watching. Lake Hood is the world's largest and busiest seaplane base, with more than 800 takeoffs and landings on a peak summer day. Merrill Field ranked 74th busiest airport in the nation in 1994, with a monthly average of 1,460 takeoffs and landings.

Alaska Aviation Heritage Museum, located on the south shore of Lake Hood at 4721 Aircraft Dr., preserves the colorful history of Alaska's pioneer bush pilots. Included are rare historical films of Alaska's pioneer aviators and an extensive photo exhibit of pioneer pilot memorabilia. The museum features a collection of 28 Alaska bush planes. RV parking. Open year-round, May 1 to Sept. 30, 9 A.M. to 6 P.M. daily; Oct. 1 to April 30, 10 A.M. to 4 P.M. Tuesday through Saturday; phone (907) 248-5325. Adults, $5.75, seniors and active military, $4.50, children 7 to 12, $2.75, children 6 and under, free. Wheelchair accessible.

Elmendorf Air Force Base Open House. This annual, day-long summer event features aerial shows, aircraft displays, ground demonstrations, booths and more. For more information, phone 3rd Wing Public Affairs (907) 552-8151.

Renown Charters & Tours offers wildlife and glacier cruises in the Kenai Fjords and in Prince William Sound. Our comfortable, new 76- and 42-passenger vessels have the speed to get you out to where the action is. Calving glaciers, whales, puffins, otters and much more. Lunch is included on all cruises. Fully narrated by a professional and friendly crew. Call 1-800-655-3806. See display ad.
[ADVERTISEMENT]

Era Helicopters. Experience a panoramic view of the Anchorage area and the unspoiled wilderness and wildlife of the Chugach Mountains. Soar through picturesque mountains, valleys and glaciers, minutes away from Alaska's largest city. One- and 2-hour tours. Phone 1-800-843-1947 or (907) 266-8351 locally. Tours also available in Juneau, Mount McKinley and Valdez.
[ADVERTISEMENT]

Kenai Fjords Tours Ltd. "Alaska's #1 Wildlife and Glacier Cruises" has a convenient reservation's office in downtown Anchorage. Located in the Hilton Hotel, Kenai Fjords Tours is just 1 block north of the Visitors' Log Cabin, on 3rd Avenue between E and F streets at 536 West 3rd Avenue. (907) 276-6249. This is the original Kenai Fjords National Park cruise you've been looking for! See display ad this section.
[ADVERTISEMENT]

Major Marine Glacier Tours. Offering Anchorage's only cruise through Prince William Sound to awesome Blackstone Glacier. Tour includes an all-you-can-eat Alaska salmon dinner with dessert bar. The leisurely 6-hour cruise is an easy day-trip from Anchorage and features abundant wildlife and up-close viewing of lots of glaciers. One of the trip's highlights is Blackstone Glacier, where you'll drift among icebergs as you enjoy a delicious salmon dinner and watch waterfalls and a calving glacier. The 100-foot boat features reserved seating, indoor heated cabins and outdoor viewing decks. Complete tours cost only $99 and depart daily from Whittier's Boat Harbor early May to mid-September. Complete rail and bus packages are available from Anchorage. Our trip is Prince William Sound's best cruise value. For reservations or free brochure, call: 1-800-764-7300 or (907) 274-7300. Major Marine Tours, 411 West 4th, Anchorage, AK 99501. [ADVERTISEMENT]

Portage Glacier Cruise. See Alaska's most popular attraction, up close from the deck of the MV *Ptarmigan*. This Gray Line of Alaska cruise takes you right to the face of imposing 10-story-high Portage Glacier. An incredible experience. Tours depart Anchorage twice daily or you may drive to Portage Glacier and board the MV *Ptarmigan* for the cruise-only portion. Tour price is $59 per person; cruise-only price is $22 per person.

The Alaska Railroad station on First Avenue in Anchorage. (© Barbara Willard)

Prices subject to change. Call (907) 277-5581. [ADVERTISEMENT]

Prince William Sound Cruise. Experience the spectacular beauty of Prince William Sound aboard the MV *Nunatac*. This Gray Line of Alaska tour cruises past Columbia Glacier, the largest glacier in Prince William Sound. Watch for abundant marine life as you travel to picturesque Valdez. Return to Anchorage via the scenic Matanuska Valley. Two days, 1 night from $265 ppdo. Prices subject to change. Tour departs Anchorage daily. Call (907) 277-5581. [ADVERTISEMENT]

Train to Denali. Ride the luxurious private domed railcars of the *McKinley Explorer* to Denali National Park from either Anchorage or Fairbanks. Overnight packages in Denali with roundtrip train service are available from only $265 ppdo. Prices subject to change. Call Gray Line of Alaska at (907) 277-5581 for train and package tour options. [ADVERTISEMENT]

Take in an Alaska Film: Alaska films can be seen at the Anchorage Museum of History and Art, 121 W. 7th Ave., at 3 P.M., daily during summer. Alaska Experience Center, located at 6th Avenue and G Street, offers "Alaska the Great Land," a 70mm film presented on a 180-degree domed screen, and a film and exhibit on the 1964 earthquake. Admission fee charged; open year-round.

Hitting the links at the Anchorage Golf Course. (© Barbara Willard)

Call (907) 276-3730 for recorded information.

Watch the Tide Come In: With frequent tidal ranges of 30 feet/9m within 6 hours, and some approaching 40 feet/12m, one of Anchorage's best nature shows is the rise and fall of the tides in both the Knik and Turnagain arms of upper Cook Inlet. Among the better vantage points along Knik Arm are Earthquake Park, Elderberry Park (at the west end of 5th Avenue), Resolution Park (near the corner of 3rd Avenue and L Street) and the Anchorage small-boat harbor.

A good overlook for the tides in Turnagain Arm is Bird Creek State Recreation Site south of Anchorage at **Milepost S 101.2** on the Seward Highway. With good timing you might see a tidal bore, an interesting phenomenon you probably won't see elsewhere. A bore tide is a foaming wall of tidal water, up to 6 feet/2m in height, formed by a flood tide surging into a constricted inlet, such as Knik or Turnagain Arm.

CAUTION: In many places the mud flats of Knik and Turnagain arms are like quicksand. Don't go wading!

Play Golf: The municipality of Anchorage maintains a 9-hole golf course at Russian Jack Springs Park, Debarr Road and Boniface Parkway, featuring artificial turf greens. It is open from mid-May through September; phone (907) 333-8338 or (907) 343-4474 for details. Alyeska Resort maintains the Anchorage Golf Course, 3651 O'Malley Road, an all-grass, 18-hole course is open from mid-May through mid-September; phone (907) 522-3363 for more information. Two military courses are open to civilians. Eagle Glen Golf Course, an 18-hole, par-72 course, is located on Elmendorf Air Force Base, near the Post Road gate. Open mid-May through September. Phone (907) 552-2773 for tee times; rentals available. Fort Richardson's 18-hole Moose Run Golf Course is the oldest golf course in Alaska. The course is accessible from Arctic Valley Road (**Milepost A 6.1** on the Glenn Highway) and is open May through September. Rentals available. Call (907) 428-0056 for tee times.

Play Tennis: The municipality of Anchorage maintains 58 tennis courts, including those in Eagle River and Girdwood. In addition, private clubs offer year-round indoor courts.

Picnic at a Park. Anchorage has several parks for picnicking. Chester Creek Green Belt, which stretches from Westchester Lagoon to Goose Lake, has a number of public parks along it and a paved bike trail (also popular with joggers) runs the length of the greenbelt. The greenbelt is accessible from several streets; Spenard Road leads to Westchester Lagoon and E Street leads to Valley of the Moon Park.

Elderberry Park, at the foot of 5th

Avenue, overlooks Knik Arm. Nearby Resolution Park, at 3rd Avenue and L Street, where a statue of Capt. James Cook stands, has terraced decks overlooking Knik Arm. The Capt. James Cook statue was dedicated in 1976 as a bicentennial project.

Tour Anchorage by Bicycle: The municipality has about 120 miles/193 km of paved bike trails (including trails in Eagle River and Girdwood) paralleling many major traffic arteries and also passing through some of the city's most beautiful greenbelt areas. Maps of the trail system are available at Anchorage Parks & Recreation, 120 South Bragaw St. Offering an especially unique experience is the 11-mile/17.7-km Tony Knowles Coastal Trail, which begins at 3rd Avenue and Christensen Drive, and follows the coast around Point Woronzof to Point Campbell and Kincaid Park. One of the most popular trails in the city, it is used by bicyclists, joggers and walkers who are treated to close-up views of Knik Arm (watch for beluga whales) and on clear days a beautiful view of the Alaska Range.

Another popular bike route for families is the Chester Creek Bike Trail from Westchester Lagoon, at 15th Avenue and U Street, to Russian Jack Springs Park. The 6.5-mile/10.5-km trail traverses the heart of Anchorage, following Chester Creek past Goose Lake, a favorite summer swimming beach.

Downtown Bicycle Rental. Bike the Coastal Trail. Nice bikes. Low rates. Free lock, cable, map. Open every day. Stay at 6th & B Bed & Breakfast and receive bikes for free. For more information please call (907) 279-5293. Or visit our web page at http://www.custom-cpu.com/commercial/bicycle. [ADVERTISEMENT]

Watch Birds: There are some surprisingly good bird-watching spots within the city limits. Lakes Hood and Spenard, for instance, are teeming with seaplanes but also, during the summer, are nesting areas for grebes and arctic loons. Also seen are wigeons, arctic terns, mew gulls, green-winged teals and sandpipers.

Another great spot is the Potter Point State Game Refuge, south of downtown on the Seward Highway at **Milepost S 117.4.** Early July evenings are best, according to local bird watchers. Forests surrounding Anchorage also are good for warblers, juncos, robins, white-crowned sparrows, varied thrushes and other species.

The Park for All People in the Chester Creek Green Belt on W. 19th Avenue near Spenard Road has a nature trail through a bird nesting area.

Go for a Hike. Hiking trails in the Anchorage area are found in Chugach State Park and in Municipality of Anchorage parks. Three popular hikes in Chugach State Park's Hillside Trail System, accessed from the Glen Alps trailhead, are Flattop Mountain, Powerline Trail and Williwaw Lakes. To reach the trailhead, take the Seward Highway south to the O'Malley exit and go east to Hillside Drive; take a right on Hillside then a left at the trailhead sign and continue to Glen Alps parking lot. The hike up Flattop Mountain begins here; elevation gain is 1,550 feet/472 m in 3.5 miles/5.6 km, hiking time is 3 to 5 hours. Also accessible from Glen Alps is the Powerline trail; total length 11 miles/18 km, elevation gain 1,300 feet/396m. Williwaw Lakes trail branches off Powerline trail to several small alpine lakes; round-trip is 13 miles/21 km with a 742-foot/226-m elevation gain. For more information phone Chugach State Park at (907) 345-5014.

Hilltop Ski Area, 4 miles/6 km east of the Seward Highway at Dimond, is the trailhead for summer hiking, biking, and horsebackriding on trails in Bicentennial and Hillside municipal parks. The trails range in length from an easy mile walk to a strenuous 16-mile/26-km hike. For more information phone Hilltop Ski Area at (907) 346-1446.

Other Anchorage parks offering hiking, jogging or biking include Kincaid Park, Russian Jack Springs Park and Far North Bicentennial Park. For more information phone Anchorage Parks and Recreation at (907) 343-4474.

Summer Solstice. Alaskans celebrate the longest day of the year with a variety of special events. In Anchorage, there's the annual Mayor's Midnight Sun Marathon, a 26-mile/42-km, 385-yard run through the city. This event is usually scheduled on the Saturday nearest summer solstice (June 20 or 21).

See a Baseball Game: Some fine semi-pro baseball is played in Anchorage. Every summer some of the nation's top college players play for the Anchorage Glacier Pilots and Anchorage Bucs, the Peninsula Oilers, the Mat–Su Miners and the Fairbanks Goldpanners. Anchorage games are played at Mulcahy Ball Park, Cordova Street and E. 16th Avenue. Check local newspapers for schedules or call the Anchorage Bucs, (907) 561-2827 or the Glacier Pilots, (907) 344-5444.

Watch a Salmon: King, coho, pink and a few chum salmon swim up Ship Creek and can be seen jumping a spillway in the dam just east of Ocean Dock Road. Watch for kings from early June until mid-July and for other species from mid-August until September. A fine wooden viewing platform has been built to make salmon watching easy.

Watch an Equestrian Event. The

William Clark Chamberlin Equestrian Center in 530-acre Ruth Arcand Park hosts a variety of equestrian events every weekend from late May through August. This public facility is open from 9 A.M. to 9 P.M. Phone (907) 522-1552.

Kayaking, Canoeing, Rafting: All are available in or near Anchorage. Guided tours from 1 to 14 days run on several rivers within 100 miles/160 km of Anchorage, including the Chulitna, Susitna, Little Susitna, Matanuska and Kenai rivers. Information on guided raft and canoe trips is available through travel agencies, local sporting goods stores and in the free *Visitors Guide* available from the Log Cabin Visitor Information Center.

Several flying services provide unguided float trips. The service flies customers to a remote river, then picks them up at a predetermined time and place downriver.

Several streams in the area make excellent canoeing and kayaking paths. Information on the Swanson River and Swan Lake canoe trails on the Kenai Peninsula is available from the Kenai National Wildlife Refuge Manager, Box 2139, Soldotna, AK 99669-2139; phone (907) 262-7021. Nancy Lake State Recreation Area, 67 miles north of Anchorage, offers a popular canoe trail system. Contact the Alaska State Parks, Mat–Su/Valdez–Copper River Area, H.C. 32, Box 6706, Wasilla, AK 99654-9719; phone

(907) 745-3975.

Sailing in the Anchorage area is limited to freshwater lakes and lagoons (usually ice free by May).

Mirror Lake, 24.5 miles/39.4 km north of Anchorage on the Glenn Highway, and Big Lake, 52.3 miles/84.2 km north of Anchorage on the George Parks Highway, are also popular spots for small sailboats.

Motorboating: Big Lake and Lake Lucille along the George Parks Highway offer motorboating. Several rivers, including the Susitna, offer riverboating, but the shallowness and shifting bottoms of most of Alaska's rivers mean a jet-equipped, flat-bottom boat is almost required.

Cruises on larger boats are available from Whittier into Prince William Sound, from Homer Spit into Kachemak Bay and Cook Inlet, and from Seward into Resurrection Bay and Kenai Fjords National Park. Venturing into those areas in small boats without a local guide with knowledge of the area can be dangerous.

Cook Inlet waters around Anchorage are

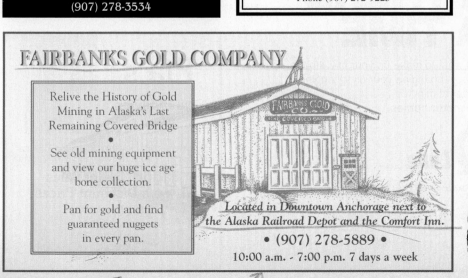

only for the experienced because of powerful bore tides, unpredictable weather, dangerous mud flats and icy, silty waters. Turnagain Arm is strictly off-limits for any boats, and Knik Arm and most of the north end of Cook Inlet is the domain of large ships and experienced skiff and dory operators.

Swimming: Anchorage Parks and Recreation can answer questions about aquatics; phone (907) 343-4476.

Goose Lake is open daily, June through August, from 10:30 A.M. to 5:30 P.M.; lifeguards, bathhouse and picnic area. It is located 3 miles/4.8 km east from downtown Anchorage on UAA Drive.

Jewel Lake, 6.5 miles/10.4 km from downtown Anchorage on W. 88th Avenue off Jewel Lake Road, is open daily June through August, from 10:30 A.M. to 5:30 P.M.; lifeguards, restrooms and covered picnic area.

Spenard Lake is open daily, June through August, from 10:30 A.M. to 5:30 P.M.; lifeguards, restrooms, picnic area. Located 3 miles/4.8 km southwest of downtown Anchorage on Spenard Road, then west on Wisconsin Street to Lakeshore Drive.

CAUTION: Do not even consider swimming in Cook Inlet! Soft mud, swift tides and icy water make this extremely dangerous!

The YMCA, 5353 Lake Otis Parkway, offers discounts to outside members with YMCA identification. Call (907) 563-3211 for pool schedule and information on other facilities.

The following pools are also open to the public: Service High School pool, 5577 Abbott Road, phone (907) 346-3040; Bartlett High School pool, 25-500 Muldoon Road, phone (907) 337-6375; West High School pool, 1700 Hillcrest Dr., phone (907) 274-5161; East High School pool, 4025 E. 24th Ave., phone (907) 278-9761; Dimond High School pool, 2909 W. 88th Ave., phone (907) 249-0356; Chugiak High School pool, South Birchwood Loop Road, off the Glenn Highway north of Anchorage, phone (907) 696-2010; and University of Alaska pool, Providence Drive, phone (907) 786-1233.

Charter Boats: Visitors must drive south to the Kenai Peninsula for charter boats. Sightseeing and fishing charters are available at Whittier, Seward and Homer.

Fishing: The Alaska Dept. of Fish and Game annually stocks about 28 lakes in the Anchorage area with rainbow trout, landlocked chinook (king) salmon, grayling and arctic char. Nearly 135,000 6- to 8-inch rainbow trout are released each year along with about 50,000 salmon. All lakes are open to the public. In addition, salmon-viewing areas and limited salmon fishing are available in the immediate Anchorage area. For specific information, check the Alaska fishing regulations book, call the agency at (907) 267-2218, or phone (907) 349-4687 for a recorded message. Urban salmon fisheries have been developed recently by the Alaska Dept. of Fish and Game in several Anchorage-area streams. King and coho salmon can be caught in **Ship Creek** in downtown Anchorage through July as well as in **Eagle River** just north of town. Coho salmon fisheries opened for the first time in 1993 in **Campbell Creek** in Anchorage and at **Bird Creek** just north of Girdwood on the Seward High-

Day Trips From Anchorage

Several interesting and memorable sights may be taken in on a day's drive from Anchorage by heading either south of downtown on the Seward Highway or north on the Glenn or George Parks highways. Following are some of the points of interest along these roads. Follow the mile-by-mile logs given in the related highway sections in *The MILEPOST*. Keep in mind that several companies offer motorcoach tours to many of these same attractions and that you can see a great many attractions in a short amount of time by taking a flight-seeing trip out of Anchorage; there's even a 1-day trip to Kotzebue from Anchorage.

South from Anchorage, the Seward Highway offers some spectacular views of Turnagain Arm less than 10 miles/16 km from downtown. Stop at one of the scenic viewpoints for photos. Other stops close to Anchorage include Potter Marsh for bird watching and the Potter Section House, which serves as the Chugach State Park Visitor Center and features displays of railroad history.

Continue south to **Milepost S 90** (37 miles/59.5 km from Anchorage) for the Girdwood/Alyeska Road turnoff. About 2 miles/3.2 km up this road, a gravel road forks to the left and leads 3.1 miles/5 km to Crow Creek Mine, a historic 1898 mining camp where visitors can pan for gold and tour the camp's old buildings. Returning from the mine to the main road, continue about another mile for Alyeska Resort.

Back out on the Seward Highway, continue south 11 miles/17.7 km to **Milepost S 79.1** and the Portage Glacier Access Road. On the 5-mile/8-km drive to the glacier, watch for salmon spawning at Williwaw Creek and look for the hanging Explorer Glacier. The Begich, Boggs Visitor Center at Portage Glacier has interpretive displays on glaciers, regular showings of films of interest and Forest Service naturalists are available to answer your questions. You can stand on the shore of Portage Lake or take a tour boat for a close-up view of Portage Glacier.

Return to the Seward Highway. Depending on your time, you may wish to head back up the highway to Anchorage (which would add up to about 114 miles/183 km total driving distance), or extend your trip farther south to take in the old gold mining town of Hope.

North from Anchorage, the Glenn and George Parks highways offer many attractions. Drive out on the Glenn Highway from downtown Anchorage to Palmer, 42 miles/67.6 km. Heart of the Matanuska–Susitna Valley, the Palmer–Wasilla area has the Alaska State Fair, Colony Village, a musk-oxen farm, Knik Museum and Mushers' Hall of Fame, Wasilla Museum and Frontier Village, and the Iditarod Trail headquarters visitor center. Drive 59 miles/95 km east on the Glenn Highway from Palmer to see the spectacular Matanuska Glacier. Several lakes in the area offer picnicking and water sports. Largest is Big Lake, a year-round recreation area accessible from Big Lake Road off the George Parks Highway, 52 miles/84 km from Anchorage. Kepler–Bradley State Recreation Area on Matanuska Lake, at **Milepost A 36.4** Glenn Highway, has canoe rentals.

You may wish to stop off at Eklutna Lake or the Eagle River Visitor Center. Also, take the Eklutna Road exit for Eklutna Village Historical Park, which features 350 years of Athabascan culture. The park includes St. Nicholas Russian Orthodox Church and spirit houses. It is open daily, 9 A.M. to 9 P.M., from the end of May to mid-September; admission charged.

---

way. Natural-run pink salmon are also available in Bird Creek.

Within a day's drive of Anchorage are several excellent fishing spots. The Kenai Peninsula offers streams where king, red, silver, pink and chum salmon may be caught during the season. Dolly Varden and steelhead also run in peninsula streams. Several lakes contain trout and landlocked salmon. In-season saltwater fishing for halibut, rockfish and several species of salmon is excellent at many spots along the peninsula and out of Whittier, Homer and Seward. For specific fishing spots both north and south of Anchorage see the Seward, Sterling, Glenn and George Parks highways sections. Because of the importance of fishing to Alaska both commercially and for sport, regulations are strictly enforced. Regulations are updated yearly by the state, often after *The MILEPOST* deadline, so it is wise to obtain a current regulations book. ◆

WINTER ATTRACTIONS

Alyeska Resort. Located in the community of Girdwood, Alyeska Resort is a 45-mile/65-km drive south from Anchorage along scenic Turnagain Arm via the Seward Highway. Judged by *Conde Nast Traveler* as having the "best view" of any U.S. ski resort,

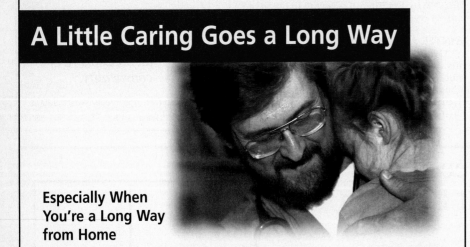

Alyeska Resort is Alaska's largest ski resort, with snow from early November to the middle of April. Night skiing is available during holiday periods in December and on Fridays and Saturdays from January through March. Ski facilities include a high-speed detachable bubble quad, 2 fixed grip quads, 3 double chair lifts and 2 pony tows. Chair 7, a fixed grip quad, added 20 acres of beginner and intermediate ski terrain to the resort's existing terrain. A 60-passenger aerial tram takes sightseers and skiers from the mountain's base at 250 feet/76m to a mountaintop facility at the 2,300-foot/701-m level. This facility, open year-round and accessible by wheelchair, features a large viewing deck, a cafeteria-style restaurant and a fine dining restaurant and lounge. Centerpiece for the resort is the 307-room, chateau-style Westin Alyeska Prince Hotel. The hotel features a fitness facility with indoor swimming pool and 16-person whirlpool, 4 restaurants and 2 lounges. For more information, phone (907) 754-1111 or 1-800-880-3880.

Alpenglow at Arctic Valley: East of downtown Anchorage in the Chugach Mountains, Alpenglow Ski Area has a 4,500-foot/1,372-m double chair lift, a 2,200-foot/671-m double chair lift, a 2,800-foot/873-m T-bar platter lift combination and a 700-foot/213-m rope tow for beginners. There is a day lodge with full cafeteria and ski shop. Cross-country skiing is available, but trails are not maintained. The ski area operates from about late October until early May. Hours are 1–9 P.M. Wednesday and Thursday, 10 A.M. to 9 P.M. Friday, Saturday and all school holidays and 10 A.M. to 6 P.M. Sunday. Drive northeast from downtown on the Glenn Highway. Just beyond Ship Creek, turn right on Arctic Valley Road and follow the main road 7.5 miles/12 km to the ski area. For more information, phone (907) 563-2524.

Hilltop Ski Area: Located 15 minutes from downtown Anchorage 4 miles/6.4 km east of the Seward Highway at Dimond, Hilltop has 2 miles/3.2 km of lighted slopes classified as beginner to intermediate. Ski facilities include a double chair lift; a beginner rope tow; 15m, 40m and 60m jumps; and certified snowboard half-pipe. Ski rentals (Alpine, Nordic and snowboards), ski school, gift shop and restaurant. The area is open daily with complete night lighting. Hours are 3–9 P.M. Monday through Friday, and 9 A.M. to 10 P.M. weekends. There are also 9 miles/15 km of cross-country ski trails in adjoining Hillside and Bicentennial parks, with 5 miles/8 km offering night lighting. For more information, phone (907) 346-1446.

Chugach State Park: Although the entire park is open to cross-country skiers, most

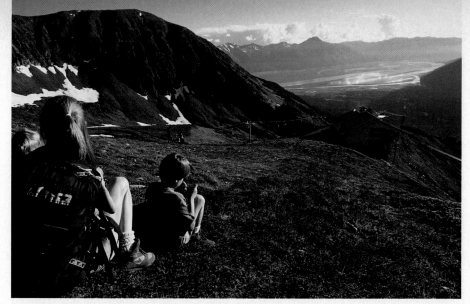

a chalet, a ski rope tow and 8 miles/13 km of cross-country ski trails, 3 miles/5 km of which are lighted. The ski area is maintained by the Municipality of Anchorage. Ski trail maps are available at Anchorage Parks and Recreation, phone (907) 343-4474.

Far North Bicentennial/Hillside Parks: Best access to this 5,000-acre tract in the eastern portion of the Anchorage bowl is via Hilltop Ski Area on Abbott Road. There are 13.7 miles/22 km of groomed cross-country ski trails, 3.9 miles/6.3 km of which are lighted. There are also 6 miles/9.7 km of multi-use trails. Cross-country skiing is allowed anywhere in the area except on dogsled trails. For further information, phone Anchorage Parks and Recreation, (907) 343-4474.

Summer hiking at Mount Alyeska ski resort. (© Michael DeYoung)

maintained ski trails are found in the Hillside Trail System/Campbell Creek area, accessible via Upper Huffman Road and Upper O'Malley Road. Skiers are encouraged to use established trails as most of Chugach State Park is prime avalanche country.

Five major areas in the park are open to snowmobiling when snow levels are deep enough: Eklutna Lake Valley, reached from the Glenn Highway via Eklutna Road; Eagle River valley, also accessible from the Glenn Highway; Bird Creek, **Milepost S 101.2** Seward Highway; Peters Creek Valley and Little Peters Creek, accessible from the Glenn Highway; and portions of the Hillside/Campbell Creek area, accessible from Upper Huffman Road. A 24–hour recorded message giving the status of all snowmobile areas is availble at (907) 694-6391.

Ski trail maps and snowmobiling information are available at the trailheads or from the park office, phone (907) 345-5014.

Russian Jack Springs: Located at DeBarr Road and Boniface Parkway. This ski area has

Chugach State Park

This 495,000-acre park flanking Anchorage to the north, east and south, offers wilderness opportunities for all seasons: hiking, mountain biking, camping, berry picking, skiing and snowmobiling. Information about the park is available from Chugach State Park, H.C. 52, Box 8999, Indian, AK 99540; phone (907) 345-5014. The Chugach State Park office, located in Potter Section House on the Seward Highway, has maps showing access to the park's recreation areas.

Between June and September, park staff offer guided nature walks and more strenuous hikes on the weekends to various points of interest in the park. The nature walks, which last about 2 hours, focus on some aspect of natural history, such as wildflower identification or bird watching. The more strenuous hikes last approximately 4 hours. Phone (907) 694-6391 for a recorded message.

There are several access points to Chugach State Park attractions from Anchorage. North from downtown on the Glenn Highway take the Eklutna Road exit (**Milepost A 26.3**) and drive in 10 miles/16 km to reach Eklutna Lake Recreation Area. Eklutna Lake is the largest lake in Chugach State Park. The recreation area has a campground, picnic area and hiking trails. Cross-country skiing and snowmobiling in winter.

You may also reach Eagle River Nature Center for Chugach State Park by driving north on the Glenn Highway and taking the Eagle River exit (**Milepost A 13.4**). Follow Eagle River Road 12.7 miles/20.4 km to reach this beautifully situated visitor center, with its views of the Chugach Mountains. Excellent wildlife displays, a nature trail, Dall sheep viewing and other summer activities make this a worthwhile stop. Cross-country skiing and snowmobiling in winter. Phone (907) 694-2108 for more information.

Another easily accessible park area from downtown is Arctic Valley. Turn off the Glenn Highway at Arctic Valley Road, **Milepost A 6.1**, and drive in 7.5 miles/ 12 km. Spectacular views of Anchorage and Cook Inlet. Good berry picking and hiking in summer; downhill and cross-country skiing in winter.

The park's hillside trailheads may be reached by driving south from downtown to the O'Malley Road exit at **Milepost S 120.8** on the Seward Highway. Follow O'Malley Road east for 4 miles/6.4 km until Hillside Drive enters from the right; turn on Hillside and proceed about 1.5 miles/2.4 km to the intersection of Upper Huffman Road and Hillside Drive. Turn left on Upper Huffman Road and continue 4 miles/6.4 km to the Glen Alps trailhead. Hiking in summer, cross-country skiing and snowmobiling in winter.

The Seward Highway south from Anchorage gives access to several Chugach State Park hiking trails.

Beach Lake Park: 10.5 miles/16.9 km of groomed cross-country ski trails with 3 miles/4.8 km lighted. There are approximately 20 miles/32 km of dog mushing trail.

Wheelchair-accessible lodge and cabins available for a minimal user fee. Outstanding views of lake and wildlife from lodge deck and cabins. Contact Eagle River Parks and Recreation, phone (907) 694-2011.

Campbell Creek Green Belt: The municipality maintains approximately 3 mile/4.8 km of multi-use ski trails in south Anchorage.

Centennial Park: 3 miles/4.8 km of wooded cross-country ski trails over some hilly terrain. Maintained by the Municipality of Anchorage and located near Glenn Highway and Muldoon Road.

Chester Creek Green Belt: Located in the heart of Anchorage, the municipality main-

tains more than 6.2 miles/10 km of cross-country ski trails.

Connors Lake Park: A popular site to learn skijoring, run in conjunction with the local skijoring club. Over 4.8 miles/7.7 km of multi-use trails.

Kincaid Park: 30 miles/48 km of cross-country ski trails are marked and maintained for novice, intermediate and expert skiers by the municipality. There are 9.9 miles/15.9 km of lighted trails and a warm-up chalet. Access is from the west end of Raspberry Road. Ski trail maps are available at Anchorage Parks and Recreation, phone (907) 343-4474; or Kincaid Park, phone (907) 343-6397.

Turnagain Pass: On the Seward Highway, about 59 miles/95 km south of downtown Anchorage. Turnagain Pass (elev. 988 feet/301m) is a popular winter recreation area in the Chugach National Forest. The west side of the pass is open to snowmobiling as soon as snow cover permits; the east side is reserved for skiers. Snow depths in this pass often exceed 12 feet/4m.

Dog Mushing begins in December. Dog mushing organizations in the Montana Creek area, Knik, Chugiak, Palmer and Anchorage sponsor races every weekend. Anchorage races usually begin in January at the Tozier Track and continue through the end of February. In addition, some of the clubs offer instruction in the sport. Several of the races are considered preliminaries to the World Championship races held during the Anchorage Fur Rendezvous.

The annual Iditarod Trail Sled Dog Race, 1,049 miles/1688.2 km to Nome, takes place in March. The race begins on 4th Avenue in downtown Anchorage and mushers on the trail can be seen along the Glenn Highway, in the Knik Bridge area about 30 miles/48 km north of Anchorage and at Knik on the west side of Knik Arm.

To find a race, watch local newspapers for times, dates and places.

Anchorage Fur Rendezvous: Major event of the winter season is the Anchorage Fur Rendezvous. Billed as the "Mardi Gras of the North," this elaborate winter festival, held in February, attracts thousands of celebrants annually.

The 10-day-long celebration dates from 1936 when it began primarily as a fur auction where trappers could bring their pelts to town and make a few extra dollars selling them to buyers from around the world. Trap-

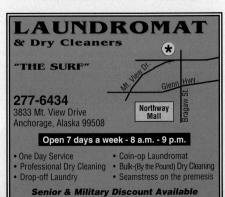

Alaska's Most Popular Day Cruise

26 GLACIER CRUISE In One Day!™

Visitors to Alaska are always humbled by the majesty of our scenery, especially the frozen rivers of ice...glaciers. Most are happy to see just one of these wonders. Imagine what you will say when you see more than 26...in one day!

Phillips' Cruises & Tours makes it possible with an exciting six hour cruise on the calm, protected waters of Prince William Sound. Sail in comfort aboard the M/V Klondike Express. Take in the beauty of rugged, snow-capped mountains, and tree-lined fjords. Experience a close-up view of an amazing array of wildlife...whales, sea otters, seals, eagles, sea birds... just to name a few.

Join us any day for this exciting 26 Glacier Cruise. See for yourself why it is called "Alaska's Most Popular Day Cruise."

Prince William Sound - Calm Waters! Wild Sights!

- Cruise the calm and protected waters of Prince William Sound
- See spectacular marine and bird life — whales, seals, sea otters, bird rookeries
- Deluxe, high-speed catamaran gives you more time at the glaciers and wildlife areas
- Three outdoor viewing decks and two inside lounges - Cruise in comfort

- Fully narrated six hour cruise
- Compare routes. See three times as much area.
- Complimentary lunch
- Operates daily from Whittier
- Easy access from Anchorage, Alyeska Resort or the Kenai Peninsula
- Money back guarantee - No motion sickness on board

"Your Best Single Day in Alaska"

$119

Per person plus tax
Cruise from Whittier includes lunch
Best Value in Alaska

Great For All Visitors The 26 Glacier Cruise

Anchorage
276-8023

Toll Free
1-800-544-0529

Phillips' CRUISES & TOURS

519 West Fourth Avenue
Anchorage, Alaska 99501

© 1996 Phillips' Cruises & Tours

pers still bring their pelts, and the fur auction, held downtown, still attracts many buyers.

Alaskans shake off cabin fever during "Rondy" (the local term for the Fur Rendezvous). There are arts and crafts exhibits, a parade, the Miners' and Trappers' Ball, a blanket toss, a carnival and pet shows. Past Rondy competitions have been unique: a beard-growing contest, a waiter and waitress race, an ice and snow sculpturing contest and a home-brew competition, to name a few.

During the first weekend of the Fur Rendezvous, the Annual World Championship Dog Weight Pulling Contest attracts several thousand spectators at Mulcahy Park, located at E. 16th Avenue and Cordova Street.

The highlight of the Fur Rendezvous, however, is dog mushing. The World Championship Sled Dog Race, held during the final 3 days, attracts dozens of mushers from Alaska, Canada and the Lower 48. Thousands of spectators line the 25-mile/40-km race course, which begins and ends on

Chugach State Park permits mountain biking on some trails. (© Barbara Willard)

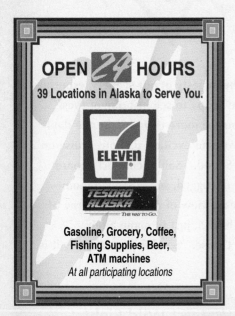
4th Avenue in downtown Anchorage. *(CAUTION: Leave pets and flashbulbs home, as they'll distract the dog teams.)* The musher with the best total elapsed time in 3 heats over 3 days is declared the winner. The women's and junior world championship sled dog races are held at Tozier Track the first weekend of the Fur Rendezvous. For more information, phone (907) 277-8615.

Ice Skating: Three municipal facilities, Ben Boeke Ice Arena (334 E. 16th Ave., phone 907/274-2767), Dempsey-Anderson Ice Arena (1741 W. Northern Lights, phone 907/277-7571) and Harry J. McDonald Center (13701 Old Glenn Highway in Eagle River, phone 907/696-0051) offer a total of 4 indoor rinks for spectator as well as participatory uses. The University of Alaska also has 1 indoor rink as does the Dimond Center shopping mall. Outdoor ice-skating areas include Cheney Lake, Chester Creek Sports Complex, Delaney Recreation Area, Goose Lake, Jewel Lake Park, Spenard Lake, Delong Lake, Tikishla Park and Westchester Lagoon.

Sledding: Popular sledding hills are at Balto Seppala Park, Centennial Park, Conifer Park, Kincaid Park, Nunaka Valley Park, Sitka Street Park, Sunset Park, Service High School and Alaska Pacific University.

Snowshoeing: Muldoon Park, Far North Bicentennial Park and Campbell Creek Green Belt are used for snowshoeing, as are backcountry areas of Chugach National Forest and Chugach State Park.

Winter Basketball. Anchorage hosts 2 major collegiate basketball events. The Great Alaska Shootout, held every Thanksgiving weekend, features 8 major college basketball teams in this well-known invitational tournament. The Northern Lights Invitational showcases women's collegiate basketball with 8 teams in a 3-day playoff the last weekend in February.

Ice Fishing: Countless lakes in the Anchorage and the Matanuska–Susitna Valley areas offer excellent ice fishing. Ice fishing is especially good in the early winter in Southcentral. Some Anchorage lakes are stocked each year with landlocked king salmon or rainbow trout. Among them: **Beach Lake, Cheney Lake, Delong Lake, Jewel Lake, Little Campbell Lake** in Kincaid Park and **Sand Lake.** For more information contact the Alaska Dept. of Fish and Game at (907) 344-0541; for a recorded message on fishing and ice conditions, phone (907) 349-4687. ✦

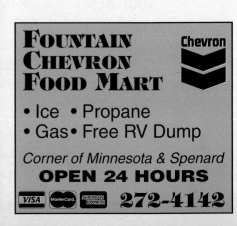

GEORGE PARKS HIGHWAY ①③

Connects: Anchorage to Fairbanks, AK   **Length:** 358 miles
Road Surface: Paved   **Season:** Open all year
Highest Summit: Broad Pass 2,300 feet
Major Attraction: Denali National Park

(See maps, pages 364–365)

	Anchorage	Denali Park	Fairbanks	Talkeetna	Wasilla
Anchorage		237	358	113	42
Denali Park	237		121	153	195
Fairbanks	358	121		245	316
Talkeetna	113	153	245		71
Wasilla	42	195	316	71	

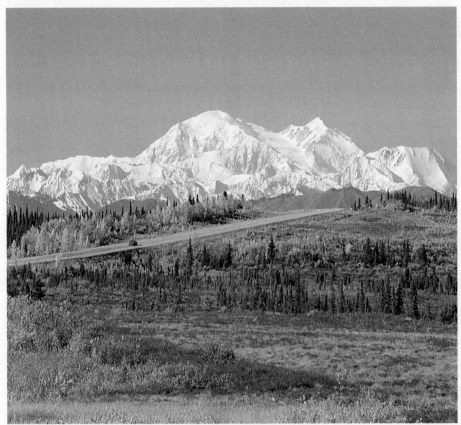

Mount McKinley looms above the George Parks Highway south of Cantwell.
(© Bruce M. Herman)

The George Parks Highway connects Anchorage and Fairbanks, Alaska's largest population centers. The route, called the Anchorage–Fairbanks Highway after its completion in 1971, was renamed in July 1975, in honor of George A. Parks (1883–1984), the territorial governor from 1925 to 1933. The highway runs 358 miles/576.1 km through some of the grandest and most rugged land that Alaska has to offer. The road is a modern paved highway, maintained year-round. The highway is mostly in good condition with some pavement breaks and frost heaves.

Motorists who plan to drive the highway during the winter (roughly from Oct. 1 to June 1) should check highway conditions before proceeding. Severe winter storms and extremely low temperatures can create hazardous driving conditions. Contact the Alaska Dept. of Transportation or the Alaska State Troopers in Anchorage or Fairbanks.

Some facilities along the highway north of the Talkeetna turnoff (**Milepost A 98.7**) and south of Nenana (**Milepost A 304.5**) are open in summer only.

From approximately **Milepost A 70** north of Anchorage there are many places where Mount McKinley—also called Denali—(elev. 20,320 feet/6,194m) is visible from the highway, weather permitting.

The George Parks Highway provides the most direct highway access to Denali National Park and Preserve (formerly Mount McKinley National Park) from either Anchorage or Fairbanks. Driving distance to the park entrance is 237.3 miles/381.9 km from Anchorage and 120.7 miles/194.2 km from Fairbanks. See DENALI NATIONAL PARK section for details.

Emergency medical services: Between the Glenn Highway junction and **Milepost A 202.1**, phone 911. Between **Milepost A 174** at Hurricane Gulch bridge and **Milepost A 224** at Carlo Creek bridge, phone the Cantwell ambulance at 768-2982 or the state troopers at 768-2202. Between **Milepost A 224** and Fairbanks, phone 911.

George Parks Highway Log

ALASKA ROUTE 1
Distance from Anchorage (A) is followed by distance from Fairbanks (F).

A 0 F 358 (576.1 km) ANCHORAGE. Follow the Glenn Highway (Alaska Route 1) north 35 miles/56.3 km to junction with the George Parks Highway. (Turn to the end of the GLENN HIGHWAY section and read log back to front from Anchorage to junction with the George Parks Highway.)

ALASKA ROUTE 3
A 35 (56.3 km) F 323 (519.8 km) Traffic light at junction of the George Parks Highway (Alaska Route 3) and the Glenn Highway (Alaska Route 1).

A 35.4 (57 km) F 322.6 (519.2 km) Trunk Road. Turn right, northbound, for Mat–Su College and the University of Alaska Fairbanks' Matanuska Research Farm. The Matanuska Research Farm conducts research in agronomy, horticulture, soil science and animal science. No formal tours are conducted.

A 35.5 (57.1 km) F 322.5 (519 km) Welcome Way; access to Mat–Su Visitors Center, operated by the Mat–Su Convention & Visitors Bureau. Open May 15 to Sept. 15, 8 A.M. to 6 P.M. daily. This large center offers a wide variety of displays and information

GEORGE PARKS HIGHWAY
Anchorage, AK, to Milepost A 169

Denali National Park and Preserve

▲ Mount McKinley
20,320 ft./6,193m

Glaciated

Mount Barrille ▲ The Mooses Tooth
7,650 ft./2,332m   10,335 ft./3,150m

Mount Hunter ▲   Mount
14,573 ft./4,442m Huntington   ▲ Mount Dickey
         12,240 ft./3,731m   9,845 ft./3,001m

Area

Buckskin Glacier

Tokositna Glacier   Ruth Glacier   Spink Lake

Kahiltna Glacier

Petersville ○

F-189/305km
A-169/271km

Eldridge Glacier

East Fork
Honolulu Creek

Little Coal Creek

Denali State Park

Fountain R.   Chulitna River   Coal River   Lucy Lake   Byers L.   Troublesome Cr.

Susitna River

The Alaska Railroad

TALKEETNA

A-134.5/216.5km Mary's McKinley View Lodge LM
A-132.8/213.7km Mt. McKinley Princess Lodge LM

Petersville Road

F-243/391km
A-115/185km

J-18.7/30.1km Forks Roadhouse ILM
J-17.2/27.7km McKinley Foothills B&B/Cabins L
J-10.5/17.3km Gate Creek Cabins L
J-2.7/5km North Country Bed & Breakfast L
A-114.8/184.7km Trapper Creek Inn & General Store CDdGILMPST
A-104/167.4km Big Su Lodge ILMPT
A-99.5/160.1km H&H Lakeview Restaurant & Lodge CDdGILMPST

Trapper Creek

A-115.7/186.2km Trapper Creek Pizza Pub M
A-115.5/185.9km Trapper Creek Trading Post CDGILMPST

Talkeetna ✳ ▲ ✚ ✝

J-3.5/5.6km Johnson Family Guitar Builders
J-3.1/5km Denali View Bed & Breakfast L
J-1/1.6km Moose Dropping Inn Bed & Breakfast L

A-99/159.3km Denali Way Auto R
A-98.8/159km Sunshine One Stop dGIMPST
A-98.7/158.8km K2 Denali Direct
Moores' Mercantile
Mary Carey's Fiddlehead Fern Farm
Talkeetna/Denali Visitor Center
A-96.6/155.5km Montana Creek Campgrounds C
A-91.5/147.3km Susitna Dog Tours & Bed and Breakfast L

Montana Cr.

Sheep Cr.

F-259/417km
A-99/159km

Sheep River

MOUNTAINS

Glaciated Area

A-88.2/142km Sheep Creek Lodge CGILMPT
A-87/140km Wolf Safari
A-85.5/137.6km Willow Wildlife Art Gallery
A-82.5/132.8km Ron's Riverboat Service & Susitna Landing
A-80/128.7km Lucky Husky Racing Kennel

Caswell Cr.   Kashwitna River

A-88.1/141.8km Cline's Caswell Lake Bed & Breakfast L

Mint Glacier

Yentna River

A-71.5/115.1km Willow Island Resort CDILST
A-71.4/114.9km Pioneer Lodge CDILMPT
A-70/112.7km Willow Air Service Inc.
A-69.5/111.8km Ruth Lake Lodge L
Willow Trading Post Lodge CDILMT
A-69/111km Willow True Value Hardware, Willow Creek Grocery, Willow Creek Service GIPrST
A-68.8/110.7km Newman's Hilltop Service dGIPST
A-66.5/107km Alaskan Hosts Bed & Breakfast L

A-71.2/114.6km Alaska Creekside Bed & Breakfast L
A-65.8/105.9km Nancy Lake Bed & Breakfast L
A-64.5/103.8km Nancy Lake Resort CGILPST
A-57.8/93km Fisherman's Choice Charters
A-57.7/92.9km Riverside Camper Park CDIT
A-57.6/92.7km Miller's Place CILMST
A-57.5/92.5km Houston Lodge IMT

Kashwitna Lake

Little Willow Cr.   Willow

Willow

Nancy L.

Kashwitna Lake

Hatcher Pass
3,886 ft./1,184m

Hatcher Pass Road

To Glennallen
(see GLENN HIGHWAY section)

Matanuska River

A-49.5/79.7km The Roadside Inn LM
A-49.4/79.5km Alaska R&R Laundry & RV Park CD
A-49/78.9km Seymour Lake Bed & Breakfast L
A-47/75.6km Museum of Alaska Transportation & Industry
A-45/72.4km Wasilla Car Wash

Houston ▲ ? ✚

Mat-Su Valley Vicinity
(see detailed map this section)

A-53.2/85.6km Plettner Kennels
A-51.3/82km Earth 'n Art Studio & Gift Shop
A-51/82km Big Lake-Susitna Veterinary Hospital

Wasilla ✳ ? ▲ ✚

Wasilla Lake

Palmer ▲ ? ✚ ✝

A-41.8/67.3km The Rock Shop
A-40.9/65.8km House of Tires, Inc. R
Pilgrims Baptist Church
The Windbreak LM
A-40.5/65.2km Northern Recreation R
A-40/64.4km Alaskan View Motel L
A-38.4/61.8km Alaska Jetboat Charters / Arctic Fox Taxidermy
A-35.5/57.1km Bestview RV Park CDIT
Matanuska–Susitna Convention & Visitors Bureau

✳ ▲ ✚ ✝ **Big Lake**
Big Lake

A-50.1/80.6km Blodgett Lake Bed & Breakfast L

Knik

Fish Creek

J-10.1/16.3km Knik Knack Mud Shack

Little Susitna River
Susitna R.

J-13.9/22.4km Knik Museum Mushers' Hall Of Fame

Knik Arm

Old Glenn Highway

F-323/519km
A-35/56km

Knik R.   Knik Glacier

Eklutna Lake

F-358/576km
A-0

Chugach State Park

Cook Inlet

Anchorage ✳ ? ▲ ✚ ✝

Glaciated Area

To Girdwood
(see SEWARD HIGHWAY section)

Map Location

Scale
0 ———— 10 Miles
0 ———— 10 Kilometres

Key to mileage boxes
miles/kilometres
miles/kilometres
from:
A- Anchorage
F- Fairbanks
J- Junction

Principal Route
Paved   Unpaved
Other Roads
Paved   Unpaved
Ferry Routes   **Hiking Trails**

✳ Refer to Log for Visitor Facilities
? Visitor Information   ✝ Fishing
▲ Campground   ✚ Airport ✝ Airstrip

Key to Advertiser Services
C -Camping
D -Dump Station
d -Diesel
G -Gas (reg., unld.)
I -Ice
L -Lodging
M -Meals
P -Propane
R -Car Repair (major)
r -Car Repair (minor)
S -Store (grocery)
T -Telephone (pay)

GEORGE PARKS HIGHWAY   *Milepost A 169 to Fairbanks, AK*

Scale

0 ⬚⬚⬚⬚⬚ 10 Miles
0 ⬚⬚⬚⬚⬚ 10 Kilometres

Key to mileage boxes

miles/kilometres
miles/kilometres from:

A- Anchorage
J- Junction
F- Fairbanks

Map Location

Principal Route

Paved
Other Roads — Unpaved
Paved
Ferry Routes — **Hiking Trails** Unpaved

Key to Advertiser Services
C - Camping
D - Dump Station
d - Diesel
G - Gas (reg., unld.)
I - Ice
L - Lodging
M - Meals
P - Propane
R - Car Repair (major)
r - Car Repair (minor)
S - Store (grocery)
T - Telephone (pay)

✵ Refer to Log for Visitor Facilities
❓ Visitor Information   ⌕ Fishing
⛺ Campground   ✚ Airport   ✦ Airstrip

To Livengood (see ELLIOTT HIGHWAY section)
To Circle (see STEESE HIGHWAY section)

F-0 A-358/576km

Murphy Dome 2,930 ft./893m ▲

A-352.5/567.3km Gold Hill dGI
Inua Wool Shoppe
Parks Highway Truck Stop dG

To Chena Hot Springs

⛺ Ester   ○

Chena R.

The Alaska Railroad

Fairbanks ✵❓⛺✚

A-351.7/566km Ester Gold Camp CDLM
Judie Gumm Designs

To Delta Junction (see ALASKA HIGHWAY section)

A-328/527.8km Skinny Dick's Halfway Inn CIT

Little Goldstream Cr.

Tanana

Wood River

✵❓⛺✚ **Nenana** ○
A-304.5/490km A-Frame Service dGIPST

F-53/86km A-305/490km

A-302.1/486.2km Finnish Alaskan Bed and Breakfast L

A-298/479.6km Tamarack Inn M

Fish Creek

Teklanika River

Anderson
✚ **Clear**

F-75/120km A-284/456km

A-283.5/456.2km Anderson Riverside Park CDT
A-280.1/450.8km Rochester Lodge CLM
A-280/450.6km Clear Sky Lodge IMPT
A-276/444.2km Tatlanika Trading Co. CD

Julius Creek

▲ Rex Dome 4,155 ft./1,266m

Jumbo Dome 4,493 ft./1,369m

▲ Walker Dome 3,942 ft./1,202m

A-248.8/400.4km Denali North Star Inn LMT
Denali Wings
Stampede Lodge & Bushmaster Grill LMT
A-248.5/399.8km Nenana Raft Adventures
A-248.4/399.8km McKinley RV & Campground CDIPST
A-248.2/399.4km Quality Services dGIPrT
A-247/397.5km Black Diamond Resort Co.
Otto Lake R.V. Park and CD
A-245.1/394.4km Denali RV Park & Motel CLT
Denali Outdoor Center

A-251.1/404.1km Earth Song Lodge L
Touch of Wilderness Bed & Breakfast L

A-249.6/401.7km Evans Industries, Inc. R
A-249.5/401.5km Motel Nord Haven L
A-249.2/401km Larry's Healy Tesoro dGIPST

Panguingue Cr.

✵ **Healy**
○ **Suntrana**
Usibelli
▲ Dora Peak 5,572 ft./1,698m

Healy Cr.

A-239.1/384.8km Alaska Cabin Nite Dinner Theatre M
Alaska Raft Adventures
McKinley Chalet Resort LM
A-239/384.6km Northern Lights Theatre and Gift Shop IS
A-238.9/384.5km Denali Outdoor Center
A-238.8/384.3km Sourdough Cabins L
McKinley Raft Tours Inc.
A-238.7/384.1km Denali Windsong Lodge LT
A-238.6/384km Denali Rainbow Village & RV Park CDM
Wolf Spirit Expeditions
A-238.5/383.8km Denali Crow's Nest Log Cabins
and Overlook Bar & Grill LMT
McKinley/Denali Cabins ILMT
McKinley/Denali Gift Shop
McKinley/Denali Steakhouse and Salmon Bake ILMT
A-238.4/383.6km Denali Bluffs Hotel LT
A-238.1/383.2km Denali Raft Adventures

Otto Lake
Dry Cr.

Sugarloaf Mountain 4,430 ft./1,356m

▲ Mount Healy 5,716 ft./1,742m

Park Road (see DENALI NATIONAL PARK section)

⛺ **Park Entrance**

F-121/194km A-237/382km

A-229.2/368.8km Denali Air

▲ Mount Fellow 4,476 ft./1,364m

Yanert Fork

▲ Pyramid Peak 5,201 ft./1,585m

A-231.1/371.9km Denali Grizzly Bear Cabins & Campground CILPST
Denali River Cabins CDLT
McKinley Village Lodge LM
A-224/360.5km The Perch LMT
McKinley Wilderness Lodge L

Denali National Park and Preserve

Fang Mountain ▲ 6,736 ft./2,053m

Kantishna ○

R A N G E

F-148/238km A-210/338km

A-210.4/338.6km Cotter's Quality Services dGIPT
A-210.2/338.3km Parkway Gift Shop

A-223.9/360.3km Carlo Creek Lodge CDILPST

Carlo Cr.

✵⛺✚ **Cantwell**

A-210.6/338.9km Lazy-J-Cabins L

A-209.7/337.4km Reindeer Mtn. Lodge L

To Paxson (see DENALI HIGHWAY section)

Nenana River

A L A S K A

Broad Pass 2,300 ft./701m

West Fork
Middle Fork

A-193/310.6km Sourdough Paul's Bed & Breakfast L
A-188.5/303.4km The Igloo dGT

East Fork

Chulitna R.

⛺

Chulitna River

Honolulu Creek

▲ Mount McKinley 20,320 ft./6,194m

Mount Huntington 12,240 ft./3,731m
The Mooses Tooth 10,335 ft./3,150m
Mount Barrille 7,650 ft./2,332m
Mount Dickey 9,845 ft./3,001m

Glaciated Area
Eldridge Glacier
Buckskin Glacier
Coal Cr.

③

F-189/305km A-169/271km

(map continues previous page)

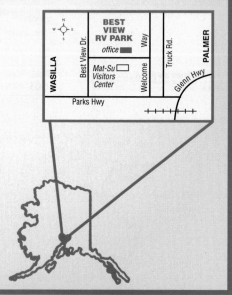
on the Mat–Su Valley; pay phone, gift shop. Write HC01, Box 6166J21, Palmer, AK 99645; or phone (907) 746-5000. The visitors bureau also operates a booking and reservation service.

Best View RV Park. See display ad this section. ▲

Matanuska–Susitna Convention & Visitors Bureau. See display ad this section.

A **36.2** (58.3 km) F **321.8** (517.9 km) Highway narrows to 2 lanes northbound.

A **37.4** (60.2 km) F **320.6** (515.9 km) Air Road; road to airstrip.

A **37.8** (60.8 km) F **320.2** (515.3 km) Hyer Road. Wasilla Creek bridge. Turnout.

A **38** (61.2 km) F **320** (515 km) Fairview Loop Road to west leads 11 miles/17.7 km to connect with Knik Road. Access to Palmer Hay Flats State Game Refuge.

A **38.4** (61.8 km) F **319.6** (514.3 km) **Alaska Jetboat Charters, Arctic Fox Taxidermy.** Fishing charters, taxidermy shop, Alaska Jetboat Charters (907) 376-4776. Offers guided full-day or half-day fishing trips for king salmon May 25 to July 14. Silver, red, pink and chum salmon July 15 to September. Arctic Fox Taxidermy, a full service taxidermy shop, specializes in Alaskan fish and big game mounts. (907) 376-4776.
[ADVERTISEMENT]

A **39.4** (63.4 km) F **318.6** (512.7 km) Seward Meridian Road, which junctions with the Palmer–Wasilla Highway, which leads east to Palmer and provides access to Finger Lake State Recreation Site (see **Milepost A 41.1**). Shopping center.

A **39.5** (63.6 km) F **318.5** (512.6 km) Wasilla city limits; medical clinic (376-1276). Wasilla shopping, services and attrac-

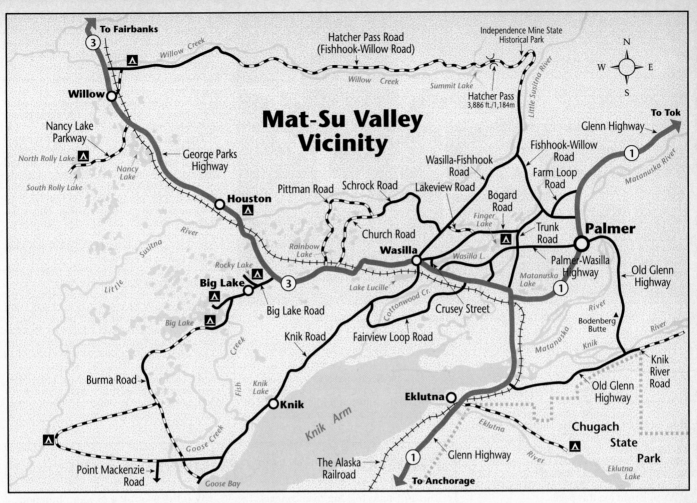

Mat-Su Valley Vicinity

tions are located along the highway (from here north to **Milepost A 45**) and at Main Street in Wasilla city center.

A 40 (64.4 km) **F 318** (511.8 km) **Alaskan View Motel.** We proudly present Wasilla's newest motel. This beautiful Alaskan log motel, complete with Alaskan decor, features a breathtaking mountain and inlet view from each of our 24 rooms. Minutes from fine dining, entertainment, shopping and theater. Welcome! (907) 376-6787. [ADVERTISEMENT]

A 40.5 (65.2 km) **F 317.5** (511 km) **Northern Recreation.** See display ad this

section.

A 40.9 (65.8 km) **F 317.1** (510 km) Tire and auto repair, church, hotel, cafe and lounge.

House of Tires, Inc. See display ad this section.

Pilgrims Baptist Temple. See display ad this section.

Wasilla visitor center is one block north of Milepost A 42.2. (© Ruth Fairall)

Palmer–Wasilla Highway, or turn east at **Milepost A 42.2** and drive 0.3 mile/0.5 km to intersection of Wasilla–Fishhook and Bogard roads, then follow Bogard Road 4.1 miles/6.6 km to Finger Lake.) Finger Lake has picnic tables, campsites, water, toilets and a boat launch. Camping fee $10. Also access to Wolf Lake state recreation site, off Bogard Road, which has picnic sites, toilets and hiking trail. ▲

The Rock Shop. Rough rock to finished gemstones. Handmade Alaskan jewelry. Original and custom designs. Native art and artifacts. Huge bead selection. Leather, feathers, furs. Hours Monday–Friday 10–7, Saturday 10–6. Day phone (907) 373-3094. Turn at Crusey Street and follow the blue highway signs off Parks Highway. [ADVERTISEMENT]

A **42** (67.6 km) F **316** (508.5 km) Art gallery and food market.

A **42.1** (67.8 km) F **315.9** (508.4 km) Boundary Street, Lake Lucille Park.

A **42.2** (67.9 km) F **315.8** (508.2 km) Wasilla's Main Street; visitor center and museum 1 block north; post office 2 blocks north (ZIP code 99687). Access to Hatcher Pass and Knik from this intersection. Turn south across railroad tracks for Knik Road to Knik, the "Dog Mushing Center of the World" (see KNIK ROAD log on page 370). Turn north on Wasilla's Main Street for downtown Wasilla and Hatcher Pass. Description of Wasilla follows. ▲

The Windbreak. See display ad this section.

A **41** (66 km) F **317** (510.1 km) Cottonwood Creek bridge.

A **41.1** (66.1 km) F **316.9** (510 km) **Junction** with Palmer–Wasilla Highway, which leads east 10 miles/16 km to the Glenn Highway at Palmer. It provides access to several businesses, Finger Lake state recreation site and a day-use area with picnic sites and playground. See PALMER–WASILLA HIGHWAY side road log this page.

A **41.7** (67 km) F **316.3** (509 km) Park with picnic shelter, restrooms, playground and swimming beach on Wasilla Lake; limited parking. Monument to George Parks.

A **41.8** (67.3 km) F **316.2** (508.9 km) Crusey Street, access to Bogard Road, a resort with motel and dining, and Finger Lake state recreation site. Turn right (northbound) and drive 3.7 miles/6 km via Crusey Street and Bogard Road to reach Finger Lake. (The recreation site is also accessible from

Palmer-Wasilla Highway Log

This 10.1 mile/16.3 km road connects the George Parks and Glenn highways (Alaska Routes 3 and 1). It provides access to a number of Wasilla and Palmer businesses. **Distance from Wasilla (W) is followed by distance from Palmer (P).**

W **0** P **10.1** (16.3 km) **Junction** with George Parks Highway at **Milepost A 41.1**. Access to drugstore, gas stations, auto body shops and other businesses.

W **0.3** (0.5 km) P **9.8** (15.8 km) Gas station.

W **0.4** (0.6 km) P **9.7** (15.6 km) Car wash.

W **0.7** (1.1 km) P **9.4** (15.1 km) Cottonwood Creek; fish viewing platform; spawning salmon.

W **0.9** (1.4 km) P **9.2** (14.8 km) Gas station.

W **1.1** (1.8 km) P **9** (14.5 km) Bed and breakfast.

W **1.6** (2.6 km) P **8.5** (13.7 km) Cottle Loop; Volunteer Park day-use area; bowling alley.

W **1.9** (3.1 km) P **8.2** (13.2 km) Fire station, gas station. **Junction** with Seward Meridian Road, which connects to George Parks Highway at **Milepost A 39.4**.

W **2.9** (4.7 km) P **7.2** (11.6 km) Bed and breakfast.

W **3** (4.8 km) P **7.1** (11.4 km) Hatcher Business Park.

W **3.2** (5.1 km) P **6.9** (11.1 km) Brentwood Plaza.

W **5.1** (8.2 km) P **5** (8 km) Valley Christian Schools.

W **5.9** (9.5 km) P **4.2** (6.8 km) Grocery store.

W **6.1** (9.8 km) P **4** (6.4 km) **Junction** with Trunk Road; access to Four Corners Mat–Su Community College. Trunk Road connects to Bogard Road, which connects Wasilla with Fishhook–Willow Road. Access to campgrounds at Finger Lake and Wolf Lake via Trunk and Bogard roads. Finger Lake SRS has 41 campsites, wheelchair-accessible toilets, picnic tables, water, hiking trails and boat launch, $10 camping fee, 7-day limit. Wolf Lake SRS has 4 campsites, picnic tables, hiking trails, no water and no camping fee. &▲

W **6.7** (10.8 km) P **3.4** (5.5 km) Four Corners Business Park.

W **7.3** (11.7 km) P **2.8** (4.5 km) Moffit Road; access to 49th Street, middle school and refuse dump.

W **7.9** (12.7 km) P **2.2** (3.5 km) Colony Plaza; pizza, chiropractor and Eagle View Car Wash.

W **8.1** (13 km) P **2** (3.2 km) Loma Prieta Road. Access to Crevasse–Moraine trailhead (5-mile/8-km loop); parking, picnic tables, fireplaces.

W **9.2** (14.8 km) P **0.9** (1.4 km) Hemmer Road; access to Palmer High School.

W **9.7** (15.6 km) P **0.4** (0.6 km) Tsunami Warning Center.

W **10.1** (16.3 km) P **0** Pioneer Square (Carr's Mall). **Junction** with Glenn Highway at **Milepost A 41.8** in Palmer (see GLENN HIGHWAY section).

Return to Milepost A 41.1
George Parks Highway or A 41.8
Glenn Highway

Wasilla–Fishhook Road leads northeast about 10 miles/16 km to junction with the Hatcher Pass (Fishhook–Willow) Road to Independence Mine State Historical Park; turn to the Hatcher Pass side road log in the GLENN HIGHWAY section, page 310, for a description of the road to Hatcher Pass from this junction (J 6.8 in that log). See also the map 367. The 49-mile/79-km Hatcher Pass Road junctions with the George Parks Highway at **Milepost A 71.2.**

Wasilla

A 42.2 (67.9 km) **F 315.8** (508.2 km). Located between Wasilla and Lucille lakes in the Susitna Valley, about an hour's drive from Anchorage. **Population:** 4,635. **Emergency Services: City Police,** phone (907) 745-2131, emergency only phone 911. **Fire Department and Ambulance,** phone (907) 376-5320, emergency only phone 911. **Hospital,** in Palmer. **Doctor** on Seward Meridian Road, **Milepost A 39.5,** phone (907) 376-1276, and at West Valley Medical Center, E. Bogard Road, phone (907) 376-5028. Chiropractic clinics, phone (907) 373-2022.

Visitor Information: At the Dorothy G. Page Museum and Old Wasilla Town Site Park on Main Street just off the George Parks Highway, phone (907) 373-9071, fax 373-9072. Or contact the chamber of commerce, Box 871826, Wasilla 99687, phone (907) 376-1299. Mat–Su Visitors Center at **Milepost A 35.5,** write Mat–Su Convention & Visitors Bureau, HC 01, Box 6166J21-MP, Palmer, AK 99645; phone (907) 746-5000.

Radio and **Television** via Anchorage sta-tions; KNBZ-FM 99.7. **Newspapers:** *The Valley Sun* (weekly); *The Frontiersman* (semiweekly). **Transportation: Air**–Charter service available. **Railroad**–Alaska Railroad. **Bus**–Matanuska Valley commuter to Anchorage.

Private Aircraft: Wasilla municipal airport,

WASILLA ADVERTISERS

Accommodations &
    Adventures ....Ph. (800) 401-7444
Alaska Kozey Cabins ....Ph. (907) 376-3190
Attainable Antique
    Bed & Breakfast...........Ph. (907) 376-3567
Campbell & Sons Tesoro ....Mile 42.5
Dorothy G. Page Museum & Visitors
    Information Center .....Ph. (907) 373-9071
Iditarod Trail
    Sled Dog Race® ....Mile 2.2 Knik Rd.
Inlet View..........................Ph. (907) 376-9675
Lake Lucille Inn ....Ph. (907) 373-1776
Lakeshore Bed and
    Breakfast.....................Ph. (907) 376-1380
Mat–Su Resort ....Ph. (907) 376-3328
Mr. Lube...................................See ad
Peak A View Bed and
    Breakfast......................Ph. (907) 376-6259
Shady Acres Inn
    Bed & Breakfast...........Ph. (907) 376-3177
Six Robblees....................Mile 40.5 Parks Hwy.
Southshore Bed &
    Breakfast ....S. Shore Lake Lucille
Tesoro 7-Eleven....................................See ad
Town Square
    Art Gallery ....Ph. (907) 376-0123
Valley Chiropractic
    Clinic, Inc. ....Ph. (907) 373-2022
Veterans of Foreign
    Wars Post #9365.............Mile 0.2 Knik Rd.
Wasilla Home Style
    Laundry ....Wasilla Shopping Center
Wasilla One-Hour
    Photo...................Wasilla Shopping Center

4.8 miles/7.7 km north on Neuser Drive; elev. 348 feet/ 106m; length 3,700 feet/1,128m; gravel; unattended. Wasilla Lake seaplane base, 0.9 mile/1.4 km east; elev. 330 feet/100m. Numerous private airstrips and lakes in vicinity.

Wasilla is one of the Matanuska–Susitna Valley's pioneer communities, supplying mines and farms in the area. Long before the George Parks Highway was built, local residents and visitors bound for Lake Lucille, Wasilla Lake, Big Lake and Knik, drove over the valley roads from Palmer to the village of Wasilla. Wasilla became a station on the Alaska Railroad about 1916.

Today, Wasilla is the largest community on the George Parks Highway between Anchorage and Fairbanks. Shopping malls and businesses here offer a wide assortment of services. NOTE: There are no banks between Wasilla and Fairbanks, but automatic teller machines are available and noted in the log.

ACCOMMODATIONS/VISITOR SERVICES

All visitor facilities are available here, including sporting goods stores, post office, gas stations, tire and RV repair, laundromats and other services. Mat–Su Ice Arena, at Bogard Road and Crusey Street, has ice skating, picnic area and fitness court. Swimming and showers are available at Wasilla High School.

Alaska Kozey Cabins & RV Rental. Modern, hand-crafted log cabins set in the state's No. 1 recreation area. Cabins feature queen and full beds, fully-equipped kitchens, bath and living rooms. Cross-country skiing, snow machining, hiking, fishing, and hunting abound. Near the official Iditarod restart. Open year-round. (907) 376-3190. See display ad this section. [ADVERTISEMENT]

Attainable Antiques Bed & Breakfast. New, spacious home on Lake Lucille; quiet, yet walking distance to town center and railroad. Flightseeing! Fishing charters! Deluxe suites, private baths, separate entrances, hot tub. Antiques for sale. Also Talkeetna cabin! Call today, reserve "3 day package." (907) 376-3567; 313 Lakeview Ave., Wasilla, AK 99654. [ADVERTISEMENT]

Lake Lucille Inn. Located 45 miles north of Anchorage on the shores of beautiful Lake Lucille. 54 deluxe rooms, suites with Jacuzzi, health club with sauna and hot tub. Boat and float plane dock, water craft rentals and

Knik Road Log

Distance is measured from the junction (J) with George Parks Highway.

J 0 Junction with George Parks Highway, **Milepost A 42.2.**

J 0.1 (0.2 km) CAUTION: Road crosses railroad tracks.

J 0.2 (0.3 km) VFW Post No. 9365.

J 0.7 (1.1 km) Glenwood Avenue, Senior center.

J 1.5 (2.4 km) Gas station.

J 2.1 (3.4 km) Smith ball fields.

J 2.2 (3.5 km) Iditarod Trail Sled Dog Race® headquarters and visitor center; historical displays, films, dogs and musher, souvenir shop. Open 8 A.M. to 5 P.M., daily in summer, weekdays the rest of the year. Adjacent Lake Lucille campground.

J 2.3 (3.7 km) **Lake Lucille** Mat–Su Borough Park Campground and day-use area 0.6 mile/1 km north via gravel road; 64 campsites, pavilion with covered picnic tables, firepits, parking. Camping fee charged. Fishing for landlocked silver salmon. Non-motorized lake access. ◄▲

J 4.1 (6.6 km) **Junction** with Fairview Loop Road, which joins the Parks Highway at **Milepost A 38**; access to Palmer Hay Flats State Game Refuge. Shopping center with gas and groceries at this junction.

J 7 (11.3 km) Knik fire hall.

J 8 (12.9 km) Settlers Bay, a housing development built around a lodge; golf course and stables.

J 10.1 (16.3 km) Turnoff for Homestead Museum, with a large collection of early Alaskan memorabilia, and gift shop.

Knik Knack Mud Shack. See display ad this section.

J 11.1 (17.9 km) Laurence airport.

J 13 (20.9 km) Knik Kennels.

J 13.3 (21.4 km) **KNIK** (area pop. 462) on Knik Lake. There is a bar here with a pay phone, a liquor store, gas station and private campground. Lake fishing for rainbow; inquire at the Knik Bar. Knik is a checkpoint on the Iditarod Trail Sled Dog Race® route and is often called the "Dog Mushing Center of the World"; many famous Alaskan dog mushers live in this area. ◄▲

J 13.9 (22.4 km) Knik Museum and Sled Dog Mushers' Hall of Fame, open noon to 5 P.M. Wednesday through Sunday, from June 1 through Aug. 31. The museum is housed in 1 of 2 buildings remaining from Knik's gold rush era (1898–1916). Regional memorabilia, artifacts, archives, dog mushing equipment, mushers' portraits and historical displays on the Iditarod Trail. Admission fee $2 for adults, $1.50 for seniors, free for children under 18. Phone (907) 376-7755, from September through May call 376-2005.

Traditional Athabascan graveyard with fenced graves and spirit houses next to Knik Museum. The gravesite can be observed from the Iditarod Trail.

Knik Museum and Sled Dog Mushers' Hall of Fame. See display ad this section.

J 16.1 (25.9 km) **Fish Creek** bridge; parking, fishing for silver salmon.

J 17.2 (27.7 km) Goose Bay Point Road to Little Susitna River public-use facility at Susitna Flats State Game Refuge (12 miles/19.3 km); 83 parking spaces, 65 campsites, boat ramps, dump station, water, tables, toilets. Also access to Point Mackenzie. Daily parking $5; boat launch, $5 (includes parking); overnight camping, $10. State parks annual pass not accepted here. For more information phone (907) 745-3975. ▲

J 18.5 (29.8 km) Pavement ends at small bar beside road. Road continues into rural area.

Return to Milepost A 42.2 George Parks Highway

lighted gazebo. Winter activities include lighted ice rink. Fine dining restaurant and lounge with pristine view. Convention and meeting facilities. [ADVERTISEMENT]

Peak A View Bed and Breakfast uniquely offers a large cozy room, ideal for families or travelers who want all the comforts of home. Two queen-size beds, day bed,

private bath, telephone, microwave and refrigerator. Enjoy the continental breakfast at your own leisure. Large deck with panoramic mountain view. 5731 Portage Dr., Wasilla, AK 99654. 1-800-776-6259. (907) 376-6259. [ADVERTISEMENT]

Valley Chiropractic Clinic Inc. Phone (907) 373-2022. 24-hour emergency service. Complete modern facility, same day emergency care. Reasonable fees with VISA and MasterCard accepted. We're accustomed to treating travelers' needs. We're located at 400 N. Main St., in Wasilla. Turn north on to Main Street from the Parks Highway and go up 2 blocks on the left, directly across the street from the post office. [ADVERTISEMENT]

ATTRACTIONS

On the town's Main Street, north of the Parks Highway, are the Dorothy G. Page Museum and Visitors Information Center, the library and the post office. The museum is open daily year-round, 10 A.M. to 6 P.M. in summer, 8 A.M. to 5 P.M. in winter; admission fees are $3 adults, $2.50 senior citizens; under 18 years free. Included in the price of admission to the museum is entrance to the Old Wasilla Town Site Park, located behind the museum. Picnic tables and museum

A young visitor plays with future Iditarod team. (© Barbara Willard)

shop on site. Local Farmer's Market on Wednesdays in summer. The historical park has 7 renovated buildings from before, during and after Wasilla's pioneer days, including Wasilla's first schoolhouse (built in 1917). Adjacent to the park is the Herning/Teeland Country Store, which is currently under restoration. The log museum building, school, store and nearby railroad depot are on the National Register of Historic Sites.

Wasilla is home to the Iditarod Trail Sled Dog Race® headquarters. The internationally known 1,150-mile Iditarod Trail Sled Dog Race® between Anchorage and Nome takes place in March. The Iditarod headquarters and visitors center is located at Mile 2.2 Knik Road. The center has historical displays on the Iditarod, videos, an Iditarod musher and dog teams, and a gift shop with unique souvenirs. Open daily in summer, weekdays in winter, from 8 A.M. to 5 P.M. Large tours are welcome, phone (907) 376-5155 in advance. Circular drive for buses and motorhomes, camping at adjacent Lake Lucille campground. No fee for museum or film. Fee charged for rides on wheeled dogsled.

Historical displays on Alaskan mushers and sled-dog trails can be found at the Knik Museum at Mile 13.9 Knik Road (see KNIK ROAD log this section). The museum is open from noon to 5 P.M. daily except Monday and Tuesday in summer. Admission fee $2 adults.

Iditarod Days is held in conjunction with the Iditarod Race in March. Other area winter events include ice golf at Mat–Su Resort and ice bowling at Big Lake. Check with the chamber of commerce about summer events.

Town Square Art Gallery. Fine art and unique gifts by Alaskan artists, jewelry and pottery. Representing the best of Alaskan,

Mill Pond Press and Greenwich Workshop artists. We gladly pack and ship. Credit cards, layaways, and phone orders are welcome. Open Monday–Friday 10–6, Saturday 10–5 and seasonally on Sundays 1–4 (summer and Christmas). Carrs Wasilla Mall. 591 E. Parks Hwy. #406, Wasilla, AK 99654. (907) 376-0123. [ADVERTISEMENT]

George Parks Highway Log
(continued)

A 42.7 (68.7 km) **F 315.3** (507.4 km) Airport Drive; food and shopping.

A 43.5 (70 km) **F 314.5** (506.1 km) Lucas Road; Hallea Lane access to Lake Lucille.

A 44.2 (71.1 km) **F 313.8** (505 km) Divided highway ends northbound.

A 44.4 (71.4 km) **F 313.6** (504.7 km) Church Road.

A 45 (72.4 km) **F 313** (503.7 km) Wasilla city limits. Shopping and services are located along the highway to **Milepost A 39.5** and at Main Street in Wasilla city center.

Wasilla Car Wash. See display ad this section.

A 46.7 (75.2 km) **F 311.3** (501 km) Highway crosses over the Alaska Railroad.

A 47 (75.6 km) **F 311** (500.5 km) Neuser Drive. Turnoff for Wasilla municipal airport and the Museum of Alaska Transportation and Industry. First annual Wasilla Airshow at the airport, June 7–8, 1997. The museum features historic aircraft, railroad equipment, old farm machinery and heavy equipment. Steam train rides on selected Saturdays. Admission fees in summer are $5 adults, $12 families. Group tours by arrangement.

Museum of Alaska Transportation & Industry. See display ad this section.

A 48.8 (78.5 km) **F 309.2** (497.6 km) Turnoff on Pittman Road to Rainbow Lake. Medical center, convenience store, gas station, cafe and Meadow Lakes post office.

A 49 (78.9 km) **F 309** (497.3 km) Seymour Lake Bed & Breakfast. See display ad this section.

A 49.4 (79.5 km) **F 308.6** (496.6 km) **Alaska R & R Laundry and RV Park.** Rose and Rich your highway hosts, invite you to stop in. Located at Mile 49.4 Parks Highway. Open 7 days a week, 8 A.M.–10 P.M. Self-serve laundry, showers, dump station, snack bar. Drop-off laundry welcome. Full hookups. P.O. Box 366, Houston, AK 99694. (907) 373-7286. [ADVERTISEMENT] ▲

A 49.5 (79.7 km) **F 308.5** (496.5 km) **The Roadside Inn.** See display ad this section.

A 50.1 (80.6 km) **F 307.9** (495.5 km) **Blodgett Lake B & B.** See display ad this section.

A 51 (82 km) **F 307** (494 km) **Big Lake–Susitna Veterinary Hospital.** See display ad this section.

A 51.3 (82.6 km) **F 306.7** (493.6 km) **Earth'n Art Studio and Gift Shop.** Located 1 block east of the Parks Highway on Spring Drive, you will find the workshop of Michael Stanelle, craftsman, ceramist and master mold maker. Manufactured on site, Michael creates individually handcrafted "Down to Earth" wind chimes, and displays them in his showroom. Other local artists are also featured in the unique, quality gift shop. Open year-round. Easy RV access. VISA and MasterCard accepted. (907) 892-7516. [ADVERTISEMENT]

A 52.3 (84.2 km) **F 305.7** (492 km) **Junction with Big Lake Road.** Meadowood shopping mall located here with a service station, hardware store, automatic teller machine, grocery and emergency phone (dial 911). See

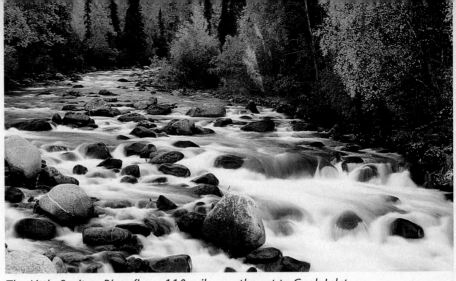

The Little Susitna River flows 110 miles southwest to Cook Inlet. *(© Tom Bol)*

BIG LAKE ROAD log on page 374.

A 53.2 (85.6 km) **F 304.8** (490.5 km) **Plettner Kennels.** A full-service Iditarod sled dog training facility. Year-round sled dog rides, guided kennel tours, play with puppies, learn to mush dogs, dog team boarding, sales and leases, sled shop and mushers newspaper. RV, tour bus and handicapped accessible. P.O. Box 878586, Wasilla, AK 99687-8586; (907) 892-6944. [ADVERTISEMENT] ♿

A 53.3 (85.8 km) **F 304.7** (490.4 km) Houston High School and Wasilla Senior Center. Turnout to west with map and infor-

Big Lake Road Log

The 6.5-mile/10.5-km Big Lake Road leads south from the George Parks Highway junction at **Milepost A 52.3** to **BIG LAKE** (pop. 2,333), a recreation area with swimming, camping, boating, fishing, jet skiing and tour boat rides in summer. Winter sports include snow machining. Businesses are found along Big Lake Road and along North Shore Drive, which forks off Big Lake Road at Mile J 3.6. Evidence of the June 1996 Big Lake wildfire, which began on Millers Reach Road, is visible from the road. Many Big Lake businesses and facilities escaped the fire, while some were partially burned or destroyed; many have rebuilt.

Distance is measured from the junction (J) with the George Parks Highway.

J 0 Junction with George Parks Highway. Meadowood Mall and gas station; automatic teller machine.

J 3.4 (5.5 km) Beaver Lake Road turnoff. Turn right here for public and private campgrounds. Drive 0.5 mile/0.8 km on Beaver Lake Road (gravel) for Rocky Lake state recreation site; 10 campsites, $10 nightly fee or annual pass, toilets, firepits, water and boat launch. ▲

J 3.5 (5.6 km) Gas station with automatic teller machine.

J 3.6 (5.8 km) Fisher's Y; gas station and Big Lake post office (ZIP code 99652). Big Lake Road forks here: Go straight ahead for North Shore Drive (description follows); keep to left for south Big Lake Road businesses and Big Lake South state recreation site (continue with this log).

North Shore Drive provides access to Klondike Inn and restaurant (1.4 miles/2.3 km) and Big Lake North state recreation site (1.6 miles/2.6 km), which has parking for 120 vehicles, overnight RV parking, tent sites, $10 nightly fee per vehicle or annual pass, covered picnic tables, water, toilets, dumpsters, boat launch ($5 fee) and sandy beach. Day-use parking $2. Pay phone. ▲

Big Lake Houseboat Rental. Watch the sunset in a secluded cove or cruise 53 miles of scenic shoreline aboard a comfortable, easy to handle houseboat. Galley, bathroom, shower. Models to accommodate 2 to 6 persons. Linens and fishing gear available. One hour north of Anchorage. VISA/MasterCard. (907) 892-9187.

E-mail:akboat@AKCashe.com. [ADVERTISEMENT]

J 3.7 (6 km) Shopping mall.

J 3.9 (6.3 km) Big Lake fire station.

J 4 (6.4 km) East Lake Mall; visitor information center, restaurant and grocery.

J 4.7 (7.6 km) Aero Drive and Big Lake airport. Big Lake is a 15-minute flight from Anchorage.

Private Aircraft: 1 mile/1.6 km southeast; elev. 150 feet/46m; length 2,400 feet/732m; gravel; fuel 100LL.

J 5 (8 km) Big Lake Motel. Bridge over Fish Creek. Fish Creek park picnic area; fish weir with salmon spawning view area. Fishing prohibited.

J 5.2 (8.4 km) Big Lake South state recreation site; 13 campsites, 6 picnic sites, toilets, water, dumpsters, boat ramp ($5 fee). Camping fee $10/night per vehicle or annual pass. Day-use fee $2. ▲

J 5.3 (8.5 km) Double-ended turnout with picnic tables and water.

J 5.7 (9.2 km) Gravel turnout, Echo Lake Road. Dog mushers' race track.

J 6.5 (10.5 km) Pavement ends. Burma Road continues into rural area, providing access to the south Big Lake area, former Point MacKenzie dairy project and the Little Susitna River public-use facility at Susitna Flats State Game Refuge (also accessible via Knik Road); parking, camping, boat ramps. Fee charged, state parks annual pass not accepted. See description and fee schedule at **Milepost J 17.2** Knik Road this section. ▲

Big Lake is connected with smaller lakes by dredged waterways. It is possible to boat for several miles in the complex. Fish in Big Lake include lake trout, Dolly Varden, rainbow, red and coho salmon, and burbot. ⊶

Return to Milepost A 52.3
George Parks Highway

Fishing at Nancy Lake recreation area, Milepost A 67.2. (© Michael DeYoung)

small weighted spoons or fresh salmon roe. No bait is allowed and artificials are required during the early weeks of the fishery in the first part of August. Also red salmon to 10 lbs., in mid-July, use coho flies or salmon eggs. Charter boats nearby. 🐟

A **57.5** (92.5 km) F **300.5** (483.6 km) **HOUSTON** (pop. 956) has a grocery store, restaurant (open daily), laundromat, gift shop, inn with food, lodging and pay phone, a campground and gas station. Post office located in the grocery store. Fishing charter operators and marine service are located here. Emergency phone at Houston fire station. ▲

Homesteaded in the 1950s, incorporated as a city in 1966. Houston is a popular fishing center for anglers on the Little Susitna River.

Houston Lodge. See display ad this section.

A **57.6** (92.7 km) F **300.4** (483.4 km) **Miller's Place.** Don't miss this stop! Groceries, post office, laundry, RV parking, cabin rentals, tenting on riverbank. Gift shop, fishing tackle and licenses, fresh salmon eggs. Ice, sporting goods sales and rental, pay phone. Fishing charters available; full day only $45. Probably the best soft ice cream and hamburgers in Alaska. Clean restrooms. Visitor information experts. Family-run Christian business. Gary and Debbie Miller. (907) 892-6129. [ADVERTISEMENT] ▲

A **57.7** (92.9 km) F **300.3** (483.3 km) **Riverside Camper Park.** See display ad this section. ▲

A **57.8** (93 km) F **300.2** (483.1 km) **Fisherman's Choice Charters.** Guided trips on the Little Susitna and Talkeetna Rivers. Trophy kings, silvers, reds and rainbow trout. Drop-offs available. May through September. We furnish the highest quality equipment available. 20 years experience. We know where the fish are, we go where the fish are. Reservations, information: (907) 892-8707. Box 940276, Houston, AK 99694. See display ad. [ADVERTISEMENT]

mation sign.

A **56.1** (90.3 km) F **301.9** (485.8 km) Miller's Reach Road. Alaska's most destructive wildfire began here in June 1996. The Big Lake wildfire burned some 37,000 acres and more than 350 homes and other buildings before it was contained.

A **56.4** (90.8 km) F **301.6** (485.4 km) *CAUTION: Railroad crossing.*

A **57.1** (91.9 km) F **300.9** (484.2 km) Bridge over the Little Susitna River; turnouts either side; toilets. This river heads at Mint Glacier in the Talkeetna Mountains to the northeast and flows 110 miles/177 km into Upper Cook Inlet.

A **57.3** (92.4 km) F **300.7** (483.9 km) Turnoff to Houston City Hall, fire station, emergency phone and city-operated Little Susitna River Campground. Large, well-maintained campground with 86 sites (many wide, level gravel sites); camping fee, water, restrooms, covered picnic area, 10-day limit. Off-road parking lot near river with access to river. Follow signs to camping and river. Day-use area with water and toilets west side of highway. ▲

The **Little Susitna River** has a tremendous king salmon run and one of the largest silver salmon runs in southcentral Alaska. Kings to 30 lbs. enter the river in late May and June, use large red spinners or salmon eggs. Silvers to 15 lbs., come in late July and August, with the biggest run in August; use

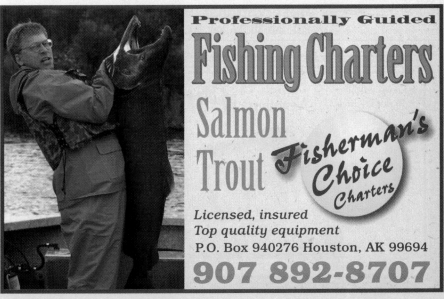

A 64.5 (103.8 km) F 293.5 (472.3 km) Nancy Lake Resort. See display ad this section.

A 65.8 (105.9 km) F 292.2 (470.2 km) **Nancy Lake Bed & Breakfast.** Great full breakfast or Continental style. Two rooms with private baths. Single, double or family welcome. Meet our Siberian husky sled dog team. Visiting dog teams welcome. Mushing,

cross-country skiing, snow machining, hiking, fishing, canoeing. Open year-round. Swiss-Canadian American hosts Romano and Maureen Conzett, Box 67, Willow, AK 99688. Phone/fax (907) 495-5845. [ADVERTISEMENT]

A 66.5 (107 km) F 291.5 (469.1 km) **Your Alaskan Hosts Bed & Breakfast.** See display ad this section.

A 66.7 (107.3 km) F 291.3 (468.8 km) Turnoff (not well marked) for Nancy Lake state recreation site; 30 campsites, 30 picnic

Bicycle tourers take a break at Willow. (© Ruth von Spalding)

sites, toilets, boat launch, horseshoe pits. Camping fee $10/night or annual pass. ▲

CAUTION: Highway crosses Alaska Railroad tracks.

A 67.2 (108.1 km) F 290.8 (468 km) Wide gravel road into Nancy Lake Recreation Area in the mixed birch and spruce forest of the Susitna River valley (good mushroom hunting area). At Mile 2.5/4 km on the access road there is a well-marked nature trail, toilets and parking area. At Mile 4.7/7.6 km there is a canoe launch, toilet and parking area. At Mile 5.7/9.2 km a hiking trail leads 3 miles/4.8 km to Chicken Lake, 5.5 miles/8.9 km to Red Shirt Lake. At Mile 6.2/10 km is South Rolly Lake overlook (day use only) with barbecues, 11 picnic tables, litter barrels and toilets. There are 106 campsites at South Rolly Lake Campground, at Mile 6.6/10.6 km, with firepits, toilets, water, canoe rentals and boat launch; firewood sometimes is provided. Camping fee $10/night or annual pass. ▲

South Rolly Lake, small population of rainbow, 12 to 14 inches. ◄

A 68.8 (110.7 km) F 289.2 (465.4 km) Miner's Last Stand Museum of Hatcher Pass, gas, diesel and gift shop.

Newman's Hilltop Service. See display ad this section.

A 69 (111 km) F 289 (465.1 km) **WILLOW** (pop. 368). Visitor facilities include 2 gas stations, grocery, hardware and notions store, air taxi service, lodges, RV parks, video rental and restaurants. The Willow civic organization sponsors an annual Winter Carnival in January.

Willow extends about 2.5 miles/4 km north along the George Parks Highway. The community is also a stop on the Alaska Railroad. Willow had its start about 1897, when gold was discovered in the area. In the early 1940s, mining in the nearby Talkeetna Mountains slacked off, leaving Willow a virtual ghost town. The community made a comeback upon completion of the Parks Highway in 1972.

In 1976, Alaska voters selected the Willow area for their new capital site. However, funding for the capital move from Juneau to Willow was defeated in the

November 1982 election.

Willow True Value Hardware, Willow Creek Grocery and **Willow Creek Service.** See display ad this section.

A 69.2 (111.4 km) **F 288.8** (464.8 km) Long Lake Road. Alternate access to Deshka Landing Cafe.

A 69.4 (111.7 km) **F 288.6** (464.4 km) Gas station, convenience store.

A 69.5 (111.8 km) 288.5 (464.3 km) Short road to Willow post office, lodge, trading post with cabins and camper spaces, and Alaska Railroad depot. ▲

Ruth Lake Lodge. See display ad this section.

Willow Trading Post Lodge. See display ad this section. ▲

A 69.6 (112 km) **F 288.4** (464.1 km) Willow elementary school.

A 69.7 (112.2 km) **F 288.3** (464 km) Willow Community Center, open daily, has a large parking area, commercial kitchen, showers, covered picnic pavilion, grills, ball court, boat launch and pay phone. (Available for rent to groups, 500-person capacity; phone 907/495-6633). Willow library.

A 69.9 (112.5 km) **F 288.1** (463.6 km) Fire station.

A 70 (112.7 km) **F 288** (463.5 km) **Private Aircraft:** Willow airport; elev. 220 feet/67m; length 4,200 feet/1,280m; gravel; fuel 100LL.

Willow Air Service Inc. See display ad this section.

A 70.8 (113.9 km) **F 287.2** (462.2 km) Willow Creek Parkway (**Susitna River** access road) to Willow Creek state recreation area (4 miles/6.4 km); camping $10/night, parking, litter barrels, trail to mouth of creek. Access to Deshka Landing boat launch. Fishing for king and silver salmon, rainbow trout. ◄▲

A 71 (114.3 km) **F 287** (461.9 km) Willow DOT/PF highway maintenance station.

A 71.2 (114.6 km) **F 286.8** (461.5 km) Junction with Hatcher Pass (Fishhook–Willow) Road. This road leads east and south across Hatcher Pass 49 miles/79 km to junction with the Glenn Highway. Independence Mine State Historical Park is 31.8 miles/51.2 km from here. Turn to the Hatcher Pass side road in the GLENN HIGHWAY section, page 310, for log of this road. (Parks Highway travelers should read that log back to front.) See also the Mat–Su Valley Vicinity map page 367. Hatcher Pass Road is mostly gravel with some steep, narrow, winding sections.

Access to Willow Creek state recreation area via Hatcher Pass Road. Deception Creek main campground, with 17 campsites, is located 1.2 miles/1.9 km from this junction via Hatcher Pass Road. Additional campsites and a picnic area are located 0.8 mile/1.3 km east. Both sites have tables, firepits and toilets. Camping fee $10/night or annual pass. Bed and breakfast located 2 miles/3.2 km east of highway past the campground. ▲

Alaska Creekside Bed & Breakfast. See display ad this section.

A 71.4 (114.9 km) F 286.6 (461.2 km) Lodge. Bridge over **Willow Creek**. This stream heads in Summit Lake, west of Hatcher Pass on the Hatcher Pass Road, and is a favorite launch site for airboat enthusiasts. Excellent king salmon fishing; also silvers, rainbow. Inquire at either lodge or resort for information. Entering Game Management Subunit 14B northbound, 14A southbound. From here to Denali National Park and Preserve watch for views of the Alaska Range to the east of the highway. ◣

Pioneer Lodge. One of Alaska's oldest, original log lodges. Restaurant with full bar overlooking Willow Creek. Liquor store. Full RV hookups $12, campground—tent sites $8, showers, laundromat, dump station. Rooms. Fishing, hunting charters, drop offs, wilderness tours, fly-ins, bank fishing—4

types of salmon, rainbows, grayling. Hiking trails. Boat launch. Bait, tackle, fishing rentals. Licenses, ice, gift shop. (907) 495-6883. See display ad. [ADVERTISEMENT] ▲

A 71.5 (115.1 km) F 286.5 (461.1 km) **Willow Island Resort**. Scenic riverside RV park, cabins and campground. Great salmon and trout fishing from the banks of crystal clear Willow Creek. Full hookups on level riverbank sites. Hot showers, laundry,

Aerial view of the Susitna River.
(© W. Wright-Diamond Photo)

dump station, tackle, mini-grocery, good water. Excellent king and silver salmon fishing. Rainbows to 10 lbs. Scenic fishing and

hunting charters. Guided fishing charters available. Close to Hatcher Pass; 3 hours from Denali National Park. Plan to stay awhile. Write: P.O. Box 85, Willow, AK 99688 or call (907) 495-6343. See display ad this section [ADVERTISEMENT] ▲

A 74.7 (120.2 km) F 283.3 (455.9 km) Bridge over **Little Willow Creek**. Parking on either side of creek; fishing for salmon and trout. ◣

A 76.4 (122.9 km) F 281.6 (453.2 km)

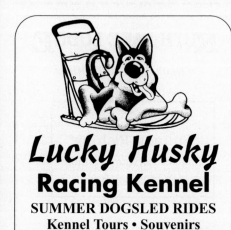

Paved double-ended turnout to west by **Kashwitna Lake.** Stocked with rainbow trout. Small planes land on lake. Good camera viewpoints of lake and Mount McKinley (weather permitting).

A 80 (128.7 km) F 278 (447.4 km) **Lucky Husky Racing Kennel.** Experience a true Alaskan lifestyle. Take an exciting summer dogsled ride! Meet the Lucky Husky family. Get dressed in original musher's clothes at the Iditarod checkpoint display. Take pictures with your favorite husky. Individuals and groups are welcome. Wir sprechen Deutsch. May–September: Open daily 10 A.M.–6 P.M. November–March: Reservation only. See display ad this section. [ADVERTISEMENT]

A 81.3 (130.8 km) F 276.7 (445.3 km) **Grey's Creek,** gravel turnouts both sides of highway. Fishing for salmon and trout. ◄

A 82.5 (132.8 km) F 275.5 (443.4 km) Susitna Landing, 1 mile/1.6 km on side road; boat launch, camping, handicap-accessible restrooms, bank fishing, riverboat service. Concessionaire-operated (ADF&G land) boat launch on **Kashwitna River,** just upstream

Sharply hooked nose of a spawning male red salmon. There are 5 species of Pacific salmon in Alaska's streams: king (also called chinook), silver (coho), red (sockeye), chum (dog, calico) and pink (humpback). (© Barbara Willard)

of the **Susitna River**; access to both rivers on site. The Susitna River heads at Susitna Glacier in the Alaska Range to the northeast and flows west then south for 260 miles/ 418 km to Cook Inlet. ⚓☕▲

Susitna Landing & Ron's Riverboat Service. See display ad this section. ⚓▲

A **83.2** (133.9 km) F **274.8** (442.2 km)

Bridge over the **Kashwitna River**; parking areas located at both ends of bridge. Salmon and trout fishing. The river heads in a glacier in the Talkeetna Mountains and flows westward 60 miles/ 96.5 km to enter the Susitna River 12 miles/19 km north of Willow. 🐟

A **84.1** (135.3 km) F **273.9** (440.8 km) Large paved turnout to west.

A **84.3** (135.7 km) F **273.7** (440.5 km) Gravel turnout to west. Walk-in for fishing at **Caswell Creek**; kings, silvers, pinks and rainbow. 🐟

A **85.1** (137 km) F **272.9** (439.2 km) Caswell Creek, large gravel turnout.

A **85.5** (137.6 km) F **272.5** (438.5 km) Gift shop and art gallery.

Willow Wildlife Art Gallery. Features Alaskan wildlife and sled dog art, as well as locally handcrafted gifts. Meet artist Dave

Totten in his home studio/gallery. "From Anchorage to Fairbanks ... best gallery," Jerry Griswold, *L.A. Times*, Aug. 1, 1993. Free coffee and wildberry muffins. (907) 495-1090. Open all year. [ADVERTISEMENT]

A **86** (138.4 km) F **272** (437.7 km) Public access road leads 1.3 miles/2.1 km to mouth of Sheep Creek public boat launch and Bluffs on Susitna. **Sheep Creek** has parking, toilets, dumpster and wheelchair-accessible trail to mouth of creek; fishing for kings, silvers, pinks and rainbow. ♿🐟

A **87** (140 km) F **271** 436.1 km) **Wolf Safari**, an educational facility and home of the "Kissing Wolves." 30 hybrid wolves on hand for your viewing and petting pleasure on a guided tour. Cameras welcome. Memento shop and free picnic area. Open every day. No backing up RV parking and pull-through. Remember, "You Gotta Pettum." (907) 495-5874. [ADVERTISEMENT]

A **88.1** (141.8 km) F **269.9** (434.4 km) **Cline's Caswell Lake Bed & Breakfast.** See display ad this section.

A **88.2** (142 km) F **269.8** (434.2 km) **Sheep Creek Lodge.** Beautiful log lodge, built with Alaskan white spruce logs, some over 200 years old. Fine dining, cocktail lounge, serving breakfast, lunch and dinner. Warm cozy cabins, creekside RV parking or camping. Excellent salmon and trout fishing within walking distance of lodge. Package liquor store, ice, fuel and propane. Gift shop featuring unique local Alaskan gifts, many Alaskan wildlife mounts and local tour information. Open year-round with winter activities including cross-country skiing, marked snow machine trails, ice fishing and dog mushing. Phone (907) 495-6227. See display ad this section. [ADVERTISEMENT]   ▲

A 88.6 (142.6 km) **F 269.4** (433.5 km) Bridge over **Sheep Creek**. Unimproved picnic area on west side below bridge by creek. Fishing for salmon and trout.   ◄●

A 91.5 (147.3 km) **F 266.5** (428.9 km) **Susitna Dog Tours & Bed and Breakfast.** Easy access to newly built log home offering a unique blend of Alaskan living and wilderness sled dog mushing or just a peaceful night's rest. Hot showers, sauna. Trails and seminars available for cross-country skiing, skijoring, dog mushing. Located within striking distance of Talkeetna and Denali National Park. Your hosts: Iditarod Veterans Bill and Rhodi Davidson and 50 sled dogs. Open year-round. Phone (907) 495-6324; e-mail: susdog@matnet.com. [ADVERTISEMENT]

A 91.7 (147.6 km) **F 266.3** (428.5 km) CAUTION: Railroad crossing.

A 93.4 (150.3 km) **F 264.6** (425.8 km) Gravel turnouts both sides of highway.

A 93.5 (150.5 km) **F 264.5** (425.7 km) **Goose Creek** culvert; gravel turnout. Fishing.   ●

A 93.6 (150.6 km) **F 264.4** (425.5 km) Goose Creek community center; park pavilion, picnic tables, grills, litter barrels.

A 95.1 (153 km) **F 262.9** (423.1 km) **Private Aircraft:** Montana Creek airstrip; elev. 250 feet/76m; length 2,400 feet/731m; gravel; fuel 80, 100.

A 96.6 (155.5 km) **F 261.4** (420.7 km) Bridge over **Montana Creek**. Homesteaders settled in the area surrounding this creek in the 1950s. Today, about 200 families live in the area. Camping and picnic areas on both sides of Montana Creek (operated by concessionaire, state park annual pass not accepted). Excellent king salmon fishing, also silvers, pinks (even-numbered years), grayling, rainbow and Dolly Varden.   ●▲

Montana Creek Campgrounds. Located on the south side of Montana Creek, all campsites in these private campgrounds are scenic, with some overlooking one of Alaska's best salmon and trout fishing streams. Picnic tables, campfires, toilets, tackle shop, tackle rentals and snacks. Only a short walk to the Susitna River. Conveniently located within 3 miles of grocery

store, cafe, laundromat and showers.   ▲
[ADVERTISEMENT]

A 97.8 (157.4 km) **F 260.2** (418.7 km) Denali Medical Center and Alaska State Troopers post (phone 907/733-2556 or 911 for emergencies).

A 98 (157.7 km) **F 260** (418.4 km) For weather information, tune your radio to 830-AM (99.7-FM).

A 98.4 (158.3 km) **F 259.6** (417.8 km) Susitna Valley High School; 3.1-mile/5-km trail for running in summer, cross-country skiing in winter. Senior Center.

A 98.7 (158.8 km) **F 259.3** (417.3 km) **Talkeetna junction.** Junction with Talkeetna Spur Road; 2 visitor information cabins. Access to hardware, lumber and feed store with automatic teller machine. Turn right northbound on paved spur road that

leads 14.5 miles/23.3 km to community of Talkeetna, an interesting side trip (description begins on page 383). See TALKEETNA SPUR ROAD log on page 383. Continue straight ahead on the George Parks Highway for Fairbanks.

Mary Carey's Fiddlehead Fern Farm. See display ad this section.

Moores' Mercantile. See display ad this section.

K2 Denali Direct. Alaska, Denali Park and Talkeetna area information and reservation service. Central booking for flightseeing statewide, McKinley scenic flights, glacier landings, fishing, rafting, Kenai Fjords tours, Arctic Circle tours, remote cabins, wilderness lodges including fly-drive-rail overnight Denali Park locations. Comfortable rest stop Mile 99 Parks, espresso, snacks, gifts, Denali art, modern restrooms. Up to the minute McKinley flightseeing reports, snow conditions and area activities. Watch for the K2

flag and office adjacent to the Talkeetna Spur Road junction. Benefit from our knowledge of the area. Write, call or stop in. Box 985, Talkeetna, AK 99676. Call 1-888-880-2580 or (907) 733-2295; fax (907) 733-2296. E-mail: ZQSH56A@prodigy.com. [ADVERTISEMENT]

Talkeetna/Denali Visitor Center. Staffed by knowledgeable local residents. Information and bookings of area recreational activities, including fishing, flightseeing, rafting, lodging and Denali Park. Statewide brochures and information. Large garden and picnic area. Public restrooms. Parks Highway at

Talkeetna Junction. Write Box 688, Talkeetna, AK 99676. Phone 1-800-660-2688 or (907) 733-2688. [ADVERTISEMENT]

A 98.8 (159 km) **F 259.2** (417.1 km) **Sunshine One Stop/Tesoro Alaska.** See display ad this section.

A 99 (159.3 km) **F 259** (416.8 km) **Denali Way Auto.** See display ad this section.

A 99.3 (159.8 km) **F 258.7** (416.3 km) **Montana and Little Montana lakes** on opposite sides of highway, stocked with rainbow. Watch for floatplanes.

A 99.5 (160.1 km) **F 258.5** (416 km) **H&H Lakeview Restaurant & Lodge,** serving travelers since 1965. Feast your senses in our spacious lakeside dining room, hidden away from the busy highway by a birch grove. You'll love our omelettes. Great hamburgers and steaks. Prime rib and seafood,

too. Our bread pudding is famous statewide. Take home a taste of Alaska in jellies from our gift shop. We make the jellies from Alaska berries, each with its own distinct flavor. Lakeside RV parking and camping. Hear the loons and watch beavers from your motorhome. Gerald and Sherry Berryman, proprietors since 1977. See display ad for details. [ADVERTISEMENT]

A 99.8 (160.6 km) **F 258.2** (415.5 km) Access road to YMCA camp on Peggy Lake.

A 100.4 (161.6 km) **F 257.6** (414.6 km) CAUTION: Railroad crossing.

A 102 (164.1 km) **F 256** (412 km) Paved double-ended turnout to east. Lakes both sides of highway.

A 102.6 (165.1 km) **F 255.4** (411 km) Turnout at Sunshine Road; access to

(Continues on page 389)

Talkeetna Spur Road Log

Distance from George Parks Highway junction (J) at Milepost A 98.7 is shown.

J 0 Junction with the George Parks Highway; visitor center.

J 1 (1.6 km) Fiddle fern farm and lodging.

Moose Dropping Inn Bed & Breakfast. See display ad this section.

J 3.1 (5 km) Turn west on Jubilee Road for bed and breakast. Turn east on Yoder Road for Benka Lake (private).

Denali View B&B. (Turn on Jubilee, St. Johns and Coffee roads.) Cozy cedar home offers hunting and fishing motif, antiques, great homemade breakfasts. Private baths. Located 12 miles south of Talkeetna, midway between Anchorage

and Denali Park. View of Denali. Lush gardens. Wonderful, friendly atmosphere. Let us book your Talkeetna experience. Book early; deposit required. Resident hosts, long-time Alaskans LesLee and Norm Solberg. HC 89 Box 8360, Talkeetna, AK 99676. Phone or fax (907) 733-2778. [ADVERTISEMENT]

J 3.5 (5.6 km) **Johnson Family Guitar Builders.** Turn on Noel Wien Drive to visit our family-owned and operated shop and showroom where we design and build fine flat-top and arch-top steel string acoustic guitars. We also handcraft the traditional classical guitar. Please stop in. We would like to meet you. (907) 733-2777. [ADVERTISEMENT]

J 5.3 (8.5 km) Answer Creek. Sunshine Community Health Center.

J 7.1 (11.4 km) Question Lake.

J 7.8 (12.6 km) Paradise Lodge.

J 9.2 (14.8 km) Fish Lake private floatplane base.

J 12 (19.3 km) Turn east on paved Comsat Road (unmarked) for **Christianson Lake**; drive in 0.7 mile/1.1 km on Comsat Road, turn left at Christianson Lake Road sign onto gravel road and drive 0.7 mile/1.1 km, turn right and follow signs to floatplane base. Fishing for silvers and rainbow. Good place to observe loons and waterfowl. ⊷

J 13 (20.9 km) Large gravel double-ended turnout with interpretive sign and viewpoint at crest of hill. Splendid views of Mount McKinley, Mount Foraker and the Alaska Range above the Susitna River. A must photo stop when the mountains are out. *CAUTION: Watch for traffic.*

J 13.3 (21.4 km) *CAUTION: Alaska Railroad crossing.*

J 13.5 (21.7 km) Talkeetna public library. Gas station.

J 13.8 (22.2 km) Restaurant and motel. VFW Post No. 3836 is 2 blocks west.

J 14 (22.5 km) East Talkeetna Road leads to state airport, municipal campground and boat launch on Talkeetna River and businesses. ▲

J 14.2 (22.9 km) Talkeetna post office (ZIP code 99676).

J 14.3 (23 km) Welcome to Beautiful Downtown Talkeetna sign and Talkeetna Historical Society visitor center log cabin; walking tour brochures available. (Description of Talkeetna follows.)

Museum of Northern Adventure. Highlighting Alaska's exciting history in 24 realistic dioramas, featuring life-sized figures and sounds. Entertaining and educational for all ages. Meander through the historic railroad building, experiencing Alaskana at every turn: homesteading, prospecting, wildlife, famous characters and more. Open daily year-round with special group/family rates. Clean restrooms. Gift shop featuring Eskimo dolls and totems. Carved grizzly and prospector outside to greet you. Main Street, Talkeetna. (907) 733-3999. Handicap accessible. [ADVERTISEMENT] ♿

J 14.5 (23.3 km) Talkeetna Spur Road ends at Talkeetna River Park.

Talkeetna

Located on a spur road, north of **Milepost A 98.7** George Parks Highway. **Population:** 441. **Emergency Services: Alaska State Troopers, Fire Department and Ambulance,** phone 911 or 733-2556. **Doctor,** phone 733-2708.

Visitor Information: Stop by the Talkeetna Historical Society Museum one block off Main Street opposite the Fairview Inn. Visitor information also available at log cabin at junction of Parks Highway and Spur Road. Or, write the Chamber of Commerce, P.O. Box 334, Talkeetna 99676.

The National Park Service maintains a ranger station that is staffed full time from mid-April through mid-September and intermittently during the winter. Mountaineering rangers provide information on Denali National Park and climbing within the Alaska Range. A reference library and video program are available to climbers. Mountaineering regulations and information may be obtained from Talkeetna Ranger Station,

Talkeetna Spur Road Log (continued)

P.O. Box 588, Talkeetna, AK 99676; phone (907) 733-2231.

Elevation: 346 feet/105m. **Radio:** KSKA-FM (PBS). **Television:** Channels 4, 6, 9.

Private Aircraft: Talkeetna airstrip (state airport), adjacent east; elev. 358 feet/109m; length 3,500 feet/1,067m; paved; fuel 100LL, Jet B. Talkeetna village airstrip on Main Street; elev. 346 feet/105m; length 1,200 feet/366m; gravel; village airstrip not recommended for transient aircraft or helicopters (watch for closures and poor conditions).

A Welcome to Beautiful Downtown Talkeetna sign is posted at the town park as you enter Talkeetna's old-fashioned Main Street, the only paved street in town. Log cabins and clapboard homes and businesses line Main Street, which dead ends at the Susitna River.

Talkeetna is the jumping-off point for many climbing expeditions to Mount McKinley. Most climbing expeditions use the West Buttress route, pioneered by Bradford Washburn, flying in specially equipped ski-wheel aircraft to Kahiltna Glacier. The actual climb on Mount McKinley is made from about 7,000 feet/ 2,134m (where the planes land) to the summit of the South Peak (elev. 20,320 feet/6,194m). Several air services based in Talkeetna specialize in the glacier landings necessary to ferry climbers and their equipment to and from the mountain. The climb via the West Buttress route usually takes 18 to 20 days. Flightseeing the mountain is also popular (and easier!).

ACCOMMODATIONS/VISITOR SERVICES

Talkeetna has 5 motels/hotels, several bed and breakfasts, 6 restaurants, 2 gas stations, laundromats, gift and clothing shops, grocery and general stores. (Nagley's Store, formerly the B&K Trading Post and the second oldest building in Talkeetna, was gutted by fire on Jan. 1. The owner plans to rebuild.) A dump station is located at Three Rivers Tesoro.

There is a campground with toilets and shelters at the public boat launch (fee charged) just beyond the Swiss Alaska Inn; take East Talkeetna Road (a right turn at Mile 14 on the Spur Road as you approach Talkeetna). ▲

Talkeetna Motel, Restaurant and Lounge. Built in 1964 by "Evil Alice" and Sherm Powell, the "Tee-Pee" (nicknamed by oldtimers) became known for its excellent food, fast service and sincere Alaskan hospitality. Today, we also offer private baths, color TV in rooms and lounge, full menu for casual and fine dining. MasterCard/VISA welcome. See display ad this section. [ADVERTISEMENT]

Talkeetna Roadhouse. Open year-

Three Rivers
Accommodations

Office at Three Rivers Tesoro
P.O. Box 525MP (907) 733-2741
Talkeetna, Alaska 99676

Trapper John's
Bed & Breakfast
Historic log cabin, 5★ outhouse
Full sourdough breakfasts!
P.O. Box 243 Talkeetna, AK 99676
(907) 733-2353   **1-800-735-2354**
Phone / Fax   In Alaska

TALKEETNA MOTEL *In Picturesque Talkeetna*

25 MODERN ROOMS
UNIQUE RESTAURANT and COCKTAIL LOUNGE
OPEN YEAR AROUND

BOX 115, TALKEETNA, AK 99676 • (907) 733-2323

Swiss-Alaska Inn

• RESTAURANT — Complete Menu
Fresh Halibut and Salmon Dinners
• COCKTAIL LOUNGE
• MOTEL — All Modern Rooms with Bath
Reasonable Prices • PAY PHONE

MasterCard VISA AMERICAN EXPRESS

EAST TALKEETNA BY BOAT LAUNCH—watch for sign
P.O Box 565, Talkeetna, AK 99676   Phone (907) 733-2424
OPEN YEAR-ROUND   Please contact: Werner Rauchenstein

CHINOOK WINDS
3 Cabins • Full Baths • Each Cabin Sleeps 5
Children Under 12 Free
Coffee, Toaster, Refrigerator
OPEN YEAR AROUND
VISA, MasterCard Accepted
Box 356, Talkeetna, Alaska 99676 • **(907) 733-1899 or 733-2369**

TALKEETNA ADVERTISERS

Alaska Bush Float
   Plane Service ....Ph. (907) 733-1693
Chinook Winds
   Cabins ....Ph. (907) 733-1899
Crowley
   Guide Service...............Ph. (907) 733-1279
Denali Dry Goods ....Main St.
Denali Floats ....Ph. (907) 733-2384
Doug Geeting
   Aviation ....Ph. (907) 733-2366
Fitzgerald
   Guide Service...............Ph. (907) 733-2704
Hudson Air
   Service, Inc. ....Ph. (907) 733-2321
K2 Aviation ....Ph. (800) 764-2291
Latitude 62°
   Lodge/Motel................Ph. (907) 733-2262
Mahay's Riverboat
   Service ....Ph. (907) 733-2223
McKinley Air Service ....State Airport
Mountain Gift Shop/Visitor
   Information Cabin.........................Main St.
Museum of Northern
   Adventure.................................Mile J 14.3
Nagley's Store...................Ph. (907) 733-3663
Paradise Cabins ....Ph. (907) 733-1471
Peak Dodger Flight Tours ....Main St.
Swiss–Alaska Inn ....Ph. (907) 733-2424
Talkeetna Air Taxi ....Ph. (907) 733-2218
Talkeetna Gifts and
   Collectables ....Mile J 14.3
Talkeetna Motel................Ph. (907) 733-2323
Talkeetna River
   Adventures ....Ph. (907) 733-2604
Talkeetna River Guides......................Main St.
Talkeetna Riverboat Service..............Main St.
Talkeetna Roadhouse........................Main St.
Three Rivers
   Accommodation ....Ph. (907) 733-2741
Three Rivers Tesoro...........................Main St.
Timberline Aviation ....Ph. (907) 733-1800
Trapper John's
   Bed & Breakfast...........Ph. (907) 733-2354
Tri–River Charters.............Ph. (907) 733-2400
Village Arts & Craft...........Ph. (907) 733-2281

Talkeetna is located at the junction of the Susitna, Talkeetna and Chulitna rivers. (© Ruth von Spalding)

ing and glacier landings are available. See ads this section.

Railroad: The Alaska Railroad.

Highway: At the end of a 14.5-mile/ 23.3-km spur road off the George Parks Highway (Alaska Route 3).

ATTRACTIONS

The **Talkeetna Historical Society Museum** is located 1 block off Main Street opposite the Fairview Inn. The original 1-room schoolhouse, built in 1936, exhibits historical items, local art, a historical library and a display on the late Don Sheldon, famous Alaskan bush pilot. In the Railroad Section House see the impressive 12-foot-by-12-foot scale model of Mount McKinley (Denali) with photographs by Bradford Washburn. A mountaineering display features pioneer and recent climbs of Mount McKinley. The Ole Dahl cabin, an early trapper/ miner's cabin located on the museum grounds, is furnished with period items. Admission: $1 adult, under 12 free. Pick up a walking tour map of Talkeetna's historic sites here. Picnic area adjacent museum. Museum buildings open 10 A.M. to 5 P.M. daily in summer. Reduced hours other seasons. Phone (907) 733-2487. Privately operated guided history tours.

Miners Day. Held the weekend

round. Located on the edge of wilderness in a living pioneer village, the Talkeetna Roadhouse (Frank Lee cabin, circa 1917) has served the territory since early gold rush days. Still family owned and operated, this historic restaurant, lodge and bakery featuring 1902 sourdough, is known worldwide for its fine home-style cooking, cinnamon rolls, and frontier hospitality. Slow down to "Talkeetna time," relax amidst the rustic charm and

listen to the stories these old walls have to tell! Rooms start at $45, bunk spaces $21. Restaurant features classic road house breakfast, daily soup and sandwich menu, supper specials and locally home-brewed beers on tap. Phone (907) 733-1351, fax (907) 733-1353. [ADVERTISEMENT]

TRANSPORTATION

Air: There are several air taxi services in Talkeetna. Charter service, flightsee-

Talkeetna Spur Road Log (continued)

before Memorial Day, this family event has a trade and craft fair, local cancan dancers, softball tournament, a thrilling outhouse race, street dance and parade.

The Talkeetna Gold Dust Dancers perform at the pavillion in the park, next to the "Welcome to Beautiful Downtown Talkeetna" sign, in summer. Made up of local women, the group won the 1995 state championship for cancan dancing. Check locally for schedule.

Annual Moose Dropping Festival is held the second Saturday in July as a fund-raising project for the museum. Activities include a 5-km run and walk, a parade, entertainment, music, barbecue, food and game booths, and, of course, a moose dropping throwing contest.

Riverboat tours up Talkeetna Canyon, Devils Canyon, Chulitna River and Tokositna River are available. Several guides also offer riverboat fishing trips from Talkeetna. Talkeetna is located at the confluence of the Susitna, Talkeetna and Chulitna rivers. Inquire locally for details and see ads this section.

Crowley Guide Service. Main Street, Talkeetna. Guided fishing for salmon, rainbow trout and arctic grayling. River transportation and camp support. Scenic and wildlife charters. Mountain biking, rentals, sales and tours. Mount McKinley scenic flights and glacier landings. International expeditions. Personalized service at reasonable rates. VISA, Master-Card. P.O. Box 431, Talkeetna, AK 99676. Phone (907) 733-1279; fax (907) 733-1278. [ADVERTISEMENT]

Hudson Air Service, Inc., Talkeetna's senior air taxi, provides unique guided tours of "Denali" with running commentary on the points of interest, wildlife

and history of the area. Cliff Hudson helped pioneer Mount McKinley flights and glacier landings. Our family-owned business, in continuous operation since 1946, now has 2 generations of pilots

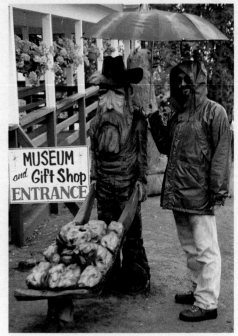

Visitor and local prospector pose for photo. (© Susan Cole Kelly)

flying. Highly skilled and knowledgeable, with many years of accident–free flying, their safety records speak for them. We specialize in scenic flights, Mount McKinley glacier landings and scenic wildlife tours. We can make your trip to Alaska and Mount McKinley a memorable one. Fly with us for a once-in-a-lifetime Alaskan experience. Reservations and information: 1-800-478-2321 or (907) 733-2321. Fax (907) 733-2333. P.O. Box 648, Talkeetna, AK 99676. [ADVERTISEMENT]

Mahay's Riverboat Service. Fish clear-water streams for all 5 species of Pacific salmon and trout. Custom-designed jet boats allow access to over 200 miles of prime fishing territory. Guided fishing charters include all equipment needed. Fishing packages are also available that include accommodations, meals and all the "extras." Spend the afternoon exploring an authentic trapper's cabin, viewing nesting bald eagles and sightseeing on the McKinley View River Cruise. Drop-off fishing also available at reasonable rates. Credit cards accepted. (907) 733-2223, fax (907) 733-2712. In Alaska, 1-800-736-2210. [ADVERTISEMENT]

Mountain Gift Shop/Visitor Information Cabin. Near the famous "Welcome to Beautiful Downtown Talkeetna" sign. Enjoy shopping for mountain theme items: books, maps, posters, T-shirts, flags, colorful gemstone necklaces and quill jewelry handmade in Alaska. Moose nugget items our specialty. Open summer 10–5:30. Free town map. Information, reservation (907) 733-1686. [ADVERTISEMENT]

Peak Dodger Flight Tours. Experience a flight with renowned glacier and flying expert Doug Geeting, who knows the climbers and all the lore and legend

of Denali (the great one). You can experience a glacier landing and look up at 5,000-foot walls of ice and rock that will astound the most world-weary traveler. This flight will definitely be the high point of all your Alaska adventures! Intercom-equipped. Group rates available. Accommodations available, $65 per night. Fly-in fishing cabins. Open year-round. For reservations and prices write or call Doug Geeting Aviation, Box 42

MP, Talkeetna, AK 99676; (800) 770-2366 or (907) 733-2366. Fax (907) 733-1000. See display ad in the DENALI NATIONAL PARK section. [ADVERTISEMENT]

Talkeetna Air Taxi. The ultimate Denali experience. Fly Mount McKinley.

Talkeetna Spur Road Log (continued)

Glacier landing, wildlife tours, aerial photography. Remote backpacking. In business since 1947. Office in log building at state airport. Write Box 73-MP, Talkeetna, AK 99676. For information, reservations, call ahead 1-800-533-2219 or (907) 733-2218. See display ad. [ADVERTISEMENT]

Talkeetna Gifts & Collectables. "One of the nicest and most complete gift shops in Alaska" located in a spacious log building with handmade keepsakes, souvenirs, jewelry, books, Alaskana, birch bowls, quilts and other treasures. Fur slippers/accessories, beautiful sweatshirts, sweaters, plush toys, puppets and huggable Eskimo dolls. Alaskan foods

Returning to Talkeetna state airport after flightseeing Mount McKinley.
(© W. Wright-Diamond Photo)

and sourdough. Suzy's exclusive "Alaska Map" cross-stitch pattern. Quality merchandise with friendly service. We mail purchases. Goldpanning, with gold guaranteed! Open daily year-round. Main Street, Talkeetna. (907) 733-2710. [ADVERTISEMENT]

Talkeetna River Guides. Fish with a recognized leader for salmon and trout in our exciting, area streams and rivers. Guided charters start at $119 and include all equipment and use of our specialized jet boats. Drop-off fishing available as well. Also, join us on a wildlife, natural history float trip. 2, 4 and 6-hour tours available daily. 1-800-353-2677. See display ad. [ADVERTISEMENT]

Timberline Aviation. Experience the highest mountain in North America while flying in the comfort and safety of our larger turbine engine aircraft. We can quickly accommodate the single pas-

senger or a very large group. Why get stuffed into the back of a small airplane? With Timberline Aviation everybody enjoys plenty of room, a large window and a headset. Relax and let our professional Airline Transport rated pilots show you the best of Mount McKinley. Trust this trip of a lifetime to us, you'll see more and spend less. We can also arrange glacier landings at the 7500-foot climber base camp or the world famous Don Sheldon Amphitheater. Bring plenty of film and fly with Alaska's mountain flying experts. Floatplane service available. Backpackers welcome. Lodging available. Seniors, children under 12, RVer's and mothers from Colorado get a 10 percent discount. Physically challenged welcome. Office located on the Talkeetna Airport. P.O. Box 1047, Talkeetna, AK 99676. Phone (907) 733-1800. [ADVERTISEMENT] ♿

Fishing. A Calico (chum) Salmon Derby is held the first 3 weeks of August. The **Susitna River** basin offers many top fishing streams and lakes, either accessible by road, plane or riverboat. 🐟

Return to Milepost A 98.7
George Parks Highway

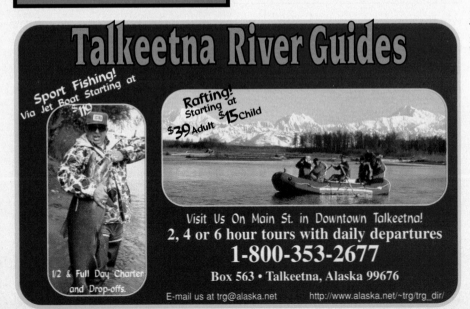

(Continued from page 382)

Sunshine Creek for fishing via dirt road. ⚓

A 104 (167.4 km) **F 254** (408.8 km) **Big Su Lodge.** See display ad this section.

A 104.2 (167.7 km) **F 253.8** (408.4 km) Entering Game Management Unit 16A, northbound, Unit 14B southbound.

A 104.3 (167.8 km) **F 253.7** (408.3 km) Bridge over Big Susitna River. State rest area to west on south bank of river; loop road, parking area, tables, firepits, toilets, no drinking water. ▲

Some of the finest stands of white birch in Alaska may be seen for several miles on both sides of the river. This area is also noted for its fiddlehead ferns. The ferns (lady fern, ostrich fern and shield fern) are harvested in the spring, when their young shoots are tightly coiled, resembling a fiddle's head. Fiddleheads should be cooked before consumption.

A 104.6 (168.3 km) **F 253.4** (407.8 km) Rabideaux Creek access; parking, 0.3 mile/0.5 km trail to mouth of creek. Watch for seasonal flooding.

A 104.8 (168.7 km) **F 253.2** (407.5 km) Double-ended turnout to west.

A 105.9 (170.4 km) **F 252.1** (405.7 km) Rabideaux Creek access and bridge.

A 107.6 (173.2 km) **F 250.4** (403 km) View of Mount McKinley for northbound travelers.

A 114.8 (184.7 km) **F 243.2** (391.4 km) Cluster of businesses serving highway travelers and Trapper Creek the next mile northbound include: lodges with gift shops, gas and restaurants; RV park; laundromats; and flightseeing service. ▲

Trapper Creek Inn & General Store. Gateway to Denali, visitors information center, Tesoro gas, diesel, deluxe lodging with Mount McKinley view, large RV campground, full hook-ups, dump station, propane, showers, restrooms, laundry, pay phone, deli, groceries, coffee, ice, etc. Fish-

ing and hunting supplies and charters. Flightseeing Mount McKinley. Major credit cards accepted. Phone (907) 733-2302. Fax (907) 733-1002. Tour buses welcome. See large display ad this section. [ADVERTISEMENT] ▲

A 114.9 (184.9 km) **F 243.1** (391.2 km) **TRAPPER CREEK** (area pop. about 700), at **junction** with Petersville Road. Trapper Creek post office (ZIP code 99683). Miners built the Petersville Road in the 1920s and federal homesteading began here in 1948, with settlement continuing through the 1950s and 1960s. The George Parks Highway opened as far as Trapper Creek in 1967. Today it is the southern gateway to Denali Park and the Alaska Range, with access via the Petersville Road (description follows). Trapper Creek businesses are located along the Parks Highway and up Petersville Road.

Petersville Road leads west and north from Trapper Creek approximately 40 miles/64 km (no winter maintenance beyond Mile 14). This scenic gravel road (with excellent views of Mount McKinley) goes through a homestead and gold mining area that also contains some new subdivisions. Berry picking in season. Lodging available at Mile 2.7, 10.5, 17.2 and 18.7. Turn down the right fork for the former mining camp of Petersville (4-wheel drive recommended). *Please respect private property.* The left fork leads 0.2 mile/0.3 km to **Peters Creek** stream. Fishing for salmon and trout. The road to Petersville is rough and used primarily by miners and trappers beyond The Forks Roadhouse at Mile 18.7. ⚓▲

North Country Bed and Breakfast (Mile 2.7 Petersville Road). Nestled on a lake with a spectacular view of Mount McKinley. Five

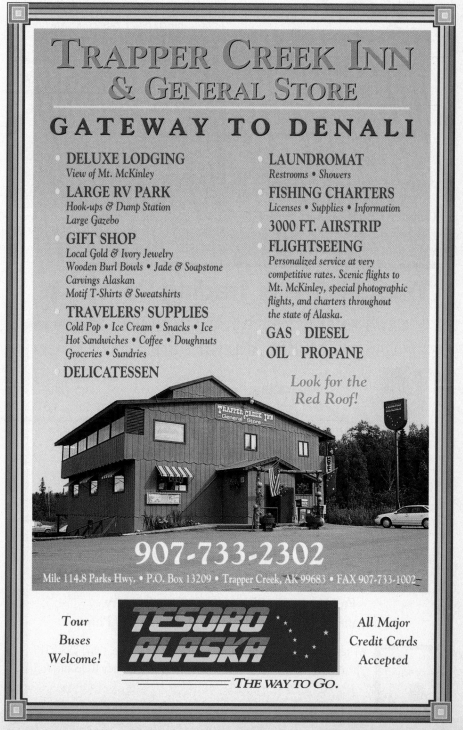

first-class rooms with private bathrooms and private entries. Mount McKinley flightseeing trips available at the lake by appointment. Bird watching, wildlife, paddleboating and horseshoes available. Open year-round. Your hosts—Mike and Sheryl Uher. Phone (907) 733-3981. [ADVERTISEMENT]

Gate Creek Cabins. Modern log cabins, equipped for comfortable stay of day, week or longer. Located Mile 10.5 on historic Petersville Road, with year around access. Furnished with linens, dishes, utensils, stove, refrigerator, TV, VCR, showers, sauna, BBQ grill. Bring your personal items, food

and recreation equipment. Fishing, mountain viewing, hiking, biking, photography, berry picking, canoeing, paddle boating on our small lake; cross-country skiing, snowmobiling, with rentals and guided tours available. Rates: $38/person/night, children 12 and under free, 5 percent bed tax. Weekly rate. Family pets welcome. Your hosts, Gary and Dorothy Rawie, reservations (907) 733-1393 (cabins), (907) 248-2765 (Anchorage). [ADVERTISEMENT]

McKinley Foothills B&B/Cabins. Off Mile 17.2 Petersville Road. Furnished,

secluded log cabins, kitchenettes. Full breakfast. Great food, Alaskan hospitality.

Great Mount McKinley views. Summer: gold panning tours, fishing nearby, birding, hiking, mountain biking. Winter: skiing, snow machining, dog mushing tours. Major credit cards. Homepage: www.matnet.com/mckinley. E-mail: mckinley@matnet.com. Phone/fax (907) 733-1454. P.O. Box 13089, Trapper Creek, AK 99683. [ADVERTISEMENT]

The Forks Roadhouse. See display ad this section.

A 115.2 (185.4 km) **F 242.8** (390.7 km) Trapper Creek community park.

A 115.5 (185.9 km) **F 242.5** (390.2 km) **Trapper Creek Trading Post.** See display ad this section. ▲

A 115.6 (186 km) **F 242.4** (390.1 km) Highway crosses Trapper Creek.

Excellent views of Mount McKinley (weather permitting) northbound.

A 115.7 (186.2 km) **F 242.3** (390 km) **Trapper Creek Pizza Pub.** See display ad this section.

A 117.3 (188.8 km) **F 240.7** (387.4 km) Turnout east; vehicle weighing.

A 121.1 (194.9 km) **F 236.9** (381.2 km) Chulitna highway maintenance camp.

A 121.5 (195.5 km) **F 236.5** (380.6 km) Easy-to-miss large paved double-ended rest area to east with tables, firepits, drinking water, toilet and interpretive bulletin board. Shade trees; cow parsnip grows lush here.

A 123.4 (198.6 km) **F 234.6** (377.5 km) Wooded area with many dead trees covered with "conks" (a term applied to a type of bracket fungus).

A 126.6 (203.7 km) **F 231.4** (372.4 km) Large paved turnout to east.

A 128.4 (206.6 km) **F 229.6** (369.5 km) Undeveloped parking area below highway by creek.

A 132 (212.4 km) **F 226** (363.7 km) Boundary of Denali State Park (see description next milepost).

A 132.7 (213.6 km) **F 225.3** (362.6 km) Denali State Park entrance sign. This 325,460-acre state park has 48 miles/77.2 km of hiking trails. Camping at Troublesome Creek (**Milepost A 137.3**), Byers Lake (**Milepost A 147**) and Denali View North (**Milepost A 162.7**). Hunting is permitted in the park, but discharge of firearms is prohibited within 0.3 mile of highway, and 0.5 mile of a developed facility or 0.5 mile of trail around Byers Lake. ▲

A 132.8 (213.7 km) **F 225.2** (362.4 km) **Chulitna River** bridge. Fishing for grayling, rainbow. Game Management Unit 13E, leaving unit 16A, northbound. ◆

Mount McKinley Princess Lodge. A brand new riverside retreat located in Denali State Park featuring spectacular views of Mount McKinley, private bungalows and a host of amenities including an array of

View of Mount McKinley and Mount Foraker from Milepost A 135.2. (Jerrianne Lowther, staff)

Curry Ridge and south to Troublesome Creek. *CAUTION: Bears frequent campground. Keep a clean camp.*　　　　&◀▲

A 147.2 (236.9 km) F 210.8 (339.2 km) Alaska Veterans Memorial turnoff. This concrete memorial honoring the armed forces was renovated in 1996 to include a park store, spotting scopes, viewing deck, visitor contact station, interpretive kiosk, picnic area and restrooms.

A 155.6 (250.4 km) F 202.4 (325.7 km) For the next mile northbound, there are views of Eldridge Glacier to the left. The face of the glacier is 6 miles/9.7 km from the road. The Fountain River heads at the terminus of the glacier and flows into the Chulitna.

A 157.7 (253.8 km) F 200.3 (322.3 km) Small paved turnout to west.

A 159.4 (256.5 km) F 198.6 (319.6 km) Double-ended paved turnout to west.

A 159.9 (257.3 km) F 198.1 (318.8 km) Parking area east side of highway by Horseshoe Creek.

A 160.8 (258.8 km) F 197.2 (317.4 km) The highway makes a steep descent northbound with moderate S-curves to Little Coal Creek.

A 161 (259.1 km) F 197 (317 km) Large gravel turnout to east.

A 162.4 (261.4 km) F 195.6 (314.8 km) Large paved turnout to west; Mount McKinley

dining options, tour desk and gift shop. Open mid-May through mid-September. Call 1-800-426-0500 year-round. See display ad in DENALI NATIONAL PARK section. [ADVERTISEMENT]

A 134.5 (216.5 km) F 223.5 (359.7 km) Mary's McKinley View Lodge. Located on Mary Carey's original homestead. Spectacular view of McKinley from every room, especially the glass-walled restaurant. Mary, famous for Alaskan books, homesteaded before the state park was created. She fought for highway completion to share her magnificent view with travelers. Enjoy dining, browse the gift shop or spend a pleasant night in the modern rooms. Call (907) 733-1555. See display ad this page. [ADVERTISEMENT]

A 134.8 (216.9 km) F 223.2 (359.2 km) Small turnout to east. Springwater piped to road. *CAUTION: Spring water is not treated. Use at own risk.*

A 135.2 (217.6 km) F 222.8 (358.6 km) Large paved turnout with toilet and view of 20,320-foot/6,194-m Mount McKinley; a display board here points out peaks. From here northbound for many miles there are views of glaciers on the southern slopes of the Alaska Range to the west. Ruth, Buckskin and Eldridge glaciers are the most conspicuous.

Ruth Glacier trends southeast through the Great Gorge for 31 miles/50 km. The glacier was named in 1903 by F.A. Cook for his daughter. The Great Gorge was named by mountain climbers in the late 1940s. Nicknamed the Grand Canyon of Alaska, peaks on either side of the gorge tower up to 5,000 feet/1,500m above Ruth Glacier. The gorge opens into Don Sheldon Amphitheater, at the head of Ruth Glacier, where the Don Sheldon mountain house sits. Donald E. Sheldon (1921–75) was a well-known bush pilot who helped map, patrol, and aid search and rescue efforts in this area.

Flightseeing trips can be arranged that take you close to Mount McKinley, into the Don Sheldon Amphitheater, through the Great Gorge and beneath the peak of The

Mooses Tooth. Inquire at Trapper Creek Inn, **Milepost A 114.8,** or with air taxi operators in Talkeetna and in the national park.

Peaks to be sighted, left to right, along the next 20 miles/32.2 km to the west are: Mount Hunter (elev. 14,573 feet/4,442m); Mount Huntington (elev. 12,240 feet/3,731m); Mount Barrille (elev. 7,650 feet/2,332m); and Mount Dickey (elev. 9,845 feet/3,001m).

A 137.3 (221 km) F 220.7 (355.1 km) Troublesome Creek bridge. Lower Troublesome Creek state recreation site has 10 campsites, $6/night camping fee per vehicle or annual pass, day-use area with sheltered picnic sites, toilets, water and litter barrels. Lower Troublesome Creek trailhead. This is usually a clear runoff stream, not silted by glacial flour. The stream heads in a lake and flows 14 miles/22.5 km to the Chulitna River.　　　　▲

Troublesome Creek, rainbow, grayling and salmon (king salmon fishing prohibited); June through September.　　🐟

A 137.6 (221.4 km) F 220.4 (354.7 km) Upper Troublesome Creek trailhead and parking area. Trails to Byers Lake (15 miles/24 km) and Tarn Point, elev. 2,881 feet/878m (10.8 miles/17.3 km). *NOTE: Trailhead and trail to Mile 5.5 closed from mid-July to Sept. 1 due to the high concentration of bears feeding on spawning salmon.*

A 139.9 (225.1 km) F 218.1 (351 km) Paved turnout to west.

A 143.9 (231.6 km) F 214.1 (344.6 km) Bridge over Byers Creek.

A 145.7 (234.5 km) F 212.3 (341.6 km) Paved turnout to west.

A 147 (236.6 km) F 211 (339.6 km) **Byers Lake** state campground with 66 sites, $12/night camping fee or annual pass, picnic tables, firepits, water, toilets (wheelchair accessible) and access to Byers Lake (electric motors permitted). Fishing for grayling, burbot, rainbow, lake trout and whitefish. Remote campsite 1.8-mile/2.9-km hike from campground (see directions posted on bulletin board). Hiking trail to

Hurricane Gulch bridge at Milepost A 174. (© Susan Cole Kelly)

viewpoint.

A 162.7 (261.8 km) F 195.3 (314.3 km) Denali View North campground; 20 sites, camping fee charged, day-use parking, toilets (wheelchair accessible), water, interpretive kiosks, spotting scope, short loop trail. Overlooks Chulitna River. Views of Denali, Mooses Tooth, Mount Huntington and Alaska Range peaks above Hidden River valley. 🚻▲

A 162.8 (262 km) F 195.2 (314.1 km) Small paved turnout to east. Watch for beaver pond to west northbound. Denali view to north.

A 163.1 (262.5 km) F 194.9 (313.6 km) Large double-ended paved turnout to west.

A 163.2 (262.6 km) F 194.8 (313.5 km) Bridge over Little Coal Creek.

Coal Creek, rainbow, grayling and salmon, July through September. 🐟

A 163.8 (263.6 km) F 194.2 (312.5 km) Little Coal Creek trailhead and parking area. According to park rangers, this trail offers easy access (1½-hour hike) to alpine country. It is a 27-mile/43.5-km hike to Byers Lake via Kesugi Ridge.

A 165.6 (266.5 km) F 192.4 (309.6 km) A small stream passes under the road; paved turnouts on both sides of highway. Good berry picking in the fall.

A 168.5 (271.2 km) F 189.5 (305 km) Denali State Park boundary sign.

A 169 (272 km) F 189 (304.2 km) *CAUTION: Railroad crossing.* A solar collector here helps power the warning signals.

Denali State Park boundary (leaving park northbound, entering park southbound).

A 170.3 (274 km) F 187.7 (302.1 km) Paved viewpoint area to west.

A 171 (275.2 km) F 187 (300.9 km) There are several small turnouts next 5 miles/8 km northbound.

A 174 (280 km) F 184 (296.1 km) Bridge over Hurricane Gulch; rest area. From the south end of the bridge, scramble through alders up the east bank of the gulch to find photographers' trail (unmarked). A 0.3-mile/0.4-km trail along edge of Hurricane Gulch offers good views of the bridge span and gulch. A pleasant walk, good berry picking in the fall. *Do not go too near the edge.* Parking areas at both ends of bridge.

Construction costs for the bridge were approximately $1.2 million. The 550-foot/168m deck of the bridge is 260 feet/79m above Hurricane Creek, not as high as the railroad bridge that spans the gulch near the Chulitna River. From this bridge the high-

way begins a gradual descent northbound to Honolulu Creek.

A 176 (283.2 km) F 182 (292.9 km) Paved turnout to east. There are several small turnouts next 5 miles/8 km southbound.

A 176.5 (284 km) F 181.5 (292.1 km) Double-ended gravel turnout to west with view of the Alaska Range. Highway descends long grade northbound.

A 177.8 (286.1 km) F 180.2 (290 km) Paved turnout and view of eroded bluffs to west.

A 178.1 (286.6 km) F 179.9 (289.5 km) Bridge over Honolulu Creek. The highway begins a gradual ascent northbound to Broad Pass, the gap in the Alaska Range crossed by both the railroad and highway. Undeveloped parking areas below highway on the creek.

A 179.7 (289.2 km) F 178.3 (286.9 km) Paved turnout to west by small lake. In early September blueberries are plentiful for the next 25 miles/40 km.

A 180 (289.7 km) F 178 (286.5 km) Small paved turnout to west by small lake. Short trail to **Mile 180 Lake**, stocked with grayling. 🐟

A 183.2 (294.8 km) F 174.8 (281.3 km) Large paved double-ended turnout to west of highway. Look to the west across the Chulitna River for dramatic view of the Alaska Range.

A 184.5 (296.9 km) F 173.5 (279.2 km) Paved turnout to west.

A 185 (297.7 km) F 173 (278.4 km) East Fork DOT/PF highway maintenance station.

A 185.1 (297.9 km) F 172.9 (278.3 km) Bridge over East Fork Chulitna River.

A 185.6 (298.7 km) F 172.4 (277.4 km) East Fork rest area (no sign at turnoff) on right northbound. A 0.5-mile/0.8-km paved loop gives access to a gravel picnic area with overnight parking, 23 tables, concrete fireplaces and picnic shelter. No restrooms or toilet facilities were open here in 1996; current status of facilities unknown. The rest area is in a bend of the East Fork Chulitna River amid a healthy growth of Alaskan spruce and birch. Cut wood is often available. ▲

A 186.4 (300 km) F 171.6 (276.2 km) Small paved turnout to east.

A 187.5 (301.8 km) F 170.5 (274.4 km) Paved double-ended turnout to west; small paved turnout east side of highway.

A 188.5 (303.4 km) F 169.5 (272.8 km) Igloo City, an Alaskan landmark, 50 miles south of entrance to Denali National Park. New ownership. Unleaded, regular and diesel fuels, propane. Ask for 5-cent discount for cash fill-ups. Caravan discounts.

Espresso, postcards, candy, snacks, soft drinks, ice, pay phone. Camping, lodging. Unique Alaskan art, gifts and souvenirs not seen elsewhere. Open 24 hours year-round. (907) 768-2622. See display ad. [ADVERTISEMENT] 🚻▲

A 189.9 (305.6 km) F 168.1 (270.5 km) Gravel double-ended turnout. Watch for beaver dam to east northbound.

A 191.5 (308.2 km) F 166.5 (267.9 km) Large paved turnout to west. Look for cotton grass.

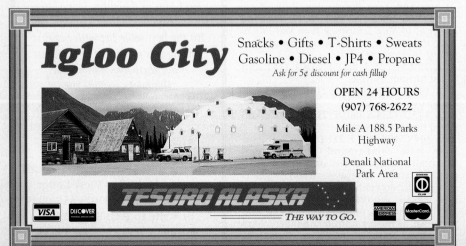

A 193 (310.6 km) **F 165** (265.5 km) **Sourdough Paul's Bed and Breakfast.** Paul can take you gold panning, sightseeing, fishing, blueberry picking, float trips. Wonderful snow machining. Enjoy a sourdough breakfast and listen to stories of yesteryear.

Experience pioneer hand-built log home. Complete with sauna, gravity shower, oil lamps and sanitized outhouse. Mount McKinley view. Hour from Denali Park. Kids stay free. Reservations toll free 1-888-287-7002 or (907) 768-2020. [ADVERTISEMENT]

A 194.3 (312.7 km) **F 163.7** (263.4 km) *CAUTION: Railroad crossing.*

A 194.5 (313 km) **F 163.5** (263.1 km) Bridge over Middle Fork Chulitna River. Undeveloped parking area southwest of bridge below the highway. *CAUTION: Windy area through Broad Pass.*

A 195 (313.8 km) **F 163** (262.3 km) Entering Broad Pass northbound. Good views of Broad Pass.

A 195.9 (315.3 km) **F 162.1** (260.9 km) Large paved trunout east; mountain views.

A 201.1 (323.6 km) **F 156.9** (252.5 km) Large paved parking area to east with mountain view.

A 201.3 (324 km) **F 156.7** (252.2 km) Summit of Broad Pass (not signed), 2,300 feet/701m. Broad Pass is one of the most beautiful areas on the George Parks Highway. A mountain valley, bare in some places, dotted with scrub spruce in others, and surrounded by mountain peaks, there's a top-of-the-world feeling for the traveler, although it is one of the lowest summits along the North American mountain system. Named in 1898 by George Eldridge and Robert Muldrow, the 2,300-foot/701m pass, sometimes called Caribou Pass, marks the divide between the drainage of rivers and streams that empty into Cook Inlet and those that empty into the Yukon River.

Orange towers of weather service station building west of highway.

A 202.3 (325.6 km) **F 155.7** (250.6 km) Boundary of Matanuska–Susitna and Denali boroughs.

A 203.1 (326.9 km) **F 154.9** (249.3 km) *CAUTION: Railroad crossing.*

A 203.6 (327.7 km) **F 154.4** (248.5 km) Paved parking area with view to east.

A 208 (334.7 km) **F 150** (241.4 km) Turnout to west at end of bridge over Pass Creek; blueberries in season.

A 209.4 (337 km) **F 148.6** (239.1 km) Large gravel parking area to east.

A 209.5 (337.1 km) **F 148.5** (239 km) Bridge over Jack River; paved turnout.

A 209.7 (337.4 km) **F 148.3** (238.7 km) **Reindeer Mtn. Lodge.** Lodging, gifts, snacks and furs. Beautiful view of Mount McKinley. Rooms have private baths and color TV. Beautiful log office has ornate wood carvings. Open year-round. Wildlife, scenery, skiing, snowmobiling, fishing, hunting, hiking or relaxing. Call (907) 768-2420 or fax (907) 768-2942. Write Box 7, Cantwell, AK 99729. [ADVERTISEMENT]

A 209.9 (337.8 km) **F 148.1** (238.3 km) **Junction** of the George Parks Highway and the Denali Highway (Alaska Route 8) and

turnoff for Cantwell (description follows). Turn west on the Denali Highway for Cantwell (1.8 miles/2.9 km from junction); turn east for Paxson (see page 468 in the DENALI HIGHWAY section for log).

Cantwell

Located 1.8 miles/2.9 km west of George Parks Highway, end of the Denali Highway. **Population: 145. Emergency Services: Alaska State Troopers,** business phone (907) 768-2202. **Fire Department,** emergency only phone (907) 768-2240. **Ambulance,** phone (907) 768-2982.

Elevation: 2,190 feet/668m. **Private Aircraft:** Cantwell airport, adjacent north; elev. 2,190 feet/668m; length 2,100 feet/640m; gravel, dirt; fuel 100LL.

Cantwell began as a railroad flag stop on the Alaska Railroad. The village was named for the Cantwell River, the original name of the Nenana River, which was named by Lt. Allen in 1885 for Lt. John C. Cantwell, of the Revenue-Cutter Service, who explored

CANTWELL ADVERTISERS

the Kobuk River region. ∎

Many of Cantwell's businesses are clustered around the intersection of the Denali and George Parks highways or on the way into downtown Cantwell. Services include food, gas, lodging and camping. ▲

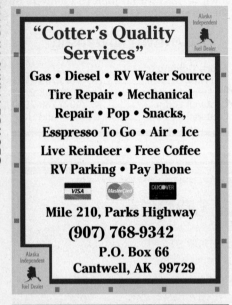
George Parks Highway Log

(continued)

A 210 (338 km) **F 148** (238.2 km) Cantwell post office (ZIP code 99729).

A 210.2 (338.3 km) **F 147.8** (237.9 km) **Parkway Gift Shop.** See display ad this section.

A 210.4 (338.6 km) **F 147.6** (237.5 km) **Cotter's Quality Services.** See display ad this section.

A 210.6 (338.9 km) **F 147.4** (237.2 km) **Lazy-J-Cabins.** Authentic Alaska log cabins, warm and cozy. 20 minutes from Denali National Park entrance and one mile from Denali Highway. Clean, modern bathhouse and laundromat. Reasonable rates. Open year-round. We specialize in winter activities. Beauty salon on site. Reservations recommended (907) 768-2415. See display ad this section. [ADVERTISEMENT]

A 211.5 (340.4 km) **F 146.5** (235.8 km) Paved double-ended parking area to west.

A 212.7 (342.3 km) **F 145.3** (233.8 km) Gravel turnout to west by Nenana River. Watch for large beaver dam to west. Slide area northbound.

A 213.9 (344.2 km) **F 144.1** (231.9 km) Paved double-ended turnout to west among tall white spruce and fireweed.

A 215.3 (346.5 km) **F 142.7** (229.6 km) Access road to Nenana River, which parallels the highway northbound.

A 215.7 (347.1 km) **F 142.3** (229 km) First bridge northbound over the Nenana River. Highway narrows northbound.

A 216.2 (347.9 km) **F 141.8** (228.2 km) Entering Game Management Unit 20A and leaving unit 13E northbound.

A 216.3 (348.1 km) **F 141.7** (228 km) Paved double-ended turnout to west. Good spot for photos of Panorama Mountain (elev. 5,778 feet/1,761m), the prominent peak visible to the east.

A 217.6 (350.2 km) **F 140.4** (225.9 km) Small gravel turnout to west.

A 218.6 (351.8 km) **F 139.4** (224.3 km) Paved double-ended turnout to west with beautiful view of Nenana River.

A 219 (352.4 km) **F 139** (223.7 km) Slide area: Watch for rocks next 0.4 mile/0.6 km northbound.

A 219.8 (353.7 km) **F 138.2** (222.4 km) Paved double-ended turnout to west overlooking Nenana River.

A 220 (354 km) **F 138** (222.1 km) Slime Creek.

A 220.2 (354.4 km) **F 137.8** (221.8 km) Wide gravel turnout to east.

A 222.2 (357.6 km) **F 135.8** (218.5 km) Large, paved double-ended turnout to west beside Nenana River slough. Snow poles beside roadway guide snowplows in winter.

A 223.9 (360.3 km) **F 134.1** (215.8 km) **Carlo Creek Lodge.** Located 12 miles south of Denali Park entrance. 32 wooded acres bordered by beautiful Carlo Creek, the Nenana River and Denali National Park.

Cozy creekside log cabins with own bathroom, showers. RV park, dump station, potable water, propane. Clean bathroom, showers. Dishwashing facility. Individual sheltered tent sites each with picnic table and firepit. Unique gift shop. Small store. Information. Pay phone. You won't be disappointed. It's a beautiful place to be. HC 2, Box 1530, Healy, AK 99743. (907) 683-2576, 683-2573. [ADVERTISEMENT] ▲

A 224 (360.5 km) **F 134** (215.7 km) **The Perch.** A beautiful, established restaurant-bar perched on a private hill. Spectacular dining, specializes in freshly baked bread,

seafood and steaks. Also, take-out giant cinnamon rolls. Breakfast 6 A.M. to 11:30 A.M.; lunch 11:30 A.M. to 2 P.M.; dinner 5 P.M. to 10 P.M., open daily mid-May through September; and Friday, Saturday, Sunday October through May. Sleeping cabins with central bath, some with private baths, beside Carlo Creek. Owners/operators, Duane and Leslie Watters. Phone (907) 683-2523. HC2 Box 1525, Healy, AK 99743. See display ad in the DENALI NATIONAL PARK section. [ADVERTISEMENT]

A 224 (360.5 km) **F 134** (215.7 km) Bridge over Carlo Creek.

McKinley Wilderness Lodge, on the banks of Carlo Creek. Cabins with private bath, economy cabins with central bath. Restaurant. Phone (907) 683-2277; fax (907) 683-1558. P.O. Box 89, Denali Park, AK 99755. See display ad in DENALI NATIONAL PARK section. [ADVERTISEMENT]

A 225 (362.1 km) **F 133** (214 km) Beautiful mountain views southbound.

A 226 (363.7 km) **F 132** (212.4 km) Fang Mountain (elev. 6,736 feet/2,053m) may be visible to the west through the slash in the mountains.

A 229.2 (368.8 km) **F 128.8** (207.3 km) Private airstrip. Flightseeing service.

Denali Air. We fly you closer to Denali's beauty on our 1-hour aerial tours of Mount McKinley and Denali National Park. Flights

PHOTO: Johnny Johnson

originate from the airstrip here. Additional bookings offices next to Denali Park railroad depot and at **Milepost A 238.7** Parks Highway. Two person minimum. Reservations: Phone (907) 683-2261. See display ad in the DENALI NATIONAL PARK section. [ADVERTISEMENT]

A 229.7 (369.7 km) **F 128.3** (206.5 km) Paved turnout to west.

A 231.1 (371.9 km) **F 126.9** (204.2 km) **McKinley Village Lodge,** is convenient to all Denali National Park activities. Located on a quiet stretch of the Nenana River, the 50-room lodge is complete with a lovely cafe, lounge, gift shop and tour desk to arrange area tour and rafting activities. Phone (800) 276-7234; in Anchorage (907) 276-7234. [ADVERTISEMENT]

Denali Grizzly Bear Cabins & Campground. South boundary Denali National Park. AAA approved. Drive directly to your individual kitchen, sleeping or tent cabin with its old-time Alaskan atmosphere overlooking scenic Nenana River. Two conveniently located buildings with toilets, sinks, coin-operated hot showers. Advance cabin reservations suggested. Tenting and RV campsites also available in peaceful lower wooded area. Hookups. Propane. Caravans welcome! Hot coffee and rolls, ice cream, snacks, groceries, ice, liquor store, Alaskan gifts. Specialty sweatshirts. VISA and MasterCard accepted. Owned and operated by a pioneer Alaskan family. Reservations (907) 683-2696 (summer); (907) 457-2924 (winter). See display ad in DENALI NATIONAL PARK section. [ADVERTISEMENT] ▲

Denali River Cabins. Located on the banks of the Nenana River, 5 minutes away from the Visitor Center, our cedar cabin resort offers the ideal base for your Denali Park experience. Our cabins are situated both on and off river with an extra large hot tub and riverside sauna. The new cozy cedar cabins are fully furnished all with private bath. There are 3 sun decks right on the riverbank, looking into Denali Park. We also offer exclusive Fairbanks day tours and Kantishna tours inside Denali National Park. (907) 683-2500 for reservations year-round. See display ad in DENALI NATIONAL PARK section. [ADVERTISEMENT] ▲

A 231.3 (372.2 km) **F 126.7** (203.9 km) Crabb's Crossing, second bridge northbound over the Nenana River. Small paved turnout with wide shoulders west side of highway.

At the north end of this bridge is the boundary of Denali National Park and Preserve. From here north for 6.8 miles/10.9 km the George Parks Highway is within the boundaries of the park and travelers must abide by park rules. No discharge of firearms permitted.

A 233.1 (375.1 km) **F 124.9** (201 km) Gravel turnout to east.

A 234.1 (376.7 km) **F 123.9** (199.4 km)

Caribou photographed near the road in Denali National Park. (© Tom Bol)

Double-ended turnout with litter barrels to east; scenic viewpoint. No overnight parking or camping. Mount Fellows (elev. 4,476 feet/ 1,364m) to the east. The constantly changing shadows make this an excellent camera subject. Exceptionally beautiful in the evening. To the southeast stands Pyramid Peak (elev. 5,201 feet/1,585m).

A 235.1 (378.4 km) **F 122.9** (197.8 km) *CAUTION: Railroad crossing.* Solar panels and wind generators provide power for crossing signals.

A 236.7 (380.9 km) **F 121.3** (195.2 km) Alaska Railroad crosses over highway. From this point the highway begins a steep descent northbound to Riley Creek.

A 237.2 (381.7 km) **F 120.8** (194.4 km) Riley Creek bridge.

A 237.3 (381.9 km) **F 120.7** (194.2 km) Entrance to **DENALI NATIONAL PARK AND PRESERVE** (formerly Mount McKinley National Park) to west. Fresh water fill-up hose and dump station 0.2 mile/0.3 km from junction on Park Road; Visitor Center is 0.5 mile/0.8 km from the highway junction. Campsites within the park are available on a first-come, first-served basis; sign up at the visitor center. You may also pick up schedules for the shuttle bus service at the visitor center (private vehicle access to the park is restricted). See DENALI NATIONAL PARK section for details.

Clusters of highway businesses north and south of the park entrance between Cantwell and Healy offer a variety of services to the highway traveler and park visitor. Services include river running, gift shops, accommodations, restaurants and entertainment.

A 238 (383 km) **F 120** (193.4 km) Third bridge northbound over the Nenana River. Era Helicopters office is located here.

The 4.8 miles/7.7 km of road and 7 bridges in the rugged Nenana Canyon cost $7.7 million to build. Sugarloaf Mountain (elev. 4,450 feet/1,356m), to the east, is closed to the hunting of Dall sheep, which are regularly sighted in the early and late

summer months. Mount Healy (elev. 5,716 feet/1,742m) is to the west.

Southbound for 6.8 miles/10.9 km the George Parks Highway is within the boundaries of Denali National Park and Preserve and travelers must abide by park rules. No discharge of firearms.

A 238.1 (383.2 km) **F 119.9** (193 km) **Denali Raft Adventures.** Come with the original Nenana River rafters! Paddleboats, too! Age 5 or older welcome, 7 departures daily. Whitewater or scenic floats. Get away

to untouched wilderness! 2-hour, 4-hour full-day and overnight trips are available. See display ad in DENALI NATIONAL PARK section. Phone (907) 683-2234. VISA, MasterCard accepted. [ADVERTISEMENT]

A 238.3 (383.5 km) **F 119.7** (192.6 km) Kingfisher Creek.

A 238.4 (383.6 km) **F 119.6** (192.5 km) **Denali Bluffs Hotel.** The newest and closest hotel to the Denali National Park and Preserve entrance. 112 rooms, each room features 2 double beds, TVs, phones and other amenities. Most of the rooms have spectacular views of the Alaska Range. The lodge features a large stone fireplace and cathedral ceilings. There are comfortable sitting areas inside the lodge or outside on the deck to enjoy the panoramic views. Gift shop and coin-operated laundry. Shuttle service to visitor center and rail depot. Complete tour and activity desk. Wheelchair accessible. Open mid-May through mid-September. Credit cards accepted. P.O. Box 72460, Fairbanks, AK 99707. Phone (907) 683-7000. Fax (907) 683-7500. See display ad in the DENALI NATIONAL PARK section. [ADVERTISEMENT] ♿

A 238.5 (383.8 km) **F 119.5** (192.3 km)

Alaska flag display features a 10-by-15-foot/3-by-5-m state flag and plaques detailing history of flag design and song.

A 238.5 (383.8 km) F 119.5 (192.3 km) McKinley/Denali Steakhouse and Salmon Bake. Satisfy that hearty Alaskan appetite at a real home-style barbecue restaurant, featuring char-broiled burgers, steaks, sandwiches,

fresh salmon and halibut, tender beef ribs, barbecued chicken with rice pilaf, baked beans, extensive salad bar, homemade soups and desserts. Cocktails. Rustic heated indoor seating with majestic view of mountains. Free shuttle from all local hotels. Sourdough breakfasts. Large selection of postcards in our upstairs gift shop. T-shirts, sweatshirts and ice for sale. Pay phone. Open daily 5 A.M. to 11 P.M. in summer. Phone (907) 683-2733. See display ad in the DENALI NATIONAL PARK section. [ADVERTISEMENT]

McKinley/Denali Gift Shop. Largest giftshop in park area—upstairs at McKinley/Denali Steakhouse and Salmon Bake. Largest selection of Mount McKinley and Denali National Park T-shirts and sweatshirts. Hundreds of souvenirs and gifts. Photo calendars and postcards. Open 5 A.M. to 11 P.M. Call for free shuttle service. [ADVERTISEMENT]

McKinley/Denali Cabins. Economy tent cabins with electric heat and lights from $65. Closest full-service facility to park entrance, wildlife shuttles. Close to raft trips, store, gift shop, gas. Beds, linens, blankets. Central showers. Pay phone. Some cabins with private baths. Shuttle to visitor center, railroad depot available. Free visitor information. Call us for reservations on many area activities. Reservations: (907) 683-2258 or 683-2733 or write: Box 90M, Denali Park, AK 99755. See display ad in DENALI NATIONAL PARK section. [ADVERTISEMENT]

Denali Crow's Nest Log Cabins and the Overlook Bar & Grill. Open mid-May to mid-September, offering the finest view in area. Close to park entrance. Authentic Alaska log cabins with hotel comforts; all rooms with private bath. Courtesy trans-

portation. Hot tub, tour bookings. Dine on steaks, seafood, burgers, salmon and halibut indoors or on the deck at The Overlook Bar & Grill. 64 varieties of beer, 6 draft beers; meals 11 A.M. to 11 P.M. Bar open till midnight. For restaurant courtesy shuttle from all local hotels, call (907) 683-2723, fax (907) 683-2323. See display ad in DENALI NATIONAL PARK section. [ADVERTISEMENT]

A 238.6 (384 km) F 119.4 (192.2 km) Denali Princess Lodge, private RV park and river rafting service.

Denali Rainbow Village & RV Park, opening May 1997, welcomes you to Denali National park. We are the closest private RV

park to the Denali Park entrance, convenient to Denali activities and services. open May 20 through September 20. Featuring: easy highway access, level pull-through sites, electric hookups, potable water, dump station, bathrooms, shower, laundry, picnic tables, log bench swings, night security, fax service, restaurant, flightseeing, river rafting, bear facts, tour arrangments, free Denali information. Other local services: grocery, gas taxi service, horseback riding, beauty salon, public telephone, film processing, camping supplies, dinner theaters. Advance reservations suggested, space is limited. MasterCard and Visa accepted. Write Box 777, Denali National Par, AK 99755 or call (907) 683- DENALI (683-3662) or fax (907) 683-PARK (683-7275). See display ad in Denali National Park section.

Denali Wilderness Lodge is Alaska's historic fly-in wilderness lodge, sometimes called the most remote hotel in America. Authentic bush homestead nestled in the pristine Wood River Valley just outside Denali National Park. Accessible only by

spectacular bush plane flight over the mountains and glaciers of the Alaska Range. Comfortable accommodations, fine dining, naturalist programs, flightseeing, horseback riding, nature/photo walks and hikes, bird-watching, wildlife museum. This will be your best memory of Alaska! Overnight packages and day trips available. Free brochure. 1-800-541-9779. See display ad in DENALI NATIONAL PARK section. [ADVERTISEMENT]

Wolf Spirit Expeditions. Unique whitewater and scenic wilderness river rafting adventures on the Nenana River bordering Denali National Park. Also guided Denali-view tundra hiking. Other rivers throughout Alaska. Visit us at Red Roof Log Cabin across from Denali Princess Lodge. RV parking available. Information and reservations (907) 683-4445 or 1-800-241-2615. [ADVERTISEMENT]

A 238.7 (384.1 km) F 119.3 (192 km) Denali Windsong Lodge, formerly McKinley Motor Lodge, we are specialists in serving the highway traveler. Thirty-six clean, modern rooms with full bath, satellite TV and beautiful mountain views. Located

near park entrance, and in the midst of restaurants and activities. Our friendly staff and reasonable rates make this the place to stay. Call 1-800-208-0200, or (907) 683-1240. See display ad in DENALI NATIONAL PARK section.

A 238.8 (384.3 km) F 119.2 (191.8 km) McKinley Raft Tours Inc. Scenic and whitewater trips on the Nenana River. Several departures daily. Float the eastern boundary of Denali National Park. An exhilarating

whitewater adventure you'll remember. Local transportation available. Reservations suggested. MasterCard, VISA, American Express, Discover accepted. Call (907) 683-2392. See display ad in DENALI NATIONAL PARK section.

Sourdough Cabins offers individually heated cabins with private bath, nestled in a spruce forest. Conveniently located within walking distance to all services. Courtesy transportation provided. Phone (907) 683-2773, fax (907) 683-2357. VISA, MasterCard, American Express accepted. See display ad in the DENALI NATIONAL PARK section. [ADVERTISEMENT] ▲

A 238.9 (384.5 km) F119.1 (191.7 km) Denali Outdoor Center. Denali's most diversified river outfitter. Oarboats, paddleboats, inflatable kayak tours and comprehensive whitewater kayak school. Whitewater or scenic wilderness trips daily. 2-hour, 4-hour, 1/2-day and full-day guided trips. All gear and custom drysuits provided! Ages 5 and up. Call for reservations (907) 683-1925. Major credit cards accepted. [ADVERTISEMENT]

A 239 (384.6 km) F 119 (191.5 km) Northern Lights Theatre and Gift Shop. Come experience the Northern Lights on a 34-foot-wide screen. This presentation is one of a kind, entertaining and informative. Stop by for show times and tickets. Don't miss Denali's largest gift shop in a beautiful,

natural log building next door, specializing in quality Alaskan gifts. Full mount, world class polar bear on display. Groceries at Denali General Store. Located 1.5 miles north of park entrance. Large parking area. Dont miss this attraction! P.O. Box 65, Denali Park, AK 99755. Phone (907) 683-4000. Mention this ad for 10 percent discount on theater admission. Courtesy for tour agents, escorts and drivers. [ADVERTISEMENT]

A 239.1 (384.8 km) F 118.9 (191.3 km) McKinley Chalet Resort, offers 343 mini-suites overlooking the Nenana River. We offer fine dining, lounge, gift shop and full service tour desk. The Chalet Center Cafe treats you to fresh muffins, sandwiches, salads, soups, a specialty drink bar, indoor pool, sauna, Jacuzzi and local artist's gallery. Also the home of Alaska Cabin Nite Dinner Theater and Alaska Raft Adventures. (800) 276-7234; in Anchorage 276-7234. [ADVERTISEMENT]

Alaska Cabin Night Dinner Theater has 2 evening shows. Expect an all-you-can-eat dinner featuring salmon and ribs, served family style followed by a rousing musical revue depicting the exciting gold rush days. Located at McKinley Chalet Resort in a beautiful handcrafted log cabin. For reservations call (800) 276-7234; in Anchorage 276-7234 or stop by the tour desk located in the lobby of the McKinley Chalet Resort. [ADVERTISEMENT]

Alaska Raft Adventures, offers 2 wonderful rafting experiences complete with experienced guides and all equipment needed to enjoy a great Nenana River adventure. Our Wilderness Run floats through a glacial valley offering unparalleled scenery. Our Canyon Run offers exciting whitewater action, (class III & IV rapids). Both adven-

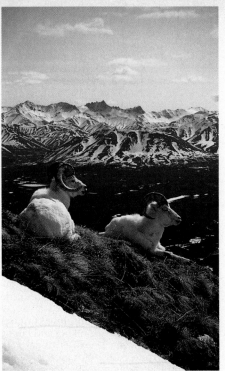

Dall sheep in Denali National Park.
(© Mike Jones)

bridge. Entering Game Management Unit 20A northbound, 20C southbound.

A 243.6 (392 km) **F 114.4** (184.1 km) Bridge over Bison Gulch. Paved viewpoint to east. A steep grade follows northbound, end wind area.

A 244.1 (392.8 km) **F 113.9** (183.3 km) Paved turnout to east. Watch for frost heaves next 1 mile/1.6 km northbound.

A 244.6 (393.6 km) **F 113.4** (182.5 km) Bridge over Antler Creek.

A 245.1 (394.4 km) **F 112.9** (181.7 km) **Denali RV Park & Motel.** 90 full and partial RV hookups, 30-amp electric. Level sites, pull-throughs, easy highway access. Individual restrooms with private showers, flush toilets. Dump station. Caravans welcome! 14 motel rooms: Central bath $45, private bath $65, family units with full kitchen $90. Outdoor cooking area, covered meeting area, pay phones, gift shop. Located 8 miles north of park entrance. Close to all park facilities. Beautiful mountain views. Hiking trails. Reasonable rates. VISA/MasterCard/Discover. Box 155, Denali Park, AK 99755. 1-907-683-1500. 1-800-478-1501. See display ad in the DENALI NATIONAL PARK section. [ADVERTISEMENT] ▲

A 245.6 (395.2 km) **F 112.4** (180.9 km) Watch for rough road, frost heaves and dips 0.4 mile/0.6 km northbound.

A 246.9 (397.3 km) **F 111.1** (178.8 km) Paved turnout to east and beautiful view of Healy area.

A 247 (397.5 km) **F 111** (178.6 km) Side road leads 1 mile/1.6 km to **Otto Lake**, 5 miles/8 km to Black Diamond Coal Mine. Primitive parking area on lakeshore (0.8-mile/1.3-km drive in) with toilet, litter barrels, shallow boat launch. Stocked with rainbow and coho. Denali hostel. Access to bed and breakfasts, golf driving range and RV park. ◂▲

Black Diamond Resort Co. Come visit us on the greens! Golf: 10 holes surrounded by the exceptional beauty of Alaska Mountain Range; or drive a bucket while you enjoy the serenity of Otto Lake. One mile west down the Otto Lake Road. Club rentals available. (907) 683-GOLF. [ADVERTISEMENT]

Otto Lake R.V. Park and Campground. Beautiful mountain views from primitive lakeside RV and tent sites, ¹/₂ mile west of Parks Highway on Otto Lake Road. Spacious and secluded sites with picnic tables, firepits, firewood, potable water, toilets, dump station and pay phone. Boat rentals. Family camping at its best, not a gravel strip. Located 9.7 miles north of Denali National Park entrance. [ADVERTISEMENT] ▲

A 248.2 (399.4 km) **F 109.8** (176.7 km) **Quality Services.** See display ad this section.

A 248.4 (399.8 km) **F 109.6** (176.4 km) **McKinley RV & Campground.** One of the nicest campgrounds around; 89 sites and utilities available. Come let our family help your family have a great vacation. We will help you experience the sights and sounds

tures depart 3 times daily, and courtesy transportation is available between area hotels and the Alaska Railroad Depot. Allow for a total of 3 hours. Call 1-800-276-7234; in Anchorage (907) 276-7234 or stop by the tour desk at the McKinley Chalet Resort. [ADVERTISEMENT]

A 240.1 (386.4 km) **F 117.9** (189.7 km) Bridge over Ice Worm Gulch. *CAUTION: Rock slide area. Slow down.* High winds in the Nenana Canyon can make this stretch of road dangerous for campers and motorhomes.

WARNING: The highway has many sharp curves. Do not park along the highway. Use the many parking areas provided.

A 240.2 (386.6 km) **F 117.8** (189.6 km) Hornet Creek bridge. Paved double-ended turnout to west beside Nenana River.

A 240.5 (387 km) **F 117.5** (189.1 km) Private RV park. ▲

A 240.7 (387.4 km) **F 117.3** (188.8 km) Paved double-ended turnout to west beside river.

A 241 (387.7 km) **F 117** (188.3 km) Paved turnout to west.

A 241.2 (388.2 km) **F 116.8** (188 km) Bridge over Fox Creek; gravel road to creek. Large gravel turnout to west. Slide area next 0.4 mile/0.6 km northbound.

A 241.7 (389 km) **F 116.3** (187.2 km) Large gravel turnout to west.

A 242.3 (389.9 km) **F 115.7** (186.2 km) Paved double-ended turnout to west.

A 242.4 (390.1 km) **F 115.6** (186 km) Dragonfly Creek bridge; paved double-ended turnout to west.

A 242.8 (390.7 km) **F 115.2** (185.4 km) Paved double-ended turnout to west. *CAUTION: Windy area next mile northbound.*

A 242.9 (390.9 km) **F 115.1** (185.2 km) Moody Bridge. This 4th bridge northbound over the Nenana River. Measures 174 feet/53m from its deck to the bottom of the canyon. Dall sheep can be spotted from the of Denali. We book camping, rafting, horseback riding, dinner, flightseeing and shows.

We offer our guests free showers, dump station, wooded landscape, a movie on Alaska, miniature golf, fax service and propane. Caravans-groups welcome. Peaceful setting, spectacular view and beautiful open skies. Come let us make you feel at home. Reservations recommended. Write Box 340MP, Healy, AK 99743. Phone: (907) 683-2379. Fax: (907) 683-2281. National (800) 478-AKOA. See display ad in the DENALI NATIONAL PARK section. [ADVERTISEMENT]

A 248.5 (399.9 km) **F 109.5** (176.2 km) Paved turnout to east. River rafting service office.

Nenana Raft Adventures. Day trips on the Nenana River. Multi-day expeditions on rivers throughout Alaska. We provide wetsuits or drysuits for all clients. Paddle rafting available. Call 1-800-789-RAFT or (907) 683-7238. Write P.O. Box 500, Healy, AK 99743. Office next to McKinley RV & Campground. See display ad, DENALI NATIONAL PARK section. [ADVERTISEMENT]

A 248.7 (400.2 km) **F 109.3** (175.9 km) Junction with spur road to community of Healy (see description following **Milepost A 248.8**). Homes and businesses of this Alaska community are dispersed along the highway from here north to **Milepost A 249.6** and in the first mile east along the spur road toward the Nenana River. Hotel and motel accommodations are available at the highway junction, and several bed and breakfasts are located along the spur road.

A 248.8 (400.4 km) **F 109.2** (175.7 km) North side of Healy Spur Road intersection.

Denali North Star Inn. Located at Healy intersection, Mile 248.8 Parks Highway. Reasonably priced rooms, finest food in Denali Park area. Information and reservations for Denali Park area tours. Shuttle service, Alaskan gifts, beauty salon, barber shop, tanning beds. Recreation and exercise

areas, saunas, self-service laundry. 11 miles to Denali Park entrance. 1-800-684-1560. See display ad in DENALI NATIONAL PARK section. [ADVERTISEMENT]

Denali Wings. The most comprehensive Air Tour of Denali National Park. Your 1-hour, 10-minute narrated fight to Mount McKinley overflies both remote and well-known areas of the Park. Views of glaciers, mountains and wildlife not seen on ground tours. When you visit Denali, See Denali!! (907) 683-2245. Reservation desk at Stampede Lodge, Mile 248.8 Parks Highway. [ADVERTISEMENT]

Stampede Lodge and Bushmaster Grill. Historic Alaskan Lodge and Restaurant completely remodeled in 1995. Warm, comfortable atmosphere located 10 minutes away from the congestion of the Park entrance. Private baths and phones in all rooms. Free train station pick-up. Restaurant open 6 A.M.– 10 P.M. 7 days a week. 1-800-478-2370, (907) 683-2242, fax (907) 683-2243. [ADVERTISEMENT]

Healy

Located on a spur road just east of the George Parks Highway **junction**. **Population:** 605. **Emergency Services: Alaska State Troopers,** phone (907) 683-2232. **Fire Department,** Tri–Valley Volunteer Fire Dept., phone 911 or (907) 683-2223. **Clinic,** Healy Clinic, located on 2nd floor of Tri–Valley Community Center at Mile 0.5 Usibelli Spur Road, phone (907) 683-2211 or 911 (open 24 hours).

Visitor Information: Available at the Healy Senior Center, located on Healy Spur Road behind the grocery store. Open 11 A.M. to 7 P.M., year-round; phone (907) 683-1317.

Elevation: 1,294 feet/394m. **Radio:** KUAC-FM 101.7. **Private Aircraft:** Healy River airstrip adjacent north; length 2,800 feet/853m; gravel; unattended.

Healy's power plant has the distinction of being the largest coal-fired steam plant in Alaska, as well as the only mine-mouth power plant. This plant is part of the Golden Valley Electric Assoc., which furnishes electric power for Fairbanks and vicinity. The

Fairbanks–Tanana Valley area uses primarily coal and also oil to meet its electrical needs.

Across the Nenana River lie the mining settlements of Suntrana and Usibelli. Dry Creek, Healy and Nenana river valleys comprise the area referred to as Tri–Valley. Coal mining began here in 1918 and has grown to become Alaska's largest coal mining operation. Usibelli Coal Mine, the state's only commercial coal mine, mines about 800,000 tons of coal a year, supplying South Korea, the University of Alaska, the military and other Fairbanks-area utilities. The Usibelli Coal Mine began a successful reclamation program in 1971; Dall sheep now graze where there was once evidence only of strip mining.

From the highway, you may see a 33-cubic-yard walking dragline (named Ace in the Hole by local schoolchildren in a contest) removing the soil, or overburden, to expose the coal seams. This 4,275,000-lb. machine, erected in 1978, moves an average of 24,000 cubic yards each 24 hours. Private vehicles are not allowed into the mining area and no tours are available.

Alaskan Chateau Bed and Breakfast, set on two wooded acres with hiking and biking trails. Just minutes to Denali National Park entrance. Private baths, entrances and sun decks, mini kitchens. Satellite TV available. Continental-plus breakfast. Families welcome. Hosts Teresa Chepoda and Alaskan-born John Usibelli will provide an environment of elegance, hospitality and congeniality. Call (907) 683-1377, fax (907) 683-1380, or write PO Box 187, Healy, AK 99743. See display ad in DENALI NATIONAL PARK section. [ADVERTISEMENT]

Denali Dome Home Bed, Breakfast and Hospitality is a 7,200-foot geodesic home run year-round by the Miller Family and located one turn and 15 minutes from Denali National Park. The Dome has 9 bedrooms, 7 baths, 2 living rooms, sauna, fireplaces, decks and large off-street parking on 2.75 wooded acres. The Millers are happy to advise or arrange your Denali Park vacation. Very reasonable rates. MasterCard and VISA accepted. Call (907) 683-1239 or write Box 262, Healy, AK 99743 for information. [ADVERTISEMENT]

Denali Suites. Located 15 minutes north of entrance to Denali National Park on Healy Spur Road. Units include 2 or 3 bedrooms, kitchen and dining area, living room with queen-sized hide-a-bed, TV and VCR, and private baths. Coin-operated laundry facilities. Clean, comfortable, affordable. Each unit accommodates up to 6 people, one accommodates 8, with 2 private baths; families welcome. VISA, MasterCard, Discover. Open all year. Call (907) 683-2848 or write Box 393, Healy, AK 99743. See display ad in the DENALI NATIONAL PARK section. [ADVERTISEMENT]

GrandView Bed & Breakfast. Located 12 miles from the entrance to Denali National Park. Relax and enjoy the spectacular view of the Alaska Range. Deck, barbecue, sitting area. Continental breakfast. Open year-round. VISA/MasterCard. Write GrandView Bed & Breakfast, Box 109, Healy, AK 99743 or call (907) 683-2468. See display ad in DENALI NATIONAL PARK section. [ADVERTISEMENT]

George Parks Highway Log
(continued)

A 248.8 (400.4 km) **F 109** (175.7 km) Healy spur road junction, north side of intersection; food and lodging.

HEALY ADVERTISERS

✓ Alaskan Chateau Bed & Breakfast	Ph. (907) 683-1377
Denali Dome Home Bed and Breakfast	Ph. (907) 683-1239
✓ Denali North Star Inn	Mile 248.8 Parks Hwy.
Denali Suites	Ph. (907) 683-2848
Denali Wings	Mile 248.8 Parks Hwy.
GrandView Bed & Breakfast	Ph. (907) 683-2468
✓ Pat & Windell's Bed and Breakfast	Ph. (907) 683-2472
✓ Stampede Lodge	Mile 248.8 Parks Hwy.
✓ Totem Inn	Ph. (907) 683-2384

A 249 (400.7 km) **F 109** (175.4 km) Suntrana Road, post office and Tri–Valley School.

A 249.2 (401 km) **F 108.8** (175.1 km) **Larry's Healy Tesoro.** See display ad this section.

A 249.3 (401.2 km) **F 108.7** (174.9 km) Dry Creek Bridge No. 1.

A 249.4 (401.4 km) **F 108.6** (174.8 km) Lester Road.

A 249.5 (401.5 km) **F 108.5** (174.6 km) **Motel Nord Haven.** Built in 1994 with your motoring family in mind. West side of highway in the trees. Peaceful and secluded. 12 miles north of Denali National Park entrance. All rooms have queen beds, private bath, television and telephone. Open year-round. MasterCard, VISA., American Express. Phone (907) 683-4500. Fax (907) 683-4503. [ADVERTISEMENT]

A 249.6 (401.7 km) **F 108.4** (174.4 km) **Evans Industries, Inc.** See display ad this section.

A 249.8 (402 km) **F 108.2** (174.1 km) Dry Creek bridge No. 2. Good berry picking area first part of August.

A 251.1 (404.1 km) **F 106.9** (172 km) Stampede Road to west. Lignite Road to east. **Earth Song Lodge,** Denali's natural retreat. Enjoy the Denali Park area without the crowds. Ten charming log cabins with private baths. Evening programs by staff naturalist at comfortable central lodge. Dog sled demonstrations and rides. Continental breakfast available. Located on scenic and historic Stampede Road, just north of the park. Wonderful views of Denali and wildlife. Phone/fax (907) 683-2863. P.O. Box 89-MP, Healy, AK 99743. See display ad in the DENALI NATIONAL PARK section. [ADVERTISEMENT]

Touch of Wilderness Bed & Breakfast. See display ad this section.

A 251.2 (404.3 km) **F 106.8** (171.9 km) Paved turnout to west. Coal seams visible in bluff to east. Cotton grass and lupine along roadside in June, fireweed in July.

A 252.4 (406.2 km) **F 105.6** (169.9 km) Gravel turnout to west.

A 252.5 (406.4 km) **F 105.5** (169.8 km) Bridge over **Panguingue Creek**; turnout at end. Moderate success fishing for grayling. This stream, which flows 8 miles/13 km to the Nenana River, was named for a Philippine card game.

CAUTION: Watch for frost heaves northbound.

A 259.4 (417.5 km) **F 98.6** (158.7 km) Large paved turnout to east. Views of Rex Dome to the northeast. Walker and Jumbo domes to the east. Liberty Bell mining area lies between the peaks and highway.

A 261.1 (420.2 km) **F 96.9** (155.9 km) Gravel turnout to east. Look for bank swallows, small brown birds that nest in clay and sand banks near streams and along highways.

A 262 (421.6 km) **F 96** (154.5 km) Watch for rough patches in pavement and gravel shoulders, northbound. Watch for frost heaves southbound.

A 263 (423.2 km) **F 95** (152.9 km) Small gravel turnout to east. Wildflowers include sweet pea and oxytrope.

A 264.5 (425.7 km) **F 93.5** (150.5 km) Paved turnout to west.

A 269 (432.9 km) **F 89** (143.2 km) June Creek rest area and picnic spot to east; large gravel parking area. Gravel road leads down to lower parking area on June Creek (trailers and large RVs check turnaround space before driving down). Wooden stairs lead up to the picnic spot and a view of the Nenana River. There are picnic tables, fireplaces, toilets, a litter bin and a sheltered table. Cut wood may be available.

A 269.3 (433.4 km) **F 88.7** (142.8 km) Bridge over Bear Creek. Gravel turnout to east.

A 271.4 (436.8 km) **F 86.6** (139.4 km) Paved turnout to west. Highway northbound leads through boggy area with few turnouts.

A 275.6 (443.5 km) **F 82.4** (132.6 km) Entering Game Management Unit 20A

northbound, 20C southbound.

A 275.8 (443.9 km) **F 82.2** (132.3 km) Rex Bridge over Nenana River.

A 276 (444.2 km) **F 82** (132 km) **Tatlanika Trading Co.** Located in a beautiful pristine wilderness setting. Tent sites and RV parking with electricity, water, dump station, showers. 39 miles from Denali National Park on the Nenana River. Our gift shop features a gathering of handmade art/crafts/artifacts from various villages. See the rare Samson fox, along with relics and antiques from Alaska's colorful past in a museum atmosphere. Many historical and educational displays. Nothing sold from overseas. Visitor information. Coffee, pop, juice, snacks. Clean restrooms. This is a must stop. See display ad this section. [ADVERTISEMENT] ▲

A 276.5 (445 km) **F 81.5** (131.2 km) *CAUTION: Railroad crossing.*

A 280 (450.6 km) **F 78** (125.5 km) Lodge with dining and a cafe/grocery.

Clear Sky Lodge. See display ad this section.

CAUTION: Watch for dips in road next

5 miles/8 km northbound.

A 280.1 (450.8 km) **F 77.9** (125.4 km) **Rochester Lodge.** See display ad this section.

A 280.4 (451.2 km) **F 77.6** (124.9 km) Entering Clear Air Force Station northbound.

A 283.5 (456.2 km) **F 74.5** (119.9 km) Access road west to **ANDERSON** (pop. 626) and **CLEAR.** Clear is a military installation (ballistic missile early warning site), and a sign at turnoff states it is unlawful to enter without permission. However, you can drive into Anderson without permission. Located 6 miles/9.7 km northwest of Clear, Anderson has a city campground in an 616-acre park with 40 sites on the Nenana River. RV dump station, toilets, showers. The community also has churches, a restaurant, softball fields and shooting range. For more information call the city office at (907) 582-2500. Emergency aid is available through the Clear Air Force Site Fire Department; phone (907) 585-6321. ▲

Anderson Riverside Park. Come enjoy our city's 616 beautiful acres located along the bank of the Nenana River! Featuring restrooms, showers, RV dump station, electrical hook-ups. Riverside campsites, rustic campsites with barbecue pits, picnic area with covered pavilion, fireplace. Shooting range, bandstand, telephone. Home of the annual Anderson Bluegrass Festival, held the last weekend in July. City of Anderson, P.O. Box 3100, Anderson, AK 99744. Phone (907) 582-2500; fax (907) 582-2496. [ADVERTISEMENT]▲

Private Aircraft: Clear airstrip, 2.6 miles/4.2 km southeast; elev. 552 feet/168m; length 3,900 feet/1,189m; gravel; unattended. Clear Sky Lodge airstrip, 4.3 miles/6.9 km south; elev. 650 feet/198m; length 2,500 feet/762m; gravel, earth.

A 285.7 (459.8 km) F 72.3 (116.3 km) Julius Creek bridge.

A 286.3 (460.7 km) F 71.7 (115.4 km) View of Mount McKinley southbound.

A 286.8 (461.5 km) F 71.2 (114.6 km) Double-ended paved parking area to east. Watch for frost heaves northbound.

A 288 (463.5 km) F 70 (112.7 km) Entering Clear Military Reservation southbound.

A 296.7 (477.5 km) F 61.3 (98.7 km) Bridge over **Fish Creek**. Small gravel turnout with litter barrels by creek. Access to creek at south end of bridge; moderate success fishing for grayling. ●

A 298 (479.6 km) F 60 (96.6 km) **Tamarack Inn.** See display ad this section.

A 302.1 (486.2 km) F 55.9 (90 km) **Finnish Alaskan Bed and Breakfast.** See display ad this section.

A 302.9 (487.4 km) F 55.1 (88.7 km) Nenana municipal rifle range.

A 303.7 (488.7 km) F 54.3 (87.4 km) Nenana airport (see Private Aircraft information in Nenana).

A 304.5 (490 km) F 53.5 (86.1 km) **A Frame Service.** See display ad this section.

Nenana

A 304.5 (490 km) F 53.5 (86.1 km) Located at the confluence of the Tanana and Nenana rivers. **Population:** 361. **Emergency Services:** Emergency only (fire, police, ambulance), phone 911. **Alaska State Troopers,** phone (907) 832-5554, at **Milepost A 310** George Parks Highway. **City Police,** phone (907) 832-5632. **Fire Department,** phone (907) 832-5632.

Visitor Information: In a picturesque log cabin with sod roof at junction of the highway and A Street, phone (907) 832-9953. Open 8 A.M. to 6 P.M., 7 days a week, Memorial Day to Labor Day. Pay phone and ice for sale. Ice Classic tickets may be purchased here.

Marge Anderson Senior Citizen Center,

FRAME SERVICE
NEAR THE 'Y' AT NENANA
MI A 304.5 PARKS HWY.

 • Chevron Gas • Diesel • Propane • Chevron Products • Kerosene • Sandwiches • Ice • Essential Groceries

Open 24 Hours Summers
(907) 832-5823

Nenana played a key role in construction of the Alaska Railroad. (© Susan Cole Kelly)

GEORGE PARKS HIGHWAY • Nenana

located on 3rd Street between Market and B streets, also welcomes visitors.

Elevation: 400 feet/122m. **Radio:** KIAM 630, KUAC-FM 91.1. **Transportation: Air**–Nenana maintains an FAA-approved airport. **Railroad**–The Alaska Railroad.

Private Aircraft: Nenana Municipal Airport, 0.9 mile/1.4 km south; elev. 362 feet/110m; length 5,000 feet/1,524m; asphalt;

fuel 100, Jet B. Floatplane and skiplane strip.

The town got its name from the Indian word *Nenana*, which means "a good place to camp between the rivers." It was first known as Tortella, a white man's interpretation of the Athabascan word *Toghotthele*. In 1902 Jim Duke built a roadhouse and trading post here, trading with Indians and supplying river travelers with goods and lodging.

Nenana boomed as a construction base for the Alaska Railroad. Today, Nenana is home port of the tug and barge fleet that in summer carries tons of freight, fuel and supplies to villages along the Tanana and Yukon rivers. Because the Tanana is a wide, shallow, muddy river, the barges move about 12 mph downstream and 5 mph upstream. The dock area is to the right of the highway northbound. Behind the Nenana visitor information center is the *Taku Chief*: This old tug, which has been renovated, once pushed barges on the Tanana.

On July 15, 1923, Pres. Warren G. Harding drove the golden spike at Nenana, signifying completion of the Alaska Railroad. A monument to the event stands east of the depot here. The Nenana Railroad Depot, located at the end of Main Street, is on the National Register of Historic Places. Built in 1923 and renovated in 1988, the depot has a pressed metal ceiling and houses the state's Alaska Railroad Museum; open 9 A.M. to 6 P.M. daily.

One block from the depot is St. Mark's Mission Church. This Episcopal church was built in 1905 upriver from Nenana; it was moved to its present location in the 1930s when riverbank erosion threatened the structure. A school was located next door to the mission until the 1940s, and pupils were brought in by tug from villages along the river. The restored log church has pews with hand-carving and an altar covered with Native beadwork-decorated moosehide.

Nenana is perhaps best known for the Nenana Ice Classic, an annual event that offers cash prizes to the lucky winners who can guess the exact minute of the ice breakup on the Tanana River. Ice Classic festivities begin the last weekend in February with the Tripod Raising Festival, and culminate at breakup time (late April or May) when the surging ice on the Tanana River dislodges the tripod. A line attached to the tripod stops a clock, recording the official breakup time.

The Alaska Come-Back Dog Sled Race is held in late March to commemorate the 1925 serum run from Nenana to Nome. Because of a diptheria outbreak in Nome, serum was brought to Nenana by train and then by dog team to Nome. The legend of sled dog "Balto"—made into a popular animated feature—is connected with this run. The Iditarod Trail Sled Dog Race between Anchorage and Nome also commemorates this event. Nenana celebrates River Daze the first weekend in June. The main event is "The Annihilator," the toughest 10-km footrace in Alaska, over Tortella Hill.

Nenana has an auto repair shop, radio station, several churches, restaurants, a laundromat, gift shops, a grocery and general store. Accommodations at motel, inn and

NENANA ADVERTISERS

bed and breakfast. RV park with hookups. Picnic tables and rest area beside the restored *Taku Chief* are behind the visitor information center. ▲

Bed & Maybe Breakfast. Step back in time and charm yourself in the atmosphere of the old railroad depot built for President Harding's historic visit in 1923. Oak or brass beds, hardwood floors and braided rugs enhance the decor of these rooms. Overlook the hustling loading dock area of the barge lines on the Tanana River. View the Native cemetery and the historic railroad bridge from your window. Credit cards accepted. Reservations: (907) 832-5272 or 832-5556. [ADVERTISEMENT]

Tripod Gift Shop and Mini Mall. "Take time to smell the flowers." Over 19,000 flowers are planted each year to enhance the beauty of one of the loveliest gift shops in Alaska. A fun stop! Enjoy old-time concertina music played by Joanne Hawkins. Take the boardwalk to our Art Lovers' Gallery, Trapper's Cabin stocked with a wide selection of local furs; king- and queen-sized shop; Bargain Corner with special prices on

T-shirts, souvenirs and mugs. Enjoy ice cream or snacks at our Sweets and Treats Shoppe and purchase our fine canned smoked salmon. Also available: ice, worldwide postcard stamps, assorted camera batteries and wildflower seeds. Complimentary gold panning with $5 purchase in any of these shops. The shops are a must, a highlight of any vacation. Interesting displays include record size moose antlers, Kodiak grizzly bear trap (largest ever manufactured), antique ice saw, working fish wheel, trapper's steam boiler, dog salmon drying rack and authentic 1997 Ice Classic tripod. Be sure to have your picture taken with Sourdough Pete and rub his head for luck. Tour operators may call ahead to reserve a guided tour of Nenana, compliments of Tripod Gift Shop. Joanne Hawkins has hosted tour groups for over 20 years at no charge. Allow 30–45 minutes if the tour is to be included with your rest stop. A little history, a little fact, a little music and a lot of fun are packed into this tour. Have a picture taken of your coach, escort and driver for our display board. Over 15 years of tour operator photos are on display. This tour is a must! Remember, reservations are necessary. Tour operators thinking about lunch can call ahead for reservations at Two Choice Cafe (907) 832-5272. Ask about our soup and sandwich special for groups of 25 or more. Complimentary RV parking for self-contained vehicles. [ADVERTISEMENT]

George Parks Highway Log
(continued)

A 305.1 (491 km) **F 52.9** (85.1 km) Tanana River bridge. Large paved turnout to west at north end of bridge. The Tanana is formed by the joining of the Chisana and the Nabesna rivers near Northway and flows

440 miles/708 km westward to the Yukon River. From the bridge, watch for freight-laden river barges bound for the Yukon River. North of this bridge, fish wheels sometimes may be seen in action and occasionally fish may be purchased from the owners of the wheels.

Entering Game Management Unit 20B northbound, 20A southbound.

A 305.5 (491.6 km) **F 52.5** (84.5 km) Paved turnout to west by Tanana River. There is a Native cemetery 0.6 mile/1 km to east on side road.

A 305.6 (491.8 km) **F 52.4** (84.3 km) Paved turnout to west overlooking Tanana River.

A 305.9 (492.3 km) **F 52.1** (83.8 km) Double-ended gravel turnout to east. RV park. ▲

A 308.9 (497.1 km) **F 49.1** (79 km) *CAUTION: Railroad crossing.*

A 314.6 (506.3 km) **F 43.4** (69.8 km) Paved double-ended turnout to west.

A 314.8 (506.6 km) **F 43.2** (69.5 km) Bridge over Little Goldstream Creek.

A 315.4 (507.6 km) **F 42.5** (68.6 km) Truck lane next 2.8 miles/4.5 km northbound.

A 318.8 (513 km) **F 39.2** (63.1 km) Paved double-ended turnout to west with scenic view. The view is mostly of bogs, small lakes and creeks, with names like Hard Luck Creek, Fortune Creek, All Hand Help Lake and Wooden Canoe Lake.

Southbound travelers will see the Tanana River on both sides of the highway. It follows a horseshoe-shaped course, the top of the closed end being the bridge at Nenana.

A 321 (516.6 km) **F 37** (59.5 km) Fairbanks-bound traffic: Highway climbs a steep

grade with sweeping curves next 1 mile/1.6 km; truck lane next mile northbound. Mount McKinley is visible to the southwest on a clear day.

A 323 (519.8 km) **F 35** (56.3 km) Tanana River visible to east in valley below highway.

A 323.8 (521.1 km) **F 34.2** (55 km) Truck lane next 0.3 mile/0.5 km northbound.

A 324.5 (522.2 km) **F 33.5** (53.9 km) Paved double-ended turnout to east with scenic view to south.

A 325 (523 km) **F 33** (53.1 km) This stretch of highway is often called Skyline Drive; views to west. Downgrade northbound.

A 325.7 (524.1 km) **F 32.3** (52 km) Entering Fairbanks North Star Borough northbound.

A 328 (527.8 km) **F 30** (48.2 km) **Skinny Dick's Halfway Inn.** See display ad this section.

A 328.3 (528.3 km) **F 29.7** (47.8 km)

Truck lane next 3 miles/4.8 km southbound.

A 331.6 (533.6 km) F 26.4 (42.5 km) Long paved double-ended turnout to east. Intermittent truck lanes northbound to Fairbanks.

A 338.2 (544.3 km) F 19.8 (31.9 km) Wide view to east. Look for Murphy Dome (elev. 2,930 feet/893m) with white communication installations on summit to west.

A 339.3 (546 km) F 19.7 (30.1 km) Viewpoint and sign to east. This is the south end of a 1-mile/1.6-km scenic loop road that rejoins the highway at Milepost A 339.9. Highway begins downgrade northbound.

A 339.9 (547 km) F 18.1 (29.1 km) Turnoff (unmarked) for Bonanza Experimental Forest via 1-mile/1.6-km loop road east; scenic viewpoint.

A 342.2 (550.7 km) F 15.8 (25.4 km) Rosie Creek Road.

A 342.4 (551 km) F 15.6 (25.1 km) Old Nenana Highway.

A 344.2 (553.9 km) F 13.8 (22.2 km) Monument in honor of George Alexander Parks, former governor of Alaska. Also here

is a Blue Star Memorial highway plaque honoring the armed forces. Viewpoint to east. Tanana River can be seen below the Parks monument.

A 349 (561.6 km) F 9 (14.5 km) Cripple Creek Road to south, Park Ridge Road to north. Truck lane next 4.2 miles/6.8 km southbound.

A 350 (563.3 km) F 8 (12.9 km) Alder Creek.

A 351.2 (565.2 km) F 6.8 (10.9 km) Old gold dredges visible to the east.

A 351.7 (566 km) F 6.3 (10.1 km) Turnoff to west for Ester (description follows).

Ester

Located 0.6 mile/1 km west of highway. **Population:** 211. **Emergency Services:** Emergency only, phone 911. **Fire Department**, phone (907) 479-6858. A former gold mining camp and current visitor attraction, Ester has a hotel, RV camping, 2 saloons, 3 gift shops and a post office. A village sign on Main Street locates these services.

Ester was a raucous mining camp in 1906, with a population of some 5,000 miners. Today a quiet bedroom community of Fairbanks, Ester's heydays are relived in music, song and dance at the Malemute Saloon. Active gold mining is still under way in the area. One of the best preserved gold dredges from the gold rush days can be seen from **Milepost A 351.2.**

Ester Gold Camp. At the turn-of-century, discovery of gold in the Ester region drew hundreds of prospectors to seek their fortunes. In 1936, the Fairbanks Exploration Company built Ester Camp to support a large scale gold dredge operation. After 20 years of operation, the camp was closed. It opened again in 1958, but this time as a summer visitor attraction. Today, Ester Gold Camp, on the National Register of Historic Places, provides services for another kind of prospector: those seeking accommodations, excellent food and a fun-filled night of entertainment. Open late May through early September. See display ad in FAIRBANKS section. [ADVERTISEMENT] ▲

Judie Gumm Designs. Noted for her sculptural interpretations of northern images, her work has been featured in many national publications. Priced moderately; easy to pack—her jewelry makes a perfect remembrance of your adventure North.

Follow the signs in Ester. Weekdays 10–6. Saturday 12–5. Catalog available. P.O. Box 169, Ester, AK 99725. Phone: (907) 479-4568. See display ad. [ADVERTISEMENT]

George Parks Highway Log
(continued)

A 351.8 (566.2 km) F 6.2 (10 km) Weigh stations.

A 352.5 (567.3 km) F 5.5 (8.8 km) Gold Hill Road.

Gold Hill. See display ad this section.

PHTS (Parks Highway Truck Stop). See display ad this section.

Inua Wool Shoppe. Turn on Gold Hill Road, go 0.3 mile left to Henderson, 1 mile to 202 Henderson Road. Inua Wool Shoppe is Interior Alaska's most complete knitting shoppe. Fabulous selection of Quiviuq and other fine wool yarns. Large selection of Alaskan, Norwegian and American patterns, needlepoints, buttons, books and needles. Come enjoy a unique knitting shoppe. Open 10–5 Monday–Saturday. (907) 479-5830 (Alaska 1-800-478-9848). VISA and Master-Card welcome. [ADVERTISEMENT]

A 353.5 (568.9 km) F 4.5 (7.2 km) Gas station and store. Public dumpster and aluminum recycling bin.

A 355.8 (572.6 km) F 2.2 (3.5 km) Sheep Creek Road and Tanana Drive. Road to Murphy Dome (a restricted military site).

A 356.8 (574.2 km) F 1.2 (1.9 km) Turnoff to University of Alaska, Geist Road, Chena Ridge Loop and Chena Pump Road.

A 357.6 (575.5 km) F 0.4 (0.6 km) Bridge over Chena River.

A 357.7 (575.6 km) F 0.3 (0.5 km) Fairbanks airport exit.

A 358 (576.1 km) F 0 Fairbanks exit; George Parks Highway (Robert J. Mitchell Expressway) continues to Richardson Highway, bypassing Fairbanks. Take Airport Way exit west for Fairbanks International Airport and Dale Road to Discovery Steamboat Landing. Exit east at Airport Way for: private campground on Boat Street; University Avenue (access to University of Alaska and Chena River state recreation site); Peger Road (access to private campground, flying service and Alaskaland); Cushman Street (access to visitor center and Alaska Railroad depot); and to connect with the Steese Expressway. (See Fairbanks Vicinity map on page 410 in the FAIRBANKS section.)

FAIRBANKS

(See maps, page 410)

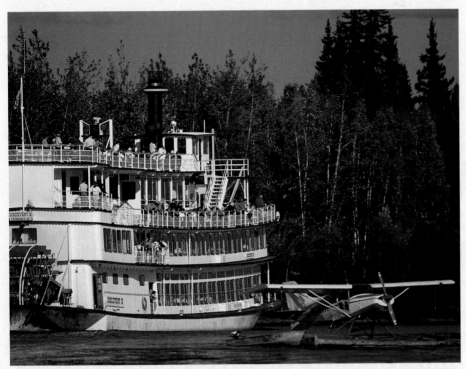

Floatplane and Discovery II *on the Chena River.* (© Roy M. Corral)

Located in the heart of Alaska's Great Interior country. By highway, it is approximately 1,488 miles/2,395 km north of Dawson Creek, BC, the start of the Alaska Highway (traditional milepost distance is 1,523 miles); 98 miles/158 km from Delta Junction (official end of the Alaska Highway); 358 miles/576 km from Anchorage via the George Parks Highway; and 2,305 miles/3,709 km from Seattle.

Population: Fairbanks–North Star Borough, 84,380. **Emergency Services: Alaska State Troopers**, 1979 Peger Road, phone (907) 451-5333; for nonemergencies, (907) 451-5100; and using TTY service, (907) 451-5344. **Fairbanks Police**, 656 7th Ave., phone 911 or, for nonemergencies, phone (907) 459-6500. **Fire Department** and **Ambulance Service**, phone 911. **Hospitals**, Fairbanks Memorial, 1650 Cowles St., phone (907) 452-8181; Bassett Army Hospital, Fort Wainwright, phone (907) 353-5143; Eielson Clinic, Eielson AFB, phone (907) 377-2259. **Women's Crisis Line**, phone (907) 452-2293. **Emergency Management**, phone (907) 459-1481 or (907) 474-7721 (24-hour line). **Borough Information**, phone (907) 459-1000.

Visitor Information: Fairbanks Visitor Information Center at 550 1st Ave. (at Cush-

man Street, where a riverside marker shows the distance of Fairbanks from some 75 cities); phone (907) 456-5774 or 1-800-327-5774. In summer, open 8 A.M. to 8 P.M. daily; in winter, open 8 A.M. to 5 P.M. weekdays, closed weekends. Phone (907) 456-INFO for daily recorded information.

Visitor information is also available at Fairbanks International Airport in the baggage claim area, at the Alaska Railroad depot at the University of Alaska Museum and at Alaskaland.

For information on Alaska's state parks, national parks, national forests, wildlife refuges and other outdoor recreational sites, visit the Alaska Public Lands Information Center downstairs in historic Courthouse Square at 250 N. Cushman St. The center is a free museum featuring films on Alaska, interpretive programs, lectures, exhibits, artifacts, photographs and short video programs on each region in the state. The exhibit area and information desk are open 7 days a week in summer; Tuesday through Saturday in winter. Phone (907) 456-0527. For recorded information on Denali National Park, phone (907) 456-0510. TDD information line is (907) 456-0532.

Elevation: 436 feet/133m at Fairbanks International Airport. **Climate:** January temperatures range from -2°F/-19°C to -19°F/-28°C. The lowest temperature ever recorded was -62°F/-52°C in December 1961. July temperatures average 62°F/17°C, with a record

high of 99°F/37°C in July 1919. In June and early July daylight lasts 21 hours—and the nights are really only twilight. Annual precipitation is 10.9 inches, with an annual average snowfall of 65 inches. The record for snowfall is 147.3 inches, set the winter of 1990–91. **Radio:** KSUA-FM, KFAR, KCBF, KAKQ, KWLF-FM, KIAK, KIAK-FM, KJNP-AM and FM (North Pole), KUAC-FM 104.7. **Television:** Channels 2, 4, 7, 9, 11, 13 and cable. **Newspapers:** *Fairbanks Daily News–Miner*.

Private Aircraft: Facilities for all types of aircraft. Consult the *Alaska Supplement* for information on the following airports: Eielson AFB, Fairbanks International, Fairbanks International Seaplane, Chena Marina Air Field and Fort Wainwright. For more information phone the Fairbanks Flight Service Station at (907) 474-0137.

HISTORY

In 1901, Captain E.T. Barnette set out from St. Michael on the stern-wheeler *Lavelle Young*, traveling up the Yukon River with supplies for his trading post, which he proposed to set up at Tanana Crossing (Tanacross), the halfway point on the Valdez–Eagle trail. But the stern-wheeler could not navigate the fast-moving, shallow Tanana River beyond the mouth of the Chena River. The stern-wheeler's captain finally dropped off the protesting Barnette on the Chena River, near the present site of 1st Avenue and Cushman Street. A year later, Felix Pedro, an Italian prospector, discovered gold about 16 miles/26 km north of Barnette's temporary trading post. The opportunistic Barnette quickly abandoned his original plan to continue on to Tanana Crossing.

In September 1902, Barnette convinced the 25 or so miners in the area to use the name "Fairbanks" for the town that he expected would grow up around his trading post. The name had been suggested that summer by Alaska Judge James Wickersham, who admired Charles W. Fairbanks, the senior senator from Indiana. The senator later became vice president of the United States under Theodore Roosevelt.

The town grew, largely due to Barnette's promotion of gold prospects and discoveries in the area, and in 1903 Judge Wickersham moved the headquarters of his Third Judicial District Court (a district which encompassed 300,000 square miles) from Eagle to Fairbanks.

Thanks to Wickersham, the town gained government offices and a jail. Thanks to Barnette, it gained a post office and a branch of the Northern Commercial Company, a large Alaska trading firm based in San Francisco. In addition, after Barnette became the first mayor of Fairbanks in 1903, the town acquired telephone service, set up fire protection, passed sanitation ordinances and contracted for electric light and steam heat.

(Continues on page 409.)

RIVERBOAT DISCOVERY • A most memorable adventure

The Riverboat Discovery is the one adventure you won't want to miss when you travel to Fairbanks. Owned and operated by the Binkley family, whose river boating experience in Alaska spans four generations and almost 100 years, the Riverboat Discovery tour has been rated the top boating attraction in North America in Travel Weekly Magazine. Captain Jim Binkley and his crew of children, grandchildren and native Alaskans takes you back to the heyday of sternwheelers, to an era when prospectors, fur traders and Native people of the Interior relied on rivers as their only link to the outside world.

Passengers relax in the comfort of glass enclosed or open decks as the Discovery III winds its way down the Chena and Tanana Rivers. Drawing on their knowledge of Alaskan history, the Binkley family entertains listeners with witty descriptions of Alaskan life during the four hour narrated cruise. The Discovery makes a brief stop at the river front home of veteran Iditarod Dog Musher Susan Butcher, where visitors hear tales of Susan's Iditarod adventures and are introduced to her champion sled dogs.

One of the highlights of the trip is a stop ashore at the Old Chena Indian Village. Here passengers disembark for a guided tour. Alaskan Natives share their culture as they recount how their ancestors hunted, fished, sewed clothing and built shelters to survive for centuries in the harsh Alaskan wilderness. At the village a dog mushing distance racing team gives passengers a "close-up" view of an actual mushing kennel.

The Discovery departs Steamboat Landing, off Dale Road, daily at 8:45 AM and 2:00 PM mid-May through mid-September.

Reservations are required. For further information call 907-479-6673.

Before or after your cruise step into the past at Steamboat Landing, one of the finest gift stores in Alaska. Stroll along the picturesque boardwalk beside the Chena River and enter any of four turn-of-the-century shops. Discovery Trading Post offers unique Alaskan gifts at great low prices. The Susan Butcher Dog Mushing gallery features mementos of the Iditarod champion's lifestyle and an exclusive line of sportswear. Susan's winning Iditarod dogsled and Iditarod trophies are conveniently located so you can take photos you'll always treasure. The Binkley and Barrington Gift Shop offers Alaskan made products, and the Pioneer Hotel is a replica of Fairbanks' first luxury hotel featuring authentic Russian collectibles. Be sure not to miss this cultural treat between Discovery III departures – you'll find an impressive selection of gifts at some of the best prices in Alaska. Open 8:00 AM to 8:00 PM daily.

The two hour tour to a working gold mine begins when passengers board the Tanana Valley Railroad for a narrated trip through the original gold fields of the Interior that were once part of Alaska's richest mining district on record.

Passengers ride the narrow gauge rails through a permaforst tunnel where miners with head lamps and pick-axes seek out the rich gold veins, reminiscent of mining days gone by. Winding through the valley, the train comes to a halt as a prospector crouches down to dip his gold pan into cold, clear waters of Fox Creek in search of the sparkle of gold.

At El Dorado Camp, local miners "Yukon Yonda" and her husband Dexter Clark are on hand to conduct a guided tour through a working gold mine. Visitors gather around to watch the operation of a modern day sluice box and enjoy stories about life in Alaskan mining camps.

A crash course in gold panning is followed by the real thing. Visitors grab a poke filled with pay dirt right from the sluice box and try their hand at panning for gold. And when they strike it rich, they keep the gold!

The next stop is the assay office where visitors, while enjoying complimentary homemade cookies and coffee, weigh their gold and assay its market value. The "all aboard" call gathers everyone onto the train for the short ride back to the station.

Daily tours for the El Dorado Gold Mine depart from the old train station at 1.3 mile Elliott Highway, just past Fox, Alaska, nine miles north of Fairbanks. For reservations call 907-479-7613.

EL DORADO GOLD MINE • Gold Mining History

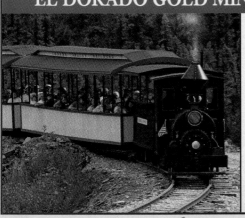

PAN for GOLD
You're guaranteed to find it!

Pan for gold at the El Dorado Gold Mine. Join the Binkley family for another Alaskan experience that can't be missed! El Dorado Gold Mine is an exciting hands-on adventure for the whole family. Visitors learn about the history of mining in Alaska, experience a modern day mining operation and pan for gold, while enjoying El Dorado Gold Mine's famous Alaskan hospitality.

Visit our web site
URL: http://www2.polarnet.com/~discovry
e-Mail: discovery @ ARIInc.com

Adventure Into Fairbanks' Gold Mining History

All Aboard.

Hop aboard our own Tanana Valley Railroad and ride the narrow gauge rails through the original gold fields of the Interior, to a present day working gold mine.

Working Gold Mine.

Modern mining equipment and techniques are demonstrated by the actual miners who work this claim.

DAILY departures. Two hour tour of an operating gold mine. Just 9 miles north of Fairbanks on the Elliott Highway.

Catch The Fever.

Pan for your own gold! We supply the rich, concentrated "pay dirt" right out of our modern sluice box. You WILL find gold. We guarantee it!

Permafrost Tunnel.

Ride the train into our permafrost tunnel. Learn about underground mining methods from the past and see prehistoric bones up to 30,000 years old.

El Dorado GOLD MINE

Call for Reservations 907-479-7613

For further information fax 907-479-4613 or write: 1975 Discovery Drive, Fairbanks, Alaska 99709

(Continued from page 405)
In 1904, Barnette started a bank.

The town of "Fairbanks" first appeared in the U.S. Census in 1910 with a population of 3,541. Miners living beside their claims on creeks north of town brought the area population figure to about 11,000.

Barnette stayed in Fairbanks until late 1910, when he resigned the presidency of the Washington–Alaska Bank and moved to California. When the bank collapsed early in 1911, the people of Fairbanks blamed Barnette. The tale of the "most hated man in Fairbanks" is told in *E.T. Barnette, The Strange Story of the Man Who Founded Fairbanks*.

ECONOMY

The city's economy is linked to its role as a service and supply point for Interior and Arctic industrial activities. Fairbanks played a key role during construction of the trans-Alaska pipeline in the 1970s. The Dalton Highway (formerly the North Slope Haul Road) to Prudhoe Bay begins about 75 miles/121 km north of town. Extractive industries such as oil and mining continue to play a

Bank shows record cold day in winter of 1989. (© Craig Brandt)

Fairbanks

To the University of Alaska

Farmers Loop Rd.

College Rd.

Tanana Valley Fairgrounds

Creamers Field Wildlife Refuge

Department of Fish and Game

College Rd.

Esquire Ave.

Noyes Slough

Noyes Slough

Aspen St.

Aurora Dr.

Danby St.

Illinois St.

Bentley Mall

Old Steese Highway

Minnie St.

Deadman Slough

Hanson Rd.

Johansen Expressway

Graehl Street Boat Landing

Gavora Mall

3 St.

Geist Rd.

Johansen Expressway

The Alaska Railroad

Clay

Steese Expressway

Chena River

Phillips Field Rd.

Chena River

Alaska Railroad Depot

Visitor Information Center

Griffin Park

Wendell

2 Ave.

Front St.

Slater Dr. W.

University Ave.

1 Ave.

5 Ave.

3 Ave.

4 Ave.

Post Office

Dunkle

Noble

Lacey

Rampart Mini Mall

6 Ave.

9 Ave.

Police & Fire Depts.

7 Ave.

8 Ave.

10 Ave.

11 Ave.

12 Ave.

Federal Building

2 Ave.

Lathrop St.

Cushman St.

9 Ave.

10 Ave.

Peger Rd.

Alaskaland

Tourist Information

Crosson Ave.

Airport Way

Cowles St.

Mary Siah Recreation Center

Gaffney Rd.

University Center Mall

Rewak Dr.

Hamme Pool

14 Ave.

15 Ave.

Wickersham St. Way

Entrance to Fort Wainwright

University Ave. S.

Kiana St.

17 Ave.

18 Ave.

19 Ave.

Gilam

16 Ave.

Eielson St.

16 Ave.

2

Alaska-Richardson Highway

Alaska State Troopers

Hospital

Cowles St.

19 Ave.

Cushman St.

Ladd

18 Ave.

21 Ave.

To Delta Junction

Hez Ray Recreation Complex and Parks & Recreation Offices

Gillam Park

21 Ave.

22 Ave.

Davis Road

Davis Road

23 Ave.

To Metro Field

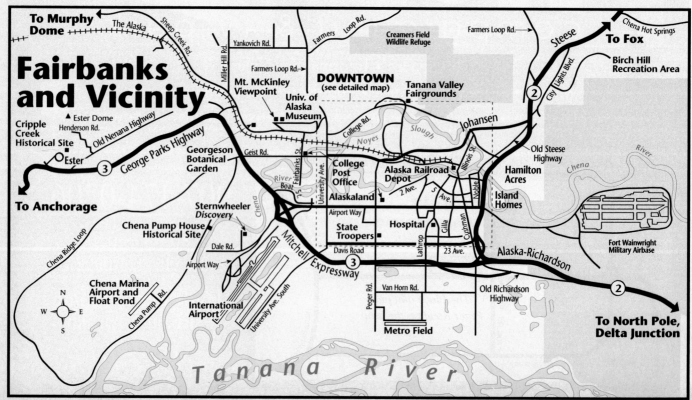

Fairbanks and Vicinity

To Murphy Dome

The Alaska

Sheep Creek Rd.

Miller Hill Rd.

Yankovich Rd.

Farmers Loop Rd.

Creamers Field Wildlife Refuge

Farmers Loop Rd.

Steese

Chena Hot Springs

To Fox

Mt. McKinley Viewpoint

Farmers Loop Rd.

DOWNTOWN (see detailed map)

Tanana Valley Fairgrounds

2

City Lights Blvd.

Birch Hill Recreation Area

Ester Dome

Henderson Rd.

Old Nenana Highway

Univ. of Alaska Museum

College Rd.

Noyes

Johansen

Slough

Illinois St.

Old Steese Highway

Chena River

Cripple Creek Historical Site

Geist Rd.

Fairbanks St.

River Boat

College Post Office

Alaska Railroad Depot

Hamilton Acres

Ester

3

George Parks Highway

Georgeson Botanical Garden

University Ave.

Alaskaland

2 Ave.

5 Ave.

Noble

Island Homes

To Anchorage

Sternwheeler Discovery

Chena

Airport Way

State Troopers

Hospital

Gilla

Cushman

Fort Wainwright Military Airbase

Chena Pump House Historical Site

Dale Rd.

Mitchell Expressway

Davis Road

Lathrop

23 Ave.

Alaska-Richardson

Chena Ridge Loop

Airport Way

3

Peger Rd.

Van Horn Rd.

Old Richardson Highway

2

Chena Marina Airport and Float Pond

Chena Pump Rd.

International Airport

University Ave. South

Metro Field

To North Pole, Delta Junction

Tanana River

RIVER'S EDGE
RV PARK & CAMPGROUND
FAIRBANKS

"River's Edge is RV heaven!"
Dr. Helen Stover of Richmond, VA

River's Edge RV Park has so much to offer!

- Full and partial hook-ups
- Pull-throughs
- 30-amp electric
- Dump station
- Dry tent sites
- FREE showers
- Laundry
- Gift shop
- Pay phones
- Car/RV wash facility

- Over 160 sites
- Walking distance to major shopping centers and groceries
- FREE shuttle service to Sternwheeler Discovery and Alaska Salmon Bake
- ★ Denali One-Day Tour
- ★ Tour Arrangements: Pt. Barrow & Arctic Circle

From Anchorage/Denali, AK3: take East Fairbanks exit, left on Sportsmans Way, left on Boat Street.

From Tok/Richardson Hwy., AK2: left on Airport Way, cross University Avenue, right on Sportsmans Way, left on Boat Street.

4140 Boat Street (off Airport Way),
Fairbanks, Alaska 99709 • 1-800-770-3343

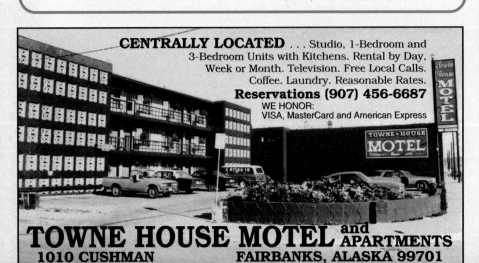
major role in the economy.

Government employment contributes significantly to the Fairbanks economy. Including military jobs, 50 percent of employment in Fairbanks is through the government. Fort Wainwright (formerly Ladd Field) was the first Army airfield in Alaska, established in 1938. The fort currently employs 4,600 soldiers and 1,600 civilians, and it houses 6,200 family members. Fort Wainwright also provides emergency services by assisting with search and rescue operations. Eielson Air Force Base, located 25 miles/40 km southeast of Fairbanks on the Richardson–Alaska Highway, also has a strong economic impact on the city. Eielson has about 2,700 military personnel and approximately 4,200 family members assigned, with about 1,200 military personnel and family members living off base.

Also boosting the Fairbanks economy are the University of Alaska Fairbanks, and trade and service industries such as retail sales and tourism.

DESCRIPTION

Alaska's second largest city and the administrative capital of the Interior, Fairbanks lies on the flat valley floor of the Tanana River on the banks of the Chena River. Good views of the valley are available from Chena Ridge Road to the west and Farmers Loop Road to the north.

The city is a blend of old and new: Modern hotels and shopping malls stand beside log cabins and historic wooden buildings.

Fairbanks is bounded to the north, east and west by low rolling hills of birch and

ver's Edge RV Park presents

BARROW

Land of the Midnight Sun

Don't stop till you reach the top!

Day or Overnight Tours from Fairbanks

featuring Boeing 737 jet service on Alaska Airlines and overnight accommodations with Top of the World Hotel.

Overnight Tour

All the excitement of the one-day tour *plus* for a few more dollars:

Stay overnight at the **Top of the World Hotel.**

Return to Fairbanks the next afternoon. River's Edge will meet you.

One-Day Tour

River's Edge takes you to the airport in the early morning for your flight on Alaska Airlines.

Receive a certificate after crossing the Arctic Circle.

Spend the day in Barrow with your own tour guide. Includes an extensive Native Culture Exhibition featuring Blanket Toss and Inupiat Eskimo Traditional Dances.

Arrive that evening in Fairbanks. River's Edge picks you up.

Barrow is only a 75 minute flight from Fairbanks.

Warm clothing is available.

In-flight breakfast and dinner snack are provided.

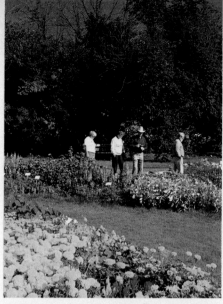

Georgeson Botanical Garden, University of Alaska. (© Harry M. Walker Photo)

white spruce. To the south is the Alaska Range and Denali National Park, about a 2½-hour drive via the George Parks Highway. The Steese and Elliott highways lead north to the White Mountains.

ACCOMMODATIONS/VISITOR SERVICES

Fairbanks has about 2 dozen hotels and motels and more than 100 bed and breakfasts during the summer. Rates vary widely, from a low of about $40 for a single to a high of $150 for a double. Reservations for accommodations are suggested during the busy summer months.

There are several private campgrounds in the Fairbanks area. Chena River recreation site, a state campground, is located on University Avenue by the Chena River bridge. The campground has 57 sites, tables, firepits, toilets, water and a dump station. Camping fee $15/night or annual pass; $3 for use of dump station; and $5 for use of boat launch.

There is overnight camping at Alaskaland for self-contained RVs only with a 4-night limit, $9 fee and use of the Borough dump station on 2nd Avenue. ▲

Fairbanks has more than 100 restaurants ranging from deluxe to fast food.

A Bed and Breakfast on Minnie is an inspected and approved home that offers lovely, clean and cozy rooms. King, queen and twin beds. Hot tub in king room. Private upstairs suite with kitchenette. Private and shared baths offered. Full or continental

breakfast. Phones, cable TV, computer hook-up, laundry facilities available. No smoking. Friendly dog on premises. Children welcome. Itinerary and tickets for Interior of Alaska events available. Rates $65–$95. 72-hour cancellation policy. Credit cards accepted. Phone (907) 456-1802. Fax (907) 451-1751. [ADVERTISEMENT]

Ah, Rose Marie Downtown Bed and Breakfast. Historic 1928 Fairbanks home. Very centrally located in downtown neighborhood. Full hearty breakfasts. Friendly cat and dog. Outdoor smoking areas. Singles,

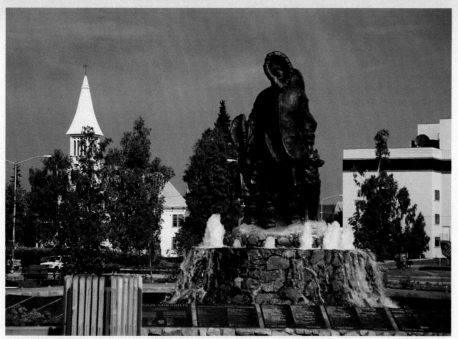

"Unknown First Family" statue at Golden Heart Park next to visitor information center on 1st Avenue. (© Barbara Willard)

couples, triples, families welcomed. Open year-round. Extraordinary hospitality. Single $50 up, doubles $65 up. Wow! John E. Davis, 302 Cowles St., Fairbanks, AK 99701. (907) 456-2040. [ADVERTISEMENT]

Applesauce Inn B&B. Small Alaskan family with 3 friendly cats welcomes you! Peaceful, woodsy neighborhood, 5-minute drive to town. Four bedrooms, 3 of them adjacent to own living room offering group/family privacy. Hearty breakfasts feature reindeer sausage. (Belgian waffles and

Arctic Slumber Downtown B&B. Ideal for walkers, convenient to local attractions, Chena River, restaurants, shopping, art galleries, visitor's center. Smoke-free. Sociable family enjoys sharing their home and excitement about living in Fairbanks. Full breakfast, Alaskan library, clean and cozy. $65 and

up. 1382 6th Ave., Fairbanks, AK 99701. (907) 451-9931. [ADVERTISEMENT]

Chena Marina RV Park guests speak: "RV having fun? Yes—Thanks to folks like you! ... 'Dankeschon' services really special ... One of the best—location, spacious, landscaped ... First-rate." Extra-wide, long pull-throughs (slide-outs welcome). Free Klondinental breakfast; on floatplane pond (fishing); laundry, free guest showers, electric, water, TV, dump, tour tickets, free RV/car wash. Mile 2.8 Chena Pump Road, watch for signs. (907) 479-GOLD (4653), 1145 Shypoke Dr., Fairbanks, AK 99709. See map in display ad for directions. Open May 1. [ADVERTISEMENT] ▲

Fairbanks Bed And Breakfast. Barbara Neubauer, hostess and 26-year resident, has many bear and gold mining tales. The quiet historical neighborhood is walking distance to town on bus route. Our home has many interesting ivory artifacts and Alaskan art. Private bath, large yard and deck. Deck smoking. Hearty breakfast and laundry facilities for fee plus ample parking. 902 Kellum St. (907) 452-4967, fax (907) 451-6955. [ADVERTISEMENT]

Fairbanks Princess Hotel. Interior Alaska's finest accommodations located on the Chena River. Featuring an array of dining options, lounge, terraced riverside deck, tour desk, gift shop, health club with steam rooms, complimentary airport shuttle, meeting facilities for groups up to 435. Open year-round. Call 1-800-426-0500 for reservations. [ADVERTISEMENT]

Fairbanks Private Vacation Homes

Tours Starting At
$19
Per Person, Including Gold

Gold Dredge No. 8

A piece of history to experience.
A piece of gold to remember it by.

Prospectors used to travel for weeks through ice and snow in hopes of coming across a mere trace of gold. Today, Gray Line of Alaska has made prospecting much easier with tours to Gold Dredge No. 8, the only gold dredge in Alaska still open to the public. Gold Dredge No. 8 offers a truly authentic gold mining experience, including a tour of the site that unearthed 7.5 million ounces of gold, as well as the opportunity to pan for guaranteed gold yourself. Afterwards enjoy the Miner's Buffet lunch for just $8, and visit the museum or gift shop for a large variety of mining souvenirs.

Open 9 a.m. to 6 p.m. every day from May 15 through September 15.
From Fairbanks, take the Steese Highway north to Goldstream Road, then follow the signs.
Gold Dredge No. 8 is approximately 10 minutes from Fairbanks.

GRAY LINE **Gray Line of Alaska**
A DIVISION OF HOLLAND AMERICA LINE-WESTOURS

Mention The MILEPOST® to our advertisers!

Network. Peaceful, quiet, wooded settings, all within 12 minutes of city center. All have clean and modern kitchens and bathrooms, phones, TV/VCRs and stock breakfast fixings. Smoking outdoors. Reasonable rates. Brochures available. Beth's Vacation Home, 1 bedroom, no pets, 1000 Bennett Rd., Fairbanks, AK 99712, (907) 457-2725; Cedar Creek Vacation Home, custom-built 2-story, 2 1/2 bedrooms, pets on approval, P.O. Box 10355, Fairbanks, AK 99710, phone (907) 457-3392, within Alaska 1-800-764-3392, fax (907) 457-3332; Gram's Cabins, on 3 riverfront acres, pets on approval, P.O. Box 58034, Fairbanks, AK 99711, phone (907) 488-6513, fax (907) 488-6593. [ADVERTISEMENT]

Fountainhead Hotels. Our hotel hotline, 1-800-528-4916, accesses more than 700 rooms at 3 of Fairbanks' best hotels: Sophie Station, Wedgewood Resort, and the Bridgewater Hotel. Varying locations and features assure that we will have the right room for you. Our staff will gladly assist you in selecting the best accommodations. Each property offers dining facilities, laundry services and free local calls. For color brochure call our hotline, or write: 1501 Queens Way, Fairbanks, AK 99701. E-mail: Fountain@Mosquitonet.com. [ADVERTISEMENT]

Geni's Bed & Breakfast. Country hospitality May to September. Large bedroom, private bath. Two bedrooms with queen-sized beds, shared full bath. No pets, smoking on deck only. Continental or full country breakfast. Affordable accommodations in woodland setting 15 minutes from Fairbanks at Mile 5.3 Chena Hot Springs Road.

Handmade Alaska crafts available. George and Nila Lyle, P.O. Box 10352, Fairbanks, AK 99710; phone (907) 488-4136. [ADVERTISEMENT]

Jan's B&B. Located halfway between downtown Fairbanks and the University. Have your choice of the private apartment (nice for families) or our solarium room with hot tub. Private or semi-private baths. Enjoy eating a gourmet breakfast on our large deck surrounded by lots of Alaskan flowers. Reasonable rates. (907) 456-5431, 1605 Marika Rd. [ADVERTISEMENT]

Marilyn's Bed and Breakfast. Located in downtown Fairbanks. Enjoy true pioneer friendliness in a comfortable, homey atmosphere. Continental breakfast with homemade jams. Perhaps you may persuade Marilyn to fix waffles made from her 1877 sourdough starter. No smoking. Off-street parking. For reservations, Marilyn Nigro, 651 9th Ave., Fairbanks, AK 99701. Phone (907) 456-1959, fax (907) 456-6624. [ADVERTISEMENT]

Norlite Campground, Inc. Centrally located within Fairbanks city limits just 0.3 mile south off Airport Road on Peger Road, Norlite is the most complete of all Fairbanks' campgrounds. City water, sewer and electric hookups, showers, dump station, tour tickets, laundry, truck/car wash, snack and ice cream bar and grocery store are all on the grounds. 30 years hosting happy visitors. (907) 474-0206, fax (907) 474-0992. (See display ad in this section.) [ADVERTISEMENT] ▲

Raven Inn Bed and Breakfast. Charming 1931 home located in the "heart" of the "Golden Heart City." Three rooms with 2 shared baths or 2-room suite with private bath and entrance. Beautiful yard, open kitchen, family and group rates available. Alaskan friendly, Alaskan proud. 409 Dunkel, Fairbanks, AK 99701. (907) 456-3088. [ADVERTISEMENT]

River's Edge RV Park & Campground. Beautiful setting on the Chena River and within walking distance of major shopping centers. 180 spacious wooded sites. Wide pull-throughs; 30-amp electric; dump station; full and partial hookups, free showers, gifts, free shuttle to Riverboat *Discovery* and Alaskaland Salmon Bake. Tour arrangements featuring Point Barrow and Arctic Circle.

Immaculate facilities. [ADVERTISEMENT] ▲

Riverview RV Park & Campground is one of the top-rated RV parks in Alaska. It is situated on 20-acres adjoining the beautiful Chena River. Total atmosphere and only 10 minutes from downtown Fairbanks. It is the only RV park with cable TV in the Fairbanks area. Call Riverview RV Park 1-800-488-6392 or (907) 488-6281. See display ad. [ADVERTISEMENT] ▲

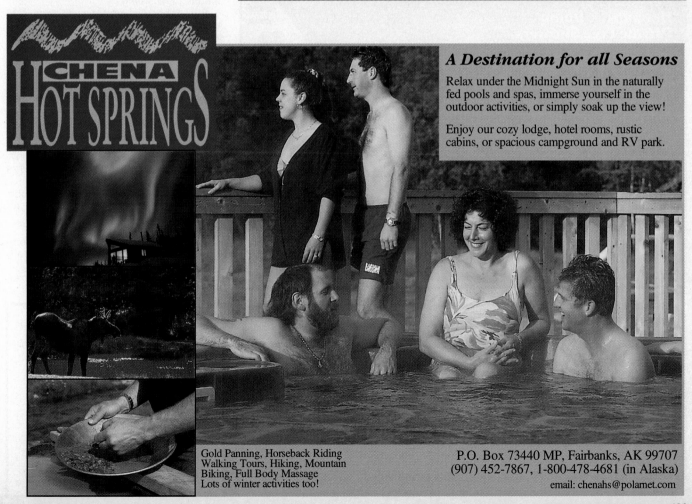

7 Gables Inn. Central to major attractions, this remodeled fraternity house is between the University campus and the airport. The spacious Tudor-style house features a floral solarium, stained-glass foyer with indoor waterfall, cathedral ceilings, banquet/conference facilities. Gourmet breakfast served daily. Cable TV, VCR, phone in each room, laundry, bikes, canoes and skis. Rates $50–120; 4312 Birch Lane, Fairbanks, AK 99709. Phone (907) 479-0751. [ADVERTISEMENT]

Uebernachtung und Fruehstueck, Bed & Breakfast. We speak English and German and provide lots of German hospitality. We have 3 trained dogs, a cat and a bird. We provide queen beds, shared or private bath and a big breakfast. You can watch German news via satellite TV. Robert and Sylvia Harris, 2402 Cowles St., Fairbanks, AK 99701. Phone (907) 455-7958, fax (907) 452-7958 [ADVERTISEMENT]

Wildview Cabin is your own log home away from home! On a private wooded 12 acre lot, your cabin is fully furnished and outfitted for short stays or long visits. Available all year round. Exceptional rates, so book early! Wildview Cabin, 891 Goldpan Rd., Fairbanks, AK 99712. (907) 457-1154. [ADVERTISEMENT]

TRANSPORTATION

Air: Several international, interstate and intra-Alaska carriers serve Fairbanks; see Air Travel in the GENERAL INFORMATION section.

Air charter services are available for flightseeing, fly-in fishing and hunting, and trips to bush villages; see ads.

Warbelow's Air Ventures, Inc. Scheduled commuter airline flying in Alaska's vast, roadless Interior. Experience Alaska first hand on one of our 14 daily Bush mail plane departures from Fairbanks. The ultimate in flightseeing excursions, including flights across the Arctic Circle. 3758 University Ave. S., Fairbanks International Airport, Fairbanks, AK 99709. (907) 474-0518, 1-800-478-0812. E-mail: WAV@polarnet.com. [ADVERTISEMENT]

Railroad: Alaska Railroad passenger depot at 280 N. Cushman St. in the downtown area. Daily passenger service in summer between Fairbanks and Anchorage with stop-overs at Denali National Park; less frequent service in winter. For details see the ALASKA RAILROAD section, or phone (800) 544-0552.

Train to Denali. Ride the luxurious private domed railcars of the *McKinley Explorer* to Denali National Park from either Anchorage or Fairbanks. Overnight packages in Denali with round-trip train service are available from only $265 ppdo. Prices subject to change. Call Gray Line of Alaska at (907) 456-7741 for train and package tour options. [ADVERTISEMENT]

Bus: Scheduled motorcoach service to Anchorage and points south. Local daily bus service by Metropolitan Area Commuter Service (MACS), and regular MACS service is also now available to North Pole weekdays; no service on Sundays and some legal holidays. Drivers do not carry change, and exact change or tokens must be used. Fares are: $1.50 or 1 token. All-day passes are $3. Tokens are available at Transit Park, the UAF Woodcenter, Fred Meyer west, Bentley Hall and North Pole Plaza. Information is available via the Transit Hotline, phone (907) 459-1011, or from MACS offices at 3175 Peger Road, phone (907) 459-1002.

Tours: Local and area sightseeing tours are available from several companies; see ads in this section.

Taxi: 9 cab companies.

Car and Camper Rentals: Several companies rent cars, campers and trailers; see ads in this section.

The Diesel Doctor. 3021 Davis Road,

Northern lights over Fairbanks, photographed from Old Steese Highway. (© Craig Brandt)

Building 2, Fairbanks. Specializing in Ford, GM and Dodge diesels, bumper-to-bumper drive train—gasoline or diesel vehicles. Big lot, plenty of room for motorhomes, overnight parking permitted in conjunction with repairs, electric and potable water (no dump). Monday–Friday 8 A.M. to 6 P.M. (907) 456-2483. [ADVERTISEMENT]

ATTRACTIONS

Get Acquainted: A good place to start is the visitor information center at 550 1st Ave., where you'll find free brochures, maps and tips on what to see and how to get there. Phone (907) 456-5774 or 1-800-327-5774. For a recording of current daily events phone (907) 456-INFO.

Next to the log cabin visitor information center is Golden Heart Park, site of the 18-

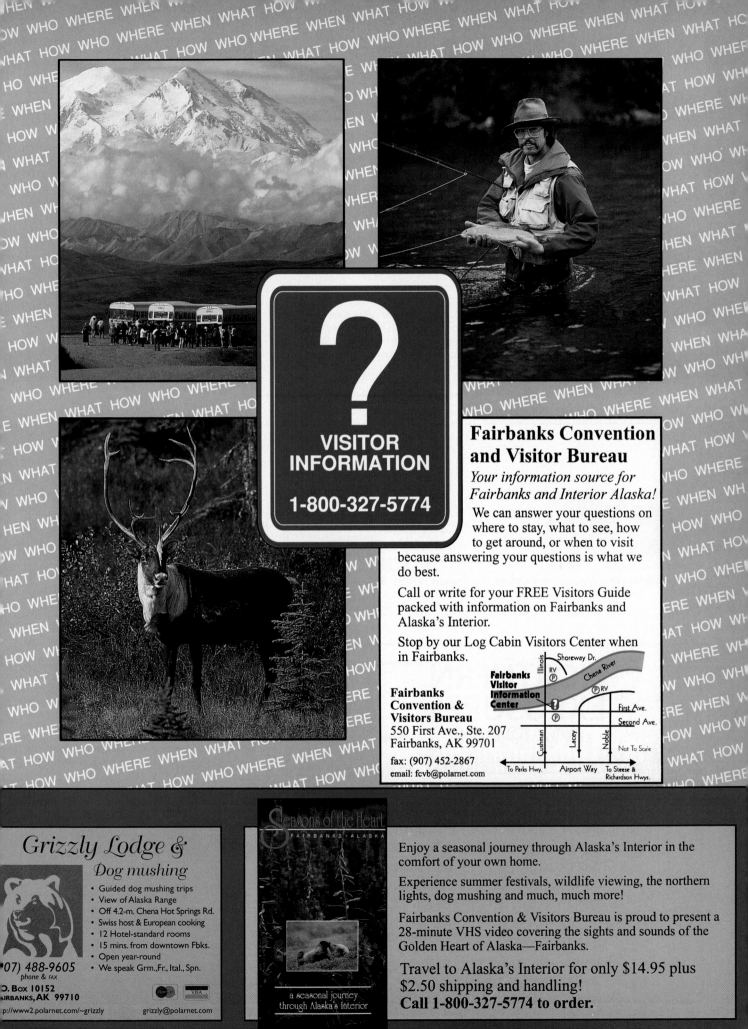

? VISITOR INFORMATION

1-800-327-5774

Fairbanks Convention and Visitor Bureau

Your information source for Fairbanks and Interior Alaska!

We can answer your questions on where to stay, what to see, how to get around, or when to visit because answering your questions is what we do best.

Call or write for your FREE Visitors Guide packed with information on Fairbanks and Alaska's Interior.

Stop by our Log Cabin Visitors Center when in Fairbanks.

Fairbanks Convention & Visitors Bureau
550 First Ave., Ste. 207
Fairbanks, AK 99701

fax: (907) 452-2867
email: fcvb@polarnet.com

foot/5-m bronze monument, "Unknown First Family." The statue, by sculptor Malcolm Alexander, and park were dedicated in July 1986 to celebrate Fairbanks' history and heritage.

The Alaska Public Lands Information Center, located in the lower level of historic Courthouse Square at 3rd Avenue and Cushman Street, is a free museum and information center featuring Alaska's natural history, cultural artifacts and recreational opportunities. In addition to detailed information on outdoor recreation in the state, the center offers films, interpretive programs, lectures and a book shop.

Tour the University of Alaska Fairbanks, situated on a 2,250-acre ridge overlooking the city and Tanana River valley. The campus has all the features of a small town, including a fire station, post office, radio and TV stations, medical clinic and a 1,000-seat concert hall.

UAF offers special tours and programs from June through August. Free guided tours of the campus are provided Monday through Friday at 10 A.M.; tours begin at the UA Museum. Also offered are tours of the Large Animal Research Station, Poker Flat Research Range, and a slide show and tour at the Geophysical Institute, where research and study range from the center of the earth to the center of the sun. Films on mining in Alaska are also shown. Visitors can take a guided tour or tour on their own at the Agricultural and Forestry Experiment Station's Georgeson Botanical Garden, which is open to the public June through September. Phone (907) 474-7581 for information on any tour.

The University of Alaska Museum is a must stop for Fairbanks visitors. The museum features cultural and natural history displays from all the state's regions. The 5 galleries explore Alaska's history, Native culture, art, natural phenomena, wildlife, birds, geology and prehistoric past. Highlights include a 36,000-year-old Steppe bison mummy, the state's largest gold display, the trans-Alaska pipeline story and a special section on the northern lights. The museum grounds hold sculptures, totem poles, a Russian blockhouse and a nature trail with signs identifying local vegetation. The museum's special summer exhibit in 1997 will be "Threads of Gold," about women in the gold rush. Free summer programs include presentations on natural and cultural history topics and Alaska Native Elders discussing traditional and contemporary lifestyles. Summer shows include "Northern Inua," a 50-minute show of northern athletic games, dance and creation stories produced by the World Eskimo-Indian Olympics, and "Dynamic

Aurora," a 50-minute show on the scientific and Alaska Native understanding of the northern lights. Admission is charged for these shows; call for times. Hours are: May and September, 9 A.M. to 5 P.M.; June through August, 9 A.M. to 7 P.M.; October through April, weekdays, 9 A.M. to 5 P.M., weekends, noon to 5 P.M. Museum admission fees: adults, $5; seniors, $4.50; youth (12 to 17), $3; children under 12, free. For 24-hour information, call (907) 474-7505.

Take in Some Local Events: Fairbanks has several unique summer celebrations. Late June is a busy time as Fairbanks celebrates the longest day of the year (summer solstice is June 21). The Midnight Sun Baseball Game will be played at 10:45 P.M. on June 21, 1997, without artificial lights. A Midnight Sun 10K Fun Run begins at 10 P.M. on June 21, 1997.

Golden Days, when Fairbanksans turn out in turn-of-the-century dress and celebrate the gold rush, is July 10–20, 1997. Golden Days starts off with a Felix Pedro look-alike taking his gold to the bank and includes a parade and rededication of the Pedro Monument honoring the man who started it all when he discovered gold in the Tanana Hills. Other events include pancake breakfasts, a dance, canoe and raft races, and free outdoor concerts.

The World Eskimo and Indian Olympics, with Native competition in such events as the high kick, greased pole walk, stick pull, fish cutting, parka contest and muktuk-eating contest will be held in mid-July 1997.

The annual Tanana Valley State Fair will be held Aug. 1–9, 1997. Alaska's oldest state fair, the Tanana Valley State Fair features agricultural exhibits, arts and crafts, food booths, a rodeo and other entertainment.

Fairbanks Summer Arts Festival, 2 weeks of workshops and concerts including music from jazz to classics, dance, theater and the visual arts, will be held July 25 to Aug. 10, 1997.

Check with the Fairbanks visitor informa-

ALASKA A TO Z is a handy reference about Alaska; ask for it in bookstores.

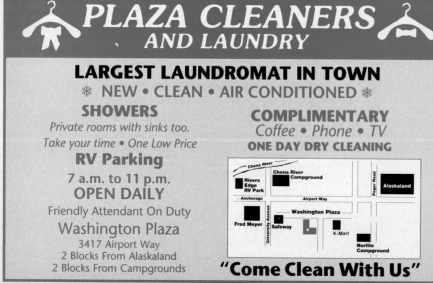
tion center for more information on local events.

Besides these special events, summer visitors can take in a semipro baseball game at Growden Park where the Fairbanks Goldpanners take on other Alaska league teams.

The Fairbanks Shakespeare Theatre, now entering their fourth season, presents "Merry Wives of Windsor." This production is held in the outdoor setting of Birch Hill Recreation Area, a few easy miles from Fairbanks off the Steese Highway. July 15–Aug. 2; shows 8 P.M. Wednesdays–Sundays. For information call 457-POET. [ADVERTISEMENT]

Visit Creamer's Field. Follow the flocks of waterfowl to Creamer's Field Migratory Waterfowl Refuge. Located 1 mile/1.6 km from downtown Fairbanks, this 1,800-acre refuge managed by the Alaska Dept. of Fish and Game offers opportunities to observe large concentrations of ducks, geese, shorebirds and cranes in the spring and fall. Throughout the summer, sandhill cranes eat in the planted barley fields.

Explore the 2-mile/3.2-km self-guided nature trail and the renovated historic farmhouse that serves as a visitor center. Stop at 1300 College Road to find the trailhead, viewing areas and brochures on Creamer's Field. For more information, phone (907) 452-5162.

Creamer's Field Migratory Waterfowl Refuge—where nature is at its best. Summer visitor center hours, 10–5, closed Sunday and Monday. June–August, guided walks leave front parking lot on College Road Tuesday and Thursday at 7 P.M.; Wednesday and Saturday at 9 A.M. No charge and the refuge is always open. (907) 452-5162. [ADVERTISEMENT]

SS *Nenana.* A premier attraction. Voices from Alaska's past echo from the 5 decks of the SS *Nenana,* a National Historic Landmark. Fully restored and permanently berthed at Alaskaland, the last overnight packet sternwheeler remaining in America has begun her final and most important voyage. By telling her story through the art form of her incredibly detailed diorama, she will transport visitors back in time from 1847 to 1932 along the mighty Yukon River system, where the lure and mystique of the North cast its spell on the early sourdoughs. Nothing will equal the unique and unforgettable experience aboard the steamer *Nenana,* the second largest wooden vessel in existence most appropriately called: "The Last Lady of the River." [ADVERTISEMENT]

Tanana Valley Farmers Market. Visit Alaska's premier Farmers Market, located next to the Fairgrounds on College Road, open from mid-May to mid-September. Vendors offer "thousands of miles fresher" Alaska grown vegetables; blue-ribbon florals; Alaskan meats, fish, honey, jams and syrups; made in Alaska handcrafts and baked goods. Look for our brochure at local Visitor's Centers. Market hours are Wednesdays 11 A.M. to 4 P.M. and Saturdays 9 A.M. to 4 P.M.; there's plenty of parking. Stop by the Market and enjoy Alaska made and grown products ... "Meet You At The Market!" [ADVERTISEMENT]

The Alaska Rag Co. A must-see for Fairbanks travelers. This unique Alaskan gift shop manufactures beautiful handwoven rag rugs from 100 percent recycled clothing. The store also features works from many Alaskan artists. Items include jewelry, pottery, paintings, stained glass, qiviut, dog hair hats, mittens and much more. Stop in, meet our weavers and see their work. 552 2nd Ave., Fairbanks, AK 99701. Phone (907) 451-4401. [ADVERTISEMENT]

The Great Alaskan Bowl Company. One of very few mills in the country still turning out nesting, 1-piece wooden bowls. Watch demonstrations using 1800's ingenuity and 1990's technology as we carve nested sets from a single block. Large viewing area. Close to airport. Open year-round. (907) 474-9663. 1-800-770-4222. P.O. Box 60598, Fairbanks, AK 99706. [ADVERTISEMENT]

Great Land Sports. Selling quality mountain bikes, parts and accessories. Excellent, fast, friendly service. We carry Fisher, LeMond, Marin, Bontrager, Klein, Fuji, Jandd, Blackburn and more. Stop by for a free map of Fairbanks' many scenic bike paths. Rental bikes available for as low as $15/day. 261 College Rd., Fairbanks, AK 99701. (907) 479-8438. [ADVERTISEMENT]

Chena Pump House National Historic Site. Built in 1931–33 by the Fairbanks Exploration Co. to pump water from the Chena River to dredging operations at Cripple Creek, the pump house was remodeled in 1978 and now houses a restaurant and saloon. The sheet metal cladding, interior roof and some equipment (such as the intake ditch) are from the original pump house, which shut down in 1958 when the F.E. Co. ceased its Cripple Creek dredging operations. The pump house is located at Mile 1.3 Chena Pump Road.

Sled Dog Racing. The Alaska Dog Mushers' Assoc. hosts a series of dog races beginning in mid-December with preliminary races, and ending in March with the Open North American Championship. The Open is a 3-day event with 3 heats (of 20, 20 and 30 miles) with teams as large as 24 dogs; this race is considered by many to be the "granddaddy of dog races." Fairbanks also hosts the 1,000-mile/1,609-km Yukon Quest Sled Dog Race between Fairbanks and Whitehorse, YT. The Yukon Quest alternates start and finish between the 2 cities. For more information, contact the Alaska Dog Mushers' Assoc. at (907) 457-MUSH, or the Yukon Quest office at (907) 451-8985.

See Bank Displays: The Key Bank, at 1st Avenue and Cushman Street, has a display of gold nuggets and several trophy animals. Mount McKinley Mutual Savings Bank features a display of McKinley prints and the original cannonball safe used when the bank opened. The bank is at 531 3rd Ave.

Visit Historic Churches: St. Matthew's Episcopal, 1029 1st Ave., was originally built in 1905, but burned in 1947 and was rebuilt the following year. Of special interest is the church's intricately carved altar, made in 1906 of Interior Alaska birch and saved from the fire.

Immaculate Conception Church, on the Chena River at Cushman Street bridge, was drawn by horses to its present location in the winter of 1911 from its original site at 1st Avenue and Dunkel Street.

See the Pipeline: Drive about 10 miles/ 16 km north from downtown on the Steese Highway to see the trans-Alaska pipeline. Clearly visible are the thermal devices used to keep the permafrost frozen around the pipeline support columns.

View Mount McKinley: The best spot to see Mount McKinley is from the University of Alaska Fairbanks campus (on Yukon

Drive, between Talkeetna and Sheenjek streets) where a turnout and marker define the horizon view of Mount Hayes (elev. 13,832 feet/4,216m); Hess Mountain (elev. 11,940 feet/3,639m); Mount Deborah (elev. 12,339 feet/3,761m); and Mount McKinley (elev. 20,320 feet/6,194m). Distant foothills are part of the Wood River Butte.

Cruise Aboard the Riverboat *Discovery*: Every day at 8:45 A.M. and 2 P.M. in summer, the riverboat *Discovery* departs for a half-day cruise on the Chena and Tanana rivers. Drive out Airport Road, turn south at Dale Road and continue 0.5 mile/0.8 km on Dale to Discovery Drive. Reservations are required, as this is one of the most popular attractions in town. For the first leg of the trip, the *Discovery* winds its way down the meandering Chena River, its banks lined by old homesteads, modern homes and bush planes. The Chena River also joins with Cripple Creek, the Interior's richest gold rush stream. On the Tanana River, fish wheels turn in the swift glacial water, scooping up salmon to be dried and smoked for winter food. Returning up the Tanana River, the boat stops at Old Chena Indian Village, where passengers have the opportunity to see Susan Butcher's Iditarod-champion dog team in action. After the demonstration, passengers disembark for a tour of the village. Guides from the *Discovery*, who are of Indian or Eskimo heritage, are on hand to explain past and present Native culture. For more information on the riverboat *Discovery*, contact Alaska Riverways, Inc., 1975 Discovery Dr., Fairbanks, AK 99709; phone (907) 479-6673, fax 479-4613.

Alaskaland log cabins house a variety of shops. (© Barbara Willard)

Visit Alaskaland Pioneer Park. Visitors will find a relaxed atmosphere at Alaskaland, a pleasant park with historic buildings, small shops, food, entertainment, playgrounds and 4 covered picnic shelters. The park—which has no admission fee—is open year-round.

To drive to Alaskaland (at Airport Way and Peger Road), take Airport Way to Wilbur, turn north onto Wilbur, then immediately west onto access road, which leads to Alaskaland enclosure.

The 44-acre historic park was created in 1967 as the Alaska Centennial Park to commemorate the 100th anniversary of U.S. territorial status. Designed to provide a taste of interior Alaska history, visitors may begin their visit at the information center, which is located just inside the park's main gate. Walk through Gold Rush Town, a narrow winding street of authentic old buildings that once graced downtown Fairbanks and

now house gift shops. Here you will find: the Kitty Hensley and Judge Wickersham houses, furnished with turn-of-the-century items; the First Presbyterian Church, constructed in 1906; and the Pioneers of Alaska Museum, dedicated to those who braved frontier life to found Fairbanks. Free guided historical walking tours take place each afternoon.

The park is home to the newly renovated SS *Nenana*, a national landmark. Cared for by the Fairbanks Historical Preservation Foundation, the *Nenana* is the largest stern-

Historic riverboat Nenana *is on display at Alaskaland.* (© Roy M. Corral)

wheeler ever built west of the Mississippi; and the second largest wooden vessel in existence. The Foundation also displays a 300-foot/91-m diorama of life along the Tanana and Yukon rivers in the early 1900s.

The top level of the Civic Center houses

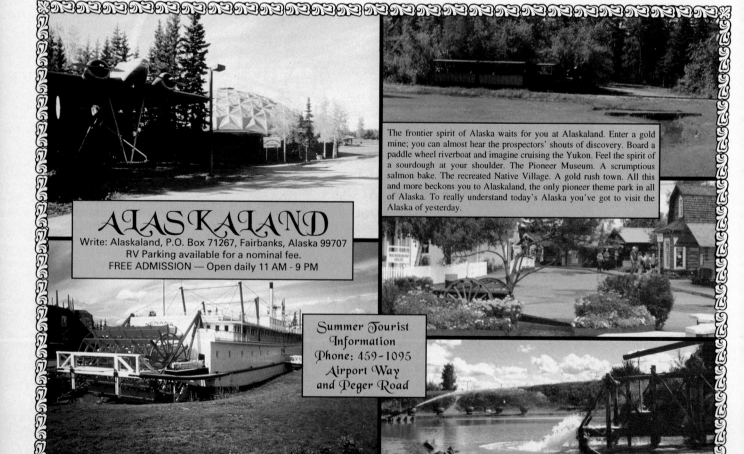

an art gallery, featuring rotating contemporary exhibits and paintings; 11 A.M. to 9 P.M. daily, Memorial Day through Labor Day; noon to 8 P.M. daily, except Monday, during the rest of the year.

Behind the Civic Center, you'll find the Pioneer Air Museum, which features antique aircraft and stories of their Alaskan pilots, with displays from 1913–48. Phone (907) 451-0037, Memorial Day through Labor Day, for information. Admission is $1.

At the rear of the park is the Native Village Museum and Kashims with Native wares, artifacts, crafts and exhibitions of Native dancing. Across from the Native Village is Mining Valley, with displays of gold-mining equipment. The Salmon Bake, with both outdoor and heated indoor seating areas, is also part of Mining Valley. A popular feature, the Salmon Bake is open daily for lunch from noon to 2 P.M. (June 10 to Aug. 15), and for dinner from 5–9 P.M. (end of May to mid-September). Salmon, barbecued ribs, halibut and 18-oz. porterhouse steaks are served, rain or shine.

There's entertainment 7 nights a week starting at 8 P.M. at the Palace Theatre & Saloon, featuring a musical comedy review about life in Fairbanks titled "Golden Heart Review." "Riversong," a musical about Native lifestyles, is performed in the Civic Center Theater at 8 P.M. Thursday through Saturday form mid-June to mid-August. The Big Stampede show in Gold Rush Town is a theater in the round presenting the paintings of Rusty Heurlin which depicts the trail of '98; narrative by Ruben Gaines.

The Crooked Creek & Whiskey Island Railroad, a 30-gauge train, takes passengers for a 12-minute ride around the park. Other types of recreational activities available at Alaskaland include miniature golf, an antique carousel and picnicking in covered shelters. A public dock is located on the Chena River at the rear of the park.

Visitors are welcome to take part in square and round dances year-round at the Alaskaland Dance Center. Phone (907) 452-5699 evenings for calendar of events. For more information about Alaskaland, phone (907) 459-1087.

Area Attractions: Fairbanks is a good jumping-off point for many attractions in Alaska's Interior. Head out the Steese Highway for swimming at Chena Hot Springs or Circle Hot Springs. At Fox, 11 miles/17.7 km north of Fairbanks, the Steese Highway intersects with the Elliott Highway, which leads to the start of the Dalton Highway (formerly the North Slope Haul Road). Popular attractions in this area include Gold Dredge Number 8 (take Goldstream Road exit to Old Steese Highway), a historic 5-deck, 250-foot dredge, and Little El Dorado Gold Mine at Mile 1.2 Elliott Highway. Both offer gold mining demonstrations and gold panning. See highway sections for details.

Denali National Park is a 2½-hour drive,

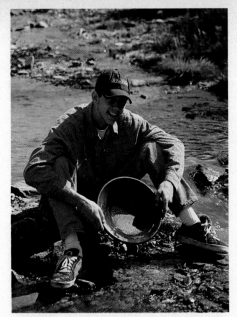

Commercial gold panning is available near Fairbanks. (© Barbara Willard)

or a 3¹/₂-hour train trip via the Alaska Railroad, from Fairbanks. Once there, take the shuttle bus or guided tour through the park. For road conditions on the George Parks Highway between Fairbanks and Denali, phone the Dept. of Transportation at (907) 451-2226.

Eielson AFB, 25 miles/40 km southeast of

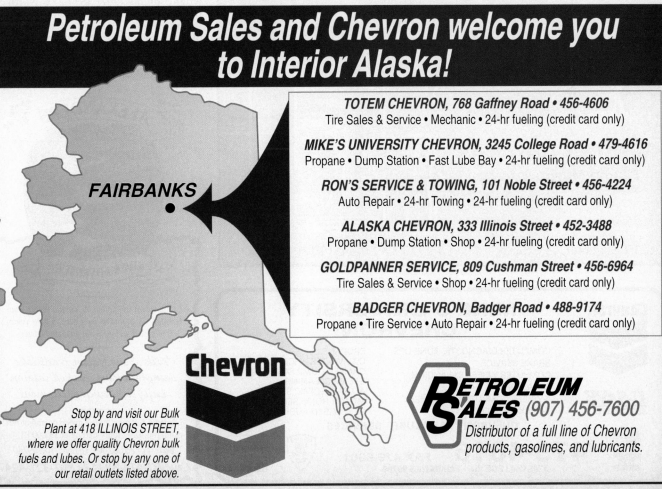

PRUDHOE BAY

A D V E N T U R E™

A three day guided roundtrip journey to the shores of the Arctic Ocean.

Experience the breathtaking beauty & solitude of Alaska's Arctic, one of the earth's last great wilderness regions •Visit the Arctic Circle Trading Post situated in the rural community of Joy, Alaska •Travel the famous Dalton Highway •Cruise the mighty Yukon River •Visit an Athabascan Indian summer fish camp •Cross the Arctic Circle in ceremonious fashion •Overnight at rustic Coldfoot •Pass through the majestic Brooks Mountain Range •Walk out on the spongy yet delicate tundra of the Arctic Coastal Plain •Overnight at and tour Prudhoe Bay, site of North America's largest oil discovery •Complete your northward journey by dipping your toe in the frigid Arctic Ocean •Extend your stay with an optional overnight in the village of Barrow •Tour the community and experience a program of traditional Inupiat culture •For further adventure continue your journey along the Arctic Coast to Kotzebue & Nome.

Northern Alaska Tour Company

Box 82991-MF97, Fairbanks AK 99708 • 907-474-8600 Fax 907-474-4767

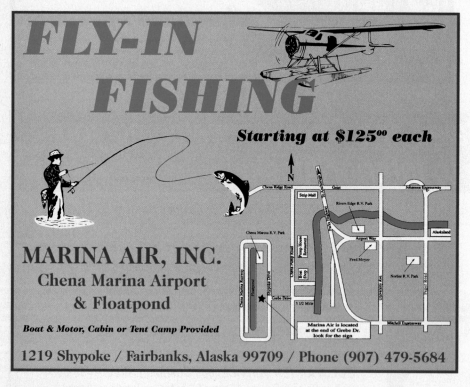

FLY-IN FISHING

Starting at $125⁰⁰ each

MARINA AIR, INC.

Chena Marina Airport & Floatpond

Boat & Motor, Cabin or Tent Camp Provided

1219 Shypoke / Fairbanks, Alaska 99709 / Phone (907) 479-5684

Fairbanks on the Richardson–Alaska Highway, was built in 1943. Originally a satellite base to Ladd Field (now Fort Wainwright) and called Mile 26, it served as a storage site for aircraft on their way to the Soviet Union under the WWII Lend–Lease program. Closed after WWII, the base was reactivated in 1946 and renamed Eielson AFB, after Carl Ben Eielson, the first man to fly from Alaska over the North Pole to Greenland. A tour of the base is offered every Friday during the summer months from 9–10 A.M.; phone the public affairs office at (907) 377-2116 for reservations and more information.

There are 1-day or longer sightseeing trips to Point Barrow, Prudhoe Bay, Fort Yukon and other bush destinations. See ads in this section or consult local travel services.

Historic Gold Dredge No. 8. Gold Dredge No. 8 is a monument to the miners who used the machinery to produce more than 7.5 million ounces of gold and the engineers who built it. Visitors tour the only dredge in Alaska open to the public. Gold panning and a "Miner's Buffet" lunch are also available at this national historic site. See advertisement on page 419 this section.
[ADVERTISEMENT]

Play Tennis: There are 6 outdoor asphalt courts at the Mary Siah Recreation Center, 1025 14th Ave. No fees or reservations. For more information phone (907) 459-1070.

Play Golf: Maintaining a scenic 9-hole course with natural greens, the Fairbanks Golf and Country Club (public is invited) is west of the downtown area at 1735 Farmers Loop Road; phone (907) 479-6555 for information and reservations. The 18-hole Chena Bend Golf Course is located on Fort Wainwright; phone (907) 353-6223. North Star Golf Club, located 10 minutes north of downtown on the Old Steese Highway, offers a regulation 9-hole course; phone (907) 457-4653 or (907) 452-2104.

Ride Bikes Around Fairbanks: There are many day-touring choices in Fairbanks. A

Canoeing the Chatanika River near Fairbanks. (© Craig Brandt)

ski out to Ester Dome.

Go Swimming. Fairbanks North Star Borough Parks and Recreation Dept. offers 3 pools: Mary Siah Recreation Center, 1025 14th Ave., phone (907) 459-1082; Robert

Northern Lights Scenic Tours, Inc.

- Offering the ultimate in Customized Scenic Flights!

- See the Interior.

- Visit Fort Yukon and Cross the Arctic Circle.

- View the Midnight Sun Over MT. McKINLEY.

- Have Dinner at Circle Hot Springs.

Call for Reservations
Phone (907) 479-0594 FAX (907) 488-2393
Write P.O. Box 60378, Fairbanks, AK 99706

round-trip tour of the city, the University of Alaska and the College area can be made by leaving town on Airport Way and returning on College Road. The Farmers Loop Road or a ride out the Old Steese Highway toward Fox are easy tours.

Go Skiing: Fairbanks has several downhill ski areas: Cleary Summit, **Milepost F 20.3** Steese Highway; Skiland, **Milepost F 20.9** Steese Highway; Eielson AFB and Fort Wainwright ski hills; Moose Mountain Ski Resort, Spinach Creek Road on Murphy Dome; and an alpine ski hill at Chena Hot Springs Resort at **Milepost J 56.5** Chena Hot Springs Road.

Cross-country ski trails are at Birch Hill Recreation Area; drive 2.8 miles/4.5 km north of Fairbanks via Steese Expressway to a well-marked turnoff, then drive in 2.3 miles/ 3.7 km. University of Alaska Fairbanks has 26 miles/42 km of cross-country ski trails. The trail system is quite extensive; you may

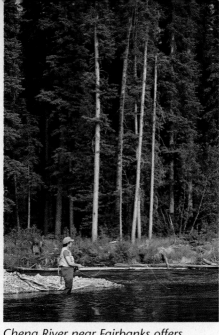

Chena River near Fairbanks offers grayling fishing. (© Robin Brandt)

Hamme Memorial Pool, 901 Airport Way, phone (907) 459-1086; and Robert Wescott Memorial Pool, 8th Avenue in North Pole, phone (907) 488-9402.

Chena Lakes Recreation Area. This 2,178-acre park, located 17.3 miles/27.8 km southeast of Fairbanks on the Richardson–Alaska Highway, offers a wide assortment of outdoor recreation. There are 86 campsites for both RV and tent camping, including campsites on an island; canoe, sailboat and rowboat rentals; bike paths and trails for nature hikes, skiing, skijoring and dog mushing; and boat ramp access to the nearby Chena River. Admission to the park, maintained by the Fairbanks North Star Borough, is $3 per vehicle between Memorial Day and Labor Day. No admission is charged the rest of the year. For more information, call (907) 488-1655.

Go Fishing: There are several streams and lakes within driving distance of Fair-

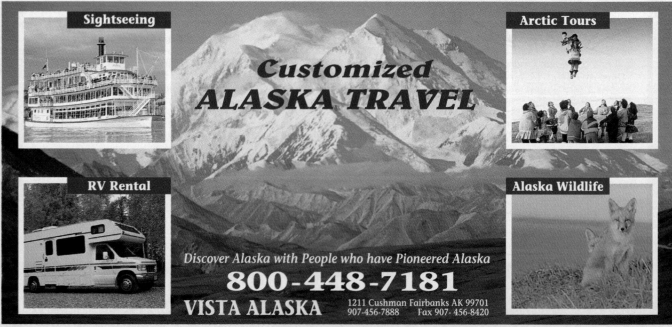

banks, and local fishing guides are available. **Chena Lake,** about 20 miles/32 km southeast of the city via the Richardson–Alaska Highway at Chena Lakes Recreation Area, is stocked with rainbow trout, silver salmon and arctic char. The **Chena River** and its tributaries offer fishing for sheefish, whitefish, northern pike and burbot. The Chena River flows through Fairbanks. Chena Hot Springs Road off the Steese Highway provides access to fisheries in the Chena River Recreation Area (see the STEESE HIGHWAY section). The Steese Highway also offers access to the **Chatanika River** for northern pike and burbot fishing. Special regulations apply in these waters for grayling and salmon fishing. Phone the ADF&G Division of Sport Fish office at (907) 465-4180.

Air taxi operators and guides in Fairbanks offer short trips from the city for rainbow trout, grayling, northern pike, lake trout, and sheefish in lakes and streams of the Tanana and Yukon river drainages. Some operators have camps set up for overnight trips while others specialize in day trips. The air taxi operators usually provide a boat and motor for their angling visitors. Rates are reasonable, and vary according to the distance from town and type of facilities offered. ✦

DENALI NATIONAL PARK

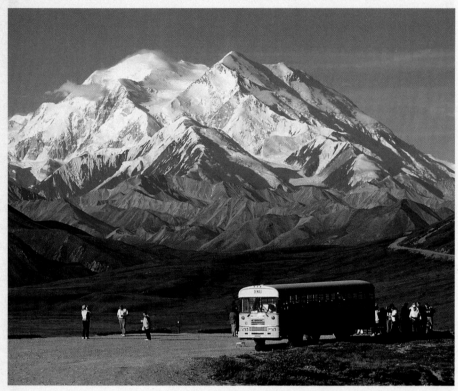

Tour bus passengers get a great view of Mount McKinley from Stony Hill Overlook.
(© Roy Corral)

Denali National Park and Preserve (formerly Mount McKinley National Park) lies on the north flank of the Alaska Range, 250 miles/402 km south of the Arctic Circle. The park entrance, accessible by highway, railroad and aircraft, is 237 highway miles/ 381 km north of Anchorage, and about half that distance from Fairbanks.

The park is open year-round to visitors, although the hotel, most campgrounds, and food and shuttle bus service within the park are available only from late May or early June to mid-September. (Opening dates for facilities and activities for the summer season are announced in the spring by the Park Service and depend mainly on snow conditions in May.)

When you arrive be sure to stop at the Visitor Center, near the park entrance. The center offers information and limited reservations for campgrounds in the park; maps, brochures and schedules of events; details on campfire talks, hikes, nature walks, sled dog demonstrations and wildlife tours; and shuttle bus schedules and ticket reservations. Also available are National Park entrance passes. The center is open daily in summer, generally from early morning into the evening.

Parking space is limited at the Visitor Center. Overflow parking is available at Riley Creek Campground (walk or mini-shuttle to Visitor Center).

Lodging and camping are available outside the park on the George Parks Highway, and there are a variety of activities—river rafting, hikes and ranger programs—to enjoy. Check with operators outside the park and with personnel at the Visitor Center about programs and activities.

First-time visitors should be particularly aware of the controlled-access system for Park Road use. Private vehicle traffic on the 92-mile/148-km road into the park is restricted beyond the Savage River check station (**Milepost J 14.8**) to registered campers. Campers may reserve campsites by phone or at the Visitor Center. The shuttle bus system and concessionaire-operated tours are available to allow visitors a means of viewing the park without disturbing the wildlife. See Accommodations/Visitor Services this section for details on the shuttle bus service and campsite reservations system.

In an effort to preserve wildlife viewing opportunities for the public, the National Park Service has set road traffic limits. Traffic will be held to the 1984 averages. Consequently, there are limited bus seats available. When planning trips to the park, visitors should reserve shuttle bus tickets in advance by phone or plan activities in the entrance area, such as attending ranger-led interpretive programs, for the first 1 or 2 days, until bus seats can be obtained.

An admission fee of $5 per person ($10 per vehicle/family) is charged to visitors traveling along the park road. The fee is collected when visitors either obtain shuttle bus tickets, campground permits or stop at the Visitor Center. Persons 16 years of age or less, and U.S. citizens 62 years or older, are exempt from the admission fee. (A $20 annual park pass and the $25 Golden Eagle Pass, are valid for admission.)

For information about the park, write Denali National Park and Preserve, Box 9, Denali Park, AK 99755; winter phone (907) 683-2294, summer phone (907) 683-1266 or 1267; Web site www.nps.gov/dena.

One of the park's best-known attractions is Mount McKinley, North America's highest mountain at 20,320 feet/6,194m. On a clear day, Mount McKinley is visible from Anchorage. However, cloudy, rainy summer weather frequently obscures the mountain, and travelers have about a 30 percent chance of seeing it in summer.

First mention of Mount McKinley was in 1794, when English explorer Capt. George Vancouver spotted a "stupendous snow mountain" from Cook Inlet. Early Russian explorers and traders called the peak *Bolshaia Gora,* or "Big Mountain." The Tanana Indian name for the mountain is *Denali,* said to mean "high one." The mountain was named McKinley in 1896 by a Princeton-educated prospector named William A. Dickey for presidential nominee William McKinley of Ohio. Even today, the mountain has two names: Mount McKinley according to USGS maps, and Denali according to the state Geographic Names Board.

The history of climbs on McKinley is as intriguing as its many names. In 1903, Judge James Wickersham and party climbed to an estimated 8,000 feet/2,438m, while Dr. Frederick A. Cook and party reached the 11,000-foot/3,353m level. In 1906, Cook returned to the mountain and made 2 attempts at the summit—the first unsuccessful, and the second (according to Cook) successful. Cook's vague description of his ascent route and a questionable summit photo led many to doubt his claim. The 1910 Sourdough Party (which included Charles McGonagall, Pete Anderson and Billy Taylor), claimed they had reached both summits (north and south peaks) but could not provide any photographic evidence. (Much later it was verified that they had reached the summit of the lower north peak.) The first complete ascent of the true summit of Mount McKinley was made in 1913 by Hudson Stuck, Harry Karstens and Walter Harper. Harper, a Native Athabaskan, was the first to set foot on the higher south peak.

Today, more than a thousand people attempt to climb Mount McKinley each year between April and June, most flying in to

Denali National Park and Preserve

N

To Paxson

To Fairbanks

Denali Highway

George Parks Highway

8

Park Entrance
See detail map below

Nenana River

To Fairbanks

Nenana River

Riley Creek

Savage River

Sanctuary River

Fang Mountain
6,736 ft. / 2,053m

Cantwell

Bull River

3

The Alaska Railroad

To Anchorage

Permit required to drive beyond this point

Park Road

Polychrome Pass
3,500 ft. / 1,067m

Sable Mountain
5,923 ft. / 1,805m

Mount Eielson
5,802 ft. / 1,768m

Sunset Peak
7,865 ft. / 2,397m

Sushana River

East Fork

Toklat River

Stony Creek

Clearwater Creek

Mount Sheldon
5,670 ft. / 1,728m

Muldrow Glacier

Gorge Glacier

Mount Deception
11,826 ft. / 3,605m

Mount Silverthrone
13,220 ft. / 4,029m

Eldridge Glacier

Buckskin Glacier

Chitsia Mountain
1,180 ft. / 360m

Kankona Peak
1,512 ft. / 461m

Park Road
(Limited Access)

Kantishna

Wonder Lake

Mt. Cloud Creek

Peters Glacier

Mount McKinley
20,320 ft. / 6,194m

Mount Hunter
14,573 ft. / 4,442m

Ruth Glacier

Tokositna Glacier

Bearpaw River

McKinley River

Slippery Creek

Mount Foraker
17,400 ft. / 5,304m

Foraker Glacier

Herron Glacier

Kahiltna Glacier

Muddy River

Birch Creek

Foraker River

Herron River

Slippet Creek

Chedotlothna Glacier

Mount Russell
11,670 ft. / 3,557m

Yenna Glacier

East Fork

Kentna River

Foraker River

Scott Fork

Slippet Creek

Swift Fork Kuskokwim River

West Fork

Scale
20 Miles
20 Kilometres

Map Location

Park Entrance Area

To Fairbanks

Nenana River

George Parks Highway

Visitor Center

Nenana River

The Alaska Railroad

3

To Anchorage

Horseshoe Lake

Riley Creek Campground

Park Road

Store
Hotel

Railroad Station

Riley Creek

Hines Creek

To Kantishna

Park Headquarters

Scale
2 Miles
2 Kilometres

The largest gold nugget found in
Alaska weighed 107 ounces.

base camp at 7,000 feet/2134m. (The first airplane landing on the mountain was flown in 1932 by Joe Crosson.) Geographic features of McKinley and its sister peaks bear the names of many early explorers: Eldridge and Muldrow glaciers, after George Eldridge and Robert Muldrow of the U.S. Geographic Service who determined the peak's altitude in 1898; Wickersham Wall; Karstens Ridge; and Mount Carpe and Mount Koven, named for Allen Carpe and Theodore Koven, both killed in a 1932 climb.

The National Park Service maintains a ranger station in Talkeetna that is staffed full time from mid-April through mid-September and intermittently during the winter. Mountaineering rangers provide information on climbing within the Alaska Range. A refer-

DENALI PARK AREA ADVERTISERS

Alaskan Chateau B & B .....Ph. (907) 683-1377
Alpenglow Tours..............Ph. 1-800-770-7275
Backwoods Lodge ....Ph. 1-800-292-2232
Beaver Lake Trail Rides ....Ph. 1-800-893-6828
Cantwell RV Park ....Mile 209.9 Parks Hwy
Carlo Creek
    Bed & Breakfast...........Ph. (907) 683-2557
Carlo Creek Lodge ....Mile 224 Parks Hwy.
Denali Air ....Ph. (907) 683-2261
Denali Backcountry
    Lodge..........................Ph. 1-800-841-0692
Denali Bluffs Hotel...........Ph. 1-800-488-7002
Denali Crow's
    Nest Cabins.............Mile 238.5 Parks Hwy.
Denali Dome Home
    Bed & Breakfast....................Healy Spur Rd.
Denali Grizzly Bear Cabins &
    Campground ....Mile 231.1 Parks Hwy.
Denali Lakeside Lodging ..Ph. (907) 683-2511
Denali Mountain Works....Ph. (907) 683-1542
Denali National Park
    Hotel..........................Ph. 1-800-276-7234
Denali National Park Wilderness
    Centers–Camp Denali..Ph. (907) 683-2290
Denali National Park Wilderness Centers–
    North Face Lodge........Ph. (907) 683-2290
Denali North Star Inn ......Ph. 1-800-684-1560
Denali Outdoor Center.....Ph. (907) 683-1925
Denali Park Resorts..........Ph. (907) 276-7234
Denali Princess Lodge......Ph. 1-800-426-0500
Denali Raft Adventures.....Ph. (907) 683-2234
Denali Rainbow Village &
    RV Park ....Ph. (907) 683-3362
Denali River Cabins...........Ph. (907) 683-2500
Denali Riverside RV Park..Ph. 1-888-778-7700
Denali RV Park & Motel...Mile 245.1 Parks Hwy.
Denali Suites ....Mile 248.8 Parks Hwy.
Denali West Lodge ....Ph. (907) 674-3112
Denali Wilderness
    Lodge..........................Ph. 1-800-541-9779
Denali Windsong Lodge...Ph. (907) 683-1240
Denali Wings...................Ph. (907) 683-2245
Destinations in Travel......Ph. 1-800-354-6020
Doug Geeting Aviation....Ph. 1-800-770-2366
Earth Song Lodge............Ph. (907) 683-2863
Era Helicopters................Ph. 1-800-843-1947
Fly Denali ....Mile 238.9 Parks Hwy.
Grandview Bed and
    Breakfast ....Ph. (907) 683-2468

Healy Heights Family
    Cabins ....Ph. (907) 683-2639
Homestead
    Bed & Breakfast...........Ph. (907) 683-2575
Kantishna Roadhouse ......Ph. 1-800-942-7420
K2 Aviation ....Ph. (907) 733-2291
Lynx Creek Pizza...........Mile 238.6 Parks Hwy.
McKinley Air Service ....Ph. 1-800-564-1765
McKinley/Denali
    Cabins ....Ph. (907) 683-2733
McKinley/Denali
    Gift Shop..................Mile 238.5 Parks Hwy.
McKinley/Denali
    Salmon Bake ....Mile 238.5 Parks Hwy.
McKinley RV &
    Campground ....Mile 248.4 Parks Hwy.
McKinley Raft Tours......Mile 238.8 Parks Hwy.
McKinley Wilderness
    Lodge..........................Ph. (907) 683-2277
Midnight Sun Express® ....Ph. 1-800-835-8907
Motel Nord Haven............Ph. (907) 683-4500
Mt. McKinley
    Gold Camp..................Ph. 1-800-770-7275
Mt. McKinley
    Princess Lodge............Ph. 1-800-426-0500
Nenana Raft
    Adventures................Mile 248.5 Parks Hwy
Northern Lights Theater and
    Gift Shop ....Ph. (907) 683-4000
Overlook Bar & Grill, The .Ph. (907) 683-2723
Otto Lake RV Park............Mile 247 Parks Hwy.
Perch, The ....Mile 224 Parks Hwy.
Red Fox Bed &
    Breakfast, The..............Ph. (907) 683-1227
Rick Swenson's Carlo Heights Bed and
    Breakfast and Sled Dog
    School ....Ph. (907) 683-1615
Rock Creek Country Inn...Mile 261 Parks Hwy.
Sourdough Cabins ....Mile 238.8 Parks Hwy.
Stampede Lodge..............Ph. 1-800-478-2370
Talkeetna Air Taxi.............Ph. (907) 733-2218
Too-Loo'-Uk River
    Guides ....Ph. (907) 683-1542
Touch of Wilderness
    Bed & Breakfast...........Ph. (907) 683-2459
Valley Vista
    Bed & Breakfast...........Ph. (907) 683-2842
White Moose Lodge .....Mile 248.1 Parks Hwy.
Wolf Spirit Expeditions....Ph. 1-800-241-2615

Moose cow with newborn calf in Denali National Park. (© Robin Brandt)

ence library and slide/tape program are available for climbers. Mountaineering regulations and information may be obtained from: Talkeetna Ranger Station, P.O. Box 588, Talkeetna, AK 99676; phone (907) 733-2231.

Timberline in the park is 2,700 feet/ 823m. The landscape below timberline in this subarctic wilderness is called taiga, a term of Russian origin that describes the scant growth of trees. Black and white spruce, willow, dwarf birch and aspen grow at lower elevations. The uplands of alpine tundra are carpeted with lichens, mosses, wildflowers and low-growing shrubs. Wildflowers bloom in spring, usually peaking by early July.

Denali National Park represents one of the last intact ecosystems in the world, according to the National Park Service. Here visitors have the opportunity to observe the natural behavior of wild animals. Grizzly

Grizzly bear sow and cubs forage for food in spring tundra. (© Craig Brandt)

bears, caribou, wolves and red foxes freely wander over the tundra. Moose wade through streams and lake shallows. A few lynx pursue snowshoe hare in taiga forests. Marmots, pikas and Dall sheep inhabit high, rocky areas. The arctic ground squirrel's sharp warning call is heard throughout the park.

Migratory bird life encompasses species from 6 continents, including waterfowl, shorebirds, songbirds and birds of prey. Ptarmigan, gray jays and magpies are year-round residents.

The park's silty glacial rivers are not an

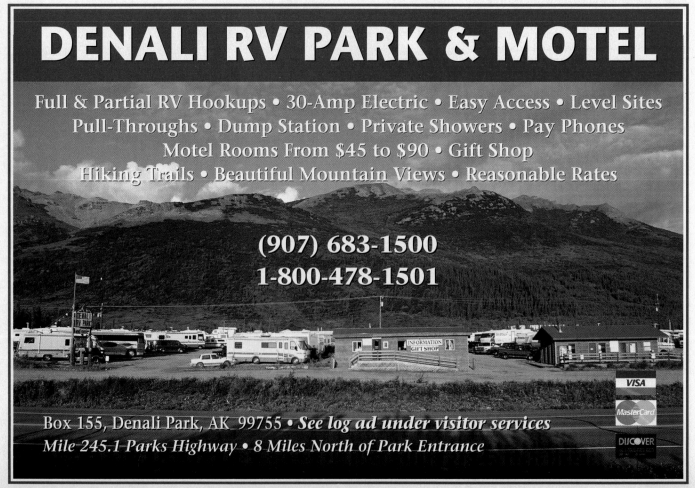

angler's delight, but grayling, Dolly Varden and lake trout are occasionally caught in the clear streams and small lakes.

Emergency Services: Within Denali National Park, phone (907) 683-2294.

ACCOMMODATIONS/VISITOR SERVICES

There is only 1 hotel within the park, but several motels are on the highway, clustered around the park entrance (turn to **Milepost A 237.3** in the GEORGE PARKS HIGHWAY section). Accommodations are also available in the Kantishna area. *NOTE: Visitors should make reservations for lodging far in advance.* The park hotel and area motels are often filled during the summer. Visitors must book their own accommodations. See ads for accommodations this section.

Visitor services are available from late May to mid-September, depending on weather. The Denali National Park Hotel has a gift shop, restaurant, snack bar and saloon. Limited groceries and showers are available at a small store near the hotel. Gas is no longer available inside the park. Gas service 1 mile/1.6 km north of the Park Road junction, May to mid-September. The post office is near the hotel. There is a dump station near Riley Creek Campground.

NOTE: There are no food services in the park

Campground	Spaces	Tent	Trailer	Pit toilets	Flush toilets	Tap water	Fee
Morino	60	•		•			$12
Riley Creek	102	•	•		•	•	$12
Savage River	33	•	•		•	•	$12
Sanctuary River	7	•		•		•	$12
Teklanika River	50	•	•	•		•	$12
Igloo Creek	7	•		•		•	$12
Wonder Lake	28	•			•	•	$12

after you leave the headquarters entrance area.

Campers should bring a gasoline or propane stove or purchase firewood from concessionaire; a tent or waterproof shelter because of frequent rains; and rain gear.

There are 7 campgrounds in the park along the 92-mile/148.1-km Park Road (see log of Park Road in this section for most locations). Wonder Lake, Sanctuary River and Igloo Creek campgrounds are tent only and accessible only by shuttle bus. Riley Creek, Savage River and Teklanika are available for both RV and tent camping. Morino is for those without vehicles only and is not on the reservation system. ▲

The campgrounds are open from about late May to early September, except for Riley Creek, which is open year-round (snow-covered and no water, flush toilets or dump station in winter). There is a fee and a 14-day limit at all campgrounds in summer.

DENALI PARK RESORTS

Come for the Mountain

Stay for the Adventure

Unbelievable scenery, amazing wildlife and exciting activities await you at Denali National Park. It is nature at its grandest. And Denali Park Resorts is dedicated to helping you enjoy everything about this majestic experience. That's why we offer you a choice of comfortable accommodations, excellent restaurants, evening entertainment, and a full range of outdoor adventures.

▲ *After an adventurous day touring the Park, unwind in our indoor swimming pool, hot tub and sauna.*
➤ *Alaska Cabin Nite Dinner Theater is a treat for all ages: songs, stories and an all-you-can eat Alaskan-style barbecue.*

Activities Abound

At Denali Park Resorts we help you experience this amazing wilderness area with a variety of entertaining and exciting activities. Photograph Alaska wildlife, massive mountains, and taiga forests on one of our special park tours. Travel a wild Alaska river by raft, flightsee, enjoy a unique dinner theater presentation. The activities are endless, simply stop by the tour desk at any of our hotels.

➤ *Guest rooms compliment the warmth and charm of the wilderness.*

▼ *There are numerous hiking and scenic spots to explore in Denali and we can show them to you.*

If you really want to enjoy the whole Denali experience, let us help. Denali Park Resorts has 20 years of experience in Alaska's premiere National Park, and we're ready to put that knowledge to work for you.

Your Wilderness Home

McKinley Chalet Resort offers you Alaskan hospitality at its best featuring more than 300 rooms with warm, pine wood interiors. Plus, a complete restaurant, dinner theater, lounge, and gift shop.

Denali National Park Hotel, with 100-rooms "inside" the Park, is the bustling center for visitor activities. In addition to our dining room, snack shop, gift shop and lounge, the hotel is home to a 300-seat auditorium for National Park Service programs.

McKinley Village Lodge rests quietly on the banks of the Nenana River. The 50-room lodge has a full-service cafe, gift shop and cozy lounge with river-rock fireplace for your relaxation.

Denali Park Resorts
For Information And Reservations
(907) 276-7234
(800) 276-7234

P.O. Box 202516
Anchorage, AK, 99520

Denali Park Resorts, managed by ARAMARK, is an authorized concessioner of the National Park Service. © 1994 Denali Park Resorts.

DENALI
PARK RESORTS

Rock ptarmigan in winter plumage. Willow ptarmigan are also common in Alaska.
(© Bill Sherwonit)

Reservations for campsites at Riley Creek, Teklanika River and Savage River campgrounds are available; see Reservation System following. There is a 3-night minimum stay requirement at Teklanika River Campground, and also a limit of one round-trip to this campground for registered campers with vehicles. Additional travel to

and from Teklanika is by shuttle bus. See chart for facilities at each campground. *(NOTE: Campground fees are subject to change!)*

Several private campgrounds are located outside the park along the George Parks Highway. See display ads this section.

For area accommodations, also turn to pages 393-398 in the GEORGE PARKS HIGHWAY section.

Shuttle bus: The National Park Service concessionaire (Denali Park Resorts) provides shuttle bus service from the Visitor Center to Toklat, Eielson Visitor Center and Wonder Lake. During peak season, bus tickets for the next day's shuttles are generally gone by mid-morning. Up to 8 tickets may be reserved in advance; see Reservation System following. Shuttle buses pick up and drop off passengers along the Park Road on a space-available basis, and stop for scenic and wildlife viewing as schedules permit. The buses generally depart the Visitor Center on the hour and half-hour between 7 A.M. and 2 P.M., May 24 to Sept. 11.

Ticket prices are $12 adult, $6 youth (13–16 years) to Toklat; $20 adult, $10 youth to Eielson; $26 adult, $13 youth to Wonder Lake; and $30 adult, $15 youth to Kantishna. Children 12 and under are free.

A round-trip between the Visitor Center and Eielson Visitor Center takes approximately 8 hours. The round-trip to Wonder Lake takes about 11 hours. Bring a lunch, camera, binoculars, extra film, warm clothes and rain gear. Buses run daily from approximately Memorial Day through Labor Day, weather permitting.

Reservation System: Park shuttle bus

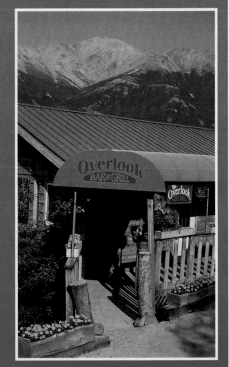

tickets and campsites may be reserved through a nationwide, toll-free number, 1-800-622-7275 (PARK). Advanced reservations (more than 2 days before departure) are available for 40 percent of the bus tickets and campsites. The remaining 60 percent are available 2 days in advance. Anchorage residents and residents of foreign countries phone (907) 272-7275 for reservations. The phone-in reservation system opens Feb. 24, 1997. The call center is open 7 A.M. to 5 P.M. (Alaska time), 7 days a week. A maximum of 8 shuttle bus tickets may be requested with each call. Shuttle bus and campsite reservations may also be faxed (907/264-4684) or mailed to Denali Park Resorts, Visitor Transportation System, 241 W. Ship Creek Ave., Anchorage, AK 99501, between Dec. 1 and Sept. 1. Mail-in requests must include a check or credit card number with expiration date, and must be received by Denali Park Resorts 30 days prior to your scheduled departure. Tickets that have been requested and paid for, prior to the date of departure, can be picked up at a dedicated window at the park visitor center. For travel prior to

7 A.M. each day, unclaimed, prepaid reserved tickets will be in the possession of the bus drivers. During peak season, campgrounds fill up by midmorning for the following day and, on occasion, the day after.

Carlo Creek Bed & Breakfast. Just outside of Denali National Park. Enjoy your own 2-story Alaskan log cabin. This creekside cabin sleeps 4, has cooking facilities, phone and a wood-fired sauna. No running water. Light breakfast included. Restaurant close by. From $57 a night. (907) 683-2557. P.O. Box 137, Denali Park, AK 99755. [ADVERTISEMENT]

Denali Backcountry Lodge. Don't pass up a visit to this lodge if you want to escape the park's crowded east entrance and immerse yourself deep within the park for a few days. The lodge is located at the end of the 97-mile park road. Full-service accommodations feature a comfortable wilderness lodge, cozy cedar cabins, dining room and lounge. One- to 4-night all-inclusive stays include round-trip transportation from the train depot, all meals and lodging, guided hikes, wildlife viewing, bicycling, photography and natural history programs. Credit cards accepted. P.O. Box 189, Denali Park,

AK 99755. Call (800) 841-0692. See display ad this section. [ADVERTISEMENT]

Denali Bluffs Hotel. The newest and closest hotel to the Denali National Park and Preserve entrance. 112 rooms, each room featuring 2 double beds, TVs, phones and other amenities. Most of the rooms have spectacular views of the Alaska Range. The lodge features a large stone fireplace and cathedral ceilings. There are comfortable sitting areas inside the lodge or outside on the deck to enjoy the panoramic views. Gift shop and coin-operated laundry. Shuttle service to visitor center and rail depot. Complete tour and activity desk. Wheelchair accessible. Open mid-May through mid-September. Credit cards accepted. P.O. Box 72460, Fairbanks, AK 99707. Phone (907) 683-7000; or fax (907) 683-7500. See display ad this section. [ADVERTISEMENT]

Denali National Park Hotel, located in park, this 100-room hotel is the bustling center for visitor activities and accommodations. The hotel is a 5 minute walk from the rail depot, provides fine dining, snack shop, gift shop, railcar lounge and grocery store (propane available). The hotel auditorium is the center for national park interpretive services. All accommodations for the hotel, McKinley Chalet (at **Milepost A 238.9** Parks Highway), McKinley Village Lodge (at **Milepost A 229** Parks Highway), wildlife and history tours, rafting adventures, dinner theater and transportation can be arranged by calling (800) 276-7234; in Anchorage 276-7234. [ADVERTISEMENT]

Denali National Park Wilderness Centers—Camp Denali. Since 1951, Alaska's premier small wilderness lodge and nature center. Log cabin lodging with unparalleled views of Mount McKinley. Natural history emphasis, guided backcountry hiking, wildlife observation, canoeing, biking. Periodic special emphasis sessions and Northern studies credit courses. Three-and four-night stays or longer include lodging, all meals and activities, round-trip transportation from park entrance. Brochure: P.O. Box 67, Denali National Park, AK 99755. (907) 683-2290. [ADVERTISEMENT]

Denali National Park Wilderness

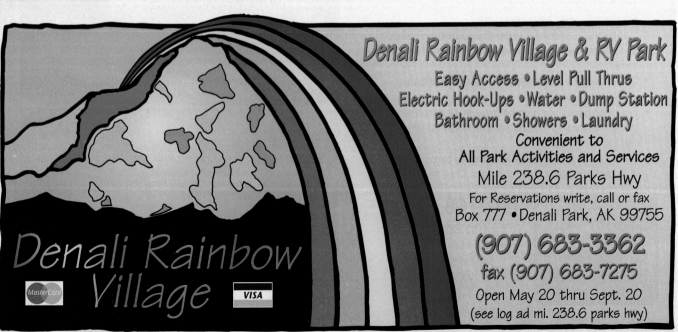

Centers—**North Face Lodge.** Small, well-appointed inn with spectacular Mount McKinley view. Located in the remote heart of the park near the end of the 90-mile park road. Natural history emphasis, guided back-country hiking, wildlife observation, canoeing, biking. Two- and three-night stays or longer include lodging, all meal and activities, round-trip transportation from park entrance. Brochure: P.O. Box 67, Denali National Park, AK 99755. (907) 683-2290. [ADVERTISEMENT]

Denali Princess Lodge. Located near the entrance to Denali National Park featuring spectacular views of the park and a host of amenities including several dining options, tour desk, gift shop, complimentary shuttle to rail depot and park activities. Open mid-May through mid-September. Call 1-800-426-0500 year-round. [ADVERTISEMENT]

Denali RV Park and Motel. 90 full and partial RV hookups, 30-amp electric. Level sites, pull-throughs, easy highway access. Individual restrooms with private showers, flush toilets. Dump station. Caravans welcome! 14 motel rooms; central bath $45, private bath $65, family units with full kitchens $90. Gift shop, covered meeting area, outdoor cooking area, pay phones. Close to all park facilities. Beautiful mountain views. Hiking trails. Reasonable rates. VISA/MasterCard/Discover. Box 155, Denali Park, AK 99755. Located 8 miles north of park entrance, Mile 245.1 Parks Highway. (907) 683-1500. 1-800-478-1501. See display ad this section. [ADVERTISEMENT] ▲

Denali Wilderness Lodge is Alaska's historic fly-in wilderness lodge, sometimes called the most remote hotel in America. Authentic bush homestead nestled in the pristine Wood River Valley. Accessible only by spectacular bush plane flight. Comfortable accommodations, fine dining, naturalist programs, flightseeing, horseback riding, nature/photo walks and hikes, bird watching, wildlife museum. This will be your best memory of Alaska! Overnight packages and day trips available. Free brochure. Phone 1-800-541-9779. See display ad this section. ▲

[ADVERTISEMENT]

Kantishna Roadhouse. Premier wilderness lodge located at the quiet west end of

Denali National Park offers opportunities to view, photograph and explore the park. Packages include comfortable log cabins with private baths, guided hiking, gold panning, horses, fishing, fine meals and Alaskan hospitality. P.O. Box 130, Denali Park, AK 99755. Phone 1-800-942-7420. [ADVERTISEMENT]

Lynx Creek Pizza. "The Best Pizza in Alaska!" We also offer Mexican specialties, hand-dipped ice cream, espresso, extensive beer/wine selection. In addition, great grocery store. Only 1 mile north of park entrance (Mile 238.6 Parks Highway). In Denali, call (907) 683-2547. [ADVERTISEMENT]

McKinley/Denali Cabins at McKinley/Denali Steakhouse and Salmon Bake. Economy tent cabins with electric heat and lights from $65. Some cabins with private baths. Closest full-service facility to park entrance, wildlife shuttles. Close to raft trips, store, gas. Largest T-shirt selection in park area on premises. Shuttle to visitor center, railroad depot available. Free visitor information. Reservations: (907) 683-2258 or (907) 683-2733 or write P.O. Box 90M, Denali Park, AK 99755. See display ad this section.

[ADVERTISEMENT]

Mt. McKinley Gold Camp, historic mining camp cabins, cabin/tents (like Yosemite) and wilderness hostel 90 miles inside Denali National Park in Kantishna. Mining trails, leading to awesome views of Mount McKinley, surround camp. Pan for and keep gold. Van (not bus) tour/transportation through park to Gold Camp. Reservations: 1-800-770-7275. [ADVERTISEMENT]

Grizzly tastes a car bumper at Eielson Visitor Center. (© Craig Brandt)

Rick Swenson's Carlo Heights Bed and Breakfast and Sled Dog School. Open year around, this establishment offers privacy, seclusion and spectacular views of the Alaska Range. Accommodations include 2 double rooms and an executive suite, full kitchen and laundry facilities. The sled dog school offers dog mushing courses and tours. Reservations recommended. Phone (907) 683-1615. [ADVERTISEMENT]

TRANSPORTATION

Highway: Access via the George Parks Highway and the Denali Highway.

The Park Road runs westward 92 miles/148.1 km from the park's east boundary to Kantishna. The road is paved only to Savage River (**Milepost J 14.7**). Private vehicle travel is restricted beyond the Savage River checkpoint at Mile 14.8. Mount McKinley is first visible at about **Milepost J 9** Park Road, but the best views begin at about **Milepost J 60** and continue with few interruptions to Wonder Lake. At the closest point, the summit of the mountain is 27 miles/43.5 km from the road. See log this section.

Air: Charter flights are available from most nearby towns with airfields, and flightseeing tours of the park are offered by operators from the park area or out of Talkeetna, Anchorage or Fairbanks. A round-trip air tour of the park from Anchorage takes 3 to 4 hours. See ads this section.

Era Helicopters. Enjoy an eagle-eye view of the grandeur of Denali National Park. Look for wildlife in the valleys and mountain sides below. Glide by numerous glaciers as Mount McKinley towers on the horizon. Guided heli-hiking tours are also available. Located at Milepost 238. Phone 1-800-843-1947 or (907) 683-2574, May to September.
[ADVERTISEMENT]

Railroad: The Alaska Railroad offers daily northbound and southbound trains between Anchorage and Fairbanks, with stops at Denali Park Station, during the summer season. For details on schedules and fares see the ALASKA RAILROAD section.

Midnight Sun Express®. Ultra Dome railcars featuring glass-domed ceilings, meals prepared to order by on-board chefs and the only outdoor viewing platforms on the

Alaska Railroad system. Daily service between Anchorage, Talkeetna, Denali National Park and Fairbanks. Packages available with overnights at the new Mount McKinley Princess Lodge and/or Denali Princess Lodge. Service mid-May to mid-September. Call 1-800-426-0500 year-round.

Bus: Daily bus service to the park is available from Anchorage and Fairbanks, and special sightseeing tours are offered throughout the summer months. A 6- to 8-hour guided bus tour of the park is offered by the park concessionaire. Tickets and information are available in the hotel lobby at the front desk tour window. For details on the park shuttle bus system, see Accommodations/Visitor Services this section.

Tours: By plane, bus and van are available. See ads this section.

Alpenglow Tours, through Denali National Park in 15-passenger van (not bus) from Fairbanks airport, Nenana, Denali area hotels/RV parks and Cantwell to Mount McKinley Gold Camp in historic Kantishna Mining District. Includes: continental breakfast, picnic lunch, snacks and beverages, plenty rest and photo stops, gold panning.

Full- and half-day tours. 1-800-770-7275.

ATTRACTIONS

Organized activities put on by the Park Service include ranger-led nature hikes; sled dog demonstrations at park headquarters; campfire programs at Riley Creek, Savage River, Teklanika River and Wonder Lake campgrounds; and interpretive programs at the hotel auditorium.

Private operators in the park offer flight-seeing tours, bus tours, raft tours and wintertime dogsled tours. Cross-country skiing and

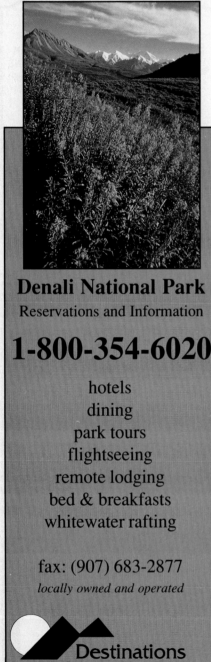
snowshoeing are also popular in winter.

There are few established trails in the park, but there is plenty of terrain for cross-country hiking. Free permits are required for any overnight hikes.

Permits and information on ranger-led hikes and other activities are available at the Visitor Center near the park entrance.

Fly Denali. Denali Park's highest rated flightseeing tour. Local, experienced pilot. Naturalists give you more than just an airplane ride. Our aircraft get you 30 miles closer than helicopters! We're located at Mile 238.9 across from the McKinley Chalets, next to Northern Lights Gift Shop. (907) 683-2889 (April–October). See display ad. [ADVERTISEMENT]

A FEW SPECIAL NOTES FOR VISITORS

The 1980 federal legislation creating a much larger Denali National Park and Preserve also changed some rules and regulations normally followed in most parks. The following list of park rules and regulations apply in the Denali Wilderness Unit—the part of the park that most visitors come to. Contact the Superintendent at Denali (Box 9, Denali Park, 99755) for more information on regulations governing the use of aircraft, firearms, snow machines and motorboats in

View of park terrain from near Eielson Visitor Center. (© J. Peery)

the park additions and in the national preserve units.

For those driving: The Park Road was built for scenic enjoyment and not for high speed. Maximum speed is 35 mph/56 kmp except where lower limits are posted.

Your pets and wildlife don't mix. Pets are allowed only on roadways and in campgrounds and must be leashed or in a vehicle at all times. Pets are not allowed on shuttle buses, trails or in the backcountry.

Hikers who stay overnight *must obtain a backcountry permit* and return it when the trip is completed. Backpacking permits must be obtained in person (no phone-ins) up to 1 day in advance at the Visitor Center, Milepost J 0.5 Park Road. There may be a fee.

Mountaineering expeditions are required to acquire a permit and pay a $150 fee before climbing Mount McKinley or Mount Foraker. Permit applications must be received at least 60 days prior to the start of the expedition. Contact the Talkeetna Ranger Station, Box 588, Talkeetna, AK 99676; phone (907) 733-2231.

Natural features: The park was established to protect a natural ecosystem. Destroying, defacing or collecting plants, rocks and other features is prohibited. Capturing, molesting, feeding or killing any animal is prohibited.

Firearms and hunting are not allowed in the wilderness area.

Fishing licenses are not required in the wilderness area; state law is applicable on all other lands. Limits for each person per day are: lake trout (2 fish); grayling and other fish (10 fish or 10 lbs. and 1 fish). Fishing is poor because most rivers are silty and ponds are shallow.

Motor vehicles of any type, including trail bikes, motorcycles and mopeds, may not leave the Park Road.

Feeding wildlife is prohibited. Wild animals need wild food; your food will not help them.

Park Road Log

Distance from the junction (J) with George Parks Highway is shown.

J 0 Junction. Turn west off the George Parks Highway (Alaska Route 3) at **Milepost**
A 237.3 onto the Park Road. The Park Road is paved to the Savage River bridge.

J 0.2 (0.3 km) Turnoff for Riley Creek Campground and overflow parking area. A dump station is also located here. ▲

J 0.5 (0.8 km) Visitor Center has information on all visitor activities as well as shuttle bus tickets and camping and overnight hiking permits. A park orientation program is available in the theater. The center is open daily. This is also the shuttle bus departure point.

J 1.2 (1.9 km) Alaska Railroad crossing. Horseshoe Lake trailhead.

J 1.4 (2.3 km) Convenience store showers.

J 1.5 (2.4 km) **Denali National Park Hotel.** Located in Denali National Park, this 100-room hotel is the bustling center for visitor activities. The hotel is proud to offer a full-service dining room, snack shop, railcar lounge and grocery store (propane available). The hotel auditorium is the center for national park interpretive services. The hotel is a 5-minute walk from the rail depot. Wilderness activities include wildlife and natural history bus tours, rafting and flightseeing. All arrangements can be made by calling (800) 276-7234; in Anchorage 276-7234, or by contacting the hotel tour desk staff. [ADVERTISEMENT]

J 1.6 (2.6 km) Denali Park Station (elev. 1,730 feet/527m), where visitors can make train connections to Anchorage and Fairbanks, daily service during the summer. Denali National Park Hotel is across from the depot. The post office and a flying service office are located in the hotel area.

Private Aircraft: McKinley Park airstrip, 1.7 miles/2.7 km northeast of park headquarters; elev. 1,720 feet/524m; length 3,000 feet/914m; gravel; unattended.

J 3.5 (5.6 km) Park headquarters. This is the administration area for Denali National Park and Preserve. In winter, information on all visitor activities can be obtained here. Report accidents and emergencies to the rangers; phone (907) 683-9100.

J 5.5 (8.9 km) Paved turnout with litter barrel. Sweeping view of countryside. There are numerous small turnouts along the Park Road.

J 12.8 (20.6 km) Savage River Camp-

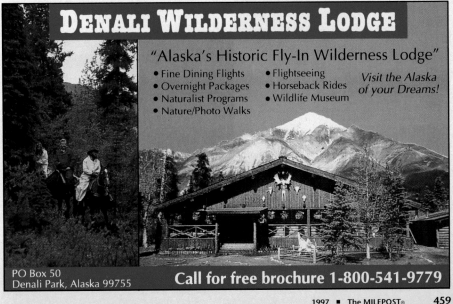

ground (elev. 2,780 feet/847m). Wildlife in the area includes moose, grizzly bear and fox.

J 14.7 (23.7 km) Bridge over the Savage River. Blacktop pavement ends. Access to river, toilet and picnic tables at east end of bridge. ▲

J 14.8 (23.8 km) Savage River check station. PERMIT REQUIRED BEYOND THIS POINT.

NOTE: Road travel permits for access to the Kantishna area are issued at park headquarters only under special conditions. However, the road may be open to all vehicles to Milepost 30 in early May and late September, weather permitting.

J 17.3 (27.8 km) Viewpoint of the Alaska Range and tundra.

J 21.3 (34.3 km) Hogan Creek bridge.

J 22 (35.4 km) Sanctuary River bridge, ranger station and campground (tents only). Wildlife: moose, fox, grizzly bear, wolf. ▲

J 29.1 (46.8 km) Teklanika River Campground (elev. 2,580 feet/786m). Grizzly bears may sometimes be seen on the gravel bars nearby. ▲

J 30.7 (49.4 km) Rest area with chemical toilets.

J 31.3 (50.4 km) Bridge over Teklanika River.

J 34.1 (54.9 km) Igloo Creek Camp-

The Denali caribou herd numbers about 2,300 animals. *(© Roy Corral)*

ground (tents only); accessible by shuttle bus only. Wildlife in the area includes Dall sheep, grizzly bear, moose, fox and wolf. ▲

J 37 (59.5 km) Igloo Creek bridge. *NOTE: The area within 1 mile/1.6 km of each side of the Park Road from Milepost J 38.3 to J 42.9 is closed to all off-road foot travel as a special*

wildlife protection area. Toklat grizzlies are often seen in the area.

J 39.1 (62.9 km) Sable Pass (elev. 3,900 feet/1,189m).

J 43.4 (69.8 km) Bridge over East Fork Toklat River. Views of Polychrome Mountain, the Alaska Range and several glaciers are visible along the East Fork, from open country south of the road.

J 45.9 (73.9 km) Summit of Polychrome Pass (elev. 3,700 feet/1,128m); rest stop with toilets. The broad valley of the Toklat River is visible below to the south. Good hiking in alpine tundra above the road. Wildlife: wolf, grizzly bear, Dall sheep, marmot, pika, golden eagle and caribou.

J 53.1 (85.5 km) Bridge over the Toklat River. The Toklat and all other streams crossed by the Park Road drain into the Tanana River, a tributary of the Yukon River.

J 53.7 (86.4 km) Ranger station.

J 58.3 (93.8 km) Summit of Highway Pass (elev. 3,980 feet/1,213m). This is the highest point on the Park Road.

J 61 (98.2 km) Stony Hill (elev. 4,508 feet/1,374m). A good view of Mount McKinley and the Alaska Range on clear days. Wildlife: grizzly bear, caribou, fox and birds.

J 62 (99.8 km) Viewpoint.

J 64.5 (103.8 km) Thorofare Pass (elev. 3,900 feet/1,189m).

J 66 (106.2 km) Eielson Visitor Center. Ranger-led hikes, nature programs, displays, restrooms and drinking water. Film, maps and natural history publications for sale. Report accidents and emergencies here.

Excellent Mount McKinley viewpoint. On clear days the north and south peaks of Mount McKinley are visible to the southwest. The impressive glacier, which drops from the mountain and spreads out over the valley floor at this point, is the Muldrow. Wildlife: grizzly bear, wolf, caribou.

For several miles beyond the visitor center the road cut drops about 300 feet/91m to the valley below, paralleling the McKinley River.

J 84.6 (136.1 km) Access road leads left, westbound, to Wonder Lake Campground (elev. 2,090 feet/637m). Tents only; campground access by shuttle bus only. An excellent Mount McKinley viewpoint. ▲

The road continues to Wonder Lake, where rafting and canoeing are permitted (no rental boats available). Wildlife: grizzly bear, caribou, moose, beaver, waterfowl.

J 85.6 (137.8 km) Reflection Pond, a kettle lake formed by a glacier.

J 86.6 (139.4 km) Wonder Lake ranger station.

J 87.7 (141.1 km) Moose Creek bridge.

J 88 (141.6 km) North Face Lodge.

J 88.2 (141.9 km) Camp Denali.

J 91 (146.4 km) **KANTISHNA** (pop. 2 in winter, 135 in summer; elev. 1,750 feet/533m). Established in 1905 as a mining camp at the junction of Eureka and Moose creeks. Most of the area around Kantishna is private property and there may be active mining on area creeks in summer. Kantishna Roadhouse, which consists of a dozen log guest cabins and a dining hall, comprise the townsite of Kantishna.

Private Aircraft: Kantishna airstrip, 1.3 miles/2.1 km northwest; elev. 1,575 feet/480m; length 1,850 feet/564m; gravel; unattended, no regular maintenance.

J 91.8 (147.7 km) Mt. McKinley Gold Camp.

J 92 (148.1 km) Denali Backcountry Lodge.

ALASKA RAILROAD

(See maps, pages 364–365 and 482)

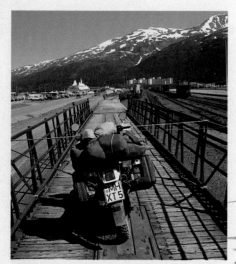

Alaska Railroad shuttle arrives in Whittier. (© Ruth von Spalding)

The Alaska Railroad operates year-round passenger and freight service between Anchorage, Fairbanks, Portage and Whittier. In summer, passenger service is available daily between Anchorage and Fairbanks via Denali Park; Portage and Whittier; and between Anchorage and Seward. For more information on the Alaska Railroad, write Passenger Services Dept., Box 107500, Anchorage 99510. Phone 1-800-544-0552 or (907) 265-2494; fax 265-2323.

Construction of the railroad began in 1915 under Pres. Woodrow Wilson. On July 15, 1923, Pres. Warren G. Harding drove the golden spike at Nenana, signifying completion of the railroad. The main line extends from Seward to Fairbanks, approximately 470 miles/756 km.

The Alaska Railroad accommodates visitors with disabilities. Six coaches feature wheelchair lifts. Coaches have provisions for occupied wheelchairs, and restrooms are accessible. With advance notice, sign language interpreters are available. ♿

Following are services, schedules and fares available on Alaska Railroad routes. Keep in mind that schedules and fares are subject to change without notice.

ANCHORAGE–DENALI PARK–FAIRBANKS (Express Service)

Passenger service between Anchorage, Denali Park and Fairbanks is offered daily from May 16 to Sept. 17, 1997. The express service operates with a food service car, a vista-dome for all passengers to share and coaches with comfortable reclining seats. Travel along the 350-mile/1563-km route between Anchorage and Fairbanks is at a leisurely pace with comfortable window seats and good views of the countryside.

Luxury railcars are available on the Anchorage–Denali Park–Fairbanks route through Gray Line of Alaska (Holland America Lines/Westours) and Princess Tours. These tour companies operate (respectively) the *McKinley Explorer* and *Midnight Sun Express.* Both cars, which are coupled onto the end of the regular Alaska Railroad train, are glass-domed and offer gourmet cuisine along with other amenities. Higher priced than the regular Alaska Railroad cars, tickets are sold on a space-available basis. Packages with a Denali Park overnight are also available. Phone Princess Tours at (800) 835-8907, or Gray Line of Alaska at (800) 544-2206 for details.

The summer schedule is: Northbound express trains depart Anchorage at 8:15 A.M., arrive Denali Park at 4 P.M., and arrive Fairbanks at 8:30 P.M. Southbound express trains depart Fairbanks at 8:15 A.M., arrive Denali Park at 12:30 P.M., and arrive Anchorage at 8:30 P.M.

One-way fares are as follows: Anchorage–Denali Park, $99; Fairbanks–Denali Park, $53; Anchorage–Fairbanks, $149. Children aged 2 through 11 ride for approximately half fare, under 2 ride free.

During fall, winter and spring, weekend-only rail service is provided between Anchorage and Fairbanks. The train travels from Anchorage to Fairbanks on Saturday and returns on Sunday.

Reservations: Reservations should be made 40 days prior to travel. Write the Alaska Railroad, Passenger Services Dept., Box 107500, Anchorage 99510; phone 1-800-544-0552 or (907) 265-2623; fax 265-2323. Your letter should include the dates you plan to travel, points of departure and destination, the number of people in your party and your home phone number. Tickets may be purchased in advance by mail if you desire.

Baggage: Each adult is allowed 2 pieces of luggage to a maximum combined weight of 100 lbs. Children are allowed 2 pieces of baggage to a maximum combined weight of 75 lbs. Excess baggage may be checked for a nominal fee. Bicycles are accepted for a charge of $20 per station, on a space-available basis on the day of travel. Keep in mind that baggage, including backpacks, must be checked before boarding, and it is not accessible during the trip. Canoes, motors, motorcycles, items weighing over 150 lbs., etc., are not accepted for transportation on passenger trains. These items are shipped via freight train.

LOCAL SERVICE

Local rural service between Anchorage and Hurricane Gulch operates Thursday, Saturday and Sunday each week between May 16 and Sept. 17, 1997. This 1-day trip takes you past breathtaking views of Mount McKinley into some remote areas and provides an opportunity to meet local residents who use the train for access. Local service uses self-propelled rail diesel cars and has vending-machine snacks available.

PORTAGE–WHITTIER

The Portage–Whittier shuttle train carries passengers and vehicles between Portage on the Seward Highway and Whittier on Prince William Sound. Portage, which has no facilities other than the railroad's vehicle loading ramp, is 47 miles/75 km south of Anchorage at **Milepost S 80.3** on the Seward Highway. Whittier, on Prince William Sound, is port to the Alaska Marine Highway's ferry MV *Bartlett,* which provides passenger and vehicle service to Cordova and Valdez. The Portage–Whittier railway line is 12.4 miles/20 km long, includes 2 tunnels (one 13,090 feet/3,990m long, the other 4,910 feet/1,497m long). Called the Whittier Cutoff, the line was constructed in 1942–43 as a safeguard for the flow of military supplies. It is a 35-minute train ride.

The shuttle makes several round trips daily between Portage and Whittier, from mid-May through mid-September, connecting with Alaska Marine Highway ferry sailings and other vessels which operate between Whittier and Valdez. (Remember that ferry tickets are purchased separately from train tickets; see MARINE ACCESS ROUTES section, Southwest Ferry System.)

Train tickets for the Whittier shuttle may be purchased from ticket sellers at Portage. Reservations are not accepted for the shuttle train, although passengers with confirmed ferry connections are given priority boarding on the 1:20 P.M. shuttle between Portage and Whittier, if vehicles are at Portage by no later than 12:30 P.M. Standard vehicles under 24 feet/7m in length are charged $70, round-trip, between Portage and Whittier; includes driver fare. Other adult passengers in the vehicle are charged $16 round-trip; children (2 through 11 years of age) pay $8 round-trip. Vehicle rates are based upon length. Some height and width restrictions apply.

During fall, winter and spring, service to Whittier is provided on Wednesday, Friday, Saturday and Sunday.

ANCHORAGE–SEWARD

Rail passenger service between Anchorage and Seward operates daily between May 17 and Sept. 1, 1997. (Weekend service to Seward is available May 10–11 and Sept. 6–7 and 13–14.) The 230-mile/370-km excursion follows Turnagain Arm south from Anchorage and passes through some of the most beautiful scenery to be found along the railroad. Travel is aboard classic passenger coaches. Food service is available in the bar/deli car. Departs Anchorage at 6:45 A.M., arrives Seward at 11 A.M. The return trip departs Seward at 6 P.M., arriving Anchorage at 10:30 P.M. Reservations are required. The round-trip fare is $80 for adults; half fare for children 2 through 11. Overnight tours which include hotel and Resurrection Bay boat excursions are available from the railroad ticket office.

DENALI HIGHWAY ⑧

Connects: Paxson to Cantwell, AK **Length:** 136 miles
Road Surface: Gravel **Season:** Closed in winter
Highest Summit: Maclaren Summit 4,086 feet
Major Attraction: Tangle Lakes–Delta River Canoe Trial

(See map, page 464)

	Cantwell	Delta Junction	Denali Park	Paxson
Cantwell		217	27	136
Delta Junction	217		244	81
Denali Park	27	244		163
Paxson	136	81	163	

Hunters park along the Denali Highway in early fall. (© James D. Ronan, Jr.)

The Denali Highway extends 135.5 miles/218.1 km from Paxson at **Milepost V 185.5** on the Richardson Highway to Cantwell, about 2 miles/3.2 km west of **Milepost A 209.9** on the George Parks Highway. The first 21 miles/33.8 km from Paxson are paved and the rest is gravel. *NOTE: Watch for road paving between **Milepost P 21** and **P 42** in 1997.* The highway is closed from October to mid-May.

The condition of the gravel portion of the highway varies, depending on highway maintenance, weather and the opinion of the driver. The road surface is rough; washboard can develop quickly. Much of the road is in need of gravel, but the roadbed is solid. This can be a dusty and bumpy drive in dry weather. Watch for potholes in wet weather.

There are dozens of primitive campsites and turnouts along the highway (heavily used by hunters in the fall). Excellent fishing in lakes and streams accessible on foot or via designated off-road vehicle trails. Highway access to the Delta River canoe trail through the Tangle Lakes, headwaters of the Delta National Wild, Scenic and Recreational River System, is at **Milepost P 21.5**. The Denali Highway is popular with mountain bikers. There are also many unmarked trails leading off into the Bush. Inquire locally and carry a good topographic map when hiking off the highway.

The Denali Highway has very beautiful scenery and some interesting geography. Glacier-formed features visible from the road include: moraines (drift deposited by glaciers); kames (conical hills or terraces of gravel and sand); kettle lakes (holes formed by blocks of ice melting); and eskers (ridges of gravel formed by streams flowing under glaciers).

Tangle Lakes Archaeological District lies between **Milepost P 17** and **P 35**. Within this 226,000-acre area, more than 400 archaeological sites chronicle man's seasonal exploitation of the local natural resources. For more than 10,000 years, hunter-gatherers have dug roots, picked berries, fished and hunted big game (primarily caribou) in this area. You may hike along the same high, gravel ridges once used by prehistoric people and used today by modern hunters, anglers and berry pickers. Off-road vehicles are permitted within the district, although some restrictions are in effect spring through fall. Information on Tangle Lakes Archaeological District and off-road vehicle use is available at the lodges along the Denali Highway and at the Bureau of Land Management office in Glennallen. Write BLM, Box 147, Glennallen, AK 99588; or phone (907) 822-3217.

The Denali Highway was the only road link to Denali National Park and Preserve (formerly Mount McKinley National Park) prior to completion of the George Parks Highway in 1972. Before the Denali Highway opened in 1957, Denali National Park was accessible only via the Alaska Railroad.

Emergency medical services: Between Paxson and **Milepost P 77.5** (Susitna Lodge), phone 911 or the state troopers at (907) 822-3263. Between **Milepost P 77.5** and Cantwell, phone the Cantwell ambulance at (907) 768-2982 or the state troopers at (907) 768-2202.

Denali Highway Log

ALASKA ROUTE 8
Distance from Paxson (P) is followed by distance from Cantwell (C).

P 0 C 135.5 (218.1 km) **PAXSON** (pop. 33; elev. 2,650 feet/808m). A lodge with restaurant, gas station, post office and small grocery store is located here. Wilderness tours; inquire at lodge. Wildlife often seen near here: grizzly bear, moose and porcupine.

Paxson Inn & Lodge. See display ad this section.

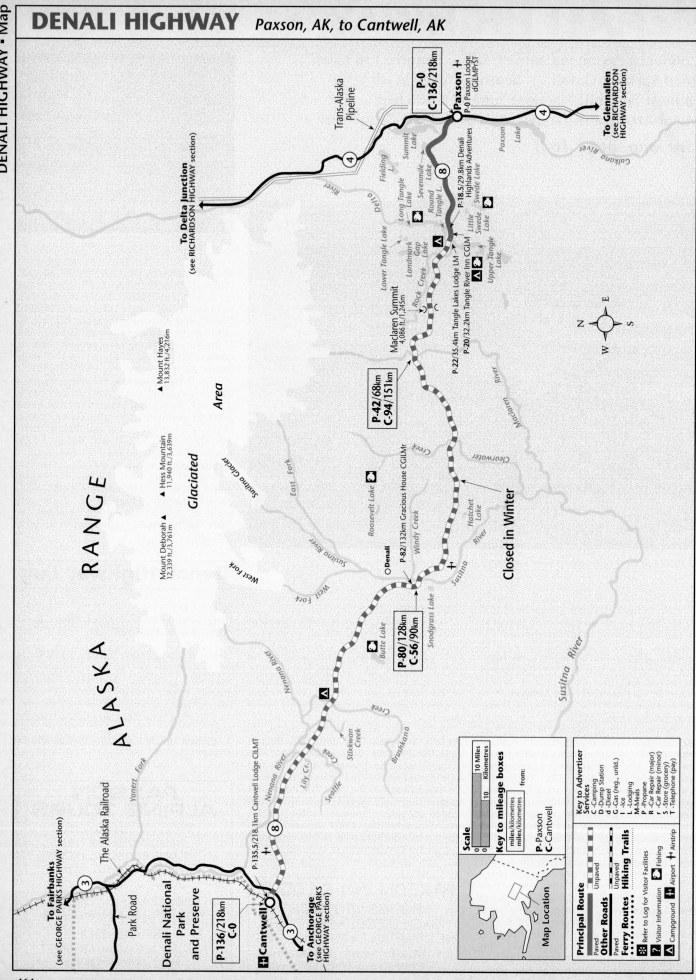

DENALI HIGHWAY

Paxson, AK, to Cantwell, AK

P-0
C-136/218km

Paxson ✈ ⊹

P-0 Paxson Lodge dGILMPST

To Glennallen
(see RICHARDSON
HIGHWAY section)

Trans-Alaska
Pipeline

Summit
Lake

Fielding
L.

Paxson
Lake

Guilkana River

To Delta Junction
(see RICHARDSON HIGHWAY section)

Long Tangle
Lake

Sevenmile
Lake

P-18.5/29.8km Denali
Highlands Adventures

Round
Lake

Tangle L.

Little
Swede
Lake

Swede
Lake

Delta River

Lower Tangle Lake

Landmark
Gap

Rock Creek
Lake

P-22/35.4km Tangle Lakes Lodge LM

P-20/32.2km Tangle River Inn CGLM

▲

▲

▲

Upper Tangle
Lake

Maclaren Summit
4,086 ft./1,245m

Maclaren River

▲ Mount Hayes
13,832 ft./4,216m

Glaciated
Area

P-42/68km
C-94/151km

Hess Mountain
11,940 ft./3,639m

Susitna Glacier

Clearwater Creek

Clearwater

Mount Deborah
12,339 ft./3,761m

East Fork

Roosevelt Lake

♣

Windy Creek

P-82/132km Gracious House CGILMr

Hatchet
Lake

Closed in Winter

West Fork

West Fork
Susitna River

○ Denali

⊹

Susitna River

Susitna River

ALASKA RANGE

Nenana River

West Fork
Nenana River

Lily Cr.

Seattle Creek

Stikkwan Creek

Brushkana Creek

Butte Lake

♣

Snodgrass Lake

P-80/128km
C-56/90km

▲

Yanert Fork

To Fairbanks
(see GEORGE PARKS HIGHWAY section)

The Alaska Railroad

Park Road

Denali National
Park and Preserve

P-136/218km
C-0

P-135.5/218.1km Cantwell Lodge CILMT

8

⊹

⊹ Cantwell

To Anchorage
(see GEORGE PARKS
HIGHWAY section)

3

3

Scale

0	10 Miles
0	10 Kilometres

Key to mileage boxes

miles/kilometres
miles/kilometres

from:

P-Paxson
C-Cantwell

Key to Advertiser Services

C -Camping
D -Dump Station
d -Diesel
G -Gas (reg., unld.)
I -Ice
L -Lodging
M -Meals
P -Propane
R -Car Repair (major)
r -Car Repair (minor)
S -Store (grocery)
T -Telephone (pay)

Principal Route

Paved
Unpaved

Other Roads

Paved
Unpaved

Ferry Routes   Hiking Trails

Refer to Log for Visitor Facilities

? Visitor Information   ⟨ Fishing
▲ Campground   ⊹ Airport/Airstrip

Map Location

Private Aircraft: Paxson airstrip, adjacent south; elev. 2,653 feet/809m; length 2,800 feet/853m; gravel; emergency fuel; attended.

P 0.2 (0.3 km) **C 135.3** (217.7 km) Gulkana River bridge; parking at west end. In season, spawning salmon may be seen here. This portion of the Gulkana River is off-limits to salmon fishing.

Paxson Alpine Tours. See display ad on page 463.

P 0.3 (0.5 km) **C 135.2** (217.6 km) Entering Paxson Closed Area westbound. This area is closed to the taking of all big game. Side road leads south to Mud Lake.

Westbound, there are many long steep upgrades and many turnouts the next 21 miles/33.8 km. Wildflowers carpet the tundra in the spring and summer.

P 1.1 (1.8 km) **C 134.4** (216.3 km) **Mud Lake** below highway; early grayling fishing.

P 3.6 (5.8 km) **C 131.9** (212.3 km) Paved turnout to south. Several more turnouts next 2.5 miles/4 km with views of Summit Lake to the north. Gakona Glacier to the northeast and Icefall Peak to the west of the glacier. West of Icefall Peak is Gulkana Glacier.

P 6.1 (9.8 km) **C 129.4** (208.2 km) Paved turnout to north; views of Gulkana and Gakona glaciers.

P 6.7 (10.8 km) **C 128.8** (207.3 km) Paved turnout to south.

P 6.8 (10.9 km) **C 128.7** (207.1 km) Access to **Sevenmile Lake** 0.8 mile/1.3 km north; excellent fishing for lake trout in summer.

P 7.1 (11.4 km) **C 128.4** (206.6 km) Paved turnout to south.

P 7.3 (11.7 km) **C 128.2** (206.3 km) Gravel turnout overlooking Sevenmile Lake. Two Bit Lake is the large lake to the north; Summit Lake is to the northeast.

P 7.5 (12.1 km) **C 128** (206 km) Paved turnout to north overlooking Sevenmile Lake. Summit Lake visible to east.

P 8.2 (13.2 km) **C 127.3** (204.9 km) Paved turnout to north; small lakes (not visible from highway) in Hungry Hollow to the south.

P 9 (14.5 km) **C 126.5** (203.6 km) Gravel turnout. Entering BLM public lands westbound.

P 10.1 (16.3 km) **C 125.4** (201.8 km) Paved turnout to south overlooking **Ten Mile Lake**. Short hike downhill to outlet. Fishing for lake trout, grayling and burbot in summer.

P 10.6 (17.1 km) **C 124.9** (201 km) Paved turnout overlooking **Teardrop Lake** to south. Short hike down steep hill to lake; lake trout, grayling and burbot in summer.

For the next 4 miles/6.4 km westbound, there are wide-open spaces with magnificent views of the great Denali country. Look for kettle lakes and kames.

P 11.1 (17.9 km) **C 124.4** (200.2 km) Paved turnout and trail to **Octopus Lake** 0.3 mile/0.5 km south; lake trout, grayling, whitefish.

P 13.1 (21.1 km) **C 122.4** (197 km) Viewpoint at summit; interpretive plaque. In the spring from this spot a traveler can count at least 40 lakes and potholes. To the southeast are Mount Sanford, Mount Drum and Mount Wrangell in the Wrangell Mountain range.

Highway begins descent westbound to Tangle Lakes area. Lupine blooms alongside the road in late June.

P 15 (24.1 km) **C 120.5** (193.9 km) Fourteenmile Lake lies about 1.5 miles/2.4 km north of the highway, beyond 8 smaller ponds.

P 16.8 (27 km) **C 118.7** (191 km) **16.8 Mile Lake** to north (walk up creek 200 yards); lake trout and grayling. **Rusty Lake**, 0.5 mile/0.8 km northwest of 16.8 Mile Lake; lake trout and grayling. Swede Lake trail, 3 miles/4.8 km long, to south; **Little Swede Lake**, 2 miles/3.2 km. This trail connects with the Middle Fork Gulkana River branch trail (access to Dickey Lake and Meier Lake trail) and the Alphabet Hills trail. **Big Swede Lake** has excellent fishing for lake trout, grayling, whitefish and burbot. Little Swede Lake excellent for lake trout. Inquire at Tangle River Inn for directions.

P 17 (27.4 km) **C 118.5** (190.7 km) 17 **Mile Lake** to north, turnout at west end of lake; lake trout and grayling fishing.

P 18.2 (29.3 km) **C 117.3** (188.8 km) Bad frost heave.

P 18.4 (29.6 km) **C 117.1** (188.4 km) Gravel turnout by **Denali–Clearwater Creek**; grayling fishing.

P 18.5 (29.8 km) **C 117** (188.3 km) **Denali Highlands Adventures.** See display ad this section.

P 20 (32.2 km) **C 115.5** (185.9 km) **Tangle River Inn** overlooking Tangle Lakes. Home-style cooking and desserts. Motel rooms starting at $45 double. Log cabin bunkhouse with restroom inside for groups. Beautiful views. Hiking and canoe trails,

Pavement extends to Milepost P 21.3 on the Denali Highway, and more paving is planned. (© Ruth Fairall)

fishing for grayling and lake trout. Local talent, prospectors, artist and "liars" on premises. Karaoke bar. See display ad. ▲

P 20.1 (32.3 km) **C 115.4** (185.7 km) Large paved turnout to north overlooking lake.

P 20.6 (33.2 km) **C 114.9** (184.9 km) Paved parking area with toilets to north.

P 21 (33.8 km) **C 114.5** (184.3 km) The Nelchina caribou herd travels through this area, usually around the end of August or early in September.

*NOTE: Watch for road paving westbound between **Milepost P 21** and **P 42**.*

P 21.3 (34.3 km) **C 114.2** (183.8 km) Pavement ends westbound.

P 21.4 (34.4 km) **C 114.1** (183.6 km) One-lane bridge over Tangle River.

P 21.5 (34.6 km) **C 114** (183.5 km) Tangle Lakes BLM campground and wayside, 0.7 mile/1.1 km north from highway on shore of Round Tangle Lake; 13 sites, toilets, boat launch, picnicking, hiking (no thick brush, good views). Blueberry picking in August. ▲

Easy access to boat launch for Delta River canoe trail, which goes north through Tangle Lakes to the Delta River. The 2- to 3-day float to the take-out point on the Richardson Highway requires 1 portage. The Delta National Wild, Scenic and Recreational River system is managed by the BLM. For details on this river trail or the Gulkana River trail, contact the BLM, Box 147, Glennallen, AK 99588; phone (907) 822-3217.

Watershed divide. The Gulkana River joins the Copper River, which flows into Prince William Sound. The Delta River joins the Tanana River, which flows into the Yukon River. The Yukon flows into the Bering Sea.

P 21.7 (34.9 km) **C 113.8** (183.1 km) Tangle River BLM campground; toilets, water pump, boat launch. Watch for caribou on surrounding hills. Watch for arctic warblers nesting along the Tangle River. ▲

The name Tangle is a descriptive term for the maze of lakes and feeder streams contained in this drainage system. Access to

Upper Tangle Lakes canoe trail, which goes south through Tangle Lakes (portages required) to Dickey Lake, then follows the Middle Fork to the main Gulkana River.

AREA FISHING: Tangle Lakes system north and south of the highway (**Long Tangle**, **Round Tangle**, **Upper Tangle** and **Lower Tangle Lake**). Good grayling, burbot and lake trout fishing. Fishing begins as soon as the ice goes out, usually in early June, and continues into September. Good trolling, and some fish are taken from the banks. Early in season, trout are hungry and feed on snails in the shallows at the outlet. Inquire at Tangle Lakes Lodge or Tangle River Inn for information and assistance in getting to where the fish are.

P 22 (35.4 km) **C 113.5** (182.6 km) **Tangle Lakes Lodge**, originally Butcher's Hunting Camp, was built in 1952, the first lodge on the Denali Highway. It is becoming a popular birding destination. Arctic warblers, Smith's longspurs, gyrfalcons and ptarmigan are local favorites. Owners Rich and Linda Holmstrom are avid birders and provide the most accurate local information available. Most of the Nelchina caribou herd can be seen nearby during most of the season, and this is a favorite moose calving area. Tangle Lakes boasts the best arctic grayling fishing you can drive to in Alaska. Discover the real Alaska. Drop by Tangle Lakes Lodge and find the finest food, local information and hospitality around. Phone (907) 688-9173; fax (907) 688-9174. See display ad.

P 22.3 (35.9 km) **C 113.2** (182.2 km) Trail to south along esker.

P 24.8 (39.9 km) **C 110.7** (178.1 km) Landmark Gap BLM trail to north open to ORVs to **Landmark Gap Lake**. Grayling in stream at trail end; trout in main lake. Mountain biking is also popular on this trail.

P 24.9 (40.1 km) **C 110.6** (178 km) **Rock Creek** 1-lane bridge; parking and informal campsites at both ends of bridge. Fair grayling fishing. Landmark Gap Lake lies north of highway between the noticeable gap in the mountains (a caribou migration route). ◂

P 28.1 (45.2 km) **C 107.4** (172.8 km) Downwind Lake north side of road.

P 30.6 (49.2 km) **C 104.9** (168.8 km) Cat trail leads 2 miles/3.2 km north to **Glacier Lake**; lake trout, grayling. ◂

P 32 (51.5 km) **C 103.5** (166.6 km) Amphitheater Mountains rise above High Valley to the north. Glacier Lake is visible in the gap in these mountains.

P 35.2 (56.6 km) **C 100.3** (161.4 km) Turnout at Maclaren Summit (elev. 4,086 feet/1,245m). Highest highway pass in Alaska (not including 4,800-foot/1,463-m Atigun Pass on the Dalton Highway, formerly the North Slope Haul Road). A profusion of flowers—notably the various heaths and frigid shooting star.

P 36 (57.9 km) **C 99.5** (160.1 km) **36 Mile Lake** 0.5-mile/0.8-km hike north; lake trout and grayling. ◂

P 36.4 (58.6 km) **C 99.1** (159.5 km) Entering Clearwater Creek controlled-use area westbound. Closed to motorized hunting.

P 36.6 (58.9 km) **C 98.9** (159.2 km) Osar Lake ORV trail south; 5 miles/8 km.

P 37 (59.5 km) **C 98.5** (158.5 km) Turnout with view of Susitna River valley, Mount Hayes and the Alaska Range. Osar Lake trail leads 5 miles/8 km south toward the Alphabet Hills; Maclaren Summit trail leads 3 miles/4.8 km north to good view of Alaska Range; mountain biking. Osar Lake was first named Asar Lake, the Scandinavian word for esker. (An esker is a ridge of sand and gravel marking the former stream channel of a glacier.)

P 39.8 (64.1 km) **C 95.7** (154 km) Sevenmile Lake ORV trail to north; 6.5 miles/10.5 km long, parallels Boulder Creek, crosses peat bog.

P 42 (67.6 km) **C 93.5** (150.5 km) Maclaren River and bridge, a 364-foot/111-m multiple span crossing this tributary of the Susitna River. Parking and litter barrels. Maclaren River Lodge west side. Look for cliff swallows nesting under bridge.

P 43.3 (69.7 km) **C 92.2** (148.4 km) Maclaren River Road leads north 12 miles/19.3 km to Maclaren Glacier; mountain biking. Maclaren River trailhead to south. The Maclaren River rises in the glaciers surrounding Mount Hayes (elev. 13,832 feet/4,216m). For the next 60 miles/96.6 km westbound, the highest peaks of this portion of the mighty Alaska Range are visible, weather permitting, to the north. From east to west: Mount Hayes, Hess Mountain (elev. 11,940 feet/3,639m) and Mount Deborah (elev. 12,339 feet/3,761m). Mount Hayes, first climbed in August 1941, is named after Charles Hayes, an early member of the U.S. Geological Survey. Mount Deborah, first climbed in August 1954, was named in 1907 by Judge Wickersham after his wife.

P 44.1 (71 km) **C 91.4** (147.1 km) Small turnout to south. Beaver lodge and dam.

P 44.6 (71.8 km) **C 90.9** (146.3 km) Highway crosses Crazy Notch gap.

P 46.9 (75.5 km) **C 88.6** (142.6 km) Road north to **46.9 Mile Lake**; fishing for grayling in lake and outlet stream. ⊶

P 47 (75.6 km) **C 88.5** (142.4 km) Beaver dam. Excellent grayling fishing in **Crooked Creek**, which parallels the highway. ⊶

P 48.6 (78.2 km) **C 86.9** (139.8 km) Informal campsite by small lake.

P 49 (78.8 km) **C 86.5** (139.2 km) The road follows an esker between 4 lakes. Parts of the highway are built on eskers. Watch for ptarmigan, swans, arctic terns, ducks and beaver. Look for a pingo (earth-covered ice hill) at lakeshore.

P 49.7 (80 km) **C 85.8** (138.1 km) Turnout to north overlooks lake. Interpretive plaque on glacial topography and wildlife, including trumpeter swans and loons.

P 51.8 (83.4 km) **C 83.7** (134.7 km) Private hunting camp to south. Trail to north.

P 56.1 (90.3 km) **C 79.4** (127.8 km) **Clearwater Creek** 1-lane bridge and rest area with toilets and litter barrels. Informal camping. Cliff swallows nest under bridge. Grayling fishing in summer. ⊶

P 58.2 (93.7 km) **C 77.3** (124.4 km) Clearwater Creek walk-in (no motorized vehicles) hunting area north of highway.

P 58.8 (94.6 km) **C 76.7** (123.4 km) Road winds atop an esker flanked by kames and kettle lakes. Watch for moose.

P 64 (103 km) **C 71.5** (115.1 km) Road descends westbound into Susitna Valley. Highest elevation of mountains seen to north is 5,670 feet/1,728m.

P 65.7 (105.7 km) **C 69.8** (112.3 km) Waterfall Creek.

P 68.9 (110.9 km) **C 66.6** (107.2 km) Raft Creek. Hatchet Lake lies about 2 miles/3.2 km south of highway. Inquire at Gracious House, **Milepost P 82**, for directions.

Beavers eat a variety of vegetation, including aspen, willow, birch and poplar. (© Mike Jones)

P 71.5 (115.1 km) **C 64** (103 km) Moose often sighted in valley below road.

P 72.2 (116.2 km) **C 63.3** (101.9 km) Nowater Creek.

P 72.8 (117.2 km) **C 62.7** (100.9 km) Swampbuggy Lake.

P 75 (120.7 km) **C 60.5** (97.4 km) Clearwater Mountains to north; watch for bears on slopes. View of Susitna River in valley below.

P 77.5 (124.7 km) **C 58** (93.3 km) Clear Water Mountain Resort, formerly Susitna Lodge; current status of services unknown.

Private Aircraft: Private airstrip, adjacent west; elev. 2,675 feet/815m; length 2,000 feet/610m; gravel.

P 78.8 (126.8 km) **C 56.7** (91.2 km) Valdez Creek Road. Former mining camp of Denali, about 6 miles/10 km north of the highway via a gravel road, was first established in 1907 after the discovery of gold in 1903. The Valdez Creek Mine operated at this site from 1990 to 1995. The mine pit was converted into a lake in 1996 as part of a reclamation project. Area mining equipment was donated to the Museum of Transportation and Industry (see **Milepost A 47** in the GEORGE PARKS HIGHWAY section). Do not trespass on private mining claims. Fair fishing reported in **Roosevelt Lake** and area creeks. Watch for bears. ⊶

P 79.3 (127.6 km) **C 56.2** (90.4 km) Susitna River 1-lane bridge, a combination multiple span and deck truss, 1,036 feet/316m long. Butte Creek trailhead.

The Susitna River heads at Susitna Glacier in the Alaska Range (between Mounts Hess and Hayes) and flows southwest 260 miles/418 km to Cook Inlet. Downstream through Devil's Canyon it is considered unfloatable. The river's Tanaina Indian name, said to mean "sandy river," first appeared in 1847

on a Russian chart.

Entering Game Management Unit 13E westbound, leaving unit 13B eastbound.

P 81 (130.4 km) **C 54.5** (87.7 km) Snodgrass Lake (elev. 2,493 feet/760m) is about 2 miles/3.2 km south of the highway. Check with Gracious House, **Milepost P 82**, for directions. *CAUTION: Watch for horses.*

P 82 (132 km) **C 53.5** (86.1 km) **Gracious House.** Centrally located on the shortest, most scenic route to Denali National Park. 16 modern cabins or motel units, most with private baths, bar, cafe featuring ice cream and home-baked pies. Tent sites, parking for self-contained RVs overlooking lake. Water, restrooms and showers available at lodge. "Cash" gas, towing, welding, mechanical repairs, tire service. Air taxi, guide service available in a variety of combinations serving the sportsman, tourist, photographer, families with tours and outings to individual desires, from campouts to guided hunts. Same owners/operators for 39 years. Reasonable rates. For brochure on hunting and fishing trips, write to the Gracious Family. Summer address: P.O. Box 88, Cantwell, AK 99729. Winter address: 859 Elaine Dr., Anchorage, AK 99504. Message phone (907) 333-3148 or call (907) 822-7307 (let ring, radio phone). [ADVERTISEMENT] ▲

P 83 (133.6 km) **C 52.5** (84.5 km) Visible across the Susitna River is Valdez Creek mining camp at the old Denali townsite. Valdez Creek Mine is operated by Cambior Alaska, Inc. *CAUTION: Watch for truck traffic.*

P 84 (135.2 km) **C 51.5** (82.9 km) **Stevenson's Lake** 0.5 mile/0.8 km south; grayling fishing. ⊶

P 88.7 (142.7 km) **C 46.8** (75.3 km) Large turnout by pond. Good stop for pictures of the Alaska Range (weather permitting).

P 90.5 (145.6 km) **C 45** (72.4 km) A major water drainage divide occurs near here. East of the divide, the tributary river system of the Susitna flows south to Cook Inlet. West of the divide, the Nenana River system flows north to the Yukon River, which empties into the Bering Sea.

P 91.2 (146.8 km) **C 44.3** (71.3 km) Turnout and access to small lake beside road.

P 93.8 (151 km) **C 41.7** (67.1 km) **Butte**

Cantwell is the western terminus of the Denali Highway. (Jerrianne Lowther, staff)

Lake, 5 miles/8 km south of highway. Motorized access by all-terrain vehicle from lodge at **Milepost P 99.5.** Best fishing June through September. Lake trout to 30 lbs., troll with red-and-white spoons or grayling remains; grayling to 20 inches, small flies or spinners; burbot to 12 lbs., use bait on bottom.

P 94.3 (151.8 km) **C 41.2** (66.3 km) Short road leads to parking area above pond. View of Monahan Flat and Alaska Range to the north. Interpretive plaque on earthquakes.

P 94.8 (152.6 km) **C 40.7** (65.5 km) Bridge over Canyon Creek.

P 96.1 (154.7 km) **C 39.4** (63.4 km) Good viewpoint of the West Fork Glacier. Looking north up the face of this glacier, Mount Deborah is to the left and Mount Hess is in the center.

P 97 (156.1 km) **C 38.5** (62 km) Looking at the Alaska Range to the north, Mount Deborah, Mount Hess and Mount Hayes are the highest peaks to your right; to the left are the lower peaks of the Alaska Range and Mount Nenana.

P 99.5 (160.1 km) **C 36** (57.9 km) **Adventures Unlimited Lodge,** now open year-round. Summer hiking, mountain biking. Fish for grayling at remote Butte Lake (access via 4-wheel ATVs, available for rent). Guided fly fishing. Winter snow machining, dog sled tours, cross-country skiing and northern lights viewing far from city lights. Cafe with home cooking, fresh-brewed coffee and homemade pies. Lodging available. Phone (907) 561-7723, fax (907) 561-2093. See display ad this section. [ADVERTISEMENT]

P 100 (160.9 km) **C 35.5** (57.1 km) Residents of this area say it is a wonderful place for picking cranberries and blueberries in August.

P 103 (165.8 km) **C 32.5** (52.3 km) Highway is built on an esker between kettle lakes.

P 104.6 (168.3 km) **C 30.9** (49.7 km) **Brushkana River** bridge and BLM campground; 12 sites beside river, tables, firepits, toilets, litter barrels and water. Fishing for grayling and Dolly Varden. Watch for moose.

P 106.6 (171.6 km) **C 28.9** (46.5 km) **Canyon Creek,** grayling fishing.

P 107.2 (172.5 km) **C 28.3** (45.5 km) **Stixkwan Creek** flows under highway in culvert. Grayling.

P 111.2 (179 km) **C 24.3** (39.1 km) **Seattle Creek** 1-lane bridge. Fishing for grayling and Dolly Varden.

P 112 (180.2 km) **C 23.5** (37.8 km) Lily Creek. Matanuska–Susitna Borough boundary.

P 113.2 (182.2 km) **C 22.3** (35.9 km) View to east of the Alaska Range and extensive rolling hills grazed by caribou.

P 115.7 (186.2 km) **C 19.8** (31.9 km) Large gravel turnout with beautiful view of the Nenana River area.

P 117.1 (188.4 km) **C 18.4** (29.6 km) Log cabin beside Nenana River.

P 117.5 (189.1 km) **C 18** (29 km) Leaving BLM public lands westbound.

P 117.7 (189.4 km) **C 17.8** (28.6 km) Highway parallels the Nenana River, which flows into the Tanana River at the town of Nenana.

P 120 (193.1 km) **C 15.5** (24.9 km) A variety of small water birds, including ducks, snipes and terns, can be observed in the marshy areas along both sides of the road for the next 1 mile/1.6 km westbound.

P 122.3 (196.8 km) **C 11.3** (18.2 km) View (westbound) of Mount McKinley.

P 125.7 (202.3 km) **C 9.8** (15.8 km) **Joe Lake,** about 0.5 mile/0.8 km long (large enough for floatplane), is south of highway. **Jerry Lake** is about 0.2 mile/0.3 km north of the highway. Two small turnouts provide room for campers and fishermen. Both lakes have grayling.

P 128.1 (206.2 km) **C 7.4** (11.9 km) Fish Creek bridge. Access to creek and informal campsite at east end of bridge.

P 128.2 (206.3 km) **C 7.3** (11.7 km) Beautiful view of Talkeetna Mountains to the south.

P 128.6 (207 km) **C 6.9** (11.1 km) Small pond just off highway. Good berry picking in the fall. Fishing for grayling in unnamed creek.

P 130.3 (209.7 km) **C 5.2** (8.4 km) The small town of Cantwell, nestled at the foot of the mountains, can be seen across a long, timbered valley dotted with lakes. Excellent view of Mount McKinley, weather permitting.

P 131.5 (211.6 km) **C 4** (6.4 km) Airstrip; current status unknown.

P 132 (212.4 km) **C 3.5** (5.6 km) Good grayling fishing in stream beside road.

P 133 (214 km) **C 2.5** (4 km) Cantwell Station highway maintenance camp.

P 133.1 (214.2 km) **C 2.4** (3.9 km) Junction with old Anchorage–Fairbanks Highway; turn right westbound for Alaska State Troopers complex located approximately 0.2 mile/0.3 km north on left side of road.

P 133.7 (215.2 km) **C 1.8** (2.9 km) Junction of Denali and George Parks highways (Alaska Routes 8 and 3). Cantwell post office and school, a lodge, rental cabins, RV park with hookups, 2 restaurants, mini-grocery, gas stations and gift shop are clustered around this intersection. Continue straight ahead 1.8 miles/2.9 km for the original town of Cantwell. Turn left (south) for Anchorage or right (north) for Denali National Park and Fairbanks. See **Milepost A 209.9** in the GEORGE PARKS HIGHWAY section for details.

P 135.5 (218.1 km) **C 0 CANTWELL** (pop. 145), western terminus of the Denali Highway. Cantwell Lodge has rooms, a campground, cafe, bar and liquor store. Flightseeing service available.

Private Aircraft: Cantwell airport, adjacent north; elev. 2,190 feet/668m; length 2,100 feet/640m; gravel, dirt; fuel 100LL.

Cantwell began as a railroad flag stop between Seward on Prince William Sound and Fairbanks on the Chena River. The Alaska Railroad now serves Cantwell several times a week on its Anchorage to Fairbanks run during summer. The village was named for the Cantwell River, which is the former name of the Nenana River.

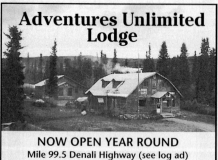

STEESE HIGHWAY ② ⑥

Connects: Fairbanks to Circle, AK   **Length:** 162 miles
Road Surface: 30% paved, 70% gravel   **Season:** Open all year
Highest Summit: Eagle Summit, 3,624 feet
Major Attractions: Hot Springs, Gold Dredge No. 8

(See map, page 470)

	Central	Chena Hot Springs	Circle	Circle Hot Springs	Fairbanks
Central		180	35	8	128
Chena Hot Springs	180		214	188	61
Circle	35	214		43	162
Circle Hot Springs	8	188	43		136
Fairbanks	128	61	162	136	

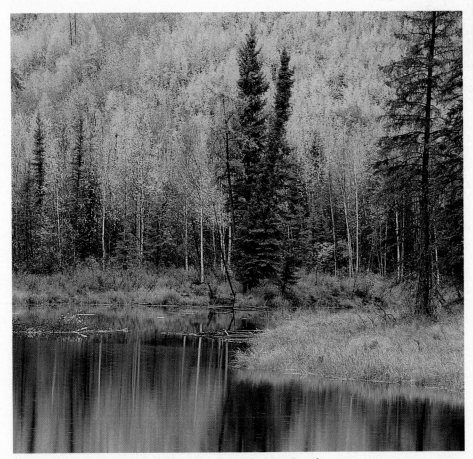

Autumn color reflections along Chena Hot Springs Road. (© Robin Brandt)

The Steese Highway connects Fairbanks with Chena Hot Springs (61.4 miles/98.8 km) via Chena Hot Springs Road; the town of Central (127.5 miles/205.2 km); Circle Hot Springs (136.1 miles/219 km) via Circle Hot Springs Road; and with Circle, a small settlement 162 miles/260.7 km to the northeast on the Yukon River and 50 miles/80.5 km south of the Arctic Circle. The scenery alone makes this a worthwhile drive. The first 44 miles/70.8 km of the Steese Highway are paved. Beyond this it is wide gravel road into Central, where there is a stretch of paved road. From Central to Circle, the highway is a narrow, winding road with gravel surface. *NOTE: Watch for road construction between Milepost F 81 and F 125 in 1997.*

The highway is open year-round; check with the Dept. of Transportation in Fairbanks regarding winter road conditions. The Steese Highway was completed in 1927 and named for Gen. James G. Steese, U.S. Army, former president of the Alaska Road Commission.

Among the attractions along the Steese are Eagle Summit, highest pass on the highway, where there is an unobstructed view of the midnight sun at summer solstice (June 21); the Chatanika River and Chena River recreation areas; and Chena and Circle hot springs.

Emergency medical services: Between Fairbanks and Circle, phone the state troopers at 911 or (907) 452-1313. Use CB Channels 2, 19, 22.

Steese Highway Log

ALASKA ROUTE 2
Distance from Fairbanks (F) is followed by distance from Circle (C).

F 0 C 162 (260.7 km) **FAIRBANKS. Junction** of Airport Way, Richardson–Alaska Highway and the Steese Expressway. Follow the 4-lane Steese Expressway north.

F 0.4 (0.6 km) C 161.6 (260.1 km) Tenth Avenue exit.

F 0.6 (1 km) C 161.4 (259.7 km) Expressway crosses Chena River.

F 0.9 (1.4 km) C 161.1 (259.3 km) Third Street exit.

F 1 (1.6 km) C 161 (259.1 km) College Road exit to west and access to Bentley Mall and University of Alaska.

F 1.4 (2.3 km) C 160.6 (258.5 km) Trainer Gate Road; access to Fort Wainright.

F 2 (3.2 km) C 160 (257.5 km) Johansen Expressway (Old Steese Highway) to west, City Lights Boulevard to east.

F 2.8 (4.5 km) C 159.2 (256.2 km) Fairhill Road; access to Birch Hill Recreation Area, 2.3 miles/3.7 km from the highway via a paved road. Access to Farmers Loop Road to west; residential areas of Birch Hill, Fairhill, Murray Highlands and View Crest to east. Birch Hill Recreation Area is mainly for winter use as a cross-country ski area; open from 8 A.M. to 10 P.M.; picnic areas, toilets, firepits and hiking trails. Day-use only.

F 4.9 (7.9 km) C 157.1 (252.8 km) Chena Hot Springs Road underpass, exits both sides of highway. Turn east at exit for Chena Hot Springs Road; see CHENA HOT SPRINGS ROAD log on pages 471–472. Turn west for grocery, gas and pay phone at Old Steese Highway.

F 6.4 (10.3 km) C 155.6 (250.4 km) Steele Creek Road. Exit for Bennett Road, Hagelbarger Road, Old Steese Highway and Gilmore trail. Exit to left northbound for scenic view of Fairbanks.

F 7 (11.3 km) C 155 (249.4 km) View of pipeline from top of hill.

F 7.6 (12.2 km) C 154.4 (248.4 km) Watch for frost heaves.

F 8 (12.9 km) C 154 (247.8 km) End 4-lane divided highway, begin 2 lanes, northbound. *CAUTION: Watch for moose.*

F 8.4 (13.5 km) C 153.6 (247.2 km) Trans–Alaska pipeline viewpoint with interpretive displays. Excellent opportunity for pipeline photos. Alyeska Pipeline Service Co. visitor center open May to September, 7 days a week. Free literature and information; phone (907) 456-9391. Highway parallels pipeline.

F 9.5 (15.3 km) C 152.5 (245.4 km) Goldstream Road exit to Old Steese Highway and Gold Dredge Number 8. The dredge, built in 1928, was added to the list of national historic sites in 1984 and designated a National Historical Mechanical Engineering Landmark in 1986. The 5-deck, 250-foot-long dredge operated until 1959; it is now pri-

STEESE HIGHWAY
Fairbanks, AK to Circle, AK

Yukon River

Circle ▲ ✈
C-0
F-162/261km

F-162/260.7km H.C. Company Store dGrST
Yukon Trading Post CGIMPST

Birch Creek

6

Crabb's Corner L
Central Motor Inn & Campground CGILMT

Medicine Lake

Circle Hot Springs ▲ ✈
J-8/13km

F-127.7/205.5km Crabb's Corner L
F-127.5/205.2km Central Motor Inn & Campground CGILMT
J-8.3/13.4km Circle Hot Springs Resort CLM

South Fork

Central ✈

Harrison Creek

C-35/56km
J-0
F-128/205km

Porcupine Creek

Deadwood Creek

Mammoth Creek

North Fork

Birch Creek

Eagle Summit
3,624 ft./1,105m

South Fork

Crooked Cr.

Albert Creek

Porcupine Dome
4,915 ft./1,498m

Pinnell Mountain
4,721 ft./1,439m

Eagle Creek

North Fork

Ptarmigan Cr.

Twelvemile Cr.

Twelvemile Summit
2,982 ft./909m

C-76/123km
F-86/138km

McManus Dome
4,184 ft./1,275m

McManus Cr.

Faith Cr.

Sourdough Cr.

Cripple Cr.

Chatanika River

TANANA HILLS

Chena Hot Springs ▲ ✈
J-57/91km

F-56.5/90.9km Chena Hot Springs Resort CDILMPT

North Fork

Monument Creek

West Fork

East Fork

Chena Hot Springs Road

Angel Cr.

Chena River

Little Chena River

Colorado Cr.

C-151/243km
F-11/18km

Jenny M Creek

F-25.9/41.7km Snowy River Bed & Breakfast L
F-23.9/38.5km Pleasant Valley RV Park CDT
F-23.5/37.8km Tack's General Store and Greenhouse Cafe dGIMST

Fish Creek

Gold Dredge Number 8

Steese Expressway

Badger Road

Nordale Road

2

North Pole

To Delta Junction
(see ALASKA HIGHWAY section)

South Fork

F-31/49.9km Farthest North Chatanika RV Park CD
F-28.6/46km Chatanika Lodge CILMPT
F-27.9/44.9km Old F.E. Gold Camp LM

McKay Cr.
Moose Cr.
Long Cr.
Grouse Cr.
Ptarmigan Cr.
Kokomo Cr.

Belle Cr.

Crooked Cr.

O Cleary

Cleary Summit
2,233 ft./681m

F-13.7/22km White Fox Inn B&B L

F-9.5/15.3km

6

Pedro Dome
2,600 ft./792m

Fox ▲

2

To Livengood
(see ELLIOTT HIGHWAY section)

F-11/17.7km Fox General Store GS
Howling Dog Saloon M

Chatanika River

C-157/253km
J-0
F-5/8km

3

Old Steese Highway

To Anchorage
(see GEORGE PARKS HIGHWAY section)

Fairbanks
? ▲ ✈
C-162/261km
F-0

Tanana River

WHITE MOUNTAINS

Trans-Alaska Pipeline

N E S W

vately owned and open to the public for tours (admission fee).

Historic Gold Dredge No. 8. Gold Dredge No. 8 is a monument to the miners who used the machinery to produce more than 7.5 million ounces of gold and the engineers who built it. Visitors tour the only dredge in Alaska open to the public. Gold panning and a Miner's buffet lunch are also available at this national historic site. See advertisement in FAIRBANKS section. [ADVERTISEMENT]

F 10.4 (16.7 km) **C 151.6** (244 km) Road to permafrost tunnel to east (research area, not open to public). Excavated in the early 1960s, the tunnel is maintained cooperatively by the University of Alaska Fairbanks and the U.S. Army Cold Regions Research and Engineering Laboratory.

F 11 (17.7 km) **C 151** (243 km) End of Steese Expressway. Weigh station. Check here for current information on Dalton Highway conditions. Turn east at this junction for continuation of Steese Highway, which now becomes Alaska Route 6 (log follows). Continue straight ahead (north) on Alaska Route 2, which now becomes the Elliott Highway, for access to a private RV park, the Dalton Highway and Manley Hot Springs (see ELLIOTT HIGHWAY section for details).

Turn west for Old Steese Highway and for **FOX,** a once famous mining camp established before 1905 and named for nearby Fox Creek. Gas, food and lodging.

Fox General Store. Located at the crossroads of Steese Expressway and Elliott Highway; the gateway to fishing, camping, hunting and mining. Last gas for 117 miles when traveling north on Steese, and next to last gas for 150 miles when traveling north on Elliott. Gas, grocery, beer, liquor, Alaskana gifts and last chance for hunting and fishing licenses. [ADVERTISEMENT]

Howling Dog Saloon. Mile 11.5, Old Steese. Farthest north rock and roll bar in the world. Genuine Alaskan atmosphere. Live music Wednesday–Sunday. Pizza Tuesday–Sunday, 4–whenever. All night volleyball and horseshoes. Famous T-shirts available in person or mail order. P.O. Box 10701, Fox, AK 99710. (907) 457-8780. [ADVERTISEMENT]

ALASKA ROUTE 6

F 13.6 (21.9 km) **C 148.4** (238.8 km) Eisele Road; turnoff on right northbound for
(Continues on page 473)

Fox General Store

Gas • Groceries • Beer
Liquor • Alaskana Gifts
Fishing licenses

Mile 11.5 Steese Highway
Fox, Alaska
Phone
(907) 457-8903
Fax
(907) 457-2014

Chena Hot Springs Road Log

This paved road, open year-round, leads 56.5 miles/90.9 km east to Chena Hot Springs, a private resort open daily year-round. Chena Hot Springs Road passes through the middle of Chena River Recreation Area, 254,000 acres of mostly undeveloped river bottom and alpine uplands. This is an exceptional year-round recreation area with picnic sites, campgrounds, hiking trails and easy access to the Chena River, one of the most popular grayling fisheries in the state. *IMPORTANT: Check current ADF&G regulations regarding the taking of any fish.*

*NOTE: Watch for paving under way between **Mileposts J 0** and **J 7** in 1997. Also watch for trucks and crews doing erosion control and flood repair work between **Mileposts J 28** and **J 48**.* (Motorists from Fairbanks or North Pole can avoid the road construction by using Badger Road from the Richardson Highway, **Milepost V 349.5** or **V 357.1**, to access Nordale Road, which connects with Chena Hot Springs Road at Milepost J 6.4.)

Distance is measured from junction with the Steese Highway (J).

J 0 Chena Hot Springs Road exit at Milepost F 4.9 Steese Highway.
J 0.5 (0.8 km) Bad frost heaves.
J 1.8 (2.9 km) Bennett Road.
J 3.5 (5.6 km) Steele Creek Road.
J 4 (6.4 km) Frost heaves.
J 5.3 (8.5 km) Eberhard Road; access to bed and breakfast.
J 6.4 (10.3 km) Nordale Road.
J 8.3 (13.4 km) Paved double-ended turnout to south.
J 10.3 (16.6 km) Mini-mart, public dumpster.
J 11.9 (19.2 km) Bridge over Little Chena River. Water gauging station in middle of bridge. This Army Corps of Engineers flood control project, completed in 1979, was designed to prevent floods such as the one which devastated Fairbanks in 1967.
J 14 (22.5 km) Bumpy paved double-ended turnout to south.
J 15 (24.1 km) Rough road next 2 miles/3.2 km eastbound.
J 18 (29 km) Watch for moose.

Camping along Chena Hot Springs Road. (© Craig Brandt)

J 18.6 (29.9 km) Two Rivers Road. Access to Two Rivers School and Two Rivers Recreation Area (maintained by Fairbanks North Star Borough) with cross-country ski and hiking trails. Public dumpster.
J 20.1 (32.3 km) Jenny M. Creek. Some 2,000 people reside along the road.
J 20.2 (32.5 km) Large, double-ended paved parking area to south.
J 23.4 (37.7 km) Grocery with gas; public dumpster.
J 23.5 (37.8 km) Store; Two Rivers post office is in store.
Tacks' General Store and Greenhouse Cafe. See display ad this section.
J 23.9 (38.5 km) **Pleasant Valley RV Park.** Quiet country setting near entrance to Chena River Recreation Area. Fishing, hiking, biking, ATV trails. All pull-throughs. Water and electric hookups, restrooms and dump station. Tent sites, firepits, free firewood. Gift shop, pay phone. Laundromat and showers available. Convenient to local amenities. P.O. Box 16019, Two Rivers,

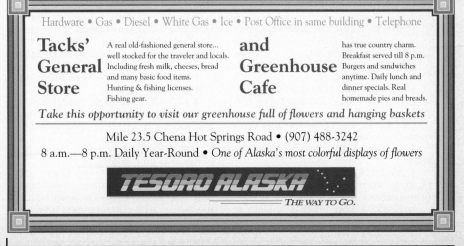

Hardware • Gas • Diesel • White Gas • Ice • Post Office in same building • Telephone

Tacks' General Store A real old-fashioned general store... well stocked for the traveler and locals. Including fresh milk, cheeses, bread and many basic food items. Hunting & fishing licenses. Fishing gear. **and Greenhouse Cafe** has true country charm. Breakfast served till 8 p.m. Burgers and sandwiches anytime. Daily lunch and dinner specials. Real homemade pies and breads.

Take this opportunity to visit our greenhouse full of flowers and hanging baskets

Mile 23.5 Chena Hot Springs Road • (907) 488-3242
8 a.m.—8 p.m. Daily Year-Round • *One of Alaska's most colorful displays of flowers*

TESORO ALASKA — THE WAY TO GO.

Route 2 • STEESE HIGHWAY • Chena Hot Springs Road

1997 ■ The MILEPOST® 471

AK 99716. Phone (907)488-8711. MasterCard, VISA accepted. [ADVERTISEMENT] ▲

J 25.6 (41.2 km) HIPAS Observatory, UCLA Plasma Physics Lab (Geophysical Institute Chena Radio Facility).

J 25.9 (41.7 km) **Snowy River Bed & Breakfast.** Mile 25.9. Attractive, clean log cabin. 35 minutes from Fairbanks in a private setting on the Chena River. Fishing, guided/unguided, hiking trails, float trips, canoe/raft rentals, wildlife viewing, photography and northern lights viewing. Available year round. No smoking/pets. B&B in a true Alaskan setting. Full breakfast available. (907) 488-7517. [ADVERTISEMENT]

J 26.1 (42 km) Entering **Chena River** Recreation Area. No shooting except at target range. Grayling fishing (check current regulations). ✦

J 26.5 (42.6 km) Flat Creek culvert.

J 26.7 (43 km) Paved turnout to south for picnic area with tables and toilets.

J 27 (43.5 km) Rosehip state campground to south; 25 sites, picnic tables, firepits, toilets, water, $8 nightly fee or annual pass. Large, flat, gravel pads and an easy 0.7-mile/1.1-km loop road make this a good campground for large RVs and trailers. ▲

Canoe exit point. The Chena is popular with paddlers, but should not be underestimated: The river is cold and the current very strong. Watch for river-wide logjams and sweepers. Secure your gear in waterproof containers. Local paddlers suggest a float from **Milepost J 39.5** to **J 37.9** for easy paddling; **J 44** to **J 37.9** for a longer float; and **J 52.3** to **J 47.3** for paddlers with more skill. Allow about an hour on the river for each road mile traveled.

J 27.5 (44.3 km) Paved turnout to south.

J 27.9 (44.9 km) Toilets and access to river via road to south which leads 0.9 mile/1.4 km to large parking area with picnic tables, dumpster, loop turnaround. Canoe exit point.

J 28.8 (46.3 km) Access road to river, drive 0.7 mile/1.1 km south to canoe launch in brushy area along river; picnic table, toilet, dumpster, parking.

J 29.4 (47.3 km) Pleasant double-ended paved turnout to south on Chena River; picnic table.

J 30 (48.3 km) Outdoor education camp (available for rent by groups). Small lake stocked with grayling. ✦

J 31.3 (50.4 km) Bridge over Colorado Creek. River access.

J 31.5 (50.7 km) River access.

J 31.8 (51.2 km) Colorado Creek ATV trail.

J 33.9 (54.6 km) Fourmile Creek flows under the road.

J 35.8 (57.6 km) Paved turnout to south.

J 36.5 (58.7 km) Target shooting range to north. ORV trails, toilets and picnic tables. Cathedral Bluffs view.

J 37 (59.5 km) Road is subject to flooding after heavy rains.

J 37.9 (61 km) First bridge over the **North Fork Chena River.** Water gauge in center of bridge. There are 3 stream flow meters on the upper Chena. Grayling fishing (check current special regulations).

Side road leaves highway to the south and forks. Left fork is a short road to the river and toilet; right fork leads 0.2 mile/0.3 km to picnic tables by the river. Canoe launch. This road is bordered by dense underbrush which may scratch wide vehicles.

J 39.2 (63.1 km) Paved turnout to south.

J 39.5 (63.6 km) Second bridge over North Fork Chena River. Loop road through Granite Tors trail state campground; 20 large sites among tall spruce trees, parking area, water, toilets, tables, firepits, $8 nightly fee or annual pass. Canoe launch. Picnic area on loop road along river. ▲

Trailhead for Granite Tors trail; follow dike (levee) on west side upstream 0.3 mile/0.5 km to trail sign. It is a 6-mile/9.7-km hike to the nearest tors, 8 miles/12.9 km to the main grouping. Tors are isolated pinnacles of granite jutting up from the tundra.

J 39.7 (63.9 km) A 0.2-mile/0.3-km side road leads south to Chena River picnic area with tables, toilets and a riverbank of flat rocks ideal for sunbathing.

J 39.8 (64.1 km) Campground loop road exit; toilet beside road.

J 41.8 (67.3 km) Paved turnout to south by slough.

J 42.1 (67.8 km) Large turnout south of road. Watch for muskrats and beaver in ponds here.

J 42.8 (68.9 km) Mile 43 Red Squirrel picnic area to north, one of the nicest on this road, with covered tables, firepits, toilets, water and dumpster. Located on edge of small lake stocked with grayling. Watch for moose. ✦

J 43.8 (70.5 km) Small lake to north stocked with grayling.

J 44.1 (71 km) Third bridge over North Fork Chena River. Picnic area with tables and toilets to north at east end of bridge. A favorite place to sunbathe and fish. Canoe launch. ✦

J 45.7 (73.5 km) Fourth bridge over North Fork Chena River.

J 46 (74 km) Paved turnout to south.

J 46.8 (75.3 km) **Chena River** flows alongside the road; good access point for fishermen. Paved parking to south opposite river. ✦

J 47.3 (76.1 km) Access to river north side of road.

J 47.9 (77.1 km) Side road leads 0.1 mile/0.2 km south to **48-Mile Pond.** Stocked with grayling; picnic tables, informal campsites. ✦

J 48.8 (78.5 km) Watch for people and horses next mile eastbound.

J 48.9 (78.7 km) Angel Rocks trailhead; table, toilet, dumpster. Angel Rocks trail is a 3.5-mile/5.6-km loop trail to spectacular rock outcroppings; strenuous hike.

J 49 (78.9 km) Fifth bridge over North Fork Chena River; parking. Excellent fishing from here. ✦

J 49.1 (79 km) Lower Chena Dome trailhead. Side road leads 0.2 mile/0.3 km north to trailhead, parking, water, dumpster and toilets.

J 49.3 (79.3 km) Cathedral Bluffs, an unusual rock formation to southeast.

J 49.9 (80.3 km) Paved turnout to north. Angel Creek, grayling 12 to 17 inches. ✦

J 50.5 (81.3 km) Chena Dome trailhead; this 29-mile/47-km loop trail exits at **Milepost J 49.1.** Angel Creek Cabin ATV trailhead (6 miles/10 km). Parking, toilets. Bring mosquito repellent!

J 50.7 (81.6 km) Chena River Recreation Area boundary.

J 52.3 (84.2 km) Bridge over West Fork Chena River. Gravel side road leads south to parking area along the river. *CAUTION: Abrupt approaches to bridge.*

J 55.3 (89 km) North Fork Chena River bridge. Double-ended paved turnout to south.

J 56.5 (90.9 km) **CHENA HOT SPRINGS:** food, lodging, camping, bar and swimming. There is an airstrip at the lodge. ▲

The Resort at Chena Hot Springs. Interior Alaska's year-round visitor destination. Relax, refresh, and rejuvenate in the natural spring-fed pool and spas. Enjoy the cozy lodge, comfortable hotel rooms, rustic cabins, spacious campground and RV parking (electric hookups, dump station and water avail

able). Each season offers unlimited recreational opportunities. Enjoy the scenic 1-hour drive from Fairbanks. Summer solstice brings gold panning, hiking, horseback riding, historical and naturalist walking excursions, and mountain biking. Plus other activities like basketball, volleyball, horseshoes and picnicking areas. Fishing and boating areas are conveniently nearby. Massage therapy sessions available all year. Winter activities feature aurora viewing, dogsled rides, cross-country skiing, ice fishing, horse-drawn sleigh rides, ice skating, snowshoeing and guided snow machine rides. P.O. Box 73440-MP, Fairbanks, AK 99707, (907) 452-7867, or instate (800) 478-4681. See display ad in FAIRBANKS section. [ADVERTISEMENT] ▲

**Return to Milepost F 4.9
Steese Highway**

Fishing for grayling along the Chatanika River. (Jerrianne Lowther, staff)

banks Exploration Co. gold camp at **CHATANIKA**, built in 1925 to support gold dredging operations in the valley. Between 1926 and 1957 the F.E. Co. removed an estimated $70 million in gold. The gold camp is on the National Register of Historic Places.

Old F.E. Gold Camp. The historic Fairbanks Exploration Co. gold camp, built in 1925 and on the National Register of Historic Places, offers food and lodging year-round at competitive rates. The original bunkhouses now house a bar, lounge and dining room with complete lunch and dinner menus, and a famous Sunday brunch. The 50-acre site has numerous trails for backpacking, bicycling and berry picking, as well as dogsled trips by local musher Beverly Tolmie from Awl Alaskan Kennels. Float the wild and scenic Chatanika River and fish for grayling. You can experience winter snow machining, cross-country skiing and spectacular northern lights viewing here at the gateway to the White Mountains wilderness area. All arrangements can be made by calling your host, Jack Chrestensen, at (907) 389-2414. See display ad. [ADVERTISEMENT]

F 28.6 (46 km) **C 133.4** (214.7 km) Old gold dredge behind tailing piles to west (private property, *DO NOT TRESPASS*). Lodge to east with meals and lodging.

Chatanika Lodge. Cafe open 9 A.M. daily (year-round). Halibut/catfish fry Friday and Saturday, country-fried chicken on Sunday,

(Continued from page 471)

NOAA/NESDIS Command and Data Acquisition Station at Gilmore Creek. This facility monitors 2 polar orbiting satellites. Tours of the satellite tracking station are available 9 A.M. to 4 P.M., Monday through Saturday, from June through August. Phone (907) 451-1200 for more information.

F 13.7 (22 km) **C 148.3** (238.7 km) White Fox Inn Bed & Breakfast. See display ad this section.

F 16.4 (26.4 km) **C 145.6** (234.3 km) Turnout by gold-bearing creek. Now privately claimed; no recreational gold panning permitted.

F 16.5 (26.6 km) **C 145.5** (234.2 km) Gravel turnout to west. Monument to Felix Pedro, the prospector who discovered gold on Pedro Creek in July 1902 and started the rush that resulted in the founding of Fairbanks.

F 17.6 (28.3 km) **C 144.4** (232.4 km) Gravel turnout to east. Winding ascent northbound to Cleary Summit area.

F 19.6 (31.5 km) **C 142.4** (229.2 km) Large gravel turnout to east.

F 20.5 (33 km) **C 141.5** (227.7 km) Cleary Summit (elev. 2,233 feet/681m) has a weekend ski area in winter. Named for early prospector Frank Cleary. On a clear day there are excellent views of the Tanana Valley and Mount McKinley to the south and the White Mountains to the north. Road north to Pedro Dome military site.

Fairbanks Creek Road to the south leads several miles along a ridge crest; access to Fish Creek Road and dirt roads leading to Solo Creek, Bear Creek and Fairbanks Creek.

Highway descends steep grade northbound. Watch for frost heaves.

F 20.6 (33.2 km) **C 141.4** (227.6 km) View of current mining operation and old buildings from early mining and dredging on Cleary Creek below.

F 21 (33.8 km) **C 141** (226.9 km) Double-ended paved turnout east.

F 23.9 (38.5 km) **C 138.1** (222.2 km) Gravel turnout to east. Watch for frost heaves.

F 27.6 (44.4 km) **C 134.4** (216.3 km) Tailings (gravel and boulders of dredged streambeds) from early mining activity which yielded millions of dollars in gold. There is quite a bit of mining in the Chatanika area now.

F 27.9 (44.9 km) **C 134.1** (215.8 km) Sharp right turn up hill for historic Fair-

Hoary marmot, a common furbearer in Alaska. (© Bill Sherwonit)

served family-style, all you can eat. Diamond Willow Lounge. Rustic atmosphere, Alaska artifacts. Historic Alaska gold dredge across from lodge, plus aurora borealis videos on big-screen TV. Good grayling fishing. Great winter snow machining on groomed trails; snow machine rentals. Rooms $45 to $50. See display ad this section. [ADVERTISEMENT]

F 29.5 (47.5 km) C 132.5 (213.2 km) Neal Brown Road to Poker Flat rocket facility; off-limits except to authorized personnel. The Poker Flat rocket range, operated by the Geophysical Institute, University of Alaska, is dedicated to unclassified auroral and upper atmospheric research. It is the only university-owned sounding rocket range in the world and the only high latitude and auroral zone launch facility on U.S. soil. Tours for interested groups may be arranged by calling (907) 474-7798.

Fishing at gravel pit ponds from here north to **Milepost F 39.5**. Ponds are stocked with grayling. (Watch for green signs at access points.) ◄●

F 31 (49.9 km) C 131 (210.8 km) **Farthest North Chatanika RV Park.** See display ad this section. ▲

F 31.4 (50.5 km) C 130.6 (210.2 km) Double-ended gravel turnout to west by pond; stocked with grayling. ◄●

F 32.3 (52 km) C 129.7 (208.7 km) Captain Creek bridge. Watch for frost heaves.

F 32.5 (52.3 km) C 129.5 (208.4 km) *CAUTION: Severe frost heaves and cracks in*

pavement next 0.2 mile/0.3 km northbound.

F 35 (56.3 km) C 127 (204.4 km) Access to Chatanika River. Double-ended paved turnout to west.

F 36.5 (58.7 km) C 125.5 (202 km) Gravel turnout alongside ponds to west. Pond stocked with grayling. ◄●

F 37.1 (59.7 km) C 124.9 (201 km) *CAUTION: Severe frost heaves and dips in pavement next 0.1 mile/0.2 km northbound.*

F 37.3 (60 km) C 124.7 (200.7 km) Kokomo Creek bridge.

F 39 (62.8 km) C 123 (197.9 km) Chatanika River bridge. Upper Chatanika River State Recreation Site, just north of the bridge, is a beautiful state campground on the riverbank. There are 25 sites with fireplaces and a gravel parking area near the bridge. A water pump is at the entrance. Firewood is usually available during the summer. Camping fee $8/night or annual pass. Look for wild roses here in June. ▲

Boats can be launched on the gravel bars by the river. Bring your mosquito repellent. This is an access point to the Chatanika River canoe trail. See **Milepost F 60** for more information on canoeing this river.

Chatanika River, grayling 8 to 20 inches, use flies or spinners, May to September. ◄●

F 39.5 (63.5 km) C 122.5 (197.1 km) **39.3 Mile Pond**, to west, is stocked with grayling. ◄●

F 40.2 (64.7 km) C 121.8 (196 km) *CAUTION: Watch for severe dips in highway surface.*

F 40.4 (65 km) C 121.6 (195.7 km) Bridge over Crooked Creek.

F 41.5 (66.8 km) C 120.5 (193.9 km) Bridge over Belle Creek. Most homes here are those of permanent residents.

F 42.7 (68.7 km) C 119.3 (192 km) Bridge over McKay Creek.

F 42.9 (69 km) C 119.1 (191.7 km) Turnout to east.

F 43.8 (70.5 km) C 118.2 (190.2 km) Pavement ends; it is good gravel road to Circle with the exception of a short stretch of blacktop at Central. Highway parallels the Chatanika River for the next 10 miles/16 km.

F 45.4 (73.1 km) C 116.6 (187.6 km) **Long Creek** bridge. Grayling 8 to 14 inches, use spinners or flies, May to September. Beautiful view of Chatanika River. ◄●

F 49 (78.9 km) C 113 (181.9 km) View down Chatanika River valley to east.

F 53.5 (86.1 km) C 108.5 (174.6 km) Ptarmigan Creek in valley below highway.

F 57.1 (91.9 km) C 104.9 (168.8 km) White Mountains National Recreation Area (BLM). Access to this area's trails and cabins is from the Elliott Highway.

F 57.3 (92.2 km) C 104.7 (168.5 km) U.S. Creek to west. The large pipe near U.S. Creek was part of the Davidson Ditch, built in 1925 by the Fairbanks Exploration Co., to carry water to float gold dredges. The 83-mile/133.6-km-long ditch, designed and engineered by J.B. Lippincott, begins near **Milepost F 64** on the Steese Highway and ends near Fox. A system of ditches and inverted siphons, the pipeline was capable of carrying 56,100 gallons per minute. After the dredges closed, the water was used for power until 1967, when a flood destroyed a bridge and flattened almost 1,000 feet/305m of pipe.

All-weather road leads 6 miles/9.7 km west to Nome Creek; recreational gold panning. There are some mining claims on

Nome Creek. No dredges allowed. The road to Nome Creek is very steep and not recommended for large or underpowered vehicles. Nome Creek is a historic mining area; additional recreational facilities are under development by the BLM.

F 59 (94.9 km) C 103 (165.8 km) Wide double-ended gravel parking area to east.

F 60 (96.6 km) C 102 (164.1 km) Cripple Creek BLM campground (7-day limit), 6 tent, 15 trailer sites; water pumps, fireplaces, toilets, tables, nature trail. Parking for walk-in campers. Firewood is usually available all summer. Recreational gold panning permitted. *Bring mosquito repellent!* ▲

Access to Cripple Creek BLM recreation cabin. Preregister and pay $10 fee at BLM office, 1150 University Ave., Fairbanks, AK 99709; phone (907) 474-2200.

Cripple Creek bridge is the uppermost access point to the Chatanika River canoe trail (follow side road near campground entrance to canoe launch site). *CAUTION: This canoe trail may not be navigable at low water.* The Chatanika River is a clear-water Class II stream. The Steese Highway parallels the river for approximately 28 miles/45 km and there are many access points to the highway downstream from the Cripple Creek bridge. No major obstacles on this canoe trail, but watch for overhanging trees. Downstream pullout points are Perhaps Creek, Long Creek and Chatanika Campground.

F 62.3 (100.3 km) C 99.7 (160.4 km) Viewpoint to east overlooking Chatanika River.

F 63.4 (102 km) C 98.6 (158.7 km) View of historic Davidson Ditch pipeline.

F 65 (104.6 km) C 97 (156.1 km) Side road east to viewpoint.

F 65.6 (105.6 km) C 96.4 (155.1 km) Sourdough Creek bridge.

F 65.7 (105.7 km) C 96.3 (155 km) Mile 66. Double-ended turnout to east; Davidson Ditch viewpoint; lodge.

F 66 (106.2 km) C 96 (154.5 km) Sourdough Creek Road (unmarked) to north.

F 69 (111 km) C 93 (149.7 km) Faith Creek bridge and road. Creek access to east at north end of bridge. Large parking area to west.

F 72 (115.9 km) C 90 (144.8 km) View ahead for northbound travelers of highway route along mountains, McManus Creek below.

F 73.8 (118.8 km) C 88.2 (141.9 km) Faith Creek Road to west.

F 79.1 (127.3 km) C 82.9 (133.4 km) Road widens for parking next 500 feet/152m.

F 80.1 (128.9 km) C 81.9 (131.8 km) Montana Creek state highway maintenance station. Montana Creek runs under road and into McManus Creek to the east. McManus Dome (elev. 4,184 feet/1,275m) to west.

F 81.2 (130.7 km) C 80.8 (130 km) Turnout to east. Spring water (untested) piped to roadside. Wide gravel highway begins ascent to Twelvemile Summit. *NOTE: Watch for road construction northbound to* **Milepost F 125** *in 1997.*

F 83 (133.6 km) C 79 (127.1 km) Sharp turn to right northbound. Watch for the hoary marmot and other small mammals.

F 85.5 (137.6 km) C 76.5 (123.1 km) Large parking area and viewpoint to east at Twelvemile Summit (elev. 2,982 feet/909m) on the divide of the Yukon and Tanana river drainages. Wildflowers carpet the alpine tundra slopes. Entering Game Management

Unit 25C, leaving unit 20B, northbound. Fairbanks–North Star Borough limits. This is caribou country; from here to beyond Eagle Summit (**Milepost F 108**) migrating bands of caribou may be seen from late July through mid-September.

Access to Pinnell Mountain national recreation trail (Twelvemile Summit trailhead). The trail is also accessible from **Milepost F 107.1**. Named in honor of Robert Pinnell, who was fatally injured in 1952 while climbing nearby Porcupine Dome. This 27-mile-/43-km-long hiking trail winds through alpine terrain, along mountain ridges and through high passes. Highest elevation point reached is 4,721 feet/1,439m. The trail is marked by rock cairns. Shelter cabins at Mile 10.7 and Mile 17.7. Vantage points along the trail with views of the White Mountains, Tanana Hills, Brooks Range and Alaska Range. Watch for willow ptarmigan, hoary marmot, rock pika, moose, wolf and caribou. Mid-May through July is the prime time for wildflowers, with flowers peaking in mid-June. Carry drinking water and insect repellent at all times. Additional information on this trail is available from the Bureau of Land Management, 1150 University Ave., Fairbanks, AK 99708-3844; phone (907) 474-2350.

F 88 (141.6 km) **C 74** (119.1 km) Twelvemile Creek to east below road.

F 88.7 (142.7 km) **C 73.3** (118 km) Bridge over Reed Creek.

F 90.5 (145.6 km) **C 71.5** (115.1 km) Double-ended turnout to east.

F 93.4 (150.3 km) **C 68.6** (110.4 km) Bridge over the North Fork Twelvemile Creek. Nice picnic spot to west below bridge.

F 94 (151.3 km) **C 68** (109.4 km) Side road leads 0.2 mile/0.3 km down to north fork of Birch Creek; parking area and canoe launch for Birch Creek canoe trail. This is the main put-in point for canoeing Birch Creek, a Wild and Scenic River. Undeveloped campsite by creek. Extensive mining in area. **Birch Creek**, grayling to 12 inches; use flies, June to October. 🐟

F 95.8 (154.2 km) **C 66.2** (106.5 km) Bridge over Willow Creek.

Much gold mining activity along this part of the highway. These are private mining claims. *IMPORTANT: Do not trespass. Do not approach mining equipment without permission.*

F 97.6 (157.1 km) **C 64.4** (103.6 km) Bridge over Bear Creek.

F 98 (157.7 km) **C 64** (103 km) Gold mine and settling ponds in creek valley to east.

F 99.7 (160.4 km) **C 62.3** (100.3 km) Bridge over Fish Creek. Privately owned cabins.

F 101.5 (163.3 km) **C 60.5** (97.4 km) Bridge over Ptarmigan Creek (elev. 2,398 feet/731m). Alpine meadows carpeted with wildflowers in spring and summer for next 9 miles/14.5 km. *NOTE: Avalanche gates may be closed if road conditions are hazardous over the summit.*

F 102.3 (164.6 km) **C 59.7** (96.1 km) Ptarmigan Creek access to west.

F 103 (165.8 km) **C 59** (94.9 km) Good view of mining operation next mile northbound.

F 104.6 (168.3 km) **C 57.4** (92.4 km) Snowpoles guide snowplows in winter.

F 105.4 (169.6 km) **C 56.6** (91.1 km) Large gravel parking area to west.

F 107.1 (172.4 km) **C 54.9** (88.4 km) Parking area to west. Pinnell Mountain trail access (Eagle Summit trailhead); see description at **Milepost F 85.5**.

F 108 (173.8 km) **C 54** (86.9 km) Eagle Summit (elev. 3,624 feet/1,105m) to the east. Steep, narrow, rocky side road leads from the highway 0.8 mile/1.3 km to the summit. This is the third and highest of 3 summits (including Cleary and Twelvemile) along the Steese Highway. *NOTE: Gates at* **Milepost F 101.5** *and* **F 114.2** *across the highway may be closed in bad weather.* Favorite spot for local residents to observe summer solstice (weather permitting) on June 21. Best wildflower viewing on Alaska highway system.

Scalloped waves of soil on hillsides to west are called solifluction lobes. These are formed when meltwater saturates the thawed surface soil, which then flows slowly downhill.

Wildflowers found here include: dwarf forget-me-nots, alpine rhododendron or rosebay, rock jasmine, alpine azalea, arctic bell heather, mountain avens, Jacob's ladder, anemones, wallflowers, Labrador tea, lupine, oxytropes, gentians and louseworts. The museum in Central has a photographic display of Eagle Summit alpine flowers to help highway travelers identify the wildflowers of this area.

F 109.2 (175.7 km) **C 52.8** (85 km) Large parking area to east with view down into Miller Creek far below. Excellent wildflower display. Highway begins steep descent northbound.

F 114.2 (183.8 km) **C 47.8** (76.9 km) Parking area to east looking down onto the Mastodon and Mammoth creeks area. Avalanche gates.

F 114.4 (184.1 km) **C 47.6** (76.6 km) Side road to east leads to Mammoth and Mastodon creeks; active gold placer mining areas.

F 116.2 (187 km) **C 45.8** (73.7 km) Road east to creek.

F 116.4 (187.3 km) **C 45.6** (73.4 km) Bridge over Mammoth Creek. Near here fossil remains of many species of preglacial Alaskan mammals have been excavated and may be seen at the University of Alaska museum in Fairbanks and at the museum in Central.

F 117 (188.3 km) **C 45** (72.4 km) Highway crosses over Stack Pup. From here the highway gradually descends to Central.

F 117.6 (189.3 km) **C 44.4** (71.5 km) Parking area to west.

F 119.1 (191.7 km) **C 42.9** (69 km) Bedrock Creek.

F 119.2 (191.8 km) **C 42.8** (68.9 km) Narrow dirt road leads to site of former Bedrock Creek BLM campground; closed.

F 121 (194.7 km) **C 41** (66 km) Bridge over Sawpit Creek.

F 122.5 (197.1 km) **C 39.5** (63.6 km) Road west to parking space by pond.

F 125.4 (201.8 km) **C 36.6** (58.9 km) Bridge over Boulder Creek.

F 126.8 (204.1 km) **C 35.2** (56.6 km) Paved highway begins and continues through Central. *NOTE: Road construction ends northbound, 1997.*

F 127.1 (204.5 km) **C 34.9** (56.2 km) Central elementary school.

F 127.5 (205.2 km) **C 34.5** (55.5 km) **CENTRAL** (pop. approximately 400 in summer, 130 in winter; elev. 965 feet/ 294m). **Radio**: KUAC-FM 91.7. This small community, formerly called Central House, is situated on Crooked Creek along the Steese Highway.

Central is the central point in the huge Circle Mining District, one of the oldest and still one of the most active districts in the state. The annual Circle Mining District Picnic for local miners and their families is held in August.

Central has many facilities for the visitor: state airstrip (see **Milepost F 128.3**), cafes and bars, motel, cabins, laundromat, showers, groceries, gas, tire repair, welding, pay phone and post office (ZIP code 99730). Report fires to BLM. Picnic area at Central Park.

The Circle District Historical Society museum has displays covering the history of the Circle Mining District and its people. Also here are a photo display of wildflowers, fossilized remains of preglacial mammals, a minerals display, library and archives, gift shop and visitor information. Admission is $1 for adults, 50¢ for children under 12; members free. Open daily noon to 5 P.M., Memorial Day through Labor Day.

Central Motor Inn and Campground. See display ad this section. ▲

F 127.7 (205.5 km) **C 34.3** (55.2 km) **Crabb's Corner.** Jim and Sandy are back in business with cabins for rent, overnight RV parking and tenting. Office in Crabb's Corner Gift Shop. Mostly locally made hand-crafted and Yukon Quest items. Visitor information from longtime local residents. Gold mining spoken here. P.O. Box 30109, Central, AK 99730; or call (907) 520-5322. [ADVERTISEMENT]. ▲

F 127.8 (205.7 km) **C 34.2** (55 km) **Junction** with Circle Hot Springs Road; see CIRCLE HOT SPRINGS ROAD log on page 476.

F 127.9 (205.8 km) **C 34.1** (54.9 km) Bridge over Crooked Creek. Site of Central House roadhouse on north side of bridge.

F 128.1 (206.2 km) **C 33.9** (54.6 km) Central DOT/PF highway maintenance station.

F 128.3 (206.5 km) **C 33.7** (54.2 km) **Private Aircraft**: Central state-maintained airstrip, adjacent north; elev. 932 feet/ 284m; length 2,700 feet/823m; gravel; unattended.

Pavement ends northbound. Watch for soft spots, curves and little or no shoulder between here and Circle; otherwise, the road is in good shape. Wildlife is frequently sighted between Central and Circle.

F 130.5 (210 km) **C 31.5** (50.7 km) Pond frequented by a variety of ducks.

F 131.2 (211.1 km) **C 30.8** (49.6 km)

Old cache at Circle Hot Springs.
(© Barbara Willard)

Circle Hot Springs Road Log

Distance is measured from junction with Steese Highway (J).

J 0 Pavement extends first 0.3 mile/ 0.5 km of road.

J 0.9 (1.4 km) Graveyard Road, 0.5 mile/0.8 km to cemetery.

J 1.9 (3.1 km) Deadwood Creek Road.

J 2.9 (4.7 km) Bridge over Deadwood Creek.

J 5.7 (9.2 km) Bridge over Ketchem Creek. Primitive camping at site of former Ketchem Creek BLM campground on right before bridge; no facilities.

J 8.3 (13.4 km) **CIRCLE HOT SPRINGS**; year-round swimming, lodging, food and RV parking. A popular spot with Alaskans.

According to research done by Patricia Oakes of Central, the hot springs were used as a gathering place by area Athabascans before the gold rush. Local prospectors probably used the springs as early as the 1890s. Cassius Monohan homesteaded the site in 1905, selling out to Frank Leach in 1909. Leach built the airstrip, on which Noel Wien landed in 1924. (Wien pioneered many flight routes between Alaska communities.)

Private Aircraft: Circle Hot Springs state-maintained airstrip; elev. 956 feet/ 291m; length 3,600 feet/1,097m; gravel; lighted, unattended.

Return to Milepost F 127.8 Steese Highway

Albert Creek bridge. Small parking area with litter barrel at end of bridge.

F 133 (214 km) **C 29** (46.7 km) Repair shop.

F 147.1 (236.7 km) **C 14.9** (24 km) One-lane bridge over Birch Creek; clearance 13 feet, 11 inches. Turnouts, undeveloped campsites, both ends of bridge. Usual take-out point for the Birch Creek canoe trail.

F 147.6 (237.5 km) **C 14.4** (23.2 km) Turnout to east.

F 148.4 (238.8 km) **C 13.6** (21.9 km) Nice stand of quaking aspen.

F 155.9 (250.9 km) **C 6.1** (9.8 km) Diamond (Bebb) willow along road. Diamond willow is used to make walking sticks.

F 156.7 (252.2 km) **C 5.3** (8.5 km) Large turnout opposite gravel pit. Look for bank swallow nests in cliffs.

F 159.6 (256.8 km) **C 2.4** (3.9 km) Old Indian cemetery to east.

F 161 (259.1 km) **C 1** (1.6 km) Circle post office (ZIP code 99733); airstrip; school.

Circle

F 162 (260.7 km) **C 0** Located on the banks of the Yukon River, 50 miles/ 80.5 km south of the Arctic Circle. The Yukon is Alaska's largest river; the 2,000-mile/3,219-km river heads in Canada and flows west into Norton Sound on the Bering Sea. **Population:** 107.

Elevation: 610 feet/186m. **Climate:** Mean monthly temperature in July 61.4°F/ 16.3°C, in January -10.6°F/-23.7°C. Record high 91°F/ 32.8°C July 1977, record low -69°F/-56°C in February 1991. Snow from October (8 inches) through April (2 inches). Precipitation in the summer averages 1.45 inches a month.

Private Aircraft: Circle City state-maintained airstrip, adjacent west; elev. 610 feet/186m; length 3,000 feet/914m; gravel; fuel 100LL.

Before the Klondike Gold Rush of 1898, Circle City was the largest gold mining town on the Yukon River. Prospectors discovered gold on Birch Creek in 1893, and the town of Circle City (so named because the early miners thought it was located on the Arctic Circle) grew up as the nearest supply point to the new diggings on the Yukon River.

Today, Circle serves a small local population and visitors coming in by highway or by river. The post office is at **Milepost F 161** just before the airstrip and school. Gas, groceries, snacks and sundries are available at 2 local stores. The trading post houses the post office, cafe and liquor store. Hunting and fishing licenses are also available at the trading post. A motel is located just beyond the trading post. There's a lot of summer river traffic here: canoeists put in and take out.

The old Pioneer Cemetery, with its markers dating back to the 1800s, is an interesting spot to visit. Walk a short way upriver (past the old machinery) on the gravel road to a barricade: You will have to cross through a private front yard (please be respectful of property) to get to the trail. Walk straight ahead on the short trail, which goes through dense under brush (many mosquitoes), for about 10 minutes. Watch for a path on your left to the graves, which are scattered among the thick trees.

Camping on the banks of the Yukon at the end of the road; tables, toilets, parking area. In 1989, when the Yukon flooded, water covered the bottom of the welcome sign at the campground entrance. From the campground you are looking at one channel of the mighty Yukon. ▲

H.C. Company Store. See display ad this section.

Yukon Trading Post. See display ad this section.

ELLIOTT HIGHWAY ②

Connects: Fox to Manley Hot Springs, AK   **Length:** 152 miles
Road Surface: Gravel   **Season:** Open all year
Major Attraction: White Mountains National Recreation Area

(See map, page 478)

Mixed spruce, birch and willow along the Elliott Highway; view from Milepost F 118. (Jerrianne Lowther, staff)

	Patton Hwy	Fairbanks	Manley	Minto
Dalton Hwy		84	79	48
Fairbanks	84		163	132
Manley	79	163		53
Minto	48	132	53	

The Elliott Highway leads 152 miles/ 244.6 km from its junction with the Steese Highway at Fox (11 miles/17.7 km north of Fairbanks) to Manley Hot Springs, a small settlement near the Tanana River with a natural hot springs. The highway was named for Malcolm Elliott, president of the Alaska Road Commission from 1927 to 1932.

The first 28 miles/45.1 km of the Elliott Highway are paved; the remaining 124 miles/200 km are gravel. The highway is wide, hard-based gravel to the Dalton Highway junction. (The road is treated with calcium chloride for dust control; wash your vehicle after travel to prevent corrosion.) From that junction until Manley, the road is narrower but fairly smooth with some soft spots and a roller-coaster section near Manley. Gas is available at Milepost F 5.5, probably at Milepost F 49.5 and at Manley.

Watch for heavy truck traffic. Drivers pulling trailers should be especially cautious when the road is wet. The highway is open year-round; check with the Dept. of Transportation in Fairbanks regarding winter road conditions.

The Elliott Highway also provides access to 4 trailheads in the White Mountains National Recreation Area. These hiking trails lead to recreation cabins; the trails and cabins are managed by the BLM in Fairbanks. For more information and cabin registration, contact the BLM office in Fairbanks at 1150 University Ave., Fairbanks, AK 99709; phone (907) 474-2350.

Emergency medical services: Between Fox and Manley Hot Springs, phone the state troopers at 911 or (907) 452-1313. Use CB channels 9, 14, 19.

Elliott Highway Log

ALASKA ROUTE 2
Distance from Fox (F) is followed by distance from Manley Hot Springs (M).

F 0 M 152 (244.6 km) FOX. Junction of the Steese Highway with the Elliott Highway. Weigh station.

F 0.2 (0.3 km) M 151.8 (244.3 km) Private RV park. ▲

F 0.4 (0.6 km) M 151.6 (244 km) Fox Spring picnic area; 2 tables, spring water.

F 1.2 (1.9 km) M 150.8 (242.7 km) Turnoff for Little El Dorado Gold Mine, a commercial gold mine offering tours and gold panning to the public; admission charged.

F 1.8 (2.9 km) M 150.2 (241.7 km) Fort Knox gold mine.

F 3.4 (5.5 km) M 148.6 (239.1 km) Rough side road leads west to Murphy Dome, 28 miles/45 km away. Road is signed "restricted military site."

F 5.5 (8.9 km) M 146.5 (235.8 km) Hilltop Truck Stop. See display ad this section.

F 7.5 (12.1 km) M 144.5 (232.5 km) Views to the east of Pedro Dome and Dome Creek. Buildings of Dome and Eldorado camps are in the valley below to the east (best view is southbound).

F 8.6 (13.8 km) M 143.4 (230.8 km) Dome Creek Road to east (right northbound).

F 9.2 (14.8 km) M 142.8 (229.8 km) Olnes, former railroad station of Tanana Valley Railroad and mining camp. Old tailings and abandoned cabins.

F 10.6 (17.1 km) M 141.4 (227.6 km) Lower Chatanika River State Recreation Area Olnes Creek Campground, 1 mile/1.6 km west of highway on loop road; 50 campsites, toilets, water, tables, group area with campfire ring and benches. Camping fee $8/night or annual pass. ▲

F 11 (17.7 km) M 141 (226.9 km) Chatanika River bridge. Lower Chatanika State Recreation Area Whitefish Campground at north end of bridge; picnic area (wheelchair accessible) with covered picnic tables, campsites, toilets, firepits, water, litter barrels, river access and boat launch. Camp-

ELLIOTT HIGHWAY *Fox, AK, to Manley Hot Springs, AK*

Map Location

Scale

10 Miles

10 Kilometres

Key to mileage boxes

from:
F- Fox
M- Manley Hot Springs

Key to Advertiser Services

C -Camping
D -Dump Station
d -Diesel
G -Gas (reg., unld.)
I -Ice
L -Lodging
M -Meals
P -Propane
R -Car Repair (major)
r -Car Repair (minor)
S -Store (grocery)
T -Telephone (pay)

Principal Route

Paved — Unpaved
Other Roads
Paved — Unpaved
Ferry Routes ......
Hiking Trails ......

Refer to Log for Visitor Facilities
Visitor Information
Campground   Fishing   Airport   Airstrip

**Map labels:**

To Circle (see STEESE HIGHWAY section)

To Chena Hot Springs (see STEESE HIGHWAY section)

To Delta Junction (see ALASKA HIGHWAY section)

M-152/245km F-0

Pedro Dome 2,600 ft./792m

Fox 6

WHITE MOUNTAINS

Willow Creek

Wickersham Dome 3,207 ft./977m

Cushman Creek

To Chena Hot Springs

Chena River   Little Chena R.

Fairbanks

Old Steese Highway

Snowshoe Creek

Washington Creek

F-5.5/8.9km Hilltop Truck Stop CdGIMPST

Murphy Dome 2,930 ft./893m

To Anchorage (see GEORGE PARKS HIGHWAY section)

The Alaska Railroad (see ALASKA RAILROAD section)

Minto Lakes

former Minto

F-49.5/79.7km The Arctic Circle Trading Post

M-124/200km F-28/45km

River

Amy Dome 2,317 ft./706m

M-81/131km F-71/114km

Livengood

Lost Creek

Hess Creek

Trans-Alaska Pipeline

To Prudhoe Bay (see DALTON HIGHWAY section) 11

M-79/127km F-73/118km

Tolovana

West Fork

Troublesome Creek

Raven Creek Hill 2,388 ft./728m

Yukon River

Ray River

Sawtooth Mountain 4,494 ft./1,370m

Cooper Lake

M-42/68km F-110/177km

Minto

Tolovana River

Chatanika River

Tatalina River

Wolverine Mountain 4,580 ft./1,396m

Elephant Mountain 3,661 ft./1,116m

Pioneer Cr.   Goff Cr.   Applegate Cr.

Eureka Cr.

Hutlinana

Eureka Dome 2,393 ft./729m

Eureka

Baker Creek

Baker Lake

Hutlinana

F-151.2/243.3km Manley Hot Springs Resort CDdGLMPT

Hot Springs Slough

Tofty

M-0 F-152/245km

Manley Hot Springs

ing fee $8/night or annual pass. &▲

F 11.5 (18.5 km) **M 140.5** (226.1 km) General store.

F 13.1 (21.1 km) **M 138.9** (223.5 km) Willow Creek bridge.

F 13.4 (21.6 km) **M 138.6** (223 km) Landmark old log cabin to west.

F 18.3 (29.5 km) **M 133.7** (215.2 km) Double-ended paved turnout to west.

F 18.5 (29.8 km) **M 133.5** (214.8 km) Washington Creek. Parking area below bridge east of road; undeveloped campsite.

F 20.1 (32.3 km) **M 131.9** (212.3 km) Beaver pond with dam and lodge to east.

F 20.3 (32.7 km) **M 131.7** (212 km) Cushman Creek Road.

F 23.5 (37.8 km) **M 128.5** (206.8 km) Large double-ended turnout with view of forested valley to west.

F 24.2 (38.9 km) **M 127.8** (205.7 km) Double-ended gravel turnout to east at top of hill. Snowshoe Creek parallels the road.

F 24.7 (39.7 km) **M 127.3** (204.9 km) Long paved double-ended turnout to east.

F 27.7 (44.6 km) **M 124.3** (200 km) Large double-ended paved turnout to west. Highway winds around the base of Wickersham Dome (elev. 3,207 feet/977m). Views of the White Mountains, a range of white limestone mountains (elev. 5,000 feet/1,524m). Entering Livengood/Tolovana Mining District northbound, Fairbanks Mining District southbound.

Trailhead for White Mountains–Wickersham Creek trail and White Mountains–Summit trail to Borealis–LeFevre BLM cabin. The Wickersham Creek route is 20 miles/32 km in length; ATVs are permitted. The Summit route is 22 miles/35.4 km long and ATVs are prohibited.

Pipeline access restricted to ensure public safety and security, and to protect the reseeding and restoration of construction areas.

F 28 (45.1 km) **M 124** (199.6 km) *NOTE: Pavement ends; chip-seal surface continues to Milepost F 30.4.*

F 29.1 (46.8 km) **M 122.9** (197.8 km) Sled Dog Rocks ahead northbound.

F 29.5 (47.5 km) **M 122.5** (197.1 km) Double-ended gravel turnout to east.

F 29.8 (48 km) **M 122.2** (196.7 km) Turnouts to west. Spring water piped to road.

F 30.4 (48.9 km) **M 121.6** (195.7 km) Rough double-ended turnout to west. Fairbanks–North Star Borough boundary. *NOTE: End of chip-seal surface northbound.*

F 31 (49.9 km) **M 121** (194.7 km) Long double-ended gravel turnout to east.

F 31.8 (51.2 km) **M 120.2** (193.4 km) Double-ended turnout to west.

F 34.7 (55.8 km) **M 117.3** (188.8 km) Good view of pipeline; creek.

F 36.4 (58.6 km) **M 115.6** (186 km) Large double-ended turnout to east.

F 37 (59.5 km) **M 115** (185.1 km) Globe Creek bridge. Steep access road to parking area next to bridge.

F 38 (61.2 km) **M 114** (183.5 km) Highway follows pipeline. View of Globe Creek canyon. Grapefruit Rocks ahead, northbound.

F 39 (62.8 km) **M 113** (181.9 km) Double-ended turnout to east.

F 39.3 (63.2 km) **M 112.7** (181.4 km) Double-ended turnout to west.

F 40.6 (65.3 km) **M 111.4** (179.3 km) Scenic view from double-ended turnout to east at top of hill.

F 41.2 (66.3 km) **M 110.8** (178.3 km) Drive-in parking area to east; no easy turn-around.

F 42.8 (68.9 km) **M 109.2** (175.7 km) Pipeline pump station No. 7 to west.

F 44.8 (72.1 km) **M 107.2** (172.5 km) Tatalina Creek bridge; rest area to east at south end of bridge. The Tatalina is a tributary of the Chatanika.

F 47.1 (75.8 km) **M 104.9** (168.8 km) Turnout to east.

F 49.5 (79.7 km) **M 102.5** (165 km) **The Arctic Circle Trading Post** (Wildwood General Store). The first stop on your journey to the Arctic Circle. Best selection of Arctic

Liz Barry Photo

Circle gifts, T-shirts, postcards, pins and much more. Dalton Highway road conditions and general information. Official Arctic Circle Registry. Stop in and get outfitted for your Arctic journey! [ADVERTISEMENT]

F 49.9 (80.3 km) **M 102.1** (164.3 km) Northern Lights School. This 2-room public school has an enrollment of 22 students.

F 51.9 (83.5 km) **M 100.1** (161.1 km) Double-ended parking area, water. View of White Mountains to northeast and the Elliott Highway descending slopes of Bridge Creek valley ahead. Bridge Creek flows into the Tolovana River.

F 52 (83.7 km) **M 100** (160.9 km) Watch for grizzly and black bear in this area.

F 57.1 (91.9 km) **M 94.9** (152.7 km) **Tolovana River** bridge. Grayling to 11 inches; whitefish 12 to 18 inches; northern pike. ◂●

Colorado Creek trail to Colorado Creek and Windy Gap BLM cabins.

F 58 (93.3 km) **M 94** (151.3 km) Highway winds around Amy Dome (elev. 2,317 feet/706m) to east. The Tolovana River flows in the valley to the southwest, paralleling the road.

F 59.3 (95.4 km) **M 92.7** (149.2 km) Parking area to west by stream.

F 59.9 (96.4 km) **M 92.1** (148.2 km) Double-ended turnout to west.

F 62.3 (100.3 km) **M 89.7** (144.4 km) Access to Fred Blixt BLM cabin, east side of road. Preregister at BLM office in Fairbanks.

F 70.1 (112.8 km) **M 81.9** (131.8 km) Livengood Creek, 2-lane bridge. Money Knob to northeast.

F 70.8 (113.9 km) **M 81.2** (130.7 km) Double-ended turnout at **junction** with Livengood access road. Drive 2 miles/3.2 km to former mining camp of **LIVENGOOD** (area pop. about 100); state highway maintenance station and EMT squad.

The settlement of Livengood began in July 1914 with the discovery of gold by Nathaniel R. Hudson and Jay Livengood. A lively mining camp until 1920, some $9.5 million in gold was sluiced out by miners. Large-scale mining was attempted in the late 1930s and again in the 1940s, but both operations were eventually shut down and Livengood became a ghost town.

With the building of the trans-Alaska pipeline and the North Slope Haul Road (now the Dalton Highway) in the 1970s, the town was revitalized as a construction camp. In 1977 a mining corporation acquired much of the gold-rich Livengood Bench. *NO TRESPASSING* on mining claims.

F 71.1 (114.4 km) **M 80.9** (130.2 km) Large double-ended turnout to south.

Overnight parking allowed.

F 73.1 (117.6 km) **M 78.9** (127 km) **Junction** with the Dalton Highway (see DALTON HIGHWAY section); turn left (west) for Manley Hot Springs.

F 74.1 (119.2 km) **M 77.9** (125.4 km) Alyeska pipeline access road (restricted). Pipeline stretches for miles to the east.

F 74.3 (119.6 km) **M 77.7** (125 km) Site of old Livengood pipeline camp.

F 74.7 (120.2 km) **M 77.3** (124.4 km) Camping spot at west end of **Tolovana River** bridge; grayling to 15 inches, use spinners or flies. ◂●▲

F 76.3 (122.8 km) **M 75.7** (121.8 km) Cascaden Ridge (low hills to north).

F 79 (127.1 km) **M 73** (117.5 km) Travelers should appreciate the abundance of dragonflies seen along the Elliott Highway: their main food is mosquitoes.

F 85.5 (137.6 km) **M 66.5** (107 km) Looking south toward the Tolovana River valley, travelers should be able to see Tolovana Hot Springs Dome (elev. 2,386 feet/727m). (Hot springs are on the other side of dome; no road access.)

F 93.7 (150.8 km) **M 58.3** (93.8 km) Watch for foxes from here to top of hill. Wild rhubarb and fireweed border roadsides for miles.

F 94.5 (152.1 km) **M 57.5** (92.5 km) Long double-ended turnout to south. Good vantage point to view Minto Flats, Tanana River and foothills of the Alaska Range to south. Many wildflowers, including arnica, Alaska spirea, mountain harebell, prickly saxifrage, elegant paintbrush.

F 97 (156.1 km) **M 55** (88.5 km) The mountains to the north are Sawtooth (elev. 4,494 feet/1,370m); Wolverine (elev. 4,580 feet/1,396m); and Elephant (elev. 3,661 feet/1,116m). To the south are Tolovana River flats and Cooper Lake. Wild rhubarb and fireweed grow in old burn area.

F 98.3 (158.2 km) **M 53.7** (86.4 km) Turnout to southwest with view of Minto Lakes.

F 100.4 (161.6 km) **M 51.6** (83 km) Turnout to east in former gravel pit.

F 106.8 (171.9 km) **M 45.2** (72.7 km) Turnout with view of Sawtooth Mountains to north.

F 110 (177 km) **M 42** (67.6 km) **Junction** with Minto Road which leads 11 miles/17.7 km to the Indian village of **MINTO** (pop. 233). The village was moved to its present location on the Tolovana River from the east bank of the Tanana River in 1971 because of flooding. Minto has a lodge with accommodations, meals and a general store. Most Minto residents make their living by hunting and fishing. Some local people also work in the arts and crafts center, making birch-bark baskets, beaded skin and fur items. Temperatures here range from 55°F/13°C to 90°F/32°C in summer, and from 32°F/0°C to -50°F/-46°C in winter. Minto Flats is one of the most popular duck hunting spots in Alaska, according to the ADF&G.

Private Aircraft: Minto airstrip 1 mile/1.6 km east; elev. 460 feet/140m; length 2,000 feet/610m; gravel; unattended.

Minto Lakes, name refers to all lakes in this lowland area. Accessible only by plane or boat; best to fly in. Pike to 36 inches, use wobblers, bait, red-and-white spoons, good all summer. Also grayling, sheefish and whitefish. ●▸

F 113 (181.9 km) **M 39** (62.8 km) Evidence of 1983 burn.

F 113.5 (182.7 km) **M 38.5** (62 km) West Fork Hutlitakwa Creek.

F 119 (191.5 km) **M 33** (53.1 km) The road travels the ridges and hills, providing a "top of the world" view of hundreds of square miles in all directions.

F 119.5 (192.3 km) **M 32.5** (52.3 km) Eureka Dome (elev. 2,393 feet/729m) to north.

F 121.1 (194.9 km) **M 30.9** (49.7 km) To the north, travelers look down into the draws of Applegate and Goff creeks.

F 123.2 (198.3 km) **M 28.8** (46.3 km) Small turnout to north. Road begins descent into the Eureka area.

F 123.7 (199.1 km) **M 28.3** (45.5 km) Dugan Hills visible to the south at this point.

F 129.3 (208.1 km) **M 22.7** (36.5 km) Hutlinana Creek bridge.

F 131.3 (211.3 km) **M 20.7** (33.3 km) Eureka Road turnoff; access to private ranch. Active mining is taking place in this area. *NO TRESPASSING* on private claims. A trail leads to the former mining camp of Eureka, at the junction of Pioneer and Eureka creeks, 3 miles/4.8 km south of Eureka Dome.

Private Aircraft: Eureka Creek airstrip; elev. 700 feet/213m; length 1,500 feet/457m; turf; unattended.

F 137.4 (221.1 km) **M 14.6** (23.5 km) One-lane bridge over **Baker Creek**. Grayling 5 to 20 inches, use flies, black gnats, mosquitoes, May 15 to Sept. 30. ✦

Winding road with many ups and downs.

F 138.4 (222.7 km) **M 13.6** (21.9 km) Highway goes over Overland Bluff and through a 1968 burn area. Bracket fungus is growing on the dead birch trees.

F 150 (241.4 km) **M 2** (3.2 km) *NOTE: This part of the road can be extremely slick after heavy rains. Drive with caution.*

F 151.1 (243.2 km) **M 0.9** (1.4 km) Manley DOT/PF highway maintenance station.

F 151.2 (243.3 km) **M 0.8** (1.3 km) **Junction** with Tofty Road, which leads 16 miles/25.7 km to former mining area of Tofty, founded in 1908 by pioneer prospector A.F. Tofty. Mining activity in area.

The hot springs are on a hillside on the

right before entering the town. One spring runs 35 gallons a minute with a temperature of 136°F/58°C, another runs 110 gallons per minute at 135°F/57°C.

F 151.2 (243.3 km) **M 0.8** (1.3 km) **Manley Hot Springs Resort.** Open year-round. Swim in hot mineral spring-fed pool. Rooms with half baths, full baths or double Jacuzzis; log cabins, restaurant, bar, RV park, dump station, laundromat, showers, gift shop. Gas and diesel, boats available for grayling, northern pike, sheefish. Riverboat charters available. All our tours are to authentic operating fish camps, gold mines. See the real Interior Alaska lifestyle. River tours include visits to fish camp (operating fish wheel). Dogsled rides cross-country in winter. Crystal clear winter nights for viewing aurora borealis. Cross-country skiing, snowshoeing, ice skating. We can accommodate up to 65 guests. Write Box 28, Manley Hot Springs Resort, Manley Hot Springs, AK 99756 or phone (907) 672-3611. Fax (907) 672-3461. [ADVERTISEMENT] ▲

Manley Hot Springs

F 152 (244.6 km) **M 0** Located at the end of the Elliott Highway on Hot Springs Slough. **Population:** 88. **Elevation:** 330 feet/101m. **Climate:** Mean temperature in July is 59°F/15°C, in January -10.4°F/-23.6°C. Record high 93°F/33.9°C in June 1969, record low -70°F/-56.7°C in January 1934. Precipitation in summer averages 2.53 inches a month. Snow from October through April, with traces in September and May. Greatest mean monthly snowfall in January (11.1 inches). Record snowfall 49 inches in January 1937.

Private Aircraft: Manley Hot Springs civil airstrip (open year-round), adjacent southwest; elev. 270 feet/82m; length 2,900 feet/884m; gravel; fuel 100.

A pocket of "Pioneer Alaska." J.F. Karshner homesteaded here in 1902, about the same time the U.S. Army Signal Corps established a telegraph station nearby. The location soon became known as Baker Hot Springs, after nearby Baker Creek. Frank Manley built a 4-story resort hotel here in 1907. The settlement's name was changed to Manley Hot Springs in 1957. Once a busy

trading center during peak activity in the nearby Eureka and Tofty mining districts, Manley Hot Springs is now a quiet settlement with a trading post, roadhouse, airfield and hot springs resort. Many residents are enthusiastic gardeners, and visitors may see abundant displays of vegetables and berries growing around homes and businesses. Outstanding display of wild irises at the airstrip in June.

A restaurant, bar and overnight accommodations are at the roadhouse. The post office, gas station and grocery are at the trading post. There is an air taxi service here and scheduled service from Fairbanks.

The Manley Roadhouse. Come visit one of Alaska's oldest original roadhouses from the gold rush era. See the many prehistoric and Alaskana artifacts on display. The Manley Roadhouse is a great place to meet local miners, dog mushers, trappers or fishermen enjoying a cup of coffee. The Manley Roadhouse specializes in traditional Alaska home-style hospitality, fresh-baked pies, giant cinnamon rolls and good food. Largest liquor selection in Alaska. Stop by and see us. See display ad this section. [ADVERTISEMENT]

Manley Hot Springs Park Assoc. maintains a public campground near the bridge in town; fee $5 (pay at roadhouse). The hot springs are a short walk from the campground. There's a nice grassy picnic area on the slough near the campground. A boat launch is also nearby. ▲

Manley Hot Springs Slough, pike 18 to 36 inches, use spinning and trolling lures, May through September. Follow the dirt road from the old Northern Commercial Co. store out of town for 2.5 miles/4 km to reach the Tanana River; king, silver and chum salmon from 7 to 40 lbs., June 15 to Sept. 30. Fish wheels and nets are used. ✦

Wood's Bush Adventures. Experience the real Alaska in the "Bush." The term "Bush" refers to the vast area of Alaska inaccessible by road, where planes, boats and dog teams are the only way around. Travel this country by boat, canoe or dog team, and get to know it with your guides Bill and Cheryl Wood. Located 12 miles from Manley on the Tanana River. Call our remote phone between 6–7 P.M. Alaska time, 7–8 P.M. Pacific time. (907) 672-3952. [ADVERTISEMENT]

Kenai Peninsula
SEWARD HIGHWAY ① ⑨

Connects: Anchorage to Seward, AK   **Length:** 127 miles
Road Surface: Paved   **Season:** Open all year
Highest Summit: Turnagain Pass 988 feet
Major Attractions: Mount Alyeska; Portage Glacier; Kenai Fjords National Park

(See map, page 482)

	Alyeska	Anchorage	Hope	Portage Glacier	Seward
Alyeska		42	56	22	95
Anchorage	42		88	54	127
Hope	56	88		46	75
Portage Glacier	22	54	46		85
Seward	95	127	75	85	

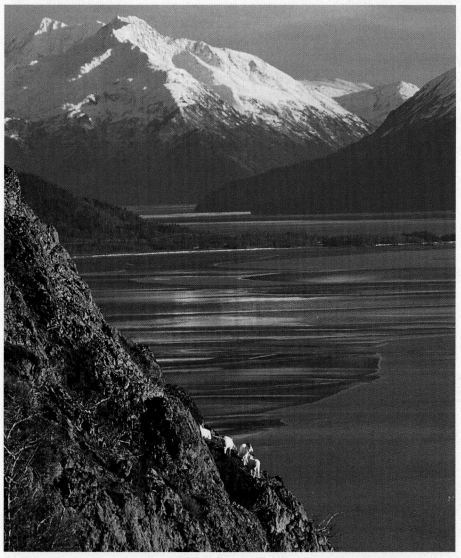

Dall sheep on cliffs above Turnagain Arm, with Kenai Peninsula peaks in background.
(© Michael DeYoung)

The 127-mile-/204-km-long Seward Highway connects Anchorage with the community of Seward on the east coast of the Kenai Peninsula. It has been called one of the most scenic highways in the country and has been designated a National Forest Scenic Byway. Leaving Anchorage, the Seward Highway follows the north shore of Turnagain Arm through Chugach State Park and Chugach National Forest, permitting a panoramic view of the south shore and the Kenai Mountains.

The Seward Highway provides access to Alyeska ski resort, the Hope Highway, Portage Glacier and Kenai Fjords National Park. There is a bike trail between Anchorage and Girdwood. The bike route is marked by signs. Numerous hiking trails branch off the highway.

The Seward Highway junctions with the other major Kenai Peninsula route, the Sterling Highway (see STERLING HIGHWAY section) at Tern Lake. Both these highways offer hiking, fishing and camping opportunities, and beautiful scenery.

Physical mileposts on the Seward Highway show distance from Seward. The Seward Highway is a paved, 2-lane highway with passing lanes. It is open all year. There are no gas stations on the Seward Highway between **Milepost S 90** (Girdwood turnoff) and **Milepost S 6.6**, just outside Seward. Some sections of the highway are subject to avalanches in winter. Check Anchorage news sources for winter road conditions. In 1997, expect major road construction projects along the Seward Highway between **Milepost S 97** and **S 90** (Girdwood turnoff) and between **Milepost S 59** and **S 53** (Hope Highway cutoff).

CAUTION: The Seward Highway from Anchorage to just past Girdwood statistically has one of the highest number of traffic accidents in the state. DRIVE CAREFULLY! Motorists must drive with headlights on at all times.

Emergency medical services: Phone 911 or use CB channels 9, 11 or 19. Cellular phone service is available as far south as Girdwood and is also available in Seward.

Seward Highway Log

ALASKA ROUTE 1
Distance from Seward (S) is followed by distance from Anchorage (A). Physical mileposts show distance from Seward.

S 127 (204.4 km) **A 0** Gambell Street and 10th Avenue in Anchorage. The Seward Highway (Gambell Street) connects with the Glenn Highway in Anchorage via 5th Avenue (westbound) and 6th Avenue (eastbound). (See map on page 322 in the ANCHORAGE section.) Follow Seward Highway signs south on Gambell.

S 126.7 (203.9 km) **A 0.3** (0.5 km) 15th Avenue (DeBarr Road).

S 126.6 (203.7 km) **A 0.4** (0.6 km) 16th Avenue; access to Sullivan sports arena, ice rinks and baseball stadium.

S 126 (202.8 km) **A 1** (1.6 km) Fireweed Lane.

S 125.8 (202.4 km) **A 1.2** (1.9 km) Northern Lights Boulevard (one-way westbound).

SEWARD HIGHWAY
Anchorage, AK, to Seward, AK

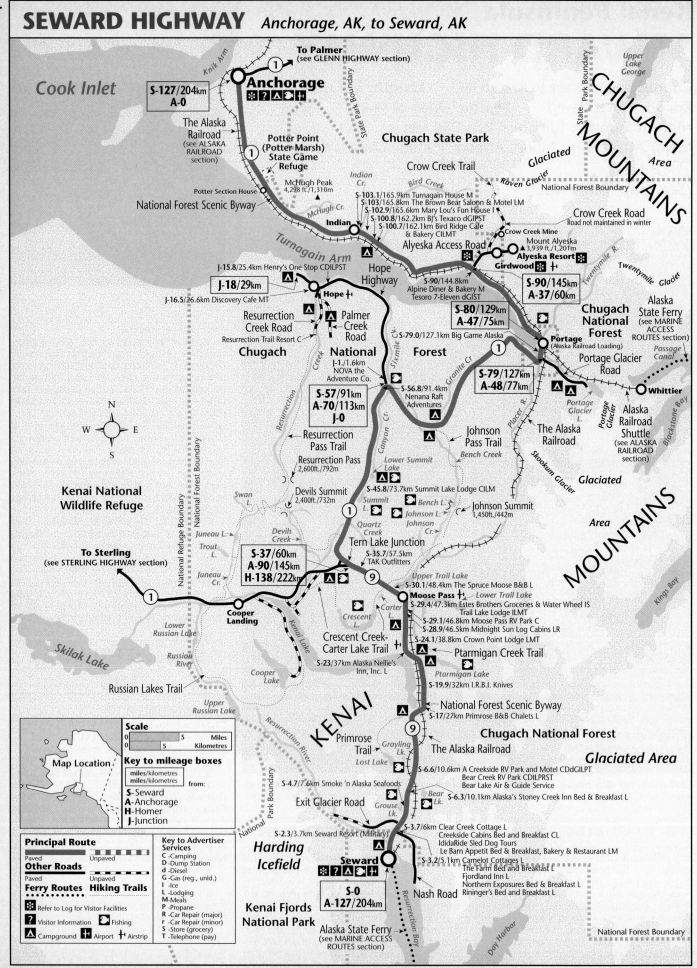

To Palmer
(see GLENN HIGHWAY section)

Cook Inlet

S-127/204km
A-0

Anchorage

The Alaska Railroad
(see ALASKA RAILROAD section)

Potter Point (Potter Marsh) State Game Refuge

National Forest Scenic Byway

Potter Section House

McHugh Peak 4,298 ft./1,310m

McHugh Cr.

Indian

Turnagain Arm

Chugach State Park

CHUGACH MOUNTAINS

Upper Lake George

State Park Boundary

Crow Creek Trail

Glaciated

Raven Glacier

National Forest Boundary

Indian Cr.
Bird Creek

S-103.1/165.9km Turnagain House M
S-103/165.8km The Brown Bear Saloon & Motel LM
S-102.9/165.6km Mary Lou's Fun House I
S-100.8/162.2km BJ's Texaco dGIPST
S-100.7/162.1km Bird Ridge Cafe & Bakery CILMT

Crow Creek Road
Road not maintained in winter

Crow Creek Mine
Mount Alyeska 3,939 ft./1,201m
Alyeska Access Road
Alyeska Resort
Girdwood

Hope Highway

Alpine Diner & Bakery M
Tesoro 7-Eleven dGIST

S-90/144.8km

S-90/145km
A-37/60km

Chugach National Forest

Alaska State Ferry
(see MARINE ACCESS ROUTES section)

Twentymile Glacier
Twentymile R.

J-15.8/25.4km Henry's One Stop CDILPST

J-18/29km

J-16.5/26.6km Discovery Cafe MT

Hope

Resurrection Creek Road
Resurrection Trail Resort C

Palmer Creek Road

Chugach

National

Forest

S-80/129km
A-47/75km

S-79.0/127.1km Big Game Alaska

Portage
(Alaska Railroad Loading)

Portage Glacier Road

Passage Canal

Whittier

S-79/127km
A-48/77km

Resurrection Creek

Canyon Cr.

Sixmile Ck.

Granite Cr.

J-1./1.6km NOVA the Adventure Co.

S-57/91km
A-70/113km
J-0

Resurrection Pass Trail

Resurrection Pass 2,600ft./792m

Devils Summit 2,400ft./732m

S-56.8/91.4km Nenana Raft Adventures

Johnson Pass Trail
Bench Creek

Placer R.

The Alaska Railroad

Portage Glacier L.

Alaska Railroad Shuttle
(see ALASKA RAILROAD section)

Skookum Glacier

Glaciated Area

Kenai National Wildlife Refuge

Swan L.
Juneau L.
Trout L.
Juneau Cr.

Devils Creek

Lower Summit Lake

S-45.8/73.7km Summit Lake Lodge CILM

Summit L.

Bench L.

Johnson L.
Johnson Cr.

Johnson Summit 1,450ft./442m

MOUNTAINS

Quartz Creek

Tern Lake Junction

S-35.7/57.5km
TAK Outfitters

Kings Bay

To Sterling
(see STERLING HIGHWAY section)

S-37/60km
A-90/145km
H-138/222km

Cooper Landing

Lower Russian Lake

Russian River

Kenai Lake

Upper Trail Lake

S-30.1/48.4km The Spruce Moose B&B L

Moose Pass

Lower Trail Lake

S-29.4/47.3km Estes Brothers Groceries & Water Wheel IS
Trail Lake Lodge ILMT
S-29.1/46.8km Moose Pass RV Park C
S-28.9/46.5km Midnight Sun Log Cabins LR
S-24.1/38.8km Crown Point Lodge LMT

Carter L.
Crescent L.

Crescent Creek-Carter Lake Trail

Ptarmigan Creek Trail

Russian Lakes Trail

Skilak Lake

Cooper Lake

Upper Russian Lake

S-23/37km Alaska Nellie's Inn, Inc. L

Ptarmigan Lake

S-19.9/32km I.R.B.I. Knives

National Forest Scenic Byway

S-17/27km Primrose B&B Chalets L

KENAI

Primrose Trail

Grayling Lk.

Chugach National Forest

The Alaska Railroad

Glaciated Area

Resurrection River

Lost Lake

S-6.6/10.6km A Creekside RV Park and Motel CDdGILPT
Bear Creek RV Park CDILPRST
Bear Lake Air & Guide Service

Bear Lk.

S-6.3/10.1km Alaska's Stoney Creek Inn Bed & Breakfast L

Exit Glacier Road

S-4.7/7.6km Smoke 'n Alaska Seafoods

Grouse Lk.

S-3.7/6km Clear Creek Cottage L
Creekside Cabins Bed and Breakfast CL
IdidaRide Sled Dog Tours
Le Barn Appetit Bed & Breakfast, Bakery & Restaurant LM

S-2.3/3.7km Seward Resort (Military)

Harding Icefield

Seward

S-0
A-127/204km

S-3.2/5.1km Camelot Cottages L
The Farm Bed and Breakfast L
Fjordland Inn L
Northern Exposures Bed & Breakfast L
Rininger's Bed and Breakfast L

Nash Road

Kenai Fjords National Park

Alaska State Ferry
(see MARINE ACCESS ROUTES section)

Resurrection Bay

Day Harbor

National Forest Boundary

Map Location

Scale
0 — 5 Miles
0 — 5 Kilometres

Key to mileage boxes
miles/kilometres
miles/kilometres from:
S-Seward
A-Anchorage
H-Homer
J-Junction

Principal Route
Paved
Unpaved
Other Roads
Paved
Unpaved
Ferry Routes   Hiking Trails

Refer to Log for Visitor Facilities
? Visitor Information   Fishing
Campground   + Airport   + Airstrip

Key to Advertiser Services
C -Camping
D -Dump Station
d -Diesel
G -Gas (reg., unld.)
I -Ice
L -Lodging
M -Meals
P -Propane
R -Car Repair (major)
r -Car Repair (minor)
S -Store (grocery)
T -Telephone (pay)

Access to shopping centers.

S 125.7 (202.3 km) **A 1.3** (2.1 km) Benson Boulevard (one-way eastbound).

S 125.4 (201.8 km) **A 1.6** (2.6 km) Southbound access only to Old Seward Highway.

S 125.3 (201.6 km) **A 1.7** (2.7 km) 36th Avenue; hospital to east.

S 125.2 (201.5 km) **A 1.8** (2.9 km) Freeway begins southbound. There are no services or facilities along the new Seward Highway. However, there are several exits in the next 7.5 miles/12.1 km to the Old Seward Highway (which parallels the new Seward Highway) where traveler services are available.

S 124.7 (200.7 km) **A 2.3** (3.7 km) Tudor Road overpass; exits both sides of highway. (Tudor Road is used as a bypass route for northbound travelers, connecting them with the Glenn Highway via Muldoon Road.)

S 124.2 (199.8 km) **A 2.8** (4.5 km) Campbell Creek bridge.

S 123.7 (199.1 km) **A 3.3** (5.3 km) Dowling Road underpass; exits on both sides of highway.

S 122.7 (197.5 km) **A 4.3** (6.9 km) 76th Avenue exit, southbound traffic only.

S 122.2 (196.7 km) **A 4.8** (7.7 km) Dimond Boulevard underpass; exits on both sides of highway.

S 120.8 (194.4 km) **A 6.2** (10 km) O'Malley Road underpass; exits on both sides of highway. Turn east on O'Malley Road and drive 2 miles/3.2 km to reach the Alaska Zoo. Turn west for access to Old Seward Highway and major shopping area on Dimond Boulevard. Views of Chugach Mountains along this stretch.

S 119.7 (192.6 km) **A 7.3** (11.7 km) Huffman Road underpass; exits on both sides of highway.

S 118.5 (190.7 km) **A 8.5** (13.7 km) De Armoun Road overpass, exits both sides of highway.

S 117.8 (189.6 km) **A 9.2** (14.8 km) Overpass: Exits both sides of highway for Old Seward Highway (west); access to Rabbit Creek Road (east). The picturesque Chapel by the Sea overlooks Turnagain Arm. The church is often photographed because of its unique setting and its display of flowers.

S 117.6 (189.3 km) **A 9.4** (15.1 km) View

Red-necked grebe's nest at Potter's Marsh, Milepost S 117.4. (© James D. Ronan)

of Turnagain Arm and Mount Spurr.

S 117.4 (188.9 km) **A 9.6** (15.4 km) Rabbit Creek Rifle Range to west. Boardwalk Wildlife Viewing exit leads east to Potter Point State Game Refuge. This is a very popular spot for bird watching. From the parking lot, an extensive boardwalk crosses Potter Marsh, a refuge and nesting area for waterfowl. The marsh was created when railroad construction dammed a small creek in the area. Today, the marsh is visited by arctic terns, Canada geese, trumpeter swans, many species of ducks and other water birds. Bring binoculars.

S 117.3 (188.8 km) **A 9.7** (15.6 km) Highway narrows to 2 lanes southbound.

S 117.2 (188.6 km) **A 9.8** (15.8 km) Small paved turnout at end of boardwalk.

S 116.1 (186.8 km) **A 10.9** (17.5 km) Paved double-ended turnout to east. Highway parallels Alaska Railroad southbound to **Milepost S 90.8.**

S 115.4 (185.7 km) **A 11.6** (18.7 km) **Junction** with Old Seward Highway; access to Potter Valley Road. Old Johnson trail begins 0.5 mile/0.6 km up Potter Valley Road; parking at trailhead. Only the first 10 miles/16 km of this state park trail are cleared. Moderate to difficult hike; watch for bears.

The natural gas pipeline from the Kenai Peninsula emerges from beneath Turnagain Arm here and follows the roadway to Anchorage.

WARNING: When the tide is out, the sand in Turnagain Arm might look inviting. DO NOT go out on it. Some of it is quicksand. You could become trapped in the mud and not be rescued before the tide comes in.

S 115.3 (185.6 km) **A 11.7** (18.8 km) Entering Chugach State Park southbound. Potter Section House, Chugach State Park Headquarters (phone 907/345-5014) to west; pay phone, large parking lot, wheelchair-accessible toilets. Open daily in summer, Monday to Friday 8 A.M. to 4:30 P.M. year-round. The renovated Potter Section House, dedicated in October 1986, was home to a small crew of railroad workers who maintained the Alaska Railroad tracks between Seward and Anchorage in the days of coal- and steam-powered locomotives. Displays

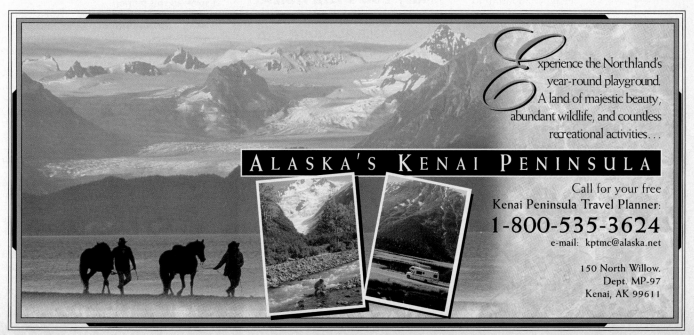

here include photographs from the National Archives, a vintage snowblower and working model railroad.

S 115.1 (185.2 km) **A 11.9** (19.2 km) Potter Creek trailhead to east. &

S 115 (185 km) **A 12** (19.3 km) Watch for rockfalls. Avalanche area and hazardous driving conditions during winter for the next 25 miles/40.2 km.

From here to **Milepost S 90** there are many turnouts on both sides of the highway, some with scenic views of Turnagain Arm. An easterly extension of Cook Inlet, Turnagain Arm was called Return by the Russians. Captain Cook, seeking the fabled Northwest Passage in 1778, called it Turnagain River, and Captain Vancouver, doing a more thorough job of surveying in 1794, gave it the present name of Turnagain Arm.

S 114.7 (184.6 km) **A 12.3** (19.8 km) Weigh station and pay phone to east.

S 114.5 (184.3 km) **A 12.5** (20.1 km) Double-ended gravel turnout to east. From here to **Milepost S 104**, patches of harebells (Bluebells of Scotland) can be seen in late July and early August.

S 113.3 (182.3 km) **A 13.7** (22.1 km) Large paved turnout for slow vehicles.

S 113.1 (182 km) **A 13.9** (22.4 km) Small gravel turnout to east at McHugh boulder area. Watch for rock climbers practicing on the steep cliffs alongside the highway. The cliffs are part of the base of McHugh Peak (elev. 4,298 feet/1,310m).

S 111.8 (179.9 km) **A 15.2** (24.5 km) McHugh Creek state wayside to east with 30 picnic sites. A stream and waterfall make this a very refreshing place to stop. *CAUTION: Steep but paved road into this picnic site. Be sure you have plenty of power and good brakes for descent, especially if you are towing a trailer.* There is also a parking area beside the highway. Good berry picking in season near the stream for wild currants, blueberries and watermelon berries. A 1-mile portion of the Old Johnson trail here is wheelchair accessible. &

S 111.6 (179.6 km) **A 15.4** (24.8 km) Double-ended gravel turnout to east. There are numerous turnouts southbound to Indian.

S 110.3 (177.5 km) **A 16.7** (26.9 km) Beluga Point scenic viewpoint and photo stop has a commanding view of Turnagain Arm. A good place to see bore tides and beluga whales. (The only all-white whale, belugas are easy to identify.) Large paved double-ended turnout to west with tables, benches, telescopes and interpretive signs on orcas, bore tides, mountain goats, etc.

WARNING: Do not go out on the mud flats at low tide. The glacial silt and water can create a dangerous quicksand.

Turnagain Arm is known for having one of the world's remarkably high tides, with a diurnal range of more than 33 feet/10m. A bore tide is an abrupt rise of tidal water just after low tide, moving rapidly landward, formed by a flood tide surging into a constricted inlet such as Turnagain Arm. This foaming wall of water may reach a height of 6 feet/2m and is very dangerous to small craft. To see a bore tide, check the Anchorage-area tide tables for low tide, then add approximately 2 hours and 15 minutes to the Anchorage low tide for the bore to reach points between 32 miles/ 51.5 km and 37 miles/59.5 km south of Anchorage on the Seward Highway. Visitors should watch for bore tides from Beluga Point south to Girdwood.

S 109.2 (175.7 km) **A 17.8** (28.6 km) Paved turnout to west. Spring water is piped to the highway.

S 108.5 (174.6 km) **A 18.5** (29.8 km) Rainbow Road to Rainbow Valley.

S 108.4 (174.4 km) **A 18.6** (29.9 km) Rainbow trailhead and parking; access to Old Johnson trail.

S 107.3 (172.7 km) **A 19.7** (31.7 km) Gravel turnout to east. Rock climbers practice on the cliffs here.

S 107 (172.2 km) **A 20** (32.2 km) From here to Girdwood, in summer when snow is still on the peaks or after heavy rainfall, watch for many small waterfalls tumbling down the mountainsides to Turnagain Arm.

S 106.9 (172 km) **A 20.1** (32.3 km) Scenic viewpoint. Double-ended paved turnout to west; Old Johnson trail access. Watch for Dall sheep near road. *NOTE: DO NOT FEED WILDLIFE.*

S 106.7 (171.7 km) **A 20.3** (32.7 km) Paved turnout to east; Windy trailhead.

S 106.6 (171.5 km) **A 20.4** (32.8 km) Large paved turnout to west; watch for Dall sheep.

S 105.7 (170.1 km) **A 21.3** (34.3 km) Falls Creek trailhead and parking to east; Old Johnson trail access.

S 104 (167.4 km) **A 23** (37 km) Indian Valley Mine National Historic Site.

S 103.9 (167.2 km) **A 23.1** (37.2 km) Indian Road and Indian Valley businesses on east side of highway.

S 103.5 (166.6 km) **A 23.5** (37.8 km) INDIAN; current status of services unknown.

S 103.1 (165.9 km) **A 23.9** (38.5 km) Bore Tide Road, also called Ocean View Road. Turnagain House restaurant.

Turnagain House, Milepost 103.1 Seward Highway at Indian, AK. Fresh Alaskan seafood, fine steaks and baby back ribs. Located 16 miles south of Anchorage. Excellent view of Turnagain Arm and bore tides. Rustic and casual atmosphere. The Turnagain House is a year-round favorite of Anchorage residents and is considered one of the finest restaurants in the area. Major credit cards accepted. Reservations: (907) 653-7500. [ADVERTISEMENT]

S 103 (165.8 km) **A 24** (38.6 km) Motel and bar. Bridge over Indian Creek.

The Brown Bear Saloon & Motel. See display ad this section.

Indian Creek, heavily fished! Pink salmon, sea-run Dolly Varden, few coho (silver) salmon and rainbow, June to September; pink salmon run from latter part of July to mid-August in even-numbered years. **Bird Creek,** same fishing as Indian Creek, except heavier run of pink salmon in July and August.

S 102.9 (165.6 km) **A 24.1** (38.8 km) Indian Creek rest area to west; wheelchair accessible toilets and parking. Bar and liquor store to east. Pay phone. &

Mary Lou's Fun House. See display ad this section.

S 102.1 (164.3 km) **A 24.9** (40.1 km) Bird Ridge trailhead and parking; Old Johnson trail access.

S 101.5 (163.3 km) **A 25.5** (41 km) Bridge over Bird Creek; parking. Watch for pedestrians next mile southbound.

S 101.2 (162.9 km) **A 25.8** (41.5 km) Bird Creek State Recreation Site with picnic sites and 19 campsites, firepits, pay phone, covered picnic tables, toilets and water. Firewood is sometimes available. Camping fee $10/night or annual pass. A pleasant camp

(Continues on page 489)

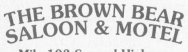

Alyeska Access Road Log

This 3-mile/4.8-km paved spur road provides access to Crow Creek Road, Girdwood, Mount Alyeska ski area and Alyeska Resort. There are many restaurants, gift shops, accommodations and attractions in the Girdwood/Alyeska area. **Distance is measured from junction with Seward Highway (J).**

J 0 Junction with Seward Highway at **Milepost S 90.** Towing service. Girdwood Station Mall: 24-hour convenience store and gas station, medical clinic with emergency services, chiropractic clinic, restaurant and a bakery.

J 0.2 (0.3 km) Bridge over Alaska Railroad tracks. Paved bike trail to Alyeska Resort begins.

J 0.4 (0.6 km) Forest Station Road. Chugach National Forest Glacier Ranger District office (P.O. Box 129, Girdwood, AK 99587; phone 907/783-3242). Open 8 A.M. to 5 P.M. Monday to Friday yearround; also 9 A.M. to 5 P.M. weekends Memorial Day through Labor Day. Maps and information available here.

J 0.5 (0.8 km) **Alaska Candle Factory.** One-half mile off Seward Highway on Alyeska. Home of handcrafted candles made in the form of Alaska wild animals.

Hand-dipped tapers and molded candles made daily. All candles have unique individual designs. Open 7 days a week, 10 A.M. to 6 P.M., in summer until 7 P.M. Visitors welcome. Phone (907) 783-2354. P.O. Box 786, Girdwood, AK 99587.
[ADVERTISEMENT]

J 1.6 (2.6 km) **Junction** with Brenner Road.

J 1.9 (3.1 km) **Junction** with Crow Creek Road. Two restaurants and Raven Glacier Lodge are located 0.2 mile/0.3 km up Crow Creek Road. This single-lane dirt road leads 3.1 miles/5 km to Crow Creek Mine, 7 Miles/11.3 km to Crow Pass trailhead. In winter, the road is not maintained past nile 0.6. Crow Creek Mine is a national historic site. The authentic gold mine and 8 other buildings at the mine are open to the public (fee charged).

Crow Creek Mine. Visit this historic 1898 mining camp located in the heart

of Chugach National Forest. Drive 3 miles up Crow Creek Road (Old Iditarod trail). Eight original buildings. Pan for gold. Visit our gift shop. Enjoy beautiful grounds, ponds, flowers. Animals and friendly people. Campground

Alyeska Access Road Log (continued)

for tents and self-contained vehicles. Open May 15–Sept. 15, 9 A.M. to 6 P.M. daily. Phone (907) 278-8060 (messages).

▲

Crow Pass and Old Iditarod trailhead at Mile 7 Crow Creek Road. Crow Pass trail climbs steeply 3 miles/4.8 km to ruins of an old gold mine and a USFS public-use cabin at Crow Pass near Raven Glacier; hiking time approximately 2¹/₂ hours. The Old Iditarod trail extends 22.5 miles/36.2 km north from Crow Pass down Raven Creek drainage to the Chugach State Park Visitor Center on Eagle River Road. All of the hiking trail, from Crow Creek Road trailhead to the state park visitor center, is part of the Iditarod National Historic Trail used in the early 1900s. Trail is usually free of snow by mid-June. Closed to motorized vehicles; horses prohibited during early spring due to soft trail conditions.

J 2 (3.2 km) California Creek bridge.

J 2.1 (3.4 km) **GIRDWOOD** (area pop. 1,500), at the junction of Alyeska access road and Hightower Road. **Emergency Services: Alaska State Troopers, EMS** and **Fire Department,** phone 911 or (907) 783-2704 (message only) or 269-5711. Located here are a post office, restaurants, vacation rental offices, grocery store with gas, a rafting business, small shops and fire hall. Girdwood is a popular resort area for winter sports enthusiasts and for summer activities. There are many fine summer homes here and a substantial year-round community.

Girdwood Community Center offers tennis courts, pay phone, Kinder Park day-care center and picnic area, and is the site of the Girdwood midsummer crafts fair. The town was named after Col. James Girdwood, who established a mining operation near here in 1901.

Alyeska Booking Co. offers free reservation service to travelers. Affordable lodging ranges from bed and breakfasts to luxury condos and chalets. The friendly, knowledgeable staff can also assist you in planning activities. Call them to arrange a glacier cruise from nearby Whittier or Seward, to arrange the flightseeing trip of a lifetime over Prince William Sound or a rafting adventure you'll long remember. Stop at the downtown Girdwood office, next to Chair Five Restaurant or call (907) 783-4386. [ADVERTISEMENT]

Chair Five Restaurant. A favorite of locals and travelers since 1983, Chair Five offers quality food at affordable prices. Renowned for its famous tundra steak with buffalo and reindeer, always fresh halibut and pasta dishes. They also offer gourmet fresh-dough pizza that gets rave reviews. Over 60 beer varieties and 30-plus single malt scotch selections round out a great cocktail menu. Open 11–11 daily. MasterCard/VISA/American Express. Phone (907) 783-2500. Mile 2.1 Alyeska Access Road; turn on Hightower Road. [ADVERTISEMENT]

J 2.3 (3.7 km) Glacier Creek bridge.

J 2.6 (4.2 km) Donner access to Airport Road. **Private Aircraft:** Girdwood landing strip; elev. 150 feet/46m; length 2,100 feet/640m; gravel; unattended.

Alpine Air Inc. Scenic flights in spacious, intercom-equipped wheel/ski planes and floatplanes into Prince

William Sound, the Chugach Mountains and Mount McKinley area. Glacier and

floatplane landings are our specialty. Guided and unguided fishing trips. Statewide charters available. Federally licensed and fully insured. Visitors welcome year-round to stop in at our hangar/office at the Girdwood airport, last blue hangar on the airport road. Phone (907) 783-2360. Internet address: http://www.alaska.net/~alpinair; e-mail: alpinair@alaska.net. [ADVERTISEMENT]

Alyeska Air Service. Chuck Sassara welcomes you to share over 40 years of flying experience in Alaska. Alaskan hospitality always on our customized fishing and photography charters. Special 1-hour Prince William Sound flightseeing tours. Breathtaking views. Stop in and have a cup of coffee, and visit with our pilots while we map out your Alaska adventure. Phone (907) 783-2163; fax (907)

GIRDWOOD / ALYESKA ADVERTISERS

Alyeska Access Road Log (continued)

783-1294. See display ad. [ADVERTISEMENT]

Fireweed Inn Bed & Breakfast. See display ad this section.

J 2.7 (4.3 km) Timberline Drive.

J 3 (4.8 km) **ALYESKA** Resort and recreation area at Mount Alyeska (elev. 3,939 feet/1,201m). Road forks: To right are the daylodge and ski lift in the base area. To the left is Alyeska business district with jade shop, gift and craft shops, restaurant and ski resort.

Alyeska Resort is Alaska's largest ski area and a year-round resort. Owned and operated by Seibu Alaska Inc. since 1980.

Ski season is generally from mid-November through mid-April. Facilities include a high-speed detachable bubble quad, 2 fixed-grip quads, 3 double chair lifts and 2 pony tows. Night skiing available during holiday periods in December, and Friday through Saturday from January through March. Ski school, ski rental shop and sports shops. Wheelchair-accessible mountaintop cafeteria, restaurant and lounge (open year-round) accessed by a 60-passenger tram, see **Milepost J4.5.** &

Winter activities include cross-country skiing, dogsled rides, heli-skiing, ice fishing and snowmachining. Summer activities available are glacier skiing, hiking,

Alyeska tramway. (Alyeska Resort)

mountain biking, flightseeing, canoeing, tennis, gold panning and river rafting.

J 3.2 (5.1 km) **Alyeska Resort.** See display ad on page 486.

J 4 (6.4 km) Parking for shuttle to hotel and tram to top of mountain and Glacier Express restaurant.

J 4.5 (7.2 km) Westin Alyeska Prince Hotel and Glacier Terminal (tram). The 307-room hotel has 4 restaurants, 2 lounges and a fitness center with indoor swimming pool. The chalet-style hotel has wood-paneled interior. For more information phone (907) 754-1111 or 1-800-880-3880.

**Return to Milepost S 90
Seward Highway**

(Continued from page 484)

ground densely wooded but cleared along the high banks of Turnagain Arm. Paved bike trail goes through campground (nice ride along Turnagain Arm). Great spot for sunbathing. This campground is full most weekends in the summer. ▲

WARNING: Do not go out on the mud flats at low tide. The glacial silt and water can create a dangerous quicksand.

S 100.8 (162.2 km) **A 26.2** (42.2 km) **BJ's Texaco.** See display ad this section.

S 100.7 (162.1 km) **A 26.3** (42.3 km) **Bird Ridge Cafe & Bakery.** See display ad this section.

S 99.8 (160.6 km) **A 27.2** (43.8 km) Paved turnout to west. Southbound traffic entering avalanche area, northbound traffic leaving avalanche area.

S 99.3 (159.8 km) **A 27.7** (44.6 km) Large gravel turnout to west with view across Turnagain Arm to the cut in the mountains where Sixmile Creek drains into the arm; the old mining settlement of Sunrise was located here. The town of Hope is to the southwest. The peak visible across Turnagain Arm between here and Girdwood is Mount Alpenglow in the Kenai mountain range. Avalanche gates.

S 99.2 (159.6 km) **A 27.8** (44.7 km) Avalanche gun emplacement (motorists will notice several of these along the highway southbound).

S 97.2 (156.4 km) **A 29.8** (48 km) Southbound traffic leaving winter avalanche area, northbound traffic entering avalanche area.

S 96.8 (155.8 km) **A 30.2** (48.6 km) *CAUTION: Watch for road construction next 7 miles/11.3 km southbound in 1997; possible traffic delays.* Winter avalanche area. There are many gravel turnouts the next 5 miles/8 km southbound.

S 95.5 (153.7 km) **A 31.5** (50.7 km) Turnout to west; avalanche gun emplacement. European elder bushes on slopes; white blossoms in spring, red berries (not edible) in fall.

S 94.4 (151.9 km) **A 32.6** (52.5 km) Turnout to west. Avalanche safety zone.

S 90.8 (146.1 km) **A 36.2** (58.3 km) *CAUTION: Railroad crossing and very bad curve.*

S 90.6 (145.8 km) **A 36.4** (58.6 km) Bridge crosses Tidewater Slough. Avalanche gun emplacement at south end of bridge.

S 90.4 (145.5 km) **A 36.6** (58.9 km) Leaving Chugach State Park southbound. The 1964 Good Friday earthquake caused land to sink in the Turnagain Arm area, particularly apparent from here to **Milepost S 74.** As a result, many trees had their root systems invaded by salt water, as seen by the stands of dead spruce trees along here. Good bird watching, including bald eagles, arctic

terns and sandhill cranes.

S 90.2 (145.2 km) **A 36.8** (59.2 km) Girdwood highway maintenance station. End avalanche area southbound. *NOTE: Major road construction northbound 1997, next 7 miles/11.3 km.*

S 90 (144.8 km) **A 37** (59.5 km) **Junction** with 3-mile/4.8-km Alyeska (pronounced al-ee-ES-ka) access road to Crow Creek road and mine, Girdwood and Alyeska Recreation Area. Worth the drive! ALYESKA ACCESS ROAD log starts on page 485. This intersection is "old" Girdwood: railroad station, school, towing service and shopping center located here. Girdwood Station Mall houses a 24-hour Tesoro 7–Eleven gas station; medical and chiropractic clinic, restaurant and a bakery. After the 1964 earthquake, Girdwood moved up the access road 2.1 miles/3.4 km.

Alpine Diner & Bakery. See display ad this section.

Tesoro 7–Eleven. See display ad this section.

NOTE: Next gas available southbound on the Seward Highway is at **Milepost S 6.6**; *next gas available westbound on Sterling Highway is at* **Milepost S 45** *(Sunrise).*

S 89.8 (144.5 km) **A 37.2** (59.9 km) Glacier Creek bridge.

S 89.1 (143.4 km) **A 37.9** (61 km) Virgin Creek bridge. View of 3 glaciers to east.

S 89 (143.2 km) **A 38** (61.2 km) Wide straight highway from here to Portage. The Alaska Railroad parallels the highway.

S 88.2 (141.9 km) **A 38.8** (62.4 km) Turnout to east.

S 87.5 (140.8 km) **A 39.5** (63.6 km) Avalanche gun emplacement.

S 86.1 (138.6 km) **A 40.9** (65.8 km) Small gravel turnout by ocean. Chugach National

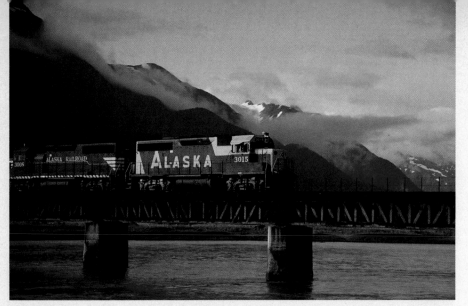

Alaska Railroad links Anchorage and Seward, with a shuttle to Whittier. (© *Barbara Willard*)

Forest boundary sign.

S 84.1 (135.3 km) A 42.9 (69 km) Peterson Creek. View of Blueberry Mountain.

S 82.3 (132.4 km) A 44.7 (71.9 km) Turnout to east.

S 81 (130.4 km) A 46 (74 km) BLM observation platform with informative plaques on Twentymile River wetlands and wildlife. Watch for dip-netters in the spring fishing for hooligan (also known as eulachon or candlefish) and smelt. Road access east to Twentymile River.

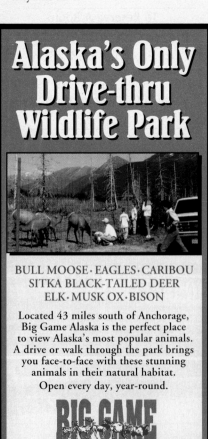
Twentymile River, good hooligan fishing in May. These smelt are taken with long-handled dip nets. Pink, red and silver (coho) salmon 4 to 10 lbs., use attraction lures, best in August. Dolly Varden 4 to 10 lbs., eggs best, good all summer in clear-water tributaries.

S 80.7 (129.9 km) A 46.3 (74.5 km) Bridge over Twentymile River, which flows out of the Twentymile Glacier and other glaciers through a long green valley at the edge of the highway. Twentymile Glacier can be seen at the end of the valley to the northeast. Twentymile River is a popular windsurfing area in summer. Gravel turnout west side of highway.

S 80.3 (129.2 km) A 46.7 (75.2 km) Access to the Alaska Railroad motor vehicle loading area for ferry traffic taking the shuttle train to Whittier. Ticket office and pay phone. Small visitor information center, gift shop and tour boat office. Connections at Whittier with Alaska Marine Highway; regular ferry service is provided across Prince William Sound past the spectacular Columbia Glacier to Valdez. For details see the ALASKA RAILROAD (page 462) and PRINCE WILLIAM SOUND (page 580) sections.

S 80.1 (128.9 km) A 46.9 (75.5 km) PORTAGE. No facilities here. The 1964 earthquake caused the land to drop between 6 and 12 feet along Turnagain Arm here. High tides then flooded the area, forcing the estimated 50 to 100 residents of Portage to move. Some old buildings are visible; more evidence of trees killed by the invading salt water. Leaving Game Management Unit 14C, entering unit 7, southbound.

S 80 (128.7 km) A 47 (75.6 km) Second access to motor vehicle loading ramps and passenger parking for Alaska Railroad shuttle train from Portage to Whittier.

S 79.4 (127.8 km) A 47.6 (76.6 km) Bridge No. 2 southbound over Portage Creek. Parking and interpretive sign to west at south end of bridge. This gray-colored creek carries the silt-laden glacial meltwater from Portage Glacier and Portage Lake to Turnagain Arm. Mud flats in Turnagain Arm are created by silt from the creek settling close to shore.

S 79 (127.1 km) A 48 (77.2 km) Bridge No. 1 southbound over Portage Creek. Drive-through wildlife park and gift shop.

Big Game Alaska. See display ad this section.

S 78.9 (127 km) A 48.1 (77.4 km) **Junction** with Portage Glacier access road. Portage Glacier is one of Alaska's most popular attractions. See PORTAGE GLACIER ROAD log on opposite page. *NOTE: There is no gas or lodging available at the glacier.* Tidewater Cafe south side of junction.

S 78.4 (126.1 km) A 48.6 (78.2 km) Bridge over Placer River; boat launch. Second bridge over Placer River at **Milepost S 77.9.** Turnouts next to both bridges. Between Placer River and Ingram Creek, there is an excellent view on clear days of Skookum Glacier to the northeast. To the north across Turnagain Arm is Twentymile Glacier. Arctic terns and waterfowl are often seen in the slough here.

Placer River has good hooligan fishing in May. These smelt are taken with long-handled dip nets. Silver salmon may be taken in August and September.

S 77.9 (125.4 km) A 49.1 (79 km) Bridge over Placer River overflow. Paved turnout to south.

S 77 (123.9 km) A 50 (80.5 km) Boundary of Chugach National Forest.

S 75.5 (121.5 km) A 51.5 (82.9 km) Paved double-ended scenic viewpoints both sides of highway.

S 75.2 (121 km) A 51.8 (83.4 km) Bridge over **Ingram Creek**; pink salmon fishing (even years).

S 75 (120.7 km) A 52 (83.7 km) Paved turnout to west. Welcome to the Kenai Peninsula sign. Highway begins ascent to Turnagain Pass southbound. Passing lane next 5 miles/8 km southbound.

S 74.5 (119.9 km) A 52.5 (84.5 km) Double-ended paved turnout to east. Several kinds of blueberries, together with false azalea blossoms, are seen along here during summer months.

S 72.5 (116.7 km) A 54.5 (87.7 km) Double-ended paved turnout to east.

S 71.5 (115.1 km) A 55.5 (89.3 km) Double-ended paved turnout to west.

S 71.2 (114.6 km) A 55.8 (89.8 km) Double-ended paved turnout to west.

S 71 (114.3 km) A 56 (90.1 km) Paved turnout to east. The many flowers seen in surrounding alpine meadows here include yellow and purple violets, mountain heliotrope, lousewort and paintbrush.

S 69.9 (112.5 km) A 57.1 (91.9 km) Scenic viewpoint with double-ended parking area to west. The highway traverses an area of mountain meadows and parklike stands of spruce, hemlock, birch and aspen, interlaced with glacier-fed streams. Lupine and wild geranium grow profusely here in the summer.

S 69.2 (111.4 km) A 57.8 (93 km) Paved turnout to east.

S 69.1 (111.2 km) A 57.9 (93.2 km) Passing lane ends southbound.

S 68.9 (110.9 km) A 58.1 (93.5 km) Divided highway begins southbound, ends northbound.

S 68.5 (110.2 km) A 58.5 (94.1 km) Turnagain Pass Recreation Area (elev. 988 feet/301m). Parking area, restrooms and dumpster (southbound lane); emergency call box. U-turn. Turnagain Pass Recreation Area is a favorite winter recreation area for snowmobilers (west side of highway) and cross-country skiers (east side of highway). Snow depths here frequently exceed 12 feet/4m.

S 68.1 (109.6 km) A 58.9 (94.8 km) Park-

Portage Glacier Road Log

Distance from the junction with the Seward Highway (J).

J 0 Junction with Seward Highway at Milepost S 78.9. *CAUTION: Alaska Railroad tracks, rough crossing.*

J 2 (3.2 km) Portage Glacier Work Center (USFS); no services available.

J 2.4 (3.8 km) Paved turnout. Explorer Glacier viewpoint on right.

J 3.1 (5 km) Bridge. Beaver dam visible from road.

J 3.7 (5.9 km) Black Bear USFS campground; 12 sites (2 will accommodate medium-sized trailers), toilets, water, firepits, dumpsters, tables, $9 fee. Pleasant wooded area. ▲

J 4.1 (6.6 km) Bridge over Williwaw Creek. USFS campground, south of road below Middle Glacier; 38 campsites, toilets, dumpsters, water, firepits, tables, $10 single, $15 double (reservations available, phone 1-800-280-CAMP). Beautiful campground. Campfire programs in the amphitheater; check bulletin board for schedule. Spawning red salmon and dog salmon can be viewed (from late July to mid-September) from Williwaw Creek observation deck near campground entrance. Self-guided Williwaw nature trail off the campground loop road goes through moose and beaver habitat. ▲

J 5.2 (8.4 km) Paved road forks at Portage Glacier Lodge; left fork leads to visitor center (description follows). Take right fork 0.8 mile/1.3 km to parking lot; 1.2 miles/1.9 km to Byron Glacier overlook; and 1.5 miles/2.4 km to MV *Ptarmigan* sightseeing boat cruise dock and passenger waiting facility.

J 5.5 (8.8 km) Begich, Boggs Visitor Center at Portage Glacier and Portage

Trail up Byron Glacier near Portage Glacier. (© Barbara Willard)

Lake. Open daily in summer (9 A.M.–6 P.M.); weekends in winter (10 A.M.–4 P.M.). Phone the visitor center at (907) 783-2326 or the U.S. Forest Service district office at (907) 783-3242 for current schedule.

Forest Service naturalists are available to answer questions and provide information about Chugach National Forest resources. There are displays on glaciers and on the natural history of the area. The award-winning film *Voices from the Ice* is shown in the theater hourly. Schedules of hikes and programs led by naturalists are posted at the center. One of the

most popular activities is the iceworm safari. (Often regarded as a hoax, iceworms actually exist; the small, black worms thrive at temperatures just above freezing.) A self-guided interpretive trail about glacial landforms begins just south of the visitor center.

Large paved parking area provides views of Portage Lake. There are several excellent spots in the area to observe salmon spawning (August and September) in Portage Creek and its tributaries.

Return to Milepost S 78.9
Seward Highway

---

ing area, restrooms and dumpster for northbound traffic. U-turn.

S 67.8 (109.1 km) **A 59.2** (95.3 km) Bridge over Lyon Creek.

S 67.6 (108.8 km) **A 59.4** (95.6 km) Divided highway ends southbound, begins northbound.

S 66.8 (107.5 km) **A 60.2** (96.9 km) Paved double-ended turnout with litter container to east.

S 65.3 (105.1 km) **A 61.7** (99.3 km) Bridge over Bertha Creek. Bertha Creek USFS campground; 12 sites, water, toilets, firepits, table, dumpsters and $9 fee. ▲

S 64.8 (104.3 km) **A 62.2** (100.1 km) Bridge over Spokane Creek.

S 64 (102.9 km) **A 63** (101.3 km) Granite Creek fireguard station.

S 63.7 (102.5 km) **A 63.3** (101.9 km) Johnson Pass north trailhead. This 23-mile-/37-km-long trail is a fairly level good family trail, which follows a portion of the Old Iditarod trail which went from Seward to Nome. See **Milepost S 32.6.**

Johnson Pass trail leads to **Bench Lake,** which has arctic grayling, and **Johnson Lake,** which has rainbow trout. Both lakes are about halfway in on trail. ◄►

S 63.3 (101.9 km) **A 63.7** (102.5 km) Bridge over Granite Creek. Traditional halfway point on highway between Anchorage

and Seward.

S 63 (101.4 km) **A 64** (103 km) Granite Creek USFS campground, 0.8 mile/1.3 km from main highway; 19 sites (most beside creek), water, toilets, dumpsters, tables, firepits and $9 fee. **Granite Creek,** small Dolly Varden. ◄►▲

S 62 (99.8 km) **A 65** (104.6 km) Bridge over East Fork Sixmile Creek.

S 61 (98.2 km) **A 66** (106.2 km) Bridge over Silvertip Creek.

S 59.7 (96.1 km) **A 67.3** (108.3 km) Gravel turnout next to Granite Creek. Excellent place to photograph this glacial stream. Beaver dam.

S 58.8 (94.6 km) **A 68.2** (109.8 km) Large gravel turnout to west. There are several turnouts along this stretch of highway.

S 57.6 (92.7 km) **A 69.4** (111.7 km) Bridge over Dry Gulch Creek.

S 57 (91.7 km) **A 70** (112.7 km) Bridge over Canyon Creek.

NOTE: Watch for road construction next 7 miles/11.3 km southbound in 1997.

S 56.8 (91.4 km) **A 70.2** (113 km) Staging area for raft trips on Sixmile Creek. **Nenana Raft Adventures, Inc.** See display ad this section.

S 56.7 (91.2 km) **A 70.3** (113.1 km) Southbound **junction** with Hope Highway to historic mining community of Hope. See

HOPE HIGHWAY log on page 492.

NOTE: Southbound travelers may find this junction confusing. Hope Highway veers right; Seward Highway veers left.

S 56.6 (91.1 km) **A 70.4** (113.3 km) Northbound **junction** with Hope Highway. Numerous gravel turnouts next 6 miles/9.7 km southbound.

S 50.1 (80.6 km) **A 76.9** (123.8 km) Begin improved highway southbound with wide shoulders and passing lanes. Winter avalanche area next 1.5 miles/2.4 km southbound.

Truck lane next 2 miles/3.2 km northbound.

S 48 (77.2 km) **A 79** (127.1 km) Fresno Creek bridge; turnout to east at south end of bridge.

S 47.6 (76.6 km) **A 79.4** (127.8 km) Double-ended paved turnout to east on lake.

S 47.2 (76 km) **A 79.8** (128.4 km) Paved

Hope Highway Log

The paved 17.7-mile/28.5-km Hope Highway leads northwest to the historic community of Hope on the south side of Turnagain Arm and provides access to the Resurrection Creek area.

Distance is measured from junction with the Seward Highway (J).

J 0 Junction with Seward Highway at **Milepost S 56.7.**

J 0.1 (0.2 km) Silvertip highway maintenance station.

J 0.7 (1.1 km) Double-ended paved turnout to east; road access to creek.

J 0.9 (1.4 km) Highway parallels Sixmile Creek, a glacial stream. There are many paved turnouts along the Hope Highway, some with views of Turnagain Arm.

J 1 (1.6 km) **NOVA the Adventure Co.** Since 1975. Sixmile Creek, Alaska's premier whitewater trip! Rated class IV and V, this is the most challenging raft trip in the state. Spectacular canyons and thrilling participatory whitewater! Granite Creek, a great first-timers whitewater, includes the Class IV canyon of the Six mile plus a very scenic float down Turnagain Pass. All river gear provided. Call 1-800-746-5753 for information and reservations. P.O. Box 1129, Chickaloon, AK 99674. [ADVERTISEMENT]

J 1.4 (2.3 km) Beaver marsh to east.

J 2.3 (3.7 km) Large paved turnout to east. Moose may often be seen in Sixmile Creek valley below. The old gold mining town of Sunrise City, with a population of 5,000, was founded in 1895 at the mouth of Sixmile Creek. The present community of Sunrise has a population of about 20.

J 3.4 (5.5 km) Large paved turnout to east; trail access to creek.

J 3.9 (6.3 km) Large paved turnout to

Resurrection Creek near Hope.
(Sharon Paul Nault)

east; trail access to creek.

J 10 (16.1 km) Double-ended paved turnout to east overlooking Turnagain Arm.

J 11.1 (17.9 km) Large paved turnout to east overlooking Turnagain Arm.

J 11.8 (19 km) Double-ended paved turnout to east overlooking Turnagain Arm.

J 15.8 (25.4 km) **Henry's One Stop.** See display ad this section. ▲

J 15.9 (25.6 km) Bear Creek Lodge.

J 16.2 (26 km) Turn left (south) for Hope airport; USFS Resurrection Pass trailhead, 4 miles/6.4 km south on Resurrection Creek Road; Resurrection Trail Resort, 4.6 miles/7.4 km; and Coeur d'Alene Campground on Palmer Creek Road, 7.6 miles/12.2 km. ▲

Resurrection Trail Resort. See display ad this section.

The 38-mile-/61-km-long Resurrection Pass USFS trail climbs from an elevation

of 400 feet/122m at the trailhead to Resurrection Pass (elev. 2,600 feet/792m) and down to the south trailhead at **Milepost S 53.1** on the Sterling Highway. There are 8 cabins on the trail. Parking area at the trailhead.

Coeur d'Alene, former USFS campground (semi-developed), has 5 sites (not recommended for large RVs or trailers); primitive camping only; no maintained facilities; no water, no camping fee. Palmer Creek Road continues past the campground to alpine country above 1,500 feet/457m elevation, and views of Turnagain Arm and Resurrection Creek valley. The road past the old campground is rough and narrow and not recommended for low-clearance vehicles. ▲

J 16.5 (26.6 km) Turn on Hope Road for downtown **HOPE** (pop. 224). Hope Road leads past the post office down to the waterfront, a favorite fishing spot near the ocean; motel, cafe, grocery store and gift shop.

This historic mining community was founded in 1896 by gold seekers working Resurrection Creek and its tributary streams. Today, many Anchorage residents have vacation homes here.

Discovery Cafe. See display ad this section.

J 17 (27.3 km) Road to historic Hope townsite. Interpretive sign at intersection. The original townsite of Hope City was founded in 1896. Portions of the town destroyed by the 1964 earthquake are marked with dotted lines on the map sign.

J 17.1 (27.5 km) Resurrection Creek bridge.

J 17.7 (28.4 km) Gas station.

J 17.8 (28.6 km) Hope Highway ends at Porcupine USFS campground; 24 sites, tables, tent spaces, toilets, firepits, dumpster, drinking water and $9 fee. Gull Rock trailhead. ▲

Return to Milepost S 56.7 Seward Highway

double-ended turnout to east next to Lower Summit Lake; a favorite photo stop. Extremely picturesque with lush growth of wildflowers in summer.

Upper and Lower Summit lakes, good spring and fall fishing for landlocked Dolly Varden (goldenfins), ranging in size from 6 to 11 inches, flies and single salmon eggs. ◂

S 46.6 (74.7 km) A 80.6 (129.7 km) Double-ended paved turnout to east on lake.

S 46 (74 km) A 81 (130.4 km) Colorado Creek bridge. Tenderfoot Creek USFS campground 0.6 mile/0.9 km from highway; 28 sites, water, toilets (wheelchair accessible), dumpsters, tables, firepits, boat launch, $9 fee. ♿▲

S 45.8 (73.7 km) A 81.2 (130.7 km) Summit Lake Lodge; open year-round. Emergency radio. Winter avalanche area begins southbound.

Summit Lake Lodge. Genuine hospitality on the north shore of Summit Lake in

Alaska's most beautiful log lodge. Located in the heart of Chugach National Forest, it is a landmark for many. The view is spectacular and the food excellent. Complete menu from eye-opening omelettes to mouthwatering steaks. Enjoy our cozy motel and relaxing lounge. Open year-round. Fishing, hiking, photography, cross-country skiing, snowmobiling. It's a must stop for every visitor in the last frontier. See display ad this section. [ADVERTISEMENT] ▲

S 45.5 (73.2 km) A 81.5 (131.2 km) Upper Summit Lake. Paved turnout to east.

S 44.5 (71.6 km) A 82.5 (132.7 km) Large paved double-ended turnout with interpretive sign to east at end of Upper Summit Lake.

S 44.3 (71.3 km) A 82.7 (133.1 km) Beaver dams.

S 44 (70.8 km) A 83 (133.6 km) Gravel turnout to east. Avalanche gun emplacement.

S 43.8 (70.5 km) A 83.2 (133.9 km) Winter avalanche area begins northbound. Avalanche gates.

S 43.7 (70.3 km) A 83.3 (134.1 km) Paved double-ended turnout to east.

S 42.6 (68.6 km) A 84.4 (135.8 km) Summit Creek bridge.

S 42.2 (67.9 km) A 84.8 (136.5 km) Quartz Creek bridge.

S 41.4 (66.6 km) A 85.6 (137.8 km) Passing lane next 1 mile/1.6 km northbound.

S 39.6 (63.7 km) A 87.4 (140.7 km) Avalanche gates.

S 39.4 (63.4 km) A 87.6 (141 km) Devils Pass trailhead; parking area and toilets to west. This USFS trail starts at an elevation of 1,000 feet/305m and follows Devils Creek to Devils Pass (elev. 2,400 feet/732m), continuing on to Devils Pass Lake and Resurrection Pass trail. Hiking time to Devils Pass is about 5½ hours.

S 39 (62.8 km) A 88 (141.6 km) Truck lane extends northbound to Milepost S 39.3.

S 38.6 (62.1 km) A 88.4 (142.3 km) Paved turnout to west adjacent **Jerome Lake**, rainbow and Dolly Varden to 22 inches, use salmon egg clusters, year-round, still fish. A sign here explains rainbow plant in lake. ◂

S 38.3 (61.6 km) A 88.7 (142.7 km) Paved

double-ended turnout to west overlooking Jerome Lake. USFS interpretive sign about sticklebacks.

S 38.2 (61.5 km) A 88.8 (142.9 km) Truck lane ends northbound.

S 37.7 (60.7 km) A 89.3 (143.7 km) **Junction.** First southbound exit (one-way road) for Sterling Highway (Alaska Route 1) on right. Continue straight ahead on Alaska Route 9 for Seward.

If you are bound for Soldotna, Homer, or other Sterling Highway communities and attractions, turn to page 513 in the STERLING HIGHWAY section and begin that log. Continue with this log if you are going to Seward.

ALASKA ROUTE 9

S 37.2 (59.9 km) A 89.8 (144.5 km) Paved turnout to west overlooking Tern Lake for Seward-bound travelers.

S 37 (59.5 km) A 90 (144.8 km) **Tern Lake Junction.** Second southbound turnoff on right (2-way road) for Sterling Highway (Alaska Route 1) and access to Tern Lake USFS campground and salmon spawning channel. To reach campground, drive 0.4 mile/0.6 km around Tern Lake; 25 sites, water, toilets, picnic tables, firepits, canoe launch, $9 fee. Tern Lake is a good spot for bird watching in summer. See STERLING HIGHWAY section. ▲

Continue straight ahead on Alaska Route 9 for Seward.

S 36.7 (59.1 km) A 90.3 (145.3 km) Truck lane begins northbound.

S 36.4 (58.6 km) A 90.6 (145.8 km) Avalanche gates.

S 35.7 (57.5 km) A 91.3 (146.9 km) Outfitter for guided horse pack trips.

TAK Outfitters. See display ad this section.

S 35.3 (56.8 km) A 91.7 (147.6 km) End avalanche area southbound.

S 35 (56.3 km) A 92 (148 km) For the next 3 miles/4.8 km many small waterfalls tumble down the brushy slopes. Winter avalanche area between **Milepost S 35.3** and **34.6.** You are driving through the Kenai mountain range.

S 33.1 (53.3 km) A 93.9 (151.1 km) Carter Lake USFS trailhead No. 4 to west; parking and toilets. Trail starts at an elevation of 500 feet/152m and climbs 986 feet/300m to **Carter Lake** (stocked with rainbow

trout). Trail is good, but steep; hiking time about 1½ hours. Good access to sheep and mountain goat country. Excellent snowmobiling area in winter. ⌐

S 32.6 (52.5 km) A 94.4 (151.9 km) Johnson Pass USFS south trailhead with parking area, toilet. North trailhead at **Milepost S 63.7.**

S 32.5 (52.3 km) A 94.5 (152.1 km) Large paved double-ended turnout; USFS information sign on life cycle of salmon; short trail to observation deck on stream where spawning salmon may be seen in August.

S 32.4 (52.1 km) A 94.6 (152.2 km) Cook Inlet Aquaculture Association. Trail Lake fish hatchery on Moose Creek; display room. Open 8 A.M. to 5 P.M. daily; phone (907) 288-3688.

S 31.8 (51.1 km) A 95.2 (153.2 km) Paved double-ended rest area to east on Upper Trail Lake; toilets, picnic tables.

Moose Pass waterwheel is a local landmark. (Jerrianne Lowther, staff)

S 30.1 (48.4 km) **A 96.9** (155.9 km) **Spruce Moose Bed and Breakfast.** Two comfortable chalet-style homes are nestled among spruce trees on a 5-acre hillside. Spectacular views of Upper Trail Lake and Lark Mountain. Each spacious chalet, which is yours exclusively, provides everything needed for a relaxing stay for up to 8 people. Available year-round. MasterCard and VISA accepted. Roseann Hetrick, P.O. Box 7, Moose Pass, AK 99631. (907) 288-3667. [ADVERTISEMENT]

S 30 (48.3 km) **A 97** (156.1 km) Short side road to large undeveloped gravel parking area on Upper Trail Lake; boat launch.

S 29.9 (48.1 km) **A 97.1** (156.3 km) Gravel turnout by Trail Lake.

S 29.4 (47.3 km) **A 97.6** (157.1 km) Large working waterwheel that turns a grindstone, built by the late Ed Estes, on way into Moose Pass. Parking area and sign at waterwheel which reads: "Moose Pass is a peaceful little town. If you have an ax to grind, do it here."

MOOSE PASS (pop. 145) has a motel, bed and breakfast, log cabins for rent, RV park, general store, gift shop, restaurant, salmon bake, post office and highway maintenance station. Pay phone outside GTE building. Alaska State Troopers, emergency only phone 911. This mountain village on Upper Trail Lake was a construction camp on the Alaska Railroad in 1912. Local resident Ed Estes attributed the name Moose Pass to a 1904 observation by Nate White of the first moose recorded in this area. Another version holds that "in 1903, a mail carrier driving a team of dogs had considerable trouble gaining the right-of-way from a giant moose." A post office was established in 1928. ▲

Moose Pass has a 1.3-mile-/2.1-km-long paved bike trail which winds along Trail Lake from the Moose Pass ball diamond to the McFadden house on the south. Gravel turnout by lake.

The main street of town is the site of the Annual Moose Pass Summer Festival, a community-sponsored event which takes place the weekend nearest summer solstice (June 21). The festival features a triathlon, arts and crafts booths, a barbecue, auction and other events.

Estes Brothers Groceries & Water Wheel. See display ad this section.

Trail Lake Lodge. Home cooking, reasonable rates, friendly staff and clean facilities welcome you to this landmark lodge.

Conveniently located in the heart of the Chugach National Forest trail system on the shores of scenic Trail Lake, a short drive to Seward and Kenai Fjords National Park. Phone 1-800-208-0200 or (907) 288-3101. See display ad in the Seward section. [ADVERTISEMENT]

S 29.1 (46.8 km) **A 97.9** (157.6 km) **Moose Pass RV Park.** New! 25 spaces and growing. Electric hookups. Scenic campground-like setting. Close to restaurant, laundromat, showers, post office, small store, telephone. Just off main highway. (907) 288-3184. [ADVERTISEMENT] ▲

S 28.9 (46.5 km) **A 98.1** (157.9 km) **Midnight Sun Log Cabins.** See display ad this section.

S 26 (41.8 km) **A 101** (162.5 km) Lower Trail Lake. Timbered slopes of Madson Mountain (elev. 5,269 feet/1,605m) to the west. Crescent Lake lies just west of Madson.

S 25.8 (41.5 km) **A 101.2** (162.9 km) Gravel turnout to west.

S 25.4 (40.9 km) **A 101.6** (163.5 km) Bridge over Trail River.

S 25 (40.2 km) **A 102** (164.1 km) Bridge over Falls Creek.

S 24.8 (39.9 km) **A 102.2** (164.5 km) Gravel turnout to west.

S 24.2 (38.9 km) **A 102.8** (165.4 km) Side road leads 1.2 miles/1.9 km to Trail River USFS campground; 64 sites, picnic tables, firepits, dumpsters, toilets, and volleyball and horseshoe area. Day-use group picnic area. Spacious, wooded campsites in tall spruce on shore of Kenai Lake and Lower Trail River. Pull-through sites available. Fee $9 single, $13 double, reservations available; phone 1-800-280-CAMP. Campground host may be in residence during summer, providing fishing and hiking information. Good spot for mushrooming and berry picking in August. ▲

Lower Trail River, lake trout, rainbow and Dolly Varden to 25 inches, July, August and September, use salmon eggs, small spinners. Access via Lower Trail River campground road. **Trail River,** Dolly Varden 12 to 20 inches, spring and fall, use fresh eggs; rainbow 12 to 20 inches, spring, use fresh eggs. ◄

S 24.1 (38.8 km) **A 102.9** (165.6 km) **Crown Point Lodge.** Let our staff plan your fishing, hunting, sightseeing or flightseeing while you dine on our true home-cooked meals, pies and breads in an Alaska setting. Clean, comfortable rooms are available at moderate costs. We offer package prices for lodging, meals and charters. Phone (907) 288-3136 or fax (907) 288-3641. Y'all come! [ADVERTISEMENT]

S 23.4 (37.7 km) **A 103.6** (166.7 km)

CAUTION: *Railroad crossing.* USFS Kenai Lake work center (no information services available). Report forest fires here.

Private Aircraft: Lawing landing strip; elev. 475 feet/144m; length 2,300 feet/701m; gravel; unattended.

S 23.1 (37.1 km) **A 103.9** (167.2 km) **Ptarmigan Creek** bridge and USFS picnic area and campground with 16 sites, water, toilets, tables, firepits and dumpsters, $9 fee (reservations available, phone 1-800-280-CAMP). Fair to good fishing in creek and in lake outlets at **Ptarmigan Lake** (hike in) for Dolly Varden. Watch for spawning salmon in Ptarmigan Creek in August. ◄▲

Ptarmigan Creek USFS trail No. 14 begins at campground (elev. 500 feet/152m) and leads 3.5 miles/5.6 km to Ptarmigan Lake (elev. 755 feet/230m). Trail is steep in spots; round-trip hiking time 5 hours. Good chance of seeing sheep, goats, moose and bears. Carry insect repellent. Trail is poor for winter use due to avalanche hazard.

S 23 (37 km) **A 104** (167.3 km) Turnoff for Alaska Nellie's Homestead. The late Nellie Neal–Lawing arrived in Alaska in 1915. Her colorful life included cooking for the railroad workers and big game hunting and guiding. She converted a roadhouse at Lawing into a museum to house the trophies and souvenirs she and her husband, Billie Lawing, gathered on their travels.

Alaska Nellie's Inn, Inc. See display ad this section.

S 22.9 (36.9 km) **A 104.1** (167.5 km) Viewpoint to west overlooking Kenai Lake. This lake (elev. 436 feet/132m) extends 24 miles/39 km from the head of the Kenai River on the west to the mouth of Snow River on the east. A sign here explains how glacier meltwater gives the lake its distinctive color.

Winter avalanche area next 3 miles/4.8 km southbound.

S 22.5 (36.2 km) **A 104.5** (168.2 km) Rough gravel double-ended turnout to east.

S 21.3 (34.3 km) **A 105.7** (170.1 km) Gravel turnout to east overlooking lake.

S 20.2 (32.5 km) **A 106.8** (171.9 km) Avalanche gun emplacement.

S 20.1 (32.3 km) **A 106.9** (172 km) Gravel turnout. Avalanche area ends southbound.

S 19.9 (32 km) **A 107.1** (172.4 km) **I.R.B.I. Knives.** See display ad this section.

S 19.5 (31.4 km) **A 107.5** (173 km) Victor Creek bridge. Victor Creek USFS trail No. 23 begins here. A 2-mile/3.2-km hike with good view of mountains.

S 17.7 (28.5 km) **A 109.3** (175.9 km) Bridge over center channel of Snow River. This river has 2 forks that flow into Kenai Lake.

S 17 (27 km) **A 110** (177 km) Primrose Road. Access to bed and breakfast. Turn west for Primrose USFS campground, 1 mile/1.6 km from the highway. (Campground access road leads past private homes. Drive carefully!) The campground, overlooking Kenai Lake, has 10 sites, toilets, dumpsters, tables, firepits, boat ramp, water, $9 fee. Primrose trail (6.5 miles/10.5 km) starts from the campground and connects with Lost Lake trail (7 miles/11.2 km). High alpine hike, trail is posted. ▲

Primrose B&B Chalets. See display ad this section.

Bridge over south channel of Snow River.

S 16.2 (26.1 km) **A 110.8** (178.3 km) Gravel turnout to east.

S 16 (25.7 km) **A 111** (178.6 km) Snow River hostel.

S 15 (24.1 km) **A 112** (180.2 km) Watch for moose in ponds and meadows.

S 14.9 (24 km) **A 112.1** (180.4 km) Gravel turnout to east.

S 14 (22.5 km) **A 113** (181.9 km) CAUTION: *Railroad crossing.*

S 13.3 (21.4 km) **A 113.7** (183 km) Grayling Lake USFS trailhead to west, large paved parking area to east. Grayling Lake trail No. 20, 1.6 miles/2.6 km, connects with trails to Meridian and Leech lakes. Good spot for photos of Snow River valley. Watch for moose. **Grayling Lake**, 6- to 12-inch grayling, use flies, May to October. ◢

S 12 (19.3 km) **A 115** (185.1 km) Alaska Railroad crosses under highway.

S 11.6 (18.6 km) **A 115.4** (185.7 km) Gravel parking area to west and USFS trail No. 6 to **Golden Fin Lake**, Dolly Varden averaging 8 inches. This is a 0.6-mile/1-km hike on a very wet trail: wear rubber footwear. ◢

S 10.8 (17.4 km) **A 116.2** (187 km) Large gravel turnout to east.

S 8.5 (13.6 km) **A 118.5** (190.7 km) Gravel turnout to west.

S 8.3 (13.4 km) **A 118.7** (191 km) Paved turnout by creek to east. Leaving Chugach National Forest land southbound.

S 8 (12.9 km) **A 119** (191.5 km) **Grouse**

Floatplane on Bear Lake outside Seward. (Jerrianne Lowther, staff)

Creek bridge. Dolly Varden fishing.

S 7.4 (11.9 km) **A 119.6** (192.5 km) **Grouse Lake** access road. Good ice fishing for Dolly Varden in winter.

S 7.1 (11.4 km) **A 119.9** (193 km) Old Mill subdivision.

S 6.6 (10.6 km) **A 120.4** (193.7 km) Bear Creek bridge and Bear Lake Road; access to gas station, 2 private RV parks, bed and breakfast, and a flying service. Drive in 0.7 mile/1.1 km on Bear Lake Road to see a state-operated fish weir. Silver and red (sockeye) salmon are trapped to provide life-cycle data and also eggs for the state's salmon stocking program.

A Creekside Park & Motel. See display ad this section.

Bear Creek RV Park, drive ½ mile on Bear Lake Road. Good Sam Park has full and partial hookups, dump station, 4 private restrooms with showers, cable TV, travelers lounge, propane, laundry, convenience store, ice, video rentals. 2 free showers per site. Pay phone inside. Excellent water. (907) 224-5725. Fax service available. Bunkhouse for rent. Free shuttle when reservations are booked through our office for glacier and fishing trips. Auto and RV repair and service.

RV and boat storage. High pressure wash. Short walk to fish weir. Bear Creek RV Park is not to be mistaken for A Creekside RV Park located at the gas station on the corner of the Seward Highway and Bear Lake Road. Internet: http://www.alaska.net/~bear. See display ad this section. [ADVERTISEMENT] ▲

Bear Lake Air & Guide Service. See display ad this section.

S 6.3 (10.1 km) **A 120.7** (194.2 km) Lake Drive; access to bed and breakfasts.

Alaska's Stoney Creek Inn Bed & Breakfast. See display ad this section.

S 5.9 (9.4 km) **A 121.1** (194.8 km) **Salmon Creek** bridge. Good fishing in stream for sea-run Dolly Varden averaging 10 inches, use single salmon eggs, begins about Aug. 1.

S 5.2 (8.4 km) **A 121.8** (196 km) Bear Creek volunteer fire department.

S 4.7 (7.6 km) **A 122.3** (196.8) Smoke 'n Alaska Seafoods. See display ad this section.

S 3.8 (6.1 km) **A 123.2** (198.3 km) Clear Creek bridge.

S 3.7 (6 km) **A 123.3** (198.4 km) Turnoff for Exit Glacier Road. Access to restaurant, health food store, dogsled rides, and bed and breakfasts; turn right onto loop road (old Exit Glacier Road) immediately after turning off highway.

The 9-mile/14.5-km Exit Glacier Road (maintained by DOT/PF May to September, depending on snow) is paved for the first 4 miles/6.4 km; expect road construction on the last 5 miles/8 km in 1997. The road ends at a parking lot with toilets and picnic area next to Exit Glacier ranger station in Kenai Fjords National Park. Look for bears high on the hillside opposite the ranger station. Walk-in campground with 9 sites (no fee, reservations). A public-use cabin is available; access in winter by cross-country skis, dogsled or snow machine; permit required, phone (907) 224-3175. ▲

The National Park Service operates a visitor center at the ranger station (seasonal). The flat, easy 0.8-mile Lower Loop trail leads through alder forest to outwash plain; pick your own route to base of glacier. The longer half-mile Upper Loop trail offers excellent views of the glacier. The first 0.2 mile/0.3 km of this trail is paved and wheelchair accessible. There is also an easy 0.8 mile/1.3 km nature trail loop with 10 interpretive signs on forest succession. A strenuous 3.5-mile/5.6-km trail leads to Harding Icefield from the parking lot (a ranger patrols this trail). Summer activities include ranger-led nature walks at 10 A.M. and 2 P.M. daily. Park Information Line: (907) 224-2132. Worth the drive to see an active glacier up close. *CAUTION: Falling ice at face of glacier, stay behind warning signs.* ♿

On the drive out, note the finger dikes

Walking trails lead to face of Exit Glacier, 9 miles from turnoff at Milepost S 3.7.
(© James Ronan)

built along the road to protect it from erosion by the Resurrection River. The trailhead for Resurrection River trail is located just before crossing the Resurrection River bridge on the access road. The 16-mile/25.7-km USFS trail ties in with the Russian Lakes trail. It is part of the 75-mile/121-km Hope-to-Seward route. *CAUTION: Black and brown bears also use this trail.*

Clear Creek Cottages. See display ad this section.

Creekside Cabins Bed & Breakfast. See display ad this section.

Le Barn Appétit Bed & Breakfast. See display ad this section.

IdidaRide Sled Dog Tours. See display ad this section.

S 3.2 (5.1 km) **A 123.8** (199.2 km) Nash Road, access to bed and breakfasts: Camelot Cottages, The Farm, Northern Exposure, Rininger's, Fjordland Inn. It is a scenic 5-mile/8-km drive out Nash Road to Seward's Marine Industrial Center in the Fourth of July Creek valley. Fine views along the way and from Kertulla Point of Resurrection Bay and the city of Seward. At Mile 2.1 Nash Road is the trailhead for the Iditarod Trail, which begins at the ferry terminal in downtown Seward. Hike to Bear Lake; from north end of lake, trail continues to Mile 12 on the Seward Highway.

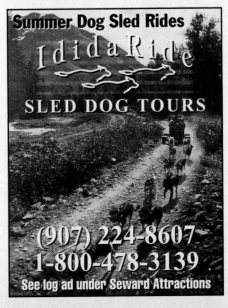

Camelot Cottages. See display ad on page 497.

The Farm Bed & Breakfast. Turn off Seward Highway onto Nash Road, turn left immediately onto Salmon Creek Road, follow signs to "The Farm." Tranquil country setting on acres of trees and lawn.

Choose from our main house ... cottages ... economy bungalow ... or kitchenette units with private phones, perfect for business travelers. Enjoy cable TV, decks, barbecue,

private baths. Freezer space, laundry facilities. Families welcome. Continental breakfast. Open year-round. VISA, MasterCard, Discover. Long-time Alaskan host Jack Hoogland, Box 305, Seward, AK 99664. Reservations suggested. (907) 224-5691. Fax (907) 224-2300. See display ad in Seward section. [ADVERTISEMENT]

Northern Exposure Bed & Breakfast. See display ad this section.

Rininger's Bed & Breakfast (Mile 1.6 Nash Road) is located on Rabbit Run Road (left at fork). Open year-round. Large, sunny room with skylights and handcrafted furnishings. Private bath and kitchenette; sleeping loft, separate entrance. Breakfast in room at your leisure. Outdoor wood-heated sauna. Hiking and cross-country ski trails nearby. A perfect weekend getaway. Families welcome. Sleeps up to 8. Kent and Lisa Rininger, P.O.

Mountain goat in Kenai Fjords National Park. (© Mike Jones)

Box 548, Seward, AK 99664. (907) 224-5918. [ADVERTISEMENT]

Fjordland Inn. See display ad this section.

S 3 (4.8 km) A 124 (199.6 km) Resurrection River; 3 channels, 3 bridges. This river flows from the Harding Icefield into Resurrection Bay just northeast of Seward. Seward city limits.

S 2.7 (4.3 km) A 124.3 (200 km) Turnoff for Seward airport.

S 2.5 (4 km) A 124.5 (200.4 km) Hemlock Street. Forest Acres municipal campground; water, flush toilets, 14-day limit. No tables.▲

S 2.3 (3.7 km) A 124.7 (200.7 km) Sea Lion Drive. U.S. Air Force and U.S. Army Seward Recreation Area.

Seward Resort (Military). See display ad this section.

S 2.1 (3.4 km) A 124.9 (201 km) Dimond Boulevard.

S 2 (3.2 km) A 125 (201.1 km) Seward Chamber of Commerce–Convention and Visitors Bureau visitor center.

S 1.8 (2.9 km) A 125.2 (201.5 km) Gas station.

S 1.7 (2.7 km) A 125.3 (201.6 km) Bear Drive; access to bed and breakfasts.

S 1.5 (2.4 km) A 125.5 (202 km) Seward High School.

S 1.2 (1.9 km) A 125.8 (202.4 km) Large parking area to west with memorial to Benny Benson, who designed the Alaska state flag.

S 1 (1.6 km) A 126 (202.8 km) Main entrance to boat harbor.

S 0.4 (0.6 km) A 126.6 (203.7 km) Madison Street. Post office one block east.

S 0.3 (0.5 km) A 126.7 (203.9 km) Intersection of 3rd Avenue (Seward Highway) and Jefferson. Hospital 2 blocks west. Information Cache railcar at intersection.

Seward

S 0 A 127 (204.4 km) Located on Resurrection Bay, east coast of Kenai Peninsula; 127 miles/204.4 km south of Anchorage by road, or 35 minutes by air. **Population: 3,500. Emergency Services: Police, Fire Department** and **Ambulance,** emergency only, phone 911. **State Troopers,** phone (907) 224-3346. **Hospital,** Providence Seward Medical Center, 1st Avenue and Jefferson Street, phone (907) 224-5205. **Maritime Search and Rescue,** phone 1-800-478-5555.

Visitor Information: Available at 2 locations, operated by the Seward Chamber of Commerce–Convention and Visitors Bureau. The visitor center at **Milepost S 2** Seward Highway (2001 Seward Highway) is open 7 days a week from Memorial Day through Labor Day, weekdays the rest of the year; phone 224-8051. The Information Cache,

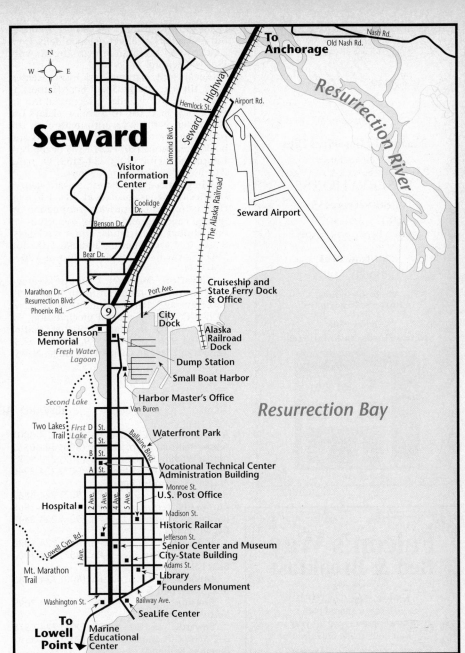

Seward map: To Anchorage, Old Nash Rd., Nash Rd., Resurrection River, Hemlock St., Airport Rd., Dimond Blvd., Seward Highway, The Alaska Railroad, Seward Airport, Visitor Information Center, Coolidge Dr., Benson Dr., Bear Dr., Marathon Dr., Resurrection Blvd., Phoenix Rd., Port Ave., Cruiseship and State Ferry Dock & Office, City Dock, Alaska Railroad Dock, Benny Benson Memorial, Fresh Water Lagoon, Dump Station, Small Boat Harbor, Harbor Master's Office, Van Buren, Resurrection Bay, Second Lake, Two Lakes Trail, First Lake, D St., C St., B St., A St., Ballaine Blvd., Waterfront Park, Vocational Technical Center Administration Building, Monroe St., U.S. Post Office, Hospital, 1 Ave., 2 Ave., 3 Ave., 4 Ave., 5 Ave., Madison St., Historic Railcar, Jefferson St., Senior Center and Museum, City-State Building, Adams St., Library, Founders Monument, Lowell Cyn. Rd., Mt. Marathon Trail, Washington St., Railway Ave., SeaLife Center, To Lowell Point, Marine Educational Center.

located in the historic railroad car *Seward* at 3rd and Jefferson Street, is open daily from 11 A.M. to 5 P.M., June through August; write Box 749, Seward, AK 99664.

Kenai Fjords National Park Visitor Center, 1212 4th Ave. (in the Small Boat Harbor), is open 8 A.M. to 7 P.M. daily, Memorial Day to Labor Day; 8:30 A.M. to 5 P.M. weekdays the remainder of the year. Information on the park, slide show, interpretive programs and bookstore. Phone (907) 224-3175 or the Park Information Line (907) 224-2132. Or write P.O. Box 1727, Seward, AK 99664.

Chugach National Forest, Seward Ranger District office, is located at 334 4th Ave. USFS personnel can provide information on hiking, camping and fishing opportunities on national forest lands. Open weekdays, 8 A.M. to 5 P.M. Mailing address: P.O. Box 390, Seward, AK 99664. Phone (907) 224-3374.

Elevation: Sea level. **Climate:** Average daily maximum temperature in July, 62°F/17°C; average daily minimum in January, 18°F/-7°C. Average annual precipitation, 67 inches; average snowfall, 80 inches. **Radio:** KSKA-FM 92, KWAVE 104.9, KPEN 102.3. **Television:** Several channels by cable. **News-**paper: *Seward Phoenix Log* (weekly).

Private Aircraft: Seward airport, 1.7 miles/2.7 km northeast; elev. 22 feet/7m; length 4,500 feet/1,371m; asphalt; fuel 80, 100, jet.

Seward—known as the "Gateway to Kenai Fjords National Park"—is a picturesque community nestled between high mountain ranges on a small rise stretching from Resurrection Bay to the foot of Mount Marathon. Thick groves of cottonwood and scattered spruce groves are found in the immediate vicinity of the city, with stands of spruce and alder growing on the surrounding mountainsides.

Downtown Seward (the main street is 4th Avenue) has a frontier-town atmosphere with some homes and buildings dating back to the early 1900s. The town was established in 1903 by railroad surveyors as an ocean terminal and supply center. The 470-mile/756-km railway connecting Fairbanks in the Interior with Seward was completed in 1923.

The city was named for U.S. Secretary of State William H. Seward, who was instrumental in arranging the purchase of Alaska from Russia in 1867. Resurrection Bay was named in 1791 by Russian fur trader and

View of Mount Marathon and downtown Seward. *(© Michael DeYoung)*

explorer Alexander Baranof. While sailing from Kodiak to Yakutat he found unexpected shelter in this bay from a storm and named the bay Resurrection because it was the Russian Sunday of the Resurrection.

Resurrection Bay is a year-round ice-free harbor and Seward is an important cargo and fishing port. The Alaska state ferry MV *Tustumena* calls at Seward.

Seward's economic base includes tourism, a coal terminal, sawmill, fisheries and government offices. The Alaska Vocational Technical Center is located here. A new marine educational center—the SeaLife Center—is under construction here; see Attractions this section for more details.

ACCOMMODATIONS/VISITOR SERVICES

All visitor facilities, including hotels, motels, bed and breakfasts, cafes and restaurants, post office, grocery stores, drugstore, travel agencies, gift shops, gas stations, bars, laundromats, churches, bowling

alley and theater.

The Harbormaster Building has public restrooms and pay showers, mailbox and pay phones. Weather information is available here during the summer. Public restrooms and pay showers on Ballaine Boulevard along the ocean between the boat harbor and town. Dump station and drinking water fill-up at the Small Boat Harbor at the end of 4th Avenue (see city map). There are picnic areas with covered tables along Ballaine Blvd., just south of the harbor, and at Adams Street.

Seward has made a good effort to provide overnight parking for self-contained RVs. There are designated camping areas along the shore south of Van Buren; camping fee charged. RV parking is marked by signs. Restrooms with coin-operated showers; water and electric hookups available at some sites. (Caravans: contact the City Parks and Recreation Dept. for reservations, phone 907/224-3331.) Forest Acres municipal campground is at **Milepost S 2.4** Seward Highway. Private RV parks at Small Boat Harbor, at **Milepost S 6.6** and on Lowell Point Road. Tent camping also available at Exit Glacier (turnoff at **Milepost S 3.7** Seward Highway). ▲

Alaska's Stoney Creek Inn Bed & Breakfast. Alaskan country comfort in a spectacular setting. Surrounded by towering spruce, snow-capped mountains and salmon-spawning streams. Deluxe, smoke-free rooms, private baths, queen beds, handmade comforters. Enjoy Alaskan hospitality with lifetime Alaskans. (907) 224-3940. See display ad at Mile 6.3 Seward Highway. [ADVERTISEMENT]

Alaska's Treehouse Bed and Breakfast. Nestled in the trees at the edge of town. Spectacular views of the Chugach Mountains from the solarium. Hiking and skiing trails at your doorstep, fishing nearby. Relax in

the hand-built, wood-fired sauna. Breakfast—hearty Alaskan sourdough pancakes and waffles with local wild berry sauces. Hosted by long-time Alaskans. Large, comfortable, smoke-free rooms. Accommodating singles to small groups. Open year-round. Phone (907) 224-3867; fax (907) 224-3978; P.O. Box 861, Seward, AK 99664. [ADVERTISEMENT]

Bay Vista Bed & Breakfast is nestled at the bottom of Mount Marathon with a spectacular panoramic view of Resurrection Bay. Two private suites with a spacious sitting

room, phone, TV/VCR, fridge, microwave and private entrance. Walk to harbor, train, bus/trolley. Shared and private baths. Doug

Best Western Hotel Seward

THE KENAI PENINSULA'S FINEST HOTEL.
LOCATED IN THE CENTER OF SEWARD.

Queen-size Beds • Executive Suites
Non-Smoking Rooms • Free In-room Movies
Cable TV and VCR in Each Room

 Highest Rating
on the Peninsula
AAA

TOLL-FREE IN ALASKA: 1-800-811-1191

PHONE: (907) 224-2378, FAX: (907) 224-3112
221 5TH AVE., P.O. BOX 670, SEWARD, ALASKA 99664

Bear's Den Bed & Breakfast

• Luxurious studio-style B&B • Sleeps up to 6 • Spectacular view of Resurrection Bay
• Guest deck • Private entry • Private bath • Kitchenette • Cable TV
• Continental breakfast • Evening popcorn • Coffee & Tea • Smoking outside only

1-800-232-7099 • (907) 224-3788
Richard & Shareen Adelmann • Box 2142, Seward, AK 99664

HARBORVIEW B&B Inn

900 3rd and "C" Street (See log ad under accommodations/visitor services)

"Best moderately priced lodging, Seward"
– Frommer's Alaska, 4th Edition

Tommy, Jerry and Jolene King, Box 1305, Seward, Alaska 99664

Phone/Fax (907) 224-3217 (year-round)

✴ New rooms ✴ Private bath ✴ Private entrances
✴ Telephones ✴ Short walk to boat harbor and downtown
✴ Color TV ✴ Non-smoking ✴ Alaskan Native fine art decor ✴
2 Bedroom Beachfront Apartments Available

MasterCard. VISA

Lechner, lifelong Seward resident. P.O. Box 1232, Seward, AK 99664. (907) 224-5880.
[ADVERTISEMENT]

Best Western Hotel Seward. Enjoy being in the center of activity, yet in a quiet setting overlooking Resurrection Bay. Our 1991 extensive expansion includes breathtaking view rooms with in-room coffee and your own refrigerator. And check this out! For your in-room entertainment, all rooms include (1) remote control TVs with cable-vision, (2) remote control VCRs with video-tape rental available and (3) 2 channels of free in-room movies featuring the latest hits! Complimentary scheduled shuttle bus service for our guests to boat harbor, train depot and airport. We accept all major credit cards. Reservations (907) 224-2378 or (800) 811-1191 inside Alaska. Fax (907) 224-3112. See display ad this section. [ADVERTISEMENT]

Bluefield Bed and Breakfast, found in a quiet neighborhood at the foot of Mount Marathon, surrounded by lovely gardens. Easy walking distance to boat harbor, railroad depot, shops and fine restaurants. Private entrance to your spacious room with king bed and double-futon sitting area. Tea cart, Jacuzzi in private bath. Breakfast table in room serving a hearty, gourmet, continental breakfast at your leisure. Liz, Duane and Darcy Harp, P.O. Box 2068, Seward, AK

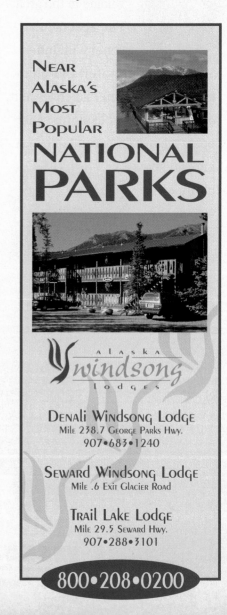

NEAR
Alaska's
MOST
Popular

NATIONAL PARKS

Windsong
l o d g e s

DENALI WINDSONG LODGE
MILE 238.7 GEORGE PARKS HWY.
907•683•1240

SEWARD WINDSONG LODGE
MILE .6 EXIT GLACIER ROAD

TRAIL LAKE LODGE
MILE 29.5 SEWARD HWY.
907•288•3101

800•208•0200

99664; (907) 224-8732. [ADVERTISEMENT]

Camelot Cottages. 1.4 Mile Salmon Creek Road: Affordable, clean, cozy furnished cabins with private baths and fully equipped kitchenettes. Hot tub. Linens, housekeeping services provided. Nestled in a natural woodland setting, the smaller cabins sleep 2–4 comfortably, the beautiful natural wood Chalet sleeps up to 8. Private, family friendly, owned and operated by longtime Alaskans. 1-800-739-3039, (907) 346-3039 Anchorage, (907) 224-3039 Seward. See display ad Mile 3.2 Seward Highway. [ADVERTISEMENT]

Clear Creek Cottage. Fully furnished smoke-free 2-bedroom cabin, full kitchen. Sleeps up to 8. Clean, comfortable, affordable rates. Perfect hideaway for couples, families, small groups. On the banks of Clear Creek, on Resurrection River Road to Exit Glacier, Mile 3.7 Seward Highway. 7 minutes to downtown Seward. (907) 224-3968. Fax (907) 224-7230. P.O. Box 241, Seward, AK 99664. [ADVERTISEMENT]

Creekside Cabins Bed & Breakfast. Clean, cozy cabins nestled in the trees, along peaceful Clear Creek. Continental breakfast. Central heated restrooms. Toasty, log sauna on the creek; tent sites. Peaceful country setting for a relaxing stay. Nonsmoking. Phone (907) 224-3834. See display ad Mile 3.7 Seward Highway. Take first right off Exit Glacier Road, 0.3 mile on right. [ADVERTISEMENT] ▲

Eagle Song Bed & Breakfast is located in a peaceful country setting in the shadow of an active bald eagle's nest, easy 15-minute

commute from Seward. We offer 4 bedrooms, with queen-size beds, 2 shared baths, full country breakfast, smoking outside, no alcohol, adults only. VISA and MasterCard. (907) 224-8755, P.O. Box 2231, Seward, AK 99664. [ADVERTISEMENT]

Fjordland Inn (formerly The White

BARDARSON STUDIO

Dot's art and gift gallery
in the Seward boat harbor.

1317 - 4th Ave., Box 630, Seward, AK 99664 ▪ (907) 224-5448

House B&B), is nestled in a mountain panorama. Country charm, smoke-free. Private or shared bath. Private entrance to guest area. Breakfast self-served in our guest kitchen. Families and groups welcome. Room rates $65 to $100. Open year-round. Winter rates. (907) 224-3614 or 1-800-785-3614. Fax (907) 224-3615. Owner-hosts Lee and Mary George. Mile 1.7 Nash Road. See display ad at Mile 3.2 Seward Highway. [ADVERTISEMENT]

Harborview B & B Inn. 900 3rd and C Street. New rooms with private entrances, private baths, color cable television, telephone, Alaska Native fine art. Just 10-minute walk to: tour boats, fishing charters, downtown and laundromat. Ask about "Seaview," our newly remodeled 2-bedroom apartments on the beachfront, breathtaking view of snowcapped mountains and bay. All non-smoking. $85. Early reservations advised. Alaska Native hostess. Phone/fax (907) 224-3217; P.O. Box 1305, Seward, AK 99664. See display ad. [ADVERTISEMENT]

Harmony Bed & Breakfast, nestled peacefully in Forrest Acres and conveniently close to town and harbor. Private entrance, private bath. Very clean, new rooms with all the comforts of home. Open year-round with reasonable rates. Call Carol for information and reservations. (907) 224-3661. P.O. Box 1606, Seward, AK 99664. [ADVERTISEMENT]

Kenai Fjords Wilderness Lodge. Located 14 miles south of Seward in scenic Resurrection Bay on Fox Island. Accessible by boat only. Stay in fully-equipped rustic cabins or main lodge for a comfortable overnight wilderness experience. Two-day/one-night packages include transportation, lodging, wildlife and glacier cruises to Kenai Fjords National Park, and delicious hearty meals. Sea kayaking, hiking available. Call toll free, 1-800-478-8068. See display ad this section. [ADVERTISEMENT]

Le Barn Appétit Restaurant, Bakery, Health Food Store and Bed and Breakfast. Creekside setting in the trees; beautiful views. Nonsmoking, nonalcoholic. Families welcome. Petting park for small children.

Giant teeter-totter. Breakfast, lunch and dinner. Continental cuisine. Omelettes, crépes, quiches, seafood specialties. European-style coffees and teas. VISA, Master-Card accepted. Your hosts: Yvon and Janet Van Driessche, P.O. Box 601, Seward, AK 99664. Phone (907) 224-8706 or (907) 224-3462. Fax (907) 224-8461. Mile 3.7 Seward Highway, first right off Exit Glacier Road. [ADVERTISEMENT]

Miller's Landing. Alaskan family operated fishing, tent/RV campground located on family homestead. Boat and pole rentals, fishing/sightseeing charters (full and half day), water taxi service to remote fishing areas, boat launch, kayak dropoffs to Aialik Glacier, Holgate Arm, Fox Island. Catch king salmon, Dolly Varden, pink, silver, chum salmon from beach, catch halibut from boat rentals or charters. Scenic campground located on Resurrection Bay. See sea otters, eagles, seals from camp. Private beaches. Hiking trail to Caine's Head State Park. Cozy cabin rentals, $40. Country store sells bait, tackle, ice, fishing licenses, T-shirts, hats, gifts. Pull-through electric RV sites, 20/30/50 amps; large tent sites. Beach sites or forested sites. Showers (included in camping cost). Phone. Mike Miller homesteaded here. He's an expert on fishing advice and visitor

information Survived 1964 earthquake. Free coffee. Fishing advice 5¢. Guaranteed effective or your nickel back! Down-home Alaskan atmosphere. Reservations accepted/advisable for guaranteed arrivals only. $12.50 dry camp, $17.50 electric. Box 81, Seward, AK 99664. Phone (907) 224-5739. [ADVERTISEMENT]   ▲

Morning Calm Bed and Breakfast. A touch of the Orient in Alaska. Quiet residential neighborhood near the visitor center, small boat harbor and railroad depot. Nonsmoking. Two rooms, queen and twin beds,

shared bath. Hot tub. In-room TV/VCR. Open year-round. The Martins, P.O. Box 816, Seward, AK 99664. (907) 224-3049. [ADVERTISEMENT]

New Seward Hotel & Saloon. Centrally located in downtown Seward, within walking distance of shops, ferry, bus terminal, boat harbor; 35 rooms featuring TV, phones, free videos. Some kitchenettes. Salmon and halibut fishing charters or Kenai Fjords tours available. Year-round service. Brochure. All major credit cards accepted. Reservations (907) 224-8001. Fax (907) 224-3112. See display ad this section. [ADVERTISEMENT]

Northern Exposure Bed & Breakfast. Clean, quiet and comfortable, 5 minutes from town. Queen and king beds, shared and private baths, cable TV, VCR and phone in common area. Continental breakfast. Smoking permitted outside. One room is a full apartment, sleeps 4, has private entrance, full private bath, TV in room and its own kitchen. (907) 224-3211. See display ad Mile 3.2 Seward Highway. [ADVERTISEMENT]

River Valley Cabins. Handcrafted cabins with bedrooms, bath, phone, sitting room, carpet, heat, continental breakfast, wilder-

ness setting. Also a cozy 2-bedroom cabin with kitchen, bath and living room is open year–round. Exit Glacier turnoff, first road to right, drive 1 mile. HCR 64, Box 3517, Seward, AK 99664. Phone (907) 224-5740, fax (907) 224-2333. [ADVERTISEMENT]

Seward Resort (Military). Motel, cabins, RV and tent sites. Charter fishing, Resurrection Bay wildlife boat tours. Open year-round. Authorized patrons: active duty military; retirees; National Guard and Reserves; DOD/NAF civilians, families and guests; federal governmental agencies. Call 1-800-770-1858; DSN 384-3474/5463. See display ad, Mile 2.3 Seward Highway. [ADVERTISEMENT]

Seward Windsong Lodge. Seward's newest lodge, overlooks the Resurrection River, not far from the only road access to

Kenai Fjords National Park and Exit Glacier. Modern, clean units with full bath in a quiet wilderness setting. Take the Exit Glacier turnoff, 1/2 mile on the right. Call 1-800-208-0200 for reservations. [ADVERTISEMENT]

Taroka Inn. Clean, 1- or 2-bedroom units featuring equipped kitchens, private bathrooms and color cable television, accommodate up to 8 persons. Smoking and nonsmoking available. Conveniently located 1 block from restaurants, shopping, theater, information, marine education center and museum. Two blocks from Alaska SeaLife Center. One mile to boat harbor. Rates among the most reasonable in Seward. (907) 224-8975. See display ad this section. [ADVERTISEMENT]

Van Gilder Hotel. Seward's favorite small hotel, built in 1916 and completely renovated for the 1990s. Now a National Historic Site, it retains its original Edwardian charm. Centrally located at 308 Adams Street in downtown Seward within easy walking distance of restaurants and shops. Clean, casual, comfortable rooms for tourists and business travelers. For hotel reservations call 1-800-204-6835. P.O. Box 2, Seward, AK, 99664. Fax (907) 224-3689. Our tour desk can book your tours, charters or complete itinerary. Tour desk: 1-800-204-2404. See display ad this section. [ADVERTISEMENT]

TRANSPORTATION

Air: Seward airport is reached by turning east on Airport Road at **Milepost S 2.7** on the Seward Highway. Scheduled daily service to Anchorage; charters also available.

Ferry: Alaska Marine Highway office on Cruise Ship Dock; phone (907) 224-5485. The Alaska ferry MV *Tustumena* departs Seward for Kodiak and Valdez. See the MARINE ACCESS ROUTES section for schedule.

Railroad: The Alaska Railroad connects Seward to Anchorage and Fairbanks. See the ALASKA RAILROAD section.

Bus: Scheduled service to Anchorage.

Seward's Charter Connection
We Put The Fun In Fishing!
Call or Write for Reservations & Our Color Brochure
Seward: 907-224-4446 • Seattle: 206-271-6106
Box 2348 • Seward, Alaska 99664

Taxi: Service available.

Highway: Seward is reached via the 127-mile/203.2-km Seward Highway from Anchorage.

Tours: Seward Trolley offers city tours 10 A.M. to 7 P.M. daily, Memorial Day through Labor Day.

ATTRACTIONS

The Railcar *Seward* houses the chamber of commerce information center. Located at 3rd and Jefferson Street, this railcar was the Seward observation car on the Alaska Railroad from 1936 until the early 1960s. Information and detailed map of the city are available.

Walking Tour of Seward encompasses more than 30 attractions including homes and businesses that date back to the early 1900s; some are still being used, while others have been restored as historic sites. A brochure containing details on all the attractions of the tour is available at the railcar information center. The complete tour covers about 2 miles/3.2 km and takes about 1 to 2 hours, depending upon how much time you wish to spend browsing.

Marine Educational Center, maintained by the University of Alaska, has laboratories, aquaculture ponds and the vessel *Alpha Helix*, which carries on oceanographic research in Alaskan waters. There is a marine display here. Open 10 A.M. to 4 P.M. Tuesday through Sunday, closed Monday, June through August.

Alaska SeaLife Center. The 7-acre waterfront construction site next to the Seward Marine Educational Center is the new Alaska SeaLife Center. The center will combine research facilities with wildlife rehabilitation and public education. Construction of the SeaLife Center is funded by the Exxon Valdez Oil Spill Restoration fund and private donations. It is scheduled to open in 1998.

Visit the Small Boat Harbor. This municipal harbor, built after the 1964 earthquake, is home port to fishing boats, charter boats and sightseeing boats. The harbor is also home to sea otters—watch for them! Visitors may notice the great number of sailboats moored here: many are members of the William H. Seward Yacht Club, which sponsors an annual sailboat and yacht show.

Seward Museum, at Jefferson and 3rd Avenue, is operated by the Resurrection Bay Historical Society (Box 55, Seward 99664). The museum features artifacts and photographs from the 1964 earthquake, WWII, the founding days of Seward and other highlights of Seward's history. Also on display is a collection of Native baskets and ivory carvings. The museum is open daily, 10 A.M. to 5 P.M., May 1 to Sept. 30. Open reduced hours remainder of year; check locally, or phone (907) 224-3902. A modest admission fee is charged.

Seward Community Library, across from the City–State Building, presents (on request) short slide/sound shows on a variety of subjects and has some informative displays. A program on the 1964 earthquake is shown daily at 2 P.M. (except Sunday) from June 15 through the first Saturday in September. Library hours are 1–8 P.M. Monday through Friday, 1–6 P.M. Saturday.

St. Peter's Episcopal Church is 3 blocks west of the museum at the corner of 2nd Avenue and Adams Street. It was built

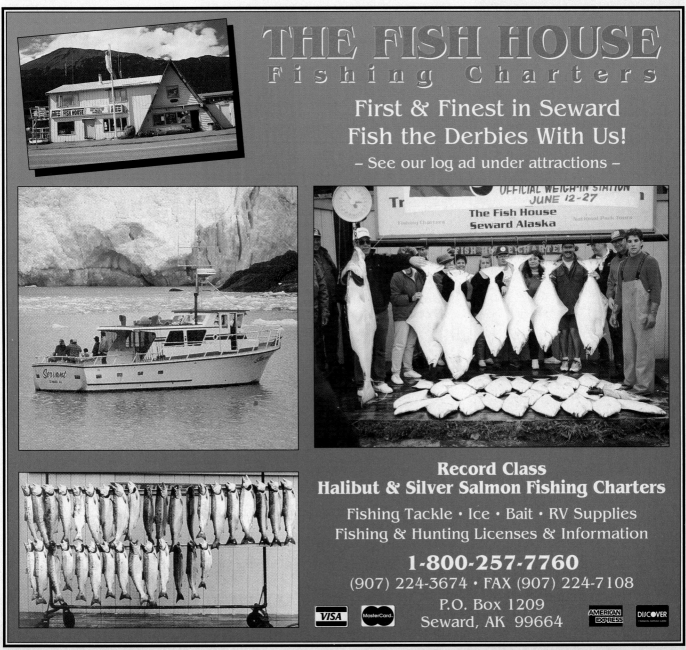

in 1906 and is considered the oldest Protestant church on the Kenai Peninsula. A feature is the unique painting of the Resurrection, for which Alaskans were used as models and Resurrection Bay as the background. Well-known Dutch artist Jan Van Emple was commissioned to paint the picture in 1925 when he was living in Seward. Obtain key to church from the Information Cache in season.

Hiking Trails. Two Lakes trail is an easy mile-long loop trail along the base of Mount Marathon. The trail passes through a wooded area and follows what used to be Hemlock Street. Beautiful view of marina below and north end of Resurrection Bay. Start at First Lake, behind the Alaska Vocational and Technical Center Administration Building at 2nd Avenue and B Street.

The National Historic Iditarod Trail begins at the ferry terminal and follows a marked course through town, then north on the Seward Highway. At Mile 2.1 Nash Road (turn off at **Milepost S 3.2** Seward Highway), the trail continues from a gravel parking area on the east side of Sawmill Creek north to Bear Lake. The trail eventually rejoins the Seward Highway at **Milepost S 12.**

Caines Head State Recreation Area, 6 miles/9.6 km south of Seward, is accessible by boat or via a 4.5-mile/7.2-km beach trail (low tide only). The trailhead/parking is located about Mile 2 Lowell Point Road. The Caines Head area has bunkers and gun emplacements that were used to guard the entrance to Resurrection Bay during WWII.

Mount Marathon Race™, Seward's annual Fourth of July endurance race to the top of Mount Marathon (elev. 3,022 feet/921m) and back down, is a grueling test for athletes. The race is said to have begun in 1909 with a wager between 2 sourdoughs as to how long it would take to run up and down Mount Marathon. The first year of the official race is uncertain: records indicate either 1912 or 1915. Fastest recorded time is 43 minutes, 23 seconds set in 1981 by Bill Spencer, who broke his own 1974 record. The descent is so steep that it's part run, part jump and part slide. The race attracts competitors from all over, and thousands of spectators line the route each year.

Annual Seward Silver Salmon Derby™ in August is one of the largest sporting events in Alaska. It is held over 9 days, starting the second Saturday in August through Sunday of the following weekend. 1997 will be the derby's 42nd year. Record derby catch to date is a 20.59-lb. salmon caught off Twin Rocks by John Westlund of Anchorage.

There is more than $240,000 in prizes for the derby, including $10,000 in cash for the largest fish. Also part of the derby are the sought-after tagged silvers worth as much as $100,000. Prizes are sponsored by various merchants and the chamber of commerce.

The town fills up fast during the derby: Make reservations! For more information

contact the Seward Chamber of Commerce; phone (907) 224-8051.

Annual Seward Halibut Jackpot Tournament runs June through July. First, second and third place prizes awarded for heaviest fish. In 1996 the winner weighed in at 326 lbs. A 360-lb. halibut was reeled in in 1993. That was the largest halibut reported caught in southcentral Alaska.

Kenai Fjords National Park. Seward is the gateway to this popular 650,000-acre national park. Dominant feature of the park is the Harding Icefield, a 700-square-mile vestige of the last ice age. Harding Icefield can be reached by a strenuous all-day hike from the base of Exit Glacier or by a charter flightseeing trip out of Seward.

The fjords of the park were formed when glaciers flowed down to the sea from the ice field and then retreated, leaving behind the deep inlets that characterize the coastline here. Substantial populations of marine mammals inhabit or migrate through the park's coastal waters, including sea otters, Steller sea lions, dolphins and whales. Icebergs from calving glaciers provide ideal refuge for harbor seals, and the rugged coastline provides habitat for more than 100,000 nesting birds. The park's spectacular scenery and wildlife may be viewed by daily private tour and charter boats or by charter planes. Four public-use cabins along the coast are available in summer by reservation; phone (907) 271-2737. Kayakers and boaters can also camp on beaches, but must be aware ahead of time of land status; 77,000 acres of coastline are owned by Native corporations and are *not* available for public camping. Maps indicating land ownership are available from the park visitor center. *NOTE: Private boaters should consult with local outfitters and charter operators for detailed information on boating conditions.*

Exit Glacier is the most accessible of the park's glaciers. Turn at **Milepost S 3.7** on the Seward Highway and follow Exit Glacier Road to the visitor center parking area. There are several trails through the outwash plain of Exit Glacier that afford excellent views of the ice and surrounding mountains. A 0.2-mile paved trail is wheelchair accessible and leads from the parking lot to an information display. Ranger-led nature walks are available in summer at Exit Glacier, where there is a picnic area and walk-in campground. Visitor information is available at the Exit Glacier ranger station and visitor center; open summer only. Exit Glacier is accessible in winter by skis, dogsled or snow machine. A public-use cabin is available by permit; phone (907) 224-3175; or the Park Information Line (907) 224-2132. *CAUTION: Active glacier with unstable ice. Do not walk past warning signs!* &

Slide programs, videos, exhibits and information on Kenai Fjords National Park and organized activities at the park are available at the park visitor center on 4th Avenue in the Small Boat Harbor area next to the Harbormaster's office. The center is open daily from Memorial Day to Labor Day; hours are 8 A.M. to 7 P.M. The remainder of the year hours are 8 A.M. to 5 P.M. (subject to change) weekdays. Phone (907) 224-3175 or write the park superintendent, Box 1727, Seward 99664.

Alaska Wildlife Cruises. Our low-priced half-day and full-day cruises of the Kenai Fjords National Park feature incredible glaciers and up-close wildlife—otters, sea lions, puffins, eagles, bird colonies, whales and more. Cruise aboard our large, comfortable boats with reserved seating and inside heated cabins. Close-up wildlife viewing and photography are easy from our outside decks. Snacks and full beverage service on board. The all-day cruise is narrated by a National Park ranger. The half-day tours

Salmon fishing at Seward small boat harbor. (© Bruce M. Herman)

depart from Seward's Boat Harbor daily at 12:45 P.M. ($59) and 6 P.M. ($59). The all-day cruises depart at 11:30 A.M. ($79). Kids 12 and under, half-price. Reservations/free brochure, call: 1-800-764-7300 or (907) 272-9775. Alaska Wildlife Cruises, 411 West 4th, Anchorage, AK 99501. [ADVERTISEMENT]

Bardarson Studio. In Seward find Bardarson Studio on the prettiest boardwalk in the boat harbor area, with the best selection of Alaska art and fine crafts set to music. Bardarson Studio recognizes that shopping is entertainment for travelers, providing a Kiddie-Kave for children, and a video room for your non-shopper. Public restroom and postal service available. 1317 4th Avenue. Phone 1-800-354-0141. [ADVERTISEMENT]

Bear Lake Air and Guide Service. Exclusive floatplane service from beautiful Bear Lake. Flightseeing, air charters, fly-in day fishing. Guiding services for big game hunting. Bunkhouse for rent. Shuttle service available. Reservations welcome, 1-800-224-5985. Bear Lake Air Service office located at Bear Creek RV Park, Mile 6.6 Seward Highway, drive ¹/₂ mile on Bear Lake Road. Internet: http://www.alaska.net/~bear. [ADVERTISEMENT]

The Fish House. First and finest fishing charter service in Seward! Record class halibut and silver salmon fishing charters available now. While fishing, enjoy the scenic beauty of the Kenai Fjords National Park—glaciers, mountains, puffins, whales, sea otters and seals. The Fish House also supplies a complete line of fishing tackle, bait, ice and outboard motor repairs. Call now for reservations or information on fishing the scenic waters surrounding Seward, Alaska. 1-800-257-7760 or (907) 224-3674. Halibut charters: April 1–Oct. 1. Salmon charters: June 1–Sept. 20. P.O. Box 1209, Seward, AK 99664. See display ad this section. [ADVERTISEMENT]

Fjordland Studio, the working studio of artist Lee George, exhibits paintings of Alaskan and marine subjects, and works of invited guest artists. Fjordland studio affords visitors an opportunity to see paintings in development, share like interests with the artist in a relaxed setting and to become

acquainted with the workings of an art studio. Original paintings and limited-edition prints available. The studio with the grand view of Resurrection Bay is located in the historic "Old Solly's" building at Railway and Washington streets, across from the future Alaska SeaLife Center. Open year-round. Phone (907) 224-6059. [ADVERTISEMENT]

IdidaRide Sled Dog Tours. Experience dog mushing, summer style, on a 2-mile wilderness dog sled ride at Iditarod racer Mitch Seavey's training location. Informative tour includes 80-husky kennel, cuddly puppies, arctic equipment demonstration. P.O. Box 2906, Seward, AK 99664. (907) 224-8607, fax (907) 224-8608. Off Exit Glacier Road. See display ad Mile 3.7 Seward Highway. [ADVERTISEMENT]

Kenai Fjords Tours Ltd. The excitement begins the moment you pull away from the Seward boat harbor! You'll be greeted by playful sea otters, look for whales and por-

poise, photograph colorful puffins, bald eagles, and watch a calving glacier. Cruising since 1974, Kenai Fjords Tours is the original Kenai Fjords National Park tour, and continues to be the most popular. Our new, comfortable cruisers have walk-around decks, so you can easily watch and photograph the magnificent scenery. Our captains are experienced naturalists, so you'll learn about this coastal wilderness from guides who really know the area. Lunch (or dinner) and beverages served on board, or many cruises include a special stop at Fox Island for our delicious all-you-can-eat salmon bake at Kenai Fjords Wilderness Lodge. Don't miss it! Call for reservations. Toll free, 1-888-4-PUFFIN (1-888-478-3346). Located at the Seward Small Boat Harbor. See display ad this section. [ADVERTISEMENT]

Major Marine Kenai Fjords National

Park Tours. Join us for Seward's famous wildlife cruises of the Kenai Fjords. We offer 2 wonderful cruise options: 1) A 4 ¹/₂-hour wildlife cruise of the Kenai Fjords, and 2) An 8-hour wildlife cruise of the Kenai Fjords National Park and Chiswell Islands National Wildlife Refuge, narrated by a Kenai Fjords National Park Ranger. Both cruises include incredible glaciers and up-close wildlife—otters, sea lions, puffins, eagles, porpoises, whales, bird colonies and more. The tour boats feature reserved table seating, inside heated cabins and multiple outside decks for close-up wildlife viewing and photography. The 4¹/₂-hour cruise features an all-you-can-eat salmon, crab and shrimp buffet with dessert bar. On the 8-hour cruise, you'll be served an all-you-can-eat salmon buffet with all the trimmings. Both cruises sail from Seward's boat harbor May to late September. The 8-hour cruise departs at 11:30 A.M. and costs $99. The 4¹/₂-hour cruise departs at 12:45 P.M. ($79) and 6 P.M. ($69). For reservations or free brochure, call: 1-800-764-7300 or (907) 274-7300. Major Marine Tours, 411 West 4th, Anchorage, AK 99501. Ticket office also located on Seward boardwalk: (907) 224-8030 (May to Sept.). [ADVERTISEMENT]

Mariah Tours. Guided natural history tours in Kenai Fjords and the Chiswell Islands Wildlife Refuge since 1981. Our custom-built 22 passenger ships offer the

small ship alternative to Kenai Fjords National Park, for a more personalized, uncrowded tour. Also featuring tours to spectacular Northwestern Glacier via Granite Passage, the most scenic area within Kenai Fjords National Park. Popular exclusive tours for birding and naturalist groups and other interested parties. Operating April 20 to Sept. 30. For reservations: 1-800-270-1238. In Anchorage: (907) 243-1238. See display ad this section. [ADVERTISEMENT]

Renown Charters & Tours offers wildlife and glacier cruises in the Kenai Fjords and in Prince William Sound. Our comfortable, new 76- and 42-passenger vessels have the speed to get you out to where the action is. Calving glaciers, whales, puffins, otters and much more. Lunch is included on all cruises. Fully narrated by a professional and friendly crew. Call 1-800-655-3806. See display ad. [ADVERTISEMENT]

Resurrection Bay Galerie. The only art gallery in Alaska devoted exclusively to original fine art—paintings and sculpture, and other fine arts. Open daily April 15 to Oct. 15. Corner of 4th and Madison, behind the red door. Phone (907) 224-3212; fax (907) 224-5990. [ADVERTISEMENT]

AREA FISHING: Resurrection Bay, coho (silver) salmon to 22 lbs., use herring, troll or cast, July to October; king salmon to 45 lbs., May to August; also bottom fish, flounder, halibut to 300 lbs. and cod, use weighted spoons and large red spinners by jigging, year-round. Charter and rental boats are available.

Kenai Peninsula
STERLING HIGHWAY ①

Connects: Seward Highway to Homer, AK　　**Length:** 143 miles
Road Surface: Paved　　**Season:** Open all year
Major Attractions: Kenai National Wildlife Refuge,
Russian Orthodox Churches, Homer Spit

(See maps, pages 514–515)

	Anchorage	Homer	Kenai	Seward	Soldotna
Anchorage		233	158	127	147
Homer	233		96	180	85
Kenai	158	96		105	11
Seward	127	180	105		94
Soldotna	147	85	11	94	

Sterling Highway Log

Distance from Seward (S) is followed by distance from Anchorage (A) and distance from Homer (H). Physical mileposts show distance from Seward.

S 37.7 (60.7 km) **A 89.3** (143.7 km) **H 141.8** (228.2 km) **Junction** with Seward Highway. First exit southbound (1-way road) for Sterling Highway.

S 37 (59.5 km) **A 90** (144.8 km) **H 142.5** (229.3 km) **Tern Lake Junction.** Second southbound exit (2-way road) for Sterling Highway. This exit provides access to Tern Lake day-use area (see description next milepost). Gravel turnout beside Tern Lake with interpretive boardwalk and viewing platforms. Information signs on area birds and wildlife.

S 37.4 (60.2 km) **A 90.4** (145.5 km) **H 142.1** (228.7 km) USFS Tern Lake day-use picnic area; toilets, water, picnic tables. USFS spawning channel for king salmon on Daves Creek at outlet of Tern Lake. Short viewing

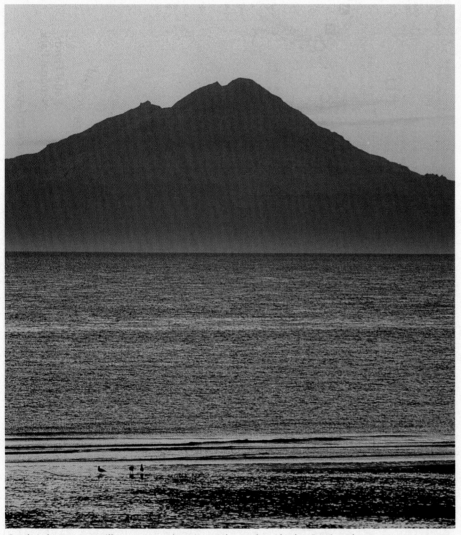

Cook Inlet sunset silhouettes volcanic peak on the Alaska Peninsula. (© Harry M. Walker Photo)

The Sterling Highway (Alaska Route 1) begins 90 miles/145 km south of Anchorage at its junction with the Seward Highway and travels 142.5 miles/229.3 km west and south to the community of Homer. The Sterling Highway junctions with several major Kenai Peninsula side roads (see logs this section): Skilak Lake Loop Road, Swanson River Road, Kenai Spur Highway, Kalifornsky Beach Road, Cohoe Loop Road and Anchor River Beach Road.

From its junction with the Seward Highway at Tern Lake (see SEWARD HIGHWAY section), the Sterling passes through Chugach National Forest and Kenai National Wildlife Refuge. The Kenai Mountains are home to Dall sheep, mountain goats, black and brown bears, and caribou. The many lakes, rivers and streams of the Kenai Peninsula are famous for their sportfishing. The highway also provides access to the Resurrection Pass Trail System.

From Soldotna south, the Sterling Highway follows the west coast of the peninsula along Cook Inlet. There are beautiful views of peaks on the Alaska Peninsula.

Physical mileposts on the Sterling Highway show distance from Seward. The Sterling Highway is a paved 2-lane highway, open year-round.

Emergency medical services: phone 911 or use CB channels 9, 11 or 19.

STERLING HIGHWAY *Tern Lake Junction to Soldotna, AK*

Chugach National Forest

Resurrection Pass Trail
Resurrection Pass
2,600ft./792m

To Anchorage
(see SEWARD HIGHWAY section)

**S-37 /60km
A-90 /145km
H-142 /229km**

To Seward
(see SEWARD HIGHWAY section)

Tern Lake Junction

Upper Trail Lake
Lower Trail Lake
Grant Lake

S-47.7/76.8km Alaskan Sourdough Bed & Breakfast L
Bruce Nelson's Float Fishing Service
Kenai Princess Lodge LMT
Kenai Princess RV Park CS
S-47.9/77.1km Kenai Lake Baptist Church
S-48.1/77.4km Cooper Landing Grocery &
   Hardware IMS
St. John Neumann Catholic Church
Sport Fishing Cabins L
S-48.2/77.6km Red Salmon Guest House L
Troutfitters Alpine Motel L
S-48.4/77.9km The Shrew's Nest C
S-48.5/78.1km Hamilton's Place CdGILMrST
S-48.8/78.5km Kenai Lake Adventures L
S-49.7/80km Miller Homestead Bed & Breakfast
   & RV Park CDL

Quartz Creek
Devils Creek
Swan Creek
Swan Lake

Juneau Creek
Juneau L.

Kenai Lake

Cooper Lake

Sunrise Inn CDdGILMT
S-45 /72.4km

Cooper Landing

Resurrection River

Kenai National Wildlife Refuge

National Forest Boundary
National Refuge Boundary

Russian Lakes Trail

Upper Russian Lake
Lower Russian Lake
Russian R.

Trout L.

S-50 /80.5km Alaska Rivers Co.
S-50.1/80.6km
Alaska Wildland Adventures L
Kenai Backcountry Lodge LM
S-52 /83.7km Gwin's Lodge,
   Restaurant & Bar CILMST
Kenai Cache IL
S-52.6/84.6km K'Beq
   Footprints

**S-58 /93km
A-111 /178km
H-121 /195km**

Kenai R.

Kenai National Wildlife Refuge

Harding Icefield
Kenai Fjords National Park
Glaciated Area

National Refuge Boundary
National Park Boundary
National Forest Boundary

Swan Lake Road

Rainbow Lake
Dolly Varden Lake

J-30 /48km

Swan Lake
Swanson River

SY-40 /64km

J-17 /28km

Swanson River Road

S-82.5/132.8km Big Sky Charter & Fish Camp L
Kenai Magic Lodge L
S-82.3/132.4km Alaska Adventure Reservations
S-82.1/132.1km Kenai Moose Bed & Breakfast L
S-82 /132km Sterling Chevron & Food Mart GM
S-81 /130.3km Bing Brown's RV Park & Motel CDILST
   Moose River Auto Parts & Towing r
S-81.7/131.5km Cook's Corner DdGIPT
   Sterling House Bed & Breakfast L
S-80.3 /129.2km Peninsula Furs
S-79.2 /127.4km Fish On Inn & RV Park CL

Moose River
Kenai River

Swanson River

Sterling

Bottlenintnin L.
Longmere Lake Lodge B&B L

Jean L.
Hidden L.
Kelly L.
Peterson L.
Engineer L.
Lower Ohmer L.
Hidden Cr.

Skilak Lake

Skilak Lake Loop Road

S-84.9/136.6km Cast Away
   Riverside RV Park CDIST
S-84.5/136km Alaskan Abode B&B L
S-84.3/135.7km Scout Lake Inn
   and Nicki's Restaurant LM
S-84 /135.2km Sterling Baptist Church
   ZIPMART dGIST
S-83.4/134.2km

S-88 /141.6km Alaskan Paradise B&B L
S-88.3 /142.1km Alaska Horn & Antler
   The Jade Shop
S-91.8 /147.7km Eagle Smokehouse
S-92.7 /149.1km Aalaska Tree Top Bed & Breakfast L
   Bill Siemp's Wild Alaska L
S-93 /149.7km Eagle's Nest Bed N' Breakfast L
S-94.1 /151.4km Through The Seasons Restaurant M

Captain Cook State Recreation Area

Daniels Lake
Island Lake
Bernice L.

Kenai Spur Highway

SY-29.7/47.8km Daniels Lake Lodge
   Bed & Breakfast L
S-84/135.2km Kenai Tesoro DdGIP

S-94.4/151.9km
S-94.7/1.6km
Soldotna Tesoro DdGIP
Eleven dGIST

Soldotna

Funny River Road

SY-11 /18km

Nikiski

Kenai

**SY-0
S-94 /152km
A-147 /237km
H-85 /137km**

SY-5.5/8.9km Alicia's Eagle Rock Lodge
   & Alaska-Pacific N.W. Fishing Adventures L

Kalifornsky Beach Road

(map continues next page)

Cook Inlet

Scale
0   5   Miles
0   5   Kilometres

Key to mileage boxes
miles/kilometres
miles/kilometres   from:
S–Seward   SY–Soldotna Y
A–Anchorage
H–Homer
J–Junction

Key to Advertiser Services
C –Camping
D –Dump Station
d –Diesel
G –Gas (reg., unld.)
I –Ice
L –Lodging
M –Meals
P –Propane
R –Car Repair (major)
r –Car Repair (minor)
S –Store (grocery)
T –Telephone (pay)

Map Location

Principal Route
Paved   Unpaved
Other Roads
Paved   Unpaved
Ferry Routes   Hiking Trails

⌘ Refer to Log for Visitor Facilities
? Visitor Information
▲ Campground   Airport + Airstrip   Fishing

STERLING HIGHWAY   *Soldotna, AK, to Homer, AK*

Map Location

Scale

0 ___ 5 Miles
0 ___ 5 Kilometres

Key to mileage boxes

miles/kilometres
miles/kilometres
from:
S-Seward
A-Anchorage   **SY**-Soldotna Y
H-Homer
K-Kasilof

Principal Route
Paved
Other Roads
Paved   Unpaved
Ferry Routes   Hiking Trails

❄ Refer to Log for Visitor Facilities
? Visitor Information   🎣 Fishing
⛺ Campground   ✈ Airport   ✛ Airstrip

Key to Advertiser Services
C -Camping
D -Dump Station
d -Diesel
G -Gas (reg., unld.)
I -Ice
L -Lodging
M -Meals
P -Propane
R -Car Repair (major)
r -Car Repair (minor)
S -Store (grocery)
T -Telephone (pay)

(map continues previous page)

Kenai Spur Highway

SY-0
S-94/152km
A-147/237km
H-85/137km

SY-11/18km

❄?⛺✈✛ Kenai
Beaver Loop Road

Kalifornsky Beach Road

(map continues previous pagee)

Kenai River

⛺ Soldotna ❄?⛺✈✛

S-3.1/5km Short Stop GIST

Funny River Road

K-22/36km
S-96/154km
A-149/240km
H-83/134km

Ski Hill Road

Funny River

K-0
S-109/175km
A-162/260km
H-71/114km

Kenai National Wildlife Refuge

S-20.3/32.7km Daily's Kasilof Bed & Breakfast L

NJ-5.6/9.0km Kasilof River Kabins L

NJ-8.6/13.8km Deal's Den Bed & Breakfast L

Kasilof ✛

Cohoe Loop Road

S-109.2/175.7km Kasilof Riverview dGIPST
S-110.8/178.3km Tustumena Lodge ILM
S-111/178.6km Crooked Creek RV Park and Guide Service CDILM
Kasilof RV Park CD
Tustumena Ridge Cabins L

Kasilof R.

SJ-0
S-114/184km
A-167/296km
H-65/105km

⛺ 🎣

Johnson Lake

Tustumena Lake

⛺🎣 Clam Gulch
S-118.2/190.2km Rod Buster Charters CL
S-118.3/190.4km Clam Shell Lodge CILMPT
S-119.6/192.5km Clam Gulch Lodge Bed & Breakfast L

S-127.1/204.5km Scenic View RV Park C

Crooked Creek

S-130.5/210km Ninilchik Point Overnighter CL
S-132.2/212.7km Heavenly Sights Charters & Campground CL

Ninilchik River

S-135.4/217.9km Hylen's Camper Park CDILT
S-135.7/218.4km Ninilchik General Store S
S-135.8/218.5km Bull Moose Gifts
S-135.9/218.7km Caribou Hills Wilderness Lodge L
Country Boy Campground CD
Reel 'Em Inn & Cook Inlet Charter CL
Homestead House B&B L

S-136/218km
A-189/303km
H-44/71km

⛺ Ninilchik ❄⛺✈
S-136/218.9km Chinook Tesoro dGIPR

National Refuge Boundary

S-136.1/219km Chihuly's Charters and Porcupine Shop L
S-136.2/219.2km Bluff House Bed & Breakfast L
S-137/220.4km Deep Creek Custom Packing, Inc. IT
Fishward Bound Adventures ILST
S-137.4/???km Roe's Charerter Service L

Deep Creek

Happy Valley

Stariski Creek

S-152.7/245.6km Eagle Crest RV Park & Cabins CL
Eagle Crest Wilderness Fishing Adventures
S-153.2/246.5km Short Stop RV Parking CDIS
S-154.1/248km Timberline Creations
S-155/249.4km Bear Paw Charters L
S-155.3/249.9km Red Door Bed & Breakfast L
S-156.3/251.5km Mugs and Jugs
Anchor River Tesoro dGIPT
The Warehouse, Inc. IS
S-156.7/252.2km Iliamna Mt. View Bed & Breakfast L
Our Front Porch Bed & Breakfast L
S-156.8/252.3km Anchor Point B&B and Clive's Fishing Guide Service IL
Anchor Point Roadhouse LM

River

Anchor Point
S-156.9/252.5km Wallin's Hilltop Bed & Breakfast L
J-0.1/0.2km Anchor River Inn ILMST
J-1.3/2.1km Kyllonen's RV Park CT

East End Road

Old Sterling Highway

Anchor River

S-165.4/266.2km Billikin Gift Shop L
S-166.8/268.4km Holland Days Bed & Breakfast L

Homer ❄?⛺✈✛
S-169.3/272.5km Village Barabara RV Park C
S-172.7/277.9km Oceanview RV Park CT
S-174.8/281.3km Homer Tesoro DdGIF

Kachemak Bay

Homer Spit

S-180/289km
A-233/374km
H-0

KENAI

Cook Inlet

Harding Icefield

Kenai Fjords National Park

National Park Boundary

Area

Glaciated

MOUNTAINS

Alaska State Ferry
(see MARINE ACCESS ROUTES section)

❄⛺🎣✈ Seldovia

National Refuge Boundary

Kenai Peninsula rivers are famous for their fishing. (© Barbara Willard)

trail with information signs illustrating use of log weirs and stream protection techniques.

S 38 (61.1 km) **A 91** (146.4 km) **H 141.5** (227.7 km) Avalanche gates. Gravel turnouts.

S 38.3 (61.6 km) **A 91.3** (146.9 km) **H 141.2** (227.2 km) Gravel turnout. Emergency call box.

S 39 (62.8 km) **A 92** (148 km) **H 140.5** (226.1 km) **Daves Creek**, an unusually beautiful mountain stream which flows west into Quartz Creek. Dolly Varden and rainbow averaging 14 inches, June through September. A good place to view spawning salmon in late July and August.

S 40.5 (65.2 km) **A 93.5** (150.5 km) **H 139** (223.7 km) Double-ended gravel turnout to south.

S 40.9 (65.8 km) **A 93.9** (151.1 km) **H 138.6** (223 km) Bridge over Quartz Creek. This stream empties into Kenai Lake. You are now entering one of Alaska's best-known lake and river fishing regions, across the center of the Kenai Peninsula. The burn on the hillsides to the south was part of a Forest Service moose habitat improvement program.

S 41.1 (66.1 km) **A 94.1** (151.4 km) **H 138.4** (222.7 km) Cooper Landing Closed Area. This area is closed to the hunting of Dall sheep. The ridges to the north are a lambing ground for Dall sheep.

S 42.8 (68.9 km) **A 95.8** (154.2 km) **H 136.7** (220 km) Gravel turnouts on Quartz Creek.

S 43.1 (69.4 km) **A 96.1** (154.6 km) **H 136.4** (219.5 km) Double-ended gravel turnout to east on Quartz Creek.

S 43.5 (70 km) **A 96.5** (155.3 km) **H 136** (218.9 km) Double-ended gravel turnout to east.

S 44 (70.8 km) **A 97** (156.1 km) **H 135.5** (218.1 km) Gravel turnout on Quartz Creek.

S 44.3 (71.3 km) **A 97.3** (156.6 km) **H 135.2** (217.6 km) Solid waste transfer site to east; public dumpsters.

S 45 (72.4 km) **A 98** (157.7 km) **H 134.5** (216.5 km) Quartz Creek Road to Quartz Creek Recreation Area. Quartz Creek Campground, 0.3 mile/0.5 km from the highway, has 31 sites, boat launch, flush toilets, firepits and a $10 camping fee. Crescent Creek Campground, 3 miles/4.8 km from the highway, has 9 sites, tables, water and pit toilets; $9 fee. Crescent Creek USFS trail leads 6.2 miles/10 km to the outlet of Crescent Lake. The trailhead is about 1 mile/ 1.6 km from Crescent Creek Campground. A public-use cabin is located at the lake; permit required for use; not accessible in winter or early spring due to extreme avalanche danger. ▲

The Sterling Highway from the junction with the Seward Highway west to the community of Sterling **(Milepost S 81)** takes the traveler through the heart of some prime fishing country, and provides access to numerous fishing lakes and rivers. *NOTE: The diversity of fishing conditions and frequent regulation changes in all Kenai waters make it advisable to consult locally for fishing news and regulations.*

Beautiful views of Kenai Lake next 3 miles/ 4.8 km westbound. The lake's unusual color is caused by glacial silt.

Quartz Creek, rainbow, midsummer; Dolly Varden to 25 inches, late May through June. **Crescent Lake**, grayling, July 1 to April 14 (2 grayling daily bag and possession limit). **Kenai Lake**, lake trout, May 15 to Sept. 30; trout, May to September; Dolly Varden, May to September. Kenai Lake and tributaries are closed to salmon fishing.

S 45 (72.4 km) **A 98** (157.7 km) **H 134.5** (216.5 km) **Sunrise Inn**. See display ad this section.

S 45.6 (73.4 km) **A 98.6** (158.7 km) **H 133.9** (215.5 km) Large turnout with toilet. This is an observation point for Dall sheep on Near Mountain and mountain

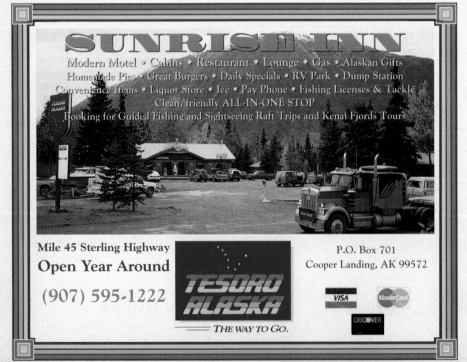

goats on Cecil Rhode Mountain (directly across Kenai Lake); use binoculars.

S 46.3 (74.5 km) **A 99.3** (159.8 km) **H 133.2** (214.4 km) Small gravel turnout to east.

S 47 (75.6 km) **A 100** (160.9 km) **H 132.5** (213.2 km) Turnout to east.

S 47.1 (75.8 km) **A 100.1** (161.1 km) **H 132.4** (213.1 km) Kenai Lake Lodge (closed 1996; current status unknown).

S 47.7 (76.8 km) **A 100.7** (162 km) **H 131.8** (212.1 km) Bean Creek Road, access to a fishing guide service, bed and breakfast and the Kenai Princess Lodge and RV Park on the Kenai River. The lodge's lobby has an interesting chandelier made from antlers. ▲

Alaskan Sourdough Bed & Breakfast. See display ad this section.

Bruce Nelson's Float Fishing Service and Eid's Cabin. See display ad this section.

Kenai Princess Lodge. A wilderness retreat overlooking the salmon-rich Kenai River featuring 70 cozy bungalows with sun porches, wood stoves, televisions and telephones. Spacious view deck, fine restaurant, lounge, gift shop, tour desk, hot tubs, exercise room. Meeting facilities. Open March to December. Call 1-800-426-0500 year-round. [ADVERTISEMENT]

Kenai Princess RV Park. At Cooper Landing on the Kenai River. Featuring 35 sites with water and power, general store, showers, laundry, septic. Use of facilities at the adjacent Kenai Princess Lodge. Open mid-May through mid-September. $20 per night. Call (907) 595-1425, March to December, for reservations. [ADVERTISEMENT] ▲

S 47.8 (76.9 km) **A 100.8** (162.2 km) **H 131.7** (211.9 km) Kenai River bridge. A new boat launch and parking area with restrooms may be under construction here in 1997; boaters may launch on the north side of the bridge at the unimproved launch.

The Kenai River flows directly alongside the highway for the next 10 miles/16 km with several gravel turnouts offering good views. (A proposed plan to reroute this portion of the Sterling Highway away from the Kenai River and into the mountains is under consideration.)

Kenai River from **Kenai Lake** to **Skilak Lake**, including Skilak Lake within a half mile of the Kenai River inlet, closed to king salmon fishing; closed to all fishing April 15 through June 10. Silver salmon 5 to 15 lbs., August through October; pink salmon 3 to 7 lbs., July and August; red salmon 3 to 12 lbs., June 11 through mid-August; rainbow and Dolly Varden, June 11 through October. *IMPORTANT: Be familiar with current regulations on closed areas; dates given here are subject to change!* ᵔ

S 47.9 (77.1 km) **A 100.9** (162.4 km) **H 131.6** (211.8 km) Snug Harbor Road. This side road leads 12 miles/19.3 km to Cooper Lake and trailhead for 23-mile/37-km USFS trail to Russian River Campground (see **Milepost S 52.6**). A Baptist church and the St. John Neumann Catholic Church, named after one of the first American saints, are on Snug Harbor Road.

Kenai Lake Baptist Church. See display ad this section.

St. John Neumann Catholic Church. See display ad this section.

S 48.1 (77.4 km) **A 101.1** (162.7 km) **H 131.4** (211.7 km) **Sport Fishing Cabins.** See display ad this section.

Cooper Landing Grocery & Hardware, the only full-service store between Anchorage and Soldotna. New owners in 1995 have made this the store to stop at on your trip through the Kenai Peninsula. Located in Cooper Landing, 1/2 mile from the bridge over the Kenai River and Lake. Friendly folks will provide you with the latest fishing news and visitor information. Hunting and fishing licenses are available, along with all the preferred tackle to fish the Kenai and Russian rivers. A large selection of groceries and fresh produce and everyday low prices eliminate the need to "stock up" before heading south from Anchorage. Ice cream parlor and deli. Fried chicken and pizza to go. RV supplies and hardware for minor repairs. VISA and MasterCard accepted at no extra charge. Wayne and Glenda Mitchell, (907) 595-1677. See display ad. [ADVERTISEMENT]

S 48.2 (77.6 km) **A 101.2** (162.9 km) **H 131.3** (211.3 km) **Red Salmon Guest House.** See display ad this section.

Troutfitters Alpine Motel. See display ad this seciton.

S 48.4 (77.9 km) **A 101.4** (163.2 km) **H 131.1** (211 km) **COOPER LANDING** (pop. 386) stretches along several miles of the highway. All visitor facilities. Cooper Landing ambulance, phone (907) 595-1255.

The Shrew's Nest, Last Resort RV Park and Landing Latté. See display ad this section. ▲

Private Aircraft: Quartz Creek (Cooper Landing) airstrip, 4 miles/6.4 km west; elev. 450 feet/137m; length 2,200 feet/671m; gravel; unattended.

S 48.5 (78.1 km) **A 101.5** (163.3 km) **H 131** (210.8 km) **Hamilton's Place** river resort, only complete stop on the upper Kenai River. Information center for

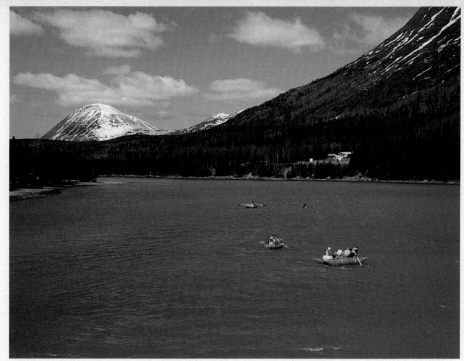

Rafting the Kenai River near Cooper Landing. (© Barbara Willard)

the famous Russian River and surrounding area. Centrally located for day trips to Seward, Soldotna/Kenai, Homer. Make us your Kenai Peninsula headquarters. Tesoro services, 24-hour recovery and transport (flatbed) service, 24-hour locksmith, propane. (All emergency road service providers.) General store, groceries, licenses, tackle, ice, liquor store. Restaurant, lounge. Hair salon. RV hookups, modern cabins with cooking facilities, laundromat, phone. Fish freezing, storage, Federal Express shipping. Hamilton's Place, serving the public since 1952, hopes to make your stay enjoyable. Phone (907) 595-1260; fax (907) 595-1530. See display ad this section. [ADVERTISEMENT] ▲

S 48.7 (78.4 km) **A 101.7** (163.7 km) **H 130.8** (210.5 km) Cooper Landing post office, located in resort; open 9 A.M. to 5 P.M. weekdays and Saturday morning. Pay phone.

S 48.8 (78.5 km) **A 101.8** (163.8 km) **H 130.7** (210.3 km) **Kenai Lake Adventures.** See display ad this section.

S 49.4 (79.5 km) **A 102.4** (164.8 km) **H 130.1** (209.4 km) Large paved turnout by Kenai River. The highway winds along the Kenai River. Many spruce trees in this area have died from spruce bark beetle infestation. Several thousand acres of spruce trees on the Kenai Peninsula may be logged as a result of this rapidly expanding infestation. The U.S. Forest Service hopes to reduce fire hazards, speed regrowth and salvage timber through selective cutting.

S 49.7 (80 km) **A 102.7** (165.3 km) **H 129.8** (208.9 km) **The Miller Homestead**

Bed & Breakfast RV Park. Make us your vacation headquarter for Kenai Peninsula adventures. We can arrange fishing for trophy rainbow trout, Russian River red salmon, Dolly Varden, Kenai River kings, silvers and halibut. Bank fishing from the park. See display ad this sectoin. [ADVERTISEMENT] ▲

S 49.8 (80.1 km) **A 102.8** (165.4 km) **H 129.7** (208.7 km) Haul road used by loggers removing dead spruce trees. Watch for trucks.

S 50 (80.5 km) **A 103** (165.8 km) **H 129.5** (208.4 km) **Alaska Rivers Co.,** right side westbound. Rafting daily on the beautiful Kenai River. Half-day scenic float, or full-day canyon trip with white water. Both trips include homemade picnic lunch, excellent viewing of wildlife, professional guides, all

equipment provided. All ages welcome. Personalized guided drift boat fishing for all species of fish. Overnight accommodations available. Family-owned and operated by Cooper Landing residents. Gary Galbraith, owner. (907) 595-1226 for reservations or just stop by. [ADVERTISEMENT]

S 50.1 (80.6 km) **A 103.1** (165.9 km) **H 129.4** (208.2 km) **Alaska Wildland Adventures.** Don't pass up taking a rafting or fishing trip with Alaska Wildland Adventures. You'll enjoy this facility's unique and

Don't pass up one of Alaska's most popular day trips while visiting the Kenai Peninsula!

KENAI RIVER TRIPS
RAFTING • FISHING

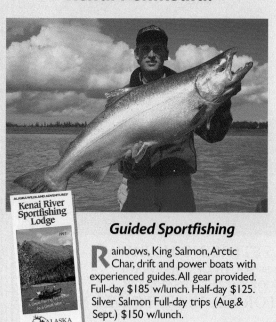

Kenai Canyon Raft Trip

A fun-filled, one day outing for those seeking adventure and majestic wilderness scenery. See the Kenai National Wildlife Refuge, shoot spirited rapids, and enjoy a gourmet lunch on a wild and scenic lakeshore. Exciting, informative, safe. Raingear and rubber boots provided. Adults $95 and kids $55. Daily departure: 11am.

See Log Ad

Guided Sportfishing

Rainbows, King Salmon, Arctic Char, drift and power boats with experienced guides. All gear provided. Full-day $185 w/lunch. Half-day $125. Silver Salmon Full-day trips (Aug. & Sept.) $150 w/lunch.

Call for a free color brochure

Natural History Float

Take a two-hour placid float. Watch for Eagles, Moose, Salmon, and Dall sheep. Enjoy the snowcapped mountain scenery. Hear the stories behind the sights. Adults $42 and kids $29. Daily departures: 9:30am, 1:00pm, 5:00pm.

Call for a free color brochure

PLEASE SEE MILEPOST MAP FOR OUR LOCATIONS

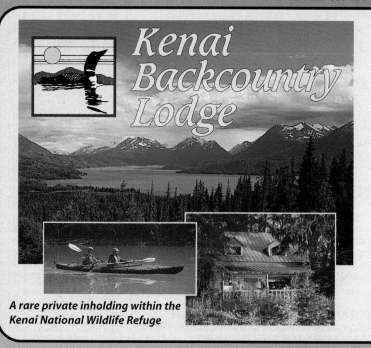

Kenai Backcountry Lodge

A rare private inholding within the Kenai National Wildlife Refuge

A Complete Wilderness Lodge Package
for Kenai Peninsula Visitors

Kenai Backcountry Lodge & Safari

KENAI BACKCOUNTRY LODGE is nestled in the heart of the Kenai National Wildlife Refuge along the wild shores of scenic Skilak Lake. The lodge, a rare private inholding, is accessed by boat. Each day of your stay is filled with adventure and activities. Naturalist/guides lead the way.

3 AND 4 DAY PACKAGES INCLUDE: Transfers to the lodge, lakeside cabins, delicious meals, rafting or boat explorations, wildlife viewing, photography, hikes led by naturalists, kayak paddling trips, and much more.

KENAI BACKCOUNTRY SAFARI -- 5 DAYS/4 NIGHTS

An exceptional value! Package combines Kenai Backcountry Lodge and Kenai Riverside Cabins plus an all-day boat tour of Kenai Fjords National Park.

Call for a free color brochure

Free Catalog - Alaska Adventure Vacations

- **Alaska Wildland Safaris**
  (5 to 12 day all-inclusive trips)
- **Unique Alaskan Lodges**
  Kenai Peninsula & Denali Nat'l Park (*see Denali Backcountry Lodge ad in Denali National Park section of this book*)
- **Other Exclusive Offerings**

OUR 21ST SEASON

ALASKA
WILDLAND
ADVENTURES

Milepost 50.1 Sterling Hwy. 1 in Cooper Landing. 2 hours south of Anchorage, or one hour from Soldotna or Seward.

 800-478-4100 Master

PO Box 389 Girdwood, Alaska 99587 Email: wildland@alaska.net scenic setting on the Kenai River. They offer daily guided raft trips along with a delicious Alaskan picnic lunch. You can expect to see wildlife and enjoy the scenery of one of the world's most beautiful rivers. If you're seeking a quality fishing experience, ask about their guided fishing trips for salmon and rainbow trout. This company is well known for its professional guides and deluxe boats. All tackle, rods and reels are furnished. Operating since 1977. Phone call toll free (800) 478-4100 for more information or reservations. See "Kenai River Trips" display ad. [ADVERTISEMENT]

Kenai Backcountry Lodge. In their 21st year, Alaska Wildland Adventures has opened their newest destination lodge. Similar to their Denali Backcountry Lodge in Kantishna, the Kenai Backcountry Lodge is another rare in-holding. It's nestled in the heart of the Kenai National Wildlife Refuge on Skilak Lake and is accessed only by boat or a scenic raft trip down the Kenai River. Dine in the newly renovated lodge first established in the 1930's and choose either a Yukon cabin tent or lakeside log cabin. This is one of those genuine Alaskan experiences you don't want to pass up. See Alaska Wildland Adventure's full-page display ad. For free brochure or reservation phone call 1-800-334-8730. [ADVERTISEMENT]

S 50.4 (81.1 km) **A 103.4** (166.4 km) **H 129.1** (207.8 km) **Juneau Creek**, Dolly Varden and rainbow, mid-June through July. 🐟

S 50.5 (81.3 km) **A 103.5** (166.6 km) **H 129** (207.6 km) Bridge over Cooper Creek. USFS Cooper Creek Campground. Camping area on the river side of highway (second entrance westbound) has 7 sites, several on the riverbank. Camping area on the other side of the highway has 23 sites. Both have tables, water and firepits. Fee is $9 single, $13 double. Reservations available, phone 1-800-280-CAMP (2267). ▲

S 52 (83.7 km) **A 105** (169 km) **H 127.5** (205.2 km) **Kenai Cache.** See display ad this section.

Gwin's Lodge, Restaurant and Bar, left side southbound. One of Alaska's few remaining traditionally built log roadhouses where Alaskans and visitors alike

always stop for food with a homemade touch and fast, courteous service. At heart of Kenai Peninsula. Closest lodge to nearby Kenai and Russian rivers confluence, Russian Lakes and Resurrection Pass trailheads. World renowned restaurant and bar, package store, modern cabins with private baths, full RV hookups, ice, fishing tackle/licenses, gifts, fish freezing/processing/smoking services. River and saltwater fishing, rafting, and goldpanning charters and booking services. VISA, MasterCard, and Discover accepted. (907) 595-1266 (voice); (907) 595-1681 (fax). [ADVERTISEMENT] ▲

S 52.6 (84.6 km) **A 105.6** (169.9 km) **H 126.9** (204.2 km) USFS Russian River Campground has 84 sites at the end of a 2-mile/3.2-km road. All have river access, toilets, water, tables and firepits. Fish cleaning stations, covered picnic tables and dump

station. The Russian River Campground is often full during the summer, particularly during the Russian River red salmon runs. Arrive early! Fees: $11 single RV occupancy, $18 double RV occupancy, $5 12-hour day-use parking, $6 dump station. Concessionaire-operated. For reservations phone 1-800-280-CAMP (2267). ▲

Bears attracted by the salmon are frequent visitors to this campground.

Russian Lakes USFS trail, trailhead and parking at Mile 0.9/1.4 km on campground road. Lower Russian Lake at Mile 2.6/4.2 km (elev. 500 feet/152m; hiking time 1¹/₂ hours). Good trail to Mile 3/4.8 km. Upper Russian Lake at Mile 12/19.3 km (elev. 690 feet/210m). Trail continues to Cooper Lake at end of Snug Harbor Road (see **Milepost S 47.9**). Public-use cabins along trail (see Cabins in the GENERAL INFORMATION section). Winter use; good snowmobiling to lower lake only, avalanche danger beyond.

CAUTION: This is brown bear country.

The **Russian River:** Closed to all fishing April 15 through June 10. Bait prohibited at all times in Russian River drainage. Check regulations for limits and other restrictions. Red (sockeye) salmon run starts mid-June. Second run begins July 20–25 and lasts about 3 weeks. Must use flies prior to Aug. 21. Silver (coho) salmon to 15 lbs., run begins mid-August. Catch-and-release only for rainbow trout in lower part of river at all times that season is open.

S 52.6 (84.6 km) **A 105.6** (169.9 km) **H 126.9** (204.2 km) Cultural heritage site of the Kenaitze Indian tribe; tours, gift shop.

K-Beq Footprints. See display ad this section.

S 53 (85.3 km) **A 106** (170.6 km) **H 126.5** (203.6 km) Bridge over Kenai River.

S 53.2 (85.6 km) **A 106.2** (170.9 km) **H 126.3** (203.3 km) Well-marked entry point to Resurrection Pass USFS trail; parking at trailhead. This 38-mile-/61-km-long trail climbs to Resurrection Pass (elev. 2,600 feet/792m) and descends to north trailhead near Hope on Turnagain Arm.

S 54.7 (88 km) **A 107.7** (173.3 km) **H 124.8** (200.8 km) Leaving Chugach

Skilak Lake Loop Road Log

The 19.1-mile/30.7-km Skilak Lake Loop Road (good gravel) loops south through the Skilak Wildlife Recreation Area to campgrounds, trails and fishing spots. *CAUTION: Do not leave valuables in unattended boats or vehicles.*

Distance from east junction (EJ) with Sterling Highway at Milepost S 58 is followed by distance from west junction (WJ) with Sterling Highway at Milepost S 75.2.

EJ 0 WJ 19.1 (30.7 km) **Junction** with Sterling Highway at **Milepost S 58.**

EJ 0.1 (0.2 km) **WJ 19** (30.5 km) Jim's Landing Day-use area on Kenai River, 0.2 mile/0.3 km from road; toilets, dumpster, tables, firepits, water, boat launch, parking area. Pavement ends westbound.

EJ 0.6 (1 km) **WJ 18.5** (29.7 km) Kenai River trail (6.3-mile/10.1-km hike); parking area.

EJ 2 (3.2 km) **WJ 17.1** (27.5 km) Pothole Lake Overlook turnout overlooks scene of Pothole Lake forest fire of 1991; interpretive sign on fire.

EJ 2.4 (3.9 km) **WJ 16.7** (26.8 km) Kenai River trail (6.3-mile/10.1-km hike); parking area.

EJ 3.6 (5.8 km) **WJ 15.5** (24.9 km) Hidden Lake Campground is an exceptionally nice camping area with 44 sites on paved loop roads. Located 0.5 mile/0.8 km in from the road on the lakeshore, it has picnic pavilions, a dump station, wheelchair-accessible toilets, tables, water, firepits and boat launch. Campfire programs in amphitheater. Observation deck for viewing wildlife.

Campground hosts in residence. Camping fee $10 for vehicles. Trailer parking area, interpretive exhibits and kitchen shelter with barbecue.　　 ⬥▲

Hidden Lake, lake trout average 16 inches and kokanee 9 inches, year-round, best from May 15 to July 1, use spoon, red-and-white or weighted, by trolling, casting and jigging. This lake is a favorite among local ice fishermen from late December through March. ◄►

EJ 4.7 (7.6 km) **WJ 14.4** (23.1 km) Hidden Creek trail (1.5-mile/2.4-km hike); parking area.

EJ 5.3 (8.5 km) **WJ 13.8** (22.2 km) Hidden Creek Overlook double-ended turnout; view of one arm of Skilak Lake; forest fire damage from 1996 fire visible.

EJ 5.5 (8.9 km) **WJ 13.6** (21.8 km) Skilak Lookout trail (2.6-mile/4.2-km hike); parking area.

EJ 6.2 (10 km) **WJ 12.9** (20.7 km) Bear Mountain trail (1-mile/1.6-km hike); parking area with firepit across from lily pond.

EJ 6.9 (11.1 km) **WJ 12.2** (19.6 km) Scenic viewpoint of Skilak Lake.

EJ 8.5 (13.6 km) **WJ 10.6** (17 km) Upper Skilak Lake Campground, drive 2 miles/3.2 km around Lower Ohmer Lake; 0.2-mile/0.3-km loop road through campground. There are 25 campsites (some sites on lakeshore), boat launch, toilets and tables; similar facilities to Hidden Lake Campground (**Milepost EJ 3.6**). Camping fee $10/vehicle, $6/tent site (walk-in). ▲

Lower Ohmer Lake, rainbow 14 to 16 inches, year-round. **Skilak Lake,** offers rainbow and Dolly Varden. Red (sockeye) salmon enter lake in mid-July. ◄►

EJ 8.6 (13.8 km) **WJ 10.5** (16.9 km) Lower Ohmer Lake, short side road to parking area on lakeshore; three campsites, toilet, boat launch, firepits and tables. ▲

EJ 9.5 (15.2 km) **WJ 9.6** (15.4 km) Short side road to **Engineer Lake,** boat launch and Seven Lakes trail; turnaround and parking area with firepits. Stocked silver salmon to 15 inches, best in July. ◄►

EJ 9.6 (15.4 km) **WJ 9.5** (15.3 km) Engineer Lake wayside; gravel turnout.

EJ 11.5 (18.5 km) **WJ 7.6** (12.2 km) Dump station on paved double-ended turnout to east.

EJ 13.8 (22.2 km) **WJ 6.3** (8.5 km) Well-marked 1-mile/1.6-km side road to Lower Skilak Lake Campground; 14 sites, tables, toilets, firepits, boat launch. ◄►

CAUTION: Skilak Lake is cold; winds are fierce and unpredictable. Wear life jackets!

EJ 14.2 (22.8 km) **WJ 4.9** (7.8 km) Fire guard station.

EJ 18.7 (30.1 km) **WJ 0.4** (0.6 km) Bottinentnin Lake; well-marked side road leads 0.3 mile/0.5 km to parking area on lakeshore. Shallow lake: No sport fish, but nice area for recreational canoeing.

EJ 19.1 (30.7 km) **WJ 0 Junction** with Sterling Highway at **Milepost S 75.2.**

Return to Milepost S 58 or S 75.2 Sterling Highway

National Forest lands westbound. Gravel turnout to east. Many turnouts and access to the Kenai River between here and **Milepost S 58.**

S 55 (88.5 km) **A 108** (173.8 km) **H 124.5** (200.4 km) Kenai–Russian River recreation area, access to Russian River ferry. During salmon season this campground, a favorite with fishermen, is heavily used; toilets, water, dumpsters, interpretive display, pay phone. Fees charged for boat launch, parking or camping. Privately operated 28-person ferry crosses the Kenai River here offering access to good fishing on opposite bank and to the mouth of the Russian River. Ferry fee is $6 adults round-trip, $4 children. ◄►▲

Leaving Game Management Unit 7, entering Unit 15 westbound. Entering Kenai National Wildlife Refuge westbound, administered by the USF&WS; contains more than 1.97 million acres of land set aside to preserve the moose, bear, sheep and other wildlife found here.

S 55.1 (88.7 km) **A 108.1** (174 km) **H 124.4** (200.2 km) Paved turnout.

S 57.1 (91.9 km) **A 110.1** (177.2 km) **H 122.4** (197 km) Fuller Lake trailhead (well marked), parking. **Lower Fuller Lake,** arctic grayling; **Upper Fuller Lake,** Dolly Varden. ◄►

S 58 (93.3 km) **A 111** (178.6 km) **H 121.5** (195.5 km) USF&WS visitor contact station opposite **junction** with Skilak Lake Loop Road. See SKILAK LAKE LOOP ROAD log this page. The information cabin is open Memorial Day through Labor Day; brochures and information on Kenai Peninsula attractions including federal, state and local recreation areas, such as Kenai National Wildlife Refuge; restrooms.

S 59 (94.9 km) **A 112** (180.2 km) **H 120.5** (193.9 km) **Milepost S 59.** Actual driving distance between here and **Milepost S 61** is 2.6 miles/4.2 km or 0.6 mile/1 km more than the posts indicate.

S 60.6 (97.5 km) **A 113.6** (182.8 km) **H 118.9** (191.3 km) **Jean Lake,** small campground (3 sites) and picnic area; boat launch, rainbow fishing. ◄►▲

S 61.4 (98.8 km) **A 114.4** (184.1 km) **H 118.1** (190.1 km) Skyline trail to north; double-ended gravel parking area to south.

S 62.3 (100.3 km) **A 115.3** (185.6 km) **H 117.2** (188.6 km) Large gravel turnout to north. Mystery Hills to the north and Hideout Hill to the south.

S 64.5 (103.8 km) **A 117.5** (189.1 km) **H 115** (185.1 km) Gravel turnout to north.

S 68.3 (109.9 km) **A 121.3** (195.2 km) **H 111.2** (179 km) Turnoff to south for Peterson Lake (0.5 mile/0.8 km) and Kelly Lake (1 mile/1.6 km) public campgrounds. Both have tables and firepits for 3 camping parties, water and boat launch, and parking space for self-contained RVs. **Kelly** and **Peterson lakes** have rainbow population.

Access to Seven Lakes trail. ◄►▲

S 70.4 (113.3 km) **A 123.4** (198.6 km) **H 109.1** (175.6 km) Egumen wayside with large parking area. East Fork Moose River and Seven Lakes trail. Half-mile marshy trail to **Egumen Lake** (lake not visible from highway); good rainbow population.

S 71.3 (114.7 km) **A 124.3** (200 km) **H 108.2** (174.1 km) Parking area at entrance to Watson Lake public campground; 0.4-mile/0.6-km drive from highway to small campground with 3 sites, toilets, picnic tables, fireplaces, water, dumpsters and steep boat launch (suitable for canoes or hand-carried boats). **Watson Lake,** rainbow. ◄►▲

S 72.8 (117.2 km) **A 125.8** (202.4 km) **H 106.7** (171.7 km) Paved double-ended turnout to south, lake to north.

S 75.2 (121 km) **A 128.2** (206.3 km) **H 104.3** (167.8 km) West **junction** with Skilak Lake Loop Road. See SKILAK LAKE LOOP ROAD log this page.

Kenai River from Skilak Lake to Soldotna. Consult regulations for legal tackle, limits and seasons. King salmon 20 to 80 lbs., use spinners, excellent fishing June to August; red salmon 6 to 12 lbs., many, but hard to catch, use flies, best from July 15 to Aug. 10; pink salmon 4 to 8 lbs., abundant fish on even years Aug. 1 to Sept. 1, spoons; silver salmon 6 to 15 lbs., use spoons, Aug. 15 to Nov. 1; rainbow, Dolly Varden 15 to 20 inches, June through September, use spinners, winged bobber, small-weighted spoon.

NOTE: *The Kenai River Special Management Area is managed by the Alaska Division of Parks and Outdoor Recreation (DPOR), and includes the waters of Kenai and Skilak lakes and the Kenai River. Motors are limited to maximum 35 horsepower on the river, and prohibited on some sections. For more information, contact DPOR at P.O. Box 1247, Soldotna, AK 99669, phone (907) 262-5581.*

S 79.2 (127.4 km) **A 132.2** (212.7 km) **H 100.3** (161.4 km) Kenai Keys Road. Divided highway begins southbound.

Fish On Inn & RV Park. See display ad this section. ▲

S 80.3 (129.2 km) **A 133.3** (214.5 km) **H 99.2** (159.6 km) Turnoff for Peninsula Furs and Bing's Landing State Recreation Site with RV and tent camping, picnic area, water, boat launch, toilets (wheelchair accessible), dumpster and access to Kenai River. Camping fee $8/night or annual pass. Boat launch fee $5 or annual boat launch pass. ♿▲

Peninsula Furs. See display ad this section.

S 80.6 (129.7 km) **A 133.6** (215 km) **H 98.9** (159.2 km) Double-ended paved turnout to east.

S 81 (130.3 km) **A 134** (215.6 km) **H 98.5** (158.5 km) STERLING (pop. 1,732; elev. 150 feet/45m). Traveler services include 2 gas stations, 2 motels, several restaurants and cafes; gift, grocery, hardware, antique, fur and furniture stores, laundromat and several campgrounds. Post office at **Milepost S 81.6**. (Businesses with a Sterling mailing address extend west to **Milepost S 85**.) Nearby recreational opportunities include fishing and the extensive canoe trail system (see description at **Milepost S 82**). Moose River Raft Race and Sterling Days held in July.

Bing Brown's RV Park & Motel. See display ad this section. ▲

Moose River Auto Parts & Towing. See display ad this section.

S 81.1 (130.5 km) **A 134.1** (215.8 km) **H 98.4** (158.4 km) Gift shop and grocery store.

S 81.6 (131.3 km) **A 134.6** (216.6 km) **H 97.9** (157.6 km) Sterling post office (ZIP code 99672).

View of Skilak Lake from overlook on Skilak Lake Loop Road. (Jerrianne Lowther, staff)

S 81.7 (131.5 km) **A 134.7** (216.8 km) **H 97.8** (157.4 km) **Cook's Corner.** See display ad this section. ▲

Sterling House Bed & Breakfast. See display ad this section.

S 82 (132 km) **A 135** (217.3 km) **H 97.5** (156.9 km) Pay phone on highway just before turnoff for Izaak Walton State Recreation Site, located at the confluence of the Kenai and Moose rivers. Paved access road, 25 campsites, parking, tables, toilets, water and dumpster. Camping fee $10/night or annual pass. Boat launch ($5 fee or annual boat launch pass) and good access to Kenai

River. A small log cabin, totem pole and an information sign about Moose River archaeological site. ▲

Sterling Chevron & Food Mart. See display ad this section.

Bridge over Moose River. *CAUTION: Drive carefully during fishing season when fishermen walk along bridge and highway.*

Canoe rentals and shuttle bus service to the head of the canoe trail system are available by the Moose River bridge. This is the terminus of the Swan Lake canoe trail. There are 2 canoe routes in Kenai National Wildlife Refuge: Swan Lake route, a 60-mile/

97-km route connecting 30 lakes; and the Swanson River route, an 80-mile/129-km route linking 40 lakes. Guided canoe tours and fishing charters are available. Portions of the canoe system may be traveled taking anywhere from 1 to 4 days. Contact Kenai National Wildlife Refuge, Box 2139, Soldotna, AK 99669 for details. See SWANSON RIVER AND SWAN LAKE ROADS log on page 525.

Moose River, 0.3 mile/0.4 km of fishing down to confluence with Kenai River. Sockeyes here in June. Big summer run of reds follows into August; silvers into October. ◄━

Kenai and **Moose rivers** (confluence), Dolly Varden and rainbow trout, salmon (king, red, pink, silver). June 15 through October for trout; year-round for Dolly Varden. King salmon from May through July, pink salmon in August and silver salmon from August through October. This is a fly-fishing-only area from May 15 through Aug. 15; closed to fishing from boats, May 15 until the end of the king salmon season or July 31, whichever is later. ◄━

S 82.1 (132.1 km) **A 135.1** (217.4 km) **H 97.4** (156.8 km) **Kenai Moose Bed & Breakfast.** See display ad this section.

S 82.3 (132.4 km) **A 135.3** (217.7 km) **H 97.2** (156.4 km) **Alaska Adventure Reser-**

Swanson River and Swan Lake Roads Log

Swanson River Road leads north 17.2 miles/27.7 km, where it junctions with Swan Lake Road, which leads east 12.7 miles/20.4 km and dead ends at Paddle Lake. Both roads provide access to fishing, hiking trails and canoe trails. *CAUTION: Do not leave valuables in vehicles at canoe trailheads.*

Distance from junction with the Sterling Highway (J) is shown.

J 0 Junction with Sterling Highway at **Milepost S 83.4.** Swanson River Road is a good gravel road but can be rough in spots; slow speeds are advised. There are numerous turnouts suitable for overnight camping in self-contained RVs.

J 0.7 (1.1 km) Robinson Loop Road; rejoins Sterling Highway at **Milepost S 87.5.**

J 1.3 (2.1 km) Airstrip.

J 4.4 (7.1 km) Entering Kenai National Wildlife Refuge.

J 7.9 (12.7 km) **Mosquito Lake**, turnout; 0.5-mile trail to lake. Rainbow trout.

J 9.1 (14.6 km) **Silver Lake** trailhead and parking: 1-mile/1.6-km hike to lake. Rainbow trout and arctic char.

J 9.8 (15.8 km) **Finger Lake** trailhead: 2.3-mile/3.7-km hike to lake. Good arctic char fishing.

J 10.6 (17.1 km) **Forest Lake** wayside, parking; 0.3-mile/0.5-km trail to lake. Rainbow trout; best fished from canoe or raft.

J 13 (20.9 km) **Weed Lake** wayside; small turnout by lake. Rainbow trout.

J 13.3 (21.4 km) **Drake** and **Skookum lakes** trailhead and parking; 2-mile/3.2-km trail. Rainbow trout and arctic char.

J 14 (22.5 km) Access to Breeze Lake.

J 14.2 (22.9 km) **Dolly Varden Lake** Campground; 15 sites, water, toilets, boat launch. Large RVs and trailers note: 0.5-mile/0.8-km access road to campground is narrow and bumpy; check turnaround space before driving in. Fishing for Dolly Varden and rainbow; best in late August and September.

J 14.9 (24 km) Access road to canoe trails to east. Oil field road to west closed to private vehicles. The Swanson River Road was originally built as an access road to the Swanson River oil field. Chevron operated the field from 1958 to 1986; it is currently operated by Unocal.

J 15.7 (25.2 km) **Rainbow Lake** Campground; small 3-unit camping area on lakeshore with toilets, water and boat launch. Fishing for Dolly Varden and rainbow trout. *CAUTION: Steep road; difficult turnaround. Large RVs: check visually before driving in.*

J 17.2 (27.7 km) **Junction** with Swan Lake Road. Continue north 0.5 mile/0.8 km for Swanson River Landing at end of Swanson River Road; camping area with picnic tables, firepits, water, toilets, boat launch, large gravel parking area. This is the terminus of the Swanson River canoe route, which begins at Paddle Lake at the end of Swan Lake Road. Log now follows Swan Lake Road east.

J 17.3 (27.8 km) Kenai National Wildlife Refuge Outdoor Environmental Education Center. Reservation required. Educational group-use permits obtained at Kenai National Wildlife Refuge Visitor Center in Soldotna.

J 20.2 (32.5 km) **Fish Lake**; 3 sites, tables, firepits, toilets. Fishing for Dolly Varden.

J 21.2 (34 km) **Canoe Lake**, parking. West entrance to Swan Lake canoe route. Fishing for Dolly Varden.

J 21.8 (35.1 km) Sucker Creek wayside; campsite, table, fireplace. **Sucker Lake**, rainbow trout.

J 23.3 (37.5 km) **Merganser Lakes**, 0.5-mile/0.8 km south; rainbow trout.

J 25.4 (40.9 km) Nest Lakes trail, 0.5-mile/0.8-km hike north.

J 26.9 (43.3 km) Large turnout and toilet to west.

J 27 (43.5 km) **Portage Lake**. East entrance to Swan Lake canoe route. Lake is stocked with coho salmon.

J 27.3 (43.9 km) Informal pullout on lake.

J 29.4 (47.3 km) Y in road; bear left.

J 29.9 (48.1 km) End of road. **Paddle Lake** entrance to Swanson River canoe route; parking, picnic table, water and toilet. Fishing for rainbow and Dolly Varden.

Return to Milepost S 83.4 Sterling Highway

---

vations. Budget camp-out fishing or wilderness trips (5 or 7 days). Guided canoe trips (3 days) and rental. Charters for salmon, halibut and trout. Fly-outs and bear camp—we do it all. 1-800-262-9666. HC1 Box 218, Sterling, AK 99672; fax (360) 638-1582. See display ad this section. [ADVERTISEMENT]

S 82.5 (132.8 km) **A 135.5** (218.1 km) **H 97** (156.1 km) Keyston Road.

Big Sky Charter & Fish Camp. See display ad this section.

Kenai Magic Lodge & Fishing Adventures. See display ad this section.

S 82.6 (132.9 km) **A 135.6** (218.2 km) **H 96.9** (155.9 km) Airstrip. Restaurant and bar.

S 82.8 (133.3 km) **A 135.8** (218.5 km)

H 96.7 (155.6 km) Truck weigh station; senior center across highway.

Highway narrows to 3 lanes southbound.

S 83.4 (134.2 km) **A 136.4** (219.5 km) **H 96.1** (154.7 km) **Junction** with Swanson River and Scout Lake Loop roads. Swanson River Road turnoff to north (see SWANSON RIVER AND SWAN LAKE ROADS log this page). Scout Lake Loop Road turns off to south and rejoins the Sterling Highway at **Milepost S 85** (see milepost for description). Sterling elementary school.

Convenience store with gas, church, laundromat and showers located on Swanson River Road, just past intersection.

Sterling Baptist Church. See display ad this section.

ZIPMART. See display ad on page 526.

S 84 (135.2 km) **A 137** (220.5 km) **H 95.5** (153.7 km) **Sterling Campground RV.** See display ads on page 526.

S 84.3 (135.7 km) **A 137.3** (221 km) **H 95.2** (153.2 km) **Scout Lake Inn and Nicki's Restaurant**, located near the Kenai and Moose rivers. Good fishing June to August 15. clean and modern rooms. Nicki's specializes in homemade cinnamon rolls, breads and pies. New RV park. Secluded private cabins with bath house. Call early to reserve your space or cabin. Visit our Alaskan gift shop. (907) 262-5898.

S 84.5 (136 km) **A 137.5** (221.3 km) **H 95** (152.9 km) **Alaskan Abode B&B.** John 14:23. 200 feet off highway. Queen-size beds. Private baths. Common living room with TV. No smoking or liquor. Continental or full breakfast, homemade breads. Porcelain doll and gift shop. Open all year. MasterCard/VISA accepted. Phone/fax (907)

262-9719. P.O. Box 684, Sterling, AK 99672.

S 84.9 (136.6km) **A 137.9** (221.9 km) **H 94.6** (152.2 km) Scout Lake State Recreation Site to south on Scout Lake Loop Road; 12 campsites, water, toilets, covered picnic shelter. Camping fee $8/night or annual pass. Scout Lake Loop Road loops south of the Sterling Highway for 7 miles/11.3 km and rejoins the Sterling Highway at **Milepost S 83.4.** Turn here and drive down Scout Lake Loop Road 1.6 miles/2.6 km to turnoff for Morgan's Landing: follow side road 2.4 miles/3.9 km to reach Morgan's Landing State Recreation Area; $10 nightly fee per vehicle or annual pass, 40 developed campsites with 10 pull-through sites and some double sites, toilets and water. Alaska State Parks area headquarters is located here.   ▲

Cast Away Riverside RV Park. See display ad this section.   ▲

Good access from Morgan's Landing to the **Kenai River**, king salmon from mid-June through July, average 30 lbs. Red (sockeye) salmon average 8 lbs., use flies in July and August; silver (coho) salmon to 15 lbs., August and September, use lure; pink salmon average 4 lbs. with lure, best in July, even-

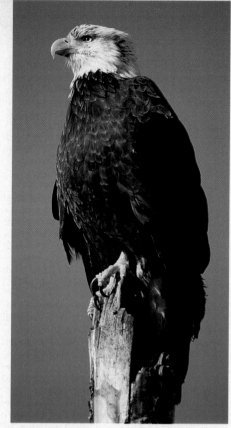

Bald eagles are common on the Kenai Peninsula. (© Tom Bol)

numbered years only; rainbow and Dolly Varden, use lure, June through August.   🐟

Divided highway ends southbound.

S 87.5 (140.8 km) **A 140.5** (226.1 km) **H 92** (148.1 km) Robinson Loop Road.

S 88 (141.6 km) **A 141** (226.9 km) **H 91.5** (147.3 km) St. Theresa's Drive.

Alaskan Paradise B&B. Spend time in Paradise with the Mains. Clean, quiet, country setting near beautiful Longmere Lake. Reasonable rates. Yummy breakfasts. Cozy beds. Private or shared baths. Sign 100-square-foot guest book. 20-foot golf practice net. Freezers, barbecue available. Outdoor smoking only. MasterCard, VISA. P.O. Box

152, Soldotna, AK 99669. Phone (907) 262-3214. [ADVERTISEMENT]

Longmere Lake Lodge B&B. One mile off Sterling Highway. Beautiful lakeside set-

ting in the comfort of spacious accommodations. Large stone fireplace and Alaskan artifacts sets the mood to relax and enjoy the scenery. Master bedrooms with full private baths or complete unit with kitchen. Guided salmon, halibut, hiking, bird watching, flightseeing arranged. Longtime Alaskan hosts. P.O. Box 1707, Soldotna, AK 99669 (907) 262-9799. [ADVERTISEMENT]

S 88.3 (142.1 km) **A 141.3** (227.4 km) **H 91.2** (146.8 km) **Alaska Horn & Antler.** See display ad this section.

The Jade Shop at Alaska Horn and Antler features raw jade, finished pieces, clocks, novelties. Also, Alaskan marble and petrified wood from Kachemak Bay. Antler buttons, bolos, earrings, letter openers, souvenir pins, antler baskets, Alaska back-scratchers. We buy antlers. Watch Tom Cooper carve here. Closed Sunday. See display ad. [ADVERTISEMENT]

S 91.3 (146.9 km) **A 144.3** (232.2 km) **H 88.2** (141.9 km) Gas station, convenience store and RV repair.

S 91.8 (147.7 km) **A 144.8** (233 km) **H 87.7** (141.1 km) **Eagle Smokehouse.** We will smoke (kipper) or pickle your salmon or halibut for you. We also vacuum pack and freeze your fresh fish. No luck fishing? We have all of the above for sale plus our smoked salmon/cream cheese spread in 2 flavors, pickled and fresh Alaskan shrimp and 4 flavors of smoked salmon jerky. All our products are all natural with no artificial colors, flavors or preservatives—no nitrites. We box and ship. Free samples. Box 4085, Soldotna, AK 99669. Phone and fax (907) 262-7007. [ADVERTISEMENT]

S 92 (148 km) **A 145** (233.3 km) **H 87.5** (140.8 km) Public golf course, driving range and cottages.

S 92.4 (148.7 km) **A 145.4** (234 km) **H 87.1** (140.2 km) State Division of Forest,

Land and Water Management. Fire danger indicator sign.

S 92.7 (149.1 km) **A 145.7** (234.5 km) **H 86.8** (139.7 km) Mackey Lake Road. Private lodging is available on this side road.

Aalaska Tree Top Bed & Breakfast. See display ad this section.

Bill Slemp's Cabin Rentals. See display ad this section.

S 93 (149.7 km) **A 146** (235 km) **H 86.5** (139.2 km) **Eagles' Nest Bed N' Breakfast.** See display ad this section.

S 93.1 (149.8 km) **A 146.1** (235.1 km) **H 86.4** (139 km) Loren Lake.

S 93.7 (150.8 km) **A 146.7** (236.1 km) **H 85.8** (138.1 km) Four-lane highway begins and leads through Soldotna.

S 94 (151.2 km) **A 147** (236.6 km) **H 85.5** (137.6 km) Traffic light to shops and gas.

S 94.1 (151.4 km) **A 147.1** (236.7 km) **H 85.4** (137.4 km) Restaurant. Turn on East Redoubt Street and follow the gravel road 0.5 mile/0.8 km for Swiftwater Park municipal campground. The municipal campground has 20 spaces on **Kenai River** (some pull-throughs), some tables, firepits,

firewood, phone, dump station, 2-week limit, litter barrels, toilets, boat landing, fee charged, good fishing. ◄▲

Through the Seasons Restaurant specializes in fine dining in pleasant surroundings. Open daily for lunch and dinner. Lunch: homemade breads, gourmet soups, sandwiches made with freshly roasted meats. Dinner: seafoods, homemade pasta, steak and

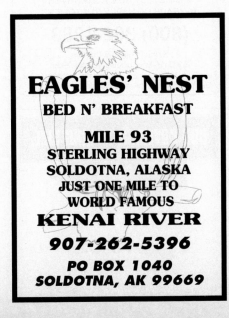

nightly specials. Through the Seasons cheesecakes. Fine wines and imported beers. See display ad in Soldotna section. [ADVERTISEMENT]

S 94.2 (151.6 km) **A 147.2** (236.9 km) **H 85.3** (137.3 km) **Junction** with Kenai Spur Highway. This junction is called the Soldotna Y.

There are 2 ways to reach the city of Kenai (see description of city on page 540): Turn right (westbound) at the Y, physical **Milepost S 94.2**, and continue 11 miles/17.7 km northwest to Kenai via the Kenai Spur Highway; or continue on the Sterling Highway to **Milepost S 96.1** and turn right (southbound) on the Kalifornsky Beach Road and continue 9.3 miles/14.9 km to Kenai via the Warren Ames Memorial Bridge. For details see KENAI SPUR HIGHWAY log on page 539 and KALIFORNSKY BEACH ROAD log on page 545. Description of Soldotna follows.

S 94.4 (151.9 km) **A 147.4** (237.2 km) **H 85.1** (137 km) Soldotna DOT/PF highway maintenance station, gas station. Turn east here for access to Soldotna Creek Park (day use only). Follow road behind restaurant.

Soldotna Tesoro. See display ad this section.

S 95 (152.9 km) **A 148** (238.2 km) **H 84.5** (136 km) Soldotna city center; Peninsula Center shopping mall. Turn on Binkley Street for access to fire station, police station and post office. See description of city following. See city map opposite page.

Homer-bound travelers continue south across the Kenai River bridge past visitor center. Turn west on Kalifornsky Beach Road for Centennial Park, the Soldotna city campground, and Soldotna Historical Society Museum.

The Slikok Valley School, the last of the Alaska Territory log schools, built in 1958, is one of the attractions at the museum's log village. Turn east off the Sterling Highway on Funny River Road for airport. See desciption at **Milepost S 96.1** on page 544.

Log of the Sterling Highway continues on page 544.

Log of the Sterling Highway continues on page 544.

Soldotna

S 95.2 (153.2 km) **A 148.2** (238.5 km) **H 84.3** (135.7 km) On the western Kenai Peninsula, the city stretches over a mile southwest along the Sterling Highway and northwest along the Kenai Spur Highway. **Population:** 3,900; Kenai Peninsula Borough 44,411. **Emergency Services:** Phone 911 for all emergency services. **Alaska State Troopers** at Mile 22 Kalifornsky Beach Road just off Sterling Highway, phone (907) 262-4453. **City Police**, phone (907) 262-4455. **Fire Department**, phone (907) 262-4792. **Ambulance**, phone (907) 262-4500. **Hospital**, Central Peninsula General, 1 mile/1.6 km north of Public Safety Building off Marydale Drive, phone (907) 262-4404.

Visitor Information: The Kenai Peninsula Visitor Information Center is located in downtown Soldotna on the Sterling Highway south of the Kenai River bridge. The center is open 7 days a week, mid-May through mid-September, 9 A.M. to 7 P.M. The remainder of the year the center is open weekdays from 9 A.M. to 5 P.M. Write: Greater Soldotna Chamber of Commerce, 44790 Sterling Highway, Soldotna, AK 99669; phone (907) 262-1337 or 262-9814, fax (907) 262-3566.

Elevation: 115 feet/35m. **Climate:** Average daily temperature in July, 63°F to 68°F/17°C to 20°C; January, 19°F to 23°F/-7°C to -5°C. Annual precipitation, approximately 18 inches. **Radio:** KGTL 620, KFQD 750, KSRM 920, KGTL-FM 100.9/103.5, MBN-FM 95.3/97.7, KWHQ-FM 1001, KPEN-FM 101-7, KZXX 980. **Television:** Channels 2, 4, 9, 12 and 13 via booster line from Anchorage, cable and KANG public education channel. **Newspapers:** *Peninsula Clarion* (daily), *The Dispatch* (weekly).

Private Aircraft: Soldotna airstrip, 0.9 mile/1.4 km southeast; elev. 107 feet/32m; length 5,000 feet/1,524m; asphalt; fuel 100LL; unattended.

The town of Soldotna was established in the 1940s because of its strategic location at the Sterling–Kenai Spur Highway junction. (Visitors may see the homestead cabin, which became Soldotna's first post office in 1949, at its original location on the Kenai Spur Highway at Corral Street.) Soldotna was named for a nearby stream; it is a Russian word meaning "soldier," although some believe the name came from an Indian word meaning the "stream fork."

Soldotna was incorporated as a first-class city in 1967. It has a council–manager form of government. Kenai Peninsula Borough headquarters and state offices of the Departments of Highways, Public Safety, Fish and Game, and Forest, Land and Water Management are located here. Soldotna is also headquarters for the Kenai Peninsula Borough school district. There are 3 elementary schools, a junior high school and 2 high schools. University of Alaska Kenai Peninsula College is also located in Soldotna.

Area terrain is level and forested, with many streams and lakes nearby. Large rivers of the area are the Swanson River, the Moose River and the Kenai River, which empties into Cook Inlet just south of Kenai. The area affords a majestic view of volcanic mountains across Cook Inlet. Always snow-covered, they are Mount Spurr (elev. 11,100 feet/3,383m), which erupted in 1992; Mount Iliamna (elev. 10,016 feet/3,053m), which has 3 smaller peaks to the left of the larger one; and Mount Redoubt (elev. 10,197 feet/3,108m), which was identified by its very regular cone shape until it erupted in December 1989.

ACCOMMODATIONS/VISITOR SERVICES

All modern conveniences and facilities are available, including supermarkets, banks, hotels/motels, restaurants and drive-ins,

Soldotna

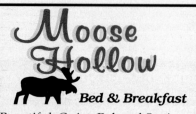
medical and dental clinics, bowling alley, golf course, veterinarians, churches and a library. Two shopping malls are located on the Sterling Highway near the center of town. Bed-and-breakfasts, cabin rentals and lodges also offer accommodations.

Accommodations Alaskan Style. Let us help book your adventure in Alaska. As year-round Alaskans we know where the bargains are and will work hard to make your vacation memorable and affordable. We book quality lodging, fishing charters, nature tours, complete packages and more. All lodging personally inspected. HC1 Box 157H, Soldotna, AK 99669. 1-800-313-3226 or 1-800-262-1421. [ADVERTISEMENT]

Alaskan Holiday Suites. Two-bedroom, 2-bath suites, with fully equipped kitchens. Suites accommodate up to 6. Convenient location, close to all services and just a short walk to the famous Kenai River. Continental breakfast. Free local calls. Cable TV. Guide reservations available. VISA/MasterCard accepted. Reservations: (907) 694-7615 or (907) 262-9635. See display ad. [ADVERTISEMENT]

Best Western King Salmon Motel, Restaurant and RV Park downtown Soldotna on Kenai Spur Highway. Large rooms, queen beds, some kitchenettes, cable TV, phones. Free in-room coffee. Restaurant serves early fisherman's breakfast, lunch, dinner. Steaks, seafood, salad bar. Beer and wine available. Fishing licenses, ice. Fish processing close by. RV park with 39 pull-through spaces, full hookups, restrooms, coin-operated showers and laundry. Phone (907) 262-5857; fax (907) 262-9441. See display ad this section. [ADVERTISEMENT] ▲

Cashman's Lodging. Finest lodging on the Kenai Peninsula. Spacious cabins on the Kenai River. Also, condos with 1 to 3 bedrooms, 1 or 2 baths, complete kitchens. Laundry facilities available. Centrally located in Soldotna. Complete services for fishing or

SOLDOTNA ADVERTISERS

hunting. Groups and combination packages our specialty. (907) 262-4359. Write Box 3143, Soldotna, AK 99669. [ADVERTISEMENT]

Diamond M Ranch. Opening June 1, 1997. Long-time Alaskans, JoAnne and Carrol Martin and family, are expanding their ranch to include a variety of accommodations for Kenai Peninsula visitors. Bed and breakfast features wild berry muffins, guest kitchen, outdoor barbecue, hot tub and sauna, large green lawn, igloo for the kids. New, hand-crafted cabins nestled in the trees, rustic or full bath and kitchenette. Variety of RV spaces, some with electricity, pull-throughs. Central shower, dump station. Magnificent view of Cook Inlet, waterfowl, moose, caribou. Hiking trails. Access to Kenai River. Minutes to airport, shopping, restaurants, churches. VISA, MasterCard. Phone (907) 283-9424. P.O. Box 1776, Soldotna, AK 99669. See display ad. ▲

[ADVERTISEMENT]

Gulls Landing B&B. Lovely Vermont-style home. Wooded Kenai River setting near Soldotna "Y." River curls around 3 viewing decks. Fishing dock planned for 1997. Separate entrance, equipped kitchenette, private river-view living room. TV/VCR. Three sizable river-view bedrooms. Queen, twin, king beds. Two bathrooms, one private. Friendly

hostess. Delicious breakfasts. VISA, Master-Card. 485 Lingonberry Lane, Soldotna, AK 99669. (907) 262-6668. [ADVERTISEMENT]

Kenai River Retreat. Vacation condos on the Kenai River are nonsmoking and include well-supplied kitchens, master bedroom, cable TV, telephone, laundry facilities, large freezer and great Alaskan hospitality! Relax on your secluded deck overlooking the river, walk down and fish from our bank or hike on nearby trails. Kenai River Retreat offers an Alaskan adventure—in style. For

reservations, call (907) 262-1361 or write 360 W. Endicott–MP, Soldotna, AK 99669. [ADVERTISEMENT]

Lottie's Place Bed and Breakfast. Located Mile 12.3 Kalifornsky Beach Road, halfway between the Kenai and Kasilof rivers. Walk the beach, relax by the fireplace. Barbecue available for your catch of the day. Continental or full breakfast. Queen–size beds, satellite TV. Honeymoon bedroom with fireplace. Owned and operated by long-time Alaskans. Reservations: phone

(907) 283-8707. See display ad in Soldotna section. [ADVERTISEMENT]

Orca Lodge. Beautiful, hand-crafted log cabins on the world-famous Kenai River near

Soldotna. Kitchens, outdoor barbecue, dock. Guided salmon, trout and halibut fishing,

raft trips, flightseeing, glacier tours. 3–7 night packages. Box 4653, Soldotna, AK 99669. Phone (907) 262-5649. Web address: http://www.alaskaOne.com/orcalodge; e-mail: fishorca@alaska.net. [ADVERTISEMENT]

RiverSide House Hotel & RV Park. Hotel, restaurant, lounge, and RV park on the banks of the Kenai River. Clean rooms, cable TV, Alaska cuisine, cocktails, dancing, fishing on premises. RV electrical hookups; water in park, showers, laundromat within half-block. Guide service, individual, groups, fishing. 44611 Sterling Highway, Soldotna, AK 99669. Phone (907) 262-0500, fax (907) 262-0406. [ADVERTISEMENT] ▲

Spruce Avenue Bed and Breakfast. Native Alaskan art decorates large, non-smoking residence. Delicious breakfasts

feature Finnish fare hosted by retired Alaskan teachers. Moderate rates $50–$80. Gift shop. Send for Recipe/Story Collection, $9 ppd. Sharon and Richard Waisanen, 35985 Pioneer Dr., Soldotna, AK 99669; (907) 262-9833. E-mail: sprucebb@alaska.net. [ADVERTISEMENT]

For Swiftwater Campground, turn on East Redoubt Street at **Milepost S 94.1** Sterling Highway. Centennial Park Campground is 0.1 mile/0.2 km from the Sterling Highway just south of the Kenai River bridge on Kalifornsky Beach Road; turn west at **Milepost S 96.1**. Both campgrounds are owned by the City of Soldotna. Register for camping at either park; camping fees charged. Dump station available at Centennial Park Campground. These campgrounds are heavily used; good idea to check in early. There are several private campgrounds located in and near Soldotna; see ads this section and contact the chamber of commerce. ▲

Across The River RV Park. Bank fishing for reds, rainbows, silvers. Guided fishing for Kenai River kings, silvers. Public boat launch close by. Fish cleaning facility, ice, freezer, water, dump station. Electric hookups, laundry, showers, phone, ice, tackle. Phone 1-800-276-2434, summer (907) 262-0458. Box 2193, Soldotna, AK 99669. Mile 13.8 Funny River Road. See display ad. [ADVERTISEMENT] ▲

Edgewater RV Park on the banks of world famous Kenai River, across from the Soldotna visitors' center. Full and partial hookups, laundry, showers, grassy sites, picnic tables, local guide service and fish cleaning facilities. Bank fishing. Walk to stores, restaurants. Reservations and information (907) 262-7733. P.O. Box 976, Soldotna, AK 99669. [ADVERTISEMENT] ▲

River Terrace RV Park features 1,100 feet of Kenai River frontage in Soldotna at the bridge. Walking distance to Kenai Peninsula Visitor Center, restaurants, groceries and downtown shopping malls. Full and partial hookups, riverfront sites. Heated

restrooms, showers with unlimited hot water, laundry. World-famous red salmon fishing from the riverbank. 1,004,214 salmon swam by our property in 1994, by Alaska State Fish and Game sonar count. Tackle shop, ice, fish processing and taxidermy available on premises. Let our park resident master guides provide custom king and silver salmon charters on the Kenai and Kasilof rivers. Reserve early to avoid disappointment. Phone (907) 262-5593; fax (907) 262-9229; write P.O. Box 322, Soldotna, AK 99669. [ADVERTISEMENT] ▲

TRANSPORTATION

Air: Charters available. Soldotna airport is south of Soldotna 2 miles/3.2 km off the Sterling Highway; at **Milepost S 96.1**, just after crossing Kenai River bridge, turn left (east) on Funny River (Airport) Road 2 miles/3.2 km.

Local: Taxi service, car rentals, vehicle leasing, boat rentals and charters.

Highway: Accessible via the Sterling Highway (Alaska Route 1), 148.2 miles/238.5 km from Anchorage.

ATTRACTIONS

Join in Local Celebrations. July's big event is the annual Soldotna Progress Days, held during the 4th weekend of the month. Activities include a parade, 2 days of rodeo, autocross competition, car show, barbecues, dance, arts and crafts show, and other events.

During the month of August the Kenai River Guides Association sponsors the annual Soldotna Silver Salmon Derby. 1997 marks the 11th year for this event. Daily prizes are awarded for the heaviest silver salmon caught, in addition to other categories. Several thousand dollars in cash and merchandise is awarded in this exciting event. The Peninsula Winter Games take place in February in Soldotna. Activities include an ice sculpture contest, cross-coun-

try ski race, ice bowling and snow volleyball.
Games, booths, concessions and demonstrations are held throughout the weekend. The
Alaska State Championship Sled Dog Races
and Dog Weight Pull Contest take place
during the Winter Games.

Donna's Country & Victorian Gifts at
Blazy's Soldotna Mall. A shopper's delight, a
fisherman's wife's revenge. This is the perfect place to spend an afternoon while your

husband goes fishing. Roomfuls of wonderful things, constantly changing. Enjoy our
cozy, relaxing atmosphere. Don't miss our
Santa room! You'll find things in our shoppe
you never thought you'd find in Alaska!
[ADVERTISEMENT]

Fish the Kenai River. Soldotna is one
of Alaska's best known sportfishing headquarters, and many claim that some of the

world's best fishing is here at the Kenai River, which flows next to town. Many charter boats and fishing guides for Kenai River fishing are located in the Soldotna area. In May 1985, Les Anderson of Soldotna landed a 97-lb., 4-oz. king salmon, a new world's record. The mounted fish is on display at the visitor center.

Soldotna gets very busy during fishing season, and for those fishermen who want a more remote fishing spot—or for visitors who want to see wildlife and glaciers—there are fly-in fishing trips for rainbow, grayling, salmon and Dolly Varden, and flightseeing trips to see Tustumena Lake, the Harding Icefield and wildlife, through local outfitters.

In Soldotna, the early run of kings begins about May 15, with the peak of the run occurring between June 12 and 20. The late run enters the river about July 1, peaking between July 23 and 31; season closes July 31. The first run of red salmon enters the river during early June and is present in small numbers through the month; the second run enters about July 15 and is present through early August. In even years pink salmon are present from early through mid-August. The early silver salmon run arrives in early August, peaks in mid-August, and is over by the end of the month. Late run silver salmon enter the Kenai in early September, peak in mid- to late-September, and continue to enter the river through October. Dolly Varden and rainbow trout

Soldotna visitor center is at the Kenai River bridge. *(Jerrianne Lowther, staff)*

can be caught all summer.

Day-use Parks. Soldotna Creek Park, located off the Sterling Highway on the Kenai River, behind Hutchings Chevrolet at the Y, has covered picnic tables, grills, playground and trails. Facilities include wheelchair-accessible toilets and a boardwalk with wheelchair accessibility for bank

fishing. Airport Rotary Park, at Mile 4 Funny River Road, also has a wheelchair-accessible boardwalk with excellent bank fishing during the red salmon run.

Central Peninsula Sports Center, on Kalifornsky Beach (K-Beach) Road, has an Olympic-sized hockey rink, a jogging track, 2 racquetball/volleyball courts, a weight and

exercise room, dressing rooms and showers. The Sports Center also has convention facilities and meeting rooms. Phone (907) 262-3150 for more information.

Soldotna Historical Society Museum, located on Centennial Park Road, features a wildlife museum and historic log village. Among the log buildings is the last territorial school (built in 1958). Soldotna's founding settlers arrived in 1947. The "habitable dwellings" that entitled 2 of these first homesteaders to 160 acres from what is now mid-town Soldotna are part of the village. How these latter-day pioneers lived is revealed in a collection of homestead artifacts and photos in the former Soldotna Chamber of Commerce log tourist center. Damon Hall, a large building constructed for the Alaska Centennial, features an outstanding display of wildlife mounts with a background mural of these species' natural habitat. Open 10 A.M. to 4 P.M., Tuesday

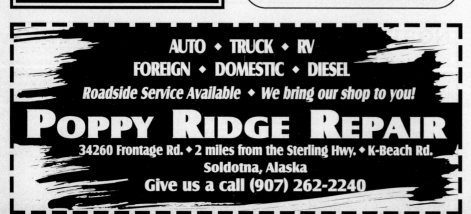

through Saturday; noon to 4 P.M. Sunday; closed Monday.

Joyce Carver Memorial Library offers temporary cards for visitors; large sunlit reading areas for both adults and children; Alaska videos on summer Saturday afternoons at 2 P.M. Open 9 A.M. to 8 P.M. Monday through Thursday, noon to 6 P.M. Friday, and 9 A.M. to 6 P.M. Saturdays. 235 Binkley St., Soldotna, phone (907) 262-4227.

Kenai National Wildlife Refuge Visitor Center, located at the top of Ski Hill Road (see **Milepost S 97.9**) and also accessible from Funny River Road (see **Milepost**

S 96.1), hosts some 25,000 visitors annually. This modern center has dioramas containing lifelike mounts of area wildlife in simulated natural settings. There is a free video about the refuge shown on the hour, between noon and 4 P.M., weekdays in summer. Free wildlife films are shown on the hour every weekend from noon to 5 P.M. Information available here on canoeing, hiking and

camping. There is a 1-mile-/1.6-km-long nature trail with an observation platform and spotting scope on Headquarters Lake. The Alaska Natural History Assoc. has a sales outlet here with books, posters and slide sets. Pay phone located in center. Open weekdays 8 A.M. to 4:30 P.M., and weekends 10 A.M. to 6 P.M. No admission fee.

The refuge was created in 1941 when

President Franklin D. Roosevelt set aside 1,730,000 acres of land (then designated the Kenai National Moose Range) to assure that the large numbers of moose, Dall sheep and other wild game would remain for people to enjoy. With the passage of the Alaska National Interest Lands Conservation Act in 1980, the acreage was increased to 1.97 million acres and redesignated Kenai National Wildlife Refuge. The area is managed by the U.S. Dept. of the Interior's Fish and Wildlife Service. Write: Refuge Manager, Kenai National Wildlife Refuge, P.O. Box 2139, Soldotna, AK 99669-2139; phone (907) 262-7021.

Take a Canoe Trip on one of several routes available in this part of the Kenai Peninsula. Enjoyment of wildlife in their natural habitat, true wilderness scenery, camping, and fishing for trout and salmon are a few highlights of a canoe trip.

Established canoe trails include the Swanson River route (80 miles/129 km) and Swan Lake route (60 miles/97 km). Complete information on Kenai Peninsula canoe trails is available at the USF&WS information cabin at Mile 58 Sterling Highway, the Kenai NWR information center in Soldotna and at chamber of commerce visitor centers in Kenai and Soldotna.

Kenai Spur Highway Log

The Kenai Spur Highway branches off the Sterling Highway at the Soldotna Y. **Distance from Soldotna Y (SY) is shown.**

SY 0 Junction with Sterling Highway at **Milepost S 94.2.**

SY 0.7 (1.1 km) Hospital, Soldotna High School.

SY 1 (1.6 km) Fishing licenses, tackle, 24-hour gas.

Tesoro 7–Eleven. See display ad this section.

SY 1.8 (2.8 km) Big Eddy Road to west. Access to Big Eddy state recreational site on Kenai River with wheelchair-accessible toilets, fishing guides, private camping, moorage, boat launches and rental facilities.   ♿▲

SY 2.2 (3.5 km) Big Eddy second access.

SY 2.5 (4 km) Sport Lake Road; access to bed and breakfast.

SY 4 (6.4 km) Kenai city limits.

SY 5.5 (8.9 km) **Alicia's Eagle Rock Lodge and Alaska–Pacific N.W. Fishing Adventures.** Expert fishing guides on the world-famous Kenai River. King salmon our specialty, mid-May through July. Silver salmon in August. Excellent lodging, economy units and 2-bedroom family units available. Free RV parking when fishing with us. 5743 Kenai Spur Highway, Kenai, AK 99611. Phone/fax (907) 283-3788. Open May 10–Sept. 5. [ADVERTISEMENT]

SY 5.9 (9.4 km) Dogwood Street.

SY 6.1 (9.8 km) Beaver Creek Park (day use only); parking, toilets, picnic tables, playground, basketball court, covered table, litter barrels.

SY 6.4 (10.3 km) Twin City Raceway. South **junction** with Beaver Loop Road: Drive 2.5 miles/4 km on Beaver Loop Road and turn south (left fork), crossing Warren Ames Memorial Bridge, to connect with Kalifornsky Beach Road. Turn north (right fork) for return to Kenai Spur Highway at Mile 10.9.

SY 8.2 (13.2 km) Begin divided 4-lane highway, 35-mph/56-kmph. Paved bike trails both sides of highway to Kenai.

SY 9.3 (14.9 km) Tinker Lane. Access to Peninsula Oilers baseball park, munici-pal golf course and junior high school.

SY 10.2 (16.4 km) Airport Road (right), Walker Road (left).

SY 10.5 (16.9 km) Bridge Access Road; north **junction** with Beaver Loop Road. Access south to Bridge Access Road and Port of Kenai; public boat launch with parking and toilets available. Road crosses Warren Ames Bridge and junctions with Kalifornsky Beach Road. Kenai River Flats state recreation site south of bridge has toilets and dumpster. Good spot to see migrating waterfowl.

SY 11 (17.7 km) **KENAI** (description of city begins on page 540). Carr's/Kmart shopping complex. Willow Street access to Kenai Municipal Airport 1 mile northeast.

SY 12.1 (19.5 km) Forest Drive. Scenic viewpoint overlooking Cook Inlet.

SY 12.4 (20 km) C Plaza; shopping.

SY 15 (24.1 km) Kenai city limits.

SY 21.3 (34.3 km) Miller Loop Road, connects with Island Lake Road.

SY 22.1 (35.5 km) **NIKISKI** (pop. 5,000). **Emergency Services**, phone 911 for fire and paramedics. Also known as Port Nikiski and Nikishka, this area was homesteaded in the 1940s and grew with the discovery of oil on the Kenai Peninsula in 1957. By 1964, oil-related industries here included Unocal Chemical, Phillips LNG, Chevron and Tesoro. Oil docks servicing offshore drilling platforms today include Rigtenders, Standard Oil, Phillips 66 and Union Collier Chemical. Commercial fishing, hunting and trapping are still a source of income for some residents.

SY 22.5 (36.2 km) Access to Nikiski Rigtenders dock; tankers may be seen next to dock.

SY 23.5 (37.8 km) North Peninsula Recreation Area and Nikiski elementary school. Dome-shaped building in trees near highway is the Nikiski recreational swimming pool, with indoor slide and hot tub; visitor observation area at pool. Other facilities include an ice rink, hiking and ski trails, a picnic area and ball fields. Phone (907) 776-8800.

SY 25.8 (41.5 km) Island Lake Road.

SY 26.6 (42.8 km) Nikishka Mall shopping, restaurant, supermarket, gas station and Nikiski branch Kenai post office.

SY 26.7 (43 km) Nikiski Beach Road; views of Nikishka Bay and Cook Inlet. Nikiski Fire Station No. 2.

SY 29.7 (47.8 km) Halbouty Road. **Daniels Lake Lodge Bed & Breakfast.** See display ad this section.

SY 30 (48.2 km) Daniels Lake.

SY 32.5 (52.3 km) Turnout west opposite Twin Lakes.

SY 35.6 (57.3 km) Entering Captain Cook State Recreation Area.

SY 35.9 (57.8 km) Bishop Creek State Recreation Site; 15 campsites, parking, toilets, water, picnic area and trail to beach. Camping fee $8/night or annual pass. Watch for spawning red salmon in creek in July and August, silvers August to September. Closed to salmon fishing.   ▲

SY 36.5 (58.7 km) Access to **Stormy Lake** swimming area, changehouse, toilet, water, parking, and rainbow and arctic char fishing.   🐟

SY 36.7 (59.1 km) Stormy Lake overlook; large paved turnout to east.

SY 36.9 (59.4 km) Stormy Lake picnic area; water, toilets, covered tables.

SY 37.8 (60.8 km) Stormy Lake boat launch; water, toilets, parking.

SY 38.6 (62.1 km) Swanson River canoe landing area; drive 0.6 mile/1 km east to parking and toilets, river access.

SY 38.7 (62.3 km) Clint Starnes Memorial Bridge crosses **Swanson River**; parking next to bridge for fishing access, toilets, view of Mount Spurr. Fishing for silver and red salmon, and rainbow.   🐟

SY 39 (62.8 km) Pavement ends at T. Take left fork for Discovery Campground (Captain Cook SRA); 53 campsites, picnic area, Maggie Yurick Memorial hiking trail, water, beachcombing for agates. Right fork leads to additional parking. Camping fee $10/night or annual pass.   ▲

SY 39.6 (63.7 km) Picnic area with tables and toilets, on bluff overlooking ocean at end of Kenai Spur Highway.

Return to Milepost S 94.2 Sterling Highway

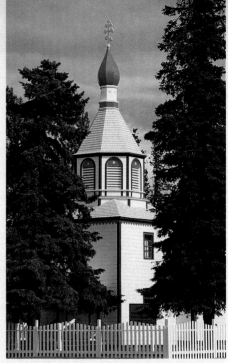

Holy Assumption Russian Orthodox Church. (© Loren Taft, Alaskan Images)

Kenai

SY 11 (17.7 km). On the western Kenai Peninsula. Reached via the Kenai Spur Highway, or 9.3 miles/ 14.9 km from Soldotna via the Kalifornsky Beach Road, 158.5 miles/255 km from Anchorage, 89.3 miles/ 143.7 km from Homer. **Population:** 6,613.

Emergency Services: Phone 911 for all emergency services. **Alaska State Troopers** (in Soldotna), phone (907) 262-4453. **Kenai City Police,** phone (907) 283-7879. **Fire** **Department** and **Ambulance,** phone 911. **Hospital** (in Soldotna), phone (907) 262-4404. **Maritime Search and Rescue,** dial 0 for Zenith 5555, toll free.

Visitor Information: The Kenai Bicentennial Visitors and Cultural Center, located in downtown Kenai, provides brochures and other visitor information. The center features a cultural museum, wildlife displays and movies (in summer). For a full list of visitor services available in Kenai, write the Kenai Visitors and Cultural Center, 11471 Kenai Spur Highway, Kenai, AK 99611; phone (907) 283-1991, fax 283-2230.

Elevation: 93 feet/28m. **Climate:** Aver- age daily maximum temperature in July, 61°F/16°C; January temperatures range from 11° to -19°F/-12° to -28°C. Lowest recorded temperature in Kenai was -48°F/-44°C. Average annual precipitation, 19.9 inches (68.7 inches of snowfall). **Radio:** KCSY 1140, KENI 550, KGTL 620, KSRM 920, KWVV 105, KGTL 100.9/103.5, MBN-FM 95.3/97.7, KENY 980, KWHQ-FM 100.1, KPEN-FM 101.7. **Television:** Several channels and cable. **Newspaper:** *Peninsula Clarion* (daily).

Private Aircraft: Kenai Municipal Airport, adjacent north; elev. 92 feet/28m; length 7,575 feet/2,309m; asphalt; fuel 100LL; attended. Transient tie-down fees $2/day. Adjacent floatplane base offers 3,500-foot/1,067-m basin with 35 slips.

Kenai is situated on a low rise overlooking the mouth of the Kenai River where it empties into Cook Inlet. It is the largest city on the Kenai Peninsula. Prior to Russian Alaska, Kenai was a Dena'ina Native commu-

nity. The Dena'ina people fished, hunted, trapped, farmed and traded with neighboring tribes here. In 1791 it became the second permanent settlement established by the Russians in Alaska, when a fortified post called Fort St. Nicholas, or St. Nicholas Redoubt, was built near here by Russian fur traders. In 1848, the first Alaska gold discovery was made on the Russian River. In 1869 the U.S. Army established Fort Kenai (Kenay); in 1899 a post office was authorized.

Oil exploration began in the mid-1950s, with the first major discovery in this area, the Swanson River oil reserves, 20 miles/ 32.2 km northeast of Kenai in 1957. Two years later, natural gas was discovered in the Kalifornsky Beach area 6 miles/9.6 km south of the city of Kenai. Extensive exploration offshore in upper Cook Inlet has established that Cook Inlet's middle-ground shoals contain one of the major oil and gas fields in the world.

The industrial complex on the North Kenai Road is the site of Unocal Chemicals, which produces ammonia and urea for fertilizer. Phillips Petroleum operates a liquid natural gas plant. Tesoro has a refinery here.

Offshore in Cook Inlet are 15 drilling platforms, all with underwater pipelines bringing the oil to the shipping docks on both sides of Cook Inlet for loading onto tankers.

Federal and state agencies based in and around Kenai contribute to the local economy. Next to oil, tourism, fishing and fish processing are the leading industries.

ACCOMMODATIONS/VISITOR SERVICES

Kenai has all shopping facilities and conveniences. Medical and dental clinics, banks, laundromats, theaters, pharmacies, supermarkets, and numerous gift and specialty shops are located on and off the highway and in the shopping malls. Several motels and hotels and about a dozen restaurants and drive-ins are located in Kenai. Local artists are featured at the Kenai Fine Arts Center on Cook Street. Showers, sauna, weight room, racquetball courts and gym at Kenai Recreation Center, on Caviar Street. Open 6 A.M. to 10 P.M. Monday through Saturday, Sunday 1 to 10 P.M. Phone (907) 283-

3855. For joggers there's the Bernie Huss Memorial Trail, a 0.5-mile jogging and exercise course located just off the Kenai Spur Highway on Main Street Loop. Dump stations located at several local service stations and city dock.

City of Kenai public boat ramp on Boat Launch Road off Bridge Access Road has 24-hour parking, restrooms with flush toilets, pay phone.

Kenai City Park has covered picnic tables and fireplaces. Arrangements for caravan camping may be made in advance through the Kenai Visitors and Cultural Center. Tent camping and private RV parks available in and near shopping areas. Ask at the visitors Center for directions. ▲

Drive north of town on the Kenai Spur Highway for more lodging and camping.

Beluga Lookout RV Park, 2 blocks from Kenai Visitors Center, downtown Kenai.

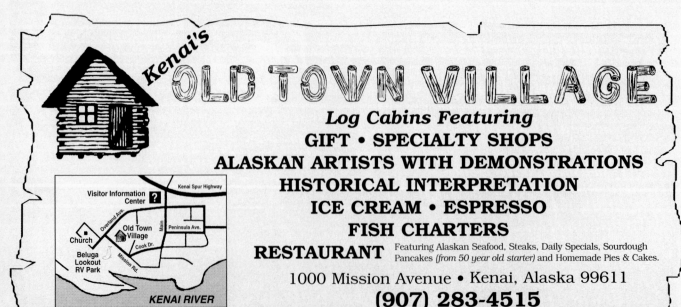

Overlooking bluff with fantastic view of beluga whales, Kenai River, Cook Inlet, Mount Redoubt. The historic Russian Orthodox Church, Fort Kenay are next door. Restaurants, shopping 2 blocks. New log lodge office, private bathrooms and hot showers, laundry, free coffee. Charter and tour bookings. Service with a smile. 75 level full-hookup spaces, cable TV, picnic tables, gas grills, pull-throughs, 30-50 amp power. Caravans welcome. Good Sam Club. VISA, MasterCard accepted. Reservations 1-800-745-5999 or (907) 283-5999. See display ad this section. [ADVERTISEMENT]

Harborside Cottages. Location! Location! Location! Spectacular view right from the deck of your private cottage. Located at the mouth of the Kenai River. Enjoy a panoramic view of the river, Cook Inlet and surrounding mountains. Walk to restaurants, shops, beach and visitor services. Cottages are self-contained with kitchenettes and barbecue area. Each cottage sleeps 2 and groups up to 10 are welcome. VISA, MasterCard accepted. (907) 283-6162. Box 942, Kenai, AK 99611. [ADVERTISEMENT]

Kenai Merit Inn. Conveniently located in downtown Kenai. $80–$90 June–August. $50–$60 September–May. Same rates single or double occupancy. Tour groups welcome year-round. Large parking area. Group meals to fit your schedule. 58 clean, quiet, comfortable rooms, cable TV, phone, private

bath. Free local calls. Full-service restaurant and lounge. Freshest salmon/halibut lunch/dinner in Kenai. Breakfast served all day. Laundromat, vehicle services nearby. Walk to see: Beluga whales in the famous Kenai River, local commercial fishing fleet, Russian Orthodox church tours, Visitor Center displays and information. 5 minutes to 18-hole golf course. 15 minutes to indoor pool. Book adventures. Credit cards accepted. 1-800-227-6131. [ADVERTISEMENT]

Kenai's Old Town Village. Dine in the beautifully refurbished 1918 cannery building, featuring Alaska seafood, steaks, home cooking. Fantastic view of Kenai River, Cook Inlet and mountains. Visit shops as they might have been in the early 1900s. Walk the boardwalk to each log cabin shop featuring local artists and craftspersons at work. Located 2 blocks from visitor center, one block from historic Russian Orthodox Church, across street from Beluga Lookout RV Park. (907) 283-4515. See display ad this section. [ADVERTISEMENT]

Lottie's Place Bed and Breakfast. Located Mile 12.3 Kalifornsky Beach Road, halfway between the Kenai and Kasilof rivers. Walk the beach, relax by the fireplace. Barbecue available for your catch of the day. Continental or full breakfast. Queen-size beds, satellite TV. Honeymoon bedroom with fireplace. Owned and operated by longtime Alaskans. Reservations: (907) 283-8707. See display ad in Soldotna section. [ADVERTISEMENT]

Overland RV Park and Gift Shop, next to Kenai Visitors Center, downtown Kenai, within a block of everything: Kenai River bluff view, Russian Orthodox Church, restaurants, shopping. 50 full hookups, 30-amp power, level spaces, pull-throughs; picnic tables at each site. Dump station, clean restrooms, hot showers, laundry for guests only. Daily, weekly, monthly rates. Caravans welcome. We can arrange fishing charters or tell you where to bank fish. Quality gifts and souvenirs at affordable prices. Alaska Native handicrafts, T-shirts and postcards, too. VISA, MasterCard accepted. (907) 283-4512 (summer); (907) 283-4227 (winter). See display ad this section. [ADVERTISEMENT] ▲

Tanglewood Bed & Breakfast. Fish king salmon from our backyard, on the lower Kenai River. View moose, caribou, bears, wolves, eagles, ducks, seals, beluga whales on regular basis. Newly remodeled. Rooms $75. Common room with fireplace. Fully equipped private suite with Jacuzzi, $125. Full breakfast. Laundry facilities. (907) 283-6771. Open year-round. See display ad. [ADVERTISEMENT]

Toyon Villa offers fully equipped apartments for motel room prices. Stay 5 nights, get 2 nights free. Make us your peninsula home base. Leave your suitcases unpacked. Privacy and freedom. Fully equipped kitchens. Located on Kenai River outlook in historic Old Town, where beluga whales frolic, eagles soar and the commercial fishing fleet passes in review. We arrange flight-seeing, guided fishing or a once-in-a-lifetime trip to a remote Alaskan homestead on a pristine, salmon-packed river. (907) 283-

4221. See display ad. [ADVERTISEMENT]

TRANSPORTATION

Air: Kenai is served by Era–Alaska. Several firms offer charter service out of Kenai. Kenai Municipal Airport (see description under Private Aircraft) is approximately 2 blocks west of the Carr's/Kmart complex on the Kenai Spur Highway.

Local: Limousine and taxi service is available as well as car rentals, vehicle leasing, boat rentals and charters.

Highway: On the Kenai Spur Highway, 11 miles/17.7 km north of Soldotna.

ATTRACTIONS

Get Acquainted. Pick up a brochure at the Kenai Visitors and Cultural Center. The center houses a cultural museum, which has wildlife displays, and information on local activities. The center also shows films on Alaska, daily in summer.

Kenai River Flats is a must stop for bird-watchers. Great numbers of Siberian snow geese and other waterfowl stop to feed on this saltwater marsh in the spring.

The state recreation site on Bridge Access Road at Warren Ames Bridge has parking and interpretive signs. Boardwalk for wildlife-watchers. Also watch for caribou on the Kenai Flats.

Beluga Whale Watching on the Kenai River beach at the west end of Main Street. Beluga whales are the only all-white whale. The beach also offers a good view of Kenai's fish-processing industry.

Watch Baseball or Play Golf. Some fine semipro baseball is played at the Peninsula Oilers ball park on Tinker Lane. Golfers may try the 18-hole Kenai golf course on Lawton Drive.

Fort Kenay was the first American military installation in the area, established in 1869. More than 100 men were stationed here in the $1\frac{1}{2}$ years it officially served to protect American citizens in the area. A replica of the fort's barracks building was built as an Alaskan Purchase Centennial project by Kenai residents in 1967. It is opeated by the Holy Assumption Russian Orthodox Church.

Holy Assumption Russian Orthodox Church is across from Fort Kenay. The original church was founded in 1846 by a Russian monk, Egumen Nicolai. The present church was built some 50 years after the original and with its 3 onion-shaped domes is considered one of the finest examples of a Russian Orthodox church built on a vessel or quadrilateral ground plan. It is one of the oldest Russian Orthodox churches in Alaska. In 1971 it was designated a national historic landmark. An 1847 edition of the book of the Holy Gospel of the 4 evangelists—Matthew, Mark, Luke and John—with 5 enameled icons on the cover, is awaiting restoration (not on display). Regular church services are held here, and tours are available; inquire at the church. Donations accepted.

St. Nicholas Chapel, built in 1906, west of the Russian church, marks the burial location of Father Egumen Nicolai and other Russian Orthodox Church workers.

Kenai Fine Arts Center. Sales gallery of original local art featuring hand-built pottery, paintings, jewelry, hand-painted silk scarves, T-shirts and much more. Pottery studio, weavers' studio, art shows, adult and children's workshops. Historic building with Kenai's original jail. Located in Old Town. 816 Cook Ave., Kenai. Phone (907) 283-7040. [ADVERTISEMENT]

Sterling Highway Log
(continued from page 528)

S **95.9** (154.3 km) A **148.9** (239.6 km) H **83.6** (134.5 km) Kenai River bridge.

Entering Soldotna northbound. Description of city begins on page 528.

S **96** (154.5 km) A **149** (239.8 km) H **83.5** (134.4 km) Soldotna visitor center at south end of Kenai River bridge.

S **96.1** (154.7 km) A **149.1** (239.9 km) H **83.4** (134.2 km) **Junction.** Funny River Road to east, Kalifornsky Beach Road to west. Kalifornsky Beach Road rejoins the Sterling Highway at **Milepost S 108.8.** (See KALIFORNSKY BEACH ROAD log on page 545.)

Centennial Park campground, 0.1 mile/0.2 km west, on the banks of the Kenai River. There are 126 campsites (some on river), tables, firepits, firewood provided, water, restrooms, dump station, pay phone, 2-week limit. Boat launch and favorite fishing site at far end of campground. Register at campground entrance.

Funny River (Airport) Road leads east

2 miles/3.2 km to Soldotna airport, 4 miles/6.4 km to Airport Rotary Park (day-use only) and 11.5 miles/18.5 km to Funny River State Recreation Site; 12 campsites, $8 nightly fee per vehicle or annual pass, picnic tables, water, toilets, river access. Salmon and trout fishing at the confluence of the **Kenai** and **Funny rivers** at the recreation area. Turn on Funny River Road and take first right (Ski Hill Loop Road) for USF&WS visitor center. Funny River Road dead ends 17.2 miles/27.7 km from the highway. Private RV park located at Mile 13.8.

S 97.9 (157.6 km) **A 150.9** (242.8 km) **H 81.6** (131.3 km) Sky View High School. Easy-to-miss turnoff for Kenai National Wildlife Refuge headquarters and information center: Turn east off highway and drive 1 mile/1.6 km on Ski Hill Road, which loops back to Funny River Road (see preceding milepost). Nature trail with wildlife observation platform and spotting scope on Headquarters Lake. The center is open 8 A.M. to 4:30 P.M. on weekdays, 10 A.M. to 6 P.M. weekends.

S 108.8 (175 km) **A 161.8** (260.4 km) **H 70.7** (113.8 km) South **junction** with Kalifornsky Beach Road. (See KALIFORNSKY BEACH ROAD log this page.) Drive west 4.8 miles/7.7 km to Beach Road for access to beach, Kasilof small-boat harbor and Kasilof River. This loop road rejoins Sterling Highway at **Milepost S 96.1.**

KASILOF (kuh-SEE-lawf; pop. 383; elev. 75 feet/23m) was originally a settlement established in 1786 by the Russians as St. George. An Indian fishing village grew up around the site, but no longer exists. Native inhabitants of the peninsula are mostly Kanai Indians, a branch of the great Athabascan family. The population is spread out over the general area which is called Kasilof. The area's income is derived from fishing and fish processing.

Kasilof River. The red salmon dip-net fishery here is open by special announcement for Alaska residents only. Check with the ADF&G for current regulations. ◄

Private Aircraft: Kasilof airstrip, 1.7 miles/2.7 km north; elev. 125 feet/38m; length 2,300 feet/701m; gravel; unattended.

S 109 (175.4 km) **A 162** (260.7 km) **H 70.5** (113.5 km) Grocery store.

S 109.2 (175.7 km) **A 162.2** (261 km) **H 70.3** (113.1 km) **Kasilof Riverview.** See display ad this section.

Kalifornsky Beach Road Log

Also called K–Beach Road, Kalifornsky Beach Road leads west and south from the Sterling Highway at Soldotna, following the shore of Cook Inlet to Kasilof. **Distance from the Sterling Highway junction at Milepost S 96.1 at Soldotna (S)** is followed by distance from Sterling Highway junction at Milepost **S 108.8 at Kasilof (K).** Mileposts run south to north.

S 0 K 22.2 (35.7 km) **Junction** with Sterling Highway at **Milepost S 96.1.**

S 0.1 (0.2 km) **K 22.1** (35.6 km) Soldotna Alaska Purchase Centennial Park Campground, operated by the city of Soldotna. Kenai River access for bank fishing, boat launch (fee charged). ◄▲

S 0.2 (0.3 km) **K 22** (35.4 km) Alaska State Troopers.

S 0.4 (0.6 km) **K 21.8** (35.1 km) Rodeo grounds.

S 0.6 (1 km) **K 21.6** (34.8 km) Central Peninsula Sports Center; hockey, ice skating, jogging track and other sports available; phone (907) 262-3150 for more information.

S 1.7 (2.7 km) **K 20.5** (33 km) Kenai Peninsula Community College access road. Also access to Slikok Creek State Recreation Site, 0.7 mile/1.1 km north; day use only with 12-hour parking, wheelchair accessible toilets, picnic tables, information kiosk and trails. No fires or ATVs. &

S 2.9 (4.7 km) **K 19.3** (31.1 km) K–Beach center. ADF&G office; stop in here for current sportfishing information.

S 3.1 (5 km) **K 19.1** (30.7 km) Poppy Lane. Grocery and gas.

Short Stop. See display ad this section.

S 3.5 (5.6 km) **K 18.7** (30.1 km) Red Diamond shopping center, Duck Inn Motel and restaurant.

S 4.6 (7.4 km) **K 17.6** (28.3 km)

Firehouse.

S 4.7 (7.6 km) **K 17.5** (28.2 km) Ciechansky Road leads 2.2 miles/3.5 km to Ciechansky State Recreation Site, a day-use only picnic area with tables, toilets, dumpster and Kenai River access. Also access to private campgrounds with RV hookups on the Kenai River. ▲

S 6 (9.7 km) **K 16.2** (26.1 km) Turnoff for city of Kenai, 3.1 miles/5 km north via the Warren Ames Memorial Bridge.

S 6.8 (10.9 km) **K 15.4** (24.8 km) Magnificent beaver dam and lodge, lupine display in June.

S 7.6 (12.2 km) **K 14.6** (23.5 km) Robinsons mini-mall.

S 7.8 (12.5 km) **K 14.4** (23.2 km) VIP Drive; Kenai Custom Seafoods.

S 8 (12.9 km) **K 14.2** (22.9 km) Cafe.

S 13 (20.9 km) **K 9.2** (14.8 km) Scenic viewpoint overlooking Cook Inlet.

S 17.4 (28 km) **K 4.8** (7.7 km) Kasilof Beach Road; access to beach, harbor, river.

S 20.1 (32.3 km) **K 2.1** (3.4 km) Kasilof Airfield Road.

S 20.3 (32.7 km) **K 1.9** (3.1 km) **Daily's Kasilof Bed & Breakfast.** Near Soldotna, Kenai, Ninilchik. Minutes from Kenai, Kasilof rivers. Fishing, tours available. Freezer space. Immaculate. Reasonable. Sleeps 9. Private or shared baths. Robes. Full or bag breakfasts. Lunches, dinners on request. Open year-round. Professional innkeeper. Look for red barrels. (907) 260-4184; fax (907) 260-4185. See display ad. [ADVERTISEMENT]

S 22.1 (35.6 km) **K 0.1** (0.2 km) Kasilof post office.

S 22.2 (35.7 km) **K 0 Junction** with Sterling Highway at **Milepost S 108.8** at Kasilof.

Return to Milepost S 96.1 or S 108.8 Sterling Highway

S 109.4 (176.1 km) A 162.4 (261.3 km) H 70.1 (112.8 km) Bridge over Kasilof River, which drains Tustumena Lake, one of the largest lakes on the Kenai Peninsula. Kasilof River State Recreation Site; 16 campsites, $8 nightly fee or annual pass, 5 picnic sites on riverbank, picnic tables, toilets and water are on the south side of the bridge. Boat launch $5 fee or annual pass. Entering Game Management Subunit 15C southbound, 15B northbound.

S 110 (177 km) A 163 (262.3 km) H 69.5 (111.8 km) Tustumena Elementary School and north end of Tustumena Lake Road. This is the first turnoff southbound for access to Johnson and Tustumena lakes. Also turn off here for picnic area with covered picnic tables, toilets (wheelchair accessible), firepits, water and dumpster. There is a huge metal T at Tustumena Lake Road, just beyond the picnic area: Turn east at the T for Johnson and Tustumena lakes. **Johnson Lake** is 0.3 mile/0.5 km from the highway. Johnson Lake state campground has 50 sites (some double and some pull-throughs), $10 nightly fee or annual pass, water, toilets, boat launch and firewood. Lake is stocked with rainbow. Watch for beaver, moose and king salmon migrating up Crooked Creek. **Tustumena Lake** is 6.4 miles/10.3 km from the highway; a campground on the Kasilof River near the lake has 10 sites, toilets and boat launch. Fishing for lake trout and salmon. Tustumena Lake is closed to king and sockeye salmon fishing. ♿🚣▲

CAUTION: This lake is 6 miles/10 km wide and 25 miles/40 km long and subject to severe winds.

S 110.5 (177.8 km) A 163.5 (263.1 km) H 69 (111 km) Double-ended paved parking by Crooked Creek.

S 110.8 (178.3 km) A 163.8 (263.6 km) H 68.7 (110.6 km) **Tustumena Lodge.** Motel, cocktail lounge, fishing guides. Phone (907) 262-4216. Clean, affordable rooms at half the price of town. Some kitchenettes. Friendly Alaskan atmosphere where a cold drink, light snack and good fish stories are always available. Monday night—prime rib, $8. Friday night—New York Steak, $7. See the world's largest razor clam. Look for a hat from your hometown among the over 10,000 hats in our pending Guinness record collection. [ADVERTISEMENT]

S 111 (178.6 km) A 164 (263.9 km) H 68.5 (110.2 km) Cohoe Loop Road north **junction** (turnoff to west). Crooked Creek State Recreation Site (camping and fishing) 1.8 miles/2.8 km west on Cohoe Loop Road. South end of Tustumena Lake Road (to east) for Johnson and Tustumena lakes (see description at **Milepost S 110**). Cohoe Loop Road rejoins the Sterling Highway at **Milepost S 114.3** (see COHOE LOOP ROAD log this section).

Just east of the highway on the Johnson and Tustumena lakes access road is Crooked Creek fish hatchery; a sign explains the chinook and sockeye salmon operation here. For further information, contact Cook Inlet Aquaculture Assoc., phone (907) 283-5761. The hatchery-produced salmon create a popular fishery at the confluence of Crooked Creek and the Kasilof River, accessible via the Cohoe Loop Road. Just past the hatchery is Crooked Creek Road, and just beyond is a huge metal T at Tustumena Lake Road. Continue past this monument for a picnic area, and return to Sterling Highway at **Milepost S 110**; turn at the T for lakes and camping. 🚣▲

Crooked Creek RV Park & Guide Service. See display ad this section. ▲

Kasilof RV Park. See display ad this section.

Tustumena Ridge Cabins, in park-like setting with quiet comfort and class. In Kasilof, convenient to all local recreational areas. See map in display ad. Nicely furnished cabins with kitchens, and supplied with a good variety of breakfast items, including fresh gourmet coffee beans. Hot tub and sauna. Private/shared bath. Open all year. (907) 262-7050, Cell #398-6407. Box 312, Kasilof, AK 99610.[ADVERTISEMENT]

S 114.3 (183.9 km) A 167.3 (269.2 km) H 65.2 (104.9 km) Cohoe Loop Road south **junction** with the Sterling Highway. The 13-mile/21-km road loops north to **Milepost S 111.** See COHOE LOOP ROAD log this page.

S 117.4 (188.9 km) A 170.4 (274.2 km) H 62.1 (99.9 km) Clam Gulch State Recreation Area (watch for easy-to-miss sign) is 0.5 mile/0.8 km from highway; picnic tables, picnic shelter, toilets, water, 116 campsites, $8 nightly fee or annual pass. *CAUTION: High ocean bluffs are dangerous.* Short access road to beach (recommended for 4-wheel-drive vehicles only, limited turnaround space). ▲

Clam digging for razor clams on most of the sandy beaches of the western Kenai Peninsula from Kasilof to Anchor Point can be rewarding. Many thousands of clams are dug each year at Clam Gulch. You must have a sportfishing license to dig, and these are available at most sporting goods stores. The bag limit is 60 clams regardless of size (always check current regulations). There is no legally closed season, but quality of the clams varies with month; check locally. Good clamming and fewer people in March and April, although there may still be ice on the beach. Any tide lower than minus 1-foot is enough to dig clams; minus 4- to 5-foot tides are best. The panoramic view of Mount Redoubt, Mount Iliamna and Mount Spurr across Cook Inlet and the expanse of beach are well worth the short side trip even during the off-season. ◄❚

S 118.2 (190.2 km) A 171.2 (275.5 km) H 61.3 (98.7 km) CLAM GULCH (pop. 79) post office and lodge.

Rod Buster Charters. Launch within minutes at Deep Creek. Covered, heated boats. Gear provided. Cabin rentals. Ocean view. RVers, tenters welcome. Gift shop, video rentals. Clamming, bank fishing, equipment rentals. Fishing and lodging packages. Unguided hunts. Reservations (907) 262-9707. P.O. Box 405, Clam Gulch, AK 99568. Fax (907) 262-6470. Credit cards accepted. See display ad. [ADVERTISEMENT]

S 118.3 (190.4 km) A 171.3 (275.7 km) H 61.2 (98.5 km) **Clam Shell Lodge.** See display ad this section.

S 119.6 (192.5 km) A 172.6 (277.8 km) H 59.9 (96.4 km) **Clam Gulch Lodge Bed and Breakfast.** Welcome to our lodge. Breathtaking view across Cook Inlet, of Mount Redoubt and Mount Iliamna, from the fireplace lounge. King-size or single beds with shared baths. Group rates. Smoke-

Cohoe Loop Road Log

The Cohoe Loop Road loops south 15.3 miles/24.7 km from **Milepost S 111** on the Sterling Highway. The popular Crooked Creek fishing and camping area is at the top or north end of the loop. The bottom (or south) 10 miles of the Cohoe Loop Road travels through mostly undeveloped parcels of land; no services, views or recreation. Motorists may wish to use the north junction approach. **Distance from north junction with the Sterling Highway (NJ) at Milepost S 111 is followed by distance from south junction (SJ) at Milepost S 114.3. Mileposts run south to north.**

NJ 0 SJ 15.3 (24.6 km) **Junction** with Sterling Highway at **Milepost S 111.**

NJ 1.8 (2.9 km) SJ 13.5 (21.7 km) Crooked Creek/Rilinda Drive; access to private RV park and Crooked Creek State Recreation Site at the confluence of Crooked Creek and the Kasilof River. The recreation site has 83 campsites, 36 day-use sites, toilets and water trails to Kasilof River for fishermen. Camping fee $8/night or annual pass, day-use fee $5/vehicle or annual pass. ▲

Fishing in **Crooked Creek** closed to king salmon fishing and closed to all fishing near hatchery. Fishing access to confluence of Crooked Creek and Kasilof River is through the state recreation site. *NOTE: Fishing access to Crooked Creek frontage above confluence is through a private RV park; fee charged.* Fishing in the **Kasilof River** for king salmon, late May through July, best in mid-June; coho salmon, mid-August to September, use salmon egg clusters, wet flies, assorted spoons and spinners. ◄❚

NJ 2.4 (3.9 km) SJ 12.9 (20.7 km) Webb–Ramsell Road. Kasilof River access across private property, fee charged.

NJ 5.3 (8.5 km) SJ 10 (16 km) Cohoe Spur Road **junction**. A post office was established in 1950 at

COHOE (area pop. 508), originally an agricultural settlement.

NJ 5.6 (9 km) SJ 9.7 (15.6 km) T intersection; go west 0.8 mile/1.3 km for beach and boat launch. Private campground on Madsen Road. Cabins for rent on St. Elias Road to right. Cohoe Loop Road continues north. Pavement begins northbound. ▲

Kasilof River Kabins. See display ad this section.

NJ 8.6 (13.8 km) SJ 6.7 (10.8 km) **Deal's Den Bed & Breakfast.** A warm, Irish welcome. Spectacular view of volcanoes. Stairway access to miles of beach-combing. Visit with the local commercial fishermen working their fish sites. Buy fresh salmon or catch your own. Three bedrooms and cabin, private or shared bath. Sourdough pancakes and reindeer sausage start your day. Tour historic sites. Open all year. Reservations: (907) 262-2643. Write: HC2 Box 525A, Kasilof, AK 99610. [ADVERTISEMENT]

NJ 15.3 (24.6 km) SJ 0 **Junction** with Sterling Highway at **Milepost S 114.3.**

**Return to Milepost S 114.3
or Milepost S 111
Sterling Highway**

free environment. Close to the best clam beach in Alaska. We offer our guests guided clam digging. Call ahead for the best tides. We arrange charters for salmon and halibut, sightseeing and raft trips. Limited RV parking with large turnaround. Reservations appreciated. Phone/fax (907) 260-3778 or

1-800-700-9555, or write P.O. Box 499, Clam Gulch, AK 99568. Internet: http://alaskan. com/vendors/clam.htm/; E-mail:clamgulch@ aol.com.[ADVERTISEMENT]

S 122.8 (197.6 km) A 175.8 (282.9 km) H 56.7 (91.2 km) Paved, double-ended turnout oceanside (no view).

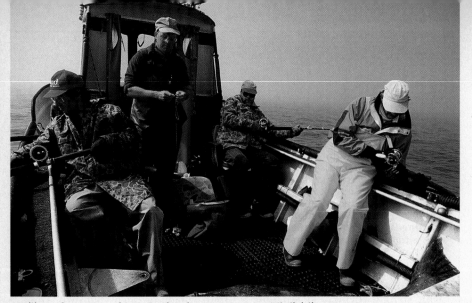

Halibut charter working Cook Inlet waters near Ninilchik. (© Bill Sherwonit)

S 124.8 (200.8 km) **A 177.8** (286.1 km) **H 54.7** (88 km) Paved, double-ended turnout oceanside with view of Cook Inlet.

S 126.8 (204.1 km) **A 179.8** (289.4 km) **H 52.7** (84.8 km) Double-ended paved scenic wayside overlooking upper Cook Inlet. Polly Creek, due west across Cook Inlet, is a popular area for clam diggers (fly in). Across the inlet is Mount Iliamna; north of Iliamna is Mount Redoubt.

S 127.1 (204.5 km) **A 180.1** (289.8 km) **H 52.4** (84.3 km) Double-ended paved scenic viewpoint to west with interpretive display on Mount Redoubt and Mount Spurr volcanoes. Private RV park. ▲

Scenic View RV Park. View Mount Redoubt, Cook Inlet. 10 minutes to clamming. Elby fishing charters for halibut and salmon, out of Deep Creek. Visit Homer, Kenai, Soldotna and return to scenic view sunsets. Hookups, tenting, showers, laundry. Weekly, monthly rates. Pay phone. 27 spaces. Friendly family atmosphere. See display ad this section. [ADVERTISEMENT] ▲

S 130.5 (210 km) **A 183.5** (295.3 km) **H 49** (78.9 km) **Ninilchik Point Overnighter.** Spacious, comfortable, home-grown log cabins. Scenic getaway. Cook Inlet view. Economy camping, with showers. One cabin self-contained with kitchen. 3-cabins served by shower house. 2-burner electric units. Bedding, linens provided. Outdoor grill. Close to famous fishing, clam beaches. Local charters. (907) 567-3423. See display ad. [ADVERTISEMENT]. ▲

S 132.2 (212.7 km) **A 185.2** (298 km) **H 47.3** (76.1 km) **Heavenly Sights Charters &**

Campgrounds. See display ad this section. ▲

S 134.5 (216.4 km) **A 187.5** (301.7 km) **H 45** (72.4 km) Ninilchik State Recreation Area. Ninilchik River Scenic Overlook: $8/camping fee, $3/day-use fee. Ninilchik River Campground: $10 camping fee, 43 sites, water, toilets and tables. Trail to **Ninilchik River;** fishing for king and silver salmon, steelhead and Dolly Varden. Ninilchik Beach Campground: $8 camping fee, 50 campsites, toilets, water. Popular beach for razor clamming. Access to the clamming beds adjacent to the campgrounds during minus tides.

CAUTION: Drownings have occurred here. Be aware of tide changes when clam digging. Incoming tides can quickly cut you off from the beach. ◄▲

S 134.7 (216.8 km) **A 187.7** (302 km) **H 44.8** (72.1 km) Coal Street; access west to Ninilchik's historic Russian Orthodox Church at top of hill; plenty of parking and turnaround space.

S 134.8 (216.9 km) **A 187.8** (302.2 km) **H 44.7** (71.9 km) Large double-ended gravel turnout.

S 135.1 (217.4 km) **A 188.1** (302.7 km) **H 44.4** (71.4 km) Double-ended gravel turnout and dumpsters at north end of Ninilchik River bridge. Side road leads to **NINILCHIK VILLAGE,** the original village of Ninilchik, and to the beach. Access to mouth of **Ninilchik River;** fishing. A short road branches off this side road and leads into the old village of Ninilchik. Continue straight on side road for motel, beach, overnight RV parking, camping and toilets (follow signs). Sea breezes here keep the beach free of mosquitoes. Historic signs near beach and at village entrance tell about Ninilchik Village, which includes several old dovetailed log buildings. A walking tour brochure is available from businesses in the village and along the highway. Present-day Ninilchik is located at **Milepost S 135.5.** ◄▲

A beautiful white Russian Orthodox church sits on a hill overlooking the sea above the historic old village. Trail leads up to it from the road into town (watch for sign just past the old village store). The church and cemetery are still in use. You are welcome to walk up to it but use the well-defined path behind the store (please do not walk through private property), or drive up using the Coal Street access at **Milepost S 134.7.**

S 135.3 (217.7 km) **A 188.3** (303 km) **H 44.2** (71.1 km) Gravel turnout to west.

S 135.4 (217.9 km) **A 188.4** (303.2 km) **H 44.1** (71 km) Kingsley Road; access to Ninilchik post office and 2 private campgrounds. Ninilchik View state campground is across the highway overlooking the village and sea; 12 campsites, water, toilets, litter disposal, 2 dump stations ($5 fee), drinking water fill-up. Camping fee $10/night or annual pass. Foot trail from campground down to beach and village. DOT/PF road maintenance station. ▲

Hylen's Camper Park. 50 full hookups, 19 partial, dry camping with full service for 40-footers to tents. Fish Deep Creek and Ninilchik River for kings, silvers; Afishunt Charters on site to fish Cook Inlet for record halibut, king salmon, May–September. Great clamming. Fish cleaning tables, smoker. Daily, weekly, monthly, seasonal-rated sites. Housekeeping cottages, showers, laundry, storage, social room. Horseshoes. Pay phone. Clean, friendly, reasonable rates. Reservations (907) 567-3393. [ADVERTISEMENT] ▲

Ninilchik

S 135.5 (218 km) A 188.5 (303.4 km) H 44 (70.8 km) Pronounced Nin-ILL-chick. **Population:** 456. **Emergency services:** Phone 911. **Clinic and ambulance,** phone (907) 567-3412. **Visitor Information:** At Kiosk, Milepost S 136.1. Local businesses are also very helpful. **Private Aircraft:** Ninilchik airstrip, 6.1 miles/9.8 km southeast; elev. 276 feet/84m; length 2,400 feet/732m; dirt; unattended.

Restaurant, lodging and charter service east side of road are part of the community of Ninilchik. Ninilchik extends roughly from Ninilchik State Recreation Area to the north to Deep Creek to the south, with services (grocery stores, gas stations, campgrounds, etc.) located at intervals along the highway. The original village of Ninilchik (signed Ninilchik Village) is reached by a side road from **Milepost S 135.1.**

On Memorial Day weekend, Ninilchik is referred to as the third biggest city in Alaska, as thousands of Alaskans arrive for the fishing (see Area Fishing following). The Kenai Peninsula Fair is held at Ninilchik the third weekend in August. Dubbed the "biggest little fair in Alaska," it features a parade, horse show, livestock competition and exhibits ranging from produce to arts and crafts. Pancake breakfasts, bingo and other events, such as the derby fish fry, are held at the fairgrounds throughout the year. The king salmon derby is held from May to June

View towards historic Ninilchik Village at Milepost S 135.1. *(© Ruth von Spalding)*

15. A halibut derby, sponsored by the Ninilchik Chamber of Commerce, runs from Father's Day through Labor Day. There is an active senior center offering meals and events. Swimming pool at the high school.

AREA FISHING: Well-known area for saltwater king salmon fishing and record halibut fishing. Charter services available. (Combination king salmon and halibut charters are available and popular.) Salt water south of the mouth of **Deep Creek** has produced top king salmon fishing in late May, June and July. Kings 50 lbs. and over are frequently caught. "Lunker" king salmon are available 1 mile/1.6 km south of Deep Creek in **Cook Inlet** from late May through July. Trolling a spinner or a spoon from a boat is the preferred method. Silver, red and pink salmon are available in salt water between Deep Creek and the Ninilchik River during July. A major halibut fishery off Ninilchik has produced some of the largest trophy halibut found in Cook Inlet, including a 466-lb. unofficial world record sport-caught halibut.

Sterling Highway Log
(continued)

S 135.6 (218.2 km) A 188.6 (303.5 km) H 43.9 (70.6 km) Ninilchik High School. Ninilchik Library, open 10 A.M. to 4 P.M. daily in the summer.

S 135.7 (218.4 km) A 188.7 (303.7 km) H 43.8 (70.5 km) **Ninilchik General Store.** Open every day for all your travel needs. Offering groceries, bait, tackle, licenses, rain gear, ice, film, gifts, books, T-shirts, gold nugget jewelry, hardware and a snack bar. Try our Fisherman's Bag Lunch. Stop in for free information packet on the Ninilchik area. You'll like our prices and service. Ask your friends who have met us. We com-

pete for your business, we don't just wait for it to happen. See display ad this section. [ADVERTISEMENT]

S 135.8 (218.5 km) A 188.8 (303.7 km) H 43.7 (70.3 km) **Bull Moose Gifts.** One of the nicest gift shops on the Kenai Peninsula, offering a wide selection of gifts and souvenirs. Alaskan and Russian arts and crafts, fine art prints, jewelry, including Alaskan gold nuggets, caps, postcards, notecards, and over 50 Alaskan designs of T-shirts and sweatshirts. Easy access for large RVs, lots of

parking and clean restroom. See display ad this section. [ADVERTISEMENT]

S 135.9 (218.7 km) A 188.9 (304 km) H 43.6 (70.2 km) **Country Boy Campground.** See display ad this section.

Homestead House B&B. See display ad this section. ▲

Caribou Hills Wilderness Lodge. Located 20 miles east of Ninilchik at the end of Oil Well Road in a unique, secluded but easily accessed setting. A pristine mountain stream runs year-round by the lodge. Fantastic views of Cook Inlet and Mount Redoubt. World-class fishing packages. Book early for best dates. Sightseeing packages, car packages. Delicious meals packed or served in the lodge. Laundry and kitchen facilities. International guests welcome. Families welcome. Airport pick-up. (907) 262-2154. See display ad. [ADVERTISEMENT]

Reel 'Em Inn/Cook Inlet Charters. East 1 mile on Oilwell Road at the Chinook Tesoro. Owned and operated by Alaskan family with the knowledge to show you how to experience the area's attractions. Full-service facility. Fishing charters, lodging, RV hookups. Equipment rental—fishing poles, raingear, boots, clam shovels. Check us out, you will not be sorry! Reservations welcome. (907) 567-7335. See display ad. [ADVERTISEMENT]

S 136 (218.9 km) **A 189** (304.1 km) **H 43.5** (70 km) **Chinook Tesoro.** Ninilchik. 24-hour card lock. Open year-round. Self-serve gasoline, propane, on-road and dyed diesel. Auto/RV mechanics, tire repair, water/air for RVs. Bait, ice, market items. Free tide books, visitor information on clamming and guided fishing. Tesoro, VISA, MasterCard, Discover. All major oil company cards welcome. See display ad this section. [ADVERTISEMENT]

S 136.1 (219 km) **A 189.1** (304.3 km) **H 43.4** (69.8 km) **Chihuly's Charters** and **Porcupine Shop.** See display ad this section.

S 136.2 (219.2 km) **A 189.2** (304.5 km) **H 43.3** (69.7 km) Peninsula Fairgrounds. Visitor Information Kiosk opposite the fairgrounds.

Bluff House Bed and Breakfast. See display ad this section.

S 136.7 (219.9 km) **A 189.7** (305.3 km) **H 42.8** (68.9 km) Bridge over Deep Creek. Developed sites on both sides of creek: Deep Creek North Scenic Overlook and Deep Creek South Scenic Overlook. Both have $8/camping fee, $3/day-use fee, restrooms, water, interpretive kiosks, tables and fireplaces. Deep Creek South offers camping May and June only, day-use only rest of summer. ▲

Freshwater fishing in **Deep Creek** for king salmon up to 40 lbs., use spinners with red bead lures, Memorial Day weekend and the 4 weekends following; Dolly Varden in July and August; silver salmon to 15 lbs., August and September; steelhead to 15 lbs., late September through October. No bait fishing permitted after Aug. 31. Mouth of Deep Creek access from Deep Creek State Recreation Area turnoff at **Milepost S 137.3.** ◄

S 137 (220.4 km) **A 190** (305.8 km) **H 42.5** (68.4 km) Cannery and sports shop with tackle and clam shovel rentals west side of road.

Fishward Bound Adventures. See display ad this section.

Deep Creek Custom Packing, Inc. Just south of Deep Creek bridge in Ninilchik. Home of the finest gourmet smoked salmon and halibut in the world. Free samples and coffee. Seafood display includes locally caught scallops, razor clams, crab, halibut and salmon. Sport fishermen take their own catch in to be hand-packed, frozen, canned or smoked to their specifications. Mail order service available for gift packs, fresh Alaskan seafood, canned salmon, smoked salmon and halibut. State-of-the-art insulated packaging. Overnight delivery, door-to-door, anywhere in the U.S. Visitor information on the best charters, clam digging and fishing. Stop in and see this truly traditional Alaskan business. See display ad this section. [ADVERTISEMENT]

S 137.3 (220.9 km) **A 190.3** (306.2 km) **H 42.2** (67.9 km) Deep Creek State Recreation Area on the beach at the mouth of Deep Creek; parking for 300 vehicles, overnight camping, water, tables, dumpsters, toilets and fireplaces. Drive 0.5 mile/0.8 km down paved road. Camping fee $10/night per vehicle or annual pass, day-use fee $5 or annual pass. Favorite area for surf fishing and to launch boats. Boat launch $5 fee or annual pass. Private boat launch service here uses tractors to launch boats from beach into Cook Inlet. Seasonal checks by U.S. Coast Guard for personal flotation devices, boating safety. Good bird watching in wetlands behind beach; watch for eagles. Good clamming at low tide. The beaches here are lined with coal, which falls from the exposed seams of high cliffs. ◄▲

CAUTION: Rapidly changing tides and weather. Although the mouth of Deep Creek affords boaters good protection, low tides may prevent return; check tide tables.

S 137.4 (221.1 km) **A 190.4** (306.4 km) **H 42.1** (67.8 km) **Roe's Charter Service.** Family owned, operated by year-round residents. Halibut, salmon combo charters, April–September. Friendly, personalized ser-

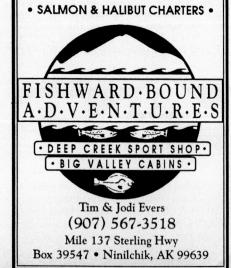

vice at our quiet location. Circle drive for RV convenience. Fish from custom built 26-foot offshore, heated cabin boat, or 20-foot open boat. Both boats outfitted with marine bathroom, comfortable seating, state of the art electronics, custom made rods, top quality gear. Free filleting. Further processing, shipping services nearby. Lodging, etc. available. (907) 567-3496. See display ad. [ADVERTISEMENT]

S 138.6 (223 km) **A 191.6** (308.3 km) **H 40.9** (65.8 km) Solid waste transfer site; public dumpsters.

S 140.3 (225.8 km) **A 193.3** (311.1 km) **H 39.2** (63.1 km) Double-ended turnout with scenic view to west.

S 142.7 (229.6 km) **A 195.7** (314.9 km) **H 36.8** (59.2 km) Double-ended paved turnout with dumpster, view of Mount Iliamna across the inlet.

S 143.8 (231.4 km) **A 196.8** (316.7 km) **H 35.7** (57.4 km) Happy Valley Creek. The area surrounding this creek is known locally as the Happy Valley community.

S 148 (238.1 km) **A 201** (323.5 km) **H 31.5** (50.7 km) Scenic viewpoint. Sign here reads: "Looking westerly across Cook Inlet, Mt. Iliamna and Mt. Redoubt in the Chigmit Mountains of the Aleutian Range can be seen rising over 10,000 feet above sea level. This begins a chain of mountains and islands known as the Aleutian Chain extending west over 1,700 miles to Attu beyond the International Date Line to the Bering Sea, separating the Pacific and Arctic oceans. Mt. Redoubt on the right, and Iliamna on the left, were recorded as active volcanoes in the mid-18th century. Mt. Redoubt had a minor eruption in 1966."

Mount Redoubt had a major eruption in December 1989. The eruptions continued through April 1990, then subsided to steam plumes. Mount Redoubt is still considered active.

S 150.9 (242.8 km) **A 203.9** (328.1 km) **H 28.6** (46 km) Bridge over Stariski Creek.

S 151.9 (244.4 km) **A 204.9** (329.7 km) **H 27.6** (44.4 km) Stariski Creek State Recreation Site on bluff overlooking Cook Inlet; 13 campsites, $10 nightly fee or annual pass, toilets (wheelchair accessible) and well water. ♿▲

S 152.7 (245.7 km) **A 205.7** (331 km) **H 26.8** (43.1 km) **Eagle Crest RV Park & Cabins**. See display ad this section. ▲

Campers line the beach at Deep Creek State Recreation Area, Milepost S 137.3.
(© Roy Corral)

Eagle Crest Wilderness Fishing Adventures. Fish for halibut and king salmon on the ocean, and fly in to Mount Iliamna area for giant rainbows, grayling, kings, reds and silver salmon. Call toll free 1-888-235-2905 or (907) 235-6851. Office at Eagle Crest RV Park and Cabins, P.O. Box 249, Anchor Point, AK 99556. [ADVERTISEMENT]

S 153.2 (246.5 km) **A 206.2** (331.8 km) **H 26.3** (42.3 km) **Short Stop RV Parking.** See display ad this section. ▲

S 154.1 (248 km) **A 207.1** (333.3 km) **H 25.4** (40.9 km) **Timberline Creations.** See display ad this section.

S 155 (249.4 km) **A 208** (334.7 km) **H 24.5** (39.4 km) **Bear Paw Charters.** This Anchor Point location is only minutes from trophy halibut and salmon fishing. All equipment provided plus free filleting. Small groups and personalized service are the focus of this family-owned and operated business. Lodging also available in private, fully equipped log cabin. You'll like

the gift shop. Phone (907) 235-5399. See display ad this section. E-mail: bearpaw@xyz.net; Web address: www.xyz.net\~bearpaw. [ADVERTISEMENT]

S 155.3 (249.9 km) **A 208.3** (335.2 km) **H 24.2** (38.9 km) **Red Door Bed & Breakfast.** See display ad this section.

S 156.3 (251.5 km) A 209.3 (336.8 km) H 23.2 (37.3 km) **Anchor River Tesoro.** See display ad this section.

Mugs and Jugs. See display ad this section.

The Warehouse, Inc. See display ad this section.

S 156.7 (252.2 km) A 209.7 (337.5 km) H 22.8 (36.7 km) Anchor Point post office at turnoff for Milo Fritz Road to west and North Fork Road to east, an 18-mile/29-km loop which rejoins the Sterling Highway at **Milepost S 164.3.** Post office is open 9 A.M. to 5 P.M. weekdays, 9 A.M. to noon Saturday.

ANCHOR POINT (pop. 866) has groceries, gas stations with major repair service, motel, restaurant and fast-food stands, liquor store, clinic, sporting goods, gift shops and ceramic studio. Volunteer fire department and ambulance, phone 911. **Visitor Information:** Located in the log cabin just off the Sterling Highway on Old Sterling Highway. Open 10 A.M. to 4 P.M., weekdays, Memorial Day to Labor Day. The center is manned by volunteers from Anchor Point Senior Citizens, Inc.

Our Front Porch Bed & Breakfast. See display ad this section.

Iliamna Mt. View Bed & Breakfast. Just one mile off the Sterling Highway. Turn on Milo Fritz Avenue, to Sand Beach Road, one block. Located on the bluffs above the mouth of the Anchor River. View soaring eagles and beautiful sunsets. Centrally located. Reasonable rates. New May 1997. (907) 235-6331. See display ad. [ADVERTISEMENT]

S 156.8 (252.3 km) A 209.8 (337.6 km) H 22.7 (36.5 km) **Anchor Point B&B, Clive's Fishing Guide Service.** Just off highway on Thurmond Street. Enjoy our quiet clean rooms with private bath and entrance. All new Beautyrest mattresses, central lounge with TV, coffee and phone. Fish for salmon and halibut on the same day, all equipment furnished. U.S. Coast Guard licensed and insured. Call (907) 235-1236. Hosts: Clive and Marilyn Talkington, Box 97, Anchor Point, AK 99556. [ADVERTISEMENT]

Anchor Point Roadhouse. See display ad this section. ▲

S 156.9 (252.5 km) A 209.9 (337.8 km) H 22.6 (36.4 km) **Junction** with Old Sterling Highway; access to Anchor River businesses and Anchor River (Beach) Road. See ANCHOR RIVER (BEACH) ROAD log on page 556.

Anchor River Inn. See display ad this section.

Kyllonen's RV Park. See display ad on page 556.

Wallin's Hilltop Bed & Breakfast. See display ad this section.

S 157.1 (252.8 km) A 210.1 (338.1 km) H 22.4 (36 km) Anchor River bridge.

S 160.9 (258.9 km) **A 213.9** (344.2 km) **H 18.6** (29.9 km) Side road to artist Norman Lowell's studio and KWLS radio station.

S 161 (259.1 km) **A 214** (344.4 km) **H 18.5** (29.8 km) Anchor River bridge.

S 164.3 (264.4 km) **A 217.3** (349.7 km) **H 15.2** (24.5 km) North Fork Loop Road to Anchor River.

S 164.8 (265.2 km) **A 217.8** (350.5 km) **H 14.7** (23.7 km) Old Sterling Highway leads 9.4 miles/15.1 km northwest in a loop to Anchor River (Beach) Road, which provides access to Cook Inlet, Anchor River recreation and Anchor Point businesses. See ANCHOR RIVER (BEACH) ROAD log on page 556 and **Milepost S 156.9.**

S 165.4 (266.2 km) **A 218.4** (351.5 km) **H 14.1** (22.7 km) **Billikin Gift Shop.** See display ad this section.

S 166.8 (268.4 km) **A 219.8** (353.7 km) **H 12.7** (20.4 km) Virginia Avenue.

Holland Days Bed & Breakfast. See display ad this section.

S 167.1 (268.9 km) **A 220.1** (354.2 km) **H 12.4** (20 km) Diamond Ridge Road.

S 168.5 (271.2 km) **A 221.5** (356.5 km) **H 11** (17.7 km) Alaska State Parks' South District office is located on the bluff here. A small parking lot is adjacent to the log office where visitors may obtain information on Kachemak Bay state park, as well as other southern Kenai Peninsula state park lands.

S 169.3 (272.5 km) **A 222.3** (357.7 km) **H 10.2** (16.4 km) Homer DOT/PF highway maintenance station. RV park. *NOTE: Watch for road construction southbound next 5 miles/8 km in 1997.*

The Village Barabara RV Park. See display ad this section. ▲

S 169.6 (272.9 km) **A 222.6** (358.2 km) **H 9.9** (15.9 km) Two viewpoints overlooking Kachemak Bay.

S 170 (273.6 km) **A 223** (358.9 km) **H 9.5** (15.3 km) Bay View Inn.

S 171.2 (275.5 km) **A 224.2** (360.8 km) **H 8.3** (13.4 km) Land fill road.

S 171.9 (276.6 km) **A 224.9** (361.9 km) **H 7.6** (12.2 km) West Hill Road; access to bed and breakfasts. Connects to Skyline Drive and East Hill Road for scenic drive along Homer Bluff.

S 172.5 (277.6 km) **A 225.5** (362.9 km) **H 7** (11.3 km) Hotel.

S 172.6 (277.8 km) **A 225.6** (363 km) **H 6.9** (11.1 km) Homer Junior High School.

S 172.7 (277.9 km) **A 225.7** (363.2 km) **H 6.8** (10.9 km) **Oceanview RV Park.** See display ad this section. ▲

S 172.8 (278.1 km) **A 225.8** (363.4 km) **H 6.7** (10.8 km) Exit onto Pioneer Avenue for downtown **HOMER** (description follows). Drive 0.2 mile/0.3 km on Pioneer Avenue and turn left on Bartlett Avenue for

the Pratt Museum (see Attractions in the Homer section) and Homer city campground (follow signs). Pioneer Avenue continues through downtown Homer to Lake Street and to East Hill Road. ▲

S 173.1 (278.6 km) **A 226.1** (363.9 km) **H 6.4** (10.3 km) Homer Chamber of Commerce Visitor Center at Main Street; access to food, lodging, dump station and other services. Bishop's Beach Park.

S 173.5 (279.2 km) **A 226.5** (364.5 km) **H 6** (9.7 km) Eagle Quality Center; shopping, groceries.

S 173.7 (279.5 km) **A 226.7** (364.8 km) **H 5.8** (9.3 km) Heath Street. Post office (ZIP code 99603).

S 173.9 (279.9 km) **A 226.9** (365.2 km) **H 5.6** (9 km) Lake Street. Access to downtown Homer and Lakeside Center.

S 174 (280 km) **A 227** (365.3 km) **H 5.5** (8.9 km) Beluga Lake floatplane base.

S 174.4 (280.7 km) **A 227.4** (366 km) **H 5.1** (8.2 km) Lambert Lane, access to floatplane base.

S 174.7 (281.1 km) **A 227.7** (366.4 km) **H 4.8** (7.7 km) Alaska Dept. of Fish and

Anchor River (Beach) Road Log

Turn off the Sterling Highway at **Milepost S 156.9** on to the Old Sterling Highway and continue past the Anchor River Inn to the Anchor River. Just beyond the bridge is the turnoff for Anchor River (Beach) Road, a 1.2-mile/1.9-km spur road providing access to Anchor River recreation area.
Distance from junction (J) is shown.

J 0 Junction of Old Sterling Highway and Sterling Highway at **Milepost S 156.9.**

J 0.1 (0.2 km) School Road. Anchor Point visitor information center. A plaque across from the visitor center marks the westernmost point on the contiguous North American Highway system.

Anchor River Inn, overlooking beautiful Anchor River and in business for 20 years, has the finest family restaurant on the peninsula, where you can see one of the largest displays of collectible plates in Alaska. Serving breakfast, lunch and dinner. Large cocktail lounge has a widescreen TV, pool tables, dance floor and video games. 20 modern motel units with phones; 10 spacious units with color TV and 2 queen-sized beds, and 10 smaller units overlooking the river. Our fully stocked liquor, grocery store and gift shop serve the Anchor Point area year-round. Write: Box 154, Anchor Point, AK 99556; phone 1-800-435-8531 in USA, or (907) 235-8531; fax (907) 235-2296. Your hosts: Bob and Simonne Clutts. [ADVERTISEMENT]

J 0.3 (0.5 km) Anchor River bridge, also known as "the erector set bridge."

J 0.4 (0.6 km) Road forks: Old Sterling Highway continues south and rejoins Sterling Highway at **Milepost S 164.8.** Turn right for Anchor River (Beach) Road.

Access to Silverking campground (Anchor River State Recreation Area); RV camping, toilets, dumpster, $8 nightly fee or annual pass. ▲

J 0.6 (1 km) Coho campground (Anchor River SRA); camping, toilets, $8 nightly fee or annual pass.

J 0.7 (1.1 km) Anchor Point Chamber of Commerce Salmon Derby Weigh-in and information.

J 0.7 (1.1 km) Tackle shop.

J 0.8 (1.3 km) Steelhead campground (Anchor River SRA); camping, toilets, $8 nightly fee or annual pass. ▲

J 1.1 (1.8 km) Slidehole campground (Anchor River SRA); 30 campsites, $10 nightly fee or annual pass, shelter with tables, public water source for campers, special senior/wheelchair camping area, large day-use parking lot, trail access to river. ♿▲

J 1.3 (2.1 km) **Kyllonen's RV Park**, a few steps from famous Anchor River and picturesque Cook Inlet. Providing spring water, electricity and sewer. Additional amenities include fish cleaning station, BBQ pits, free firewood and picnic tables. Showers, restrooms. Gift shop and Espresso Bar. Fishing licenses. We book fishing charters and area sightseeing tours. May through September. Year-round area information center, phone/fax (907) 235-7762, fax (907) 235-6435. See display ad this section. [ADVERTISEMENT]

J 1.5 (2.4 km) Halibut campground (Anchor River SRA); camping, toilets, $8 nightly fee or annual pass. ▲

J 1.6 (2.6 km) Road deadends on shore of Cook Inlet; beach access, 12-hour parking. Private tractor boat launch service. Signs here mark the most westerly point on the North American continent accessible by continuous road system and depict outlines of Cook Inlet volcanoes.

The Anchor Point area is noted for seasonal king and silver salmon, steelhead and rainbow fishing. Saltwater trolling for king salmon to 80 lbs., halibut to 200 lbs., spring through fall. **Anchor River**, king salmon fishing permitted only on 5 consecutive weekends, beginning Memorial Day weekend; trout and steelhead from July to October; closed to all fishing Dec. 31 to June 30, except for king salmon weekends. Excellent fishing for 12- to 24-inch sea-run Dollies in July and late summer. During August silver runs, fish high tides. Anchor River King Salmon Derby is usually held the last weekend in May and the first 4 weekends in June. A silver salmon derby is held in August. 🐟

Return to Milepost S 156.9
Sterling Highway

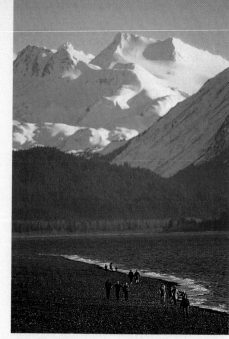

Walking Homer Spit on Kachemak Bay.
(© Roy Corral)

Game office.

S 174.8 (281.3 km) **A 227.8** (366.6 km) **H 4.7** (7.6 km) **Homer Tesoro.** See display ad this section.

S 175 (281.6 km) **A 228** (366.9 km) **H 4.5** (7.2 km) Airport Road. Sterling Highway crosses onto Homer Spit.

A series of boardwalks along the Spit house shops, charter services, food outlets, etc. Also on the Spit: a resort hotel, restaurants, seafood markets, private campgrounds, and public camping areas (check in with camping registration office on the Spit); the harbormaster's office, small boat basin, shore fishing for salmon in the Fishing Hole, Alaska Marine Highway ferry terminal and a boat ramp. ▲

S 179.5 (288.9 km) **A 232.5** (374.2 km) **H 0** Sterling Highway ends at Land's End Resort and Campground at the tip of Homer Spit.

Homer

Located on the southwestern Kenai Peninsula on the north shore of Kachemak Bay at the easterly side of the mouth of Cook Inlet; 226 miles/364 km by highway or 40 minutes by jet aircraft from Anchorage. **Population:** 4,133. **Emergency Services:** Phone 911 for all emergency services. **City Police**, phone (907) 235-3150. **Alaska State Troopers**, in the Public Safety Bldg., phone (907) 235-8239. **Fire Department** and **Ambulance**, phone (907) 235-3155. **Coast Guard**, phone Zenith 5555. (Coast Guard Auxiliary, phone (907/235-7277.) **Hospital**, South Peninsula, phone (907) 235-8101. **Veterinary Clinic**, phone (907) 235-8960.

Visitor Information: Chamber of Commerce Visitor Center is located on the Homer Bypass at Main Street. Open year-round. Contact the Homer Chamber of Commerce, Box 541, Homer 99603; phone during business hours (907) 235-7740 or 235-5300.

The Pratt Museum is open daily 10 A.M. to 6 P.M. from May through September; open noon to 5 P.M. Tuesday through Sunday from October through April; closed in January. Contact the Pratt Museum, 3779 Bartlett St., Homer 99603. Phone (907) 235-8635.

Elevation: Sea level to 800 feet/244m. **Climate:** Winter temperatures occasionally fall below zero, but seldom colder. The Kenai Mountains north and east protect Homer from severe cold, and Cook Inlet provides warming air currents. The highest temperature recorded is 81°F/27°C. Average annual precipitation is 27.9 inches. Prevailing winds are from the northeast, averaging 6.5 mph/10.5 kmph. **Radio:** KGTL 620, KWAV 103.5/104.9/106.3, MBN-FM 107.1/96.7/95.3, KBBI 890, KPEN-FM 99.3/100.9/102.3, KWHQ-FM 98.3. **Television:** KTUU, KTBY, KTVA, KAKM, KIMO. **Newspaper:** *Homer News* (weekly), *Homer Tribune* (weekly).

Private Aircraft: Homer airport, 1.7 miles/2.7 km east; elev. 78 feet/24m; length

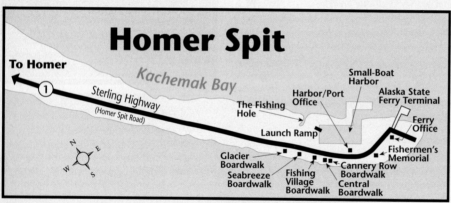

7,400 feet/2,255m; asphalt; fuel 100LL, Jet A; attended.

In the late 1800s, a coal mine was operating at Homer's Bluff Point, and a railroad carried the coal out to the end of Homer Spit. (The railroad was abandoned in 1907.) Gold seekers debarked at Homer, bound for the goldfields at Hope and Sunrise. The community of Homer was established about 1896 and named for Homer Pennock.

Coal mining operations ceased about WWI, but settlers continued to trickle into the area, some to homestead, others to work in the canneries built to process Cook Inlet fish.

Today, Homer's picturesque setting, mild climate and great fishing (especially for halibut) attract thousands of visitors each year. In addition to its tourist industry and role as a trade center, Homer's commercial fishing industry is an important part of its economy. Homer calls itself the "Halibut Fishing Capital of the World." Manufacturing and seafood processing, government offices, trades and construction are other key industries.

Homer is host to a large artist community. Potters, sculptors, painters and jewelers practice their craft and sell their goods in local shops and galleries. The local theater group provides live performances year-round.

Rising behind the townsite are the gently sloping bluffs which level off at about 1,200 feet/366m to form the southern rim of the western plateau of the Kenai. These green slopes are tinted in pastel shades by acres of wildflowers from June to September; fireweed predominates among scattered patches of geranium, paintbrush, lupine, rose and many other species. Two main roads (East Hill Road and West Hill Road) lead from the Homer business section to the "Skyline Drive" along the rim of the bluffs, and other roads connect with many homesteads on the "Hill."

The name *Kachemak* (in Aleut dialect said to mean "smoky bay") was supposedly derived from the smoke which once rose from the smoldering coal seams jutting from the clay bluffs of the upper north shore of Kachemak Bay and the cliffs near Anchor Point. In the early days many of the exposed coal seams were slowly burning from causes unknown. Today the erosion of these bluffs drops huge fragments of lignite and bituminous coal on the beaches, creating a plentiful supply of winter fuel for the residents. There are an estimated 400,000,000 tons of coal deposit in the immediate vicinity of Homer.

Kachemak is a magnificent deep-water bay that reaches inland from Cook Inlet for 30 miles/48.3 km, with an average width of 7 miles/11.3 km. The bay is rich in marine life. The wild timbered coastline of the south shore, across from Homer, is indented with many fjords and inlets, reaching far into the rugged glacier-capped peaks of the Kenai Mountains.

Jutting out for nearly 5 miles/8 km from the Homer shore is the Homer Spit, a long, narrow bar of gravel. The road along the backbone of the Spit connects with the main road through Homer (all the Sterling

Highway). The Spit has had quite a history, and it continues to be a center of activity for the town. In 1964, after the earthquake, the Spit sank 4 to 6 feet, requiring several buildings to be moved to higher ground. Today, the Spit is the site of a major dock facility for boat loading, unloading, servicing and refrigerating. The deep-water dock can accommodate up to 2 340-foot vessels with 30-foot drafts at the same time, making it accessible to cruise and cargo ships. It is also home port to the Alaska Marine Highway ferry MV *Tustumena*. The small-boat harbor on the Spit has a 5-lane load/launch ramp. Also in the small-boat harbor area are the harbormaster's office, canneries, parking/camping areas, charter services, small shops, live theatre, galleries, restaurants, motels and bed and breakfasts.

In summer, the Homer Spit bustles with activity: people fish from its shores for-

HOMER ADVERTISERS

Alaska Coastal Journeys ....Ph. (907) 235-2228
Alaska Coastal Marine
   Service Co. ....Ph. (907) 262-4359
Alaska Luxury Charters .....Ph. (907) 235-6259
Alaska Maritime Tours.............Homer Spit Rd.
Alaska Wild Berry
   Products ....528 E. Pioneer Ave.
Alaska Woodside
   Lodging ....Ph. (907) 235-8389
Alaska's Pioneer Inn ....244 Pioneer Ave.
All Points North Travel .....Ph. (907) 235-7362
Almost Home
   B&B Cabins ....Ph. 1-800-478-2352
Art Shop Gallery ....Ph. 800-478-7076
Arctic Sun Lodging ....Ph. (907) 235-2283
B & C Charters ....Ph. (907) 235-7916
Bald Mountain Air ....Ph. (907) 235-7969
Bay View Inn ....Mile 170 Sterling Hwy.
Bayview RV Park ....Ph. XXX-XXX-XXXX
Beary Patch Bed &
   Breakfast, The..............Ph. (907) 235-2483
Beeson's Bed &
   Breakfast......................Ph. (907) 235-3757
Blue Sky Bed &
   Breakfast......................Ph. (907) 235-4383
Bob's Trophy Charters......Ph. (907) 235-6544
Bookstore, The.................Eagle Quality Center
Central Charters Booking
   Agency, Inc. ....Ph. (907) 235-7847
Chocolate Drop B & B ......Ph. (907) 235-3668
Cloudy Mountain
   Inn B & B ....Ph. (907) 235-2254
Coal Point Trading Co. ....Ph. 1-800-325-3877
Coastal Outfitters ....Ph. (907) 235-8492
Copper Helmet B & B ....Ph. (907) 235-5608
Crane's Crest B & B ....Ph. (907) 235-2969
Dovetail B&B.....................Ph. (907) 235-3426
Driftwood Inn & RV Park..Ph. (907) 235-8019
Eagle View, The ....Ph. (907) 235-8996
Fishing Hole R.V. Park
   and Campground ....Homer Spit Rd.
Forest Light Cottage........Ph. (907) 235-2313
Garden of Eden, The ....Ph. (907) 235-8996
Halcyon Heights B & B .....Ph. (907) 235-2148
Halibut Cove Cabins....................Halibut Cove
Heritage Hotel-Lodge.......Ph. (907) 235-7787
Holland Days Bed and
   Breakfast......................Ph. (907) 235-7604
Homer Alaska Referral
   Agency/Seekins ....Ph. (907) 235-8996
Homer B&B.......................Ph. (907) 235-2176
Homer Chamber of Commerce Jackpot
   Halibut Derby ....Ph. (907) 235-7740

Homer Ocean
   Charters, Inc. ......Cannery Row, Homer Spit
Homer Spit Campground
   & Lodging.................................Homer Spit
Homer Tesoro ....1554 Homer Spit Rd.
Inlet Charters.....................Ph. (907) 235-6126
Island Watch
   Bed & Breakfast...........Ph. (907) 235-2265
J.P.'s B&B............................Ph. (907) 235-7362
Journeymen's B & B ....Ph. (907) 235-8238
Kachemak Air
   Service, Inc. ....Ph. (907) 235-8924
Kachemak Bay Lynx ....Ph. 1-800-235-5969
Kachemak Goldsmith,
   The ....105 W. Pioneer Ave.
Kachemak Kiana Bed and
   Breakfast......................Ph. (907) 235-8824
Kachemak Shores Bed and
   Breakfast......................Ph. (907) 235-6864
Kenai Fjords Outfitters..................Beluga Lake
Land's End Resort ....End of Homer Spit
Land's End RV Park ....End of Homer Spit
Lucky Pierre Charters........Ph. (907) 235-8903
Morning Glory Bed & Breakfast/
   Charters.......................Ph. (907) 235-8084
NOMAR (Northern Marine
   Canvas Products) ....104 E. Pioneer Ave.
North Country Halibut Charters ....Cannery
                     Row Boardwalk, Homer Spit
Ocean Shores Motel ....Ph. (907) 235-7775
Oceanview RV Park...........Ph. (907) 235-3951
Old Town
   Bed & Breakfast...........Ph. (907) 235-7558
Pier One Theatre ....Homer Spit
Pratt House Inn.................Ph. (907) 235-4090
Salty Dawg Saloon.........................Homer Spit
Silver Fox Charters.......................Homer Spit
Sorry Charlie Charters......Ph. (907) 235-2553
Sportsman's Supply ....Ph. (907) 235-8206
Spruce Acres Bed &
   Breakfast......................Ph. (907) 235-8388
Staghorn Ranch ....Ph. (907) 235-4127
Sundmark's B & B ....Ph. (907) 235-5188
SunSpin Guest House ....Ph. (907) 235-6677
Tacklebuster Halibut
   Charters.......................Ph. (907) 235-7847
3 Moose Meadow
   Wilderness B & B...........Ph. (907) 235-0755
Trail's End Horse
   Adventures ....Ph. (907) 235-6393
Washboard, The ....Ph. (907) 235-6781
Wild Rose Bed & Breakfast
   & Private Cabins ....Ph. (907) 235-8780

salmon; fishermen come and go in their boats; cars, trucks and trailers line the road; tent camps are set up on the beach; and boat builders and repairers are busy at their craft. Fresh crab, shrimp and halibut, as well as smoked fish, can be purchased from seafood shops on the Spit or sometimes from the fishermen themselves. Seafood processors on Homer Spit offer custom smoking, freezing and air shipping for sport-caught fish. It is also possible to trade your sport-caught fish for similar fish already processed and ready to ship or take with you.

ACCOMMODATIONS/VISITOR SERVICES

Homer has hundreds of small businesses offering a wide variety of goods and services. There are many hotels, motels, bed and breakfasts, and private campgrounds (reservations advised in summer). Nearly 40 restaurants offer meals ranging from fast food to fine dining. Homer has a post office, library, museum, laundromats, gas stations with propane and dump stations, banks, a hospital and airport terminal. There are many boat charters, boat repair and storage facilities, marine fuel at Homer marina, bait, tackle and sporting goods stores, and also art galleries, gift shops and groceries. City campground accessed via Bartlett Avenue (follow signs).

Homer Spit has both long-term parking and camping. Camping and parking areas are well-marked. Camping fees are $7 per night for RVs and $3 per night for tents. Camping permits are available at the camper registration office on the Spit. There is a 14-day limit; restrooms, water and garbage available. Check with the harbormaster's office or the camper registration office on the Spit if you have questions on rules and regulations pertaining to camping, campfires, long-term parking, boat launching and moorage. ▲

Following are paid advertisements for campgrounds and lodging. A number of other services and stores are listed under Attractions.

Homer Spit Campground and Lodging. Beachfront and ocean view campsites surrounded by breathtaking views of Kachemak Bay. Harbor, restaurants and boardwalk shops close by. Electric hook-ups, dump station, showers, supplies, gifts, B&B. Trailer rentals on site. Bookings for halibut charters, boat tours and all recreational activities. Visitor information. Our 23rd year of dependable service. P.O. Box 1196, Homer, AK. (907) 235-8206. [ADVERTISEMENT] ▲

Land's End RV Park. On the water's edge, at the tip of Homer Spit. Truly the most spectacular spot on the Kenai Peninsula. Gorgeous mountain views and sunsets. Minutes from the Spit's boardwalks and small-boat harbor. Electric hookups, laundry. Showers, ice, sundries. Open May through September. (907) 235-2525. P.O. Box 273, Homer, AK 99603. [ADVERTISEMENT] ▲

Oceanview RV Park just past Best Western Bidarka Inn on your right coming into Homer. Spectacular view of Kachemak Bay, beachfront setting. 85 large pull-through spaces in terraced park. Full/partial hookups, heated restrooms, free showers, laundry, pay phone, free cable TV, picnic area. Walking distance to downtown Homer. Special hal-

ibut charter rates for park guests. Phone (907) 235-3951. See display ad at Mile 172.7 Sterling Highway. [ADVERTISEMENT]

Alaska's Pioneer Inn. 244 Pioneer Ave., in downtown Homer. Clean, comfortable 1-bedroom suites with private baths and furnished kitchens. Sleeps up to 4. Complimentary coffee. Single guest rooms available.

Year-round. Homer's best value. Credit cards accepted. Brochure: P.O. Box 1430, Homer, AK 99603. (907) 235-5670. Toll free from continental U.S. 1-800-STAY-655. In Alaska, 1-800-478-8765. [ADVERTISEMENT]

Alaska Woodside Lodging. Your host, Merle Meisinger, a 28-year Alaska resident, will welcome you with hospitality and a wealth of local information. Offering plush, spacious condos for your comfort, with furnished kitchens and bathrooms, linens, phones and TV. Laundry facilities. Conveniently located right in downtown Homer. Bed and breakfast rooms also available. ▲

Quiet, reasonable rates. We can make all your reservations for halibut or salmon fishing, lodging, sightseeing or wildlife tours. All you need for your Alaskan adventure. Southbound on Sterling Highway, turn left onto Pioneer Avenue, immediately turn left on Woodside Avenue (behind Intermediate School). See Homer map. Phone: (907) 235-8389. See display ad. [ADVERTISEMENT]

Almost Home B&B/Cabins. Nestled in the trees on the bluff overlooking the mountains and the bay. Two B&B rooms have private entrance, mini-kitchen, shared bath and continental breakfast. Or, choose our

cabin with complete kitchen, living room, bath and 2 bedrooms. Clean, comfortable, affordable and friendly! Halibut and salmon charters available. Reservations recommended. (907) 235-2553, fax (907) 235-0553. In Alaska: 1-800-478-2352; 1269 Upland Court, Homer, AK 99603. [ADVERTISEMENT]

Bay View Inn. Spectacular panoramic view from the top of the hill as you enter Homer. Every room overlooks the shimmering waters of Kachemak Bay and the Kenai Mountains. Immaculately clean rooms, non-smoking, firm comfortable beds, color TV, private bathrooms and outside entrances. Options include kitchenettes, suite with fireplace and separate honeymoon cottage. Serene setting, spacious lawn, picnic tables, Adirondack chairs and freshly brewed morning coffee. Friendly staff offering local tour information and activity recommendations. Mile 170 Sterling Highway. P.O. Box 804, Homer, AK 99603. Phone (907) 235-8485. Fax (907) 235-8716. In Alaska only 1-800-478-8485. See display ad this section. [ADVERTISEMENT]

Cloudy Mountain Inn B&B. Hospitality-plus awaits you at our B&B. We have a beautiful panoramic view of the mountains and glaciers from our large deck and hot tub. We offer a two-bedroom apartment with private deck and barbecue. Immaculate rooms with sunshine-fresh linens, include a jacuzzi suite or bedrooms with shared and private baths.

Fresh baked bread daily, with full breakfasts for all, including early morning fisherfolks. Freezer space available. Located 5 minutes from downtown. Hosts Gary and Treania Stegall, P.O. Box 3801, Homer, AK 99603. (907) 235-2254, fax (907) 235-6471. [ADVERTISEMENT]

Cranes' Crest B&B. Crandall the Crane and I welcome you to our home. Unobstructed panoramic view of Kachemak Bay, mountains, five glaciers, from 1200-foot elevation. Breathtaking, awe-inspiring. Sandhill cranes, moose, coyotes, visit regularly for your viewing pleasure. Wildflowers and birds abound. Two rooms, shared bath, ADA approved for folks who need extra care. One queen bedroom with private bath. Continental breakfast. Open year-round. 59830 Sanford Drive. (907) 235-2969. [ADVERTISEMENT] &

Dovetail B&B. Unique lodging in a hand-hewn dovetail log home built by the owners. We're located in a serene setting just outside of Homer. Enjoy view of 3

glaciers and Kachemak Bay. Explore the undiscovered beauty of this area where the end of the road begins. Deluxe continental breakfast. Open year-round. Also home of Great Northern log homes. P.O. Box 15023, Fritz Creek, AK 99603. Phone (907) 235-3426. [ADVERTISEMENT]

Driftwood Inn and RV Park. Charming, historic beachfront hotel/motel, B&B, RV parking. Spectacular view overlooking beautiful Kachemak Bay, mountains, glaciers. Quiet in town location. Immaculately clean, unique rooms. Free coffee, tea, local information. Comfortable common areas with

Homer calls itself "Halibut Fishing Capital of the World." (© Barbara Willard)

TV, fireplace, library, microwave, refrigerator, barbecue, shellfish cooker, fish cleaning area, freezer, picnic and laundry facilities. Continental breakfast available. Full hookup

FRESH CAUGHT SEAFOOD

You never know who may stop in for dinner . . .

◆ Fresh seafood always available

◆ Seafood Lover's Gift Pack for those special people and special occasions

◆ After your fishing charter, we will process, freeze, pack and ship your fish anywhere

◆ Open all year. Phone orders welcome

Ask for the best, ask for . . .

COAL POINT TRADING CO.

Don't forget about our Seafood Gift Packs!

4306 Homer Spit, Homer, AK 99603
Phone (907) 235-3877 ~ Fax (907) 235-5330

(800) 325-3877

RV park with 20-/30-/50-amp electric, water, sewer. Phone and cable available. Friendly, knowledgeable staff, specializing in helping make your stay in Homer the best possible. Reasonable, seasonal rates. Open year-round. Write, call for brochure. 135 W. Bunnell Ave., MP, Homer, AK 99603. (907) 235-8019. 1-800-478-8019. [ADVERTISEMENT] ▲

Heritage Hotel-Lodge. One of Alaska's finest log hotels, conveniently located in the heart of Homer. Walking distance to beach, shops, museum. Accommodations: 36 rooms including suite with 2-person Jacuzzi. Reasonable rates. Color TV, movie channels. Phones, free local calls. Courtesy coffee. Restaurants adjacent. Alaskan hospitality. Open year-round. 147 E. Pioneer Ave., phone (907) 235-7787. Reservations 1-800-380-7787. Fax (907) 235-2804. See display ad this section. [ADVERTISEMENT]

Holland Days Bed and Breakfast offers charming cabins for your stay in the Homer area. Guests enjoy a hearty breakfast, or for those who have an early fishing charter, a breakfast can be packed to go. These fine Alaskan cabins, which have a touch of Holland, are nestled in the beautiful Alaska countryside surrounded by vegetable and floral gardens. Located 1/4 mile off the Sterling Highway. Turn on Virginia Avenue. (907) 235-7604. See display ad. [ADVERTISEMENT]

Homer Alaska Referral Agency. We do it all with one phone call. Your reservation specialists for bed and breakfasts, lodging, halibut and salmon fishing, wildlife viewing, adventures and Kenai Fjords glacier trips. Bookings made at no expense to client for Anchorage, Seward, Homer and all the Kenai

Peninsula. For free information, reservations (907) 235-8996 or fax (907) 235-2625. Box 1264, Homer, AK 99603. Established by Seekins, Alaskan residents since 1969. Your reliable source for making Alaskan dreams come true. Call today. [ADVERTISEMENT]

Journeymen's B & B. Join us, Ron and Gay Pendleton, for some down-Homer hospitality in our spacious 1-level home, Mile 3.8 East Road. Nonsmoking, no alcohol. Homebaked goodies. Fresh raspberries in August. Third night half-price. Winter rates. Phone (907) 235-8238; P.O. Box 3106-MP, Homer, AK 99603. See display ad. [ADVERTISEMENT] &

Kachemak Shores Bed and Breakfast. On Kachemak Drive, convenient to airport. Apartment-size units. Kitchenette, satellite TV. Can accommodate parties of 1 to 7 persons. Beach access. Captivating view of Kachemak Bay, romantic harbor lights, glaciers. Watch seals and majestic bald eagles from your window or deck. Reservations: (907) 235-6864 or (907) 235-8234 or 1-800-245-8234. See Kachemak Shores display ad this section. E-mail: nebroke@ptia/aska.net. [ADVERTISEMENT]

Land's End Resort. Open year-round! Homer Spit's only hotel, on the water, at the tip of Homer Spit. Breathtaking views! Watch seals, otters, various seabirds and other sea life as you have lunch or cocktails on our spacious outdoor deck. The Chartroom restaurant is famous for its locally caught seafood. The Wheelhouse Lounge provides lighter meals. Rates are 30 percent off between Oct. 1 and April 30. Truly an Alaskan landmark! (907) 235-2500 or 1-800-478-0400 (AK). 4786 Homer Spit Rd., Homer, AK 99603. [ADVERTISEMENT]

Ocean Shores Motel. 22 brand new spacious, seaside rooms located above our beautiful, private beach. Each unit has a balcony and 7-foot picture window with spectacular views of the ocean, mountains and glaciers. Cable TV, phones, 5-star queen beds, kitchenette and handicap-accessible rooms. Three

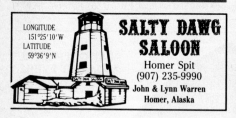

LONGITUDE 151°25'10"W LATITUDE 59°36'9"N

SALTY DAWG SALOON

Homer Spit
(907) 235-9990
John & Lynn Warren
Homer, Alaska

Dog mushing is the official Alaska state sport.

UNIQUE GOLD NUGGET JEWELRY...

ALASKAN GIFTS & ARTWORK

GOLD & SILVER JEWELRY, IVORY & GEMSTONES. WE SHIP ANYWHERE

The *Kachemak Goldsmith*
2 LOCATIONS IN HOMER

4470 SPIT ROAD · 235-7903   105 W. PIONEER AVE. · 235-7803

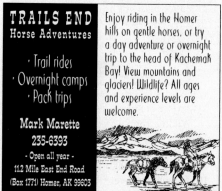

TRAILS END Horse Adventures

· Trail rides
· Overnight camps
· Pack trips

Mark Marette
235-6393
- Open all year -
11.2 Mile East End Road
(Box 1771) Homer, AK 99603

Enjoy riding in the Homer hills on gentle horses, or try a day adventure or overnight trip to the head of Kachemak Bay! View mountains and glaciers! Wildlife? All ages and experience levels are welcome.

Fishing Hole R.V. Park & Campground
HOMER SPIT

• Across from Homer's own fishing hole.

• Beach front spaces with picnic tables.

• Electric hookups $12 • Dry Camp $8.

• Reservations available.

• Mile 3.5 Homer Spit Rd. (907) 235-8928 P.O. Box 1597, Homer, AK 99603

HALIBUT FISHING
SALTWATER SALMON TROLLING
COMPLETE VACATION PACKAGES
MULTI-DAY KAYAK TRIPS
PO Box 2543, Homer AK 99603
(800) 426-6212
(907) 235-6212
Internet access: http://www.xyz.net/~hoc/

HOMER OCEAN CHARTERS
Since 1979

FUN IN HOMER!
at Alaska Wild Berry Products

Delicious
JAMS, JELLIES & WILD BERRY CANDIES

No visit to Alaska Wild Berry would be complete without a pause at the taster's stand, where you can dip into savory, free samples of jams and jellies. How about a slice of fresh fudge or Wild Berry candy?
(Taster's stand open May - September.)

See our jams, jellies and chocolates hand made the old-fashioned way.

GIFT SHOP & ALASKAN RELICS

Take some time to browse through our unique gift shop, featuring fine jewelry, souvenirs, and Alaska crafts. Also view the fascinating bits of Alaska's rich heritage collected over our 50 years in business in Homer.

VISIT US SOON!

Alaska Wild Berry Products is located in Homer on Beautiful Kachemak Bay at the southern tip of the Kenai Peninsula. The drive south from Anchorage takes you through some of the most spectacular countryside in America. Once in Homer, turn left onto Pioneer Avenue and look for our log cabin store. We'll be waiting to greet you.

Don't leave Homer without it!!

Alaska Wild Berry Products

Large parking lot. Picnic area. Open year-round. Long summer hours, 7 days a week. For more information call (907) 235-8858 in Homer. For free mail order catalog write Alaska Wild Berry Products, 5225 Juneau Street, Anchorage, Alaska 99518. Also visit our downtown Anchorage outlet at Fifth Avenue Mall and our main store and wild berry kitchens on International Airport Road between Old and New Seward Highways. (907) 562-8858.

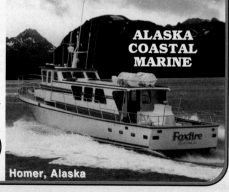
blocks to downtown Homer, adjacent to restaurants, quiet location and reasonable rates, all make this the best location in Homer. Highway Frontage #451, Sterling Highway. (907) 235-7775 or 1-800-770-7775. E-mail: oceanshs@alaska.net [ADVERTISEMENT]

Old Town Bed & Breakfast. In the restored historic Inlet Trading Post on the shore of Kachemak Bay. Sunny, clean and elegant, our antique-appointed rooms, reasonable rates and old-fashioned hospitality welcome you. Bunnell Street Gallery and Two Sisters Bakery downstairs. The perfect beachwalkers retreat. 106-D West Bunnell Ave., Homer, AK 99603, (907) 235-7558.
[ADVERTISEMENT]

Sundmark's B&B (formerly Seekins Homer B&B). Our guests enjoy one of Homer's best views of the Homer Spit, Kachemak Bay and the mountains and glaciers beyond. Our accommodations vary to meet the needs of our guests. Private cabin, private apartments, rooms with shared or private bath, furnished kitchens, cable TV. We serve a large, hearty breakfast every day. Children welcome. Reasonable rates. Nonsmoking. Open year-round. Hosts: Teresa, Dean and Dillon Sundmark, and friendly dog, Jessi. Brochure available. P.O. Box 375, Homer, AK 99603. (907) 235-5188 phone/fax. 2 miles up East Hill Road.
[ADVERTISEMENT]

3 Moose Meadow Wilderness B&B has taken the bed and breakfast to a new level. Understanding that travelers to Alaska want to experience Alaska, we offer a newly constructed log cabin in a wilderness setting. Your cozy cottage is nestled in the woods and overlooks a meadow with snow-capped mountains beyond. It's very private, has a kitchen and bath, wood stove, large deck and even a porch swing. Also included is a homemade breakfast guaranteed not to leave you hungry. Our weekly rates make it ideal for an extended stay in Homer. We also offer guided coastal rainforest and glacier hikes in beautiful Kachemak Bay State Park. For brochure or reservations call (907) 235-0755.

TRANSPORTATION

Air: Regularly scheduled air service to Anchorage. Several charter services also operate out of Homer.

Ferry: The Alaska State ferry *Tustumena* serves Seldovia, Kodiak, Seward, Port Lions, Valdez and Cordova from Homer with a limited schedule to Sand Point, King Cove and Dutch Harbor. Natural history programs offered on ferry in summer by Alaska Maritime National Wildlife Refuge naturalists. See MARINE ACCESS ROUTES section for details, or contact the offices of the Alaska Marine Highway System at the City Dock, phone (907) 235-8449. Tour boats offer passenger service to Seldovia and Halibut Cove.

Local: 3 rental car agencies and several taxi services.

ATTRACTIONS

The **Pratt Museum**, focusing on the natural and cultural history of southcentral Alaska, is located at 3779 Bartlett St. Exhibits include artifacts from the area's first Native people, thousands of years ago, to home-

Hiking in Kachemak Bay State Park. (© Ruth von Spalding)

steaders of the 1930s and 1940s. Excellent aquariums and a tide pool tank feature live Kachemak Bay sea creatures. Also exhibited are Alaskan birds and land and sea mammals, including the complete skeletons of a Bering Sea beaked whale and a beluga whale. Displays also feature local fish industry ves-

sels and the recently restored Harrington homesteader cabin.

Changing exhibits feature Alaskan artwork and other topics of special interest. Beautiful handmade quilts depict local natural history themes. Summer visitors may take a self-guided tour through the botanical

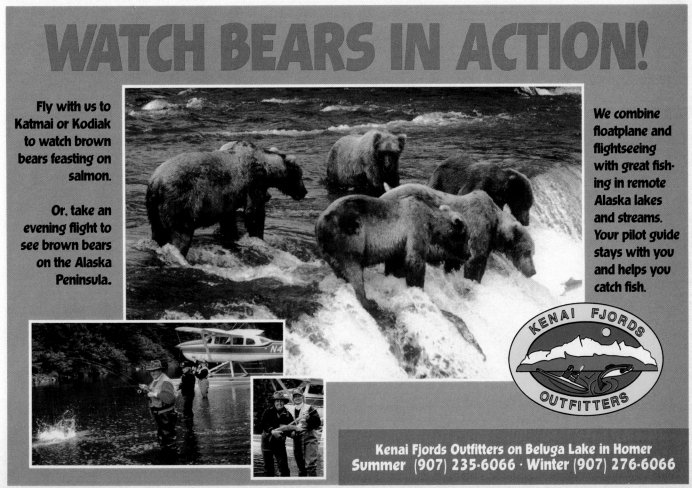

garden. This forest trail includes interpretive panels on local wild plants and the homesteader's cabin in the museum yard. The Museum Store features books and Alaskan collectibles.

The Pratt Museum is sponsored by the Homer Society of Natural History. All facilities are wheelchair accessible. $4 admission charged. Summer hours (May through September), 10 A.M. to 6 P.M. daily. Winter hours (October through April), noon to 5 P.M., Tuesday through Sunday. Closed January. Phone (907) 235-8635.

The U.S. Fish and Wildlife Alaska Mar-itime **National Wildlife Refuge** protects the habitats of seabirds and marine mammals on 3,500 islands and rocks along the coastline from Ketchikan to Barrow. The visitor center is open in summer from 9 A.M. to 6 P.M. daily. The center has displays focusing on the marine environment, videos and a small shop selling books and pamphlets. Wildlife programs include guided bird walks and beach walks, special slide presentations and a children's nature hour. Join the naturalists at the visitor center for an informative day. Naturalists are also on board the state ferry runs to Seldovia, Dutch Harbor and Kodiak.

Information on the latest bird sightings can be obtained by calling the Bird Hotline at (907) 235-PEEP (7337). The visitor center is located at 509 Sterling Highway, Homer, AK 99603; phone (907) 235-6961.

The Kachemak Bay Shorebird Festival celebrates the arrival of 100,000 migrating shorebirds to the tidal flats of Kachemak Bay. The 5th annual festival is scheduled for May 8–11, 1997. The event promotes awareness of this critical shorebird habitat that provides a feeding and resting place for at least 20 species of shorebirds on the last leg of their journey from Central and South America to breeding grounds in western and northen Alaska. Festival highlights include guided bird walks, classes for beginning and advanced birders, children's activities and more. Sponsored by the Homer Chamber of Commerce and U.S. Fish & Wildlife Service; phone (907) 235-7740 for more details.

Fish the Homer Halibut Derby. The annual Jackpot Halibut Derby, sponsored by the Homer Chamber of Commerce, runs from May 1 through Labor Day. The state's largest cash halibut derby ($85,000) provides 4 monthly cash prizes, tagged fish and final jackpot prize. Tickets are $7 and available at the Jackpot Halibut Derby headquarters on Homer Spit, visitor center or local charter service offices. Phone (907) 235-7740.

Charter Boats, operating out of the boat harbor on Homer Spit, offer sightseeing and halibut fishing trips. (Charter salmon fishing trips, clamming, crabbing, and sightseeing charters are also available.) These charter operators provide gear, bait and expert knowledge of the area. Homer is one of Alaska's largest charter fishing areas (most charters are for halibut fishing). Charter boats for halibut fishermen cost about $120 to $155 a day. Several sightseeing boats operate off the Homer Spit, taking visitors to view the bird rookery on Gull Island, to Halibut Cove and to Seldovia. (Most sightseeing trips are available Memorial Day to Labor Day). Watch for whales, puffins, sea

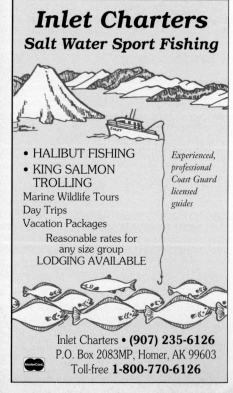

otters, seals and other marine wildlife.

AREA FISHING: The Kachemak Bay and Cook Inlet area is one of Alaska's popular spots for halibut fishing, with catches often weighing 100 to 200 lbs. Guides and charters are available locally. Halibut up to 350 lbs. are fished from June through September, fish the bottom with herring. Year-round trolling for king salmon is popular, use small herring. King salmon may also be taken during late May and June in area streams. Pink salmon (4 to 5 lbs.) may be caught in July and August; use winged bobbers, small weighted spoons and spinners. Similar tackle or fresh roe will catch silver salmon weighing 6 to 8 lbs. in August and September. Dolly Varden are taken throughout the area April to October; try single eggs or wet flies. Steelhead/rainbow are available in local streams, but for conservation purposes, must be immediately released unharmed.

Fishermen have had great success in recent years casting from the shore of Homer Spit for king salmon. The Fishing Hole (also referred to as the Fishing Lagoon or Spit Lagoon) on the Homer Spit supports a large run of hatchery-produced kings and silvers beginning in late May and continuing to September. Kings range from 20 to 40 lbs. The fishery is open 7 days a week in season.

Regulations vary depending on species and area fished, and anglers are cautioned to consult nearby tackle shops or Fish and Game before fishing.

Take a Scenic Drive. East Road, a 20-mile/32-km drive from downtown Homer, climbs through hills and forests toward the head of Kachemak Bay; pavement ends at Mile 12.5, beautiful views of the bay. Or turn off East Road on to East Hill Road and drive up the bluffs to Skyline Drive; beautiful views of the bay and glaciers. Return to town via West Hill Road, which intersects the Sterling Highway at **Milepost S 167.1.**

The glaciers that spill down from the Harding Icefield straddling the Kenai Mountains across the bay create an ever-changing panorama visible from most points in Homer, particularly from the Skyline Drive. The most spectacular and largest of these glaciers is Grewingk Glacier in Kachemak Bay State Park, visible to the east directly across Kachemak Bay from Homer. The glacier was named by Alaska explorer William H. Dall in 1880 for Constantin Grewingk, a German geologist who had published a work on the geology and volcanism of Alaska. The Grewingk Glacier has a long gravel bar at its terminal moraine, behind which the water draining from the ice flows into the bay. This gravel bar, called Glacier Spit, is a popular excursion spot, and may be visited by charter plane or boat. (There are several charter plane operators and charter helicopter services in Homer.) Portlock and Dixon glaciers are also visible directly across from the spit.

Kachemak Bay State Park is located on the south shore of the bay and includes glaciers, alpine tundra, forests, fjords, bays and high-country lakes. Recently the state enlarged this park by the purchase of 23,802 additional acres of land with funds from the settlement of the Exxon Valdez oil spill. The existing trail system offers hiking from Glacier Spit to China Poot Peak. An extensive new trail system is under construction. Campsites are currently available on Glacier Spit, Halibut Cove Lagoon and China Poot Lake. Additional campsites and public-use cabins are planned. Inquire locally about transportation to the park. Daily ferry service and water taxis are available to take you to trailheads. The bay shoreline offers excellent kayaking, clamming, tide pooling and beach combing opportunities. Phone the district office at (907) 235-7024 for more information or stop by the state park office at **Milepost S 168.5.**

McNeil River State Game Sanctuary/ Katmai National Park. Homer is the main base for visitors flying across Cook Inlet to both locations, where the world's largest concentration of bears in a natural area this size is found. Brown bears congregate near the mouth of the McNeil River, where a falls slows down migrating salmon, making fishing easy for the bears. Visits to the game sanctuary are on a permit basis; a drawing for the limited number of permits is held in March each year. Permit applications are available from the Alaska Dept. of Fish and Game, Attn: McNeil River, 333 Raspberry Road, Anchorage 99518. Phone (907) 267-2180.

Katmai National Park offers viewing platforms for close (and safe!) brown bear view-

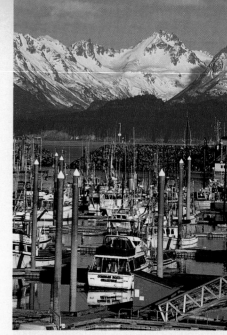

Small-Boat Harbor on Homer Spit.
(© Tom Bol)

ing. Several area outfitters provide service, including overnight stays and access to remote areas of the park.

Study Marine Environment. The Center for Alaskan Coastal Studies is located across Kachemak Bay from Homer. Volunteer naturalists lead a day tour which includes Gull Island bird rookery, coastal forest and intertidal areas. Write the Center for Alaskan Coastal Studies, P.O. Box 2225-MP, Homer 99603; phone (907) 235-6667. Reservations, phone (907) 235-7272.

Alaska Coastal Journeys. Immerse yourself in abundant wildlife on the shores and in the rainforest of Kachemak Bay. Our unique 3- and 5-day adult learning adventure programs include bird and marine mammal watching, intertidal exploration and sea kayaking, including instruction, all with Alaskan naturalists. Box 2094, Homer, AK 99603. (907) 235-2228. [ADVERTISEMENT]

Alaska Maritime Tours. Enjoy the only half-day wildlife tour from Homer to Seldovia which includes Gull Island bird rookery. Top quality, personal service is provided aboard the 50-foot MV *Denaina*. Two daily departures: 8 A.M. and 1:30 P.M. Weekly all-day birding trips to Barren Islands scheduled June–August. Bring camera, extra film, warm jacket, light rain gear to be prepared to spend time outside on deck for close-up views of puffins, sea otters and occasional whales. Located on Homer Spit Road. Call (907) 235-2490 or in Alaska 1-800-478-2490 for reservations or brochure. See display ad this section. [ADVERTISEMENT]

Alaska Wild Berry Products, celebrating more than 50 years in downtown Homer, invites you to see our wild berry jams, jellies and chocolates handmade the old-fashioned way. Delicious free samples at our taster's stand. Gift shop. Picnic area. Open year around, 528 East Pioneer Avenue. See display ad this section. [ADVERTISEMENT]

Art Shop Gallery, where Homer shops for art. Open year-round. Original works, prints, posters by local, Alaskan and nationally recognized artists. Alaska Native art, jewelry, dolls, pottery, Christmas tree ornaments by Alaskan artists. Homer's premier gallery. A must see. World-wide shipping. Eagle Quality Center on the bypass. (907) 235-7076 or 1-800-478-7076. [ADVERTISEMENT]

Bald Mountain Air. All-day brown bear photo safari from Homer via floatplane landing in Katmai National Park. Let life-long Alaskans, Gary and Jeanne Porter, give you an unforgettable adventure. Scenic wildlife glacier tours. See the best of Alaska! Hunting and fishing also. P.O. Box 3134, Homer, AK 99603. 1-800-478-7969. [ADVERTISEMENT]

The Bookstore, located in Eagle Quality Center, specializes in Alaskan, nature, cooking and children's books. It is acclaimed as one of the nicest bookstores in the state. Besides a great selection of paperback books, it features the most original card selection on the Peninsula (many by local artists) and a very special kids' corner. While browsing, check out the view. Hours 10 A.M. to 7 P.M. 436 Sterling Highway. (907) 235-7496 or toll free in continental U.S.A. and Alaska 1-888-635-BOOK.. [ADVERTISEMENT]

Coastal Outfitters: Experience the best wilderness adventure and photographic opportunity for all that Alaska has to offer. Fly from Homer, via floatplane, over ocean, volcanoes, glaciers and coastline en route to our vessel located in the pristine waters along Katmai National Park. Stay overnight or longer aboard our vessel for exclusive bear viewing and halibut fishing tours. You will thrill to the exposure of the magnificent Alaskan brown bears up close, while surrounded by breath-taking scenery, a multitude of sea birds and marine mammals. See display ad. (907) 235-8492, fax (907) 235-2967. [ADVERTISEMENT]

Kachemak Air Service, Inc. offers 2 unique opportunities: Fly over the glaciers across Kachemak Bay with Bill deCreeft in his 1929 Travel Air S6000B floatplane

"Limousine of the Air", large, mahogany-framed windows for each passenger; or fly out for the day in Kachemak Air Service, Inc.'s deHavilland Otter floatplane with Chris Day for a day trip viewing brown bears. P.O. Box 1769, Homer, AK 99603. (907) 235-8924. [ADVERTISEMENT]

NOMAR (Northern Marine Canvas Products) began business the summer of 1978 in a yellow school bus! Today, visit our manufacturing facility and manufacturer's outlet store at 104 E. Pioneer Ave., downtown Homer. NOMAR manufactures a wide variety of products for our Alaskan lifestyles. Warm NOMAR fleece clothing to keep you warm, no matter what the adventure. Soft-sided 'Laska Luggage® that's stuffable and floatplane friendly. Watertight bags for kayak tours or whitewater expeditions, and well-made Homer-made, packable, mailable, useful gifts for everyone on the "list." Park in our spacious, paved parking lot and take a walk around our town. We'll gladly ship your purchases for you. See display ad this section. [ADVERTISEMENT]

North Country Charters, on the Homer Spit. Sean and Gerri Martin, original owners since 1979. We have an excellent catch record with prize-winning derby fish, bringing in some of the largest halibut in Homer. Three 6-passenger and one 16-passenger boat for halibut fishing along with a saltwater salmon trolling boat. All vessels are Coast Guard equipped, heated cabins, full restrooms. 1-800-770-7620. See display ad. [ADVERTISEMENT]

Pier One Theatre. Local talent lights up an intimate stage in an Alaskan-friendly waterfront atmosphere halfway out the Homer Spit. Plays, new productions, readings, dance theatre, musicals. Offered summer weekends with some midweek

shows. Season information available locally. Phone (907) 235-7333. [ADVERTISEMENT]

Sorry Charlie Charters/B&B. Come and enjoy fantastic halibut fishing aboard a clean, comfortable 28-foot six-passenger *Baha* with heated cabin. Your captain has over 13 years experience and believes in providing quality, personalized service at an affordable rate. Accommodation packages also available. Reservations recommended. (907) 235-2553. Fax (907) 235-0553. In Alaska: 1-800-478-2352. 1269 Upland Court, Homer, AK 99603. [ADVERTISEMENT]

Seldovia

Reached by air, tour boat or ferry. Located on the southwestern Kenai Peninsula on Seldovia Bay, an arm of Kachemak Bay, 16 miles/25.7 km southwest of Homer. **Population: 403. Emergency Services: City Police, Ambulance, Fire** and **Rescue,** emergency only, phone 911, monitor CB Channel 9. **Seldovia Medical Clinic,** phone (907) 234-7825. Seldovia has a resident doctor and visiting dentists.

Visitor Information: Seldovia Chamber of Commerce, Drawer F, Seldovia, AK 99663. Phone (970) 234-7612; Web page: www.xyz.net\~seldovia. Information cache at Synergy Art Works on Main Street, across from the boat harbor. You may also stop by the Seldovia Native Assoc. office on Main Street. The office features a small museum with Native artifacts.

Elevation: Sea level. **Climate:** Rather mild for Alaska, with a year-round average temperature of about 39°F/4°C. Annual precipitation, 28 inches. Wind is a small factor due to the protecting shield of the Kenai Mountains. **Radio:** Homer stations. **Television:** KENI Channel 2, KTVA Channel 4, KAKM Channel 7, KIMO Channel 13.

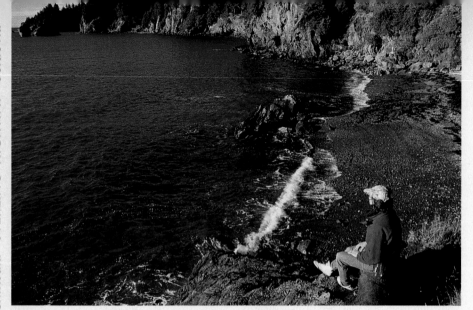

Listening to the waves at Seldovia Bay. (© Bill Sherwonit)

Harmony Point Wilderness Lodge. Easily reached by sea or air from Homer. We offer sea kayaking, boating, mountain biking, fishing, hiking, wildlife, sauna and fun. Private guest cabins and local seafood served in a new, handcrafted lodge. Come, explore or relax. Call (907) 234-7858 or write Box 110, Seldovia, AK 99663. [ADVERTISEMENT]

Seldovia, City of Secluded Charm, is still the unspoiled Alaska you dream of. Easily reached by commercial tour boat, airline or state ferry, Seldovia is an affordable step beyond the end of the road. For brochure, information call (907) 234-7612 or write Seldovia Chamber of Commerce, Drawer F, Seldovia, AK 99663. [ADVERTISEMENT]

Undeveloped campground for tent camping only at Outside Beach; picnic tables, litter containers, pit toilet. RV camping at the city-owned Seldovia Wilderness Park located just outside the city. From downtown, drive 1 mile/1.6 km out via Anderson Way to fork in road; turn left and drive 0.9 mile/1.4 km to beach. ▲

TRANSPORTATION

Air: Scheduled and charter service available.

Ferry: Alaska's Southwestern Marine Highway system serves Seldovia, with connections to and from Homer, Port Lions, Kodiak, Valdez, Cordova and Seward. See MARINE ACCESS ROUTES section.

Charter and Tour Boats: Available for passenger service; inquire locally and in Homer.

ATTRACTIONS

Special Events. Just about the whole town participates in Seldovia's old-fashioned Fourth of July celebration. The holiday includes food booths, parade, games and contests. Check with the chamber of commerce for details.

Scenic Drives. Outside Beach, a beautiful spot with undeveloped tent camping, beachcombing, surf fishing, rockhounding, and a view of Kachemak Bay and the volcanoes St. Augustine, Mount Iliamna and Mount Redoubt, is 1.9 miles/3.1 km from town. Drive out Anderson Way from downtown 1 mile/1.6 km to a fork in the road by a gravel pit; turn left and drive 0.9 mile/1.4 km to beach.

Continue on Anderson Way (past the Outside Beach turnoff) to hilly and unpaved Jakolof Bay Road, which offers panoramic views of Kachemak Bay, McDonald Spit, Jakolof Bay and Kasitsna Bay. At Mile 7.5, steps lead down to 1.5-mile-long McDonald Spit, a favorite spot for seabirds and marine life. Spend an afternoon exploring the spit, or continue out to Jakolof Bay, where the road offers many opportunities to get onto the beach. The road becomes impassable to vehicles at Mile 13.

It is a pleasant drive out to Seldovia's refuse dump, with wonderful blueberry picking in the fall. From downtown, cross the bridge over Seldovia Slough; then turn right on North Augustine Avenue, then left on Rocky Street for the dump. This is a 1.4-mile/2.3-km drive.

Fishing: Kachemak Bay, king salmon, January through August; halibut May through October; Dolly Varden, June through September; silver salmon in August and September; red salmon, July through August. **Seldovia Bay,** king, silver and red salmon, also halibut, May through September. Excellent bottom fishing. 🐟

Private Aircraft: Seldovia airport, 0.6 mile/1 km east; elev. 29 feet/9m; length 2,000 feet/610m; gravel; unattended.

Seldovia is a small community connected to Homer by the Alaska Marine Highway Southwest ferry system. Because it is removed from Kenai Peninsula highways, Seldovia has retained much of its old Alaska charm and traditions (its historic boardwalk dates from 1931). There are some areas just outside town, accessible by car, that have been called "Alaska's hidden paradises." A good place to observe bald eagles, seabirds, and sea otters, Seldovia is included as a stop on some tour boat cruises out of Homer.

The name Seldovia is derived from Russian *Seldevoy,* meaning "herring bay." Between 1869 and 1882, a trading station was located here. A post office was established in Nov. 1898.

ACCOMMODATIONS/VISITOR SERVICES

Seldovia has most visitor facilities, including 2 hotels, 12 bed and breakfasts, a lodge, general store, 3 restaurants and a variety of shops. The post office is in the center of town. Public restrooms, showers, and pay phone in front of the boat harbor near town center. Pay phones are also located at the ferry dock outside ferry office, at the airport, and library.

Seldovia Boardwalk Hotel. Waterfront view. 14 lovely rooms with private baths. Large harbor view deck. In-room phones. Near bike rental and Otterbahn Trail. Free airport or harbor pickup. Friendly service. Romantic getaway. Package prices from Homer. P.O. Box 72, Seldovia, AK 99663. (907) 234-7816. [ADVERTISEMENT]

Gerry's Place. Bed and breakfast 1 block from harbor. Convenient for fishermen and divers. Private entrance. Close to everything. Air fills available. Rates for families. Freshly baked continental breakfast. Accommodates 6, share bathroom. Box 33, Seldovia, AK 99663. (907) 234-7471. [ADVERTISEMENT]

SELDOVIA ADVERTISERS

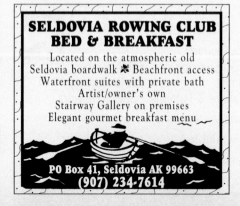

KODIAK

(See map, page 578)

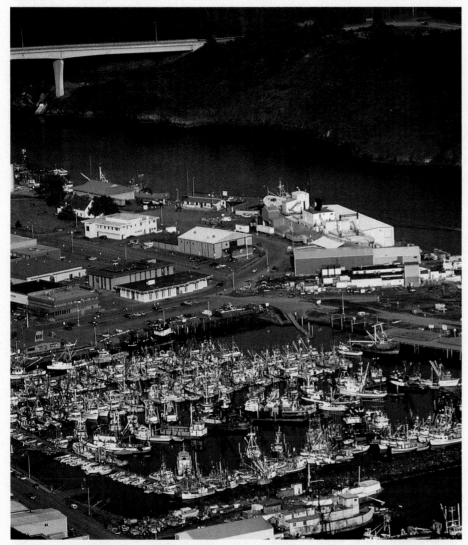

Kodiak is one of the largest commerical fishing ports in the U.S. *(© Harry M. Walker Photo)*

The Kodiak Island group lies in the Gulf of Alaska, south of Cook Inlet and the Kenai Peninsula. The city of Kodiak is located near the northeastern tip of Kodiak Island, at the north end of Chiniak Bay. By air it is 1 hour from Anchorage. By ferry from Homer it is 10 hours.

Population: 15,575 Kodiak Island Borough. **Emergency Services in Kodiak:** Dial 911 for emergencies. **Alaska State Troopers,** phone (907) 486-4121. **Police,** phone (907) 486-8000. **Fire Department,** phone (907) 486-8040. **Hospital,** Kodiak Island Hospital, Rezanof Drive, phone (907) 486-3281. **Coast Guard,** Public Affairs Officer, phone (907)

487-5542. **Crime Stoppers,** phone (907) 486-3113.

Visitor Information: Located at 100 Marine Way; open year-round. Hours in June, July and August are: 8 A.M. to 5 P.M. weekdays, 10 A.M. to 3 P.M. Saturday, 1–5 P.M. Sunday (and later for arriving ferries). Knowledgeable local staff will answer your questions and help arrange tours and charters. Free maps, brochures, hunting and fishing information. For information, contact the Kodiak Island Convention & Visitors Bureau, Dept. MP, 100 Marine Way, Kodiak 99615; phone (907) 486-4782.

Elevation: Sea level. **Climate:** Average daily temperature in July is 54°F/12°C; in January 30°F/-1°C. September, October and May are the wettest months in Kodiak, with each month averaging more than 6 inches of rain.

Radio: KVOK 560, KMXT-FM 100.1, KJJZ-FM 101.1, KPEN-FM 102.3, KWVV-FM 105. **Television:** Via cable and satellite. **Newspapers:** *The Kodiak Daily Mirror* (daily except Saturday and Sunday).

Private Aircraft: Kodiak state airport, 3 miles/4.8 km southwest; elev. 73 feet/22m; length 7,500 feet/2,286m; asphalt; fuel 100LL, Jet A-1. Kodiak Municipal Airport, 2 miles/3.2 km northeast; elev. 139 feet/42m; length 2,500 feet/762m; paved; unattended. Kodiak (Lilly Lake) seaplane base, 1 mile/1.6 km northeast; elev. 130 feet/40m. Inner Harbor seaplane base, on east side of Near Island at Trident Basin, unattended, docks; no fuel.

Gravel airstrips at Akhiok, length 3,000 feet/914m; Karluk, length 1,900 feet/579m; Larsen Bay, length 2,400 feet/732m; Old Harbor, length 2,000 feet/610m; Ouzinkie, length 2,500 feet/762m; and Port Lions, length 2,600 feet/792m.

Kodiak Island, home of the oldest permanent European settlement in Alaska, is about 100 miles/161 km long. Known as "the emerald isle," Kodiak is the largest island in Alaska and the second largest island in the United States (after Hawaii), with an area of 3,588 square miles and about 87 miles/140 km of road (see logs this section). The Kodiak Island Borough includes some 200 islands, the largest being Kodiak, followed in size by Afognak, Sitkalidak, Sitkinak, Raspberry, Tugidak, Shuyak, Uganik, Chirikof, Marmot and Spruce islands. The borough has only one unincorporated townsite, **KARLUK** (pop. 65), located on the west coast of Kodiak Island, 75 air miles/121 km from Kodiak.

The 6 incorporated cities in the Kodiak Island Borough are: **KODIAK** (pop. 7,428) on Chiniak Bay, with all visitor services (see Visitor Services, Transportation and Attractions this section); **AKHIOK** (pop. 86) at Alitak Bay on the south side of Kodiak Island, 80 miles/129 km southwest of Kodiak; **LARSEN BAY** (pop. 153) on the northwest coast of Kodiak Island, 62 miles/100 km southwest of Kodiak; **OLD HARBOR** (pop. 311) on the southeast side of Kodiak Island, 54 miles/87 km from Kodiak; **OUZINKIE** (pop. 221) on the west coast of Spruce Island; and **PORT LIONS** (pop. 264) on Settler Cove on the northeast coast of Kodiak Island.

Kodiak Island was originally inhabited by the Alutiiq people, who were maritime hunters and fishermen. More than 7,000 years later, the Alutiiq still call Kodiak home.

In 1763, the island was discovered by Stephen Glotov, a Russian explorer. The name Kodiak, of which there are several variations, was first used in English by Captain Cook in 1778. Kodiak was Russian Alaska's first capital city, until the capital was moved to Sitka in 1804.

Kodiak's turbulent past includes the 1912 eruption of Novarupta Volcano, on the nearby Alaska Peninsula, and the tidal wave of 1964. The Novarupta eruption covered the island with a black cloud of ash. When the cloud finally dissipated, Kodiak was buried under 18 inches of drifting pumice. On Good Friday in 1964 the greatest earthquake ever recorded in North America (9.2 on the Richter scale) shook the Kodiak area. The tidal wave that followed virtually leveled downtown Kodiak, destroying the fishing fleet, processing plants, canneries and 158 homes.

Because of Kodiak's strategic location for defense, military facilities were constructed on the island in 1939. Fort Abercrombie, now a state park and a national historic landmark, was one of the first secret radar installations in Alaska. Cement bunkers still remain for exploration by the curious.

The Coast Guard occupies the old Kodiak Naval Station. Kodiak is the base for the Coast Guard's North Pacific operations; the U.S. Coast Guard cutters *Storis*, *Ironwood* and *Firebush* patrol from Kodiak to seize foreign vessels illegally fishing U.S. waters. (The 200-mile/322-km fishing limit went into effect in March 1977.) A 12-foot star, situated halfway up the side of Old Woman Mountain overlooking the base, was rebuilt and rededicated in 1981 in memory of military personnel who have lost their lives while engaged in operations from Kodiak. Origi-

nally erected in the 1950s, the star is lit every year between Thanksgiving and Christmas.

Kodiak's St. Paul and St. Herman harbors are home port to 800 local fishing boats and serve about 2,000 outside vessels each year.

Commercial fishing is the backbone of Kodiak's economy. Kodiak is one of the largest commercial fishing ports in the U.S. Some 3,000 commercial fishing vessels use the harbor each year, delivering salmon, shrimp, herring, halibut and whitefish, plus king, tanner and Dungeness crab to the 15 seafood processing companies in Kodiak. Cannery tours are not available. Kodiak's famous seafood is premarketed, with almost all the commercially caught seafood exported. (Kodiak is the only city in Alaska with more tonnage exported than imported.) You can celebrate Kodiak's main industry at the Kodiak Crab Festival, May 22–26, 1997.

Kodiak is also an important cargo port and transshipment center. Container ships stop here to transfer goods to smaller vessels bound for the Aleutians, the Alaska Peninsula and other destinations.

ACCOMMODATIONS/VISITOR SERVICES

There are 4 hotels/motels in Kodiak and more than a dozen bed and breakfasts. A variety of restaurants offers a wide range of menus and prices. Shopping is readily available for gifts, general merchandise and sporting goods. There is a movie theater and 750-seat performing arts center.

There are 3 state campgrounds: Fort Abercrombie, north of town (see Rezanof–Monashka Bay Road log); Buskin River state recreation site, south of town (see Chiniak Road log); and Pasagshak River state recreation site at the end of Pasagshak Bay Road (see log). City campground (established for transient process workers) at Gibson Cove has showers and restrooms, $2 per person/night camping fee. ▲

Dump stations are located at the Buggy Banya station on Mill Bay Road, at the Union 76 service station in downtown Kodiak, and at Buskin River state recreation site at Mile 4.4 Chiniak Road.

There are 23 remote fly-in hunting and fishing lodges in the Kodiak area; several roadhouses on the island road system; public-use cabins available within Kodiak National Wildlife Refuge, Shuyak Island and Afognak Island state parks; and private wilderness camps and cabin rentals available throughout the Kodiak area.

TRANSPORTATION

Air: Scheduled service via Era Aviation and Alaska Airlines.

Ferry: The Alaska state ferry MV *Tustumena* serves Kodiak from Homer (9½-hour ferry ride) and Seward (13 hours). It also stops at Port Lions. Ferry terminal is downtown; phone (907) 486-3800 or toll free in the U.S. 1-800-526-6731. See MARINE ACCESS ROUTES section for details.

Highways: There are 4 roads on Kodiak Island (see logs this section). The 11.3-mile/18.2-km Rezanof–Monashka Bay Road leads from downtown Kodiak north to Fort Abercrombie and Monashka Bay. Chiniak Road leads 42.8 miles/68.9 km south from Kodiak along the island's eastern shore to Chiniak Point and Chiniak Creek (it is a beautiful drive!). Anton Larsen Bay Road leads 11.8 miles/19 km from junction with Chiniak Road near Kodiak airport to Anton Larsen Bay. Pasagshak Bay Road branches off Chiniak Road and leads 16.5 miles/26.6 km to Fossil Beach at Pasagshak Point.

IMPORTANT: Most of the land along the road system is privately owned. Using land owned by Leisnoi, Inc. requires a nonfee user permit, available at the Leisnoi office in Kodiak at 202 Center Ave.; phone (907) 486-8191.

Car Rental and Taxi: Available.

ATTRACTIONS

State Fair and Rodeo held Labor Day weekend, at the fairgrounds in Womens Bay, includes all-state competitions in crafts, gardening, 4-H livestock raising and home products. Stock car races are held at the fairgrounds on weekends during the summer.

St. Herman's Day, Aug. 9, is of particular significance to the Kodiak community as Father Herman, the first saint of the Russian Orthodox Church in North America, was canonized in Kodiak in 1970. Father Herman arrived in Kodiak in 1794.

The Baranov Museum (Erskine House), maintained by the Kodiak Historical Society (101 Marine Way, Kodiak 99615; phone 907/486-5920), is open in summer, 10 A.M. to 4 P.M. daily. (Winter hours 11 A.M. to 3 P.M. weekdays, except Thursday and Sunday, and noon to 3 P.M. Saturday. Closed in February.) The building was originally a

fur warehouse built in the early 1800s by Alexsandr Baranov. It is one of just 4 Russian-built structures in the United States today. Purchased by the Alaska Commercial Co. around 1867, the building was sold to W.J. Erskine in 1911, who converted it into a residence; it was then referred to as the Erskine House. In 1962 it was declared a national historic landmark. Many items from the Koniag and Russian era are on display. In the gift shop, Russian samovars, Russian Easter eggs, Alaska Native baskets and other items are for sale. Donations accepted, $2 per adult, children under 12 free.

Picnic on the Beach. There are some outstandingly beautiful beaches along Chiniak Road (see log this section). These unpopulated beaches are also good for beachcombing. Watch for Sitka deer and foxes.

Go for a Hike. Hiking trails around the Kodiak area provide access to alpine areas, lakes, coastal rainforests and beaches. Trail guide available for $5 at the visitors center, (907) 486-4782. Pay attention to notes regarding footwear and clothing, tides, bears, trailhead access and weather conditions.

Go Mountain Biking. Kodiak is fast becoming known for its premier mountain biking, attracting racers and enthusiasts from around the country. Bike rentals are available year-round for half-days, weekends and weekly rates. For information on upcoming bike races, call (907) 486-4219.

Kodiak Tribal Council's Barabara sod house is an authentic Alutiiq dwelling that features presentations of Alutiiq dancing. The Kodiak Alutiiq Dancers form the only

Alutiiq dance group in Alaska. The dances have been re-created from stories passed down through generations of the Alutiiq people, who have inhabited Kodiak Island for more than 7,000 years. Dance performances are held in summer, Monday through Saturday at 3:30 P.M., at the barabara located at 713 Rezanof Drive. Phone (907) 486-4449 to confirm performance times.

City Parks and Recreation Department maintains a swimming pool year-round, and the school gyms are available on a year-round basis for community use. The town has 8 parks and playgrounds including the 7-acre Baranof Park with 4 tennis courts, baseball field, track, playgrounds and picnic areas.

Bear Valley Golf Course. The 9-hole Bear Valley Golf Course is located on the Anton Larsen Bay Road. Owned and operated by the U.S. Coast Guard, the course has a driving range, putting green and pro shack. The course is open to the public from approximately June until October, depending on weather. The pro shack carries golf clothing, items and rental equipment, and serves food and beer. Hours of operation vary according to weather and daylight hours. Call (907) 486-7561 or 487-5108.

Fort Abercrombie State Park. Site of a WWII coastal fortification, bunkers and other evidence of the Aleutian campaign. The park is located north of Kodiak on scenic Miller Point. Picnicking and camping in a setting of lush rain forest, wildflowers, seabirds and eagles.

The U.S. Coast Guard Winter Recre-

ation Area is located on the Anton Larsen Bay Road and has a lighted downhill ski slope with rope-tow lift, a separate sledding area and a ski chalet that serves refreshments. Open to the public, depending on weather and snow conditions. Call (907) 487-5108.

Alutiiq Museum Archaeological Repository Center in downtown Kodiak houses artifacts from coastal sites around Kodiak Island. The Alutiiq are descendants of the Pacific Eskimos, whom Russian explorers encountered and referred to as the Koniag people, many of whom lived in the Karluk area on Kodiak's west coast around 1200 A.D. However, some of the items found date to 3,000 and even 7,000 years ago. The Karluk area is billed as one of the most amazing archaeological finds in Alaska because of the level of preservation of the artifacts and because of the abundance of items used in daily life.

Shuyak Island State Park encompasses 11,000 acres and is located 54 air miles north of Kodiak. Access is by boat or by plane only. Hunting, fishing and kayaking are the major recreational activities. Four public-use cabins are available at $30 per night, December through May, and $50 per night, June through November. Cabins are 12 feet by 20 feet and sleep up to 8 people. Reservations accepted up to 6 months in advance with a full nonrefundable payment. Call (907) 486-6339 or 762-2261.

Holy Resurrection Russian Orthodox Church. Orthodox priests, following Russian fur traders from Siberia, arrived in Kodiak and established the first Russian Orthodox Church in North America in September 1794. The original church was built on a bluff overlooking St. Paul Harbor in 1796. A second church was built on the same location. The bluff was leveled during reconstruction following the earthquake and tsunami in 1964.

Three churches have been built on the present site. The first appears on an 1869 map of Fort Kodiak. Another church was begun in 1874 and survived until destroyed by fire in 1943. The present church was built in 1945 and is listed on the National Register of Historic Places.

The church interior provides a visual feast, and the public is invited to attend services. Visitors may visit on weekdays in summer between 1–3 P.M.; donation $1. (The church will close to visitors during special services.) In winter, call the parish priest at (907) 486-3854 to arrange for a tour.

A scale replica of the original (1796) church building was completed in May 1994 and is located on the grounds of St. Herman's Theological Seminary on Mission Road.

Arrange a Boat or air charter, or guide for fishing and hunting trips, adventure tours, sightseeing and photography. There are several charter services in Kodiak.

See Kodiak by Kayak. One of the best ways to experience Kodiak's beautiful coastline, and view marine mammals and seabirds, is from a kayak. Day tours around the nearby islands are available for all skill levels, or schedule an extended tour.

Kodiak National Wildlife Refuge encompasses 2,812 square miles on Kodiak Island, Uganik Island, Afognak Island and Ban Island. The refuge was established in 1941 to preserve the natural habitat of the famed Kodiak bear and other wildlife. Biologists estimate that more than 3,000 bears inhabit Kodiak Island. Most bears enter dens by December and remain there until April. Bears are readily observable on the refuge in July and August when they congregate along streams to feed on salmon. At other times they feed on grasses or berries.

Native wildlife within the refuge includes the red fox, river otter, short-tailed weasel, little brown bat and tundra vole. Introduced mammals include the Sitka black-tailed deer, beaver, snowshoe hare and mountain goat. On Afognak Island, an introduced herd of elk share the island with the bears. The coastline of Kodiak refuge shelters a large population of waterfowl and marine mammals. Bald eagles are common nesting birds on the refuge, along with 215 other bird species that have been seen on the island.

Visitors to the refuge typically go to fish, observe/photograph wildlife, backpack, kayak, camp and hunt.

NOTE: The refuge is accessible only by float-plane or boat. There are primitive public-use cabins available; applications must be made in advance to the refuge manager. For more information contact the Kodiak National Wildlife Refuge Manager, 1390 Buskin River Road, Kodiak, AK 99615; phone (907) 487-2600. You may also stop by the U.S. Fish and Wildlife Service Visitor Center at Mile 4.4 Chiniak Road. The center features exhibits and films on Kodiak wildlife, and is open weekdays year-round, and also Saturdays April through September; hours are variable.

Wildlife Watching. The best time to observe animals is when they are most active: at daybreak. Bald eagles can be seen near the city of Kodiak from January through March, and nesting near water in the summer. Peregrine falcons are spotted frequently from the road in October. In the summer, puffins can be seen at Miller Point on calm days. Narrow Cape, Spruce Cape and Miller Point are good stakeout points in the spring for those in search of gray whales. Womens Bay is home to a variety of migrating geese in April.

Kodiak is a gateway to Katmai National Park and Preserve, well-known for its bear-viewing and sportfishing, as well as for an abundance of other wildlife and activities. There is a National Park Service information office in Kodiak, and local air taxi operators offer direct flights to King Salmon and also to the remote Katmai coast.

Bear-viewing Trips. To see brown bears, it's best to leave the road system and travel to the Bush by plane or boat. Almost all the air charter services offer some sort of bear-viewing excursion, ranging from half-day trips to multiple-day visits in cabins or tent-camps. Many lodge operations and licensed guides/outfitters also provide bear-viewing trips.

AREA FISHING: Kodiak Island is in the center of a fine marine and freshwater fishery and possesses some excellent fishing for rainbow, halibut, Dolly Varden and 5 species of Pacific salmon. Visiting fishermen will have to charter a boat or aircraft to reach remote lakes, rivers and bays, but the island road system offers many good salmon streams in season. Roads access red salmon fisheries in the Buskin and Pasagshak rivers. Pink and silver salmon are also found in the **Buskin** and **Pasagshak rivers**, and **Monashka, Pillar, Russian, Salonie, American, Olds, Roslyn** and **Chiniak creeks**.

Afognak and Raspberry islands, both approximately 30 air miles/48 km northeast of Kodiak, have lodges and offer excellent remote hunting and fishing. Both islands are brown bear country. Hikers and fishermen should make noise as they travel and carry a .30–06 or larger rifle. Stay clear of bears. If you take a dog, make sure he is under control. Dogs can create dangerous situations with bears. ⌐

CAUTION: A paralytic-shellfish-poisoning alert is in effect for all Kodiak Island beaches. This toxin is extremely poisonous. There are no approved beaches for clamming on Kodiak Island. For more current information, call the Dept. of Environmental Conservation in Anchorage at (907) 349-7343.

View from Pillar Mountain on a clear day. (© Rich Reid)

boat launch ramp, fish-cleaning station; and Fishery Industrial Technology Center, phone (907) 486-1500 for tours. Also access to Trident Basin seaplane base, located beyond the Technology Center on Trident Way.

K 1.5 (2.4 km) Kodiak Island Hospital on left.

K 2 (3.2 km) Benny Benson Drive. Turnoff left to Kodiak College and beginning of paved bicycle trail, which parallels main road to Fort Abercrombie State Historic Park.

Excellent for walking, jogging and bicycling.

K 3.4 (5.5 km) Turnout and gravel parking area to right for Mill Bay Park. Scenic picnic spot with picnic tables, barbecue grates. Good ocean fishing from beach. ⌐

K 3.9 (6.3 km) Road right to Fort Abercrombie State Historic Park. Drive in 0.2 mile/0.3 km to campground; 13 campsites with 7-night limit at $10 per night, water, toilets, fishing, swimming and picnic shelter. Extensive system of scenic hiking

Rezanof–Monashka Bay Road Log

Distance is measured from the junction of Rezanof Drive and Marine Way in downtown Kodiak (K).

K 0.1 (0.2 km) Mill Bay Road access to library, post office and Kodiak businesses.

K 0.4 (0.6 km) Entrance to Near Island bridge to North End Park, a city park with trails and picnic areas; St. Herman Harbor,

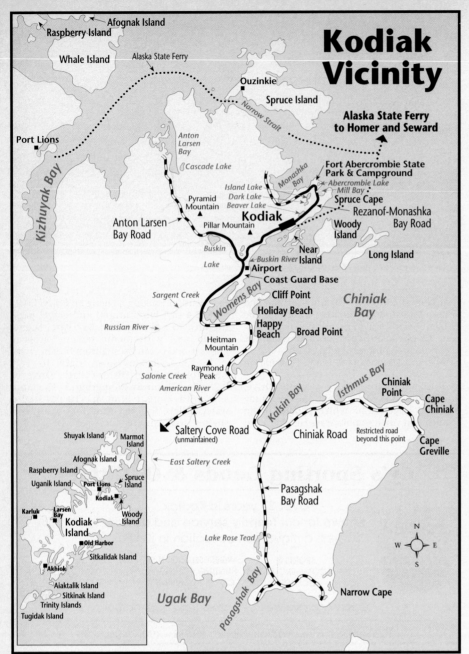

Kodiak Vicinity

Afognak Island
Raspberry Island
Whale Island
Alaska State Ferry
Port Lions
Kizhuyak Bay
Ouzinkie
Spruce Island
Narrow Strait

Alaska State Ferry to Homer and Seward

Anton Larsen Bay
Cascade Lake
Monashka Bay

Fort Abercrombie State Park & Campground
Abercrombie Lake
Mill Bay

Pyramid Mountain
Island Lake
Dark Lake
Beaver Lake

Spruce Cape

Anton Larsen Bay Road
Pillar Mountain
Kodiak

Rezanof-Monashka Bay Road

Buskin Lake
Woody Island

Near Island

Buskin River
Airport
Coast Guard Base

Long Island

Sargent Creek
Cliff Point
Womens Bay
Holiday Beach
Happy Beach

Chiniak Bay

Russian River
Heitman Mountain
Broad Point

Raymond Peak
Salonie Creek
American River

Kalsin Bay
Isthmus Bay
Chiniak Point
Cape Chiniak

Saltery Cove Road (unmaintained)
East Saltery Creek

Chiniak Road
Restricted road beyond this point
Cape Greville

Pasagshak Bay Road
Lake Rose Tead

N
W E
S

Ugak Bay
Pasagshak Bay
Narrow Cape

Shuyak Island
Marmot Island
Afognak Island
Raspberry Island
Uganik Island
Port Lions
Spruce Island
Karluk
Larsen Bay
Kodiak
Woody Island
Kodiak Island
Old Harbor
Sitkalidak Island
Akhiok
Aiaktalik Island
Sitkinak Island
Trinity Islands
Tugidak Island

---

trails. No off-road biking. View of bay and beach, WWII fortifications. Miller Point Bunker open Monday, Friday and Sunday at 2:30 P.M. for public viewing. Saturday evening naturalist programs June 1 to Aug. 30. Just beyond the campground entrance is the Alaska State Parks ranger station, open weekdays 8 A.M. to 5 P.M.; pay phone, public restrooms, park information. ▲

K 4.6 (7.4 km) Monashka Bay Park left at junction with Otmeloi Way. Playground equipment, covered picnic area, barbecue grates.

K 6.3 (10.1 km) Kodiak Island Borough baler/landfill facility. Recycling center.

K 6.4 (10.3 km) Pavement ends. Excellent gravel road.

K 6.8 (10.9 km) Gravel turnout to right.

K 6.9 (11.1 km) Good view of Three Sisters mountains.

K 7.1 (11.4 km) Road on right leads to VFW RV park with camping facilities, scenic views, restaurant and lounge, (907) 486-3195; Kodiak Island Sportsman's Association shooting range, (907) 486-8566. ▲

K 7.6 (12.2 km) Pillar Creek bridge and Pillar Creek Hatchery to left.

K 8.3 (13.3 km) Road to right leads to Pillar Beach. Beautiful black-sand beach at mouth of creek. Scenic picnic area. Dolly Varden fishing. 🐟

K 9.2 (14.8 km) Pullout to right. Scenic overlook and panoramic views of Monashka Bay and Monashka Mountain.

K 10.1 (16.3 km) Gravel pullout and parking to right. Access to North Sister trailhead directly across road.

K 11.2 (18 km) Bridge over Monashka Creek.

K 11.3 (18.2 km) Road ends. Large turnaround parking area. Paths to right lead through narrow band of trees to secluded Monashka Bay beach. Large, sweeping sandy beach. Excellent for picnics. Fishing off beach for Dolly Varden, pink salmon. To north of parking area is trailhead for Termination Point hike, a beautiful 6-mile loop trail along meadows and ocean bluffs, and dense Sitka spruce forest. *NOTE: Leisnoi user-permit required to hike this trail.* 🐟

Chiniak Road Log

Distance from Kodiak's U.S. post office building (K).

K 0 Kodiak U.S. post office building.

K 2.2 (3.5 km) Gibson Cove campground, operated by City Parks & Recreation, with showers and restrooms. Fee $2 per person/night; $3/vehicle; $5/trailer. ▲

K 2.4 (3.9 km) Gravel turnout to left with panoramic view of Kodiak, Chiniak Bay and nearby islands.

K 3.8 (6.1 km) **Boy Scout Lake**, stocked; gravel turnout and parking to left. 🐟

K 4.4 (7.1 km) U.S. Fish and Wildlife Service Visitor Center and Kodiak National Wildlife Refuge headquarters; open weekdays year-round, 8 A.M. to 4:30 P.M., weekends, noon to 4:30 P.M. Exhibits and films on Kodiak wildlife. Road on left to Buskin River state recreation site; 15 RV campsites with a 14-night limit at $10/night, picnic tables and shelter, water, pit toilets, trails, beach access and dump station. Fishing along **Buskin River** and on beach area at river's mouth for red, silver and pink salmon and trout. Wheelchair accessible fishing platform. Parking for fishermen. ♿🐟

K 5 (8 km) Unmarked turnoff on right for Anton Larsen Bay Road (see log this section).

K 5.1 (8.2 km) Kodiak airport.

K 5.5 (8.9 km) *CAUTION: Jet blast area at end of runway. Stop here and wait if you see a jet preparing for takeoff.*

K 5.7 (9.2 km) Gravel turnout and limited parking to access Barometer Mountain. Steep, straight, well-trodden trail to 2,500-foot peak. Beautiful panoramic views. To access trailhead, cross paved road and walk halfway back to jet blast area.

K 6.6 (10.6 km) Entrance to U.S. Coast Guard station.

K 7.2 (11.6 km) Road continues around Womens Bay. The drive out to Chiniak affords excellent views of the extremely rugged coastline of the island.

K 9.3 (15 km) Turnoff to right to state fair and rodeo grounds. Excellent bird watching on tideflats to Salonie Creek.

K 10.1 (16.3 km) **Sargent Creek** bridge. Good fishing for pink salmon in August. 🐟

K 10.3 (16.6 km) Russian River and Bell Flats Road.

K 10.6 (17.1 km) Pavement ends; gravel begins. *NOTE: Be sure you have a spare tire. It is the law in Alaska to drive with headlights on at all times.*

K 10.7 (17.2 km) Grocery and liquor store, diesel and unleaded gas.

K 10.8 (17.4 km) View of Bell Flats.

K 10.9 (17.5 km) Store and gas station (diesel and unleaded), tire repair.

K 12 (19.3 km) Salonie Creek.

K 12.4 (20 km) Kodiak Island Sportsman's Association rifle range turnoff to right.

K 12.6 (20.3 km) Pull off to left; beach access.

K 12.8 (20.6 km) Remnants on beach of WWII submarine dock. Begin climb up Marine Hill.

K 13.6 (21.9 km) Good turnout to left with panoramic view of Mary Island, Womens Bay, Bell Flats, Kodiak. Mountain goats visible with binoculars in spring and fall in mountains behind Bell Flats.

K 14.4 (23.2 km) Pullout and limited parking at **Heitman Lake** trailhead. Beautiful views. Stocked with rainbow trout. 🐟

K 15 (24.1 km) View of Long Island.

K 16.2 (26 km) Turnout to left.

K 16.7 (26.9 km) Road east to Holiday Beach. Closed to public. Permission by USCG required for access.

K 17.1 (27.5 km) USCG communication facility; emergency phone.

K 17.8 (28.6 km) View of Middle Bay.

K 19 (30.6 km) Undeveloped picnic area in grove of trees along beach of Middle Bay; easy access to beach. Watch for livestock.

K 19.6 (31.5 km) Small Creek bridge.

K 20 (32.2 km) Salt Creek bridge. Excellent bird watching on tideflats to left.

K 20.8 (33.5 km) American River bridge. River empties into Middle Bay.

K 20.9 (33.6 km) Unimproved road on right, marginal for 4-wheel-drive vehicles, leads toward Saltery Cove. *NOTE: NOT RECOMMENDED FOR MOST VEHICLES AND DRIVERS. Check in Kodiak for road conditions before driving.*

K 21 (33.8 km) Felton Creek Bridge.

K 23.2 (37.3 km) Pullout to left. Foot access to gravel beach; nice picnic site.

K 24.1 (38.8 km) *CAUTION: Steep switchbacks. Slow to 10 mph.*

K 24.5 (39.4 km) Pullout to right, limited parking. Access to Mayflower Lake. Stocked with landlocked silver salmon. ◄

K 24.6 (39.6 km) Mayflower Beach.

K 25.3 (40.7 km) View of Kalsin Bay.

K 27.1 (43.6 km) Turnout to right.

K 28.2 (45.4 km) Steep, narrow, winding road drops down to head of Kalsin Bay; sheer cliffs on both sides of road.

K 28.9 (46.5 km) Kalsin Bay Inn; food, bar, laundromat, showers, tire repair; open year-round. ▲

K 29.2 (47 km) Deadman Creek Bridge.

K 29.9 (48.1 km) Olds River.

K 30.2 (48.6 km) Kalsin River (creek) bridge. Slow down for cattle guard in road just before bridge.

K 30.6 (49.2 km) Road forks: Turn left for Chiniak, right for Pasagshak Bay. See Pasagshak Bay Road log this section.

K 30.9 (49.7 km) Kalsin Pond on right; excellent silver salmon fishing in fall. ◄

K 31.1 (50 km) Turnoff to left; access to mouth of Olds River and beach.

K 31.5 (50.7 km) Highway maintenance station.

K 32 (51.5 km) Picnic area beside Kalsin Bay.

K 33.2 (53.4 km) Turnoff Myrtle Creek, picnic site.

K 34.9 (56.2 km) Thumbs Up Cove. Unimproved boat launch ramp.

K 35.1 (56.5 km) Chiniak post office. Window hours Tuesday and Thursday 4 to 6 P.M., Saturday noon to 2 P.M.

K 35.9 (57.8 km) Brookers Lagoon. Access to gravel beach.

K 36.9 (59.4 km) Roslyn River. Access to Roslyn Bay beach, a beautiful area with picnic tables.

K 37.6 (60.5 km) Access to mouth of Roslyn River.

K 39.6 (63.7 km) Access to a beautiful point overlooking the sea; site of WWII installations. Good place for photos.

K 39.9 (64.2 km) Twin Creeks Beach, beautiful dark-sand and rolling breakers. Park in pullout area. Do not drive onto soft beach sand.

K 40.4 (65 km) Twin Creek.

K 40.7 (65.5 km) Silver Beach.

K 40.8 (65.7 km) **Pony Lake** (stocked). ◄

K 41.3 (66.4 km) Chiniak wayside, a borough park; benches, beautiful setting.

K 41.5 (66.8 km) Chiniak school, public

library, playground and ballfield. Baseball diamond, play area, picnic tables.

K 41.7 (67.1 km) Turnoff to right onto King Crab Way. Location of Tsunami Evacuation Center.

K 42.4 (68.2 km) Road's End lounge and restaurant. Excellent whalewatching for gray whales in April, across road from restaurant.

K 42.5 (68.4 km) Chiniak Point, also known as Cape Chiniak, is the south point of land at the entrance to Chiniak Bay. Capt. Cook named the point Cape Greville in 1778, but the name is now applied to that point of land 2 miles southeast of here. State-maintained road ends. Unmaintained road continues as public easement across Leisnoi Native Corp. land. Public access discouraged beyond Chiniak Creek.

K 42.8 (68.9 km) Public road ends at **Chiniak Creek.** Pink salmon fishing in midsummer. View of Chiniak Point. Turnaround point. ◄

Pasagshak Bay Road Log

Distance is measured from junction with Chiniak Road (J).

J 0 Turn right at **Milepost K 30.6** Chiniak Road for Pasagshak Bay. Road leads up the valley of Kalsin Creek past a private ranch.

J 0.1 (0.2 km) Northland Ranch Resort; lodging, food, lounge.

J 1.2 (1.9 km) Pull off to right to access Kalsin River, good picnic area.

J 4.5 (7.2 km) Top of Pasagshak Pass; scenic views.

J 6.8 (10.9 km) Road crosses Lake Rose Tead on causeway. Good fishing in river from here to ocean. Good place to view spawning salmon and eagles late summer through fall. ◄

J 7.1 (11.4 km) Combined barn and single aircraft hangar to right. Remnant of Joe Zentner Ranch, established in the 1940s.

J 8.4 (13.5 km) Derelict wooden bridge once connected old road to Portage Bay, now an easy hiking trail. Trailhead begins across the river.

J 8.9 (17.5 km) Pasagshak River State Recreation Site: 7 campsites with a 14-night limit (no fee), toilets, water, picnic sites, fishing and beach access. ◄▲

J 9.3 (15 km) Mouth of Pasagshak River, view of Pasagshak Bay.

J 9.6 (15.4 km) Turnout at Boat Bay, traditional gravel boat launch ramp and mooring area. Four-wheel drive vehicles required to use launch ramp.

J 10.3 (16.6 km) Turnoff to right takes you to Pasagshak Point, 2 trout lakes, nice vistas.

J 11.1 (17.9 km) Entrance to Kodiak Cattle Co. grazing lease. Public land—hunting, fishing, hiking, but keep vehicle on road. ◄

J 11.4 (18.3 km) Turnout to right provides panoramas of Narrow Cape, Ugak Island, Pasagshak Point, Sitkalidik Island. Good beachcombing on sandy beaches.

J 12.3 (19.8 km) Beach access to the right. *CAUTION: Do not approach free-ranging buffalo on foot. They can be dangerous.*

J 14.6 (23.5 km) Entrance to Kodiak Cattle Co. Ranch; guided horseback riding,

fishing, camping, hunting. ◄▲

J 14.9 (24 km) Entrance at right to USCG Narrow Cape Loran Station. No public access. *NOTE: Minimal road maintenance from here to end of road. Drive with caution and have a good spare tire.*

J 16.2 (26.1 km) **Twin Lakes** to the left and right of road. Trout in lake to the left. ◄

J 16.5 (26.6 km) Road ends at Fossil Cliffs. Fossils imbedded in cliffs are visible along Fossil Beach to left and right. *CAUTION: Cliffs are extremely unstable. Do not approach cliff face, and watch for falling rocks at all times.* Beautiful vistas and views of WWII observation bunkers on Narrow Cape to the left.

Anton Larsen Bay Road Log

Distance is measured from the turnoff (T) at Milepost K 5 Chiniak Road.

T 0 Unmarked turnoff for Anton Larsen Bay Road at **Milepost K 5** on Chiniak Road immediately before crossing the Buskin River bridge.

T 0.6 (1 km) **Buskin River** bridge No. 6. Parking area to left accessing fishing along river. Road to the right leads to good fishing holes. ◄

T 0.7 (1.1 km) Pavement ends.

T 0.9 (1.4 km) Enter posted restricted-access area in USCG antenna field. Do not leave road for approximately next 1.5 miles.

T 1.5 (2.4 km) **Buskin River** bridge No. 7. Turnoff to left before crossing bridge accesses river and outlet of Buskin Lake. Good fishing for Dolly Varden, salmon. ◄

T 1.6 (2.6 km) Immediately after crossing bridge, paved road to right leads to USCG communications site. Turn on gravel road to left to Anton Larsen Bay. Beautiful drive, berry picking, mountain views, wildflowers, boat launch ramp. Excellent kayaking in bay and around outer islands.

T 2 (3.2 km) High hill on right is Pyramid Mountain (elev. 2,420 feet/738m).

T 2.4 (3.9 km) End restricted access area.

T 2.9 (4.7 km) Bear Valley Golf Course. Driving range, parking on left. Nine-hole course operated by USCG. Open to the public April to October, weather permitting. Phone (907) 486-7561 or 486-4782.

T 3.2 (5.1 km) Turnout to left to unimproved trailhead of Buskin Lake. Watch for bears.

T 4.2 (6.8 km) Steep switchback.

T 5.8 (9.3 km) Buskin Valley Winter Recreation Area. Phone (907) 487-5274 or 486-4782. To right is large parking area and trailhead to top of 2,400-foot Pyramid Mountain. Trail follows ridgeline. Great vistas from top.

T 7.3 (11.7 km) Red Cloud River bridge. Small, unimproved campsite is adjacent to river on right.

T 9 (14.5 km) **Cascade Lake** trail to right. Approximately 5 miles round-trip. Rubber boots recommended to cross tidal areas. Watch for bears. Lake is stocked. ◄

T 9.3 (15 km) Head of Anton Larsen Bay. Fox, land otters and deer can be seen in this area. Good bird watching along tidal flats.

T 10.1 (16.3 km) Public small-boat launch adjacent to road. Road continues on left side of bay for about 1.5 miles/2.4 km.

T 11.8 (19 km) Road ends. A foot-path continues beyond this point. Parking area to right.

PRINCE WILLIAM SOUND

(See map, page 624)

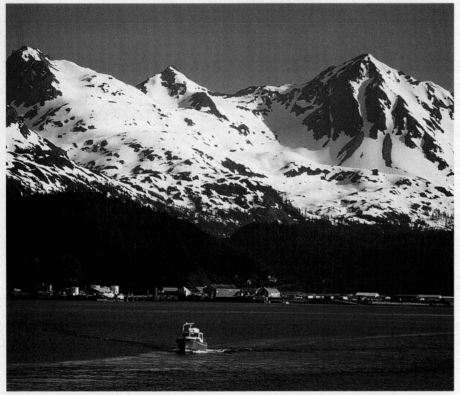

Approaching Cordova, located on the east side of Prince William Sound, by ferry.
(Jerrianne Lowther, staff)

Southcentral Alaska's Prince William Sound lies at the north extent of the Gulf of Alaska. It is just as spectacular as southeastern Alaska's Inside Passage. The area is also rich in wildlife. Visitors may see Dall sheep, mountain goats, sea lions, sea otters, whales, harbor seals, bald eagles and other birds. The waters carry all species of Pacific salmon; king, Dungeness and tanner crab; halibut; and rockfish.

This section includes: Columbia Glacier; Whittier; Valdez, start of the Richardson Highway; and Cordova, start of the Copper River Highway.

There are several ways to explore Prince William Sound. From Anchorage, drive south on the Seward Highway 47 miles/75.6 km to Portage and board the Alaska Railroad shuttle train for a 35-minute ride to Whittier (presently there is no road connection to Whittier); see the ALASKA RAILROAD section on page 462. You may also start your trip across Prince William Sound from Valdez. Drive 304 miles/498.2 km from Anchorage to Valdez via the Glenn and Richardson highways (see GLENN HIGHWAY and RICHARDSON HIGHWAY sections).

From Whittier or Valdez, board the ferry or one of the privately operated excursion boats to tour Prince William Sound. Flightseeing trips are also available. Depending on your itinerary and type of transportation, you may see the glacier and return to Anchorage in a day or have to stay overnight along the way. All-inclusive tours of Prince William Sound are available out of Anchorage.

Plan your trip in advance. Reservations for the ferry or cruise boats are necessary. The Alaska Railroad does not take reservations, although passengers with confirmed ferry reservations are given first priority when loading.

Columbia Glacier

Star attraction of Prince William Sound is Columbia Glacier, one of the largest and most magnificent of the tidewater glaciers along the Alaska coast. The Columbia Glacier has an area of about 440 square miles/1144 square km. The glacier is more than 40 miles/64 km long; its tidewater terminus, which visitors to Prince William Sound will see, is about 3 miles/4.8 km across. Columbia Glacier has receded more than 5 miles/8 km since the early 1980s, and is expected to leave behind a 26-mile/42-km-long fiord. A bay has formed between its face and terminal moraine (where it rested prior to retreat). This bay has been filled with ice during the retreat, keeping boats away from the glacier's face. In late 1995, the icebergs had cleared enough so that boats were able to approach and visitors could watch ice calving from the face. However, the bay again filled with ice in early 1996, blocking access to the glacier's face.

The face of the glacier varies in height above sea level from 25 to 200 feet/8 to 61m, and reaches 1,000 feet/305m or more below sea level. An abundance of plankton thrives here attracting great numbers of fish which attract bald eagles, kittiwakes, gulls and harbor seals. Seals can usually be seen resting on ice floes or swimming in the icy waters.

The glacier was named by the Harriman Alaska expedition in 1899 for Columbia University in New York City. The glacier's source is Mount Einstein (elev. 11,552 feet/3,521m) in the Chugach Mountains.

There are daily and weekly charters by yacht or sailboat and flightseeing trips over the glacier. (See the ads in Whittier, Valdez and Cordova in this section for charter boats offering sightseeing trips and flying services offering flightseeing trips.) See the MARINE ACCESS ROUTES section for ferry schedule.

Whittier

Located at the head of Passage Canal on Prince William Sound, 75 miles/121 km southeast of Anchorage. **Population:** 290. **Emergency Services: Police, Fire** and **Medical,** phone (907) 472-2340. **Visitor Information:** Information kiosk at the Harbor Triangle.

Elevation: 30 feet/9m. **Climate:** Normal daily temperature for July is 56°F/13°C; for January, 25°F/-4°C. Maximum temperature is 84°F/29°C and minimum is -29°F/-2°C. Mean annual precipitation is 174 inches, including 260 inches of snow. Winter winds can reach 60 mph.

Private Aircraft: Airstrip adjacent northwest; elev. 30 feet/9m; length 1,100 feet/335m; gravel; no fuel; unattended.

Named after the poet John Greenleaf Whittier, the community of Whittier is nestled at the base of mountains that line Passage Canal, a fjord that extends eastward into Prince William Sound. Whittier is connected to the Seward Highway by railroad and to other Prince William Sound communities by ferry and charter air service. No roads lead to Whittier, although a plan for an access road extending the existing Portage Glacier Road to connect with Whittier via the railroad tunnel is under consideration.

Whittier was created by the U.S. Army during WWII as a port and petroleum delivery center tied to bases farther north by the Alaska Railroad and later a pipeline. The railroad spur from Portage was completed in 1943, and Whittier became the primary debarkation point for cargo, troops and dependents of the Alaska Command. Construction of the huge buildings that dominate Whittier began in 1948 and the Port of Whittier, strategically valuable for its ice-free deep-water port, remained activated until 1960, at which time the population was

Alaska state ferry Bartlett *unloads at Whittier.* (© Rich Reid)

1,200. The city of Whittier was incorporated in 1969. The government tank farm is still located here.

The 14-story Begich Towers, formerly the Hodge Building, houses more than half of Whittier's population. Now a condominium, the building was used by the U.S. Army for family housing and civilian bachelor quarters. The building was renamed in honor of U.S. Rep. Nick Begich of Alaska, who, along with Rep. Hale Boggs of Louisiana, disappeared in a small plane near here in 1972

WHITTIER ADVERTISERS

while on a campaign tour.

The Buckner Building, completed in 1953, was once the largest building in Alaska and was called the "city under one roof." It is now privately owned and is to be renovated.

Whittier Manor was built in the early 1950s by private developers as rental units for civilian employees and soldiers who were ineligible for family housing elsewhere. In early 1964, the building was bought by another group of developers and became a condominium, which now houses the remainder of Whittier's population.

Since military and government activities ceased, the economy of Whittier rests largely on the fishing industry, the port and increasingly on tourism.

Annual events in Whittier include a Fourth of July parade, barbecue and fireworks; a Fish Derby, held Memorial Day weekend to Labor Day weekend; and Regatta, at the end of April or beginning of May, when residents boat to Valdez for Game Night and then bus or fly back to Whittier.

Whittier has 2 inns providing accommodations, a bed and breakfast, several restaurants, 2 bars, gift shops, laundry facilities, 2 general stores, video rental, gas station, post office, library and a school (preschool through grade 12), and a camper park for tents and self-contained RVs ($5 nightly fee). Fishing licenses may be purchased locally. There is no bank in Whittier. ▲

Whittier also has a harbor office, marine services and repairs, marine supply store, boat launch and lift, freight services, dry storage and self-storage units.

Alaska Trail and Sail Adventures. Morning, afternoon and full-day guided sailing and sea kayaking. Get up close with otters, eagles, glaciers, salmon and kittiwakes. All necessary gear and instruction is provided. Paddling is easy and fun! Beginners welcome. Kayak rentals for experienced paddlers. Group discounts are available. Phone/fax (907) 346-1234. [ADVERTISEMENT]

Valdez

Located on Port Valdez (pronounced val-DEEZ), an estuary off Valdez Arm in Prince William Sound. Valdez is 115 air miles/ 185 km and 304 highway miles/489 km from Anchorage, 368 highway miles/592 km from Fairbanks. Valdez is the southern terminus of the Richardson Highway and the trans-Alaska pipeline. **Population:** 4,068.

Emergency Services: Alaska State Troopers, phone (907) 835-4359 or 835-4350. **City Police**, **Fire Department** and **Ambulance**, emergency only phone 911. **Hospital**, Valdez Community, phone (907) 835-2249. **Maritime Search and Rescue**, dial 0 for Zenith 5555, toll free. Report oil spills to Dept. of Environmental Conservation, dial 0 and ask for Zenith 9300.

Visitor Information: The visitor information center, located opposite city hall at 200 Chenega St., is open 7 days a week from 8 A.M. to 8 P.M. The visitor center offers a self-guided tour map of historic homes moved from old Valdez. Write: Valdez Convention and Visitors Bureau, Box 1603-MP, Valdez 99686; or phone (907) 835-2984, fax 835-4845. Visitors may also check the community calendar at the Valdez Civic Center by phoning the hotline at (907) 835-3200.

Elevation: Sea level. **Climate:** Record high was 81°F/27°C in August 1977; record low -20°F/-29°C in January 1972. Normal daily maximum in January, 30°F/-1°C; daily minimum 21°F/-6°C. Normal daily maxi-

Trans-Alaska oil pipeline terminal at Valdez. (© Chris Sharp)

mum in July, 61°F/16°C; daily minimum 46°F/8°C. Average snowfall in Valdez from October to May is 303 inches, or about 25 feet. (By comparison, Anchorage averages about 6 feet in that period.) New snowfall records were set in January 1990, with snowfall for one day at 47¹/₂ inches. Record monthly snowfall is 180 inches in February 1996. Windy (40 mph/64 kmph) in late fall. **Radio:** KCHU 770, KVAK 1230. **Television:** Many channels via cable and satellite. **Newspapers:** *Valdez Vanguard* (weekly) and *Valdez Star* (weekly).

Private Aircraft: Valdez, 3 miles/4.8 km east; elev. 120 feet/37m; length 6,500feet/ 1,981m; asphalt; fuel 100LL, Jet B; attended.

Flanked by the Alp-like Chugach Mountains, Valdez is often called Alaska's "Little Switzerland." The city lies on the north shore of Port Valdez, an estuary named in

1790 by Spanish explorer Don Salvador Fidalgo for Antonio Valdes y Basan, a Spanish naval officer.

Valdez was established in 1897–98 as a port of entry for gold seekers bound for the Klondike goldfields. Thousands of stampeders arrived in Valdez to follow the Valdez trail to the Eagle mining district in Alaska's Interior, and from there up the Yukon River to Dawson City and the Klondike. The Valdez trail was an especially deadly route, the first part of it leading over Valdez Glacier, where the early stampeders faced dangerous crevasses, snowblindness and exhaustion.

Copper discoveries in the Wrangell Mountains north of Valdez in the early 1900s brought more development to Valdez, and conflict. A proposed railroad from tidewater to the rich Kennicott copper mines at McCarthy began a bitter rivalry between Valdez and Cordova for the railway line. The Copper River & Northwestern Railway eventually went to Cordova, but not before Valdez had started its own railroad north. The Valdez railroad did not get very far: The only trace of its existence is an old hand-drilled railway tunnel at **Milepost V 14.9** on the Richardson Highway.

The old gold rush trail out of Valdez was developed into a sled and wagon road in the early 1900s. It was routed through Thompson Pass (rather than over the Valdez Glacier) by Captain Abercrombie of the U.S. Army, who was commissioned to connect Fort Liscum (a military post established in 1900 near the present-day location of the pipeline terminal) with Fort Egbert in Eagle. Colonel Wilds P. Richardson of the Alaska

Aerial view of Valdez and harbor area. (© Gene & Judy Wright, Diamond Photo)

Valdez

VALDEZ ADVERTISERS

Road Commission further developed the wagon road, building an automobile road from Valdez to Fairbanks which was completed in the early 1920s.

Old photos of Valdez show Valdez Glacier directly behind the town. This is because until 1964 Valdez was located about 4 miles east of its present location, closer to the glacier. The 1964 Good Friday earthquake, the most destructive earthquake ever to hit southcentral Alaska, virtually destroyed Valdez. The quake measured between 8.4 and 8.6 on the Richter scale (since revised to 9.2) and was centered in Prince William Sound. A series of local waves caused by massive underwater landslides swept over Valdez wharf and engulfed the downtown area. Afterward, it was decided that Valdez would be rebuilt at a new townsite. By late August 1964, reconstruction projects had been approved for Valdez and relocation was under way. The last residents remaining at "old" Valdez moved to the new town in 1968.

Since its days as a port of entry for gold seekers, Valdez has been an important gateway to Interior Alaska. As the most northerly ice-free port in the Western Hemisphere, and connected by the Richardson Highway to the Alaska highway system, Valdez has

evolved into a shipping center, offering the shortest link to much of interior Alaska for seaborne cargo.

Construction of the trans-Alaska pipeline was begun in 1974 and completed in 1977 (the first tanker load of oil shipped out of Valdez on Aug. 1, 1977). The 1,000-acre site at Port Valdez was chosen as the pipeline terminus; tours of the marine terminal are available (see Attractions).

From Prudhoe Bay on the Arctic Ocean, the 48-inch-diameter, 800-mile-/1287-km-long pipeline follows the Sagavanirktok River and Atigun Valley, crossing the Brooks Mountain Range at 4,739-foot/1,444m Atigun Pass. South of the Brooks Range it passes through Dietrich and Koyukuk valleys and crosses the hills and muskeg of the Yukon–Tanana uplands to the Yukon River. South of the Yukon the line passes through more rolling hills 10 miles/16 km east of

Fairbanks, then goes south from Delta Junction to the Alaska Range, where it reaches an elevation of 3,420 feet/1,042m at Isabel Pass before descending into the Copper River basin. It crests the Chugach Mountains at Thompson Pass (elev. 2,812 feet/857m) and descends through the Keystone Canyon to Valdez, where it is fed by gravity into tanks or directly into waiting oil tankers at the marine terminal.

Because of varying soil conditions along its route, the pipeline is both above and below ground. Where the warm oil would

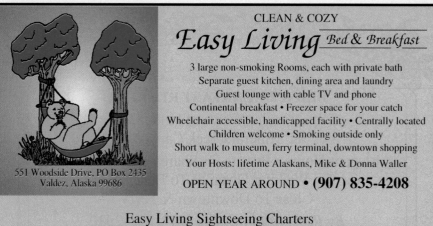

cause icy soil to thaw and erode, the pipeline goes above ground to avoid thawing. Where the frozen ground is mostly well-drained gravel or solid rock, and thawing is not a problem, the line is underground.

The line was designed with 11 pump stations (although Pump Station 11 was never built) and numerous large valves to control the flow of oil. The entire system can operate on central computer control from Valdez or independent local control at each pump station.

National attention was focused on Valdez and the pipeline when the oil tanker *Exxon Valdez* ran aground in March 1989, causing an 11-million-gallon oil spill.

Valdez's economy depends on the oil industry, the Prince William Sound fishery and tourism. The city limits of Valdez comprise an area of 274 square miles, and include all surrounding mountains to timberline. Valdez has long been known for its beautiful setting, with the Chugach Mountains rising behind the city, and the small-boat harbor in front. The town has wide streets and open spaces, with the central residential district built around a park strip which runs from the business district almost to the base of the mountains behind town.

ACCOMMODATIONS/VISITOR SERVICES

Services in Valdez include several restaurants and bars, grocery stores, sporting goods stores, gift shops, 4 service stations, hardware, hair stylists, 1 drugstore, 2 pharmacies and numerous churches.

Valdez has 7 motel/hotel facilities and numerous bed and breakfasts. You are advised to make reservations well in advance. Summer tourist season is also the peak work season, and accommodations fill up quickly. Expect to pay $100 and up for a double motel room with bath, $65 to $85 for a bed and breakfast.

Casa de LaBellezza Bed & Breakfast in Valdez. Elegant, first-class, nonsmoking, accommodations located within the city; straight up the street from the ferry dock. Friendly, comfortable, quiet, peaceful, immaculate rooms. Queen beds. (Twin, family only.) Private or shared bath. Beautiful, private backyard and deck. Gourmet breakfast at your convenience. Homemade pastries and pizzelles. We aspire to make your stay in Valdez a memorable one. Phone (907) 835-4489. Fax (907) 835-5450. See display ad this section. [ADVERTISEMENT]

Downtown B & B Inn. Motel accommodations, 113 Galena Dr. Centrally located near small boat harbor, museum, ferry terminal, downtown shopping. View rooms, private and shared baths, coin-op laundry, TV and phones in rooms. Wheelchair accessible. Complimentary breakfast. Reasonable rates. Single, double, family rooms. (800) 478-2791 or (907) 835-2791. See display ad this section. [ADVERTISEMENT] ♿

Keystone Hotel. Located downtown (corner of Egan and Hazelet) within walking

distance to ferry terminal, shops and restaurants. 107 rooms with private baths, cable TV, phones, nonsmoking or smoking, handicap access, coin-op laundry facilities. Continental breakfast included with room. Comfortable, clean rooms at reasonable rates. (907) 835-3851. See display ad this section. [ADVERTISEMENT] ♿

The Lake House Bed & Breakfast. Comfortable and quiet, this very large home is located only 10 minutes from Valdez's city center. Excellent bird and wildlife viewing and dramatic alpine scenery. Spacious rooms, most with private bath. Continental breakfast. Brochure available. P.O. Box 1499, Valdez, AK 99686; phone (907) 835-4752.

Mile 6 Richardson Highway. [ADVERTISEMENT]

One Call Does It All. Free reservation service for Valdez, Kennicott, Cordova and the Greater Copper Valley. Lodging, glacier cruises, extended cruises, fishing charters.

Flightseeing, rafting, kayaking, car and RV rentals. VISA, MasterCard accepted. For the spectacular Prince William Sound, One Call Does It All! (907) 835-4988. See display ad this section. [ADVERTISEMENT]

Totem Inn, completely remodeled restaurant and lounge featuring an Old Town look with a New Town taste. Diners are surrounded by famous works of Alaska art. Restaurant opens at 5 A.M., serving breakfast, lunch and dinner. The lounge offers tall tales and a wide variety of libations. The motel provides deluxe rooms with private baths, satellite TV, phones, handicap access. Ask for rooms or suites in our brand new annex. Motel reservations suggested. Ample parking available. Open year-round. Phone (907) 835-4443, fax (907) 835-5751. See display ad this section. [ADVERTISEMENT]

Valdez Village Inn, downtown Valdez: 100 modern rooms. Cable TV, private baths. Wheelchair access. Fitness center, sauna, Jacuzzi, beauty shop, espresso bar. Casa Valdez Restaurant & Sugarloaf Saloon. Room/Glacier Cruise packages. Phone (907) 835-4445, fax (907) 835-2437. See display ad this section. [ADVERTISEMENT]

There are 5 private RV parks with hookups near the small-boat harbor. Dump station and diesel at Valdez Tesoro. Dump

station at Bear Paw R.V. Park for registered guests.

The nearest public campground is Valdez Glacier campground, at the end of the airport road, about 6 miles/9.7 km from town; turn left on Airport Road at **Milepost NV 3.4** Richardson Highway. This city-owned and privately-operated campground has 101 sites, tent-camping areas, picnic areas, firepits, tables, litter barrels, water and toilets; 15-day limit, $10 fee charged. ▲

Bear Paw R.V. Park, centrally located on scenic North Harbor Drive overlooking the boat harbor, puts you within easy walking distance of museums, shops, restaurants, entertainment, charter boats—no need to unhook and drive to grocery stores or points

of interest. Full, partial or no hookups; immaculate private restrooms with hot, unmetered showers. Dump station and coin-operated launderette with irons and ironing boards available for guests. Also available, for adults only: waterfront full-hookup RV sites and very nice, quiet, wooded tent sites, some platforms, among the salmonberries on Porcupine Hill. Tables, fire pots and freezer available. Campfire wood for sale. Full discount coupons available. Don't miss the Bear Paw Trading Post Gift Shop. Let us book your glacier tour with Stan Stephens Cruises at the reservations desk in our spacious office lounge. We also book raft trips, flightseeing and pipeline terminal tours. Advance reservations recommended: (907) 835-2530. (Bear Paw does fill up!) The coffee pot is always on at Bear Paw. Let us know if you're coming in on the evening ferry and we'll be there to help you get parked. See our large display ad this section. [ADVERTISEMENT] ▲

Eagle's Rest RV Park, the newest RV park in downtown Valdez, offers you Good Sam Park service with a smile. Let Herb, Jeff or Laura take care of all your bookings on

cruises, tours and charters. Enjoy the beautiful panoramic view of our mountains and glaciers right off our front porch! We also can let you know where the hottest fishing spots are or the quietest walking trails! Fish-cleaning table and freezer available. Capt'n Joe's Tesoro next door offers gas,

diesel, propane; free sewer dump with fill-up. Parking with us puts you within walking distance of our museum, gift shops, banks and even the largest grocery store on our same block. Shuttle service for glacier cruises. No charge to wash your RV at your site. Call us for reservations, 1-800-553-7275 or (907) 835-2373. Fax (907)

835-KAMP (835-5267). Stay with us and leave feeling like family. See display ad this section. [ADVERTISEMENT] ▲

TRANSPORTATION

Air: Daily scheduled service via Alaska Airlines and Era Aviation. Air taxi and helicopter services available.

Ferry: Scheduled state ferry service to Cordova, Whittier and Seward. Phone (907) 835-4436. Reservations are a must! See MARINE ACCESS ROUTES section.

Bus: Regularly scheduled service to Anchorage and Fairbanks.

Taxi: One local taxi service.

Car Rental: Two companies offer car rentals; available at airport terminal.

Highway: The Richardson Highway extends north from Valdez to the Glenn Highway and the Alaska Highway. See the RICHARDSON HIGHWAY section.

ATTRACTIONS

Celebrate Gold Rush Days. Held Aug. 6–10, 1997, this celebration includes a parade, contests and a game night. During the celebration cancan girls meet the cruise ships and a jail is pulled through town by "deputies" who arrest citizens without beards and other suspects.

Visit Valdez Museum, located at 217 Egan Dr. Exhibits depict lifestyles and workplaces from 1898 to present. Displays include a beautifully restored 1907 Ahrens steam fire engine, the original Cape Hinchinbrook lighthouse lens, a Civil War-era field cannon and an illuminated model of the Alyeska Marine Terminal. Interpretive exhibits explain the impact of the 1964 earthquake, the construction of the trans-Alaska oil pipeline and the 1989 *Exxon Valdez* oil spill cleanup. Visitors can touch Columbia Glacier ice, play slot machines (for entertainment only!), sing along with the jukebox in the Pinzon Bar exhibit, and feel the luxurious softness of a sea otter pelt. The museum's William A. Egan Commons provides a showcase setting for the Ahrens steam fire engine, models of antique aircraft and the lighthouse lens. Outside exhibits include displays of local wildflowers, an oil pipeline "pig" and a unique snow tractor. Valdez Museum is open year-round: daily during summer months (May to September);

Tuesday through Saturday during off-season (October to April). Children free; $2 for adults (18 and older). Call (907) 835-2764 for more information.

Tour the oil pipeline terminus. The marine terminal of the Alyeska pipeline is across the bay from the city of Valdez. Bus tours of the pipeline terminal are available daily, from May to September, from Valdez Tours Co.; fee charged, reservations suggested, cameras welcome. Phone (907) 835-2686 for details.

While entry to the terminal is restricted to authorized bus tours only, the drive out to the terminal is worthwhile. From Meals Avenue drive 6.8 miles/10.9 km out the Richardson Highway and turn right on the terminal access road (Dayville exit). The 5.4-mile/8.7-km road leading to the terminal

passes Solomon Gulch dam and a spectacular view of Solomon Gulch Falls. There is also excellent fishing in season at Allison Point for pink and silver salmon. Entrance to the pipeline terminal is at the end of the road.

Outside the marine terminal gate is a bronze sculpture commemorating the efforts of men and women who built the trans-Alaska oil pipeline. Dedicated in September 1980, the sculpture was created by Californian Malcolm Alexander. It is composed of 5 figures representing various crafts and skills employed in the construction project. The work is the focal point of a small park from which visitors can watch tankers loading Alaska crude oil at the terminal. A small parking lot accommodates about 30 cars, and a series of signs explains the pipeline

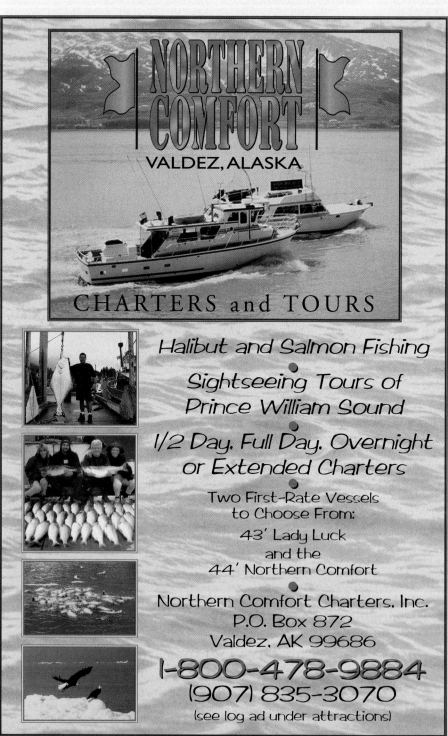

and terminal operations.

Take a boat tour to see Columbia Glacier, Shoup Glacier and other Prince William Sound attractions. Columbia Glacier, a tidewater glacier in Columbia Bay 28 miles/45 km southwest of Valdez, has become one of Alaska's best-known attractions. See ads in this section.

Raft and kayak trips of Prince William Sound, Keystone Canyon and surrounding rivers are available.

Go flightseeing and see Columbia Glacier, spectacular Prince William Sound and the surrounding Chugach Mountains from the air. There are several air charter services and 2 helicopter services in Valdez; see ads in this section.

Our Point of View, an observation platform offering views of the original Valdez townsite, pipeline terminal and the town, is located by the Coast Guard office.

Valdez Consortium Library, located on Fairbanks Street, has a magazine and paperback exchange for travelers. A trade is appreciated but not required. The library also has music listening booths, public computers, typewriters and a photocopier. Wheelchair accessible. Open Monday and Friday 10 A.M. to 6 P.M., Tuesday through Thursday, 10 A.M. to 8 P.M., and Saturday, noon to 6 P.M.

Visit Prince William Sound Community College, located at 303 Lowe St. Two huge wooden carvings on campus (1 located in the dorms on Pioneer Street), by artist Peter Toth, are dedicated to the Indians of America. Four Elderhostel programs are held at Prince William Sound Community College in June and July. This educational program (college credit given) is available for people over age 55. Subjects include Alaska history, wildlife and fisheries of Prince William Sound, and Alaska literature. Contact Elderhostel, 80 Boylston St., Suite 400, Boston, MA 02116, for more information on its Alaska programs. The fifth annual Edward Albee Theatre Conference sponsored

by the college will be held Aug. 11–17, 1997, at the Valdez Convention and Civic Center. Past visiting playwrights at the conference have included Edward Albee and Arthur Miller. For more information contact PWSCC, P.O. Box 97, Valdez, AK 99686.

View salmon spawning at Crooked Creek. From Meals Avenue drive 0.9 mile/ 1.4 km out the Richardson Highway to the Crooked Creek salmon spawning area and hatchery. A U.S. Forest Service information station, open Memorial Day to Labor Day, has interpretive displays, and information on cultural history and recreation. An observation platform gives a close-up look at salmon spawning in midsummer and fall. This is also a waterfowl sanctuary and an excellent spot for watching various migrating birds.

Fish a Derby. The Valdez Chamber of Commerce holds a halibut, silver salmon and pink salmon derby every year, with cash prizes awarded to the first through third place winners for all 3 derbies. For further information contact the Valdez Chamber of Commerce at (907) 835-2330.

Drive Mineral Creek Road. A 5.5-mile/ 8.9-km drive behind town leading northwest through the breathtaking alpine scenery along Mineral Creek. *Drive carefully!* This is a narrow road; conditions depend on weather and how recently the road has been graded. Bears are frequently sighted here. To reach Mineral Creek Road drive to the end of Hazelet Street toward the mountains and turn left on Hanagita then right on Mineral Creek Road. Excellent view of the city from the water tower hill just to the right at the start of Mineral Creek Road.

Valdez Arm supports the largest sport fishery in Prince William Sound. Important species include pink salmon, coho (silver) salmon, halibut, rockfish and Dolly Varden. Charter boats are available in Valdez. A hot fishing spot near Valdez accessible by road is the **Allison Point** fishery (or "Winnebago Point" as it is known locally) created by the Solomon Gulch Hatchery, which produces major pink and silver salmon returns annually. Turn off the Richardson Highway at **Milepost V 2.9**. It is one of the largest pink salmon fisheries in the state. Pink salmon returns are best in odd years, but with hatchery production good pink runs are anticipated every year. Pinks average 3 to 5 lbs., from late June to early August. Silvers from 6 to 10 lbs., late July into September. ◄

Anadyr Adventures offers 3-hour to 10-day guided sea kayaking eco-tours throughout Prince William Sound. Paddle amongst icebergs. See whales, otters, seals, birds. Hike, fish, beachcomb. Lodge, cabin,

motor vessel-support. Kayak rentals. No experience necessary. Children welcome. 203 N Harbor Drive, Box 1821, Valdez, AK 99686. Phone/fax (907) 835-2814 or 1-800-TO-KAYAK. Internet address: http://www.alaska.net/~anadyr/anadyr.index.html. E-mail: anadyr@alaska.net. [ADVERTISEMENT]

Bear Paw Trading Post Gift Shop, next to Bear Paw RV Park on Harbor Drive, features fine Alaska Native arts and crafts. Carved walrus ivory, scrimshaw, soapstone carvings, Native masks, fur items. Gold nugget jewelry, jade, hematite. Prints and books by Doug Lindstrand. Film, postcards, souvenirs, Alaska books. VISA, MasterCard accepted. Phone (907) 835-2530. [ADVERTISEMENT]

Era Helicopters. Fly over Valdez and the Prince William Sound with Alaska's most experienced helicopter company. Soar over the breathtaking Columbia Glacier. Land at the face of Shoup Glacier or feast on Alaskan

seafood at a rustic island camp. Phone (800) 843-1947 or (907) 835-2595 locally. Tours also available in Anchorage, Juneau and Mount McKinley. [ADVERTISEMENT]

Ketchum Air Service, Inc. Alaska's outdoor specialists. Floatplane tours/charters into Prince William Sound, Wrangell–St. Elias park. Day fishing/fully equipped. Columbia Glacier tour. Drop-off cabins. Kennecott Mine visit! Floatplane tour office located small-boat harbor Valdez. Call or write for brochure. VISA, MasterCard. Phone (907) 835-3789 or (800) 433-9114. Box 670, Valdez, AK 99686. [ADVERTISEMENT]

Lu-Lu Belle. The motor yacht *Lu-Lu Belle* is probably the cleanest, plushest tour vessel you will ever see! We cater to adult travelers. When you come aboard and see all the teak,

mahogany and oriental rugs, you will understand why Captain Rodolf asks you to wipe your feet before boarding. The *Lu-Lu Belle* has wide walk-around decks thus assuring

Tour boats get close to kittiwake colonies like this one. (© Ruth Fairall)

everyone ample opportunity for unobstructed viewing and photography, and is equipped with 110-volt outlets for battery chargers. Captain Fred Rodolf has logged over 2,600 Columbia Glacier cruises since 1979 and he will personally guide and narrate every cruise. The Columbia Glacier wildlife cruise of Prince William Sound is awesome. Puffins, Steller sea lions, sea otters, seals and bald eagles are seen on every cruise. Dall porpoise, orca, humpbackand minke whales, black bear, Sitka black-tail deer, Dall sheep and mountain goats are often seen as the *Lu-Lu Belle* cruises from Valdez to Columbia Glacier on the protected, calm waters of the Sound. We guarantee no "sea sickness." Boarding at 1:45 P.M. each day from Memorial Day to Labor Day. (No morning cruise on Sunday.) During the busier part of the season, an 8 A.M. cruise is added. The cost is $60 per person (with a cash discount price of $55). The cruise is approximately 5 hours. During the trip the crew prepares fresh-baked goods in the galley. Friendliness and gracious hospitality on a beautiful yacht with small intimate groups. No wonder people refer to the *Lu-Lu Belle* as the limousine of Prince William Sound. Join us for an extra special day and see why Captain Rodolf refers to Switzerland as being the "Valdez of Europe!" We offer Good Sam discount at our office only. Call 1-800-411-0090 or (907) 835-5141. Winter phone (206) 842-9123. [ADVERTISEMENT]

Northern Comfort Charters operates 2 boats designed for your fishing comfort and pleasure. For halibut (and a wide variety of other bottom-feeding fish) the 43-ft. Lady Luck features a comfortable warm cabin, full restroom and a 360 degree all-around fishing deck. The 44-ft. Northern Comfort is more suitable for 2-day overnight charters and is an excellent boat for silver salmon fishing featuring a full fishing deck cover, large comfortable cabin and full restroom. Go with us and enjoy the excellent fishing offered by Prince William Sound as well as the abundant sea life, glaciers, majestic mountains and waterfalls. Phone (907) 835-2331. See our display ad this section. [ADVERTISEMENT]

Northern Magic Charters and Tours offers one of the finest personalized tours in Valdez. You'll enjoy the spacious luxury of our custom-built, 43-foot ship, the *Viking*. The 360-degree wrap-around deck makes it ideal for close-up wildlife viewing and photography. See it up close and in comfort aboard our 20-passenger vessel for a more relaxed, uncrowded tour. It's the small ship alternative. Two of our more popular sightseeing and wildlife tours are the 2¹/₂ hour Shoup Glacier and Port of Valdez historic harbor tour or our 5¹/₂ hour Columbia Glacier tour. We also offer customized tours and halibut fishing throughout Prince William Sound. Locally owned and operated. For more information or reservations, call 1-800-443-3543 or (907) 835-4433. Or write P.O. Box 1559, Valdez, AK 99686. See display ad. [ADVERTISEMENT]

Prince William Sound Cruise. Experience the spectacular beauty of Prince William Sound aboard the *MV Nunatak*. This Gray Line of Alaska tour cruises past Columbia Glacier, the largest glacier in Prince William Sound. Watch for abundant marine life as you travel round-trip between Valdez and Whittier. Two meals are included. This 12-hour tour departs daily from Valdez and costs $110 per person. Prices subject to change. Call (907) 835-2357. [ADVERTISEMENT]

Raven Sailing Charters. Cruise in comfort aboard our handsome 50-foot ketch on 1–10 day trips personalized to fulfill your interests. View wildlife, marine life, glaciers and secluded bays. Involve yourself in wilderness hiking, photography and beachcombing. Hot showers, prepared meals, fresh linens and central heating are some of the amenities offered aboard. Complete safety and navigation equipment. Small group of 1–6 persons. (907) 835-5863, (907) 835-4960 message. See display ad this section. [ADVERTISEMENT]

Cordova

Located on the east side of Prince William Sound on Orca Inlet. **Population:** 2,585. **Emergency Services: Alaska State Troopers,** phone (907) 424-7331, emergency phone 911. **Police, Fire Department, Ambulance,** phone (907) 424-6100, emergency phone 911. **Hospital,** phone (907) 424-8000.

Visitor Information: Information kiosk at the ferry office. Chamber of Commerce office on 1st Street inside the Union Hall Building; phone (907) 424-7260 or write Box 99, Cordova, AK 99574. There is also a visitor information center at the museum. A one-hour audiotaped, self-guided walking tour of downtown Cordova is available for rent from the Chamber of Commerce. A self-guided walking tour map of Cordova historic sites, prepared by the Cordova Historical Society, is also available.

Chugach National Forest Cordova Ranger District office is located at 612 2nd St. USFS personnel can provide information on trails, cabins and other activities on national forest lands. The office is open weekdays from 8 A.M. to 5 P.M. Write P.O. Box 280, Cordova 99574, or phone (907) 424-7661.

Elevation: Sea level to 400 feet/122m. **Climate:** Average temperature in July is 54°F/12°C, in January 21°F/-6°C. Average annual precipitation is 167 inches. Prevailing winds are easterly at about 4 knots. **Radio:** KLAM-AM, KCHU-FM (National Public Radio). **Television:** Cable. **Newspaper:** *Cordova Times* (weekly).

Private Aircraft: Merle K. "Mudhole" Smith Airport, 11.3 miles/18.2 km southeast; elev. 42 feet/13m; length 7,500 feet/ 2,286m; asphalt; attended. Cordova Municipal (city air field), 0.9 mile/1.4 km east; elev. 12 feet/4m; length 1,900 feet/579m; gravel; fuel 100, 100LL; unattended. Eyak Lake seaplane base, 0.9 mile/1.4 km east.

It was the Spanish explorer Don Salvador Fidalgo who named the adjacent water Puerto Cordoba in 1790. The town was named Cordova by Michael J. Heney, builder of the Copper River & Northwestern Railway. By 1889, the town had grown into a fish camp and cannery site. A post office was established in 1906. Cordova was incorporated in 1909.

One of the first producing oil fields in Alaska was located at Katalla, 47 miles/ 76 km southeast of Cordova on the Gulf of Alaska. The discovery was made in 1902 and the field produced until 1933.

The town was chosen as the railroad terminus and ocean shipping port for copper ore shipped by rail from the Kennecott mines near Kennicott and McCarthy. The railroad and town prospered until 1938 when the mine closed.

Commercial fishing has now supplanted mining as the basis of the town's economy. The fishing fleet can be seen at Cordova harbor, home port of the MV *Bartlett* and the USCG cutter *Sweetbrier*. Also at the harbor is the Cordova Fishermen's Memorial, *The Southeasterly*.

The fishing and canning season for salmon runs from about May to September, with red, king and silver (coho) salmon taken from the Copper River area, chum, red and pink salmon from Prince William Sound. Black cod, crab and shrimp season runs during winter. Dungeness crab season runs during the summer and early fall

CORDOVA ADVERTISERS

months. Razor clams, halibut and scallops are also processed.

ACCOMMODATIONS/VISITOR SERVICES

Cordova has 2 motels and 2 hotels, 10 bed and breakfasts, 12 restaurants, 2 laundromats and a variety of shopping facilities.

Cordova Rose Lodge. Historical 1924 landlocked barge and lighthouse. Former fishtrap setter, cannery, recluse home, machine shop and houseboat. Unique B&B in barge decor; nautical artifacts with a touch of whimsy. Guests from around the world "cruise" on the renovated barge. Alaskan ambiance and hospitality the moment you go on board. (907) 424-7673; 1315 Whitshed Road. See display ad. [ADVERTISEMENT]

Cordova has one campground, Odiak Camper Park, located on Whitshed Road and operated by the city. The camper park has 24 RV sites and a tenting area. Free shower tokens are available for paying campers. Contact Cordova's city hall at (907) 424-6200.

The historic Skater's Cabin on Eyak Lake is available for rent from the city. The rustic cabin has a woodstove and outhouse. The fee is $25 per night. Contact Bidarki Recreation Center, phone (907) 424-7282.

The U.S. Forest Service maintains 17 cabins in the Cordova district. Three are accessible by trail, the rest by boat or plane. Phone (907) 424-7661 for current fees, reservations and information. ▲

TRANSPORTATION

Air: Scheduled service via Alaska Airlines and Era Aviation. Several air taxi services based at the municipal airport, Mile 13 airport, and Eyak Lake offer charter and flightseeing service.

Ferry: The Alaska Marine Highway system ferries connect Cordova with Valdez, Whittier and Seward. Phone (907) 424-7333. See the MARINE ACCESS ROUTES section for details.

Taxi: Local service available.

Car Rental: Available locally.

Highways: The Alaska state highway system does not connect to Cordova. The Copper River Highway leads 48 miles/77 km east and north of Cordova, ending at the Million Dollar Bridge and Childs Glacier. (See the COPPER RIVER HIGHWAY section.)

Private Boats: Cordova has an 850-slip boat harbor serving recreational boaters as well as the commercial fishing fleet. Berth arrangements may be made by contacting the harbormaster's office at (907) 424-6400 or on VHF Channel 16.

ATTRACTIONS

Cordova's Museum and Library, at 622 1st St., are connected by a central entryway. "Where Cultures Meet" is the theme of the museum. Native artifacts such as stone implements, a dugout canoe and skin bidarka (kayak) represent the rich Native culture. One display tells of early explorers to the area, including Vitus Bering, who claimed Alaska for Russia in 1741. Exhibits

Photographing western sandpipers during Copper River Delta spring migration, Cordova. (© Roy Corral)

of the later mining and railroad era explain the development of the copper mines and of the town. Exhibits include a diorama of a vintage fishing vessel. The museum displays original work by Alaskan artists Sydney Laurence, Eustace Ziegler and Jules Dahlager, who all worked in Cordova. The Cordova Historical Society operates a small gift shop at the museum, featuring books of local interest and Alaskan crafts.

Admission to the museum is $1. Open 10 A.M.–6 P.M. Monday through Saturday; 2–4 P.M. on Sunday; other times on request. Tours can be arranged. Write P.O. Box 391 or phone (907) 424-6665 for more information. Library hours are 1–8 P.M. Tuesday through Saturday.

Swim in the Bob Korn Memorial Swimming Pool, Cordova's Olympic-sized pool, located on Railroad Avenue below Main Street. Open year-round to the public. Check locally for hours.

Mount Eyak. Ski Hill on Mount Eyak offers summer chair lift rides for sightseeing, June through August. Fee charged: $7 adults, $5 students, under 12 years free. Phone (907) 424-7766 for days and hours of operation. To reach the chair lift from 4th Avenue, take Council Avenue 1 block, then follow Ski Hill Road to top (about 1 mile/ 1.6 km from Main Street).

The single chair lift rises 880 feet/268m up Mount Eyak and overlooks the town and harbor from 1,600 feet/488km. Walk up,

take a cab, take the tour bus or drive your own vehicle.

Ski Hill is usually open for skiing mid-December to the end of April, depending on weather. The winter schedule is Wednesday (adults only), Saturday, Sunday and holidays, 9 A.M. to dusk.

Visit the USFS office on the 3rd floor of the USFS Building at 612 2nd St. Erected in 1925, it is the original federal building for the town of Cordova. Natural history display in 2nd floor Interpretive Center. The USFS office is next to the old courtroom and jail. Open weekdays 8 A.M. to 5 P.M.

Copper River Delta Shorebird Festival, held in May, offers 5 days of birding along the tidal mudflats and wetlands of the Copper River Delta and the rocky shoreline of Prince William Sound. The festival will include workshops, community activities and numerous field trip opportunities. Contact the Chamber of Commerce, Box 99, Cordova 99574, for details; phone (907) 424-7260.

Salmon Derbies. Silver Salmon Derby in August offers cash and merchandise prizes. Contact the Chamber of Commerce, Box 99, Cordova 99574, for details. Tackle, licenses and supplies may be purchased locally. You can fish from the beach (the Fleming Creek area near the ferry terminal is especially popular). The King Salmon Derby will be held in June at Fleming Spit/Orca Inlet.

Attend the Iceworm Festival: Held February 7–9, 1997, this festival offers a parade, art show, dances, craft show, ski events, survival suit race, beard judging and a King and Queen of Iceworm contest. Highlight is the 100-foot-/30-m-long "iceworm" that winds its way through the streets of Cordova. Contact Barbara Beedle at (907) 424-3527 for more information.

Whitshed Road leads out past the lighthouse (Mile 0.4) to a large mudflat at Hartney Bay (Mile 5.5). The lighthouse is privately owned and maintained by the Gleins, who also operate a bed and breakfast in their home: a converted barge. Hartney Bay is part of the 300,000-acre Copper River Delta mudflats. The delta is one of the most important stopover places in the Western Hemisphere for the largest shore-

bird migration in the world. Birders can view up to 31 different species as millions of shorebirds pass through the delta each spring.

Power Creek Road, from the corner of Lake and Chase avenues, leads out past the municipal airport to Crater Lake trailhead and Skaters Cabin picnic area (Mile 1.2), continues to Hatchery Creek salmon spawning channel (Mile 5.7), and ends at the Power Creek trailhead (Mile 6.9). The Crater Lake trailhead is directly northwest of the Eyak Lake Skaters Cabin. The 2.4-mile/ 3.8-km trail climbs to 1,500 feet/457m. Excellent views, alpine lake with fishing for cutthroat trout. Watch for bears. Visitors may view spawning salmon at the Hatchery Creek channel in July and August. Power Creek trail, 4.2 miles/6.7 km long, accesses both the USFS public-use cabin in Power Creek Basin and a ridge that connects with the Crater Lake trail creating a 12-mile/ 19.3-km loop. Power Creek trail offers spectacular scenery, with waterfalls, hanging glaciers and views of Power Creek Basin (called "surprise valley" by locals), the Chugach Range and Prince William Sound. Excellent berry picking. Watch for bears.

Drive the Copper River Highway to see the Million Dollar Bridge, Childs Glacier and the Copper River Delta. The 48-mile/77-km highway leads east from Cordova through the Delta to the historic Million Dollar Bridge, built in 1909–10, and Childs Glacier. Viewing platform and picnic area at Childs Glacier. Wildlife seen along the highway includes brown and black bear, moose, beaver, mountain goats, trumpeter swans and numerous other species of birds. See COPPER RIVER HIGHWAY section for log of road.

AREA FISHING: According to the ADF&G, "Saltwater fishing in **Orca Inlet** and adjacent western Prince William Sound is accessible from Cordova. Species include halibut, rockfish and 5 species of salmon. Trolling for salmon is best for kings in the winter and spring, and silvers in the summer and fall. Boat charters are available locally. Road-accessible fishing opportunities exist for salmon in salt water at **Fleming Spit/ Lagoon,** near the ferry terminal off Orca Bay Road. Strong runs of hatchery-enhanced kings (in the spring) and silvers (August and September) return to this terminal fishery. The Chamber of Commerce sponsors a fishing derby for both the king and silver fisheries. Road-accessible freshwater fishing is also good in the Cordova Area. **Eyak Lake** and **Eyak River** support strong returns of sockeye during June and July and silvers in August and September. The area at the outlet of the lake, where the road crosses, is fly-fishing only. Several streams along the **Copper River** Highway between Eyak Lake and the Million Dollar Bridge also support runs of sockeye and coho. These streams include **Clear Creek, Alaganik Slough, Eighteen-mile Creek** and **Twenty-mile Creek.** In addition, cutthroat trout and Dolly Varden are present in most of these streams. Lake fishing for sockeye salmon, Dolly Varden and cutthroat trout is available in **McKinley Lake** and the **Pipeline Lake** system. Arctic grayling are stocked in several gravel-pit ponds developed by the U.S. Forest Service. Fly-out fishing from Cordova is also popular for salmon, Dolly Varden and cutthroat trout. Charter operators are available locally." See also the COPPER RIVER HIGHWAY section for area fishing.

RICHARDSON HIGHWAY

Connects: Valdez to Fairbanks, AK   **Length:** 368 miles
Road Surface: Paved   **Season:** Open all year
Highest Summit: Isabel Pass 3,000 feet
Major Attractions: Trans-Alaska Pipeline, Worthington Glacier
(See map, pages 600)

	Anchorage	Delta Jct.	Glennallen	Paxson	Valdez
Anchorage		340	189	260	308
Delta Jct.	340		151	80	270
Glennallen	189	151		71	119
Paxson	260	80	71		190
Valdez	308	270	119	190	

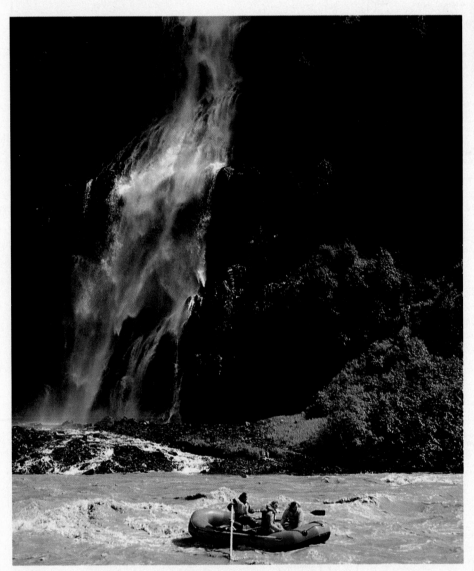

Rafting the Lowe River in Keystone Canyon. (© Bruce M. Herman)

The Richardson Highway (Alaska Route 4) extends 368 miles/592 km from Valdez to Fairbanks. This section logs the first 270 miles/434.5 km of the Richardson Highway from Valdez to Delta Junction (the remaining 98 miles/157.7 km from Delta Junction to Fairbanks are logged in the ALASKA HIGHWAY section).

The Richardson is a wide paved highway in good condition except for sporadic frost heaving. A new section of highway completed in 1989 bypasses the historic community of Copper Center. *The MILEPOST®* logs the old highway through town. The "new" Richardson Highway (bypass route) is of equal distance—6.5 miles/10.5 km—with no notable features. You must exit the highway (watch for signs) to see Copper Center.

The Richardson Highway is a scenic route through the magnificent scenery of the Chugach Mountains and Alaska Range. It passes many fine king salmon streams, including the Gulkana and Tonsina rivers.

The Richardson Highway was Alaska's first road, known to gold seekers in 1898 as the Valdez to Eagle trail. The gold rush trail led over the treacherous Valdez Glacier, then northeast to Eagle and the Yukon River route to the Klondike goldfields. Captain W.R. Abercrombie of the U.S. Army rerouted the trail in 1899 through Keystone Canyon and over Thompson Pass, thus avoiding the glacier. As the Klondike Gold Rush waned, the military kept the trail open to connect Fort Liscum in Valdez with Fort Egbert in Eagle. In 1903, the U.S. Army Signal Corps laid the trans-Alaska telegraph line along this route.

Gold stampeders started up the trail again in 1902, this time headed for Fairbanks, site of a big gold strike. The Valdez to Fairbanks trail became an important route to the Interior, and in 1910 the trail was upgraded to a wagon road under the direction of Gen. Wilds P. Richardson, first president of the Alaska Road Commission. The ARC updated the road to automobile standards in the 1920s. The Richardson Highway was hard-surfaced in 1957.

Emergency medical services: Phone 911 anywhere along the highway.

Richardson Highway Log

Mileposts on the Richardson Highway were erected before the 1964 Good Friday earthquake and therefore begin 4 miles/6.4 km from present-day downtown Valdez near the Old Valdez townsite (destroyed during the earthquake).
Distance from New Valdez (NV) is followed by distance from Old Valdez (OV).

NV 0 OV 4 (6.4 km) Intersection of Meals Avenue and the Richardson Highway.

NV 0.4 (0.6 km) **OV 3.6** (5.8 km) Paved double-ended turnout to north with Valdez information kiosk, maps, brochures, pay phones.

NV 0.5 (0.8 km) **OV 3.5** (5.6 km) DOT/PF district office.

NV 0.6 (1 km) **OV 3.4** (5.5 km) Valdez highway maintenance station.

NV 0.9 (1.4 km) **OV 3.1** (5 km) Double-ended turnout to north at Crooked Creek salmon spawning area and hatchery. Viewing platform offers close-up look at salmon spawning in midsummer and fall. U.S. Forest Service information station is staffed Memorial Day through Labor Day; interpretive displays, history and recreation. Migrating birds

RICHARDSON HIGHWAY
Valdez, AK, to Delta Junction, AK

To Fairbanks (see ALASKA HIGHWAY section)

V-266/428km
F-98/158km

Delta Junction

Fort Greely

ALASKA

Delta Creek

Bolio L.

To Tok (see ALASKA HIGHWAY section)

Donnelly Dome▲
3,910 ft./1,192m

Mount Deborah ▲
12,339 ft./3,761m

Hess Mount
11,940 ft./3,639m

▲ Mount Hayes
13,832 ft./4,216m

Glaciated

Black Rapids Glacier

Delta River

Jarvis Creek

Tanana River

RANGE

Glaciated

Area

Gulkana Glacier

Fielding L.

Isabel Pass
3,000 ft./914m

V-195/313.8km Hines Site 20/20 Bed & Breakfast L
V-191.4/308km Water's Edge B&B CL
V-185.7/298.5km Paxson Alpine Tours
V-185.5/298.5km Paxson Lodge CDdGILMPrST

Summit L.

To Cantwell
(see DENALI HIGHWAY section)

Paxson

V-186/299km
F-179/287km

Trans-Alaska Pipeline

Paxson Lake

V-170/273.6km Meier's Lake Roadhouse CdGILMPST

miles/kilometres
miles/kilometres from:

V-Old Valdez
NV-Valdez
F-Fairbanks

Gulkana River

Copper River

National Park Boundary

▲ Hogan Hill
2,647 ft./807m

Sourdough

Sourdough Cr.

Gakona Cr.

To Tok (see GLENN HIGHWAY section)

Principal Route
Paved — Unpaved
Other Roads
Paved — Unpaved
Ferry Routes ··· Hiking Trails ···

Refer to Log for Visitor Facilities
? Visitor Information
Campground + Airport + Airstrip
Fishing

Key to Advertiser Services
C -Camping
D -Dump Station
d -Diesel
G -Gas (reg., unld.)
I -Ice
L -Lodging
M -Meals
P -Propane
R -Car Repair (major)
r -Car Repair (minor)
S -Store (grocery)
T -Telephone (pay)

Tok Cutoff

Gakona

V-129/207km
F-235/379km

V-128.6/206.9km Line Camp CILrS

▲ Mount Sanford
16,237 ft./4,949m

Gulkana

Moose Creek

Gakona Junction

V-115.5/185.9km Glennallen Quick Stop Truck Stop dGIST
Rendezvous Cafe IMT

Mount Drum 12,010 ft./3,661m

To Palmer (see GLENN HIGHWAY section)

Glennallen

V-115/185km The Hub of Alaska dGIPRST

V-111.2/179km Tazlina River Trading Post & Western Auto GIST
V-110.5/177.8km Tazlina River RV Park CDT
V-101.8/163.8km Wild River Gallery
V-101.5/163.3km Copper River Cash Store IST
V-101.1/162.7km Copper Center Lodge L

Tazlina River

Glaciated Area

▲ Mount Wrangell
14,163 ft./4,317m

V-115/185km
F-249/401km

Tazlina Lake

Copper Center

V-100.8/162.2km Mtn. View Liquor & Gas dGIPST
V-100.7/162.1km Klutina Salmon Charters CDI
V-100.6/161.9km Grove's Klutina River Charters and Fish Camp CDI
V-92.7/149.2km Grizzly Pizza & Gift Shop CGMT

Klutina River

Willow Cr.

Willow Lake

Pippin L.

CHUGACH

Klutina Lake

V-83/133km
F-281/453km

V-82.3/132.4km Ruthe's Handcrafted Gifts
V-81/130.4km Alaskan House dG
V-79.5/127.9km Squirrel Creek Store GIPST

Squirrel Cr. River

To McCarthy
(see EDGERTON HIGHWAY section)

Wrangell-St. Elias National Park and Preserve

Tonsina River

Little Tonsina River

Trans-Alaska Pipeline

Area

Glaciated

Tonsina Lake

V-56/90.1km Tiekel River Lodge CGLMT

Stuart Cr.

Tiekel River

Copper River

V-0
NV-4/6km
F-364/586km

Chugach National

Valdez Glacier

Mineral Creek

Girls Mountain
6,134 ft./1,870m

Worthington Gl.

Sheep Cr.

Tsaina R.

Forest

Valdez

Old Valdez

Robe L.

Lowe R.

Thompson Pass
2,771 ft./845m

V-34.7/55.8km Tsaina Lodge LMT

Chugach National Forest

MOUNTAINS

Pipeline Terminal

V-0.1/0.2km Big Wheel Services dGPr

NV-3.4/5.5km ABC Liquors ST
Acres Kwik Trip ST

Alaska State Ferry
(see MARINE ACCESS ROUTES section)

V-4/6km
NV-0

Tasnuna River

Glaciated Area

Prince William Sound

such as Canada geese and various ducks are often here. It is a game sanctuary; no shooting is allowed. Good spot for pictures.

NV 1.3 (2.1 km) **OV 2.7** (4.3 km) Paved turnout to south.

NV 2 (3.2 km) **OV 2** (3.2 km) Paved turnout to south.

NV 2.1 (3.4 km) **OV 1.9** (3.1 km) Mineral Creek Loop Road through business and residential area on outskirts of Old Valdez comes out at **Milepost NV 3.4.** Access to Port of Valdez container terminal and grain elevators.

NV 3.4 (5.5 km) **OV 0.6** (1 km) Airport Road; deli, market, liquor store, laundromat. Turn off to north for Valdez Airport (0.6 mile/ 1 km), Valdez Glacier campground (2 miles/ 3.2 km) and Valdez Glacier (3.9 miles/ 6.3 km). Parking area next to glacial moraine; good views of the glacier area are *not* available from this spot, nor is Valdez Glacier a very spectacular glacier. Valdez Glacier campground has 101 sites, tent camping, covered picnic area, litter barrels, water, toilets and fireplaces; 15-day limit, camping fee. *CAUTION: Beware of bears.* ▲

ABC Liquors. See display ad this section.
Acres Kwik Trip. See display ad this section.

Mineral Creek Loop Road leads south to the original townsite of Valdez, destroyed during the Good Friday earthquake on March 27, 1964. A few homes and businesses are here now; there is little evidence of the earthquake's destruction.

NV 4 (6.4 km) **OV 0** Former access road to Old Valdez, now blocked off. Milepost 0 of the Richardson Highway is located here.

(Southbound travelers note: Physical mileposts end here, it is 4 miles/6.4 km to downtown Valdez.)
Distance from Old Valdez (V) is followed by distance from Fairbanks (F). Physical mileposts begin northbound showing distance from Old Valdez.

V 0 F 364 (585.8 km) **Milepost 0** of the Richardson Highway is located here at the former access road to Old Valdez.

V 0.1 (0.2 km) **F 363.9** (585.6 km) **Big Wheel Services.** See display ad this section.

V 0.9 (1.4 km) **F 363.1** (584.4 km) The highway passes over the terminal moraine of the Valdez Glacier, bridging several channels and streams flowing from the melting ice.

V 1.4 (2.3 km) **F 362.6** (583.5 km) Valdez Trapshooting Range.

V 1.5 (2.4 km) **F 362.5** (583.4 km) City of Valdez Goldfields Recreation Area; trails, ponds, swimming, picnic sites, baseball field.

V 2.2 (3.5 km) **F 361.8** (582.2 km) Dylen Drive.

V 2.4 (3.9 km) **F 361.6** (581.9 km) Paved turnout to west.

V 2.5 (4 km) **F 361.5** (581.8 km) Valdez cemetery to east.

V 2.7 (4.3 km) **F 361.3** (581.5 km) Large paved double-ended turnout to west beside Robe River. During August and early September watch for pink and silver salmon spawning in roadside creeks and sloughs. *DO NOT* attempt to catch or otherwise disturb spawning salmon. *CAUTION: Beware of bears.*

V 2.9 (4.7 km) **F 361.1** (581.1 km) Turnoff for Old Dayville Road to Trans-Alaska Pipeline Valdez Marine Terminal and access to Allison Point fishery. This 5.4-mile/8.7-km paved road (open to the public) crosses the Lowe River 4 times. At Mile 2.4/3.9 km the road parallels the bay

and there is excellent fishing in season at Allison Point, especially for pink and silver salmon; also watch for sea otters and bald eagles along here. At Mile 4.1/6.6 km is the Solomon Gulch water project and a spectacular view of Solomon Gulch Falls; a fish hatchery is located across from the water project. Entrance to the pipeline terminal is at the end of the road. Supertankers load oil pumped from the North Slope to this facility via the trans-Alaska pipeline. Bus tours of the terminal are available; see the VALDEZ section for details.

V 3 (4.8 km) **F 361** (581 km) Weigh station.

V 3.4 (5.5 km) **F 360.6** (580.3 km) A 0.5-mile/0.8-km gravel road to Robe Lake and floatplane base. Watch for cow parsnip and river beauty (dwarf fireweed). Also watch for bears!

V 4.7 (7.5 km) **F 359.3** (578.2 km) Turnout to east. Access to **Robe River**; Dolly Varden, red salmon (fly-fishing only, mid-May to mid-June). ⊷

V 5.3 (8.5 km) **F 358.7** (577.3 km) Salmonberry Ridge ski area road to west.

V 7.3 (11.7 km) **F 356.7** (574 km) Lowe River parallels the highway next mile northbound.

V 9.6 (15.4 km) **F 354.4** (570.3 km) Fire station.

V 11.6 (18.7 km) **F 352.4** (567.1 km) Large paved turnout to east.

V 12.8 (20.6 km) **F 351.2** (565.2 km) Here the Lowe River emerges from Keystone Canyon. The canyon was named by Captain William Ralph Abercrombie, presumably for Pennsylvania, the Keystone State. In 1884, Abercrombie had been selected to lead an exploring expedition up the Copper River to the Yukon River. Although unsuccessful in his attempt to ascend the Copper River, he did survey the Copper River Delta and a route to Port Valdez. He returned in 1898 and again in 1899, carrying out further explorations of the area. The Lowe River is named for Lt. Percival Lowe, a member of his expedition. Glacier melt imparts the slate-gray color to the river.

V 13.5 (21.7 km) **F 350.5** (564.1 km) Horsetail Falls; large paved turnout to west. *CAUTION: Watch for pedestrians.*

V 13.7 (22 km) **F 350.3** (563.7 km) Goat trail is visible on the west side of the highway; see description of this landmark at **Milepost V 15.2.**

V 13.8 (22.2 km) **F 350.2** (563.6 km) Bridal Veil Falls; large paved turnout to west.

V 14.9 (24 km) **F 349.1** (561.8 km) Lowe River bridge (first of 3 bridges northbound); view of Riddleston Falls. About 175 yards east of this bridge and adjacent to the highway is an abandoned hand-drilled tunnel. Large paved turnout with historical marker. Sign reads: "This tunnel was hand cut into the solid rock of Keystone Canyon and is all that is left of the railroad era when 9 companies fought to take advantage of the short route from the coast to the copper country. However, a feud interrupted progress. A gun battle was fought and the tunnel was never finished."

V 15.2 (24.5 km) **F 348.8** (561.3 km) Small gravel turnout. On the far side just above the water are the remains of the old sled trail used in the early days. This trail was cut out of the rock just wide enough for 2 horses abreast. 200 feet above can be seen "the old goat trail." This road was used until 1945.

V 15.3 (24.6 km) **F 348.7** (561.2 km) Lowe River bridge No. 2, built in 1980,

replaced previous highway route through the long tunnel visible beside highway. Turnout at south end of bridge. Traces of the old trail used by horse-drawn sleds can be seen about 200 feet/61m above the river.

V 15.9 (25.6 km) **F 348.1** (560.2 km) Leaving Keystone Canyon northbound, entering Keystone Canyon southbound. Raft trips of Keystone Canyon are available; check with visitor center in Valdez.

V 16.2 (26.1 km) **F 347.8** (559.7 km) Avalanche gun emplacement.

V 16.3 (26.2 km) **F 347.7** (559.6 km) Lowe River bridge No. 3.

V 18 (29 km) **F 346** (556.8 km) Large paved turnouts both sides of road.

V 18.6 (29.9 km) **F 345.4** (555.8 km) Sheep Creek bridge.

Truck lane begins northbound as highway ascends 7.5 miles/12 km to Thompson Pass. This was one of the most difficult sections of pipeline construction, requiring heavy blasting of solid rock for several miles. The pipeline runs under the cleared strip beside the road. Low-flying helicopters often seen along the Richardson Highway are usually monitoring the pipeline.

V 21.6 (34.8 km) **F 342.4** (551 km) Paved turnout to east.

V 22.2 (35.7 km) **F 341.8** (550.1 km) Snow poles along highway guide snow plows in winter.

V 23 (37 km) **F 341** (548.8 km) Large gravel turnout to east.

V 23.4 (37.7 km) **F 340.6** (548.1 km) Large paved turnout to east with view.

V 23.6 (38 km) **F 340.4** (547.8 km) Loop road past Thompson Lake to Blueberry Lake and state recreation site; see **Milepost V 24.1.**

V 23.8 (38.3 km) **F 340.2** (547.5 km) Small paved turnout to east.

V 24.1 (38.8 km) **F 339.9** (547 km) Loop road to Blueberry Lake State Recreation Site; drive in 1 mile/1.6 km. Tucked into an alpine setting between tall mountain peaks,

Worthington Glacier view from Milepost V 30.2 Richardson Highway. (Jerrianne Lowther, staff)

this is one of Alaska's most beautifully situated campgrounds; 10 campsites, 4 covered picnic tables, toilets, firepits and water. Camping fee $10/night or annual pass. ▲

Blueberry Lake, and **Thompson Lake** (formerly Summit No. 1 Lake). Good grayling and rainbow fishing all summer. 🐟

V 24.4 (39.3 km) **F 339.6** (546.5 km) Large paved turnout to west. Bare bone peaks of the Chugach Mountains rise above the highway. Thompson Pass ahead; Marshall Pass is to the east.

During the winter of 1907, the A.J. Meals Co. freighted the 70-ton river steamer *Chitina* (or *Chittyna*) from Valdez over Marshall Pass and down the Tasnuna River to the Copper River. The ship was moved piece by piece on huge horse-drawn freight sleds and assembled at the mouth of the Tasnuna. The 110-foot-/34-m-long ship navigated 170 miles/274 km of the Copper and Chitina rivers above Abercrombie Rapids, moving supplies for construction crews of the Copper River & Northwestern Railway. Much of the equipment for the Kennicott mill and tram was moved by this vessel.

V 25.5 (41 km) **F 338.5** (544.7 km) Large paved turnout to west. Entering Game Management Unit 13D, leaving unit 6D, northbound.

V 25.7 (41.4 km) **F 338.3** (544.4 km) Large paved turnout to west with view; Keystone Glacier to the south.

V 26 (41.8 km) **F 338** (543.9 km) Thompson Pass (elev. 2,678 feet/816m) at head of Ptarmigan Creek. Truck lane ends northbound; begin 7.5-mile/12-km descent southbound.

Thompson Pass, named by Captain Abercrombie in 1899, is comparatively low elevation but above timberline. A wildflower lover will be well repaid if he rambles over the rocks in this area: tiny alpine plants may be in bloom, such as Aleutian heather and mountain harebell.

The National Climatic Center credits snowfall extremes in Alaska to the Thompson Pass station, where record measurements are: 974.5 inches for season (1952–53); 298 inches for month (February 1953); and 62

inches for 24-hour period (December 1955). Snowpoles along the highway mark the road edge for snow plows.

Private Aircraft: Thompson Pass airstrip; elev. 2,080 feet/634m; length 2,500 feet/762m; turf, gravel; unattended.

V 27 (43.5 km) **F 337** (542.3 km) Thompson Pass highway maintenance station.

V 27.5 (44.3 km) **F 336.5** (541.5 km) Steep turnout to east by **Worthington Lake;** rainbow fishing. 🐟

V 27.7 (44.6 km) **F 336.3** (541.2 km) Good viewpoint of 27 Mile Glacier.

V 28 (45.1 km) **F 336** (540.7 km) Paved turnout to east. Entering winter avalanche area southbound.

V 28.6 (46 km) **F 335.4** (539.8 km) Paved turnout to west.

V 28.7 (46.2 km) **F 335.3** (539.6 km) Worthington Glacier State Recreation Site; large viewing shelter, interpretive displays, toilets, picnic sites, parking and pay phone. According to state park rangers, this is the most visited site in the Copper River Basin. The glacier, which heads on Girls Mountain (elev. 6,134 feet/1,870m), is accessible via a short road to the left. It is possible to drive almost to the face of the glacier. Care should be exercised when walking on ice because of numerous crevasses.

NOTE: Watch for road upgrading under way in 1997.

V 30.2 (48.6 km) **F 333.8** (537.2 km) Large paved turnout both sides of highway. Excellent spot for photos of Worthington Glacier.

V 31.1 (50 km) **F 332.9** (535.7 km) Small turnout to east. Avalanche gun emplacement.

V 32 (51.5 km) **F 332** (534.3 km) Highway parallels Tsaina River. Long climb up to Thompson Pass for southbound motorists.

V 33.6 (54.1 km) **F 330.4** (531.7 km) Tsaina River access to west.

V 34.7 (55.8 km) **F 329.3** (529.9 km) **Tsaina Lodge.** Treat yourself to a fine dining experience in the comforting, rustic charm of the hand-hewn log interior. View the spectacular Worthington Glacier surrounded by snow-capped peaks while relaxing in a museum of treasured relics from times long past. Modern gourmet food prepared the old-fashioned way, using fresh local ingredients. Specialties include Alaska seafood, homemade pastas, soups, desserts and fresh baked goods daily. Full-service bar and wine list. The spring helicopter ski operation attracts the world's finest skiers. Summer activities are many, ranging from berry picking and fishing to rafting and paragliding. Real Alaskan hospitality. New hand-crafted log cabins, yurts and a bunkhouse. (907) 835-3500. See display ad this section.

[ADVERTISEMENT]

V 36.5 (58.7 km) **F 327.5** (527 km) Pipeline runs under highway.

V 37 (59.5 km) **F 327** (526.2 km) Entering BLM public lands northbound.

V 37.3 (60 km) **F 326.7** (525.8 km) Tsaina River bridge at Devil's Elbow; turnout at south end of bridge.

V 38 (61.2 km) **F 326** (524.6 km) Crest of hill. Beautiful views southbound.

V 40.5 (65.2 km) **F 323.5** (520.6 km) Pipeline passes under highway. Avalanche gun emplacement.

V 40.8 (65.7 km) **F 323.2** (520.1 km) Gravel turnout to west.

V 42 (67.6 km) **F 322** (518.2 km) Buried pipeline. View of waterbars (ridges on slope designed to slow runoff and control erosion).

V 43.3 (69.7 km) **F 320.7** (516.1 km) Long double-ended turnout.

V 43.5 (70 km) **F 320.5** (515.8 km) Wide shoulder eastside of highway.

V 45.6 (73.4 km) **F 318.4** (512.4 km) Large paved turnout to east at north end of Stuart Creek bridge.

V 45.8 (73.7 km) **F 318.2** (512.1 km) Copper River Valley welcome sign. Watch for moose next 20 miles/32 km northbound.

V 46.9 (75.5 km) **F 317.1** (510.3 km) **Tiekel River** bridge; small Dolly Varden. Small turnout at north end of bridge. ⊶

V 47.9 (77.1 km) **F 316.1** (508.7 km) Large paved rest area by Tiekel River; covered picnic sites, toilets, no drinking water. Viewpoint and historical sign for Mount Billy Mitchell.

Lieutenant William "Billy" Mitchell was a member of the U.S. Army Signal Corps, which in 1903 was completing the trans-Alaska telegraph line (Washington–Alaska Military Cable and Telegraph System) to connect all the military posts in Alaska. The 2,000 miles/3,200 km of telegraph wire included the main line between Fort Egbert in Eagle and Fort Liscum at Valdez, and a branch line down the Tanana River to Fort Gibson and on to Fort St. Michael near the mouth of the Yukon and then to Nome. Mitchell was years later to become the "prophet of American military air power."

V 50.7 (81.6 km) **F 313.3** (504.1 km) Bridge over Tiekel River. Dead spruce trees in this area were killed by beetles.

V 53.8 (86.6 km) **F 310.2** (499.2 km) Squaw Creek culvert.

V 54.1 (87.1 km) **F 309.9** (498.7 km) Large paved turnout to east by Tiekel River. Look for lupine in June, dwarf fireweed along river bars in July.

V 54.3 (87.4 km) **F 309.7** (498.4 km) Old beaver lodge. Beaver may inhabit the same site for generations.

V 54.5 (87.7 km) **F 309.5** (498.1 km) Moose often seen here in the evenings.

V 55.1 (88.7 km) **F 308.9** (497.1 km) Large paved turnout to east by Tiekel River.

V 56 (90.1 km) **F 308** (495.7 km) **Tiekel River Lodge.** See display ad this section.

V 56.3 (90.6 km) **F 307.7** (495.2 km) Large paved turnout to east by Tiekel River.

V 57 (91.7 km) **F 307** (494.1 km) Old beaver lodge and dams in pond to east. Tireless and skillful dam builders, beavers construct their houses in the pond created by the dam. Older beaver dams can reach 15 feet in height and may be hundreds of feet long. The largest rodent in North America, beavers range south from the Brooks Range. They eat a variety of vegetation, including aspen, willow, birch and poplar.

V 58.1 (93.5 km) **F 305.9** (492.3 km) Wagon Point Creek culvert.

V 60 (96.6 km) **F 304** (489.2 km) Large paved turnout to east. Highway parallels **Tiekel River**; fishing for small Dolly Varden. ⊶

V 62 (99.7 km) **F 302** (486 km) Ernestine Station highway maintenance camp.

V 62.4 (100.4 km) **F 301.6** (485.4 km) Boundary for Sport Fish Management areas. Entering Upper Susitna/Copper River Area N northbound, Prince William Sound southbound.

V 64.7 (104.1 km) **F 299.3** (481.7 km) Pump Station No. 12 to east. Interpretive viewpoint and parking to west. Short walk to viewpoint from parking area.

V 65 (104.6 km) **F 299** (481.2 km) Little Tonsina River.

V 65.1 (104.8 km) **F 298.9** (481 km) **Little Tonsina River** State Recreation Site with 10 campsites, firepits, water, litter barrels and toilets. Camping fee $6/night or annual pass. Dolly Varden fishing. Road to right as you enter wayside dead ends, road to left goes to the river (no turnaround space); follow loop road for easy access. Good berry picking in fall. *CAUTION: Beware of bears!* ⊶▲

Watch for moose next 20 miles/32 km southbound.

V 66.2 (106.5 km) **F 297.8** (479.2 km) Double-ended gravel turnout to west.

V 68.1 (109.6 km) **F 295.9** (476.2 km) Site of former Tonsina Camp (Alyeska Pipeline Service Co.) used during pipeline construction. These camps have been completely removed.

V 70.5 (113.5 km) **F 293.5** (472.3 km) Trans-Alaska pipeline follows base of mountains across valley.

V 71.2 (114.6 km) **F 292.8** (471.2 km) Long double-ended paved turnout to east.

V 72 (115.9 km) **F 292** (469.9 km) Double-ended paved turnout to west. Leaving BLM public lands northbound. View of trans-Alaska pipeline across the valley.

V 74.4 (119.7 km) **F 289.6** (466.1 km) Paved double-ended turnout to west. Vehicle access to Little Tonsina River.

V 78.9 (127 km) **F 285.1** (458.8 km) Bernard Creek trail. According to the BLM, this 15-mile loop road—which was originally part of the WAMCATS line—provides mountain bikers with an uphill ride on hard-pack dirt to near Kimball Pass.

V 79 (127.1 km) **F 285** (458.7 km) Tonsina Lodge. **Private Aircraft:** (Upper) Tonsina airstrip, adjacent south of lodge; elev. 1,500 feet/457m; length 1,400 feet/426m; turf; fuel 80; unattended.

V 79.2 (127.5 km) **F 284.8** (458.3 km) Bridge over Tonsina River, which rises in Tonsina Lake to the southwest.

V 79.5 (127.9 km) **F 284.5** (457.8 km) **Squirrel Creek Store.** See display ad this section.

V 79.6 (128.1 km) **F 284.4** (457.7 km) Bridge and Squirrel Creek state campground.

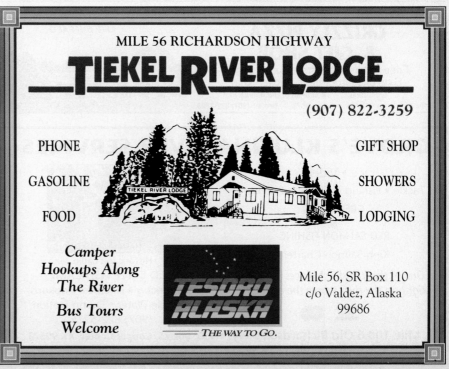

Pleasant campsites on the bank of Squirrel Creek, some pull-through spaces; $10/night or annual pass; dumpster, boat launch, water, toilets and firepits. Rough access road through campground; low-clearance vehicles use caution. Large vehicles note: Limited turnaround on back loop road. ▲

Mouth of **Squirrel Creek** at Tonsina River. Some grayling and salmon; grayling, small, use flies or eggs, all season; salmon, average size, egg clusters and spoons, all season. Also try the gravel pit beside the campground; according to state park rangers, some fishermen have good luck catching rainbow and grayling here using flies, eggs and spinners. ⚓

V 79.7 (128.3 km) **F 284.3** (457.5 km) Begin 1.3-mile/2.1-km truck lane northbound up Tonsina Hill. Hill can be slippery in winter. Watch for severe frost heaves.

V 81 (130.4 km) **F 283** (455.4 km) **Alaskan House.** See display ad this section.

V 82.3 (132.4 km) **F 281.7** (453.3 km) **Ruthe's Handcrafted Gifts.** Stop by our cabin, and see quilts and critters, one-of-a-kind wearing apparel, and many other functional and attractive gifts. For a unique remembrance of Alaska, take home a cup, tee or sweatshirt with your picture in an Alaskan setting using our computer portrait imaging equipment. We also have a very large inventory of antique and collectable bottles. [ADVERTISEMENT]

V 82.6 (132.9 km) **F 281.4** (452.9 km) **Junction** with the Edgerton Highway. The Edgerton Highway leads east to Chitina and connects with the McCarthy Road to McCarthy in Wrangell–St. Elias National

Copper Center

To Glennallen

Milepost V 106

New Richardson Highway

Milepost V 101.1 — Post Office

Old Richardson Highway

Lodge

Museum

Loop Road

Milepost V 100.8 — Klutina River

4

Milepost V 100.2

To Valdez

N / W / E / S

Park and Preserve (see EDGERTON HIGHWAY section).

V 83 (133.6 km) **F 281** (452.2 km) Small paved turnout to west beside Pippin Lake.

V 87.7 (141.1 km) **F 276.3** (444.6 km) Paved double-ended turnout to east at Willow Lake. On a clear day this lake mirrors the Wrangell Mountains which lie within Wrangell–St. Elias National Park and Preserve. The park visitor center is at **Milepost V 105.1** and there is a good mountain viewpoint at **V 112.6**.

V 88.5 (142.4 km) **F 275.5** (443.4 km) Pipeline parallels road. Interpretive viewpoint to west on pipeline (1 of 3 Alyeska pipeline displays along this highway). National Park Service plaque with schematic diagram of Wrangell Mountains.

V 90.8 (146.1 km) **F 273.2** (439.7 km) Large paved turnout to west by Willow Creek culvert; thick patches of diamond willow in woods off highway (and thick clouds of mosquitoes!).

V 91.1 (146.6 km) **F 272.9** (439.2 km) Turnoff to east is an 8-mile/12.9-km gravel cutoff that intersects Edgerton Highway at **Milepost J 7.3**. This is a drive through the rolling hills of homestead country and heavy thickets of birch and spruce.

V 92.7 (149.2 km) **F 271.3** (436.6 km) **Grizzly Pizza & Gift Shop.** See display ad this section.

V 98.1 (157.9 km) **F 265.9** (427.9 km) Microwave tower.

V 100.2 (161.2 km) **F 263.8** (424.5 km) IMPORTANT: South **junction** with Copper Center Bypass (New Richardson Highway). Northbound travelers TURN OFF onto Old Richardson Highway for scenic route through historic Copper Center (log and description follow). *The MILEPOST®* does not log the bypass route (New Richardson Highway), which is the same distance as the old highway (6.5 miles/10.5 km) with no notable features. Although according to the BLM, there is an old 4-wheel-drive road to Klutina Lake (25 miles/40 km) which is appropriate for mountain bikes. Turn west at Brenwick–Craig Road sign on the bypass and cross under pipeline. The old highway rejoins the bypass route at **Milepost V 106**.

V 100.6 (161.9 km) **F 263.4** (423.9 km)

Grove's Klutina River Charters and Fish Camp. One of the friendliest places around. Great king and red salmon fishing. Also Dolly Varden, grayling and lake trout. Camping and RV parking on the south bank of the Klutina River. Electrical hookups, dump station, potable water. Headquarters in historic log cabin on premises. Call 1-800-770-5822. See Grove's Klutina River Services ad on opposite page. [ADVERTISEMENT] ▲

V 100.7 (162.1 km) **F 263.3** (423.7 km) Klutina River bridges. Excellent fishing in the **Klutina River** for red (sockeye) and king (chinook) salmon. Also grayling and Dolly Varden. Kings to 50 lbs., average 30 lbs.; from June 15 to Aug. 10, peaking in mid-July. Red's peak run is from late June to early August; fish from either bank downstream from the new bridge to the mouth of the Copper River. *NOTE: Most riverfront property is privately owned. Inquire at the tackle shop about river access.* Two campgrounds and fishing charter services are located here. ◄▲

Klutina Salmon Charters. See display ad this section. ▲

V 100.8 (162.2 km) **F 263.2** (423.6 km) Copper Center (description follows); loop road opposite gas station provides access to lodge and museum.

Mtn. View Liquor & Gas. See display ad this section.

Copper Center

V 100.8 (162.2 km) **F 263.2** (423.6 km) Located on the Klutina River, 1 mile/1.6 km west of its junction with the Copper River; 104.8 miles/168.6 km north of Valdez via Alaska Route 4. An inner loop road leads through Copper Center and rejoins the Richardson Highway at **Milepost V 101.1. Population:** 449. **Emergency Services:** Phone 911. Ambulance in Glennallen, phone 911. **Elevation:** 1,000 feet/305m.

Private Aircraft: Copper Center NR 2 airstrip, 1 mile/1.6 km south; elev. 1,150 feet/351m; length 2,500 feet/762m; gravel; unattended.

Facilities include lodging, private campgrounds, meals, groceries, liquor store, gas station, general store, post office, laundromat and gift shops. Fishing charters, tackle, riverboat services and guides available.

With the influx of gold seekers following the trail from Valdez to the Klondike, a trading post was established in Copper Center in 1898. A telegraph station and post office were established in 1901 and Copper Center

COPPER CENTER ADVERTISERS

George I. Ashby museum displays pioneer artifacts. (© Susan Cole Kelly)

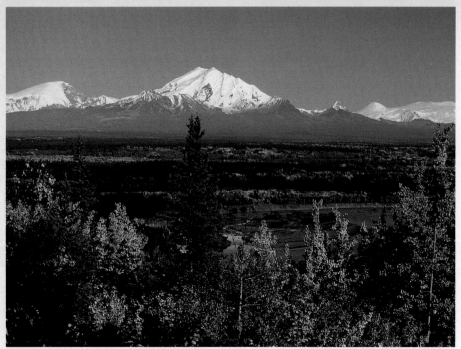

View of Mount Sanford and Mount Drum from Milepost V 112.6 Richardson Highway. (Jerrianne Lowther, staff)

became the principal settlement and supply center in the Nelchina–Susitna region.

Copper Center Lodge on the inner loop road, selected by the Alaska Centennial Commission as a site of historic importance

(a plaque is mounted to the right of the lodge's entrance), had its beginning as the Holman Hotel and was known as the Blix Roadhouse during the gold rush days of 1897–98. It was the first lodging place in the Copper River valley and was replaced by the Copper Center Lodge in 1932.

The George I. Ashby Memorial Museum, operated by the Copper Valley Historical Society, is housed in the bunkhouse annex at the Copper Center Lodge. It contains early Russian religious articles, Athabascan baskets, telegraph and mineral displays, copper and gold mining memorabilia, and trapping articles from early-day Copper Valley. Hours vary. Donations appreciated.

Historic buildings in Copper Center are located on private property. Please do not trespass.

The Copper River reportedly carries the highest sediment load of all Alaskan rivers. The river cuts through the Chugach Moun-

tains and connects the interior of southcentral Alaska with the sea; it is the only corridor of its kind between Cook Inlet and the Canadian border.

Richardson Highway Log

(continued)

V 101 (162.5 km) **F 263** (423.3 km) A visitor attraction in Copper Center is the log Chapel on the Hill built in 1942 by Rev. Vince Joy with the assistance of U.S. Army volunteers stationed in the area. The chapel is open daily and there is no admission charge. A short slide show on the Copper River area is usually shown to visitors in the chapel during the summer. A highway-level parking lot is connected to the Chapel on the Hill by stairs.

V 101.1 (162.7 km) **F 262.9** (423 km) Inner loop road to historic Copper Center Lodge George I. Ashley Memorial Museum and other businesses.

Copper Center Lodge. Beautifully rustic historic landmark, serving the public since 1898; 21 rooms, private or shared baths. Century-old sourdough starter hotcakes, homemade pies. Restaurant serving breakfast, lunch, dinner. Wine and beer served. Located near the base of the Wrangell–St. Elias National Park and next to the Copper and Klutina rivers. See display ad. [ADVERTISEMENT]

V 101.4 (163.2 km) **F 262.6** (422.6 km) Post office to east; outside mailbox.

V 101.5 (163.3 km) **F 262.5** (422.4 km) **Copper River Cash Store**, established in 1896, sits on part of the first farm started in Alaska. The center of the building is the original structure. Behind the store is the old jail, bars still on windows. Open 6 days a week, all year. Complete line of groceries, general merchandise, RV supplies, video rentals. [ADVERTISEMENT]

V 101.8 (163.8 km) **F 262.2** (422 km) **Wild River Gallery.** All Alaskan handmade art and gifts, paintings, ceramics, beaded and ivory jewelry, furs, paper creations, baskets, beadwork, weaving, dolls, clothing and cards. Open 10 A.M. to 6 P.M. Monday through Saturday in Historic Copper Center, Alaska. Old Richardson Highway Loop Road. Major credit cards accepted. Phone (907) 822-5344. [ADVERTISEMENT]

V 101.9 (164 km) **F 262.1** (421.8 km) Parking area. Historical marker about Copper Center reads: "Founded in 1896 as a government agriculture experiment station, Copper Center was the first white settlement in this area. The Trail of '98 from Valdez over the glaciers came down from the mountains and joined here with the Eagle Trail to Forty Mile and Dawson. 300 miners, destitute and lonely, spent the winter here. Many suffered with scurvy and died. Soon after the turn of the century, the Washington–Alaska Military Cable and Telegraph System, known as WAMCATS, the forerunner of the Alaska communications system, operated telegraph service here between Valdez and Fairbanks."

V 102 (164.1 km) **F 262** (421.6 km) Brenwick–Craig Road. Access to Klutina River Bed & Breakfast.

V 102.2 (164.5 km) **F 261.8** (421.3 km) Copper Center Community Chapel and Indian graveyard.

V 102.5 (165 km) **F 261.5** (420.8 km) Fish wheel may sometimes be seen here operating in Copper River to east. The old school is a local landmark.

V 104 (167.4 km) **F 260** (418.4 km)

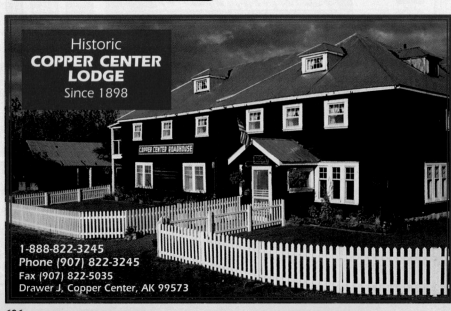

Ahtna building houses Copper River Native Assoc.

V 104.5 (168.2 km) **F 259.5** (417.6 km) Silver Springs Road. Copper Center school.

V 104.8 (168.7 km) **F 259.2** (417.1 km) Paved turnout to east. Watch for horses.

V 105.1 (169.1 km) **F 258.9** (416.6 km) National Park Service headquarters and visitor center for Wrangell–St. Elias National Park and Preserve. Access to Wrangell–St. Elias National Park and Preserve is via the Edgerton Highway and McCarthy Road (see EDGERTON HIGHWAY section) and the Nabesna Road off the Tok Cutoff (see the GLENN HIGHWAY section). Ranger on duty, general information available. A 10-minute video is shown; additional video programs shown on request. Maps and publications are for sale. Open 8 A.M. to 6 P.M. daily, Memorial Day through Labor Day. Winter hours are 8 A.M. to 5 P.M. weekdays. For more information write P.O. Box 439, Copper Center, AK 99573; or phone (907) 822-5234.

V 106 (170.6 km) **F 258** (415.2 km) IMPORTANT: North **junction** with Copper Center Bypass (New Richardson Highway). Southbound travelers TURN OFF on to Old Richardson Highway for scenic route through historic Copper Center (see description this section). *The MILEPOST®* does not log the bypass route (New Richardson Highway), which is the same distance as the old highway (6.5 miles/10.5 km) but without notable features. The old highway rejoins the bypass route at **Milepost V 100.2.**

V 110 (177 km) **F 254** (408.8 km) Dept. of Highways Tazlina station and Dept. of Natural Resources office. Report forest fires here or phone (907) 822-5533.

V 110.5 (177.8 km) **F 253.5** (408 km) Pipeline storage area. Turn west on pipeline storage area road and take second right for private RV park.

V 110.5 (177.8 km) **F 253.5** (408 km) **Tazlina River RV Park.** See display ad this section. ▲

V 110.6 (178 km) **F 253.4** (407.8 km) Rest area to east on banks of Tazlina River; large paved surface, 2 covered picnic tables, water, toilets.

V 110.7 (178.2 km) **F 253.3** (407.6 km) Tazlina River bridge. *Tazlina* is Indian for "swift water." The river flows eastward from the glacier of the same name into the Copper River.

V 111.2 (179 km) **F 252.8** (406.8 km) Community college and trading post; groceries and gas.

Tazlina River Trading Post & Western Auto. See display ad this section.

V 111.7 (179.8 km) **F 252.3** (406 km) Copperville access road. Developed during pipeline construction, this area has a church and private homes. Glennallen fire station.

V 112.3 (180.7 km) **F 251.7** (405 km) Steep grade southbound from Tazlina River to the top of the Copper River bluffs.

V 112.6 (181.2 km) **F 251.4** (404.6 km) Paved parking area with historical information sign on the development of transporta-

tion in Alaska. Short (0.1 mile) walk to good viewpoint on bluff with schematic diagram of Wrangell Mountains: Mount Sanford (elev. 16,237 feet/4,949m); Mount Drum (elev. 12,010 feet/3,661m); Mount Wrangell (elev. 14,163 feet/4,317m); and Mount Blackburn (elev. 16,390 feet/4,996m).

Sign at viewpoint reads: "Across the Copper River rise the peaks of the Wrangell Mountains. The 4 major peaks of the range can be seen from this point, with Mount Drum directly in front of you. The Wrangell Mountains, along with the St. Elias Mountains to the east, contain the most spectacular array of glaciers and ice fields outside polar regions. The Wrangell Mountains are part of Wrangell–St. Elias National Park and Preserve, the nation's largest national park. Together with Kluane National Park of Canada, the park has been designated a World Heritage site by the United Nations."

Visitor information for Wrangell–St. Elias National Park is available at **Milepost V 105.1** Old Richardson Highway.

V 115 (185 km) **F 249** (400.7 km) **South**

junction of Richardson and Glenn highways at Glennallen. Greater Copper Valley Visitor Information Center at service center at junction, open daily in summer; pay phone, gas, groceries. The town of Glennallen extends west along the Glenn Highway from here, with businesses located at the junction and along the Glenn Highway. Anchorage is 189 miles/304 km, Tok 139 miles/224 km, from here.

Offices of the Alaska State Troopers (phone 907/822-3263), Dept. of Fish and Wildlife, Dept. of Motor Vehicles, Alaska Court and community college located on east side of highway.

For the next 14 miles/22.5 km northbound the Richardson and Glenn highways share a common alignment. They separate at **Milepost V 128.6.**

NOTE: Anchorage- or Tok-bound travelers turn to **Milepost A 189** *in the GLENN HIGHWAY section on page 295. Valdez- or Fairbanks-bound travelers continue with this log.*

The Hub of Alaska and Maxi Mart. See display ad this section.

V 115.5 (185.9 km) **F 248.5** (399.9 km) **Rendezvous Cafe.** See display ad this section.

V 115.5 (185.9 km) **F 248.5** (399.9 km) **Glennallen Quick Stop Truck Stop.** Stop for friendly family service. Gas, diesel. Convenience store contains ice, pop, snacks,

postcards, ice cream, specialty items, pay phone and free coffee. Senior citizen, truck and caravan discounts. Several interesting items on display include an authentic Native Alaskan fish wheel. Full-service restaurant adjacent. [ADVERTISEMENT]

V 118 (189.9 km) **F 246** (395.9 km) Dry Creek State Recreation Site; 51 campsites, walk-in tent camping, water, tables, toilets, firepits, 15-day limit. Camping fee $10/night or annual pass. *Bring mosquito repellent!* Old ore car here was once used to haul gravel to Tonsina. ▲

V 118.1 (190.1 km) **F 245.9** (395.7 km) **Private Aircraft**: Gulkana airport; elev. 1,579 feet/481m; length 5,000 feet/1,524m; asphalt; fuel 100.

V 123.2 (198.3 km) **F 240.8** (387.5 km) Large paved turnout to east and well-defined 1.5-mile/2.4-km trail east side of road to the mouth of the **Gulkana River** (see **Milepost V 126.9** for details on access and permits). Excellent fishing mid-June to mid-July for king salmon to 50 lbs. (average is 30 lbs.), and red salmon to 6 lbs. Use bright colored yarn or flies, half-inch hook. Heavy tackle with 25- to 30-lb.-test line recommended for kings. Check special regulations before fishing the Gulkana River. ◄►

V 126 (202.8 km) **F 238** (383 km) Paved double-ended turnout to west.

V 126.8 (204.1 km) **F 237.2** (381.7 km) Gulkana River bridge. Entering Game Management Unit 13B, leaving unit 13A, northbound.

V 126.9 (204.2 km) **F 237.1** (381.6 km) Access road to **GULKANA** (pop. 100) on the bank of the Gulkana River. Camping is permitted along the river by the bridge. ▲

NOTE: Gulkana River frontage from 2 miles/3.2 km downstream of Sourdough Campground to the mouth of the Gulkana River is owned by Gulkana Village and managed by Ahtna, Inc. There are public easements along the Richardson Highway between Sourdough Campground and the bridge.

V 128.6 (206.9 km) **F 235.4** (378.8 km) **North junction** (Gakona Junction) of the Richardson Highway and Tok Cutoff (Glenn Highway), known locally as Gulkana Junction. Gas, food and lodging. Tok Cutoff leads east 125 miles/201 km to Tok on the Alaska Highway. The Richardson Highway crosses the Gulkana River bridge and continues straight ahead north.

Line Camp (at junction with Tok Cutoff). Groceries, ice, sporting goods, minor repairs, welding. 2 bed and breakfast units (2 bedrooms and kitchen in each). RV parking. Tourist information, guided king salmon on the Gulkana River. Specialized tours available. Phone (907) 822-3508 or (907) 822-5723; P.O. Box 255, Glennallen, AK 99588. [ADVERTISEMENT]

*NOTE: Tok-bound travelers turn to **Milepost A 203** on page 295 in the GLENN HIGHWAY section. Valdez- or Fairbanks-bound travelers continue with this log.*

V 129.2 (207.9 km) **F 234.8** (377.9 km) Pond with lily pads and occasionally a floatplane.

V 129.4 (208.2 km) **F 234.6** (377.5 km) Paved turnout to west. Sailor's Pit (gravel pit opposite lake to west); BLM trail across to **Gulkana River.** Fishing for rainbow trout, grayling, king and red salmon. Highway follows the Gulkana River. ◄►

V 132.1 (212.6 km) **F 231.9** (373.2 km) Paved turnout to west.

V 134.6 (216.6 km) **F 229.4** (369.2 km) Paved double-ended turnout with view of Gulkana River to west.

V 135.5 (218.1 km) **F 228.5** (367.7 km) Watch for caribou.

V 135.8 (218.5 km) **F 228.2** (367.2 km) Paved turnout to east. Old beaver pond; 1 mile/1.6 km winter trail to Gulkana River.

V 136.4 (219.5 km) **F 227.6** (366.3 km) Coleman Creek bridge.

V 136.7 (220 km) **F 227.3** (365.8 km) Side road west to **Gulkana River** fishing access: Poplar Grove/Gulkana River BLM-marked vehicle trail, 1 mile/1.6 km. Informal campsites along river. ◄►

V 138.1 (222.2 km) **F 225.9** (363.5 km) **Poplar Grove Creek** bridge; spring grayling fishing. Paved turnout to west at north end of bridge. ◄►

V 139 (223.7 km) **F 225** (362.1 km) Watch for frost heaves.

V 139.4 (224.3 km) **F 224.6** (361.4 km) Paved turnout to west with view of Gulkana River.

V 140.6 (226.3 km) **F 223.4** (359.5 km) Paved turnout to east.

V 141.2 (227.2 km) **F 222.8** (358.6 km) Side road west to Gulkana River fishing access. Informal campsites along river. ◄►

V 141.4 (227.6 km) **F 222.6** (358.2 km) Paved double-ended scenic viewpoint to west. One-mile/1.6-km trail to Gulkana River.

V 146 (234.9 km) **F 218** (350.8 km) Lakes and potholes next 9 miles/14.5 km northbound; watch for waterfowl. Views of Chugach Mountains southbound.

V 146.4 (235.6 km) **F 217.6** (350.2 km) Entering BLM public lands northbound.

V 147.1 (236.7 km) **F 216.9** (349.1 km) Double-ended paved scenic viewpoint.

V 147.6 (237.5 km) **F 216.4** (348.3 km) **SOURDOUGH.** BLM Sourdough Creek Campground; 60 sites, good king salmon fishing. Access to **Gulkana River**, marked trail to Sourdough Creek. Across the bridge (load limit 8 tons) and to the right a road leads to parking, toilets and boat launch on river. Watch for potholes in access roads. Native lands; check for restrictions. ◄►▲

The Sourdough Roadhouse, destroyed by fire in December 1992, stood next to the creek. It was established in 1903. A gas station was operating here in 1996. The old Valdez trail runs 150 yards/137m behind the few buildings left standing.

The Gulkana River is part of the National Wild and Scenic Rivers System managed by the BLM. A popular float trip for experienced canoeists begins at Paxson Lake and ends at Sourdough Campground. See description at **Milepost V 175.**

Gulkana River above Sourdough Creek, grayling 9 to 21 inches (same as Sourdough Creek below), rainbow 10 to 24 inches, spinners, June through September; red salmon 8 to 25 lbs. and king salmon up to 62 lbs., use streamer flies or spinners, mid-June through mid-July. **Sourdough Creek,** grayling 10 to 20 inches, use single yellow eggs or corn, fish deep early May through first week in June, use spinners or flies mid-June until freezeup. ◄►

V 150.7 (242.5 km) **F 213.3** (343.3 km) Large gravel turnout to east.

V 151 (243 km) **F 213** (342.8 km) Private gravel driveway to west by large pond; please do not trespass.

V 153.8 (247.5 km) **F 210.2** (338.3 km) Highway passes through boggy terrain; watch for caribou. *CAUTION: No turnouts, little shoulder. Watch for dips and rough patches in highway next 10 miles/16 km northbound.*

V 154.2 (248.2 km) **F 209.8** (337.6 km) Double-ended gravel turnout to east.

V 156.4 (251.7 km) **F 207.6** (334.1 km) As the highway winds through the foothills of the Alaska Range, over a crest called Hogan Hill (elev. 2,647 feet/807m), there are magnificent views of 3 mountain ranges: the Alaska Range through which the highway leads, the Wrangell Mountains to the southeast and the Chugach Mountains to the southwest. To the west is a vast wilderness plateau where the headwaters of the Susitna River converge to flow west and south into Cook Inlet, west of Anchorage.

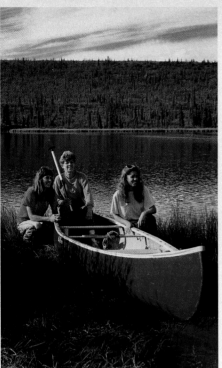

Family of canoeists pose for photo at Paxson Lake. (© Craig Brandt)

V 156.7 (252.2 km) **F 207.3** (333.6 km) Good view of pothole lakes to west.

V 157 (252.7 km) **F 207** (333.1 km) Good long-range viewpoints from highway. Moose and other game may be spotted from here (use binoculars).

V 158.9 (255.7 km) **F 205.1** (330.1 km) Sweeping view of the Glennallen area to the south.

V 160.7 (258.6 km) **F 203.3** (327.2 km) **Haggard Creek** BLM marked trailhead; grayling fishing. Access to Gulkana River 7 miles/11.3 km to west. ◄

V 162.2 (261 km) **F 201.8** (324.8 km) Double-ended gravel turnout to east.

V 166.5 (267.9 km) **F 197.5** (317.8 km) Jane Lake trail; 1 mile/1.6 km to west.

V 168.1 (270.5 km) **F 195.9** (315.3 km) **Gillespie Lake** trailhead and parking to west. Walk up creek 0.3 mile/0.5 km to lake; grayling fishing. ◄

V 169.3 (272.5 km) **F 194.7** (313.3 km) Large gravel pit. Turnout to west.

V 169.4 (272.6 km) **F 194.6** (313.2 km) Middle Fork BLM-marked trail to Meier's Lake and Middle Fork Gulkana River.

V 170 (273.6 km) **F 194** (312.2 km) Roadhouse with gas, food, lodging and camping. **Meier's Lake**; parking area, good grayling fishing. ◄▲

Meier's Lake Roadhouse. See display ad this section. ▲

V 171.6 (276.2 km) **F 192.4** (309.6 km) Gravel turnout by river to west. Long upgrade begins northbound.

V 172.7 (277.9 km) **F 191.3** (307.9 km) Small turnout to west, view of pipeline to east.

V 173.3 (278.9 km) **F 190.7** (306.9 km) **Dick Lake** to the east via narrow side road (easy to miss); no turnaround space. Good grayling fishing in summer. View of trans-Alaska oil pipeline across the lake. Good spot for photos.

V 175 (281.6 km) **F 189** (304.2 km) BLM Paxson Lake Campground turnoff. Wide gravel road (full of potholes if not recently graded) leads 1.5 miles/2.4 km to large camping area near lakeshore; 50 campsites, some pull-throughs, spaces for all sizes of vehicles but some sites on slope (RVs may need leveling boards); toilets, water, tables, firepits, dump station and concrete boat launch. Parking for 80 vehicles. Bring mosquito repellent. *CAUTION: Watch for bears.* Fishing in **Paxson Lake** for lake trout, grayling and red salmon. ◄▲

This is the launch site for floating the Gulkana River to Sourdough Campground at **Milepost V 147.6.** Total distance is about 50 miles/80 km and 4 days travel, according to the BLM, which manages this national wild river. While portions of the river are placid, the Gulkana does have Class II and III rapids, with a gradient of 38 feet/mile in one section. Canyon Rapids may be Class IV depending on water levels (there is a portage). Recommended for experienced boaters only. For further information on floating the Gulkana, contact the BLM at Box 147, Glennallen 99588, or phone (907) 822-3217.

V 177.1 (285 km) **F 186.9** (300.8 km) Small gravel turnout to west with view of Paxson Lake.

V 177.5 (285.7 km) **F 186.5** (300.1 km) Turnout to east. Trans-Alaska oil pipeline may be seen on the ridge northwest of the highway.

V 178.7 (287.6 km) **F 185.3** (298.2 km) Small gravel turnout to east.

V 179 (288.1 km) **F 185** (297.7 km) Gravel turnout overlooking Paxson Lake. The lake was named for the former owner of the roadhouse (still Paxson Lodge) about 1906.

V 179.2 (288.4 km) **F 184.8** (297.4 km) Gravel turnout to west overlooking Paxson Lake.

V 182.1 (293 km) **F 181.9** (292.7 km) Large gravel turnout at head of Paxson Lake. Rough gravel trail to lake.

V 183.2 (294.8 km) **F 180.8** (291 km) Entering Paxson Closed Area northbound (closed to taking of all big game).

V 184.4 (296.8 km) **F 179.6** (289 km) Large gravel turnout to west.

V 184.7 (297.2 km) **F 179.3** (288.6 km) One Mile Creek bridge.

V 185.5 (298.5 km) **F 178.5** (287.3 km) **Junction** with Denali Highway to Denali National Park and George Parks Highway (see DENALI HIGHWAY section for details) at **PAXSON** (pop. 33), site of a lodge with gas station (open year-round), restaurant and small grocery store. Wilderness tours, inquire at lodge. Sled dog racing first weekend in April. Paxson Mountain (elev. 5,200 feet/1,585m) is 3 miles/4.8 km west-southwest.

Paxson Inn & Lodge. See display ad this section.

Private Aircraft: Paxson airstrip (Hufman Field), adjacent south; elev. 2,653 feet/809m; length 2,800 feet/853m; gravel; emergency fuel; attended.

V 185.7 (298.9 km) **F 178.3** (286.9 km) Site of original Paxson Lodge.

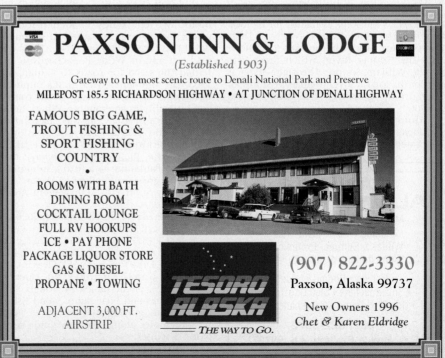

Paxson Alpine Tours. See display ad this section.

V 185.8 (299 km) F 178.2 (286.8 km) Paxson Station highway maintenance camp.

V 186.4 (300 km) F 177.6 (285.8 km) Leaving BLM public lands northbound.

V 188.3 (303 km) F 175.7 (282.8 km) Large paved double-ended rest area to east across from Gulkana River; tables, fireplaces, toilets, dumpster and water. The Gulkana River flows south to the Copper River.

V 189.6 (305.1 km) F 174.4 (280.7 km) Long paved double-ended turnout to west.

V 190.4 (306.4 km) F 173.6 (279.4 km) Paved parking area by Gulkana River with picnic tables, dumpster and view of Summit Lake and pipeline. Access to Summit Lake. Interpretive sign about red salmon. Salmon spawning area; fishing for salmon prohibited. Access to **Fish Creek** at north end of turnout; grayling fishing. Access to Fish Lake is via trail paralleling creek for 2 miles/3.2 km, according to the ADF&G.

V 191 (307.4 km) F 173 (278.4 km) Summit Lake to west; turnout at head of stream.

V 191.1 (307.5 km) F 172.9 (278.2 km) Double-ended turnout to west.

V 191.4 (308 km) 172.6 (277.8 km) **Water's Edge B&B** on Summit Lake. Extra nice cabins and rooms, some with cooking facilities. Tent and motorhome spaces, showers. Quiet setting, breathtaking view. Good fishing, birding, berry picking, wildflowers, lots of wildlife, unique flower garden. Excellent winter snowmobiling. Hosts are longtime Alaskans. Write P.O. Box 3020, Paxson, AK 99737. Phone/fax (907) 482-9001. [ADVERTISEMENT]

V 192.2 (309.3 km) F 171.8 (276.5 km) Turnout with table and boat launch on **Summit Lake;** lake trout, grayling, burbot and red salmon.

V 192.6 (310 km) F 171.4 (275.8 km) Large gravel turnout on Summit Lake.

V 193.3 (311.1 km) F 170.7 (274.7 km) Gravel turnout to west by Summit Lake.

V 194.1 (312.4 km) F 169.9 (273.4 km) Gravel turnout on Summit Lake.

V 195 (313.8 km) F 169 (271.9 km) Large gravel turnout at **Summit Lake** (elev. 3,210 feet/978m). Bed and breakfast. This lake, 7 miles/11.3 km long, is named for its location near the water divide between the Delta and Gulkana rivers. The Gulkana River flows into the Copper River, which flows into Prince William Sound. The Delta River is part of the Yukon River drainage. Fishing for lake trout, grayling, red salmon and burbot.

Hines Site 20/20 Bed and Breakfast overlooks Summit Lake. Five new beautifully decorated, non-smoking view rooms with

Fall colors brighten steep hills along Richardson Highway near Milepost V 207.
(© Bruce M. Herman)

private baths. Continental breakfast. Quiet, peaceful environment. Good fishing and

snow machining. Open year around. Your host: "Boots" Hines, HC 72 Box 7195, Delta Junction, AK 99737. Reservation phone (907) 388-8299. Or just truck on in. [ADVERTISEMENT]

V 195 (313.8 km) F 169 (272 km) Summit Lake Lodge; burned down in November 1993. Current status unknown.

V 196.8 (316.7 km) F 167.2 (269.1 km) Gunn Creek bridge. View of Gulkana Glacier to the northeast. This glacier, perched on 8,000-foot/2,438m Icefall Peak, feeds streams that drain into both Prince William Sound and the Yukon River.

V 197.6 (318 km) F 166.4 (267.8 km) Large gravel turnout. Memorial monument honoring Gen. Wilds P. Richardson, for whom the highway is named, at summit of Isabel Pass (elev. 3,000 feet/914m). Sign here reads: "Captain Wilds P. Richardson presented the need for roads to Congress in 1903. His familiarity with Alaska impressed Congress with his knowledge of the country and his ability as an engineer. When the Act of 1905 became a law, he was placed at the head of the Alaska Road Commission in which position he served for more than a decade. The Richardson Highway, from Valdez to Fairbanks, is a fitting monument to the first great road builder of Alaska."

Entering Sport Fish Management Area C southbound.

V 198.5 (319.4 km) F 165.5 (266.3 km) Gravel turnout to west.

V 200.4 (322.5 km) F 163.6 (263.3 km) Gravel side road leads west 1.5 miles/2.4 km to **Fielding Lake** Campground. Pleasant area above tree line; 7 campsites, no water, no camping fee, picnic tables, pit toilets, large parking areas and boat ramp. Good fishing for lake trout, grayling and burbot.

Snow poles along highway guide snowplows in winter.

V 201.5 (324.3 km) F 162.5 (261.5 km) Phelan Creek bridge. Buried section of

pipeline to west is a large animal crossing.

V 202 (325.1 km) F 162 (260.7 km) Trans-Alaska oil pipeline parallels the highway above ground here. Entering BLM public lands northbound.

V 202.5 (325.9 km) F 161.5 (259.9 km) McCallum Creek bridge, highway follows Phelan Creek northbound. This stream heads in Gulkana Glacier and flows northwest to the Delta River.

V 203.5 (327.5 km) F 160.5 (258.3 km) Watch for beaver ponds (and beaver); lupine in June.

V 204 (328.3 km) F 160 (257.5 km) Spring water piped to east side of highway; paved turnout.

V 204.7 (329.4 km) F 159.3 (256.4 km) Large gravel turnouts both sides of highway.

V 205.3 (330.4 km) F 158.7 (255.4 km) Small gravel turnout by stream. Good place for pictures of the pipeline up a steep hill.

V 206.4 (332.2 km) F 157.6 (253.6 km) Double-ended turnout with picnic tables, litter barrels and view of mineralized Rainbow Ridge to northeast. Wildflowers include yellow arnica and sweet pea.

V 207 (333.1 km) F 157 (252.7 km) Good gravel turnout to west. There are frequent turnouts the next 6 miles/9.6 km northbound.

V 207.8 (334.4 km) F 156.2 (251.4 km) Turnout. Rock slide and avalanche area next mile northbound; watch for rocks on road.

V 208.1 (334.9 km) F 155.9 (250.9 km) Turnout to west by creek. Look for wild, or Alaskan, rhubarb (*P. alaskanum*), a member of the buckwheat family. Grows to 6 feet with showy clusters of small yellowish-white flowers.

V 211.7 (340.7 km) F 152.3 (245.1 km) Side roads signed APL are Alyeska pipeline access roads and closed to the public.

V 213.2 (343.1 km) F 150.8 (242.7 km) Gravel turnout to west along Phelan Creek.

V 213.6 (343.7 km) F 150.4 (242 km) Gravel turnout and road to gravel pit to east. Avalanche area ends northbound.

V 214 (344.4 km) F 150 (241.4 km) Double-ended paved turnout with picnic tables and litter barrels. Highway follows Delta River northbound, Phelan Creek southbound.

V 215.1 (346.2 km) F 148.9 (239.6 km) Pipeline crosses Miller Creek right next to bridge. Parking at both ends of bridge, access to creek.

V 215.9 (347.4 km) **F 148.1** (238.3 km) Pipeline interpretive viewpoint with information sign.

V 216.3 (348.1 km) **F 147.7** (237.7 km) Gravel turnout to east.

V 216.7 (348.7 km) **F 147.3** (237 km) Lower Miller Creek. Turnouts at both ends of bridge. This is one of the best spots on the highway to photograph the pipeline.

V 217.2 (349.5 km) **F 146.8** (236.2 km) Castner Creek; parking at both ends of bridge, west side of road.

V 218.2 (351.1 km) **F 145.8** (234.6 km) Trims Station DOT/PF highway maintenance camp.

V 218.8 (352.1 km) **F 145.2** (233.7 km) Bridge over Trims Creek, parking. Wildflowers in the area include lupine, sweet pea and fireweed. Watch for caribou on slopes.

V 219.2 (352.8 km) **F 144.8** (233 km) Access to Pipeline Pump Station No. 10.

V 219.3 (352.9 km) **F 144.7** (232.9 km) Small gravel turnout. Note the flood control dikes (also called finger dikes) in stream to slow erosion. Alyeska Pipeline calls these "river training structures."

V 219.9 (353.9 km) **F 144.1** (231.9 km) Michael Creek bridge; parking at both ends of bridge. Buried pipeline to west. Southbound drivers have a spectacular view of Pump Station No. 10 and the surrounding mountains.

V 220.9 (355.5 km) **F 143.1** (230.3 km) Flood Creek bridge; parking.

V 223 (358.9 km) **F 141** (226.9 km) Whistler Creek bridge; parking. Watch for frost heaves.

V 223.8 (360.2 km) **F 140.2** (225.6 km) Boulder Creek bridge; parking.

V 224.5 (361.3 km) **F 139.5** (224.5 km) Lower Suzy Q Creek bridge; parking.

V 224.8 (361.8 km) **F 139.2** (224 km) Suzy Q Creek bridge. Double-ended gravel turnout.

V 225.2 (362.4 km) **F 138.8** (223.4 km) Large gravel turnout to east.

V 225.4 (362.7 km) **F 138.6** (223.1 km) Double-ended paved turnout with picnic table and litter barrels to west. Historical marker here identifies the terminal moraine of Black Rapids Glacier to the west. Currently a retreating glacier with little ice visible, this glacier was nicknamed the Galloping Glacier when it advanced more than 3 miles/4.8 km during the winter of 1936–37.

Black Rapids Lake trail begins across from historical sign (0.3 mile/0.4 km to lake). Look for river beauty and wild sweet pea blooming in June.

Private Aircraft: Black Rapids airstrip, adjacent north; elev. 2,125 feet/648m; length 2,200 feet/671m; gravel.

V 226 (363.7 km) **F 138** (222.1 km) Good gravel turnout by river to west.

V 226.3 (364.2 km) **F 137.7** (221.6 km) Falls Creek bridge.

V 226.7 (364.8 km) **F 137.3** (221 km) Black Rapids U.S. Army training site at Fall Creek. Boundary between Game Management Units 20D and 13.

V 227 (365.3 km) **F 137** (220.5 km) Gunnysack Creek. View of Black Rapids Glacier to west.

V 227.4 (366 km) **F 136.6** (219.8 km) Old Black Rapids Lodge. Dirt airstrip.

V 228.4 (367.6 km) **F 135.6** (218.2 km) Parking beside One Mile Creek bridge.

V 230.4 (370.8 km) **F 133.6** (215 km) Large paved turnout overlooks Delta River.

V 231 (371.7 km) **F 133** (214 km) Darling Creek. Gravel turnout to east.

V 233.3 (375.5 km) **F 130.7** (210.3 km) Bear Creek bridge; turnouts at either end, access to creek. Wildflowers include pale oxytrope, yellow arnica, fireweed, wild rhubarb and cow parsnip.

V 234.2 (376.9 km) **F 129.8** (208.9 km) Double-ended gravel turnout to east.

V 234.5 (377.4 km) **F 129.5** (208.4 km) Paved turnout to west. Pipeline access road. Pipeline comes up out of the ground here and goes through forest.

V 234.8 (377.9 km) **F 129.2** (207.9 km) Ruby Creek bridge; parking to west.

V 237.9 (382.9 km) **F 126.1** (202.9 km) Loop road (watch for potholes) through Donnelly Creek State Recreation Site; 12 campsites, tables, firepits, toilets and water. Camping fee $8/night or annual pass. ▲

V 238.7 (384.1 km) **F 125.3** (201.6 km) Watch for frost heaves northbound.

V 239.1 (384.8 km) **F 124.9** (201 km) Small gravel turnout to east.

V 241.3 (388.3 km) **F 122.7** (197.5 km) Large paved turnout to west.

V 242 (389.5 km) **F 122** (196.3 km) Pipeline parallels highway. Donnelly Dome ahead northbound. Watch for pavement dips.

V 242.1 (389.6 km) **F 121.9** (196.2 km) Coal Mine Road (4-wheel-drive vehicles only) leads east to fishing lakes; **Last Lake**, arctic char; **Coal Mine No. 5 Lake**, lake trout; **Brodie Lake** and **Pauls Pond**, grayling and lake trout. Check with the ADF&G for details. ⬖

V 243.4 (391.7 km) **F 120.6** (194.1 km) Pipeline viewpoint with interpretive signs. Good photo stop.

V 243.9 (392.5 km) **F 120.1** (193.3 km) Paved double-ended turnout to east. The trans-Alaska oil pipeline snakes along the ground and over the horizon. Zigzag design of pipeline converts pipe thermal expansion, as well as movement from other forces (like earthquakes), into a controlled sideways movement. A spectacular view to the southwest of 3 of the highest peaks of the Alaska Range. From west to south they are: Mount Deborah (elev. 12,339 feet/3,761m); Hess Mountain (elev. 11,940 feet/3,639m), center foreground; and Mount Hayes (elev. 13,832 feet/4,216m).

In spring look for wild sweet pea, chiming bells, lupine, lousewort and bluebell for the next 3 miles/4.8 km.

V 244.3 (393.2 km) **F 119.7** (192.6 km) Gravel turnout to east. Trail to **Donnelly Lake**; king and silver salmon, rainbow trout. Donnelly Dome ahead northbound.⬖

V 246 (395.9 km) **F 118** (189.9 km) Donnelly Dome immediately to the west (elev. 3,910 feet/1,192m), was first named Delta Dome. For years the mountain has been used to predict the weather: "The first snow on the top of the Donnelly Dome means snow in Delta Junction within 2 weeks."

V 246.9 (397.3 km) **F 117.1** (188.4 km) Gravel turnout to east.

V 247 (397.5 km) **F 117** (188.3 km) Cutoff to Old Richardson Highway loop to west; access to fishing lakes.

V 247.3 (398 km) **F 116.7** (187.8 km) From here northbound the road extends straight as an arrow for 4.8 miles/7.7 km.

V 249.3 (401.2 km) **F 114.7** (184.6 km) Bear Drop Zone. Military games area. Controlled access road: No trespassing.

V 252.8 (406.8 km) **F 111.2** (179 km) Scenic viewpoint to west with picnic tables and litter barrels.

Trans-Alaska pipeline parallels the Richardson Highway to Valdez.
(© Susan Cole Kelly)

V 253.9 (408.6 km) **F 110.1** (177.2 km) Good view of Pump Station No. 9 if southbound.

V 256 (412 km) **F 108** (173.8 km) Fort Greely Ridge Road to west.

V 257.6 (414.6 km) **F 106.4** (171.2 km) Entrance to U.S. Army Cold Regions Test Center at Fort Greely.

Meadows Road (4-wheel-drive vehicles only) leads west to fishing lakes. Access to **Bolio Lake**; grayling, rainbow, lake trout. Rainbow-producing **Mark Lake** is 4.5 miles/ 7.2 km along this road. Meadows Road junctions with the Old Richardson Highway loop. Check with the ADF&G for details on fishing lakes. ⬖

V 258.3 (415.7 km) **F 105.7** (170.1 km) Pump Station No. 9 access road to east. Tours of Pump Station 9 are offered daily from June to August. Phone (907) 869-3270 or 456-9391 for more information and tour reservations.

V 261.2 (420.3 km) **F 102.8** (165.4 km) **FORT GREELY** (restricted area) main gate. Fort Greely was named for A.W. Greely, arctic explorer and author of *Three Years of Arctic Service.*

V 262.6 (422.6 km) **F 101.4** (163.2 km) Double-ended paved turnout with scenic view. Watch for bison. Wind area next 2 miles/3.2 km northbound.

V 262.7 (422.8 km) **F 101.3** (163 km) FAA buildings. Big Delta.

V 264.9 (426.3 km) **F 99.1** (159.5 km) Jarvis Creek, rises near Butch Lake to the east and flows into the Delta River. Buffalo (bison) may be seen in this area.

V 266 (428 km) **F 98** (157.7 km) **Junction** of the Richardson Highway and the Alaska Highway, **Milepost DC 1422**, at Delta Junction. Visitor center is located at junction. Turn to page 183 for description of Delta Junction services and continuation of highway log to Fairbanks (the remaining 98 miles/157.7 km of the Richardson Highway leading into Fairbanks are logged in the ALASKA HIGHWAY section).

EDGERTON HIGHWAY/ McCARTHY ROAD ⑩

Connects: Richardson Highway Junction to McCarthy, AK
Length: 93 miles   **Road Surface:** 40% paved 60% gravel
Season: McCarthy Road not maintained in winter
Major Attraction: Wrangell–St. Elias National Park & Preserve

(See map, page 613)

	Chitina	McCarthy	Richardson Hwy.
Chitina		60	33
McCarthy	60		93
Richardson Hwy.	33	93	

Historic Kennecott mine is about a 4 1/2-mile walk from McCarthy. There is a lodge nearby. (©Susan Cole Kelly)

The Edgerton Highway, known locally as the Edgerton Cutoff, is a scenic paved road leading 35.1 miles/56.5 km east from its junction with the Richardson Highway to Chitina, then across the Copper River bridge to the start of the McCarthy Road. The gravel McCarthy Road leads 58.3 miles/93.8 km east and dead ends at the Kennicott River, about 1 mile/1.6 km west of the settlement of McCarthy. Total driving distance from the Richardson Highway turnoff to the end of the McCarthy Road is 93.4 miles/150.3 km.

The Edgerton Highway is paved with some long, steep grades. From **Milepost R 7.3**, the Edgerton Highway follows the approximate route of the old pack trail that once connected Chitina with Copper Center. The Edgerton Highway is named for U.S. Army Maj. Glenn Edgerton of the Alaska Territorial Road Commission.

The McCarthy Road is recommended for the adventurous traveler and only in the summer. Allow 4 hours driving time, with a maximum speed of 20 mph/32 kmph. Maintained by the state Dept. of Transportation, the road is suitable for most vehicles to **Milepost J 13.3** (Strelna Creek). The road is very narrow and may be dusty in dry weather and muddy in wet weather.

Increased tourist and truck traffic on the McCarthy Road resulted in alternate hourly closures of the road to passenger vehicles and logging trucks in summer 1996 to avoid collisions. Also be aware that the Kennicott River crossing is by hand-pulled cable tram. There is currently no vehicle access across the river; see description at **Milepost J 58.2**. Keep in mind that there may be long lines at the tram crossing on holiday weekends. The state plans to install a footbridge here in 1997.

Motorists with large vehicles or trailers exercise caution, especially in wet weather. Watch for old railroad spikes in roadbed. Unless recently graded, watch for potholes, soft spots and severe washboard. Tire repair and mechanical light-towing service are available at Silver Lake Campground, **Milepost J 9.3**. The National Park Service ranger station in Chitina has information on current road conditions and also on backcountry travel in Wrangell–St. Elias National Park and Preserve. Most land along the McCarthy Road is either privately- or publicly-held. Local residents have asked that visitors please help protect water sources from contamination.

The McCarthy Road follows the right-of-way of the old Copper River & Northwestern Railway. Begun in 1907, the CR&NW (also referred to as the "can't run and never will") was built to carry copper ore from the Kennecott Mines to Cordova. It took 4 years to complete the railway. The railway and mine ceased operation in 1938.

The solitude and scenery of McCarthy, along with the historic Kennecott Mine and surrounding wilderness of Wrangell–St. Elias National Park and Preserve, have drawn increasing numbers of visitors to this area. It is a 126-mile/202-km drive from Glennallen to McCarthy, 315 miles/507 km from Anchorage.

Emergency medical services: Between the junction of the Richardson and Edgerton highways and McCarthy, contact the Copper River EMS in Glennallen, phone 911 or (907) 822-3203.

Edgerton Highway Log

Distance from junction with Richardson Highway (R) is followed by distance from junction with McCarthy Road (M).

R O M 35.1 (56.5 km) **Junction** at **Milepost V 82.6** Richardson Highway. Begin long down-grade eastbound. Watch for horses.

Excellent view of Mount Drum (to the northeast), a 12,010-foot/3,661-m peak of the Wrangell Mountains. Mount Wrangell

▲ Mount Wrangell
14,163 ft./4,317m

WRANGELL

MOUNTAINS

Mount Blackburn ▲
16,390 ft./4,996m

Glaciated Area

Scale

0 _____ 10 Miles
0 ____ 10 Kilometres

Map Location

Key to mileage boxes

miles/kilometres
miles/kilometres from:

J-Junction   **R**-Richardson
M-McCarthy   Highway
Road   Junction
Junction   **RE**-Road End

To Glennallen
(see RICHARDSON HIGHWAY section)

● Copper Center

Klutina R.

Copper

National Park Boundary

Willow Creek

Willow Lake

Pippin Lake

Squirrel Creek

Tonsina

Kenny Lake

River

4

R-0
M-35/57km
RE-93/150km

Lower Tonsina

Liberty Creek

Twomile L.

Trans-Alaska Pipeline

To Valdez
(see RICHARDSON HIGHWAY section)

Old Edgerton Loop Road

R-5.2/8.4km Rather Rough-It Adventures
R-7.2/11.6km Kenny Lake Mercantile & RV Park CDGIPST

R-13/20.9km Tonsina Native Arts & Crafts

Chetaslina River

Cheshnina R.

Tonsina R.

Kossina R.

Kuskulana River

Strelna L.

Van Lake

Silver Lake

Sculpin Lake

▲ Chitina

R-33/53.1km Chitina Fuel & Grocery
& Chitina Motel dGILPS
Spirit Mountain Artworks

R-33/53km
M-2/3km

Copper River

Glaciated

Area

R-35/57km
M-0
J-0
RE-58/94km

J-9.3/15km Silver Lake Campground Clr

J-15/24.1km McCarthy Road
Farm and Rides CL

The McCarthy Road

Long Lake

Chitina River

Wrangell-St. Elias National Park and Preserve

Glaciated Area

Kennicott Glacier

Kennicott Cr.

Nizina River

● Kennicott

J-58.3/93.8km Roadside Potatohead M
J-58.2/93.7km Copper Oar Rafting

J-58/94km
RE-0

▲ ● McCarthy

J-58/93.3km Glacier View Campground
and Glacier Wings Helicopter Tours C

J-57.7/92.9km McCarthy Trailrides B&B L

J-55.2/88.8km Willow Herb
Mountain Depot Lr

Kennicott River

N
W E
S

Principal Route

Paved — Unpaved ▪▪▪

Other Roads

Paved — Unpaved ▪▪▪

Ferry Routes •••••   **Hiking Trails** ——

⊡ Refer to Log for Visitor Facilities

❓ Visitor Information   ⊡ Fishing

▲ Campground   ✈ Airport   ✝ Airstrip

Key to Advertiser Services

C - Camping
D - Dump Station
d - Diesel
G - Gas (reg., unld.)
I - Ice
L - Lodging
M - Meals
P - Propane
R - Car Repair (major)
r - Car Repair (minor)
S - Store (grocery)
T - Telephone (pay)

(elev. 14,163 feet/4,317m) and Mount Blackburn (elev. 16,390 feet/4,996m) are visible straight ahead.

R 5.2 (8.4 km) **M 29.9** (48.1 km) Kenny Lake School.

Rather Rough-It Adventures. See display ad this section.

R 5.3 (8.5 km) **M 29.8** (48 km) Paved turnout to north.

R 7.2 (11.6 km) **M 27.9** (44.9 km) Grocery store with gas, laundromat, showers, camping, gift shop and pay phone.

Kenny Lake Mercantile & RV Park. See display ad this section.

R 7.3 (11.7 km) **M 27.8** (44.7 km) Old Edgerton Loop Road (gravel) leads from here 8 miles/12.9 km through homestead and farm country to the Richardson Highway at **Milepost V 91.1.**

R 7.5 (12.1 km) **M 27.6** (44.4 km) Kenny Lake community hall, fairgrounds.

R 7.7 (12.4 km) **M 27.4** (44.1 km) Spacious double-ended paved rest area to south with picnic table on shore of Kenny Lake.

R 12.3 (19.8 km) **M 22.8** (36.7 km) Paved turnout to south. Tonsina River BLM trailhead, 2 miles/3.2 km (marked, brushed trail; good hike).

R 12.5 (20.1 km) **M 22.6** (36.4 km) Paved turnout to north. Copper River BLM trailhead, 5 miles/8 km.

R 13 (20.9 km) **M 22.2** (35.7 km)

Tonsina Native Arts & Crafts. See display ad on page 614.

R 18 (29 km) **M 17.1** (27.5 km) Steep downhill grade eastbound. Views of the Copper River and bluffs.

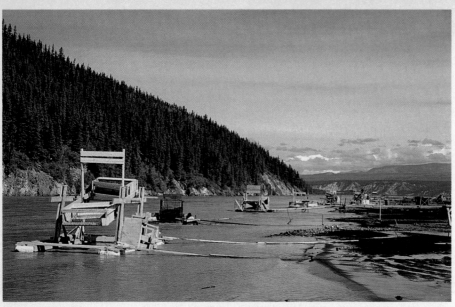

Fish wheels are used for subsistence salmon fishing on the Copper River.
(© Barbara Willard)

R 19.3 (31 km) **M 15.8** (25.4 km) Site of the settlement of Lower Tonsina, formerly a roadhouse for travelers using the Copper River. Tonsina and Copper rivers are visible here. Beyond are the Wrangell Mountains.

The road continues from here east up a steep bluff. Much of the highway has been hewn from solid rock, leaving great cuts on either side. Pockets of pure peat moss are evident in breaks in the rock walls along the road. *CAUTION: Peat fires can be a serious problem; be careful with campfires.*

R 19.4 (31.2 km) **M 15.7** (25.3 km) Tonsina River bridge. Former Lower Tonsina townsite to west of bridge.

R 19.5 (31.4 km) **M 15.6** (25.1 km) Turnout to south.

R 19.6 (31.5 km) **M 15.5** (24.9 km) Double-ended turnout at lake to north.

R 21 (33.8 km) **M 14.2** (22.9 km) Gravel turnout to north overlooking the Copper River.

R 21.6 (34.8 km) **M 13.5** (21.7 km) Paved viewpoint to north above Copper River.

R 21.9 (35.2 km) **M 13.3** (21.4 km) Small gravel turnout to north.

R 22 (35.4 km) **M 13.1** (21.1 km) Top of hill, steep descents both directions.

R 23.5 (37.8 km) **M 11.6** (18.7 km) Liberty Falls Creek BLM trailhead to south.

R 23.7 (38.1 km) **M 11.4** (18.3 km) Liberty Creek bridge (8-ton load limit) and Liberty Falls State Recreation Site. The campground is just south of the highway on the banks of Liberty Creek, near the foot of the thundering falls. Scenic spot. Loop road through campground (large RVs and trailers check road before driving in); 5 sites, no water, no camping fee. Berry picking; watch for bears. ▲

R 28.4 (45.7 km) **M 6.7** (10.8 km) Small gravel turnout to north overlooking river.

R 28.5 (45.9 km) **M 6.6** (10.6 km) Pavement break. Side road north to Chitina DOT/PF maintenance station and airstrip. ADF&G office.

Private Aircraft: Chitina Municipal Airfield; elev. 556 feet/169m; length 2,800 feet/853m; gravel; unattended.

R 29.5 (47.5 km) **M 5.7** (9.2 km) Small gravel turnout by Threemile Lake.

R 29.7 (47.8 km) **M 5.4** (8.7 km) Paved turnout by **Threemile Lake**; good grayling and rainbow trout fishing.

R 30.1 (48.4 km) **M 5** (8 km) Small turnout to south by **Twomile Lake**; good grayling and rainbow trout fishing, canoe launch.

R 30.6 (49.2 km) **M 4.5** (7.2 km) Large paved turnout at end of Twomile Lake.

R 31.9 (51.3 km) **M 3.2** (5.1 km) Onemile Lake (also called First Lake). Access road to boat launch at east end of lake.

Chitina

R 33 (53.1 km) **M 2.1** (3.4 km). Located about 120 miles/193 km northeast of Valdez, and about 66 miles/106 km southeast of Glennallen. **Population:** 49. **Emergency Services:** Copper River EMS, phone (907) 822-3203.

Visitor Information: National Park Service ranger station for Wrangell–St. Elias National Park and Preserve in Chitina. Hours were 10 A.M. to 6 P.M., daily, in 1996; hours may vary. Open Memorial Day to Labor Day. A slide show on the McCarthy Road

Dogs wait for their owner to return outside Spirit Mountain Artworks.
(© Ruth von Spalding)

and video programs are available. Write Box 439, Copper Center, AK 99573, or phone (907) 822-5234 (park headquarters); Chitina ranger station, phone (907) 823-2205.

Chitina has a post office, grocery, gas, motel, restaurant, tire repair service and phone service. (The Chitina Saloon, the town's only bar, burned down in December 1996.) The National Park Service ranger station is housed in a historic cabin. Follow signs to public well and toilets. One of the first buildings in Chitina, a hardware and sheet metal shop now on the National Register of Historic Places, houses Spirit Mountain Artworks. Pay phone next to highway between the ranger station and Town Lake.

Chitina (pronounced CHIT-na) was established about 1908 as a railroad stop on the Copper River & Northwestern Railway and as a supply town for the Kennecott Copper Mines at McCarthy. The mine and railroad were abandoned in 1938. The McCarthy Road east of town follows the old railroad bed, which is listed on the National Register of Historic Places.

Inquire locally about informal camping areas: Much of the land around Chitina is owned by the Chitina Native Corp. and is posted no trespassing. Primitive camping is available along the Edgerton Highway at Onemile and Twomile lakes. There is an 8-site state campground east of Chitina across the Copper River bridge and a private campground on the McCarthy Road. ▲

A big attraction in Chitina for fishermen and spectators is the seasonal salmon run (reds, kings or silvers), which draws hundreds of dip-netters to the **Copper River.** The dip-net fishery for salmon runs June through September (depending on harvest levels), and it's worth the trip to see fish wheels and dip nets in action. O'Brien Creek Road provides a state right-of-way access to popular fishing areas on large sandbars along the Copper River. This fishery is open only to Alaska residents with a personal-use or subsistence permit. Check with the Chitina ADF&G office for details and current regulations. ◄►

Chitina Fuel & Grocery and Chitina Motel. See display ad this section.

Spirit Mountain Artworks. See display ad this section.

Edgerton Highway Log

(continued)

R 33.6 (54.1 km) **M 1.6** (2.6 km) Pavement ends eastbound. No road maintenance east of here between Oct. 15 and May 15.

R 33.8 (54.4 km) **M 1.4** (2.3 km) Turnout overlooking the Copper River.

R 34.1 (54.9 km) **M 1.1** (1.8 km) Turnout overlooking the Copper River. Access to river.

R 34.7 (55.8 km) **M 0.5** (0.8 km) Copper River bridge. Completed in 1971, this 1,378-foot/420-m steel span was designed for year-round use. The $3.5 million bridge re-established access across the river into the McCarthy–Kennicott area.

R 35.1 (56.5 km) **M 0 Junction** with McCarthy Road (log follows). Dept. of Transportation campground on the **Copper River;** 8 sites, picnic tables, fireplaces, toilets, boat launch, no water. Fishing for red and king salmon. Travelers are now within Wrangell–St. Elias National Park and Preserve. ◄►▲

McCarthy Road Log

Distance from junction with the Edgerton Highway (J) is followed by distance from road end (RE). Traditional mileposts used by local residents are indicated in the log.

J 0 RE 58.3 (93.8 km) **Junction** with the Edgerton Highway.

J 3.7 (6 km) **RE 54.6** (87.9 km) Turnout overlooking the Chitina River.

J 8.3 (13.4 km) **RE 50** (80.5 km) **Milepost 10.** Physical mileposts indicate distance from Chitina. Trail opposite homestead leads 0.3 mile/0.5 km north to **Strelna Lake;** rainbow trout and silver salmon. (Private property adjacent trail.) ◄►

J 9.3 (15 km) **RE 49** (78.9 km) **Milepost 11.** Private campground on **Silver Lake;** rainbow trout fishing, boat and canoe rentals, boat launch, tire repair. Trail access to **Van Lake,** located south of Silver Lake; good rainbow trout fishing. ◄►▲

Silver Lake Campground. Gene and Edith Coppedge invite you to fish for rainbow trout or just relax at beautiful Silver Lake. Bring your camera. RV or tent spaces, motorboat, rowboat and canoe rentals. New tires, tire repairs, fishing tackle, cold pop and candy, ice, bottled drinking water. See display ad. [ADVERTISEMENT] ▲

J 10.8 (17.4 km) **RE 47.5** (76.4 km) **Milepost 12. Sculpin Lake** (also known as Nelson Lake); rainbow trout fishing. ◄►

J 13 (20.9 km) **RE 45.3** (72.9 km) Access road leads north 2.5 miles/4 km to trailheads for Dixie Pass, Kotsina and Nugget Creek trails. *NOTE: Access road crosses private homesteads. Please do not trespass.*

J 13.3 (21.4 km) **RE 45** (72.4 km) **Milepost 15. Strelna Creek** (culvert); fair fishing for Dolly Varden. ◄►

J 15 (24.1 km) **RE 43.3** (69.7 km) **McCarthy Road Farm and Rides.** Take a break from bumpy McCarthy Road, visit us at our year-round home, Mile 15. Guided horseback trail rides, private wooded campground with electric and water. Debra's Store: snacks, microwave meals, sodas, etc. Guest house sleeps 6 for $75/night. Especially great for families. Riding and cabin packages available. Write P.O. Box 14, Chitina, AK 99566. [ADVERTISEMENT] ▲

J 16 (25.7 km) **RE 42.3** (68.1 km) Kuskulana bridge. This old railroad bridge (built in 1910) is approximately 525 feet/160m long and 385 feet/117m above the river. It is a narrow 3-span steel railway bridge with wood decking. Rehabilitated in 1988 for vehicle traffic.

Large gravel turnout at east end of bridge, small turnout at west end.

J 22.3 (35.9 km) **RE 36** (57.9 km) Large gravel turnout to south with view of Wrangell Mountains. There are several turnouts between here and the Kennicott River.

J 22.5 (36.2 km) **RE 35.8** (57.6 km) Boundary between park and preserve lands (unmarked). Wrangell–St. Elias National Park and Preserve allows sport hunting with a valid Alaska state license.

J 23.5 (37.8 km) **RE 34.8** (56 km) **Lou's Lake** to north; silver salmon and grayling fishing. ◄►

J 25.5 (41 km) **RE 32.8** (52.8 km) Chokosna River bridge.

J 27.7 (44.6 km) **RE 30.6** (49.2 km) One-lane bridge over Gilahina River. Old railroad trestle and parking.

J 40.3 (64.9 km) **RE 18** (29 km) Crystal Lake.

J 41.4 (66.6 km) **RE 16.9** (27.2 km) Double-ended turnout with view to south.

J 42.9 (69 km) **RE 15.4** (24.8 km) One-lane bridge over Lakina River, access to river at east end.

J 44.1 (71 km) **RE 14.2** (22.9 km) Long Lake Wildlife Refuge next 2.6 miles/4.2 km eastbound.

J 44.2 (71.1 km) **RE 14.1** (22.7 km) Watch for salmon spawning in Long Lake outlet (no fishing at outlet within 300 feet/91m of weir).

J 44.7 (71.9 km) **RE 13.6** (21.9 km) Turnout on **Long Lake**; lake trout, silver salmon, grayling, Dolly Varden, burbot. ◣

J 54.9 (88.4 km) **RE 3.4** (5.5 km) Swift Creek culvert.

J 55.2 (88.8 km) **RE 3.1** (5 km) **Willow Herb Mountain Depot.** Enjoy true Alaskan hospitality at our gift shop and B&B. McCarthy/Kennicott visitor information and assistance with local, year-round residents. Stop and chat about log building or winter life here. We specialize in local artwork and hand-crafted items from around Alaska. Also USGS maps, books, cards and more. Rent our beautiful, handscribed log cabin by the night. Secluded, wood heat, light breakfast provided. Tire repair available. Terry and Dee Frady, proprietors. MasterCard, VISA. (907) 554-4420. [ADVERTISEMENT]

J 57.7 (92.9 km) **RE 0.6** (1.0 km) **McCarthy Trailrides B&B** is conveniently located on the McCarthy Road ¹/₂ mile from the Kennicott River. Lodging is provided in private cabins. Your host provides you with a hot breakfast in his home and can arrange tours of the area. Contact John Adams, P.O. Box MXY, Glennallen, AK 99588. Phone (907) 554-4433. [ADVERTISEMENT]

J 58 (93.3 km) **RE 0.3** (0.5 km) **Glacier View Campground and Glacier Wings Helicopter Tours.** Less than ¹/₂ mile from the tram, our scenic and private campsites offer breathtaking views of the Root Glacier and surrounding Wrangell Mountains. Take a "thrill-a-minute" helicopter ride over timeless ice and then enjoy live jazz and your favorite beverage on our spacious sun deck. At Glacier View we strive to make your ultimate road trip unforgettable. Phone (907) 554-4490. [ADVERTISEMENT] ▲

J 58.1 (93.5 km) **RE 0.2** (0.3 km) Local parking lot for Kennicott and McCarthy residents.

J 58.2 (93.7 km) **RE 0.1** (0.2 km) Parking lot and Tram Station for visitors crossing Kennicott River; $5/day for parking, $10/day for parking and camping. ▲

The Tram Station, constructed from salvaged timbers from the Nizina River railroad bridge, houses the parking concession, tour booking service, snack shop and gift shop.

A hand-pulled, open-platform, cable tram carries passengers across the first part of the Kennicott River. (There is a footbridge across the river's second channel, unless it has been washed out.) The state plans to install a footbridge over the main channel in 1997. If the tram is still in use, keep in mind that you must pull yourself across 300 feet of river. It takes about ¹/₂ hour, less time if someone helps from the other bank; it is customary to help. (Kids were helping for tips in 1996.) Wear gloves. The tram is open 24-hours a day. Expect long lines Fourth of July weekend and other holidays. *CAUTION: DO NOT attempt to wade across this glacial river; strong currents and cold water make it extremely treacherous.*

A CB radio at the Tram Station has instructions for calling businesses in McCarthy and Kennicott (they monitor Channel 5 when the Tram Station is closed).

Parking on the riverbank is not recommended in July or early August because of sudden flooding when an ice-dammed lake breaks free upstream.

Copper Oar Rafting. See display ad this section.

J 58.3 (93.8 km) **RE 0** McCarthy Road dead ends at Kennicott River. On the east side of the river, follow the road for about ¹/₂ mile to a fork; the right fork leads to McCarthy (less than a mile) and the left fork goes to Kennicott (about 5 miles).

Roadside Potatohead, a welcome sight after your adventurous journey down the McCarthy Road. Your hosts, Kathleen and Denise, offer great food that won't bust your budget. Specialties ... fresh-cut fries, homemade burritos, hamburgers, Starbucks coffee and more. Catering to vegetarians and wranglers. Open 7 days. Visit the unique "Home of the Flying Potato." [ADVERTISEMENT]

McCarthy

Located across the Kennicott River and about 1.5 miles/2.4 km by road from the end of the McCarthy Road; within Wrangell–St. Elias National Park and Preserve; approximately 60 miles/96.5 km east of Chitina. **Population:** 25.

Transportation: Air—Charter service between Chitina, McCarthy and Kennicott. Van—Scheduled service between Glennallen, McCarthy/Kennicott and Valdez; daily shuttle to Chitina; shuttle service between McCarthy and Kennicott; phone (907) 822-5292. **Radio:** KCAM (Glennallen).

Lodging is available in McCarthy at the McCarthy Lodge, which also offers food service and a bar. The McCarthy area has flightseeing services, a bed and breakfast, a pizza restaurant and an operating gold mine. Check with lodges about activities in the area. Two wilderness guide services operate here. McCarthy has cellular phone service and some businesses can send and receive e-mail and faxes. McCarthy does not have a post office, school or television.

Private Aircraft: McCarthy airstrip, 1 mile/1.6 km south; elev. 1,494 feet/455m; length 1,400 feet/427m; turf, gravel; unattended. McCarthy Nr 2, 1 mile/1.6 km northeast; elev. 1,531 feet/467m; length 3,400 feet/1,036m; gravel; unattended.

The town of McCarthy is in a beautiful area of glaciers and mountains. The Kennicott River flows by the west side of town and joins the Nizina River which flows into the Chitina River. The local museum, located in the railway depot, has historical artifacts and photos from the early mining days.

It is 4.5 miles/7.2 km from McCarthy at

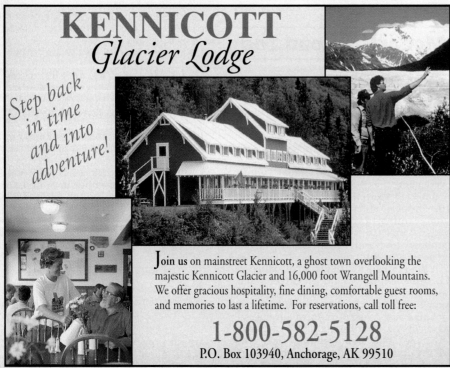

the end of the CR&NW railroad bed to the old mining town of **KENNICOTT** (pop. 8 to 15). Perched on the side of a mountain next to Kennicott Glacier, the town was built by Kennecott Copper Corp. between 1910 and 1920. (An early-day misspelling made the mining company Kennecott, while the region and settlement are Kennicott.) The richest copper mine in the world until its closure in 1938, Kennicott's mill processed more than 591,535 tons of copper ore and employed some 800 workers in its heyday. Today, a lodge is located here. The 3 dozen barn-red mine buildings are on private land. Kennecott Copper Mine is a National Historic Site.

Kennicott Glacier Lodge, located in the ghost town of Kennicott, offers the area's finest accommodations and dining. Built in 1987, this new lodge has 25 clean, delightful guest rooms, 2 living rooms, a spacious dining room, and a 180-foot front porch with a spectacular panoramic view of the Wrangell Mountains, Chugach Mountains and Kennicott Glacier. The homemade food, served family-style, has been called "wilderness gourmet dining." Guest activities at this destination resort include glacier trekking, flightseeing, photography, alpine hiking, historical and nature tours, rafting. May 15 to Sept. 20. (800) 582-5128. See display ad.
[ADVERTISEMENT]

McCarthy lies within **WRANGELL–ST. ELIAS NATIONAL PARK AND PRESERVE.** This 13.2 million acre park encompasses the southeast corner of the Alaska mainland, stretching from the Gulf of Alaska to the Copper River basin. Access to the park is by way of the McCarthy Road, the Nabesna Road (off the Tok Cutoff) and out of Yakutat. This vast unspoiled wilderness offers backpacking, mountaineering, river running, hunting and sportfishing. For more information, contact: Superintendent, Wrangell–St. Elias National Park and Preserve, P.O. Box 439, Copper Center, AK 99573; phone (907) 822-5234.

Wrangell Mountain Air offers daily flights to Kennicott and McCarthy as a convenient alternative to driving the McCarthy Road. Park your car or RV in Chitina at the end of the paved road and enjoy a spectacular flight through the Wrangell Mountains. Affordable fly-drive day trips are offered for the first time this year. Call for details.

McCarthy offers food, lodging and wilderness guide and air services.
(© James D. Ronan)

Along with world-class flightseeing, fly-in hiking, rafting, glacier trekking are also available. Aircraft are high wing for great viewing and equipped with intercom and headsets for each passenger. Call free for reservations and information: 1-800-478-1160 or (907) 554-4411. See display ad.
[ADVERTISEMENT]

COPPER RIVER HIGHWAY ⑩

Connects: Cordova to Million Dollar Bridge, AK   **Length:** 48 miles
Road Surface: 25% paved, 75% gravel
Season: Not maintained in winter
Major Attraction: Childs Glacier

	Cordova	Alaganik Slough	Million Dollar Bridge
Cordova		17	48
Alaganik Slough	17		31
Million Dollar Bridge	48	31	

The north span of the Million Dollar Bridge collapsed during the 1964 earthquake.
(© Ruth Fairall)

The Copper River Highway leads 48.1 miles/77.4 km northeast from Cordova to the Million Dollar Bridge at the Copper River.

Construction of the Copper River Highway began in 1945. Built along the abandoned railbed of the Copper River & Northwestern Railway, the highway was to extend to Chitina (on the Edgerton Highway), thereby linking Cordova to the Richardson Highway.

Construction was halted by the 1964 Good Friday earthquake, which severely damaged the highway's roadbed and bridges. The quake also knocked the north span of the Million Dollar Bridge into the Copper River and distorted the remaining spans. The 48 miles of existing highway have been repaired and upgraded since the earthquake, but repairs to the Million Dollar Bridge remain temporary and travel across the bridge and beyond is not recommended.

Copper River Highway Log

Distance is measured from Cordova (C).

C 0 CORDOVA. See description on page 596 in the PRINCE WILLIAM SOUND sec-tion. The Copper River Highway starts at the ferry terminal and leads east through town.

C 1.3 (2.1 km) Hollis Hendricks Park.

C 1.4 (2.3 km) Whitshed Road on right leads 0.5 mile/0.8 km to Odiak municipal camper park (24 sites, tenting area, obtain shower tokens at City Hall), 5.5 miles/8.9 km to **Hartney Bay.** Fishing from Hart-ney Bay bridge for Dolly Varden from May; pink and chum salmon, mid-July through August; closed for salmon upstream of bridge. Use small weighted spoons, spinners and eggs. Clam digging at low tide (license required). Shorebird migration in early spring. ◄▲

C 2.1 (3.4 km) Powder House Bar and Liquor Store (restaurant) overlooking Eyak Lake. Site of CR&NW railway powder house.

C 2.3 (3.7 km) Paved turnout to north by Eyak Lake. Heney Range to the south. Mount Eccles (elev. 2,357 feet/718m) is the first large peak. Pointed peak beyond is Heney Peak (elev. 3,151 feet/960m).

C 3.7 (5.9 km) Large paved turnout Eyak Lake.

C 4.1 (6.6 km) Historical marker on left gives a brief history of the CR&NW railway. Also here is a monument erected by the rail-road builder M.J. Heney in memory of those men who lost their lives during construction of the CR&NW. Begun in 1907 and com-pleted in 1911, the CR&NW railway con-nected the port of Cordova with the Kennecott Copper Mines near Kennicott and McCarthy. The mine and railway ceased operation in 1938.

For the next 2 miles/3.2 km, watch for bears during early morning and late evening (most often seen in June).

C 5.3 (8.5 km) Paved turnout at lake to north.

C 5.6 (9 km) Paved turnout at lake to north.

C 5.7 (9.2 km) Bridge over Eyak River, access to Eyak River trail. This is a good spot to see waterfowl feeding near the outlet of Eyak Lake. An estimated 100 trumpeter swans winter on Eyak Lake.

Eyak River trailhead is on the west bank of the river. The 2.2-mile/3.5-km trail, much of which is boardwalk over muskeg, is popu-lar with fishermen.

C 6 (9.7 km) **Eyak River**, toilet and boat launch. Dolly Varden; red salmon, June–July; silvers, August–September. Also pinks and chums. Use Vibrax spoon, spinner or salmon eggs. Fly-fishing only for salmon within 200 yards of weir. ◄►

C 7.4 (11.9 km) Paved turnout. *CAUTION: High winds for next 4 miles/6.4 km.* In January and February, these winds sweep across this flat with such velocity it is safer to pull off and stop.

C 7.6 (12.2 km) Bridge over slough.

C 7.7 (12.4 km) First bridge across Scott River.

C 8.1 (13 km) Bridge over slough waters. Gravel turnout; access to slough.

C 8.4 (13.5 km) Scott River bridge.

C 9 (14.5 km) Between **Mileposts 9** and **10** there are 4 bridges across the Scott River and the slough. Sloughs along here are from the runoff of the Scott Glacier, visible to the northeast. Bear and moose are often seen, especially in July and August. In May and August, thousands of dusky Canada geese nest here. This is the only known nesting area of the dusky geese, which winter in Oregon's Willamette Valley. Also watch for swans.

Moose feed in the willow groves on either side of the highway. Moose are not native to Cordova; the mountains and glaciers prevent them from entering the delta country. Today's herd stems from a transplant of 26 animals made between 1949 and 1959.

C 10.4 (16.7 km) Scott River bridge. Watch for old and new beaver dams and lodges beside the highway.

C 10.7 (17.2 km) U.S. Forest Service information pavilion (8 interpretive plaques) and large paved turnout with litter barrel to south. Game management area, 330,000 acres. Trumpeter swans and Canada geese.

COPPER RIVER HIGHWAY Cordova, AK, to Million Dollar Bridge

Principal Route

Paved   Unpaved

Other Roads

Paved   Unpaved

Ferry Routes   **Hiking Trails**

❄ Refer to Log for Visitor Facilities

❓ Visitor Information   ⊶ Fishing

⛺ Campground   ✈ Airport   ✦ Airstrip

Key to Advertiser Services
C -Camping
D -Dump Station
d -Diesel
G -Gas (reg., unld.)
I -Ice
L -Lodging
M -Meals
P -Propane
R -Car Repair (major)
r -Car Repair (minor)
S -Store (grocery)
T -Telephone (pay)

Scale

Map Location

Key to mileage boxes

miles/kilometres
miles/kilometres
from:

C-Cordova

Allen Glacier

Copper River

Area

Million Dollar Bridge

C-48/77km

Childs Glacier

Miles Lake   Miles Glacier

Glaciated Area

CHUGACH MOUNTAINS

Scott Glacier

Goodwin Glacier

Glaciated

▲ Mount Murchison
6,263 ft./1,909m

Goat Mountain
4,370 ft./1,332m

Chugach National Forest

Alaska State Ferry
(see MARINE ACCESS ROUTES section)

Sheridan Glacier

Sherman Glacier

Orca Bay

Eyak Lake

Cabin Lake

McKinley Peak
2,351 ft./717m

C-28/44km

Hotcake Channel

Long Island

Chugach National Forest

C-0

❄⛺✈✦ **Cordova**

Hawkins Island

Mount Eccles
2,357 ft./718m

(10)

Pipeline Lake

McKinley Lake

Round Island

Heart Island

Orca Inlet

Heney Peak
3,151 ft./960m

Eyak R.

C-12/20km

Hartney Bay →

HENEY RANGE

Aleganik Slough

Copper River Delta

Martin River

Castle Island Slough

Gulf of Alaska

Castle Island

Storey Slough

N
W   E
S

1997 ■ The MILEPOST®   619

Look for arctic terns.

C 10.8 (17.4 km) Bridge, beaver lodge.

C 11.1 (17.9 km) Elsner River bridge.

C 11.5 (18.5 km) Look for brown bears feeding in the outwash plains of Scott Glacier. Thousands of salmon swim up nearby rivers to spawn. There are numerous beaver lodges on both sides of the highway.

C 11.8 (19 km) State of Alaska Cordova highway maintenance station to northeast. U.S. Coast Guard station.

C 12.1 (19.5 km) Cordova airport and access to Cabin Lake Recreation Area. Drive north 2.8 miles/4.5 km for recreation area (gravel access road forks 0.3 mile/0.5 km in; right fork leads to gravel pit, continue straight ahead for recreation area). *CAUTION: Narrow road, no directional signs, active logging and logging trucks.* Picnic tables, toilet, litter barrel and firepits at **Cabin Lake**; cutthroat fishing.   ⊶

C 12.4 (20 km) Pavement ends, gravel begins. Watch for potholes.

C 13 (20.9 km) Keep a lookout for snowshoe hare and birds of prey.

C 13.7 (22 km) Sheridan Glacier access road leads 4.3 miles/6.9 km to the terminus of Sheridan Glacier. *CAUTION: Narrow road, watch for logging trucks.* The glacier was named by U.S. Army explorer Capt. Abercrombie for Gen. Philip H. Sheridan of Civil War fame. Sheridan Mountain trailhead, several picnic tables, litter barrels and a partial view of the glacier are available at the end of the access road. It is about a 0.5-mile/0.8-km hike to the dirt-covered glacial moraine.

C 14.8 (23.8 km) Bridge over Sheridan

River. Raft takeout point. View of Sheridan Glacier. To the east of Sheridan Glacier is Sherman Glacier.

Winter moose range next 8 miles/13 km eastbound.

C 15 (24.1 km) Silver salmon spawn during September and October in the stream beside the highway.

C 16 (25.7 km) Beautiful view of Sheridan Glacier to the northeast.

C 16.3 (26.2 km) Second bridge over Sheridan River.

C 16.9 (27.2 km) Turnoff for **Alaganik Slough**, Chugach National Forest Recreation Area. Drive south 3 miles/4.8 km via gravel road; picnic tables, firepits, wheelchair accessible toilets, litter barrel, information kiosk and boat launch. Wheelchair-accessible interpretive boardwalk with viewing blind for watching birds and other wildlife. No water, informal camping. Interpretive plaque on side road reads: "Why are Delta moose the largest and healthiest? This moose herd, first introduced in 1949, maintains its vitality primarily due to its abundant willow supply. As part of a normal cycle, accelerated by the 1964 earthquake, much of the willow is becoming unavailable to moose. As the willow grows tall, the moose can no longer reach the tender new shoots. In the future this could cause a decrease in the numbers of moose on the delta. To slow the cycle down, the Forest Service is experimenting in this area, cutting back the shrubs. This should increase the amount of available willow browse. Biologists will evaluate the response of moose to new willow growth."

Fishing for Dolly Varden, sockeye (July) and silver salmon (August and September).⛺⊶▲

C 17.4 (28 km) Trumpeter swans may be seen in pond beside highway. One of the largest of all North American waterfowl (6 to 8 foot wingspan), it has been almost completely eliminated in the Lower 48 and Canada. Alaska harbors more than 80 percent of breeding trumpeters and more than 7 percent of the world population breeds in the Copper River Delta.

C 18 (29 km) For the next mile look for silver salmon spawning in streams during September. To the left and on the slopes above timberline mountain goats may be seen. The mountain to the left of the road ahead eastbound is McKinley Peak (elev. 2,351 feet/717m).

C 18.1 (29.1 km) Entering Chugach National Forest eastbound.

C 18.5 (29.8 km) Road narrows. *NOTE: Road not maintained in winter (after Nov. 1) beyond this point.*

C 18.8 (30.3 km) Turnout to north access to Muskeg Meander cross-country ski trailhead; length 2.5 miles/4 km. According to the USFS district office, this trail offers a beautiful view of the Copper River Delta.

C 19.2 (30.9 km) Haystack trailhead to south. Easy 0.8-mile/1.2-km trail leads to delta overlook with interpretive signs. Excellent place to see moose and bear according to the USFS district office in Cordova.

C 20.1 (32.3 km) Large gravel turnout to south; beaver dam, fishing.   ⊶

C 21.4 (34.4 km) **Pipeline Lakes** trailhead to north, parking to south. The

View of Sheridan Glacier from Milepost 16 on the Copper River Highway. (© Ruth Fairall)

1.8-mile/2.9-km trail was originally built as a water pipeline route to supply locomotives on the CR&NW railway. Segments of the pipeline are still visible. Fishing for grayling and cutthroat, fly or bait. Trail joins McKinley Lake trail. Rubber boots are necessary. ➤

C 21.6 (34.8 km) **McKinley Lake** trail to north; easy 2.1-mile/3.4-km hike with excellent fishing for sockeye, Dolly Varden and cutthroat. Access to USFS public-use cabins: McKinley Trail cabin (100 yards from highway) and McKinley Lake cabin (45-minute walk in from highway; also accessible by boat via Alaganik Slough). ➤

C 22 (35.4 km) Double-ended turnout to north.

C 22.1 (35.5 km) **Alaganik Slough** boat ramp, picnic tables, firepits, toilets, litter barrel, wildflowers, interpretive signs on local cultural history and fishing access to south at west side of Alaganik Slough river bridge. Sockeye (red) and coho (silver) salmon, July to September. Also boat access to McKinley Lake. ➤

C 23.4 (37.7 km) Salmon Creek bridge, parking; creek access.

C 24.6 (39.6 km) One-mile/1.6-km road north leads to Saddlebag Glacier trailhead and parking area; access to canoe route. According to the USFS office in Cordova, this is an easy 3-mile/4.8-km trail to Saddlebag Lake. View of Saddlebag Glacier and icebergs; look for goats on surrounding mountains. *CAUTION: Watch for bears.*

C 24.8 (39.9 km) Channel to beaver pond for spawning salmon. A plaque here reads: "Pathway to salmon rearing grounds. Channel provided access to beaver pond (north side of road) for coho fry. Beaver pond can support up to 25,400 young salmon. Fallen trees and brush provide cover from predators."

C 25.4 (40.9 km) Small gravel turnout by 2 spawning channels with weirs. Interpretive signs along a short trail here explain the project: "Channel built by USDA Forest Service to provide high quality spawning habitat for coho and sockeye salmon. Before construction, the streambed was muddy and the stream dried up during low flow periods. Fish spawned in the streams but few eggs survived. Improved channel is deeper and ensures a consistent flow. Adjustable weirs control water depth. Clean gravels placed in

the channel make better spawning conditions while large rip-rap on streambanks prevent erosion.

"Can you see small circles of gravel which appear to have been turned over? These are salmon 'redds,' or nests in which female salmon lay their eggs. Female salmon create the redds by digging with their tails. Environmental conditions and predators take a heavy toll on salmon eggs and small fry. Of the 2,800 eggs which the average female coho salmon lays, only about 14 will survive to adulthood. Most of these will then be caught by commercial, sport or subsistence fishermen. Only 2 salmon from each redd will actually return to spawn and complete their life cycle."

Near here was the cabin of Rex Beach, author of *The Iron Trail,* a classic novel about the building of the CR&NW railway.

C 26.4 (42.5 km) Flag Point. Turnout with view of the Copper River which empties into the Gulf of Alaska. Downriver to the southwest is Castle Island Slough. Storey Slough is visible a little more to the south. Castle Island and a number of small islands lie at the mouth of the Copper River. Monument on the riverbank is dedicated to the men who built these bridges and "especially to the crane crew who lost their lives on July 21, 1971."

CAUTION: Extreme high winds next 10 miles/16 km in fall and winter. Stay in your vehicle.

C 26.7 (43 km) Two bridges cross the Copper River to Round Island, a small island with sand dunes and a good place to picnic.

In midsummer the Copper River has half a million or more red (sockeye) and king salmon migrating 300 miles/483 km upstream to spawn in the river's clear tributaries. There is no sportfishing in this stretch of the Copper River because of glacial silt.

Candlefish (eulachon) also spawn in the Copper River. Candlefish oil was once a significant trade item of the Coastal Indians. These fish are so oily that when dried they can be burned like candles.

C 27.5 (44.3 km) Copper River Bridge No. 3 from Round Island to Long Island. The 6.2 miles/10 km of road on Long Island pass through a sandy landscape dotted with dunes. Long Island is in the middle of the Copper River.

C 28.5 (45.9 km) Lake to south is stocked with grayling. ➤

C 30.8 (49.5 km) Watch for nesting swans, other birds and beaver in slough to south of road. NOTE: *Use extreme caution if you drive off road: sandy terrain.*

C 31 (49.9 km) Lakes to south stocked with grayling. ➤

C 33 (53.1 km) View of 2 glaciers to the northwest; nearest is Goodwin, the other is Childs.

C 33.3 (53.6 km) First bridge leaving Long Island. View to south down Hotcake Channel to Heart Island. Road built on top of a long dike which stretches across the Copper River Delta. From here to **Milepost C 37.7** there are 7 more bridges across the delta. The Copper River channels have changed and many bridges now cross almost dry gulches.

C 34.2 (55 km) Large gravel turnout to north.

C 34.3 (55.2 km) Copper River bridge.

C 35.7 (57.5 km) Large gravel turnout to north.

C 36.8 (59.2 km) Bridge crossing main flow of the Copper River (this is the 5th bridge after leaving Long Island eastbound). Access to river at east end of bridge.

C 37.4 (60.2 km) Bridge, river access.

C 37.8 (60.8 km) Bridge, river access, large gravel turnout to north.

C 38.8 (62.4 km) Childs Glacier directly ahead.

C 39.7 (63.9 km) Milky glacial waters of Sheep Creek pass through large culvert under road.

C 40.5 (65.2 km) **Clear Creek;** Dolly Varden, cutthroat, red salmon (July) and silvers (August–September). Use flies, lures, spinners or eggs. Watch for bears. ➤

C 41.1 (66.1 km) Park on old railroad grade to south for access to Clear Creek.

C 41.7 (67.1 km) Goat Mountain (elev. 4,370 feet/1,332m) rises to the east of the highway. To the west parts of the Sherman and Goodwin glaciers flow down the sides of Mount Murchison (elev. 6,263 feet/1,909m).

C 42.1 (67.7 km) Side road to gravel pit, pond, informal camping and picnic site by Goat Mountain.

C 48 (77.2 km) Access to Childs Glacier Recreation Area with wheelchair-accessible covered viewing platform, picnic sites, covered tables, toilets and trails. No water. Limited RV parking. U.S. Forest Service hosts on site in summer. Childs Glacier was named by Capt. W.R. Abercrombie (1884 expedition) for George Washington Childs of Philadelphia. The glacier face is approximately 350 feet/107m high and very active. *CAUTION: Calving ice may cause waves to break over the beach and into the viewing area. Be prepared to run to higher ground!* ♿

C 48.1 (77.4 km) The Million Dollar Bridge; viewing platform. The north span collapsed during the 1964 earthquake. Temporary repairs were made and people have been driving across it, but driving across the bridge and beyond is definitely a "drive at your own risk" venture. Primitive road extends only about 10 miles/16 km beyond the bridge to the Allen River. Heavy snow blocks road in winter; road may not be open until June. Proposed extension of the Copper River Highway to Chitina is currently under debate.

From here there is a view of Miles Glacier to the east. This glacier was named by Lieutenant Allen (1885 expedition) for Maj. Gen. Nelson A. Miles.

MARINE ACCESS ROUTES

Alaska ports via BC Ferries, Alaska State Ferries and Cruise Ships

(See maps, pages 622–624)

Marine access to Alaska from Canada and the Lower 48 is primarily by cruise ship and ferry from west coast ports via the Inside Passage. The Inside Passage is the route north along the coast of British Columbia and through southeastern Alaska that uses the protected waterways between the islands and the mainland. (Inside Passage is also commonly used to refer to Southeast Alaska and its communities; see page 647.)

Historically, this famed water route was used by early explorers (Vancouver, Cook) in the 18th century and by gold stampeders during the 19th century. The water passage travels along hundreds of miles of forested coastline, passing deep fjords and the steep, snow-capped peaks of the Coast Range.

Marine access to Alaska by ferry is provided by the Alaska Marine Highway, which is the name of the Alaska state ferry system and also refers to the water route the ferries follow from Bellingham, WA, to Skagway, AK. The Alaska Marine Highway actually operates 2 ferry systems, one in Southeast Alaska and one in Southcentral/Southwest Alaska, but they do not connect with one another.

The Alaska state ferries on the Southeast system depart from Bellingham, WA, and Prince Rupert, BC, for Southeast Alaska communities from Ketchikan to Skagway. These ferries do not cross the Gulf of Alaska to Anchorage or other Southcentral ports.

If traveling to Alaska by ferry, visitors may make their way up the Inside Passage to

Alaska state ferry heads down Lynn Canal from Haines. (© Derby Photography)

any Southeast Alaska community on the ferry system. (Descriptions of southeastern Alaska communities begin on page 655.)

Only 2 mainline ports, Haines and Skagway, are connected to the inland highway system.

(Continues on page 624)

MARINE ACCESS ROUTES
Washington and British Columbia from Puget Sound to Hecate Strait

To Alaska
(map continues next page)

Pitt Island

Banks Island

Hecate Strait

Grenville Channel

Otter Pass

Butedale

Princess Royal Channel

Queen Charlotte Islands

Klemtu

Mathieson Channel

Ocean Falls

Shearwater

Dean Channel

Bella Coola

Bella Bella

Milbanke Sound

Kunghit Island

Cape St. James

Hunter Island

Namu

Bute Channel

Rivers Inlet

Calvert Island

Queen Charlotte Sound

Knight Inlet

BRITISH COLUMBIA

N
W   E
S

Queen Charlotte Strait

Bute Inlet

Port Hardy

Bear Cove

Alert Bay

Hardwicke Island

Sonora Island

Malcolm Island

19

Kelsey Bay

Johnstone Strait

Discovery Passage

Quadra Island

Redonda Islands

Campbell River

Cortes Island

Powell River

Saltery Bay

Earls Cove

Texada Island

Vancouver Island

Courtenay

19

Langdale

Horseshoe Bay

Highway to Horseshoe Bay

Port Alberni

Nanaimo

1

Strait of Georgia

Vancouver

Tsawwassen

CANADA
U.S.A.

Bellingham

Saltspring Island

Swartz Bay

Sidney

Anacortes

Victoria

San Juan Islands

5

Pacific Ocean

CANADA
U.S.A.

Strait of Juan de Fuca

Port Angeles

Everett

WASHINGTON

Seattle

Puget Sound

Scale
0   20   Miles
0   20   Kilometres

Map Location

Highways
Alaska Ferry Routes
Cruise Ship and Other Ferry Routes

MARINE ACCESS ROUTES

British Columbia and Southeastern Alaska from Prince Rupert, BC, to Skagway, AK

To Alaska Highway

Haines Highway
(see HAINES
HIGHWAY section)

To Alaska Highway

Klondike Highway 2
(see KLONDIKE HIGHWAY 2 section)

Skagway

White Pass & Yukon Route

Haines

CANADA
U.S.A.

Glaciated Area

Glacier Bay National Park and Preserve

Glacier Bay

Bartlett Cove

Gustavus

Auke Bay Ferry Terminal

Juneau

Lynn Canal

Glaciated Area

BRITISH
ALASKA

Taku Inlet

Pelican

Hoonah

Douglas Island

Gastineau Channel

Icy Strait

Chichagof Island

Admiralty Island

Tracy Arm

Tenakee Springs

Endicott Arm

Stephens Passage

Angoon

Chatham Strait

Sitka

Baranof Island

Frederick Sound

Kake

Kupreanof Island

BRITISH COLUMBIA

Stikine River

Kuiu Island

Petersburg

Mitkof Island

Zarembo Island

Wrangell

Summer Strait

Wrangell Island

Etolin Island

BRITISH COLUMBIA
ALASKA

Map Location

Scale
0   20   Miles
0   20   Kilometres

Highways

Alaska Ferry Routes

Cruise Ship and Other Ferry Routes

N
W   E
S

Misty Fiords

Hyder

Thorne Bay

Revillagigedo Island

Klawock

Hollis

National

Craig

Hydaburg

Prince of Wales Island

Ketchikan

Clarence Strait

Gravina Island

Revillagigedo Channel

Belm Canal

Portland Canal

Monument

Metlakatla

Annette Island

U.S.A.
CANADA

Chatham Sound

Dixon Entrance

Dundas Island

Prince Rupert

16

Yellowhead Highway 16
(see YELLOWHEAD HIGHWAY 16 section)

Skeena River

Pacific Ocean

Masset

Graham Island

Porcher Island

Kitimat

Grenville Channel

Hecate Strait

Queen Charlotte Islands

Queen Charlotte City

Skidegate

Sandspit

Banks Island

Pitt Island

Morseby Island

Otter Pass

(map continues previous page)

SOUTHCENTRAL/SOUTHWEST FERRY SYSTEM

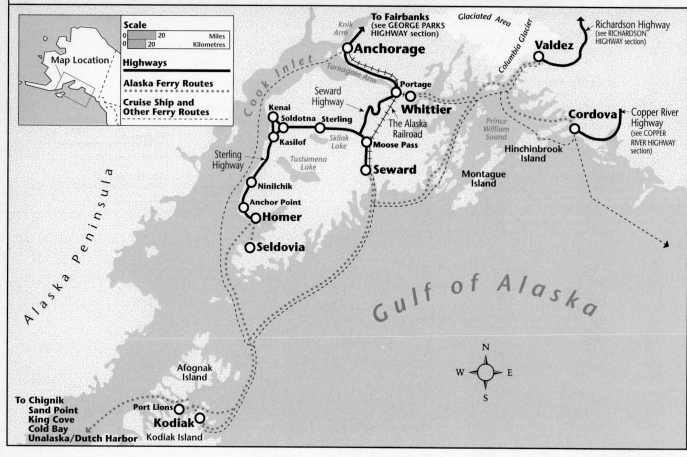

(Continued from page 621)

Motorists often use the Alaska Marine Highway northbound or southbound as an alternative to driving all of the Alaska Highway and its access routes. By using the Alaska state ferry one way to transport themselves and their vehicles between Bellingham or Prince Rupert and Skagway or Haines, travelers can eliminate between 700- and 1,700-miles of highway driving (depending on their itinerary), avoid covering the same ground twice, and have the opportunity to take in the magnificent scenery and picturesque communities of the Inside Passage.

The Alaska Marine Highway also provides marine access for passengers and vehicles to various communities in Southcentral/Southwest Alaska (see map above).

Complete details on the Alaska state ferry system begin on page 626. Ferry schedules begin on page 628.

BC Ferries also serves the Inside Passage, providing marine transportation for passengers and vehicles between Port Hardy and Prince Rupert, BC. Port Hardy is located at the north end of Vancouver Island. Prince Rupert is the western terminus of Yellowhead Highway 16 and the southern port for 3 Alaska state ferries serving southeastern Alaska. Prince Rupert is also the farthest north

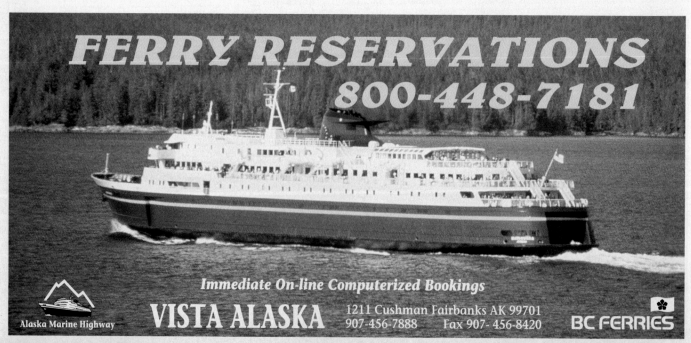

of the 46 ports served by BC Ferries. For complete details on BC Ferries , see below.

Cruise ships provide passenger service only from West Coast ports through the Inside Passage to Southeast Alaska ports of call. Several cruise ships also provide marine access across the Gulf of Alaska to Southcentral ports of call. See Cruise Lines on page 644 for more information on this travel option.

BC Ferries

BC Ferries provides year-round service on 25 routes throughout coastal British Columbia, with a fleet of 40 passenger- and vehicle-carrying ferries. BC Ferries "Inside Passage" service between Port Hardy and Prince Rupert offers Alaska-bound travelers a convenient connection with the Alaska Marine Highway at Prince Rupert.

Port Hardy is approximately 307 miles/494 km north of Victoria via Trans-Canada Highway 1 and BC Highway 19. From Nanaimo it is 236 miles/380 km—or about 5 hours' driving time—to Port Hardy. If you are driving from Victoria, allow at least 8 hours (the route is almost all 2-lane highway between Victoria and Campbell River). The Port Hardy ferry terminal is located at Bear Cove, 4 miles/7 km south of downtown Port Hardy.

Prince Rupert is located 450 miles/724 km west of Prince George via the Yellowhead Highway (see YELLOWHEAD HIGHWAY 16 section).

Summer service between Port Hardy and Prince Rupert is aboard the *Queen of the North,* which carries 750 passengers and 157 vehicles. The ferry has a cafeteria, buffet dining room, news/gift shop, licensed and view lounges, children's playroom, day cabins and staterooms (for round-trip use). Summer service on this route is during daylight hours to make the most of the scenery, so cabins are not necessary.

Reservations: Strongly recommended for passengers and required for vehicles on the Inside Passage route. For reservations (7 A.M. to 10 P.M. daily) and recorded schedule information (24-hours) phone (604) 669-1211 in Vancouver; (250) 386-3431 in Victoria; and 1-888-223-3779 elsewhere in British Columbia. Or fax (250) 381-5452. Reservations may also be made on-line at http://bcferries.bc.ca/ferries. The Internet site also has rates, schedules and fleet profiles. Or contact BC Ferries at 1112 Fort St., Victoria, BC V8V 4V2.

Schedules and fares: The 1997 Inside Passage sailing schedule is shown here. Schedules are subject to change without notice. Rates current at time of printing (subject to change) are as follows (1-way, in Canadian funds): Adult passenger, $100; child (5 to 11 years), $50; car, $206;

MARINE ACCESS ADVERTISERS

BC FERRIES 1997 INSIDE PASSAGE SCHEDULE
PORT HARDY TO PRINCE RUPERT

NORTHBOUND
Departs: Port Hardy 7:30 A.M.
Arrives: Prince Rupert 10:30 P.M.
Dates: May (2 sailings weekly May 1–25);
May 26, 28, 30
June, July, September (odd-numbered days)
August (even-numbered days)
Late October through April (one sailing weekly)

SOUTHBOUND
Departs: Prince Rupert 7:30 A.M.
Arrives: Port Hardy 10:30 P.M.
Dates: May (2 sailings weekly May 1–25);
May 27, 29, 31
June, July, September (even-numbered days)
August (odd-numbered days)
Late October through April (one sailing weekly)

Northbound positioning cruise between Tsawwassen and Port Hardy: May 25.
Southbound positioning cruise between Prince Rupert and Port Hardy, Sept. 28; between Port Hardy and Tsawwassen, Sept. 29.

camper/RV (up to 20 feet in length, over 6 feet 8 inches in height), $344; additional length, $17.20 per foot; motorcycle, $103; bicycle, $6.50. Service during the fall, winter and spring is less frequent and fares are reduced. Contact BC Ferries for details.

Check-in time is 1 hour before sailing. Cancellations made less than 30 days prior to departure are subject to a cancellation fee.

Connecting routes: BC Ferries also provides year-round service on the 3 major routes that link lower mainland British Columbia and Vancouver Island. These are Tsawwassen–Swartz Bay, Tsawwassen–

Nanaimo, and Horseshoe Bay–Nanaimo. Reservations are not accepted for passengers or vehicles on these routes.

To reach either the Tsawwassen or Horseshoe Bay terminals on the mainland, take BC Highway 99. Turn off Highway 99 approximately 17 miles/27 km north of the U.S. border for the Tsawwassen terminal and service to Swartz Bay near Victoria (1½-hour crossing) and to Nanaimo (2-hour crossing). There are a minimum of 16 round trips daily during summer between Tsawwassen and Swartz Bay, and 8 round trips daily year round between Tsawwassen and Nanaimo. Continue on Highway 99 through Vancouver for the Horseshoe Bay terminal, 13 miles/21 km northwest of the city, and ferry service to Nanaimo (crossing time: 1½ hours).

There are several ways to reach Vancouver Island from Washington. If you are traveling with a vehicle, you can take the Washington state ferry from Anacortes, WA, to Sidney, BC (near Victoria), cruising through the San Juan Islands; or you can take the MV *Coho* from Port Angeles, WA, to Victoria. Reservations are not accepted for passengers or vehicles on either service. Anacortes is 85 miles/137 km north of Seattle, WA, via Interstate 5. Port Angeles is about 2 hours west of Seattle by ferry and highway. The Anacortes crossing to Sidney is approximately 3 hours. The Port Angeles crossing is 1½ hours. For the Washington state ferries, phone (206) 464-6400 in Seattle or 1-800-843-3779 state-wide. For the MV *Coho*, contact Black Ball Transport, 430 Belleville St., Victoria, BC V8V 1W9; phone (206) 622-2222 in the Seattle area, (360) 457-4491 in

Port Angeles, or (250) 386-2202 in Victoria.

Bus service is available between Vancouver and Victoria, from Pacific Coach Lines, 150 Dunsmuir St., Vancouver; phone (604) 662-8074. Bus service between Victoria and Port Hardy is provided by Island Coach Lines, 700 Douglas St., Victoria, BC V8W 2B3; phone (250) 385-4411. Canadian Regional Airlines, Orca Air and Pacific Coastal Airlines have scheduled air service to Port Hardy.

Alaska State Ferries

The main office of the Alaska Marine Highway is in Juneau. Write P.O. Box 25535, Juneau, AK 99802-5535; phone toll free 1-800-642-0066, TDD 1-800-764-3779; fax (907) 277-4829. Local reservation numbers in Juneau (907/465-3941) and in Anchorage (907/272-7116). Or via Internet: www.dot.state.ak.us/external/amhs/home.html.

The Alaska State Ferry System is divided into 2 different systems serving 2 different areas: Southeast and Southcentral/Southwest. These 2 systems *DO NOT* connect.

The Alaska state ferries on the Southeast system depart from Bellingham, WA (85 miles north of Seattle on Interstate 5, Exit 250), or Prince Rupert, BC (450 miles/724 km west of Prince George, BC, or approximately 1,000 miles/1,609 km by highway from Seattle, WA) for Southeast Alaska communities.

Bellingham is accessible by Amtrak and bus. Fairhaven Station transportation center, next to the Bellingham Cruise Terminal at

401 Harris Ave. in south Bellingham, provides a central location for rail, bus, airporter, taxi and ferry services.

Alaska state ferries out of Bellingham do not stop in Canada. Ferries out of Prince Rupert follow the same route as the ferries out of Bellingham from Chatham Sound north. Ketchikan (the first stop for both) is a 36-hour ferry ride from Bellingham and about 6 hours by ferry from Prince Rupert. The ferries stop at mainline Southeast Alaska port cities from Ketchikan to Skagway.

Remember that only 2 major Southeast communities are connected to the Alaska Highway: Haines, via the Haines Highway; and Skagway, via Klondike Highway 2. (See the HAINES HIGHWAY and KLONDIKE HIGHWAY 2 sections.)

The Southeast system also includes feeder service between Ketchikan and Stewart/Hyder; Ketchikan and Hollis; Ketchikan and Metlakatla; and Juneau and Pelican. See Inside Passage/Southeast Alaska schedules this section.

The Southcentral/Southwest ferry system of the Alaska Marine Highway serves coastal communities from Prince William Sound to the Aleutian Islands. Southcentral communities on the ferry system that are also accessible by highway are Valdez, Seward and Homer. Southcentral communities accessible only by ferry are Cordova, Seldovia and Kodiak. Whittier is accessible only via shuttle train (see the ALASKA RAILROAD section). All communities on the Southwest system are accessible only by ferry or by air.

Travel on the Alaska state ferries is at a leisurely pace, with observation decks, food service (hot meals, snacks and beverages) and vehicle decks on all ferries. Cabins are available only on 4 Southeast ferries and 1 Southwest ferry.

Keep in mind that the state ferries are not cruise ships: They do not have beauty salons, gift shops, deck games, telephones and the like. The small stores on the larger ferries are open limited hours and sell a limited selection of items.

It's a good idea to bring your own snacks, books, games and toiletries, since these are not always available on board.

Season: The Alaska Ferry System has 2 seasons—May 1 to Sept. 30 (summer), when sailings are most frequent, and Oct. 1 to April 30 (fall/winter/spring), when departures are somewhat less frequent. Schedules and information appearing in this section are for the summer season only.

Contact the Alaska Marine Highway office for fall/winter/spring schedules, fares and information. Special fares may be available and crowds are virtually nonexistent.

Reservations: Required on all vessels for passengers, vehicles and cabins. The Alaska state ferries are very popular in summer. Reservations should be made as far in advance as possible to get the sailing dates you wish. Cabin space on summer sailings is often sold out by early December on the Bellingham sailings (see Deck Passage). Requests for space are accepted year-round and held until reservations open (see Waitlist/Standby). For reservations, write the Alaska Marine Highway, P.O. Box 25535, Juneau, AK 99802-5535; phone toll free 1-800-642-0066, or fax (907) 277-4829.

Reservation requests (see page 643) must include departure dates and ports of embarkation/debarkation; full names of all members of the party, and the ages of those under 12 years; width, height and overall length (including hitch if with trailer) of

(Continues on page 636)

RECORDED ARRIVAL / DEPARTURE INFORMATION

Southeast Alaska Offices

Bellingham ....(360) 676-8445	Petersburg ....(907) 772-3855
24-hour recorded info. ..(360) 676-0212	Sitka ....(907) 747-3300
Prince Rupert ....(250) 627-1744	Juneau ....(907) 465-3940
Ketchikan ....(907) 225-6181	Haines ....(907) 766-2113
Wrangell ....(907) 874-3711	Skagway ....(907) 983-2229

Southcentral / Southwest

Anchorage ....(907) 272-4482
Cordova ....(907) 424-7333
Homer ....(907) 235-8449
Kodiak ....(907) 486-3800
Seldovia ....(907) 234-7868
Seward ....(907) 224-5485
Valdez ....(907) 835-4436

HOW TO READ YOUR SCHEDULE

1. Reading across the top of each page, find the month you wish to travel, and refer to either the Northbound or Southbound schedule. (Using the example of traveling from Skagway to Juneau/Auke Bay, you would read the Southbound schedule on the right-hand page.)
2. Reading across the top of the schedule, find the city from which you wish to depart (e.g. Leave Skagway).
3. Read down the column to locate your desired departure date. For example: Leave Skagway SU2 (Sunday, the 2nd) 8:45 p.m..

4. Beginning with departure date, read horizontally from left to right for dates and times of departure from various ports. For example: After departing Skagway, ferry will dock in Haines, and after a short time in port it will depart Haines on SU2 (Sunday, the 2nd) at 11:15 p.m. for Juneau/Auke Bay. Refer to the Running Time Table on page 643 to calculate the time in port and approximate unlisted arrival time.
5. The color of the horizontal bars indicates the ship on which you will travel.

Example

LEAVE SKAGWAY		HAINES		JUNEAU/ AUKE BAY		HOONAH	TENAKEE	ANGOON	ARRIVE SITKA		KAKE		PETERSBURG		WRANGELL		HOLLIS	KETCHIKAN		METLAKATLA	ARRIVE STEWART/HYDER	ARRIVE PRINCE RUPERT		ARRIVE BELLINGHAM
F31	6:00P	F31	8:30P	S1	2:30A								S1	11:30A	S1	3:30P		S1	11:00P			SU2	6:00A
S1	1:45P	S1	4:15P	S1	10:15P				SU2	7:45A	SU2	7:45P	M3	12:30A	M3	4:15A		M3	11:15A			M3	6:15P
SU2	8:45P	SU2	11:15P	M3	5:15A								M3	1:45P	M3	5:30P		T4	1:15P			T4	8:30P

Day of week ⟶
Day of month ⟶
⟵ AM or PM
⟵ Time

VESSEL COLOR CODING

■ Aurora ■ Columbia ■ Le Conte ■ Malaspina ■ Matanuska ■ Taku

1997 Alaska Marine Highway Summer Schedules

May 1997 Northbound Schedule – Inside Passage/Southeast Alaska

LEAVE BELLINGHAM	LEAVE PRINCE RUPERT	LEAVE STEWART/HYDER	METLAKATLA	KETCHIKAN	HOLLIS	WRANGELL	PETERSBURG	KAKE	ARRIVE SITKA	ANGOON	TENAKEE	HOONAH	JUNEAU/ AUKE BAY	HAINES	ARRIVE SKAGWAY
				T29 11:30P	W30 3:15A			W30 12:30P	W30 6:30P						
									TH1 2:30A	TH1 11:00A	TH1 2:15P	TH1 6:30P	F2 12:45A	F2 6:15A	F2 7:15A
				TH1 6:15P	TH1 9:00P										
	F2 4:30P		F2 2:15P	F2 6:15P	F2 9:00P										
				S3 1:00A		S3 8:00A	S3 11:55A		S3 11:15P				SU4 12:15P	SU4 5:45P	SU4 6:45P
			S3 8:15A	S3 10:30A	S3 1:15P										
F2 6:00P			S3 8:45P	S3 11:00P	SU4 1:45A										
									Lv. Sitka S3 1:15P	S3 7:30P	S3 10:45P	SU4 3:00A	SU4 6:15A		
				SU4 10:45A		SU4 6:45P	SU4 10:45P						M5 9:15A	M5 3:15P	M5 4:15P
			SU4 2:15P	SU4 6:15P	SU4 9:00P										
	M5 9:00A			M5 3:15P		M5 10:00P	T6 2:45A								
			M5 2:15P	M5 6:15P	M5 9:00P										
									Lv. Sitka M5 3:00P	M5 9:15P	T6 12:30A	T6 4:45A	T6 8:00A		
	T6 10:30A			T6 5:00P		W7 12:15A	W7 4:00A						T6 11:55A	T6 5:30P	T6 6:30P
				T6 9:00P	T6 9:00P										
			W7 2:15P	W7 6:15P	W7 9:00P								W7 1:45P	W7 7:45P	W7 8:45P
								W7 6:00P	TH8 12:45A	TH8 8:45A	TH8 5:00P	TH8 10:00P			
	TH8 11:15A			TH8 5:30P		F9 12:15A	F9 5:00A	F9 3:45P							
				TH8 6:15P	TH8 9:00P								F9 2:15P	F9 7:45P	F9 8:45P
	F9 2:00P		F9 2:15P	F9 6:15P	F9 9:00P								S10 5:30A	S10 11:00A	S10 11:55A
				F9 9:00P		S10 4:00A	S10 9:00A		S10 10:30P						
			S10 8:15A	S10 10:30A	S10 1:15P										
F9 6:00P			S10 8:45P	S10 11:00P	SU11 1:45A								SU11 11:55A	SU11 5:45P	SU11 6:45P
									Lv. Sitka S10 12:45P	S10 6:45P	S10 10:00P	SU11 2:15A	SU11 5:30A		
				SU11 6:45A		SU11 1:15P	SU11 5:15P						M12 2:15A	M12 8:45A	M12 9:45A
			SU11 2:15P	SU11 6:15P	SU11 9:00P					Lv. Pelican SU11 3:00P			SU11 9:30P		
			M12 2:15P	M12 6:15P	M12 9:00P				Lv. Sitka M12 8:15P	T13 2:30A	T13 5:45A	T13 10:00A	T13 1:15P		
	M12 9:15A			M12 3:45P		M12 10:30P	T13 3:15A						T13 12:45P	T13 6:15P	T13 7:15P
	T13 11:30A	T13 3:45P		T13 6:00P		W14 2:30A	W14 5:00A						W14 2:45P	W14 8:45P	W14 9:45P
			W14 2:15P	W14 6:15P	W14 9:00P		W14 5:15A								
							*TH15 1:15A	TH15 6:45A	TH15 2:45P	TH15 11:30P		F16 4:30A	F16 8:45A	F16 2:15P	F16 3:15P
	*TH15 11:45A			TH15 6:00P		F16 12:45A	F16 5:15A	F16 4:30P					S17 6:00A	S17 11:55A	S17 1:00P
				TH15 6:15P	TH15 9:00P										
	*F16 4:30P		F16 2:15P	F16 6:15P	F16 9:00P										
				S17 12:30A		S17 8:00A	S17 11:55A		S17 10:45P				SU18 12:30P	SU18 6:00P	SU18 7:00P
			S17 8:15A	S17 10:30A	S17 1:15P										
*F16 6:00P			S17 8:45P	S17 11:00P	SU18 1:45A				Lv. Sitka S17 7:00P	SU18 1:15A	SU18 4:30A	SU18 8:45A	SU18 11:55A		
				SU18 7:30A		SU18 1:45P	SU18 6:15P						M19 3:15A	M19 9:15A	M19 10:15A
			SU18 2:15P	SU18 6:15P	SU18 9:00P				Lv. Sitka M19 8:15A	M19 2:30P	M19 5:45P	M19 10:00P	T20 1:15A		
	M19 9:00A			M19 3:45P		M19 10:30P	T20 3:15A						T20 12:45P	T20 6:15P	T20 7:15P
	T20 11:15A	T20 3:45P		T20 5:45P		W21 2:30A	W21 4:45A						W21 2:30P	W21 8:30P	W21 9:30P
			W21 2:15P	W21 6:15P	W21 9:00P	W21 12:45A									
							*W21 12:15P	W21 5:15P	TH22 1:15A	TH22 10:00A			TH22 10:00P	F23 3:30A	F23 4:30A
	TH22 11:55A			TH22 6:30P		F23 1:15A	F23 6:00A	F23 8:15P				TH22 3:00P	S24 10:00A	S24 4:00P	S24 5:00P
				TH22 6:15P	TH22 9:00P										
	*F23 3:15P		F23 2:15P	F23 9:15P	F23 9:00P								SU25 10:45P	SU25 5:15P	SU25 6:15P
				S24 10:30A	S24 1:15P	S24 4:00A	S24 11:30A		S24 9:30P						
			S24 8:15A	S24 11:00P	SU25 1:45A										
F23 6:00P			S24 8:45P			SU25 12:45P	SU25 4:30P		Lv. Sitka S24 11:15A	S24 5:30P	S24 8:45P	SU25 1:00A	SU25 4:15A	M26 1:30A	M26 7:30A	M26 8:30A
			SU25 2:15P	SU25 6:30A	SU25 9:00P										
				SU25 6:15P					Lv. Sitka M26 6:45P	M26		Lv. Pelican SU25 3:30P	SU25 10:00P		
	M26 10:30A		M26 2:15P	M26 5:15P	M26 9:00P	M26 11:55P	T27 4:45A		T27 1:00A	T27 4:15A	T27 8:30A	T27 11:45A		
	T27 12:45P			M26 6:15P	T27 9:00P								T27 2:15P	T27 7:45P	T27 8:45P
			W28 2:15P	T27 6:15P											
				T27 7:15P	W28 9:00P	W28 2:15A	W28 6:15A						W28 4:00P	W28 10:00P	W28 11:00P
				W28 6:15P								F30 3:00A	F30 6:15A		
	TH29 1:30P			TH29 6:15P	TH29 9:00P	W28 11:45P	TH29 5:30A	TH29 1:30P	TH29 10:00P						
				TH29 8:15P									S31 10:45A	S31 4:15P	S31 5:15P
			F30 2:15P	F30 6:15P	F30 9:00P	F30 3:00A	F30 7:45A	F30 9:00P							
			S31 8:15A	S31 10:30A	S31 1:15P										
			S31 8:45P	S31 11:00P	SU1 1:45A				Lv. Sitka S31 6:15P	SU1 12:30A	SU1 3:45A	SU1 8:00A	SU1 11:15A		
F30 6:00P	S31 10:00A			S31 4:30P		S31 11:15P	SU1 3:00A						SU1 2:45P	SU1 9:15P	SU1 10:15P
				SU1 10:00A		SU1 4:15P	SU1 8:15P		M2 5:15A				M2 7:15P	T3 2:15A	T3 3:15A

* The following events may affect availability of space: Little Norway Festival May 15-18 - Petersburg; High School Track & Field Meet May 23-24 - Juneau; Craft, Beer & Home Brew Festival May 16-18 - Haines

ALL TIMES ARE LOCAL TIMES

Vessel legend: ▪ Aurora ▪ Columbia ▪ Le Conte ▪ Malaspina ▪ Matanuska ▪ Taku

Alaska state ferry schedules reprinted courtesy of Alaska Marine Highway

May 1997 Southbound Schedule – Inside Passage/Southeast Alaska

LEAVE SKAGWAY	HAINES	JUNEAU/ AUKE BAY	HOONAH	TENAKEE	ANGOON	ARRIVE SITKA	KAKE	PETERSBURG	WRANGELL	HOLLIS	KETCHIKAN	METLAKATLA	ARRIVE STEWART/HYDER	ARRIVE PRINCE RUPERT	ARRIVE BELLINGHAM
										TH1 9:15A	TH1 11:55A				
F2 9:45A	F2 11:45A	F2 6:30P	F2 10:45P	S3 2:45A	S3 6:00A	S3 11:00A				F2 6:15P	F2 12:15P	F2 1:30P			
										F2 10:00P	S3 6:15A	S3 7:30A			
SU4 9:45P	SU4 11:45P	M5 5:15A						M5 1:45P	M5 5:30P	T6 12:30A				T6 7:30A	
										S3 2:15P	S3 6:45P	S3 8:00P			
										SU4 6:15A	SU4 12:15P	SU4 1:30P			
M5 7:15P	M5 9:45P	SU4 8:15P	M5 12:30A	M5 4:30A	M5 7:45A	M5 12:45P									F9 6:15A
		T6 4:45A						T6 1:00P	W7 3:15A	W7 7:45A	M5 6:15A	M5 12:15P	M5 1:30P		
T6 9:30P	T6 11:30P	T6 11:30A	T6 3:45P		T6 8:45P	W7 1:45A	W7 1:15P	W7 5:15P		T6 9:15A	TH8 1:00A			TH8 8:15A	
		W7 5:00A						W7 2:00P	W7 6:00P	T6 11:55A	T6 11:55A				
W7 11:45P	TH8 2:15A	TH8 8:45A						TH8 5:15P	TH8 9:00P	F9 4:00A				F9 11:00A	
										W7 6:15A	W7 12:15P	W7 1:30P			
										TH8 9:15A	TH8 11:55A				
F9 10:15A	F9 12:15P	F9 5:45P	F9 10:00P	S10 2:00A	S10 5:15A	S10 10:15A								M12 6:00A	
S10 3:00P	S10 5:00P	S10 10:30P						SU11 7:30A	SU11 12:15P	SU11 10:00P					
										F9 6:15A	F9 12:15P	F9 1:30P			
										F9 10:00P	S10 6:15A	S10 7:30A			
SU11 9:45P	SU11 11:55P	M12 5:45A						M12 2:30P	M12 6:30P	T13 1:30A				T13 8:30A	
										S10 2:15P	S10 6:45P	S10 8:00P			
										SU11 6:15A	SU11 12:15P	SU11 1:30P			
M12 12:45P	M12 3:15P	SU11 6:30A	Ar. Pelican	SU11 1:00P		T13 6:00A		W14 1:45A	W14 5:45A	W14 4:15P					F16 6:15A
		M12 9:45P													
		M12 1:30A	M12 5:45A	M12 9:45A	M12 1:00P	M12 6:00P				M12 6:15A	M12 12:15P	M12 1:30P			
										M12 10:00P	T13 1:45A		T13 1:00P		
		*T13 5:00P	T13 9:15P		W14 2:15A	W14 7:15A	W14 7:15P	W14 11:15A							
T13 10:15P	W14 12:15A	W14 5:45A						W14 2:30P	W14 6:30P	TH15 1:30A				TH15 8:45A	
*TH15 12:45A	TH15 3:15A	TH15 9:45A						TH15 6:30P	TH15 10:30P	F16 6:30A				F16 1:30P	
										W14 6:15A	W14 12:15P	W14 1:30P			
										TH15 9:15A	TH15 11:55A				
*F16 4:45P	F16 6:45P	S17 12:15A	S17 4:30A	S17 8:30A	S17 11:45A	S17 4:45P				SU18 9:45P				M19 6:00A	
*S17 4:00P	S17 6:00P	S17 11:30P						SU18 8:45A	SU18 12:45P						
										F16 6:15A	F16 12:15P	F16 1:30P			
										F16 10:00P	S17 6:15A	S17 7:30A			
*SU18 10:00P	SU18 11:55P	M19 5:30A						M19 2:15P	M19 6:15P	T20 1:15A				T20 8:15A	
										S17 2:15P	S17 6:45P	S17 8:00P			
										SU18 6:15A	SU18 12:15P	SU18 1:30P			
		SU18 1:30P	SU18 5:45P	SU18 9:45P	M19 1:00A	M19 6:00A		W21 1:45A	W21 6:15A	W21 4:15P					F23 6:15A
M19 1:15P	M19 3:45P	M19 10:00P				T20 6:15A									
		T20 4:30A	T20 8:45A		T20 1:45P	T20 6:45P	W21 6:15A	W21 10:15A		M19 6:15A	M19 12:15P	M19 1:30P			
T20 10:15P	W21 12:15A	W21 5:45A						W21 2:45P	W21 6:45P	TH22 1:45A				TH22 9:00A	
										M19 10:00P	T20 1:45A		T20 1:00P		
*TH22 12:30A	TH22 3:00A	TH22 9:30A						TH22 6:15P	TH22 10:15P	F23 5:15A				F23 12:15P	
										W21 6:15A	W21 12:15P	W21 1:30P			
										TH22 9:15A	TH22 11:55A				
F23 6:00A	F23 8:00A	F23 4:30P	F23 8:45P	S24 12:45A	S24 4:00A	S24 9:00A		SU25 1:00P	SU25 5:15P	M26 12:15A				M26 7:30A	
S24 8:00P	S24 10:30P	SU25 4:00A								F23 6:15A	F23 12:15P	F23 1:30P			
										F23 10:00P	S24 6:15A	S24 7:30A			
*SU25 9:15P	SU25 11:45P	M26 6:15A						M26 3:00P	M26 7:00P	T27 2:45A				T27 9:45A	
										S24 2:15P	S24 6:45P	S24 8:00P			
										SU25 6:15A	SU25 12:15P	SU25 1:30P			
M26 11:30A	M26 2:00P	SU25 7:00A	Ar. Pelican	SU25 1:30P		T27 4:30A		W28 12:30A	W28 5:00A	W28 4:00P					F30 6:15A
		M26 8:15P								M26 6:15A	M26 12:15P	M26 1:30P			
		SU25 11:55P	M26 4:15A	M26 8:15A	M26 11:30A	M26 4:30P									
		*T27 12:45P	T27 7:45A		W28 12:45A	W28 5:45A	W28 5:45P	W28 9:45P							
T27 11:45P	W28 1:45A	W28 7:15A						W28 4:15P	W28 8:15P	TH29 3:15A				TH29 10:30A	
										T27 9:15A	T27 11:55A				
										W28 6:15A	W28 12:15P	W28 1:30P			
TH29 2:00A	TH29 4:30A	TH29 11:00A						TH29 7:45P	TH29 11:45P	F30 7:45A				F30 2:45P	
										TH29 9:15A	TH29 11:55A				
		F30 5:00P	F30 9:15P	S31 1:15A	S31 4:30A	S31 9:30A				F30 6:15A	F30 12:15P	F30 1:30P			
										M2 12:15A				M2 7:30A	
S31 8:15P	S31 10:45P	SU1 4:15A						SU1 1:15P	SU1 5:15P	F30 10:00P	S31 6:15A	S31 7:30A			
										S31 2:15P	S31 6:45P	S31 8:00P			

June 1997 Northbound Schedule – Inside Passage/Southeast Alaska

Left margin: MARINE ACCESS ROUTES • Alaska State Ferries

Handwritten notes (top): (? TRAIN To Bellingham; Ferries to Skagway?) (for Drive Prince Rupert?) (? or Drive Port Hardi?) (& Ferry to P. Rup.)

Handwritten note (left, lower): OR Leave Mon 23rd 9:30AM Pr. Rup — Arrive Skagway Tu 24th 9 P.M. — 35½ Hrs.

LEAVE BELLINGHAM	LEAVE PRINCE RUPERT	LEAVE STEWART/HYDER	METLAKATLA	KETCHIKAN	HOLLIS	WRANGELL	PETERSBURG	KAKE	ARRIVE SITKA	ANGOON	TENAKEE	HOONAH	JUNEAU/AUKE BAY	HAINES	ARRIVE SKAGWAY
		SEE M/V AURORA SCHEDULE BELOW	SEE M/V AURORA SCHEDULE BELOW		SEE M/V AURORA SCHEDULE BELOW				Lv. Sitka S31 6:15P	SU1 12:30A	SU1 3:45A	SU1 8:00A	SU1 11:15A		
F30 6:00P	S31 10:00A			S31 4:30P		S31 11:15P	SU1 3:00A						SU1 2:45P	SU1 9:15P	SU1 10:15P
	SU1 9:00P			SU1 10:00A		SU1 4:15P	SU1 8:15P	M2 5:15A		M2 5:15A			M2 7:15P	T3 2:15A	T3 3:15A
				M2 3:00A		M2 10:00A	M2 2:00P						M2 8:15P		
	M2 10:30A			M2 5:00P		M2 11:30P	T3 4:00A		M2 8:15P	T3 6:15A	T3 2:45P	T3 7:45P	W4 1:00A	W4 7:00A	W4 8:00A
	T3 9:15P			W4 5:15A		W4 12:15P	W4 4:15P						W4 1:30P	W4 7:00P	W4 8:00P
	W4 8:45A			W4 3:15P		W4 10:00P	TH5 1:45A	TH5 6:45A					TH5 2:00A	TH5 9:00A	TH5 10:00A
	TH5 12:15P			TH5 6:30P		F6 1:00A	F6 5:30A		Lv. Sitka TH5 4:00P	TH5 10:15P	F6 1:30A	F6 5:45A	TH5 6:15P	F6 12:45A	F6 1:45A
									F6 8:30P				F6 9:00A		
	S7 10:15A			S7 6:15P		SU8 1:15A	SU8 5:00A		Lv. Sitka S7 11:15A	S7 5:30P	S7 8:45P	SU8 1:00A	S7 10:15A	S7 4:15P	S7 5:15P
F6 6:00P	SU8 10:00P			SU8 8:00A		SU8 2:45P	SU8 6:30P	M9 3:45A					SU8 4:15A	SU8 11:45P	M9 12:45A
				M9 4:00A		M9 11:00A	M9 3:00P		Lv. Pelican SU8 3:30P				SU8 4:45P		
	M9 11:00A			M9 5:45P		T10 12:30A	T10 5:00A		M9 6:45P	T10 1:00A		T10 6:00A	SU8 10:00P	T10 12:45A	T10 1:45A
	T10 11:45P			W11 5:45A		W11 12:30P	W11 4:15P						M9 5:45P	T10 5:45P	T10 6:45P
	W11 10:45A			W11 5:15P		W11 11:55P	TH12 3:45A	TH12 8:30A					M9 10:45P	T10 8:00P	T10 9:00P
									Lv. Sitka TH12 2:30A	TH12 8:45A	TH12 12:15P	TH12 5:00P	T10 12:15P		
	TH12 1:45P			TH12 8:30P		F13 3:15P	F13 8:00A		F13 8:00P				T10 2:30P	TH12 9:00A	TH12 10:00A
									Lv. Sitka S14 11:15A	S14 5:30P	S14 8:45P	SU15 1:00A	TH12 2:00A	F13 2:30A	F13 3:30A
	S14 9:00A			S14 3:00P		S14 10:00P	SU15 1:45A						TH12 8:00P	S14 3:45P	S14 4:45P
F13 6:00P				SU15 8:15A		SU15 3:00P	SU15 6:45P	M16 4:00A		M16 4:00A			S14 9:45A	SU15 4:00P	SU15 5:00P
	SU15 10:15P			M16 4:15A		M16 11:15A	M16 3:15P						SU15 4:15A	M16 6:30A	M16 7:30A
	M16 9:45A			M16 4:30P		M16 11:15P	T17 3:30A		T17 5:15A	T17 1:45P		T17 6:45P	SU15 10:30A	T17 1:00A	T17 2:00A
	T17 9:15P			W18 3:15A		W18 10:15A	W18 2:15P						M16 1:00A	W18 6:00A	W18 7:00A
	W18 10:00A			W18 4:30P		W18 11:15P	TH19 3:00A	TH19 8:00A					M16 6:00P	T17 6:30P	T17 7:30P
													T17 11:55P		
	TH19 11:45A			TH19 6:00P		F20 12:30A	F20 4:45A		Lv. Sitka TH19 3:00P	TH19 9:15P	F20 12:30A	F20 4:45A	T17 1:00P	TH19 9:00A	TH19 10:00A
									F20 7:30P				TH19 1:30A	TH19 10:00P	TH19 11:00P
	*S21 9:00A			S21 5:00P		S21 11:55P	SU22 3:45A		Lv. Sitka S21 10:15A	S21 4:30P	S21 7:45P	S21 11:55P	TH19 4:30P	F20 11:30A	F20 12:30P
F20 6:00P													F20 8:00A		
													S21 9:15A	S21 3:15P	S21 4:15P
	SU22 11:00P			SU22 7:30A		SU22 1:45P	SU22 5:30P	M23 2:45A		M23 2:45A			SU22 3:15A	SU22 6:00P	SU22 7:00P
				M23 5:00A		M23 5:00A	M23 4:00P		Lv. Pelican SU22 2:30P				SU22 12:30P		M23 9:30A
	M23 9:30A	6:45 Hrs.		M23 4:15P		M23 11:00P	T24 3:45A		Lv. Sitka M23 5:45P	M23 11:55P		T24 5:00A	M23 4:30A	M23 11:45P	T24 12:45A
	T24 10:45P			W25 4:45A	7 Hrs.	W25 11:45A	W25 ...						SU22 9:00P	W25 10:15A	W25 11:15A
	*W25 10:00A			W25 4:30P		W25 11:15P	TH26 3:00A	TH26 8:00A					M23 4:45P	T24 8:00P	T24 9:00P
								3:45 Hrs.	Lv. Sitka M23 8:45P	F27 3:00A	F27 6:15A	F27 10:30A	M23 11:00P	TH26 8:45A	TH26 9:45A
	TH26 1:30P			TH26 8:15P		F27 3:00A	F27 7:15A	12 Hrs.	TH26 8:45P				W25 4:15A	TH26 10:00P	TH26 11:00P
									M23 7:15P				T24 2:30P	F27 6:00A	F27 12:30P
	*S28 9:00A			S28 3:30P		S28 10:15P	SU29 2:00A		Lv. Sitka S28 4:30P	S28 10:45P	SU29 2:00A	SU29 6:15A	TH26 1:45A	F27 11:30A	F27 12:30P
F27 6:00P									17 Hrs.				TH26 10:30P		
													F27 6:00A		
													F27 1:45P	S28 3:30P	S28 4:30P
	SU29 10:15P			SU29 8:30A		SU29 2:45P	SU29 6:30P	M30 3:45A		M30 3:45A			S28 9:30A	SU29 4:15P	SU29 5:15P
				M30 4:15A		M30 11:15A	M30 3:15P				2 Hrs.		SU29 9:30A	M30 6:45A	M30 7:45A
	M30 9:15A			M30 3:45P		M30 10:30P	M30 7:00P		T1 5:00A	T1 1:30P		T1 6:30P	SU29 10:45A	T1 12:45A	T1 1:45A
								T1 2:45A					M30 1:15A	W2 5:45A	W2 6:45A
													M30 5:45P	T1 5:45P	T1 6:45P
													M30 11:00P		
													T1 11:45P		
													T1 12:15P		

* The following event may affect availability of space: Kluane to Chilkat Bike Relay June 21-22 - Haines; Gold Rush Days June 27-29 - Juneau

ALL TIMES ARE LOCAL TIMES

M/V AURORA SOUTHERN PANHANDLE SUMMER 1997 - EFFECTIVE JUNE 1 - SEPTEMBER 10

How To Use This Schedule

The M/V AURORA operates a daily schedule between Ketchikan, Metlakatla and Hollis (Gateway to Prince of Wales Island). There are several sailings to and from these communities each day. To determine the best one for your trip, use this table. Please allow enough time to make appropriate connections with the mainline sailings from Ketchikan (see tables above).

SUN			MON			*TUE		
Lv Hollis	6:15AM		Lv Hollis	6:15AM		Lv Hollis	9:15AM	
Ar Ketchikan	9:00AM		Ar Ketchikan	9:00AM		Ar Ketchikan	11:55AM	
Lv Ketchikan	12:15PM		Lv Ketchikan	12:15PM		Lv Ketchikan	6:15PM	
Ar Metlakatla	1:30PM		Ar Metlakatla	1:30PM		Ar Hollis	9:00PM	
Lv Metlakatla	2:15PM		Lv Metlakatla	2:15PM		WED Lv Hollis	6:15AM	
Ar Ketchikan	3:30PM		Ar Ketchikan	3:30PM		Ar Ketchikan	9:00AM	
Lv Ketchikan	6:15PM		Lv Ketchikan	6:15PM		Lv Ketchikan	12:15PM	
Ar Hollis	9:00PM		Ar Hollis	9:00PM		Ar Metlakatla	1:30PM	
						Lv Metlakatla	2:15PM	
						Ar Ketchikan	3:30PM	

* See STEWART/HYDER TRIPS on next page

 Aurora   ✓ Columbia   ✓ Le Conte   ✓ Malaspina   ✓ Matanuska   ✓ Taku

June 1997 Southbound Schedule – Inside Passage/Southeast Alaska

MARINE ACCESS ROUTES • Alaska State Ferries

LEAVE SKAGWAY	HAINES	JUNEAU/AUKEBAY	HOONAH	TENAKEE	ANGOON	ARRIVE SITKA	KAKE	PETERSBURG	WRANGELL	HOLLIS	KETCHIKAN	METLAKATLA	ARRIVE STEWART/HYDER	ARRIVE PRINCE RUPERT	ARRIVE BELLINGHAM
S31 8:15P	S31 10:45P	SU1 4:15A						SU1 1:15P	SU1 5:15P		M2 12:15A				M2 7:30A
		SU1 1:15P	SU1 5:30P	SU1 9:30P	M2 12:45A	M2 5:45A		M2 6:30P							
M2 6:15A	M2 9:15A	M2 6:15P						T3 2:45A			T3 11:15A			T3 6:15P	
T3 6:15A	T3 9:45A	T3 4:15P				W4 12:30A		W4 1:45P	W4 5:30P		W4 11:55P				F6 9:00A
		M2 11:45P						T3 1:00P	T3 4:45P		T3 11:45P			W4 6:45A	
W4 10:30A	W4 1:00P	W4 11:30P	TH5 3:45A		TH5 8:45A	TH5 1:45P									
T3 11:00P	W4 1:00A	W4 6:30A					T3 8:15A	W4 3:30P	W4 7:30P		TH5 2:15A			TH5 9:30A	
TH5 1:00P	TH5 4:00P	TH5 10:30P						F6 10:45A	F6 3:15P		S7 12:15A			S7 7:15A	
F6 12:15P	F6 3:45P	F6 4:30P	F6 8:45P	S7 12:45A	S7 4:00A	S7 9:00A	S7 8:30P	SU8 1:15A	SU8 5:00A		SU8 11:55A			SU8 7:00P	
						S7 9:00A									
S7 8:15P	S7 10:45P	SU8 4:45A						SU8 1:45P	SU8 5:45P		M9 12:30A			M9 8:00A	
		SU8 7:00A	Ar. Pelican	SU8 1:30P											
M9 8:45A	M9 12:15P	M9 9:15P						T10 5:45A			T10 2:15P			T10 9:15P	
		SU8 11:55P	M9 4:15A	M9 8:15A	M9 11:30A	M9 4:30P									
T10 4:45A	T10 8:15A	T10 2:00P				T10 11:30P					TH12 1:00A			W11 7:45A	F13 10:00A
		T10 12:45A					T10 9:15A	W11 2:45P	W11 6:30P		W11 12:45A				
T10 9:00P	T10 11:00P	W11 10:00A	W11 2:15P			W11 7:15P	TH12 12:15A	T10 2:00P							
T10 11:55P	W11 2:00A	W11 7:45A						W11 4:45P	W11 8:45P		TH12 3:30A			TH12 10:45A	
TH12 1:00P	TH12 4:30P	F13 1:00A						F13 9:45A	F13 1:45P		F13 10:00P			S14 6:00A	
F13 2:00P	F13 5:30P	F13 11:30P				S14 8:30A	S14 8:15P	SU15 1:00A	SU15 4:45A		SU15 12:15P			SU15 7:15P	
		F13 3:30A	F13 2:15P	F13 6:15P	F13 9:30P	S14 2:30A									
S14 7:45P	S14 10:15P	SU15 3:30A						SU15 12:30P	SU15 4:30P		SU15 11:30P			M16 6:45A	
		SU15 11:55A	SU15 4:15P	SU15 8:15P	SU15 11:30P	M16 4:30A		M16 5:00P							
		SU15 11:30P													
SU15 6:30P	M16 12:45P	M16 6:15P						T17 2:45A			T17 11:15A			T17 6:15P	
M16 10:30A		M16 6:15A						W18 12:30P	W18 4:30P		W18 11:00P				F20 8:00A
T17 5:00A	T17 8:30A	T17 3:00P			T17 11:15P	TH19 12:45A									
W18 9:30A	W18 11:55A	W18 10:30P	TH19 2:45A		TH19 7:45A	TH19 12:45A		T17 9:30A							
		W18 1:00A						T17 2:15P	T17 6:00P		W18 1:00A			W18 8:00A	
T17 10:30P	W18 12:30A	W18 6:15A						W18 3:00P	W18 7:00P		TH19 1:45A			TH19 9:00A	
TH19 2:00P	TH19 6:30P	F20 2:30A						F20 11:00A	F20 3:00P		F20 10:30P			S21 6:00A	
TH19 11:55P		F20 5:00A													
F20 3:30P	F20 5:30P	F20 11:00P				S21 8:00A	S21 7:30P	SU22 12:15A	SU22 4:00A		SU22 1:00P			SU22 8:00P	
		F20 3:30P	F20 7:45P	F20 11:45P	S21 3:00A	S21 8:00A									
S21 7:15P	S21 9:45P	SU22 3:00A						SU22 11:55A	SU22 4:15P		SU22 11:15P			M23 6:30A	
		SU22 6:00A	Ar. Pelican	SU22 12:30P											
*SU22 8:30P	SU22 10:30P	M23 3:00A						T24 4:45A			T24 1:15P			T24 8:15P	
M23 12:30P	M23 2:30P	M23 8:00P	M23 3:15A	M23 7:15A	M23 10:30A	M23 3:30P									
		SU22 11:00P				T24 10:30P		T24 2:15P	T24 6:00P		TH26 1:00A			W25 8:00A	F27 10:00A
T24 3:45A	T24 7:15A	T24 1:00P					T24 9:30A								
		T24 1:00A	TH26 4:15A	TH26 8:30A		TH26 1:30P	TH26 6:30P								
W25 1:45P	W25 4:15P	TH26 4:15A						W25 4:30P	W25 8:30P		TH26 3:15A			TH26 10:30A	
T24 11:55P	W25 2:00A	W25 7:30A						F27 9:30A	F27 1:30P		F27 10:00P			S28 6:00A	
TH26 12:45P	TH26 4:15P	F27 12:45A													
*TH26 11:55P		F27 5:00A				S28 8:00A	S28 7:45P	SU29 12:30A	SU29 4:15A		SU29 12:15P			SU29 7:15P	
F27 3:30P	F27 5:30P	F27 11:00P	F27 8:00P	F27 11:55P	S28 3:15A	S28 8:15A									
		F27 3:45P						SU29 12:15P	SU29 4:15P		SU29 11:00P			M30 6:30A	
*S28 7:30P	S28 9:45P	SU29 3:15A						SU29 12:30A							
SU29 6:45P	SU29 11:45P	SU29 11:45A	SU29 4:00P	SU29 8:00P	SU29 11:15P	M30 4:15A		M30 4:45P							
M30 10:45A	M30 1:15P	SU29 11:45P													
		M30 7:45P						T1 7:15A			T1 3:45P			T1 10:45P	

(In the HOLLIS, METLAKATLA and ARRIVE STEWART/HYDER columns: "SEE M/V AURORA SCHEDULE BELOW")

ALL TIMES ARE LOCAL TIMES

M/V AURORA SOUTHERN PANHANDLE SUMMER 1997 – EFFECTIVE JUNE 1 - SEPTEMBER 10

THU Lv Ketchikan 6:15PM	Ar Ketchikan 3:30PM	**SAT** Lv Ketchikan 10:30AM	
Ar Hollis 9:00PM	Lv Ketchikan 6:15PM	Ar Hollis 1:15PM	
THU Lv Hollis 9:15AM	Ar Hollis 9:00PM	Lv Hollis 2:15PM	
Ar Ketchikan 11:55AM	Lv Hollis 10:00PM	Ar Ketchikan 5:00PM	
Lv Ketchikan 6:15PM	**SAT** Ar Ketchikan 12:45AM	Lv Ketchikan 6:45PM	
Ar Hollis 9:00PM		Ar Metlakatla 8:00PM	
	SAT Lv Ketchikan 6:15AM	Lv Metlakatla 8:45PM	
FRI Lv Hollis 6:15AM	Ar Metlakatla 7:30AM	Ar Ketchikan 10:00PM	
Ar Ketchikan 9:00AM	Lv Metlakatla 8:15AM	Lv Ketchikan 11:00PM	
Lv Ketchikan 12:15PM	Ar Ketchikan 9:30AM	**SUN** Ar Hollis 1:45AM	
Ar Metlakatla 1:30PM			
Lv Metlakatla 2:15PM			

*STEWART/HYDER TRIPS
TUESDAY - JUN 3, 17

MON	Lv Hollis	10:00PM
TUE	Ar Ketchikan	12:45AM
	Lv Ketchikan	1:45AM
	Ar Hyder	1:00PM
	Lv Hyder	3:45PM
WED	Ar Ketchikan	1:30AM
	Lv Ketchikan	2:30AM
WED	Ar Hollis	5:15AM

MARINE ACCESS ROUTES ▪ Alaska State Ferries

For the STEWART/HYDER, METLAKATLA, and HOLLIS columns: **SEE M/V AURORA SCHEDULE BELOW**

LEAVE BELLINGHAM	LEAVE PRINCE RUPERT	LEAVE STEWART/HYDER	METLAKATLA	KETCHIKAN	HOLLIS	WRANGELL	PETERSBURG	KAKE	ARRIVE SITKA	ANGOON	TENAKEE	HOONAH	JUNEAU/AUKE BAY	HAINES	ARRIVE SKAGWAY
F27 6:00P				SU29 8:30A		SU29 2:45P	SU29 6:30P		M30 3:45A				M30 5:45P	T1 12:45A	T1 1:45A
							M30 7:00P		T1 5:00A	T1 1:30P		T1 6:30P	T1 11:45P	W2 5:45A	W2 6:45A
	M30 9:15A			M30 3:45P		M30 10:30P	T1 2:45A						T1 12:15P	T1 5:45P	T1 6:45P
	W2 1:45A			W2 7:45A		W2 2:45P	W2 6:45P						TH3 5:00A	TH3 11:55A	TH3 1:00P
	W2 10:00A			W2 4:30P		W2 11:15P	TH3 3:00A	TH3 8:00A					TH3 4:30P	TH3 10:00P	TH3 11:00P
													F4 6:00A	F4 11:30A	F4 12:30P
	TH3 10:45A			TH3 5:15P		TH3 11:55P	F4 4:15A		Lv.Sitka TH3 3:15P	TH3 9:30P	F4 12:45A	F4 5:00A	F4 8:15A		
									F4 7:30P				S5 9:30A	S5 3:30P	S5 4:30P
	S5 9:00A			S5 3:30P		S5 10:30P	SU6 2:15A		Lv.Sitka S5 10:30A	S5 4:45P	S5 8:00P	SU6 12:15A	SU6 3:30A		
F4 6:00P													SU6 11:00A	SU6 4:30P	SU6 5:30P
	SU6 11:00P			SU6 7:30A		SU6 1:45P	SU6 5:30P	M7 2:45A					M7 1:30A	M7 7:00A	M7 8:00A
				M7 5:00A		M7 11:55A	M7 4:00P						SU6 9:00P		
									Lv.Pelican SU6 2:30P				M7 4:45P	M7 11:15P	T8 12:15A
	M7 10:00A			M7 4:45P		M7 11:30P	T8 4:15A		Lv.Sitka M7 5:45P	M7 11:55P			M7 11:45P		
	T8 10:00P			W9 4:00A		W9 11:00A	W9 3:00P					T8 5:00A	W9 4:15A	W9 10:15A	W9 11:15A
	W9 10:45A			W9 5:15P		W9 11:55P	TH10 3:45A	TH10 8:45A					T8 1:45P	T8 7:15P	T8 8:15P
													TH10 12:15A	TH10 7:15A	TH10 8:15A
	TH10 1:15P			TH10 7:45P		F11 2:30A	F11 7:00A		Lv.Sitka TH10 8:00P	F11 2:15A	F11 5:30A	F11 9:45A	TH10 5:15P		
									F11 6:00P				F11 8:00A	F11 2:30P	F11 3:30P
									Lv.Sitka S12 3:15P				F11 1:00P		
	S12 9:00A			S12 5:00P		S12 11:55P	SU13 3:45A		S12 3:15P	S12 9:30P	SU13 12:45A	SU13 5:00A	S12 8:15A	S12 2:15P	S12 3:15P
													SU13 8:15A		
F11 6:00P							M14 4:45P		T15 3:30A				SU13 12:30P	SU13 6:00P	SU13 7:00P
	M14 1:00A			SU13 7:15A		SU13 1:30P	SU13 5:15P	M14 2:30A	T15 2:30A				T15 10:15P	W16 4:15A	W16 5:15A
	M14 9:15A			M14 7:00A		M14 1:45P							M14 4:15P	M14 11:15P	T15 12:15A
													T15 1:15A		
	T15 11:30P			M14 4:00P		M14 10:45P	T15 3:30A						T15 1:15P	T15 6:45P	T15 7:45P
	W16 11:55A			W16 5:30A		W16 12:30P	W16 4:30P						TH17 2:00A	TH17 9:00A	TH17 10:00A
				W16 6:00P		TH17 1:00A	TH17 7:30A	TH17 12:30P					TH17 9:00P		
									Lv.Sitka TH17 2:00P	TH17 8:15P	TH17 11:30P	F18 3:45A	F18 11:00A	F18 4:30P	F18 5:30P
	TH17 12:30P			TH17 7:15P			F18 3:15A		F18 6:30P				F18 7:00A		
									Lv.Sitka S19 9:15A				S19 8:00A	S19 1:45P	S19 2:45P
	S19 9:00A			S19 5:00P		S19 11:55P	SU20 3:45A		S19 9:15A	S19 3:30P	S19 6:45P	S19 11:00P	SU20 2:15A		
F18 6:00P													M21 3:00A	M21 8:30A	M21 9:30A
	SU20 10:00P			SU20 6:30A		SU20 1:00P	SU20 4:45P	M21 2:00A	Lv.Pelican SU20 2:45P				SU20 9:15P		
				M21 4:00A		M21 10:15A	M21 2:30P						M21 3:45P	M21 10:45P	M21 11:45P
													M21 10:15P		
	M21 8:45A			M21 3:30P		M21 10:15P	T22 3:00A		Lv.Sitka M21 11:00P	T22 5:15A		T22 10:15A	W23 3:30A	W23 9:30A	W23 10:30A
	T22 11:30P			W23 5:30A		W23 12:30P	W23 4:30P				T22 12:45P		T22 12:45P	T22 6:15P	T22 7:15P
	W23 9:15A			W23 3:45P		W23 10:30P	TH24 2:15A	TH24 7:00A					TH24 1:45A	TH24 8:45A	TH24 9:45A
													TH24 3:30P	TH24 9:00P	TH24 10:00P
									Lv.Sitka TH24 7:30P	F25 1:45A	F25 5:00A	F25 9:15A	F25 5:00A	F25 10:30A	F25 11:30A
									F25 5:45P				F25 12:30P		
	TH24 12:45P			TH24 7:30P		F25 2:15A	F25 6:30A		Lv.Sitka S26 3:15P				S26 8:15A	S26 2:15P	S26 3:15P
	S26 9:00A			S26 3:00P		S26 9:45P	SU27 2:45A		S26 9:30P	SU27 12:45A		SU27 5:00A	SU27 11:30A	SU27 5:00P	SU27 6:00P
F25 6:00P													M28 1:30A	M28 7:00A	M28 8:00A
	SU27 9:45P			SU27 7:00A		SU27 1:15P	SU27 5:00P	M28 2:15A					M28 4:15P	M28 11:15P	T29 12:15A
				M28 3:45A		M28 10:45A	M28 2:45P						M28 10:30P		
							M28 5:30P		T29 3:30A		T29 12:15P		T29 10:00P	W30 4:00A	W30 5:00A
	M28 8:15A			M28 3:00P		M28 9:30P	T29 2:00A					T29 5:15P	T29 11:45A	T29 5:15P	T29 6:15P
	T29 11:45P			W30 5:45A		W30 12:45P	W30 4:45P						TH31 2:15A	TH31 9:15A	TH31 10:15A
	W30 9:30A			W30 4:00P		W30 10:45P	TH31 2:30A	TH31 7:15A					TH31 3:45P	TH31 9:15P	TH31 10:15P
									Lv.Sitka TH31 2:00P	TH31 8:15P	TH31 11:30P	F1 3:45A	F1 7:00A		
	TH31 11:00A			TH31 5:30P		TH31 11:55P	F1 4:00A		F1 6:45P				S2 8:30A	S2 2:15P	S2 3:15P

ALL TIMES ARE LOCAL TIMES

M/V AURORA SOUTHERN PANHANDLE SUMMER 1997 EFFECTIVE JUNE 1 – SEPTEMBER 10

How To Use This Schedule

The M/V AURORA operates a daily schedule between Ketchikan, Metlakatla and Hollis (Gateway to Prince of Wales Island). There are several sailings to and from these communities each day. To determine the best one for your trip, use this table. Please allow enough time to make appropriate connections with the mainline sailings from Ketchikan (see tables above).

SUN
Lv Hollis 6:15AM
Ar Ketchikan 9:00AM
Lv Ketchikan 12:15PM
Ar Metlakatla 1:30PM
Lv Metlakatla 2:15PM
Ar Ketchikan 3:30PM
Lv Ketchikan 6:15PM
Ar Hollis 9:00PM

MON
Lv Hollis 6:15AM
Ar Ketchikan 9:00AM
Lv Ketchikan 12:15PM
Ar Metlakatla 1:30PM
Lv Metlakatla 2:15PM
Ar Ketchikan 3:30PM
Lv Ketchikan 6:15PM
Ar Hollis 9:00PM

*TUE
Lv Hollis 9:15AM
Ar Ketchikan 11:55AM
Lv Ketchikan 6:15PM
Ar Hollis 9:00PM

WED
Lv Hollis 6:15AM
Ar Ketchikan 9:00AM
Lv Ketchikan 12:15PM
Ar Metlakatla 1:30PM
Lv Metlakatla 2:15PM
Ar Ketchikan 3:30PM
Lv Ketchikan 6:15PM
Ar Hollis 9:00PM

THU
Lv Hollis 9:15AM
Ar Ketchikan 11:55AM
Lv Ketchikan 6:15PM
Ar Hollis 9:00PM

FRI
Lv Hollis 6:15AM
Ar Ketchikan 9:00AM
Lv Ketchikan 12:15PM
Ar Metlakatla 1:30PM
Lv Metlakatla 2:15PM
Ar Ketchikan 3:30PM
Lv Ketchikan 6:15PM
Ar Hollis 9:00PM
Lv Hollis 10:00PM
Ar Ketchikan 12:45AM

SAT
Lv Ketchikan 6:15AM

*See STEWART/HYDER TRIPS on next page

■ Aurora   ■ Columbia   ■ Le Conte   ■ Malaspina   ■ Matanuska   ■ Taku

July 1997 Southbound Schedule – Inside Passage/Southeast Alaska

MARINE ACCESS ROUTES ▪ Alaska State Ferries

LEAVE SKAGWAY	HAINES	JUNEAU/ AUKE BAY	HOONAH	TENAKEE	ANGOON	ARRIVE SITKA	KAKE	PETERSBURG	WRANGELL	HOLLIS	KETCHIKAN	METLAKATLA	ARRIVE STEWART/HYDER	ARRIVE PRINCE RUPERT	ARRIVE BELLINGHAM
M30 10:45A	M30 1:15P	M30 7:45P						TI 7:15A			TI 3:45P			TI 10:45P	
		TI 1:00A					TI 9:30A	TI 2:15P	TI 6:00P		W2 1:00A			W2 8:00A	
TI 4:45A	TI 8:00A	TI 3:00P				TI 11:15P		W2 12:30P	W2 4:15P		W2 11:00P				F4 8:00A
W2 9:15A	W2 11:45A	W2 10:45P	TH3 3:00A		TH3 8:00A	TH3 1:00P									
TI 9:45P	TI 11:45P	W2 5:15A						W2 2:00P	W2 6:00P		TH3 12:45A			TH3 8:00A	
TH3 4:00P	TH3 7:30P	F4 2:30A						F4 11:15A	F4 3:15P		F4 10:45P			S5 6:00A	
TH3 11:55P		F4 5:00A													
F4 3:30P	F4 5:30P	F4 11:00P				S5 8:00A	S5 7:30P	SU6 12:15A	SU6 4:00A		SU6 1:00P			SU6 8:00P	
		F4 3:45P	F4 8:00P	F4 11:55P	S5 3:15A	S5 8:15A									
S5 7:30P	S5 10:00P	SU6 3:30A						SU6 12:30P	SU6 4:30P		SU6 11:30P			M7 7:00A	
		SU6 6:00A	Ar. Pelican SU6 12:30P												
SU6 7:00P		SU6 11:55P													
M7 11:00A	M7 1:30P	M7 7:00P						T8 3:30A			T8 11:55A			T8 7:00P	
		SU6 11:00P	M7 3:15A	M7 7:15A	M7 10:30A	M7 3:30P									
T8 3:15A	T8 6:15A	T8 12:15P				T8 10:00P		W9 1:45P	W9 6:00P		TH10 12:30A			W9 8:45A	FI1 9:30A
		T8 1:45A					T8 10:15A	T8 3:00P	T8 6:45P		W9 1:45A				
W9 1:45P	W9 4:15P		TH10 7:15A		TH10 12:15P	TH10 5:15P									
T8 11:15P	W9 1:15A	W9 7:00A						W9 4:00P	W9 8:00P		TH10 2:45A			TH10 10:15A	
TH10 11:15A	TH10 2:45P	TH10 11:15P						FI1 8:00A	FI1 12:30P		FI1 10:00P			S12 6:00A	
FI1 12:45A		FI1 5:45A													
FI1 6:30P	FI1 9:30P	FI1 4:00A				S12 1:00P	SU13 12:30A	SU13 5:15A	SU13 9:00A		SU13 4:00P			SU13 11:00P	
		FI1 2:00P	FI1 6:15P	FI1 10:15P	S12 1:30A	S12 6:30A									
S12 6:15P	S12 8:45P	SU13 2:45A						SU13 11:45A	SU13 3:45P		SU13 10:45P			M14 6:15A	
		SU13 10:15A	SU13 2:30P	SU13 6:30P	SU13 9:45P	M14 2:45A		M14 3:15P							
SU13 8:30P		M14 1:30A													
M14 12:30P	M14 3:00P	M14 8:30P						T15 5:00A			T15 1:30P			T15 8:30P	
W16 7:45A	W16 10:15A	W16 9:30P	TH17 1:45A		TH17 6:45A	TH17 11:45A									
T15 3:15A	T15 6:45A	T15 1:30P				T15 9:45P									
		T15 3:15A					T15 11:30A	W16 11:15A	W16 10:00P		W16 10:00P			W16 10:00A	FI8 10:00A
T15 10:45P	W16 12:45A	W16 6:15A						W16 4:15P	W16 8:00P		TH17 2:00A			TH17 9:30A	
TH17 1:00P	TH17 4:30P	FI8 1:00A						W16 3:15P	W16 7:15P		TH17 2:00A			S19 6:00A	
FI8 4:30A		FI8 9:30A						FI8 9:45A	FI8 1:45P		FI8 10:45P				
FI8 8:30P	FI8 10:30P	S19 4:00A				S19 1:00P		SU20 2:15A	SU20 6:00A		SU20 1:00P			SU20 8:00P	
		FI8 2:30P	FI8 6:45P	FI8 10:45P	S19 2:00A	S19 7:00A									
S19 5:45P	S19 8:15P	SU20 1:45A						SU20 11:15A	SU20 3:30P		SU20 10:30P			M21 6:00A	
		SU20 6:15A	Ar. Pelican SU20 12:45P												
SU20 8:30P		M21 1:30A													
M21 12:30P	M21 3:00P	M21 8:30P						T22 5:00A			T22 1:30P			T22 8:30P	
		SU20 10:15P	M21 2:30A	M21 6:30A	M21 9:45A	M21 2:45P									
T22 2:45A	T22 6:15A	T22 12:15A				T22 9:30P		W23 1:30P	W23 5:30P		W23 11:55P			W23 7:15A	F25 9:00A
		T22 12:15A					T22 8:45A	T22 1:30P	T22 5:15P		W23 12:15A				
W23 1:00P	W23 3:30P	TH24 2:45A	TH24 7:00A		TH24 11:55A	TH24 5:00P									
T22 10:15P	W23 12:45A	W23 6:30A						W23 3:30P	W23 7:45P		TH24 2:30A			TH24 9:45A	
TH24 12:45P	TH24 4:15P	TH24 11:15P						F25 8:00A	F25 12:30P		F25 10:00P			S26 6:00A	
TH24 11:00P		F25 4:00A													
F25 2:15P	F25 4:15P	F25 9:45P				S26 6:45A	S26 6:15P	S26 11:00A	SU27 2:45A		SU27 11:45A			SU27 6:45P	
		F25 2:00P	F25 6:15P	F25 10:15P	S26 1:30A	S26 6:30A									
S26 6:15P	S26 8:45P	SU27 2:00A						SU27 11:00A	SU27 3:00P		SU27 10:00P			M28 5:15A	
		SU27 10:15A	SU27 2:30P	SU27 6:30P	SU27 9:45P	M28 2:45A		M28 3:15P							
SU27 7:30P		M28 12:30A													
M28 11:00A	M28 1:30P	M28 7:00P						T29 5:15A			T29 1:45P			T29 8:45P	
T29 3:15A	T29 6:45A	T29 1:45P				T29 10:00P		W30 11:15A	W30 3:30P		W30 10:30P			W30 7:30A	FI 9:30A
		T29 12:30A					T29 9:00A	W30 1:45P	W30 5:30P		W30 12:30A			W30 7:30A	
W30 7:30A	W30 10:00A	W30 9:30P	TH31 1:45A		TH31 6:45A	TH31 11:45A									
T29 9:15P	T29 11:45P	W30 5:15A						W30 2:15P	W30 6:15P		TH31 1:00A			TH31 8:15A	
TH31 1:15P	TH31 4:45P	FI 1:15A						FI 10:00A	FI 2:00P		FI 11:00P			S2 6:00A	
TH31 11:15P		FI 4:15A													

(Center columns HOLLIS, METLAKATLA, STEWART/HYDER marked: **SEE M/V AURORA SCHEDULE BELOW**)*

ALL TIMES ARE LOCAL TIMES

M/V AURORA SOUTHERN PANHANDLE SUMMER 1997 EFFECTIVE JUNE 1 - SEPTEMBER 10

	Ar Metlakatla	7:30AM
	Lv Metlakatla	8:15AM
	Ar Ketchikan	9:30AM
SAT	Lv Ketchikan	10:30AM
	Ar Hollis	1:15PM
	Lv Hollis	2:15PM
	Ar Ketchikan	5:00PM
	Lv Ketchikan	6:45PM
	Ar Metlakatla	8:00PM
	Lv Metlakatla	8:45PM
	Ar Ketchikan	10:00PM
	Lv Ketchikan	11:00PM
SUN	Ar Hollis	1:45AM

LOGGING SHOW & FAIR June 26-27 - Hollis (Thorne Bay)

SAT	Lv Ketchikan	6:15AM	SUN	Lv Ketchikan	6:15AM
	Ar Hollis	9:00AM		Ar Hollis	9:00AM
	Lv Hollis	10:00AM		Lv Hollis	10:00AM
	Ar Ketchikan	12:45PM		Ar Ketchikan	12:45PM
	Lv Ketchikan	1:45PM		Lv Ketchikan	1:45PM
	Ar Hollis	4:30PM		Ar Hollis	4:30PM
	Lv Hollis	6:00PM		Lv Hollis	6:00PM
	Ar Ketchikan	8:45PM		Ar Ketchikan	8:45PM
	Lv Ketchikan	9:30PM		Lv Ketchikan	9:30PM
	Ar Metlakatla	10:45PM		Ar Metlakatla	10:45PM
	Lv Metlakatla	11:30PM		Lv Metlakatla	11:30PM
SUN	Ar Ketchikan	12:45AM	MON	Ar Ketchikan	12:45AM
				Lv Ketchikan	1:30AM
				Ar Hollis	4:15AM

*STEWART/HYDER TRIPS
TUESDAY - JUL 1, 15, 29

MON	Lv Hollis	10:00PM
TUE	Ar Ketchikan	12:45AM
	Lv Ketchikan	1:45AM
	Ar Hyder	1:00PM
	Lv Hyder	3:45PM
WED	Ar Ketchikan	1:30AM
	Lv Ketchikan	2:30AM
WED	Ar Hollis	5:15AM

MARINE ACCESS ROUTES • Alaska State Ferries

LEAVE BELLINGHAM	LEAVE PRINCE RUPERT	LEAVE STEWART/HYDER	METLAKATLA	KETCHIKAN	HOLLIS	WRANGELL	PETERSBURG	KAKE	ARRIVE SITKA	ANGOON	TENAKEE	HOONAH	JUNEAU/AUKE BAY	HAINES	ARRIVE SKAGWAY
													F1 5:15A	F1 10:45A	F1 11:45A
									Lv. Sitka TH31 2:00P	TH31 8:15P	TH31 11:30P	F1 3:45A	F1 7:00A		
	TH31 11:00A			TH31 5:30P		TH31 11:55P	F1 4:00A		F1 6:45P				S2 8:30A	S2 2:15P	S2 3:15P
	S2 9:00A			S2 5:00P		S2 11:55P	SU3 3:45A		Lv. Sitka S2 9:30A	S2 3:45P	S2 7:00P	S2 11:15P	SU3 2:30A		
													SU3 12:30P	SU3 6:00P	SU3 7:00P
													M4 3:00A	M4 8:30A	M4 9:30A
F1 6:00P		SEE M/V AURORA SCHEDULE BELOW	SEE M/V AURORA SCHEDULE BELOW	SU3 6:45P	SU3 1:15P	SU3 5:00P			M4 2:00A	Lv. Pelican SU3 2:30P			SU3 9:00A		
	SU3 8:15P			M4 2:15A	M4 9:15A	M4 1:15P							M4 3:45P	M4 10:30A	M4 11:30A
									Lv. Sitka M4 10:45P	T5 5:00A		T5 10:00A	M4 9:00P		
*M4 8:45A				M4 3:30P	M4 10:15P	T5 3:00A							W6 3:15A	W6 9:15A	W6 10:15A
*T5 11:30P				T5	W6 12:30P	W6 4:30P							T5 12:45P	T5 6:15P	T5 7:15P
*W6 8:00A				W6 2:00P	W6 8:45P	TH7 12:30A	TH7 5:15A						TH7 1:45A	TH7 8:45A	TH7 9:45A
													TH7 1:45P	TH7 7:15P	TH7 8:15P
	TH7 12:30P			TH7 6:45P		F8 1:30A	F8 6:00A		*Lv. Sitka TH7 6:30P F8 4:45P	F8 12:45A		F8 5:45A	*F8 3:15A	F8 8:45A	F8 9:45A
	S9 9:00A			S9 5:00P		S9 11:55P	SU10 3:45A		Lv. Sitka S9 1:15P	S9 7:30P	S9 10:45P	SU10 3:00A	F8 10:00A	F8 2:30P	
													S9 6:45A	S9 12:45P	S9 1:45P
													SU10 7:15A	SU10 12:45P	SU10 1:45P
													SU10 12:30P		SU10 5:30P
F8 6:00P				SU10 8:45P	SU10 4:15P	SU10 8:15P		M11 6:15A					M11 3:00A	M11 8:30A	M11 9:30A
	SU10 8:30P			M11 2:30A	M11 9:15A	M11 1:00P							M11 8:00P	T12 3:30A	T12 4:30A
									Lv. Sitka M11 9:45P	T12 4:00A	T12 7:15A	T12 11:30A	M11 8:45P		
M11 8:15A				M11 3:00P	M11 9:45P	T12 2:00A							W13 2:45A	W13 8:45A	W13 9:45A
T12 11:30P				W13 5:30P	W13 12:45P	W13 4:30P							T12 11:30A	T12 5:00P	T12 6:15P
W13 7:45A				W13 2:00P	W13 8:45P	TH14 12:45A	TH14 5:45A						TH14 1:45A	TH14 8:45A	TH14 9:45A
													TH14 2:15P	TH14 7:45P	TH14 8:45P
													F15 3:45A	F15 9:15A	F15 10:15A
TH14 10:45A				TH14 5:00P		TH14 11:30P	F15 3:30A		Lv. Sitka TH14 6:30P F15 5:15P	F15 12:45A	F15 4:00A	F15 8:15A	F15 11:30A		
S16 9:00A				S16 5:00P		S16 11:55P	SU17 3:45A		Lv. Sitka S16 2:15P	S16 8:15P	S16 11:30P	SU17 3:45A	S16 7:15A	S16 1:15P	S16 2:15P
													SU17 7:00A		
													SU17 12:30P	SU17 6:00P	SU17 7:00P
										Lv. Pelican SU17 4:30P			M18 3:00A	M18 8:30A	M18 9:30A
													SU17 11:00P		
F15 6:00P				SU17 7:30A	SU17 2:30P	SU17 8:45P		M18 7:00A					M18 7:45P	T19 3:15A	T19 4:15A
	SU17 6:45P			M18 12:45A	M18 9:30A	M18 1:30P							M18 9:15P		
									Lv. Sitka M18 9:45P	T19 4:00A		T19 9:00A	W20 8:15A	W20 2:15P	W20 3:15P
M18 8:30A				M18 3:15P	M18 10:00P	T19 2:45A							T19 12:30P	T19 6:00P	T19 7:00P
T19 11:00P				W20 5:30P	W20 12:30P	W20 4:15P							TH21 2:00A	TH21 9:00A	TH21 10:00A
W20 8:15A				W20 2:45P	W20 9:30P	TH21 1:15A	TH21 6:00A						TH21 2:30P	TH21 9:00P	TH21 9:00P
													F22 4:00A	F22 9:30A	F22 10:30A
TH21 12:30P				TH21 6:45P		F22 1:15A	F22 5:15A		F22 4:30P	F22 6:30A	F22 9:45A	F22 2:00P	S23 6:45A	S23 12:45P	S23 1:45P
									Lv. Sitka F22 12:15A Lv. Sitka S23 8:00P	S23 2:15A	S23 5:30A	S23 9:45A	F22 5:15P		
S23 9:15A				S23 5:15P		S23 11:55P	SU24 4:00A						SU24 1:00P		
													SU24 12:45P	SU24 6:15P	SU24 7:15P
													M25 3:15A	M25 8:45A	M25 9:45A
F22 6:00P				SU24 8:45P	SU24 4:15P	SU24 8:45P		M25 7:00A					M25 8:45P	T26 3:45A	T26 4:45A
	SU24 8:15P			M25 2:15A	M25 9:00A	M25 12:45P							M25 8:45P		
								M25 10:00P	T26 1:00A	T26 8:00A	T26 5:00P		T26 10:00P	W27 2:45A	W27 8:45A	W27 9:45A
M25 8:00A				M25 2:30P	M25 9:00P	T26 1:00A							T26 10:45A	T26 4:45P	T26 5:45P
T26 11:45P				W27 5:45A	W27 1:00P	W27 5:00P							TH28 2:15A	TH28 9:00A	TH28 10:00A
W27 7:30A				W27 2:00P	W27 8:45P	TH28 12:30A	TH28 5:30A						TH28 2:00P	TH28 8:30P	TH28 8:30P
													F29 4:00A	F29 9:30A	F29 10:30A
TH28 11:30A				TH28 6:15P		F29 2:30A			Lv. Sitka TH28 1:15P F29 5:30P	TH28 7:30P	TH28 10:45P	F29 3:00A	F29 6:15A		
S30 9:00A				S30 5:00P		S30 11:55P	SU31 3:45A		Lv. Sitka S30 8:15A	S30 2:30P	S30 5:45P	S30 10:00P	S30 7:30A	S30 1:30P	S30 2:30P
													SU31 1:15A		
										Lv. Pelican SU31 3:30P			SU31 12:30P	SU31 6:00P	SU31 7:00P
SU31 9:30P				M1 3:30A	M1 10:15A	M1 2:00P							SU31 10:00P		
													M1 9:45P		
F29 6:00P				SU31 6:15P	SU31 11:55P	SU31 3:45P		M1 1:00A					M1 2:45P	M1 9:45P	M1 10:45P

* The Following event may affect availability of space : Southeast Alaska State Fair August 6-10 - Haines   ALL TIMES ARE LOCAL TIMES

M/V AURORA SOUTHERN PANHANDLE   SUMMER 1997   EFFECTIVE JUNE 1- SEPTEMBER 10

How To Use This Schedule

The M/V AURORA operates a daily schedule between Ketchikan, Metlakatla and Hollis (Gateway to Prince of Wales Island). There are several sailings to and from these communities each day. To determine the best one for your trip, use this table. Please allow enough time to make appropriate connections with the mainline sailings from Ketchikan (see tables above).

SUN
Lv Hollis 6:15AM
Ar Ketchikan 9:00AM
Lv Ketchikan 12:15PM
Ar Metlakatla 1:30PM
Lv Metlakatla 2:15PM
Ar Ketchikan 3:30PM
Lv Ketchikan 6:15PM
Ar Hollis 9:00PM

MON
Lv Hollis 6:15AM
Ar Ketchikan 9:00AM
Lv Ketchikan 12:15PM
Ar Metlakatla 1:30PM
Lv Metlakatla 2:15PM
Ar Ketchikan 3:30PM
Lv Ketchikan 6:15PM
Ar Hollis 9:00PM

*TUE
Lv Hollis 9:15AM
Ar Ketchikan 11:55AM
Lv Ketchikan 6:15PM
Ar Hollis 9:00PM

WED
Lv Hollis 6:15AM
Ar Ketchikan 9:00AM
Lv Ketchikan 12:15PM
Ar Metlakatla 1:30PM
Lv Metlakatla 2:15PM
Ar Ketchikan 3:30PM

* See STEWART/HYDER TRIPS on next page

Aurora   Columbia   Le Conte   Malaspina   Matanuska   Taku

August 1997 Southbound Schedule – Inside Passage/Southeast Alaska

MARINE ACCESS ROUTES • Alaska State Ferries

LEAVE SKAGWAY	HAINES	JUNEAU/ AUKE BAY	HOONAH	TENAKEE	ANGOON	ARRIVE SITKA	KAKE	PETERSBURG	WRANGELL	HOLLIS	KETCHIKAN	METLAKATLA	ARRIVE STEWART/HYDER	ARRIVE PRINCE RUPERT	ARRIVE BELLINGHAM
TH31 1:15P	TH31 4:45P	FI 1:15A						FI 10:00A	FI 2:00P		FI 11:00P				S2 6:00A
TH31 11:15P		FI 4:15A													
FI 2:45P	FI 4:45P	FI 10:15A				S2 7:15A	S2 6:45P	S2 11:30P	SU3 3:15A		SU3 10:15A			SU3 5:15P	
		FI 2:30P	FI 6:45P	FI 10:45P		S2 2:00A / S2 7:00A									
S2 6:15P	S2 8:45P	SU3 2:15A						SU3 11:15A	SU3 3:15P		SU3 10:15A				M4 5:45A
		SU3 6:00A	Ar. Pelican SU3 12:30P												
SU3 8:30P		M4 1:30A						T5 5:00A			T5 1:30P				T5 8:30P
M4 12:30P	M4 3:00P	M4 8:30P													
		SU3 10:00P	M4 2:15A	M4 6:15A	M4 9:30A	M4 2:30P		W6 12:45P	W6 4:30P		W6 11:00P				F8 10:00A
T5 2:30A	T5 6:00A	T5 12:45P				T5 9:00P		T5 12:15P	T5 4:00P		T5 11:00P			W6 6:00A	
		M4 11:00P					T5 7:30A								
W6 12:45P	W6 3:15P	TH7 1:45A	TH7 6:00A		TH7 11:00A	TH7 4:00P					TH7 2:15A			TH7 9:30A	
T5 10:15P	W6 12:45A	W6 6:30A						W6 3:30P	W6 7:30P		F8 10:00P			S9 6:00A	
TH7 12:45P	TH7 4:15P	TH7 11:15A						F8 8:00A	F8 12:30P						
TH7 9:15P		F8 2:15A				S9 5:00A	S9 4:30P	S9 10:00P	SU10 3:00A		SU10 10:00A			SU10 5:00P	
F8 12:30P	F8 2:30P	F8 8:00P													
	F8 3:30P	F8 9:00P	S9 1:15A		S9 6:00A	S9 11:00A									
*S9 4:45P	S9 7:15P	SU10 12:45A						SU10 9:45A	SU10 2:15P		SU10 9:45A			MI1 5:15A	
*SU10 3:45P	SU10 5:45P	M11 2:15A	MI1 6:30A	MI1 10:30A	MI1 1:45P	MI1 6:45P									
*SU10 7:00P	SU10 9:00P	M11 1:30A						T12 5:00A			T12 1:30P			T12 8:30P	
M11 12:30P	M11 3:00P	M11 3:00P						W13 3:45A	W13 7:45A		TH14 2:00A			W13 5:45A	
T12 7:30A	T12 11:30A	T12 6:30P				W13 2:45A		T12 11:55A	T12 3:45P		T12 10:45P				
		M11 10:45P					T12 7:15A								
W13 12:15P	W13 2:45P	TH14 2:00A	TH14 6:15A		TH14 11:15A	TH14 4:15P		W13 1:30P	W13 5:30P		TH14 12:15A			TH14 7:30A	
T12 8:45P	T12 11:00P	W13 4:30A						F15 9:30A	F15 1:30P		F15 10:00P			S16 6:00A	
TH14 12:45P	TH14 4:15P	F15 12:45A													
TH14 9:45P		F15 2:45A				S16 5:45A	S16 5:15P	S16 10:00P	SU17 1:45A		SU17 8:45A			SU17 3:45P	
F15 1:15P	F15 3:15P	F15 8:45P	F15 11:45P	S16 3:45A	S16 6:45A	S16 11:45A									
		SU17 1:45A						SU17 10:45A	SU17 3:15P		SU17 10:30P			MI8 6:00A	
S16 5:15P	S16 7:45P	SU17 8:00A	Ar. Pelican SU17 2:30P												
		M18 1:30A						T19 4:30A			T19 1:00P			T19 8:00P	
SU17 8:30P		M18 8:00P								SEE M/V AURORA SCHEDULE BELOW		SEE M/V AURORA SCHEDULE BELOW	SEE M/V AURORA SCHEDULE BELOW		
M18 12:30P	M18 2:30P	M18 3:00A	M18 7:15A	M18 11:15A	M18 2:30P	M18 7:30P		W20 3:30P	W20 7:15P		TH21 1:30A				F22 10:45A
T19 7:15A	T19 11:15A	T19 6:15P				W20 2:30A		T19 12:30P	T19 4:15P		T19 11:15P			W20 6:15A	
		M18 11:15P					T19 7:45A								
W20 5:45P	W20 8:15P	TH21 7:45A	TH21 11:55A		TH21 5:00P	TH21 10:00P		W20 2:15P	W20 6:15P		TH21 2:30A			TH21 9:45A	
T19 9:45P	T19 11:45P	W20 5:15A						F22 12:15P	F22 4:15P		F22 11:15P			S23 6:15A	
TH21 1:00P	TH21 4:30P	F22 1:00A													
TH21 10:00P		F22 3:00A				S23 5:15A	S23 4:15P	S23 9:00P	SU24 2:45A		SU24 9:45A			SU24 4:45P	
F22 12:45P	F22 2:45P	F22 8:15P						SU24 10:00A	SU24 2:30P		SU24 9:45P			MI25 5:15A	
S23 4:45P	S23 7:15P	SU24 1:00A	F22 11:00P	S23 3:00A	S23 6:15A	S23 11:15A									
		F22 6:45P													
SU24 8:45P		SU24 2:30P	SU24 6:45P	SU24 10:45P	M25 2:00A	M25 7:00A		M25 7:45P							
M25 12:45P	M25 3:15P	M25 1:45A						T26 5:15A			T26 1:45P			T26 8:45P	
T26 7:45A	T26 11:15A	M25 8:45P				W27 3:00A		W27 4:00P	W27 7:45P		TH28 2:00A			W27 5:30A	
		T26 6:15P					T26 7:00A	T26 11:45A	T26 3:30P		T26 10:30P				F29 11:00A
W27 12:15P	W27 2:45P	M25 10:30P	TH28 12:30A		TH28 5:30A	TH28 10:30A									
T26 8:45P	T26 11:00P	W27 8:15P						W27 1:45P	W27 5:45P		TH28 12:45A			TH28 8:00A	
TH28 1:00P	TH28 4:30P	W27 4:30A						F29 9:45A	F29 1:45P		F29 9:45P			S30 6:00A	
TH28 9:30P		F29 1:00A													
F29 1:30P	F29 3:30P	F29 9:00P				S30 6:00A	S30 5:30P	S30 10:15P	SU31 2:00A		SU31 11:00A			SU31 6:00P	
		F29 1:30P	F29 5:45P	F29 9:45P	S30 1:00A	S30 6:00A									
S30 5:30P	S30 8:00P	SU31 1:30A						SU31 10:30P	SU31 3:00P		SU31 10:30P			MI 6:00A	
		SU31 7:00A	Ar. Pelican SU31 1:30P												
SU31 8:30P		MI 1:30A													

ALL TIMES ARE LOCAL TIMES

M/V AURORA SOUTHERN PANHANDLE SUMMER 1997   EFFECTIVE JUNE 1- SEPTEMBER 10

THU Lv Ketchikan 6:15PM	Ar Ketchikan 3:30PM	**SAT** Lv Ketchikan 10:30AM
Ar Hollis 9:00PM	Lv Ketchikan 6:15PM	Ar Hollis 1:15PM
Lv Hollis 9:15AM	Ar Hollis 9:00PM	Lv Hollis 2:15PM
Ar Ketchikan 11:55AM	Lv Hollis 10:00PM	Ar Ketchikan 5:00PM
Lv Ketchikan 6:15PM	**SAT** Ar Ketchikan 12:45AM	Lv Ketchikan 6:45PM
Ar Hollis 9:00PM	**SAT** Lv Ketchikan 6:15AM	Ar Metlakatla 8:00PM
FRI Lv Hollis 6:15AM	Ar Metlakatla 7:30AM	Lv Metlakatla 8:45PM
Ar Ketchikan 9:00AM	Lv Metlakatla 8:15AM	Ar Metlakatla 10:00PM
Lv Ketchikan 12:15PM	Ar Ketchikan 9:30AM	Lv Ketchikan 11:00PM
Ar Metlakatla 1:30PM		**SUN** Ar Hollis 1:45AM
Lv Metlakatla 2:15PM		

*STEWART/HYDER TRIPS
TUESDAY - AUG 12, 26

MON	Lv Hollis	10:00PM
TUE	Ar Ketchikan	12:45AM
	Lv Ketchikan	1:45AM
	Ar Hyder	1:00PM
	Lv Hyder	3:45PM
WED	Ar Ketchikan	1:30AM
	Lv Ketchikan	2:30AM
WED	Ar Hollis	5:15AM

September 1997 Northbound Schedule – Inside Passage/Southeast Alaska

LEAVE BELLINGHAM	LEAVE PRINCE RUPERT	LEAVE STEWART/HYDER	METLAKATLA	KETCHIKAN	HOLLIS	WRANGELL	PETERSBURG	KAKE	ARRIVE SITKA	ANGOON	TENAKEE	HOONAH	JUNEAU/AUKE BAY	HAINES	ARRIVE SKAGWAY
F29 6:00P				SU31 6:15A		SU31 11:55A	SU31 3:45P	MI 1:00A					MI 2:45A	MI 8:15A	MI 9:15A
			SU31 2:15P	SU31 6:15P	SU31 9:00P								MI 2:45P	MI 9:45P	MI 10:45P
											Lv. Pelican SU31 3:30P		SU31 10:00P		
	SU31 9:30P			MI 3:30A		MI 10:15A	MI 2:00P						MI 9:45P		
	MI 9:00A		MI 2:15P	MI 6:15P	MI 9:00P										
				MI 3:45P		MI 10:30P	T2 2:30P						T2 12:15P	T2 5:45P	T2 6:45P
									Lv. Sitka MI 9:45P	T2 4:00A		T2 9:00A	W3 8:15A	W3 2:15P	W3 3:15P
	T2 11:15P	T2 3:45P		W3 2:30A	W3 5:15A	W3 12:15P	W3 4:15P								
	W3 9:15A			W3 5:15A									TH4 1:30A	TH4 8:30A	TH4 9:30A
				W3 3:15P		W3 10:00P	TH4 1:45A	TH4 6:45A					TH4 3:15P	TH4 9:15P	TH4 10:15P
			W3 2:15P	W3 6:15P	W3 9:00P								F5 6:15A	F5 12:15P	F5 1:15P
				TH4 6:15P	TH4 9:00P										
	TH4 12:30P			TH4 7:15P		F5 2:00A	F5 7:00A		F5 9:30P	F5 5:30A	F5 8:45A	F5 1:00P	S6 11:30A	S6 5:30P	S6 6:30P
			F5 2:15P	F5 6:15P	F5 9:00P										
			S6 8:15A	S6 10:30A	S6 1:15P										
			S6 8:45P	S6 11:00P	SU7 1:45A										
	S6 9:00A			S6 3:00P		S6 9:45P	SU7 1:30A			Lv. Sitka S6 6:30P	SU7 12:45A	SU7 4:00A	SU7 11:30A	SU7 4:15P	SU7 5:15P
				SU7 9:45A		SU7 3:45P	SU7 7:30A	MB 4:45P				SU7 8:15A	SU7 10:45A	T9 1:30A	T9 2:30A
			SU7 2:15P	SU7 6:15P	SU7 9:00P								T9 12:30A		
	SU7 11:15P			MB 5:45A		MB 12:45P	MB 4:45P								
			MB 2:15P	MB 6:15P	MB 9:00P			MB 7:45P		T9 5:45A	T9 2:30A		W10 12:45A	W10 6:45A	W10 7:45A
	MB 1:00P		Ar. Ketchikan MB 6:15P									T9 7:30P	W10 12:45A	W10 6:15P	W10 7:15P
	T9 9:00A			T9 4:30P		T9 11:30P	W10 3:30A								
		T9 3:45P	W10 2:15P	W10 2:30A	W10 5:15A										
	*W10 2:30P			W10 6:15P / W10 8:30P	W10 9:00P / TH11 12:15A	TH11 7:00A	TH11 10:45A		TH11 8:45P		FI2 6:00A	FI2 11:00A	FI2 9:45A / FI2 2:15P	FI2 3:15P	FI2 4:15P
	FI2 11:45A			FI2 5:30P		S13 12:15A	S13 6:45A		S13 4:45P / Lv. Sitka S13 1:00P	S13 7:15A	S13 10:30P	SU14 2:45A	SU14 6:00A / SU14 6:00A	SU14 11:55A	SU14 1:00P
F12 6:00P				SU14 5:00A		SU14 10:45A	SU14 2:30P	SU14 11:45P			Lv. Pelican SU14 3:30P		SU14 10:00P		
	SU14 12:45P			SU14 8:15P	SU14 11:55P	MI5 6:45A	MI5 10:30A						MI5 1:30P	MI5 8:30P	MI5 9:30P
	T16 9:00A			T16 3:00P		T16 9:45P	W17 1:30A						MI5 7:30P	T16 1:30A	T16 2:30A
			W17 7:15A	W17 9:30A / W17 5:30P	W17 12:15P								W17 10:15A	W17 3:45P	W17 4:45P
	W17 7:15P			TH18 3:00A	TH18 6:45A	TH18 1:30P	TH18 5:15P	TH18 6:45A	TH18 2:45P / TH18 11:15P	FI9 2:30A	FI9 6:45A		FI9 10:00A	FI9 9:15P	FI9 10:15P
	FI9 9:15A			FI9 6:15P		S20 1:45A	S20 6:15A	FI9 3:15A	S20 7:00P	SU21 1:15A	SU21 4:30A	SU21 8:45A	FI9 3:45P / SU21 6:00A	SU21 11:55A	SU21 1:00P
F19 6:00P				SU21 9:15A		SU21 4:00P	SU21 8:00P	M22 5:15A					SU21 11:55A	T23 1:45A	T23 2:45A
	SU21 5:45P			SU21 11:45P	M22 3:30A	M22 10:15A	M22 2:00P						M22 7:15P	T23 4:45A	T23 5:45A
	T23 9:00A		T23 1:00P	T23 3:15P / T23 3:30P	T23 6:00P	T23 10:30P	W24 2:30A						M22 10:45P		
			W24 12:45A	W24 3:00A / W24 1:15P	W24 5:45A / W24 5:00P			TH25 7:15A					W24 11:15A	W24 4:45P	W24 5:45P
	W24 9:00P			TH25 3:00A	TH25 6:45A	TH25 1:45P	TH25 5:45P		TH25 3:15P / TH25 11:45P	F26 3:00A	F26 7:15A		F26 4:30P	F26 10:00P	F26 11:00P
F26 6:00P	F26 11:55A			F26 6:30P		S27 1:15A	S27 6:15A		S27 1:15P / Lv. Sitka S27 1:15P	S27 7:30P	S27 10:45P	SU28 3:00A	F26 10:30A / SU28 6:45A	SU28 12:45P	SU28 1:45P
	SU28 6:30P			SU28 7:30A		SU28 2:15P	SU28 7:15P	M29 6:00A			Lv. Pelican SU28 3:45P		SU28 6:15A / SU28 10:15P		
				M29 12:30A	M29 4:15A	M29 11:00A	M29 2:45P						M29 7:15P / T30 1:15P	T30 2:15A	T30 3:15A
														T30 6:45P	T30 7:45P

* The Following event may affect availability of space: Klondike Trail of '98 International Road Relay September 12-13 – Skagway   ALL TIMES ARE LOCAL TIMES

Legend: ▪ Aurora   ▪ Columbia   ▪ Le Conte   ▪ Malaspina   ▪ Matanuska   ▪ Taku

---

(Continued from page 627)

vehicles; mailing address and phone number; alternate dates in the event cabin or vehicle space is not available on your first choice; and approximate date you will be leaving home.

Persons with disabilities requiring special accommodations should include this information when making reservations. Also notify the purser upon boarding the vessel. ⚓

Waitlist/Standby: If you are unable to obtain space on the sailing you want, reservation personnel may place your request on a waitlist. A limited number of requests will be added to the waitlist, which is checked on a regular basis. If a cancellation occurs for the sailing you want, you will be notified of confirmation of space. NOTE: *Do not send payment for waitlisted space until confirmed.*

If you have passenger space but do not have a confirmed cabin space, you may sign up on the purser's "Standby" list on board. If your vehicle space has not been confirmed, you must sign up on the "Standby" list at the ferry terminal. Standbys literally stand in line until all reserved passengers and vehicles are on board; if there is space, standbys may board. Standbys are subject to off-loading at each port of call.

Deck Passage: If cabin space is filled, or you do not want a cabin, you may go deck passage. This means you'll be sleeping in one of the reclining lounge chairs or rolling out your sleeping bag in an empty corner or even out on deck. There is a limited number of recliner chairs and spaces to roll out sleep-

ing bags. Small, free-standing tents are permitted on back decks if space allows. Beware of wind. Pillows and blankets are available for rent from the purser on most sailings. Public showers are available on all vessels except the *Bartlett*.

Fares and fare payment: See page 638 for Southeast passenger and vehicle tariffs, see page 639 for cabin tariffs; see page 641 for Southcentral/Southwest passenger and vehicle tariffs, page 640 for cabin tariffs.. Fares are charged for passengers, vehicles and cabins on a port-to port basis. If you are traveling from Ketchikan to Skagway with a stopover at Juneau, you are charged from Ketchikan to Juneau and Juneau to Skagway, with the total ticket cost being slightly higher than if you were not stopping off in

September 1997 Southbound Schedule – Inside Passage/Southeast Alaska

Leave Skagway	Haines	Juneau/Auke Bay	Hoonah	Tenakee	Angoon	Arrive Sitka	Kake	Petersburg	Wrangell	Hollis	Ketchikan	Metlakatla	Arrive Stewart/Hyder	Arrive Prince Rupert	Arrive Bellingham
S30 5:30A	S30 8:00A	SU31 1:30A						SU31 10:30A	SU31 3:00P		SU31 10:30P			M1 6:00A	
SU31 8:30P	M1 1:30A	M1 8:15P						T2 4:45A	W3 11:45A W3 3:45P		T2 1:15P			T2 8:15P	
M1 12:15P	M1 2:45P	M1 8:15P						W3 11:45A	W3 3:45P		W3 10:15P				F5 7:15A
T2 1:45A	T2 5:15A	T2 11:45A					T2 8:00P								
		M1 3:00A	M1 7:15A	M1 11:15A	M1 2:30P	M1 7:30P				M1 6:15A	M1 12:15P	M1 1:30P			
		M1 11:45P					T2 8:15A	T2 1:00P	T2 4:45P		T2 11:45P			W3 6:45A	
										M1 10:00P	T2 1:45A		T2 1:00P		
T2 9:45P	T2 11:55P	W3 5:30A						W3 2:30P	W3 7:15P		T2 2:15A			TH4 9:30A	
W3 5:45P	W3 8:15P	TH4 6:45A	TH4 11:00A		TH4 4:00P	TH4 9:00P									
										W3 6:15A	W3 12:15P	W3 1:30P	W3 1:30P		
TH4 12:30P	TH4 4:00P	F5 12:30A								F5 10:45A	F5 10:00P			S6 6:00A	
TH4 11:45P		F5 4:45A							F5 2:45P						
F5 4:15P	F5 6:45P	S6 12:45A			S6 9:45A	S6 9:30A		SU7 2:15A	SU7 6:00A		SU7 1:15P			SU7 8:15P	
										TH4 9:15A	TH4 11:55A				
		F5 5:15P	F5 9:30P	S6 1:30A	S6 4:45A	S6 9:45A				F5 6:15A	F5 12:15P	F5 1:30P			
S6 9:30P	S6 11:55P	SU7 6:00A						SU7 3:15P	SU7 7:30P					M8 10:00A	
										F5 10:00P	S6 6:15A	S6 7:30A			
										S6 2:15P	S6 6:45P	S6 8:00P			
										SU7 6:15A	SU7 12:15P	SU7 1:30P			
		SU7 12:30P	SU7 4:45P	SU7 8:45P	SU7 11:55P	M8 5:00A		M8 5:30A							
SU7 8:15P	SU7 10:15P	M8 3:45A						M8 12:15P	M8 4:00P		M8 11:00P			T9 6:00A	
T9 5:30A	T9 9:00A	T9 4:15P						W10 1:45P	W10 5:45P		TH11 12:15A				F12 9:15P
		T9 2:30A					T9 11:00A	T9 3:45P	T9 7:30P		M8 6:15A M8 12:15P	M8 1:30P			
											W10 2:30A			W10 9:30A	
										M8 10:00P	T9 1:45A		T9 1:00P		
W10 10:15A	W10 12:45P	TH11 6:30A	TH11 10:45A		TH11 3:45P	TH11 8:45P									
W10 10:15P	TH11 12:15A	TH11 6:15A						TH11 3:00P	TH11 6:45P	W10 6:15A TH11 9:15A	W10 12:15P TH11 11:55A	W10 1:30P		F12 1:45A F12 8:45P	
F12 7:15P	F12 9:15P	S13 2:45A						S13 11:15A	S13 3:00P	S13 10:00P	SU14 2:45A			SU14 9:45A	
	F12 6:15P	F12 10:30P	S13 2:30A	S13 5:45A	S13 10:45A			M15 9:30A	M15 1:15P		M15 10:15P			T16 6:00A	
*SU14 4:00P	SU14 6:30P	M15 1:00A													
	SU14 7:00A	Ar. Pelican SU14 1:30P													
	M15 2:00A	M15 6:15A	M15 10:15A	M15 1:30P	M15 6:30P		T16 6:00A	T16 10:45A		T16 8:15P	W17 5:15A	W17 6:30A			F19 7:00A
T16 12:30A	T16 4:00A	T16 10:45A				T16 7:00P		W17 11:30A	W17 3:30P		W17 10:00P			W17 4:15P	
T16 5:30A	T16 8:00A	T16 2:00P						T16 10:30P	W17 2:15A		W17 9:15A			F19 6:15A	
W17 7:45P	W17 9:45P	TH18 3:15A						TH18 11:45A	TH18 3:45P		TH18 11:15P				
										W17 1:45P	W17 4:30P				
		F19 5:45P	F19 10:00P	S20 2:00A	S20 5:15A	S20 10:15A									
S20 1:15A	S20 3:15A	S20 8:45A						S20 5:15P	S20 9:00P	SU21 4:00A	SU21 7:45A			SU21 2:45P	
SU21 4:00P	SU21 6:30P	M22 1:00A						M22 9:45A	M22 2:00P		M22 10:00P			T23 6:00A	
		SU21 1:00P	SU21 5:15P	SU21 9:15P	M22 12:30A	M22 5:30A	M22 5:00P	M22 9:45P		T23 7:15A	T23 11:00A	T23 12:15P			
T23 5:45A	T23 9:15A	T23 5:00P				W24 1:15A		W24 2:45P	W24 6:45P		TH25 1:15A			W24 6:00P	F26 10:15A
T23 8:15A	T23 10:15A	T23 3:45P				W24 12:15A		W24 12:15A	W24 4:00A		W24 11:00A				
										T23 7:00P	T23 10:45P	T23 11:55P		F26 9:00A	
W24 8:45P	W24 11:15P	TH25 5:45A						TH25 2:30P	TH25 6:30P		F26 2:00A				
										W24 6:45A	W24 9:30A				
		F26 6:30P	F26 10:45P	S27 2:45A	S27 6:00A	S27 11:00A								SU28 3:30P	
S27 2:00A	S27 4:00A	S27 9:30A						S27 6:00P	S27 9:45P	SU28 4:45A	SU28 8:30A				
SU28 4:45P	SU28 7:15P	M29 1:15A						M29 10:00A	M29 2:00P		M29 9:45P			T30 4:45A	
		SU28 7:15A	Ar. Pelican SU28 1:45P												
T30 6:15A	T30 9:45A	SU28 4:45P				W1 1:00A		W1 2:15P	W1 6:00P		TH2 12:30A				F3 9:30A
		SU28 11:15P	M29 6:15A	M29 10:15A	M29 1:30P	M29 6:30P	T30 6:00A	T30 10:45A		T30 8:15P	T30 11:00P			TH2 8:30A	
T30 10:45P	W1 12:45A	W1 6:15A						W1 3:00P	W1 6:45P		TH2 1:30A				

ALL TIMES ARE LOCAL TIMES

Juneau.

Special fares are available for senior citizens and persons with disabilities. Contact the Alaska Marine Highway System for fares and restrictions.

Full payment is required on or before the due date stated at the time of reservations. Bookings will be cancelled if reservations are not paid for by the payment due date. Payment may be made by mail with certified or cashier's check, or money order. Personal checks are not accepted unless written on an Alaska bank. Credit cards (VISA, MasterCard, American Express, Discover and Diners Club) are accepted at all terminals and by phone (some restrictions may apply).

Cancellation fees are charged if a change or cancellation is made within 14 days of sailing.

Vehicle tariffs depend on the size of vehicle. You are charged by how much space you take up, so a car with trailer is measured from the front of the car to the end of the trailer, including hitch space.

Bicycles, kayaks and inflatables are charged a surcharge. Check the Alternate Means of Conveyance charges in the tariff section.

Passenger tariffs are charged as follows: adults and children 12 and over, full fare; children 2 to 11, approximately half fare; children under 2, free. Passenger fares do not include cabins or meals. Special passes and travel rates are available to senior citizens (over 65) and persons with disabilities. Check with the Alaska Marine Highway or consult the official Marine Highway schedule for costs and restrictions.

Cabin rates depend on vessel, size of cabin and facilities. Cabins are sold as a unit. Only 5 vessels have cabins available.

Surcharges are assessed on pets ($25 to/from Bellingham, $10 to/from Prince Rupert and to/from Stewart/Hyder) and unattended vehicles ($50 to/from Bellingham, $20 to/from Prince Rupert and to/from Stewart/Hyder, and $10 to/from other ports). The Marine Highway does not provide for loading and off-loading of unattended vehicles.

Check-in times: Summer check-in times for reserved vehicles prior to departure are: Bellingham and Prince Rupert, 3 hours; Ketchikan, Juneau, Haines, Skagway, Homer, Seward, Kodiak, 2 hours; Petersburg, 1 1/2 hours; all other ports, 1 hour. Call the Sitka terminal for check-in time (907/747-3300). Passengers without vehicles must check in 1 hour prior to departure at all ports except Bellingham, where check-in is 2 hours prior to departure. For MV *Bartlett* departures from Whittier, check-in time at the Portage train loading ramp 1 hour prior to train departure.

Local times are shown on all Alaska Marine Highway schedules: Alaska time for Alaska ports on the Southeast and Southcentral/Southwest schedules, Pacific time for Prince Rupert, BC, Bellingham, WA, and Stewart/Hyder on the Southeast schedules.

Stopovers: In-port time on all vessels is

1997 Inside Passage/Southeast Alaska Passenger & Vehicle Tariffs

MARINE ACCESS ROUTES · Alaska State Ferries

ADULT 12 YEARS OR OVER (Meals and Berth NOT included) — ITEM ADT

BETWEEN AND	BELLINGHAM	PRINCE RUPERT	STEWART/HYDER	KETCHIKAN	METLAKATLA	HOLLIS	WRANGELL	PETERSBURG	KAKE	SITKA	ANGOON	HOONAH	JUNEAU	HAINES	SKAGWAY
KETCHIKAN	164	38	40												
METLAKATLA	168	42	44	14											
HOLLIS	178	52	54	20	22										
WRANGELL	180	56	58	24	26	24									
PETERSBURG	192	68	70	38	42	38	18								
KAKE	202	80	82	48	52	48	34	22							
SITKA	208	86	88	54	58	54	38	26	24						
ANGOON	222	100	102	68	72	68	52	40	28	22					
HOONAH	226	104	106	74	78	74	56	44	38	24	20				
JUNEAU	226	104	106	74	78	74	56	44	44	24	24	20			
HAINES	240	118	120	88	92	88	70	58	58	40	38	34	20		
SKAGWAY	246	124	126	92	96	92	76	64	64	44	42	40	26	14	
PELICAN	248	126	128	96	100	96	78	66	52	40	38	22	32	46	54
TENAKEE	226	104	106	74	78	74	56	44	32	22	16	32	34	40	32

CHILD 2 THROUGH 11 YEARS (Under 2 Transported Free) — ITEM CHD

BETWEEN AND	BELLINGHAM	PRINCE RUPERT	STEWART/HYDER	KETCHIKAN	METLAKATLA	HOLLIS	WRANGELL	PETERSBURG	KAKE	SITKA	ANGOON	HOONAH	JUNEAU	HAINES	SKAGWAY
KETCHIKAN	82	18	20												
METLAKATLA	84	20	22	8											
HOLLIS	88	26	28	12	14										
WRANGELL	90	28	30	12	14	12									
PETERSBURG	96	34	36	20	22	20	10								
KAKE	102	40	42	24	26	24	18	12							
SITKA	104	42	44	26	28	26	20	14	12						
ANGOON	110	50	52	34	36	34	26	20	14	12					
HOONAH	114	52	54	38	40	38	28	22	20	12	10				
JUNEAU	114	52	54	38	40	38	28	22	22	12	12	10			
HAINES	120	60	62	44	46	44	36	30	30	20	18	10			
SKAGWAY	124	62	64	46	48	46	38	32	32	22	22	20	14	8	
PELICAN	126	64	66	48	50	48	40	34	26	20	18	12	16	24	28
TENAKEE	114	52	54	38	40	38	28	22	16	12	8	16	18	20	16

ALTERNATE MEANS OF CONVEYANCE (Bicycles-Small Boats-Inflatables) — ITEM AMC

BETWEEN AND	BELLINGHAM	PRINCE RUPERT	STEWART/HYDER	KETCHIKAN	METLAKATLA	HOLLIS	WRANGELL	PETERSBURG	KAKE	SITKA	ANGOON	HOONAH	JUNEAU	HAINES	SKAGWAY
KETCHIKAN	28	10	11												
METLAKATLA	29	11	12	7											
HOLLIS	30	12	13	8	9										
WRANGELL	31	13	14	9	10	9									
PETERSBURG	32	14	15	11	12	11	8								
KAKE	34	16	17	12	13	12	10	8							
SITKA	35	17	18	13	14	13	11	9	8						
ANGOON	37	19	20	15	16	15	13	11	9	7					
HOONAH	38	20	21	16	17	16	14	12	11	8	8				
JUNEAU	38	20	21	16	17	16	14	12	12	8	8	8			
HAINES	39	22	23	18	19	18	16	14	14	11	10	10	8		
SKAGWAY	40	23	24	19	20	19	17	15	15	12	11	11	9	7	
PELICAN	41	23	24	19	20	19	17	15	13	11	10	8	10	12	13
TENAKEE	38	20	21	16	17	16	14	12	10	8	7	9	10	11	10

TWO WHEELED MOTORCYCLES (No Trailers - Driver NOT included) — ITEM 705

BETWEEN AND	BELLINGHAM	PRINCE RUPERT	STEWART/HYDER	KETCHIKAN	METLAKATLA	HOLLIS	WRANGELL	PETERSBURG	KAKE	SITKA	ANGOON	HOONAH	JUNEAU	HAINES	SKAGWAY
KETCHIKAN	133	28	31												
METLAKATLA	140	32	35	8											
HOLLIS	146	40	44	16	17										
WRANGELL	150	45	47	20	23	20									
PETERSBURG	160	54	58	30	33	30	14								
KAKE	169	66	68	40	44	40	26	17							
SITKA	174	70	72	45	48	45	30	20	18						
ANGOON	186	82	84	56	60	56	43	32	22	16					
HOONAH	191	86	89	61	64	61	46	36	30	18	15				
JUNEAU	191	86	89	61	64	61	46	36	36	20	18	15			
HAINES	204	98	100	72	76	72	58	47	47	30	26	15			
SKAGWAY	208	104	105	77	81	77	62	53	53	36	35	31	20	8	
PELICAN	210	106	107	79	82	79	64	55	43	31	30	17	28	32	44
TENAKEE	191	86	89	61	64	61	46	36	25	17	13	13	17	28	32	26

All motorcycles must be fully secured on the car deck with tie-downs. It is the responsibility of the owner to ensure this is completed properly. Rope may be obtained from car deck personnel for lashing purposes.

VEHICLES UP TO 10 FEET (Driver NOT Included) — ITEM 710

BETWEEN AND	BELLINGHAM	PRINCE RUPERT	STEWART/HYDER	KETCHIKAN	METLAKATLA	HOLLIS	WRANGELL	PETERSBURG	KAKE	SITKA	ANGOON	HOONAH	JUNEAU	HAINES	SKAGWAY
KETCHIKAN	218	45	50												
METLAKATLA	223	56	56	14											
HOLLIS	238	66	71	26	29										
WRANGELL	243	73	76	31	38	31									
PETERSBURG	259	89	94	49	54	49	23								
KAKE	275	105	110	65	71	65	43	28							
SITKA	284	114	118	73	79	73	49	33	30						
ANGOON	303	133	136	91	96	91	69	53	36	26					
HOONAH	310	140	144	99	105	99	75	59	49	30	25				
JUNEAU	310	140	144	99	105	99	75	59	59	33	30	24			
HAINES	330	160	163	118	124	118	94	76	76	49	43	25			
SKAGWAY	338	168	170	125	131	125	101	85	85	59	56	51	33	14	
PELICAN	341	169	171	129	129	104	86	59	43	63	71	53	43		
TENAKEE	310	140	144	99	105	99	75	59	43	20	20	20	45	53	43

VEHICLES UP TO 15 FEET (Driver NOT Included) — ITEM 715

BETWEEN AND	BELLINGHAM	PRINCE RUPERT	STEWART/HYDER	KETCHIKAN	METLAKATLA	HOLLIS	WRANGELL	PETERSBURG	KAKE	SITKA	ANGOON	HOONAH	JUNEAU	HAINES	SKAGWAY
KETCHIKAN	374	75	83												
METLAKATLA	372	84	95	21											
HOLLIS	394	107	119	41	46										
WRANGELL	405	117	129	51	61	51									
PETERSBURG	433	145	158	80	90	80	35								
KAKE	460	174	187	109	119	109	70	44							
SITKA	473	187	200	122	132	122	80	52	49						
ANGOON	505	220	233	155	164	155	116	86	60	41					
HOONAH	534	240	246	168	177	168	126	98	82	49	39				
JUNEAU	534	240	246	168	177	168	126	98	98	52	47	38			
HAINES	568	273	278	200	210	200	158	129	129	85	80	71	39		
SKAGWAY	581	286	291	213	224	213	172	143	143	99	94	85	53	21	
PELICAN	570	286	298	220	176	147	114	86	80	47	70	104	119		

(Unable to off-load vehicles longer than ten feet)

VEHICLES UP TO 19 FEET (Driver NOT Included) — ITEM 719

BETWEEN AND	BELLINGHAM	PRINCE RUPERT	STEWART/HYDER	KETCHIKAN	METLAKATLA	HOLLIS	WRANGELL	PETERSBURG	KAKE	SITKA	ANGOON	HOONAH	JUNEAU	HAINES	SKAGWAY
KETCHIKAN	445	90	99												
METLAKATLA	443	100	113	25											
HOLLIS	470	128	141	49	55										
WRANGELL	482	139	153	61	73	61									
PETERSBURG	515	172	188	95	107	95	42								
KAKE	548	207	223	130	141	130	83	52							
SITKA	563	223	238	145	157	145	96	63	58						
ANGOON	602	261	277	184	196	184	138	103	71	49					
HOONAH	636	285	292	200	211	200	150	117	97	58	47				
JUNEAU	636	285	292	200	211	200	150	117	117	62	56	45			
HAINES	676	325	331	238	250	238	188	154	154	101	95	84	46		
SKAGWAY	692	341	347	254	267	254	205	171	171	117	112	101	63	25	
PELICAN	679	339	354	261	271	210	175	136	103	95	56	83	124	141	

(Unable to off-load vehicles longer than ten feet)

VEHICLES UP TO 21 FEET (Driver NOT Included) — ITEM 721

BETWEEN AND	BELLINGHAM	PRINCE RUPERT	STEWART/HYDER	KETCHIKAN	METLAKATLA	HOLLIS	WRANGELL	PETERSBURG	KAKE	SITKA	ANGOON	HOONAH	JUNEAU	HAINES	SKAGWAY
KETCHIKAN	557	112	127												
METLAKATLA	572	129	145	31											
HOLLIS	606	164	182	62	70										
WRANGELL	622	179	197	78	93	78									
PETERSBURG	665	222	242	122	137	122	53								
KAKE	707	267	287	167	182	167	107	67							
SITKA	727	287	307	187	202	187	123	80	74						
ANGOON	777	337	357	237	252	237	177	132	91	63					
HOONAH	821	368	377	257	272	257	193	150	125	74	60				
JUNEAU	821	368	377	257	272	257	193	150	150	79	72	57			
HAINES	872	419	427	307	322	307	242	198	198	130	122	108	59		
SKAGWAY	893	440	447	327	344	327	264	220	220	151	144	130	81	31	
PELICAN	877	437	457	337	350	337	270	225	175	132	122	71	107	159	182

(Unable to off-load vehicles longer than ten feet)

HOW TO DETERMINE FARES

TARIFFS — All fares are one-way. Fares for passengers, vehicles and staterooms are all calculated separately and must be added together to determine the total cost of your travel.

Passage and vehicle fares are charged from the port of embarkation to the port of debarkation. Stateroom fares are calculated according to the route taken, and may vary from the printed rates depending on the ship and schedules.

PETS — Dogs, cats, and other household pets are charged $25 to/from Bellingham, and $10 to/from Prince Rupert and Stewart/Hyder. There is no charge for a certified service animal traveling with a disabled person.

VEHICLE FARES — Vehicle fares are determined by the vehicle's overall length and width. Vehicles 8-1/2 to 9 feet wide will be charged approximately 125% of the listed fare. Vehicles over 9 feet wide will be charged approximately 150% of the listed fare. If you are towing a vehicle, the overall connected length is used to determine fares.

VEHICLES OVER 21 FEET — Contact any Marine Highway office for fares. Vessels in Southeast Alaska can load vehicles up to 70 feet long with special arrangements. Fares for towed vehicles or trailers are calculated at their combined connected length. Vehicles may not be disconnected for travel at separate rates on the same sailing.

MINIMUM 25' RATE — Vehicles with high centers of gravity (commercial highway vans, loaded flat bed trailers) are charged at the 25 ft. rate unless the vehicle is over 25 ft.in which case the appropriate rate for the vehicle length applies. Contact the commerical booking desk (907) 465-8816 for information and reservations.

ALL TARIFFS AND RATES ARE QUOTED IN U.S. DOLLARS

1997 Inside Passage/Southeast Alaska Cabin Tariffs

Chose Highest Rate

Four Berth Cabin/Sitting Room - Outside/Complete Facilities
M/V COLUMBIA - M/V MALASPINA — ITEM 4BS

BETWEEN AND	BELLINGHAM	PRINCE RUPERT	KETCHIKAN	HOLLIS	WRANGELL	PETERSBURG	KAKE	SITKA	JUNEAU	HAINES
KETCHIKAN	272	63		N			N			
WRANGELL	300	89	58	0			0			
PETERSBURG	318	103	71		47					
SITKA	351	128	91	S	71	60	S			
JUNEAU	371	145	107	T	91	78	T	54		
HAINES	392	164	129	0	108	97	0	74	51	
SKAGWAY	392	164	129	P	108	97	P	74	51	39

Four Berth Cabin - Outside/Complete Facilities
M/V COLUMBIA - M/V MALASPINA - M/V MATANUSKA - M/V TAKU — ITEM 4BF

BETWEEN AND	BELLINGHAM	PRINCE RUPERT	KETCHIKAN	HOLLIS	WRANGELL	PETERSBURG	KAKE	SITKA	JUNEAU	HAINES
KETCHIKAN	248	58								
HOLLIS	266	71	48							
WRANGELL	274	80	53	50						
PETERSBURG	289	92	65	56	41					
KAKE	304	104	75	65	53	48				
SITKA	319	114	84	74	64	55	50			
JUNEAU	337	128	100	90	80	69	63	48		
HAINES	362	152	121	110	100	90	77	67	45	
SKAGWAY	362	152	121	110	100	90	77	67	45	35

Four Berth Cabin - Inside/Complete Facilities
M/V COLUMBIA - M/V MALASPINA - M/V MATANUSKA - M/V TAKU — ITEM 4BI

BETWEEN AND	BELLINGHAM	PRINCE RUPERT	KETCHIKAN	HOLLIS	WRANGELL	PETERSBURG	KAKE	SITKA	JUNEAU	HAINES
KETCHIKAN	210	50								
HOLLIS	229	57	42							
WRANGELL	233	69	48	43						
PETERSBURG	250	80	57	49	39					
KAKE	262	90	64	56	46	40				
SITKA	275	100	75	65	56	48	42			
JUNEAU	292	112	88	78	69	60	55	42		
HAINES	311	131	106	96	88	79	69	59	39	
SKAGWAY	311	131	106	96	88	79	69	59	39	31

Three Berth Cabin - Outside/Complete Facilities
M/V COLUMBIA - M/V MATANUSKA — ITEM 3BF

BETWEEN AND	BELLINGHAM	PRINCE RUPERT	KETCHIKAN	HOLLIS	WRANGELL	PETERSBURG	KAKE	SITKA	JUNEAU	HAINES
KETCHIKAN	202	45		N			N			
WRANGELL	222	63	44	0			0			
PETERSBURG	232	72	52		35					
SITKA	254	90	67	S	52	45	S			
JUNEAU	271	102	77	T	62	55	T	40		
HAINES	294	119	91	0	74	67	0	53	37	
SKAGWAY	294	119	91	P	74	67	P	53	37	30

Two Berth - Outside/Complete Facilities
M/V COLUMBIA - M/V MALASPINA - M/V MATANUSKA - M/V TAKU — ITEM 2BF

BETWEEN AND	BELLINGHAM	PRINCE RUPERT	KETCHIKAN	HOLLIS	WRANGELL	PETERSBURG	KAKE	SITKA	JUNEAU	HAINES
✓ KETCHIKAN	177	43								
HOLLIS	188	50	35							
✓ WRANGELL	193	58	37	36						
✓ PETERSBURG	204	67	46	44	33					
KAKE	216	76	54	46	40	34				
✓ SITKA	227	84	61	58	47	40	36			
✓ JUNEAU	243	97	72	70	58	50	45	37		
✓ HAINES	263	113	84	82	69	62	60	48	34	
✓ SKAGWAY	263	113	84	82	69	62	60	48	34	27

Two Berth Cabin - Inside/Complete Facilities
M/V COLUMBIA - M/V MALASPINA - M/V MATANUSKA - M/V TAKU — ITEM 2BI

BETWEEN AND	BELLINGHAM	PRINCE RUPERT	KETCHIKAN	HOLLIS	WRANGELL	PETERSBURG	KAKE	SITKA	JUNEAU	HAINES
KETCHIKAN	156	38								
HOLLIS	164	44	27							
WRANGELL	174	53	34	28						
PETERSBURG	180	60	41	36	29					
KAKE	189	68	48	42	36	30				
SITKA	199	74	53	47	41	35	32			
JUNEAU	211	83	63	60	51	44	40	33		
HAINES	227	98	76	73	63	57	56	44	31	
SKAGWAY	227	98	76	73	63	57	56	44	31	25

ALL TARIFFS AND RATES ARE QUOTED IN U.S. DOLLARS

---

only long enough to unload and load. A stopover is getting off at any port between your point of origin and final destination and taking another vessel at a later time. For travelers with vehicles and/or cabins this can be done as long as reservations to do so have been made in advance. For example, travelers with a camper may wish to go from Prince Rupert to Haines but stopover at Petersburg for 2 days before continuing to Haines. As long as reservations for Prince Rupert to Petersburg and Petersburg to Haines are made before leaving Prince Rupert, there will be no problems. But you cannot change your mind once you are loaded and under way. Passenger, vehicle and cabin fares are charged on a point-to-point basis, and stopovers will increase the total ticket cost.

NOTE: Check the schedules carefully. Ferries do NOT stop at all ports daily, and northbound and southbound routes vary. You may have to wait 3 to 4 days for the next ferry. Also keep in mind that ferries may be late; do not schedule connections too close together.

Cabins: All cabins on the Southeast system ferries have a toilet and shower. Linens (towels, sheets, blankets) are provided. Restrooms and shower facilities are available for deck-passage (walk-on) passengers. Pick up cabin keys from the purser's office when you board. Cabins are sold as a unit, not on a per berth basis. In other words, the cost of the cabin is the same whether 1 person occupies it or 10 people share it.

Vehicles: Reservations are required. Any vehicle that may be driven legally on the highway is acceptable for transport on the 4 larger vessels. Most vessels on the Southeast system can load vehicles up to 70 feet/21m long with special arrangements. Maximum length on the *Tustumena* is 40 feet/12m. Vehicle fares are determined by the overall length and width of the vehicle. Vehicles from 8½ to 9 feet wide are charged 125 percent of the fare listed for the vehicle length. Vehicles over 9 feet in width are charged 150 percent of the fare listed for vehicle length.

Passengers traveling with RVs do not have access to their vehicle on the car deck while the vessel is underway. RVs can not be used as dining or sleeping facilities while on the ferries.

Motorcycles, motorscooters, bicycles and kayaks are charged.

Hazardous materials may not be transported on the ferries. Bottled gas containers must be turned off. Portable containers of fuel are permitted but must be stored with vessel personnel while en route.

The state assumes no responsibility for the loading and unloading of unattended vehicles. If you ship a vehicle on the ferry you must make your own arrangements for loading and unloading. Unaccompanied vehicles are assessed a surcharge of $50 to or from Bellingham, $20 to or from Prince Rupert and Stewart/Hyder and $10 to or from all other ports..

Food Service: Food service varies from vessel to vessel. There's dining room service on the *Columbia, Tustumena* and *Bartlett.*

The *Columbia* also has a 24-hour snack bar. Cafeteria service is available on all other ferries. Alcoholic beverages are available on some vessels.

The cost of meals is not included in passenger, cabin or vehicle fares.

Luggage: You are responsible for your own luggage! Foot passengers may bring hand luggage only (not to exceed 100 lbs.). There is no limit on luggage carried in a vehicle. Coin-operated storage lockers are available aboard most ships, and baggage carts are furnished on the car deck. Baggage handling is NOT provided by the Marine Highway. Bicycles, small boats and inflatables are not considered baggage and will be charged a fare.

Vehicle deck restrictions: U.S. Coast Guard regulations prohibit passenger access to the vehicle deck while under way, so plan on bringing up items you will need for the voyage soon after boarding the vessel. Passengers can gain access to their vehicle by (Continued on 643)

Cruise line passengers go ashore in Lynn Canal for a hike. (© Jason Paur)

M/V TUSTUMENA
Cabin Tariffs

FOUR BERTH CABIN - OUTSIDE/COMPLETE FACILITIES — ITEM 4BF

BETWEEN AND	UNALASKA	AKUTAN	FALSE PASS	COLD BAY	KING COVE	SAND POINT	CHIGNIK	KODIAK	PORT LIONS	SELDOVIA	HOMER	SEWARD
AKUTAN	23											
FALSE PASS	80	57										
COLD BAY	109	86	29									
KING COVE	122	129	72	43								
SAND POINT	152	165	108	79	68							
CHIGNIK	194	210	153	124	113	80						
KODIAK	282	295	238	209	194	166	124					
PORT LIONS	282	295	238	209	194	166	124	43				
SELDOVIA	337	350	293	264	250	216	182	96	96			
HOMER	328	342	285	256	242	209	175	88	88	43		
SEWARD	349	362	305	276	262	228	194	98	98	163	155	
VALDEZ	(NO DIRECT SAILINGS)						164	164	216	209	91	

FOUR BERTH CABIN - INSIDE/NO FACILITIES — ITEM 4NO

BETWEEN AND	UNALASKA	AKUTAN	FALSE PASS	COLD BAY	KING COVE	SAND POINT	CHIGNIK	KODIAK	PORT LIONS	SELDOVIA	HOMER	SEWARD
AKUTAN	19											
FALSE PASS	66	47										
COLD BAY	91	72	25									
KING COVE	102	108	61	36								
SAND POINT	127	138	91	66	57							
CHIGNIK	162	175	128	103	94	67						
KODIAK	235	246	199	174	162	138	103					
PORT LIONS	235	246	199	174	162	138	103	36				
SELDOVIA	281	292	245	220	208	180	152	80	80			
HOMER	274	285	238	213	202	174	146	73	73	36		
SEWARD	291	302	255	230	218	190	162	82	82	136	129	
VALDEZ	(NO DIRECT SAILINGS)						137	137	180	174	76	

TWO BERTH CABIN - OUTSIDE/NO FACILITIES — ITEM 2NO

BETWEEN AND	UNALASKA	AKUTAN	FALSE PASS	COLD BAY	KING COVE	SAND POINT	CHIGNIK	KODIAK	PORT LIONS	SELDOVIA	HOMER	SEWARD
AKUTAN	13											
FALSE PASS	47	33										
COLD BAY	64	51	17									
KING COVE	75	79	45	28								
SAND POINT	100	97	63	46	40							
CHIGNIK	129	129	95	78	68	43						
KODIAK	179	192	158	141	130	110	76					
PORT LIONS	179	192	158	141	130	110	76	28				
SELDOVIA	213	226	192	175	164	140	115	56	56			
HOMER	208	221	187	170	159	136	111	52	52	28		
SEWARD	218	230	196	179	168	144	119	60	60	101	96	
VALDEZ	(NO DIRECT SAILINGS)						103	103	144	140	54	

M/V TUSTUMENA
Aleutian Chain Trips

LV KODIAK	WED	4:55 PM		LV UNALASKA	SAT	11:45 AM
LV CHIGNIK	THU	1:00 PM		LV AKUTAN	SAT	4:00 PM
LV SAND POINT	THU	12:30 AM		LV COLD BAY	SUN	4:45 AM
LV KING COVE	FRI	9:00 AM		LV KING COVE	SUN	7:15 AM
LV COLD BAY	FRI	11:55 AM		LV SAND POINT	SUN	3:00 PM
LV FALSE PASS	FRI	5:30 PM		LV CHIGNIK	MON	1:45 AM
AR UNALASKA	SAT	6:30 AM		AR KODIAK	MON	8:15 PM

REFER TO COLOR CODED BARS ON M/V TUSTUMENA SCHEDULE BEGINNING AND ENDING AT KODIAK

M/V BARTLETT / AK RAILROAD SCHEDULE
Effective May 1, 1997

The M/V BARTLETT serves the port of Whittier using the Alaska Railroad shuttle between Portage and Whittier. In Portage, passengers and their vehicles load on an Alaska Railroad flatcar for a 40 minute sight-filled trip through mountain tunnels to Whittier, a former military town. Ferry service from Whittier is available to Cordova and Valdez.

PORTAGE TO WHITTIER*

LV	PORTAGE	10:15 AM
AR	WHITTIER	10:55 AM
LV	PORTAGE	1:20 PM
AR	WHITTIER	2:00 PM

WHITTIER TO PORTAGE

LV	WHITTIER	3:30PM
AR	PORTAGE	4:10PM
LV	WHITTIER	6:15 PM
AR	PORTAGE	6:55 PM

THE STATE OF ALASKA RESERVES THE RIGHT TO ALTER, REVISE OR CANCEL SCHEDULES AND RATES WITHOUT PRIOR NOTICE AND ASSUMES NO RESPONSIBILITY FOR DELAYS AND/OR EXPENSES DUE TO SUCH MODIFICATIONS.

*Check-in time in Portage is one hour earlier than departure.

RAILROAD SHUTTLE FARES

Prices not available at press time. Contact any Alaska Marine Highway office for rates and reservations.

SOUTHCENTRAL/SOUTHWEST ALASKA - M/V BARTLETT SCHEDULE

EFFECTIVE MAY 2 — MAY 29, 1997 AND AUGUST 29 — SEPTEMBER 13, 1997

MON	LV	CORDOVA	7:00 AM
	AR	WHITTIER	2:00 PM
	LV	WHITTIER	2:45 PM
	AR	CORDOVA	9:45 PM
TUE	LV	CORDOVA	12:30 AM
	AR	VALDEZ	6:15 AM
	LV	VALDEZ	7:15 AM
	AR	WHITTIER	2:00 PM
	LV	WHITTIER	2:45 PM
	AR	VALDEZ	9:30 PM
WED	LV	VALDEZ	6:45 AM **
	AR	CORDOVA	2:30 PM
	LV	CORDOVA	6:30 PM **
THU	AR	VALDEZ	2:15 AM
THU	LV	VALDEZ	7:15 AM
	AR	WHITTIER	2:00 PM
	LV	WHITTIER	2:45 PM
	AR	VALDEZ	9:30 PM

*FRI	LV	VALDEZ	12:15 AM ###
	AR	CORDOVA	6:00 AM
	LV	CORDOVA	7:00 AM
	AR	WHITTIER	2:00 PM
	LV	WHITTIER	2:45 PM
	AR	CORDOVA	9:45PM
SAT	LV	CORDOVA	12:30 AM ***
	AR	VALDEZ	6:15 AM
	LV	VALDEZ	7:15 AM
	AR	WHITTIER	2:00 PM
	LV	WHITTIER	2:45 PM
	AR	VALDEZ	9:30 PM
SUN	LV	VALDEZ	7:15 AM
	AR	WHITTIER	2:00 PM
	LV	WHITTIER	2:45 PM
	AR	VALDEZ	9:30 PM
	LV	VALDEZ	11:45 PM
MON	AR	CORDOVA	5:30 AM

EFFECTIVE MAY 29, 1997 — AUGUST 29, 1997

MON	LV	VALDEZ	7:15 AM
	AR	WHITTIER	2:00 PM
	LV	WHITTIER	2:45 PM
	AR	CORDOVA	9:45 PM
MON	LV	CORDOVA	10:45 PM **
TUE	AR	VALDEZ	6:15 AM
	LV	VALDEZ	7:15 AM
	AR	WHITTIER	2:00 PM
TUE	LV	WHITTIER	2:45 PM
	AR	VALDEZ	9:30 PM
	LV	VALDEZ	11:45 PM
WED	AR	CORDOVA	5:30 AM
WED	LV	CORDOVA	7:00 AM
	AR	WHITTIER	2:00 PM
	LV	WHITTIER	2:45 PM
	AR	VALDEZ	9:30PM

THU	LV	VALDEZ	7:15 AM
	AR	WHITTIER	2:00 PM
	LV WHITTIER		2:45 PM +++
	AR	VALDEZ	9:30 PM
FRI	LV	VALDEZ	5:00 AM **
	AR	CORDOVA	12:45 PM
	LV	CORDOVA	6:30 PM
SAT	AR	VALDEZ	12:15 AM
SAT	LV	VALDEZ	7:15 AM
	AR	WHITTIER	2:00 PM
	LV	WHITTIER	2:45 PM
	AR	VALDEZ	9:30 PM
SUN	LV	VALDEZ	7:15 AM
	AR	WHITTIER	2:00 PM
	LV	WHITTIER	2:45 PM
	AR	VALDEZ	9:30 PM

**THU MAY 1   LV CORDOVA 2:45PM
AR VALDEZ 8:30PM**

*   Schedule begins here May 2, 1997.
**   Tatitlek Whistle Stops available by notifying Valdez or Cordova terminal.
+++ Switch to this schedule at Whittier, Thursday May 29.
Switch to this schedule at Valdez, Friday August 29

*** PRINCE WILLIAM SOUND GOLD RUSH REGATTA MAY 10, 1997

| SAT | LV | CORDOVA | 12:30 AM | | SAT | LV | WHITTIER | 11:00 AM |
| | AR | WHITTIER | 7:30 AM | | | AR | VALDEZ | 6:00 PM |

1997 Southcentral/Southwest Alaska Passenger & Vehicle Tariffs

MARINE ACCESS ROUTES • Alaska State Ferries

PASSENGER 12 YEARS & OVER (Meals and Berths NOT included) — ITEM ADT

BETWEEN AND	UNALASKA	AKUTAN	FALSE PASS	COLD BAY	KING COVE	SAND POINT	CHIGNIK	KODIAK	PORT LIONS	SELDOVIA	HOMER	SEWARD	WHITTIER	VALDEZ	TATITLEK
AKUTAN	16														
FALSE PASS	46	34													
COLD BAY	62	50	18												
KING COVE	74	66	34	18											
SAND POINT	98	90	58	42	32										
CHIGNIK	132	124	92	76	66	42									
KODIAK	202	194	162	146	136	112	76								
PORT LIONS	202	194	162	146	136	112	76	20							
SELDOVIA	246	240	208	192	180	156	122	52	52						
HOMER	242	236	204	188	176	152	118	48	48	18					
SEWARD	250	242	210	194	184	160	124	54	54	100	96				
WHITTIER	316	308	276	260	250	226	190	120	120	166	162				
VALDEZ	292	286	254	238	226	202	168	98	98	142	138	58	58		
TATITLEK	292	286	254	238	226	202	168	98	98	142	138	58	58	30	
CORDOVA	292	286	254	238	226	202	168	98	98	142	138	58	58	30	30

CHILDREN 2 THROUGH 11 YEARS OLD (Under 2 Transported Free) — ITEM CHD

BETWEEN AND	UNALASKA	AKUTAN	FALSE PASS	COLD BAY	KING COVE	SAND POINT	CHIGNIK	KODIAK	PORT LIONS	SELDOVIA	HOMER	SEWARD	WHITTIER	VALDEZ	TATITLEK
AKUTAN	8														
FALSE PASS	24	18													
COLD BAY	32	26	10												
KING COVE	38	34	18	10											
SAND POINT	50	46	30	22	16										
CHIGNIK	66	62	46	38	34	22									
KODIAK	102	98	82	74	68	56	38								
PORT LIONS	102	98	82	74	68	56	38	10							
SELDOVIA	124	120	104	96	90	78	62	26	26						
HOMER	122	118	102	94	88	76	60	24	24	10					
SEWARD	126	122	106	98	92	80	62	28	28	50	48				
WHITTIER	158	154	138	130	126	114	96	60	60	84	82				
VALDEZ	146	144	128	120	114	102	84	50	50	70	70	30	30		
TATITLEK	146	144	128	120	114	102	84	50	50	70	70	30	30	16	
CORDOVA	146	144	128	120	114	102	84	50	50	70	70	30	30	16	16

ALTERNATE MEANS OF CONVEYANCE (Bicycles-Kyaks-Inflatables) — ITEM AMC

BETWEEN AND	UNALASKA	AKUTAN	FALSE PASS	COLD BAY	KING COVE	SAND POINT	CHIGNIK	KODIAK	PORT LIONS	SELDOVIA	HOMER	SEWARD	WHITTIER	VALDEZ	TATITLEK
AKUTAN	6														
FALSE PASS	10	8													
COLD BAY	12	10	8												
KING COVE	14	12	10	6											
SAND POINT	18	16	12	9	8										
CHIGNIK	23	18	14	15	13	9									
KODIAK	33	23	18	25	23	20	15								
PORT LIONS	33	23	23	25	23	20	15	6							
SELDOVIA	40	33	23	32	30	26	21	11	11						
HOMER	39	40	33	31	29	26	21	10	10	5					
SEWARD	40	39	40	32	30	77	22	11	11	18	17				
WHITTIER	50	44	42	42	40	37	31	21	21	28	27				
VALDEZ	47	54	52	38	37	33	28	18	18	24	24	10	8		
TATITLEK	47	54	52	38	37	33	28	18	18	24	24	10	8	8	
CORDOVA	47	54	52	38	37	33	28	18	18	24	24	10	8	8	8

TWO-WHEELED MOTORCYCLES (No Trailers-Driver not included) — ITEM 705

BETWEEN AND	UNALASKA	AKUTAN	FALSE PASS	COLD BAY	KING COVE	SAND POINT	CHIGNIK	KODIAK	PORT LIONS	SELDOVIA	HOMER	SEWARD	WHITTIER	VALDEZ	TATITLEK
FALSE PASS	38	N													
COLD BAY	52	O	14												
KING COVE	61		28	14											
SAND POINT	197	V	48	35	25										
CHIGNIK	227	E	78	64	55	35									
KODIAK	171	H	139	125	115	209	64								
PORT LIONS	171	I	139	125	115	209	64	15							
SELDOVIA	210	C	176	162	153	132	102	43	43						
HOMER	207	L	174	160	151	130	99	39	39	12					
SEWARD	213	E	178	164	155	135	105	45	45	84	81				
WHITTIER	265	S	232	219	209	189	160	100	100	139	135				
VALDEZ	246		213	199	190	169	139	82	82	121	118	40	29		
TATITLEK	246		213	199	190	169	139	82	82	121	118	40	29	24	
CORDOVA	246		213	199	190	169	139	82	82	121	118	40	29	24	24

VEHICLES UP TO 10 FEET (Driver NOT included) — ITEM 710

BETWEEN AND	UNALASKA	AKUTAN	FALSE PASS	COLD BAY	KING COVE	SAND POINT	CHIGNIK	KODIAK	PORT LIONS	SELDOVIA	HOMER	SEWARD	WHITTIER	VALDEZ	TATITLEK
FALSE PASS	61	N													
COLD BAY	84	O	23												
KING COVE	99		45	23											
SAND POINT	133	V	79	56	41										
CHIGNIK	181	E	128	105	90	56									
KODIAK	279	H	225	203	188	154	105								
PORT LIONS	279	I	225	203	188	154	105	25							
SELDOVIA	341	C	286	264	249	215	166	69	69						
HOMER	335	L	281	259	214	210	161	64	64	19					
SEWARD	345	E	290	268	253	219	170	73	76	136	131				
WHITTIER	436	S	383	360	345	311	263	165	165	229	223				
VALDEZ	405		350	328	313	279	230	133	133	196	191	68	49		
TATITLEK	405		350	328	313	279	230	133	133	196	191	68	49	39	
CORDOVA	405		350	328	313	279	230	133	133	196	191	68	49	39	39

VEHICLES UP TO 15 FEET (Driver NOT included) — ITEM 715

BETWEEN AND	UNALASKA	AKUTAN	FALSE PASS	COLD BAY	KING COVE	SAND POINT	CHIGNIK	KODIAK	PORT LIONS	SELDOVIA	HOMER	SEWARD	WHITTIER	VALDEZ	TATITLEK
FALSE PASS	104	N													
COLD BAY	142	O	38												
KING COVE	168		72	34											
SAND POINT	226	V	131	93	67										
CHIGNIK	311	E	215	177	151	93									
KODIAK	480	H	384	346	320	262	177								
PORT LIONS	480	I	384	346	320	262	177	39							
SELDOVIA	587	C	492	454	428	369	285	116	116						
HOMER	577	L	482	444	418	359	275	106	106	29					
SEWARD	593	E	498	460	434	376	291	122	122	233	223				
WHITTIER	753	S	657	619	593	535	450	281	281	392	382				
VALDEZ	697		602	564	538	480	395	226	226	337	327	112	72		
TATITLEK	697		602	564	538	480	395	226	226	337	327	112	72	64	
CORDOVA	697		602	564	538	480	395	226	226	337	327	112	72	64	64

VEHICLES UP TO 19 FEET (Driver NOT included) — ITEM 719

BETWEEN AND	UNALASKA	AKUTAN	FALSE PASS	COLD BAY	KING COVE	SAND POINT	CHIGNIK	KODIAK	PORT LIONS	SELDOVIA	HOMER	SEWARD	WHITTIER	VALDEZ	TATITLEK
FALSE PASS	123	N													
COLD BAY	169	O	46												
KING COVE	200		87	41											
SAND POINT	269	V	156	110	80										
CHIGNIK	370	E	257	211	180	110									
KODIAK	571	H	458	412	381	312	211								
PORT LIONS	571	I	458	412	381	312	211	46							
SELDOVIA	699	C	586	540	509	439	339	138	138						
HOMER	687	L	574	528	497	428	327	126	126	35					
SEWARD	706	E	594	548	517	447	347	145	145	277	265				
WHITTIER	896	S	783	737	706	637	536	335	335	467	455				
VALDEZ	830		718	672	641	571	470	269	269	401	389	134	85		
TATITLEK	830		718	672	641	571	470	269	269	401	389	134	85	76	
CORDOVA	830		718	672	641	571	470	269	269	401	389	134	85	76	76

VEHICLES UP TO 21 FEET (Driver NOT included) — ITEM 721

BETWEEN AND	UNALASKA	AKUTAN	FALSE PASS	COLD BAY	KING COVE	SAND POINT	CHIGNIK	KODIAK	PORT LIONS	SELDOVIA	HOMER	SEWARD	WHITTIER	VALDEZ	TATITLEK
FALSE PASS	158	N													
COLD BAY	217	O	59												
KING COVE	257		111	52											
SAND POINT	347	V	201	142	102										
CHIGNIK	477	E	331	272	232	142									
KODIAK	737	H	591	532	492	402	272								
PORT LIONS	737	I	591	532	492	402	272	59							
SELDOVIA	902	C	756	697	657	567	437	177	177						
HOMER	887	L	741	682	642	552	422	162	162	44					
SEWARD	912	E	766	707	667	577	447	187	187	357	342				
WHITTIER	1157	S	1011	952	912	822	692	432	432	602	587				
VALDEZ	1072		926	867	827	737	607	347	347	517	502	172	110		
TATITLEK	1072		926	867	827	737	607	347	347	517	502	172	110	97	
CORDOVA	1072		926	867	827	737	607	347	347	517	502	172	110	97	97

All motorcycles must be fully secured on the car deck with tie-downs. It is the responsibility of the owner to ensure this is completed properly. Rope may be obtained from car deck personnel for lashing purposes.

ALL TARIFFS AND RATES ARE QUOTED IN U.S. DOLLARS

TARIFFS — All fares are one-way. Fares for passengers, vehicles and staterooms are all calculated separately and must be added together to determine the total cost of your travel.

Passage and vehicle fares are charged from the port of embarkation to the port of debarkation. Stateroom fares are calculated according to the route taken, and may vary from the printed rates depending on the ship and schedules.

VEHICLE FARES — Vehicle fares are determined by the vehicle's overall length and width. Vehicles 8-1/2 to 9 feet wide will be charged approximately 125% of the listed fare. Vehicles over 9 feet wide will be charged approximately 150% of the listed fare. If you are towing a vehicle, the overall connected length is used to determine fares.

VEHICLES OVER 21 FEET — Contact any Marine Highway office for fares. The M/V TUSTUMENA can load vehicles to a maximum length of 40 feet. The M/V BARTLETT will accept vehicles up to 60 feet in length. Please notify your reservation agent at the time of booking if your vehicle is over 6 foot 6 inches in height. Fares for towed vehicles or trailers are calculated at their combined connected length. Vehicles may not be disconnected for travel at separate rates on the same sailing.

MINIMUM 25' RATE — Vehicles with high centers of gravity (commercial highway vans, loaded flat bed trailers) are charged at the 25 ft. rate unless the vehicle is over 25 ft.in which case the appropriate rate for the vehicle length applies. Contact the commerical booking desk (907) 465-8816 for information and reservations.

M/V TUSTUMENA Southcentral/Southwest Alaska Schedule

MAY EASTBOUND

Leave SELDOVIA	Leave HOMER	PORT LIONS	Arrive KODIAK	Leave SEWARD	Arrive VALDEZ
T29 6:00P	T29 9:55P	W30 8:30A	Lv.W30 4:00P	Ar.TH1 5:15A	
SU4 6:00A	SU4 9:30A		SU4 7:00P		
	M5 10:30A		M5 8:00P		
T6 6:00P	T6 11:30P		W7 9:00A		
	FROM ALEUTIAN CHAIN TRIP		M12 8:15P		
T13 6:00P	T13 9:55P	W14 8:30A	Lv.W14 4:55P	TH15 6:15A	
SU18 6:00A	SU18 9:30A		SU18 7:00P		
	M19 10:30A		M19 8:00P		
*T20 5:00P	W21 1:30A		Lv.W21 4:00P	TH22 9:45A	TH22 11:00P
SU25 5:00A	SU25 8:00A		SU25 5:30P		
	*M26		M26 7:00P		
T27 7:00P	T27 9:55P	W28 8:30A	Lv.W28 4:00P	TH29 9:45A	TH29 11:00P

* Kodiak King Crab Festival   May 20 - 26

MAY WESTBOUND

Leave VALDEZ	Leave SEWARD	Leave KODIAK	PORT LIONS	Leave HOMER	Arrive SELDOVIA
	F2 9:30P	S3 12:45P	S3 3:45P	SU4 3:30A	SU4 4:55A
	SU4 10:30P			Ar.M5 8:00A	
		M5 11:00P		T6 12:30P	T6 2:00P
		W7 4:55P	***TO ALEUTIAN CHAIN TRIP***		
		M12 11:00P		T13 12:30P	T13 2:00P
	F16 9:30P	S17 12:45P	S17 3:45P	SU18 3:30A	SU18 4:55A
	SU18 10:30P			Ar.M19 8:00A	
		M19 11:00P		T20 12:30P	T20 2:00P
F23 5:00P	F23 8:00P	S24 11:30A	S24 2:30P	SU25 2:30A	SU25 4:00A
	SU25 10:30P			Ar.M26 8:00A	
		M26 11:55P		T27 2:00P	T27 3:30P
F30 6:30P	F30 8:30P	S31 12:45P	S31 3:45P	SU1 3:30A	SU1 4:55A

JUNE EASTBOUND

Leave SELDOVIA	Leave HOMER	PORT LIONS	Arrive KODIAK	Leave SEWARD	Arrive VALDEZ
SU1 6:00A	SU1 9:30A		SU1 7:00P		
	M2 10:30A		M2 8:00P		
T3 6:00P	T3 9:55P	W4 8:30A	Lv.W4 4:00P	TH5 9:45A	TH5 11:00P
SU8 6:00A	SU8 9:30A		SU8 7:00P		
	M9 10:30A		M9 8:00P		
T10 6:00P	T10 11:30P		W11 9:00A		
	FROM ALEUTIAN CHAIN TRIP		M16 8:15P		
T17 6:00P	T17 9:55P	W18 8:30A	Lv.W18 4:00P	TH19 9:45A	TH19 11:00P
SU22 6:00A	SU22 9:30A		SU22 7:00P		
	M23 10:30A		M23 8:00P		
T24 6:00P	T24 9:55P	W25 8:30A	Lv.W25 4:00P	TH26 9:45A	TH26 11:00P
SU29 6:00A	SU29 9:30A		SU29 7:00P		
	M30 10:30A		M30 8:00P		

JUNE WESTBOUND

Leave VALDEZ	Leave SEWARD	Leave KODIAK	PORT LIONS	Leave HOMER	Arrive SELDOVIA
	SU1 10:30P			Ar.M2 8:00A	
		M2 11:00P		T3 12:30P	T3 2:00P
F6 6:30P	F6 9:30P	S7 12:45P	S7 3:45P	SU8 3:30A	SU8 4:55A
	SU8 10:30P			Ar.M9 8:00A	
		M9 11:00P		T10 12:30P	T10 2:00P
		W11 4:55P	***TO ALEUTIAN CHAIN TRIP***		
		M16 11:00P		T17 12:30P	T17 2:00P
F20 6:30P	F20 9:30P	S21 12:45P	S21 3:45P	SU22 3:30A	SU22 4:55A
	SU22 10:30P			Ar.M23 8:00A	
		M23 11:00P		T24 12:30P	T24 2:00P
F27 6:30P	F27 9:30P	S28 12:45P	S28 3:45P	SU29 3:30A	SU29 4:55A
	SU29 10:30P			Ar.M30 8:00A	
		M30 11:00P		T1 12:30P	T1 2:00P

JULY EASTBOUND

Leave SELDOVIA	Leave HOMER	PORT LIONS	Arrive KODIAK	Leave SEWARD	Arrive VALDEZ
T1 6:00P	T1 9:55P	W2 8:30A	Lv.W2 4:00P	TH3 9:45A	TH3 11:00P
SU6 6:00A	SU6 9:30A		SU6 7:00P		
	M7 10:30A		M7 8:00P		
T8 6:00P	T8 11:30P		W9 9:00A		
	FROM ALEUTIAN CHAIN TRIP		M14 8:15P		
T15 6:00P	T15 9:55P	W16 8:30A	Lv.W16 4:00P	TH17 9:45A	TH17 11:00P
SU20 6:00A	SU20 9:30A		SU20 7:00P		
	M21 10:30A		M21 8:00P		
T22 6:00P	T22 9:55P	W23 8:30A	Lv.W23 4:00P	TH24 9:45A	TH24 11:00P
SU27 6:00A	SU27 9:30A		SU27 7:00P		
	M28 10:30A		M28 8:00P		
T29 6:00P	T29 9:55P	W30 8:30A	Lv.W30 4:00P	TH31 9:45A	TH31 11:00P

JULY WESTBOUND

Leave VALDEZ	Leave SEWARD	Leave KODIAK	PORT LIONS	Leave HOMER	Arrive SELDOVIA
F4 6:30A	F4 9:30P	S5 12:45P	S5 3:45P	SU6 3:30A	SU6 4:55A
	SU6 10:30P			Ar.M7 8:00A	
		M7 11:00P		T8 12:30P	T8 2:00P
		W9 4:55P	***TO ALEUTIAN CHAIN TRIP***		
		M14 11:00P		T15 12:30P	T15 2:00P
F18 6:30A	F18 9:30P	S19 12:45P	S19 3:45P	SU20 3:30A	SU20 4:55A
	SU20 10:30P			Ar.M21 8:00A	
		M21 11:00P		T22 12:30P	T22 2:00P
F24 6:30A	F24 9:30P	S25 12:45P	S25 3:45P	SU26 3:30A	SU26 4:55A
	SU27 10:30P			Ar.M28 8:00A	
		M28 11:00P		T29 12:30P	T29 2:00P
F1 6:30A	F1 9:30P	S2 12:45P	S2 3:45P	SU3 3:30A	SU3 4:55A

AUGUST EASTBOUND

Leave SELDOVIA	Leave HOMER	PORT LIONS	Arrive KODIAK	Leave SEWARD	Arrive VALDEZ
SU3 6:00A	SU3 9:30A		SU3 7:00P		
	M4 10:30A		M4 8:00P		
T5 6:00P	T5 11:30P		W6 9:00A		
	FROM ALEUTIAN CHAIIN TRIP		M11 8:15P		
T12 6:00P	T12 9:55P	W13 8:30A	Lv.W13 4:00P	TH14 9:45A	TH14 11:00P
SU17 6:00A	SU17 9:30A		SU17 7:00P		
	M18 10:30A		M18 8:00P		
T19 6:00P	T19 9:55P	W20 8:30A	Lv.W20 4:00P	TH21 9:45A	TH21 11:00P
SU24 6:00A	SU24 9:30A		SU24 7:00P		
	M25 10:30A		M25 8:00P		
T26 6:00P	T26 9:55P	W27 8:30A	Lv.W27 4:00P	TH28 9:45A	TH28 11:00P
SU31 6:00A	SU31 9:30A		SU31 7:00P		

AUGUST WESTBOUND

Leave VALDEZ	Leave SEWARD	Leave KODIAK	PORT LIONS	Leave HOMER	Arrive SELDOVIA
	SU3 10:30P			Ar.M4 8:00A	
		M4 11:00P		T5 12:30P	T5 2:00P
		W6 4:55P	***TO ALEUTIAN CHAIN TRIP***		
		M11 11:00P		T12 12:30P	T12 2:00P
F15 6:30A	F15 9:30P	S16 12:45P	S16 3:45P	SU17 3:30A	SU17 4:55A
	SU17 10:30P			Ar.M18 8:00A	
		M18 11:00P		T19 12:30P	T19 2:00P
F22 6:30A	F22 9:30P	S23 12:45P	S23 3:45P	SU24 3:30A	SU24 4:55A
	SU24 10:30P			Ar.M25 8:00A	
		M25 11:00P		T26 12:30P	T26 2:00P
F29 6:30A	F29 9:30P	S30 12:45P	S30 3:45P	SU31 3:30A	SU31 4:55A
	SU31 10:30P			Ar.M1 8:00A	

SEPTEMBER EASTBOUND

Leave SELDOVIA	Leave HOMER	PORT LIONS	Arrive KODIAK	Leave SEWARD	Leave CORDOVA	Arrive VALDEZ
	M1 10:30A		M1 8:00P			
T2 6:00P	T2 9:55P	W3 8:30A	Lv.W3 4:00P	TH4 9:45A		TH4 11:00P
SU7 6:00A	SU7 9:30A		SU7 7:00P			
	M8 10:30A		M8 8:00P			
T9 6:00P	T9 11:30P		W10 9:00A			
	FROM ALEUTIAN CHAIN TRIP		M15 8:15P			
T16 6:00P	T16 9:00P	W17 7:30A	Lv.W17 4:00P	TH18 9:45A	TH18 11:45P	F19 7:30A
					S20 9:55P	SU21 3:30A
					TH25 11:45P	F26 7:30A
T23 2:00P	T23 7:30P	W24 6:00A	Lv.W24 4:00P	TH25 9:45A	S27 9:55P	SU28 3:30A

SEPTEMBER WESTBOUND

Leave VALDEZ	Arrive CORDOVA	Leave SEWARD	Leave KODIAK	PORT LIONS	Leave HOMER	Arrive SELDOVIA
			M1 11:00P		T2 12:30P	T2 2:00P
F5 6:30A		F5 9:30P	S6 12:45P	S6 3:45P	SU7 3:30A	SU7 4:55A
			SU7 10:30P		Ar.M8 8:00A	
			M8 11:00P		T9 12:30P	T9 2:00P
			W10 4:55P	***TO ALEUTIAN CHAIN TRIP***		
			M15 11:00P		T16 12:30P	T16 2:00P
F19 9:00A	F19 2:30P					
SU21 4:30A	SU21 1:45P	M22 2:15A	M22 4:55P	M22 7:55P	T23 8:30A	T23 10:00A
F26 9:00A	F26 2:30P					
SU28 4:30A	SU28 1:45P	M29 2:15A	M29 4:55P	M29 7:55P	T30 8:30A	T30 10:00A

Whistle stops at Chenega Bay are on Thursdays Between Seward and Valdez arriving Chenega Bay at 2:15PM leaving at 2:45PM. Vessel will not stop if there are no reservations.

(Continued from page 639)

applying to the purser's desk for an escort. Regulations prohibit sleeping in your vehicle while the vessel is under way.

Weapons: It is illegal to carry hand weapons to or through Canada. Any person arriving at a Canadian port of entry with a restricted weapon will be required to return it to the U.S. (officials will not hold weapons pending your return). Within Alaska, ferry travelers may keep unloaded firearms locked in their vehicle. Walk-on passengers are required to check firearms with vessel personnel.

Pet policy: Dogs and other pets are not allowed in cabins and must be transported on the vehicle deck only—*NO EXCEPTIONS.* (There are special accommodations for animals aiding disabled passengers. Proper paperwork is required.) Animals and pets are to be transported inside a vehicle or in suitable containers furnished by the passenger. Animals and pets must be cared for by the owner. Passengers who must visit pets or animals en route should apply to the purser's office for an escort to the vehicle deck. (On long sailings the purser periodically announces "cardeck calls.") You may walk your pet at port stops. Keep in mind that some port stops are very brief and that sailing time between some ports will be as long as 36 hours (Bellingham to Ketchikan).

Dogs, cats, or larger animals are assessed a charge of $25 to or from Bellingham and

$10 to or from Prince Rupert and to or from Stewart/Hyder. This surcharge applies even if the animal is traveling inside the owner's vehicle.

Animal's owner or attendant must possess a current health certificate (within 30 days) for the animal in order to transport it

through Canada and into Alaska. (See Customs Requirements in the GENERAL INFORMATION section.)

Crossing the U.S.–Canada border: If any part of your trip is to, from or through Canada, you must report to customs at the port of entry. No passport is required for

RUNNING TIME TABLE

INSIDE PASSAGE ROUTE:

Bellingham — Ketchikan	37 hrs.
Prince Rupert — Ketchikan	6 hrs.
Stewart/Hyder — Ketchikan	9 hrs. 45 min.
Ketchikan — Wrangell	6 hrs.
Wrangell — Petersburg	3 hrs.
Petersburg — Sitka	10 hrs.
Petersburg — Juneau/Auke Bay	8 hrs.
Sitka — Juneau/Auke Bay	8 hrs. 45 min.
Juneau/Auke Bay — Haines	4 hrs. 30 min.
Haines — Skagway	1 hr.

SOUTHCENTRAL ROUTE:

Whittier — Valdez	6 hrs. 45 min.
Valdez — Cordova	5 hrs. 30 min.
Cordova — Whittier	7 hrs.
Cordova — Seward	11 hrs.
Valdez — Seward	11 hrs.
Homer — Seldovia	1 hr. 30 min.

SOUTHCENTRAL/SOUTHWEST ROUTE:

Homer — Kodiak	9 hrs. 30 min.
Homer — Port Lions	10 hrs.
Seward — Kodiak	13 hrs. 15 min.

SOUTHWEST ROUTES:

Kodiak — Port Lions	2 hrs. 30 min.
Kodiak — Chignik	18 hrs. 30 min.
Chignik — Sand Point	9 hrs. 15 min.
Sand Point — King Cove	6 hrs. 30 min.
King Cove — Cold Bay	2 hrs.
Cold Bay — False Pass	4 hrs. 15 min.
False Pass — Akutan	10 hrs. 30 min.
Akutan — Unalaska	3 hrs. 30 min.

Note: Running times are approximate. For more accurate arrival times, please contact the local Marine Highway office on the day of arrival.

Mail form to: Alaska Marine Highway, P.O. Box 25535, Juneau, AK 99802-5535
Or fax to: (907) 277-4829

REQUEST FOR RESERVATIONS

DO NOT SEND PAYMENT UNTIL RESERVATIONS ARE CONFIRMED

SPECIAL CUSTOMER NO. (if any)

Full Name

Travel Agency Name (if applicable)

Mailing Address

City, State, Zip Code

Daytime Phone ( )   FAX ( )

VEHICLE INFORMATION

- ☐ Passenger car/truck
- ☐ Truck/camper
- ☐ Camper Van
- ☐ Motorhome
- ☐ Vehicle with trailer
- ☐ Other (describe)

NUMBER AND NAMES OF PERSONS TRAVELING:

_____ Under 2 yrs

_____ 2-11 yrs

_____ 12 yrs and over

Veh. Height	Veh. Width	Veh. Length*

*This figure should reflect the total vehicle length, including hitch and trailer, if any.

_____ Number of Pets

If a cabin is NOT available, are you willing to travel without one? ☐ Yes ☐ No

Approximate date you will _____ be departing your area.

TRAVEL DATE & SHIP (if important)	FROM	TO	CABIN (yes or no)	ALTERNATE TRAVEL DATES

Do you want to receive free information about products and travel-related services? ☐ Yes ☐ No

FAX to: 1-907-277-4829

Cruise ship docked at Ketchikan, AK. (© George Wuerthner)

citizens of either country, but you will be required to furnish proof of citizenship, financial responsibility, and vehicle registration, ownership and liability coverage. Special restrictions govern firearms and animals. (See Customs Requirements in the GENERAL INFORMATION section.)

Information aboard state ferries: Pursers provide general information, and there are also U.S. Forest Service interpreters on duty in summer aboard most vessels to answer questions and provide information about points of interest.

Cruise Lines

From May through September, large luxury cruise ships and small explorer-class ships carry visitors to Alaska from West Coast ports via the Inside Passage. Most ships depart from Vancouver, BC. Other ports of departure include San Francisco and Seattle.

There are 42 ships to choose from and almost as many itineraries. There's also a bewildering array of travel options. Both round-trip and one-way cruises are available, or a cruise may be sold as part of a packaged tour that includes air, rail and/or motorcoach transportation. Various shore excursions may be included in the cruise price or offered to passengers for added cost. Ports of call may depend on length of cruise, which ship you choose, time of sailing or debarkation point. Because of the wide variety of cruise trips available, it is wise to work with your travel agent.

Following is a list of cruise lines serving Alaska in 1997. Included are the names of the line's ships (passenger capacity is shown in parentheses) and proposed Alaska ports of call. Not all ships have the same itinerary;

see chart on page 646. Contact the cruise line directly or your travel agent for more details.

Alaska Sightseeing/Cruise West, 4th & Battery Bldg., Suite 700, Seattle, WA 98121-1438; phone 1-800-426-7702 or (206) 441-8687, fax (206) 441-4757. *Spirit of Glacier Bay* (58 passengers); *Sheltered Seas* (90 passengers, no cabin space); *Spirit of Alaska* (82 passengers); *Spirit of Discovery* (84 passengers), and *Spirit of '98* (101 passengers), *Glacier Seas* (85 passengers) and *Spirit of Endeavor* (107 passengers). Ports of call: Anchorage, Glacier Bay, Haines, Juneau, Ketchikan, Misty Fiords, Petersburg, Sitka, Skagway, Tracy Arm, Valdez, Wrangell.

Carnival Cruise Line, Carnival Place, 3655 NW 87th Ave., Miami, FL 33178-2428; phone (305) 599-2600. *Tropicale* (1,428 passengers). Ports of call: College Fjord, Haines, Hubbard Glacier, Juneau, Ketchikan, Seward, Sitka, Skagway, Tracy Arm, Valdez.

Celebrity Cruises, Inc., 5200 Blue Lagoon Dr., Miami, FL 33126; phone (305) 262-6677. *Horizon* (1,354 passengers) and *Galaxy* (1,870 passengers). Ports of call: College Fjord, Glacier Bay, Haines, Hubbard Glacier, Juneau, Ketchikan, Misty Fiords, Seward, Sitka, Skagway, Tracy Arm, Valdez.

Clipper Cruise Lines, Windsor Bldg., 7711 Bonhomme Ave., St. Louis, MO 63105-1956; phone 1-800-325-0010 or (314) 727-2929, fax (314) 727-6576. *Yorktown Clipper* (138 passengers). Ports of call: Glacier Bay, Haines, Juneau, Ketchikan, Misty Fiords, Petersburg, Sitka, Skagway, Tracy Arm, Wrangell.

Crystal Cruises, 2121 Avenue of the Stars, Los Angeles, CA 90067; phone 1-800-446-6620, (310) 785-9300. *Crystal Symphony* (960 passengers). Ports of call: Glacier Bay, Hubbard Glacier, Juneau, Ketchikan, Misty Fiords, Seward, Sitka, Skagway, Tracy Arm.

Cunard Line Ltd., 555 5th Ave., New York, NY 10017-2453; phone 1-800-5-CUNARD or (212) 949-0915. *Sea Goddess II* (116 passengers). Ports of call: Anchorage, College Fjord, Glacier Bay, Homer, Hubbard Glacier, Juneau, Ketchikan, Misty Fiords, Petersburg, Seward, Sitka, Skagway, Tracy Arm, Valdez, Wrangell.

Glacier Bay Tours & Cruises, 520 Pike St., Suite 1400, Seattle, WA 98101; phone 1-800-451-5952 or (206) 623-2417, fax (206) 623-7809. *Executive Explorer* (49 passengers), *Wilderness Explorer* (36 passengers) and the *Wilderness Adventure* (80 passengers). Glacier Bay, Haines, Juneau, Ketchikan, Misty Fiords, Wrangell, Petersburg, Tracy Arm, Sitka, Skagway.

Hanseatic Cruises GmbH, Nagelsweg 55, 20097 Hamburg, Germany; phone 49-40-231603. *Hanseatic.* Ports of call: College Fjord, Glacier Bay, Haines, Juneau, Ketchiakn, Misty Fiords, Seward, Sitka, Skagway, Tracy Arm, Wrangell.

Holland America Westours, 300 Elliott Ave. W., Seattle, WA 98119; phone (206) 281-3535, fax (206) 283-2687. *Statendam* (1,266 passengers), *Nieuw Amsterdam* (1,214 passengers), *Noordam* (1,214 passengers), *Ryndam* (1,266 passengers), *Rotterdam* (1,075 passengers), *Veendam* (1,266 passengers). Ports of call: College Fjord, Glacier Bay, Hubbard Glacier, Skagway, Juneau, Ketchikan, Seward, Sitka, Valdez.

Majestic Cruise Line, P.O. Box 025420, Miami, FL.; phone (305) 530-8900. *Crown Majesty* (1,600 passengers). Ports of call: Ketchikan, Sitka, Juneau, Glacier Bay, Hubbard Glacier, Seward, Skagway, Tracy Arm, Wrangell.

Norwegian Cruise Lines, 95 Merrick Way, Coral Gables, FL 33134; phone 1-800-327-7030, (305) 447-9660. *Windward* (1,246 passengers). Ports of call: Glacier Bay, Haines, Juneau, Ketchikan, Sitka, Skagway, Tracy Arm.

Princess Cruises, 10100 Santa Monica Blvd., Los Angeles, CA 90067; phone (310) 553-1770, fax (310) 277-6175. *Regal Princess* and *Crown Princess* (1,590 passengers), *Star Princess* (1,490 passengers), *Golden Princess* (830 passengers), *Sky Princess* (1,200 passengers) *Dawn Princess* (,1950 passengers) and *Sun Princess* (1,950 passengers). Ports of call: College Fjord, Glacier Bay, Hubbard Glacier, Juneau, Ketchikan, Seward, Sitka, Skagway, Haines.

Royal Caribbean Cruise Line, 1050 Caribbean Way, Miami, FL 33132; phone 1-800-327-6700. *Legend of the Seas* (1,808 passengers), and *Rhapsody of the Seas* (2,400 passengers). Ports of call: Haines, Hubbard Glacier, College Fjord, Glacier Bay, Juneau, Ketchikan, Misty Fiords, Sitka, Skagway.

Royal Cruise Line, 1 Maritime Plaza, San Francisco, CA 94111; phone (305) 447-9660, fax (305) 436-4127. *Royal Odyssey* (1,716 passengers). Ports of call: College Fjord, Glacier Bay, Hubbard Glacier, Juneau, Ketchikan, Seward, Sitka, Skagway, Tracy Arm.

Seabourn Cruise Line, 55 Francisco St., San Francisco, CA 94133; phone (415) 391-7444. *Seabourne Pride* (200 passengers) and *Seabourne Legend* (200 passengers). Ports of call: College Fjord, Glacier Bay, Haines, Hubbard Glacier, Juneau, Ketchikan, Misty Fiords, Petersburg, Seward, Sitka, Skagway, Tracy Arm.

Society Expeditions, 2001 Western Ave., Suite 300, Seattle, WA 98121; phone (206) 728-9400. *World Discoverer* (138 passengers). Ports of call: College Fjord, Homer, Hubbard Glacier, Ketchikan, Misty Fiords, Seward, Sitka, Tracy Arm.

Unicom Management Services, Oasis Center, 2nd Floor, Gladstone and Karaiskakis Sts., P.O. Box 6674, Bonn, Germany; phone 49-228-726280. *Maxim Gorkiy*. Ports of call: College Fjord, Glacier Bay, Hubbard Glacier, Juneau, Ketchikan, Misty Fiords, Sitka, Skagway, Valdez, Wrangell.

Wilderness Cruises, 1415 Western Ave., Suite 700, Seattle, WA 98101; phone (206) 382-9593. *Sea Bird* and *Sea Lion* (70 passengers). Ports of call: Haines, Juneau, Ketchikan, Sitka, Tracy Arm, Petersburg.

World Explorer Cruises, 555 Montgomery St., Suite 1400, San Francisco, CA 94111; phone 1-800-854-3835, (415) 393-1565. *Universe Explorer* (550 passengers). Ports of call: Glacier Bay, Hubbard Glacier, Juneau, Ketchikan, Seward, Sitka, Skagway, Valdez, Wrangell.

Cruise Highlights

The list of ports of call given under Cruise Lines hardly does justice to the experience of cruising Alaska. Following are more informative descriptions of just a few of the highlights on these Alaska cruises. Add in the smell of the sea and forest; the sounds of calving glacier ice and sea gulls; the feel of fresh ocean breezes; the taste of cruise ship cuisine; and the sight of a land still as pristine as early explorers saw it, and you have a better idea of the experience.

All of the coastal communities listed in the cruise ship itineraries are covered in detail in *The MILEPOST®* (see the Index in the back of the book to locate any community). You may also read through the INSIDE PASSAGE section that starts across from the cruise ship chart on the 646. This section describes each of the Southeast Alaska communities that appear on the cruise ship itineraries, and also covers Glacier Bay in detail (see page 689).

College Fjord is an 18-mile-long estuary that extends northeast off Port Wells, another estuary, in the northwest corner of Prince William Sound, near Whittier.

Glaciers cascade down the west side of College Fjord; some cutting a wide, white swath to the sea; others long, narrow ribbons of ice. Sailing up College Fjord on a clear day, the glaciers and their attendant ice floes glisten in the sun, brilliant white tinged with blue.

A breathtaking surprise comes at the north end of the College Fjord, where a large black island of rock divides Harvard Arm, to the left, from Yale Arm, to the right. At the head of each arm, a magnificent tidewater glacier. These "twin glaciers" were named by members of the Harriman Alaska Expedition in 1899.

Cruiseship passengers can stand at the bow of the ship and see both glaciers: the darkly striated Harvard glacier, marked by its winding moraines; and the softly white Yale Glacier.

Hubbard Glacier heads in an icefield in Canada and trends some 80 miles to tidewater, about 34 miles northeast of Yakutat. Hubbard Glacier is tucked into the corner of the Alaska coastline as it

Cruising the face of Hubbard Glacier. (© George Wuerthner)

curves around the Gulf of Alaska between the panhandle and the main body of Alaska. In recent years, Hubbard Glacier has become a popular port of call with cruise ships crossing the Gulf of Alaska between Southeast Alaska's Inside Passage and Southcentral Alaska's Prince William Sound.

Framed by snow-covered mountains, Hubbard Glacier rolls toward the sea like a blue-white breaking wave. The glacier made headlines in June 1986, when it surged, damming Russell Fiord. The ice dam eventually weakened and broke, but scientists predict the glacier will again close off the fjord. Russell Fiord extends more than 35 miles inland from Disenchantment Bay. It is located within Russell Fiord Wilderness Area.

Misty Fiords is a national monument encompassing more than 2 million acres of Southeast Alaska. The major waterway cutting through the monument, Behm Canal, is more than 100 miles long and extraordinary among natural canals for its length and depth. The scenery is dramatic: thick rainforest, vertical granite cliffs and snowy peaks. Waterfalls plunge to salt water along the steep-walled waterways, fed by lakes and streams which absorb an annual rainfall in excess of 14 feet.

Misty Fiords takes its name from the constant precipitation characteristic of this coastal rainforest environment, and the myriad fiord-like inlets, bays, arms and coves that cut into the coastline. The monument's waters are a popular destination with boaters and kayakers out of Ketchikan, 30 miles to the west. The large cruise ships sail the deep waters of Behm Canal and Rudyerd Bay.

Tracy Arm, and adjoining Endicott Arm, are both long, deep, narrow fjords that extend more than 30 miles into the heavily glaciated Coast Mountain Range. At the head of each arm are active tidewater glaciers, which continually calve icebergs into the fjords: Sawyer and South Sawyer glaciers at the head of Tracy Arm; Dawes Glacier at the head of Endicott Arm.

Both are located within the Tracy Arm–Fords Terror Wilderness Area in Tongass National Forest, about 50 miles southeast of Juneau (see map on page 652). Fords Terror is a small fjord off Endicott Arm, with a narrow entrance and sheer rock walls. In 1889, a crew member (named Ford) of a naval vessel moored in Endicott Arm, rowed into the narrow fjord and was caught in its turbulent, iceberg-filled waters for 6 "terrifying" hours when the tide changed.

1997 Alaska Cruise Ship Ports of Call

Color indicates port of call; number* represents estimated port-calls in 1997 (if available)

Cruise Lines

Cruise Ship	Wrangell	Valdez	Tracy Arm	Skagway	Sitka	Seward	Petersburg	Misty Fiords	Ketchikan	Juneau	Hubbard Glacier	Homer	Haines	Glacier Bay	College Fjord	Anchorage
Crown Majesty	7		7	8	8	7		1	18	17	14			9	18	
Crown Princess				18		9			18	18			1	18		
Crystal Symphony			2	6	6			4	6	6				6		
Dawn Princess				16		8			16	16				16	16	
Executive Explorer				19					19	19			8	8		
Galaxy				19	1			1	19	19	12		8	8		
Glacier Seas**																
Golden Princess																
Hanseatic	1		1	1	1	1		1	1	1	14		1	1	1	
Horizon		7	11	19	8	7			19	19	13		19	7	7	
Legend of the Seas				19				19	19	19				7	7	
Nieuw Amsterdam				18					18	19				19	19	
Noordam		13		1	18	9			19	13	13			6	6	
Regal Princess					19				1	19				1	19	
Rhapsody of the Seas				13	14			14	14	13						
Rotterdam		16			16	8			16	16	16			16	16	
Royal Odyssey		4			19	10			19	19	4					
Ryndam			14						2	8				16	19	
Sea Bird													13			
Sea Goddess II																
Sea Lion			13		8		1		2	7			11	1	1	
Seabourne Legend			5	4	5	1	5	5	6	5	1		4	1	1	
Seabourne Pride							5									
Sheltered Seas**																
Sky Princess				8	4	2			12	11	11			2	2	
Spirit of Alaska																
Spirit of Endeavor																
Spirit of Glacier Bay																
Spirit of '98																
Star Princess				18		9			19	18	16			2	18	
Statendam				19					19	19				19		
Sun Princess				18		9			18	18				18	18	
Tropicale		10	10	19	10	10			19	19	10				19	
Universe Explorer	8	8		8	8	8			8	8	8			8		
Veendam				19					19	19				19		
Wilderness Adventure																
Windward			6	19					19	19			19	13		
World Discoverer					16		1	9	9	16						
Yorktown Clipper	7		16	9						16			9			

* Courtesy of Cruise Line Agencies of Alaska. ** Denotes overnight on land. Not shown: Spirit of Discovery (Whittier, College Fiord), Wilderness Explorer: Maxim Gorky.

INSIDE PASSAGE

Southeastern Alaska communities from Ketchikan to Skagway
(See maps, pages 649–653)

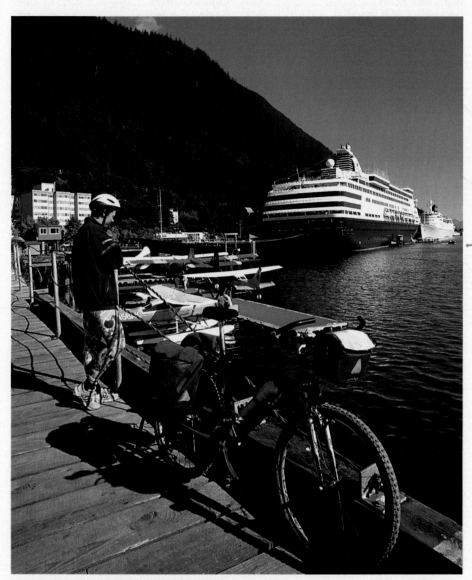

Bicycling tourist Ruth von Spalding near Juneau cruise ship dock. (© Ruth von Spalding)

Southeastern Alaska lies between 54°40' and 60° north latitude, the same as Scotland, Denmark and southern Sweden. The latitude of Scotland's Loch Ness is slightly north of the latitude at Wrangell Narrows. Stockholm and Skagway share the same latitude, and Ketchikan's latitude is a little south of Copenhagen's.

Warmed by ocean currents, this region experiences mild, warm summers, with July temperatures averaging around 60°F/16°C. An occasional heat wave may reach the high 80s. Winters are cool, alternating snow, rain and sunshine; January temperatures average 20° to 40°F/-7° to 4°C. Sub-zero winter temperatures are uncommon. The region receives considerable annual rainfall, from 80 to more than 200 inches (heaviest in late fall, lightest in summer). Populated areas receive 30 to 200 inches of snow annually; the high mountains more than 400 inches a year.

The majority of southeastern Alaska lies within Tongass National Forest, the largest national forest in the United States. (Southeastern Alaska has over 5.6 million acres of wilderness lands.) The forests historically have provided one of the region's major industries; timber harvesting primarily supplies area sawmills.

Commercial fishing and fish processing is another of Southeast's major industries. The numerous rivers and streams, mountains, valleys, melting glaciers and frequent rainfall create ideal spawning grounds for salmon. Local waters harbor an abundance of sea-life, including crab, shrimp, halibut, herring and black cod.

Government is a significant employer throughout the region with federal, state and local government providing the majority of jobs. Juneau serves as the state's capital. Tourism is another major contributor to the region's economy, providing both jobs and revenue.

About 69,000 people live along the Inside Passage, according to 1990 U.S. Census figures. About 70 percent live in the 5 major communities of Juneau (29,755), Ketchikan (15,082), Sitka (9,194), Petersburg (3,350) and Wrangell (2,400). More than 20 percent

Alaska's Inside Passage, located in the southeastern section of the state, is referred to by many of its residents simply as "Southeast." It is a unique region where industry, transportation, recreation and community planning are dictated by spectacular topography.

The region is accessible by air, land or sea. Jet service is available to Juneau, Ketchikan, Wrangell, Petersburg, Sitka and Gustavus. Smaller communities are served by local commuter aircraft. The port communities of Haines and Skagway offer road connections to the Alaska Highway system via the Haines Highway and Klondike Highway 2. The Alaska Marine Highway moves people and vehicles between ports, and connects the Inside Passage with Prince Rupert, BC, and Bellingham, WA. Several cruise ship lines ply the waterways of the Inside Passage and offer a variety of cruising opportunities. (For details on ferry and cruise ship travel, see the MARINE ACCESS ROUTES section.)

Measuring about 125 by 400 miles/200 by 650 km, 60 percent of the region consists of thousands of islands covered with dense forests of spruce, hemlock and cedar, a result of the mild, moist coastal climate. These islands make up the Alexander Archipelago, and include Prince of Wales Island, the third largest island in the United States (the Big Island of Hawaii is first, followed by Kodiak). The Coast Mountains form the mainland portion of southeastern Alaska.

are Native, mostly Tlingit (KLINK it) Indian, plus Haida (HI duh) and Tsimshian (SHIM shian).

Alaska's Natives, famous for their totem poles, weaving, beading, basketry and dancing, occupied the region long before Vitus

Bering discovered Alaska in 1741.

Russia controlled Alaska from the turn of the 19th century until 1867, centering its extensive fur-trading empire in Sitka, the Russian capital of Alaska. Sitka was a port of international trade, controlling trading posts

from California to the Aleutians, and was considered cultured because of European influence. At a time when San Francisco was a crude new boom town, Sitka was called the "Paris of the Pacific."

(Continues on page 654)

INSIDE PASSAGE ADVERTISERS

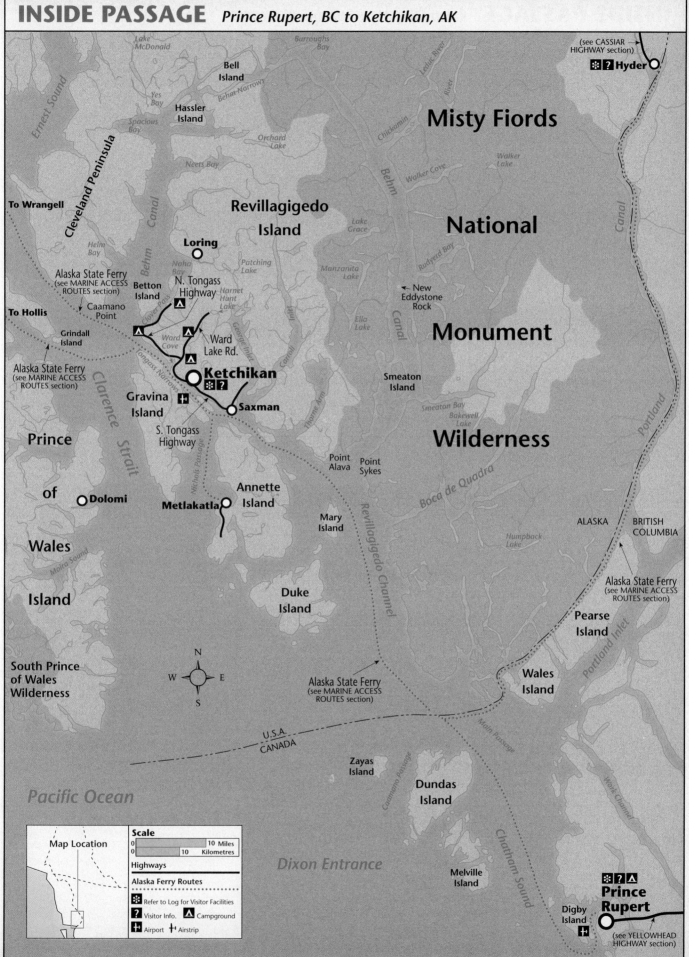

INSIDE PASSAGE *Prince Rupert, BC to Ketchikan, AK*

Lake
McDonald

Burroughs
Bay

(see CASSIAR
HIGHWAY section)

❊ ? **Hyder**

Bell
Island

Ledulc River

River

Yes Bay

Behm Narrows

Hassler
Island

Spacious
Bay

Orchard
Lake

Chickamin

Misty Fiords

Walker
Lake

Ernest Sound

Cleveland Peninsula

Behm Canal

Neets Bay

Behm

Walker Cove

**Revillagigedo
Island**

Lake
Grace

National

To Wrangell

Helm
Bay

Loring

Naha
Bay

Patching
Lake

Manzanita
Lake

Rudyerd Bay

Canal

← New
Eddystone
Rock

Alaska State Ferry
(see MARINE ACCESS
ROUTES section) ↓

**Betton
Island**

**N. Tongass
Highway**

Harriet
Hunt
Lake

Monument

Caamano
Point

⛺

Ella
Lake

To Hollis

Clover Pass

⛺

George Inlet

Ward
Cove

Ward
Lake Rd.

Ketchikan ❊ ?

Carroll Inlet

**Smeaton
Island**

Wilderness

Grindall
Island

Tongass Narrows

⛺

Alaska State Ferry
(see MARINE ACCESS
ROUTES section)

Clarence Strait

**Gravina
Island** ✚

Saxman

S. Tongass
Highway

Smeaton Bay

Bakewell
Lake

Prince

Dolomi

Metlakatla

**Annette
Island**

Nichols Passage

Point
Alava

Point
Sykes

Thorne Arm

of

**Mary
Island**

Boca de Quadra

Portland

Humpback
Lake

Wales

Revillagigedo Channel

ALASKA / BRITISH
COLUMBIA

**Duke
Island**

Alaska State Ferry
(see MARINE ACCESS
ROUTES section) ↗

Island

Moira Sound

**Pearse
Island**

Portland Inlet

**South Prince
of Wales
Wilderness**

Alaska State Ferry
(see MARINE ACCESS
ROUTES section)

N
W ✦ E
S

**Wales
Island**

U.S.A.
CANADA

Caamano Passage

**Zayas
Island**

Main Passage

Work Channel

Pacific Ocean

**Dundas
Island**

Chatham Sound

❊ ? ⛺

**Prince
Rupert**

Dixon Entrance

**Melville
Island**

Digby
Island ✚

(see YELLOWHEAD
HIGHWAY section)

Map Location

Scale
0 ———— 10 Miles
0 —— 10 Kilometres

Highways

Alaska Ferry Routes ·········

❊ Refer to Log for Visitor Facilities

? Visitor Info.   ⛺ Campground

✚ Airport   ✞ Airstrip

INSIDE PASSAGE
Ketchikan, AK to Wrangell, AK

Map Location

Scale
0   10Miles
0   10   Kilometres

Highways
Alaska Ferry Routes
✳ Refer to Log for Visitor Facilities
? Visitor Info.   ⛺ Campground
✈ Airport   ✚ Airstrip

To Petersburg

To LeConte Bay

Stikine
LeConte
Wilderness

Stikine River

BRITISH COLUMBIA
ALASKA

Mitkof Island

Crystal Lake

Glaciated Area

Alaska State Ferry
(see MARINE ACCESS
ROUTES section)

✳ ? ✚ **Wrangell**

Kupreanof Island

Pt. Barrien

Strait Island

Sumner Strait

Pt. Baker

Zarembo Island

Woronkofski Island

Chichagof Pass

⛺ Zimovia Highway

Wrangell Island

Virginia Lake

N
W   E
S

Port Protection

Red Bay

Pt. Colpoys

Stikine Strait

Zimovia Strait

Marten Lake

Harding River

Labouchere Bay

North Island Road

Salmon Bay Lake

Calaer Bay

Thoms Lake

Bradfield Canal

Anan Bay

✦ **Anan Bear Observatory**

Barrier Islands

El Capitan Peak ▲

Neck Lake

Kashevarof Islands

Etolin Island

Anan Lake

Shakan Bay

El Capitan Passage

Kashevarof Passage

Deer Island

Kosciusko Island

Whale Pass ✳

South Etolin Wilderness

Lake McDonald

Prince

Coffman Cove

Luck Lake

Clarence

Spacious Bay

Sea Otter Sound

Naukati

Tuxekan ⛺

of

Ernest Sound

Tuxekan Island

⛺

Heceta Island

Wales

Thorne River

Thorne Bay Road

Narrow Pt.

Cleveland Peninsula

Maurelle Islands Wilderness

⛺

Island

⛺ **Thorne Bay** ✳

Big Salt Road

Control Lake

Strait

Karta River Wilderness

Salmon Lake

Karta Bay

Naha Bay

San Alberto Bay

✈✚ **Klawock** ✳⛺

Hollis-Klawock-Craig Road

Kasaan

North Tongass Highway

⛺

San Fernando Island

Noyes Island

Lulu Island

Klawock Lake

Hollis

Kasaan Bay

Ward Lake Rd.

⛺

Outside Islands Wilderness

San Juan Bautista Island

Craig ✳

Grindall Island

Vallenar Bay

⛺

Baker Island

Hydaburg Road

Alaska State Ferry
(see MARINE ACCESS
ROUTES section)

✳ ? ✈ **Ketchikan**

Bucareli Bay

Trocadero Bay

South Tongass Highway

To Prince Rupert

Waterfall

Chasina Pt.

Gravina Island

Suemez Island

Soda Bay

Windy Pt.

Cholmondeley Sound

Nichols Passage

Cape Bartolome

Hydaburg

Dolomi

Quarry

INSIDE PASSAGE *Angoon, AK to Juneau, AK*

Stephens *Passage*

To Petersburg

Tracy Arm

Port Snettisham

Holkham Bay

Alaska State Ferry
(see MARINE ACCESS
ROUTES section)

The Brothers

Indian Lake

Long Lake

Crater Lake

Lake Dorothy

Turner Lake

Stephens

Glass Peninsula

Admiralty Island National Monument Wilderness

Pleasant Bay

Mole Harbor

Gambier Bay

Pybus Bay

Seymour Canal

Juneau Veterans
Memorial Highway

Juneau ⊛ ? ✚
Mt. Juneau ▲
Thane ○
Gastineau
Douglas ○ Douglas
Point Hilda
Douglas Island
Point Young

To Haines

Stephens Passage

Point Arden

Doty Cove

Pack Creek Bear
Observatory ○

Admiralty

Hasselborg Lake

Lake Guerin

Lake Davidson

Mitchell Bay

Distin Lake

Kanalku Bay

Young Lake

Young Bay

Lake Kathleen

Lake Florence

Angoon ○

Killisnoo Harbor

Chatham Strait

To Kake

Barlow Cove

Mansfield Peninsula

Hunter Bay

To Juneau

Chatham

Florence Bay

Point Thatcher

Catherine Island

Kelp Bay

Portage Arm

Alaska State Ferry
(see MARINE ACCESS
ROUTES section)

The Sisters

Freshwater Bay

East Point

S. Passage Point

Little Basket Bay

Sitkoh Bay

Kook Lake

Chatham ○

Peril Strait

Lake Eva

Baranof

Island

Porpoise Island

Alaska State Ferry
(see MARINE ACCESS
ROUTES section)

Point Sophia

Hoonah ○

Tenakee Springs ○

Tenakee Inlet

MOUNTAINS

Icy Strait

Point Adolphus

Chichagof

Island

MOORE

Hoonah Sound

To Sitka

Lemesurier Island

Goose Island

Mud Bay

Pelican ⊛

Chichagof

Yakobi Wilderness

Petersburg Bay

Elfin Cove ○

Port Althorp

West Chichagof Wilderness

Goulding Lakes

Cape Spencer

Cross Sound

Lisianski Inlet

Lisianski Strait

Yakobi Island

Point Theadore

White Sulphur Springs

Gulf of Alaska

N
W   E
S

Map Location

Scale
0 — 10 Miles
0 — 10 Kilometres

Highways

Alaska Ferry Routes

⊛ Refer to Log for Visitor Facilities

? Visitor Info.   ▲ Campground

✚ Airport   ✈ Airstrip

INSIDE PASSAGE *Juneau, AK to Skagway, AK*

Map Location

Scale
10 Miles
Kilometres
0   10

Highways
Alaska Ferry Routes
❓ Refer to Log for Visitor Facilities
❓ Visitor Info. ▲ Campground
Airport ✈ Airstrip

Devils Paw ▲

Taku River

CANADA
U.S.A.

Mt. Ogilvie ▲
Mt. Bressier ▲
Mt. Nesselrode ▲

Mt. Poletica ▲

Chilkoot Range

Coast Mountains

Juneau Icefield

Mt. Canning ▲

N E W S

BRITISH COLUMBIA
ALASKA

Mt. Bagot ▲

Ketchin River

Meade Glacier

Berners River

Kakuhan Range

Point St. Mary

Berners Bay

Echo Cove

Juneau Veterans' Memorial Highway

Windfall Lake

Mendenhall Glacier

North Douglas Highway

Juneau ❓❓
Auke Bay ▲ ✈
Favorite Channel

Shelter Island

Douglas

To Kake and Petersburg

Mt. Ogilvie

Skagway ❓✈▲
Klondike Highway 2

Taiya Inlet

Ferebee River

Haines ❓✈▲
Port Chilkoot ❓✈▲

Chilkoot Inlet

Chilkat Inlet

Pyramid Harbor

Seduction Point

Chilkat Island

Sullivan Island

Eldred Rock

Lynn Canal

Lincoln Island

Ralston Island

Point Retreat

Barlow Cove

Admiralty Island

Chilkat Range

To Hoonah and Angoon

Alaska State Ferry (see MARINE ACCESS ROUTES section)

Haines Highway

Klehini River

Chilkoot River
Chilkoot Lake

Tsirku River
Takhin River
Chilkat Lake

Takhinsha Mountains

Berg Mtn. ▲

Endicott River Wilderness

Glacier Bay

National

Park

Mt. Wright ▲

Muir Inlet

Muir Glacier

Glacier Bay

Queen Inlet

Excursion Inlet ✈

Gustavus ❓✈

Bartlett Cove

Icy Passage

Pleasant Island

Porpoise Island

Point Gustavus

Point Adolphus

Chichagof Island

Icy Strait

Lemesurier Island

Dundas Bay

To Pelican

Turner Lake
Taku Inlet

(Continued from page 648)

Commercial interest in southeastern Alaska declined with the fur trade, following Alaska's purchase by the United States. Interest in Southeast was rekindled by the salmon industry as canneries were established, the first at Klawock in 1878. Salmon canning peaked in the late 1930s and then declined from overfishing.

But the first significant white populations arrived because of gold. By the time thousands of gold seekers traveled through the Inside Passage in 1898 to Skagway and on to Canada's Klondike (sparking interest in the rest of Alaska), the largest gold ore mine of its day, the Treadwell near Juneau, had been in operation for years.

Juneau became Alaska's capital in 1906, and Southeast remained Alaska's dominant region until WWII, when military activity and the Alaska Highway shifted emphasis to Anchorage and Fairbanks.

Additional population growth came to Southeast with new timber harvesting in the 1950s. Increased government activities, as a result of Alaska statehood in 1959, brought even more.

Today, visitors enjoy the many wonders the area offers. Spectacular scenery greets the eye at every turn. Glacier Bay National Park and Preserve, Misty Fiords and Admiralty Island national monuments, Mendenhall Glacier at Juneau, LeConte Glacier near Petersburg and the Stikine River near Wrangell are just a few of the attractions.

The Inside Passage is the last stronghold of the American bald eagle. More than 20,000 eagles reside in the region, and sightings are frequent. Humpback and killer whales, porpoises, sea lions and seals are often observed from ferries, cruise ships and charter boats. Bear viewing opportunities are offered at Pack Creek on Admiralty Island and Anan Creek near Wrangell.

Activities and attractions include Russian and Tlingit dance performances; salmon bakes; historical melodramas; festivals; glaciers and icefield flightseeing; sportfishing and wilderness adventure tours by kayak, canoe and raft. Among other attractions are museums, totem poles, hiking trails, colorful saloons and fine dining.

The following sections describe the communities and attractions of Southeast with the exception of Hyder, which is accessible by highway from British Columbia and is included in the CASSIAR HIGHWAY section.

Fishing Southeastern Alaska

The biggest challenge for fishermen visiting southeastern Alaska is the sheer number—and variety—of fishing opportunities available. The following information is designed to help you figure out the what, when, where and how of a fishing trip to Southeast Alaska.

Fishermen are advised to first identify whether they want to fish fresh water or salt water and their desired species. Southeast Alaska is perhaps best known for its saltwater sportfishing, although freshwater angling and fly-fishing are also excellent along the Inside Passage. The region also offers a wide range of species.

Salmon are the most popular sport fish in Southeast, with all 5 species of Pacific salmon found here: King (chinook), silver (coho), pink (humpy), chum (dog) and red (sockeye). Salmon are anadromous, spawning in fresh water and maturing in the sea. King salmon fishing in Southeast is restricted to salt water. Silver and pink salmon can be taken in fresh water and salt water. Reds are taken in freshwater streams. Landlocked red salmon, called kokanee, are also available in Southeast.

Other popular sport fish found in Southeast include halibut, rainbow trout and steelhead, Dolly Varden, cutthroat and brook trout. Halibut, a saltwater fish that can weigh more than 300 pounds, is the largest fish in Alaska that a fisherman is likely to catch. Rainbows are a fresh water trout, the sea-run of which is the steelhead. Cutthroat are the common trout of Southeast Alaska, present in both fresh water and salt water. Eastern brook trout is an introduced species to Southeast Alaska freshwater lakes. Dolly Varden, which spawn in streams and migrate to sea in the spring to feed, are primarily a saltwater sportfish here.

If you know what kind of fish you want, that may also determine when to go. Although most fishing enthusiasts focus their trips to Southeast between April and October, when the weather is generally more mild, the fish have something to say about timing. King salmon are present year-round in the sheltered marine waters of Southeast, although the best period for big kings is from mid-April to mid-June, when mature fish are moving through. Pink salmon fishing is good in July and August. Silver salmon are available from July through September, peaking in August. Chum salmon are available in Southeast waters from July to September. Red salmon are available in June and July. The various trout are present throughout the spring and summer. Steelhead are a spring fish in Southeast, with steelhead runs at more than 300 streams in the spring. (A notable exception is the fall run on the Situk River at Yakutat.) Dollies are best in salt water along the shoreline from May through July, and in coastal streams in August and September.

Where to fish is probably the most difficult choice, with the number of fishing destinations available well beyond the capability of most anglers to visit. The list of possible fishing spots is also beyond our capability to list here, although many favorite fishing spots are mentioned under Area Fishing in the Attractions section of each southeastern Alaska community covered in this section. The Alaska Dept. of Fish and Game is the source for much of this information, and they have literally hundreds of pamphlets on fishing regional waters. Particularly helpful is their "Sportfishing Alaska" brochure, which shows run times and also lists area office phone numbers. ADF&G area offices are also listed in the community descriptions in this section. Or write the Sport Fish Division, Box 25526, Juneau, AK 99802-5526; phone (907) 465-4180; internet www.state.ak.us/local/akpages/FISH.GAME.adfghome.htm.

While you can arrive in any Southeast community and fish from the pier, the shore, or at a nearby lake or river that is accessible by road, the majority of southeastern Alaska's best fishing locations are accessible only by plane or boat. You can book these fishing charters yourself in nearly every community in Southeast. Many fishing guides and charter operators advertise in The MILEPOST®; see ads this section. Local visitor bureaus and chambers of commerce can direct you to certified operators and provide details for independent trip planning. See Visitor Information under each community in this section for chamber and bureau addresses and phone numbers.

It is possible to fly out of any Southeast community, fish for cutthroat trout on a remote lake, and fly back to town, all within 3 hours. Charter planes charge an hourly rate, either per plane load or per passenger, or may offer a fixed-rate fishing charter that may or may not include guide services and fishing gear. Fly-in fishing operators may offer lodge accommodations or only provide drop-off and pickup service, with the client either camping or overnighting at a U.S. Forest Service cabin. (Many of these cabins are located on fishing lakes with skiffs available; see Cabins in GENERAL INFORMATION for details.)

Charter boats are available for half-, full- or multi-day fishing trips. Multi-day fishing boat charters may overnight on board yachts or in floating lodges. Boat charters for saltwater sportfishing average $185 per person per day, based on a shared charter boat. Rates often include gear, license, bait, fish processing and land transportation, but ask ahead of time. Clients may have a destination in mind, or depend on the charter boat operator for guiding services.

There are also numerous fishing lodges in Southeast. Full-service lodges generally offer food and lodging, guide service, boats for saltwater fishing and daily fly-outs for freshwater fishing. Rates range anywhere from $300 to $800 per person per day, and include transportation to the lodge, accommodations, meals, guide services, fishing license and equipment, and fish processing. Refreshments, gratuities and personal items are extra. Again, the visitor bureaus and chambers of commerce in all communities can provide information on area fishing lodges; also see ads in this section.

When, where and how you fish Southeast Alaska requires some careful thought and planning, but the rewards are well worth it.

Ketchikan
(See map, pages 649–650)

Located on Revillagigedo Island, 235 miles/378 km south of Juneau, 90 miles/145 km north of Prince Rupert, BC. **Population:** Ketchikan Gateway Borough and city, 15,082. **Emergency Services: Alaska State Troopers**, phone (907) 225-5118. **City Police**, phone (907) 225-6631, or 911 for all emergency services. **Fire Department, Ambulance** and **Ketchikan Volunteer Rescue Squad**, phone (907) 225-9616. **Hospital**, Ketchikan General at 3100 Tongass Ave., phone (907) 225-5171. **Maritime Search and Rescue**, call the Coast Guard at (907) 225-5666.

Visitor Information: Ketchikan Visitors Bureau office is located on the downtown dock, open during daily business hours and weekends May through September. Write them at 131M Front St., Ketchikan 99901; phone (907) 225-6166 or 1-800-770-2200; fax (907) 225-4250. U.S. Forest Service office for Misty Fiords National Monument and Ketchikan Ranger District is located at 3031 Tongass Ave.; open 8 A.M. to 4:30 P.M. weekdays; phone (907) 225-2148. The Southeast Alaska Visitor Center, located at 50 Main St., is open May 1 to Sept. 30, 8:30 A.M to 4:30 P.M. daily; Oct. 1 to April 30, 8:30 A.M. to 4:30 P.M., Tuesday through Saturday; phone (907) 228-6214, fax 228-6234.

Elevation: Sea level. **Climate:** Rainy. Yearly average rainfall is 162 inches and snowfall is 32 inches. Average daily maximum temperature in July 65°F/18°C; daily minimum 51°F/11°C. Daily maximum in January 39°F/4°C; daily minimum 29°F/-2°C. **Radio:** KTKN 930, KRBD-FM 105.9, KGTW-FM 106.7, KFMJ-FM 99.9. **Television:** CFTK (Prince Rupert, BC) and 27 cable channels. **Newspapers:** *Ketchikan Daily News* (daily); *Southeastern Log* (monthly); *New Alaskan* (monthly).

Private Aircraft: Ketchikan International Airport on Gravina Island; elev. 88 feet/27m; length 7,500 feet/2,286m; asphalt; fuel

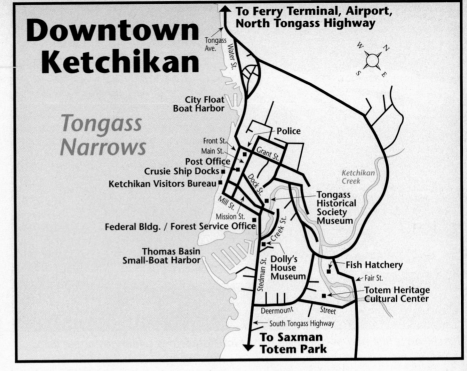

Downtown Ketchikan

Tongass Narrows

To Ferry Terminal, Airport, North Tongass Highway

Tongass Ave.
Water St.
City Float Boat Harbor
Police
Front St.
Main St.
Grant St.
Post Office
Dock St.
Crusie Ship Docks
Ketchikan Visitors Bureau
Mill St.
Ketchikan Creek
Tongass Historical Society Museum
Mission St.
Federal Bldg. / Forest Service Office
Creek St.
Thomas Basin Small-Boat Harbor
Stedman St.
Dolly's House Museum
Fish Hatchery
Fair St.
Totem Heritage Cultural Center
Deermount Street
South Tongass Highway
To Saxman Totem Park

100LL, A. Ketchikan Harbor seaplane base downtown; fuel 80, 100, A.

Ketchikan is located on the southwest side of Revillagigedo (ruh-vee-uh-guh-GAY-doh) Island, on Tongass Narrows opposite Gravina Island. The name Ketchikan is derived from a Tlingit name, Kitschk-Hin, meaning the creek of the "thundering wings of an eagle." The creek flows through the town, emptying into Tongass Narrows. Before Ketchikan was settled, the area at the mouth of Ketchikan Creek was a Tlingit Indian fish camp. Settlement began with interest in both mining and fishing. The first salmon cannery moved here in 1886, operating under the name of Tongass Packing Co. It burned down in August 1889. Gold was discovered nearby in 1898. This, plus resid-

ual effects of the gold, silver and copper mines, caused Ketchikan to become a booming little mining town. It was incorporated in 1901.

As mining waned, the fishing industry began to grow. By the 1930s more than a dozen salmon canneries had been built; during the peak years of the canned salmon industry, Ketchikan earned the title of "Salmon Capital of the World." Overfishing caused a drastic decline in salmon by the 1940s, and today only 4 canneries and a cold storage plant operate. Trident Seafoods Corp., owner of Ketchikan's oldest and largest cannery, provides lodging for 200-plus salmon processors in a floating bunkhouse. An industry under development is the commercial harvest of abalone near

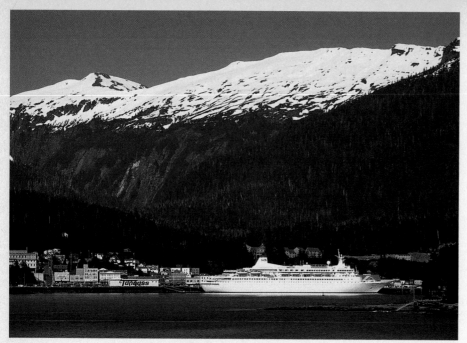

Ketchikan is first port of call in Southeast for state ferries and many cruise ships.
(© Rich Reid)

Ketchikan.

As fishing reached a low point, the timber industry expanded. The first sawmill was originally built in 1898 at Dolomi on Prince of Wales Island to cut timber for the Dolomi Mine. It was dismantled and moved to Ketchikan and rebuilt in 1903. A large pulp mill was constructed in 1953 at Ward Cove, a few miles northwest of town. It is scheduled to close in 1997.

Tourism is a very important industry here; Ketchikan is Alaska's first port of call for cruise ships and Alaska Marine Highway vessels.

Ketchikan is Alaska's southernmost major city and the state's fourth largest (after Anchorage, Fairbanks and Juneau). The closest city in British Columbia is Prince Rupert. Ketchikan is a linear waterfront city, with much of its 3-mile/5-km-long business district suspended above water on pilings driven into the bottom of Tongass Narrows. It clings to the steep wooded hillside and has many homes perched on cliffs that are reached by climbing long wooden staircases or narrow winding streets.

The area supports 4 public grade schools, 4 parochial grade schools, a junior high school, 2 high schools and a University of Alaska Southeast campus.

ACCOMMODATIONS/VISITOR SERVICES

Accommodations in Ketchikan include bed and breakfasts (see ads following) and several motels/hotels. Major downtown lodgings include Best Western's The Landing (800/428-8304), Gilmore Hotel (800/275-9423), Ingersoll Hotel (800/478-2124), Super 8 Motel (800/800-8000) and the Westmark Cape Fox Lodge (800/544-0970). The major shopping areas are downtown and the west end.

Blueberry Hill Bed & Breakfast. Enjoy simple, peaceful charm within walking distance of downtown Ketchikan. Forested hillside setting with wonderful views from every window. Relax in spacious living room, and watch ever-changing picturesque scenes of Ketchikan's waterways. Or, take a short stroll to museums, galleries, shops and restaurants. Treat yourself to Blueberry Hill's scrumptious homemade breads! Box 9508, Ketchikan, AK 99901. (907) 247-2583. [ADVERTISEMENT]

Innside Passage Bed & Breakfast. Close to downtown; 1½ miles from airport/ferries. Outstanding breakfasts served with an incredible view. Hadley room appointed with antiques, double bed, beautiful view. Orca room has two comfortable twins—one built into the eve. Apartment Elyssa fully outfitted, separate entrance, exceptional view. Phone, cable TV, double bed plus futon (sleeps two). Late night arrivals with prior arrangement. Year-round. 114 Elliot Street Stairway, Ketchikan, AK 99901. (907) 247-3700. [ADVERTISEMENT]

Ketchikan AYH hostel is located at the First United Methodist Church, Grant and Main streets; write Box 8515, Ketchikan, AK 99901; phone (907) 225-3319 (summer only). Open June 1 to Aug. 31, the hostel has showers, sleeping pads (bring sleeping bag) and kitchen facilities. Check-in time is 6 to 11 P.M. Reservations strongly recommended. Cost is $8 per night for members (AYH membership passes may be purchased at the hostel), $11 for nonmembers.

There are 5 campgrounds (4 public campgrounds and a private resort) north of the city on North Tongass Highway and Ward Lake Road. See highway logs in this section. Dump station located at Ketchikan Public Works office, 2 blocks north of state ferry terminal. Contact the visitors bureau for brochure on RV use and parking. ▲

TRANSPORTATION

Air: Daily scheduled jet service is provided from the Ketchikan International Airport by Alaska Airlines to other Southeast cities, Anchorage and Seattle, WA. Commuter and charter service to other Southeast communities is available via Ketchikan Air, Taquan Air and Pro-Mech Air. Taquan Air (800/770-8800) has daily scheduled flights to Prince Rupert, BC.

Airport terminal, across Tongass Narrows on Gravina Island, is reached via shuttle ferry (10-minute ride, $2.50 per person, $5 per vehicle, one way) departing from the ferry terminal on North Tongass Avenue at half-hour intervals. Airport ferry terminal on Revillagigedo Island is 2.7 miles/4.3 km from downtown. Airporter service between downtown and airport is $11 to $12 (includes ferry fare). Shuttle and taxi service is also available between downtown and the airport.

Ferry: Alaska Marine Highway vessels connect Ketchikan with all mainline southeastern Alaska port cities, Prince Rupert, BC, and Bellingham, WA. There are also daily state ferry connections via the MV *Aurora* between Ketchikan and Metlakatla (1 hr. 15 min.), and Ketchikan and Hollis (2 hrs 45 min.). The *Aurora* also sails between Ketchikan and Stewart/Hyder (11 hrs. 15 min.) 2 to 3 times a month in summer. See MARINE ACCESS ROUTES section for schedules.

Terminal building with waiting room, ticket counter and loading area is on North Tongass Avenue (Highway), 2 miles/3.2 km north of downtown. Phone (907) 225-6181. Foot passengers can walk from the ferry to a post office, restaurant and grocery store if stopover time permits. Taxi service available.

Bus: Daily municipal bus service, stops at every stop within the city limits at half-hour intervals; schedules available at visitors bureau. Fares is $1 one way.

Car Rental: Available at airport and downtown locations from Alaska Car Rental (907) 225-5000, Avis Rent-A-Car (907) 225-

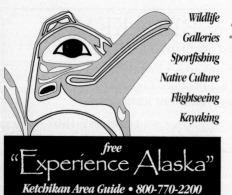

Wildlife
Galleries
Sportfishing
Native Culture
Flightseeing
Kayaking

4515 and Payless Car Rental (907) 225-6004.

Taxi: Taxi cabs meet ferry and airport arrivals.

Highways: North Tongass and South Tongass highways and Ward Lake Road (see logs this section).

Cruise Ships: Ketchikan is the first port of call for many cruise ships to Alaska. Cruises depart from U.S. West Coast ports and Vancouver, BC. Two cruise lines depart from Ketchikan.

Private Boats: Two public docks downtown, Thomas Basin and City Float, provide transient moorage. In the West End District, 1 mile/1.6 km from downtown, Bar Harbor has moorage, showers. No gas available. Permits required. Moorage space in Ketchikan is limited; all private boats should contact the harbormaster's office at (907) 225-3610 prior to arrival to secure a spot.

ATTRACTIONS

Ketchikan's waterfront is the center of the city. A narrow city on a mountainside, Ketchikan has a waterfront that runs for several miles and consists of docks, stores on pilings, seaplane floats, 3 picturesque boat harbors, a seaplane base and ferry terminal. There is constant activity here as seaplanes take off and vessels move in and out of the harbor. Walking-tour maps are available at the visitors bureau and at the ferry terminal.

Plaza, the. Southeast Alaska's premier shopping center. Two comfort-controlled levels feature a variety of national and local retail shops and services for complete one-stop shopping. Plenty of free parking. Less than a mile south of the ferry terminal. Open every day except major holidays.

[ADVERTISEMENT]

Fish Pirate's Daughter, a well-done local musical-comedy melodrama, portrays Ketchikan's early fishing days, with some of the city's spicier history included. Performed 7 P.M. and 8:45 P.M. Fridays, July through August. Contact First City Players, 338 Main St., phone (907) 225-4792 or 225-2211, for more information. Admission fee.

Tongass Historical Museum, located in the Centennial Building on Dock Street in central downtown, explores the rich culture of the Tlingit, Haida and Tsimshian people, and the history of settlement in this area, in the exhibit "Salmon, Cedar and Gold: The History of Ketchikan." Open in summer from 8 A.M to 5 P.M. daily. Winter (October to mid-May) hours are 1–5 P.M. Wednesday through Friday, 1–4 P.M. Saturday and Sunday. The Raven Stealing the Sun totem stands just outside the entrance. Salmon viewing platforms. Admission fee is $2 for adults; free admission Sunday afternoons. Phone (907) 225-5600 for more information.

Creek Street is Ketchikan's famous "redlight district," where Black Mary, Dolly, Frenchie and others plied their trade for over half a century until 1954. Nearly 20 houses lined the far side of Ketchikan Creek; many have been restored. There are also several art and gift shops. Dolly's House, a former brothel, is open during the summer. Admission charged. Creek Street is a wooden street on pilings that begins just past the bridge on Stedman (South Tongass Highway). Watch for salmon in the creek below the bridge in late August. Also look for the metal sculpture paying tribute to the salmon; it's a local landmark.

Totem Heritage Center, at 601 Deermount St., houses 33 totem poles and fragments retrieved from deserted Tlingit and Haida Indian villages. This national landmark collection comprises the largest exhibit of original totems in the United States. Facilities include craft exhibits, craft classes for children and reference library. Gift shop, craft demonstrations and guided tours during summer months. Summer admission fee $4. No admission charged off-season. Summer hours are 8 A.M. to 5 P.M. daily. Winter hours (October through mid-May) are 1–5 P.M. Tuesday through Friday. Phone (907) 225-5900.

Deer Mountain Hatchery is located in the city park within walking distance of downtown (take the bridge across Ketchikan Creek from the Totem Heritage Center). The hatchery produces about 100,000 king, 150,000 coho, 30,000 rainbow trout and 6,500 steelhead fingerlings annually. Observation platforms and information signs provide education on the life cycles of salmon. Open from 8 A.M. to 4:30 P.M. daily late May to late September.

The Ketchikan Mural on Stedman Street was created by 21 Native artists in 1978. The 125-by-18-foot/38-by-4-m design is collectively entitled *The Return of the Eagle.*

Fourth of July is a major celebration in Ketchikan. The Timber Carnival takes place over the Fourth of July with events such as ax throwing and chopping, power saw bucking and a tug-of-war. There are also fireworks, the Calamity Race (by canoe and kayak, bicycle and on foot), a parade and other events.

The Blueberry Arts Festival, on Aug. 9, 1997, features arts and crafts, the performing arts and plenty of homemade blueberry pies, blueberry crêpes, blueberry cheesecakes and other culinary delights. Events include a slug race, bed race, pie-eating contest, trivia contest and spelling bee. A juried art show, funrun and dance are also part of the festival. Sponsored and coordinated by the Ketchikan Area Arts and Humanities Council, Inc. (338 Main St., Ketchikan 99901; 907/225-2211).

Saxman Totem Park, Milepost 2.5 South Tongass Highway, is included in local sightseeing tours. Open year-round. There is no admission charge, but there is a fee for guided tour (offered May through September). The totem park has 28 totems. The tour includes demonstrations at the Carving Center and performances by the Cape Fox Dancers at the Beaver Tribal House. For more information on hours, tours and events, phone the Cape Fox Tours office at (907) 225-5163, ext. 301 or 304.

Totem Bight community house and

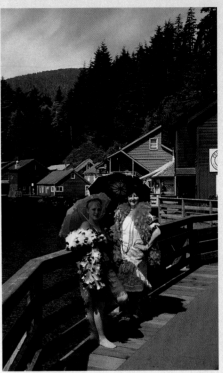

Creek Street was Ketchikan's famous redlight district. (© Michael Dill)

totem park, Milepost 9.9 North Tongass Highway, contains an excellent model of a Tlingit community house and a park with 13 totems.

Misty Fiords National Monument, 30 miles/48 km east of Ketchikan, encompasses more than 2 million acres of pristine coastal rain forest and glacially carved fjords. Rich in forests, marine wildlife, waterfalls and spectacular geologic features, the monument offers great scenic and scientific interest for visitors from May to September. The Forest Service maintains 25 miles/40 km of trails and several public-use cabins available for rent. Access to the monument is by boat or floatplane from Ketchikan. Floating dock at Naha Bay is 17 miles/27 km north of Ketchikan. Sea kayaking is a popular means of exploring the coastlines and venturing into remote areas. A system of 9 marine buoys is available to saltwater boaters on a first-come, first-served basis; fishing and photography are favorite pastimes in the monument. Cabin reservations, maps and

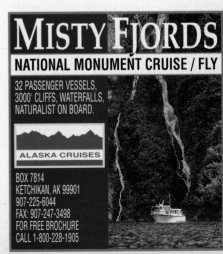

natural history publications are available from the Ketchikan Ranger District, 3031 Tongass Ave., Ketchikan, AK 99901; phone (907) 225-2148.

Charter boats: About 120 vessels operate out of Ketchikan for half-day, all-day or overnight sightseeing or fishing trips and transport to USFS public-use cabins and outlying communities. See advertisements this section and check with the visitors bureau or at the marinas.

Fishing lodges and resorts in the area offer sportfishing for steelhead, salmon, halibut, trout, lingcod and red snapper. Resorts near Ketchikan include Mink Bay Lodge, Salmon Falls Resort and Yes Bay Lodge. There are several fishing lodges on Prince of Wales Island, including Waterfall Resort, which is housed in a renovated fish cannery.

Charter planes operate from the airport and from the waterfront on floats and are available for fly-in fishing, flightseeing or service to lodges and smaller communities.

Picnic areas include Settlers Cove by Settlers Cove Campground, **Milepost 18.2** North Tongass Highway; Refuge Cove, **Milepost 8.7** North Tongass Highway; Rotary Beach at **Milepost 3.5** South Tongass Highway; and Grassy Point and Ward Lake, **Milepost 1.1** Ward Lake Road.

Hiking trails include Deer Mountain trail, which begins at the corner of Fair and Deermount streets. The 3-mile/4.8-km, 3,001-foot/915-m ascent gives trekkers an excellent vantage of downtown Ketchikan and Tongass Narrows. Good but steep trail. Access to Deer Mountain cabin, the only USFS public-use cabin accessible by trail from Ketchikan. Cabin reservations are required. Perseverance Lake trail, 2.4 miles/3.8 km from Ward Lake to Perseverance Lake. Connell Lake trail, about 1.5 miles/2.4 km along north shore of Connell Lake, is in poor condition. Silvis Lakes trail, about 2 miles/3.2 km up to Lower Silvis Lake and picnic area. Trail continues to Upper Silvis Lake and Deer Mountain trail, but is very difficult. An easy and informative 1-mile/1.6-km nature trail circles Ward Lake.

Southeast Alaska Visitor Center, 50 Main St., features exhibits on Native cultures, ecosystems, resources and the rainforest in Southeast Alaska. Also 13-minute, award-winning "Mystical Southeast Alaska" audio visual program and Alaska Public Lands trip planning room. Open 8:30 A.M. to 4:30 P.M., daily in summer, Tuesday through Saturday in winter.

USFS public-use cabins are available for $25 a night. There are 48 cabins in the Ketchikan management area of the Tongass National Forest. Most are accessible by floatplane, with some accessible by hiking or by boat. Reservations may be made at Southeast Alaska Visitor Center, 50 Main St.; office hours are 8:30 A.M. to 4:30 P.M. daily. Phone (907) 228-6214. For additional information see Cabins in the GENERAL INFORMATION section. ▲

AREA FISHING: Check with the Alaska Dept. of Fish and Game at 2030 Sea Level Dr., Suite 215, or phone (907) 225-2859 for details on fishing in the Ketchikan area. Good fishing spots range from Mountain Point, a 5-mile/8-km drive from Ketchikan on South Tongass Highway, to streams, lakes, bays, and inlets 50 miles/80 km away by boat or by air. Half-day and longer charters and skiff rentals available out of Ketchikan. There are fishing resorts at Yes

Ketchikan cannery workers sort salmon. (© Michelle Arab)

Bay, Clover Pass and at the entrance to Behm Canal (Salmon Falls Resort); and 13 fishing resorts on Prince of Wales Island. Fish include salmon, halibut, steelhead, Dolly Varden, cutthroat and rainbow, arctic grayling, eastern brook trout, lingcod and rockfish; shellfish include dungeness crab and shrimp. Ketchikan has 2 king salmon derbies, a silver salmon derby and a halibut derby in summer. ⬿

North Tongass Highway Log

The North Tongass Highway is 18.4 miles/29.6 km long with 15.2 miles/24.5 km paved. It begins at the corner of Mill Street and Stedman (at the Federal Bldg.) and proceeds north to Ward Lake Road, Totem Bight, Clover Pass and Settlers Cove Campground.

0 Federal Building on left with area information display. Proceeding on Mill Street.

0.1 (0.2 km) Southeast Alaska visitor center with information on federal lands in Alaska.

0.2 (0.3 km) Turning right onto Front Street, cruise ship dock on left where passengers disembark from major ships.

0.3 (0.5 km) Tunnel. North of this, Front Street becomes Water Street.

0.5 (0.8 km) City Float on left. Note older vessels, some dating back to the early 1900s.

0.7 (1.1 km) Highway turns left, then right, and becomes Tongass Avenue.

1.2 (1.9 km) West end shopping area begins.

1.7 (2.7 km) Bar Harbor boat basin on left.

2 (3.2 km) Ketchikan General Hospital on right, Ketchikan Ranger Station and Misty Fiords National Monument on left, northbound.

2.3 (3.7 km) Ferry terminals for Alaska Marine Highway.

2.4 (3.9 km) Main branch post office.

2.6 (4.2 km) Carlanna Creek and bridge.

2.7 (4.3 km) Airport shuttle ferry.

3.2 (5.1 km) Almer Wolfe Memorial view-

point of Tongass Narrows. 24-hour RV parking. Airport terminal is visible across the narrows on Gravina Island.

4 (6.4 km) Hillside on right is a logged area, an example of clear-cut logging method and regrowth.

4.4 (7.1 km) Alaska State Troopers and Highway Dept.

5.5 (8.8 km) Small paved viewpoint overlooking Tongass Narrows and floatplane dock.

6 (9.6 km) Ward Cove Cannery next to road. Cannery Creek and bridge.

6.8 (10.9 km) **Junction** with Ward Lake Road (see log this section).

7 (11.3 km) Ward Creek and bridge; Ketchikan sawmill, owned by Ketchikan Pulp Co.; see Mile 7.8.

7.3 (11.7 km) **WARD COVE.** Post office, gas station and grocery.

7.8 (12.5 km) Ketchikan Pulp Co. pulp mill was built in 1953; it is scheduled to close in 1997.

8.7 (14 km) Refuge Cove state recreation site with 14 picnic sites.

9.4 (15.1 km) Mud Bight; "float houses" rest on mud at low tide and float during high tide.

9.9 (15.9 km) Totem Bight state historical park; parking area, restrooms and phones. A short trail leads through the woods to Totem Bight community house and totem park. A striking setting. Don't miss this!

10.8 (17.4 km) Grocery store and gas station.

12.9 (20.8 km) Scenic viewpoint overlooking Guard Island lighthouse built in 1903 and manned until 1969 when finally automated.

14.2 (22.9 km) Clover Pass Resort turnoff. Left, North Point Higgins Road leads 0.6 mile/1 km to turnoff to resort; food, lodging, camping.

Left, then immediately right, is Knudson Cove Road, leading 0.4 mile/0.6 km to Knudson Cove Marina with public float, boat launch and boat rentals. Road rejoins North Tongass Highway at **Milepost 14.8.** ▲

14.8 (23.8 km) Knudson Cove Marina to left 0.5 mile/0.8 km.

15.2 (24.5 km) Pavement ends.

16.6 (26.8 km) Salmon Falls Resort; private fishing lodge with restaurant and boat rentals.

18.2 (29.3 km) Settlers Cove state campground, parking area and picnic area; 13 tent/trailer campsites; 2 covered picnic pavilions flanked by 12 picnic units are along the beach on either side of the campground. Camping fee $6/night. Tables, water, pit toilets. Open year-round. Good gravel beach for kids and boats. To right of beach is **Lunch Creek** (pink salmon in August), falls and trail. ◄🐟▲

18.4 (29.6 km) Road end.

Ward Lake Road Log

An 8.3-mile/13.4-km road off the North Tongass Highway leading to Ward Lake Recreation Area. (Access to Harriet Hunt Road to Harriet Hunt Lake at **Milepost 7.1**). Motorists and hikers should be aware of private property boundaries, posted by Cape Fox Corp. (CFC), and logging and trucking activities. Campers should be aware of USFS regulations in the Ward Lake Recreation Area: Camping is restricted to developed campgrounds and limited to 7 nights.

0 Right turn northbound from North Tongass Highway at **Milepost 6.8.**

0.1 (0.2 km) Tongass National Forest boundary.

0.4 (0.6 km) Small scenic turnout on right. Pond with lily pads surrounded by pine in muskeg.

0.7 (1.1 km) Signal Creek USFS campground on left; 24 sites with tables, water and pit toilets. Open Memorial Day to Sept. 30. Camping fee charged. Situated among large trees on the shore of Ward Lake. One end of a nature trail around Ward Lake begins here and encircles the lake; it is a 30- to 50-minute easy walk on well-graveled path. Some campsites can be reserved; phone 1-800-280-2267 (CAMP) or TDD 1-800-879-4496. ▲

0.9 (1.4 km) Beginning of Perseverance Lake trail on right. Trailhead is within 100 feet of CCC Campground with parking across road. Site of WWII Aleut internment camp. The 2.4-mile/3.9-km boardwalk trail leads to **Perseverance Lake** (elev. 518 feet/158m); brook trout fishing. 🐟

1 (1.6 km) CCC (or Three C's) USFS campground entrance on right; 4 campsites, camping fee, open mid-May to October. ▲

1.1 (1.8 km) Ward Creek bridge. Grassy Point USFS picnic area. Several walk-in picnic sites with tables and shelters near road. Footbridge across Ward Creek leads to **Ward Lake** trail; good fly-fishing for steelhead, salmon and Dolly Varden.

Ward Creek and **Ward Lake**, cutthroat and Dolly Varden year-round, best March to June; steelhead to 16 lbs.; silver salmon to 18 lbs. and pink salmon to 5 lbs., August to October. (Hatchery-raised coho salmon; bring head of tagged fish to ADF&G.) 🐟

1.3 (2.1 km) Ward Lake USFS picnic area; beach, parking area and picnic shelters. One end of nature trail around Ward Lake.

2.9 (4.7 km) Right, Last Chance USFS campground; 19 spaces, tables, pit toilets, water, camping fee. Open mid-June to Sept. 30. ▲

3 (4.8 km) Connell Lake Road, on right, a narrow gravel road extending 0.6 mile/1 km to Connell Lake Reservoir. At Mile 0.4 Connell Lake Road, a bridge passes over large pipe, which carries water from the reservoir to the pulp mill at Ward Cove. Connell Lake trail at reservoir.

3.3 (5.3 km) Turnout.

7.1 (11.4 km) **Junction** with 2.4-mile/3.9-km Harriet Hunt Lake Road. Harriet Hunt Lake Road dead ends at **Harriet Hunt Lake** Recreation Area; parking area, pit toilets; rainbow to 20 inches, May to Nov. Road is on Cape Fox Corp. lands. Watch for logging trucks.

8.3 (13.4 km) End public highway. Private logging road begins.

South Tongass Highway Log

The 12.9-mile/20.8 km South Tongass Highway leads from the corner of Mill and Stedman streets south to Saxman Totem Park. First 8.5 miles/13.7 km are paved.

0 Federal Building on right.

0.1 (0.2 km) Ketchikan Creek and bridge. Beginning of Creek Street boardwalk on left next to bridge.

0.2 (0.3 km) Thomas Street begins on right, a boardwalk street where old-time businesses are located. Thomas Basin boat harbor.

0.5 (0.8 km) Cannery and cold storage plant.

0.9 (1.4 km) U.S. Coast Guard base.

2.5 (4 km) **SAXMAN** (pop. 389) was founded in 1896 by Tlingit Alaska Natives and named after a Presbyterian missionary who served the Tlingit people. The Native village of Saxman has a gas station and convenience store and is the site of Saxman Totem Park. Developed by Cape Fox Corp., this popular attraction includes a carving center and tribal house. Guided tours available from Cape Fox Tours.

2.7 (4.3 km) Gas station.

3.5 (5.6 km) Rotary Beach, public recreation area, contains a shelter and table.

5 (8.1 km) Mountain Point, suburb of Ketchikan. Parking area and access to good salmon fishing from shore in July and August. 🐟

5.6 (9 km) Boat ramp on right.

8.2 (13.2 km) Herring Cove bridge and sawmill. Private hatchery for chum, king and coho salmon on short road to left; no tours.

8.5 (13.7 km) Pavement ends.

8.8 (14.2 km) Whitman Creek and bridge.

9 (14.5 km) Scenic turnout on right. Note different shades of green on trees across the water. Light green are cedar; medium, hemlock; and the darker are spruce. Species grow intermixed.

10.3 (16.6 km) Left, scenic waterfall.

11 (17.7 km) Scenic turnout.

11.8 (19 km) Lodge.

12.9 (20.8 km) Road end, view of power plant, an experimental sockeye salmon hatchery (no tours) and an abandoned cannery. Two-mile/3.2-km walk up gravel road leads to Lower Silvis Lake picnic area. Trail continues to Upper Silvis Lake and joins Deer Mountain trail, which connects to John Mountain National Recreation trail. Trail between Upper and Lower Silvis lakes is very difficult.

Metlakatla
(See map, page 649)

Located on the west coast of Annette Island, 15 miles/24 km south of Ketchikan, Southeastern Alaska's southernmost community. **Population:** 1,673. **Emergency Services: Police, fire and ambulance,** emergency only, phone 911. **Visitor Information:** Tours to Metlakatla depart daily from Ketchikan; reservations are required. Contact the Community Tour Office at 1-800-643-4898 for scheduling information. The Metlakatla tour and salmon bake operates from early-May to October. A permit from Metlakatla Indian Community is required for long-term visits to Annette Island.

Elevation: Sea level. **Climate:** Mild and moist. Summer temperatures range from 36°F/12°C to 65°F/18°C; winter temperatures from 28°F/-2°C to 44°F/7°C. Average annual precipitation is 115 inches: October is the wettest month with a maximum of 35 inches of rainfall. Annual snowfall averages 61 inches. **Radio:** KTKN 930 (Ketchikan). **Television:** 20 channels via cable.

Private Aircraft: Floatplane services.

Transportation: Air—Charter and scheduled floatplane service. Ferry—Daily state ferry service in summer via MV *Aurora* from Ketchikan; crossing time 1 hour 15 minutes.

Overnight accommodations, restaurant, groceries and banking services available.

Metlakatla was founded in 1887 by William Duncan, a Scottish-born lay minister, who moved here with several hundred Tsimshian Indians from a settlement in British Columbia after a falling-out with church authorities. Congress granted reservation status and title to the entire island in 1891, and the new settlement prospered under Duncan, who built a salmon cannery and sawmill.

Today, fishing and lumber continue to be the main economic base of Metlakatla. The community and island also retain the status of a federal Indian reservation, which is why Metlakatla has the only salmon fish traps in Alaska. (Floating fish traps were outlawed by the state shortly after statehood.)

The well-planned community has a town hall, a recreation center with an Olympic-sized swimming pool, well-maintained wood-frame homes, a post office, 2 lumber mills and cold storage. The Metlakatla Indian Community is the largest employer in town,

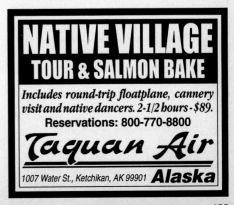

with retail and service trades the second largest. Many residents also are commercial fishermen. Subsistence activities remain an important source of food for residents, who harvest seaweed, salmon, halibut, cod, clams, dungeness crab and waterfowl.

The Duncan Museum in Metalkatla is located in the original cottage occupied by founder Father William Duncan until his death in 1918. There is also a replica of the turn-of-the-century William Duncan Memorial Church here, built after the original was destroyed by fire in 1948.

Prince of Wales Island

(See map, page 650)

Includes Coffman Cove, Craig, Hollis, Hydaburg, Klawock, Thorne Bay and Whale Pass

View from ferry on Clarence Strait of east coast of Prince of Wales Island. (Staff)

About 15 miles/24.1 km west of Ketchikan. **Population:** Approximately 6,300. **Emergency Services: Alaska State Troopers,** in Klawock, phone (907) 755-2918. **Police,** in Craig, phone (907) 826-3330; in Klawock, phone (907) 755-2777; emergencies only, phone 911; **Village Public Safety Officers** in Thorne Bay, phone (907) 828-3905; in Hydaburg, phone (907) 285-3321; in Klawock, phone (907) 755-2906. **Ambulance,** Hydaburg, Hydaburg emergency response team, phone 911. **Health Clinics** for all emergencies, phone 911; in Craig, phone (907) 826-3257; in Kla-

wock, phone (907) 755-4800; in Thorne Bay, phone (907) 828-3906; in Hydaburg, phone (907) 285-3462. **Maritime Search and Rescue,** call the Coast Guard at 1-800-478-5555.

Elevation: Sea level to 4,000 feet/1,219m. **Climate:** Mild and moist, but variable due to the island's size and topography. Rainfall in excess of 100 inches per year, with modest snowfall in winter at lower elevations. **Radio:** KRSA 580 (Petersburg), KTKN 930 (Ketchikan), KRBD-FM 90.1 (Ketchikan). **Television:** Via satellite. **Newspaper:** *Island News* (Thorne Bay, weekly).

Private Aircraft: Klawock airstrip, 2 miles/3.2 km northeast; elev. 50 feet/15m; length 5,000 feet/1,524m; lighted and paved; fuel 100LL. Seaplane bases adjacent to all the largest communities and in several bays.

Heavily forested with low mountains, Prince of Wales Island measures roughly 135 miles/217 km north–south by 45 miles/72 km east–west. The third largest island under the American flag (Kodiak is second, the Big Island of Hawaii is first), it is 2,231 square miles/5,778 square km. The 4 major communities on the island—Craig (the

largest with 1,946 residents), Klawock, Thorne Bay and Hydaburg—and the smaller camps and communities of Coffman Cove, Whale Pass, Labouchere Bay and Naukati are connected by road. Kasaan, a small Haida village at the head of Kasaan Bay, was connected to the road system in 1996. **PORT PROTECTION** and **POINT BAKER,** both at the northwest tip of the island, are not connected by road (see *The ALASKA WILDERNESS GUIDE* for details on these communities).

Prince of Wales Island has been the site of several lumbermills and mining camps since the 1800s. But it was salmon that led to permanent settlement on the island. Klawock was the site of one of Alaska's first canneries, built in 1878. In the following years, some 25 canneries were built on the island to process salmon. Today, logging is prevalent on the island.

Prince of Wales Island offers uncrowded backcountry, fishing for salmon and trout, kayaking and canoeing waters, opportunities for viewing wildlife (black bears, Sitka black-tailed deer, bald eagles), adequate visitor facilities and some historical attractions. Most of the island is national forest land. The Forest Service manages 5 large, designated wilderness areas on Prince of Wales Island. There are also some Native corporation and private land holdings. Respect No Trespassing signs.

There are several roadside fishing spots on Prince of Wales Island. See the road logs in this section for details. Lakes and streams support red, pink and silver salmon, cutthroat, rainbow trout and Dolly Varden. ◆

ACCOMMODATIONS

Prince of Wales has several hotels and lodges located in Craig and Klawock. Lodging in Craig includes Haida Way Lodge (907/826-3268), Sunnahae Lodge (907/826-4000), Ruth Ann's Hotel and Shelter Cove. In Klawock, Fireweed Lodge (907/755-2930) and the Columbine Inn (907/755-2287). Other lodges and resorts on the island include Deer Creek Cottage (800/830-3393), Windy Way Lodge (907/826-3084), McFarland's Floatel, Wooden Wheel Cove Lodge and Waterfall Resort.

Cabins are available at Coffman Cove

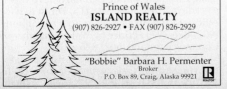

Cabins (907/329-2251) and Whale Pass Gas and Grocery. Log Cabin RV Park & Resort at Klawock offers camping and cabins.

There are also more than 20 USFS cabins (accessible by plane, boat or on foot) available for public use; reservations and a fee are required. Contact the USFS office in Ketchikan or the local ranger districts at Craig (907/826-3271) and Thorne Bay (907/828-3304). Also see Cabins in the GENERAL INFORMATION section.

There is one developed USFS campground on the island—Eagle's Nest on Thorne Bay Road ($8 camping fee)—and several undeveloped dispersed camping sites accessible via the island road system. See road logs this section. ▲

TRANSPORTATION

Air: All communities on the island are served by floatplane, most daily. Wheel planes land at Klawock. Daily scheduled service by Taquan Air (800/770-8800), Ketchikan Air and Pro–Mech from Ketchikan.

Ferry: Alaska state ferry MV *Aurora* from Ketchikan to Hollis; crossing time 2 hours, 45 minutes. Phone Craig office at (907) 826-3432, Hollis terminal at (907) 530-7115. See MARINE ACCESS ROUTES section for rates and schedule. Van taxi service meets ferry at Hollis and offers service to Craig and Klawock. See list of taxi services following.

Taxi: No free public transport meets the ferry at Hollis. Arrangements with taxis can be made. According to the chamber of commerce, the fare ranges from about $25 per person to $50–$60 to charter a taxi (which is usually a van for several people). Available in Klawock from Irish Setter Cab (907/755-2217), Jackson Cab (907/755-2557) and Screaming Eagle (907/755-2699). Available in Craig from Chief Wiah Cab (907/826-3375) and Craig–Klawock Taxi (907/755-2217).

Car rental: in Klawock at Practical Rent-A-Car (907/755-2424); in Craig at Wilderness Rent-A-Car (907/826-2205) and Craig Car Rentals (907/826-3701).

Highways: Prince of Wales Island has the most extensive road network in Southeast Alaska. Over 1,100 miles/1,770 km of road allows access to most areas of the island. The island's main roads are the Hollis–Klawock–Craig Highway, Big Salt Road, Thorne Bay Road, Hydaburg Road, Coffman Cove Road and North Island Road (USFS Road No. 20) to Labouchere Bay. See road logs in this section for details.

DRIVER CAUTION: Watch for heavily loaded logging trucks while driving; they have the right-of-way. CB radios are helpful. Carry a spare tire and spare gas. (Gas is available in Coffman Cove, Hydaburg, Craig, Klawock, Whale Pass and Thorne Bay.) Use turnouts and approach hills and corners on your side of the road. Spur roads are *NOT* recommended for large RVs or cars with trailers. Some side roads may be closed intermittently during logging operations or highway construction. Watch for signs posted when roads are closed and expect delays.

ATTRACTIONS

El Capitan Cave. Located just north of Whale Pass off the North Island Road, people have been visiting El Capitan Cave for many years. El Capitan's pit is one of the deepest known in the U.S. Northern Prince of Wales has extensive limestone cave systems. Significant scientific discoveries have

been found in these caves, including grizzly bear bones dating back 12,295 years, and black bear bones dating back 11,565 years.

There is a steep trail (more than 300 steps) leading to the cave entrance. Because of damage to cave formations, a gate has been installed to regulate visitation. There is open visitation to the gate some distance within the cave; guided tours beyond the gate. The 2-hour guided tours departed at 8 A.M., 10 A.M., 1 P.M. and 3 P.M., Wednesdays through Sundays, from mid-May to September in 1996; call for 1997 schedule. For guided tours, group size is limited to 6. For reservations write Thorne Bay Ranger District, Box 19001, Thorne Bay 99919; phone (907) 828-3304. There are vault toilets, a government dock, and a floatplane and boat tie-up at this U.S. Forest Service-administrated site.

AREA FISHING: Most fish in streams on the island are anadromous (travel upstream to spawn). Try **Klawock Lake** for trout and salmon; **Klawock River** downstream from the hatchery good for trout, steelhead and salmon; **Thorne River** for Dolly Varden and trout; and **Sarkar River** for trout, steelhead and salmon. Fresh and saltwater guiding services are available.

World-class saltwater sportfishing abounds immediately offshore and throughout the many smaller islands surrounding Prince of Wales Island. Most communities have boat ramps. For those traveling without a boat, quality half-, full- and multi-day fishing trips are available through many of the local charter operators. 100-lb. halibut, 50-lb. king (chinook) salmon and 15-lb. silver (coho) salmon are not considered uncommon in the sport season, usually May through August due to the weather and fish migration patterns. Abundant bottom fish, including lingcod and red snapper, reside throughout these waters year-round. 🐟

DESCRIPTION AND VISITOR SERVICES

COFFMAN COVE (pop. 254), 53 miles/85 km north of Klawock. Formerly one of the largest independent logging camps in Southeast, Coffman Cove is now a second-class city. Recreation includes hunting (deer and bear), good freshwater and saltwater fishing, boating, hiking, and also cable TV and VCRs. Canoe Lagoon Oyster Co. here is the state's oldest and largest oyster producer; fresh oysters available at the Riggin' Shack.

Coffman Cove has a general store, gift shop, gas pump, playground and ballfield. Tire repair available. There is a dock and a small beach with access to salt water for canoes and cartop boats. Rental cabins are available. EMTs dispatch from Riggin' Shack.

CRAIG (pop. 1,946), 31 miles/50 km from Hollis, is on the western shore of Prince of Wales Island. The original townsite, on Craig Island, is now connected to Prince of Wales by a short causeway. Craig has several hotels and lodges (see Accommodations this section), bed and breakfasts, and restaurants and fast food outlet. There is a grocery store, clothing and general merchandise stores, a gas station, a laundromat, gift shops, liquor stores, bars, beauty and barber shops, a library and 2 banks (one with automatic teller machine). There is a school, grades K through 12. An indoor community swimming pool was completed in 1995. Propane, towing and auto repair available.

Free RV dump facilities on Cold Storage Road. Contact City Public Works at (907) 826-3405 during business hours for key. Evenings and weekends, contact the police

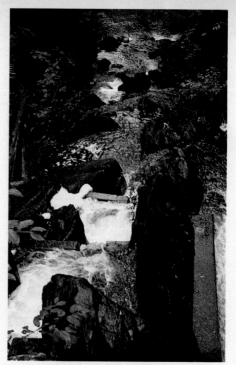

Lush vegetation at Cable Creek on Hydaburg Road. (Judy Parkin)

department at (907) 826-3330.

Craig Primary Health Care Facility, commonly known as the Craig clinic, is located just up the hill from the city municipal offices and is currently managed by the Craig Health Corp. The facility is approximately 4,300 square feet and is occupied by a physician and staff, public health nurses and the Craig Native health aide.

Physician services are generally available 24 hours a day except for brief periods of time when the physician is unavailable. An emergency room is provided at the clinic for treatment, minor surgery and stabilization of patients. Medications, emergency pharmaceuticals and medical supplies are available through the clinic (by doctor's prescription only; no retail pharmacies are located on the island). The clinic can take routine X-rays. Clinic hours are 9 A.M. to 5 P.M. Monday through Saturday in the summer; 9 A.M. to 5 P.M. weekdays in winter. Emergency Medical Services are available full-time at 911, or call Craig PD at (907) 826-3330. The Craig Native health aide and public health nurse are available weekdays from 9 A.M. to 4 P.M. Craig also has a chiropractic office and 2 dental clinics.

Craig has 2 modern boat harbors, North Cove and South Cove, located on either side of the causeway, a seaplane float, fuel dock, city dock and float, 2 fish-buying docks and an old cannery dock. The Craig harbormaster's office, with public showers and restrooms, is located on the corner close to South Cove; phone (907) 826-3404, VHF Channel 16.

Visitor information is available from Craig City Hall, phone (907) 826-3275, open weekdays 8 A.M. to 5 P.M.; U.S. Forest Service office, open weekdays 8 A.M. to 5 P.M., phone (907) 826-3271; Prince of Wales Chamber of Commerce, phone (907) 826-3870.

Craig was once a temporary fish camp for the Tlingit and Haida Natives of the area. In 1907, with the help of local Natives, William

D. Craig Millar established a mildcure station known as Fish Egg for nearby Fish Egg Island. The Tlingit name for Fish Egg Island is "Sheenda" and the townsite was "Sheen-sit," which is now used by the Native Shaan-Seet Corp. Between 1908 and 1911, a permanent saltery and cold storage facility, along with about 2 dozen homes, were built on the city's present location and named for founder Craig Millar. In 1912, the post office was established, E.M. Streeter opened a sawmill and Craig constructed a salmon cannery. Both businesses peaked during WWI. Craig was incorporated in 1922, and grew throughout the 1930s, with some families relocating from the Dust Bowl.

Although the salmon industry has both prospered and floundered over the years, fishing and fish processing still account for an important part of area employment. In recent years timber harvesting on the island has contributed many jobs in logging and timber processing. The Viking Lumber Co. mill, located between Craig and Klawock, provides year-round employment, producing moulding, window and door stock for the domestic market, and high-grade cants for export. The mill also produces wood chips for the manufacture of pulp. Timber will continue to be a viable economic influence on the island's economy for many years. Mining, transportation and tourism have the potential to become major employers in the foreseeable future. Construction and government jobs will increase as the island and its economy develop.

Craig is the home port of many commercial fishing and charter sportfishing boats due to its proximity to the fertile fishing grounds off the west coast of the island. Halibut, coho and chinook salmon, lingcod and red snapper (yelloweye) are the primary target species. Craig and Klawock host the annual Craig–Klawock King Salmon Derby from April to July 3, followed by a big Fourth of July parade and celebration. In early August the P.O.W. Chamber of Commerce sponsors its annual Fish Egg Seafest, an arts and crafts celebration of the fishing industry.

In 1996 the Healing Heart totem pole was raised in Craig. The totem was carved by Tsimshian master carver, Stan Marsden, in memory of his son.

HOLLIS (pop. 111), 25 road miles/40 km from Klawock, 35 nautical miles/56 km west of Ketchikan. Hollis was a mining town with a population of 1,000 from about 1900 to 1915. In the 1950s, Hollis became the site of Ketchikan Pulp Co.'s logging camp and served as the base for timber operations on Prince of Wales Island until 1962, when the camp was moved to Thorne Bay. Recent state land sales have spurred the growth of a small residential community here.

NOTE: Although Hollis is identified in the state ferry schedules as the port of call on Prince of Wales Island for the MV *Aurora* from Ketchikan, the ferry actually docks at Clark Bay, several miles from Hollis.

HYDABURG (pop. 406), 36 miles/58 km from Hollis, 45 miles/72 km from Craig. Hydaburg was founded in 1911, and combined the populations of 3 Haida villages: Sukkwan, Howkan and Klinkwan. President William Howard Taft established an Indian reservation on the surrounding land in 1912, but, at the residents' request, most of the land was restored to its former status as part of Tongass National Forest in 1926. Hydaburg was incorporated in 1927, 3 years after its people became citizens of the United States.

Most of the residents are commercial fishermen, although there are some jobs in construction and the timber industry. Subsistence is also a traditional and necessary part of life here. Hydaburg has an excellent collection of restored Haida totems. The totem park was developed in the 1930s by the Civilian Conservation Corps, which brought in poles from the three abandoned Haida villages. There is also good salmon fishing here in the fall.

Four boardinghouses provide rooms and meals for visitors. Groceries, hardware and sundry items available locally. There are a gift shop, gas station, public telephones, video store and cafe. Cable television is available.

KLAWOCK (pop. 759), 24 miles/39 km from Hollis. Klawock originally was a Tlingit Indian summer fishing village; a trading post and salmon saltery were established here in 1868. Ten years later a salmon cannery was built—the first cannery in Alaska and the first of several cannery operations in the area. Over the years the population of Klawock, like other Southeast communities, grew and then declined with the salmon harvest. The local economy is still dependent on fishing, along with timber cutting and sawmilling. A fish hatchery operated by Prince of Wales Hatchery Assoc. is located on Klawock Lake, very near the site of a salmon hatchery that operated from 1897 until 1917. Visitors are welcome. Klawock Lake offers good canoeing and boating.

Recreation here includes good fishing for salmon and steelhead in Klawock River, saltwater halibut fishing, and deer and bear hunting. Klawock's totem park contains 21 totems—both replicas and originals—from the abandoned Indian village of Tuxekan (developed by the Civilian Conservation Corps in 1938–40). A 5-year restoration project to restore and replace totems in the park was begun in 1995.

Groceries and gas are available in Klawock. Laundromat at Black Bear Quick Stop. Automatic teller machine located in A&P grocery store. Accommodations and meals available at Fireweed Lodge, Sunneyhae Lodge, Columbine Inn and Log Cabin Resort. Log Cabin Resort also offers RV campsites. Towing service available. Boat charters and rentals are also available. ▲

THORNE BAY (pop. 650), 59 miles/95 km from Hollis. Thorne Bay was incorporated in 1982, making it one of Alaska's newest cities. The settlement began as a logging camp in 1962, when Ketchikan Pulp Co. (a subsidiary of Louisiana Pacific Corp.) moved its operations from Hollis. Thorne Bay was connected to the island road system in 1974. Camp residents created the community—and gained city status from the state—as private ownership of the land was made possible under the Alaska Statehood Act. Employment here depends mainly on the lumber company and the U.S. Forest Service, with assorted jobs in municipal government and in local trades and services. Thorne Bay is centrally located between 2 popular Forest Service recreation areas: Eagle's Nest Campground and Sandy Beach picnic area. The Thorne River offers excellent canoeing and kayaking, and the bay offers excellent sailing and waterskiing (wet suit advised).

There are grocery and hardware stores, gas stations, small-boat repair, a tackle shop and a gift shop. Tire repair available. Accommodations available at several bed and breakfasts, lodges and rental cabins. Propane is available. Fuel oil is also available. Boat charters and rentals are available. Fuel for boats may be purchased at the Tackle Shack float (unleaded) and JC's float (diesel, unleaded). The Tackle Shack is open Monday through Saturday, 8 A.M. to 6 P.M., and 9 A.M. to 4 P.M. on Sunday. JC's is open daily, 7 A.M. to 6 P.M. Aviation fuel available through Petro Alaska. City-operated RV dump station. Facilities include boat dock (with potable water, power, sewer pumpout station and fish cleaning facilities), cement boat-launch ramp, helicopter landing pad, and floatplane float and parking facility. ▲

There is scheduled floatplane service to Thorne Bay from Ketchikan.

WHALE PASS (pop. 92), accessible by loop road from the North Island Road, was the site of a floating logging camp. The camp moved out in the early 1980s, but new residents moved in with a state land sale. The community has a small grocery store and gas pump; cabins and freezer space available. There is also a school, post office and floatplane dock there. Accommodations at Whale Pass Lodge and a bed and breakfast. Good fishing on the loop road into Whale Pass.

Hollis–Klawock–Craig Highway Log

This highway, 31.5 miles/50.7 km long, begins at the ferry landing at Hollis and heads west through Klawock then south to Craig, taking motorists through the temperate rainforest environment typical of Southeast Alaska. It is a wide, paved road. Posted speed is 35 to 50 mph/56 to 80 kmph. Many roads and trails off highway lead to private property; please respect barricades and No Trespassing signs. *CAUTION: Watch for logging trucks.*

Distance from Hollis (H) is followed by distance from Craig (C). Physical mileposts show distance from Craig.

H 0 C 31.5 (50.7 km) Alaska Marine Highway, Hollis ferry terminal at Clark Bay, open during ferry arrivals and departures only (phone 907/530-7115, or in Craig 826-3432)). Pay phone; no other services.

H 0.2 (0.3 km) **C 31.3** (50.4 km) Clark Bay subdivision access to right.

H 1.4 (2.3 km) **C 30.1** (48.4 km) Left 0.3 mile to Hollis townsite. School and USFS office, city harbor and float, floatplane dock, post office, telephone; no other services.

H 2 (3.2 km) **C 29.5** (47.5 km) Alaska Power and Telephone power plant and Alascom satellite station to left. Hollis Fire Department and EMS garage to right.

H 2.4 (3.9 km) **C 29.1** (46.8 km) **Maybeso Creek**, cutthroat; Dolly Varden; pink and silver salmon; steelhead run begins in mid-April. Pools offer the best fishing. Walking good along streambed but poor along bank. Watch for bears. ⬱

H 4.2 (6.8 km) **C 27.3** (43.9 km) Turnout left, view of mouth of the Harris River.

H 4.8 (7.7 km) **C 26.7** (43 km) Head left for lower Harris subdivision.

H 5.2 (8.4 km) **C 26.3** (42.3 km) Turnout, one of several slide-damaged areas from October 1993 storm that dumped 11 inches of rain in 24 hours.

H 6.4 (10.3 km) **C 25.1** (40.4 km) Entering Tongass National Forest.

H 6.5 (10.5 km) **C 25** (40.2 km) Head left for upper Harris subdivision.

H 7.7 (12.4 km) **C 23.8** (38.3 km) Turnout, slide damage repaired.

H 8.4 (13.5 km) **C 23.1** (37.2 km) USFS hiking trail to **Harris River** fishing: cutthroat; steelhead run mid-April; salmon and Dolly Varden run beginning in mid-July. Easy walking on the gravel bars in the middle of 1.3-mile/2.1-km-long river. 🐟

H 8.5 (13.7 km) **C 23** (37 km) Turnout, slide damage repaired.

H 10.5 (16.9 km) **C 21** (33.8 km) **Junction** with Hydaburg Road; see log page 665.

H 11.2 (18 km) **C 20.3** (32.7 km) USFS trailhead for 20 Mile Spur Trail (approximately 3 miles/4.8 km long).

H 11.3 (18.2 km) **C 20.2** (32.5 km) Harris River bridge.

H 12.4 (20 km) **C 19.1** (30.7 km) End of Harris River valley. Island divide is here at 500 feet/152m elev.; streams now flow west. Turnout state DOT gravel storage area.

H 12.6 (20.3 km) **C 18.9** (30.4 km) Leaving Tongass National Forest.

H 13.6 (21.9 km) **C 17.9** (28.8 km) East end of Klawock Lake, about 7 miles/11 km long and up to 1 mile/1.6 km wide. Lake borders the road on the left at several places. Private property; contact Heenya Corp. in Klawock.

H 16.1 (25.9 km) **C 15.4** (24.8 km) Turnout left, boat launch for Klawock Lake.

H 16.2 (26.1 km) **C 15.3** (24.6 km) 35 mph curve; believe the sign.

H 17.6 (28.3 km) **C 13.9** (22.4 km) Turnout left, view of Klawock Lake.

H 20.1 (32.3 km) **C 11.4** (18.3 km) Turnout right, view of Klawock Lake.

H 22 (35.4 km) **C 9.5** (15.3 km) Klawock Hatchery, operated by the city of Klawock and supported by island fishermen and businesses.

H 22.1 (35.6 km) **C 9.4** (15.1 km) Klawock-Heenya Trailer Court to right; turnout left for trail access to Klawock River sportfishing.

H 22.2 (35.7 km) **C 9.3** (15 km) Turnout left, access to Klawock River fishing.

H 22.3 (35.9 km) **C 9.2** (14.8 km) Turnout left, access to Klawock River fishing.

H 22.4 (36 km) **C 9.1** (14.6 km) Turnout left, access to Klawock River fishing.

H 22.5 (36.2 km) **C 9** (14.5 km) Klawock Lake Hatchery, operated by the Prince of Wales Assoc. The hatchery produces sockeye, coho and steelhead. Visitors welcome Monday through Friday, 8 A.M. to 4:30 P.M.

H 23.3 (37.5 km) **C 8.2** (13.2 km) Belltower Mall, grocery store, liquor store, gift shop, toy store, Papa's Pizza, arcade.

H 23.4 (37.7 km) **C 8.1** (13 km) **Junction** with Big Salt Road; access to Thorne Bay, Coffman Cove, Naukati, Whale Pass and the north end of the island.

H 23.5 (37.8 km) **C 8** (12.9 km) Turnoff right, services available.

H 23.7 (38.1 km) **C 7.8** (12.6 km) Fireweed Lodge to left, St. John's by the Sea Catholic Church to right. St. John's was designed and built with local lumber and materials by the local church community. The stained-glass designs, representing all known Native tribes, were designed and built by local artists. This is a "must-see" structure. Father Jim Blaney and Sister Tish

welcome the opportunity to show the church. Good eagle viewing in Klawock River estuary during salmon season.

H 23.8 (38.3 km) **C 7.7** (12.4 km) Loop road with 21 totem poles.

H 23.9 (38.5 km) **C 7.6** (12.2 km) Klawock-Heenya Corp. offices.

H 24.2 (38.9 km) **C 7.3** (11.7 km) **Klawock River** bridge spans tidal estuary where river meets salt water.

H 24.3 (39.1 km) **C 7.2** (11.6 km) Klawock Fuels (gas and diesel), Alaska State Troopers and Alaska Dept. of Fish and Game to left. Alesha Roberts Center.

H 24.5 (39.4 km) **C 7** (11.3 km) Entering village of **KLAWOCK**. State troopers in building on left.

H 24.6 (39.6 km) **C 6.9** (11.1 km) Turnoff right to Phoenix log sort yard, Phoenix shop and Klawock Indian Corp. dock. Ocean-going vessels load locally harvested logs for worldwide transport.

H 25 (40.2 km) **C 6.5** (10.5 km) Viking Lumber Co. mill; produces moulding, window and door stock for the domestic market and high-grade cants for export.

H 26.6 (42.8 km) **C 4.9** (7.9 km) Turnout right, scenic view of Klawock Inlet and San Alberto Bay.

H 27.9 (44.9 km) **C 3.6** (5.8 km) On left is landfill operated by city of Klawock. Bears can usually be seen here.

H 29.1 (46.8 km) **C 2.4** (3.9 km) Crab Creek subdivision.

H 29.3 (47.2 km) **C 2.2** (3.5 km) Crab Creek bridge.

H 29.8 (48 km) **C 1.7** (2.7 km) Shaan-Seet Trailer Court and St. Nicholas Road to left. St. Nicholas Road, which extends 14 miles/22.5 km around Port St. Nicholas, is scenic but in very poor condition.

H 30.2 (48.6 km) **C 1.3** (2.1 km) Craig schools to left, post office, bank and Thompson House supermarket on right.

H 30.3 (48.8 km) **C 1.2** (1.9 km) Cold Storage Road. Dmp station on right, behind supermarket.

H 30.4 (48.9 km) **C 1.1** (1.8 km) North and South Cove Harbors operated by the city of Craig. Turn left for Cemetery Island, ballpark and archaeological dig.

H 30.7 (49.4 km) **C 0.8** (1.3 km) Stop sign, downtown **CRAIG**. Turn left 1 block for Craig municipal offices and city gym. Craig clinic is on left, half block past city office. End of highway is 3 blocks right.

H 31 (49.9 km) **C 0.5** (0.8 km) Road dead ends.

Big Salt Road Log

Big Salt Road begins at **Milepost C 8.1** on the Hollis–Klawock–Craig Highway and extends 17.1 miles/27.5 km, ending at its junction with Thorne Bay Road. It is a gravel road with much logging traffic; scheduled for paving in 1997. Top speed for much of the road is 25 mph/40 kmph. Good berry picking for blueberries and huckleberries along the road.

Distance is measured from Klawock.

0 Black Bear Quick Stop: grocery store, laundromat and gas station.

0.1 (0.2 km) Klawock city trailer park on right with some overnight sites; obtain permits from the city clerk. A camping fee is charged. ▲

0.4 (0.6 km) Log Cabin R.V. Park &

Resort: tackle store, skiff rentals, lodging and campground. ▲

0.9 (1.4 km) Airport turnoff. Pavement ends.

8.7 (14 km) Big Salt Lake, actually a saltwater body protected by small islands but permitting tidal flow in and out, is visible to the left from several spots along road. Waterfowl and bald eagles are often observed here. Wreckage of a military aircraft can be seen across lake. The plane crashed in 1969 en route to Vietnam; all aboard survived.

8.9 (14.3 km) Boat ramp and canoe launching area on Big Salt Lake. If boating on this tidal lake, be aware of strong currents.

9.7 (15.6 km) **Black Bear Creek**, cutthroat; Dolly Varden; red, pink, dog and silver salmon, run mid-July to mid-September. Except for the lower 2 miles/3.2 km, creek can be fished from the bank. Best at the mouth of stream, 200 yards/183m upstream from the bridge or in large meadow, 1.5 miles/2.4 km from the mouth. Road on right leads to Black Lake. Watch for heavy equipment. 🐟

12.6 (20.3 km) **Steelhead Creek**, cutthroat; Dolly Varden; steelhead; pink, dog and silver salmon. Creek can be reached by boat through south entrance to Big Salt Lake. Lake should only be entered during high and low slack tides due to the strong tidal currents. High tide in lake is delayed 2 hours from outside waters. Bank fishing restricted by undergrowth. 🐟

15 (24.1 km) Lovely muskeg on right.

16.6 (26.7 km) Short boardwalk on right leads to **Control Lake**, cutthroat; Dolly Varden; pink and silver salmon; good red salmon stream in August. USFS cabin on other side is available for public use. Skiff docked at end of boardwalk is for registered cabin users. Wolf population in area. 🐟

17.1 (27.5 km) **Control Lake Junction.** End of Big Salt Road (SR 929); **junction** with Thorne Bay Road (USFS Road No. 30) and North Island Road (USFS Road No. 20). Road to Thorne Bay (log follows) is on the right. Road to Labouchere Bay, with access to Whale Pass and Coffman Cove, is on the left; see North Island Road log this section. Turn right for Eagle's Nest Campground. ▲

Thorne Bay Road Log

Thorne Bay Road extends 18 miles/29 km to Thorne Bay logging camp.
Physical mileposts show distance from Thorne Bay post office.

18 (29 km) **Junction** with Big Salt Road and North Island Road.

16.6 (26.7 km) Eagle's Nest USFS campground; 12 sites, tables, water, hand pump, toilet and canoe launch. Camping fee $8. **Balls Lake**, cutthroat; Dolly Varden; red, pink and silver salmon. 🐟▲

13 (20.9 km) Bridge. **Rio Roberts** and **Rio Beaver** creeks, cutthroat; pink and silver salmon. A 0.7-mile/1.1-km cedar-chip and double-plank boardwalk leads to a viewing deck overlooking falls and Rio Roberts Fish Pass. 🐟

10.7 (17.2 km) Rio Beaver Creek bridge.

6.7 (10.8 km) **Goose Creek**, cutthroat;

pink and silver salmon. Excellent spawning stream. Good run of pink salmon in mid-August. Lake Ellen Road on right leads 4.5 miles/7.2 km south to Lake No. 3 USFS campsite; space to accommodate up to 2 RVs, pit toilet, 2 fire rings and 2 picnic tables. No water or garbage. Road continues beyond campsite to lake and hiking trail to Salt Chuck. Abandoned Salt Chuck Mine is located here. ◂▲

6.5 (10.5 km) **Thorne River** runs beside road for the next 0.5 mile/0.8 km. Cutthroat; Dolly Varden; steelhead; rainbow; red, pink, dog and silver salmon. Excellent fishing reported from **Milepost 4.9 to 2.1.**◂

4.9 (7.9 km) Thorne River bridge. Thorne River now follows road on right.

4.1 (6.6 km) Falls Creek.

4 (6.4 km) Gravelly Creek USFS picnic area; walk in to picnic area on the bank of Thorne River at the mouth of Gravelly Creek; 3 tables, fire rings, vault toilet and open-sided shelter. This site was logged in 1918. Note the large stumps with notches. Notches were used by old-time loggers for spring boards to stand on while sawing or chopping.

3.7 (5.9 km) Gravelly Creek.

2.1 (3.4 km) Right, mouth of Thorne River.

1.3 (2.1 km) Log sorting area. Here different species of logs are sorted for rafting and transporting to mills or for export.

1.2 (1.9 km) Log raft holding area. After logs are sorted and tied into bundles, the bundles are chained together into a raft suitable for towing by tugboat.

0.7 (1.1 km) Dump station on Shoreline Drive just past Bayview Tire; $5 charge.

0 THORNE BAY. The road extends about 10 miles/16 km beyond the community to Sandy Beach day-use area with picnic shelter, 6 tables, fire rings, vault toilet and RV parking. Good view of Clarence Strait.

Hydaburg Road Log

The Hydaburg Road is 24 miles/38.6 km long and begins 11 miles/17.7 km west of the Hollis main ferry terminal on the Hollis–Klawock–Craig Highway. Opened in 1983, the road has been much improved. Road construction may be under way. Some sections of the road are heavily used by logging trucks. The road is scheduled for paving in 1997.

0 Junction with Hollis–Klawock–Craig Highway at **Milepost H 10.5.**

1.1 (1.8 km) Harris River bridge.

2.6 (4.2 km) Trailhead for One Duck 1.3-mile/2.1-km-long trail to alpine area and shelter. Contact the USFS office for more information on all trails along the Hydaburg Road.

4.6 (7.4 km) Bridge over Trocadero Creek.

8.9 (14.3 km) Cable Creek fish pass. Boardwalk to viewing area overlooking stream.

9.3 (15 km) Trocadero trailhead, gravel pullout.

9.5 (15.2 km) Trocadero picnic area. Picnic tables and fire grills; no toilets, trash service or water. Good view of Trocadero Valley.

9.9 (15.9 km) Road on left leads to Twelvemile Arm. This logging road leads to Polk Inlet. Watch for logging and construction activity.

12.3 (19.8 km) Trailhead for Soda Springs trail, 2.5 miles/4 km long.

13.9 (22.4 km) North Pass.

15.6 (25.1 km) Natzuhini logging camp.

15.9 (25.6 km) Natzuhini River bridge.

16.8 (27 km) Road winds along Natzuhini Bay.

21.9 (35.2 km) Hydaburg River bridge.

22.3 (35.9 km) Quarry Road to right.

23.6 (38 km) T-junction: right to Hydaburg, left to Saltery Point. Private land. No trespassing.

24 (38.6 km) **HYDABURG.**

North Island Road Log

Signed as USFS Road No. 20, this narrow 2-lane road leads north 79.5 miles/127.9 km from its junction with Big Salt and Thorne Bay roads near Control Lake to Labouchere Bay on the northwest corner of the island. The road has a fair to excellent gravel surfacing and some steep grades. Slow down for approaching vehicles. Posted speed is 25 mph/40 kmph. Gas is available at Whale Pass and Coffman Cove.

0 Control Lake Junction, junction with Big Salt and Thorne Bay roads near Control Lake.

3.1 (5 km) Drinking water on right (from hose); clearcut area.

4.8 (7.7 km) USFS Road No. 2050 leads west to upper Staney Creek/Horseshoe Hole and loops back to Road No. 20. Access to Staney Bridge campsite. ▲

7.4 (11.9 km) Rock quarry to east.

10.9 (17.5 km) USFS Road No. 2054 leads west to Staney Creek campsite, Staney Creek cabin and access to salt water. ▲

15.5 (24.9 km) **Junction** with Coffman Cove Road (see log on page 666).

18.4 (29.6 km) Naukati Creek.

19.2 (30.9 km) View to west of Tuxekan Island and Passage.

21 (33.8 km) Logging road leads west to Naukati Bay.

21.4 (34.4 km) Yatuk Creek bridge.

23.3 (37.5 km) **NAUKATI**, established and operating as a mining camp, is 3 miles/4.8 km west. The population has grown due

to a state land sale. Liquor, grocery, gas, boat rentals and boat repair available.

CAUTION: Road narrows northbound

26.5 (42.6 km) **Sarkar Lake** to east. Fishing and boat launch. USFS public-use cabin at east end of lake. Public toilets. Skiff docked at end of dock for registered cabin users only. ◂

27.9 (44.9 km) Bridge over Sarkar Lake outlet to salt water. Good spot to see eagles and sea lions during salmon season.

39.7 (63.9 km) USFS Road No. 25 leads east 7 miles/11.3 km past Neck Lake to small settlement of **WHALE PASS**; groceries and gas available, 4 cabins, floatplane dock, post office and school (1 teacher, 13 grades). Whale Pass Road loops back to the main North Island Road at **Milepost 48.6.**

40 (64.4 km) View of Neck Lake to east.

48.6 (78.2 km) Whale Pass loop road to east. Whale Pass is 8 miles/12.9 km from here; Exchange Cove is 16 miles/25.7 km from here.

50.3 (80.9 km) View of El Capitan Passage and Kosciusko Island to west.

51 (82.1 km) Side road leads west 1 mile/1.6 km to USFS El Cap Work Center; access to El Capitan Cave. Public toilets.

55.5 (89.5 km) Summit of the North Island Road (elev. 907 feet/276m). Keep an eye out for highbush cranberries.

59.5 (95.8 km) Rough road, heavy truck traffic and 1-lane bridges north from here.

60.6 (97.5 km) Red Creek 1-lane bridge.

61.7 (99.3 km) Big Creek 1-lane bridge.

63.9 (102.8 km) View of Red Bay to north; Red Lake is to the south.

67.6 (108.8 km) Buster Creek 1-lane bridge.

68.3 (109.9 km) Shine Creek 1-lane bridge.

72 (115.9 km) Flicker Creek 1-lane bridge.

72.1 (116 km) Memorial Beach picnic area 1.7 miles/2.7 km north; follow signs to parking area. A short trail leads to picnic tables, pit toilet, memorial plaque and beach. Good view of Sumner Strait and Kupreanof Island. This site is a memorial to 12 victims of a 1978 air crash.

79.5 (127.9 km) **LABOUCHERE BAY,** a small logging camp (no facilities) owned and operated by Louisiana Pacific Corp. The road continues several miles and dead ends at the base of Mount Calder.

Black bears may be seen on Prince of Wales Island. (© Roy Corral)

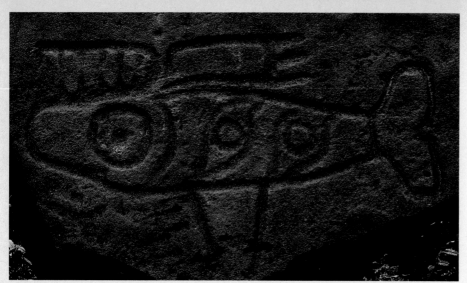

Petroglyphs are found on the beach in Wrangell. (© Kathleen Menke, Crystal Images)

Coffman Cove Road Log

Coffman Cove Road branches off the North Island Road (No. 20) at **Milepost 15.5** and leads east and north 20.5 miles/33 km to the logging camp of Coffman Cove. Watch for heavy truck traffic; 25 mph/40 kmph. Slow down for approaching vehicles.

0 Junction with North Island Road.

4.4 (7.1 km) Side road on left (USFS Road No. 30) leads 5 miles/8 km through clear-cut and dead ends.

4.5 (7.2 km) **Logjam Creek** bridge; cutthroat and steelhead; Dolly Varden; pink, silver and sockeye salmon.

9.1 (14.6 km) **Hatchery Creek** bridge; fishing same as Logjam Creek. Trailhead for canoe route to Thorne Bay.

9.4 (15.1 km) Bumpy road on right leads 13 miles/20.9 km to USFS access site; parking area and canoe launch (no trailers) on Luck Lake. Side road then loops north along Clarence Strait to Coffman Cove.

12.1 (19.5 km) View of Sweetwater Lake to left. USFS access site: parking area for Sweetwater public-use cabin, located 0.5 mile/0.8 km along west shore of lake.

17 (27.4 km) Coffman Creek bridge.
19.5 (31.4 km) Chum Creek bridge.
20.2 (32.5 km) **Junction** with Luck Lake loop road.
20.3 (32.7 km) Chum Creek bridge.
20.5 (33 km) **COFFMAN COVE**, a logging and fishing community; groceries, gas, cafe, rental cabins, gifts and local fresh oysters.

Wrangell
(See map, page 650)

Located at northwest tip of Wrangell Island on Zimovia Strait; 2.5 miles/4 km south of the Stikine River delta; 3 hours by ferry or 32 air miles/51 km southeast of Petersburg, the closest major community; and 6 hours by ferry or 85 air miles/136 km north of Ketchikan. **Population:** 2,400. **Emergency Services:** Phone 911 for all emergencies. **Police**, phone (907) 874-3304. **Fire Department** and Am-

bulance, phone (907) 874-2000. **Hospital**, Wrangell General, 310 Bennett St. just off Zimovia Highway, phone (907) 874-3356. **Maritime Search and Rescue**, contact the Coast Guard at 1-800-478-5555.

Visitor Information: Center located in the Stikine Inn Building at 107 Stikine Ave., near the cruise ship dock; phone 1-800-367-9745 or (907) 874-3901, fax (907) 874-3905, Internet: www.wrangell.com, e-mail: wrangell@wrangell.com. Write: Chamber of Commerce, Box 49MP, Wrangell 99929. Information is also available at the Wrangell Museum, 318 Church St.

The U.S. Forest Service maintains several recreation sites and trails along the Wrangell Island road system, as well as wilderness cabins. Contact the USFS office in Wrangell at (907) 874-2323.

Elevation: Sea level. **Climate:** Mild and moist with slightly less rain than other Southeast communities. Mean annual precipitation is 79.2 inches, with 63.9 inches of snow. Record monthly precipitation, 20.43 inches in October 1961. Average daily maximum temperature in June is 61°F/16°C; in July 64°F/18°C. Daily minimum in January is 21°F/-6°C. **Radio:** KSTK-FM 101.7. **Television:** Cable and satellite. **Newspaper:** *Wrangell Sentinel* (weekly).

Private Aircraft: Wrangell airport, adjacent northeast; elev. 44 feet/13m; length 6,000 feet/1,829m; paved; fuel 100LL, A.

Wrangell is the only Alaskan city to have existed under 4 nations and 3 flags—the Stikine Tlingits, the Russians, Great Britain and the United States. Wrangell began in 1834 as a Russian stockade called Redoubt St. Dionysius, built to prevent the Hudson's Bay Co. from fur trading up the rich Stikine River to the northeast. The Russians, in a change of policy, leased the mainland of southeastern Alaska to Hudson's Bay Co. in 1840. Under the British the stockade was called Fort Stikine.

The post remained under the British flag until Alaska was purchased by the United States in 1867. A year later the Americans established a military post here, naming it Fort Wrangell after the island, which was named by the Russians after Baron von Wrangel, a governor of the Russian–American Co.

Its strategic location near the mouth of the Stikine River, the fastest free-flowing navigable river in North America, made Wrangell an important supply point not only for fur traders but also for gold seekers following the river route to the goldfields. Today, the Stikine River is a popular hunting and recreation area. Currently, there is an active hard rock mine on the largest tributary of the Stikine, the Iskut. They are extracting gold, silver, copper and traces of other minerals from the site.

Wrangell serves as a hub for goods, services and transportation for outlying fishing villages, and logging and mining camps. The town depended largely on fishing until Japanese interests arrived in the mid-1950s and established a mill downtown (now

Wrangell

Sun totem on Wrangell's Shakes Island.

(© James D. Ronan, Jr.)

closed). A small, locally owned mill is now in operation 2 miles/3.2 km beyond the end of Zimovia Highway, off Forest 6265. Fishing is one of Wrangell's largest industries, with salmon the major catch.

ACCOMMODATIONS/VISITOR SERVICES

Wrangell has several motels including the Stikine Inn (907/874-3388) and Hardings Old Sourdough Lodge (907/874-3613). There are also several bed and breakfasts.

The Wrangell Hostel is located in the Presbyterian church, about ¼ mile from the ferry terminal, next to the Wrangell Museum. Open from June 9 to Labor Day, 5 P.M. to 9 A.M.; $10/night; phone (907) 874-3534.

There are 4 restaurants downtown, as well as service stations, hardware and appliance stores, banks, drugstore, laundromat, grocery stores (1 with a bakery and deli), a fish market and gift shops. Bed-and-breakfasts are available. Lodges with restaurants are located on Peninsula Street and at Mile 4.4 Zimovia Highway.

RV camping and picnic area at Shoemaker Bay, **Milepost 4.9** Zimovia Highway. Dump stations located at Shoemaker Bay and downtown at the corner of Front Street and Case Avenue. City Park, at **Milepost 1.9** Zimovia Highway, has tent sites, picnic area with tables, flush toilets, shelters and playground. ▲

TRANSPORTATION

Air: Daily scheduled jet service is provided by Alaska Airlines to other Southeast cities with through service to Seattle and Anchorage. Scheduled commuter air service to Petersburg, Kake and Ketchikan. Charter service available.

Airport terminal is 1.1 miles/1.8 km from ferry terminal or 1.1 miles/1.8 km from

Zimovia Highway on Bennett Street. Hotel courtesy vans are available from the airport to downtown. Taxi service is also available for about $5.

Ferry: Alaska Marine Highway vessels connect Wrangell with all Southeastern Alaska ports plus Prince Rupert, BC, and Bellingham, WA. See MARINE ACCESS ROUTES section for details. Ferry terminal is at the north end of town at the end of Zimovia Highway (also named Church or 2nd Street at this point). Walk or take a taxi from terminal to town for approximately $4. Tours for independent travelers are available downtown. Terminal facilities include ticket office, waiting room and vehicle waiting area. Phone (907) 874-3711.

Car Rental: Available from Practical Rent-A-Car (907) 874-3975.

Taxi: Available to/from airport and ferry terminal. Approximate cost is $4 and $5.

Highways: Zimovia Highway (see log this section). Logging roads have opened up most of Wrangell Island to motorists. Check with the USFS office at 525 Bennett St. for a copy of the Wrangell Island Road Guide map. (Write USDA Forest Service, Wrangell Ranger District, Box 51, Wrangell, AK 99929; phone 907/874-2323.) City maps are also available at the Chamber of Commerce Visitor Center downtown.

Cruise Ships: Wrangell is a regular port of call in summer for several cruise lines.

Private Boats: Transient floats are located downtown and 4.5 miles/7.2 km south of Wrangell on Zimovia Highway at Shoemaker Bay Harbor. Reliance Float is located near Shakes Tribal House.

ATTRACTIONS

Shakes Island and Tribal House, in Wrangell Harbor, is reached by boardwalk. It is the site of several excellent totem poles. The replica tribal house contains Indian working tools, an original Chilkat blanket design carved on a house panel and other cultural items. It is listed on the National Register of Historic Places. Open irregular hours when cruise ships are in port during summer (May to September) or by appointment; phone (907) 874-3747 or u874-2023. Admission $1.50.

Totem Poles. The last original totems standing in Wrangell were cut down in November 1981 and removed for preservation. A totem restoration project funded by both state and federal agencies was initiated, and replicas of original totems can be found at Kiksadi Totem Park at the corner of Front and Episcopal streets.

Wrangell Museum, at 318 Church St., features local history and includes displays representing Tlingit, Russian, British, Chinese, Japanese and American influences in Wrangell. Gold rush, trapping, logging and fishing industry exhibits depict Wrangell's boom and bust economy. May to September hours are: 10 A.M. to 5 P.M. weekdays, 1–5 P.M. Saturdays. October to April hours are: 10–11:30 A.M., 12:30–4 P.M. Tuesday through Friday, closed Saturday and Sunday. Open for cruise ships and ferries in port longer than one hour on Saturdays and Sundays when staffing available. Phone (907) 874-3770; fax (907) 874-3785. Admission for adults, $2; children 16 and under, free.

Our Collections Museum, located on Evergreen Avenue, is a private collection of antiques and Alaska memorabilia. Open when cruise ships and ferries are in port and

by special request. Phone (907) 874-3646. Donations accepted.

Sightseeing Tours of attractions and fish bakes are available upon request. Sightseeing buses meet some ferries and cruise ships. Inquire at the visitor center or Wrangell Museum. Flightseeing and jetboat excursions available to Stikine River, Stikine Icefield, Anan Wildlife Observatory and other remote locations.

Celebrations in Wrangell include a big Fourth of July celebration which begins with a salmon bake. The annual Tent City Festival, celebrated the first weekend in February, commemorates Wrangell's gold rush days. The Garnet Festival, celebrated the third week of April, marks the arrival of spring and the annual bald eagle migration on the Stikine River. The festival celebrates the arts with family activities, and includes a golf tournament at Muskeg Meadows.

Petroglyphs are ancient designs carved into rock faces, usually found between low and high tide marks on beaches. Petroglyph Beach is located 0.7 mile/1.1 km from the ferry terminal; a boardwalk trail leads to the head of the beach from the left of the road. Turn right as you reach the beach and look for petroglyphs between there and a rock outcrop several hundred feet away; at times as many as 40 can be seen. Petroglyphs are also located on the library lawn and are on display in the museum.

Muskeg Meadows. By summer 1998, Wrangell will have a 9-hole, 36-acre regulation golf course and driving range. Six holes and the driving range are currently playable. Annual tournaments have been inaugurated. Contact the Wrangell Golf Assoc., Box 2199, Wrangell, AK 99929, or association president Hartshorn, phone (907) 874-3989.

Anan Observatory, managed by the U.S. Forest Service, is located 35 miles/56 km southeast of Wrangell; accessible by boat or plane only. During July and August, visitors can watch bears catch pink salmon headed for the salmon spawning grounds. Bald eagles, ravens, crows and seals are frequently seen feeding on the fish. Contact the visitor center for list of guides permitted to transport visitors to Anan (1-800-367-9745).

Wrangell Salmon Derby runs from mid-May to Memorial Day weekend. Kings weighing more than 50 lbs. are not unusual.

Garnet Ledge, a rocky outcrop on the right bank of the Stikine River delta at Garnet Creek, is 7.5 miles/12.1 km from Wrangell Harbor, reached at high tide by small boat. Garnet, a semiprecious stone, can be found embedded in the ledge here. The garnet ledge is on land deeded to the Southeast Council of the Boy Scouts of America and the children of Wrangell by the late Fred Hanford (former mayor of Wrangell). The bequest states that the land shall be used for scouting purposes and the children of Wrangell may take garnets in reasonable quantities (garnets are sold by children at the docks when ships and ferries are in port). Contact the Wrangell Museum (Box 1050, Wrangell 99929; phone 907/874-3770) for information on digging for garnets.

The Stikine River delta lies north of Wrangell within the Stikine–LeConte Wilderness. It is accessible by boat or by plane only. The delta is habitat for migrating waterfowl, eagles, bears and moose. During the spring run, the second largest concentration of bald eagles in the world can be seen in the Stikine River delta. Also watch for seals resting on ice floes from LeConte Glacier. The glacier is at the head of LeConte Bay, just north of the delta. It is the southernmost tidewater glacier in North America. It is also an actively calving glacier, known for its prodigious iceberg production.

USFS trails, cabins and recreation sites on Wrangell Island and in the surrounding area are a major attraction here. Nemo Campsites, for example, only 14 miles/22.5 km south of Wrangell, provides spectacular views of Zimovia Strait and north Etolin Island. No reservations or fees required. Parking areas, picnic tables, fire grills and outhouses at each campsite.

USFS public-use cabins in the Wrangell district are accessible by air or by boat. The 22 USFS cabins are scattered throughout the region. See also Cabins in the GENERAL INFORMATION section.

For details on these sites and others, contact the Forest Service district office at (907) 874-2323, or stop by the USFS office at 525 Bennett St. You may also write the Wrangell Ranger District at Box 51, Wrangell, AK 99929. White courtesy phone located in the ferry terminal building.

AREA FISHING: The Wrangell Island forest road system provides access to several recreation sites and trails with fishing. For more information contact the USFS office in Wrangell at (907) 874-2323.

Fly in to **Thoms Lake, Long Lake, Marten Lake, Salmon Bay, Virginia Lake** and **Eagle Lake.** Thoms Lake and Long Lake are also accessible via road and trail. **Stikine River** near Wrangell (closed to king salmon fishing), Dolly Varden to 22 inches, and cutthroat to 18 inches, best in midsummer to fall; steelhead to 12 lbs., use bait or lures; coho salmon 10 to 15 lbs., use lures, September and October. Saltwater fishing near Wrangell for king salmon, 20 to 40 lbs., best in May and June. Stop by the Dept. of Fish and Game at 215 Front St. for details. ⟻

Zimovia Highway Log

Zimovia Highway leads south from the ferry terminal to Pat Creek at Mile 11, where it connects with island logging roads.

0 Alaska Marine Highway ferry terminal, ticket office and waiting area. There is a bike path to Mile 1.9.

0.3 (0.5 km) St. Rose of Lima Catholic Church, the oldest Roman Catholic parish in Alaska, founded May 2, 1879.

0.4 (0.6 km) First Presbyterian Church has a red-lighted cross, 1 of 2 in the world that serve as navigational aids. This was the first church in Wrangell and is one of the oldest Protestant churches in Alaska (founded in 1877 and built in 1879).

Wrangell Museum interim location situated between the church and Wrangell High School.

0.6 (1 km) Bennett Street (Airport Road) loops north 2.2 miles/3.5 km to the airport and back to the ferry terminal.

0.7 (1.1 km) Public Safety Bldg.

1.9 (3.1 km) City park. Picnic area with shelters, firepits, restrooms, litter barrels. Tent camping only allowed; 24-hour limit. ▲

3.6 (5.8 km) Turnout with beach access. Several turnouts along the highway here offer beach access and good spots for bird watching.

4.4 (7.1 km) Lodge on left with restaurant and lounge.

4.9 (7.9 km) Shoemaker Bay small-boat harbor, boat launch, picnic, camping and parking area. Camping area has tent sites, 29 RV sites ($10 per night, with hookups), water, dump station and restrooms. Tennis court, horseshoe pits and children's playground nearby. Rainbow Falls trailhead; 0.7-mile/1.1-km trail to scenic waterfall. Institute Creek trail intersects with Rainbow Falls trail Mile 0.6 mile and leads 2.7 miles/4.3 km to viewpoint and shelter overlooking Shoemaker Bay and Zimovia Strait. ▲

6.5 (10.5 km) Alaska Pulp Corp. (not operating).

7.3 (11.7 km) Milepost 7, scenic turnout.

8 (12.9 km) Turnout.

8.5 (13.7 km) Turnout, beach access (8 Mile Beach undeveloped recreation area).

10.8 (17.4 km) Access road west to Pat Creek Log Transfer Facility and small boat launch. Road east (Pat Creek Road) is a 1-lane, maintained, crushed rock road with turnouts. It leads 0.3 mile/0.5 km to Pat's Lake, and continues approximately 6 miles/10 km northeast through both old and active logging areas.

Pat Creek and **Pat's Lake**, cutthroat, Dolly Varden, pink and silver salmon, spinning gear or flies.

11 (17.7 km) Pat Creek camping area (unmaintained, no facilities); parking for self-contained vehicles. ▲

11.1 (17.9 km) State-maintained highway ends. Begin 1-lane Forest Development Road No. 6265 connecting with other Forest Service roads (map showing many island recreation sites and trails available from USFS office in Wrangell). Watch for logging trucks and other heavy equipment.

14 (22.5 km) **Junction** with USFS Road 6267, which leads to the Nemo campsites. Spectacular views of Zimovia Strait and north Etolin Island, parking areas, picnic tables, fire grills and outhouses at each site. No reservations or fees required. ▲

Petersburg
(See map, page 657)

Located on the northwest tip of Mitkof Island at the northern end of Wrangell Narrows, midway between Juneau and Ketchikan. **Population:** 3,350. **Emergency Services:** Phone 911. **Alaska State Troopers,** phone (907) 772-3100. **City Police, Poison Center, Fire Department** and **Ambulance,** phone (907) 772-3838. **Hospital,** Petersburg General, 1st and Fram streets, phone (907) 772-4291. **Maritime Search and Rescue:** contact the Coast Guard at 1-800-478-5555. Harbormaster, phone (907) 772-4688, CB Channel 9, or VHF Channel 16.

Visitor Information: Chamber of Commerce/USFS Information Center located at 1st and Fram streets; open daily from 9 A.M. to 5 P.M. spring and summer, 10 A.M. to 2 P.M. fall and winter. Write: Chamber of Commerce, Box 649MP, Petersburg 99833; phone/fax (907) 772-3646. For national forest information, write Petersburg Visitor Information Center, Box 1328, Petersburg 99833; phone (907) 772-4636. Petersburg Museum, 2nd and Fram streets, open daily in summer, limited winter hours; phone (907) 772-3598. Alaska Dept. of Fish and Game, State Office Building, Sing Lee Alley; open 8 A.M. to 4:30 P.M., Monday through Friday.

Elevation: Sea level. **Climate:** Average daily maximum temperature in July, 64°F/18°C; daily minimum in January, 20°F/-7°C. All-time high, 84°F/29°C in 1933; record low, -19°F/-28°C in 1947. Mean annual precipitation, 105 inches; mean annual snowfall, 119 inches. **Radio:** KRSA 580, KFSK-FM 100.9. **Television:** Alaska Rural Communication Service, Channel 15; KTOO (PBS) Channel 9 and cable channels. **Newspaper:** *Petersburg Pilot* (weekly).

Private Aircraft: James A. Johnson Airport, 1 mile/1.6 km southeast; elev. 107 feet/33m; length 6,000 feet/1,829m; asphalt; fuel 100, A. Seaplane base 0.5 mile/0.8 km from downtown.

Petersburg was named for Peter Buschmann, who selected the present townsite for a salmon cannery and sawmill in 1897. The sawmill and dock were built in 1899, and the cannery was completed in 1900. He was followed by other Norwegian–Americans who came to fish and work in the cannery and sawmill. Since then the cannery has operated continuously (with rebuilding, expansion and different owners) and is now known as Petersburg Fisheries Inc., a division of Icicle Seafoods Inc.

Today, Petersburg boasts the largest home-based halibut fleet in Alaska and is also well known for its shrimp, crab, salmon, herring and other fish products. Most families depend on the fishing industry for livelihood. Sportfishing questions should be directed to the Alaska Dept. of Fish and Game's Division of Sportfishing in Ketchikan, phone (907) 225-2859.

ACCOMMODATIONS/VISITOR SERVICES

Petersburg has a hotel and several motels, including Scandia House (907/772-4301), Tides Inn (907/772-4288) and Narrows Inn. There are also bed and breakfasts, many restaurants and several fast-food outlets downtown. The 5-block-long commercial area on Main Street (Nordic Drive) has grocery stores, marine and fishing supply stores, hardware, drugstores, travel agency, public showers, banks, gift and variety stores specializing in both Alaskan and Scandinavian items, city hall, post office, gas stations, cocktail bars, a community gym with racquetball courts and a public swimming pool. Petersburg has 13 churches.

There are 3 RV parks, dump station, hookups, showers, laundry; fee charged. There is a tent campground (known locally as Tent City) on Haugen Drive; it is often filled to capacity in summer with young cannery workers. Public campgrounds (1 developed, several undeveloped) are located on Mitkof Highway south of town. ▲

TRANSPORTATION

Air: Daily scheduled jet service by Alaska Airlines to major Southeast cities and Seattle, WA, with connections to Anchorage and Fairbanks. Local and charter service available.

The airport is located 1 mile/1.6 km from the Federal Building on Haugen Drive. It has a ticket counter and waiting room. There is no shuttle service to town; hotel courtesy vans and taxis are available for a fee.

Ferry: Alaska Marine Highway vessels connect Petersburg with all Southeastern Alaska cities plus Prince Rupert, BC, and Bellingham, WA. (See MARINE ACCESS

ROUTES section for schedules.) Terminal at **Milepost 0.8** Mitkof Highway, includes dock, ticket office with waiting room, and parking area. Phone (907) 772-3855.

NOTE: RVs arriving late at night are allowed to park free for up to 8 hours at the south boat harbor parking lot just north of the ferry terminal.

Car Rental: Avis Rent-A-Car at Tides Inn, (907/772-4716), and All Star, Scandia House, (907/772-4281).

Taxi: There are 2 taxi companies. Cab service to and from the airport and ferry terminal.

Highways: Mitkof Highway, Sandy Beach Road and Three Lakes Loop Road (see logs this section).

Cruise Ships: Smaller cruise ships dock ¼ mile from town. Vans take passengers to town.

Private Boats: Boaters must check with harbormaster for moorage assignment.

ATTRACTIONS

Little Norway Festival is scheduled for May 15–18, 1997, as a celebration for Norwegian Independence Day. Pageantry, old-country dress, contests, Vikings, a Viking ship, dancing and a Norwegian "fish feed" for locals and visitors are featured.

Clausen Memorial Museum, 203 Fram St., features Petersburg area history. On display are artifacts representing the cannery and fisheries, a world-record 126.5-lb. king salmon, the Cape Decision light station lens, a Tlingit canoe and the wall piece "Land, Sea, Sky." Open Wednesday and Saturday, 12:30–4:30 P.M., Oct. 1 to April 30. Open daily, 9:30 A.M. to 4:30 P.M., May 1 to Sept. 21. Phone (907) 772-3598 for programs, updated visitor information and to

Petersburg

Cork floats decorate a house in Petersburg. (© Rich Reid)

leave messages. Accessible for movement-impaired visitors.   &

The Fisk (Norwegian for fish), a 10-foot/3-m bronze sculpture commemorating Petersburg's fishing tradition, stands in a working fountain in front of the museum. It was completed during the Alaska centennial year of 1967 by sculptor Carson Boysen.

Sons of Norway Hall, on the National Register of Historic Places, was built in 1912. Situated on pilings over Hammer Slough (a favorite photography subject), its window shutters are decorated with rosemaling (Norwegian tole painting).

LeConte Glacier, in LeConte Bay, 25 miles/40 km east of Petersburg, is the continent's south-ernmost tidewater glacier. Fast-moving, the glacier continu-ally "calves," crea-ting ice falls from its face into the bay. Seals and porpoises are common; whales are often seen. Helicopters, small aircraft and boats may be chartered in Petersburg or Wrangell to see LeConte Glacier.

Salmon migration and spawning are best observed in the Petersburg area July though September Falls Creek bridge and fish ladder is a good location (silver and pink) as are Blind Slough and the Blind River Rapids area, Petersburg Creek and Ohmer Creek (king, silver, pink and chum).

Crystal Lake Fish Hatchery is at **Milepost 17.5** Mitkof Highway. This hatchery for coho, king and steelhead is operated by the state and used for fish-stocking projects in southeastern Alaska. It is open for visits, and hatchery personnel will explain the operation, though formal guided tours are not available. Best time to visit is between 8 A.M. and 4 P.M., Monday through Friday.

Falls Creek fish ladder is at **Milepost 10.8** Mitkof Highway. The ladder helps migrating salmon bypass difficult falls on the way to spawning grounds in Falls Creek. It can be observed from the creek bank just off the roadside. Best time is late summer and early fall to observe coho and pink salmon.

Petersburg King Salmon Derby is scheduled for Memorial Day weekend May 23–26, 1997; $30,000 in prizes is awarded. Check with the chamber of commerce for details.

Charter a Boat or Plane. There are charter boat services in Petersburg for guided salt- and freshwater fishing trips. Inquire at the visitor information center. Charter floatplanes and helicopters are available for flightseeing, including whale watching, fly-in fishing and transportation.

Kaleidoscope Cruises specializes in glacier ecology, whale-watcing, custom sightseeing and fishing. Professional biologist and naturalist, Barry Bracken, skipper of the comfortable 28-foot *Island Dream,* has over 25 years experience in Southeast Alaskan waters, conducting biological research, exploring, and sportfishing. Half-day, full-day, overnight tours. 1-800-TO-THE-SEA. [ADVERTISEMENT]

AREA FISHING: Salmon, steelhead, cutthroat and Dolly Varden at **Falls Creek, Blind Slough** and **Blind River Rapids**; see log of Mitkof Highway this section. Salmon can be caught in the harbor area and **Scow Bay** area. (Rapid tidal currents in front of the town necessitate the use of an outboard motor.) **Petersburg Creek**, directly across Wrangell Narrows from downtown within Petersburg Creek–Duncan Salt Chuck Wilderness Area, also offers good fishing. Blind Slough, located 15 miles/24 km south of the ferry terminal, offers good drive-up fishing for king salmon. Dolly Varden can be caught from the beach north of town and from downtown docks. Sportfishing opportunities for halibut, rockfish, crab and shrimp. Harvest of mussels, clams and the like is not recommended because of the possibility of paralytic shellfish poisoning. Contact the Sport Fish Division of the Alaska

Dept. of Fish and Game (907/225-2859) for additional information.   📣

Wrangell Narrows is a 23-mile-/37-km-long channel between Mitkof and Kupreanof islands. The channel was dredged in the 1940s to a depth of 26 feet/42m. Extremely narrow in places and filled with rocky reefs, islands and strong currents, the narrows is navigated by ships and ferries with the aid of dozens of markers and flashing lights. The $1^1/_2$-hour run through Wrangell Narrows begins immediately on ferries departing Petersburg southbound, or about $1^1/_2$ hours after departing Wrangell northbound.

Cabins, canoe/kayaking routes and hiking trails managed by the U.S. Forest Service are all within reach of Petersburg, which is the administrative center for the Stikine Area of Tongass National Forest. Stop by the USFS office in the Federal Building, or phone (907) 772-3871 for detailed information on cabins and trails. Also consult *The ALASKA WILDERNESS GUIDE.* See also Cabins in the GENERAL INFORMATION section. Information for canoers and kayakers interested in the Stikine River delta or Tebenkof Bay is also available here or at the USFS office in Wrangell.

Sandy Beach Road Log

From Federal Building, drive north through town; road leads to Sandy Beach Recreation Area.

0 Federal Building and post office.

0.1 (0.2 km) Petersburg boat harbor 1 block to left, contains one of Alaska's finest fishing fleets.

0.2 (0.3 km) Downtown Petersburg.

0.3 (0.5 km) Petersburg Fisheries Inc., the city's largest processing plant.

Eagles Roost Park. Eagles feed on beach at low tide; best viewing in early summer.

1.2 (1.9 km) Eagle observation point. Eagles can be seen nesting nearby and fishing in Wrangell Narrows. To the northeast is Frederick Sound and the mainland.

2 (3.2 km) Bed and breakfast, sightseeing cruises.

2.8 (4.5 km) Sandy Beach Recreation Area on left; picnic tables, playground, volleyball court, shelter, toilets, limited parking, no camping. **Junction** with Haugen Drive, which loops to airport and back to town.

Just past Sandy Beach Recreation Area is the Fredrick Point boardwalk, a 1-mile/1.6-km trail that leads through the woods to the beach near Fredrick Point. This trail is very popular in summer.

Mitkof Highway Log

The major road on the island, Mitkof Highway leads 33.8 miles/54.4 km south from the Federal Building to the Stikine River delta at the south end of Mitkof Island. The highway is paved to **Milepost 17.5**; good wide gravel to road end.

0 Federal Building and post office.

0.1 (0.2 km) Bridge over Hammer Slough, an intertidal estuary.

0.5 (0.8 km) Harbor parking and RV staging area (8-hour RV parking).

0.6 (1 km) Pier and floatplane base.

0.8 (1.3 km) Alaska Marine Highway ferry terminal, office and waiting area on right.

2.8 (4.5 km) Muskeg meadows on left. Muskeg is a grassy bog, common in Alaska.

2.9 (4.6 km) **Scow Bay**, a wide portion of Wrangell Narrows with king salmon fishing in spring. Scow Bay is noted traditionally as the first election precinct to report its vote in statewide elections. Scow Bay Loop Road rejoins highway at **Milepost 3.1**. ⚓

4 (6.4 km) Lodging on right.

4.3 (6.9 km) Turnout on right with view of Wrangell Narrows.

7.5 (12.1 km) Twin Creek RV Park, private campground, small store and phone. ▲

10.7 (17.2 km) North exit to Three Lakes Loop Road (see log this section).

10.8 (17.4 km) **Falls Creek** and fish ladder. Steelhead, April and May; pink salmon below falls in August; coho, August and September; Dolly Varden and cutthroat late summer and fall. No fishing within 300 feet of fish ladder. ⚓

11 (17.7 km) Road on right leads 0.5 mile/0.8 km to Papke's Landing; transient boat moorage and boat ramp. USFS Log Transportation Facility.

14.3 (23 km) Entering Tongass National Forest.

14.5 (23.3 km) Blind River Rapids parking area and trail; new outhouse. 0.3-mile/0.4-km boardwalk trail through muskeg meadow to **Blind River Rapids**, hatchery steelhead, mid-April to mid-May; king salmon, June to late July; coho, mid-August to October. Also Dolly Varden and cutthroat trout. ⚓

16.3 (26.2 km) Blind Slough waterfowl viewing area on right. Covered platform with interpretive sign on area waterfowl. Trumpeter swans winter in this area.

17.5 (28.2 km) Pavement ends; wide, hard-packed gravel to end of road. Short road leads to Crystal Lake Fish Hatchery and **Blind Slough** Recreation Area with picnic tables, shelter and pit toilets; no overnight camping. Hatchery is open for visiting, though no scheduled tours are available. Fishing for steelhead, best in May; cutthroat and Dolly Varden in summer; coho salmon, mid-August to mid-September; king salmon in June and July. ⚓

20 (32.2 km) **Manmade Hole** picnic area with tables, firepits, swimming and short trail. Ice skating in winter. Fishing for cutthroat and Dolly Varden year-round; best in summer and fall. ⚓

20.6 (33.1 km) Three Lakes Loop Road begins on left leading to Three Lakes on other side of Mitkof Island, looping back to Mitkof Highway at **Milepost 10.7** near Falls Creek bridge.

21.4 (34.4 km) Woodpecker Cove Road (1-lane) leads about 15 miles/24 km along south Mitkof Island to Woodpecker Cove and beyond. Good views of Sumner Strait. Watch for logging trucks.

21.5 (34.6 km) Ohmer Creek interpretive trail, 0.1 mile/0.2 km long; handicapped accessible. ♿

21.7 (34.9 km) Ohmer Creek Campground, 10 sites (2 are wheelchair accessible), toilets, parking area, picnic tables, drinking water and firepits. Set in meadow area among trees. Open spring to fall; no fee, no restrictions. ♿▲

24 (38.6 km) Blind Slough USFS Log Transportation Facility. Excellent fishing from skiff for king salmon in June and July; coho salmon, mid-August to mid-September. ⚓

26.1 (42 km) Narrow 0.7-mile/1.1-km road on right to Sumner Strait Campground,

locally called Green's Camp (undeveloped); must walk in, no facilities. May be inaccessible at high tide. ▲

27 (43.4 km) View of city of Wrangell.

28 (45 km) Wilson Creek state recreation area (undeveloped); picnic tables, parking, outhouse. Good view of Sumner Strait.

28.6 (46 km) Banana Point, boat ramp, outhouse.

31 (49.9 km) Stikine River mud flats, visible on right at low tide. Part of the Stikine River delta, this is the area where Dry Strait meets Sumner Strait.

33.8 (54.4 km) Road ends with turnaround.

Three Lakes Loop Road Log

Access to this 21.4-mile-/34.4-km-long, 1-lane loop road is from **Mileposts 10.7** and **20.6** on the Mitkof Highway. *CAUTION: No services; use turnouts.*

0 Junction at **Milepost 10.7** Mitkof Highway; turn east.

1.4 (2.3 km) View of Wrangell Narrows to west. Older clear-cuts; this area was logged between 1964 and 1968.

4.4 (7.1 km) Falls Creek bridge.

7 (11.3 km) Second-growth stand of spruce–hemlock. First growth was destroyed by fire or wind throw more than 180 years ago. This second-growth stand serves as an example of what a logging unit could look like a century or two after clear-cutting.

9.7 (15.6 km) Directly south is a 384-acre clear-cut logged in 1973 under a contract predating the current policy, which usually limits clear-cut tracts to 100 acres.

10.2 (16.4 km) **Big Creek**; steelhead in April and May; coho late August and September; cutthroat and Dolly Varden, best late summer and fall. ⚓

12.3 (19.8 km) Muskeg; view of Frederick Sound.

14.2 (22.8 km) Sand Lake trail. Short boardwalk trail leads to each of the Three Lakes. Tennis shoes are ideal for these short walks, but for areas around the lakes it is advisable to wear rubber boots. A 0.7-mile/1.1-km connecting trail to Hill Lake.

14.7 (23.6 km) Hill Lake trail.

15.1 (24.3 km) Crane Lake trail, 1.3 miles/2.1 km to lake; connecting trail to Hill Lake. USFS skiffs and picnic platforms are located at Sand, Hill and Crane lakes.

Sand, **Hill** and **Crane** lakes, cutthroat from May through Sept. ⚓

16.4 (26.4 km) Dry Straits Road.

21.4 (34.4 km) Second **junction** with Mitkof Highway, at **Milepost 20.6**.

St. Michael's Cathedral is a Sitka landmark. (© James D. Ronan, Jr.)

Sitka

(See map, page 651)

Located on west side of Baranof Island, 95 air miles/153 km southwest of Juneau, 185 air miles/298 km northwest of Ketchikan; 2 hours flying time from Seattle, WA. **Population:** City and Borough, 9,194. **Emergency Services: Alaska State Troopers, City Police, Fire Department,** and **Ambulance,** phone 911. **Hospital,** Sitka Community, 209 Moller Ave., phone (907) 747-3241; Mount Edgecumbe, 222 Tongass Dr., phone (907) 966-2411. **Maritime Search and Rescue,** phone the Coast Guard at 1-800-478-5555.

Visitor Information: Contact the Sitka Convention and Visitors Bureau at Box 1226-MP, Sitka, AK 99835; phone (907) 747-5940. Also available at the Isabel Miller

Sitka

To Sandy Beach, Harbor Mountain, Halibut Point Wayside, Ferry Terminal, Old Sitka and Starrigavan Campground

Russian Alaska. Baranof was governor from 1790 to 1818. A statue of the Russian governor was unveiled in 1989; it is located outside of the Centennial Building. Castle Hill in Sitka is where Alaska changed hands from Russia to the United States in 1867. Salmon was the mainstay of the economy from the late 1800s until the 1950s, when the salmon population decreased. A pulp mill operated at nearby Silver Bay from 1960 to 1993. Today, tourism, commercial fishing, cold storage plants and government provide most jobs.

ACCOMMODATIONS/VISITOR SERVICES

Sitka has several hotels/motels, most with adjacent restaurants, including: Cascade Inn and Boat Charters (907/747-6804), Potlatch Motel (907/747-8611), Sitka Hotel (907/747-3288), Super 8 Hotel (907/747-8804) and Westmark Shee Atika (907/747-6241). Bed and breakfasts are also available; see ads this section.

Alaska Ocean View Bed & Breakfast. You'll enjoy casual elegance at affordable rates at this superior, quality B&B where guests experience a high degree of personal comfort, privacy and friendly, knowledgeable hosts. Open your day with the tantalizing aroma of fresh bread, fresh ground coffee and a delicious, generous breakfast and close your day with a refreshing soak in the bubbling patio spa. Open year-round, credit cards, smoke-free, on airporter/ferry shuttle route. Business travelers and vacationers rate this lodging a 12 plus! "Delighted beyond our expectations!" Brochure and reservations: 1101 Edgecumbe Drive, Sitka, AK 99835; phone (907) 747-8310. See display ad this section. [ADVERTISEMENT]

Sitka Youth Hostel is located in the United Methodist Church, 303 Kimsham St. (1½ blocks north of McDonald's on Halibut Point Road). Send correspondence to Box 2645, Sitka, AK 99835. Open June 1 to Aug. 31; 20 beds, showers, kitchen facilities, sleeping pads required; $7/member; $10/nonmembers. Phone (907) 747-8661.

An array of businesses cluster in the downtown area, which saw its first traffic light installed in 1992. Services in Sitka's downtown area include restaurants, a laundromat, drugstore, clothing and grocery stores, and gift shops. Shopping and services are also available along Sawmill and Halibut Point roads. Dump stations are located at the Wastewater Treatment Plant on Japonski Island.

Four campgrounds are available in the Sitka area. From the ferry terminal north they are Starrigavan, Sitka Sportsman's, Sealing Cove and Sawmill Creek. Starrigavan Campground (USFS) at **Milepost 7.8** Halibut Point Road, has 32 sites, 2 picnic sites, artesian water, tables, vault toilets, 14-day limit, $8 fee, available first-come, first-served only; phone (907)747-6671. Sitka Sportsman's Assoc. RV Park, located 1 block south of the ferry terminal on Halibut Point Road, has 16 RV sites, water and electrical hookups, $14.50 fee, reservations accepted; phone (907)747-6033. Sealing Cove, operated by

Museum in the Centennial Building on Harbor Drive. Museum hours are 8 A.M. to 5 P.M. in summer, extended hours to accommodate ferry passengers; phone (907) 747-6455. For USDA Forest Service information write the Sitka Ranger District,t 201 Katlian, Suite 109, Sitka, AK 99835; phone (907) 747-6671. For information on Sitka National Historical Park, write 106 Metlakatla St., Sitka, AK 99835; phone (907) 747-6281.

Elevation: Sea level. **Climate:** Average daily temperature in July, 55°F/13°C; in January, 33°F/1°C. Annual precipitation, 95 inches. **Radio:** KIFW 1230, KRSA-FM 94.9, KSBZ-FM 103.1, KCAW-FM 104.7. **Television:** Cable channels. **Newspaper:** *Daily Sitka Sentinel.*

Private Aircraft: Sitka airport on Japonski Island; elev. 21 feet/6m; length 6,500 feet/1,981m; asphalt; fuel 100, A1. Sitka seaplane base adjacent west; fuel 80, 100.

One of the most scenic of southeastern Alaska cities, Sitka rests on the ocean shore protected at the west by myriad small islands and Cape Edgecumbe. Mount Edgecumbe, the Fuji-like volcano (dormant), is 3,201 feet/976m high.

The site was originally occupied by Tlingit Indians. Alexander Baranof, chief manager of the Russian–American Co. with headquarters in Kodiak, built a trading post and fort (St. Michael's Redoubt) north of Sitka in 1799. Indians burned down the fort and looted the warehouses. Baranof returned in 1804, and by 1808 Sitka was capital of the City and Borough of Sitka, is located adjacent Sealing Cove Boat Harbor on Japonski Island; overnight parking for 26 RVs, water and electrical hookups, 15-night limit, $16 fee. Sawmill Creek Campground (USFS) is located at **Milepost 5.4** Sawmill Creek Road; 11 tent sites, vault toilet, boil water, no garbage service, no fee, 14-day limit. ▲

TRANSPORTATION

Air: Scheduled jet service by Alaska Airlines. Charter and commuter service also available. The airport is on Japonski Island, across O'Connell Bridge, 1.7 miles/2.7 km from downtown. Airport facilities include ticket counters, rental cars, small gift shop, restaurant and lounge. Van and taxi service to downtown hotels available.

Ferry: Alaska Marine Highway ferry terminal is located at **Milepost 7** Halibut Point Road; phone (907) 747-8737. Buses for downtown meet all ferries. Van and taxi service also available. Sitka is connected via the Marine Highway to other Southeast ports, Prince Rupert, BC, and Bellingham, WA (see MARINE ACCESS ROUTES section).

Bus: Available to downtown hotels.

Car Rental: Available from A&A Car Rental–Baranof Motors Inc. (907/747-8228), Advantage Car Rentals (907/747-7557) and Avis Rent-A-Car (907/966-2404).

Taxi: Local service is available.

Highways: Halibut Point Road, 7.9 miles/ 12.7 km, and Sawmill Creek Road, 7.4 miles/11.9 km; see logs this section.

Cruise Ships: Sitka is a popular port of call for several cruise lines.

Private Boats: Transient moorage available at ANB Harbor, located downtown next to the fuel dock; Thomsen Harbor on Katlian Street, 0.6 mile/1 km from city center; and Sealing Cove on Japonski Island. Moorage is limited during the summer.

ATTRACTIONS

St. Michael's Cathedral is the focal point of Sitka's history as the capital of Russian Alaska. Built in 1844–48 under the direction of Bishop Innocent Veniaminov of the Russian Orthodox Church, one of the finest examples of rural Russian church architecture for 118 years. It was destroyed by fire on Jan. 2, 1966. Priceless icons, some predating 1800, were saved by townspeople and are now back in place in the rebuilt cathedral (an exact replica).

St. Michael's is located in the center of Lincoln Street downtown; a donation is requested when entering to view icons. Open daily June 1 to Sept. 30, 11 A.M. to 3 P.M. St. Michael's currently serves a Russian Orthodox congregation of about 100 families. Visitors are reminded that this is an active parish conducting weekly services.

Castle Hill (Baranof Castle Hill Historic Site) is where Alaska changed hands from Russia to the United States on Oct. 18, 1867. Castle Hill was the site of Baranof's castle. Walkway to site is located on the south side by the bridge (look for sign).

Sitka Pioneers' Home, near the waterfront at Lincoln and Katlian streets, was built in 1934. Pioneers welcome visitors, and handicrafts made by the residents are sold in the gift shop located on the first floor of the west wing.

Totem Square is across Katlian Street from the Pioneers' Home and contains a totem, petroglyphs, Russian cannon and 3 large anchors found in Sitka Harbor and

Wonderful view of Sitka Sound and Mount Edgecumbe from Harbor Mountain Road. (© Ruth von Spalding)

believed to be 18th century English.

Russian Blockhouse beside Pioneers' Home is a replica of the blockhouse that separated Russian and Tlingit sections of Sitka after the Tlingits moved back to the area 20 years after the 1804 battle. (See model of early Sitka in Centennial Building.)

New Archangel Russian Dancers, a group of local women, perform authentic Russian dances in authentic costumes. Performances are scheduled to coincide with the arrival of cruise ships. Fee charged. Inquire at the Centennial Building for details.

Old Russian Cemetery is located behind Pioneers' Home and includes graves of such notables as St. Iahov Netsvetov, a recently canonized saint of the Russian Orthodox Church, who was a priest in Russian Alaska for over 40 years.

The Finnish Lutheran Cemetery, dedicted in 1841, is located on Princess Way next to the Russian cemetery. Just a few steps up the hill from Sitka Lutheran Church, it holds the grave of Princess Maskutov, wife of Alaska's last Russian governor, and other important personages.

Sitka National Cemetery, Milepost 0.5 Sawmill Creek Road, is open 8 A.M. to 5 P.M. daily (maintained by the Veterans Administration). It was known locally as Military Cemetery. In 1924 Pres. Calvin Coolidge designated the site as Sitka National Cemetery, and until WWII it was the only national cemetery west of the Rockies. Civil War veterans, veterans of the Aleutian Cam-

paign in WWII and many notable Alaskans are buried here. One gravestone is dated December 1867, 2 months after the U.S. purchase of Alaska from Russia.

Whale Watching. During the summer, whales are often found in Sitka Sound. During the winter, up to 80 whales are near Sitka from mid-September to mid-January. Whale Park, 4.4 miles/7 km from town on Sawmill Creek Road, has stationary binoculars for whale viewing.

Alaska Day Celebration, Oct. 14–18, celebrates the transfer of Alaska from Russia to the United States with a reenactment of the event, complete with Sitka's own 9th (Manchu) Infantry, authentic uniforms and working muskets of the period. Period costumes and beards are the order of the day. Events ranging from pageant to costume ball and parade highlight the affair.

Annual Sitka Summer Music Festival (June 6–27, 1997). Concerts on Tuesday, Friday and some Saturday evenings in the Centennial Bldg., praised for its excellent acoustics. Emphasizing chamber music, an international group of professional musicians give evening concerts during the festival, plus open rehearsals. Advance tickets are a good idea; the concerts are popular. Dress is informal and concert-goers may have the opportunity to talk with the musicians. Children under 6 years not admitted.

Centennial Building, by the boat harbor on Harbor Drive, is used for Russian dance performances, music festivals, banquets and conventions. Its glass-fronted main hall overlooks Sitka Sound. The Isabel Miller Museum is located here. Nearby is a large hand-carved Tlingit canoe made from a single log. The Southeast Alaska Native Dancers also perform, in full regalia, in the Centennial Building. Contact the Sitka tribe of Alaska for details at (907) 747-7290.

Isabel Miller Museum, located in the Centennial Building, has permanent exhibits highlighting the history of Sitka and its people. Russian tools, paintings from all eras, fishing, forestry, tourism, and Alaska Purchase exhibits, and an 8-foot-square scale model of Sitka in 1867 are among the displays. Operated by the Sitka Historical Society; hosts are available to answer questions. Open year-round; free admission. Hours are 9 A.M. to 5 P.M. daily in summer; 10 A.M. to 4 P.M. Tuesday through Saturday during the winter. Phone (907) 747-6455.

Sitka Lutheran Church, downtown on Lincoln Street, has a small historical display. Established in 1840, it was the first Protestant church organized on the west coast of North America.

Sitka National Historical Park reflects both the community's rich Tlingit Indian heritage and its Russian-ruled past. The park consists of 2 units—the Fort Site, located at the end of Lincoln Street, 0.5 mile/0.8 km from town, and the Russian Bishop's House, located on Lincoln Street near Crescent Harbor.

At the Fort Site stood the Tlingit fort, burned to the ground by Russians after the 1804 Battle of Sitka; this was the last major stand by the Tlingits against Russian settlement. For Alexander Baranof, leader of the Russians, the battle was revenge for the 1802 destruction of Redoubt St. Michael by the Tlingits. There is a visitor center here with audiovisual programs and exhibits of Indian artifacts. The Southeast Alaska Indian Cultural Center has contemporary Tlingit artists demonstrate and interpret various traditional arts for visitors.

There is a self-guiding trail through the park to the fort site and battleground of 1804. The National Park Service conducts guided walks; check for schedule. The park's totem pole collection stands near the visitor center and along the trail. The collection includes original pieces collected in 1901–03, and copies of originals lost to time and the elements. The pieces, primarily from Prince of Wales Island, were collected by Alaska Gov. John Brady (now buried in Sitka National Cemetery). The originals were exhibited at the 1904 St. Louis Exposition.

The Russian Bishop's House was built by the Russian–American Co. in 1842 for the first Russian Orthodox Bishop to serve Alaska. It was occupied by the church until

1969, and was added to Sitka National Historical Park in 1972. The house is 1 of 2 Russian log structures remaining in Sitka, and 1 of 4 remaining in North America.

The park's visitor center is open daily, 8 A.M. to 5 P.M., June through September; weekdays, 8 A.M. to 5 P.M., October through May. The park grounds and trails are open daily, 5 A.M. to 10 P.M. in summer; shorter hours in winter. Russian Bishop's House open 9 A.M. to 5 P.M. daily, closed from 1–2 P.M. for lunch; other times by appointment; hours subject to change. The visitor center is closed Thanksgiving, Christmas and New Year's. Admission fee $3 per person. Phone (907) 747-6281 for more information.

Sheldon Jackson Museum, 104 College Dr., on the Sheldon Jackson College campus, contains some of the finest Native arts and crafts found in Alaska. Much of it was collected by missionary Sheldon Jackson and is now owned by the state of Alaska. Museum shop specializes in Alaska Native arts and crafts: ivory, dolls, masks, silver jewelry, baskets and beadwork. Admission $3, students under 18 free, annual pass $10. Open in summer 8 A.M. to 5 P.M. daily. Winter hours: Tuesday through Saturday, 10 A.M. to 4 P.M. Phone (907) 747-8981.

The Prospector is a 13¹⁄₂-foot/4-m clay and bronze statue in front of the Pioneers' Home. Sculpted by Alonzo Victor Lewis, the statue was dedicated on Alaska Day in 1949. Lewis's model was a genuine pioneer, William "Skagway Bill" Fonda.

Blarney Stone, across from Sheldon Jackson College. Believed to originally have been called Baranof's stone and used as a resting stop by Russian–American Co. chief manager Alexander Baranof.

O'Connell Bridge, 1,225 feet/373m long, connecting Sitka with Japonski Island, was the first cable-stayed, girder-span bridge in the United States. It was dedicated Aug. 19, 1972. You'll get a good view of Sitka and the harbors by walking across this bridge.

Old Sitka, at **Milepost 7.5** Halibut Point Road, is a registered national historic landmark and the site of the first Russian settlement in the area in 1799, known then as Fort Archangel Michael. In 1802, in a surprise attack, the Tlingit Indians of the area destroyed the fort and killed most of its occupants, driving the Russians out until Baranof's successful return in 1804.

Visit the Alaska Raptor Rehabilitation Center, located at 1101 Sawmill Creek Road (**Milepost 0.9**) just across Indian River, within easy walking distance of downtown Sitka. This unique facility treats injured eagles, hawks, owls and other birds. Visitors will have the opportunity to see American bald eagles and other raptors close up, review case histories of birds treated at the center and observe medical care being administered to current patients. From May 15 through September the facility is open daily for tours and educational programs; limited hours October to May 15. Phone (907) 747-8662 or fax 747-8397 for times. Admission charged.

St. Lazaria Island is host to one of the largest seabird colonies in Southeast Alaska. This 65-acre volcanic island was set aside as a wildlife refuge in 1909. A half-million seabirds representing 11 different species breed here. Landing on the island or explor-

ing the island is not advisable because foot traffic damages nesting burrows. Boat charters are available in Sitka for viewing from the water. The best time to visit is May through June. For more information, contact the Refuge Manager, Alaska Maritime National Wildlife Refuge, 2355 Kachemak Bay Dr., Suite 101, Homer, AK 99603; phone (907) 235-6546.

Hiking Trails. The Sitka Ranger District office at 201 Katlian, Suite 109, provides information sheets and maps for area trails and remote cabins. Trails accessible from the road include Harbor Mountain Ridge trail; Mount Verstovia trail; the easy 5-mile/8-km Indian River trail; and the short Beaver Lake trail off Sawmill Creek Road on Blue Lake Road.

AREA FISHING: Sitka holds an annual salmon derby Memorial Day weekend and the weekend following (May 24–26 and May 31–June 1, 1997). Contact the Sitka Convention and Visitors Bureau for more information; phone (907) 747-5940. Saltwater fishing charters available locally. There are also many lakes and rivers on Baranof Island with good fishing; these range from **Katlian River**, 11 miles/17.7 km northeast of Sitka by boat, to more remote waters such as **Rezanof Lake**, which is 40 air miles/64 km southeast of Sitka. USFS public-use cabins at some lakes (see Cabins in the GENERAL INFORMATION section). Stop by the Dept. of Fish and Game office at 304 Lake St. for details on fishing. ⚓

Sawmill Creek Road Log

Sawmill Creek Road is a 7.4-mile/11.9-km road, paved for the first 5.4 miles/8.7 km, which begins at Lake Street and ends beyond the pulp mill (closed) at Silver Bay.

0 Intersection of Lake Street (Halibut Point Road) and Sawmill Creek Road.

0.5 (0.8 km) Sitka National Cemetery.

0.7 (1.1 km) Indian River bridge. Beginning of Indian River trail on left.

0.9 (1.4 km) Alaska Raptor Rehabilitation Center.

1 (1.6 km) Post office.

1.7 (2.7 km) Mount Verstovia trail on left next to supper club. The trail extends 2.5 miles/4 km to summit of Mount Verstovia; strenuous hike, great views.

3.6 (5.8 km) Thimbleberry Creek bridge.

3.7 (6 km) On left past bridge is start of Thimbleberry Lake and Heart Lake trail. Hike in 0.5 mile/0.8 km to **Thimbleberry Lake**, brook trout to 12 inches, May to September. *NOTE: Recent changes in regulations make it illegal to use bait in fresh water, except from Sept. 15 to Nov. 15.* Trail continues 1 mile/1.6 km past Thimbleberry Lake to **Heart Lake**, brook trout. ⚓

4.4 (7.1 km) Scenic Whale Park viewpoint turnout; stationary binoculars for whale watching.

5.3 (8.5 km) Alaska Pulp Corp. (closed).

5.4 (8.7 km) Blue Lake Road on left. Pavement ends on Sawmill Creek Road. Blue Lake Road (narrow dirt) leads 2.2 miles/3.5 km to small parking area and short downhill trail to Blue Lake (no recreational facilities; check with city for information). At Mile 1.5 on right is Sawmill Creek USFS campground (unmaintained). **Blue Lake**, rainbow, May to September; use flies or lure, do not use bait. Lightweight skiff or rubber boat recommended. ⚓▲

5.7 (9.2 km) Sawmill Creek and bridge.

7.2 (11.6 km) Public road ends at Herring Cove near mouth of Silver Bay (boat tours of the bay available in Sitka). City road to hydroelectric power plant continues.

7.4 (11.9 km) Gate marking boundary of city road. No vehicles beyond this point; access for hikers and bicyclists only. No guardrails or road signs to road end.

10.5 (16.9 km) Fish hatchery and gate. Steep grades; watch for rocks on road.

13.7 (22 km) Road end. Green Lake Power Plant.

Halibut Point Road Log

Halibut Point Road (paved) leads northwest from the intersection of Harbor Drive and Lincoln Street past Old Sitka to Starrigavan Creek Campground.

0 Harbor Drive and Lincoln Street. Proceed northwest (road is now Lake Street).

0.1 (0.2 km) Fire station. Intersection with Sawmill Creek Road; keep left.

0.3 (0.5 km) **Swan Lake** to right of road, rainbow from 12 to 14 inches.

0.6 (1 km) Katlian Street on left leads to boat ramp and then to downtown. Hospital to the right.

1.8 (2.9 km) Pioneer Park picnic and day-use area with beach access; parking available.

2.2 (3.5 km) Cascade Creek bridge.

2.3 (3.7 km) Tongass National Forest work center.

2.4 (3.9 km) Sandy Beach; good swimming beach, ample parking, view of Mount Edgecumbe. Whales are sometimes sighted.

3.8 (6.1 km) Viewpoint. On a clear day you can see for 50 miles/80 km.

4.2 (6.8 km) Harbor Mountain Road; steep gravel, accessible to cars. Road leads 5 miles/8 km to road end and Harbor Mountain Ridge trail to lookout at 2,300 feet/701m. Great view of Sitka Sound.

4.4 (7.1 km) Granite Creek bridge. Just beyond the bridge on left is Halibut Point state recreation site with swimming beach, shelters, tables, fireplaces and toilets.

7 (11.3 km) Alaska Marine Highway ferry terminal on left.

7.3 (11.7 km) Boat ramp, litter barrel and pit toilet to left.

7.5 (12.1 km) Old Sitka State Historical Site at left, and Starrigavan Creek bridge just ahead. Old Sitka was the site of the Russian Fort Archangel Michael, established in 1799. Commemorative plaque and historical markers. The site is a registered national historic landmark.

7.6 (12.2 km) Narrow road on right runs along the bank of Starrigavan Creek, where pink salmon spawn in August and September, and continues several miles through Starrigavan River valley. Off-road vehicles permitted.

7.7 (12.4 km) USFS estuary life trail, Starrigavan Recreation Area; bird watching. Wheelchair access, vault toilets, trails, parking adjacent.

7.8 (12.6 km) Turnoff for Starrigavan USFS campground and picnic area; artesian well with excellent drinking water. Hiking trail to Mosquito Cove. Forest and muskeg nature trail, across from boat ramp, connects with Estuary life trail. Access to beach. **Starrigavan Bay,** Dolly Varden; pink and silver salmon, May to October.

7.9 (12.7 km) Road ends.

Charter and scheduled floatplane service is available throughout Southeast.

(© Jason Paur)

Kake

(See map, page 651)

Located on the northwest coast of Kupreanof Island; Petersburg is 40 air miles/64 km or 65 miles/105 km by boat; Juneau is 95 air miles/153 km northeast. **Population:** 820 (approximately 85 percent Native). **Emergency Services:** for all emergencies, 911. **Police,** phone (907) 785-3393. **Public Health Center,** phone (907) 785-3333. **Maritime Search and Rescue,** phone the Coast Guard at 1-800-478-5555 or (907) 785-3500.

Visitor Information: City of Kake, Box 500, Kake 99830.

Elevation: Sea level. **Climate:** Less than average rainfall for southeastern Alaska, approximately 50 inches annually. Mild temperatures. January average temperatures are around freezing. Slightly warmer than nearby Petersburg, Kake is noted for being in the "banana belt" of Southeast.

Private Aircraft: Kake seaplane base, located adjacent southeast; fuel 100. Airstrip 1 mile/1.6 km west; elev. 148 feet/45m; length 4,000 feet/1,219m; asphalt; unattended.

Transportation: Air—Scheduled service from Petersburg (15-minute flight), Juneau (45 minutes), Wrangell and Sitka. Scheduled daily charter service provided by Ketchikan Air and L.A.B. Flying Service. **Ferry**—Alaska Marine Highway vessel from Petersburg and Sitka. See MARINE ACCESS ROUTES section for schedule.

Accommodations at local inn and bed and breakfast. There are general, variety and video stores, a cafe and other services. Church groups include Baptist, Salvation Army, Presbyterian and Assembly of God. Kake has an accredited high school, junior high school and elementary.

The town is a permanent village of the Kake (pronounced cake) tribe of the Tlingit Indians. The Tlingits from Kake had a well-earned reputation for aggression in the 18th and 19th centuries. In 1869, the Kakes

murdered 2 Sitka traders in revenge for the shooting of a Native by a Sitka sentry. Reprisals taken by the United States resulted in the shelling and destruction of 3 Kake villages.

The tribe eventually settled at the present-day site of Kake, where the government established a school in 1891. Residents have historically drawn ample subsistence from the sea. However, with the advent of a cash economy, the community has come to depend on commercial fishing, fish processing (there is a cannery) and logging. The post office was established in 1904, and the city was incorporated in 1952. The city's claim to fame is its totem, reputedly the world's tallest one-piece pole at 132 feet, 6 inches. It was carved for the 1967 Alaska Purchase Centennial Celebration.

Kake Dog Salmon Festival, July 26–27, 1997, celebrates the return of the salmon. Originally a picnic for cannery workers, nearly 700 people joined in the festivities in 1996, which included events such as a giant canoe race called "The Challenge of the Chums." Contact Kake Tribal Corp. for more information, phone (907) 785-3221.

Angoon

(See map, page 652)

Located on the west coast of Admiralty Island on Chatham Strait, at the mouth of Kootznahoo Inlet. Peril Strait is across Chatham Strait from Angoon. Juneau is 60 air miles/97 km northeast. Sitka is 41 miles/66 km southwest. **Population:** 750. **Emergency Services: Police,** phone (907) 788-3631. **Clinic,** phone (907) 788-3633.

Visitor Information: Local people are happy to help. You may also contact the USFS Admiralty Island National Monument office in Angoon (phone 907/788-3166) or the city of Angoon (phone 907/788-3653).

Elevation: Sea level. **Climate:** Moderate weather with about 40 inches of annual

Crumbling cabin along Pack Creek on the east coast of Admiralty Island.

(© Ruth von Spalding)

rainfall and mild temperatures.

Private Aircraft: Angoon seaplane base; 0.9 mile/1.4 km southeast; unattended.

Transportation: Air—Scheduled seaplane service from Juneau. **Ferry**—Alaska Marine Highway service. See MARINE ACCESS ROUTES section for schedule.

Accommodations available at a motel and 2 bed and breakfasts. There are 2 general stores. Fuel service available. There are no RV facilities. Canoes and 12 charter boats available. Transient moorage for private boats also available.

Angoon is a long-established Tlingit Indian settlement at the entrance to Kootznahoo Inlet. It is the only permanent community on Admiralty Island. On Killisnoo Island, across the harbor from the state ferry landing, a community of mostly summer homes has grown up along the island beaches. The lifestyle of this primarily Tlingit community is heavily subsistence: fish, clams, seaweed, berries and venison. Fishing, mostly hand trolling for king and coho salmon, is the principal industry.

The scenery of Admiralty Island draws many visitors. All but the northern portion of the island was declared a national monument in December 1980 and is jointly managed by the U.S. Forest Service and Kootznoowoo Inc., the local Native corporation. Kootznahoo Inlet and Mitchell Bay near Angoon offer a network of small wooded islands, reefs and channels for kayaking. Mitchell Bay and Admiralty Lakes Recreational Area are the 2 major recreational attractions within the monument. Pack Creek, on the east-coast of the island, is a well-known bear viewing spot (best mid-July to late August); permit required. Admiralty Island's Indian name, *Kootznoowoo*, means "Fortress of Bears". There are 12 USFS cabins available for public use in the monument; contact the U.S. Forest Service in Angoon. (Also see Cabins in the GENERAL INFORMATION section.)

Local residents can provide directions to the interesting old Killisnoo graveyards, located both on the island and on the Angoon shore of the old Killisnoo settlement, which once was one of the larger communities in southeastern Alaska.

Fishing for salmon is excellent in the Angoon area. (Record kings have been caught in nearby Kelp Bay and in Angoon harbor.) There is also excellent halibut and

other bottom fish fishing. Trout (cutthroat and Dolly Varden) fishing in the lakes and streams on Admiralty Island; fair but scattered. ◂━━

Tenakee Springs
(See map, page 652)

Located on the north shore of Tenakee Inlet on Chichagof Island, 50 miles/81 km northeast of Sitka. **Population:** 107. **Visitor Information:** Can be obtained from city hall, phone (907) 736-2207, or from the town's store, phone (907) 736-2205. **Elevation:** Sea level. **Climate:** Average rainfall 63.2 inches annually, with moderate snowfall. **Private Aircraft:** Seaplane base.

Transportation: Air—Scheduled and charter service available through Wings of Alaska out of Juneau. **Ferry**—Alaska Marine Highway service from Sitka and Juneau. See MARINE ACCESS ROUTES section for schedule.

Tenakee Springs has 1 street—Tenakee Avenue—which is about 3 miles/5 km long and 4 to 12 feet wide. Many residents use 3-wheel motor bikes for transportation, some ride bicycles, but most walk the short distances between buildings. There are a store, cafe, clinic, post office, library, sawmill and city hall. Accommodations at 7 rental cabins (bring your sleeping bag) are available at Snyder Mercantile, and Tenakee Hot Springs Lodge offers guided sportfishing and sightseeing; phone (907) 736-2400. Tenakee Springs became a city in 1971 and has a mayor, council and planning commission.

The word Tenakee comes from the Tlingit word *tinaghu*, or "Coppery Shield Bay." This refers to 3 copper shields, highly prized by the Tlingits, which were lost in a storm.

The hot springs (temperature from 106°F to 108°F/41°C to 42°C) brought people to Tenakee at the turn of the century. A bathhouse, completed in 1940, located on the waterfront posts times of use for men and women. The facility is maintained by contributions from residents and visitors.

The major industry at Tenakee might be

described as relaxation, as many retirees have chosen to live here, away from the bustle of other Southeast cities. There are many summer homes along Tenakee Avenue. During the summer, watch for whales in Tenakee Inlet, which are sometimes spotted from town.

Some logging is under way in the area around Tenakee. Tenakee Inlet produces salmon, halibut, Dungeness and king crab, red snapper and cod. A small fleet of fishing vessels is home-ported in Tenakee's harbor, located about 0.5 mile/0.8 km east of town. Although many visitors come to Tenakee to hunt and fish, there are no hunting guides or rental boats available locally. There are 3 fishing and sightseeing charter services.

Pelican
(See map, page 652)

Located on the east shore of Lisianski Inlet on the northwest coast of Chichagof Island; 70 air miles/113 km north of Sitka and 70 air miles/113 km west of Juneau. **Population:** 209. **Emergency Services: Public Safety Officer** and **Fire Department**, phone 911. **Clinic**, phone (907) 735-2250. **Elevation:** Sea level. **Climate:** Average winter temperatures from 21°F/-6°C to 39°F/4°C; summer temperatures from 51°F/11°C to 62°F/17°C. Total average annual precipitation is 127 inches, with 120 inches of snow.

Visitor Information: Contact the Pelican Visitor Assoc., Box 737, Pelican, AK 99832; phone (907) 735-2282 or 735-2259.

Private Aircraft: Seaplane base; fuel 80, 100. **Transportation: Air**—Scheduled air service from Juneau via Loken Air and Wings of Alaska. Scheduled service from Sitka via Taquan Air. Seaplanes land within walking distance to downtown. **Ferry**—Alaska Marine Highway serves Pelican; terminal is approximately ¼ mile from downtown boardwalk. There are no cars or taxis in Pelican, which is fine, as the town is not very big. Bring a good pair of walking shoes. Four-wheels are available. See MARINE ACCESS ROUTES section for schedules.

Pelican has 2 bar-and-grills (1 with 4 rooms for rent) and a cafe. Accommodations available at a lodge, 2 seasonal lodges, and bed and breakfast. There is a grocery and dry goods store, laundromat and 2 liquor stores. There is a small-boat harbor, marine repair and a fuel dock.

Established in 1938 by Kalle (Charley) Raataikainen, and named for Raataikainen's fish packer, *The Pelican,* Pelican relies on commercial fishing and seafood processing. Pelican Seafoods processes salmon, halibut, crab, herring, black cod, rockfish, sea urchin and sea cucumber, and is the primary year-round employer. Pelican has dubbed itself "closest to the fish," a reference to its close proximity to the rich Fairweather salmon grounds. Salmon trolling season is from about June to mid-September, and the king salmon winter season is from October through April. Pelican's population increases greatly when nonresident fishers work during the salmon seasons. Pelican was incorporated in 1943. Most of Pelican is built on pilings over tidelands. A wooden boardwalk extends the length of the community, and there are about 2 miles of gravel road.

Local recreation includes kayaking, hiking, fishing, and watching birds and marine mammals.

Otter Cove Bed and Breakfast. Explore Pelican's boardwalk, then relax in this secluded, beach retreat room with private bath. Spectacular mountain and water views, and home-cooked breakfasts are yours at a reasonable price. Guided activities like kayaking, fishing, wildlife viewing and hiking. Relax and refresh yourself in this quiet fishing village. $90–$200. [ADVERTISEMENT]

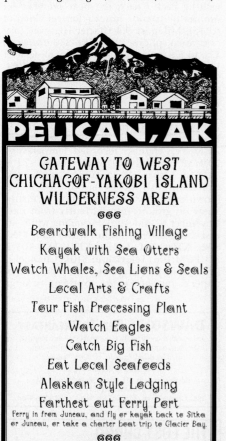
Hoonah
(See map, page 652)

Located on the northeast shore of Chichagof Island, about 40 miles/64 km west of Juneau and 20 miles/32 km south across Icy Strait from the entrance to Glacier Bay. **Population:** 903. **Emergency Services: Alaska State Troopers** and **Hoonah City Police,** phone (907) 945-3655; emergency only phone 911. **Maritime Search and Rescue,** call the Coast Guard at 1-800-478-5555.

Visitor Information: Local business people, city office staff (907/945-3663, weekdays 8 A.M. to 4:30 P.M.) and the postmaster are happy to help. The U.S. Forest Service office in Hoonah (Box 135, Hoonah, AK 99829, phone 907/945-3631) also has visitor information, including a $3 Hoonah area road guide showing forest roads on Chichagof Island and a $4 Tongass National Forest map.

Elevation: Sea level. **Climate:** Typical Southeastern Alaska climate, with average annual precipitation of 70 inches. Average daily temperature in July, 57°F/13°C; in January, 35°F/1°C. Prevailing winds are southeasterly.

Private Aircraft: Hoonah airport, adjacent southeast; elev. 30 feet/9m; length 3,000 feet/914m; paved. Seaplane base adjacent.

Transportation: Air–Scheduled and charter service from Juneau. Airport is located about 3 miles/5 km from town. **Ferry**–Alaska Marine Highway vessel serves Hoonah. See MARINE ACCESS ROUTES section.

Accommodations at Hoonah Lodge. Occasional room rentals and bed-and-breakfast lodging are also available. Hoonah has 2 restaurants, 2 grocery stores, a hardware store, a gift shop, a variety store, bank, a marine fuel docks, a gas pump and 3 flying services. The marina, with showers and a laundromat, is a popular layover for boaters awaiting permits to enter Glacier Bay.

Hoonah is a small coastal community with a quiet harbor for the seining and trolling fleets. The most prominent structures are a cold storage facility, the lodge, bank, post office and the public school. The village has been occupied since prehistory by the Tlingit people. In the late 1800s, missionaries settled here. Canneries established in the area in the early 1900s spurred the growth of commercial fishing, which remains the mainstay of Hoonah's economy. During the summer fishing season, residents work for nearby Excursion Inlet Packing Co. or Hoonah Cold Storage in town. Halibut season begins in May, and salmon season opens in midsummer and runs through Sept. Logging also contributes to the economy, with employment loading log ships and other industry-related jobs. Subsistence hunting and fishing remain an important lifestyle here, and many families gather food in the traditional way: catching salmon and halibut in summer, shellfish and bottom fish year-round; hunting deer, geese and ducks; berry picking in summer and fall.

Hunting and fishing are the main attractions for visitors. Charter fishing is available locally, with good seasonal king and coho (silver) salmon and halibut fishing as well as crabbing. Guide services are available.

Hoonah is the starting point for an extensive logging and forest road system for northwest Chichagof Island. Island road maps ($3) are available through the USFS in Hoonah, Sitka and Juneau.

Juneau
(See maps, pages 652–653)

Located on Gastineau Channel; 900 air miles/1,448 km (2 hours, 10 minutes flying time) from Seattle, WA, 650 air miles/1,046 km (1 hour, 25 minutes by jet) from Anchorage. **Population:** Borough 29,755. **Emergency Services:** Phone 911 for all emergencies. **Police,** phone (907) 586-2780. **Fire Department,** phone (907) 586-5245. **Alaska State Troopers,** phone (907) 465-4000. **Poison Center** and **Hospital,** Bartlett

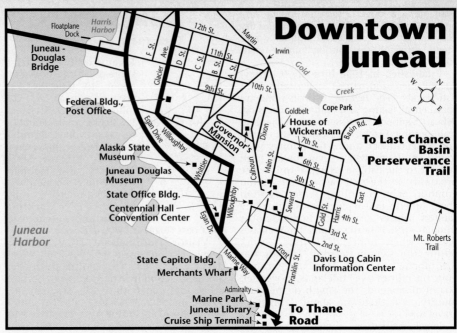

Memorial, 3260 Hospital Dr., phone (907) 586-2611. **Maritime Search and Rescue**, Coast Guard, phone (907) 463-2000 or 1-800-478-5555.

Visitor Information: Juneau Convention & Visitors Bureau, Davis Log Cabin Information Center, 134 3rd St., phone (907) 586-2201 or 586-2284; open year-round 8 A.M. to 5 P.M. Monday through Friday; additional hours during the summer, 9 A.M. to 5 P.M. Saturday, Sunday and holidays. To find out about current events in Juneau, phone (907) 586-JUNO for a recorded message. Visitor information kiosk located in Marine Park on waterfront near Merchants Wharf, usually open daily 8:30 A.M. to 6 P.M., from about mid-May to mid-September. Information booth at the airport terminal. Visitor information is also available at the cruise ship terminal on S. Franklin Street when cruise ships are in port, and at the Auke Bay ferry terminal. Large groups contact the Davis Log Cabin Information Center in advance for special assistance.

USFS Information Center at Centennial Hall, 101 Egan Dr.; open 8 A.M. to 5 P.M. daily from mid-May to mid-September; 9 A.M. to 5 P.M. Monday through Friday the rest of the year. Phone (907) 586-8751. U.S. Park Service office here open in summer. The center has seasonal features of natural history films. USFS cabins may also be reserved here. The center issues permits for visiting Pack Creek, the bear preserve on Admiralty Island. Juneau Ranger District (USFS), **Milepost 9.4** Glacier Highway (airport area), phone (907) 586-8800; open 8 A.M. to 5 P.M. weekdays. Mendenhall Glacier Visitor Center (USFS), phone (907) 789-0097, open 8:30 A.M. to 5:30 P.M. daily in summer, 9 A.M. to 4 P.M. weekends only in winter.

Elevation: Sea level. **Climate:** Mild and wet. Average daily maximum temperature in July, 63°F/17°C; daily minimum in January, 20°F/-7°C. Highest recorded temperature, 90°F/32°C in July 1975; the lowest -22°F/-30°C in January 1972. Average annual precipitation, 56.5 inches (airport), 92 inches (downtown); 103 inches of snow annually. Snow on ground intermittently from mid-November to mid-April. Prevailing winds are east-southeasterly. **Radio:** KJNO 630, KINY 800, KTOO-FM 104.3, KTKU-FM 105.1, KSUP-FM 106. **Television:** KJUD Channel 8; JATV cable; KTOO (public television). **Newspapers:** *Juneau Empire* (Sunday through

Mount Roberts tram departs cruise ship dock. (© David J. Job)

Friday) and *Capital City Weekly*.

Private Aircraft: Juneau International Airport, 9 miles/14.5 km northwest; elev. 18 feet/5m; length 8,456 feet/2,577m; asphalt; fuel 100LL, Jet A. Juneau harbor seaplane base, due east; restricted use, no fuel. International seaplane base, 7 miles/11.3 km northwest; 5,000 feet/1,524m by 450 feet/137m, avgas, Jet A. For more information, phone the Juneau Flight Service Station at (907) 789-6124.

HISTORY AND ECONOMY

In 1880, nearly 20 years before the great gold rushes to the Klondike and to Nome, 2 prospectors named Joe Juneau and Dick Harris found "color" in what is now called Gold Creek, a small, clear stream that runs through the center of present-day Juneau. What they found led to the discovery of one of the largest lodes of gold quartz in the world. Juneau (called Harrisburg the first year) quickly boomed into a gold rush town as claims and mines sprang up in the area.

For a time the largest mine was the Treadwell, across Gastineau Channel south of Douglas (which was once a larger town than Juneau), but a cave-in and flood closed the mine in 1917. In 36 years of operation, Treadwell produced $66 million in gold. The Alaska–Gastineau Mine, operated by Bart Thane in 1911, had a 2-mile shaft through Mount Roberts to the Perseverance Mine near Gold Creek. The Alaska–Juneau (A–J) Mine was constructed on a mountain slope south of Juneau and back into the heart of Mount Roberts. It operated until 1944, when it was declared a nonessential wartime activity after producing over $80 million in gold. Post–WWII wage and price inflation and the fixed price of gold prevented its reopening.

In 1900, the decision to move Alaska's capital to Juneau was made because of the city's growth, mining activity and location on the water route to Skagway and the Klondike; the decline of post-Russian Sitka, as whale and fur trading slackened, secured Juneau's new status as Alaska's preeminent city.

Congress first provided civil government for Alaska in 1884. Until statehood in 1959 Alaska was governed by a succession of presidential appointees, first as the District of Alaska, then as the Territory of Alaska. Between 1867 (when the United States purchased Alaska from Russia) and 1884, the military had jurisdiction over the District of Alaska, except for a 3-year period (1877–79) when Alaska was put under control of the U.S. Treasury Dept. and governed by U.S. Collectors of Customs.

With the arrival of Alaska statehood in 1959, Juneau's governmental role increased even further. In 1974, Alaskans voted to move the capital from Juneau to a site between Anchorage and Fairbanks, closer to the state's population center. In 1976, Alaska voters selected a new capital site near Willow, 65 road miles/105 km north of Anchorage on the George Parks Highway. However, in November 1982, voters defeated funding for the capital move.

Today, government (federal, state and local) comprises an estimated half of the total basic industry. Tourism is the largest employer in the private sector.

DESCRIPTION

Juneau, often called "a little San Francisco," is nestled at the foot of Mount Juneau (elev. 3,576 feet/1,091m) with Mount Roberts (elev. 3,819 feet/1,164m) rising immediately to the east on the approach up Gastineau Channel. The residential community of Douglas, on Douglas Island, is south of Juneau and connected by a bridge. Neighboring residential areas around the airport, Mendenhall Valley and Auke Bay lie north of Juneau on the mainland.

Shopping is in the downtown area and at suburban malls in the airport and Mendenhall Valley areas.

Juneau's skyline is dominated by several government buildings, including the Federal Building (1962), the massive State Office Building (1974), the State Court Building (1975) and the older brick, and marble-columned Capitol Building (1931). The modern Sealaska Plaza is headquarters for Sealaska Corp., 1 of the 13 regional Native corporations formed after congressional passage of the Alaska Native Claims Settlement Act in 1971.

To explore downtown Juneau, it is best to park and walk; distances are not great. The streets are narrow and congested with pedestrians and traffic (especially rush hours), and on-street parking is scarce. Visitors should check at the Davis Log Cabin and at the police station to see whether parking permits are available. Public parking lots are located across from Merchants Wharf Mall at Main Street and Egan Drive and south of Marine Park at the Marine Park parking garage; fee required.

The Juneau area supports 35 churches, a high school, 2 middle schools, several elementary schools and a University of Alaska Southeast campus at Auke Lake. There are 3 municipal libraries and the state library. The Perseverance Theatre, which was established in 1978, provides Juneau with classical and original works, September through May.

The area is governed by the unified city and borough of Juneau, which encompasses 3,108 square miles/8,060 square km. It is the first unified government in the state, combining the former separate and overlapping jurisdictions of the city of Douglas, city of Juneau and greater Juneau borough.

ACCOMMODATIONS/VISITOR SERVICES

Juneau has several hotels and motels, most of them downtown. These include: Alaska Hotel & Bar (907/586-1000), Best Western Country Lane Inn (907/789-5005), Breakwater Inn (907/586-6303), Driftwood Lodge Motel (907/586-2280), Prospector Hotel (907/586-3737), Super 8 Motel (907/789-4858), Travelodge (907/789-9700), Westmark Baranof (907/586-2660) and Westmark Juneau (907/586-6900). There are also numerous bed and breakfasts; see ads this section.

The Juneau International Hostel is located at 614 Harris St. (Juneau 99801), 4 blocks northeast of the Capitol Bldg. All ages are welcome. Check-in time is 5–11 P.M. during summer, 5–10:30 P.M. the rest of the year. Showers, cooking, laundry and storage facilities are available. Cost for members is $7, nonmembers $10, children accompanied by parent $5. Groups welcome. Open year-round. Phone (907) 586-9559.

More than 60 restaurants offer a wide variety of dining. Also watch for sidewalk food vendors downtown in summer.

Juneau also has a microbrewery. The Alaskan Brewing Co., located at 5429 Shaune Dr. in the Lemon Creek area, produces Alaskan Amber Beer and Alaskan Pale

Ale. Free tours available. Phone (907) 780-5866 for more information.

Fireweed House Bed & Breakfast with spectacular view of the Thomas Glacier on Lemon Creek. Situated in rural setting on Douglas Island, only 8 minutes from downtown Juneau. Ideal base for your Juneau stay. Choose from quality accommodations: 3 well-appointed bedrooms, each with private sitting area; a separate apartment; or executive-style, 2-bedroom house. Private and shared baths. Enjoy resident and migrating birds, regular sightings of small mammals and the occasional bear. On-site blueberry picking in late summer. Regardless of departure time, you will be treated to a delicious full-service breakfast. Arrangements for tours and charters. On-premise freezers.

Nonsmoking. Children welcome. Join the family in the open and spacious living room, and enjoy the feel of wood surroundings and the high, 2-story cathedral ceiling. Evening conversation to explore the specialties of Juneau. Toll free 1-800-586-3885. Phone (907) 586-3885; fax (907) 586-3885. 8530 North Douglas Highway-MP, Juneau, AK 99801. For reservation information contact us at www.wetpage.com/fireweed. [ADVERTISEMENT]

Mt. Juneau Inn is where you'll find comfort and hospitality that makes you feel right at home. From the warm, familiar feel of a plush robe, to the comfortable parlour filled with Native art, books and videos, you're assured that your stay here will be a relaxed and memorable one. But if it's our view of the great outdoors that inspires you, we'll provide bikes, gear and guidance to help you enjoy all that Alaska offers. (See display ad this section.) [ADVERTISEMENT]

Pearson's Pond Luxury Inn. Looking for the perfect getaway? You'll find it at this breathtaking waterfront retreat where you can relax in comfort away from the crowds. Soothe your cares in a starlit spa amid lush gardens, sparkling fountains and a peaceful duck pond left by the retreating, world-famous Mendenhall Glacier. Bike the adjacent trail, photograph wildlife between naps on the dock and enjoy a massage. Your convenient suite retreat is an exceptional value and has all the private comforts of home and stocked kitchenettes. Dine ensuite or alfresco as you enjoy the healing sounds of nature. Guests say it is the highest combination of privacy, beauty, comfort and warmth. An excellent value and year-round, smoke- and pet-free experience. Ski and spa packages available. 4541-MP Sawa Circle, Juneau, AK 99801-8723. Phone (907) 789-3772, fax (907) 789-6722. E-mail: pearsons.pond@juneau.com. Website: juneau.com/pearsons.pond. AAA/ABBA Excellence Awards. Frommer's Best of Alaska choice. Book far ahead, as the place is earning a deserved reputation. A definite 10! [ADVERTISEMENT]

The Whale's Eye Lodge is a taste of the Alaskan wilderness in comfort. Located on Shelter Island, a 30-minute boat ride from Juneau. You will find us tucked in the old growth forest on the Inside Passage. Whales, sea lions and eagles can be viewed right from the lodge windows. Private cabins allow you to harmonize with your surroundings. Our charter boat awaits you for excellent salmon and halibut fishing and wildlife excursions. Home cooked meals with fresh baked goods and seafood are on the menu daily. We cater to only 4–6 guests at a time

for a personal experience. Phone (907) 723-2920, fax (907) 723-2921. Bookings: 1-800-478-9188. P.O. Box 210166, Auke Bay, AK 99821. www.juneau.com/Whale's Eye.

The city and borough of Juneau offers limited RV overnight parking spaces at the Juneau Yacht Club (turnoff at **Milepost 1.7** Egan Drive/Glacier Highway) and at Savikko Park/Sandy Beach (**Milepost 2.5** Douglas Highway); $5 per space, per night, paid at the harbormaster's office. For parking at both yacht club and park, sign in at the harbormaster's office (across from high school on Egan Drive). Contact the visitor information center (907/586-2201) for a brochure on RV facilities. Dump stations are located at Mendenhall Lake campground, Mapco Service Station, Valley Tesoro at Mendenhall Center shopping mall in the Mendenhall Valley, and Savikko Park in Douglas.

There are 2 USFS campgrounds and 1 private RV park north of Juneau via the Glacier Highway. The USFS campgrounds are Mendenhall Lake (turn off Glacier Highway at **Milepost 9.4** or **12.2** and continue to Montana Creek Road) and Auke Village (**Milepost 15.4** Glacier Highway). Mendenhall Lake has 60 sites (16 sites accommodate vehicles longer than 20 feet), water, pit toilets, dump station. Ten sites can be reserved; phone 1-800-280-CAMP. Auke Village Campground, 1.5 miles/2.4 km west of the ferry terminal, has 12 campsites, flush and pit toilets, water and firewood: first-come, first-served. The private RV park, with hookups, is located at **Milepost 12.3** Glacier Highway; phone (907) 789-9467. ▲

TRANSPORTATION

Air: Juneau Municipal Airport turnoff is at **Milepost 8.8** Egan Drive (Glacier Highway). Airport terminal contains ticket counters, waiting area, gift shop, rental cars, restaurant, lounge and information booth.

The city express bus stops at the airport

Hillside homes and spire of St. Nicholas Orthodox Church. (© Derby Photography)

weekdays from 8 A.M. to 5 P.M. A shuttle and taxi and van service to downtown are also available. Shuttle service $7 1-way per person, $5 each for groups of 3 or more. Taxi service approximately $15 to $20. Courtesy vans to some hotels.

Alaska Airlines serves Juneau daily from Seattle, WA, Anchorage, Fairbanks, Ketchikan, Sitka, Yakutat, Cordova, Petersburg and Wrangell. Delta Airlines serves Juneau from Seattle and Fairbanks in summer. Scheduled commuter service to Haines, Skagway, Sitka, Angoon and other points via several air services. Scheduled service by Summit Air between Juneau and Whitehorse, YT, year-round and between Juneau and Atlin, BC, in summer.

Charter air service (wheel and floatplanes and helicopters) for hunting, fishing, sightseeing and transportation to other communities (see ads in this section).

Loken Aviation, Inc. provides experienced floatplane service to wilderness cabins, Native villages, and fishing lodges in Southeast Alaska. Thirty years of flying experience guarantees personalized, professional sightseeing and wildlife tours. Visit our ticket counter in the Juneau International Airport or phone (907) 789-3331 for further information. [ADVERTISEMENT]

Ferry: Juneau is served by Alaska Marine Highway ferries. See MARINE ACCESS

ROUTES section for schedule and fares.

Alaska state ferries dock at the Auke Bay terminal at **Milepost 13.9** Glacier Highway; phone (907) 465-3941 or 789-7453. Taxi service and private shuttle bus is available from Auke Bay terminal to downtown Juneau. Shuttle service runs mid-May to mid-October; $5 each way. There is also a bus stop 1.5 miles/2.4 km toward town from the ferry terminal (see following).

Bus: Capital Transit city bus system runs from the cruise ship terminal downtown and includes Juneau, Douglas, Lemon Creek, Mendenhall Valley and airport area, Auke Bay (the community, which is about 1.5 miles/2.4 km south of the ferry terminal). Hourly service Monday through Saturday, year-round; limited service on Sundays. Route map and schedule available at the visitor information center. Flag buses at any corner except in downtown Juneau, where bus uses marked stops only.

Highways: Longest road is Glacier Highway, which begins in downtown Juneau and leads 40.5 miles/65.3 km north to Echo Cove. Other major roads are Mendenhall Loop Road and Douglas and North Douglas highways. See logs this section.

Taxi: Four companies.

Cruise Ships: Juneau is southeastern Alaska's most frequent port of call. There were 487 port calls by cruise ships in 1996.

The tour boat MV *Fairweather* offers scenic cruises of Lynn Canal between Juneau and Skagway mid-May to mid-Sept. Offered on package tours by Gray Line of Alaska, seats are sold on a space-available basis to visitors not on a package tour. Contact their Juneau office in the Baranof Hotel lobby, phone (907) 586-3773. The MV *Fairweather* departs from Yankee Cove, **Milepost 33** Glacier Highway.

Car Rental: Several car rental agencies are available at the airport and vicinity, including All Star/Practical Rent-A-Car (907/790-2414); Avis Rent-A-Car (907/789-9450), Evergreen/Ford–Lincoln–Mercury (907/789-9386), Hertz (907/789-9494), Mendenhall Auto Center (907/789-1386), National Car Rental (907/789-9814) and

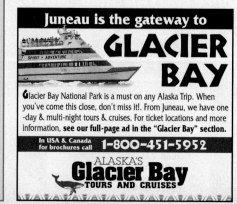

Rent-A-Wreck (907/789-4111).

There are no car rental agencies downtown, but most rental agencies will take you to their offices (sometimes at an extra charge). Best to reserve ahead of time because of the great demand for cars.

Private Boats: Transient moorage is available downtown at Harris and Douglas floats and at Auke Bay. Most boaters use Auke Bay. For more information call the Juneau harbormaster at (907) 586-5255 or hail on Channel 16 UHF.

ATTRACTIONS

Juneau walking-tour map (in English, French, Spanish, German, Chinese or Japanese) is available from the Davis Log Cabin Information Center at 134 3rd St. and from other visitor information sites and from hotels. See Juneau's many attractions—the St. Nicholas Orthodox Church, totems, Capitol Building, Governor's Mansion, historic graves, monuments, state museum, city museum, hatchery and others.

Charter a Boat for salmon and halibut fishing or sightseeing. The visitor information center can provide a list of charter operators; also see ads in this section.

Charter a Plane for fly-in fishing, hunting, transportation to remote lodges and longer flightseeing trips.

Take a Tour. Tours of Juneau and area attractions—by boat, bus, plane and helicopter—can be arranged. These tours range from sightseeing trips out to Mendenhall Glacier to river trips on the Mendenhall River.

Era Helicopters. Soar over the massive Juneau Icefield, viewing 4 unique and distinctive glaciers. Land on a glacier and explore the ancient ice. Fly past historical gold mining areas. Personalized tour with Alaska's most experienced helicopter company. Phone 1-800-843-1947 or (907) 586-2030 locally. Tours also available in Anchorage, Mount McKinley and Valdez.
[ADVERTISEMENT]

Visit the Juneau Library. Built on top of the 4-story public parking garage in downtown Juneau, this award-winning library designed by Minch Ritter Voelckers Architects is well worth a visit. Take the elevator to the 5th floor and spend a morning or afternoon reading in this well-lit and comfortable space with a wonderful view of Juneau, Douglas and Gastineau Channel. Located at South Franklin and Admiralty Way, between Marine Park and the cruise ship terminal.

Juneau–Douglas City Museum, located in the Veteran's Memorial Building across from the State Capitol Building at 4th and Main streets, offers exhibits and audiovisual presentations on the Juneau–Douglas area, featuring gold mining and local cultural history. Displays include a turn-of-the-century store and kitchen, a large relief map, a hands-on history room that's fun for kids of all ages and a special summer exhibit. Free historical walking-tour maps of Juneau are available. Museum gift shop. Summer hours are 9 A.M. to 5 P.M. weekdays, 10 A.M. to 5 P.M. weekends, mid-May to mid-September Limited hours in winter. Admission $1. Phone (907) 586-3572 or write Parks and Recreation, Attn: Juneau–Douglas City Museum, 155 S. Seward St., Juneau, AK 99801, for more information.

State Capitol Building, at 4th and Main streets, contains the legislative chambers and the governor's office. Free tours available from capitol lobby; most days in summer on the half-hour from 9 A.M. to 5 P.M. The **State Office Building,** one block west, houses the State Historical Library and Kimball theater organ (free organ concerts at noon Fridays).

Alaska State Museum is a major highlight of Juneau located downtown at 395 Whittier St. Exhibits include dioramas and contain materials from Alaska's Native groups; icons and other artifacts from Russian–America days; and a popular life-size eagle nesting tree surrounded by a 2-story high mural of a Southeast Alaska scene. A replica of Capt. George Vancouver's ship, *Discovery,* is located in the children's room for kids to explore. During the summer of 1997, there will be a photographic exhibition by Alaskan photographer Bradford Washburn. There will also be a retrospective exhibition of Tlingit artist James Schoppert's art work. The museum store carries Alaska Native crafts and Alaska books and gifts for all ages. Summer hours are 9 A.M. to 6 P.M. Monday through Friday and 10 A.M. to 6 P.M. weekends. Winter hours are 10 A.M. to 4 P.M. Tuesday through Saturday. General admission is $3. Visitors 18 and under, students with current I.D. cards and members of the Friends of the Alaska State Museum are admitted free. A $10 museum pass is also available. Phone (907) 465-2901; Internet http://ccl.alaska.edu/local/museum/home.htm/.

The House of Wickersham, 213 7th St., has an important historical collection dating to the days of the late Judge James Wickersham, one of Alaska's first federal judges, who collected Native artifacts and baskets, as well as many photographs and historical documents concerning Native culture, during his extensive travels throughout the territory early in the century. Afternoon visiting hours in summer except Sunday. Phone (907) 586-9001 for more information.

(Steep climb up to Seventh Street.)

The Governor's Mansion at 716 Calhoun Ave. has been home to Alaska's chief executives since it was completed in 1913. The 2½-story structure, containing 12,900 square feet of floor space, took nearly a year to build. Tours may be possible by advance arrangement. Phone (907) 465-3500.

The Gastineau Salmon Hatchery, operated by Douglas Island Pink and Chum, Inc., is located on Channel Drive 2.5 miles from downtown. The hatchery offers visitors a chance to see adult spawning salmon, over 100 species of Southeast Alaska sea-life in saltwater aquariums, aquaculture displays, and other seasonal activities. A variety of salmon products is also available for purchase. Visitor center open in summer 10 A.M. to 6 P.M. Monday through Friday; noon to 5 P.M. Saturday and Sunday. Incubation-room tours available May 15 through June 30; spawning salmon sights and hatchery operations tour July 1 through Oct. 1. Educational tours provided; nominal admission fee. Phone (907) 463-5114.

See Old Mine Ruins. Remnants from the Treadwell Mine may be seen from a marked trail that starts just south of Sandy Beach on Douglas Island. The impressive remains of the A–J mine mill are located on the hillside along Gastineau Channel just south of downtown Juneau; good views from Douglas Island and from the water. Evidence of the Alaska–Gastineau Mine can be seen south of town along Thane Road. Walking-tour maps of the Treadwell area are available from the city museum and the Davis Log Cabin.

Marine Park, located at foot of Seward Street, has tables, benches, information kiosk and lighterage facilities for cruise ship launches. The Ed Way bronze sculpture, "Hard Rock Miner," is located at Marine Park. Free concerts on Friday evenings in summer.

Thane Ore House, Mile 4.4 Thane Road, home of the *Gold Nugget Revue,* featuring the adventures of Joe Juneau, lively cancan dancers and a red hot mama! Enjoy a sumptuous all-you-can-eat buffet of halibut, salmon and BBQ beef ribs, homemade baked beans, corn bread, salad bar and coffee or soft drink. Beer and wine available. Enjoy the indoor/outdoor beachfront facility, a mining museum, horseshoes, beachcombing, nearby fish hatchery, or sitting by the fireplace. The Thane Ore House is open from noon 'til 9 P.M., daily from May through September. The "Gold Nugget Revue," a Janice D. Holst production, is great family entertainment. 6:30 P.M. showtime! Bring your camera! For information phone (907) 586-3442 or 586-1462. [ADVERTISEMENT]

Thane Road is a wide, straight paved road beginning just south of downtown Juneau and extending 5.5 miles/8.9 km along Gastineau Channel. Good views of the channel and old mines. Excellent viewpoint for spawning salmon at Sheep Creek bridge and falls, Mile 4.3, in summer.

Mount Juneau Waterfall, scenic but difficult to photograph, descends 3,576 feet/ 1,091m from Mount Juneau to Gold Creek behind the city. Best view is from Basin Road. The waterfall is also visible from Marine Park.

Mount Roberts Tramway. Sixty-passenger tram cars depart from base facility on

cruise ship dock every 8 to 10 minutes. Passengers are delivered to a 3,500-square-foot observation deck, 2,000 feet/610m above Juneau. There are signed interpretive trails, a restaurant, gift shops and a theater showing "Seeing Daylight." Open to the public from 8 A.M. to 10 P.M. daily, early May through the end of September. Phone (907) 463-3412 for more information on fees and special promotions.

Mount Roberts Trail Observation Point offers an elevated view of Juneau. Though the trail extends to the 3,819-foot/1,164m summit, an excellent observation point above Juneau is reached by a 20-minute hike from the start of Mount Roberts trail at the top of Starr Hill (6th Street).

Mendenhall Glacier is about 13 miles/ 21 km from downtown Juneau at the end of Mendenhall Glacier Spur Road. Turn right northbound at **Milepost 9.4** Egan Drive (Glacier Highway), and then drive straight for 3.6 miles/5.8 km to the glacier and visitor center. There is a large parking area, and trails lead down to the edge of the lake (a sign warns visitors to stay back; falling ice can create huge waves). The visitor center, a short walk up a paved switchback path (accessible, although steep, for wheelchairs) from the parking area, is open daily from Memorial Day week through September, 8:30 A.M. to 5:30 P.M.; weekends only October to May. The visitor center has glacier view and daily video programs in summer; phone (907) 789-0097 or 586-8800. A 0.5-mile/0.8-km nature trail starts behind the visitor center. Trailheads for 2 longer trails— East Glacier and Nugget Creek—are a short walk from the visitor center. Programs and guided hikes with Forest Service interpreters are offered in summer.

Bike Paths. There are designated bike routes to Douglas, to Mendenhall Valley and Glacier, and to Auke Bay. The Mendenhall Glacier route starts at the intersection of 12th Street and Glacier Avenue; total biking distance is 15 miles/24.1 km. Bikes can be rented downtown and in the vicinity of the airport. Bike-route map and hiking information are available at the Davis Log Cabin.

Glacier Bay National Park contains some of the most impressive tidewater glaciers in the world. Juneau is located about 50 miles/80 km east of the bay and is subsequently the main jumping-off point for many Glacier Bay visitors. There are several local businesses offering 1- and 2-day or longer boat and air packages to the park. The state ferries do not service Glacier Bay, but there is a private ferry service available. Contact AUK NU Tours for information on the Glacier Bay Ferry; write 76 Egan Dr., Juneau, AK 99801, or phone 1-800-820-2628, (907) 586-8687, fax (907) 586-1337. See GLACIER BAY NATIONAL PARK and GUSTAVUS sections for more information.

Tracy Arm. Located 50 miles/80 km southeast of Juneau, Tracy Arm and adjoining Endicott Arm are the major features of the Tracy Arm–Fords Terror Wilderness Area. Both Tracy and Endicott arms are long, deep and narrow fjords that extend more than 30 miles/48 km into the heavily glaciated Coast Mountain Range. Active tidewater glaciers at the head of these fjords calve icebergs into the fjords.

Fords Terror, off of Endicott Arm, is an area of sheer rock walls enclosing a narrow entrance into a small fjord. The fjord was named in 1889 for a crew member of a naval vessel who rowed into the narrow canyon at

slack tide and was caught in turbulent icy currents for 6 terrifying hours when the tide changed.

Access to this wilderness area is primarily by boat or floatplane from Juneau. Large cruise ships and small cruise ships and charter boats include Tracy Arm and Endicott Arm in their itineraries. It is also a popular destination for sea kayakers.

Tracy Arm Fjord–Adventure Bound, Alaska's greatest combination of mountains, wildlife, icebergs and tidewater glaciers. Best viewed from the *Adventure Bound.* Juneau's favorite because the Weber family doesn't overcrowd and is noted for making people feel welcome. The personal touch makes the difference. Office: 245 Marine Way. Reservations: (907) 463-2509, 1-800-228-3875. [ADVERTISEMENT]

Greatland Guides. Sea kayak among whales, porpoise, sea lions and glaciers with an Alaskan naturalist. Stay at B&B's or camp in Alaskan wilderness. Variety of learning adventures from 1–7 days. College credit available. Beginners and custom groups our specialty. For brochure: P.O. Box 22820, Juneau, AK 99802. (907) 463-4397. Internet: http://www.empnet.com/greatland. [ADVERTISEMENT]

Juneau Icefield, immediately to the east of Juneau, is a 1,500-square-mile/2414 km expanse of glaciated mountains that is the source of all the glaciers in the area, including Mendenhall, Taku, Eagle and Herbert. Best way to experience and photograph it is via charter flightseeing. Flights usually take 30 to 60 minutes. Helicopter tours, which land on the glacier, are also available. Helicopter tours last from about 45 minutes to 1½ hours.

Ski Eaglecrest, Juneau's downhill and cross-country ski area on Douglas Island. Built and maintained by the city of Juneau, the area features a day-lodge, cafeteria, ski school, ski patrol, ski rental shop, 2 chair lifts, a surface lift and runs for experienced, intermediate and beginning skiers. Three miles/5 km of maintained cross-country trails available. Open 5 days a week, Dec. to mid-April. The view from the top of the chair lift (operating during ski season only) is worth the visit—Mendenhall Glacier, Juneau Icefield, Lynn Canal, Stephens Passage and more. Drive North Douglas Highway to turnoff left at Eaglecrest sign, then 5.3 miles/8.5 km up the Eaglecrest access road to the lodge. For more information, phone (907) 586-5284 (790-2000 during ski season), or phone (907) 586-5330 for a recorded message about ski conditions.

St. Nicholas Orthodox Church, 5th and Gold streets, a tiny structure built in 1894, is now the oldest original Russian Orthodox church in southeastern Alaska. Visitors are welcome to Sunday services; open daily for summer tours. Phone (907) 586-1023.

Chapel-by-the-Lake (Presbyterian), **Milepost 11.6** Glacier Highway, is a log structure perched above Auke Lake. Its front, made entirely of glass, frames the scenic lake, Mendenhall Glacier and mountains. Popular marriage chapel.

Shrine of St. Terese (Catholic), **Milepost 23.1** Glacier Highway, is a natural stone chapel on its own island, connected to shore by a gravel causeway. A 1 P.M. Sunday mass is during the summer.

Golden North Salmon Derby is a 3-day derby (Aug. 22–24, 1997).

Hiking Trails. *Juneau Trails,* a guidebook of 20-plus area hikes, can be purchased for

$4 at Davis Log Cabin Information Center or USFS Information Center in Centennial Hall. Juneau Parks and Recreation Dept. offers free organized hikes Wednesday and Saturday, April through October; phone (907) 586-5226 for information.

Alaska Fly 'N' Fish Charters. Have the Alaskan experiences others only dream about. Explore Southeast's pristine beauty from a floatplane and on foot, with your own personal pilot and wilderness guide. Various fly-in guided adventures to suit every interest: wildlife safaris, bear watching, freshwater fishing, scenic flighseeing and more! Small groups ensure personalized attention and undisturbed wilderness enjoyment. "The highlight of our Alaskan vacation!" Free brochure: 9604 Kelly Court, Juneau, AK 99801. (907) 790-2120. [ADVERTISEMENT]

AREA FISHING: (Several special sport-fishing regulations are in effect in the Juneau area; consult current regulations booklet.) Good Dolly Varden fishing available along most saltwater shorelines in Juneau area; king salmon best from mid-May to mid-June, pink salmon available about mid-July through August, silver salmon, best August to mid-September. Good fishing by boat from Juneau, Auke Bay or Tee Harbor in **Favorite** and **Saginaw** channels, **Chatham Strait** and near mouth of **Taku Inlet**, for salmon, Dolly Varden and halibut. USFS public-use cabins available (see Cabins in the GENERAL INFORMATION section).

For up-to-date angling data in the Juneau area, phone (907) 465-4116 for recorded Alaska Dept. of Fish and Game message (April through Oct.). For specific angling information or for a copy of the local sport-fishing guide, contact the ADF&G, Division of Sport Fish, Area Management Biologist, P.O. Box 20, Douglas 99824; phone (907) 465-4270. A list of charter boats is available from the Juneau Convention and Visitors Bureau (phone 907/586-2201). Also see ads this section. ➤

Egan Drive and Glacier Highway/Juneau Veterans' Memorial Highway Log

Egan Drive from downtown Juneau proceeds north to **Milepost 9.4**, then becomes Glacier Highway. Egan Drive is named for William A. Egan (1914–84), first governor of the state of Alaska. From **Milepost 12.2** to road end, Glacier Highway has been renamed the Juneau Veterans' Memorial Highway. The highway ends 40.5 miles/65.3 km north of Juneau near Echo Cove on Berners Bay. It is a scenic drive northward along Favorite Channel.

0 Cruise ship terminal.

0.3 (0.5 km) Parking garage, 3-hour limit.

0.5 (0.8 km) Stoplight. Marine Way and Main Street. Egan Drive begins here.

0.7 (1.1 km) Alaska State Museum, exit east onto Whittier Street.

1.2 (1.9 km) Stoplight. Tenth Street exit east. For access to Douglas Highway and North Douglas Highway, turn west across Juneau–Douglas bridge (see logs this section).

1.3 (2.1 km) Turn west (left northbound) for Harris Harbor for small boats.

1.5 (2.4 km) Juneau–Douglas High School to east (right northbound).

1.7 (2.7 km) Aurora Basin small-boat

harbor to west (left northbound). Access to Juneau Yacht Club on Harbor Way Road; 10 RV sites, portable toilet and dumpster. No fee; May 1 through Sept.; sign-in at Harbormaster's office for permit (907/586-5255).

3.9 (6.3 km) Stoplight. Picnic tables at Twin Lakes to east. Also exit east for Bartlett Memorial Hospital and Alaska Native Health Center; access to Old Glacier Highway and residential area. Gastineau salmon hatchery to west.

5.5 (8.9 km) Stoplight. Lemon Creek area.

5.9 (9.5 km) Lemon Creek passes beneath highway.

6.1 (9.8 km) Mendenhall Wetlands viewing area; great place to see eagles and waterfowl.

6.7 (10.7 km) Access to Old Glacier Highway and Switzer Creek; exit east. Department store; service station with gas, propane, dump station.

8.1 (13 km) Airport access road.

8.2 (13.2 km) Fred Meyer shopping center.

8.8 (14.2 km) Stoplight; McDonald's. Airport turnoff and access to Nugget Mall and Airport Shopping Center to west. A 0.3-mile/0.5-km loop road (Old Glacier Highway) provides access to malls and to Juneau International Airport. Access to Mendenhall Wetlands State Game Refuge dike trail via Berners Avenue. Loop road rejoins Egan Drive at **Milepost 9.4.**

9.4 (15.1 km) Stoplight. South **junction** with Mendenhall Loop Road. Turn west for airport. Turn east for Mendenhall Center shopping mall and post office (just east of junction), and Mendenhall Glacier and visitor center (3.6 miles/5.8 km from junction).

Mendenhall Loop Road is a paved 6.8-mile/10.9-km loop that rejoins Glacier Highway at **Milepost 12.2.** To reach Mendenhall Glacier from here, drive east 2.2 miles/3.5 km and take spur road another 1.4 miles/2.2 km to the glacier and visitor center. The visitor center is open daily in summer from 8:30 A.M. to 5:30 P.M.; weekends only in winter, 9 A.M. to 4 P.M.

Continue on Mendenhall Loop Road past glacier spur road turnoff for Montana Creek Road (3.7 miles/6 km from junction) and access to Mendenhall Lake USFS campground, at Mile 0.4 Montana Creek Road. The campground has 60 sites, tables, fireplaces, water, pit toilets and dump station. Reservations available for some sites; phone 1-800-280 (CAMP). $8 fee. Montana Creek Road dead ends 3.5 miles/5.6 km from Mendenhall Loop Road. ▲

9.7 (15.6 km) Airport area access for southbound travelers via Old Glacier Highway.

9.9 (15.9 km) Mendenhall River and Brotherhood Bridge. The bridge was named in honor of the Alaska Native Brotherhood and is lined with bronze plaques symbolizing the Raven and Eagle clans.

10 (16.1 km) Mendenhall Glacier viewpoint to east; parking area with sign about Brotherhood Bridge and short walking trail.

10.5 (16.9 km) State troopers office.

10.8 (17.4 km) The 2.1-mile/3.4-km Mendenhall Peninsula Road, a 2-lane gravel road, to west. About halfway along this road, Engineer's Cutoff leads 0.3 mile/0.5 km to Fritz Cove Road.

11.4 (18.3 km) Auke Lake scenic wayside to east. Good view of Mendenhall Glacier reflected in the lake. This is one of the most photographed spots in Alaska. Red, pink and

This Mendenhall Glacier view is a short walk from parking area. (© David J. Job)

coho salmon spawn in Auke Lake system July to September (only limited fishing, for coho in September). Chum salmon are primarily from Auke Creek hatchery program.

11.5 (18.5 km) Fritz Cove Road (paved) leads 2.6 miles/4.2 km west and dead ends at Smuggler's Cove; excellent small-boat anchorage. Scenic viewpoint on Fritz Cove Road at Mile 1.2; Engineer's Cutoff at Mile 1.9 extends 0.3 mile/0.5 km to Mendenhall Peninsula Road.

11.6 (18.7 km) Turnoff to east for Chapel-by-the-Lake and to southeastern branch of University of Alaska.

11.8 (19 km) Short road west to National Marine Fisheries Service biological laboratory (self-guided walking tours between 8 A.M. and 4:30 P.M. Monday through Friday).

12.2 (19.6 km) **North junction** with Mendenhall Loop Road to west. Glacier Highway becomes Juneau Veterans' Memorial Highway and curves around Auke Bay to west. A small-boat harbor with snack shop, skiff and tackle rentals, and boat launch located at the head of the bay. Private ferry service (AUK NU) to Glacier Bay departs from here.

The 6.8-mile/10.9-km Mendenhall Loop Road rejoins Glacier Highway at **Milepost 9.4.** Motorists may turn east here and follow loop road 3.1 miles/5 km to Montana Creek Road and access to Mendenhall Lake USFS campground, or drive 4.6 miles/7.4 km and turn off on Mendenhall Glacier spur road, which leads another 1.4 miles/2.2 km to the glacier and visitor center. Parking area at Mendenhall Glacier; short, steep path to visitor center. The center is open daily in summer from 8:30 A.M. to 5:30 P.M. ▲

12.3 (19.8 km) Private RV park.

12.4 (20 km) Auke Bay post office to west.

12.6 (20.3 km) Spaulding trailhead to east; 3.5 miles/5.6 km long. Access to John Muir USFS cabin.

12.8 (20.6 km) Waydelich Creek and bridge.

13.8 (22.2 km) Auke Bay ferry terminal vehicle exit. *Watch for construction in 1997.*

13.9 (22.4 km) Auke Bay ferry terminal entrance. *LeConte* ferry passengers use parking area and terminal on right; all others use parking area and large terminal on left.

Visitor information counter staffed in summer; open only for ferry arrivals and departures.

15.1 (24.3 km) Auke Village Recreation Area begins northbound; 5 beachside picnic shelters accessible to west of highway (park on highway shoulder).

15.3 (24.6 km) Auke Village totem pole to east.

15.4 (24.8 km) Auke Village USFS campground; 14 picnic units, 12 campsites, tables, fireplaces, water, flush and pit toilets. $8 fee. Open May 1 to Sept. 30. ▲

16.5 (26.6 km) Lena Point Road, south entrance to loop road.

17 (27.3) Lena Point Road, north entrance to loop road.

17.4 (28.1 km) Lena Beach picnic area.

18.4 (29.6 km) Tee Harbor–Point Stevens Road (gravel) leads 0.3 mile/0.6 km west to public parking area and a private marina and fuel float.

19.2 (30.9 km) Inspiration Point turnout to west with view of the Chilkat Range, and over Tee Harbor and Shelter Island across Favorite Channel. Once a bread-and-butter commercial fishing area, hence the name "The Breadline" for this stretch of shoreline, it is now a popular sportfishing area. ◄

23.1 (37.3 km) Short road west to Catholic Shrine of St. Terese, located on a small island reached by a causeway.

23.3 (37.5 km) Turnout to west and view of island on which Shrine of St. Terese is situated.

23.9 (38.5 km) Peterson Lake trailhead to east; 4 miles/6.4 km long. Access to Peterson Lake USFS cabin. This trail connects with the Spaulding trail (see **Milepost 12.6**).

24.2 (39 km) **Peterson Creek** bridge. View spawning salmon here in late summer and early fall. Trout fishing. Black and brown bears in area. ◄

24.8 (40 km) Gravel road leads 0.6 mile/1 km west to Amalga Harbor; dock, boat launch, bait-casting area. Fireplace and chimney near end of road are remains of an old trapper's cabin.

27.1 (43.7 km) Windfall Lake trailhead to east; 3 miles/4.8 km long.

27.2 (43.9 km) Herbert River bridge.

27.4 (44.2 km) Herbert Glacier trailhead to east; 5 miles/8 km long.

27.7 (44.7 km) Eagle River bridge. Amalga trailhead just across bridge to east; 4 miles/6.4 km long.

28.4 (45.8 km) Eagle Beach picnic area with beachside picnic shelter and 8 picnic sites. View of Chilkat Range across Lynn Canal. Duck hunting on flats in low tide during open season.

28.7 (46.2 km) Scenic viewpoint to west.

29.3 (47.2 km) Scenic viewpoint to west.

32.7 (52.8 km) Turnout to west with view of Benjamin Island to southwest; just beyond it is Sentinel Island lighthouse. Visible to the northwest is North Island and northwest of it is Vanderbilt Reef, site of a great sea disaster. The SS *Princess Sophia,* carrying 288 passengers and 61 crew, ran aground on the Vanderbilt Reef early in the morning of Oct. 24, 1918. All aboard perished when a combination of stormy seas and a high tide forced the *Sophia* off the reef and she sank early in the evening of Oct. 25. The Vanderbilt Reef is now marked by a navigation light.

32.8 (52.9 km) Pavement ends northbound; 2-lane gravel extension of the Glacier Highway begins.

33 (53.1 km) Scenic viewpoint to west.

Berners Bay is a popular destination for Juneau paddlers. (© David J. Job)

Yankee Cove and beach below this point. The MV *Fairweather*, which cruises between Juneau and Skagway, docks at Yankee Cove.

35.4 (57.1 km) Sunshine Cove public beach access.

37.6 (60.7 km) North Bridget Cove beach access, Point Bridget State Park. The 2,850-acre park offers meadows, forests, rocky beaches, salmon streams and a trail system. Area is popular for cross-country skiing. Fires allowed on beach.

39 (62.8 km) Point Bridget trailhead; 3.5-mile/5.6-km hike to Point Bridget (7 hours round-trip); panoramic view of Lynn Canal and Chilkat Mountains from point.

39.4 (63.5 km) Cowee Creek bridge. Large parking area to west.

40.4 (65 km) Access left to Echo Cove beach. Park area.

40.5 (65.3 km) Road dead ends near Echo Cove on Berners Bay. Berners Bay is a popular destination for Juneau paddlers. It is 3 miles across and 34 miles northwest of Juneau.

Douglas Highway Log

Douglas Highway is a 3-mile/4.8-km paved road beginning on the Juneau side of the Douglas Bridge, crossing to Douglas Island, turning southeast, passing through the city of Douglas to road end and beginning of Treadwell Mine area.

0 Intersection of Egan Drive and Douglas Bridge.

0.5 (0.8 km) Right, Cordova Street leads to Dan Moller trail.

1.5 (2.4 km) Lawson Creek bridge.

2 (3.2 km) Tlingit Indian cemetery and grave houses.

2.5 (4 km) Turn left to boat harbor; dump station and Savikko Park with 4 overnight RV parking spaces without hookups. $5 per night, 3-day limit; obtain permit from Harbormaster's office at 1600 Harbor Way. Short gravel road leads to Juneau Island U.S. Bureau of Mines headquarters. Sandy Beach Recreation Area with water, toilets, play area, tennis courts, track, 2 ball fields, picnic tables, shelters and children's playground. Aptly named, this is one of the few sandy beaches in southeastern Alaska. Highway becomes St. Ann's Avenue.

3 (4.8 km) Road end.

North Douglas Highway Log

North Douglas Highway begins after crossing Douglas Bridge from Juneau and immediately turning right, northwest. **Milepost 1** appears at small bridge on this turn.

0 Intersection of Egan Drive and Douglas Bridge.

0.5 (0.8 km) Right, Cordova Street leads to Dan Moller trail.

1.5 (2.4 km) Lawson Creek bridge.

2 (3.2 km) Tlingit Indian cemetery and grave houses.

2.5 (4 km) Turn left to boat harbor; dump station and Savikko Park with 4 overnight RV parking spaces without hookups. $5 per night, 3-day limit; obtain permit from Harbormaster's office at 1600 Harbor Way. Short gravel road leads to Juneau Island U.S. Bureau of Mines headquarters. Sandy Beach Recreation Area with water, toilets, play area, tennis courts, track, 2 ball fields, picnic tables, shelters and children's playground. Aptly named, this is one of the few sandy beaches in southeastern Alaska. Highway becomes St. Ann's Avenue.

3 (4.8 km) Road end.

North Douglas Highway Log

North Douglas Highway begins after crossing Douglas Bridge from Juneau and immediately turning right, northwest. **Milepost 1** appears at small bridge on this turn.

0 Douglas Bridge.

0.3 (0.5 km) **Junction** of Douglas Highway and North Douglas Highway.

4.4 (7.1 km) Heliport to right.

6.9 (11.1 km) Eaglecrest Ski Area turnoff on left; drive 5.3 miles/8.5 km on gravel road to ski area. Good blueberry picking in August.

8.3 (13.5 km) Fish Creek bridge. Large parking area on right of bridge. This is a popular roadside fishing spot.

8.6 (13.9 km) Ninemile trail on right; small parking area.

9.5 (15.3 km) Scenic turnout and parking area with excellent view of Mendenhall Glacier; litter barrel. Boat ramp; launch permit required (contact harbormaster before arrival).

10.3 (16.6 km) Small waterfall on left.

11.4 (18.4 km) False Outer Point public beach access. Scenic view of Favorite Channel and Lynn Canal; parking area on right. Near the northern tip of Douglas Island, this is an excellent spot to observe marine activity and eagles.

12.3 (19.8 km) Outer Point trailhead on right.

13.1 (21 km) Road end.

Glacier Bay National Park and Preserve

What Tlingit Indians called "Big Ice-Mountain Bay" in naturalist John Muir's day (1879) is today one of southeastern Alaska's most dramatic attractions, Glacier Bay National Park and Preserve. Muir described Glacier Bay as "a picture of icy wildness unspeakably pure and sublime."

There are no roads to Glacier Bay National Park, except for a 10-mile/16-km stretch of gravel road connecting Bartlett Cove with Gustavus airport. Bartlett Cove is the site of a ranger station and Glacier Bay Lodge. Park naturalists conduct daily hikes and other activities from the visitor center at the lodge, and the excursion boat departs from there. Airlines service Gustavus airport. See Accommodations/Visitor Services and Transportation under Gustavus in this section.

Visitors should contact the Superintendent, Glacier Bay National Park and Preserve, Gustavus, AK 99826-0140, for more information, or check with Glacier Bay tour operators. The national park's headquarters is at Bartlett Cove; phone (907) 697-2230.

Glacier Bay National Park, at the northwest end of Alexander Archipelago, includes not only tidewater glaciers but also Mount Fairweather in the Fairweather Range of the St. Elias Mountains, the highest peak in southeastern Alaska, and also the U.S. portion of the Alsek River.

With passage of the Alaska National Interest Lands Conservation Act in December 1980, Glacier Bay National Monument, established in 1925 by Pres. Calvin Coolidge, became a national park. Approximately 585,000 acres were added to the park/preserve to protect fish and wildlife habitat and migration routes in Dry Bay and along the lower Alsek River, and to include the northwest slope of Mount Fairweather. Total acreage is 3,328,000 (3,271,000 in park, 57,000 in preserve) with 2,770,000 acres des-

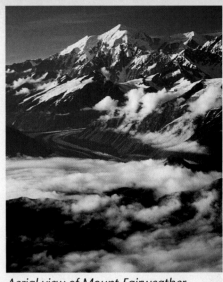

Aerial view of Mount Fairweather.
(©Michael DeYoung)

ignated wilderness.

When the English naval explorer Capt. George Vancouver sailed through the ice-choked waters of Icy Strait in 1794, Glacier Bay was little more than a dent in the coastline. Across the head of this seemingly minor inlet stood a towering wall of ice marking the seaward terminus of an immense glacier that completely filled the broad, deep basin of what is now Glacier Bay. To the north, ice extended more than 100 miles/160 km into the St. Elias Mountains, covering the intervening valleys with a 4,000-foot-/1,219-m-deep mantle of ice.

During the century following Vancouver's explorations, the glacier retreated some 40 miles/64 km back into the bay, permitting a spruce–hemlock forest to gradually fill the land. By 1916, the Grand Pacific Glacier, which once occupied the entire bay, had receded some 65 miles/105 km from the position observed by Vancouver in 1794. Nowhere else in the world have glaciers been observed to recede at such a rapid pace.

Today, few of the many tributary glaciers that once supplied the huge ice sheet extend to the sea. Glacier Bay National Park encloses 12 active tidewater glaciers, including several on the remote and seldom-visited western edge of the park along the Gulf of Alaska and Lituya Bay. Icebergs, cracked off from near-vertical ice cliffs, dot the waters of Glacier Bay.

A decline in the number of humpback whales using Glacier Bay for feeding and calf-rearing led the National Park Service to limit the number of boats visiting Glacier Bay from June to August. These regulations affect all motorized vessels. Check with the National Park Service for current regulations.

Glacier Bay National Park is approximately 100 miles/160 km from Juneau by boat. A $5 per person recreation use fee is charged on arrival at the park. Park rangers at Bartlett Cove are available to assist in advising visitors who wish to tour Glacier Bay in private boats or by kayak. Permits are required for motorized pleasure boats between June 1 and Aug. 31. The permits are free. A limited number are available, but rarely are boaters turned away. Permits must be obtained prior to entry into Glacier Bay and Bartlett Cove. Request permits no more than 2 months in advance by writing the National Park Service, Gustavus, AK 99826-0140. For more information, phone (907) 697-2627 (May 1 to Sept. 7).

Glacier Bay Lodge is the only accommodation within the national park, although nearby Gustavus (see description this section) has a number of lodges, inns, bed and breakfasts and rental cabins. Contact Glacier Bay Lodge Inc., 1-800-451-5952, for more information on the concessionaire-operated Glacier Bay Lodge and excursion boat cruises offered from the lodge.

Gasoline and diesel fuel may be purchased at Bartlett Cove, where a good anchorage is available. There are no other public facilities for boats within park boundaries; Sandy Cove, about 20 miles/32 km from Bartlett Cove, is a popular anchorage. Gustavus has a dock and small-boat harbor.

CAUTION BOATERS: No attempt should be made to navigate Glacier Bay without appropriate charts, tide tables and local knowledge. Floating ice is a special hazard. Because of the danger from waves caused by falling ice, small craft should not approach closer than 0.5 mile/0.8 km from tidewater glacier fronts.

Wildlife in the national park area is protected and hunting is not allowed. Firearms are illegal. CAUTION: Brown and black bears are present.

Fishing for silver and king salmon, Dolly Varden and halibut is excellent. A valid Alaska fishing license is required. Charter fishing trips are available.

There is an established campground at Bartlett Cove with 25 sites. Wilderness camping is also available throughout the park. ▲

Gustavus

(See map, page 653)

Gateway to Glacier Bay National Park and Preserve, the small community of Gustavus is located just outside the park boundary at the mouth of the Salmon River on the north shore of Icy Passage, 48 miles northwest of Juneau. It is 10 miles/16 km by road from Gustavus to Bartlett Cove within the park. **Population:** 380. **Emergency Services:** Phone 911. **Visitor Information:** Gustavus Visitors Assoc., Box 167, Gustavus 99826.

Private Aircraft: Gustavus airport, adjacent northeast; elev. 36 feet/11m; length 6,700 feet/2,042m; asphalt; fuel 100LL, A. Landing within the park is restricted to salt water (Adams Inlet is closed to aircraft landing).

Surrounded on 3 sides by the snow-covered peaks of the Chilkat Range and the Fairweather Mountains, Gustavus offers miles of level land with expansive sandy beaches, farmland and forest. Homesteaded in 1914

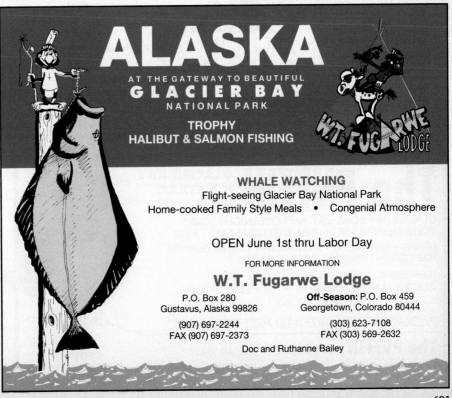

as a small agricultural community, the area was once named Strawberry Point because of its abundant wild strawberries. Today, most residents maintain gardens and make their living by fishing (commercial and subsistence), fish processing, tourism, arts and crafts, and working for the National Park Service and in various local trades.

Besides its proximity to the national park, Gustavus offers a number of attractions. Local charter boats—sometimes called "6 packs" because they carry about 6 passengers—are available for sportfishing (salmon, halibut), sightseeing Icy Strait and Glacier Bay, and whale watching. Whale sightings are almost guaranteed at Point Adolphous, where there is a resident pod. A paved road in town is great for bike riding.

There are extensive beaches in Gustavus which are great for beachwalking. Flat land walking is possible in the fen wetland environment, which also offers good bird watching for sandhill cranes and other birds. Be sure to bring rubber boots.

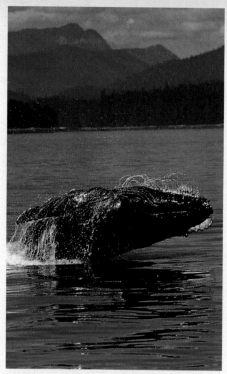

Whale watching is a popular activity out of Gustavus. (©Michael DeYoung)

ACCOMMODATIONS/VISITOR SERVICES

Accommodations in Gustavus include several inns, lodges, bed and breakfasts, and self-sufficient cabins. There are 2 restaurants. The lodges and inns serve meals for guests; drop-in customers check for space-available

meal reservations.

Businesses in Gustavus include a grocery store, art gallery, cafe, gift shop, hardware/building supply store, gas station, auto repair shop and fish-processing facilities. Fishing supplies and licenses may be purchased locally. A smokehouse is available for fishermen.

Annie Mae Lodge. Old-fashioned good food and good company. Three fine family-style meals using home-baked bread and pastries, fresh caught seafood, berries off the bush, and garden vegetables. We offer beautiful comfortable rooms, peace, quiet, abundant wildlife, wilderness, sportfishing, kayak trips, whale watching. Glacier Bay boat/plane tours. Box 80, Gustavus, AK 99826. Phone (907) 697-2346, fax (907) 697-2211. [ADVERTISEMENT]

Glacier Bay Country Inn and Grand Pacific Charters. Peaceful, storybook accommodations in a wilderness setting. Cozy comforters, warm flannel sheets, private baths. Superb dining features local seafoods, fresh produce, homebaked breads, spectacular desserts. Fishing, whale watching, sightseeing. Glacier Bay boat/plane tours. Courtesy van, bikes. Box 5MP, Gustavus, AK 99826. Phone (907) 697-2288 or 1-800-628-0912, fax (907) 697-2289. [ADVERTISEMENT]

Gustavus Inn. Country living, family-style gourmet local seafood meals, cozy bar, kitchen garden, bikes, trout fishing poles, courtesy van, afternoon park naturalist trip. Family-run since 1965. Custom fishing and Glacier Bay sightseeing packages arranged. For map, brochures, please write: Gustavus Inn, Box 60-MP, Gustavus, AK 99826 or call 1-800-649-5220. [ADVERTISEMENT]

The Puffin. See nearby Glacier Bay and Icy Strait. Stay in your own modern, comfortable, attractively decorated cabin with electricity on quiet wooded homestead. New picturesque central lodge. Complete country breakfast. Bicycles included. Children, pets welcome. Reservations for all charters, Glacier Bay tours. Qualified captains guide fishing, sightseeing charters. Friendly, personal attention. (907) 697-2260, fax (907) 697-2258, e-mail 73654.550@compuserve.com. [ADVERTISEMENT]

Spirit Walker Expeditions. Paddle with whales in Icy Strait! Premium guided sea kayaking trips are the perfect way to really experience Alaska's wilderness scenery, solitude and wildlife. Superb meals, all gear, instruction included. One to 7 days. Beginners, families, custom trips our specialties. Box 240MP, Gustavus, AK 99826. (907) 697-2266 or (800) KAYAKER. [ADVERTISEMENT]

TRI Bed and Breakfast of Glacier Bay. Visit us in our secluded rainforest homesite. Full breakfast with daily fresh eggs, homemade bread/jam. Deluxe and spacious individual cottages with insuite bath. Hiking, kayaking, whale watching, beachcombing, sportfishing, the Glacier Bay day boat or just getting here from Juneau, let us arrange your trip to Glacier Bay/Gustavus. P.O. Box 214MP, Gustavus, AK 99826. Phone (907) 697-2425; Fax (907) 697-2450. [ADVERTISEMENT]

Whalesong Lodge. Full-service lodge close to the beach and amenities. B&B accommodation with optional American plan. Also, condominium rental with full meal packages available. Unforgettable day or overnight tours of Glacier Bay, whale watching, sport fishing, kayaking, hiking. Airport transfers. Complimentary bicycles. Box 5-MP, Gustavus, AK 99826. Phone (907)

TRANSPORTATION

Ferry: *NOTE: There is no state ferry service to Glacier Bay.* Closest port of call for state ferries is Hoonah. (Kayakers getting off at Hoonah can expect a 2-day paddle across Icy Strait.

Private ferry services Gustavus from Juneau; contact AUK NU Tours, 76 Egan Dr., Juneau, AK 99801; phone (907) 586-8687 or toll free 1-800-820-2628, fax (907) 586-1337. One-way fare is $45.

Air: Glacier Bay may be reached by Alaska Airlines daily jet flights from Juneau; summer service begins June 1. Charter service available from Juneau, Sitka, Haines and Skagway to Gustavus airport. Charter air service available in Gustavus. Bus service between the airport and Bartlett Cove is available for arriving jet flights. Taxi service to local facilities and courtesy van service for some lodges are also available.

Many Gustavus bed and breakfasts will make transportation arrangements for guests from Juneau, Haines and Skagway.

Rental Cars: There is one car rental company in Gustavus, BW Rent-A-Car, phone (907) 697-2403.

Boat Service: Excursion boats operated by the park concession depart daily from Bartlett Cove. You may also charter a boat in Gustavus for sightseeing or fishing. Overnight cruise tours are available from Juneau.

Cruise Ships: Several cruise ships include Glacier Bay cruising in their itineraries. See Cruise Lines in the MARINE ACCESS ROUTES section.

Yakutat

Located on the Gulf of Alaska coast where Southeastern Alaska joins the major body of Alaska to the west; 225 miles/362 km northwest of Juneau; 220 miles/354 km southeast of Cordova and 380 miles/611 km southeast of Anchorage. **Population:** 801. **Emergency Services: Dept. of Public Safety,** phone (907) 784-3206. **Fire Department,** phone 911. **Yakutat Health Center,** phone (907) 784-3275. **Maritime Search and Rescue,** contact the Coast Guard at 1-800-478-5555.

Visitor Information: Inquire at one of the lodges, at the USFS office, or the chamber of commerce office (write Chamber of Commerce, Box 234, Yakutat, AK 99689). For sportfishing information, stop by the ADF&G office at Mile 0.5 Cannon Beach Road, or write Sport Fish Division, Box 49, Yakutat 99689, phone (907) 784-3222. For information about the National Park Service, contact the visitor center at Box 137, Yakutat, AK 99689; phone (907) 748-3295. Interpretive programs are offered daily at 2 P.M. from June through August.

Elevation: Sea level. **Climate:** Similar to the rest of coastal southeastern Alaska: mild in summer, winters are moderate. Average annual snowfall is 216 inches. Total annual precipitation is about 130 inches. Normal daily maximum in August, 60°F/16°C; minimum in January, 17°F/-8°C. Prevailing winds

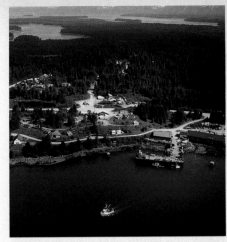

Yakutat is located on Monti Bay.

(© David J. Job)

are southeasterly.

Private Aircraft: Yakutat airport, 3 miles/4.8 km southeast; elev. 33 feet/10m; length 7,700 feet/2,347m; asphalt; fuel 100, A1. Seaplane base 1 mile/1.6 km northwest.

Transportation: Air—Daily jet service from Seattle, Juneau, Anchorage and Cordova. Charter air service available.

Yakutat has 3 lodges, 1 inn, 4 bed and breakfasts, a restaurant, cafe, 2 gift shops, bank, 2 grocery stores, 2 hardware stores, post office, clinic and gas station. Boat rentals, car rentals and cab service are available.

Yakutat Bay is one of the few refuges for vessels along this long stretch of coast in the Gulf of Alaska. The site was originally the principal winter village of the local Tlingit Indian tribe. Sea otter pelts brought Russian to the area in the 19th century. Fur traders were followed by gold seekers, who came to work the black sand beaches. Commercial salmon fishing developed in this century, and the first cannery was built here in 1904. Today's economy is based primarily on fishing and fish processing. Salmon, halibut, crab and black cod make up the fishery. Government and local businesses employ most residents. Subsistence activities are primarily fishing (salmon and shellfish), hunting (moose, bear, goats, ducks and small game), and gathering seaweed and berries. The soil is not suitable for agriculture, and a vegetable garden requires a great deal of preparation to produce small quantities.

While hunting and fishing in particular draw visitors to Yakutat, the surge of Hubbard Glacier in June 1986, which sealed off the mouth of Russell Fiord, drew national attention. Malaspina Glacier, largest on the North American continent, is northwest of town. Nearer to town, Cannon Beach has good beachcombing and a picnic area.

AREA FISHING: Yakutat is considered a world-class sportfishing destination. Steelhead fishing is among the finest anywhere. King and silver (coho) salmon run in abundance in Yakutat area salt water, rivers and streams May through September. The area also boasts red and pink salmon and smelt in season. USFS cabins available on some rivers; check with the Forest Service (907/784-3359).

Lost River and **Tawah Creek**, 10 miles/16 km south of Yakutat on Lost River Road, silver (coho) salmon to 20 lbs., mid-August through September. **Situk River**, 12 miles/19.3 km south of Yakutat on the Lost River Road (also accessible by Forest Highway 10), is one of Alaska's top fishing spots spring and fall for steelhead and silver salmon and has one of the best sockeye (red) salmon runs in the state, late June through August; steelhead averaging 10 lbs., April 1 toMay 30 for spring run, October and November for fall run; king salmon to 45 lbs., mid-June through July; silver salmon to 23 lbs., mid-August through September; pink salmon run

View from Mount Ripinski of Haines and Chilkat and Chilkoot inlets. (© Crystal Images, Kathleen Marie Menke)

in August, yields Dolly Varden also. **Yakutat Bay**, king salmon 30 to 50 lbs., May through June; silver salmon to 20 lbs., late August through September. ✦

Haines

(See map, page 653)

Located on Portage Cove, Chilkoot Inlet, on the upper arm of Lynn Canal, 80 air miles/129 km northwest of Juneau; 151 road miles/243 km southeast of Haines Junction, YT. Southern terminus of the Haines Highway. NOTE: Although Haines is only 13 miles/21 km by water from Skagway, it is 359 miles/578 km by road! **Population:** 1,363. **Emergency Services: Alaska State Troopers,** phone (907) 766-2552. **City Police,** phone (907) 766-2121. **Fire Department** and **Ambulance,** emergency only phone 911. **Doctor,** phone (907) 766-2521. **Maritime Search and Rescue,** contact the Coast Guard at 1-800-478-5555.

Visitor Information: At 2nd and Willard streets. There are free brochures for all of Alaska and the Yukon. Open daily, 8 A.M. to 8 P.M., June through August; 8 A.M. to 5 P.M. weekdays, September through May. Phone (907) 766-2234; toll free 1-800-458-3579; Internet: www.haines.ak.us; e-mail: haine-

sak@wwa.com.. Write the Haines Visitor Bureau at Box 530, Haines, AK 99827. Phone the Alaska Dept. of Transportation at (907) 766-2340.

Elevation: Sea level. **Climate:** Average daily maximum temperature in July, 66°F/19°C; average daily minimum in January, 17°F/-8°C. Extreme high summer temperature, 90°F/32°C; extreme winter low, -16°F/-27°C; average annual precipitation, 59 inches. **Radio:** KHNS-FM 102.3. **Television:** 12 cable channels. **Newspaper:** *Chilkat Valley News* (weekly).

Private Aircraft: Haines airport, 3 miles/4.8 km west;.elev. 16 feet/5m; length 3,000 feet/914m; asphalt; fuel 100; unattended.

The original Indian name for Haines was *Dtehshuh,* meaning "end of the trail." It was a trading post for both Chilkat and Interior Indians. The first white man to settle here was George Dickinson, who came as an agent for the North West Trading Co.

The following year S. Hall Young, a Presbyterian missionary, came into Chilkat Inlet with his friend, naturalist John Muir. They planned to build a Christian town, offering the Chilkat people a missionary and teacher. The site chosen was on the narrow portage between the Chilkat River and Lynn Canal. By 1881, with financial help from Sheldon Jackson, the mission was established. The town was named for Mrs. F.E. Haines, secretary of the Presbyterian National Committee of Home Missions, which raised funds for the new mission.

In 1884 the Haines post office was established, although the settlement was still known locally as Chilkoot. The town became an important outlet for the Porcupine Mining District, producing thousands of dollars' worth of placer gold at the turn of the century. Haines also marked the beginning of the Dalton Trail, which crossed the Chilkat mountain pass to the Klondike goldfields in the Yukon.

Just to the south of Haines city center is Port Chilkoot on Portage Cove. The U.S. government established a permanent military post here in 1904 and called it Fort William H. Seward, in honor of the secretary of state who negotiated the purchase of Alaska from Russia in 1867.

In 1922, the fort was renamed Chilkoot Barracks, after the mountain pass and the Indian tribe on the Chilkoot River. (There are 2 tribes in this area: the Chilkat and the Chilkoot.) Until WWII this was the only U.S. Army post in Alaska. Chilkoot Barracks was deactivated in 1946 and sold in 1947 to a group of enterprising U.S. veterans who had designs of creating a business cooperative on the site. Their original plans were never fully realized, but a few stayed on to convert some of the houses on Officers' Row into permanent homes.

In 1970, Port Chilkoot merged with Haines to become a single municipality, the city of Haines. Two years later, the post was designated a national historic site and became officially known, again, as Fort William H. Seward (although many people still call it Port Chilkoot).

Fishing and gold mining were the initial industries of the Haines area. Haines is also remembered for its famous strawberries, developed by Charles Anway about 1900. His Alaskan hybrid, *Burbank,* was a prize winner at the 1909 Alaska–Yukon–Pacific Exposition in Seattle, WA. A strawberry festival was held annually in Haines for many years, and this local event grew into the Southeast Alaska State Fair, which each summer draws thousands of visitors. Today, halibut and gill-net salmon fishing, lumbering and tourism are the basis of the economy. Haines is an important port on the Alaska Marine Highway System as the southern terminus of the Haines Highway, 1 of the 2 year-round roads linking southeastern Alaska with the Interior.

ACCOMMODATIONS/VISITOR SERVICES

Haines offers travelers accommodations at several hotels and motels, including Captin's Choice Motel (907/766-3111), Eagle's Nest Motel (907/766-2891), Halsingland Hotel (907/766-2000), Mountain View Motel (907/766-2900) and Thunderbird Motel (907/766-2131). There are also 7 bed and breakfasts and 2 apartment/condo rentals. See ads this section.

There is a youth hostel (families welcome) with cabin accommodations on Small Tracts Road.

Haines has all traveler facilities, including hardware and grocery stores, gift shops and art galleries, automotive repair, laundry, post office and bank. Gift shops and galleries feature the work of local artisans. There are several restaurants, cafes and taverns.

Alaskan Sugar Bush, located in Haines, is the only commercial birch syrup production site in Southeast Alaska, one of 7 in the state. The making of syrup from the sap of birch trees is a new and growing cottage industry. Birch Boy Products, a family-owned and operated facility, has produced over 1500 gallons of birch syrup at 18 Mile Haines Highway. Look for Birch Boy Alaskan birch syrup and other Birch Boy gourmet syrups in downtown Haines. [ADVERTISEMENT]

State campgrounds in the area include

Portage Cove, Chilkat State Park, Chilkoot Lake and Mosquito Lake.

Portage Cove State Recreation Site offers 9 tent sites, half-mile past Fort Seward on Portage Cove. Water and toilets available. Campers enjoy view of the Coast Range and Lynn Canal. Watch for cruise ships, ferries, eagles, whales and porpoises. *NOTE: This site*

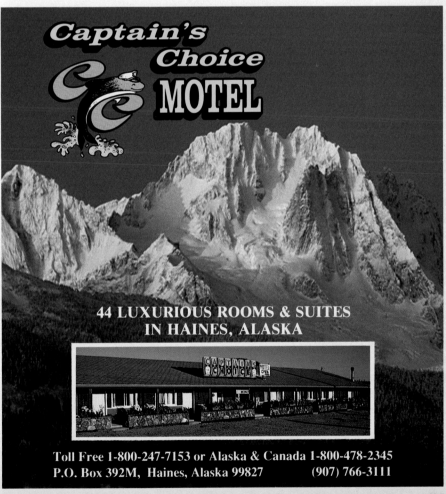

HAINES
Valley of the Eagles

The beauty of Southeast Alaska is waiting for you in Haines
Enjoy unique cultural attractions such as the Chilkat Bal
Eagle Preserve, Fort William H. Seward—a National Histori
Landmark, the Chilkat Indian Dancers, Totem Pole Carvers, Sheldon Museum and Cultura
Center, American Bald Eagle Foundation, many talented Alaskan Artists and each fall th
Alaska Bald Eagle Festival.

ACCOMMODATIONS/RESTAURANTS

(1) **BAMBOO ROOM RESTAURANT** Famous for our halibut fish 'n chips, Home-made soups & pies. Daily specials. Seafood & Steaks. Espresso. Open 6 a.m. year round. Full service bar & liquor store. Second Avenue. (907) 766-2800 or 766-2474.

(2) **BEAR CREEK CABINS** 1.5 Miles from downtown on Small Tracts Rd. FAMILY CABINS @ $38.00 Children under 6 stay free! Clean, modern kitchen & bath facilities. Coin-op laundry, store on premises. Bike and hot tub rentals. (907) 766-2259.

(3) **CAPTAIN'S CHOICE INC. MOTEL** Haines finest & most comfortable lodging. Featuring Car Rentals, Room Service, Tour Bookings, Courtesy Transfers. Centrally located. See our display ad. (907) 766-3111 or 800-247-7153 or 800-478-2345 Alaska & Yukon. FAX 766-3332.

(4) **CHILKAT BAKERY & RESTAURANT** Bakery products fresh daily. Breakfast-Lunch-Dinner. 7 a.m. - 9 p.m. Plenty of parking. 5th Avenue.

(5) **CHILKAT VALLEY INN BED & BREAKFAST** 8 miles from downtown Haines on the edge of the Eagle Preserve. 1959 homestead overlooks the Chilkat River Valley. Year round accessibility in a wilderness setting. Ideal location for wildlife photography or quiet retreat. P.O. Box 861, Haines, AK 99827 (8.5 Mile Haines Highway). (907) 766-3331.

(6) **FORT SEWARD CONDOS** Located in former officers' quarters at historic Fort Seward overlooking Lynn Canal and mountains beyond. Completely furnished, spacious apartments, 1 & 2 bedroom units, full kitchens, bath and laundry facilities. 2 day minimum rental. Families welcome. NO PETS. #3 Ft. Seward Dr., P.O. Box 75, Haines, AK 99827. (907) 766-2425.

(7) **FT. SEWARD LODGE & RESTAURANT** Affordable lodging, ocean view kitchenettes, restaurant-saloon, Alaskan cuisine and decor. Military & senior discounts. 1-800-478-7772 (good in Yukon/B.C./AK/& Continental U.S.). See our display ad.

(8) **SUMMER INN BED & BREAKFAST** Charming, historic house. Open year round. Full, homemade breakfast, centrally located, mountain & ocean views. Ask about our winter rates for wildlife photographers and eagle watchers. See our display ad. 117 Second Avenue North, P.O. Box 1198, Haines, AK 99827. Phone/Fax (907) 766-2970.

ART GALLERIES/GIFT SHOPS

(9) **BELL'S STORE** For the very best Alaskan gifts and a unique shopping experience. FTD service and Fresh Flowers too. OPEN ALL YEAR. 18 Second Ave.

(10) **KING'S STORE** "Same day" Photo Center. Alaskan ivory, gifts, gems & minerals, unique printwear. A BROWSER'S PARADISE. On Main St. across from museum. Open all year. (907) 766-2336.

(11) **SEA WOLF GALLERY** Artists at work at this fine studio-gallery. Wood carving, prints, jewelry by local artist, Tresham Gregg. Located at Totem Village, Fort Seward Parade Field. (907) 766-2558.

(12) **WHALE RIDER GALLERY** Local artist gallery featuring wood carvings, paintings, jewelry, prints and Alaskan clothing. Located at 20 Portage St., Fort Seward. (907) 766-2540.

ATTRACTIONS

(13) **ALASKA BALD EAGLE FESTIVAL** November 7-9, 1997. See the world's largest gathering of bald eagles in the Chilkat Bald Eagle Preserve. Festival highlights include: Release of wild rehabilitated eagles, slide shows by well-known authors and photographers, art show, naturalist guided transportation to the preserve, live bird presentations, visit the American Bald Eagle Foundation natural history display and diorama. For information call 1-800-246-6268 or (907) 766-2202. P.O. Box 1449, Haines, AK 99827. E-mail: chamber@seaknet.alaska.edu.

(14) **ALASKA INDIAN ARTS/CHILKAT DANCERS** Traditional Northwest Coast totem carvers, silversmiths & printmakers at work. Home of the Chilkat Dancers who perform several times each week during the summer. At Fort Seward. P.O. Box 271, Haines, AK 99827. Phone/FAX (907) 766-2160.

(15) **FORT WILLIAM H. SEWARD NATIONAL HISTORIC LANDMARK** First Army Post built in Alaska. Totem Village & Arts and Cultural Center. Walking tours available.

(16) **SHELDON MUSEUM & CULTURAL CENTER** See Chilkat Blankets, the lens from Eldred Rock Lighthouse, carved halibut hooks (designed to catch only certain size fish) and many other fascinating items as you experience the Tlingt Indian Culture and Pioneer History of our valley. Alaska Book & Gift Store. 11 Main St., P.O. Box 269, Haines, AK 99827. (907) 766-2366 or FAX (907) 766-2368.

(17) **SOUTHEAST ALASKA STATE FAIR & ALASKAN BALD EAGLE MUSIC FESTIVAL** 2nd Weekend in August 1997. Great Music, Parade, 27th Annual Horse Show, Exhibits, Logging Show, Kid's Events, Food & Trade Booths. For more information call (907) 766-2476.

AUTO SERVICE

(18) **BIGFOOT AUTO SERVICE** NAPA Parts, Welding & Towing, A.S.E. Technicians, Gas, Diesel, Goodyear Sales & Service. 1 Mile Haines Highway. (907) 766-2458/2459.

(19) **BUSHMASTER SERVICE & REPAIR** Four wheel alignment, suspension, brakes major engine & driveline work, electronic engine controls. FACTORY WARRANTY for your new vehicle. Guaranteed service. 4th & Union St. (907) 766-3217.

(20) **CHARLIE'S REPAIR SERVICE** Auto, marine, R.V., welding; free RV water and dump. 24 Hour Gas with MC-VISA. 225 Second Ave. N. (907) 766-2494.

(21) **THE PARTS PLACE** Auto-RV-Marine. If you need it, we have it or will get it. 104 3rd Ave. S. (907) 766-2940.

(22) **TESORO ALASKA** Gas and diesel. Free coffee, RV water and dump. Propane. MasterCard/VISA accepted. At intersection of the Haines Hwy./Main Street. (907) 766-2194.

CAMPER PARKS

(23) **HAINES HITCH-UP RV PARK** 92 Full Service Sites. 20 Pull-thrus. Level Grassy 25' wide lots. Cable TV. Immaculate Restrooms & Showers for our guests. Laundromat and gift shop. P.O. Box 383, Haines, AK, 99827. (907) 766-2882.

(24) **OCEANSIDE RV PARK** Beautiful Ocean View. 23 Spaces. Full service includes TV Hook-up. Adjacent to laundry & showers. Downtown on the waterfront, close to the Small Boat Harbor. P.O. Box 149, Haines, AK 99827. (907) 766-2444.

FISHING CHARTERS/LODGES

(25) **BIRCH ISLAND LODGE** Chilkat Lake. Good fishing and good times. All gear provided. P.O. Box 1276, Haines, AK 99827. (907) 767-5656.

© 1991 Tresham

GROCERIES/SEAFOOD

㉖ ALASKAN & PROUD SUPERMARKET We're here to serve the weary traveler with the finest selection of groceries, freshest meats, produce and dairy products available in Haines. Enjoy our famous Alaskan Hospitality! Open 8 a.m.-8 p.m. Mon.-Sat., 10 a.m.-7 p.m. Sundays. 3rd & Dalton Street. (907) 766-2181.

㉗ BELL'S SEAFOOD Alaskan Seafood at its very Best!!! We Pack to Ship. 2nd Avenue next to Bell's Store. Downtown Haines, Alaska. AK 561 • 18 Second Ave., P.O. Box 1189, Haines, AK 99827. (907) 766-2950.

㉘ HAINES QUICK SHOP/OUTFITTER SPORTING GOODS Groceries, Videos, Ice, Fishing, Licenses, Tackle & Sporting Goods. Next to Post Office. Open daily 7 a.m. to Midnight. Mile 0 Haines Highway.

㉙ HOWSERS SUPERMARKET One Stop Shopping, Groceries, Fresh Meat, Dairy, ICE, Deli, Natural Foods, Sandwiches & Pizzas, Toys, and much more. Main Street.

㉚ MOUNTAIN MARKET NATURAL FOOD STORE & DELI Espresso Bar • Deli • Fresh Baked Goods • Sandwiches • Fresh Soups • Natural & Organic Foods • Vitamins • Health Care Products • Located at the corner of 3rd Avenue & Haines Hwy. (907) 766-3340.

㉛ OUTFITTER LIQUOR STORE Cold beer, wide variety of liquors & wines. Ice. Open daily 8 a.m. to midnight. Next to Post Office. Mile 0 Haines Highway.

RESORTS

㉜ WEEPING TROUT SPORTS RESORT Chilkat Lake. Fly fishing, Executive golf, meals, lodging & leisure on 20 beautiful acres. Naturalists, photographers & artists welcome. P.O. Box 129, Haines, AK 99827. Phone (907) 766-2827, Fax 766-2824, Resort 766-3369 User #11.

SERVICES

㉝ E.D. & D. Cable TV, Computers, Video Tapes, Electronic Parts and Service. Radio Shack Dealer, Cellular One Agent. Mile 1 Haines Highway. (907) 766-2337 or 766-2137.

SIGHTSEEING/TRANSPORTATION

✓ **㉞ ALASKA NATURE TOURS** Fun & informative excursions into the Chilkat Bald Eagle Preserve guided by top local naturalists. Hiking adventures, wildlife photography, bus & walking tours since 1985. Located behind the Visitor's Center, 130 Second Ave. South, P.O. Box 491, Haines, AK 99827. Phone/FAX (907) 766-2876.

✓ **㉟ CHILKAT GUIDES** Daily 3 1/2 hour float trips through the Bald Eagle Preserve. Also overnight float trips & hiking adventures. (907) 766-2491.

㊱ HAINES AIRWAYS Spectacular flightseeing tours from Haines and Juneau. Scheduled service to Juneau, Haines, Gustavus & Hoonah. (907) 766-2646 or 789-2336.

㊲ HAINES-SKAGWAY WATER TAXI Two roundtrips daily between downtown Haines and Skagway. Departures from the Small Boat Harbor. Ask about our discount railroad package to Skagway. $29 RT; $18 OW, Children Under 12 half-price, Bikes $5. P.O. Box 246, Haines, AK 99827. Call (907) 766-3395.

✓ **㊳ RIVER ADVENTURES** Daily River tours available. Join us as we take you on a journey through the Bald Eagle Preserve and into the wilderness of Alaska. P.O. Box 556, Haines, AK 99827. (907) 766-2050, FAX 766-2051.

㊴ SOCKEYE CYCLE - Alaska Bicycle Tours - Daily 1-3 HR Guided Tours through the Bald Eagle Preserve in the Chilkat Valley. Multi day fully supported Mtn. Bike Tours in British Columbia and the Yukon. 2 Full Service bike shops in Haines and Skagway, rentals, sales, service. Brochure, MP. Box 829, 24 Portage Dr., Haines, AK 99827. Phone/FAX (907) 766-2869. E-mail: cycleak@ibm.net.

㊵ TANANI BAY KAYAK AND CANOE RENTALS Sea kayak and canoe rentals. Quality at low prices. Pick-up and delivery available to Chilkoot Lake and other sights in the Lynn Canal area. On Front Street near the corner of Union & Front. Near downtown. 209 Front Street. (907) 766-2804.

㊶ THE TRAVEL CONNECTION Glacier Bay Headquarters, ferry reservations, local tours, custom tours for all of Alaska. P.O. Box 645, Haines, AK 99827 (across from the Visitors Center). 800-572-8006 or (907) 766-2681.

Lynn Canal

Haines is waiting for you ... Sponsored by Haines Chamber of Commerce (907) 766-2202

is for walk-in and bicyclist camping only. ▲

Chilkat State Park, with 32 RV sites and 3 tent sites, is about 8 miles/13 km from Haines on Mud Bay Road (from the Haines Highway, bear right at the Y by the Welcome to Haines sign; continue straight past the high school and up the hill, where the road bends to the right; follow signs from hill to Chilkat State Park). See MUD BAY ROAD log this section.

Chilkoot Lake Campground (32 sites) is approximately 10 miles/16 km from Haines on Lutak Road (6 miles/10 km past the ferry terminal; turn right when exiting the ferry for Chilkoot Lake); see LUTAK ROAD log this section. There are 5 private campgrounds in Haines. ▲

Mosquito Lake State Recreation Site is located on Mosquito Lake Road, 3 miles/6.5 km north of Mile 27 Haines Highway. It has 6 campsites nestled in a wooded setting around Mosquito Lake. Toilets, drinking water, a picnic shelter, fishing and boat launch are available. Small store and softball diamond at Mile 27. See the HAINES HIGHWAY section. ▲

Eagle Camper RV Park, located at 755 Union St. in beautiful Haines, Alaska. 30 full hookups with cable TV, tents welcome. Lawn with barbecues and picnic tables. Laundromat (for registered guests only). Public showers and propane. This RV park is just blocks from town and is located on 3¹/₂ acres with grass and trees. It has a circle drive for easy entrance to all spaces. Senior discounts, 60 years or older. P.O. Box 28, Haines, AK 99827. Phone (907) 766-2335, fax (907) 766-2335. Good Sam Park. [ADVERTISEMENT]

Haines Hitch-Up RV Park offers easy access to 92 full hookups (30 amps), 25-foot-wide, grassy, level sites. 20 pull-throughs. Cable TV. Immaculate restrooms for registered guests only. Gift shop and laundromat. Located at the junction of Haines Highway and Main Street. From ferry proceed to junction of 2nd Avenue and Main Street then west 0.5 mile on Main Street. P.O. Box 383, Haines, AK 99827. (907) 766-2882. [ADVERTISEMENT] ▲

A Sheltered Harbor Bed & Breakfast. Waterfront accommodation in Haines, located in historic Fort Seward across from the cruise ship dock providing a panoramic view of the Lynn Canal. Five spacious rooms, each with a private bath, color cable TV with remote, phone and generous hot home-style breakfast. Charter fishing and sightseeing tours available, along with vacuum-packing and freezing of your catch. Browse our gift shop featuring Alaska-made and local arts and crafts. Open year-round. VISA/MasterCard accepted. Reservations: (907) 766-2741. [ADVERTISEMENT]

TRANSPORTATION

Air: Haines is served regularly by L.A.B. Flying Service, Haines Airways and Wings of Alaska. Haines airport is 3.5 miles/5.6 km from downtown. Commercial airlines provide transportation to and from motels, and some motels offer courtesy car pickup.

Bus: Local bus service to ferry terminal and guided sightseeing tours are available. Two companies also offer service to and from Anchorage, Fairbanks and Whitehorse, YT, via the Alaska Highway.

Car Rental: Available at Avis Rent-A-Car, Halsingland Hotel (907/766-2733), Captain's Choice Motel (907/766-3111), and Eagle's Nest Motel (907/766-2891).

Taxi: 24-hour service to ferry terminal and airport.

Highways: The Haines Highway connects Haines, AK, with Haines Junction, YT. It is maintained year-round. See HAINES HIGHWAY section for details.

Ferry: Alaska Marine Highway vessels serve Haines from southeastern Alaska, Prince Rupert, BC, and Bellingham, WA. Alaska state ferries run year-round; phone (907) 766-2111. See MARINE ACCESS ROUTES section for details. Ferries unload at the terminal on Lutak Road, 4.5 miles/7.2 km from downtown Haines. Bus/van service meets all ferries in summer.

Water-taxi: The Haines/Skagway Water Taxi provides water-taxi service to Skagway twice daily during the summer; phone (907) 766-3395.

Cruise Ships: Twelve cruise ships make Haines a port of call.

Private Boats: Transient moorage is available at Letnikof Cove and at the small-boat harbor downtown. Contact the harbormaster, phone (907) 766-2448.

ATTRACTIONS

Take the walking tour of historic Fort William H. Seward; details and map are available at the visitor information center and at other businesses. Historic buildings of the post include the former cable office; warehouses and barracks; "Soapsuds Alley," the housing for noncommissioned officers whose wives did washing for the soldiers; the former headquarters building, now a residence, fronted by a cannon and a totem depicting a bear and an eagle; Officers' Row at the "Top O' the Hill," restored houses now rented as apartments; the commanding officers' quarters, now the Halsingland Hotel, where Elinor Dusenbury (who later wrote the music for "Alaska's Flag," which became the state song) once lived; the

Sunset silhouettes cyclist on dock at Chilkat State Park. (© Ruth von Spalding)

fire hall; the guard house (jail); the former contractor's office, then plumber's quarters; the post exchange (now a lodge), gymnasium, movie house and the mule stables. Look for historic and interpretive signs.

Visit the Chilkat Center for the Arts at the auditorium at Fort Seward. Here, the Chilkat Dancers interpret ancient Tlingit Indian legends. Check with the visitor information center or Alaska Indian Arts Inc. for schedule of performances.

Totem Village, on the former post parade ground, includes a replica of a tribal ceremonial house and a trapper's cabin and cache. There is a salmon bake, the Port Chilkoot Potlatch, held nightly in summer next to the tribal house; reservations recommended. Prior to the establishment of the fort, this area was part of an ancient portage route for Tlingit Indians transporting canoes from the Chilkat River to Lynn Canal.

See the Welcome Totems located at the Y on the Haines Highway. These poles were created by carvers of Alaska Indian Arts Inc. *The Raven* pole is symbolic of Raven, as founder of the world and all his great powers. The second figure is *The Whale*, representing Alaska and its great size. The bottom figure is the head of *The Bear*, which shows great strength. *The Eagle* pole tells of his feeding grounds (the Haines area is noted for its eagles). Top figure is *The Salmon Chief*, who provides the late run of salmon to the feeding grounds. *The Eagle Chief*, head of the Eagle clan, is the third figure, and the bottom figure is *The Brown Bear*, which also feeds on salmon and is a symbol of strength. Inquire at the visitor information center about location of poles.

The Sheldon Museum and Cultural Center is located on the old Haines Mission property at the end of Main Street by the boat harbor. Exhibits present the pioneer history of the Chilkat Valley and the story and culture of the Tlingit Native people. Chilkat blankets, Russian trunks, blue dishes, mounted eagles, Jack Dalton's sawed-off shotgun, photographs and a video on eagles make a fascinating history lesson. Children's "discovery" sheet available. Open daily 1–5 P.M. in summer, plus many mornings and evenings; winter, 1–4 P.M Sunday, Monday and Wednesday, 3–5 P.M. Tuesday, Thursday and Friday. Admission fee $3; children free. Phone (907) 766-2366.

Mountain Flying Service/Tickets & Tours. Located 3 doors south of the visitors' center, specializing in flights over and into Glacier Bay as well as Alaska ferry reservations and all Haines/Glacier Bay tour sales. We provide the highest quality high wing "Bush" aircraft and experienced pilots to give you the best flight in all of Alaska. Mountain Flying Service (907) 766-3007. Tickets & Tours 1-800-954-8747, Box 1404, Haines, AK 99827. [ADVERTISEMENT]

Enjoy the Fourth of July celebration, which includes canoe and kayak races on Chilkoot Lake, logging events, bicycle and foot races, pie-eating and other contests, parades and performances at the Chilkat Center for the Arts.

The Southeast Alaska State Fair, held at the fairgrounds in Haines (Aug. 6–10, 1997), features agriculture, home arts, and fine arts and crafts. A big event at the fair is the Bald Eagle Music Festival. There are exhibits

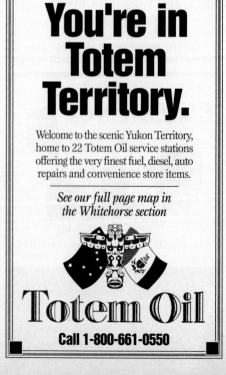

of flowers, livestock, baked goods, beer and wine, needlework, quilting, woodworking and over a dozen other categories. There are also a parade, horse show and other events, including pig racing for cookies. Brochures available from the Fair offices. Write to Box 385, Haines 99827, or (907) 766-2476.

American Bald Eagle Foundation is Haines' newest attraction. Interpretive center shows visitors how the bald eagle interacts with its environment through exhibits; mounted eagles, a wide variety of mammals, and fish and undersea life. Admission is free, donations welcomed. Open daily 10 A.M. to 6 P.M. in summer. Located at the Haines Highway and 2nd Street, just across 2nd Street from the city/municipal building.

Bald Eagle Festival. The festival includes release of wild rehabilitated eagles, live bird presentations, art exhibits, naturalist-guided tours to bald eagle preserve, exhibits and more. The events take place Nov. 7–9, 1997, and coincide with "the gathering," when eagles congregate to feed on late fall run salmon (see following). Contact the chamber of commerce at 1-800-246-6268 for more information.

Alaska Chilkat Bald Eagle Preserve, where the world's greatest concentration of American bald eagles takes place October through January on Chilkat River flats below Klukwan. The eagle viewing area begins at **Milepost H 17** on the Haines Highway. The 48,000-acre Alaska Chilkat Bald Eagle Preserve was established in 1982. The Chilkat Valley at Haines is the annual gathering site of more than 3,000 bald eagles, which gather to feed on the late run of chum salmon in the Chilkat River.

Dalton City, opened in 1992, is housed in the "White Fang" Disney film set. It is located at the fairgrounds.

Visit the small-boat harbor at the foot of Main Street for an interesting afternoon outing. Watch gill-net and crab fishermen setting out from here. Good views from Lookout Park and also from the shoreline between Haines and Portage Cove Campground.

Visit State Parks. Chilkoot Lake, at the end of Lutak Road, is worth a visit. Beautiful setting with a picnic area, campground and boat launch. Watch for brown bears in nearby waters in the fall, attracted by spawning salmon. (Private boat tours of Chilkoot Lake are available; check in town.) Chilkat State Park on Mud Bay Road is also a scenic spot with hiking trails, beach access, views of glaciers (Rainbow and Davidson), fishing, camping and picnicking. Both parks are within 10 miles/16 km of downtown Haines.

Go Flightseeing. Local air charter opera-

tors offer flightseeing trips for spectacular close-up views of glaciers, ice fields, mountain peaks and bald eagles. Glacier Bay is just west of Haines.

Charter boat operators in Haines offer fishing, sightseeing and photography trips.

Watch totem carvers at the Alaska Indian Arts Inc. workshop, located in the restored hospital at Fort Seward. This nonprofit organization is dedicated to the revival of Tlingit Indian art. Craftsmen also work in silver and stone, and sew blankets. Visitor hours 9 A.M. to noon and 1–5 P.M. weekdays year-round.

Hike Area Trails. Mount Ripinski trail is a strenuous all-day hike, with spectacular views from the summit of mountains and tidal waters. Start at the end of 2nd and Young streets; follow pipeline right-of-way about 1.3 miles/2.1 km to trail, which climbs 3.6 miles/5.8 km to the 3,610-foot/1,100-m summit. *CAUTION: This is an unmaintained trail, recommended for experienced hikers only.*

Battery Point trail starts 1 mile/1.6 km beyond Portage Cove Campground and leads about 2 miles/3 km to a primitive camping site on Kelgaya Point overlooking Lynn Canal.

Mount Riley (elev. 1,760 feet/536m) has 3 routes to the summit. The steepest and most widely used trail starts at Mile 3 Mud Bay Road and climbs 2.1 miles/3.4 km to the summit. A second route starts at the end of F.A.A. Road and leads 2 miles/3.2 km along the city water-supply route to connect with the trail from Mud Bay Road to the summit. A third route follows the Battery Point trail for approximately 2 miles/3.2 km, then forks right for a fairly steep climb to the summit of Mount Riley.

Seduction Point, at the southern tip of the Chilkat Peninsula, is accessible from Chilkat State Park via a 6-mile/9.7-km trail; a rolling forest and beach walk. Views of Davidson and Rainbow glaciers.

AREA FISHING: Local charter boat operators and freshwater fishing guides offer fishing trips. A sportfishing lodge at Chilkat Lake offers good fishing in a semi-remote setting. Good fishing in the spring for king salmon in **Chilkat Inlet**. Halibut best in summer in **Chilkat**, **Lutak** and **Chilkoot** inlets. Dolly Varden fishing good in all lakes and rivers, and along marine shorelines from early spring to late fall. Great pink salmon fishing in August along the marine shoreline of **Lutak Inlet** and in the **Chilkoot River.** Sockeye salmon in the **Chilkoot River**, late June through August. Coho salmon in the **Chilkoot** and **Chilkat rivers**, mid-September through October. Cutthroat trout year-round at **Chilkat** and **Mosquito lakes.** **Herman Lake** is full of hungry grayling

stocked there in the mid-1970s. The lake is located off the Sunshine Mountain Road (watch out for logging trucks) accessed from the steel bridge across the Klehini River at **Milepost H 26.3** Haines Highway; get directions locally. For more information, contact the Alaska Dept. of Fish and Game at (907) 766-2625. ✐

Mud Bay Road Log

Mileposts on Mud Bay Road measure distance from its junction with the Haines Highway near Front Street to road end at Mud Bay, a distance of 8 miles/13 km. This road, first paved, then wide gravel, leads to Chilkat State Park, following the shoreline of Chilkat Inlet to Mud Bay on Chilkoot Inlet. **Distance is measured from junction with Haines Highway.**

0.1 (0.2 km) Hotel on left, motel and private camper park on right. ▲

0.2 (0.3 km) **Junction** with 3rd Street, which leads back to town.

0.5 (0.8 km) Small Tract Road on left, a 1.9-mile/3.1-km loop road which rejoins Mud Bay Road at **Milepost 2.3.** Small Tract

Road leads to private residences and to Bear Creek Camp and Youth Hostel (dorms, cabins and tent camping).

Mud Bay Road leads to the right, following the shoreline of Chilkat Inlet, with views of Pyramid Island. Excellent area for eagle pictures.

2.3 (3.7 km) Stop sign at T intersection: go right for state park, left to return to town via Small Tracts Road.

3 (4.8 km) Mount Riley trail on left, parking area on right.

3.9 (6.3 km) View of Pyramid Island and Rainbow Glacier across Chilkat Inlet. Rainbow Glacier, so named because someone once saw a rainbow over it, is a hanging glacier. The ice field moved out over a cliff rather than moving down a valley to the sea. Davidson Glacier is about 2 miles/3.2 km south of Rainbow Glacier.

4.9 (7.9 km) Boat dock on right for small boats (summer tie-off only), boat ramp and pit toilets.

5.2 (8.4 km) Pavement ends, gravel begins.

5.3 (8.5 km) Private road on right to cannery on Letnikof Cove.

6.7 (10.8 km) Turn right and drive in 1.2 miles/1.9 km to entrance of Chilkat State Park (camping area 0.5 mile/0.8 km beyond entrance): 32 campsites, 3 tent sites on beach, $6 nightly fee or annual pass, picnic sites, pit toilets and boat launch. Access road paved and graveled, grades to 11 percent. Drive carefully. Beach access, view

of glaciers and hiking trail to Seduction Point at southern tip of Chilkat Peninsula. ▲

8 (12.9 km) Mud Bay Road turns east and crosses Chilkat Peninsula to Flat Bay (commonly called Mud Bay) on Chilkoot Inlet. Road ends at Mud Bay; short walk to rocky beach.

Lutak Road Log

Lutak Road begins at Front Street, and leads north along Chilkoot Inlet past the Alaska Marine Highway ferry terminal, then northwest along Lutak Inlet past Chilkoot Lake Campground to road end, a distance of 10 miles/16 km.

Distance is measured from the junction of Front Street with Lutak Road.

0 Junction, Front Street and Lutak Road.

0.1 (0.2 km) Turnout on right with view of Fort Seward and Lynn Canal.

1.6 (2.6 km) Turnouts along road from here to Mile 7 allow good view of gill-net fleet, July through Sept.

2.4 (3.9 km) Government tank farm, petroleum distribution terminal and beginning of an oil pipeline to Fairbanks. No entry.

3.2 (5.1 km) Dock for oil tankers on right.

3.6 (5.8 km) Alaska Marine Highway ferry terminal on right.

3.8 (6.1 km) City dock on right is used for shipping lumber and also for docking barges.

4.4 (7.1 km) Sawmill.

8.3 (13.4 km) Road on left follows a wide stretch of the Chilkoot River for 1 mile/1.6 km to Chilkoot Lake picnic area and boat launch; state campground with 32 sites just beyond picnic area, 7-day limit, $10 nightly fee or annual pass. ▲

8.4 (13.5 km) Bridge over the mouth of the **Chilkoot River**. Good salmon fishing June through August. Watch for bears. 🐟

In 1983, the Chilkoot tribe dedicated Deer Rock here as a historic reminder of the original location of their village.

Road continues to private homes and dead ends; no turnaround.

Skagway
(See map, page 653)

Located on the north end of Taiya Inlet on Lynn Canal, 90 air miles/145 km northwest of Juneau; 108 road miles/174 km south of Whitehorse, YT. The northern terminus of the Alaska Marine Highway Southeast ferry system and southern terminus of Klondike Highway 2 which connects with the Alaska Highway. *NOTE: Although Skagway is only 13 miles/21 km by water from Haines, it is 359 miles/578 km by road!* **Population:** 767. **Emergency Services: Skagway Police Department,** phone (907) 983-2232. **Fire Department** and **Ambulance,** phone 911. **Clinic,** phone (907) 983-2255. **Maritime Search and Rescue,** contact the Coast Guard at 1-800-478-5555.

Visitor Information: Write the Skagway Convention and Visitors Bureau, Box 415MP, Skagway, AK 99840. Phone (907) 983-2854, fax 983-3854. Klondike Gold Rush National Historical Park Visitor Center has exhibits and films on the history of the area and information on hiking the Chilkoot Trail; write Box 517, Skagway, AK 99840; phone (907) 983-2921. Located in the restored railroad depot on 2nd Avenue and Broadway, it is open daily in summer.

Elevation: Sea level. **Climate:** Average daily temperature in summer, 57°F/14°C; in winter, 23°F/-5°C. Average annual precipitation is 29.9 inches. **Radio:** KHNS-FM 91.9. **Newspaper:** *Skagway News* (biweekly).

Private Aircraft: Skagway airport, adjacent west; elev. 44 feet/13m; length 3,700 feet/1,128m; asphalt; fuel 100LL; attended.

The name Skagway (originally spelled Skaguay) is said to mean "home of the north wind" in the local Tlingit dialect. It is the oldest incorporated city in Alaska (incorporated in 1900). Skagway is also a year-round port and 1 of the 2 gateway cities to the Alaska Highway in Southeast Alaska: Klondike Highway 2 connects Skagway with

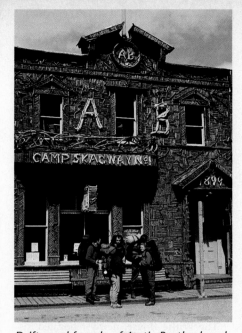

Driftwood facade of Arctic Brotherhood Hall. (© Crystal Images, Kathleen Marie Menke)

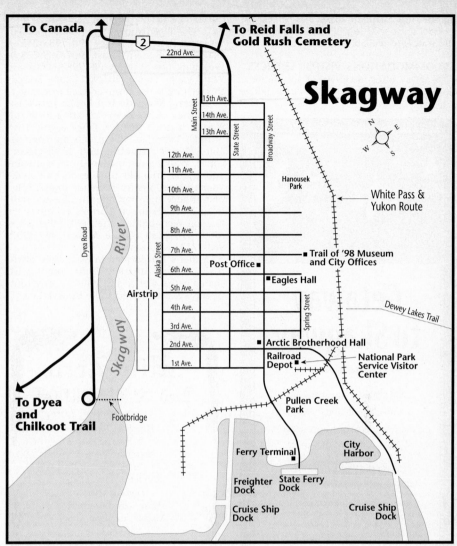

the Alaska Highway. (The other gateway city is Haines, connected to the Alaska Highway via the Haines Highway.)

The first white residents were Capt. William Moore and his son, J. Bernard, who settled in 1887 on the east side of the Skagway River valley (a small part of the Moore homesite was sold for construction of a Methodist college, now the city hall).

But Skagway owes its birth to the Klondike Gold Rush. Skagway, and the once-thriving town of Dyea, sprang up as thousands of gold seekers arrived to follow the White Pass and Chilkoot trails to the Yukon goldfields.

In July 1897, the first boatloads of stampeders bound for the Klondike landed at Skagway and Dyea. By October 1897, according to a North West Mounted Police report, Skagway had grown "from a concourse of tents to a fair-sized town, with well-laid-out streets and numerous frame buildings, stores, saloons, gambling houses, dance houses and a population of about 20,000." Less than a year later it was reported that "Skagway was little better than a hell on earth." Customs office records for 1898 show that in the month of February alone 5,000 people landed at Skagway and Dyea.

By the summer of 1899 the stampede was all but over. The newly built White Pass & Yukon Route railway reached Lake Ben-

nett, supplanting the Chilkoot Trail from Dyea. Dyea became a ghost town. Its post office closed in 1902, and by 1903 its population consisted of one settler. Skagway's population dwindled to 500. But Skagway persisted, both as a port and as terminus of the White Pass & Yukon Route railway, which connected the town to Whitehorse, YT, in 1900. Cruise ships, and later the Alaska State Ferry System, brought tourism and business to Skagway. Scheduled state ferry service to southeastern Alaska began in 1963.

Today, tourism is Skagway's main eco-

nomic base, with Klondike Gold Rush National Historical Park Skagway's major visitor attraction. Within Skagway's downtown historical district, false-fronted buildings and boardwalks dating from gold rush times line the streets. The National Park Service, the city of Skagway and local residents have succeeded in retaining Skagway's Klondike atmosphere.

Skagway has modern schools, churches, a clinic, bank and post office. U.S. customs office is located at Mile 6.8 Klondike Highway 2; phone or fax (907) 983-2325. The boat

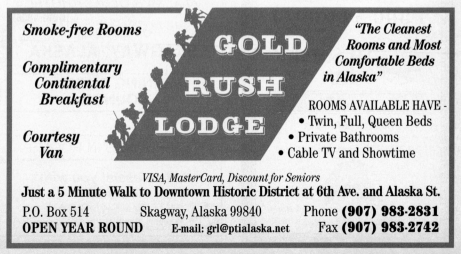

harbor and seaplane base has space for cruisers up to 100 feet/30m. Gas, diesel fuel and water are available.

ACCOMMODATIONS/VISITOR SERVICES

Skagway offers a variety of accommodations, including the Gold Rush Lodge

Getaway to Skagway

Add Skagway's breathtaking mountains, fjords and spectacular 'Days of 98' gold rush atmosphere to your northern adventure.

Visit the Westmark Inn Skagway near scenic Lynn Canal where you'll find comfortable lodging and fine dining in a setting reminiscent of those days gone by.

· 96 rooms and suites ·

· Dining room, coffee shop & lounge ·

· Gift shop · Hair salon ·

· Free parking ·

Ask about our Summer Value Rates from $79*

*Certain restrictions apply.

Central Reservations:

1-800-544-0970

Westmark Inn

S K A G W A Y

OPEN SEASONALLY
Third and Spring Streets
P.O. Box 515, Skagway, Alaska 99840

Come be our guest at Westmark Hotels throughout Alaska & the Yukon.

(907/983-2831), Golden North Hotel (907/983-2294), Miner's Inn (907/983-3303), Sergeant Preston's Lodge (907/983-2521), Skagway Bed & Breakfast (907/983-2289), Westmark Inn–Skagway (907/983-6000) and Wind Valley Lodge (907/983-2236). See ads this section. Reservations advised in summer.

Historic Skagway Inn Bed & Breakfast, established 1897, located at 7th and Broadway in historic district. Once a gold rush brothel, Victorian-style rooms are comfortable. Hearty breakfast and fresh-ground coffee. Walking distance to shops, museums and trails. Friendly innkeepers can make your reservations for railroad, shows, tours plus arrange transportation to Chilkoot trailhead. Fine dining at Lorna's evenings; Le Cordon Bleu–trained chef. (907) 983-2289. (800) 478-2290 (inside Alaska), fax (907) 983-2713. [ADVERTISEMENT]

Miner's Inn located in Skagway's downtown historic district. Eight rooms with shared baths. Coffee and hot tea. Ferry shuttle service. Established 1898. Reservations: 1-

Mile Zero Bed & Breakfast

New (1995)
Spacious Rooms
Private baths
Separate entrances
Central location
Continental breakfast
Handicap access
Luxurious queen beds
Majestic mountain view
Non-smoking
Skagway, AK. 99840
P.O. Box 165
Phone (907) 983-3045
Fax (907) 983-3046

800-764-7670 or (907) 983-3303. Fax (907) 983-3304. Major credit cards accepted. Box 589-MP, Skagway, AK 99840. [ADVERTISEMENT]

Sergeant Preston's Lodge. Rooms are almost impossible to get in Skagway without reservations. If you are lucky enough to have a choice, Sergeant Preston's Lodge is the best buy for your money. Though we were told to ask for their new section, we ended up with the old and were delighted with everything. The room was spotless, roomy and comfortable with the full facilities. In fact, as it turned out, it was the best rest of our vacation. Also, not only are they located right downtown, which was handy for the whole family, but everything is ground level, so Grandma's bad knee was no problem. The lobby area offers Sergeant Preston's gifts, bags, ice, soda pop, complimentary coffee, reservations and tickets to local shows and trains, and even, which made our son's day, Internet access for guests. The staff are genuinely happy to see and help you. They made us glad we came. We highly recommend this place. Phone (907) 983-2521. Fax (907) 983-3500. [ADVERTISEMENT]

The White House, newly renovated historical accommodations located in a neighborhood setting, one block from historic district. Offering private baths, off-street parking, independent room climate control, queen-size beds, telephones and breakfast

BACK TRACK CAMPER PARK

Electric & Water Hookups
Dry Sites, RV Wash & TV
Showers & Restrooms
Laundromat & Dump Station

In wooded area within walking distance to downtown historic Skagway

12th & Broadway
PO Box 375M, Skagway, AK 99840
(907) 983-3333

TRADITIONAL HOST TO ADVENTURERS SINCE THE DAYS OF THE GOLD RUSH

GOLDEN NORTH HOTEL

ALASKA'S OLDEST HOTEL
(Built 1898)

On Broadway
SKAGWAY, ALASKA

DINING ROOM
• LOUNGE •

TELEPHONES IN ROOMS

Let us assist you with tours of:
HOTEL • SKAGWAY
DYEA • WHITE PASS

FOR RESERVATIONS, WRITE
Box 343, Skagway, Alaska 99840
OR CALL **(907) 983-2451** • **(907) 983-2294**
FAX (907) 983-2755
OPEN YEAR-ROUND (winter rates)

Linger awhile

SKAGWAY

Visit Historic Skagway:

Gateway to the Klondike

Garden City of Alaska

Northern Terminus of the
Alaska Marine Highway System

Home of the Klondike Gold Rush
National Historical Park

SKAGWAY CONVENTION AND VISITORS BUREAU
P.O. Box 415 • Skagway, AK 99840 • (907) 983-2854 • Fax (907) 983-3854 • http://www.skagway.org

served year-round. This family run business operates 24 hours a day. Call (907) 983-9000. Address: 8th & Main, P.O. Box 41, Skagway, AK 99840. [ADVERTISEMENT]

There are several restaurants, cafes and bars, grocery, hardware and clothing stores, and many gift and novelty shops offering Alaska and gold rush souvenirs, photos, books, records, gold nugget jewelry, furs and ivory. Propane, marine and automobile gas are available, as is diesel fuel.

There is 1 bank in town (National Bank of Alaska), located at 6th and Broadway; open 10 A.M. to 5 P.M. Monday through Friday in summer. Automatic teller machines at bank and next to the Trail Bench gift shop on Broadway between 2nd and 3rd avenues.

There are several private campgrounds in Skagway offering hookups, tent sites, restrooms and showers, dump stations and laundromats. A campground for backpackers is located at the Chilkoot Trail trailhead near Dyea. ▲

TRANSPORTATION

Air: Daily scheduled service between Skagway and Haines and Juneau via L.A.B. Flying Service, Skagway Air and Wings of Alaska. Charter service also available between towns and for flightseeing via Skagway Air. Temsco provides helicopter tours. Transportation to and from the airport is provided by the flight services and local hotels in the summer.

Bus: Bus/van service to Anchorage, Fairbanks, Haines and Whitehorse, YT.

Car Rental: Available from Avis Rent-A-Car (907/983-2247) and Sourdough Car & Van Rental (907/983-2523).

Taxi: Service in Skagway is tour-oriented. Point-to-point service is limited and not available in winter. Service to Chilkoot Trail trailhead is available.

Highway: Klondike Highway 2 was completed in 1978 and connects Skagway to the Alaska Highway. It is open year-round. See KLONDIKE HIGHWAY 2 section.

Railroad: White Pass & Yukon Route offers 3-hour excursions from Skagway to White Pass Summit and return. Through rail/bus connections are also available daily between Skagway and Whitehorse. See WHITE PASS & YUKON ROUTE section for details.

Ferry: Alaska Marine Highway vessels call regularly year-round, as Skagway is the northern terminus of the Southeast ferry system. See MARINE ACCESS ROUTES section for schedules. The ferry terminal is in the large building on the waterfront (see city map this section); restrooms, pay phone and lockers inside. Ferry terminal office hours vary: opening hours are usually posted at the front door. Phone (907) 983-2941 or 983-2229. It's an easy walk into town, but hotel and motel vans do meet ferrys.

Water-taxi: Service is available between Haines and Skagway. For schedules and rates, phone (907) 983-2083 in Skagway; (907) 766-3395 in Haines.

Cruise Ships: Skagway is a regular port of call for cruise ships. Downtown is not far from the dock, but shuttle service is available between the dock and downtown from May to mid-September for about $1 each way. Tours can be purchased dockside and at downtown offices.

The excursion boat MV *Fairweather* cruises to Juneau daily, mid-May to mid-Sept. Operated by Gray Line of Alaska for their package tours, seats may be purchased by the general public on a space-available basis. Contact their Skagway office at the Westmark Hotel (phone 907/983-6000).

Private Boats: Transient moorage is available at the Skagway small-boat harbor.

Contact the harbormaster at (907) 983-2628.

ATTRACTIONS

Trail of '98 Museum is temporarily relocated in the Arctic Brotherhood Hall on Broadway Street between 2nd and 3rd avenues, while its original home, McCabe College Building/City Hall, is being renovated. The Arctic Brotherhood Hall's facade has almost 10,000 pieces of driftwood sticks arranged in a mosaic pattern, with the brotherhood's AB letters and symbols, a gold pan with nuggets. The museum's primary interest is to help preserve Alaskan historical material and to display Alaskan pioneer life. The museum is open daily May through October, 9 A.M. to 5 P.M.; contact the museum for winter hours. Phone (907) 983-2420.

McCabe College Building/City Hall is the first granite building constructed in Alaska. It was built by the Methodist Church as a school in 1899–1900 to be known as McCabe College, but public-school laws were passed that made the enterprise impractical, and it was sold to the federal government. For decades it was used as U.S. District Court No. 1 of Alaska, but as the population of the town declined, the court was aban-

doned, and in 1956 the building was purchased by the city. The main floor is occupied by City of Skagway offices. From the waterfront, walk up Broadway and turn right on 7th Avenue.

See the show *The Days of 1898 Show With Soapy Smith.* This show, produced by Gold Rush Productions, is put on several times a day; summer evening performances (subject to cruise ship arrivals) in Eagles Hall. Check the billboard in front of the hall for show times. The show relates the history of Skagway, from the days of the notorious Soapy Smith. Phone (907) 983-2545.

This show is good family entertainment; bring your camera, gamble with funny money (during evening show only), and enjoy this well-done historical musical comedy. Admission fee charged.

Alaska Wildlife Adventure displays Alaska wildlife mounts and has an extensive and ecclectic collection of Alaskana memorabilia. Gift shop and donut shop. Admission fee charged.

Klondike Gold Rush National Historical Park was authorized in 1976 to preserve and interpret the history of the Klondike Gold Rush of 1897–98. The park, managed by the National Park Service, consists of 4 units: a 6-block historical district in Skagway's business area; a 1-mile-/1.6-km-wide, 17-mile-/27.4-km-long corridor of land comprising the Chilkoot Trail; a 1-mile-/1.6-km-wide, 5-mile-/8-km-long corridor of land comprising the White Pass Trail; and a visitor center at 117 S. Main St. in Seattle, WA.

In Skagway, the National Park Service offers a variety of free programs in summer. There are daily, guided walking tours of downtown Skagway and ranger talks on a variety of topics. Films are also shown.

Check with the Park Service's visitor center in the restored railroad depot on 2nd Avenue and Broadway. Summer (June through August) hours are 8 A.M. to 6 P.M.

McFarlane Trading Co. Alaska. Skagway has a truly excellent shopping district. In terms of diversity, convenience and quality, it is unequaled in Alaska. You find items from all over Alaska in this little port city cradled at the foot of the White Pass and Chilkoot Trail. Among all these "emporia," just 1 door from Skagway's incredible ice cream store, you'll find McFarlane's Trading Company Alaska—a gift shop you must not miss! They have a wide range of genuine Alaskana in jewelry, crafts and carvings, and since Heather McFarlane was a librarian, most items have printed information to go with them. Their special pride is a fantastic collection of scrimshaw, an early American whalers' folk art refined to today's fine art, on fossilized walrus ivory or even mammoth ivory. McFarlane's also has masks and sculptures by Alaska's Eskimos, made from ancient mineralized whalebone, excavated from remote St. Lawrence Island. They also attempt to maintain a wide range of traditionally created Eskimo dolls from all over Alaska. In the summer of 1995, McFarlane's plans to acquire a few fine ivory carvings from Alaska's Eskimo villages. Finally, you'll find dog fur sweaters created by Tagish's Claudia McPhee. McFarlane's has chosen to travel a middle road in terms of price, finding that this is the best way to continue to carry truly Alaskan-made products. (If you are related to the McFarlane Clan, this shop has information on U.S. Clan McFarlane Societies.) [ADVERTISEMENT]

Skagway is located at the head of Taiya Inlet on Lynn Canal. *(Earl L. Brown, staff)*

tusk. The museum is open in summer. Free admission.

Picnic at Pullen Creek Park. This attractive waterfront park has a covered picnic shelter, 2 footbridges and 2 small docks. It is located between the cruise ship and ferry

Hike the Chilkoot Trail. This 33-mile/53-km trail begins on Dyea Road (see log this section) and climbs Chilkoot Pass (elev. 3,739 feet/1,140m) to Lake Bennett, following the historic route of the gold seekers of 1897–98. The trail is arduous but offers both spectacular scenery and historical relics. There are several campgrounds and shelters along the route. Hikers planning to take the Chilkoot Trail should check with Klondike Gold Rush NHP in Skagway, phone (907) 983-2921. Detailed information and maps of the trail are available from the National Park Service (Box 517, Skagway, AK 99840). *The ALASKA WILDERNESS GUIDE* also has details on the Chilkoot Trail, and "Chilkoot Pass" by Archie Satterfield is a good hiking and history guide to the trail.

Corrington Museum of Alaska History, located at 5th and Broadway, offers a unique record of events from prehistory to the present. Each of the 40 exhibits at the museum features a scene from Alaska history hand-engraved (scrimshawed) on a walrus

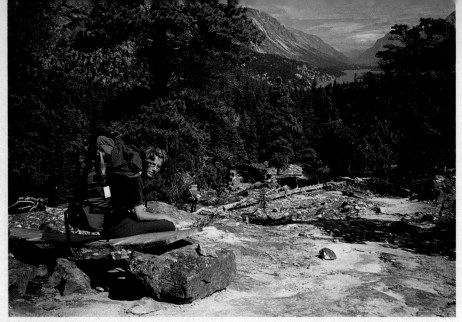

Chilkoot Trail hiker takes a break above Lake Bennett. (© Ruth von Spalding)

docks, behind the White Pass & Yukon Route depot. Watch for pink salmon in the intertidal waters in August, silver salmon in September.

Helicopter and airplane tours of Skagway and White Pass are available in summer.

Gold Rush Cemetery is 1.5 miles/2.4 km from downtown and makes a nice walk. Go north on State Street to a sign pointing to the cemetery. Follow dirt road across tracks into railroad yard, follow posted direction signs, then continue about 0.4 mile/0.6 km farther to the cemetery. If you drive in, a circular road around the cemetery eliminates having to back up to get out. A path on left at the end of the road leads to the cemetery where the graves of both "bad guy" Soapy Smith and "good guy" Frank Reid are located (both men died in a gunfight in July 1898). Smith's original gravestone was whittled away by souvenir hunters, and the resting place of the feared boss of Skagway is now marked by a metal marker.

Reid Falls are located near Gold Rush Cemetery, and it is only a short hike from Frank Reid's grave to view them.

AREA FISHING: Local charter boat operators offer fishing trips. The ADF&G Sport Fish Division recommends the following areas and species. Dolly Varden: Fish the shore of Skagway Harbor, Long Bay and Taiya Inlet, May through June. Try the Taiya River by the steel bridge in Dyea in early spring or fall; use red and white spoons or salmon eggs. Pink salmon fishing is good at the small local hatchery. Fish Skagway Harbor and Pullen Creek in town, July and August; use flashing lures. Coho and chum salmon near the steel bridge on the Taiya River, mid-Sept. through Oct. Trolling in the marine areas is good but often dangerous for small boats. Trout: A steep trail near town will take you to Dewey lakes, which were stocked with Colorado brook trout in the 1920s. Lower Dewey Lake, 1/2-hour to 1-hour hike; heavily wooded shoreline, use raft. The brook trout are plentiful and grow to 16 inches but are well fed, so fishing can be frustrating. Upper Dewey Lake, a steep 2 1/2-hour to 4-hour hike to above tree line, is full of hungry brook trout to 11 inches. Use salmon eggs or size #10 or #12 artificial flies. Lost Lake is reached via a rough trail near Dyea (ask locals for directions). The lake lies at about elev. 1,300 feet/396m and has a good population of rainbow trout. Use small spinners or spoons. For more information, contact the ADF&G office in Haines at (907) 766-2625. ◄

Dyea Road Log

The Dyea Road begins at Milepost S 2.3 on Klondike Highway 2. It leads southwest toward Yakutania Point, then northwest past Long Bay and the Taiya River to the beginning of the Chilkoot Trail and to a side road leading to the old Dyea townsite and Slide Cemetery. The Dyea Road is a narrow winding gravel road.

Distance is from the junction with Klondike Highway 2.

0 Junction.

0.1 (0.2 km) Old cemetery on right.

0.4 (0.6 km) View of Reid Falls east across the Skagway River.

1.4 (2.3 km) A scenic wayside with platform on left southbound affords view of Skagway, Taiya Inlet and the Skagway River.

1.7 (2.7 km) A steep, primitive road on left southbound descends 0.4 mile/0.6 km toward bank of the Skagway River, with a view of the Skagway waterfront and Taiya Inlet.

Drive to parking area and walk 0.2 mile/0.3 km to Yakutania Point; horse trail beyond parking area. Bridge at base of hill leads to a short trail back to town. Dyea Road turns northwest along Long Bay at this point.

1.9 (3.1 km) Skyline trailhead (poorly signed). This trail leads to top of AB Mountain (elev. 5,000 feet/1,524m).

2.1 (3.4 km) Head of Long Bay.

4 (6 km) City dump.

4.3 (6.9 km) Taiya Inlet comes into view on left northbound as the road curves away from Long Bay.

5.1 (8.2 km) View of the old pilings in Taiya Inlet. The docks of Dyea used to stretch from the trees to beyond the pilings, which are still visible. These long docks were needed to reach deep water because of the great tidal range in this inlet.

5.7 (9.2 km) Hooligan (smelt) run here in the Taiya River in May and early June. Local swimming hole across the road.

6.5 (10.5 km) Dyea information display.

6.7 (10.8 km) Chilkoot Trail trailhead campground, parking area and ranger station.

7.2 (11.6 km) The Chilkoot Trail begins on right northbound. Bridge over Taiya River.

7.4 (11.9 km) A primitive road on left northbound leads southwest to Slide Cemetery (keep right at forks and follow signs) and old Dyea townsite. The cemetery, reached by a short unmarked path through the woods, contains the graves of men killed in the Palm Sunday avalanche, April 3, 1898, on the Chilkoot Trail. At Dyea townsite, covered with fireweed and lupine in summer, hardly a trace remains of the buildings that housed 8,000 people here during the gold rush. About 30 people live in the valley today.

8.4 (13.5 km) Steel bridge across West Creek. Four-wheel drive recommended beyond this point.

KLONDIKE HIGHWAY 2

Connects: Skagway, AK, to Alaska Hwy., YT   **Length:** 99 miles
Road Surface: Paved   **Season:** Open all year
Highest Summit: White Pass 3,290 feet
Major Attraction: Klondike Gold Rush National Historical Park

(See map, page 712)

	Alaska Hwy. Jct.	Atlin	Carcross	Skagway	Whitehorse
Alaska Hwy. Jct.		125	33	99	10
Atlin	125		92	158	81
Carcross	33	92		66	43
Skagway	99	158	66		109
Whitehorse	10	81	43	109	

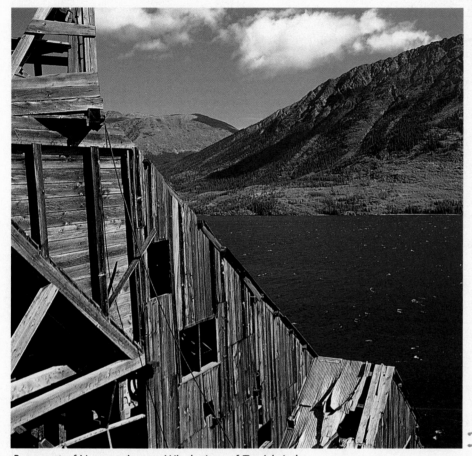

Remnant of Venus mine on Windy Arm of Tagish Lake. (© George Wuerthner)

The 98.8-mile-/159-km-long Klondike Highway 2 (also known as the Skagway–Carcross Road and South Klondike Highway) connects Skagway, AK, with the Alaska Highway at Milepost 874.4 south of White-horse. The highway between Skagway and Carcross (referred to locally as the Skagway Road) was built in 1978 and formally dedicated on May 23, 1981. The highway connecting Carcross with the Alaska Highway (referred to locally as the Carcross Road) was built by the U.S. Army in late 1942 to lay the gas pipeline from Skagway to Whitehorse.

Klondike Highway 2 is a 2-lane, asphalt-surfaced road, open year-round. The road has been improved in recent years and is fairly wide. There is a steep 11.5-mile/18.5-km grade between Skagway and White Pass.

IMPORTANT: If you plan to cross the border between midnight and 8 A.M., call ahead or inquire locally regarding customs stations' hours of operation.

Klondike Highway 2 is one of the two highways connecting ferry travelers with the Alaska Highway; the other is the Haines Highway out of Haines. Klondike Highway 2 offers some spectacular scenery and adds only about 55 miles/89 km to the trip for Alaska-bound motorists compared with the Haines Highway. (The distance from Haines to Tok, AK, is approximately 445 miles/716 km; the distance from Skagway to Tok is 500 miles/805 km.) Klondike Highway 2, like the Haines Highway, crosses from Alaska into British Columbia, then into Yukon Territory.

Klondike Highway 2 continues north of Whitehorse, turning off the Alaska Highway to Dawson City. See the KLONDIKE LOOP section for the log of Klondike Highway 2 between the Alaska Highway and Dawson City.

CAUTION: Watch for ore trucks, 85-foot-long, 8-axle vehicles carrying up to 50 tons of lead–zinc concentrates from Faro mine on the Campbell Highway to Skagway.

Emergency medical services: Between Skagway and the BC–YT border, phone the Skagway Fire Department at (907) 983-2300. Between the border and the Alaska Highway, phone the Whitehorse ambulance at 1-403-667-3333, RCMP at 1-403-667-5555. Police monitor CB Channel 9. *NOTE: Yukon Territory area code changes from (403) to (867) in October 1997.*

Klondike Highway 2 Log

Mileposts in Alaska and kilometreposts in Canada reflect distance from Skagway. The kilometre distance from Skagway in *The MILEPOST®* log reflects the location of the physical kilometreposts, and is not necessarily an accurate conversion of the mileage figure.
Distance from Skagway (S) is followed by distance from Alaska Highway (AH).

S 0 AH 98.8 (159 km) Ferry terminal in **SKAGWAY,** northern terminus of the Alaska Marine Highway. Skagway owes its birth to the Klondike Gold Rush; see the description of Skagway beginning on page 702.

S 1.6 (2.6 km) **AH 97.2** (156.4 km) Skagway River bridge.

S 2.3 (3.7 km) **AH 96.5** (155.3 km) **Junction** with Dyea Road.

S 2.6 (4.2 km) **AH 96.2** (154.8 km) Highway maintenance camp.

S 2.8 (4.5 km) **AH 96** (154.5 km) Plaque to east honoring men and women of the Klondike Gold Rush, and access to parklike area along Skagway River.

S 2.9 (4.7 km) **AH 95.9** (154.3 km) Access road east to Skagway River. Highway begins steep 11.5-mile/18.5-km ascent northbound from sea level to 3,290 feet/1,003m at White Pass.

S 4.7 (7.6 km) **AH 94.1** (151.4 km) Turnout to west.

S 5 (8 km) **AH 93.8** (151 km) Turnout to east with view across canyon of White Pass & Yukon Route railway tracks and bridge. The narrow-gauge WP&YR railway was completed in 1900 (see the WHITE PASS & YUKON ROUTE section).

S 5.5 (8.8 km) **AH 93.3** (150.1 km) Turnout to west with historical information signs.

S 6 (9.6 km) **AH 92.8** (149.3 km) Turnout

KLONDIKE HIGHWAY 2
Skagway, AK, to Junction with Alaska Highway (includes Tagish and Atlin Roads)

To Carmacks
(see KLONDIKE LOOP section)

To Haines Junction
(see ALASKA HIGHWAY section)

Whitehorse ✳ ❓ ✚

S-99/159km
AH-0

White Pass & Yukon Route
(see WHITE PASS & YUKON ROUTE section)

Kookatsoon Lake

Cowley

The Alaska Highway

Cowley Lake

Klondike Highway 2

Robinson

Bear Cr.

Marsh Lake

Two Horse Cr.

Lewes L.

Lewes Cr.

To Johnson's Crossing
(see ALASKA HIGHWAY section)

Jake's Corner

Needle Mountain ▲

Watson River

Mount Gillam ▲

Annie L.

Watson R.

Tagish Road

Tagish

C-34/54km
J-0

Caribou Mountain
5,645 ft./1,721m

Spirit L.

8

Tagish River

Little Atlin Lake

AH-33/53km
J-34/54km
C-0
S-66/106km

S-72.1/115km Spirit Lake Wilderness Resort CdDGILMPr
S-71.9/115.7km Cinnamon Cache Bakery and Coffee Shop M
S-67.9/108.6km Frontierland M

Crag Lake

Chootula Lake

Nares Lake

▲ **Carcross**

J-7.8/12.6km Pride of the Yukon C

Atlin Road

Tagish Lake

7

Snafu Lake

J-23.8/38.3km Tagish Lake Adventure Resort C

S-66.2/106.5km Montana Services & RV Park CDGIMPST
Top of the World Gold

Bove Island

▲ Lime Mountain
5,225 ft./1,593m

Lubbock River

Snafu Creek

Montana Mountain
7,280 ft./2,219m

Toku Arm

Tarfu Lake

Tarfu River

Lake Bennett

J-23.6/38km The Hitching Post CL

YUKON TERRITORY
BRITISH COLUMBIA

YUKON TERRITORY
BRITISH COLUMBIA

Mount ▲ Racine

AH-49/78km
S-50/81km

Mount Minto ▲
6,913 ft./2,107m

Hitchcock Creek

White Pass & Yukon Route
(Currently does not operate past this point)

Mount Conrad ▲

J-33/53km

Bennett

Indian Lake

▲ **Tutshi Lake**

Tagish Lake

Indian Creek

Gladys Lake

▲ Jack Peak
7,050 ft./2,149m

Chilkoot Trail

Log Cabin

Klondike Highway 2

Toku Arm

Atlin Lake

McDonald Lake

Surprise Lake

CANADA

UNITED STATES

Chilkoot Pass
3,739 ft./1,140m

Bernard Lake

Fourth of July Cr.

Summit Lake

Glaciated Area

AH-85/136km
S-14/23km

White Pass
3,290 ft./1,003m

Scotia

Discovery

Discovery Road

White Pass Fork

White Pass & Yukon Route
(see WHITE PASS & YUKON ROUTE section)

Pine Creek

Dyea Road

Goat Lake

✳ ▲ ✚ **Atlin**

Spruce Creek

Skagway River

AH-99/159km
S-0

✳ ❓ ▲ ✚ **Skagway**

J-58/93km

McKee Creek

Warm Bay Road

BRITISH COLUMBIA
ALASKA

Birch Mountain ▲
6,755 ft./2,060m

Palmer L.

To Haines Junction
(see HAINES HIGHWAY section)

Lutak Inlet

Teresa Island

Wilson Creek

O'Donnel River

Haines

Lynn Canal

COAST MOUNTAINS

RANGES

BOUNDARY

Glaciated Area

Taiya Inlet

Chilkat Inlet

Atlin Provincial Park

Provincial Park Boundary

Alaska State Ferry
(see MARINE ACCESS ROUTES section)

Llewellyn Glacier

Scale
0 — 10 Miles
0 — 10 Kilometres

Key to mileage boxes
miles/kilometres
miles/kilometres from:
S-Skagway
AH-Alaska Highway
J-Junction
C-Carcross

Map Location

Principal Route
Paved — Unpaved
Other Roads
Paved — Unpaved
Ferry Routes — Hiking Trails

✳ Refer to Log for Visitor Facilities
❓ Visitor Information
Fishing
▲ Campground
✚ Airport / Airstrip

Key to Advertiser Services
C -Camping
D -Dump Station
d -Diesel
G -Gas (reg., unld.)
I -Ice
L -Lodging
M -Meals
P -Propane
R -Car Repair (major)
r -Car Repair (minor)
S -Store (grocery)
T -Telephone (pay)

N / E / W / S

to east.

S 6.8 (10.9 km) AH 92 (148 km) U.S. customs station; open 24 hours in summer (manned 8 A.M. to midnight, video camera reporting midnight to 8 A.M.). Phone (907) 983-3144 for border crossing (immigration); phone (907) 983-2325 for customs in Skagway. All travelers entering the United States must stop. Have identification ready. Residents of North America must present birth certificate, driver's license or voter registration. All other foreign visitors must have a passport. Identification is also required for children. See also Customs Requirements in the GENERAL INFORMATION section.

S 7.4 (11.9 km) AH 91.4 (147.1 km) View to east of WP&YR railway line.

S 7.7 (12.4 km) AH 91.1 (146.6 km) Good photo stop for Pitchfork Falls, visible across the canyon. Pitchfork Falls flows from Goat Lake.

S 8.1 (13 km) AH 90.7 (146 km) Turnout to east.

S 9.1 (14.6 km) AH 89.7 (144.4 km) Paved turnout to east with historical interest signs about the Klondike Gold Rush trail. Viewpoint looks across the gorge to the WP&YR railway tracks.

S 9.9 (15.9 km) AH 88.9 (143.1 km) Truck runout ramp to west for large transport units that may lose air brakes on steep descent southbound.

S 11.1 (17.9 km) AH 87.7 (141.1 km) Captain William Moore Bridge. This unique cantilever bridge over Moore Creek spans a 110-foot-/34-m-wide gorge. Just north of the bridge to the west is a large waterfall. The bridge is named for Capt. Billy Moore, a riverboat captain and pilot, prospector, packer and trader, who played an important role in settling the town of Skagway. Moore helped pioneer this route over White Pass into the Yukon and was among the first to realize the potential of a railroad across the pass.

S 11.6 (18.7 km) AH 87.2 (140.3 km) Turnouts to east with view of Skagway River gorge, Captain William Moore Bridge and waterfalls, next 0.1 mile/0.2 km northbound.

S 12 (19.3 km) AH 86.8 (139.7 km) Truck runout ramp to west.

S 12.6 (20.3 km) AH 86.2 (138.7 km) Posts on east side of road mark highway shoulders and guide rails for snowplows.

S 14.4 (23.2 km) AH 84.4 (135.8 km) White Pass Summit (elev. 3,290 feet/ 1,003m). Turnout to west.

CAUTION: Southbound traffic begins steep 11.5-mile/18.5-km descent to Skagway.

Many stampeders on their way to the Klondike goldfields in 1898 chose the White Pass route because it was lower in elevation than the famous Chilkoot Pass trail, and the grade was not as steep. But the White Pass route was longer and the final ascent to the summit treacherous. Dead Horse Gulch (visible from the railway line) was named for the thousands of pack animals that died on this route during the gold rush.

The North West Mounted Police were stationed at the summit to meet every stampeder entering Canada and ensure that each carried at least a year's provisions (weighing about a ton).

S 14.5 (23.3 km) AH 84.3 (135.7 km) Paved turnout to west.

S 14.9 (24 km) AH 84 (135.2 km) U.S.–Canada (AK–BC) border. Turnout to west. Monument to east. TIME ZONE CHANGE: Alaska observes Alaska time; British Columbia and Yukon Territory observe Pacific time. See Time Zones in the GENERAL INFORMATION section.

S 16.2 (26.1 km) AH 82.6 (133 km) Highway winds through rocky valley of Summit Lake (visible to east). Several small gravel turnouts next 6 miles/9.6 km northbound.

S 18.1 (29.1 km) AH 80.7 (129.9 km) Summit Creek bridge.

S 18.4 (29.6 km) AH 80.4 (129.4 km) Summit Lake to east.

S 19.3 (31.1 km) AH 79.5 (128 km) North end of Summit Lake.

S 21.4 (34.4 km) AH 77.4 (124.5 km) Creek and railroad bridge to east.

S 22.5 (36.2 km) AH 76.3 (122.8 km) Canada customs at FRASER (elev. 2,400 feet/732m), open 24 hours; phone (403) 821-4111. Pay phone. All travelers entering Canada must stop. See Customs Requirements in the GENERAL INFORMATION section.

Old railroad water tower to east, highway maintenance camp to west.

S 22.6 (36.4 km) AH 76.2 (122.7 km) Beautiful deep-green Bernard Lake to east.

S 22.8 (36.7 km) AH 76 (122.3 km) Large double-ended turnout with 2 interpretive panels on area attractions and the WP&YR .

S 24.2 (38.9 km) AH 74.6 (120.1 km) Turnout to east.

S 25.1 (40.4 km) AH 73.7 (118.6 km) Shallow Lake to east.

S 25.5 (41 km) AH 73.3 (118 km) Old cabins and buildings to east.

S 25.9 (41.7 km) AH 72.9 (117.3 km) A-frame structure to east.

S 26.6 (42.8 km) AH 72.2 (116.2 km) Turnout to east. Beautiful view of Tormented Valley, a rocky desolate "moonscape" of stunted trees and small lakes east of the highway.

S 27.3 (43.9 km) AH 71.5 (115 km) Highway crosses tracks of the White Pass & Yukon Route at LOG CABIN. With completion of the railway in 1900, the North West Mounted Police moved their customs checkpoint from the summit to Log Cabin. There is nothing here today.

NOTE: There are numerous turnouts along the highway between here and Carcross. Turnouts may be designated for either commercial ore trucks or passenger vehicles.

S 30.7 (49.4 km) AH 68.1 (109.6 km) Tutshi (too-shy) River turnout to east.

S 31.1 (50 km) AH 67.7 (108.9 km) Highway parallels Tutshi Lake for several miles northbound. Excellent fishing for lake trout and grayling early in season. Be sure you have a British Columbia fishing license. ✦

S 40.1 (64.5 km) AH 58.7 (94.5 km) Short, narrow gravel access road to picnic area with pit toilet on Tutshi Lake. Large vehicles check turnaround space before driving in.

S 40.7 (65.5 km) AH 58.1 (93.5 km) Good views of Tutshi Lake along here.

S 43.7 (70.5 km) AH 55.1 (88.7 km) Turnout to east with view of Tutshi Lake.

S 46.4 (75.1 km) AH 52.4 (84.3 km) To the east is the Venus Mines concentrator, with a capacity of 150 tons per day. A drop in silver prices caused the Venus mill's closure in October 1981.

S 48.5 (78.1 km) AH 50.3 (81 km) South end of Windy Arm, an extension of Tagish Lake.

S 49.2 (79.2 km) AH 49.6 (79.9 km) Viewpoint to east.

S 49.9 (80.5 km) AH 48.9 (78.7 km) Dall Creek.

S 50.2 (81 km) AH 48.6 (78.2 km) BC–YT border. Turnout with picnic table and litter barrel to east overlooking Windy Arm.

View from Milepost S 7.7 of WP&YR at Pitchfork Falls. (Earl L. Brown, staff)

S 51.9 (83.5 km) AH 46.9 (75.5 km) Large turnout to east with litter barrel, picnic table and historical information sign about Venus Mines.

The first claim on Montana Mountain was staked by W.R. Young in 1899. By 1904 all of the mountain's gold veins had been claimed. In 1905, New York financier Col. Joseph H. Conrad acquired most of the Montana Mountain claims, formed Conrad Consolidated Mines, and began exploration and mining. A town of about 300 people sprang up along Windy Arm and an aerial tramway was built from the Conrad townsite up the side of Montana Mountain to the Mountain Hero adit. (This tramline, visible from the highway, was completed in 1906 but was never used to ship ore because the Mountain Hero tunnel did not find a vein.) More tramways and a mill were constructed, but by 1911 Conrad was forced into bankruptcy: The ore was not as rich as estimated and only a small quantity of ore was milled before operations ceased.

Small mining operations continued over the years, with unsuccessful startups by various mining interests. United Keno Hill Mines (Venus Division) acquired the mining claims in 1979, constructed a 100-ton-per-day mill and rehabilitated the old mine workings in 1980.

S 52.9 (85.1 km) AH 45.9 (73.8 km) Pooly Creek and canyon, named for J.M. Pooly who staked the first Venus claims in 1901.

Access road east to Pooly Point and Venus Mines maintenance garage, trailers and security station. No services, facilities or admittance.

S 54.2 (87.2 km) AH 44.6 (71.8 km) Venus Mines ore storage bin and foundation of old mill to east. The mill was built in the late 1960s, then disassembled and sold

Unique Carcross desert at Milepost S 67.3. (Earl L. Brown, staff)

about 1970. A sign here warns of arsenic being present: Do not pick or eat berries.

S 55.7 (89.6 km) **AH 43.1** (69.4 km) Tramline support just east of highway.

S 59.5 (95.8 km) **AH 39.3** (63.3 km) Turnout with historic information sign about Bove Island. Magnificent views along here of Windy Arm and its islands (the larger island is Bove Island). Windy Arm is an extension of Tagish Lake. Lime Mountain (elev. 5,225 feet/1,593m) rises to the east beyond Bove Island.

S 63.5 (102.2 km) **AH 35.3** (56.8 km) Sections of the old government wagon roads that once linked Carcross, Conrad and other mining claims, visible on either side of the highway.

S 65.3 (105.1 km) **AH 33.5** (53.9 km) Private road west to homes, Carcross Tagish First Nation's Band office and Carcross cemetery. Buried at the cemetery are the famous gold discoverers, Skookum Jim, Dawson (or Tagish) Charlie and Kate Carmack; pioneer missionary Bishop Bompas; and Polly the parrot. (Cemetery is closed to visitors during services.)

S 65.8 (104.3 km) **AH 33** (52.8 km) Small

Native-operated convenience store.

S 65.9 (106 km) **AH 32.9** (52.9 km) Access road west to Montana Mountain.

S 66 (106.2 km) **AH 32.8** (52.7 km) Nares Bridge crosses the narrows between Lake Bennett to the west and Tagish Lake to the east. Nares Lake remains open most winters, despite air temperatures that drop well below -40°F/-40°C. The larger lakes freeze to an ice depth of more than 3 feet/1m.

Caribou Mountain (elev. 5,645 feet/1,721m) is visible to the east.

S 66.2 (106.5 km) **AH 32.6** (52.4 km) Turnoff west for Carcross (description follows).

Carcross

On the shore of Lake Bennett, 44 miles/71 km southeast of Whitehorse. **Population:** 421. **Emergency Services: Police,** phone (403) 821-5555. **Fire Department,** phone (403) 821-2222. **Ambulance,** phone (403) 821-

3333. **Health Centre,** phone (403) 821-4444.

Visitor Information: Carcross Visitor Reception Centre, operated by Tourism Yukon, is located in the old White Pass & Yukon Route train station. Model train and lifeboat display. The centre operates daily from 8 A.M. to 8 P.M., mid-May to mid-September; phone (403) 821-4431. Ferry schedules, maps and information on Yukon, British Columbia and Alaska available. Yukon attractions may be previewed on laser disc. Get your Yukon Gold Explorer's Passport stamped here.

Elevation: 2,175 feet/663m. **Climate:** Average temperature in January, -4.2°F/-20.1°C; in July, 55.4°F/13°C. Annual rainfall 11 inches, snowfall 2 to 3 feet. Driest month is April, wettest month August. **Radio:** 590-AM, CHON-FM 90.5, CKRW, CKYN-FM 96.1 visitor information station. **Television:** CBC. **Transportation: Bus**—Scheduled bus service by Atlin Express Service, between Atlin and Whitehorse via Tagish and Carcross, 3 times weekly.

Private Aircraft: Carcross airstrip, 0.3 mile/0.5 km north of town via highway; elev. 2,161 feet/659m; length 2,000 feet/610m.

There are a hotel, general store, gift shops with Native handicrafts, snack bar and RV park. Gas station with gifts, groceries and cafe located on the highway by the airstrip. ▲

Carcross was formerly known as Caribou Crossing because of the large numbers of caribou that traversed the narrows here between Bennett and Nares lakes. It became a stopping place for gold stampeders on their way to the Klondike goldfields. Carcross was a major stop on the White Pass & Yukon Route railroad from 1900 until 1982, when the railroad ceased operation. (The WP&YR currently operates a limited excursion service; see WHITE PASS & YUKON ROUTE section for details.) Passengers and freight transferred from rail to stern-wheelers at Carcross. One of these stern-wheelers, the SS *Tutshi* (too-shy), was a historic site here in town until it burned down in July 1990.

A cairn beside the railroad station marks the site where construction crews laying track for the White Pass & Yukon Route from Skagway met the crew from Whitehorse. The golden spike was set in place when the last rail was laid at Carcross on July 29, 1900. The construction project had begun May 27, 1898, during the height of the Klondike Gold Rush.

Other visitor attractions include St. Saviour's Anglican Church, built in 1902; the Royal Mail Carriage; and the little locomotive *Duchess*, which once hauled coal on Vancouver Island. Frontierland, 2 miles/3.2 km north of town on the highway, is also a popular attraction. On sunny days you may sunbathe and picnic at Sandy Beach on Lake Bennett. Behind the post office there is a footbridge across Natasaheenie River. This small body of water joins Lake Bennett and Nares Lake. Check locally for boat tours and boat service on Bennett Lake.

Fishing in **Lake Bennett** for lake trout, northern pike, arctic grayling, whitefish and cisco. 🐟

Montana Services & RV Park. See display ad this section.

Top Of The World Gold. A short stroll from downtown Carcross will bring you to our shop overlooking historic Lake Bennett. We find our gold with shovel, sluice and pan—the old-fashioned way. We make our nugget jewellery and souvenirs by hand—

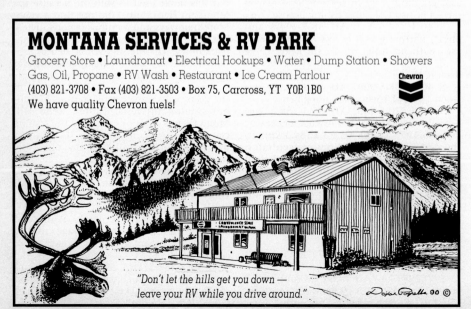

the old-fashioned way. And you'll be welcomed like friends—the old-fashioned way. So drop in for a visit … We look forward to meeting you, and we're sure you'll find something of interest. Open from mid-June. VISA/MasterCard. Phone (403) 821-3702.

[ADVERTISEMENT]

Klondike Highway 2 Log
(continued)

S 66.4 (106.9 km) **AH 32.4** (52.1 km) Airstrip to east. Turn on access road directly north of airstrip for Carcross Yukon government campground; 14 sites, picnic tables, firewood, drinking water, outhouses, camping fee. ▲

S 66.5 (107 km) **AH 32.3** (52 km) **Junction** with Yukon Highway 8 which leads east to Tagish, Atlin Road and the Alaska Highway at Jake's Corner (see TAGISH ROAD log on page 717). Turn east here for alternate access to Alaska Highway and for Yukon government campground on Tagish Road.

S 67.3 (108.3 km) **AH 31.5** (50.7 km) Turnout with point of interest sign about Carcross desert. This unusual desert area of sand dunes, seen east of the highway between Kilometreposts 108 and 110, is the world's smallest desert and an International Biophysical Programme site for ecological studies. The desert is composed of sandy lake-bottom material left behind by a large glacial lake. Strong winds off Lake Bennett have made it difficult for vegetation to take hold here; only lodgepole pine, spruce and kinnikinnick survive. (Kinnikinnick is a low trailing evergreen with small leathery leaves; used for tea.)

S 67.9 (108.6 km) **AH 30.9** (49.7 km) Frontierland (formerly the Museum of Yukon Natural History) features a Yukon wildlife museum, gift shop and coffee house. Displays include a saber-toothed tiger and the world's largest mounted bear—a polar bear. Flightseeing tours available.

Frontierland. See display ad this section.

S 70.3 (112.3 km) **AH 28.5** (45.9 km) Dry Creek.

S 71.2 (113.8 km) **AH 27.6** (44.4 km) Carl's Creek.

S 71.9 (115.7 km) **AH 26.9** (43.3 km) **Cinnamon Cache Bakery Coffee Shop.** See display ad this section.

S 72.1 (115 km) **AH 26.7** (43 km) Spirit Lake Wilderness Resort east side of road with food, gas, propane, repairs, lodging, camping and ice cream. Access road east to public use area on Spirit Lake. ▲

Spirit Lake Wilderness Resort. See display ad this section. ▲

S 73.2 (116.8 km) **AH 25.6** (41.2 km) Spirit Lake is visible to the east.

S 73.5 (117.3 km) **AH 25.3** (40.7 km) Large turnout with point of interest sign to west overlooking beautiful Emerald Lake, also called Rainbow Lake by Yukoners. (Good view of lake by climbing the hill across from the turnout.) The rainbowlike colors of the lake result from blue-green light waves reflecting off the white sediment of the lake bottom. This white sediment, called marl, consists of fragments of decomposed shell mixed with clay; it is usually found in shallow, freshwater lakes that have low oxygen levels during the summer months.

S 75.4 (120.3 km) **AH 23.4** (37.7 km) Highway follows base of Caribou Mountain (elev. 5,645 feet/1,721m). View of Montana Mountain to south, Caribou Mountain to east and Gray Ridge Range to the west

between Kilometreposts 122 and 128. Flora consists of jack and lodgepole pine.

S 79.8 (127.1 km) **AH 19** (30.6 km) Highway crosses Lewes Creek.

S 85.4 (136.3 km) **AH 13.4** (21.6 km) Access road west leads 1 mile/1.6 km to Lewes Lake.

S 85.6 (136.5 km) **AH 13.2** (21.2 km) Rat Lake to west.

S 86.7 (138.2 km) **AH 12.1** (19.4 km) Bear Creek.

S 87 (140 km) **AH 11.8** (19 km) Access to bed and breakfast and Bear Creek Dog Sled Kennels.

S 87.3 (139.1 km) **AH 11.5** (18.5 km) Access road west to large gravel pull-through with historic information sign about Robinson and view of Robinson. In 1899, the White Pass & Yukon Route built a railroad siding at Robinson (named for Stikine Bill Robinson). Gold was discovered nearby in the early 1900s and a townsite was surveyed. A few buildings were constructed and a post office—manned by Charlie McConnell—operated from 1909 to 1915. Low mineral yields caused Robinson to be abandoned, but postmaster Charlie McConnell stayed and established one of the first ranches in the Yukon. Robinson is accessible from Annie Lake Road (see next milepost).

S 87.5 (139.4 km) **AH 11.3** (18.2 km) Road west to Annie Lake (turn left after crossing the railroad tracks to reach Robinson).

Annie Lake Road (can be rough) leads 0.8 mile/1.4 km to Annie Lake golf course, 1.9 miles/3.1 km to McConnell Lake and 11 miles/17.7 km to Annie Lake. Beyond Annie Lake the road crosses the Wheaton River. The Wheaton Valley–Mount Skukum area has seen a surge of mineral exploration by private prospectors and mining compa-

nies in recent years. For the adventuresome, this is beautiful and interesting country. There are no facilities along Annie Lake Road. *CAUTION: Annie Lake Road can be very muddy during spring breakup or during rain.*

S 93 (148.5 km) **AH 5.8** (9.4 km) Turnoff west for Cowley and for access to Cowley Lake (1.6 miles/2.6 km).

S 95.5 (154.2 km) **AH 3.3** (5.3 km) Turnoff east for Kookatsoon Lake. There is a Yukon government picnic area at Kookatsoon Lake (day use only). The lake is shallow and usually warm enough for swimming in summer. Picnic tables, firepits and pit toilets. Canoe launch.

S 98.4 (156.5 km) **AH 0.4** (0.7 km) Rock shop on east side of road.

S 98.8 (157.1 km) **AH 0 Junction** with the Alaska Highway. Turn left (north) for Whitehorse, right (south) for Watson Lake. Turn to **Milepost DC 874.4** (page 126) in the ALASKA HIGHWAY section: Whitehorse-bound travelers continue with that log; travelers heading south down the Alaska Highway read that log back to front.

Restored steam engine No. 73 in Skagway. (©Harry M. Walker)

The White Pass & Yukon Route (WP&YR) is a narrow-gauge (36-inch) privately owned railroad built in 1898 at the height of the Klondike Gold Rush. Between 1900 and 1982, the WP&YR provided passenger and freight service between Skagway, AK, and Whitehorse, YT. The WP&YR no longer offers rail service to Whitehorse.

The WP&YR now operates a 3-hour round-trip train excursion between Skagway and the White Pass Summit, an 8-hour steam excursion between Skagway and Lake Bennett, and a combination train and bus trip between Skagway and Whitehorse.

Construction of the WP&YR began in May 1898. The railroad reached White Pass in February 1899 and Whitehorse in July 1900. It was the first railroad in Alaska and at the time the most northern of any railroad in North America. The White Pass & Yukon Route was declared an International Historic Civil Engineering Landmark, one of only 22 in the world, in 1994.

The railroad follows the old White Pass trail. The upper section of the old "Deadhorse" trail near the summit (Mile 19 on the WP&YR railway) is visible beside the tracks. During the Klondike Gold Rush, thousands of men took the 40-mile/64-km White Pass trail from Skagway to Lake Bennett, where they built boats to float down the Yukon River to Dawson City and the goldfields.

The WP&YR has one of the steepest railroad grades in North America. From sea level at Skagway the railroad climbs to 2,885 feet/879m at White Pass in only 20 miles/32 km of track. Currently, the railroad offers daily train service between Skagway and Fraser, BC, mid-May to mid-September, and a limited number of steam trips to Lake Bennett in summer.

Following are services, schedules and fares (U.S. funds) for White Pass & Yukon

Route in 1997. All times indicated in schedules are local times (Skagway is on Alaska Time, which is 1 hour earlier than Whitehorse, which is on Pacific Time.) Children 12 and under ride for half fare when accompanied by an adult. Children under 2 years ride free if not occupying a seat; half fare for separate seat. Reservations are required. (Tuesdays, Wednesdays and Thursdays are especially busy days.) For reservations and information, contact the White Pass & Yukon Route, Box 435, Skagway, AK 99840. Phone toll free in the U.S. and Canada 1-800-343-7373 or (907) 983-2217 in Skagway.

SUMMIT EXCURSION

This approximately 3-hour round-trip excursion features the most spectacular part of the WP&YR railway, including the steep climb to White Pass Summit, Bridal Veil Falls, Inspiration Point and Dead Horse Gulch. Offered twice daily from May 14 to Sept. 25, 1997, the morning train departs Skagway at 8:30 A.M. and returns at 11:45 A.M.; the afternoon train departs Skagway at 1 P.M. and returns at 4:15 P.M. Fares are $78 for adults and $39 for children 12 and under.

SKAGWAY TO WHITEHORSE

Through-service between Skagway, AK, and Whitehorse, YT, is offered daily from May 21 to Sept. 14, 1997. Through passengers travel 28 miles/45km by train between Skagway, AK, and Fraser, BC, and then 87 miles/140 km by bus between Fraser and Whitehorse, YT. The train portion of this trip takes passengers over historic White Pass Summit. Northbound service departs Skagway at 12:40 P.M., and arrives Whitehorse at 5:30 P.M. Southbound service departs Whitehorse at 8 A.M. and arrives Skagway at noon. One-way fares are $95 for adults and $47.50 for children 12 and under.

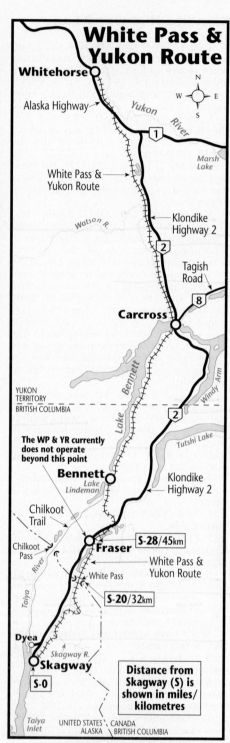

LAKE BENNETT STEAM EXCURSION

Steam travel returns to the White Pass & Yukon Route with limited summer runs to beautiful Lake Bennett. This 80-mile/128.7-km round-trip takes 8 hours and includes a layover at a restored 1903 station. St. Andrews Presbyterian Church, built in 1898, is an easy visit from the station. Steam trips are scheduled for June 14 and 28, July 12 and 26, August 9 and 23, and Sept. 1, 1997. Departs Skagway at 8:10 A.M. Fares are $150 for adults and $75 for children 12 and under.

TAGISH ROAD

Connects: Alaska Hwy. to Carcross, YT
Road Surface: 40% gravel, 60% paved

Length: 34 miles
Season: Open all year

(See map, page 712)

Fishing from Tagish bridge, Milepost J 13.1. (Staff)

The Tagish Road was built in 1942 to lay a gas pipeline. It leads south from the Alaska Highway junction at Jake's Corner (**Milepost DC 836.8**) through the settlement of Tagish to Carcross. This was the original route of the Alaska Highway in 1942. This 33.8-mile/54.4-km road connects the Alaska Highway with Klondike Highway 2. The road is good gravel from the Alaska Highway junction to Tagish, asphalt-surfaced between Tagish and Carcross.

If you are traveling Klondike Highway 2 between Skagway and Whitehorse, Tagish Road provides access to Atlin Road and also makes a pleasant side trip. Travelers may wish to use Tagish Road as an alternate route if there is road construction on Klondike Highway 2 between Carcross and the Alaska Highway. This is also a very beautiful drive in the fall; good photo opportunities.

Emergency medical services: Phone the RCMP, 1-403-667-5555; ambulance, phone 1-403-667-3333.

Tagish Road Log

Kilometreposts measure east to west from Alaska Highway junction to Carcross turn-off; posts are up about every 2 kilometres.
Distance from the junction (J) is followed by distance from Carcross (C).

J 0 C 33.8 (54.4 km) **Junction** with the Alaska Highway at Jake's Corner, **Milepost DC 836.8** (see page 125 in the ALASKA HIGHWAY section). Drive south 1.1 miles/1.8 km to junction of Tagish Road and Atlin Road (Highway 7).

J 1.1 (1.8 km) **C 32.7** (52.6 km) **Junction** of Tagish and Atlin roads. Turn southeast for Atlin, BC (see ATLIN ROAD section); head west for Tagish and Carcross.

J 8.8 (14.2 km) **C 25** (40.2 km) For several miles, travelers may see the NorthwesTel microwave tower on Jubilee Mountain (elev. 5,950 feet/ 1,814m) to the south between Little Atlin Lake and Tagish River. Jubilee Mountain was named by Dr. G.M. Dawson in 1887 in honor of Queen Victoria's Jubilee.

J 12.8 (20.6 km) **C 21** (33.8 km) Tagish Yukon government campground, on **Six Mile River** between Marsh Lake to the north and Tagish Lake to the south. Good fishing, boatlaunch, picnic area, playground, kitchen shelter, 28 campsites with firepits and tables, drinking water and toilets. Camping fee $8. *CAUTION: Watch for black bears.* ◄▲

J 13 (20.9 km) **C 20.8** (33.5 km) Marina on north side of road at east end of Tagish bridge has bait, tackle, fishing licenses, boat rental. Gas, oil, minor repairs, snacks and post office. Pay phone on road.

J 13.1 (21 km) **C 20.7** (33.3 km) Tagish bridge. Good fishing is a tradition here; Tagish bridge has an anglers' walkway on the north side. **Tagish River**, lake trout, arctic grayling, northern pike, whitefish and cisco. ◄

West end of bridge has a day-use area with parking, 4 picnic sites and water pump. Gravel ends, pavement begins, westbound.

J 13.5 (21.7 km) **C 20.3** (32.6 km) Improved gravel road leads through parklike area to settlement of **TAGISH** (pop. about 134) on Tagish River between Marsh and Tagish lakes. Express bus service between Atlin and Whitehorse stops here and in Carcross 3 times weekly. Tagish means "fish trap" in the local Indian dialect. It was traditionally an Indian meeting place in the spring on the way to set up fish camps and again in the fall to celebrate the catch. Post office at Tagish Service at east end of Tagish bridge. Wilderness lodge on Taku Arm of Tagish Lake.

Two miles/3.2 km south of Tagish on the Tagish River is **TAGISH POST**, originally named Fort Sifton, the Canadian customs post established in 1897. Two of the original 5 buildings still stand. The North West Mounted Police and Canadian customs collected duties on thousands of tons of freight carried by stampeders on their way to the Klondike goldfields between September 1897 and February 1898.

J 16.3 (26.2 km) **C 17.5** (28.1 km) Side road leads 1.2 miles/2 km to Tagish Lake and homes.

Tagish Lake, fishing for trout, pike and grayling. ◄

J 23 (37 km) **C 10.8** (17.4 km) Bryden Creek.

J 23.8 (38.3 km) **C 10** (16.1 km) **Tagish Lake Adventure Resort.** See display ad this section. ▲

J 24.8 (39.9 km) **C 9** (14.4 km) Crag Lake. Road now enters more mountainous region westbound. Caribou Mountain (elev. 5,645 feet/1,721m) on right.

J 27.2 (43.8 km) **C 6.6** (10.6 km) Porcupine Creek.

J 27.5 (44.3 km) **C 6.3** (10.1 km) **Historic Milepost 7.**

J 28.4 (45.7 km) **C 5.4** (8.7 km) Pain Creek.

J 30.2 (48.6 km) **C 3.6** (5.8 km) Side road to Chooutla Lake.

J 31 (49.9 km) **C 2.8** (4.5 km) First glimpse westbound of Montana Mountain (elev. 7,230 feet/2,204m) across narrows at Carcross.

J 33.8 (54.4 km) **C 0 Junction** with Klondike Highway 2. Westbound travelers turn left for Carcross, right for Whitehorse. See **Milepost S 66.5** (page 715) in the KLONDIKE HIGHWAY 2 section.

ATLIN ROAD

Connects: Tagish Road Jct. to Atlin, BC
Road Surface: 60% gravel, 40% paved
Major Attraction: Atlin Lake

Length: 58 miles
Season: Open all year

(See map, page 712)

	Atlin	Carcross	Jake's Corner	Skagway	Whitehorse
Atlin		92	59	158	106
Carcross	92		35	66	43
Jake's Corner	59	35		101	47
Skagway	158	66	101		109
Whitehorse	106	43	47	109	

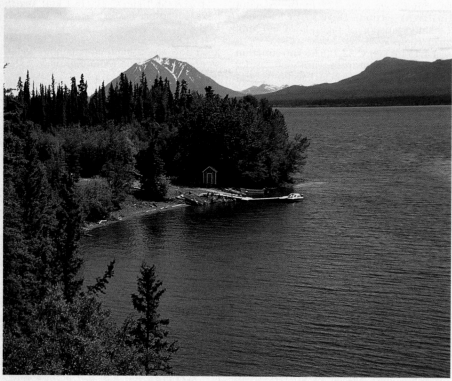

Boating and camping are available on Little Atlin Lake. (Earl L. Brown, staff)

This 58-mile/93.3-km all-weather road leads south to the pioneer gold mining town of Atlin. Built in 1949 by the Canadian Army Engineers, Atlin Road is a good road, usually in excellent condition, with some winding sections. The first 40 miles/64.4 km are gravel, with the remaining 18 miles/29 km into Atlin paved. Watch for slippery spots in wet weather.

To reach Atlin Road, turn south at Jake's Corner. **Milepost 836.8** on the Alaska Highway; drive 1.1 miles/1.8 km to the junction of Atlin Road (Highway 7) and Tagish Road (Highway 8); turn left (south) for Atlin.

It is about a 2½-hour drive to Atlin from Whitehorse and the lake scenery from the village is well worth the trip. For more information contact the Atlin Visitors Assoc., Box 365-M, Atlin, BC V0W 1A0; fax (250) 651-7721. Or phone the Atlin museum at (250) 651-7522 for visitor information.

Atlin Road Log

Physical kilometreposts in Yukon Territory and mileposts in British Columbia show distance from Tagish Road junction.
Distance from Tagish Road junction (J) is shown.

J 0 Junction of Tagish and Atlin roads.
J 1.4 (2.3 km) Fish Creek crossing. The road is bordered by many low-lying, boggy areas brilliant green with horsetail (*equisetium*).
J 1.8 (2.9 km) Side road west to Little Atlin Lake. Atlin Road descends along east shoreline of Little Atlin Lake approximately 7.6 miles/12.2 km southbound. During midsummer, the roadsides are ablaze with fire-

weed and wild roses.
J 2.4 (3.9 km) Large turnout to west on Little Atlin Lake; informal boat launch and camping area. Mount Minto (elev. 6,913 feet/2,107m) can be seen to the southwest. Road climbs southbound.
J 2.8 (4.5 km) Turnout to west. Watch for bald eagles.
J 5 (8 km) Information sign to east about 1983–84 mountain goat transplant. The 12 goats were brought from Kluane National Park. They may be observed on the mountainsides.
J 7.8 (12.6 km) Private campground, cabins and boat rentals. ⊶▲
Pride of the Yukon. See display ad this section. ▲
J 8.1 (13 km) Greenhouse and farm, roadside vegetable stand in season. Haunka Creek. Turnout to west.
J 8.9 (14.3 km) Good view of Mount Minto ahead southbound.
J 13.8 (22.2 km) Unmarked side road leads 2.4 miles/3.9 km to **Lubbock River**, which connects Little Atlin Lake with Atlin Lake. Excellent for grayling from breakup to mid-September.
J 15.5 (24.9 km) Snafu Creek. Turnout to west, north of bridge. According to R. Coutts, author of "Yukon Places & Names," the creek name is an acronym bestowed by army crews who built the road. It stands for Situation Normal—All Fouled Up. (Mr. Coutts resides in Atlin.)
J 16.4 (26 km) Access road leads 0.7 mile/1.1 km to **Snafu Lake** Yukon government campground; 4 sites, $8 camping fee, pit toilets, tables, gravel boat ramp, good fishing. ⊶▲
J 18.6 (29.9 km) Tarfu Creek. Small turnout to east, north of bridge. Creek name is another army acronym. This one stands for Things Are Really Fouled Up.
J 18.7 (30 km) Abandoned cabin and turnout to west.
J 20.4 (32.8 km) Turnoff to east for **Tarfu Lake** Yukon government campground via 2.4-mile/3.8-km side road; 6 sites, $8 camping fee, pit toilets, fishing. Steep grade near campground; not recommended for large RVs or trailers. ⊶▲
J 20.5 (33 km) Short narrow side road leads east to Marcella Lake; good lake for canoeing.
J 21.8 (35.1 km) Turnout to west with view of Atlin Lake, which covers 307 square miles/798 square km and is the largest natu-

ral lake in British Columbia. Coast Mountains to the southwest.

J 23.6 (38 km) The Hitching Post. See display ad this section. ▲

J 25.8 (41.5 km) BC–YT border. Road follows east shoreline of Atlin Lake into Atlin.

J 27 (43.5 km) Mount Minto to west, Black Mountain to east, and Halcro Peak (elev. 5,856 feet/1,785m) to the southeast.

J 28.5 (45.8 km) Slow down for sharp curve.

J 32 (51.5 km) Excellent views of Coast Mountains, southwest across Atlin Lake, next 6 miles/9.7 km southbound.

J 32.7 (52.6 km) Hitchcock Creek, grayling to 2 lbs. ◀

J 32.8 (52.7 km) Campground on Atlin Lake; 6 sites, pit toilets, tables, ramp for small boats. ▲

J 36.3 (58.4 km) Turnout with litter barrel to west, south side of Base Camp Creek.

J 36.8 (59.2 km) Historic Milepost 38.

J 40 (64.4 km) Indian River. Pull-through turnout south of creek. Highway is paved from here to Atlin.

J 40.2 (64.7 km) Big-game outfitter/guest ranch to east.

J 45.3 (72.9 km) Turnout to west.

J 49.8 (80.1 km) Burnt Creek.

J 49.9 (80.3 km) Davie Hall Lake and turnout to west. Waterfowl are plentiful on lake.

J 51.2 (82.4 km) Watch for horses.

J 51.6 (83 km) Ruffner Mine Road leads east 40 miles/64.4 km. Access to **MacDonald Lake,** 2 miles/3.2 km east; bird watching and lake trout fishing from spit. ◀

J 52.8 (85 km) Fourth of July Creek.

J 53.4 (85.9 km) Spruce Mountain (elev. 5,141 feet/1,567m) to west.

J 55.1 (88.7 km) Road skirts east shore of Como Lake next 0.6 mile/1 km southbound.

J 55.2 (88.8 km) Turnout with litter barrel to west on **Como Lake;** good lake for canoeing, also used by floatplanes. Stocked with rainbow. ◀

J 55.7 (89.6 km) South end of Como Lake; boat ramp.

J 57.1 (91.9 km) Atlin city limits.

J 58 (93.3 km) Junction of Atlin Road with Discovery Road. Turn right (west) on Discovery Avenue for town of Atlin; description follows. Turn left (east) for Discovery Road and Warm Bay Road (see page 721).

Boat and air charters may be found at Atlin waterfront. *(Earl L. Brown, staff)*

Atlin

The most northwesterly town in British Columbia, located about 112 miles/180 km southeast of Whitehorse, YT. **Population:** 500. **Emergency Services: Police,** phone (250) 651-7511. **Fire Department,** phone (250) 651-7666. **Ambulance,** phone (250) 651-7700. Red Cross outpost clinic, phone (250) 651-7677.

Visitor Information: Contact the Atlin Visitors Assoc., P.O. Box 365-M, Atlin, BC V0W 1A0, fax (250) 651-7721, phone (250) 651-7522.

Elevation: 2,240 feet/683m. **Radio:** CBC on FM-band. **Television:** 3 channels (CBC,

BCTV and the Knowledge Network).

Private Aircraft: Peterson Field, 1 mile/1.6 km northeast; elev. 2,348 feet/716m; length 3,950 feet/1,204m; gravel.

Transportation: Air—Regular service from Juneau via Summit Aviation. **Bus**—Ser-

ATLIN ADVERTISERS

Apex Air Charters ....Ph. (250) 651-0025
Atlin General Store ....Ph. (250) 651-7555
Dragon Studio ....Ph. (250) 651-7785
Fireweed Inn, The ....Ph. (250) 651-7729
M.V. *Tarahne*.....................Ph. (250) 651-7512
M.V. *Teresa Isle*.................Ph. (250) 651-0012
Noland House, The ....Ph. (250) 651-7585
Norseman
   Adventures Ltd. ....Ph. (250) 651-7535
Northern Place, The ....Ph. (250) 651-7503
Pine Tree Services.............Ph. (250) 651-7636
Quilts & Comforts.............Ph. (250) 651-7476
Simply Gold ....Ph. (250) 651-7708

vice from Whitehorse 3 times a week.

Referred to by some visitors as Shangri-la, the village of Atlin overlooks the crystal clear water of 90-mile/145-km-long Atlin Lake and is surrounded by spectacular mountains. On Teresa Island in Atlin Lake is Birch Mountain (elev. 6,755 feet/ 2,060m), the highest point in fresh water in the world.

Atlin was founded in 1898. The name was taken from the Indian dialect and means Big Water. The Atlin Lake area was one of the richest gold strikes made during the great rush to the Klondike in 1897–98. The first claims were registered here on July 30, 1898, by Fritz Miller and Kenneth McLaren.

VISITOR SERVICES/ACCOMMODATIONS

The village has a hotel, inns, cottages, bed and breakfasts, laundromat (with showers), restaurants, gas stations (propane, diesel and unleaded available), grocery, government liquor store and general stores, and a post office. Atlin branch of Bank of Montreal located at Government Agents

Office on 3rd Street; open weekdays 10 A.M. to noon and 1–3 P.M. Dump station at Mile 2.3 Discovery Road. The museum and several shops feature local gold nugget jewelry, arts and crafts, and other souvenirs. Air charter service for glacier tours and fly-in fishing trips. Charter boats and fishing charters available. Bus tours are welcome, but phone ahead so this small community can accommodate you.

The Noland House. This historic home has been restored to provide luxurious accommodations for 4 guests. Host residence is next door. Private baths and sitting rooms, complimentary wine and snacks, fully equipped kitchen, lake and mountain views, airport and floatplane dock pickup. Single $85, double $95, open May–October. Box 135, Atlin, BC V0W 1A0. Phone/fax: (250) 651-7585. [ADVERTISEMENT]

RV park with electric and water hookups, showers and laundry, pay phone and boat moorage downtown on lake. There are several camping areas on Atlin Road, Discovery Road and Warm Bay Road (see logs this section). Atlin community operates the Pine Creek campground at **Milepost J 1.6** Warm Bay Road; 14 sites, $5 fee (pay at any downtown business or at the museum). ▲

ATTRACTIONS

The MV *Tarahne* (Tah-ron) sits on the lakeshore in the middle of town. Tours daily in summer at 3 P.M.; admission by donation. Built at Atlin in 1916 by White Pass & Yukon Route, she carried passengers and freight from Atlin to Scotia Bay until 1936. (Scotia Bay is across the lake from Atlin and slightly north.) A 2-mile/3.2-km railway connected Scotia Bay on Atlin Lake to Taku Landing on Tagish Lake, where passengers arrived by boat from Carcross, YT. The *Tarahne* was the first gas-driven boat in the White Pass fleet. After she was lengthened by 30 feet in 1927, she could carry up to 198 passengers. In recent years, Atlin

residents have launched a drive to restore the boat; they hope to eventually refloat the vessel and offer tours of Atlin Lake.

Atlin Historical Museum, open weekends during June and September, daily July through August. Located in Atlin's original 1-room schoolhouse, the museum has mining artifacts and photo exhibits of the Atlin gold rush. Gift shop features the work of local artisans. Walking-tour guide of Atlin available here. Admission fee; phone (250) 651-7522.

Dragon Studio, located in downtown Atlin above Eggert's Clock, displays original works of art by visual artist Meshell Melvin. Visitors will be welcomed by the brightly coloured characters, in a multitude of mediums. These figures of wonder invite the audience to share in the adventure of the creative mind. Works for sale or commission. Stop in, or call (250) 651-7785 for appointment. [ADVERTISEMENT]

Visit the mineral springs at the north end of town, where you may have a drink of sparkling cold mineral water. The gazebolike structure over the springs was built by White Pass in 1922. Picnic area nearby.

The Pioneer Cemetery, located at **Milepost J 1.1** Discovery Road, contains the weathered grave markers of early gold seekers, including Fritz Miller and Kenneth McLaren, who made the first gold discovery in the Atlin area in July 1898. Also buried here is Walter Gladstone Sweet, reputed to have been a card dealer for Soapy Smith in Skagway.

Public Gold Panning Area has been set aside on Spruce Creek. Turn off Discovery Road at **Milepost J 3.6.** Check at the museum for details. Gold pans available locally for rent or purchase.

Take a Hike. At **Milepost J 2.3** Warm Bay Road are 2 trails: the 3-mile/4.8-km Monarch trail and the short, easy Beach trail. The Monarch trail is a moderately strenuous hike with a steep climb at the end to a bird's-eye view of the area.

Weekend guided nature walks are available at Warm Bay and Warm Springs, late-May to early-September. Fee charged. Inquire locally for details.

Tours and Rentals. Motorbike rentals, houseboat rentals, boat tours of Atlin and Tagish lakes, guided fishing trips and marine gas are available. Helicopter service, floatplanes for charter hunting and fishing trips and flightseeing trips of Llewellyn Glacier and the Atlin area are also available.

M.V. *Teresa Isle*. Gourmet charters on Atlin Lake. An elegant and unforgettable gastronomical experience on the 40-foot houseboat M.V. *Teresa Isle*. Dinner, lunch, dessert or snack cruises. Perhaps a peaceful meandering among historic Scotia Bay's Islands plus a stop for dinner. Phone Birch Mountain Gallery at (250) 651-0012 or (250) 651-7467

or write Box 165, Atlin, BC for more information on advanced bookings. VISA and MasterCard. [ADVERTISEMENT]

Atlin Provincial Park, accessible by boat or plane only (charters available in Atlin). Spectacular wilderness area; varied topography; exceptional wildlife habitat.

Take a Drive. 13-mile/21-km Discovery Road and 16.5-mile/26.5-km Warm Bay Road are both suitable for passenger cars and RVs, and both offer sightseeing and recreation. See side road logs this section for details.

Atlin Art Centre, located at **Milepost J 2** Warm Bay Road, offers alpine hiking, boating and canoeing adventures to the general public from June to September. The centre is also a summer school and retreat for artists and students, run by Gernot Dick. The centre is designed to allow participants to distance themselves from urban distractions and focus

on the creative process. Contact Atlin Art Centre, Monarch Mountain, Atlin, BC V0W 1A0; (800) 651-8882 for more information. Currently, a number of talented artists, authors and other creative people make their home in Atlin.

AREA FISHING: The Atlin area is well known for its good fishing. Fly-in fishing for salmon, steelhead and rainbow, or troll locally for lake trout. Grayling can be caught at the mouths of most creeks and streams or off Atlin docks. Public boat launch on Atlin Lake, south of the MV *Tarahne*. Boat charters available. For information on fishing in the area, contact local businesses. British Columbia fishing licenses are available from the government agent and local outlets. Fresh and smoked salmon may be available for purchase locally in the summer. Annual fishing derby held in June. ⌐■►

Discovery Road Log

Discovery Road begins 0.4 mile/0.6 km from Atlin's business district at junction with Atlin Road and leads east 13 miles/20.9 km. This is a good, wide, gravel road, bumpy in spots. Posted speed limit is 50 mph/80 kmph, but 40 mph/60 kmph or less is recommended. There is active gold mining under way along the road; watch for large trucks. Beyond Surprise Lake Dam bridge, the road becomes steep and winding for 1.2 miles/1.9 km to road end (large RVs use caution).
Distance is measured from junction with Atlin Road (J).

J 0 Junction of Atlin Road and Discovery Avenue.

J 0.3 (0.5 km) **Junction** with Warm Bay Road.

J 1.1 (1.8 km) Atlin airport to east. Pioneer cemetery to west contains grave markers and monuments to many of Atlin's historical figures.

J 2.3 (3.7 km) Dump station to south.

J 3.5 (5.6 km) Turnout to south with view of Pine Creek and falls.

J 3.6 (5.8 km) Spruce Creek Road leads south 0.9 mile/1.4 km to designated public recreational gold panning area and 1.5 miles/2.4 km to active gold mining on Spruce Creek (no tours but operations can be photographed from the road). This side road is signed as rough and narrow; suitable for cars, vans and pickups.

J 3.9 (6.3 km) Winding road next 1 mile/1.6 km.

J 5.4 (8.7 km) Former townsite of Discovery, originally called Pine Creek, now a ghost town. In its boom days, the town supplied miners working in the area.

J 7 (11.2 km) Active gold mining operation to south can be photographed from the road.

J 8.6 (13.8 km) Slow down for Pine Creek 1-lane bridge. Road follows creek

drainage from here to Surprise Lake.

J 9.2 (14.8 km) Small lake to east usually has waterfowl.

J 10.7 (17.2 km) View west of mining road switchbacks on mountainside.

J 11.2 (18 km) Road forks: bear to left. Small lake to west.

J 11.8 (19 km) Surprise Lake Dam bridge. Turnout east side of bridge with litter barrel and view of Surprise Lake.

CAUTION: Steep and winding road next 1.2 miles/1.9 km eastbound to road end.

J 12 (19.3 km) **Surprise Lake** recreation site. One campsite near main road. Steep, bumpy access road leads to more campsites near lake. Pit toilets, picnic tables, firepits. Boat launch for cartop boats and canoes. A gold mining operation is visible across the lake. Fishing for arctic grayling. ⌐■▲

J 13 (20.9 km) Road forks and both forks dead end along Boulder Creek. Ample turnaround space for vehicles.

Warm Bay Road Log

Warm Bay Road leads south 16.5 miles/26.5 km to numerous points of interest and 5 camping areas. Warm Bay Road begins at **Milepost J 0.3** Discovery Road, 0.7 mile/1.1 km east of Atlin business district.
Distance is measured from junction with Discovery Road (J).

J 0 Junction with Discovery Road.
J 0.3 (0.5 km) Atlin School.
J 1.5 (2.4 km) Pine Creek 1-lane bridge.
J 1.6 (2.6 km) Pine Creek Campground and picnic area; 14 campsites, tenting area, pit toilets, picnic tables, firepits, some firewood and water. Camping fee $5; pay at any Atlin business. Short trail to Pine Creek and Pine Creek Falls. ▲
J 2 (3.2 km) Atlin Art Centre (see Attractions in Atlin).
J 2.3 (3.7 km) Trailheads either side of road. Monarch trail is a moderately

strenuous 3-mile/4.8-km hike through meadows to scenic vista of Atlin area. Some steep sections; summit of Monarch Mountain at elev. 4,723 feet/1,439m. Beach trail is short and easy.
J 2.5 (4 km) Drinking water from pipe beside road.
J 5.7 (9.2 km) Lina Creek.
J 7 (11.2 km) Viewpoint with litter barrel. Llewellyn Glacier and Atlin Lake are to the southwest. Good photo spot.
J 7.3 (11.7 km) Bed and breakfast, canoe rentals.
J 9.5 (15.3 km) McKee Creek 1-lane bridge. The McKee Creek area has been mined since the 1890s. In July 1981, 2 area miners found what has been dubbed the "Atlin nugget," a 36.86-troy-ounce, hand-sized piece of gold.
J 11.3 (18.2 km) Palmer Lake to east.
J 11.9 (19.1 km) **Palmer Lake** recreation site to east; camping, fishing, picnic tables, pit toilets. No camping fee. ⌐■▲

J 13.9 (22.3 km) Warm Bay recreation site on **Atlin Lake**; camping, fishing, picnic tables, pit toilets. No camping fee. Boat launch for small boats. ⌐■▲
J 14.4 (23.2 km) Warm Springs to north. This is a small and shallow spring, good for soaking road-weary bones. Large grassy camping area, pit toilet. No camping fee. The meadow streams are lined with watercress. Guided nature walks available; inquire locally for details. ▲
J 16.3 (26.2 km) Grotto recreation site; 2 campsites, picnic tables, pit toilets, firepits, litter barrel. ▲
J 16.4 (26.4 km) "The Grotto" to north. Large turnaround. Water flows through a hole in the rocks from an underground stream. Locals report this is a good place to obtain drinking water.
J 16.5 (26.5 km) Maintained road ends. Steep, bumpy and narrow road continues beyond this point; not recommended for travel.

HAINES HIGHWAY ⑦ ④ ③

Connects: Haines, AK, to Haines Junction, YT   **Length:** 152 miles
Road Surface: Paved   **Season:** Open all year
Highest Summit: Chilkat Pass 3,493 feet
Major Attraction: Chilkat Bald Eagle Preserve

	Beaver Creek	Haines	Haines Jct.	Tok	Whitehorse
Beaver Creek		335	184	113	283
Haines	335		152	449	252
Haines Jct.	184	152		297	100
Tok	113	449	297		396
Whitehorse	283	252	100	396	

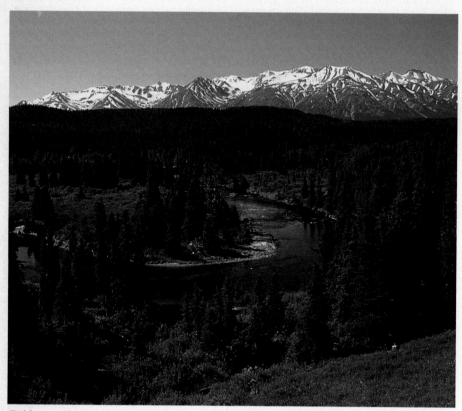

Takhanne River and Kluane Range seen from the Haines Highway. (Earl L. Brown, staff)

The paved 151.6-mile-/244-km-long Haines Highway connects Haines, AK (on the state ferry route), at the head of Lynn Canal with the Alaska Highway at Haines Junction, YT. The highway is open year-round. Allow about 4 hours' driving time. Watch for logging and fuel trucks. *NOTE: In summer, gas is available along the highway only at 33 Mile Roadhouse and at Kathleen Lake Lodge,* **Milepost H 135.2.**

Noted for the grandeur and variety of its alpine scenery, the highway leads from coastal forests near Haines through the Chilkat Eagle Preserve up over the backbone of the St. Elias Mountains, skirting Tatshenshini–Alsek Wilderness Provincial Park, and running along the eastern border of Kluane National Park Reserve and down into the valleys of the Yukon basin. Information on Kluane National Park Reserve is available in Haines Junction, YT.

Part of what is now the Haines Highway was originally a "grease trail" used by the coastal Chilkat Indians trading eulachon oil for furs from the Interior. In the late 1880s, Jack Dalton developed a packhorse trail to the Klondike goldfields along the old trading route. The present road was built in 1943 as a military access highway during WWII to provide an alternative route from the Pacific tidewater into Yukon Territory.

This historic corridor is celebrated each year during Dalton Trail Days, July 1–4. Watch for bikes on the highway during the annual Kluane/Chilkat International Bike Race (June 21, 1997). Some 850 cyclists participated in 1996.

U.S. and Canada customs stations are located about 40 miles/64 km north of Haines. U.S. customs is open from 7 A.M. to 11 P.M. (Alaska time); Canada customs is open from 8 A.M. to midnight (Pacific time). There are no facilities or accommodations at the border. All travelers must stop.

A valid Alaska fishing license is required for fishing along the highway between Haines and the international border at **Milepost H 40.7.** The highway then crosses the northern tip of British Columbia into Yukon Territory. You must have valid fishing licenses for both British Columbia and Yukon Territory if you fish these areas, and a national park fishing license if you fish waters in Kluane National Park.

If you plan to drive the Haines Highway in winter, check road conditions before starting out and carry adequate emergency equipment. In Haines Junction check with the maintenance garage (403/634-2227) or the RCMP (403/634-5555).

Emergency medical services: Between Haines and the U.S.–Canada border at **Milepost H 40.7,** phone 911. Between the U.S.–Canada border and Haines Junction, phone the RCMP at (403) 634-5555. *NOTE: Yuklon Territory area code changes from (403) to (867) in October 1997.*

Haines Highway Log

ALASKA ROUTE 7

Driving distance is measured in miles from Haines, AK. Mileposts are up along the Alaska portion of the highway. The kilometre figures on the Canadian portion of the highway reflect the physical kilometre-posts and are not an accurate metric conversion of the mileage figure.

Distance from Haines (H) is followed by distance from Haines Junction (HJ).

H 0 HJ 151.6 (244 km) HAINES. See HAINES section for accommodations and facilities.

H 0.2 (0.3 km) HJ 151.4 (243.7 km) Front Street.

H 0.4 (0.6 km) HJ 151.2 (243.4 km) Second Street. Turn right northbound (left southbound) for visitor information center and downtown Haines.

H 0.5 (0.8 km) HJ 151.1 (243.2 km) Third Street. Turn right northbound (left southbound) for downtown Haines.

H 1 (1.6 km) HJ 150.6 (242.4 km) Haines Hitch-Up RV Park. ▲

H 1.2 (1.9 km) HJ 150.4 (242.1 km) Main Street Y. If southbound, turn right to Fort William H. Seward, left to downtown Haines.

H 1.3 (2.1 km) HJ 150.3 (241.9 km) Eagle's Nest Motel.

H 3.3 (5.3 km) HJ 148.3 (238.7 km) Indian graveyard on the right northbound.

H 3.5 (5.6 km) HJ 148.1 (238.3 km) Private Aircraft: Haines airport; elev. 16 feet/5m; length 3,000 feet/914m; asphalt; fuel 100; unattended.

The Chilkat River estuary, which the highway parallels for the next 15 miles/24 km, flows into Chilkat Inlet of Lynn Canal, a massive fjord about 60 miles/

HAINES HIGHWAY *Haines, AK, to Haines Junction, YT*

To Beaver Creek
(see ALASKA HIGHWAY section)

To Whitehorse
(see ALASKA HIGHWAY section)

Haines Junction

HJ-0
H-152/246km

Pine Lake

Dezadeash River

Kathleen R.

Kathleen Lake

Jo Jo Lake

H-135.2/220.3km Kathleen Lake Lodge GILM

Sixmile Lake

ST. ELIAS

Kluane National Park Reserve

MOUNTAINS

River

Dezadeash Lake

Kusawa Lake

Klukshu Lake
Klukshu

Klukshu R.

Dalton Post

Takhanne R.

HJ-64/103km
H-88/145km

YUKON TERRITORY
BRITISH COLUMBIA

Lake Bennett

National Park Boundary
Provincial Park Boundary

Alsek

Tatshenshini River

Blanchard R.
Stanley Cr.

▲ Mount Mansfield
6,232 ft./1,900m

Kelasll Lake

Tatshenshini-Alsek Wilderness Provincial Park

Glaciated Area

← *Nadahini Creek*

Nadahini Mountain
6,809 ft./2,075m ▲

Chilkat Pass
3,493 ft./1,065m

Samuel Glacier

Stonehouse

BRITISH COLUMBIA
ALASKA

Glaciated Area

Chilkat River

Three Guardsmen Pass
3,215 ft./980m

Copper Butte ▲

C
Creek

Seltat

Kehsal River

▲Three Guardsmen Mountain
6,300 ft./1,920m
Big Boulder

To Carcross
(see KLONDIKE HIGHWAY 2 section)

Cr.

BOUNDARY RANGE

Mount McDonell ▲
8,509 ft./2,594m

Jarvis Glacier

Little Boulder Cr.

Mosquito Lake

Skagway

HJ-111/178km
H-41/72km

Saksaia Glacier

Klehini River

Klukwan

HJ-152/244km
H-0

H-27.3/43.9km
Swan's Rest RV Park

Chilkat Lake

Chilkat River

Chilkoot Inlet

Haines

Glaciated Area

TAKHINSHA

CANADA
UNITED STATES

MOUNTAINS

▲Mount Emmerich

▲Mount Krause

Chilkat Inlet

Alaska State Ferry
(see MARINE ACCESS
ROUTES section)

Lynn Canal

Provincial Park Boundary
National Park Boundary

Glaciated Area

Glacier Bay National Park and Preserve

Scale
0 —— 10 Miles
0 —— 10 Kilometres

Map Location

Key to mileage boxes
miles/kilometres
miles/kilometres
from:
H-Haines
HJ-Haines Junction

Principal Route
Paved   Unpaved
Other Roads
Paved   Unpaved
Ferry Routes   **Hiking Trails**

❄ Refer to Log for Visitor Facilities
? Visitor Information   Fishing
▲ Campground   Airport   Airstrip

Key to Advertiser Services
C -Camping
D -Dump Station
d -Diesel
G -Gas (reg., unld.)
I -Ice
L -Lodging
M -Meals
P -Propane
R -Car Repair (major)
r -Car Repair (minor)
S -Store (grocery)
T -Telephone (pay)

N
W   E
S

96.5 km long. Lynn Canal was named by English explorer Captain Vancouver for his birthplace (King's Lynn) in England. The yellow signs along the highway indicate mileages on the U.S. Army oil pipeline. The pipeline formerly pumped oil from Haines over the St. Elias Mountains to the Alaska Highway at Haines Junction, YT. These signs were used for aerial checking and monitoring of the line.

H 4.3 (6.9 km) **HJ 147.3** (237 km) Turnout along river.

H 6 (9.6 km) **HJ 145.6** (234.3 km) Picnic spot next to Chilkat River and a clear creek.

H 6.6 (10.6 km) **HJ 145** (233.3 km) Mount Ripinski trailhead.

H 8 (12.8 km) **HJ 143.6** (231.1 km) Watch for subsistence fish camps along the highway in June. Also watch for fish wheels on the river.

H 9.2 (14.8 km) **HJ 142.4** (229.2 km) Entering Alaska Chilkat Bald Eagle Preserve northbound. Established in 1982, the 48,000-acre preserve is the seasonal home to more than 3,000 bald eagles, which gather each year to feed on the late run of chum salmon. Eagle-viewing area begins at **Milepost H 19**; best viewing is mid-October to January.

H 9.6 (15.4 km) **HJ 142** (228.5 km) Magnificent view of Takhinsha Mountains across Chilkat River. This range extends north from the Chilkat Range; Glacier Bay is on the other side. Prominent peaks are Mount Krause and Mount Emmerich (elev. 6,405 feet/1,952m) in the Chilkat Range.

H 14.7 (23.6 km) **HJ 136.9** (220.3 km) Watch for mountain goats on the ridges.

H 17.6 (28.3 km) **HJ 134** (215.6 km) Rustic barn and old cabins. Good photo shots.

H 18.8 (30.3 km) **HJ 132.8** (213.7 km) Slide area.

H 19 (30.6 km) **HJ 132.6** (213.4 km) Begin eagle viewing area (northbound) on Chilkat River flats. Best viewing is mid-October to January. *CAUTION: Eagle watchers, use turnouts and park well off highway!*

H 21.4 (34.4 km) **HJ 130.2** (209.5 km) Turnoff to Indian village of **KLUKWAN**. Gravel access road dead ends at village. No visitor facilities.

H 22 (35.4 km) **HJ 129.6** (208.5 km) Second access northbound to Klukwan (steep grade).

H 23.8 (38.3 km) **HJ 127.8** (205.6 km) Chilkat River bridge. Highway now follows Klehini River. Watch for eagles beginning in late summer.

H 26.3 (42.3 km) **HJ 125.3** (201.6 km) Road west leads across Klehini River; turn off here for jet boat landing on Tsirku River for Birch Island Lodge on Chilkat Lake.

H 27.3 (43.9 km) **HJ 124.3** (200 km) Mosquito Lake State Recreation Site campground; 10 sites, tables, water, toilets, $6/night or annual pass. Mosquito Lake general store. Access to private RV park. ▲

Swan's Rest RV Park. Quiet location near eagle preserve. 12 large RV sites situated on lakeshore with full hook-ups. Hot showers. Coin laundry. Tenters welcome. Cabin for rent (proposed for 1997). Good fishing. Row boats for rent. Nesting swans and eagles. Wildlife. Great photo opportunities. At end of road, just 3 miles from highway. (907) 767-5662. [ADVERTISEMENT]

H 28.8 (46.3 km) **HJ 122.8** (197.6 km) Muncaster Creek bridge.

H 30.9 (49.7 km) **HJ 120.7** (194.2 km) Leaving Alaska Chilkat Bald Eagle Preserve

Fisherman at Mosquito Lake, Milepost S 27.3. (© Derby Photography)

northbound.

H 31.6 (50.9 km) **HJ 120** (193.1 km) Bridge over Little Boulder Creek.

H 33.2 (53.4 km) **HJ 118.4** (190.5 km) 33 Mile Roadhouse; gas and phone. Store. *NOTE: Last available gas northbound until Kathleen Lake Lodge. Check your gas tank.*

H 33.8 (54.4 km) **HJ 117.8** (189.6 km) Bridge over Big Boulder Creek. Watch for salmon swimming upstream during spawning season. Closed to salmon fishing.

H 36.2 (58.3 km) **HJ 115.4** (185.7 km) View of Saksaia Glacier.

H 40.4 (65 km) **HJ 111.2** (179 km) U.S. customs, Dalton Cache station. All travelers entering United States MUST STOP. Open year-round 7 A.M. to 11 P.M., Alaska time. Restrooms, large parking area.

Jarvis Glacier moraine is visible from the old Dalton Cache (on the National Register of Historic Places), located behind the customs building.

H 40.7 (65.5 km) **HJ 110.9** (178.5 km) U.S.–Canada border. Last milepost marker is Mile 40, first kilometrepost marker is Kilometrepost 74, northbound.

TIME ZONE CHANGE: Alaska observes Alaska time, Canada observes Pacific time. See Time Zones in the GENERAL INFORMATION section.

BC HIGHWAY 4

H 40.8 (71.8 km) **HJ 110.8** (178.3 km) Canada Customs and Immigration office at Pleasant Camp. All travelers entering Canada MUST STOP. Office is open daily year-round, 8 A.M. to midnight, Pacific time. No public facilities.

H 44.9 (78.5 km) **HJ 106.7** (171.7 km) Bridge over Fivemile Creek.

H 49.4 (80.3 km) **HJ 102.2** (164.5 km) Large gravel double-ended turnout at **Historical Mile 48**; information panels on Haines Road history.

Good viewpoint for Tatshenshini–Alsek Wilderness Provincial Park. This park, established in 1993, encompasses the rugged northwest corner of British Columbia and is dominated by the St. Elias Mountains. It is also habitat for grizzly bears, Dall sheep, the rare "glacier" bear and also rare birds such as the king eider and Stellar's eider. The Tat-shenshini and Alsek rivers are famous for their river rafting and sightseeing opportunities.

H 49.7 (86 km) **HJ 101.9** (164 km) Highway crosses Seltat Creek. This is eagle country; watch for them soaring over the uplands. Three Guardsmen Mountain (elev. 6,300 feet/1,920m) to the east.

H 53.9 (92 km) **HJ 97.7** (157.2 km) Three Guardsmen Lake to the east. Glave Peak, part of Three Guardsmen Mountain, rises directly behind the lake.

H 55.1 (94.6 km) **HJ 96.5** (155.3 km) Three Guardsmen Pass to the northeast, hidden by low hummocks along the road. Stonehouse Creek meanders through a pass at the base of Seltat Peak to join the Kelsall River about 6 miles/10 km to the east. To the north is the Kusawak Range; to the south is Three Guardsmen Mountain. The tall poles along the highway indicate the edge of the road for snowplows.

H 55.8 (95.8 km) **HJ 95.8** (154.2 km) Stonehouse Creek culvert.

H 56.2 (96.3 km) **HJ 95.4** (153.5 km) Clear Creek culvert.

H 59.8 (102.1 km) **HJ 91.8** (147.7 km) Double-ended paved turnout on west side of highway at Chilkat Pass, highest summit on this highway (elev. 3,493 feet/1,065m). White Pass Summit on Klondike Highway 2 is 3,290 feet/1,003m. The wind blows almost constantly on the summit and causes drifting snow and road closures in winter. The summit area is a favorite with snow machine and cross-country ski enthusiasts in winter. Snow until late May.

The Chilkat Pass was one of the few mountain passes offering access into the Yukon from the coast. The Chilkat and the Chilkoot passes were tenaciously guarded by Tlingit Indians. These southern Yukon Indians did not want their lucrative fur-trading business with the coastal Indians and Russians jeopardized by white strangers. But the gold rush of 1898, which brought thousands of white people inland, finally opened Chilkat Pass, forever altering the lifestyle of the Interior Natives.

From the Chilkat Pass over Glacier Flats to Stanley Creek, the highway crosses silt-laden streams flowing from the Crestline

Glacier. Nadahini Mountain (elev. 6,809 feet/2,075m) to the northwest. Three Guardsmen Mountain to the southeast.

H 63 (107 km) **HJ 88.6** (142.6 km) Chuck Creek culvert.

H 64.4 (109.3 km) **HJ 87.2** (140.3 km) Nadahini River culvert.

H 67.8 (114.7 km) **HJ 83.8** (134.8 km) **Private Aircraft:** Mule Creek airstrip; elev. 2,900 feet/884m; length 4,000 feet/1,219m; gravel. No services.

H 68.9 (116.4 km) **HJ 82.7** (133 km) Mule Creek.

H 73.6 (124.2 km) **HJ 78** (125.5 km) Goat Creek bridge. Watch for horses on road.

H 75.7 (127.3 km) **HJ 75.9** (122.1 km) Holum Creek.

H 80.1 (128.9 km) **HJ 71.5** (115.1 km) Mansfield Creek.

H 81.3 (136.3 km) **HJ 70.3** (113.1 km) Stanley Creek bridge.

H 86.5 (143.6 km) **HJ 65.1** (104.8 km) Blanchard River bridge.

H 87.1 (144.5 km) **HJ 64.5** (103.8 km) Welcome to Yukon sign.

H 87.4 (145 km) **HJ 64.2** (103.3 km) Entering Kluane Game Sanctuary northbound.

H 87.5 (145.2 km) **HJ 64.1** (103.1 km) BC–YT border. Former U.S. Army Alaska–Blanchard River Petroleum pump station, now a highway maintenance camp.

YUKON HIGHWAY 3

H 90.7 (150.7 km) **HJ 60.9** (98 km) Blanchard River Gorge to west.

H 91 (146.4 km) **HJ 60.6** (97.5 km) Large paved turnout.

H 96.2 (159.4 km) **HJ 55.4** (89.1 km) Yukon government Million Dollar Falls Campground on opposite side of Takhanne River; follow access road 0.7 mile/1.1 km west. Boardwalk trail and viewing platform of scenic falls. View of the St. Elias Mountains. Two kitchen shelters, tenting and group firepit, 27 campsites, 8 tent-only sites, $8 fee, playground and drinking water (boil water). Hiking trails in area. ▲

Good fishing below **Takhanne Falls** for grayling, Dolly Varden, rainbow and salmon. **Takhanne River**, excellent king salmon fishing in early July. ⊶

CAUTION: The Takhanne, Blanchard, Tatshenshini and Klukshu rivers are grizzly feeding areas. Exercise extreme caution when fishing or exploring in these areas.

H 96.3 (159.5 km) **HJ 55.3** (89 km) Takhanne River bridge.

H 96.4 (159.7 km) **HJ 55.2** (88.8 km) Parking area at Million Dollar Falls trailhead to west.

H 98.3 (162.6 km) **HJ 53.3** (85.8 km) Large paved turnout with good view of Kluane Range; viewing platform, litter barrels, outhouse.

H 99.5 (164.5 km) **HJ 52.1** (83.8 km) Turnoff to historic Dalton Post, a way point on the Dalton Trail. Steep, narrow, winding access road; four-wheel drive recommended in wet weather. Road not recommended for large RVs or trailers at any time. Several old abandoned log cabins and buildings are located here. Indians once formed a human barricade at Dalton Post to harvest the Klukshu River's run of coho salmon.

Fishing for chinook, coho, sockeye salmon in **Village Creek**. Grayling, Dolly Varden and salmon in **Klukshu River.** Fishing restrictions posted. *CAUTION: Watch for bears.* ⊶

H 103.4 (169.7 km) **HJ 48.2** (77.5 km) Viewpoint with information sign to west.

Alsek Range to southwest.

H 104 (170.7 km) **HJ 47.6** (76.6 km) Motheral Creek culvert.

H 106.1 (174 km) **HJ 45.5** (73.2 km) Vand Creek.

H 110.8 (181.6 km) **HJ 40.8** (65.6 km) Klukshu Creek.

H 111.6 (183 km) **HJ 40** (64.4 km) Turnoff for **KLUKSHU**, an Indian village, located 0.5 mile/0.8 km off the highway via a gravel road. This summer fish camp and village on the banks of the Klukshu River is a handful of log cabins, meat caches and traditional fish traps. Steelhead, king, sockeye and coho salmon are taken here. Each autumn, families return for the annual catch. The site is on the old Dalton Trail and offers good photo possibilities. Museum, picnic spot, souvenirs for sale. Information panels on First Nations heritage and traditional fishing techniques.

Kluane National Park Reserve borders the highway to the west from here to Haines Junction (the visitor centre there has information on the park). Watch for signs for hiking trails, which are posted 3.1 miles/5 km before trailheads. For more information on the park, contact Kluane National Park Reserve, Parks Canada, Box 5495, Haines Junction, YT Y0B 1L0, phone (403) 634-7209, fax (403) 634-7208. Also visit the park information centre in Haines Junction. Open daily, May to September, the centre has excellent interpretive displays.

H 112.8 (185 km) **HJ 38.8** (62.4 km) Gribbles Gulch.

H 114 (187 km) **HJ 37.6** (60.5 km) Parking area at St. Elias Lake trailhead (4.5-mile/7.2-km round-trip). Novice and intermediate hiking trail winds through subalpine meadow. Watch for mountain goats.

H 117.8 (193 km) **HJ 33.8** (54.4 km) Dezadeash Lodge (closed in 1996, current status unknown). Historically, this spot was known as Beloud Post and is still noted as such on some maps. Mush Lake trail (13.4 miles/21.6 km long) begins behind lodge. It is an old mining road.

NOTE: Watch for horses on highway.

H 119.3 (195 km) **HJ 32.3** (52 km) Turnout along Dezadeash Lake, one of the earliest known features in the Yukon, which parallels the highway for 9 miles/14.5 km northbound, and Dezadeash mountain range. Dezadeash (pronounced DEZ-dee-ash) is said to be the Indian word describing their fishing method. In the spring, the Indians built small fires around the bases of large birch trees, peeled the heat-loosened bark and placed it, shiny white side up, on the bottom of the lake near shore, weighted with stones. From log wharfs built over the white bark, Indians waited with spears for lake trout to cross the light area. Another interpretation of Dezadeash relates that Chilkat Indians referred to it as *Dasar-ee-ASH*, meaning "Lake of the Big Winds." Entire tribes were annihilated during mid-19th century Indian wars here.

Dezadeash Lake offers good trolling, also fly-fishing along the shore where feeder streams flow into the lake. There are northern pike, lake trout and grayling in Dezadeash Lake. *CAUTION: This is a mountain lake and storms come up quickly.* ⊶

H 119.7 (195.7 km) **HJ 31.9** (51.3 km) Entrance to Yukon government Dezadeash

Lake Campground; 20 campsites, $8 fee, kitchen shelter, picnic area, boat launch, no drinking water, pit toilets. ▲

H 123.9 (202.3 km) **HJ 27.7** (44.6 km) Rock Glacier trailhead to west; short 0.5-mile/0.8-km self-guiding trail, partially boardwalk. Interesting walk, some steep sections. Parking area and viewpoint.

H 126.2 (206.9 km) **HJ 25.4** (40.8 km) Dalton Trail Lodge to east with food, lodging and boat rentals.

H 134.7 (216.8 km) **HJ 16.9** (27.2 km) Access to bed and breakfast.

H 134.8 (219 km) **HJ 16.8** (27 km) Access road west to Kathleen Lake, a glacier-fed turquoise-blue lake, nearly 400 feet/122m deep. Access to Kathleen Lake Campground, the only established campground within Kluane National Park; 42 sites and a kitchen area; day-use area with boat launch at lake; campfire programs by park staff. Fees charged for camping ($10). Campfire talks and backcountry registration. The 53-mile/85-km Cottonwood loop trail begins here. ▲

NOTE: National parks fishing license required. **Kathleen Lake**, lake trout average 10 lbs., use lures, June and July; kokanee average 2 lbs., June best; grayling to 18 inches, use flies, June to September. **Kathleen River**, rainbow to 17 inches, June to September; grayling to 18 inches, July and August; lake trout average 2 lbs., best in September. ⊶

H 135.2 (220.3 km) **HJ 16.4** (26.4 km) Kathleen Lake Lodge; food, gas and lodging. ⊶

NOTE: Last available gas southbound for next 102 miles. Check your gas tank.

Kathleen Lake Lodge. Clean restaurant with good home cooking, mouthwatering pies, hard ice cream. Try our polar burger. Quiet motel, reasonable daily or weekly rates. Showers. Fishing supplies and licenses. Access to beautiful Kathleen Lake, excellent scenery, hiking and fishing. Unleaded gas. Ice. Open mid-May to mid-September. Phone (403) 634-2319. [ADVERTISEMENT]

H 135.8 (220.5 km) **HJ 15.8** (25.4 km) **Kathleen River** bridge; a popular spot for rainbow, lake trout and grayling fishing. Some kokanee. ⊶

H 139.2 (227 km) **HJ 12.4** (20 km) Turnout to west. Good view of Kathleen Lake. Information plaque on Kluane and Wrangell–St. Elias national parks.

H 143.4 (233.5 km) **HJ 8.2** (13.2 km) Quill Creek trailhead to west (7-mile/11-km trail).

H 147.1 (239.1 km) **HJ 4.5** (7.2 km) Parking area to west at Auriol trailhead (9.3-mile/15-km loop trail); skiing and hiking.

H 148.8 (241.1 km) **HJ 2.8** (4.5 km) Rest stop to east with litter barrels and pit toilets. View of community of Haines Junction and Shakwak Valley.

H 151 (245 km) **HJ 0.6** (1 km) Bridges over Dezadeash River. This river is part of the headwaters system of the Alsek River, which flows into the Pacific near Yakutat, AK.

H 151.6 (246 km) **HJ 0 HAINES JUNCTION,** turn left for Alaska, keep straight ahead for Whitehorse. Turn to Haines Junction (page 147 in the ALASKA HIGHWAY section) for description of town and highway log. Whitehorse-bound travelers read log back to front, Alaska-bound travelers read log front to back.

Approximate driving distances from Haines Junction are: Whitehorse 100 miles/161 km; Tok 297 miles/475 km; Fairbanks 503 miles/805 km; and Anchorage 625 miles/1000 km.

Connects: Watson Lake, YT, to Klondike Hwy.　**Length:** 373 miles
Road Surface: 85% gravel, 15% paved　**Season:** Open all year
Major Attraction: Faro Mine

	Carmacks	Dawson City	Faro	Ross River	Watson Lake
Carmacks		225	115	150	375
Dawson City	225		338	373	598
Faro	115	338		32	271
Ross River	150	373	32		239
Watson Lake	375	598	271	239	

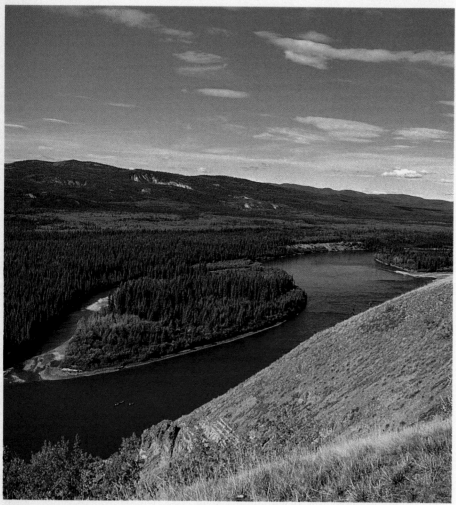

View of the Yukon River from Milepost WL 356.2 on the Campbell Highway.
(Earl L. Brown, staff)

Campbell Highway Log

YUKON HIGHWAY 4
Mileages reflect the location of physical kilometreposts; driving distance may vary from log.
Distance from Watson Lake (WL) is followed by distance from junction with the Klondike Highway just north of Carmacks (J).

WL 0 J 373 (600.2 km) **Junction** of the Campbell Highway with the Alaska Highway at Watson Lake (see description of Watson Lake beginning on page 112 in the ALASKA HIGHWAY section). The famous sign forest is located at this junction. In the parking area off the Campbell Highway (also called Airport Road) is a point of interest sign relating the highway's history. Also located at this junction is the Alaska Highway Interpretive Centre and visitor information.
WL 0.6 (1 km) **J 372.4** (599.3 km) Hospital on right northbound.
WL 4.3 (6.9 km) **J 368.7** (593.3 km) Access road on right northbound to Mount Maichen ski hill.
WL 6.3 (10.1 km) **J 366.7** (590.1 km) Airport Road left to Watson Lake airport. Pavement ends, hard-packed gravel begins, northbound.
WL 6.7 (10.8 km) **J 366.3** (589.5 km) Watson Creek. The highway begins to climb to a heavily timbered plateau and then heads north following the east bank of the Frances River. Tamarack is rare in Yukon, but this northern type of larch can be seen along here. Although a member of the pine family, it sheds its needles in the fall.
WL 10.4 (16.7 km) **J 362.6** (583.5 km) MacDonald Creek.
WL 22.5 (36.2 km) **J 350.5** (564.1 km) Tom Creek, named after an Indian trapper whose cabin is at the mouth of the stream.
WL 27.3 (44 km) **J 345.7** (556.3 km) Sa Dena Hes Mine access.
WL 36.1 (58.1 km) **J 336.9** (542.2 km) Frances River bridge. Turnout at north end of bridge; picnic spot. The highway crosses to west bank and follows the river northward. Named by Robert Campbell for the

Named for Robert Campbell, the first white man to penetrate what is now known as Yukon Territory, this all-weather, mostly gravel road leads 373 miles/600.2 km northwest from the Alaska Highway at Watson Lake, to junction with the Klondike Highway 2 miles/3.2 km north of Carmacks (see the KLONDIKE LOOP section). Gas is available at Watson Lake, Ross River, Faro and Carmacks.

The highway is gravel with the exception of stretches of pavement at Watson Lake, Ross River and the Klondike Highway junction (see map). There is a working mine at Faro; watch for large ore trucks between Faro and Carmacks. Drive with your headlights on at all times.

The Campbell Highway is an alternative route to Dawson City. It is about 20 miles/ 32 km shorter than driving the Alaska Highway through to Whitehorse, then driving up the Klondike Highway to Dawson City.

The Robert Campbell Highway was completed in 1968 and closely follows sections of the fur trade route established by Robert Campbell. Campbell was a Hudson's Bay Co. trader who was sent into the region in the 1840s to find a route west into the unexplored regions of central Yukon. Traveling from the southeast, he followed the Liard and Frances rivers, building a chain of posts along the way. His major discovery came in 1843, when he reached the Yukon River, which was to become the major transportation route within the Yukon.

Emergency medical services: Phone the RCMP or ambulance in Watson Lake, Ross River or Carmacks. Or phone toll free, Yukon-wide, the RCMP at 1-403-667-5555, or the ambulance at 1-403-667-3333. *NOTE: Yukon Territory area code changes from (403) to (867) in October 1997.*

CAMPBELL HIGHWAY

*Watson Lake, YT, to Junction with Klondike Loop
(includes Nahanni Range Road)*

To Tungsten

CJ-125/201km

Flat River

Little Hyland River

MACKENZIE MOUNTAINS

NORTHWEST TERRITORIES

YUKON TERRITORY

MOUNTAINS

LOGAN MOUNTAINS

Hyland River

Nahanni Range Road

Mount Billings 6,909 ft./2,106m

Mount Murray 7,093 ft./2,162m

10

WL-69/110km J-305/490km CJ-0

WL-0 J-373/600km

Watson Lake

To Fort Nelson (see ALASKA HIGHWAY section)

Dease River

To Stewart (see CASSIAR HIGHWAY section)

1

Watson Lake

Frances River

4

To Whitehorse (see ALASKA HIGHWAY section)

Miner's Junction

Simpson Lake

Lucky Cr.

Simpson Cr.

Tuchitua R.

Liard River

SIMPSON RANGE

CAMPBELL RANGE

Frances Lake

Finlayson River

Finlayson Lake

Money Cr.

WL-158/254km J-215/346km

Campbell Cr.

Big Campbell Cr.

Mink Cr.

Hoole River

Pelly River

To Northwest Territories (see CANOL ROAD section)

Dragon Lake

Ross River

6

Ross River Free Ferry

Horton Creek

Starr Cr.

Ketza R.

4

MOUNTAINS

WL-227/366km J-146/235km

Bruce Cr.

Lapie River

Lapie Lakes

6

To Johnson's Crossing (see CANOL ROAD section)

Quiet Lake

N E W S

Scale
Miles 20
Kilometres 20

Key to mileage boxes
miles/kilometres
miles/kilometres from:

WL-Watson Lake
J-Junction
CJ-Campbell Highway Junction

Map Location

WL-266/427km J-108/173km

Faro 2

WL-265.5/427.3km Discovery Store/ The Case Place IS Town of Faro

ANVIL RANGE

Crew Cr.

Buttle Cr.

Fisheye

Fisheye L.

WL-299.3/481.7km Little Salmon Lake Lodge & Fishing Charters LMS

Pelly River

Drury Lake

Magundy River

Little Salmon Lake

PELLY MOUNTAINS

BIG SALMON RANGES

Teslin River

Lake Laberge

Yukon River

WL-373/600km J-0

Frenchman Lake

Bearfeed Creek

Little Salmon R.

4

To Dawson City (see KLONDIKE LOOP section)

2

Carmacks

Yukon River

2

To Whitehorse (see KLONDIKE LOOP section)

Principal Route
Paved
Unpaved

Other Roads
Paved
Unpaved

Ferry Routes

Hiking Trails

•••••••• Refer to Log for Visitor Facilities

2 Visitor Information

▲ Campground

✈ Airport

+ Airstrip

Key to Advertiser Services
C –Camping
D –Dump Station
d –Diesel
G –Gas (reg., unld.)
I –Ice
L –Lodging
M –Meals
P –Propane
R –Car Repair (major)
r –Car Repair (minor)
S –Store (grocery)
T –Telephone (pay)

♦ Fishing

✈ Airport + Airstrip

Nahanni Range Road Log

The Nahanni Range (Tungsten) Road branches off the Campbell Highway at **Milepost WL 68.5** and leads 125 miles/201.2 km northeast to the former mining town of Tungsten, NWT. The road is gravel surfaced with some washouts and soft steep shoulders. *CAUTION: The Yukon government does not recommend this road for tourist travel due to lack of services and maintenance.*

Construction of the Nahanni Range Road was begun in 1961 to provide access to the mining property. The road was completed in 1963 with the bridging of the Frances and Hyland rivers. **Distance from Campbell Highway junction (CJ) is shown.**

CJ 0 Junction with Campbell Highway.

CJ 5.1 (8.2 km) **Upper Frances River** bridge; good grayling fishing in stream on southeast side. ◂

CJ 7.4 (11.9 km) Good grayling fishing at confluence of **Sequence Creek** and **Frances River.** ◂

CJ 11.8 (19 km) Queen Creek.

CJ 13.1 (21.1 km) King Creek.

CJ 14.2 (22.8 km) Road passes between Mount Billings to the north (elev. 6,909 feet/2,106m) and Mount Murray to the south (elev. 7,093 feet/2,162m).

CJ 20.3 (32.7 km) Short access road to **Long Lake**, grayling fishing. ◂

CJ 21.5 (34.6 km) Long Lake Creek. There are a few private log cabins along here.

CJ 24.1 (38.8 km) Dolly Varden Creek.

CJ 28.4 (45.7 km) French Creek.

CJ 28.9 (46.5 km) Road enters the narrow Hyland River valley through the Logan Mountains.

CJ 32.6 (52.4 km) South Bridge Creek.

CJ 33.2 (53.4 km) North Bridge Creek.

CJ 38.1 (61.3 km) Jackpine Creek.

CJ 40.6 (65.3 km) **Spruce Creek**, good glides and broken pools upstream for grayling fishing. ◂

CJ 42.8 (68.9 km) Short access road to Hyland River.

CJ 45.8 (73.7 km) **Conglomerate Creek**, scenic spot to picnic. Good grayling fishing near small waterfall.

CJ 48 (77.2 km) Mining road to west.

CJ 52.1 (83.8 km) South Moose Creek.

CJ 52.2 (84 km) Yukon government campground (unmaintained); 10 sites, kitchen shelter, picnic tables. ▲

CJ 52.5 (84.5 km) North Moose Creek.

CJ 62.4 (100.4 km) **Flood Creek**, good grayling fishing. ◂

CJ 68.4 (110.1 km) Hyland River bridge; turnout with litter barrel.

CJ 71 (114.2 km) Emergency airstrip to west.

CJ 75.9 (122.1 km) Ostensibility Creek.

CJ 82 (132 km) **Piggott Creek**, good grayling fishing. Outhouse. ◂

CJ 116.8 (188 km) YT–NWT border.

CJ 125 (201.2 km) **TUNGSTEN**, which was the company town for one of the richest mines in the world and Canada's only tungsten producer, was originally called Cantung (Canada Tungsten Mining Corp. Ltd.). Open-pit mining began here in the early 1960s with the discovery of scheelite in the Flat River area. Scheelite is an ore of tungsten, an oxide used for hardening steel and making white gold. The mine shut down in 1986, and the population of 500 moved out. Only a security staff remains. Hot springs in area.

Return to Milepost WL 68.5 Campbell Highway

---

wife of Sir George Simpson, governor of the Hudson's Bay Co. for 40 years, the Frances River is a tributary of the Liard River. Robert Campbell ascended the Liard River to the Frances River and then went on to Frances Lake and the Pelly River. The Frances River was part of Hudson's Bay Co.'s route into central Yukon for many years before being abandoned because of its dangerous rapids and canyons.

WL 47.2 (76 km) **J 325.8** (524.3 km) Lucky Creek.

WL 49.6 (79.8 km) **J 323.4** (520.4 km) Simpson Creek.

WL 51.8 (83.4 km) **J 321.2** (516.9 km) Access road leads west 1 mile/1.6 km to **Simpson Lake** Yukon government campground: 19 campsites, $8 fee, boat launch, dock, swimming beach, playground, kitchen shelter and drinking water (boil water). Excellent fishing for lake trout, arctic grayling and northern pike. ◂▲

WL 58.5 (94.2 km) **J 314.5** (506.1 km) Large turnout with litter barrels.

WL 58.7 (94.5 km) **J 314.3** (505.8 km) Access road west to Simpson Lake.

WL 68.5 (110.2 km) **J 304.5** (490 km) **Miner's Junction**, junction with Nahanni Range Road (formerly known as Cantung Junction); no services. Nahanni Range Road leads 125 miles/201 km northeast to Tungsten; see NAHANNI RANGE ROAD log this section. The road is not maintained and is not recommended for tourist traffic.

WL 70.3 (113.2 km) **J 302.7** (487.1 km) Yukon government Tuchitua River maintenance camp to east.

WL 70.5 (113.4 km) **J 302.5** (486.8 km) One-lane bridge over Tuchitua River.

WL 91.7 (147.6 km) **J 281.3** (452.7 km) Jules Creek.

WL 100 (160.9 km) **J 273** (439.3 km) 99 Mile Creek.

WL 106.6 (171.6 km) **J 266.4** (428.7 km) Caesar Creek.

WL 107.1 (172.4 km) **J 265.9** (427.9 km) View of Frances Lake to east, Campbell Range of the Pelly Mountains to west.

WL 108.9 (175.3 km) **J 264.1** (425 km) Access road east leads 0.6 mile/1 km to **Frances Lake** Yukon government campground: 19 campsites, $8 fee, boat launch, kitchen shelter, drinking water (boil water). The solitary peak between the 2 arms of Frances Lake is Simpson Tower, elev. 5,500 feet/1,676m). It was named by Robert Campbell for Hudson's Bay Co. Governor Sir George Simpson. Fishing for lake trout, grayling and northern pike. ◂▲

WL 109.1 (175.5 km) **J 263.9** (424.7 km) Money Creek, which flows into the west arm of Frances Lake, one of the Yukon's largest lakes. The creek was named for Anton Money, a mining engineer and prospector who found and mined placer gold in this area between 1929 and 1946. Money later operated "The Village" service station at Mile 442 on the Alaska Highway. He died in 1993, in Santa Barbara, CA.

WL 109.4 (176 km) **J 263.6** (424.2 km) Gravel turnout. View southbound of Frances Lake.

WL 113.8 (183.2 km) **J 259.2** (417.1 km) Dick Creek.

WL 123.8 (199.2 km) **J 249.2** (401 km) Highway descends Finlayson River valley northbound, swinging west away from Frances Lake and following the Finlayson River that may be seen occasionally to the east for about the next 20 miles/32 km. Mountains to the west are part of the Campbell Range.

WL 126.4 (203.5 km) **J 246.6** (396.9 km) Light Creek.

WL 129.1 (207.7 km) **J 243.9** (392.5 km) Van Bibber Creek.

WL 134.1 (215.8 km) **J 238.9** (384.5 km) Wolverine Creek.

WL 147.5 (237.4 km) **J 225.5** (362.9 km) Finlayson Creek, which flows into the river of the same name, drains Finlayson Lake into Frances Lake. Named by Robert Campbell in 1840 for Chief Factor Duncan Finlayson, who later became director of the Hudson's Bay Co. Placer gold mined at the mouth of Finlayson River in 1875 is believed to be some of the first gold mined in the territory. Finlayson Lake (elev. 3,100 feet/945m), on the Continental Divide, separates watersheds of Mackenzie and Yukon rivers.

WL 148.1 (238.4 km) **J 224.9** (361.9 km) Access road north to Finlayson Lake picnic area; litter barrels. To the southwest are the Pelly Mountains.

WL 149 (239.8 km) **J 224** (360.5 km) Turnout with observation platform and information panel on Finlayson caribou herd.

WL 158.1 (254.5 km) **J 214.9** (345.8 km) **Private Aircraft**: Finlayson Lake airstrip to south; elev. 3,300 feet/1,006m; length 2,100 feet/640m; gravel. No services.

WL 163.7 (263.5 km) **J 209.3** (336.8 km) Nancy J. Creek.

WL 164.4 (264.5 km) **J 208.6** (335.7 km) Little Campbell Creek. Robert Campbell followed this creek to the Pelly River in 1840.

WL 170.4 (274.2 km) **J 202.6** (326 km) Bridge over Big Campbell Creek, which flows into Pelly River at Pelly Banks. Robert Campbell named the river and banks after Hudson's Bay Co. Governor Sir John Henry Pelly. Campbell built a trading post here in 1846; never successful, it burned down in 1849. Isaac Taylor and William S. Drury later operated a trading post at Pelly Banks, one of a string of successful posts established by their firm in remote spots throughout the Yukon from 1899 on.

The highway follows the Pelly River for the next 90 miles/145 km.

WL 179 (288.1 km) **J 194** (312.2 km) Mink Creek culvert.

WL 193.9 (312 km) **J 179.1** (288.2 km) Bridge over Hoole Canyon; turnout to north. Confluence of the Hoole and Pelly rivers. Campbell named the Hoole River after his interpreter, Francis Hoole, a half-

Iroquois and half-French Canadian employed by the Hudson's Bay Co. Dig out your gold pan—this river once yielded gold.

WL 199.8 (321.6 km) **J 173.2** (278.7 km) Starr Creek culvert.

WL 206.5 (332.3 km) **J 166.5** (267.9 km) Horton Creek.

WL 210.7 (339 km) **J 162.3** (261.2 km) Bruce Lake to south.

WL 211.8 (340.8 km) **J 161.2** (259.4 km) Bruce Creek.

WL 214.9 (345.8 km) **J 158.1** (254.4 km) Pavement begins, gravel ends, westbound.

WL 215.4 (346.6 km) **J 157.6** (253.6 km) Private side road leads south 27.3 miles/44 km to Ketza River Project. The first gold bar was poured at Ketza River mine in 1988. The Ketza River hard-rock gold deposit was first discovered in 1947, but the mine was only recently developed. No visitor facilities.

WL 217.9 (350.7 km) **J 155.1** (249.6 km) Ketza River. St. Cyr Range to southwest.

WL 219.4 (353 km) **J 153.6** (247.2 km) Ketza Creek.

WL 221.4 (356.3 km) **J 151.6** (244 km) Beautiful Creek culvert.

WL 224.8 (361.8 km) **J 148.2** (238.5 km) **Coffee Lake** to south; local swimming hole, picnic tables, trout fishing (stocked). 🐟

WL 227.3 (365.8 km) **J 145.7** (234.5 km) **Junction** with South Canol Road (see CANOL ROAD section) which leads south 129 miles/207 km to Johnson's Crossing and the Alaska Highway. Ross River Flying Service; floatplane base on Jackfish Lake here.

WL 227.5 (366.1 km) **J 145.5** (234.1 km) Unmaintained side road on right westbound is continuation of Canol Road to Ross River. Use the main Ross River access road next milepost.

WL 232.3 (373.8 km) **J 140.7** (226.4 km) Access road leads 7 miles/11.2 km to Ross River (description follows). Rest area with toilets on highway just north of this turnoff.

Ross River

Located on the south west bank of the Pelly River. **Population:** about 400. **Emergency Services: RCMP,** phone (403) 969-5555. **Hospital,** phone (403) 969-2222. **Radio:** CBC 990, local FM station. **Transportation:** Scheduled air service via Trans North Air.

Private Aircraft: Ross River airstrip; elev. 2,408 feet/734m; length 5,500 feet/1,676m; gravel; fuel 40.

A point of interest sign on the way into

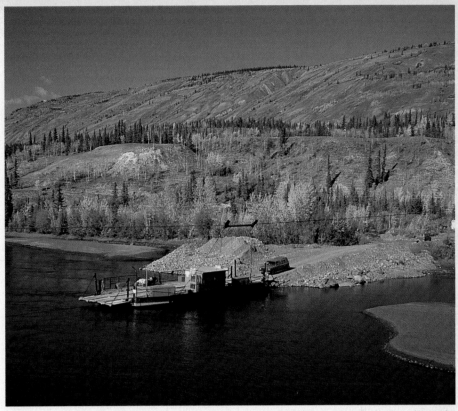

Free ferry at Ross River provides access across the Pelly River to North Canol Road.

(Earl L. Brown, staff)

Ross River relates that in 1843, Robert Campbell named Ross River for Chief Trader Donald Ross of the Hudson's Bay Co. From 1903, a trading post called Nahanni House (established by Tom Smith and later owned by the Whitehorse firm of Taylor and Drury) located at the confluence of the Ross and Pelly rivers supplied the Indians of the area for nearly 50 years. With the building of the Canol pipeline service road in WWII and the completion of the Robert Campbell Highway in 1968, the community was

linked to the rest of the territory by road. Originally situated on the north side of the Pelly River, the town has been in its present location since 1964. Today, Ross River is a supply and communication base for prospectors testing and mining mineral bodies in this region.

Ross River has gas stations with diesel, mechanical and tire repair, grocery stores, 2 motels with dining, and a bed and breakfast. The nearest campground is Lapie Canyon (see **Milepost WL 233.5**). Self-contained RVs may overnight at the gravel parking lot at the end of the pedestrian suspension bridge on the Ross River side.

Ross River is also a jumping-off point for big game hunters and canoeists. There are 2

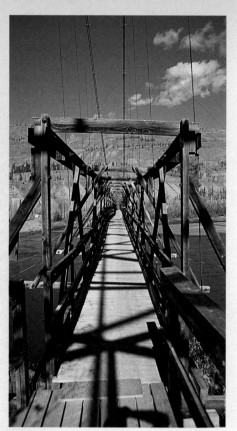

Pedestrians can use footbridge across Pelly River. (Earl L. Brown, staff)

registered hunting outfitters here. Canoeists traveling the Pelly River can launch just downriver from the ferry crossing. Experienced canoeists recommend camping on the Pelly's many gravel bars and islets to avoid bears, bugs and the danger of accidentally setting tundra fires. The Pelly has many sweepers, sleepers and gravel shallows, some gravel shoals, and extensive channeling. There are 2 sets of rapids between Ross River and the mouth of the Pelly: Fish Hook and Granite Canyon. Water is potable (boil), firewood available and wildlife plentiful. Inquire locally about river conditions before setting out.

Rock hounds watch for coal seams on

the access road into Ross River. Also check Pelly River gravels for jaspers and the occasional agate.

The suspension footbridge at Ross River leads across the Pelly River to the site of an abandoned Indian village 1 mile/1.6 km upstream at the mouth of the Ross River.

A government ferry crosses the Pelly River daily in summer, from 8 A.M. to noon and 1–5 P.M. Across the river, the North Canol Road leads 144 miles/232 km to Macmillan Pass at the Northwest Territories border. See the CANOL ROAD section for details.

Campbell Highway Log

(continued)

WL 232.3 (373.8 km) **J 140.7** (226.4 km) Access road leads 7 miles/11.2 km to Ross River (see preceding description).

WL 232.5 (374.2 km) **J 140.5** (226.1 km) Rest area with toilets.

WL 233.4 (375.6 km) **J 139.6** (224.6 km) Lapie River bridge crosses deep gorge of Lapie River, which flows into the Pelly River from Lapie Lakes on the South Canol Road. Highway continues to follow the Pelly River and Pelly Mountains.

WL 233.5 (375.8 km) **J 139.5** (224.5 km) Turnoff to left (south) to Lapie Canyon Yukon government campground adjacent Lapie River: short scenic trails, viewpoint, picturesque canyon; kitchen shelters, firewood, group firepit and picnic area; walk-in tent sites, 14 campsites, $8 fee, drinking water (boil water); boat launch. ▲

WL 236.3 (380.3 km) **J 136.7** (220 km) Danger Creek. In 1905, naturalist Charles Sheldon named this creek after his horse, Danger, supposedly the first horse in this area.

WL 237.1 (381.6 km) **J 135.9** (218.7 km) Pavement ends, gravel begins, westbound.

WL 239.9 (386 km) **J 133.1** (214.2 km) Panoramic view of the Pelly River valley just ahead westbound.

WL 243.6 (392 km) **J 129.4** (208.2 km) *CAUTION: Hill and bad corner.*

WL 244.2 (393 km) **J 128.8** (207.3 km) Highway narrows over Grew Creek, no guide rails. This creek was named for Hudson's Bay Co. trader Jim Grew, who trapped this area for many years before his death in 1906.

WL 249.6 (km) **J 123.4** (km) Pavement begins and extends approximately 1 mile/1.6 km westbound.

WL 251 (404 km) **J 122** (196.3 km) Turnout to north.

WL 260.4 (419 km) **J 112.6** (181.2 km) Buttle Creek, named for Roy Buttle, a trapper, prospector and trader who lived here in the early 1900s, and at one time owned a trading post at Ross River.

WL 264.7 (426 km) **J 108.3** (174.3 km) Across the wide Pelly River valley to the north is a view of the mining community of Faro.

WL 265.5 (427.3 km) **J 107.5** (173 km) Access road on right westbound leads 5.6 miles/9 km to Faro. Point of interest sign about Faro at intersection. Rest area with toilets and litter barrels to south just west of this junction.

Faro

Located in east-central Yukon Territory, 220 road miles/354 km from Whitehorse. **Population:** 1,500. **Emergency Services:** RCMP, phone (403) 994-5555. **Fire Department,** phone (403) 994-2222. **Hospital,** phone (403) 994-4444.

Visitor Information: Centre at the municipal-operated John Connelly RV Park, open June through August. A tourist information phone line has details on wildlife viewing, hiking, biking, horseback trails, town facilities and services, special events and individual businesses; phone (403) 994-2288, fax (403) 994-3311.

Climate: Temperatures range from -51°F/-46°C in winter to a summer maximum of 84°F/29°C. **Radio:** CBC-FM 105.1, CKRW-FM 98.7. **Television:** CBC and 7 cable channels. **Transportation:** Scheduled air service to Whitehorse and Ross River via Alcan Air. Floatplane service from Horizons North.

Private Aircraft: Faro airstrip; 1.5 miles/2.4 km south; elev. 2,351 feet/717m; length 3,000 feet/914m; gravel; fuel 100.

The town of Faro lies on a series of benches or terraces on the northern escarpment of the Tintina Trench. Many places in town offer a commanding view of the Pelly River.

There are 3 restaurants in town: the Faro Hotel, Redmond's (known locally as Cranky Frank's) and Sally's Road House. Both Redmond's and Sally's Road House offer motel accommodations. RV camping and dump station at municipal and private campgrounds. The service station has gas, diesel, propane and full garage services. The area offers excellent fly-in fishing. Other services in town include a large grocery, liquor store, video rental, post office, public library, art gallery, movie theatre and recreation centre with indoor swimming pool, squash courts and outdoor tennis courts. Catholic and Protestant Sunday services are available. ▲

Faro is named after the card game. The Cyprus Anvil mining and milling operation began producing lead–silver and zinc concentrates in 1969; operation was shut down

View of open pit lead-zinc mine at Faro. (Earl L. Brown, staff)

in 1982 because of depressed metal prices and a poor economic market. Mothballing of the mine began in the spring of 1985, but the mine was reopened in 1986 by Curragh Resources Inc. It closed down again in 1993 and was purchased in June 1994 by Anvil Range Mining Corp. Reopened in 1995, the Faro mine is one of the western world's largest producers of lead and zinc concentrates. Tours are available, phone first to John Connelly RV Park, (403) 994-2288.

Attractions include an all-season observation cabin and isolated photographer's blind, built in 1994, for wildlife viewing. Viewing areas are accessible via a gravel road skirting the Fannin sheep grazing area and are within 4 miles/6.4 km of town. A public boat ramp and canoe rentals are available for exploring the Pelly River.

Discovery Store/The Case Place. See display ad this section.

Town of Faro See display ad this section.

Campbell Highway Log
(continued)

WL 268.4 (432 km) **J 104.6** (168.3 km) Johnson Lake Yukon government campground; 15 sites (7 pull-throughs), $8 fee, toilets, water pump, firewood, picnic shelter, boat launch. Watch for livestock. ▲

Westbound, the Campbell Highway follows the Magundy River. There are several turnouts.

WL 285.8 (460 km) **J 87.2** (140.3 km) Magundy River airstrip to north; summer use only. Watch for livestock.

WL 288.1 (463.7 km) **J 84.9** (136.6 km) First glimpse of 22-mile-/35-km-long Little Salmon Lake westbound.

WL 299.3 (481.7 km) **J 73.7** (118.6 km) East end of **Little Salmon Lake**. Highway follows north shore. Lodge with meals, groceries, fishing licenses, guided fishing charters and boat rentals. Fishing for northern pike, grayling, lake trout. 🐟

Little Salmon Lake Lodge & Fishing Charters. Featuring home cooked meals and bakery items, licensed dining, off sales, gifts and groceries. (Emergency fuel available.) Open year-round. Guided fishing charters and boat rentals, half- and full-day tours on beautiful Little Salmon Lake. Fish for northern pike, lake trout and arctic grayling. Complete fishing, meals and accommodation packages available. Contact Little Salmon Lake Lodge & Fishing Charters, General Delivery, Faro, Yukon Y0B 1K0. (Mobile radio 2M5172, on the Salmon Channel.) [ADVERTISEMENT]

WL 300.1 (483 km) **J 72.9** (117.3 km) Short access road south to Drury Creek Yukon government campground, situated on the creek at the east end of **Little Salmon Lake**: boat launch, fish filleting table, kitchen shelter, group firepit, 18 campsites, $8 fee, drinking water. Good fishing for northern pike, grayling, whitefish, lake trout 2 to 5 lbs., June 15 through July. ▲

WL 300.4 (483.5 km) **J 72.6** (116.8 km) Turnout at east end Drury Creek bridge. Yukon government maintenance camp to north.

WL 308.2 (496 km) **J 64.8** (104.3 km) Turnout overlooking lake.

WL 311.3 (501 km) **J 61.7** (99.3 km) *CAUTION: Slow down for curves.* Highway follows lakeshore; no guide rails. Turnouts overlooking Little Salmon Lake next 8.5 miles/13.6 km westbound.

WL 316.9 (510 km) **J 56.1** (90.3 km) **Private Aircraft:** Little Salmon airstrip; elev. 2,200 feet/671m; length 1,800 feet/549m; sand and silt.

WL 321.4 (517.3 km) **J 51.6** (83 km) Steep, narrow, winding road south leads to Yukon government **Little Salmon Lake** campground; boat launch, fishing, 12 campsites, $8 fee, drinking water, picnic tables, outhouses, firepits and kitchen shelter. ▲

WL 323.5 (520.6 km) **J 49.5** (79.7 km) Pavement begins, gravel ends, westbound.

WL 324.7 (522.6 km) **J 48.3** (77.7 km) Bearfeed Creek, a tributary of Little Salmon River, named because of the abundance of bears attracted to the berry patches in this area. Access to creek to north at west end of bridge.

Highway follows Little Salmon River (seen to south) for about 25 miles/40 km westbound.

WL 341 (548.7 km) **J 32** (51.5 km) *CAUTION: Slow down for hill.*

WL 343.8 (553.2 km) **J 29.2** (47 km) Picnic spot on Little Salmon River, which flows into the Yukon River.

WL 347.3 (559 km) **J 25.7** (41.4 km) Access road leads 4.9 miles/8 km north to **Frenchman Lake** Yukon government campground (10 sites), 5.6 miles/9 km to photo viewpoint of lake, and 9.3 miles/15 km to Nunatak Yukon government campground (10 sites, $8 fee). Access road narrows and surface deteriorates beyond Frenchman Lake Campground. South end of this 12-mile/19-km-long lake offers good fishing for trout, pike and grayling. ▲

WL 348.4 (560.7 km) **J 24.6** (39.6 km) Pavement ends, gravel begins, westbound.

WL 349.5 (562.4 km) **J 23.5** (37.8 km) Turnoff to south for 0.9-mile/1.4-km gravel road to Little Salmon Indian village near confluence of Little Salmon River and Yukon River. There are some inhabited cabins in the area and some subsistence fishing. Private lands, no trespassing.

WL 356.2 (573.2 km) **J 16.8** (27 km) Turnout with point of interest sign overlooking Eagles Nest Bluff (formerly called Eagle Rock), well-known marker for river travelers. One of the worst steamboat disasters on the Yukon River occurred near here when the paddle-wheeler *Columbian* blew up and burned after a crew member accidentally fired a shot into a cargo of gunpowder. The accident, in which 6 men died, took place Sept. 25, 1906.

WL 356.7 (574 km) **J 16.3** (26.2 km) View of the Yukon River. At this point Whitehorse is about 160 miles/258 km upstream and Dawson City is about 300 miles/483 km downriver.

WL 360.4 (580 km) **J 12.6** (20.3 km) Northern Canada Power Commission's transmission poles and lines can be seen along highway. Power is transmitted from Aishihik dam site via Whitehorse dam and on to Cyprus Anvil mine and Faro. Orange balls mark lines where they cross river as a hazard to aircraft.

WL 370 (595.4 km) **J 3** (4.8 km) **Private Aircraft:** Carmacks airstrip to south; elev. 1,770 feet/539m; length 5,200 feet/1,585m; gravel.

WL 370.7 (596.5 km) **J 2.3** (3.7 km) Tantalus Butte coal mine on hill to north overlooking junction of Campbell and Klondike highways. The butte was named by U.S. Army Lt. Frederick Schwatka in 1883, because of its tantalizing appearance around many bends of the river before reaching it.

WL 373 (600.2 km) **J 0 Junction** with the Klondike Highway (Yukon Highway 2) at **Milepost J 104.4.** Turn south on the Klondike Highway for Carmacks (2 miles/3.2 km) and Whitehorse (115 miles/184 km); turn north for Dawson City (223 miles/357 km). Turn to page 265 in the KLONDIKE LOOP section highway log.

CANOL ROAD ⑥

Connects: Alaska Hwy. to NWT Border   **Length:** 286 miles
Road Surface: Gravel   **Season:** Closed in winter
Highest Summit: Big Salmon Summit 4,000 feet
Major Attraction: Canol Heritage Trail

(See map, page 733)

	Alaska Hwy. Jct.	Ross River	NWT Border
Alaska Hwy. Jct.		142	286
Ross River	142		144
NWT Border	286	144	

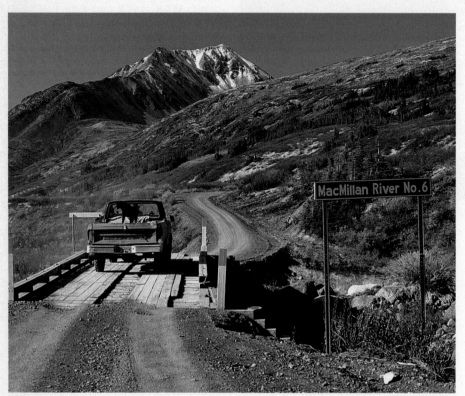

One-lane bridge over Macmillan River on the North Canol Road. (© Lyn Hancock)

The 513-mile-/825-km-long Canol Road (Yukon Highway 6) was built to provide access to oil fields at Norman Wells, NWT, on the Mackenzie River. Conceived by the U.S. War Dept. to help fuel Alaska and protect it from a Japanese invasion, the Canol (Canadian Oil) Road and a 4-inch-diameter pipeline were constructed from Norman Wells, NWT, through Macmillan Pass, past Ross River, to Johnson's Crossing on the Alaska Highway. From there the pipeline carried oil to a refinery at Whitehorse.

Begun in 1942 and completed in 1944, the Canol Project included the road, pipeline, a telephone line, the refinery, airfields, pumping stations, tank farms, wells and camps. Only about 1 million barrels of oil were pumped to Whitehorse before the war ended in 1945 and the $134 million Canol Project was abandoned. (Today, Norman Wells, pop. 757, is still a major supplier of oil with a pipeline to Zama, AB, built in 1985.) The Canol Road was declared a National Historic Site in 1990.

Since 1958, the Canol Road between Johnson's Crossing on the Alaska Highway and Ross River on the Campbell Highway (referred to as the South Canol Road) and between Ross River and the YT–NWT border

(referred to as the North Canol Road) has been rebuilt and is open to summer traffic. It is maintained to minimum standards.

The 136.8-mile/220.2-km South Canol Road is a narrow winding road which crests the Big Salmon Range and threads its way above Lapie Canyon via a difficult but scenic stretch of road. Reconstruction on the South Canol has replaced many old bridges with culverts, but there are still a few 1-lane wooden bridges. Driving time is about 4 hours one way. Watch for steep hills and bad corners. There are no facilities along the South Canol Road, and it is definitely not recommended for large RVs or trailers. Not recommended for any size vehicle in wet weather. Inquiries on current road conditions should be made locally or with the Yukon Dept. of Highways in Whitehorse (403/667-8215) before driving this road.

The 144.2-mile/232-km North Canol Road is also a narrow, winding road which some motorists have compared to a roller coaster. All bridges on the North Canol are 1-lane, and the road surface can be very slippery when wet. Not recommended during wet weather and not recommended for large RVs or trailers. If mining is under way along the North Canol, watch for large transport

trucks. *NOTE: Drive with headlights on at all times!*

Our log of the North Canol ends at the YT–NWT border, where vehicles may turn around. Road washouts prohibit travel beyond this point. From the border to Norman Wells it is 230 miles/372 km of unusable road that has been designated the Canol Heritage Trail by the NWT government. Northwest Territories Tourism recommends contacting the Norman Wells Historical Centre (phone 403/587-2415, fax 403/587-2469) for current description of trail conditions and recommended precautions.

WARNING: The only facilities on the Canol Road are at Ross River and at Johnson's Crossing on the Alaska Highway.

Emergency medical services: In Ross River, phone (403) 969-2222; or phone the RCMP, (403) 969-5555, or 1-403-667-5555. *NOTE: Yukon Territory area code changes from (403) to (867) in October 1997.*

South Canol Road Log

YUKON HIGHWAY 6
Kilometre figures in the log from the Alaska Highway junction reflect the location of physical kilometreposts when they occur. **Distance from the junction with the Alaska Highway (J) is followed by distance from the Campbell Highway junction (C).**

J 0 C 136.8 (220.2 km) **Junction** of the Canol Road (Yukon Highway 6) with the Alaska Highway. Food, gas and camping at Johnson's Crossing at the southwest end of the Teslin River bridge, 0.7 mile/1.1 km from Canol Road turnoff.

J 0.2 (0.3 km) **C 136.6** (219.8 km) Information panel on the history and construction of Canol Road. A short, dirt road (on left, northbound) leads to an auto "boneyard" that includes several WWII Canol Project trucks (all have been significantly cannibalized). Limited turnaround area, not suitable for trailers. Not recommended for any vehicle in wet weather.

J 3.9 (6.2 km) **C 132.9** (213.8 km) Fourmile Creek. Road begins ascent across the Big Salmon Range to the summit (elev. about 4,000 feet/1,219m). Snow possible at summit early October to late spring.

J 6.2 (10 km) **C 130.6** (210.1 km) Beaver Creek.

J 13.9 (22.4 km) **C 122.9** (197.8 km) Moose Creek. Small gravel turnout with

CANOL ROAD *Alaska Highway Junction, YT, to NWT Border*

SELWYN MOUNTAINS

BACKBONE

R-144/232km

Macmillan Pass

Tsichu River

Keele River

RANGES

ITSI RANGE

Macmillan River

North Macmillan River

South Macmillan River

Mount Sheldon ▲
6,937 ft./2,114m

Ross River

NORTHWEST TERRITORIES

YUKON TERRITORY

Sheldon Lake

Lewis Lake

Dragon Lake

Pup Cr.

Caribou Cr.

Tay Cr.

6

LOGA MOUNTAINS

Pelly River

River

ANVIL RANGE

Beaver Creek

Pelly

To Carmacks
(see CAMPBELL HIGHWAY section)

4

R-0

Tenas Cr.

Orchie L.

Majorie L.

North Canol Road

C-0
J-137/220km

Free Ferry
Ross River ✈

Fox Creek

Lapie River

4

To Watson Lake
(see CAMPBELL HIGHWAY section)

PELLY

Lapie Pass

Lapie Lakes

Pony Cr.

Ground Hog Creek

Caribou Mountain ▲
6,905 ft./2,105m

▲ Pass Peak
7,194 ft./2,193m

MOUNTAINS

CAMPBELL RANGE

BIG SALMON RANGE

Upper Sheep Creek

Rose River

Mount St. Cyr ▲
6,725 ft./2,050m

Nisutlin River

Nisutlin Lake

Teslin River

Quiet Lake

Cottonwood Cr. ▲

South Canol Road

Sidney Creek

Sidney Lake

Evelyn Cr.

Murphy Cr.

6

Nisutlin River

▲ Johnson's Crossing

1

C-137/220km
J-0

To Whitehorse
(see ALASKA HIGHWAY section)

Teslin Lake

1

To Teslin
(see ALASKA HIGHWAY section)

Map Location

Scale
0 ___ 10 Miles
0 ___ 10 Kilometres

Key to mileage boxes
miles/kilometres
miles/kilometres from:

C-Campbell Highway
J-Junction
R-Ross River

Principal Route
Paved   Unpaved
Other Roads
Paved   Unpaved
Ferry Routes   **Hiking Trails**

✱ Refer to Log for Visitor Facilities
❓ Visitor Information   ⟳ Fishing
▲ Campground   ✈ Airport   ✈ Airstrip

Key to Advertiser Services
C -Camping
D -Dump Station
d -Diesel
G -Gas (reg., unld.)
I -Ice
L -Lodging
M -Meals
P -Propane
R -Car Repair (major)
r -Car Repair (minor)
S -Store (grocery)
T -Telephone (pay)

litter barrels.

J 17.2 (27.6 km) **C 119.6** (192.4 km) Seventeenmile Creek.

J 19.4 (31.2 km) **C 117.4** (188.9 km) Murphy Creek.

J 19.8 (32 km) **C 117** (188.3 km) Pelly Mountains can be seen in distance northbound.

J 27 (43.4 km) **C 109.8** (176.7 km) One-lane wooden bridge over Evelyn Creek.

J 28.7 (46.2 km) **C 108.1** (174 km) Two-lane bridge over Sidney Creek.

J 30.6 (49.2 km) **C 106.2** (170.9 km) Access road on right northbound leads to Sidney Lake. Nice little lake and good place to camp.

From here northbound the South Canol follows the Nisutlin River, which is to the east and can be seen from the road the next 30 miles/48 km until the road crosses the Rose River beyond Quiet Lake.

J 30.9 (49.7 km) **C 105.9** (170.4 km) Turnout with litter barrel to east.

J 36.7 (59 km) **C 100.1** (161.1 km) Coyote Creek, culverts.

J 39.1 (62.9 km) **C 97.7** (157.2 km) Good view of Pelly Mountains ahead. Road crosses Cottonwood Creek.

J 42 (67.6 km) **C 94.8** (152.5 km) Access road on right northbound leads 0.4 mile/0.6 km to Nisutlin River. Good place to camp with tables and outhouse.

J 47.8 (76.9 km) **C 89** (143.2 km) Quiet Lake Yukon government campground; 20 sites, $8 fee, boat launch, picnic tables, kitchen shelter, firewood. Watch for steep hills northbound to Quiet Lake. ▲

J 54.7 (88 km) **C 82.1** (132.1 km) Lake Creek. Road now follows **Quiet Lake** to west; good fishing for lake trout, northern pike and arctic grayling. ⬅🐟

J 56 (90.1 km) **C 80.8** (130 km) Turnout with litter barrels and point of interest sign overlooking Quiet Lake. This is the largest of 3 lakes that form the headwaters of the Big Salmon River system. The 17-mile-/28-km-long lake was named in 1887 by John McCormack, 1 of 4 miners who prospected the Big Salmon River from its mouth on the Yukon River to its source. Although they did find some gold, the river and lakes have become better known for their good fishing and fine scenery. Until the completion of the South Canol Road in the 1940s, this area was reached mainly by boating and portaging hundreds of miles up the Teslin and Nisutlin rivers.

J 61.2 (98.5 km) **C 75.6** (121.6 km) Turnoff on left northbound (west) for **Quiet Lake**, day-use area with picnic sites, water, boat launch and fishing. Entry point for canoeists on the Big Salmon River. ⬅🐟

J 61.5 (99 km) **C 75.3** (121.2 km) Yukon government Quiet Lake maintenance camp on left northbound. A vintage Canol Project dump truck and pull grader is on display in front of the camp.

J 62.6 (100.7 km) **C 74.2** (119.4 km) Distance marker indicates Ross River 126 km.

J 63.7 (102 km) **C 73.1** (117.6 km) Steep hill and panoramic view of mountains and valley.

J 65.5 (105.4 km) **C 71.3** (114.7 km) One-lane Bailey bridge across Rose River No. 1. The road now follows the valley of the Rose River into Lapie Pass northbound. According to R.C. Coutts in "Yukon Places and Names," Oliver Rose prospected extensively in this area in the early 1900s. He came to the Yukon from Quebec, and was known as a hard-working, solitary and respected man.

J 70.4 (113.3 km) **C 66.4** (106.8 km) Canol Creek culvert.

J 71.9 (115.7 km) **C 64.9** (104.4 km) Deer Creek.

J 75.7 (121.8 km) **C 61.1** (98.3 km) Gravel Creek culvert.

J 81.1 (130 km) **C 55.7** (89.6 km) Road crosses creek (name unknown) in culvert.

J 83.7 (134 km) **C 53.1** (85.4 km) Dodge Creek culvert.

J 87.1 (140 km) **C 49.7** (80 km) Rose River No. 2 culvert.

J 89.7 (144.3 km) **C 47.1** (75.8 km) Rose River No. 3 culverts.

J 91.5 (147.2 km) **C 45.3** (72.9 km) Rose River No. 4 culverts.

J 93.8 (151 km) **C 43** (69.2 km) Rose River No. 5 culverts.

J 94.1 (151.4 km) **C 42.7** (68.7 km) Distance marker indicates Ross River 76 km.

J 95.1 (153 km) **C 41.7** (67.1 km) Upper Sheep Creek joins the Rose River here. To the east is Pass Peak (elev. 7,194 feet/ 2,193m).

J 96.4 (155.1 km) **C 40.4** (65 km) Rose River No. 6.

J 97.1 (156.2 km) **C 39.7** (63.9 km) Rose Lake to east.

J 97.5 (156.9 km) **C 39.3** (63.2 km) Pony Creek. Caribou Mountain (elev. 6,905 feet/ 2,105m) to west.

J 101.1 (162.7 km) **C 35.7** (57.4 km) Lakes to west are part of Lapie Lakes chain, headwaters of the Lapie River. These features were named by Dr. George M. Dawson of the Geological Survey of Canada in 1887 for Lapie, an Iroquois Indian companion and canoeman of Robert Campbell, who was the first to explore the Pelly River area in 1843 for the Hudson's Bay Co.

J 101.2 (162.8 km) **C 35.6** (57.3 km) Ground Hog Creek.

J 102.5 (165 km) **C 34.3** (55.2 km) Access road on left northbound leads west a short distance to Lapie Lakes. Good place to camp.

J 107.4 (172.8 km) **C 29.4** (47.3 km) Lapie River No. 1 culverts. Ponds reported good for grayling fishing. Watch for horses on the road. ⬅🐟

J 107.5 (173 km) **C 29.3** (47.1 km) Ahead northbound is Barite Mountain (elev. about 6,500 feet/1,981m).

J 110 (177 km) **C 26.8** (43.1 km) Gold Creek.

J 111.4 (179.2 km) **C 25.4** (40.8 km) Bacon Creek.

J 113.4 (182.5 km) **C 23.4** (37.6 km) Boulder Creek.

J 115.6 (186 km) **C 21.2** (34.1 km) Road runs to the east side of Barite Mountain.

J 120.2 (193.4 km) **C 16.6** (26.7 km) Fox Creek culverts.

J 120.7 (194.2 km) **C 16.1** (25.9 km) The road follows the Lapie River Canyon for about the next 11 miles/18 km, climbing to an elevation of about 500 feet/152m above the river. Narrow road, watch for rocks.

J 123.3 (198.4 km) **C 13.5** (21.7 km) Kilometrepost 200. Distance marker indicates Ross River 26 km. Lapie River runs to right side of road northbound.

J 124.7 (200.6 km) **C 12.1** (19.4 km) Glacier Creek.

J 126.3 (203.2 km) **C 10.5** (16.9 km) Turnouts on right side of road northbound overlooking Lapie River Canyon.

J 132.3 (212.9 km) **C 4.5** (7.2 km) Narrow 1-lane bridge over Lapie River No. 2. Point of interest sign on north end of bridge about the Lapie River Canyon. Approximately 100 million years ago, flat horizontal layers of

rock were buried several kilometres below the surface of the earth. Movement by rigid plates of the earth's crust subjected the rock to massive compression and strain, and it was deformed into folds. Over millions of years, the rocks rose, exposing the folds in the canyon wall.

J 133 (214 km) **C 3.8** (6.1 km) Erosional features called hoodoos can be seen in the clay banks rising above the road.

J 133.3 (214.5 km) **C 3.5** (5.6 km) Ash layer can be seen in clay bank on right side of road.

J 135.6 (218.2 km) **C 1.2** (1.9 km) Jackfish Lake, below on left northbound, is used for docking floatplanes.

J 136.8 (220 km) **C 0 Junction** of South Canol Road with the Campbell Highway. Approximately straight ahead northbound, across the Campbell Highway, a poorly maintained section of the Canol Road continues to Ross River. Motorists bound for Ross River or the North Canol Road are advised to turn left (west) on the Campbell Highway from the South Canol and drive about 5 miles/8 km to the main Ross River access road (see map).

North Canol Road Log

The North Canol Road leads 144.2 miles/232 km to the NWT border. Physical kilometreposts along the North Canol Road reflect distance from the Alaska Highway junction. *WARNING: There are no services along this road.*

Distance from Ross River (R) is shown.

R 0 ROSS RIVER (see page 729 in the CAMPBELL HIGHWAY section). Yukon government Ross River ferry (free) crosses the Pelly River. Ferry operates from 8 A.M. to noon and 1–5 P.M. daily from late May to mid-October. Those who miss the last ferry crossing of the day may leave their vehicles on the opposite side of the river and use the footbridge to walk into Ross River; vehicles can be brought over in the morning.

R 0.4 (0.6 km) Stockpile to west is barite from the Yukon Barite Mine.

R 0.6 (1 km) Road to east leads to original site of Ross River and Indian village.

R 0.9 (1.4 km) Second access road east to old Ross River and Indian village. Canol Road follows the Ross River.

R 2.1 (3.4 km) *CAUTION: Slide area, watch for falling rocks.*

R 4.7 (7.6 km)) Raspberry patch. Good pickings.

R 6.8 (10.9 km) One-lane bridge over Tenas Creek.

R 10.6 (17 km) Gravel pit to west.

R 17 (27.3 km) Deep Creek.

R 20.9 (33.6 km) **Marjorie Creek.** Locals report good grayling fishing. 🐟

R 21 (33.8 km) Access road to west leads to Marjorie Lake. Access road not recommended for large RVs.

R 21.7 (34.9 km) Marjorie Lake to west.

R 27 (43.4 km) Unnamed lake to east.

R 28.1 (45.2 km) Boat launch on Orchie Lake to west.

R 29.8 (48 km) Distance marker indicates

NWT border 195 km, Ross River 50 km.

R 31.9 (51.3 km) One-lane bridge over Gravel Creek. The next 15 miles/24 km are excellent moose country.

R 33.4 (53.7 km) One-lane bridge over Flat Creek.

R 37 (59.5 km) One-lane bridge over Beaver Creek.

R 41.8 (67.2 km) One-lane bridge over 180 Mile Creek.

R 43.9 (70.6 km) One-lane bridge over Tay Creek.

R 46.3 (74.5 km) One-lane bridge over Blue Creek.

R 48.1 (77.4 km) Kilometrepost 306. Flood Creek culvert.

R 57.6 (92.7 km) Clifford's Slough to the east.

R 58.6 (94.3 km) Steep hill to 1-lane bridge over Caribou Creek.

R 61.1 (98.3 km) Distance marker indicates NWT border 145 km, Ross River 100 km.

R 61.8 (99.4 km) **B 82.4** (132.6 km) One-lane bridge over Pup Creek.

R 64.8 (104.3 km) Turnout to west. Steep hill.

R 65.1 (104.7 km) Turnout to **Dragon Lake**; overnight parking, litter barrels. Locals report that early spring is an excellent time for pike and trout in the inlet. Rock hounds check roadsides and borrow pits for colorful chert, which can be worked into jewelry. ⚓

R 65.4 (105.2 km) Kilometrepost 334. Large, level, gravel turnout to west overlooking Dragon Lake; boat launch.

R 69.6 (112 km) Wreckage of Twin Pioneer aircraft to west. WWII remnants can be found in this area.

R 69.9 (112.5 km) Road to Twin Creek.

R 70.8 (113.9 km) Airstrip.

R 71 (114.2 km) One-lane bridge over Twin Creek No. 1. Yukon government maintenance camp.

R 71.1 (114.4 km) One-lane bridge over Twin Creek No. 2. Good views of Mount Sheldon.

R 75.1 (120.8 km) Kilometrepost 350. Mount Sheldon ahead, located 3 miles/4.8 km north of Sheldon Lake; a very beautiful and distinguishable feature on the Canol Road (elev. 6,937 feet/2,114m). In 1900, Poole Field and Clement Lewis, who were fans of writer Rudyard Kipling, named this peak Kipling Mountain and the lake at its base Rudyard. In 1907, Joseph Keele of the Geological Survey of Canada renamed them after Charles Sheldon, a well-known sheep hunter and naturalist who came to the area to collect Stone sheep specimens for the Chicago Natural History Museum in 1905.

R 76.4 (123 km) Kilometrepost 352. Of the 3-lake chain, Sheldon Lake is farthest north, then Field Lake and Lewis Lake, which is just visible from here. Lewis Lake is closest to the confluence of the Ross and Prevost rivers.

Field Lake and Lewis Lake were named in 1907 by Joseph Keele of the Geological Survey of Canada after Poole Field and Clement Lewis. The 2 partners, who had prospected this country, ran a trading post called Nahanni House at the mouth of the Ross River in 1905.

R 77.6 (124.9 km) Kilometrepost 354. One-lane bridge over Riddell Creek. Tip of Mount Riddell (elev. 6,101 feet/1,859m) can be seen to the west.

R 78.8 (126.8 km) View of Sheldon Lake ahead, Field Lake to right northbound.

R 79.8 (128.4 km) Access road east to Sheldon Lake.

R 82.7 (133.1 km) One-lane bridge over Sheldon Creek. Road climbs, leaving Ross River valley and entering Macmillan Valley northbound.

R 89.3 (143.7 km) Height of land before starting descent northbound into South Macmillan River system.

R 89.7 (144.3 km) Steep hill. Road may wash out during heavy rains. Deep ditches along roadside help channel water.

R 91.4 (147.1 km) One-lane bridge over Moose Creek.

R 91.6 (147.4 km) **B 52.6** (84.6 km) Milepost 230.

R 92.3 (148.5 km) Kilometrepost 378. Peaks of the Itsi Range ahead. Rugged, spectacular scenery northbound.

R 92.7 (149.1 km) Distance marker indicates NWT border 95 km, Ross River 150 km.

R 93.8 (151 km) First of several WWII vehicle dumps to west. To the east is a wannigan, or skid shack, used as living quarters by Canol Road workers during construction of the road. It was too far to return to base camp; these small buildings were strategically located along the route so the workers had a place to eat and sleep at night.

R 94 (151.3 km) To east are remains of a maintenance depot where heavy equipment was repaired. Concrete foundations to west. First glimpse of the South Macmillan River northbound.

R 94.7 (152.4 km) Kilometrepost 382. Another Canol project equipment dump to explore. Watch ditches for old pieces of pipeline.

R 97.8 (157.4 km) One-lane bridge over Boulder Creek.

R 98.5 (158.5 km) Access road west to South Macmillan River where boats can be launched. Locals advise launching boats here rather than from the bridge at **Milepost R 113.6**, which washes out periodically and leaves dangerous debris in the river.

R 100.8 (162.5 km) Kilometrepost 392. Itsi Range comes into view ahead northbound. Itsi is said to be an Indian word meaning "wind" and was first given as a name to Itsi Lakes, headwaters of the Ross River. The road dips down and crosses an unnamed creek.

R 104.5 (168.2 km) Kilometrepost 398. View of the South Macmillan River from here.

R 105.3 (169.4 km) View of Selwyn Mountains, named in 1901 by Joseph Keele of the Geological Survey of Canada for Dr. Alfred Richard Selwyn (1824–1902), a distinguished geologist in England. Dr. Selwyn later became director of the Geological Survey of Australia and then director of the Geological Survey of Canada from 1869 until his retirement in 1895.

R 111 (178.6 km) One-lane bridge over Itsi Creek.

R 112.2 (180.5 km) One-lane bridge over Wagon Creek.

R 113.6 (182.8 km) Turnout to east on South Macmillan River. Good place for a picnic but not recommended as a boat launch. One-lane Bailey bridge over South Macmillan River No. 1.

Robert Campbell, a Hudson's Bay Co. explorer on a journey down the Pelly River in 1843, named this major tributary of the Pelly after Chief Factor James McMillan, who had sponsored Campbell's employment with the company.

R 115.1 (185.2 km) Access road on left northbound leads about 7 miles/11 km to Yukon Barite Mine. Barite is a soft mineral that requires only crushing and bagging before being shipped over the Dempster Highway to the Beaufort Sea oil and gas wells, where it is used as a lubricant known as drilling mud.

R 117.2 (188.6 km) Access road on right northbound to gravel pit.

R 118.8 (191.2 km) Dept. of Public Works maintenance camp; status unknown.

R 118.9 (191.3 km) One-lane bridge over Jeff Creek.

R 121.2 (195 km) One-lane bridge over Hess Creek. Bears in area.

R 123.2 (198.3 km) Gravel turnout on left northbound with RCMP trailer. Distance marker indicates NWT border 45 km, Ross River 200 km. One-lane bridge over Dewhurst Creek.

R 127.5 (205.2 km) Entering Macmillan Pass. At "Mac Pass," the road climbs to elevations above 4,480 feet/1,366m.

R 129.4 (208.2 km) One-lane bridge over Macmillan River No. 2.

R 129.5 (208.4 km) Abandoned Army vehicles from the Canol Project on left northbound.

R 129.6 (208.6 km) Abandoned Army vehicles from the Canol Project on right northbound.

R 133.6 (215 km) To the west is Cordilleran Engineering camp, managers of the mining development of Ogilvie Joint Venture's Jason Project. The Jason deposit is a zinc, lead, silver, barite property. The deposit's size is still uncertain.

One-lane bridge over Sekie Creek No. 1.

R 134.4 (216.3 km) Fuel tanks on left northbound.

R 136.3 (219.3 km) Sekie Creek No. 2 culvert.

R 136.4 (219.5 km) Access to Macmillan airstrip on left northbound. Access road to right to Hudson Bay Mining & Smelting's Tom lead–zinc mineral claims. The Tom is a stratabound silver–lead–zinc deposit and the size is yet to be determined. At one time it was considered to be 9 million tons of 16 percent combined lead–zinc.

R 137.7 (221.6 km) One-lane bridge over Macmillan River No. 3.

R 141.8 (228.2 km) One-lane bridge over Macmillan River No. 4.

R 142.9 (230 km) One-lane bridge over Macmillan River No. 5.

R 144.1 (231.9 km) One-lane bridge over Macmillan River No. 6.

R 144.2 (232 km) YT–NWT border. Sign cautions motorists to proceed at their own risk. The road is not maintained and bridges are not safe beyond this point. Vehicles turn around here.

Ahead is the Tsichu River valley and the Selwyn Mountains. The abandoned North Canol Road continues another 230 miles/372 km from the YT–NWT border to Norman Wells, NWT. Designated the Canol Heritage Trail, and set aside as a territorial park reserve, the trail is currently under development. Some river crossings required; large stretches deemed dangerous and arduous. It passes through mountains, tundra and forest, and past many relics of the Canol Project. The Historical Centre museum in Norman Wells features the history of the Canol Project and has outdoor displays of Canol vehicles.

SILVER TRAIL HIGHWAY ⑪

Connects: Klondike Hwy. to Keno City, YT   **Length:** 69 miles
Road Surface: 50% paved, 50% gravel
Season: Open all year to Mayo
Major Attraction: Keno Mining Museum

	Keno City	Klondike Hwy. Jct.	Mayo
Keno City		69	37
Klondike Hwy. Jct.	69	32	
Mayo	37	32	

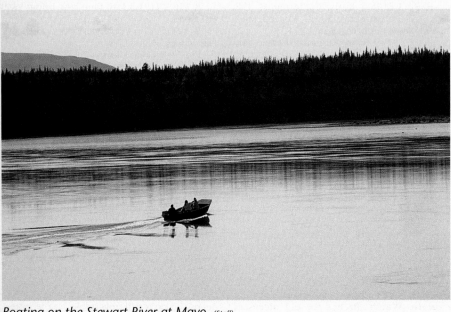

Boating on the Stewart River at Mayo. (Staff)

The Silver Trail leads northeast from the Klondike Highway (see **Milepost J 214.4** in the KLONDIKE LOOP section) to Mayo, Elsa and Keno City. From its junction with the Klondike Highway (Yukon Highway 2), the Silver Trail (Yukon Highway 11) leads 31.9 miles/51.3 km to Mayo; 60.3 miles/97 km to Elsa; and 69.1 miles/111.2 km to Keno City. The Silver Trail also provides access to Duncan Creek Road, the original Silver Trail. It is approximately 140 miles/225 km round-trip to Keno City and an easy day trip for motorists. The road is asphalt-surfaced to Mayo, hard-packed gravel from Mayo to Keno. Watch for soft shoulders, especially in wet weather. The highway is open all year to Mayo; unmaintained winter road to Keno City. Gas is available only at Mayo and at Stewart Crossing.

There is an unmanned information kiosk on the Klondike Highway at the south end of Stewart River bridge. Stop at the kiosk for information on the Silver Trail, or visit Binet House in Mayo. Or write Silver Trail Tourism, Box 268, Mayo, YT Y0B 1M0; phone (in summer) (403) 996-2926, winter phone (403) 996-2290. Information on the Silver Trail is also available from a 5-minute recorded broadcast on 93.3-FM near Stewart Crossing on the Klondike Highway.

The Silver Trail to Mayo follows the Stewart River through what has been one of the richest silver mining regions in Canada.

Emergency medical services: In Mayo, phone (403) 996-4444; or phone the RCMP toll free, Yukon-wide, at 1-403-667-5555. *NOTE: Yukon Territory area code changes from (403) to (867) in October 1997.*

Silver Trail Log

Distance is measured from the junction with the Klondike Highway (J).

J 0 Junction of Silver Trail (Yukon Highway 11) and Klondike Highway.

J 0.2 (0.3 km) Marker shows distance to Mayo 51 km, Elsa 97 km, Keno 110 km.

J 1.2 (2 km) Stewart River to the south.

J 3 (4.8 km) Bad curve. Turnout to south.

J 9.6 (15.4 km) Large gravel pit turnout to south.

J 12 (19.2 km) Large double-ended turnout with litter barrrels overlooking the Stewart River.

J 27.4 (44.1 km) Pull-through rest area; outhouses, litter barrel, picnic tables.

J 30.7 (49.5 km) Winding descent for northeast-bound traffic; good view of valley.

J 31.2 (50.2 km) McIntyre Park picnic area to south on banks of the Mayo River; 9 picnic sites and a shelter.

J 31.3 (50.3 km) **Mayo River** bridge. Good fishing from bridge for grayling. 🐟

J 31.9 (51.3 km) **Junction** with access road to Mayo (description follows). Turn right (south) for Mayo, keep left (north) for road to Elsa and Keno City.

Heartland Services–Mayo Chevron. Beautiful view of Mount Haldane rising 6,023 feet above sea level. Free coffee, tourist information, clean restroom, full-service gasoline and diesel. Fishing licenses, soft drinks and snacks. Open 7 days a week, 8 A.M.–8 P.M., May 15–Sept. 30. Closed on Sundays from Oct. 1–May 15. Major cards accepted. Phone (403) 996-2329; fax (403) 996-2503. [ADVERTISEMENT]

Mayo

Located on the bank of the Stewart River near its confluence with the Mayo River. **Population:** 500. **Emergency Services:** RCMP, phone (403) 996-5555. **Ambulance,** phone (403) 996-4444. **Visitor Information:** At Binet House Interpretive Centre, open 10:30 A.M. to 6 P.M. in summer, phone (403) 996-2926. Exhibits include floral and mineral displays, silver and galena samples, and information panels on mining and geology. Yukon Gold Explorer's Passport stamped here. **Elevation:** 1,650 feet/503m. **Climate:** Residents claim it's the coldest and hottest spot in Yukon. Record low, -80°F/-62.2°C (February 1947); record high, 97°F/36.1°C (June 1969). **Radio:**

SILVER TRAIL HIGHWAY *Klondike Highway Junction to Keno City, YT*

Map Location

Scale
0 _____ 10 Miles
0 _____ 10 Kilometres

Key to mileage boxes
miles/kilometres
miles/kilometres
from:
J-Junction

Principal Route
Paved   Unpaved
Other Roads
Paved   Unpaved
Ferry Routes   Hiking Trails

⊞ Refer to Log for Visitor Facilities
? Visitor Information   ⊠ Fishing
△ Campground   ✈ Airport ✈ Airstrip

Key to Advertiser Services
C -Camping
D -Dump Station
d -Diesel
G -Gas (reg.. unld.)
I -Ice
L -Lodging
M-Meals
P -Propane
R -Car Repair (major)
r -Car Repair (minor)
S -Store (grocery)
T -Telephone (pay)

J-69/111km

GUSTAVUS MOUNTAIN RANGE

J-48/77km
Mt. Haldane ▲ 6,032 ft./1,839m
Elsa
11 Duncan Creek Road
Keno City △

Halfway Lakes
Minto Lake Road

Mayo River

Mayo Lake

J-43/69km

Minto Lake
Wareham Lake
Williamson Lake

J-32/51km
Janet Lake
J-31.9/51.3km Heartland Services–Mayo Chevron dGT

The Silver Trail Tourism Association
Mayo ✚

11

To Dawson City
(see KLONDIKE LOOP section)

Stewart Crossing

J-0

Stewart River

Ethel Lake

To Whitehorse
(see KLONDIKE LOOP section)

N W E S

CBC 1230, CHON-FM 98.5. **Television:** CBC Anik, Channel 7. **Transportation:** Charter floatplane and helicopter service available. Scheduled bus service.

Private Aircraft: Mayo airstrip, 4 miles/ 6.5 km north; elev. 1,653 feet/504m; length 4,850 feet/1,478m; gravel; fuel 100, Jet B.

Mayo has most traveler facilities including overnight accommodations at Bedrock Motel and bed and breakfasts; food service at motel and a cafe; laundromat; full-service gas and diesel, fishing licenses and snack at Heartland Services–Mayo Chevron; hardware, grocery and variety stores (closed Sunday). Tire repair and minor vehicle repair are available. Post office, liquor store and library located in the Territorial Building. Bank service available 10 A.M. to 1 P.M. Monday, Wednesday and Friday.

Mayo was formerly known as Mayo Landing and began as a river settlement and port for silver ore shipments to Whitehorse. It is now a service centre for mineral exploration in the area. Yukon Electrical Co. Ltd. operates a hydroelectric project here.

Canoeists can put in at Mayo on the Stewart River for a paddle to Stewart Crossing or Dawson City.

The Silver Trail Tourism Association. See display ad this section.

Silver Trail Log

(continued)

J 32.8 (52.8 km) Mayo airport, built in 1928 by the Treadwell Mining Co.

J 34.9 (56.2 km) Side road to Mayo hydro dam, built in 1951 and completed in 1952.

J 35.8 (57.6 km) Turnoff to west for Five Mile Lake Yukon government campground; 20 sites, boat launch, picnic tables, firepits.   ▲

J 36.1 (58.1 km) Five Mile Lake day-use area. Pavement ends, gravel begins, northbound.

J 37.6 (60.5 km) Wareham Lake to east, created by the Mayo River power project.

J 38.2 (61.4 km) Survival shelter to east.

J 42.9 (69 km) **Junction** of Yukon Highway 11 with Minto Lake Road and Duncan Creek Road. Turn west (left) and drive 12 miles/19 km for **Minto Lake;** good fishing for lake trout and grayling. Also access to Highet Creek.   ◄

Turn east (right) at junction for Duncan Creek Road, which leads to Mayo Lake and Keno City. The original Silver Trail, Duncan Creek Road was used by Treadwell Yukon during the 1930s to haul silver ore from Keno into Mayo, where it was loaded onto riverboats.

This 25-mile/40-km back road is mostly good hard-packed gravel. Motorists note, however, that the last 10 miles/16 km into Keno City via Duncan Creek Road are narrow and winding, slippery when wet and not recommended for large vehicles or trailers. Heading northeast on Duncan Creek Road, travelers will see the site of Fields Creek Roadhouse at Mile 5, and Stones Roadhouse at Mile 11. At Mile 14 Duncan Creek Road junctions with a 6-mile/10-km side road which leads to **Mayo Lake;** there is good fishing along the **Mayo River** to the dam at the west end of Mayo Lake. At Mile 14.2 there is a private gold mine. At Mile 18 are the remains of the Van Cleaves Roadhouse. At Mile 25 Duncan Creek Road junctions with Highway 11 at Keno City.   ◄

J 47.1 (77 km) Watch for turnoff for Mount Haldane trail; follow gravel road 2 miles/3.2 km to trailhead. This 4-mile-/6.4-km-long trail leads to summit, elev. 6,023 feet/1,836m.

J 48 (77.2 km) **Halfway Lakes;** fishing for northern pike. Silver Trail Inn; food and lodging in summer.   ◄

J 49 (78.8 km) Mount Haldane Lions survival shelter.

J 54.9 (88.3 km) South McQuesten River Road.

J 60.3 (97 km) **ELSA** (pop. 10) was a company town for United Keno Hill Mines, formerly one of the largest silver mines in North America and one of the Yukon's oldest, con-

tinuously operating hardrock mines until its closure in 1989. The Elsa claim is a well-mineralized silver vein, located on Galena Hill and named for the sister of prospector Charlie Brefalt, who received $250,000 for Treadwell Yukon's richest mine. A plaque here commemorates American engineer Livingston Wernecke, who came to the Keno Hill area in 1919 to investigate the silver–lead ore discoveries for Treadwell–Yukon Mining Co.

J 63.8 (102.6 km) Side road leads north to Hanson Lakes and McQuesten Lake. Galena Mountains to east. An information sign marks the Wind River trail, a former winter road to oil and mining exploration sites, which leads 300 miles/483 km north to the Bell River. The twin towers are abandoned telephone relays.

J 69.1 (111.2 km) **KENO CITY** (pop. about 50). Originally called Sheep Hill by the early miners, it was renamed Keno—a gambling game—after the Keno mining claim that was staked by Louis Bouvette in July 1919. This enormously rich discovery of silver and galena sparked the interest of 2 large mining companies, the Guggenheims and Treadwell Yukon, who set up camps in the area. During the 1920s, Keno City was a boom town.

Keno has a hotel with a unique bar (no food service available), a coffee shop, and washers, dryers and showers available for the public. There is a city campground located on Lightning Creek.   ▲

Well worth a visit here is the Keno Mining Museum, phone (403) 995-2792, fax 395-2730. Photographs and tools recall the mining history of the area. It is open 10 A.M. to 6 P.M. in summer. Be sure to get your Yukon Gold Explorer's Passport stamped at the museum—its location makes it the most exclusive of the 14 passport stamps.

There are a number of hiking trails in the Keno area; inquire at the museum. The Summit trail (can be driven) leads 6.5 miles/ 10.5 km to the milepost sign on top of Keno Hill, elev. 6,065 feet/1,849m.

DEMPSTER HIGHWAY

Connects: Klondike Hwy. to Inuvik, NWT   **Length:** 456 miles
Road Surface: Gravel   **Season:** Open all year
Highest Summit: North Fork Pass 4,265 feet
Major Attractions: Lost Patrol Gravesite, Mackenzie River Delta

	Dawson City	Ft. McPherson	Inuvik	Klondike Hwy.
Dawson City		367	481	25
Ft. McPherson	367		114	342
Inuvik	481	114		456
Klondike Hwy.	25	342	456	

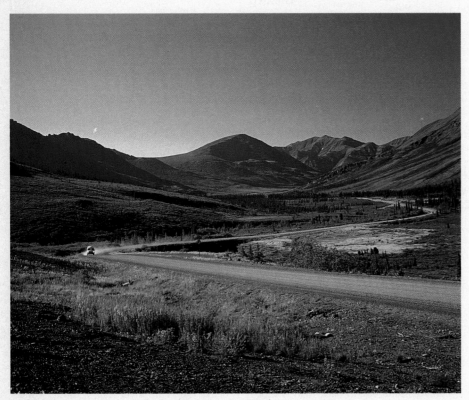

Vehicle churns up dust along the Dempster Highway. (Earl L. Brown, staff)

Territories is available by calling the Arctic Hotline at 1-800-661-0788. For recorded messages on ferry service, road and weather conditions, phone 1-800-661-0752. If you are in Dawson City, the Western Arctic Visitor Centre has information on Northwest Territories and the Dempster Highway. Located in the B.Y.N. Building on Front Street, across from the Yukon Visitor Centre, it is open 9 A.M. to 9 P.M., June to September; phone (403) 993-6167. Or write the Western Arctic Tourism Assoc., Box 2600MP, Inuvik, NT X0E 0T0; phone (403) 979-4321, fax (403) 979-2434 for more information.

NOTE: Yukon Territory area code changes from (403) to (867) in October 1997.

The Dempster Highway (Yukon Highway 5, NWT Highway 8) begins 25 miles/40.2 km east of Dawson City, YT, at its junction with Klondike Highway 2 (see **Milepost J 301.6** in the KLONDIKE LOOP section), and leads 456.3 miles/734.3 km northeast to Inuvik, NWT.

Construction of the Dempster Highway began in 1959, under the Road to Resources program, and was completed in 1978. A 5-year major reconstruction and surfacing program on the highway concluded in 1988, although freezing weather and heavy truck traffic may erode both road base and surfacing in areas. Calcium chloride is used in some areas to reduce dust and as a bonding agent; wash your vehicle as soon as practical.

The Dempster is a gravel road. There are stretches of clay surface that can be slippery in wet weather. Summer driving conditions on the Dempster vary depending on weather and maintenance. Generally, road conditions range from fair to excellent, with highway speeds attainable on some sections.

Facilities are still few and far between on the Dempster. Full auto services are available at Klondike River Lodge at the Demp-ster Highway turnoff on Klondike Highway 2. Gas, propane, food and lodging, and car repair are also available at Eagle Plains Hotel, located at about the halfway point on the Dempster. Gas, food and lodging are also available in Fort McPherson. Gas up whenever possible.

The Dempster is open year-round. The highway is fairly well-traveled in summer: A driver may not see another car for an hour, and then pass 4 cars in a row. Locals say the highway is smoother and easier to drive in winter, but precautions should be taken against cold weather, high winds and poor visibility; check road conditions before proceeding in winter. It is strongly recommended motorists carry at least 2 spare tires while traveling the Dempster. DRIVE WITH YOUR HEADLIGHTS ON!

There are 2 ferry crossings on the Dempster, at **Milepost J 334.9** (Peel River crossing) and **J 377.9** (Mackenzie River and Arctic Red River crossings). Free government ferry service is available 15 hours a day (9 A.M. to 1 A.M. Northwest Territories time, 8 A.M. to midnight Yukon time) during summer (from about June to mid-October). Cross by ice bridge in winter.

General information on Northwest

DEMPSTER HIGHWAY *Klondike Highway Junction to Inuvik, NWT*

Noell Lake

Sitidgi Lake

Mackenzie

I-0
J-456/734km

Inuvik ❊ ? △ ✛

Delta

Dolomite Lake

Campbell Lake

Caribou Lake

△

Caribou Creek

YUKON TERRITORY

NORTHWEST TERRITORIES

Bell River

Mackenzie River

Rengleng River

◗

Frog Creek

I-115/184km
J-342/550km

Fort McPherson ❊

Free Ferry

△

Peel

Arctic Red River

Free Ferry

Arctic Red River

Old Crow

Porcupine River

I-167/269km
J-289/465km

Shiltee Rock ✕

8

Rock River

△

5

Eagle River

ARCTIC CIRCLE

✛

I-204/329km
J-252/406km

YUKON TERRITORY

NORTHWEST TERRITORIES

△

J-229.3/369km Eagle Plains Hotel CDdGILMPrST

Peel River

Hart River

N
W ⊕ E
S

I-335/539km
J-122/194km

◗
△

Engineer Creek

Blackstone River

Ogilvie River

OGILVIE

✛

Chapman Lake

◗

West Fork

East Fork

△

5

MOUNTAINS

Tombstone Mountain ▲

North Fork

Bensen Creek

Yukon River

To Boundary, AK
(see KLONDIKE LOOP
HIGHWAY section)

Free Ferry

❊ ? △ ✛
Dawson City

2

I-456/734km
J-0

Klondike River

2

To Carmacks
(see KLONDIKE LOOP HIGHWAY section)

J-0 Klondike River Lodge
CDdGILMPrST

RICHARDSON MOUNTAINS

Scale

| 0 | | 20 | Miles |

| 0 | 20 | | Kilometres |

Key to mileage boxes

| miles/kilometres |
| miles/kilometres |

from:

J-Junction
I-Inuvik

Map Location

Principal Route

Paved — Unpaved

Other Roads

Paved — Unpaved

Ferry Routes — **Hiking Trails**

❊ Refer to Log for Visitor Facilities
? Visitor Information
◗ Fishing
△ Campground ✛ Airport ✛ Airstrip

Key to Advertiser Services

C -Camping
D -Dump Station
d -Diesel
G -Gas (reg., unld.)
I -Ice
L -Lodging
M -Meals
P -Propane
R -Car Repair (major)
r -Car Repair (minor)
S -Store (grocery)
T -Telephone (pay)

Dempster Highway Log

YUKON HIGHWAY 5

Driving distance is measured in miles. The kilometre figure on the Yukon portion of the highway reflects the physical kilometreposts and is not necessarily an accurate metric conversion of the mileage figure. Kilometreposts are green with white lettering and are located on the right-hand side of the highway, northbound.

Distance from junction with Klondike Highway 2 (J) is followed by distance from Inuvik (I).

J 0 I 456.3 (734.3 km) **Junction** of Yukon Highways 2 and 5, 25 miles/40.2 km east of Dawson City, also known as Dempster Corner. Lodge with food, gas, propane, lodging, camping, and tire repair and sales; open all year.

Klondike River Lodge. See display ad this section. ▲

J 0.1 (0.2 km) **I 456.2** (734.2 km) Dempster Highway monument with information panels on history and culture, wildlife, ecology and driving tips.

J 0.2 (0.3 km) **I 456.1** (734 km) One-lane wood-planked bridge over Klondike River. The road follows the wooded (spruce and poplar) North Klondike River valley.

J 0.9 (1.4 km) **I 455.4** (732.9 km) Distance marker shows Eagle Plains 363 km (226 miles), Inuvik 735 km (457 miles).

J 3 (5 km) **I 453.3** (729.5 km) Burn area from 1991 fire that burned 5,189 acres/2,100 hectacres.

J 4 (6.4 km) **I 452.3** (727.9 km) The North Fork Ditch channeled water from the North Klondike River to a power plant 15.5 miles/25 km farther west for nearly 60 years, until the 1960s, and it helped to provide electricity and water for huge gold-dredging operations farther down the valley. Watch for salmon migrating upstream from late July through August.

J 6.5 (10.5 km) **I 449.8** (723.9 km) Antimony Mountain (elev. 6,693 feet/2,040m) about 18.5 miles/30 km away, is one peak of the Ogilvie Mountains and part of the Snowy Range.

J 12.4 (20 km) **I 443.9** (714.4 km) North Klondike Range, Ogilvie Mountains to the west of the highway lead toward the rugged, interior Tombstone Range. These mountains were glaciated during the Ice Age.

J 15.4 (24.5 km) **I 440.9** (709.5 km) Glacier Creek.

J 16.6 (26.7 km) **I 439.7** (707.6 km) Pullout to west.

J 18.1 (29 km) **I 438.2** (705.2 km) Bensen Creek.

J 25.6 (41 km) **I 430.7** (693.1 km) Pea Soup Creek.

J 29.8 (48 km) **I 426.5** (686.4 km) Scout Car Creek.

J 31.7 (51 km) **I 424.6** (683.3 km) Wolf Creek. Private cabin beside creek.

J 34.7 (55.8 km) **I 421.6** (678.5 km) Highway follows North Fork Klondike River.

J 36.6 (58.9 km) **I 419.7** (675.4 km) Grizzly Creek. Mount Robert Service to right northbound.

J 39.6 (63.7 km) **I 416.7** (670.6 km) Mike and Art Creek.

J 40.4 (65 km) **I 415.9** (669.3 km) Klondike Camp Yukon government high-way maintenance station. No visitor services but may provide help in an emergency.

J 41.8 (67.3 km) **I 414.5** (667.1 km) First crossing of the North Fork Klondike River. The highway now moves above tree line and on to tundra northbound. At an elevation of approximately 4,003 feet/1,220m, you'll cross the watershed between the Yukon and Mackenzie basins.

J 43 (69.2 km) **I 413.3** (665.2 km) Spectacular first view of Tombstone Range northbound.

J 44.4 (71.5 km) **I 411.9** (662.9 km) Tombstone Mountain Yukon government campground (3,392 feet/1,034m above sea level) with 31 sites, $8 fee, shelter, fireplaces, water from the river, tables, pit toilets. Designated cyclist camping area with bear-proof food cache available. Interpretive centre located at campground, open 10 A.M. to 10 P.M., mid-June to early September; fossil displays, resource library, handouts with area information, campfire talks and nature walks. Good hiking trail begins past the outhouses and leads toward the headwaters of the North Fork Klondike River. ▲

J 46 (74 km) **I 410.3** (660.3 km) Large double-ended pullout. Good views of North Fork Pass and river. To the southwest is Tombstone Mountain (7,195 feet/2,193m). Outstanding aerial view of the mountain available through flightseeing trip out of Dawson City. To the north is the East Fork Blackstone River valley; on each side are the Ogilvie Mountains, which rise to elevations of 6,890 feet/2,100m.

J 48.4 (77.9 km) **I 407.9** (656.4 km) Blackstone River culvert. Tundra in the region indicates permafrost.

J 51 (82 km) **I 405.3** (652.2 km) North Fork Pass Summit, elev. 4,265 feet/1,300m, is the highest point on the Dempster Highway. Wildflowers abundant late June–early July. Descent to the Blackstone River. Good bird-watching area. A hike up to the lower knoll to the right of the main mountain increases chances of seeing pika and marmots.

J 52.2 (84 km) **I 404.1** (650.3 km) Anglecomb Peak (also called Sheep Mountain) is a lambing and nursery habitat for Dall sheep during May and June, as well as a frequent nesting area for a pair of golden eagles.

J 54.2 (87.2 km) **I 402.1** (647.1 km) First crossing of East Fork Blackstone River.

J 56.5 (91 km) **I 399.8** (643.4 km) The Blackstone Uplands, stretching from North Fork Pass to Chapman Lake, are a rich area for birdlife (long-tailed jaegers, gyrfalcons, peregrine falcons, red-throated loons, Whimbrels, upland sandpipers and old-squaw ducks) and big game hunting for Dall sheep and grizzly bear.

J 63.4 (102 km) **I 392.9** (632.3 km) Distance marker shows Eagle Plains 261 km (162 miles), Inuvik 633 km (393 miles), Dawson 142 km (88 miles), Whitehorse 600 km (373 miles).

J 66.9 (107.6 km) **I 389.4** (626.7 km) Large gravel pullout with litter barrels. Access to Blackstone River.

J 71.5 (115 km) **I 384.8** (619.3 km) First crossing of West Fork Blackstone River. Watch for arctic terns. Good fishing for Dolly Varden and grayling a short distance downstream where the west and east forks of the Blackstone join to form the **Blackstone River**, which the road now follows. After the river crossing, 2 low, cone-shaped mounds called pingos are visible upriver about 5 miles/8 km. ⊷

J 72.1 (116 km) **I 384.2** (618.3 km) Commemorative road sign about sled dog patrols of the Royal North West Mounted Police. Also a sign: Watch for horses. View over Chapman Lake, one of the few lakes close to the highway that is large enough to permit floatplane operations. Porcupine caribou herd sometimes crosses the highway in this area in mid-October.

J 77.3 (124.4 km) **I 379** (609.9 km) **Private Aircraft:** Government airstrip (road is part of the strip); elev. 3,100 feet/945m; length 3,000 feet/914m.

J 96 (154.5 km) **I 360.3** (579.8 km) Northbound, highway passes through barren gray hills of Windy Pass. The mountain ridges are the breeding habitat for some species of butterflies and moths not known to exist anywhere else.

J 106 (169.7 km) **I 350.3** (563.7 km) Creek culvert is red from iron oxide. Sulfurous smell is from nearby sulfur springs. Watch for interesting geological features in hills along road.

J 108.1 (173 km) **I 348.2** (560.4 km) Views of red-coloured Engineer Creek, and also erosion pillars and red rock of nearby hills between here and Kilometrepost 182.

J 121.7 (194 km) **I 334.6** (538.5 km) Sapper Hill, named in 1971 in honour of the 3rd Royal Canadian Engineers who built the Ogilvie River bridge. "Sapper" is a nickname for an army engineer. **Engineer Creek** Yukon government campground; 15 sites, $8 fee, fireplaces, water, tables, pit toilets. Grayling fishing. ⊷▲

J 122.9 (195.7 km) **I 333.4** (536.5 km) The 360-foot/110-m Jeckell Bridge spans the Ogilvie River here. Built by the Canadian Armed Forces Engineers as a training exercise, it is named in honour of Allan Jeckell, controller of the Yukon from 1932 to 1946. Fossil coral may be visible in limestone outcrops to the northeast of the bridge.

The Ogilvie River and Ogilvie Mountains were named in honour of William Ogilvie, a highly respected Dominion land surveyor and commissioner of the Yukon during the Klondike Gold Rush.

J 123 (195.8 km) **I 333.3** (536.4 km) Ogilvie grader station, Yukon government maintenance camp is on north side of the river.

For the next 25 miles/40 km, the highway follows the narrow valley of the Ogilvie River. For the first 12 miles/20 km, talus slopes edge the road, and game trails are evident along their precipitous sides.

J 124.3 (197.7 km) **I 332** (534.3 km) View of castlelike outcroppings of rock, known as tors, on mountaintops to north.

J 131.9 (209.5 km) **I 324.4** (522.1 km) Between here and Kilometrepost 216, watch for bird nests in the shale embankments along the highway and unusual rock outcroppings and erosion pillars in surrounding hills. Highway crosses rolling plateau country near Kilometrepost 218.

J 137.5 (221.2 km) **I 318.8** (513 km) Small turnout with litter barrels. Easy access to **Ogilvie River**. Good grayling fishing. Elephant Rock may be viewed from right side of road northbound. Fascinating mountain of broken rock and shale near Kilometrepost 224. ⊷

J 137.6 (221.5 km) **I 318.7** (512.9 km) Davies Creek.

J 149.1 (235.8 km) **I 307.2** (494.4 km) Ogilvie airstrip, status unknown. The great gray owl, one of Canada's largest, is known to nest as far north as this area.

J 154.4 (244 km) I 301.9 (485.8 km) Highway climbs away from the Ogilvie River, following a high ridge to the Eagle Plains plateau. One of the few unglaciated areas in Canada, this country is shaped by wind and water erosion rather than by ice. Views of Mount Cronkhite and Mount McCullum to the east.

Seismic lines next 62 miles/100 km provide hiking paths across the tundra. This was the major area of oil and gas exploration activity for which the road was originally built. In season, fields of cotton grass and varieties of tundra plants make good photo subjects. The road continues to follow a high ridge (elev. 1,969 feet/600m) with broad sweeps and easy grades.

J 160.9 (259 km) I 295.4 (475.4 km) Large double-ended turnout. Panoramic Ogilvie–Peel viewpoint. Lowbush cranberries in August. Outhouse, litter barrels.

J 171.7 (270.6 km) I 284.6 (458 km) Highway begins descent northbound and crosses fabulous high rolling country above tree line.

J 175.6 (276.7 km) I 280.7 (451.7 km) Gravel pit full of old oil drums.

J 187.7 (302 km) I 268.6 (432.3 km) Forest fire burn area; 13,590 acres/5,500 hectacres burned in July–August 1991.

J 204.5 (321 km) I 256.3 (412.5 km) Road widens to become part of an airstrip.

J 215.6 (347 km) I 240.7 (387.4 km) Richardson Mountains to the northeast. The thick blanket of rock and gravel that makes up the roadbed ahead is designed to prevent the underlying permafrost from melting. The roadbed conducts heat more than the surrounding vegetation does and must be extra thick to compensate. Much of the highway was built in winter.

J 229.3 (369 km) I 227 (365.3 km) Milepost 231. **EAGLE PLAINS;** hotel, phone (403) 979-4187, fax (403) 979-4187; food, gas, propane, aviation fuel, diesel, lodging and camping. Open year-round. ▲

Built in 1978, just before completion of the Dempster Highway, the hotel here was an engineering challenge. Engineers considered the permafrost in the area and found a place where the bedrock was at the surface. The hotel was built on this natural pad, thus avoiding the costly process of building on pilings as was done at Inuvik.

Eagle Plains Hotel. See display ad this section. ▲

J 234.8 (377.8 km) I 221.5 (356.5 km) Short side road to picnic site with information sign about Albert Johnson, "The Mad Trapper of Rat River." Something of a mystery man, Johnson killed one mounted policeman and wounded another in 2 sepa-

rate incidents involving complaints that Johnson was tampering with Native trap lines. The ensuing manhunt became famous in the North, as Johnson eluded Mounties for 48 days during the winter of 1931–32. Johnson was killed in a shoot-out on Feb. 17, 1932. He was buried at Aklavik, a community located 36 miles/58 km by air west of Inuvik.

Dick North, author of 2 books on Johnson (and also author of *The Lost Patrol*), was quoted in the *New York Times* (June 3, 1990) as being 95 percent certain that Johnson, whose true identity has not been known, was a Norwegian–American bank robber named Johnny Johnson.

J 234.9 (378 km) I 221.4 (356.3 km) **Eagle River** bridge. Like the Ogilvie bridge, it was built by the Dept. of National Defence as a training exercise. In contrast to the other rivers seen from the Dempster, the Eagle is a more sluggish, silt-laden stream with unstable banks. It is the main drainage channel for the western slopes of the Richardson Mountains. It and its tributaries provide good grayling fishing. Canoeists leave here bound for Alaska via the Porcupine and Yukon rivers. 🐟

J 239.4 (385.3 km) I 216.9 (349.1 km) Views of the Richardson Mountains (elev. 3,937 feet/1,200m) ahead. Named for Sir John Richardson, surgeon and naturalist on both of Sir John Franklin's overland expeditions to the Arctic Ocean.

J 241.7 (389 km) I 214.6 (345.4 km) **Private Aircraft:** Emergency airstrip; elev. 2,365 feet/721m; length 2,500 feet/762m; gravel. Used regularly by aircraft hauling freight to Old Crow, a Kutchin Indian settlement on the Porcupine River and Yukon's most northerly community.

J 252 (405.5 km) I 204.3 (328.8 km) Large double-ended turnout. On June 21, the sun does not fall below the horizon for 24 hours at this latitude. Picnic tables, litter barrels, outhouses nearby. Sign marks Arctic Circle crossing, 66°33′N. Highway crosses arctic tundra on an elevated berm beside the Richardson Mountains; sweeping views.

J 277 (445.8 km) I 179.3 (288.5 km) Rock River Yukon government campground; 18 sites, $8 fee, tables, kitchen shelter, water, firepits, outhouses. Black flies prevalent; bring repellent. ▲

J 280.1 (450.8 km) I 176.2 (283.6 km) Turnout. Northbound, the highway winds toward the Richardson Mountains, crossing them at George's Gap near the YT–NWT border. Good hiking area and excellent photo possibilities.

J 288 (463.5 km) I 168.3 (270.8 km) Turnout; good overnight spot for self-contained vehicles.

J 288.5 (464.3 km) I 167.8 (270 km) Plaque about Wright Pass, named for Al Wright, a highway engineer with Public Works Canada who was responsible for the routing of the Dempster Highway.

J 288.9 (465 km) I 167.4 (269.4 km) YT–NWT border. Historical marker. Continental Divide in the Richardson Mountains: West of here, water flows to the Pacific Ocean. East of here, water flows to the Arctic Ocean. Good photo spot.

TIME ZONE CHANGE: Yukon Territory observes Pacific standard time; Northwest Territories is on Mountain time.

NWT HIGHWAY 8
IMPORTANT: Kilometreposts northbound (with white letters on a blue background) indicate

Rocky outcroppings on mountaintops near Milepost J 124.3. (Earl L. Brown, staff)

distance from YT–NWT border and are indicated at intervals in our log. Highway descends, road narrows, northbound.

J 297.6 (479 km) I 158.7 (255.4 km) Kilometrepost 14. **James Creek;** good fishing. Highway maintenance camp. Good spot to park overnight. 🐟

J 299 (481.2 km) I 157.3 (253.1 km) Sign advises no passing next 4.3 miles/7 km; climb to Wright Pass summit.

J 303.7 (488.7 km) I 152.6 (245.6 km) Wright Pass Summit. From here northbound, the Dempster Highway descends 2,300 feet/853m to the Peel River crossing, 32 miles/51 km away.

J 316.3 (509 km) I 140 (225.3 km) Kilometrepost 44. Side road leads down to Midway Lake.

J 319.4 (514 km) I 136.9 (220.3 km) **Private Aircraft:** Highway widens to form Midway airstrip; length 3,000 feet/914m.

J 329.3 (530 km) I 127 (204.4 km) View of Peel River Valley and Fort McPherson to north. Litter barrels.

J 332.4 (535 km) I 123.9 (199.4 km) Kilometrepost 70. Highway begins descent northbound to Peel River.

J 334.9 (539 km) I 121.4 (195.4 km) Peel River crossing, locally called Eightmile because it is situated 8 miles/12.8 km south of Fort McPherson. Free government ferry service 15 hours a day during summer (from about early or mid-June to mid-October). Double-ended cable ferry: Drive on, drive off. Light vehicles cross by ice bridge in late November; heavier vehicles cross as ice thickens. *No crossing possible during freezeup or breakup.* Phone (toll free) 1-800-661-0752 for information on ferry crossings, road conditions and weather.

The level of the Peel River changes rapidly in spring and summer in response to meltwater from the mountains and ice jams on the Mackenzie River. The alluvial flood plain is covered by muskeg on the flats, and scrubby alder and stunted black spruce on the valley sides.

Indians from Fort McPherson have summer tent camps on the Peel River. The Indians net whitefish and sheefish (inconnu) then dry them on racks or in smokehouses for the winter.

About 4 miles/6.4 km south upstream is a trail leading to Shiltee Rock, which gives excellent views of the Peel River and the southern end of the Mackenzie.

J 335.9 (540.6 km) **I 120.4** (193.8 km) Nitainilall territorial campground with 20 sites. (Campground name is from the Gwich'in term *Noo-til-ee*, meaning "fast flowing waters." Information centre open daily June to September. Camping permits, potable water, firewood, pit toilets and kitchen shelter available. ▲

J 337.4 (543 km) **I 118.9** (191.3 km) Kilometrepost 78.

J 340.4 (547.8 km) **I 115.9** (186.5 km) Access road right to Fort McPherson airport.

J 341.8 (550 km) **I 114.5** (184.3 km) Side road on left to Fort McPherson (description follows).

Fort McPherson

Located on a flat-topped hill about 100 feet/30m above the Peel River, 24 miles/38 km from its junction with the Mackenzie River; 100 miles/160 km southwest of Aklavik by boat along Peel Channel, 31 miles/50 km directly east of the Richardson Mountains. **Population:** 632. **Emergency Services: RCMP**, phone (403) 952-2551. **Health Center**, phone (403) 952-2586.

Visitor Information: Located in a restored log house, the former home of elder Annie G. Robert; open daily, early June through mid-September, 9 A.M. to 9 P.M. **Radio:** CBC 680.

Transportation: Air—Aklak Air provides scheduled air service from Inuvik.

Private Aircraft: Fort McPherson airstrip; 67°24'N 134°51'W; elev. 142 feet/43m; length 3,500 feet/1,067m; gravel.

This Déné Indian settlement has a public phone, cafe, bed and breakfast, 2 general stores and 2 service stations (1 with tire repair). A co-op hotel here offers 8 rooms and a restaurant. Arts and crafts include beadwork and hide garments. Wildlife watching, adventure tours and canoe trips are popular along the Peel River.

Fort McPherson was named in 1848 for Murdoch McPherson, chief trader of the Hudson's Bay Co., which had established its first posts in the area 8 years before. Between 1849 and 1859 there were frequent feuds with neighboring Inuit, who later moved farther north to the Aklavik area, where they established a fur-trading post.

In addition to subsistence fishing and hunting, income is earned from trapping (mostly muskrat and mink), handicrafts, government employment, and commercial enterprises such as Fort McPherson Tent and Canvas factory, which specializes in travel bags, tents and tepees. Tours during business hours, 9 A.M. to 5 P.M. weekdays;

FORT McPHERSON ADVERTISERS

Ch'ii Adventures . . . . . .Ph. (403) 952-2442
Fort McPherson Tent and
   Canvas . . . . .Ph. (403) 952-2179
Tetlichi's Bed
   & Breakfast . . . . . . .Ph. (403) 952-2148

(403) 952-2179 fax (403) 952-2718.

Photos and artifacts depicting the history and way of life of the community are displayed in the Chief Julius School. Buried in the cemetery outside the Anglican church are Inspector Francis J. Fitzgerald and 3 men from the ill-fated North West Mounted Police patrol of 1910–1911 between Fort McPherson and Dawson.

Inspector Fitzgerald and the men had left Fort McPherson on Dec. 21, 1910, carrying mail and dispatches to Dawson City. By Feb. 20, 1911, the men had not yet arrived in Dawson, nearly a month overdue. A search party led by Corporal W.J.D. Dempster was sent to look for the missing patrol. On March 22, 1911, Dempster discovered their frozen bodies only 26 miles from where they had started. Lack of knowledge of the trail, coupled with too few rations, had doomed the 4-man patrol. One of the last entries in Fitzgerald's diary, quoted in Dick North's *The Lost Patrol*, an account of their journey, read: "We have now only 10 pounds of flour and 8 pounds of bacon and some dried fish. My last hope is gone. ... We have been a week looking for a river to take us over the divide, but there are dozens of rivers, and I am at a loss."

Fort McPherson Tent & Canvas. Be sure to visit our factory north of the Arctic Circle ... One of the most unique businesses in Canada. See our wide array of products from tents to our renowned travel bags to custom work, crafted by dedicated all-aboriginal staff with individual attention to detail. Take home one of our high quality cordura nylon bags: backpacks, totebags, attaches and elite dufflebags with their lifetime guarantee of workmanship using only the best and toughest of materials. (Catalogue available.) You'll enjoy your factory tour, and we look forward to meeting you! P.O. Box 58, Fort McPherson, NWT X0E 0J0. Phone (403) 952-2179. Fax (403) 952-2718.
[ADVERTISEMENT]

Dempster Highway Log
(continued)

J 342.4 (551 km) **I 113.9** (183.3 km) Kilometrepost 86.

J 365.1 (587.6 km) **I 91.2** (146.8 km) **Frog Creek.** Grayling and pike. Road on right northbound leads to picnic area. 🐟

J 377.1 (606.8 km) **I 79.2** (127.5 km) Mackenzie River wayside area.

J 377.9 (608.2 km) **I 78.4** (126.2 km) Mackenzie River crossing. Free government ferry service available 15 hours a day during summer (from about early or mid-June to early October). Double-ended ferry: Drive on, drive off. Light vehicles may cross by ice bridge in late November; heavier vehicles can cross as ice thickens. *No crossing possible during freezeup and breakup.*

The ferry travels between landings on either side of the Mackenzie River and also provides access to **TSIIGEHTCHIC** (formerly **ARCTIC RED RIVER**), a small Athapaskan community (pop. 140) located at the confluence of the Mackenzie and Arctic Red rivers. Tsiigehtchic has a community-owned grocery store and cafe. The Sunshine Inn provides accommodations for up to 8 people. Boat tours are available through the Band Store or local operators. For more information on lodging or tours call (403) 953-3003 or fax (403) 953-3906.

Tsiigehtchic, which means "mouth of iron river," is one of 4 communities in the Gwich'in Settlement Area. The residents

speak a dialect of Gwich'in, one of the Athapaskan languages. They refer to themselves as the Gwichya Gwich'in or "People of the flat land." The Gwich'in Social & Cultural Institute here was formed at an annual assembly in Fort McPherson in 1992 in response to people's concern about the loss of their culture and language.

The Arctic Red River (Tsiigehnjik) was declared a Canadian Heritage River in 1993. Tsiigehnjik, the Gwich'in name for the river, winds it way out of the Mackenzie Mountains and flows into the Mackenzie River at Tsiigehtchic. The Gwichya Gwich'in have long used and travelled the river for fishing, hunting and trapping.

J 399.6 (643 km) **I 56.7** (91.2 km) **Rengling River**, grayling fishing. 🐟

J 404.4 (650.8 km) **I 51.9** (83.5 km) Beginning of 13-mile/21-km straight stretch.

J 409.7 (659.3 km) **I 46.6** (75 km) Distance marker shows Inuvik 75 km.

J 426.3 (686 km) **I 30** (48.3 km) Vadzaih Van Tshik picnic and camping area. ▲

J 431.4 (694.3 km) **I 24.9** (40.1 km) Campbell Lake and Campbell escarpment ahead northbound. Good place to glass for peregrine falcons.

J 440.6 (709 km) **I 15.7** (25.3 km) Ehjuu Njk picnic spot; pit toilets.

J 442.4 (712 km) **I 13.9** (22.4 km) Nihtak campground picnic area; pit toilets. Good fishing for pike and whitefish, some sheefish (inconnu). Creek leads a short distance to Campbell Lake. Boat launch. Bring mosquito repellent.

J 449.9 (724 km) **I 6.4** (10.3 km) Airport Road turnoff; pavement begins.

J 451 (725.8 km) **I 5.3** (8.5 km) Food, gas, and lodging.

J 451.7 (727 km) **I 4.6** (7.4 km) Kilometrepost 262.

J 454 (730.6 km) **I 2.3** (3.7 km) Chuk Park territorial campground; 38 campsites, 20 pull-through, electric hookups, firewood, water, showers, $15 fee. Lookout tower. Interpretive information available. ▲

J 456.3 (734.3 km) **I 0** Turn left northbound for Inuvik town centre (description follows).

Inuvik

Situated on a flat wooded plateau on the east channel of the Mackenzie River, some 60 air miles/96 km south of the Beaufort Sea, 36 air miles/58 km and 70 water miles/113 km from Aklavik on the western edge of the delta. **Population:** 3,206, Déné, White

and Inuvialuit.

Emergency Services: RCMP, phone (403) 979-2935. **Hospital**, Inuvik General, phone (403) 979-2955.

Visitor Information: Western Arctic Regional Visitors Centre is located on Mackenzie Road across from the hospital. The centre is open mid-May to mid-September and features interactive displays. Phone (403) 979-4727. Or contact the Western Arctic Tourism Assoc., Box 2600MP, Inuvik, NT X0E 0T0, phone (403) 979-4321, fax (403) 979-2434. Visitors are also welcomed to stop by the Ingamo Hall Friendship Centre.

Elevation: 224 feet/68m. **Climate:** Weather information available by calling (403) 979-4381. May 24 marks 57 days of midnight sun. The sun begins to set on July 19; on Dec. 6, the sun sets and does not rise until Jan. 6. Average annual precipitation 4 inches rainfall, 69 inches snowfall. July mean high 67°F/19°C, mean low 45°F/7°C. January mean high -11°F/-24°C, mean low is -30°F/-35°C. **Radio** and **Television:** CBC and local. **Newspaper:** *The Drum* (weekly).

Private Aircraft: Inuvik airstrip; elev. 224 feet/68m; length 6,000 feet/1,829m; asphalt; fuel 80, 100. Townsite airstrip; elev. 10 feet/3m; length 1,800 feet/549m; gravel; fuel 80, 100, Jet B, F40. High pressure refueling.

Inuvik, meaning "The Place of Man," is the largest Canadian community north of the Arctic Circle, and the major government, transportation and communication centre for Canada's western arctic. Construction of the town began in 1955 and was completed in 1961. It was the main supply base for the petrochemical exploration of the delta until Tuktoyaktuk took over that role as activity centered in the Beaufort Sea. In Inuvik some

hunting, fishing and trapping is done, but most people earn wages in government and private enterprises, particularly in transportation and construction. With the delta one of the richest muskrat areas in the world, Inuvik is the western centre for shipping furs south.

The town's official monument says, in part, that Inuvik was "the first community north of the Arctic Circle built to provide the normal facilities of a Canadian town."

TRANSPORTATION

Air: Aklak Air provides scheduled service between Inuvik and Tuktoyaktuk, Sachs Harbour, Fort McPherson and Paulatuk. Scheduled service to Whitehorse and Old Crow, YT, via Alkan Air. Scheduled service to Edmonton, AB, and to Yellowknife, NWT, via NWT Air and Canadian Airlines International. Scheduled service to Aklavik and Tuktoyaktuk via Arctic Wings. Several air charter services operate out of Inuvik, offering flights to delta communities and charter service for hunting, fishing and camping trips.

Highways: Dempster Highway from Dawson City. Winter roads (December into April) to Aklavik and Tuktoyaktuk.

Bus: Service from Dawson City to Inuvik 2 times a week via Arctic Tour Co., phone (403) 979-4100.

Taxi and **rental cars:** Available.

ACCOMMODATIONS/VISITOR SERVICES

Visitors will find most facilities available, although accommodations should be reserved in advance. Inuvik has 3 hotels, all with dining lounges, and bed and breakfasts. There are also a laundry, post office, territorial liquor store, banks and churches. There are 3 gas stations and a car wash; propane, auto repair and towing are available. Hardware, grocery and general stores, and gift shops are here.

Happy Valley territorial campground; 38 RV sites, electrical hookups, 10 tent pads, hot showers, firewood, water, dump station, fee. Chuk Park territorial campground; 36 sites, electrical hookups, firewood, water, showers, $10 fee.　▲

ATTRACTIONS

Igloo Church, painted white with lines to simulate snow blocks, is on Mackenzie Road as you drive in to Inuvik. Inside the church is Inuit painter Mona Thrasher's interpretation of the Stations of the Cross. Visitors are welcome.

Ingamo Hall is a 2-story log community hall that serves the social and recreational needs of Native families. Visitors are welcome. The hall was built by Allan Crich over a 3-year period, using some 1,020 logs that were cut from white spruce trees in the southern part of the Mackenzie River valley and floated down the river to Inuvik.

Tour Western Arctic Communities: Air charter service is available to **AKLAVIK** (pop. 800), an important centre for muskrat harvesting; **TUKTOYAKTUK** (pop. 950), an Inuit village on the Arctic coast and site of oil development; **SACHS HARBOUR** (pop. 158) on Banks Island, an Inuit settlement supported by trapping and some big game outfitters; **PAULATUK** (pop. 255), an Inuit settlement supported by hunting, fishing, sealing and trapping; and **HOLMAN** (pop. 360), an Inuit community on the west coast of Victoria Island, famous for its printmaking. Scheduled air service is also available to **OLD CROW** (pop. 267), an Indian settlement on the Porcupine River in Yukon Territory.

The **Mackenzie River delta**, one of the largest deltas in North America and an important wildlife corridor to the Arctic, is 40 miles/64 km wide and 60 miles/97 km long. A maze of lakes, channels and islands, the delta supports a variety of bird life, fish and muskrats. Boat tours of the Mackenzie River are available.

Arctic Nature Tours, beside the Igloo Church, Arctic wildlife displays, local artwork and crafts. Fly to Tuktoyaktuk on the Arctic coast for a guided tour. Fly to Herschel Island Yukon Park, rich in history and a naturalist's delight. Toast the midnight sun while cruising the Mackenzie River. Try fishing. Call (403) 979-3300, fax (403) 979-3400 or write Box 1530(M), Inuvik, NWT X0E 0T0. [ADVERTISEMENT]

Boreal Books carries a full range of northern books on history, Native studies, exploration and wildlife. Full selection of area postcards, northern posters and local music. Authorized agent for topo maps, marine charts and air charts. Heritage books. Catalogue available. Mail orders welcome. Open all week. Phone (403) 979-3748, fax (403) 979-4429. [ADVERTISEMENT]

Special Events. The annual Northern Games are held in Inuvik or other western Arctic communities in summer. Visitors are welcome to watch participants compete in traditional Inuit and Déné sports; dances, and crafts are also part of the festival. For information, write Northern Games Assoc., Box 1184, Inuvik, NT X0E 0T0.

The 9th annual Great Northern Arts Festival is scheduled for July 18–27, 1997. The festival features exhibitions, demonstrations, workshops and art sales by Northern artists. For more information contact the Arts Festival, Box 2921, Inuvik, NT X0E 0T0; phone (403) 979-3536.

INUVIK ADVERTISERS

DALTON HIGHWAY ⑪

Connects: Elliott Hwy. to Deadhorse, AK **Length:** 414 miles
Road Surface: Gravel **Season:** Open all year
Highest Summit: Atigun Pass 4,800 feet
Major Attraction: Trans-Alaska Pipeline

(See map, page 746)

	Coldfoot	Deadhorse	Fairbanks
Coldfoot		239	259
Deadhorse	239		498
Fairbanks	259	498	

Sukakpak Mountain on the Dalton Highway. *(Jerrianne Lowther, staff)*

Highway maintenance camps can provide help only in the event of an accident or medical emergency, they cannot fix flat tires nor do they provide gas. Keep in mind that towing fees by private wrecker service can cost $5 a mile, each way.

Road conditions vary depending on weather, maintenance and time of year, but in general the road has a reputation for being rough. Watch for ruts, rocks, dust, soft shoulders and trucks. Calcium chloride is used on the road to control dust; it is corrosive to vehicles and slippery when wet. There are several steep (10 to 12 percent) grades. Drive with your headlights on at all times. Slow down and pull over to the side of the road when meeting oncoming trucks. Stop only at turnouts. Carry spare tires.

The Dalton Highway is unique in its scenic beauty, wildlife and recreational opportunities. Travelers are requested to stay on the road and to use the formal turnouts and campgrounds provided to avoid permanently scarring the fragile tundra. Report wildlife violations to Fish and Game at Coldfoot.

All waters between the Yukon River

The 414-mile/666.3-km Dalton Highway (still referred to as the "Haul Road") begins at **Milepost F 73.1** on the Elliott Highway and ends—for the general public—at Deadhorse, a few miles from Prudhoe Bay and the Arctic Ocean. (Access to Prudhoe Bay, the largest oil field in North America, is available only through commercial tour operators; private vehicles are not permitted on the oil field.) Permits are no longer required to drive the highway to Deadhorse.

The highway is named for James William Dalton, an arctic engineer involved in early oil exploration efforts on the North Slope. It was built as a haul road between the Yukon River and Prudhoe Bay during construction of the trans-Alaska pipeline, and was originally called the North Slope Haul Road. Construction of the road began April 29, 1974, and was completed 5 months later. The road is 28 feet/9m wide with 3 to 6 feet/1 to 2m of gravel surfacing. Some sections of road are underlain with plastic foam insulation to prevent thawing of the permafrost.

Construction of the 800-mile-/1,287-km-long pipeline between Prudhoe Bay and Valdez took place between 1974 and 1977. The 48-inch-diameter pipeline, of which slightly more than half is above ground, has 10 operating pump stations. The control center is in Valdez. Design, construction and operation of the pipeline are managed by Alyeska Pipeline Service Company, a consortium of 7 oil companies (BP, ARCO, Exxon, Mobil, Amerada Hess, Phillips and Unocal). For more information, contact Public Affairs Dept., Alyeska Pipeline Service Co., 1835 S. Bragaw St., Anchorage, AK 99512.

The Bureau of Land Management (BLM) manages 2.1 million acres of public land along the Dalton Highway between the Yukon and Pump Station No. 3. For information on BLM lands, contact: Arctic District, BLM, 1150 University Ave., Fairbanks, AK 99709; phone (907) 474-2301.

Services along the Dalton Highway are limited. Shop for groceries before departing Fairbanks. There are no convenience stores or grocery stores along the highway or in Deadhorse. Gas, diesel fuel, tire repair, restaurant, motel, phone and emergency communications are available at **Milepost J 56**, just past the Yukon River bridge, and at Coldfoot, **Milepost J 175**. The last dump station northbound is also located at Coldfoot. (Please do NOT dump holding tanks along the road.) Phones at both locations are for credit card and collect calls only. Public phone at Wiseman. Alyeska pump stations do not provide any public services.

IMPORTANT: For emergency services contact the Alaska State Troopers via CB radio, Channel 19, or contact any state highway maintenance camp along the highway.

DALTON HIGHWAY
Milepost F 73.1 Elliott Highway to Deadhorse, AK

(map continues at right)

Arctic Ocean

Gates of the Arctic
National Park
and
Preserve

Disaster Cr.

Dietrich
Camp

J-209/337km
D-205/330km

Headwaters of Middle
Fork Koyukuk River

Hammond
River

Bettles River

▲ Poss Mountain
6,180 ft./1,884m
▲ Wiehl Mountain 4,000 ft./1,219m
▲ Sukakpak Mountain
4,000 ft./1,219m

Gold Cr.

Minnie Cr.

Mario Cr.

Koyukuk River

State Creek

N
W   E
S

Wiseman

Emma Dome ▲
5,680 ft./1,731m

Coldfoot
J-175/281.6km Coldfoot Services and Arctic Acres Inn CDdGLMPRST

Twelvemile Mountain
3,190 ft./972m ▲

Cathedral Mountain
3,000 ft./914m

Middle Fork

Chapman
Lake

Grayling Lake

South Fork

River

Pump Station No. 5
prospect Cr.

Prospect Camp

Jim

North Fork

Gobblers Knob
1,500 ft./457m

South Fork

Bonanza Cr.

Connection
Rock

Fish
Creek

J-115/185km
D-299/481km

ARCTIC CIRCLE

Kanuti
National
Wildlife
Refuge

Old Man Camp
J-102.3/164.6km Arctic Circle
Bed & Breakfast L

Kanuti R.

Caribou
Mountain
3,183 ft./970m

Olsons
Lake

Finger Rock

Yukon Flats National
Wildlife Refuge

Trans-Alaska
Pipeline

No Name
Creek

Fort
Hamlin
Hills

Stevens Village

River

Ray River

J-56/90km
D-358/576km

Five Mile Camp
J-56/90.1km Yukon River Tours
Yukon Ventures Alaska
CDdGILMPrST

Pump Station
No. 6

Hess Creek

J-0
D-414/666km

Livengood

Yukon

Rampart

Raven Creek Hill ▲
2,388 ft./728m

Troublesome Creek

Erikson Creek

Lost Creek

2

Sawtooth Mountain ▲
4,494 ft./1,370m

Wolverine Mountain ▲
4,580 ft./1,396m

West Fork Tolovana River

River

To Fairbanks
(see ELLIOTT HIGHWAY
section)

Tolovana River

2

To Manley Hot Springs
(see ELLIOTT HIGHWAY section)

Principal Route
Paved   Unpaved
Other Roads
Paved   Unpaved
Ferry Routes   Hiking Trails

Refer to Log for Visitor Facilities

Visitor Information   Fishing

Campground   Airport   Airstrip

Right map

J-414/666.3km Deadhorse–Prudhoe Bay Tesoro DGT
Tour Arctic/Arctic Caribou Inn LM

J-414/666km
D-0

Deadhorse

Prudhoe Bay

Trans-Alaska
Pipeline

11

Franklin Bluffs Camp
▲ Franklin
Bluffs

Sagavanirktok River

Ivishak River

N
W   E
S

J-334/538km
D-80/128km

Pump Station No. 2

Happy Valley Camp

▲ Sagwon
▲ Bluffs

Kuparuk River

Toolik

▲ Kakuktukruich
Bluff

Pump Station No. 3

Slope Mountain ▲
4,010 ft./1,222m

River

Slope Mountain Camp

Arctic
National
Wildlife
Refuge

Toolik Lake

11

Galbraith
Lake

Atigun
Canyon

Galbraith Camp

Pump Station
No. 4

Atigun River

BROOKS   RANGE

CONTINENTAL DIVIDE

Atigun Camp

Atigun Pass
4,800 ft./1,463m

Chandalar Camp

Chandalar
Shelf
▲ Table Mountain

Hammond R.

Dietrich River

J-209/337km
D-205/330km

▲ Snowden Mountain
5,775 ft./1,760m

Dietrich
Camp   (map continues at left)

Key to Advertiser Services
C - Camping
D - Dump Station
d - Diesel
G - Gas (reg., unld.)
I - Ice
L - Lodging
M - Meals
P - Propane
R - Car Repair (major)
r - Car Repair (minor)
S - Store (grocery)
T - Telephone (pay)

Map Location
above right
above left

Scale
0   10   Miles
0   10   Kilometres

Key to mileage boxes
miles/kilometres
miles/kilometres
from:
J - Junction
D - Deadhorse

bridge and Dietrich River are part of the Yukon River system, and most are tributaries of the Koyukuk River. Fishing for arctic grayling is especially good in rivers accessible by foot from the highway. The large rivers also support burbot, salmon, pike and whitefish. Small Dolly Varden are at higher elevations in streams north of Coldfoot. Fishing for salmon is closed within the trans-Alaska pipeline corridor. According to the Dept. of Fish and Game, anglers should expect high, turbid water throughout much of June as the snowpack melts in the Brooks Range, with the best fishing occurring during July and August.

Dalton Highway Log

Distance from junction with Elliott Highway (J) is followed by distance from Deadhorse (D).

J 0 D 414 (666.3 km) **Junction** with Elliott Highway at **Milepost F 73.1.**

J 1 (1.6 km) **D 413** (664.6 km) Dalton Highway sign.

J 2 (3.2 km) **D 412** (663 km) Pipeline passes under highway.

J 2.9 (4.7 km) **D 411.1** (661.6 km) Turnout to west.

J 4 (6.4 km) **D 410** (659.8 km) Highway descends steeply into the Lost Creek valley. Lost Creek flows into the West Fork Tolovana River. Pipeline is visible stretching across the ridges of the distant hills.

J 5 (8 km) **D 409** (658 km) Yellow numbered signs mark oil spill containment site.

Materials are stockpiled here for use in case of an oil spill.

J 5.6 (9 km) **D 408.4** (657.2 km) Lost Creek culvert. Steep hills north- and southbound. Pipeline access road; no public admittance. There are many of these access roads along the highway; most are closed to the public for security and safety concerns. Please do not block road access.

J 8.3 (13.4 km) **D 405.7** (652.9 km) Entering game management unit 20 northbound.

J 9.8 (15.8 km) **D 404.2** (650.5 km) Road follows a high ridge with spectacular view of

Erickson Creek area and pipeline.

J 11 (17.7 km) **D 403** (648.5 km) Begin steep (12 percent) downgrade northbound.

J 12 (19.3 km) **D 402** (646.9 km) Small gravel turnouts to west.

J 12.1 (19.5 km) **D 401.9** (646.8 km) Erickson Branch; creek culvert.

J 18.6 (29.9 km) **D 395.4** (636.3 km) Bypass route for steep grade.

J 20.9 (33.6 km) **D 393.1** (632.6 km) Steep double-ended turnout at gravel pit to west.

J 21 (33.8 km) **D 393** (632.5 km) Descent to Hess Creek begins northbound.

J 23.6 (38 km) **D 390.4** (628.3 km) Pipeline access road, pond.

J 23.8 (38.3 km) **D 390.2** (627.9 km) **Hess Creek** bridge. Campsite in trees. Large gravel bar along creek at north end of bridge. *CAUTION: Sandpit at entrance to gravel bar is an easy place to get stuck.* Bring your mosquito repellent. Whitefish and grayling fishing. Hess Creek, known for its colorful mining history, is the largest stream between the junction and the Yukon River bridge. ⬤▲

J 23.9 (38.5 km) **D 390.1** (627.8 km) Road to west leads 0.2 mile/0.3 km to pond with parking space adequate for camping.

J 25 (40.2 km) **D 389** (626 km) Double-ended rough turnout. Good view of pipeline and remote-operated valve site as the highway crosses Hess Creek and valley.

J 26 (41.8 km) **D 388** (624.4 km) Pipeline parallels highway about 250 feet/76m away.

J 26.5 (42.6 km) **D 387.5** (623.6 km) Turnout.

J 27 (43.4 km) **D 387** (622.8 km) Evidence of lightning-caused forest fires.

J 33.7 (54.2 km) **D 380.3** (612 km) Turnout at tributary of Hess Creek. Chiming

bells bloom in June.

J 35.5 (57.1 km) **D 378.5** (609.1 km) Rough turnout at gravel pit.

J 38.1 (61.3 km) **D 375.9** (604.9 km) Pipeline goes under road. Evidence of the revegetation project undertaken by the oil companies.

J 40.7 (65.5 km) **D 373.3** (600.7 km) Double-ended turnout. Overview of Troublesome and Hess creeks areas. Brush obscures sweeping views.

J 42 (67.6 km) **D 372** (598.7 km) Turnout; outcrop of dark gabbroic rock.

J 43.1 (69.4 km) **D 370.9** (596.9 km) Isom Creek culvert. Steep ascent from valley north- and southbound.

J 44.6 (71.8 km) **D 369.4** (594.5 km) Turnout with litter barrel at viewpoint.

J 47.5 (76.4 km) **D 366.5** (589.8 km) Yukon radio repeater tower.

J 47.9 (77.1 km) **D 366.1** (589.2 km) Highway begins descent to Yukon River.

J 48.5 (78.1 km) **D 365.5** (588.2 km) Pipeline access road. Goalpost-like structures, called "headache bars," guard against vehicles large enough to run into and damage the pipeline.

J 50.1 (80.6 km) **D 363.9** (585.6 km) Turnout.

J 50.4 (81.1 km) **D 363.6** (585.1 km) Turnout; pond to east.

J 51 (82.2 km) **D 362.9** (584 km) Rough side road leads east 5.4 miles/8.7 km to Yukon River.

J 53.2 (85.6 km) **D 360.8** (580.6 km) First view northbound of the Yukon River. As road drops, you can see the pipeline crossing the river. Fort Hamlin Hills are beyond the river.

J 54 (86.9 km) **D 360** (579.3 km) **PUMP STATION NO. 6**. Alyeska pump stations monitor the pipeline's oil flow on its journey from Prudhoe Bay to Valdez. No public facilities.

J 54.3 (87.4 km) **D 359.7** (578.9 km) Highway passes over pipeline.

J 54.5 (87.7 km) **D 359.5** (578.5 km) Turnout to west.

J 55.6 (89.5 km) **D 358.4** (576.8 km) Yukon River bridge (formally the E.L. Patton Bridge, named for the president of the Alyeska Pipeline Service Co. after his death in 1982). This wood-decked bridge, completed in 1975, is 2,290 feet/698m long and has a 6 percent grade. The deck was replaced in 1993.

J 56 (90.1 km) **D 358** (576.1 km) Gas, diesel, tire repair, restaurant, motel, phone and emergency communications available at Yukon Ventures Alaska. Next services northbound: 120 miles/193 km. Tours and charters of the Yukon River include dinner cruise and visit to a working Native fish camp.

Yukon Ventures Alaska. See display ad this section.

Yukon River Tours—Tours and charters on the Yukon River from the Yukon Crossing daily from June 1 to September 1. Stop at our office just below the bridge. Enjoy a lunch cruise, visit a Native fishcamp, explore this historic part of Alaska. Since 1990. (907) 452-7162. 214 2nd Avenue, Fairbanks, AK 99701-4811. [ADVERTISEMENT]

This is the southern boundary of BLM-managed lands. The Yukon Crossing Visitor Contact Station here, managed and staffed by the BLM, is open 7 days a week, June through August. There is also an Alyeska pipeline interpretive display here with information on the Yukon River, pipeline construction and related subjects. Birch forest along river. East of the highway is a camping area with litter barrels. Road closed east of campsite. ▲

J 60.6 (97.5 km) **D 353.4** (568.7 km) Site of **FIVE MILE CAMP**, a former pipeline construction camp. No structures remain at these former construction camps. There is an undeveloped campsite here and a toilet. Water is available from an artesian well. Highway crosses over buried pipeline.

J 60.8 (97.8 km) **D 353.2** (568.4 km) Five Mile airstrip (length 3,500 feet/1,067m); controlled by Alyeska Security. *CAUTION: Be prepared to stop at control gates at both ends of airstrip.*

J 61.3 (98.7 km) **D 352.7** (567.6 km) Airstrip control tower.

J 61.6 (99.1 km) **D 352.4** (567.1 km) View of Fort Hamlin Hills to north, pump station No. 6 to south.

J 61.9 (99.6 km) **D 352.1** (566.6 km) Sevenmile DOT/PF highway maintenance camp.

J 66.8 (107.5 km) **D 347.2** (558.7 km) Turnout to west.

J 68.4 (110.1 km) **D 345.6** (556.2 km) Highway crosses over buried pipeline.

J 69.2 (111.4 km) **D 344.8** (554.9 km) Double-ended turnout at crest of hill overlooking the Ray River to the north. Pipeline goes underground.

J 70 (112.7 km) **D 344** (553.6 km) **Ray River** overlook and double-ended turnout. Scenic view of the Ray Mountains to the west. Burbot, grayling and northern pike fishing. ⬤

J 72.5 (116.7 km) **D 341.5** (549.6 km) Fort Hamlin Hills Creek bridge and turnout. Winter trail scars are visible just beyond the bridge.

J 73.5 (118.3 km) **D 340.5** (548 km) Begin steep 0.5-mile/0.8-km ascent of Sand Hill northbound.

J 74.8 (120.4 km) **D 339.2** (545.9 km) Steep descent northbound followed by steep

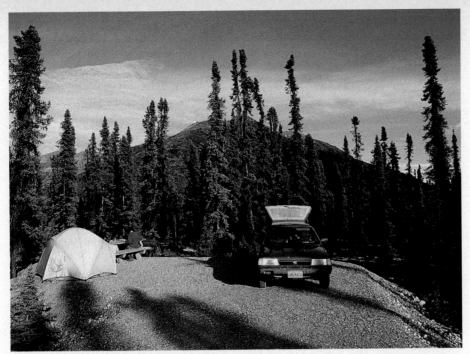

BLM campsite near Coldfoot is one of 2 government campgrounds along the Dalton Highway. (© Bill Sherwonit)

ascent; dubbed the Roller Coaster. Pipeline to east.

J 79.1 (127.3 km) **D 334.9** (539 km) **No Name Creek** and turnout east side at south end of bridge; burbot, grayling and whitefish.

J 81.6 (131.3 km) **D 332.4** (534.9 km) Fort Hamlin Hills are visible to the southeast. Tree line on surrounding hills is about 2,000 feet/610m.

J 86.5 (139.2 km) **D 327.5** (527 km) Scenic overlook 1 mile/1.6 km west with view of tors to northeast, Yukon Flats Wildlife Refuge to east and Fort Hamlin Hills to southeast. Tors are high, isolated pinnacles of jointed granite jutting up from the tundra and are a residual feature of erosion.

J 88.5 (142.4 km) **D 325.5** (523.8 km) Mackey Hill. Entering Game Management Unit 25D northbound, Unit 20F southbound. The high, unnamed hill east of the road is 2,774 feet/846m in elevation.

J 90.2 (145.2 km) **D 323.8** (521.1 km) Double-ended turnouts both sides of highway. A good photo opportunity of the road and pipeline to the north. The zig-zag design allows the pipeline to flex and accommodate temperature changes. The small green structure over the buried pipe is a radio-controlled valve, allowing the pipeline oil flow to be shut down when necessary.

J 91.1 (146.6 km) **D 322.9** (519.6 km) Culvert directs water from branch of west fork of Dall Creek. Watch for soft spots in road.

J 94 (151.3 km) **D 320** (515 km) Turnout at former gravel pit road to west.

J 96 (154.5 km) **D 318** (511.8 km) The road lies above tree line for about 5 miles/ 8 km. Good opportunities for photos, berry picking (blueberries, lowbush cranberries), wildflower viewing and hiking. Northbound, the terrain becomes more rugged and scenic.

J 97.5 (156.9 km) **D 316.5** (509.3 km) Finger Rock (signed Finger Mountain), a tor, is visible east of the road and most easily seen to the south. Tors are visible for the next 2 miles/3.2 km. Prehistoric hunting sites are numerous in this region. Please do not collect or disturb artifacts.

J 98.2 (158 km) **D 315.8** (508.2 km) Finger Mountain wayside; toilet, parking, interpretive trail. Caribou Mountain is in the distance to the northwest. Olsens Lake, Kanuti Flats, Kanuti River drainage and site of former Old Man Camp are visible ahead northbound. The road descends and passes through several miles of valley bottom with excellent mountain views.

J 100.7 (162.1 km) **D 313.3** (504.2 km) Pipeline passes under highway.

J 102.3 (164.6 km) **D 311.7** (501.6 km) **Arctic Circle Bed & Breakfast.** See display ad this section.

J 105.8 (170.3 km) **D 308.2** (496 km) **Kanuti River**, crossing and turnout; burbot, grayling. Abandoned airstrip to east. Pipeline emerges from underground. ◄━

J 107 (172.2 km) **D 307** (494.1 km) Site of **OLD MAN CAMP**, a former pipeline construction camp.

J 108.4 (174.4 km) **D 305.6** (491.8 km) Highway crosses pipeline.

J 109.8 (176.7 km) **D 304.2** (489.5 km) Turnout at Beaver Slide. *CAUTION: Road descends very steeply northbound. Watch for soft spots. Slippery when wet.*

J 110 (177 km) **D 304** (489.2 km) First view of Brooks Range northbound.

J 111.5 (179.4 km) **D 302.5** (486.8 km) View of valley and Fish Creek to the north.

J 112.2 (180.6 km) **D 301.8** (485.7 km) Turnout at pipeline access road. Moose and bear frequent willow thickets here.

J 113.9 (183.3 km) **D 300.1** (483 km) Evidence of old winter trail to Bettles is visible here.

J 114 (183.5 km) **D 300** (482.8 km) **Fish Creek** bridge and turnout; grayling 12 to 18 inches. ◄━

J 115.3 (185.5 km) **D 298.7** (480.7 km) The Arctic Circle, north latitude 66°33'. BLM wayside with tables, grills, toilets and interpretive display. Stop and have your picture taken with the sign. This is also a good photo point, with views to the south and to the

west. Follow road off turnout 0.6 mile/ 1 km for primitive campsites (pull-throughs, nice views). If you reach the Alyeska access gate you've gone too far.

J 116.2 (187 km) **D 297.8** (479.2 km) Turnout to east (can be soft).

J 120.7 (194.2 km) **D 293.3** (472 km) Connection Rock; north and south road-building crews linked up here.

J 124.7 (200.7 km) **D 289.3** (465.6 km) Turnout to east at **South Fork Bonanza Creek**; burbot, grayling, whitefish. ◄━

J 125.7 (202.3 km) **D 288.3** (464 km) Turnout to east at **North Fork Bonanza Creek**; historic gold mining area; burbot, grayling, whitefish. ◄━

J 127.1 (204.5 km) **D 286.9** (461.7 km) Turnout.

J 127.7 (205.5 km) **D 286.3** (460.7 km) Paradise Hill; blueberries and lowbush cranberries in season.

J 128.9 (207.4 km) **D 285.1** (458.8 km) Primitive campsite at gravel pit.

J 129.3 (208.1 km) **D 284.7** (458.2 km) *CAUTION: Long ascent northbound with a short stretch that is very steep. Give trucks plenty of room here!*

J 131.3 (211.3 km) **D 282.7** (454.9 km) Solar-powered communications tower to west.

J 131.5 (211.6 km) **D 282.5** (454.6 km) View of pump station No. 5 to north.

J 132 (212.4 km) **D 282** (453.8 km) Turnout with litter barrels and toilet at Gobblers Knob (elev. 1,500 feet/457m) overlooking the Jack White Range, Pope Creek Dome (the dominant peak to the northwest), Prospect Creek drainage, pump station No. 5, Jim River drainage, South Fork Koyukuk drainage and the Brooks Range on the northern horizon.

J 134.7 (216.8 km) **D 279.3** (449.5 km) Pipeline access road.

J 135.1 (217.4 km) **D 278.9** (448.8 km) **Prospect Creek**; grayling, whitefish and pike. Active gold mining area. ◄━

J 135.7 (218.4 km) **D 278.3** (447.9 km) Old winter road goes up creek to mines. Turn left for site of **PROSPECT CAMP**, which holds the record for lowest recorded temperature in Alaska (-80°F/-62°C, Jan. 23, 1971). Rough road leads 0.5 mile/0.8 km to Claja Pond; beaver, ducks. Undeveloped campsite on Jim River. Old winter road to Bettles crosses river here.

J 137.1 (220.6 km) **D 276.9** (445.6 km) **PUMP STATION NO. 5** (signed incorrectly as Prospect Camp). No public access. Side road leads to well. Pump station No. 5 is not actually a pump station, but a "drain down" or pressure relief station to slow the gravity-fed flow of oil descending from Atigun Pass in the Brooks Range. Glacial moraine marks the southern boundary of Brooks Range glaciers during the most recent ice age.

Private Aircraft: Airstrip; length 5,000 feet/1,524m; lighted runway. This airstrip is used as a BLM fire fighting staging area.

J 138.1 (222.2 km) **D 275.9** (444 km) Jim River DOT/PF highway maintenance camp EMT squad. Site of 1988 burn.

J 139 (223.7 km) **D 275** (442.6 km) Road to gravel pit.

J 140.1 (225.5 km) **D 273.9** (440.8 km) **Jim River** Bridge No. 1; narrow bridge, turnouts. Burbot, chum and king salmon, grayling, pike, whitefish. *CAUTION: Bears here for fall salmon run.* ☞

J 141 (226.9 km) **D 273** (439.3 km) **Jim River** Bridge No. 2; narrow bridge, turnouts. See fishing previous milepost. ☞

J 141.8 (228.2 km) **D 272.2** (438.1 km) Douglas Creek; blueberries and lowbush cranberries in season.

J 144.1 (231.9 km) **D 269.9** (434.4 km) **Jim River** Bridge No. 3 (main channel); turnout to east at south end of bridge. See **Milepost J 140.1** for fishing. ☞

J 145.6 (234.3 km) **D 268.4** (431.9 km) Pipeline passes under road. First views northbound of Brooks Range foothills to the north.

J 150.3 (241.9 km) **D 263.7** (424.4 km) **Grayling Lake** to east has good grayling fishing in open water season. ☞

J 150.8 (242.7 km) **D 263.2** (423.6 km) Turnout on Grayling Lake. The road is passing through the foothills of the Brooks Range. There is an active gold mining area behind the hills to the west.

J 155.2 (249.8 km) **D 258.8** (416.5 km) Overlook for the South Fork Koyukuk River valley.

J 156 (251.1 km) **D 258** (415.2 km) Turnout with toilet at the **South Fork Koyukuk River** bridge; grayling, whitefish,

chum and king salmon. Active gold mining downstream. 🐟

This large river flows past the villages of Bettles, Allakaket, Hughes and Huslia before draining into the Yukon River near Koyukuk.

J 159.1 (256 km) **D 254.9** (410.2 km) Bridge over pipeline; large animal crossing over pipeline.

J 160 (257.5 km) **D 254** (408.8 km) Good view of Chapman Lake 0.5 mile/0.8 km west of road. Old mine trail is visible from the road.

The 2 mountains visible to the north are Twelvemile Mountain (elev. 3,190 feet/972m), left, and Cathedral Mountain (elev. 3,000 feet/914m), on right. The foothills of the Brooks Range are also to the north.

J 161.2 (259.4 km) **D 252.8** (406.8 km) Road to west leads to gold claim.

J 163.3 (262.8 km) **D 250.7** (403.5 km) Turnout to west.

J 164.6 (264.9 km) **D 249.4** (401.3 km) Example of a "sag bend," a short section of buried pipeline that allows large animals to cross.

J 165.1 (265.7 km) **D 248.9** (400.6 km) Turnout to west with view of pipeline.

J 165.7 (266.7 km) **D 248.3** (399.6 km) Turnout on west side of road overlooking Middle Fork Koyukuk River.

J 167.2 (269.1 km) **D 246.8** (397.2 km) Old winter trail to Tramway Bar. "River training structures" in place direct water away from the pipeline and highway during floods.

J 175 (281.6 km) **D 239** (384.6 km) **COLDFOOT**, site of a historic mining camp at the mouth of Slate Creek on the east bank

of the Middle Fork Koyukuk River. Coldfoot Services (phone 907/678-5201) offers 3 motels, a 24-hour restaurant, gift shop, general store, trading post, laundromat, fuel facility with gas, diesel and avgas; tire repair, minor vehicle repair; RV park with hookups and dump station; post office, phone and emergency medical service. It is also home of the "farthest North saloon in North America" with "readable walls." Next services northbound: 244 miles/392.7 km. Area tours and guided hunting and fishing trips available. ▲

There is a 3,500-foot/1,067-m runway to west, maintained by the state. An Alaska State Trooper, a Fish and Wildlife officer and BLM field station are located at Coldfoot. A visitor center here, operated by the BLM, USF&WS and National Park Service, offers travel information and nightly presentations on the natural and cultural history of the Arctic. It is open from June 1 through Labor Day. Topographic maps for sale.

Originally named Slate Creek, Coldfoot reportedly got its name in 1900 when gold stampeders got as far up the Koyukuk as this point, then got cold feet, turned and departed. The old cemetery still exists. Emma Dome (elev. 5,680 feet/1,731m) is to the west.

Coldfoot Services and Arctic Acres Inn. See display ad this section.

J 175.7 (282.8 km) **D 238.3** (383.5 km) Radio repeater site on mountains to east.

J 179.9 (289.5 km) **D 234.1** (376.7 km) Marion Creek Campground; 27 sites, $6 camping fee, tables, grills, firepits, water, toilets, bear-proof litter containers, resident campground host, information kiosk, RV parking. Dump station at Coldfoot services. Marion Creek trailhead. ♿▲

J 184.4 (296.7 km) **D 229.6** (369.5 km) Scenic overlook. Excellent view of Middle Fork Koyukuk River; small slumps and rock slide on adjacent mountain.

J 186 (299.3 km) **D 228** (366.9 km) The historic mining community of Wiseman can be seen across the Koyukuk River to the west. Access to Wiseman from **Milepost J 188.6.**

J 186.7 (300.5 km) **D 227.3** (365.8 km) Turnouts both sides of highway.

J 187.2 (301.3 km) **D 226.8** (365 km) Turnout to west at **Minnie Creek**; burbot, grayling, whitefish. ☞

J 188.5 (303.4 km) **D 225.5** (362.9 km) **Middle Fork Koyukuk River** Bridge No. 1; turnout. Dolly Varden, grayling, whitefish. ☞

J 188.6 (303.5 km) **D 225.4** (362.7 km) Improved access road to **WISEMAN**, a historic mining town. The heyday of Wiseman came in about 1910, after gold seekers abandoned Coldfoot. The Wiseman Trading Co. still stands and houses the town's museum, featuring old photos and mining equipment. About 25 residents live here year-round today, and the population increases in the summer with the arrival of miners. (Note that this is an active mining area and all buildings are privately owned.) Wiseman has a general store, public phone and campground. ▲

J 189 (304.2 km) **D 225** (362.1 km) Spur (finger) dikes keep river away from highway and pipeline.

J 190.5 (306.6 km) **D 223.5** (359.7 km) Narrow bridge over Hammond River; gold mining area upstream.

J 190.8 (307.1 km) **D 223.2** (359.2 km) Middle Fork Koyukuk River Bridge No. 2. "Guide banks," another example of river training structures.

J 192.8 (310.3 km) **D 221.2** (356 km) Link Up, where 2 sections of road constructed by different crews were joined.

J 194 (312.2 km) **D 220** (354 km) First view northbound of Sukakpak Mountain (elev. 4,000 feet/1,219m) to north. Sukakpak Mountain is sometimes said to mark a traditional boundary between Eskimo and Athabascan Indian territories. Wiehl Mountain (elev. 4,000 feet/1,219m) is east of Sukakpak. The high mountain just to the west of the road is unnamed.

J 195 (313.8 km) **D 219** (352.4 km) Pipeline close to road is mounted on sliding shoes to allow flexing.

J 197 (317 km) **D 217** (349.2 km) Old cabin just west of road is reported to have been constructed in the early 1900s; private property. Gold Creek bridge.

J 197.3 (317.5 km) **D 216.7** (348.7 km) Cat trail to gold mining area.

J 197.5 (317.8 km) **D 216.5** (348.4 km) Linda Creek in culvert.

J 197.7 (318.2 km) **D 216.3** (348.1 km) Turnout east and view of Wiehl Mountain. Gates of the Arctic to west.

J 200 (321.9 km) **D 214** (344.4 km) View of the Middle Fork Koyukuk River, a typical braided river exhibiting frequent changes of the streambed during high water.

J 203.5 (327.5 km) **D 210.5** (338.7 km) Turnout and 0.5-mile/0.8-km footpath to Sukakpak Mountain. The short mounds of earth between the road and Sukakpak are palsas, formed by ice beneath the soil pushing the vegetative mat and soil upward.

J 203.8 (328 km) **D 210.2** (338.3 km) Turnouts next 0.6 mile/1 km northbound.

J 204.3 (328.8 km) **D 209.7** (337.5 km) Middle Fork Koyukuk River bridge No. 3; turnout with toilets and litter barrels to east.

J 204.5 (329.1 km) **D 209.5** (337.1 km) Middle Fork Koyukuk River bridge No. 4.

J 205.3 (330.4 km) **D 208.7** (335.9 km) Turnout to west. Good view of north side of Sukakpak Mountain.

J 206 (331.5 km) **D 208** (334.7 km) View of Wiehl Mountain.

J 207 (333.1 km) **D 207** (333.1 km) **Dietrich River** bridge, turnout to west at south end; burbot, grayling, whitefish and Dolly Varden. ◄═►

J 207.5 (333.9 km) **D 206.5** (332.3 km) Small, unnamed lake on east side of road with nice view of Sukakpak Mountain. Dillon Mountain (proposed name) is just to the north.

J 208.2 (335.1 km) **D 205.8** (331.2 km) Unnamed creek in culvert.

J 209.1 (336.5 km) **D 204.9** (329.7 km) Site of **DIETRICH CAMP**, a former pipeline construction camp.

J 211 (339.6 km) **D 203** (326.7 km) Disaster Creek. Turnout with bear-proof litter container to east.

J 216.2 (347.9 km) **D 197.8** (318.3 km) Snowden Creek culvert. Panorama of Dietrich River valley and Brooks Range north and west of the road.

J 217.1 (349.4 km) **D 196.9** (316.9 km) Rock spire to east is Snowden Mountain (elev. 5,775 feet/1,760m). Cirque above highway was carved by a glacier; hike up to waterfall.

J 221.6 (356.6 km) **D 192.4** (309.6 km) Turnout to east is quarry of black marble with white calcite veins.

J 224 (360.5 km) **D 190** (305.8 km) Turnout at gravel pit.

J 225 (362.1 km) **D 189** (304.2 km) River

bars; very braided stream.

J 226 (363.7 km) **D 188** (302.5 km) Pipeline remote valve just west of road. The arch-shaped concrete "saddle weights" keep pipeline buried in areas of possible flooding.

J 227.3 (365.8 km) **D 186.7** (300.5 km) Nutirwik Creek culvert.

J 228 (366.9 km) **D 186** (299.3 km) Highway parallels Dietrich River.

J 231.4 (372.4 km) **D 182.6** (293.9 km) Small turnouts both sides of highway. Pipeline is buried under river.

J 234.6 (377.5 km) **D 179.4** (288.7 km) Pipeline emerges from under river.

J 234.9 (378 km) **D 179.1** (288.2 km) Entering North Slope Borough boundary northbound. Borough offices are located in Barrow.

J 235.3 (378.7 km) **D 178.7** (287.6 km) Large turnout with litter barrel at foot of Chandalar Shelf and beginning of a long, steep (10 percent) grade. Truck chain-up area. The farthest north spruce tree along the highway is located just south of the turnout. No trees beyond here.

J 237.1 (381.6 km) **D 176.9** (284.7 km) Turnout at top of Chandalar Shelf; former checkpoint. Headwaters of the Chandalar River are to the east. Table Mountain (elev. 6,425 feet/1,958m) is to the southeast. Dietrich River valley to south.

NOTE: Many mileposts are missing on Atigun Pass. Physical mileposts remaining may not reflect actual driving distance between posts.

J 239 (384.6 km) **D 175** (281.6 km) Brown net structure west of road is called a Wyoming Gage; it is used to measure precipitation. Sponsored by the Natural Resources Conservation Service.

J 239.2 (384.9 km) **D 174.8** (281.3 km) Site of **CHANDALAR CAMP**, a former pipeline construction camp, now used as a BLM field station.

J 239.4 (385.3 km) **D 174.6** (281 km) Chandalar highway maintenance station on west side of highway.

J 240.2 (386.6 km) **D 173.8** (279.7 km) Avalanche gun emplacement; DOT/PF materials storage site.

J 242.2 (389.8 km) **D 171.8** (276.5 km) West Fork Chandalar River bridge.

J 242.5 (390.2 km) **D 171.5** (276 km)

Begin long, steep climb northbound toward Atigun Pass. Winter avalanche area. Slide area next 5 miles/8 km northbound.

J 244.7 (393.8 km) **D 169.3** (272.5 km) Turnout at top of Atigun Pass (elev. 4,800 feet/1,463m), highest highway pass in Alaska; Continental Divide. A Wyoming Gage to measure moisture is located here. Nice example of a cirque, an amphitheater-shaped bowl or depression caused by glacier erosion, in mountain east of road. Endicott Mountains are to the west, Phillip Smith Mountains to the east. James Dalton Mountain is to the left ahead northbound.

Highway descends steeply toward the North Slope. Many mountains in the area exceed 7,000 feet/2,134m in elevation. The pipeline is in a buried, insulated concrete cribbing to the east to protect it from rock slides and avalanches, and to keep the ground frozen. Construction in this area was extremely complex, difficult and dangerous.

J 248.4 (399.8 km) **D 165.6** (266.5 km) Turnouts both sides of highway. Good spot to view Dall sheep.

J 250 (402.3 km) **D 164** (263.9 km) Bridge over Spike Camp Creek. Highway crosses buried pipeline.

J 250.2 (402.6 km) **D 164.2** (264.2 km) Site of **ATIGUN CAMP**, a former pipeline construction camp. Turnouts both sides of highway. View of Atigun River valley. Another Wyoming Gage is located here.

J 251.5 (404.7 km) **D 162.5** (261.5 km) Turnouts next 0.3 mile/0.5 km northbound.

J 253.1 (407.3 km) **D 160.9** (258.9 km) Atigun River crossing No. 1. Highway crosses buried pipeline. *CAUTION: Grizzly bears in area.*

J 254 (408.8 km) **D 160** (257.5 km) Mountains to north exhibit extreme folding of sedimentary rock layers.

J 257.6 (414.6 km) **D 156.4** (251.7 km) Check valves on the pipeline keep oil from flowing backwards in the event of a leak.

J 258.4 (415.8 km) **D 155.6** (250.4 km) Trevor Creek bridge.

J 258.6 (416.2 km) **D 155.4** (250.1 km) Turnout.

J 261.4 (420.7 km) **D 152.6** (245.6 km) Turnout.

Dalton Highway traveler scans the landscape from a knoll in the Brooks Range.
(© Bill Sherwonit)

Manmade forest greets visitors to treeless North Slope. (© Bill Sherwonit)

J 265 (426.5 km) **D 149** (239.8 km) Roche Moutonnee Creek bridge.

J 267.5 (430.5 km) **D 146.5** (235.8 km) Bridge over Holden Creek.

J 268 (431.3 km) **D 146** (235 km) Good view of pump station No. 4.

J 269.3 (433.4 km) **D 144.7** (232.9 km) **PUMP STATION NO. 4.** This station has the highest elevation of all the pipeline stations (2,760 feet/841m), and is also a launching and receiving station for special measuring and cleaning devices called "pigs." A scraper pig consists of spring-mounted scraper blades and/or brushes on a central body which moves through the pipe, cleaning accumulated wax from interior walls and monitoring conditions inside the pipe. There are "dumb" pigs and "smart" pigs. Dumb pigs clean out wax deposits in the line. Smart pigs scan the pipeline to check welds, wall thickness and other properties to help insure the integrity of the piping and identify maintenance needs.

J 269.5 (433.7 km) **D 144.5** (232.5 km) Highway bridge passes over pipeline.

J 270 (434.5 km) **D 144** (231.7 km) Salty rocks attract Dall sheep to slopes above highway.

J 270.5 (435.3 km) **D 143.5** (230.9 km) Small lakes both sides of highway.

J 270.9 (436 km) **D 143.1** (230.3 km) Atigun River crossing No. 2. The Arctic National Wildlife Refuge boundary is located 3 miles/4.8 km east along the Atigun gorge. Galbraith Lake may be seen to the west. There are a large number of archaeological sites in this vicinity.

J 272.9 (439.2 km) **D 141.1** (227.1 km) Look for Dall sheep on mountains to east.

J 274 (440.9 km) **D 140** (225.3 km) View of Galbraith Lake and Galbraith camp.

J 274.7 (442.1 km) **D 139.3** (224.2 km) Road access to **GALBRAITH CAMP**, a construction camp; toilet, litter barrel. USF&WS field station. Nice wildflowers in season.

J 276.5 (445 km) **D 137.5** (221.3 km) Island Lake.

J 284.3 (457.5 km) **D 129.7** (208.7 km) Toolik Lake west of road. A former construction camp, it is now the site of Toolik Lake Research Camp, run by the Institute of Arctic Biology of the University of Alaska Fairbanks. The field station conducts global warming studies and has no public facilities or services.

J 286.2 (460.6 km) **D 127.8** (205.7 km) Turnout to east at high point in road. View of Brooks Range south and east. Philip Smith Mountains to west; panoramic views; caribou.

J 288.8 (464.8 km) **D 125.2** (201.5 km) Kuparuk River bridge.

J 289.3 (465.6 km) **D 124.7** (200.7 km) Pipeline crossing. Short, buried section of pipeline to west is called a sag bend and is to allow for wildlife crossing. Watch for caribou northbound.

J 290.4 (467.3 km) **D 123.6** (198.9 km) Turnout to east; road to materials site.

J 290.6 (467.7 km) **D 123.4** (198.6 km) Toolik Creek.

J 294.4 (473.8 km) **D 119.6** (192.5 km) Second sag bend northbound.

J 297.8 (479.2 km) **D 116.2** (187 km) Oksrukukuyik Creek culvert. Small turnout to east.

J 298.3 (480.1 km) **D 115.7** (186.2 km) Turnout on top of moraine; first view of Sagavanirktok Valley.

J 301 (484.4 km) **D 113** (181.8 km) Turnout. Slope Mountain (elev. 4,010 feet/1,222m) is just west of road. Watch for Dall sheep. This is the northern boundary of BLM-managed land. Land north of here is managed by the state.

J 302 (486 km) **D 112** (**180.2 km**) "Sag bend" large animal crossing.

J 305.7 (492 km) **D 108.3** (174.3 km) Site of **SLOPE MOUNTAIN CAMP**, a former pipeline construction camp, now Sag River highway maintenance station.

J 306 (492.4 km) **D 108** (173.8 km) Pipeline underground; oil spill containment site.

J 309 (497.3 km) **D 105** (169 km) Highway parallels Sagavanirktok River.

J 311.8 (501.8 km) **D 102.2** (164.5 km) **PUMP STATION NO. 3**; mobile construction camp facility.

J 313.7 (504.8 km) **D 100.3** (161.4 km) Oksrukukuyik Creek in culvert.

J 319.8 (514.7 km) **D 94.2** (151.6 km) Turnout to east at Oil Spill Hill.

J 320 (515 km) **D 94** (151.3 km) The long range of hills east of the road is the Kakuktukruich Bluff.

J 325 (523 km) **D 89** (143.2 km) Turnout; public river access from pipeline access road.

J 325.1 (523.2 km) **D 88.9** (143.1 km) Jerry Hubbard's "national forest" of willow

saplings on revegetated materials site.

J 325.3 (523.5 km) **D 88.7** (142.7 km) Turnout with litter barrel to east at the top of a steep grade called Ice Cut.

J 326.2 (525 km) **D 87.8** (141.3 km) Pipeline crossing on bridge.

J 330.7 (532.2 km) **D 83.3** (134.1 km) Dan Creek bridge.

J 334.4 (538.1 km) **D 79.6** (128.1 km) Site of **HAPPY VALLEY CAMP**, a former pipeline construction camp, now a Fish and Game field station.

J 345.5 (556 km) **D 68.5** (110.2 km) Grant Creek in culvert.

J 347.6 (559.4 km) **D 66.4** (106.9 km) Sagwon airstrip. The airstrip is currently not in use in order to protect nesting peregrine falcons in the area.

J 350.5 (564.1 km) **D 63.5** (102.2 km) View of Sagwon Bluffs to the east. The road passes over several low hills that offer views of the surrounding terrain.

J 353 (568 km) **D 61** (98.2 km) Wyoming Gage west of road on hill.

J 355.1 (571.5 km) **D 58.9** (94.8 km) Turnout with litter barrel to east.

J 358.8 (577.4 km) **D 55.2** (88.8 km) **PUMP STATION NO. 2** to the east.

NOTE: The worst winter weather conditions on the Dalton Highway are experienced the next 38 miles/61 km northbound. Blowing snow may obscure visibility and block road.

J 364 (585.8 km) **D 50** (80.5 km) Low hills to the north are the Franklin Bluffs. East of the road, the Ivishak River empties into the Sagavanirktok River on its journey to the Arctic Ocean.

J 365.1 (587.6 km) **D 48.9** (78.7 km) Turnout by pond to west; watch for nesting waterfowl.

J 366 (589 km) **D 48** (77.2 km) Large animal crossing in pipeline for caribou.

J 376 (605.1 km) **D 38** (61.2 km) The small hill that rises abruptly on the horizon about 5 miles/8 km west of the road is called a pingo. Pingos often form from the bed of a spring-fed lake that has been covered by vegetation. Freezing of the water can raise the surface several hundred feet above the surrounding terrain.

J 377.3 (607.2 km) **D 36.7** (59.1 km) Turnout to east at site of **FRANKLIN BLUFFS CAMP**, a former pipeline construction camp. Winter equipment is stored here in summer. *CAUTION: Watch for loose, coarse gravel on road.*

J 383 (616.4 km) **D 31** (49.9 km) Franklin Bluffs to the east and a pingo to the west.

J 398.7 (641.6 km) **D 15.3** (24.6 km) Underground pipeline crossing.

J 413.3 (665.1 km) **D 0.7** (1.1 km) Turnout with Prudhoe Bay and Deadhorse maps at former highway checkpoint. Oil field activity and equipment become visible along the horizon.

Deadhorse

J 414 (666.3 km) **D 0** Northern end of Dalton Highway, security gate; travel beyond this point is on oil company roads. **Population:** 25; area pop. 2,500. About 2 miles/3.2 km ahead is the Deadhorse Airport and the public-access portion of the Prudhoe Bay oil field. A number of oil fields make up the Prudhoe Bay industrial area: Kuparuk, Milne Point, Point McIntyre, Prudhoe Bay, Niakuk and Endicott.

Deadhorse was established to support oil development in the surrounding area; it is not a town in the traditional sense. Deadhorse takes its name from the airport, which was named after the construction company that built it. Most buildings are modular, pre-fab-type construction, situated on gravel pads on tundra bog. Virtually all the businesses here are engaged in oil field or pipeline support activities, such as drilling, construction, maintenance, telecommunications, warehousing and transportation. Oil field employees work a rotation such as 2 weeks on the job, then 2 weeks off. While on rotation, workers typically work 7 days a week, 10 to 12 hours each day.

There is scheduled jet service to Deadhorse/Prudhoe Bay from Anchorage (flying time from Anchorage is 1 hour, 35 minutes), Fairbanks and Barrow. Packaged tours of the North Slope area are available from Anchorage and Fairbanks. Air taxi service is available at Deadhorse Airport for sightseeing, hunting or rafting parties, and trips to outlying Native villages.

Accommodations are available at the Arctic Caribou Inn, Arctic Oilfield Hotel (Veco Camp), Peak Base Camp or Prudhoe Bay Hotel. All serve meals; however, only snacks or salad bars may be available at times other than breakfast 5:30–8 A.M., lunch noon to 1 P.M., and dinner 5–8 P.M. There is a general store, auto parts/hardware store and post office.

Regular unleaded gasoline and No. 1 diesel are available at Nana or the local Tesoro station. Nana is open from 7 A.M. until 5 P.M., with a callout charge after hours. Tesoro is a 24-hour self-serve station; an attendant is available and cash accepted from 7 A.M. until 6 P.M. There is a public phone, toilet and overnight parking with limited services available at Tesoro.

Tire and vehicle repairs are available at either Prudhoe Bay Fleet Shop or the Veco Light Vehicle Shop. Make sure to carry an extra tire, as well as the usual 2 mounted spares, because tire stock is limited. You could wait several days if a tire has to be ordered. The local auto parts store has an assortment of filters, oil, windshield wipers, headlights, etc.

Public access beyond Deadhorse is restricted. For security reasons, travel north of Deadhorse, including visits to the Arctic Ocean, is limited to commercial tours. Tour information is available at either the Arctic Caribou Inn or the Prudhoe Bay Hotel. Aerial tours may be arranged with one of the air-

craft or helicopter charter services located at the Deadhorse Airport.

Deadhorse–Prudhoe Bay Tesoro. See display ad this section.

Tour Arctic invites you to tour Prudhoe Bay, May 25–Sept. 8. Providing guided tours since 1975. Tour includes Milepost 0 at Pump Station 1. See oil rigs and Oilfield Visitor Center, and oil field informative video presentation and exhibits. Walk on the beach at the Arctic Ocean. Arctic Caribou Inn. Clean comfortable rooms. Buffet service, laundry and shower facilities. Summer phone (907) 659-2368. Winter phone (907) 659-2840. Tour Arctic/Arctic Caribou Inn, fax (907) 659-2289. Mailing address: P.O. Box 340112, Prudhoe Bay, AK 99734. [ADVERTISEMENT]

Deadhorse/Prudhoe Bay

Map showing Deadhorse/Prudhoe Bay area with Lake Colleen, Dalton Highway, Sagavanirktok River, Deadhorse Airport, and various locations including West Security Gate, East Security Gate, Peak, Arctic Oilfield Hotel, VECO Fleet Services, Tesoro, North Slope Borough, NAPA/Brooks Range Supply, Prudhoe Bay Fleet Services, General Store Post Office, Arctic Caribou Inn, Prudhoe Bay Hotel, NANA. To Arctic Ocean, To Pump Station #1, To Fairbanks, Road Closed.

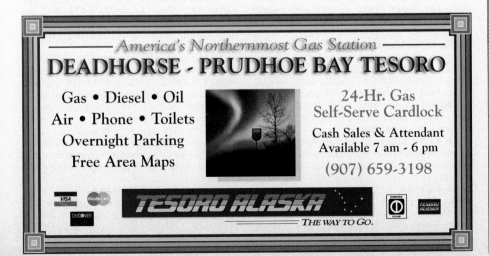

GENERAL INFORMATION

Air Travel

SCHEDULED AIR SERVICE TO ALASKA

Alaska Airlines, American West, Asiana Airlines, Continental Airlines, Delta Air Lines, Northwest Airlines, Reno Air and United Airlines all provide scheduled passenger jet service between Alaska and the Lower 48. Aeroflot Russian Airlines, Alaska Airlines, Cathay Pacific Airways, China Airlines and Korean Air fly to Anchorage with scheduled passenger jet service from other countries. Belair, Condor and World Airways travel to Anchorage from other countries from May to September.

Between Alaska and Canada, Air North connects Fairbanks and Juneau with Yukon Territory communities. Era Aviation connects Anchorage, AK, with Whitehorse, YT. Taquan Air connects Southeast Alaska communities with Prince Rupet, BC.

Contact your travel agent for current schedules and fares for all carriers.

SCHEDULED AIR SERVICE WITHIN ALASKA

Following are listed by region the carriers offering intrastate scheduled air service. Interline service available to most rural Alaska points; check with carriers. Also check local air taxi operators for charter and commuter service to any Alaskan community.

SOUTHCENTRAL/SOUTHWESTERN

Delta Air Lines, Anchorage International Airport; phone (800) 221-1212—To Anchorage and Fairbanks, and summer flights to Juneau.

Era Aviation (Alaska Airlines commuter), 6160 Carl Brady Dr., Anchorage, AK 99502; phone (800) 866-8394—From Anchorage to Cordova, Kenai, Homer, Kodiak, Valdez and Iliamna. Plus 17 southwestern Alaska villages from Bethel. Charter service available statewide. Also service between Anchorage and Whitehorse, YT (begins May 1997).

Gulkana Air Service, Box 342, Glennallen, AK 99588; phone (907) 822-5532—Serves Wrangell–St. Elias National Park and all the Copper River Basin.

PenAir (Alaska Airlines commuter), 4851 Aircraft Dr., Anchorage, AK 99502; phone (800) 448-4226—To Anchorage, Unalakleet, Dillingham, King Salmon, Dutch Harbor, Akutan, St. Mary, Aniak, Cold Bay and the Pribilof Islands.

Reeve Aleutian Airways Inc., 4700 W. International Airport Rd., Anchorage, AK 99502; phone (907) 243-1112—To Anchorage, Bethel, King Salmon, Port Heiden, Sand Point, Cold Bay, Unalaska/Dutch Harbor, Adak, Dillingham and St. Paul (special Pribilof Islands tours in summer).

Reno Air, Anchorage International Airport; phone (800) 736-6247—To Anchorage and Fairbanks.

Floatplane lands at Lake Hood, the world's busiest seaplane base. *(© Michael DeYoung)*

INTERIOR/ARCTIC/WESTERN

Arctic Circle Air Service, P.O. Box 60049, Fairbanks, AK 99706; phone (907) 474-0112, fax 474-0116—To Fairbanks, Fort Yukon, Arctic Village, Venetie, Chalkyitsik, Allakaket, Anaktuvuk Pass, Bettles, Tanana, Kaltag, Nulato, Huslia, Hughes, Rampart and Eagle.

Bering Air Inc., Box 1650, Nome, AK 99762; phone (907) 443-5464, fax 443-5919—From Nome and Kotzebue to western Alaska points and Russian Far East.

Cape Smyth Air Service, Box 549, Barrow, AK 99723; phone (907) 852-8333—Barrow service to Atqasuk, Wainwright, Point Lay, Point Hope, Nuiqsut, Deadhorse (Prudhoe Bay) and Barter Island. Also office in Kotzebue; phone (907) 442-3020, with service to Buckland, Deering, Ambler, Kiana, Kivalina, Kobuk, Noatak, Noorvik, Point Hope, Selawik and Shungnak. Office in Nome; phone (907) 443-5125, with service to St. Michael, Shishmaref, Stebbins, Teller, Unalakleet, Wales, Shaktoolik, White Mountain, Koyuk, Golovin, Elim, Brevig Mission, Gambell and Savoonga.

Delta Air Lines, Anchorage International Airport; phone (800) 221-1212—To Anchorage and Fairbanks, and summer flights to Juneau.

40-Mile Air, 6250 Old Airport Way, Fairbanks, AK 99706; phone (907) 474-0018, fax 474-8954, e-mail 40air@polar.com—To Fairbanks, Delta, Tok, Tetlin, Chisana, Chicken, Eagle, Boundary and Northway.

Frontier Flying Service, 3820 University

Ave., Fairbanks, AK 99709; phone (907) 474-0014, fax 474-0774, e-mail: frontier@polarnet.com—From Fairbanks to 23 Interior and Arctic villages including Gates of the Arctic National Park and the Arctic National Wildlife Refuge.

Larry's Flying Service Inc., 3822 University Ave., Fairbanks, AK 99709; phone (907) 474-9169, e-mail: larrys@imagi.net—To Fairbanks, Anaktuvuk Pass, Bettles, Fort Yukon and 13 more villages.

Reno Air, Anchorage International Airport; phone (800) 736-6247—To Anchorage and Fairbanks.

Tanana Air Service, Box 60713, Fairbanks, AK 99706; phone (907) 474-0301, fax 474-9311—Scheduled service from Fairbanks to 32 communities along the Yukon, Tanana and Kuskokwim rivers.

Warbelow's Air Ventures Inc., 3758 University Ave. S., Fairbanks, AK 99709; phone (800) 478-0812 or (907) 474-0518—Scheduled service to Alaska's Interior; Bush mailplane trips, Arctic Circle Tours, hot-springs fly-ins and sightseeing charters also available.

Wright Air Service, Box 60142, Fairbanks, AK 99706; phone (907) 474-0502, fax 474-0375—From Fairbanks to 8 communities along the Yukon River and north of the river.

SOUTHEAST

Air North, 1873 Shell Simmons Dr., Juneau, AK 99801; phone (907) 789-2007—To Juneau, Whitehorse, Dawson City, Old Crow and Inuvik.

Haines Airways, Box 470, Haines, AK

99827; phone (907) 766-2646—To Juneau, Hoonah, Haines and Gustavus/Glacier Bay.

Ketchikan Air Service, 1600 International Airport, Ketchikan, AK 99901; phone (800) 656-6608—To Ketchikan, Juneau, Kake, Craig, Klawock, Wrangell, Petersburg, Coffman Cove, Thorne Bay and other southeastern points.

L.A.B. Flying Service (Alaska Airlines mileage partner), Box 272, Haines, AK 99827; phone (800) 426-0543 or (907) 776-2222—To Juneau, Petersburg, Hoonah, Haines, Skagway, Kake and Gustavus/Glacier Bay.

Loken Aviation, 8995 Yandukin Dr., Juneau, AK 99801; phone (907) 789-3331—Scheduled and charter service to Angoon, Pelican, Elfin Cove, Tenakee and Hobart Bay.

Skagway Air Service, Box 357, Skagway, AK 99840; phone (907) 983-2218, fax 983-2948—To Juneau, with stops in Haines, Hoonah and Gustavus/Glacier Bay.

Taquan Air Service Inc., 1007 Water St., Ketchikan, AK 99901; phone (907) 225-9668, fax 225-0522—To Metlakatla, Prince Rupert (BC), Craig, Thorne Bay, Hydaburg, Coffman Cove, Nankati, Edna Bay, Hyder and other destinations.

Wings of Alaska Flightseeing and Charters, 1873 Shell Simmons Dr., Juneau, AK 99801; phone (907) 789-0790—To Haines, Hoonah, Skagway, Pelican, Elfin Cove, Angoon, Tenakee and Gustavus/Glacier Bay.

ALL REGIONS

Alaska Airlines, 4750 W. International Airport Road, Anchorage, AK 99502; phone (800) 426-0333—To Anchorage, Fairbanks, Prudhoe Bay, Cordova, Yakutat, Juneau, Sitka, Wrangell, Petersburg, Ketchikan, Nome, Kotzebue, Bethel, Dillingham, Dutch Harbor, King Salmon, Kodiak, Barrow and Gustavus/Glacier Bay (summer only).

SCHEDULED AIR SERVICE TO/IN YUKON AND WESTERN CANADA

Air North, Box 4998, Whitehorse, YT Y1A 4S2; phone (403) 668-2228—Between Whitehorse, Dawson City, Fairbanks, Juneau, Inuvik, Mayo and Old Crow.

AirBC, 5520 Miller Rd., Richmond, BC V7B 1L9; for reservations phone Air Canada in British Columbia at (604) 688-5515 or in the United States at 1-800-776-3000—Western Canadian service and service from Vancouver to U.S. destinations of Seattle, Spokane and Portland.

Alkan Air, P.O. Box 4008, Whitehorse, YT Y1A 3S9; phone (403) 668-2107, fax (403) 667-6117—Between Whitehorse, Dawson City, Old Crow and Inuvik, NWT.

Canadian Airlines International, 206–1030 W. Georgia St., Vancouver, BC V6E 2Y2; phone (604) 279-6611—To Calgary, Edmonton, Vancouver, Prince George, Prince Rupert, Fort St. John, Fort Nelson, Watson Lake, Whitehorse and numerous other points.

NWT Air, Postal Service 9000, Yellowknife, NT X1A 2RS; phone (403) 920-2500, fax (403) 920-4274, e-mail: xdmclrk@ssimicro.com—To Whitehorse, Vancouver, Edmonton, Yellowknife, Inuvik and other points.

CHARTER/AIR TAXI SERVICE WITHIN ALASKA

In addition to scheduled air service, there are more than 200 certified charter/air taxi operators in Alaska.

Air taxi operators conduct their business from a specific base of operations, primarily through the charter of aircraft. Any pilot flying for hire is required to hold a commercial or airline transport pilot certificate. The customer can and should be protected by having the pilot show his/her credentials. A pilot with the necessary credentials will be glad to show them. Do not fly with a pilot who cannot produce certification.

Air taxi rates may vary from carrier to carrier. Most operators charge an hourly rate either per plane load or per passenger; others may charge on a per-mile basis. Flightseeing trips to area attractions are often available at a fixed price per passenger.

Sample per-hour fares for charter planes with varied wheel, float and ski capabilities (luggage space limited and dependent on number of passengers): PA 18 (1 passenger), $160; Cessna 185 (5 passengers), $220; PA 32 (6 passengers), $280; Cessna 207 (6 passengers), $230; Beaver DHC2 (7 passengers), $300; and Otter DHC3 (10 passengers), $500.

PRIVATE AIRCRAFT

The MILEPOST® logs include the location of most airstrips along the Alaska Highway, in Alaskan communities and along other highways in Alaska and northwestern Canada. Airstrips in British Columbia and Alberta are too numerous to be included. Aircraft symbols corresponding to airstrip locations are included on the highway strip maps. The map symbols are a white plane for airports with scheduled service, and a black plane for airstrips with no scheduled service and limited facilities.

Private aircraft information in these logs includes only the name and location of the airstrip, the elevation, length and surface material of the longest runway and the availability of fuel. Many Northland pilots fly jet craft. Jet and other fuel is available at many airports. Fuel sold in Alaska and Canada is almost exclusively 100LL; 80 octane fuel is no longer available, though some airports offer car gasoline.

There are literally thousands of landing areas in the North for amphibious aircraft; *The MILEPOST®* does not include these in the log copy. A Water Aerodrome Supplement is available from the Canada Map Office, Departmentt of Energy, Mines and Resources, 130 Bentley Ave., Nepean, ON K1A 0E9. Phone 1-800-465-6277 or fax 1-800-661-6277.

CAUTION: The brief description of airstrips given in The MILEPOST® *is in no way intended as a guide for pilots flying in the North.* In Alaska, up-to-date information on airstrips, fuel, service and radio facilities is published every 8 weeks in accordance with specifications and agreements by the U.S. Dept. of Defense, the Federal Aviation Administration and the Dept. of Commerce. In Canada, this is done by the Minister of Transport and the Chief of the Defense Staff.

Pilots should obtain the latest U.S. government flight information publication, *Alaska Supplement*, by writing: National Oceanic and Atmospheric Administration, N/ACC3, Distribution Division, 6501 Lafayette Ave., Riverdale, MD 20737. Phone 1-800-638-8972 in the United States or (301) 436-8301; fax (301) 436-6829. Pilots should obtain the Canadian DND flight information publication, *Canada Flight Supplement*, by contacting the Canada Map Office. World Aeronautical Charts and catalogs of charts and related publications are also available from NOAA and CMO. Sectional maps are usually available at aviation stores along the way.

For a packet of free brochures including *Flight Tips for Pilots in Alaska*, write the Federal Aviation Administration, 222 W. 7th Ave., Anchorage, AK 99513.

Pilots may also get in touch with the Alaska Airmen's Assoc., Inc., P.O. Box 241185, Anchorage, AK 99524, phone (907) 272-1251, to buy a copy of the *Alaska Airmen's Logbook for Alaska, Northwest Canada and Russia*.

Two free Canadian publications of interest are *Air Tourist Information—Canada* and *Flying the Alaska Highway in Canada*. Both are available from Transport Canada (AANDHD), Ottawa, ON K1A 0N8.

Alcoholic Beverages

Alaska: Legal drinking age is 21. Packaged liquor, beer and wine are sold by licensed retailers rather than in state liquor stores. The sale and/or importation of alcoholic beverages is prohibited in some 70 bush communities.

Alberta: Legal age is 18. Liquor, beer and wine are sold in private liquor stores open daily. Beer and liquor (take out) are also sold in some taverns.

British Columbia: Legal age is 19. Packaged liquor, beer and wine are sold in government liquor stores (open daily except Sunday and holidays) and in licensed private stores 7 days a week. Sunday serving laws in licensed premises vary from community to community.

Northwest Territories: Legal age is 19. Packaged liquor, beer and wine are sold in government liquor stores at Hay River, Pine Point, Fort Simpson, Fort Smith, Yellowknife, Norman Wells and Inuvik. Beer-only agencies are located in some other places. You can purchase liquor in most hotels for consumption on the premises. The sale and possession of alcohol is prohibited in several

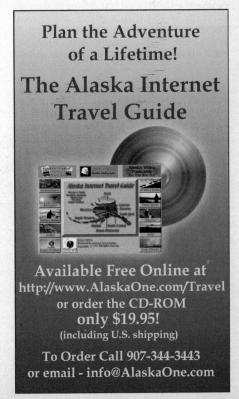

communities.

Yukon Territory: Legal age is 19. Packaged liquor, beer and wine are sold in government liquor stores at Watson Lake, Whitehorse, Dawson City, Haines Junction, Faro and Mayo. Some licensed premises have beer and wine for takeout sale.

Arctic Circle

The latitude of the Arctic Circle is approximately 66°33' north from the equator. We say "approximately" because the Arctic Circle varies a few seconds in latitude from year to year.

During summer solstice, June 20 or 21, the sun does not set at the Arctic Circle (it appears not to set for 4 days because of refraction). Farther north, at Barrow, the sun does not set from May 10 to Aug. 2.

At winter solstice, Dec. 21 or 22, the sun does not rise for 1 day at the Arctic Circle. At Barrow, the sun does not rise for 67 days.

Two highways cross the Arctic Circle. The Dalton Highway starts near Fairbanks and ends at Prudhoe Bay on the Arctic Ocean. The public may travel as far north as Dietrich, 100 miles/161 km north of the Arctic Circle. The Dempster Highway starts near Dawson City, YT, crosses the Arctic Circle after 250 miles/402 km, and ends at Inuvik, NWT, 200 miles/322 km north of the Arctic Circle.

Bears

In Alaska and in Canada, you are treading on bear territory. A true part of this wild country, bears can be a fearsome foe—never a friend. *CAUTION: Do not feed bears!*

There are 3 types of bears found in Alaska: the black bear, brown/grizzly bear and polar bear. Black bears range throughout most of the state, with highest densities in Southeast, Prince William Sound and Southcentral. Black bears can be brown in color, and may be confused with a grizzly, although they are normally smaller than a grizzly, with a more pointed head. Brown/grizzly bears range in color from black to blond, and range over most of the state. Alaska's coastal brown/grizzly bear is the world's largest carnivorous land mammal. (While polar bears are as large or larger, they actually live at sea on the ice, rather than on land.) Grizzlies have a distinct shoulder hump and larger head than black bears. Visitors are most likely to see grizzlies in Denali National Park, McNeil River State Game Sanctuary or Katmai National Park. Brown bear viewing is available on Kodiak Island, at Anan Bear Observatory near Wrangell and Pack Creek on Admiralty Island.

Bears are large, powerful animals, both unpredictable and dangerous. They will defend their territory, themselves and their young. Like any animal, survival is their most compelling instinct. Avoid surprising them. Avoid close encounters.

They may be any place—in campgrounds, highway rest stops or along hiking trails—so you must always be cautious and alert. Each bear has individual characteristics and behavior, and there are no formulas that apply to all bears.

If you are careless and disrespectful you increase the possibility of conflict between people and bears. If you use reasonable judgment and precaution you can reduce the risk

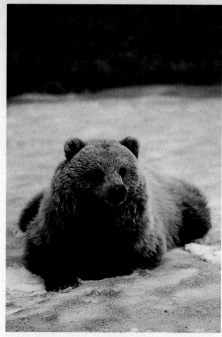

Grizzly bear photographed at Denali National Park. (© Roy M. Corral)

to yourself and to the bear.

When hiking, make a lot of noise and avoid dense brush. Hike in the open if possible. Let the bears know where you are. Bears will normally avoid people. Even though their vision is poor, their senses of smell and hearing are excellent. Surprise meetings can occur. Wind and rivers may muffle your noises, and you could surprise a bear.

Make noise by talking, ringing a bell or shaking a few pebbles in a can. Make a variety of noises. Talking or singing out loud is one of the best ways to let a bear know you are around.

Dogs are not permitted in national park backcountry. In bear country they can be a liability. Even wolves have difficulty driving bears away. Your pet, when hard pressed, may run to you with a grizzly in close pursuit.

Trouble between you and the grizzly bear can be caused by:

1. Cubs—A small, cuddly looking cub means that a protective mother is usually nearby. She aggressively protects her young, so don't approach.

2. Photography—Taking a close-up photo could lead to disaster. Keep your distance and use a telephoto lens.

3. Camps—Keep your campsite clean. Bears are omnivorous—they eat almost anything. Food and its accompanying odors attract bears. Do not bury trash—carry out everything you carry in.

In campgrounds, store food in vehicles or storage lockers (where provided). When in the backcountry, use bear-resistant food containers for all food and trash. Do not store food in your tent. Eliminate food odor from your camp and from yourself. Wash hands and face before retiring. (*Based on a National Park Service publication.*)

Bicycling in Alaska

Road conditions vary throughout Alaska, from newly paved highways to unimproved

dirt roads. In planning your bicycling routes, read the highway logs in *The MILEPOST®* carefully. Abrupt changes in road conditions are generally noted in the log, as are steep grades and whether or not there are shoulders. With the recent popularity of mountain bikes, additional routes are available to the rider who can travel on unimproved dirt roads and trails. Bicyclists will have to share the highways with vehicles, but traffic can be avoided by riding in the early morning and on weekdays. One advantage of touring Alaska in summer is the long daylight hours.

At press time, there were no laws governing bicyclists other than normal vehicle laws. Helmets are recommended.

Boating, Canoeing and Kayaking

Thousands of miles of waterways for both marine boating and lake- and river-boating are available to visitors to the North.

For marine sailors, southeastern Alaska's Inside Passage offers both recreational boating and a sheltered transportation route. There are numerous marine charter services throughout Southeast for visiting boaters. Most offer sportfishing or sightseeing tours, others have marine craft for charter (most skippered, some bare-boat). Boaters wishing to sail their own craft to Southeast should have the appropriate nautical charts and pilot guides. For U.S. waters, check locally for authorized nautical chart dealers or contact the National Oceanic and Atmospheric Administration; or write NOAA, N/ACC3, Distribution Division, 6501 Lafayette Ave., Riverdale, MD 20737. Phone 1-800-638-8972 in the United States or (301) 436-8301; fax (301) 436-6829.

For Washington and Alaska waters you'll also need the *United States Coast Pilot* (Books 8 and 9). For British Columbia waters you'll need the *British Columbia Sailing Directions* (Volumes I and II). You can get these as well as charts of Canadian coastal waters, tidal tables and other information. A free catalog of products is also available from the Canadian Hydrographic Service, Chart Sales Office, P.O. Box 6000, 9860 W. Saanich Rd., Sidney, BC V8L 4B2, phone (604) 363-6358, fax (604) 363-6841, Internet www.ios.bc.ca/ios/chs.

Marine travelers may also check local bookstores for Alaska cruising titles. Bluewater paddlers should have with them NOAA Tidal Current Tables. Contact the State of Alaska Dept. of Transportation and Public Facilities, Engineering and Operations Division, 3132 Channel Dr., Juneau, AK 99801, for a directory of harbor facilities.

Keep in mind that U.S. visitors entering Canada by private boat must report to Canadian customs immediately upon arrival.

It is possible to travel thousands of miles on Northland river systems by boat, canoe, kayak or raft. In Alaska and Yukon Territory, the Yukon River system provides such an opportunity. In Northwest Territories, the Mackenzie River system provides endless waterways to explore.

River travelers: Keep in mind that proper planning, good skills and common sense can help lessen the chance of capsizing and possible injury or loss of equipment. It is always a good idea to check with local sources, such as sporting goods stores or state and federal agencies, for current information on river conditions.

Canoe trails have been established on Alaskan rivers and lakes near Fairbanks and Anchorage, on Prince of Wales Island and on the Kenai Peninsula.

The Bureau of Land Management maintains 6 rivers that are part of the National Wild and Scenic Rivers System: Birch Creek, Beaver Creek, Forty Mile River, Delta River, Gulkane River, Unalakleet River. These rivers offer a variety of float trips. Five rivers are in Interior Alaska, near Fairbanks, and 1 is in western Alaska. A 7th river, near Kotzebue in the northwest, is being studied for possible inclusion into the system. BLM offers brochures on the river trails including access points, portages and scale of difficulty. For details on these rivers, write the Bureau of Land Management, 1150 University Ave., Fairbanks, AK 99709-3899, phone (907) 474-2251.

The Alaska Public Lands Information Centers in Fairbanks, Anchorage, Tok and Ketchikan have information on many of Alaska's navigable rivers. Paddling guides, river logs and maps are available. Visit the centers or contact the Alaska Public Lands Information Center at: 250 Cushman St., Suite 1A, Fairbanks, AK 99701, phone (907) 456-0527; 605 W. 4th Ave., Suite 105, Anchorage, AK 99501, phone (907) 271-2737, TDD (907) 271-2738; Box 359, Tok, AK 99780, phone (907) 883-5667; or 50 Main St., Ketchikan, AK 99901, phone (907) 225-8131.

Canoe trails have been established on Prince of Wales Island along the Honker Divide and at Sarkar Lakes. Outstanding sea kayaking opportunities are also available on the west coast of Prince of Wales Island. Contact Craig Ranger District, Tongass National Forest, Box 145, Craig, AK 99921, phone (907) 826-3271. For maps and information contact the Thorne Bay Ranger District, Tongass National Forest, Box 19001, Thorne Bay, AK 99919, phone (907) 828-3304.

Canoeing on the Kenai Peninsula's Swan Lake and Swanson River canoe trails starts about late May and continues until late October. For details on the trails write the Refuge Manager, Kenai National Wildlife Refuge, Box 2139, Soldotna, AK 99669.

A sea kayaking/camping map and brochure is available from Misty Fiords National Monument, Tongass National Forest, 3031 Tongass Ave., Ketchikan, AK 99901, phone (907) 225-2148.

In Yukon Territory there are more than a dozen rivers and lakes suitable for canoeing. Write Tourism Yukon, Box 2703, Whitehorse, YT Y1A 2C6.

For information on canoeing in the tundra and subarctic regions of Northwest Territories and the Mackenzie River system write to NWT Toursim Information, The North Group, Box 2107(EX), Yellowknife, NT X1A 2P6.

Bus Lines

Independent travelers wishing to travel by public bus within Alaska and Yukon Territory will generally find routes and services much more limited than in the Lower 48. Scheduled bus service is available within Alaska and Yukon Territory, but scheduled direct bus service to Alaska from the Lower 48 is not available, unless you wish to join an escorted motorcoach tour. If your schedule allows, you can travel from the Lower 48 to Alaska via public bus service by using several carriers. Most scheduled bus service in the North is seasonal.

Contact the following companies for current schedules:

Alaska Direct Bus Line, 102 Wood St., Whitehorse, YT Y1A 2E3, phone (800) 770-6652 or (403) 668-4833. Service from Anchorage to Fairbanks, Tok, Whitehorse, Dawson City, Skagway and Denali.

Alaska Sightseeing/Cruise West, 4th and Battery Building, Suite 700, Seattle, WA 98121, phone (907) 276-1305 (summer) or (800) 426-7702 year-round. Motorcoach trips connect Anchorage and Denali National Park.

Denali Express Alaska Tours, 405 L St., Anchorage, AK 99501, phone (800) 327-7651 or (907) 274-8539. Service between Anchorage and Denali Park; group tours and special itineraries.

Gray Line of Alaska/Alaskon Express, 300 Elliott Ave. W., Seattle, WA 98119, phone (800) 544-2206 or fax (206) 281-0621. Scheduled service to Anchorage, Fairbanks, Skagway, Whitehorse, Haines and most communities en route. Motorcoach tours to Anchorage, Denali National Park, Fairbanks, Prudhoe Bay, Prince William Sound, Seward and Portage Glacier.

Greyhound Lines of Canada, 2191 2nd Ave., Whitehorse, YT Y1A 3I8, phone (403) 667-2223, fax (403) 633-6858. Scheduled service to Whitehorse from all U.S.–Canada border crossings; also the Whitehorse depot has carriers to Dawson City and Alaska destinations.

Norline Coaches (Yukon) Ltd., 2191 2nd Ave., Whitehorse, YT Y1A 4T8, phone (403) 668-3355. Service between Whitehorse, Mayo, Carmacks and Dawson City.

Parks Highway Express, Box 82884, Fairbanks, AK 99708, phone (907) 479-3065, (888) 600-6001. Service between Anchorage, Denali Park and Fairbanks.

Princess Tours®, 2815 2nd Ave., Suite 400, Seattle, WA 98121, phone 1-800-835-8907. Motorcoach tours include the Klondike in Canada's Yukon, Anchorage, the Kenai Peninsula, Denali National Park, Fairbanks and Prudhoe Bay.

Seward Bus Line, Box 1338, Seward, AK 99664, phone (907) 224-3608, fax (907) 244-7237. Daily, year-round service between Anchorage and Seward.

Cabins

If you've ever wanted to try living in a log cabin in the wilderness, the USDA Forest Service gives you the opportunity for $25 per night per cabin. There are approximately 200 of these public-use cabins scattered throughout Tongass and Chugach national forests.

Cabins are accessible by air, boat or trail. Average size is 12 by 14 feet. Most cabins have wood stoves, some have oil stoves. Check with the Forest Service to determine what type of stove is provided. All cabins have tables and sleeping room for 4 or more people. You must supply bedding, cookware, stove oil (if necessary) and food. Splitting mauls are provided on site for cutting firewood. There are pit toilets but no garbage dumps (pack garbage out). Skiffs are provided at some cabins.

Permits for use of recreation cabins are issued on either a first-come, first-served basis, or by lottery in the Tongass National Forest. Applications for permits may be made in person or by mail up to 180 days in advance. You must have a permit for the specific length of occupancy. There is a 7-day limit on other cabins in the Tongass National Forest from April 1 to Oct. 31, and a 10-day limit Nov. 1 to March 31.

For reservations and information on Tongass National Forest cabins, contact one of the following area offices: Southeast Alaska Visitor Center, 50 Main St., Ketchikan, AK 99901, phone (907) 225-8131; Petersburg Ranger District, Box 309, Petersburg, AK 99833, phone (907) 772-3841; or Sitka Ranger District, 204 Siginaka Way, Sitka, AK 99833, phone (907) 747-6671.

For information on Chugach National Forest cabins, contact the Chugach National Forest, 3301 C Street, Suite 300, Anchorage, AK 99503; phone (907) 271-2500. Reservations for the 42 public recreation cabins in Chugach National Forest may be made by calling 1-800-280-2267 (TDD/TTY 1-800-879-4496). Nightly cabin rental fee is $25, and there is a reservation service fee of $8.25 for each cabin reserved. There are no special drawings or lotteries. Reservations can be made up to 180 days in advance, from March 1 to mid-September, 1997; 5 A.M. to 5 P.M., Alaska time, Monday–Friday, and 7 A.M. to 3 P.M. Saturday and Sunday; after mid-September 1997, call for hours of operation. Credit cards (VISA, MasterCard, Discover) are accepted. Full refunds are given if cancellations are 14 or more days in advance, minus a cancellation fee of $8.25. For cancellations 13 days or less before arrival, you get a refund minus the first night's cabin fee ($25).

The Bureau of Land Management has public recreation cabins in Alaska, all within 75 miles/120 km of Fairbanks. Cabins must be reserved prior to use and a fee is required. Two are road accessible year-round, 1 can be reached with a 6-mile hike, and 8 are primarily accessed by snow machine, dog team, cross-country skis or snowshoes in winter.

Contact the Bureau of Land Management, 1150 University Ave., Fairbanks, AK 99709-3899, phone (907) 474-2251.

The U.S. Fish and Wildlife Service maintains public-use cabins within Kodiak National Wildlife Refuge. Contact the refuge manager, 1390 Buskin River Rd., Kodiak, AK 99615, phone (907) 487-2600.

The Alaska Division of Parks and Outdoor Recreation maintains 35 public-use cabins scattered throughout the state. Cost ranges from $25–$50 per night. For reservations and information, contact the DNR Public Information Center: Alaska Parks Cabins, 3601 C Street, Suite 200, Anchorage, AK 99503-5929, phone (907) 269-8400.

Calendar of Events—1997

Travelers may wish to take into account some of the North's major celebrations when planning their visit. Following are some of these events listed by month and by place. Additional events are detailed under Attractions for the communities covered in the highway logs. In 1997, watch for events throughout the North that celebrate the centennial of the Klondike Gold Rush.

FEBRUARY
Anchorage—Fur Rendezvous. Cordova—Iceworm Festival. Fairbanks/Whitehorse, YT—Yukon Quest Sled Dog Race; Yukon Sourdough Rendezvous. Nenana—Tripod Raising Festival. Whitehorse, YT—Sourdough Rendezvous.

MARCH
Anchorage—Iditarod Trail Sled Dog Race. Bethel—Camai Native Dance Festival. Fairbanks—Winter Carnival; North American Sled Dog Championships. Nome—Bering Sea Ice Classic Golf Tournament; month of Iditarod events. North Pole—Winter Carnival. Yellowknife, NT—Caribou Carnival.

APRIL
Girdwood—Alyeska Spring Carnival. Juneau—Alaska Folk Festival.

MAY
This month is a busy one for fishing derbies for halibut (Homer, Seldovia and Valdez) and salmon (Ketchikan, Petersburg, Seldovia and Sitka).
Dawson City, YT—International Gold Show. Delta Junction—Buffalo Wallow Square Dance Jamboree. Kodiak—Crab Festival. Nome—Polar Bear Swim. Petersburg—Little Norway Festival. Talkeetna—Miners Day Festival.

JUNE
Anchorage—Mayor's Midnight Sun Marathon. Fairbanks—Midnight Sun Baseball Game. Nenana—River Daze. Nome—Midnight Sun Festival. Palmer—Colony Days. Sitka—Summer Music Festival. Whitehorse, YT—Yukon International Storytelling Festival.

JULY
Chugiak/Eagle River—Bear Paw Festival. Dawson City, YT—Canadian Airlines International Midnight Dome Race; Yukon Gold Panning Championships. Delta Junction—Deltana Fair. Fairbanks—Golden Days; World Eskimo–Indian Olympics. Inuvik, NT—Great Northern Arts Festival. Seward—Mount Marathon Race. Soldotna—Progress Days. Talkeetna—Moose Dropping Festival.

AUGUST
Dawson City and Watson Lake, YT—Discovery Days. Fairbanks—Tanana Valley State Fair. Haines—Southeast Alaska State Fair. Kodiak—State Fair and Rodeo. Ninilchik—Kenai Peninsula State Fair. Palmer—Alaska State Fair. Seward—Silver Salmon Derby. Whitehorse/Dawson City, YT—Annual Sourdough Rendezvous Gold-Rush Bathtub Race; Klondyke Harvest Fair.

SEPTEMBER
Dawson City, YT—Great Klondike Outhouse Race and Bathroom Wall Limerick Contest. Fairbanks—Equinox Marathon. Nome—Great Bathtub Race. Seldovia—Blueberry Festival. Skagway—Klondike Trail of '98 Road Relay to Whitehorse, YT. Whitehorse, YT, —Klondike Trail of '98 International Road Relay to Skagway, AK.

OCTOBER
Anchorage—Oktoberfest. Sitka—Alaska Day Festival.

NOVEMBER
Anchorage—Great Alaska Shootout.

Camping

The MILEPOST® indicates both private and public campgrounds with tent symbols in the highway logs and on the strip maps for Alaska, Yukon Territory, Northwest Territories, and parts of Alberta and British Columbia. Federal, state and provincial agencies offering camping areas are listed here. Reservations are not accepted at any state campgrounds. Keep in mind that government campgrounds do not maintain dump stations (except some British Columbia provincial parks) and few offer electrical hookups. Season dates for most campgrounds in the North depend on weather. Check the highway logs for private campgrounds in the North. For more information on private campgrounds in Alaska, contact the Alaska Campground Owners Assoc. (ACOA), Box 100746, Anchorage, AK 99510, phone (907) 349-1601, fax (907) 349-8010.

NOTE: Campers are urged to use established campgrounds. Overnighting in rest areas and turnouts is illegal unless otherwise posted, and may be unsafe. ▲

ALASKA
Alaska Public Lands Information Centers in Anchorage, Fairbanks, Tok and Ketchikan provide information on all state and federal campgrounds in Alaska, along with state and national park passes and details on wilderness camping. Visit the centers, or contact the Alaska Public Lands Information Center at: 605 W. 4th Ave., Suite 105, Anchorage, AK 99501, phone (907) 271-2737, TDD (907) 271-2738; 250 Cushman St., Suite 1A, Fairbanks, AK 99701, phone (907) 456-0527; P.O. Box 359, Tok, AK 99780, phone (907) 883-5667; or 50 Main St., Ketchikan, AK 99901, phone (907) 228-6219.

Alaska Division of Parks and Outdoor Recreation maintains an extensive system of roadside campgrounds and waysides. All are available on a first-come, first-served basis. There is a $6 to $10 per night camping fee charged at all developed state campgrounds, except for $12 at Byers Lake Campground and $15 at Eagle River and Chena River campgrounds. (NOTE: Rates are subject to change.) An annual pass, good for unlimited camping in a calendar year, is available for $75 for Alaska residents and $200 for nonresidents. The pass is a windshield decal and is not transferable. There is a day-use parking fee of $3 or $5 per vehicle at a small number of state park facilities, including

some picnic sites, trailheads and fishing access sites. A full-year parking pass may be purchased for $25. To obtain camping or parking passes, send check or money order payable to the State of Alaska. Mail to Alaska Camping Pass, Division of Parks and Outdoor Recreation, 3601 C Street, Suite 200, Anchorage, AK 99503-5929.

USDA Forest Service provides numerous camping areas in Chugach and Tongass national forests. Most USFS campgrounds charge a fee of under $10 per night depending on facilities. There is a 14-day limit at most campgrounds; this regulation is enforced. For further information write the Office of Information, USDA Forest Service, Box 21628, Juneau, AK 99802.

Bureau of Land Management maintains about 12 campgrounds; fees are charged on some. Unless otherwise posted, all undeveloped BLM public lands are open to free camping, usually for a maximum of 14 days per stay. Write the Bureau of Land Management, 1150 University Ave., Fairbanks, AK 99709-3899, phone (907) 474-2251.

National Park Service maintains 7 campgrounds in Denali National Park and Preserve (see DENALI NATIONAL PARK section for details). There are established hike-in campgrounds at Glacier Bay and Katmai national parks and preserves, and wilderness camping in other national parks and preserves in Alaska. For more information, contact any of the Alaska Public Lands Information Centers previously mentioned.

On-line information on national parks in Alaska is available at the following locations: Aniakchak National Monument, www.nps.gov/ania; Bering Land Bridge National Monument, www.nps.gov/bela; Cape Krusenstern National Monument, www.nps.gov/noaa; Denali National Park, www.nps.gov/dena; Gates of the Arctic National Park, www.nps.gov/gaar; Glacier Bay National Park, www.nps.gov/glba; Katmai National Park, www.nps.gov/katm; Kenai Fjords National Park, www.nps.gov/kefj, Klondike Gold Rush National Historical Park, www.nps.gov/klgo; Kobuk Valley National Park, www.nps.gov/noaa; Lake Clark National Park and Preserve, www.nps.gov/lacl; Sitka National Historical Park, www.nps.gov/sitk; Wrangell–St. Elias National Park and Preserve, www.nps.gov/wrst; and Yukon–Charley Rivers National Preserve, www.nps.gov/yuch.

U.S. Fish & Wildlife Service manages several camping areas within Kenai National Wildlife Refuge. Contact the Refuge Manager, Kenai National Wildlife Refuge, Box 2139, Soldotna, AK 99669, phone (907) 262-7021.

Two special passes for federal recreation areas are available to U.S. citizens. The Golden Age Passport is for persons 62 and older and costs a one time fee of $10. The Golden Access Passport is free for persons with blindness or another permanent disability. Both provide lifetime admittance to federally operated parks, monuments, historic sites, recreation areas and wildlife refuges that charge entrance fees. Accompanying passengers in a private car enter without charge as well. The passport bearer also receives a 50 percent discount on federal use fees charged for facilities and services such as camping, boat launching and parking (exceptions to the 50 percent discount may apply in government facilities operated by concessionaires, such as the Russian River ferry). These passes must be obtained in person by showing proof of age for a Golden

Age Passport, or proof of being medically diagnosed with blindness or another permanent disability for the Golden Access Passport. The passports are available at most of the federal recreation areas where they may be used, so travelers do not need to obtain them in advance. They also can be obtained at Alaska Public Lands Information Centers in Anchorage and Fairbanks.

CANADA

National park campgrounds generally have a per-night fee. Per-night fees range from $6.50 for a tent site to $17 for a full-service site with individual water, sewer and electrical hookups. In addition, a park motor-license sticker is required for motorists staying overnight in the national parks. Electrical service is standard 60 cycle. Wood for campfires is supplied free to all camping and picnicking grounds. Bring your own ax to split kindling. "Serviced" campgrounds have caretakers.

Provincial park campgrounds. Alberta has 67 provincial park campgrounds, some with limited facilities, others with picnic tables, electrical hookups, flush toilets, barbecues and nature programs. There is a fee ranging from $10 to $20 per night for provincial parks, and some accept reservations for an extra fee. There are also limited camping facilities at many of the 236 provincial recreation areas, which have toilets, picnic tables and litter barrels. A nominal fee is charged. Private and public campgrounds are listed in *Alberta Campground Guide*, available from Travel Alberta (phone 1-800-661-8888).

British Columbia has 156 provincial park campgrounds with vehicle/tent campsites. Provincial park campgrounds in British Columbia are indicated 1.2 miles/2 km and 1,312 feet/400m before the entrance along the highways by blue-and-white signs. They are serviced from spring to early fall (however, they may be used throughout the year). Fees range from $6 to $15.50 per night. Gates close from 11 P.M. to 6 A.M. in some parks.

Reservations are accepted at 41 British Columbia provincial parks for camping between March 15 and Oct. 15. Reservations are taken between March 1 and Sept. 15 and may be made from 3 months in advance to within 2 days prior to arrival. Phone Discover Camping at 1-800-689-9025 between 8 A.M. and 6 P.M. (PST) from anywhere in Canada and the United States; in Vancouver phone (604) 689-9025.

Territorial campgrounds in Northwest Territories charge $12 or $15 per night, depending upon the site, in attended campgrounds and parks with facilities. Campground-use firewood is available for a fee.

Yukon Territory has 43 Yukon government campgrounds located along its road system. There is a per night fee of $8 charged for nonresidents. These well-maintained campgrounds often have kitchen shelters (which may not be used as sleeping accommodations) and free firewood for use at the campground. There is a 14-day limit.

Customs Requirements

Crossing the border between the U.S. and Canada is usually not a problem. However, travelers are reminded that all persons and their vehicles are subject to search and seizure at the border according to the laws of whichever country they are entering. Vehicles may be searched at the discretion of the customs officials, whether or not the traveler feels that he or she has complied with customs requirements.

Customs agents in both Canada and the U.S. are charged with enforcing a daunting number of regulations. These regulations affect agricultural products, commercial goods, alcohol, tobacco and firearms, among other things. Canada vigorously enforces its firearms importation laws, and border officials may—at their discretion—search any vehicle for handguns. If you plan to travel with a firearm, read the requirements on transporting firearms through Canada.

Certain items, mainly crafts and souvenirs made from parts of wild animals, have caused some problems for travelers to the North in recent years. An item which may be purchased legally in Alaska, for example carved ivory, can be brought back into the Lower 49 but may not be permitted transit through Canada without a permit. Some items which may be purchased legally in parts of Canada may not be allowed into the United States. For example, a seal-fur doll purchased in Inuvik, NWT, would be confiscated by the U.S. Fish and Wildlife Service or U.S. customs because the import of seal products is prohibited except by special permit.

IMPORTANT: You cannot cross the border unless the customs office for the country you are entering is open. Severe fines are levied for crossing without clearing customs. Officials at Canadian customs are concerned about child abductions. If you are traveling with children, remember to bring identification for them.

Read through the following information and contact Canadian Customs or U.S. Customs offices directly.

ENTRY INTO CANADA FROM THE UNITED STATES

General information for U.S. visitors entering Canada is available from the Canadian Tourism Commission, Tourism Reference and Documentation Centre, 235 Queen St., 400 D, Ottawa, ON K1A 0H6; request their Travel Information brochure. Canadian Consulates may also answer general questions or direct your queries to a more specific source. In the U.S., Canadian consulates are located in Atlanta, Boston, Buffalo, Chicago, Cincinnati, Dallas, Detroit, Los Angeles, Miami, Minneapolis, New York, Pittsburgh, San Francisco, Seattle and Washington, DC.

Canada Customs stations along the U.S. border can more directly address many customs-related questions. You may phone them directly. Contact the customs office nearest you or the one you will be using to cross into Canada. Call Canadian information in that community and ask for the phone number of Canada Customs. In the Pacific Northwest, for example, the Douglas–Blaine Peace Arch crossing (open 24-hours) may be reached at (604) 535-9754; Specific questions on importing guns may also be addressed to Environment Canada, Customs and Excise, Ottawa, ON K1A 1G2; phone (613) 954-7142.

Identification: Citizens or permanent residents of the United States do not require passports or visas to enter Canada. However, native-born U.S. citizens should carry some identifying paper that shows their citizenship, in case they are asked for it. This would include a driver's license and voters registration (together), passport, or some employment cards with description and photo. Social security cards or driver's licenses alone are not positive identification. Birth certificates of children are sometimes required. Proof of residence may also be required. Naturalized U.S. citizens should carry a naturalization certificate or some other evidence of citizenship. Permanent residents of the United States who are not U.S. citizens are advised to have their Resident Alien Card (U.S. Form 1-151 or Form 1-551).

NOTE: Canada has been increasingly concerned about child adbuction. Consequently, travelers should carry identification for children, similar to those mentioned above; have a letter of permission from the child's parent or legal guardian when traveling with children who are not legally their own; carry copies of legal documents regarding custody rights if they share custody; and have their own children in the same vehicle, if traveling in a group of vehicles, when they arrive at the border.

All persons other than U.S. citizens or legal residents, and residents of Greenland, require a valid passport or an acceptable travel document.

Visitors of the United States who have a single-entry visa should check with an office of the U.S. Immigration and Naturalization Service to ensure that they have all the papers needed to return to the United States.

Persons temporarily in the United States who would require visas if coming to Canada directly from their countries of origin should contact the Canadian Embassy, Consulate or Office of Tourism in their home country before departure for the United States.

Persons under 18 years of age who are not accompanied by an adult should bring a letter with them from a parent or guardian giving them permission to travel into Canada.

Although there is no set standard for monies required for entrance into Canada, the visitor must have sufficient funds to cover his cost of living per day for the planned length of stay. Consideration in assessing "sufficient funds" includes the locale in which the visitor plans to stay and whether he will be staying with a friend or relative. (Readers report being turned back for lacking $150 in cash; one customs official suggests $500 as an appropriate amount.) The visitor must also have return transportation fare to his country of origin.

Vehicles: The entry of vehicles and trailers into Canada for touring purposes, for periods up to 12 months, is generally a quick, routine matter, without payment of a customs assessment, and any necessary permits are issued at the port of entry. Rental trailers of the U-Haul luggage variety may be subject to a nominal deposit, which is refundable on proof of exportation of trailer. Motor vehicle registration forms should be carried and, if the vehicle is rented from a car rental company, a copy of the rental contract stipulating use in Canada. If a tourist enters Canada using a vehicle not registered in his name, he should carry a letter from its registered owner authorizing the use of the vehicle.

U.S. motorists planning to travel in Canada are advised to obtain a Canadian Nonresident Interprovincial Motor Vehicle Liability Insurance Card, which provides evidence of financial responsibility. This card is available only in the United States through

U.S. insurance companies or their agents. All provinces in Canada require visiting motorists to produce evidence of financial responsibility should they be involved in an accident. Financial responsibility limits vary by province.

All national driver's licenses are valid in Canada.

Trailers: If you plan to leave your vacation trailer in Canada for a season while returning home from time to time, ask Canada customs at the time of entry for a wallet-sized special permit—an E99. Post the permit inside the trailer so that it can be seen easily from outside. You may not store a vacation trailer in Canada during the off-season.

Entry by private boat: Visitors planning to enter Canada by private boat should contact customs in advance for a list of ports of entry that provide customs facilities and their hours of operation. Immediately upon arrival, visitors must report to customs and complete all documentation. In emergency situations, visitors must report their arrival to the nearest regional customs office or office of the RCMP.

Baggage: The necessary wearing apparel and personal effects in use by the visitor are admitted free of duty. Up to 50 cigars, 200 cigarettes (1 carton) and 14 ounces of loose tobacco, 400 tobacco sticks, and up to 40 ounces of spirituous liquor or wine *OR* 24 12-ounce cans or bottles of beer or ale may be allowed entry in this manner. Additional quantities of alcoholic beverages up to a maximum of 2 gallons may be imported into Canada (except the Northwest Territories) on a payment of duty and taxes plus charges for a provincial permit at port of entry. To import tobacco products a person must be 18 years of age or over in most jurisdictions, 19 years in British Columbia, Ontario, Newfoundland, New Brunswick, and Nova Scotia. To import alcoholic beverages the importer must be at least 19 years of age in most jurisdictions, 18 years in Alberta, Manitoba and Quebec.

Recreational Equipment: Visitors may also bring in sporting outfits and other equipment for their own use by declaring them at entry. These can include fishing tackle, portable boats, outboard motors, snowmobiles, equipment for camping, golf, tennis and other games, radios and portable or table-model television sets, musical instruments, typewriters, personal computers and cameras (with a reasonable amount of film and flashbulbs) in their possession on arrival. Although not a requirement, it may facilitate entry if visitors have a list (in duplicate) of each item, including serial numbers when possible. All such articles must be identified and reported when leaving Canada.

Transporting goods through Canada: U.S. citizens from the Lower 49 who wish to transport personally their household or personal effects to Alaska when such goods are not intended for use in Canada, may obtain a temporary admission permit at the border to facilitate the in-transit movements of goods through Canada. A refundable security deposit may be required at time of entry. The traveler should prepare a list of the goods in triplicate, indicating values and serial numbers where applicable.

Firearms: Firearms are divided into 3 categories—prohibited, restricted and long guns (unrestricted).

The *only* category of gun a U.S. visitor may bring into Canada is a long gun, which is a regular hunting rifle or shotgun with a barrel at least 18 1/2 inches/47 cm, and an overall length of 26 inches/66 cm, and which does not fall into the category of a prohibited or restricted firearm.

Long guns may be imported and moved in transit through Canada provided they are securely packed; they are for sporting or competition use; and the person is over 16 years of age. Long guns are *not* allowed in national parks and may not be carried in or through a Canadian national park unless they have been dismantled

Handguns for personal protection are a restricted firearm and are not allowed to cross the border. Competitive marksmen competing in a recognized event may import handguns by obtaining a permit in advance.

A restricted firearm is described as any firearm that is not a prohibited weapon, has a barrel less than 18 1/2 inches/47 cm in length and is capable of discharging center-fire ammunition in a semiautomatic manner, or is designed or adapted to be fired when reduced to a length less than 26 inches/66 cm by folding, telescoping or otherwise. Also included would be any firearm designed, altered or intended to be aimed and fired by the action of 1 hand, such as revolvers and handguns (including antique handguns that use rimfire or centre-fire ammunition that is commonly available in Canada).

A prohibited firearm includes any firearm that is capable of firing bullets in rapid succession during 1 pressure of the trigger; any firearm adapted from a rifle or shotgun whether by sawing, cutting or other alteration or modification, that as so adapted, has a barrel that is less than 18 inches/46 cm in length, or that is less than 26 inches/66 cm in overall length; any firearm that is specifically designed as a prohibited weapon. By Order in Council (effective Jan. 1, 1995), a number of assault pistols, combat shotguns, assault riffles and carbines become prohibited. Such weapons are not permitted entry into Canada.

The following quantities of explosives (not including hollow-point handgun ammunition) may enter Canada for personal use by hunters and competitive marksmen without a permit issued by the Explosives Branch of the Dept. of Energy, Mines and Resources: 5,000 safety cartridges; 5,000 primers for safety cartridges; 5,000 empty primed safety cartridge cases; 17.6 pounds/8 kg smokeless powder (small-arms nitro compound).

Nonresidents arriving at a Canada customs port must declare all their firearms. Anyone who illegally carries a firearm into Canada is subject to a number of penalties, including seizure of the weapon and the vehicle in which it is carried. All firearms must be transported unloaded.

NOTE: Personal protection devices such as stun-guns, mace and pepper spray are prohibited entry into Canada.

Plants, fruit and vegetables: House plants may be imported without a permit. Some fruits and vegetables may be restricted entry into Canada and all are subject to inspection at the border.

Animals: Dogs and cats (over 3 months of age) from the United States must be accompanied by a certificate issued by a licensed veterinarian of Canada or the United States certifying that the animal has been vaccinated against rabies during the preceding 36 months; such a certificate shall describe the animal and date of vaccination and shall be initialed by inspectors and returned to the owner.

Up to 2 pet birds per family may be imported into Canada. Parrot and song birds may be admitted when accompanied by the owner, if the owner certifies in writing that, upon entering the country, the birds have not been in contact with any other birds during the preceding 90 days and have been in the owner's possession for the entire period. All birds of the parrot family, except budgies, cockatiels and Rose-ringed parakeets, are on the CITES endangered species list and require at the minimum a U.S. CITES export permit with some species requiring an additional Canadian CITES import permit. For U.S. CITES export permit information contact the U.S. Office of Management Authority, 4401 N. Fairfax Dr., Room 420, Arlington, VA 22202; phone (703) 358-2104. The temporary movement of all parrots through Canada requires a CITES Temporary Import Certificate from the Canadian Wildlife Service. Contact Canadian Wildlife Service, Ottawa, ON K1A 0H3, phone (819) 997-1840.

Endangered species: With limited exception, all wildlife and wildlife products imported and exported from the United States must be declared to the U.S. Fish and Wildlife Service or the U.S. Customs Service. This applies to live animals as well as any recognizable by-product made of the fur, skin, feathers, bone, etc. of any wildlife (domestic dogs, cats, chickens, horses, etc. are exempted). The importation of certain animals and plants that are on the endangered species list is prohibited. Other species of wildlife, although not listed as endangered or threatened, require a permit in order to be lawfully transported to or through Canada. For example, U.S. citizens transporting carved ivory or parts of lynx, otter, brown/grizzly bear, black bear or wolf through Canada must first obtain a CITES export permit or Personal Effects Exemption Certificate from the U.S. Fish and Wildlife Service. Permits and certificates are available at the USF&WS Import/Export office in Anchorage, phone (907) 271-6198; the regional USF&WS office in Anchorage, phone (907) 786-3311; the Fairbanks Senior Resident Agent office in Fairbanks, phone (907) 456-0255; and several wildlife refuge offices in Alaska.

The importation of any marine mammal or its products is prohibited. Many of the shops selling walrus ivory handicrafts are able to issue certificates for walrus ivory upon request. To avoid the need for any permits or certificates, individuals should mail the items to the Lower 48 or take them with them in their personal luggage when flying back to the Lower 48.

Obtain all necessary permits before importing or exporting the species or products. Request a list of restricted items from the U.S. Fish and Wildlife Service's Import/Export office at (907) 271-6198, and the Convention Administrator, Canadian Wildlife Service, Environment Canada, Ottawa, ON K1A 0H3.

RE-ENTRY INTO THE UNITED STATES

It is, of course, the responsibility of the traveler to satisfy U.S. immigration authorities of his right to re-enter the United States.

Canadian immigration officers may caution persons entering from the United States if they may have difficulty in returning.

Re-entry to the United States can be simplified if you list all your purchases before you reach the border, keep sales receipts and invoices handy, and pack purchases separately.

Within 48 Hours: Residents of the United States visiting Canada for less than 48 hours may take back for personal or household use merchandise to the fair retail value of $200, free of U.S. duty and tax. Any or all of the following may be included, so long as the total value does not exceed $200; 50 cigarettes, 10 cigars (non-Cuban in origin), 4 ounces/150 ml of alcoholic beverages or alcoholic perfume.

If any article brought back is subject to duty or tax, or if the total value of all articles exceeds $200, no article may be exempted from duty or tax. Members of a family household are not permitted to combine the value of their purchases under this exemption.

Persons crossing the International Boundary at one point and re-entering the United States in order to travel to another part of Canada should inquire at U.S. customs regarding special exemption requirements.

After More Than 48 Hours: U.S. residents returning from Canada may take back, once every 30 days, merchandise for personal or household use to the value of $400 free of U.S. duty and tax, provided they have remained in Canada 48 hours. The exemption will be based on the fair retail value of the articles acquired, and goods must accompany the resident upon arrival in the United States. Members of a family household traveling together may combine their personal exemptions—thus a family of 5 would be entitled to a total exemption of $2,000.

Duty on goods valued at more than $400 but less than $1,000 is taxed at a flat rate of 10 percent.

Up to 100 cigars (non-Cuban in origin) per person may be imported duty-free into the United States by U.S. residents, and also 1 liter of alcoholic beverages if the resident has attained the age of 21 years, and up to 200 cigarettes.

Federal wildlife laws affect what U.S. citizens may bring back into the United States from Canada. The list is extensive, and U.S. visitors to Canada should be particularly aware that items purchased, found and/or received in Canada made from the following wildlife species are strictly prohibited from importation to the U.S.: marine mammals (including seals, whales, walrus, sea otters and polar bears); most wild birds (including hawks, owls, eagles, ravens and song birds) whether mounted, skins or feathers (except legally harvested migratory water fowl and game birds). Thus, an item that may be purchased legally in parts of Canada, such as a seal-fur doll, whale bone carving or walrus ivory carving, would be prohibited from importation to the United States. Also, be aware that wildlife parts and products, whether you bought, found or hunted them, may be restricted from Canadian export without a permit. For a complete list of restricted items and information on import permits, contact the nearest U.S. Fish and Wildlife Service office and/or the Fish and Wildlife Service, Import/Export office, phone (907) 271-6198.

Animals, including those taken out of the country and being returned, must have a valid veterinarian health certificate. Particularly, dogs must have proof of rabies vaccination.

For further information contact the nearest U.S. customs office or write U.S. Customs Service, Box 7407, Washington, D.C., 20229.

Daylight Hours

SUMMER MAXIMUM

	Sunrise	Sunset	Hrs. of daylight
Barrow	May 10	Aug. 2	84 days continuous
Fairbanks	2:59 A.M.	12:48 P.M.	21:49 hours
Anchorage	4:21 A.M.	11:42 P.M.	19:21 hours
Juneau	3:51 A.M.	10:09 P.M.	18:18 hours
Ketchikan	4:04 A.M.	9:32 P.M.	17:28 hours
Adak	6:27 A.M.	11:10 P.M.	16:43 hours

WINTER MINIMUM

	Sunrise	Sunset	Hrs. of daylight
Barrow	Jan. 24 noon	Nov. 18 noon	none
Fairbanks	10:59 A.M.	2:41 P.M.	3:42 hours
Anchorage	10:14 A.M.	3:42 P.M.	5:28 hours
Juneau	8:46 A.M.	3:07 P.M.	6:21 hours
Ketchikan	8:12 A.M.	3:18 P.M.	7:05 hours
Adak	9:52 A.M.	5:38 P.M.	7:46 hours

Disabled Visitor Services

Accommodations and other facilities (public and private) that are equipped for the traveler in a wheelchair are noted with the wheelchair icon &. Travelers should be aware, however, that not all facilities carrying this symbol may indeed be wheelchair accessible, and that facilities not carrying this icon may be wheelchair accessible. *The MILEPOST®* is in the process of adding this information to the logs. Readers can help by telling us about disabled visitor services.

For travel to and within Alaska, it is wise to call ahead. With prior notice, most forms of transportation and accommodations are able to facilitate travel, depending upon the flexibility of all parties involved. The Alaska Railroad, the Alaska Marine Highway, many coach services and cruise ships, and some taxi, charter boat and flightseeing services are equipped with wheelchair lifts and accessible restrooms. Some businesses offer sign language interpreters, typed transcripts of tours, discounts, ramps, closed caption service, elevators and other enablers. The number of tour companies catering to the disabled is increasing as well.

Alaska Public Lands Information Centers, phone (907) 271-2737 or TDD (907) 271-2738, offer a map and campgrounds guide listing wheelchair-accessible campsites and restrooms. APLIC can also provide Golden Age and Golden Access passes for senior citizens and qualifying persons with disabilities. Access Alaska, 3710 Woodland Dr., Suite 900, Anchorage, AK 99517-2564, phone (907) 248-4777, provides a free packet of information on accessible services and locations within Alaska.

Relay Alaska is a service of GCI, a long-distance telephone carrier certified by the Alaska Public Utilities Commission to provide Telecommunications Relay Service in Alaska. This service for persons with hearing and speech disabilities allows text and voice telephone users to communicate with each other through specially trained GCI assistants. For additional information, phone GCI (800) 770-2234 V/TTY or AT&T Alascom 0 (700) 889-6737. &

Driving Information

Driving to the North is no longer the ordeal it was in the early days. Those old images of the Alaska Highway with vehicles stuck in mud up to their hubcaps are far removed from the asphalt-surfaced Alaska Highway of today.

Motorists can still expect road construction and some rough road, but have patience! Ongoing projects like the Shakwak Highway Reconstruction Project on the Alaska Highway between Beaver Creek, YT, and the Alaska border, for example, are helping to improve severely deteriorated sections of road.

Highways in the North range from multi-laned paved freeways to 1-lane dirt and gravel roads. Major highways in Alaska are paved with the exception of the following highways that are at least partially gravel: Steese Highway (Alaska Route 6), Taylor Highway (Alaska Route 5), Elliott Highway (Alaska Route 2), Dalton Highway (Alaska Route 11) and Denali Highway (Alaska Route 8).

In Yukon Territory, the Alaska Highway, the Haines Highway and the Klondike Highway from Skagway to Dawson City are asphalt-surfaced. All other roads are either dust-controlled or gravel. NOTE: Highway reconstruction and straightening on the Alaska Highway in Yukon Territory has resulted in the displacement or absence of many kilometreposts.

Major routes through Alberta and British Columbia are paved, with the exception of the Cassiar Highway (BC Highway 37). Although almost completely paved or seal-coated, the Cassiar still has 81 miles/130 kms of gravel. It is an increasingly popular route for many Alaska travelers.

All highways within Northwest Territories are mostly gravel roads, although paving continues on many routes. Most gravel roads in the North are well-maintained and treated with calcium chloride as a dust-control measure (wash your vehicle as soon as practical).

RV owners should be aware of the height of their vehicles in metric measurements, as bridge heights in Canada are noted in meters.

Know your vehicle and its limitations. Some Northern roads may not be suitable for a large motorhome or trailer, but most roads will present no problem to a motorist who allots adequate time and uses common sense.

Also safeguard against theft while at campgrounds, rest stops or in the cities. Always lock your vehicle, be sure valuables are out of sight in an unattended vehicle and report any thefts to the authorities.

NOTE: Driving with the headlights on at all times is the law in Yukon Territory and on posted roads in Alaska.

AUTO PREPARATION

The following recommendations for driving in the North Country in summer are from our *MILEPOST®* field editors. One thing to keep in mind is the variable nature of road conditions: Some sections of road may be in poor condition because of construction or weather; other highways—particularly gravel roads closed in winter—may be either very rough or very smooth, depending on when maintenance crews last worked on the road. Another thing to remember is the wide range of roads in the North, from multi-laned freeways to narrow gravel roads. When driving paved rural highways, beware of "frost heaves" caused by subsidence of the ground under the road. The more remote roads, such as the Dempster or Dalton highways, are gravel. Motorists are much farther from assistance and more preparation is required for these roads.

There are some simple preparations that motorists can make for their trip North to make driving easier. First make sure your vehicle and tires are in good condition. An inexpensive and widely available item to include is a set of clear plastic headlight covers (or black metal matte screens). These protect your headlights from flying rocks and gravel. You might also consider a wire-mesh screen across the front of your vehicle to protect paint, grill and radiator from flying rocks. The finer the mesh, the more protection from flying gravel. For those hauling trailers, a piece of quarter-inch plywood fitted over the front of your trailer offers protection.

There is practically no way to protect the windshield, although some motorists have experimented with screen shields that do not seriously impair their vision. These are not recommended nor do you see many of them in the North, but it is, of course, up to the individual motorist whether these are worthwhile.

Crankcases are seldom damaged, but gas tanks can be harmed on rough gravel roads. Sometimes rocks work their way in between the plate and gas tank, wearing a hole in the tank. You may wish to insert a rubber mat between the gas tank and securing straps. However, drivers maintaining safe speeds should have no problems with punctured gas tanks. A high vehicle clearance is best for some of the rougher gravel roads.

Also keep in mind the simple precautions that make driving easier. A visor or tinted glass helps when you're driving into the sun. Good windshield wipers and a full windshield washer (or a bottle of wash and a squeegee) make life easier. Many motorists also find bug screens to be a wise investment.

Dust and mud are generally not a major problem on Northern roads, though you may run into both. Heavy rains combined with a gravel road or roadbed torn up for construction make mud. Mud flaps are suggested. Many gravel roads in the North (such as the Dalton Highway) are treated with calcium chloride as a dust-control measure. Because calcium chloride tends to eat into paint and metal parts on your vehicle, be sure to thoroughly wash your vehicle. Dust can seep into everything and it's difficult if not impossible to keep it out. Remember to close the windows on your trailer or camper when on a dusty road. It also helps to keep clothes, food and bedding in sealed plastic bags. Also check your air filter periodically.

Driving at slow, safe speeds not only keeps down the dust for drivers behind you, it also helps prevent you from spraying other vehicles with gravel.

Drive with your headlights on at all times. This allows you to be seen easier, especially in dusty conditions, or when approaching vehicles are driving into the sun. It is also the law in the Yukon and posted roads in Alaska.

NOTE: If driving on a paved surface, it is still necessary to observe "Loose Gravel" signs. Drive slowly.

Although auto shops in Northern com-

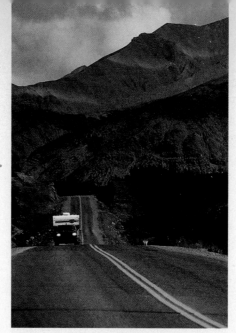

Drive with your headlights on at all times. (Earl L. Brown, staff)

munities are generally well-stocked with parts, carry the following for emergencies and on-the-spot repairs: flares; first-aid kit; trailer bearings; bumper jack with lug wrench; electrician's tape; assortment of nuts and bolts; fan belt; 1 or 2 spare tires (2 spares for remote roads); and a tool set including crescent wrenches, socket and/or open-end wrenches, hammer, screwdrivers, pliers, wire, and prybar for changing the fan belt.

If you are driving a vehicle which may require parts not readily available up North, add whatever you think necessary. You may wish to carry an extra few gallons of gas, water, and fluid for brakes, power steering and automatic transmissions.

If your vehicle should break down on the highway and tow truck service is needed, normally you will be able to flag down a passing motorist. Travelers in the North are generally helpful in such situations (traditionally, the etiquette of the country requires one to stop and provide assistance). If you are the only person traveling in the disabled vehicle, be sure to leave a note on your windshield indicating when you left the vehicle and in what direction you planned to travel.

GASOLINE

Unleaded gas is widely available in Alaska and is the rule in Canada. Diesel fuel is also commonly available. In Alaska, check with the Alaska State Troopers, and in Canada the RCMP or Visitor Information Centres, about fuel availability. Good advice for Northern travelers: gas-up whenever possible.

In the North as elsewhere, gas prices vary (see chart on page 8). Generally, gas prices are slightly higher in Canada and Alaska than the Lower 48, but this is not a hard and fast rule. You may find gas in Anchorage or elsewhere at the same price—or even lower—than at home. A general rule of thumb is the more remote the gas station, the higher the price. Gas prices may vary considerably from service station to service station within the same community.

It is a good idea to carry cash, since some gas stations in Alaska are independents and do not accept credit cards. Most Chevron, Texaco and Tesoro stations will accept VISA

or MasterCard. Also watch for posted gas prices that are for *cash*, but not noted as such. Besides double-checking the posted price before filling up, also ask the attendant which pump is for unleaded, regular or diesel, depending on what you want.

Keep in mind that Canadian gas stations have converted to the metric system; quantity and price are based on liters (see Gas Cost in U.S. Funds Per Gallon chart on page 8). There are 3.785 liters per U.S. gallon, 4.5 liters per imperial gallon. See Liters to Gallons conversion chart above.

INSURANCE

Auto insurance is mandatory in all Canadian provinces and territories. Drivers should carry adequate car insurance before entering the country. Visiting motorists are required to produce evidence of financial responsibility should they be involved in an accident. There is an automatic fine if visitors are involved in an accident and found to be uninsured. Your car could be impounded for this. Your insurance company should be able to provide you with proof of insurance coverage (request a Canadian Nonresident Interprovincial Motor Vehicle Liability Insurance Card) that would be accepted as evidence of financial responsibility.

The minimum liability insurance requirement in Canada is $200,000 Canadian, except in the Province of Quebec where the limit is $50,000 Canadian. Further information regarding automobile insurance in Canada may be obtained from The Insurance Bureau of Canada, 181 University Ave., Toronto, ON M5H 3M7. Phone (416) 362-2031 or fax (416) 362-2602.

TIRES

On gravel, the faster you drive, the faster your tires will wear out. So take it easy and you should have no tire problems, provided you have the right size for your vehicle, with the right pressure, not overloaded, and not already overly worn. Belted bias or radial ply tires are recommended for gravel roads.

Carry 1 good spare. Consider 2 spares if you are traveling remote gravel roads such as the Dempster or Dalton highways. The space-saver doughnut spare tires found in some passenger cars are not adequate for travel on gravel roads.

LITERS TO GALLONS					
Liters	Gallons	Liters	Gallons	Liters	Gallons
1	.3	21	5.5	41	10.8
2	.5	22	5.8	42	11.1
3	.8	23	6.1	43	11.4
4	1.1	24	6.3	44	11.6
5	1.3	25	6.6	45	11.9
6	1.6	26	6.9	46	12.2
7	1.8	27	7.1	47	12.4
8	2.1	28	7.4	48	12.7
9	2.4	29	7.7	49	12.9
10	2.6	30	7.9	50	13.2
11	2.9	31	8.2	51	13.5
12	3.2	32	8.5	52	13.7
13	3.4	33	8.7	53	14.0
14	3.7	34	9.0	54	14.3
15	4.0	35	9.2	55	14.5
16	4.2	36	9.5	56	14.8
17	4.5	37	9.8	57	15.0
18	4.8	38	10.0	58	15.3
19	5.0	39	10.3	59	15.6
20	5.3	40	10.6	60	15.9

For more precise conversion: 1 liter equals .2642 gallons; 1 gallon equals 3.785 liters.

RULES AND REGULATIONS

Regulations common to Alaska, Alberta, British Columbia, Northwest Territories and Yukon Territory include: Right turn on red permitted after complete stop, unless prohibited by sign; transporting open alcoholic beverage containers within a motor vehicle is prohibited.

Following are rules and regulations in effect in Alaska and northwestern Canada at our presstime:

ALASKA

Division of Motor Vehicles, Dept. of Public Safety, 5700 E. Tudor Rd., Anchorage, AK 99507; phone (907) 269-5551.

Road Condition Report: For summer road construction advisories in Southcentral Alaska, phone 24-hour rcorded roadwork hot line in Anchorage at (907) 273-6037 or toll-free (in Alaska) 1-800-478-7675; Internet www.dot.state.ak.us. If you are traveling to Fairbanks, Tok or Valdez, phone (907) 456-7623. In Southeast Alaska, phone (907) 465-2484.

Headlight use: One-half hour after sunset to one-half hour before sunrise. Driving with headlights on during all hours of the day is permitted. Headlights required at all times on designated roadways where speed is in excess of 45 mph.

Minimum driver's age: 16 years; 14 accompanied by a licensed driver 19 years or older, and driver's permit.

Rest area camping: Permitted as posted.

Studded tires: Permitted from Sept. 15 to May 1 (Sept. 30 to April 15 south of 60°N).

Motorcycles: Safety helmet required.

CB Radio: The following channels may be monitored: 2,9,11,14,19, 21 and 22.

Firearms: Permitted. Unlawful to discharge firearm on, from or across the driveable portion of any roadway including roadway shoulders.

ALBERTA

Alberta Transportation and Utilities, Twin Atria Building, 4999-98 Ave., Edmonton, AB T6B 2X3; phone (403) 427-7944, fax (403) 422-1070.

Road Condition Report: 1-800-642-3810 (in Alberta).

Headlight use: When light conditions restrict visibility to 500 feet/150m or less. Driving with headlights on during all hours of the day is permitted.

Minimum driver's age: 16 years; 14 to receive learner's permit.

Rest area camping: Prohibited unless otherwise designated.

Studded tires: Permitted year-round but only where marked or posted within federal parks.

Motorcycles: Safety helmet required.

CB Radio: Channel 9 is monitored for emergencies.

Firearms: Rifles must be unloaded and safely stored in trunk. Pistols must be carried in a secure storage box, unloaded, trigger locked and safely stored in trunk.

BRITISH COLUMBIA

Superintendent, Motor Vehicle Branch, 2631 Douglas St., Victoria, BC V8T 5A3; phone (250) 387-3140, fax (250) 387-1169.

Road Condition Report: For 24-hour detailed report (toll calls), phone 1-900-565-4997 in British Columbia; 1-900-451-4997 or (604) 420-4997 outside of British Columbia. Or call the Talking Yellow Pages in Victoria (250) 953-9000 ext. 7623; Vancouver (604)

299-9000 ext. 7623. For the Alaska Highway in British Columbia, phone (604) 774-7447.

Minimum driver's age: Driver's license divided into 6 classes—age 19 for class 1, 2 and 4; 18 for class 3; 16 for classes 5 and 6.

Rest area camping: Prohibited.

Studded tires: Permitted from Oct. 1 to April 30.

Motorcycles: Safety helmet required.

CB Radio: Not monitored for emergencies.

Firearms: All rifles and shotguns must be declared at the border. Pistols are prohibited; strictly enforced.

NORTHWEST TERRITORIES

Motor Vehicle Division, P.O. Box 1320, Yellowknife, X1A 2L9; phone (403) 873-7406, fax (403) 873-0120.

Road Condition Report: For the South Mackenzie, phone 1-800-661-0750 in NWT; for the North Mackenzie, 1-800-661-0752 in NWT.

Minimum driver's age: 16 years, 15 with learner's permit.

Rest area camping: Prohibited.

Studded tires: Tires that are manufactured as studded tires are permitted year-round for passenger vehicles.

Motorcycles: Safety helmet required for driver and passenger.

CB Radio: Channel 9 or 19 is monitored for emergencies.

Firearms: Contact the Canadian Firearms Centre, phone 1-800-731-4000.

YUKON TERRITORY

Dept. of Motor Vehicles, Box 2703, Whitehorse, YT Y1A 2C6; phone (403) 667-5315, fax (403) 393-6220.

Road Condition Report: (403) 667-8215.

Minimum driver's age: 16 years, 15 with learner's permit.

Rest area camping: Prohibited.

Studded Tires: No restrictions.

Motorcycles: Safety helmet required.

CB Radio: Channel 9 may be monitored for emergencies.

Firearms: No regulations on firearms in vehicles.

WINTER DRIVING

In addition to the usual precautions taken when driving in winter, such as keeping the windshield clear of ice, checking antifreeze and reducing driving speeds on icy pavement, equip your vehicle with the following survival gear: traction material (ashes, kitty litter, wood chips); chains (even with snow tires); first-aid kit; shovel, ice scrapper, flashlight, flares; fire extinguisher; extra warm clothing (including gloves and extra socks), blankets or sleeping bags; food; tools; and an extension cord to plug car into block heater. Other items which may be added to your survival gear are a tow rope or cable, ax, jumper cables and extra gas.

Extremely low temperatures occur in the North. A motorist may start out in -35° to -40°F weather and hit cold pockets along the road where temperatures drop to -60°F or more. If you do become stranded in weather like this, do not leave your vehicle; wait for aid. DO NOT attempt to drive unmaintained secondary roads or highways in winter (i.e. Denali Highway, Top of the World Highway), even if the roads look clear of snow.

Call ahead for road conditions and weather reports. See preceding Rules and Regulations for Road Conditions phone numbers. For recorded weather information

for the Alaska Highway in British Columbia, phone (604) 774-6461; for the Alaska Highway in Yukon, phone (403) 668-6061; and for the Alaska Highway in Alaska, phone (907) 456-7623 or (907) 883-5125.

Emergency Medical Services

Phone numbers of emergency medical services (if available), such as ambulance and hospital, are listed along with police and fire departments at the beginning of each town or city description in *The MILEPOST*®. Emergency medical services along highways are listed in the highway introductions.

In addition, travelers should note that CB Channels 9 and 11 are monitored for emergencies in most areas, Channels 14 and 19 in some areas. Recommendations for emergency equipment and a list of emergency medical services on Alaska's highways are detailed in a free brochure called *Help Along The Way*, available from the Emergency Medical Services Section, Division of Public Health, Dept. of Health and Social Services, Box 110616, Juneau 99811-0616.

Employment

It is a popular misconception that Alaska has a surplus of high-paying jobs. Work in many industries is seasonal, with long periods of inactivity. There is currently an oversupply of unskilled labor in Alaska, and adequate numbers of skilled and semi-skilled workers for present positions. Looking over the job situation during a vacation is a good approach. For more information write to the Alaska Dept. of Labor, P.O. Box 25509, Juneau, AK 99802; phone (907) 465-8900, Internet www.state.ak.us.

Fishing

Throughout *The MILEPOST*® you will find this ⬥ friendly little symbol. Wherever you see one, you will find a description of the fishing at that point.

Following is a brief summary of fishing license fees, rules and regulations for Alaska and Canada. It is not possible to list all the latest regulations in *The MILEPOST*®, so we urge you to obtain up-to-date information.

Alaska: A nonresident fishing license, valid for the calendar year issued, costs $50. A 1-day nonresident fishing license may be purchased for $10, a 3-day license for $15 and a 14-day license for $30. All anglers fishing for king salmon must also purchase a current year's king salmon tag. A 1-day tag is $10, a 3-day tag is $15 and 14-day/annual tag is $35. Nonresidents under 16 years of age do not need a fishing license or a king salmon tag. Alaska has no discount for senior citizens.

Resident sportfishing licenses cost $15; the king salmon tag is $10 for residents. A resident is a person who has maintained a permanent place of abode within the state for the previous 12 consecutive months and has continuously maintained his voting residence in the state, and any member of the military service who has been stationed in the state for the immediately preceding 12 months.

Nearly all sporting goods stores in Alaska sell fishing licenses. They may also be purchased through the mail by writing or calling the Alaska Dept. of Fish and Game, Licensing Section, Box 25526, Juneau 99802-5526, phone (907) 465-2376. For a variety of information, write the Division of Sport Fish at the above address; phone (907) 465-4180; Internet www.state.ak.us/local/akpages/FISH.GAME.adfghome.htm. You may contact any regional Sport Fish office throughout Alaska. Be sure you have the most recent edition of the ADF&G regulations booklets for information on bag limits and special permits. The state has 5 separate regional booklets.

The Bureau of Land Management has a free brochure, "Alaska Freshwater Fishing" featuring fishing opportunities on BLM-managed public lands. To request the brochure, contact the BLM, 1150 University Ave., Fairbanks, AK 99709-3899, phone (907) 494-2251.

Canada: A special fishing license is necessary for fishing in Canadian national parks and is good for the entire season in all national parks. These are on sale at park gates.

Alberta: Annual nonresident license (season), $36; limited (5-day) nonresident, $24. Licenses not required for anglers under 16 or residents 65 years of age or more.

British Columbia: Annual nonresident, non-Canadian angler's license, $40; nonresident short-term fishing license, valid for 1 or 8 consecutive days and not valid for steelhead fishing, $10 or $25 respectively. Licenses not required for nonresident anglers under 16 years of age who are accompanied by someone with a license. Special permits required for steelhead and for nonresident fishing lakes and streams classified as "Special Water." Freshwater and saltwater fishing licenses are required of all anglers 16 and older; both are renewable on March 31.

Northwest Territories: Annual nonresident fishing license (season), $40; 3-day nonresident license, $30. Nonresident anglers under 16 years of age do not need a license when accompanied by a licensed angler. Fishing licenses are available from the visitor information center at the Alberta–Northwest Territories border on the Mackenzie Highway and in most communities from hardware and sporting goods stores, fishing lodges, RCMP and government wildlife offices.

Yukon Territory: Season fishing license fee for a nonresident is $35, or $20 for 6 days. A 1-day nonresident license is also available for $5. Canadian resident season fee is $25, $15 for 6 days and $5 for one day. All persons 16 years of age or over must have a license.

Gold Panning

If you are interested in gold panning, sluicing or suction dredging in Alaska—whether for fun or profit—you'll have to know whose land you are on and familiarize yourself with current regulations. Recreational gold panning is allowed on some state and federal lands. Regulations on use of gold pans and hand shovels, nonmechanized sluice boxes and suction dredges vary depending on where you are.

Throughout Alaska, there are 2 sets of mining regulations to be familiar with—state and federal. Free pamphlets describing the respective requirements of each can be obtained from the Bureau of Land Manage-

ment. Contact them at: 222 W. 7th Ave. #13, Anchorage, AK 99513-7599, phone (907) 271-5960 or 1150 University Ave., Fairbanks, AK 99709-3899, phone (907) 474-2251. Also contact the Alaska Public Lands Information centers

Panning, sluicing and suction dredging on private property, established mining claims or Native lands is considered trespassing unless you have the consent of the owner.

You can pan for gold for a small fee by visiting one of the commercial gold panning resorts in Alaska and the Yukon. These include Crow Creek Mine (off Alyeska Access Road, see SEWARD HIGHWAY section); Gold Dredge No. 8 near Fairbanks (see STEESE HIGHWAY section); Little El Dorado, also near Fairbanks (see ELLIOTT HIGHWAY section); and GuggieVille and commercial operations on Bonanza Creek Road outside Dawson City, YT (see the KLONDIKE LOOP section). These resorts rent gold pans and let you try your luck in gold-bearing creeks and streams on their property.

In 1997, look for events throughout the North celebrating the centennial of the discovery of gold in the Klondike.

Hiking

The Alaska Public Lands Information Center, 605 W. 4th, Anchorage, AK 99501, has general information on hiking in all of the National Park Service–administered national parks, preserves and monuments in Alaska.

The State Division of Parks and Outdoor Recreation has hiking opportunities in several parks. Chena River State Recreation Area, Denali State Park, Chugach State Park and Kachemak Bay State Park each offer several miles of trails. For brochures to any of these 4 parks, contact the Dept. of Natural Resources Public Information Center, Alaska State Park Information, 3601 C Street, Suite 200, Anchorage, AK 99503-5929, phone (907) 269-8400. For visitors to Anchorage, Chugach State Park offers nearby, easily accessible wilderness for day hikes and wildlife viewing.

U.S. Fish and Wildlife Service, 1011 E. Tudor Road, Anchorage, AK 99503, has brochures about the 16 wildlife refuges throughout the state. Only 2 Alaska refuges are accessible by road.

The Bureau of Land Management, 1150 University Ave., Fairbanks, AK 99709-3899, phone (907) 474-2251, has brochures on hiking trails and areas, and opportunities in a national recreation area.

The USDA Forest Service Supervisor and District Ranger offices have trail maps and detailed information on hiking trails in Tongass and Chugach national forests.

An extensive system of hiking trails on the Kenai Peninsula is maintained by the Glacier and Seward Ranger districts of the Chugach National Forest. The most popular trail is the Resurrection Pass trail, a 38.6-mile/62.1-km trail that follows Resurrection Creek from Hope up Resurrection Pass then down Juneau Creek to the Sterling Highway. Other popular Kenai Peninsula trails are Johnson Pass, Crow Pass, Russian Lakes and Ptarmigan Creek. There are public-use cabins along many of the trails; these must be reserved in advance. Check trail conditions before hiking. Many trails may have been damaged by flooding or other natural events,

and may still be under repair. For general information, write Chugach National Forest, 3301 C St., Suite 300, Anchorage, AK 99503. (For specific information on trails and cabins in Chugach and Tongass national forests, see area office addresses in Cabins this section.)

Yukon Territory has established wilderness trails, too. Information about hiking in Kluane National Park Reserve is available from Parks Canada, Canadian Heritage, 300 Main St., Room 105, Whitehorse, YT Y1A 2B5. For other hiking trails in the Yukon contact Tourism Yukon, Box 2703, Whitehorse, YT Y1A 2C6, phone (403) 667-5340.

Holidays–1997

The following list of observed holidays in Alaska and Canada can help you plan your trip. Keep in mind that banks and other agencies may be closed on these holidays and traffic may be heavier.

ALASKA

New Year's Day	Jan. 1
Martin Luther King Day	Jan. 15
Presidents' Day	Feb. 17
Seward's Day	March 24
Easter Sunday	March 30
Memorial Day	May 26
Independence Day	July 4
Labor Day	Sept. 1
Columbus Day	Oct. 13
Alaska Day	Oct. 18
Veterans Day	Nov. 11
Thanksgiving Day	Nov. 27
Christmas Day	Dec. 25

CANADA

New Year's Day	Jan. 1
Yukon Heritage Day	Feb. 28
Good Friday	March 28
Easter Monday	March 31
Victoria Day	May 19
Canada Day	July 1
Alberta Heritage Day	Aug. 4
British Columbia Day	Aug. 4
Discovery Day (YT)	Aug. 18
Labour Day	Sept. 1
Thanksgiving Day	Oct. 13
Remembrance Day	Nov. 11
Christmas Day	Dec. 25
Boxing Day	Dec. 26

Hostels

In Alaska, there are 9 AYH (American Youth Hostels) hostels. They are located in Anchorage, Seward, Juneau, Delta Junction, Girdwood, Ketchikan, Ninilchik, Palmer, Sheep Mountain, Sitka and Tok. Other private hostel-style accommodations are available throughout the state.

In Canada, Hostelling International–Canada (HI-C) has 75 hostels coast to coast, with more than a dozen each in Alberta and British Columbia. Yukon Territory has 1 hostel, the Dawson City River hostel in Dawson City. Many hostels in Canada accept advance reservations and payment by credit card. Check with regional hostelling offices or any gateway hostel for details. Keep in mind that you should have a valid hostelling membership from the hostelling association in your own country before you visit Canada. Once in Canada, you can get a free copy of the Hostelling North America official guide to hostels in both Canada and the United States.

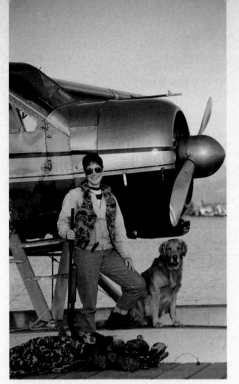

Fly-in hunting trips are common in Alaska. (© Barbara Willand)

For further information, write Hostelling International–Anchorage, 700 H St., Anchorage 99501, phone (907) 276-3635; Hostelling International–U.S.A., Box 37613, Washington, DC 20013-7613, phone (202) 783-6161; Hostelling International–Canada, National Office, 205 Catherine St., Suite 400, Ottawa, ON K2P 1C3, (613) 237-7884.

Hunting

Obtain up-to-date information on fees, licenses, seasons, bag limits and regulations from the following government agencies for Alaska, Alberta, British Columbia, Northwest Territories and Yukon Territory.

Alaska: Alaska Dept. of Fish and Game, Box 25526, Juneau, AK 99802. A complete list of registered Alaska guides is available for $5 from the Dept. of Commerce and Economic Development, Division of Occupational Licensing, Box 110806, Juneau 99811-0806.

Alberta: Environmental Protection Branch, Information Centre, 9920 108 St., Edmonton, AB T5K 2M4.

British Columbia: Fish and Wildlife Branch, Ministry of Environment, 780 Blanshard St., Victoria, BC V8V 1X4.

Northwest Territories: Dept. of Economic Development and Tourism, Tourism Development and Marketing, Box 1320, Yellowknife, NT X1A 2L9, phone 1-800-661-0788.

Yukon Territory: Yukon Government, Dept. of Renewable Resources, Fish and Wildlife Branch, P.O. Box 2703, Whitehorse, YT Y1A 2C6, phone (403) 667-5221.

Information Sources

Contact the following state and provincial tourism agencies and private associations for free maps and brochures and for travel-related questions.

Alaska: Alaska Division of Tourism, Box 110801, Juneau 99811-0801, phone (907) 465-2010.

Alaska Campground Owners Assoc., P.O. Box 100746, Anchorage, AK 99510; phone (907) 349-1601, fax (907) 349-8010.

Alaska Native Tourism Council, 1577 C Street, Suite 304, Anchorage, AK 99501; phone (907) 274-5400.

Alaska Wilderness Recreation & Tourism Assoc., P.O. Box 22827, Juneau, AK 99802; phone (907) 463-3038, fax (907) 463-3280.

Bed & Breakfast Association of Alaska, (907) 272-5909.

Alberta: Travel Alberta, 3rd Floor, 10155 102 St., Edmonton, AB T5J 4G8, phone 1-800-661-8888.

British Columbia: Tourism British Columbia, Parliament Building, Victoria, BC V8V 1X4, phone 1-800-663-6000.

Northwest Territories: Dept. of Economic Development and Tourism, Tourism Development and Marketing, Box 1320, Yellowknife, NT X1A 2L9, phone 1-800-661-0788.

Yukon Territory: Tourism Yukon, Box 2703, Whitehorse, YT Y1A 2C6, phone (403) 667-5340; Internet: www.touryukon.com.

Wilderness Tourism Assoc. of the Yukon, P.O. Box 3960, Whitehorse, YT Y1A 3M6; phone (403) 668-3180.

Maps

Best source for topographic maps is the U.S. Geological Survey. USGS topographic maps are available in scales. For Alaska, the standard scale is 1:63, 360, 15 minute series, 1-inch to 1 mile. Maps are available by mail from the USGS Distribution Section, Box 25286, Federal Center, Denver, CO 80225. Write for an index of maps for Alaska; the index shows available topographic maps, quadrangle location, name and survey date. (The index and a booklet describing topographic maps are free.)

Sales counters are maintained at USGS offices throughout the country; check the phone book to see if there's an office near you. In Alaska, USGS maps may be purchased over the counter or through the mail from the USGS office located at 4230 University Dr., Room 101, Anchorage, AK 99508-4664, phone (907) 786-7011, fax (907) 786-7050. The cost is $4 per map, plus $3.50 shipping/handling per order. Alaska map indexes are also available at no charge. Many commercial dealers also sell USGS maps.

Chugach National Forest maps are available for a small fee from the USDA Forest Service, 3301 C St., Suite 300, Anchorage 99503. Tongass National Forest maps are available from the USDA Forest Service, Box 21628, Juneau 99802. The Alaska Natural History Assoc., 605 W. 4th Ave. Suite 85, Anchorage, AK 99501, also carries Chugach and Tongass National Forest maps, as well as USGS and other recreational maps.

Topographic maps of Canada are available from the Canada Map Office, 130 Bentley Ave., Nepean, ON K1A 0E9. Index maps showing the published topographic maps are available free of charge: Eastern Canada–Index 1, Western Canada–Index 2, Northern Canada–Index 3. Also available is a list of authorized topographic map dealers for each province.

Metric System

Canada has converted to the metric system. Inches have been replaced with centimeters, feet and yards with meters, miles with kilometers and Fahrenheit with Celsius. Miles, feet, yards and temperatures in all sections of *The MILEPOST®* are followed by the equivalent metric measure. (Equivalents are: 1 mile=1.609 kilometers; 1 kilometer=0.62 miles; 1 yard=0.9144 meters; 1 meter=39.37 inches.) See the chart below.

METRIC CONVERSIONS
Temperatures, distance and speed limits

Fahrenheit	Celsius	Miles = Kilometers		Kilometers = Miles	
122°	50°	1	1.6	1	0.6
120°	49°	2	3.2	2	1.2
110°	43°	3	4.8	3	1.9
104°	40°	4	6.4	4	2.5
100°	38°	5	8.0	5	3.1
90°	32°	6	9.6	6	3.7
86°	30°	7	11.3	7	4.3
80°	27°	8	12.9	8	5.0
70°	21°	9	14.5	9	5.6
68°	20°	10	16.1	10	6.2
60°	16°	20	32.2	20	12.4
50°	10°	30	48.3	30	18.6
40°	4°	40	64.4	40	24.8
32°	0°	50	80.5	50	31.1
30°	-1°	60	96.5	60	37.3
20°	-7°	70	112.6	70	43.5
14°	-10°	80	128.7	80	49.7
10°	-12°	90	144.8	90	55.9
0°	-18°	100	160.9	100	62.1
-4°	-20°				
-10°	-23°				
-20°	-29°				
-22°	-30°				
-30°	-34°				
-40°	-40°				

Kilometers Per Hour 30 50 70 90 100
Miles Per Hour 20 30 40 55 60

Money/Credit Cards

The money system in Canada is based on dollars and cents, but the Canadian dollar and the American dollar are separate currencies and the rate of exchange varies. U.S. currency is accepted as payment in Canada, but the best advice for visitors is: exchange your currency for Canadian funds at a bank in Canada. The visitor is then assured of receiving the rate of exchange prevailing on that day. Although businesses in Canada will accept American dollars, they will often give a lower rate of exchange than banks or no exchange rate. However, businesses in some Yukon Territory communities such as Whitehorse participate in the Fair Exchange Program, in which they provide travelers with an exchange rate within 4 percent of the banks.

As you travel north, away from the more populated areas, you will find banks located only in the major cities. Smaller communities may be served by traveling banks or banks open only 1 to 3 days a week for limited hours. Banks in Whitehorse and Dawson City, YT, Yellowknife, NT, and major Alaskan cities are open generally 10 A.M. to 3 P.M. weekdays (open until 6 P.M. on Friday). Also, some Canadian holidays differ from U.S. holidays; see list under Holidays in this section.

Major American bank and credit cards, including most oil company cards and those of retailers who do business in both countries, are accepted in Canada. Credit card purchases are billed at the U.S. dollar equivalent of the Canadian price at the full exchange rate for the day of billing.

Many cities in Alaska and Canada have automated teller machines (ATMs). The MasterCard/Cirrus ATM Network, for example, lists ATMs in 32 Alaska cities, from Ketchikan to Nome, and numerous cities in Alberta and British Columbia. In Yukon Territory, there are ATMs in Whitehorse, Dawson and Watson Lake, and Northwest Territories shows 3 (Fort Smith, Inuvik and Yellowknife).

To find the ATM nearest you, or for a global directory of ATMs, phone 1-800-THE-PLUS.

It is a good idea to carry cash, since some gas stations in Alaska are independents and do not accept oil company credit cards or major-bank credit cards.

Tourists to Canada may be eligible for a rebate on the Goods and Services Tax (GST) paid on certain goods and short-term accommodation. Short-term means accommodation for no more than 30 days at any 1 location. The purchase must be for a minimum of $100 to qualify for a refund. You must keep all receipts and tax mut be greater than $3.50 per receipt to receive refund. Check with tourism or customs authorities for more information.

Mosquitoes

Mosquitoes emerge from hibernation before the snow has entirely disappeared. They peak in about June but continue to harass humans through the fall. Mosquitoes are especially active in the early morning and at dusk. Mosquitoes hatch their eggs in water, so the North—with its marshy tundra and many lakes—is a good breeding ground.

The female mosquito penetrates the skin with a hollow snout to draw blood to nourish her eggs. Mosquito saliva, injected into the wound, is what causes the itch, redness and swelling. Mosquitoes rely on their antennae to smell and are attracted to warmth, moisture, carbon dioxide and dark colors, among other things. Mosquitoes fly into the wind, relying on their senses to pick up a potential meal. They then must home in to within a few inches of the object to determine if it is a good meal. Insect repellents work by jamming the mosquitoes' sensors so they can't tell if you are a meal.

You can't plan your summer vacation around the mosquito. You can take steps to avoid them. The USDA recommends a lightweight parka, tight fitting at the wrists, with a drawstring hood fit snugly around the face, and trousers tucked securely in socks, to reduce biting. Mosquitoes can bite through thin material (such as a cotton shirt), so wear some heavier protection when and where mosquitoes are active. Choose a campsite away from mosquito-breeding areas. According to the USDA, a 5 mph wind velocity grounds most mosquitoes, so locating your campsite where you'll catch a breeze also helps.

According to the USDA, mosquito repellents containing diethyl-meta-toluamide (DEET) are most effective. Make sure you apply repellent to all exposed skin, including hands, ears and feet.

National Parks, Preserves and Monuments

The Alaska National Interest Lands Conservation Act, passed in December 1980, placed more than 97 million acres into new or expanded national parks, monuments, preserves and wildlife refuges. Denali and Glacier Bay national parks and preserves are covered in detail in *The MILEPOST®*. For general information on all of Alaska's national and state parks, refuges and forests, contact the Alaska Public Lands Information Centers either in Anchorage, AK at 605 W. 4th Ave., Suite 105, Anchorage 99510, phone (907) 271-2737; Fairbanks, AK at 250 Cushman St., Suite 1A, Fairbanks 99701, phone (907) 456-0527; Tok at Box 359, Tok, AK 99780, phone (907) 883-5667; or Ketchikan at 50 Main St., Ketchikan, AK 99901, phone (907) 228-6219.

Pets

Many people travel to the North with their pets, and it is generally not a problem. Keep your pet in your vehicle at highway businesses; local dogs can be aggressive. Also, never approach a chained village dog.

You must have a veterinarian health certificate for your pet to cross the U.S.–Canada border. See Customs Requirements in this section.

Keep your dog on a leash, both for its safety and as a courtesy to other travelers. Dogs are not allowed on national park hiking trails and must be on a leash near your vehicle or confined in your vehicle elsewhere in national parks. Some hotels and motels accept pets, others do not.

Do have identification on your pet should it get lost. However, the best idea is to keep your pet on a leash. There is a great deal of wilderness up North and the chances of recovering a lost dog are slim.

Also keep in mind that not all communities in the North have a resident veterinarian. Pet emergency phone numbers are listed in some places in *The MILEPOST®*.

If you are traveling with your pet on the Alaska state ferry, read the information on pets in the MARINE ACCESS ROUTES section.

Police

Alaska: The Alaska State Troopers are the primary police force in Alaska, and there are city police departments in each of the towns. You will find their phone numbers listed throughout *The MILEPOST®*.

Canada: The Royal Canadian Mounted Police (RCMP) is the primary police force and public safety organization throughout western Canada, although cities and towns in Alberta and British Columbia have their own city or municipal police department. If you are involved in an automobile accident within the city limits of a town in British Columbia, for instance, report the accident to the city police. Outside a city, you should report to the RCMP. The RCMP is the only police force in Yukon Territory and Northwest Territories.

The RCMP plays a major role in relaying urgent messages to visitors; if you need to locate someone in Canada, contact them.

Postal Rates

Alaska: Rates are the same as for all other U.S. states.

Canada: Rates at press time were 45¢ first class (30 grams, about 1 ounce) within Canada, and 52¢ (30 grams) to the United States. U.S. postage stamps may not be used for mailings sent from Canada.

Shipping

Vehicles: Carriers that will ship cars, campers, trailers and motorhomes from Anchorage to Seattle include: Alaska Railroad, Box 107500, Anchorage, AK 99510-7500, phone (907) 265-2490; Alaska Vehicle Transport, Inc., phone 1-800-422-7925; Sea–Land Freight Service, Inc., 1717 Tidewater Ave., Anchorage, AK 99501, phone 1-800-478-2671 or (907) 274-2671; and Totem Ocean Trailer Express (TOTE), 2511 Tidewater, Anchorage, AK 99501, phone (907) 276-5868 or toll free 1-800-234-8683.

In the Seattle, WA, area, contact A.A.D.A. Systems, Box 2323, Auburn 98071, phone (206) 762-7840 or 1-800-929-2773; Alaska Railroad, 2203 Airport Way S., Suite 215, Seattle, WA 98134, phone (206) 624-4234 or in Washington, 35050 Pacific Hightway S., Federal Way, WA 98003, phone (206) 874-9919; Sea–Land Service, Inc., 3600 Port of Tacoma Road, Tacoma, WA 98424, phone (206) 593-8100 or 1-800-426-4512 (outside the Tacoma area); or Totem Ocean Trailer Express (TOTE), Box 24908, Seattle, WA 98124, phone (206) 628-9280 or 1-800-426-0074.

Vehicle shipment between southeastern Alaska and Seattle is provided by Alaska Marine Lines, 5615 W. Marginal Way SW, Seattle, WA 98106, phone (206) 763-4244 or toll free (800) 950-4AML (direct service to Ketchikan, Wrangell, Prince of Wales Island, Kake, Petersburg, Sitka, Juneau, Haines,

Skagway, Yakutat, Excursion Inlet and Hawk Inlet). Boyer Alaska Barge Line, 7318 4th Ave. S., Seattle, WA 98108, phone (206) 763-8575 (serves Ketchikan, Metlakatla, Prince of Wales Island and Wrangell).

Persons shipping vehicles between Seattle/Tacoma and Anchorage are advised to shop around for the carrier that offers the services and rates most suited to the shipper's needs. Not all carriers offer year-round service, and freight charges vary greatly depending upon the carrier and the length and height of the vehicle. Rates increase frequently and the potential shipper is cautioned to call carriers' rate departments for those rates in effect at shipping time. An approximate sample fare from Seattle/Tacoma to Anchorage to ship a 4-door sedan one-way is $1,141; for a truck, you might pay $1,332. From Anchorage to Seattle/Tacoma, it is approximately $738 for a vehicle and $919 to ship a truck.

Not all carriers accept rented moving trucks and trailers, and a few of those that do, require authorization from the rental company to carry its equipment to Alaska. Check with the carrier and your rental company before booking service.

Book your reservation at least 2 weeks in advance and 3 weeks during summer months, and prepare to have the vehicle at the carrier's loading facility 2 days prior to sailing. Carriers differ on what non-vehicle items they allow to travel inside, from nothing at all to goods packaged and addressed separately. Coast Guard regulations forbid the transport of vehicles holding more than one-quarter tank of gas, and none of the carriers listed above allow owners to accompany their vehicles in transit. Remember to have fresh antifreeze installed in your car or truck prior to sailing!

You may ship your vehicle aboard a state ferry to southeastern ports (at a lesser rate), however, you must accompany your vehicle or arrange for someone to drive it on and off the ferry at departure and arrival ports. See MARINE ACCESS ROUTES section.

Household Goods and Personal Effects: Most moving van lines have service to and from Alaska through their agency connections in most Alaska and Lower 48 cities. To initiate service contact the van line agents nearest your origin point.

Northbound goods are shipped to Seattle and transferred through a port agent to a water vessel for carriage to Alaska. Few shipments go over the road to Alaska. Southbound shipments are processed in a like manner through Alaska ports to Seattle, then on to destination.

U-Haul provides service into the North Country for those who prefer to move their goods themselves. There are 53 U-Haul dealerships in Alaska and northwestern Canada for over-the-road service. In Alaska, there are 8 dealerships in Anchorage, 6 in Fairbanks, 2 in Soldotna, 2 in Eagle River and 1 in each of the following communities: Homer, Juneau, Ketchikan, Delta Junction, Kenai, Palmer, Petersburg, Seward, Tok, Valdez, Wasilla, Sitka and North Pole. In Canada, there are dealerships and ready stations in Dawson City (summer only), Fort St. John, Fort Nelson, Whitehorse and at other locations along the Alaska Highway. There is a dealership in Watson Lake, YT. There are also breakdown stations for service of U-Haul vehicles in Beaver Creek, Swift River and the Kluane Wilderness Area.

It's also possible to ship a rented truck or trailer into southeastern Alaska aboard the water carriers that accept privately owned vehicles (see Shipping Vehicles). A few of the water carriers sailing between Seattle and Anchorage also carry rented equipment. However, shop around for this service, for this has not been common practice in the past, and rates can be very high if the carrier does not yet have a specific tariff established for this type of shipment. You will not be allowed to accompany the rented equipment. Be aware, however, that U-Haul allows its equipment to be shipped on TOTE or Sea-Land, resulting in a 30 percent savings over the price of driving it between Seattle and Anchorage.

Telecommunications

Area Codes: Following are telephone area codes for Alaska and western Canada: **Alaska** (907); **Alberta** (403); **British Columbia** (604) for Vancouver and Lower Mainland area (including Hope, Whistler and Powell River areas), (250) rest of province; **Northwest Territories** (403) for communities included in *The MILEPOST*®, changes to (867) in October 1997; **Yukon Territory** (403) changes to (867) in October 1997.

CB Radio: There is no standard or uniform channel in Alaska for general communication with others. Often RVers, if caravanning, will select a channel. CB Channels 9 and 11 may be monitored for emergencies in most areas, Channels 14 and 19 in other areas.

Cell phone: Cell phone coverage is available in Alaska and northwestern Canada, though readers have noted that outside of major communities, coverage is unreliable.

Internet: *The MILEPOST*® includes Internet addresses where available. Generally we will not include "http://" with World Wide Web addresses in editorial.

Telegrams: Telegrams, cablegrams, mailgrams, telex and fax can be sent by telephone from anywhere in Alaska through Western Union. Money transfers can also be sent and received within 15 minutes through Western Union agencies, many with extended hours of operation. Western Union branch offices are located throughout the state and continental United States. To find the Western Union location nearest you, and for hours of operation, phone 1-800-325-6000.

Persons wishing to send telegrams to or from Canada, as well as needing money transfer services, should contact the offices of Western Union at 1-800-325-6000 (the number is valid from the United States and Canada).

Time Zones

All of Alaska is on Alaska time, or 1 hour earlier than Pacific time, except for the 4 western Aleutian Island communities of Atka, Adak, Shemya and Attu, which are on Aleutian–Hawaii time (2 hours earlier than Pacific time).

British Columbia is on Pacific time (daylight saving time in summer), the same as Yukon Territory, except for the area around Dawson Creek and Fort St. John and south from Valemount through Cranbrook, which are on Mountain time. All of Alberta and western Northwest Territories are on Mountain time and observe daylight saving time.

Water

Purify all surface water that is to be used for drinking or cooking. Northern lakes, streams and rivers may be contaminated by the Giardia organism, which can cause the intestinal disorder giardiasis. Giardiasis is characterized by diarrhea, gas, loss of appetite, abdominal cramps and bloating. These symptoms may appear from a few days to a few weeks after ingestion of the organism. To purify water, boil for at least 10 minutes at a full rolling boil. It is a good idea to treat even piped water at campgrounds to be on the safe side. Iodine and chlorine tablets are not effective unless the water is first filtered and allowed to stand for half an hour.

It is also recommended that travelers carry drinking water, and refill containers at safe sources whenever available. RV travelers should consider carrying buckets and funnels for filling tanks at campgrounds with non-standard water faucets.

Swimmers should inquire locally before taking a dip in any gravel pits or roadside lakes. Some of the northern ponds are host to the larvae of schistosomes, which cause "swimmer's itch." Symptoms are redness and itching of the skin, beginning immediately and lasting up to a week.

When to go/What to wear

One of the most often asked questions is "when is the best time to travel?" The high season is June through August, generally the warmest and sunniest months in the North, although July is often one of the wettest months in some regions. The weather is as variable and unpredictable in the North as anywhere else (see Climate Averages chart below). Go prepared for sunny hot days and cold rainy days. Waterproof footwear is always a good idea, as are a warm coat and rain gear. Generally, dress is casual. Comfortable shoes and easy-care clothes are best. There are stores in the North—just like at home—where you can buy whatever you forgot to bring along. There are laundromats (some with showers) in most communities and dry cleaners in the major cities and some smaller towns.

Because most people travel in the summer, filling up hotels, motels, campgrounds and ferries, you might consider an early spring (April or May) or fall (late August into October) trip. There's usually more room at the lodges and campgrounds and on the ferries in these shoulder seasons. The weather can also be quite beautiful in early spring and in the fall. Keep in mind that some tours, attractions, lodges and other businesses operate seasonally. Check the advertisements in *The MILEPOST*® for details on months of operation or call ahead if in doubt.

Normally, May through October is the best time to drive to Alaska. A severe winter or wet spring may affect road conditions and there may be some rough road (especially on highways that are closed in winter) until road maintenance crews get out to upgrade and repair. Motels, hotels, gas stations and restaurants are open year-round in the cities and on many highways. On more remote routes, such as the Cassiar Highway, not all businesses are open year-round. Check ahead for accommodations and gas if traveling these roads in winter.

ZIP Codes in Alaska

Afognak 99697
Akhiok 99615
Akiachak ....■99551
Akiak 99552
Akutan 99553
Alakanuk 99554
Aleknagik 99555
Alexander Creek 99695
Alifak 99697
Allakaket 99720
Ambler 99786
Amook 99697
Anaktuvuk Pass 99721
Anchor Point 99556
Anchorage:
　General Delivery 99501
　See street listings in
　official ZIP code directory.
Anderson 99744
Angoon 99820
Aniak 99557
Anvik 99558
Arctic Village 99722
Atka 99547
Atmautluak 99559
Attu 99502
Auke Bay 99821
Baranof 99850
Barrow 99723
Beaver 99724
Bell Island 99950
Bethel 99559
Bettles Field 99726
Big Lake 99652
Bird Creek 99540
Border 99764
Brevig Mission 99785
Buckland 99727
Cantwell 99729
Cape Pole 99950
Cape Yakataga 99695
Central 99730
Chalkyitsik 99788
Chatham 99850
Chefornak 99561
Chevak 99563
Chickaloon 99674
Chicken 99732
Chignik 99564
Chignik Lagoon 99565
Chignik Lake 99548
Chisana 99790
Chitina 99566
Chuathbaluk 99557
Chugiak 99567
Circle 99733
Clam Gulch 99568
Clarks Point 99569
Clear 99704
Coffman Cove 99918
Cold Bay 99571
Coldfoot 99701
College 99701
　P.O. Boxes 99708
Cooper Landing 99572
Copper Center 99573
Cordova 99574
Craig 99921
Crooked Creek 99575
Deep Bay 99950
Deering 99736
Delta Junction ....■99737
Denali National Park 99755
Dillingham 99576
Dolomi 99950
Dot Lake 99737
Douglas 99824
Driftwood Bay 99695
Dutch Harbor ....■99692
Eagle 99738
Eagle River 99577
Eek 99578

Egegik 99579
Eielson AFB 99702
Ekuk 99695
Ekwok 99580
Elfin Cove 99825
Elim 99739
Elmendorf AFB 99506
Emmonak 99581
English Bay 99603
Ester 99725
Excursion Inlet 99850
Fairbanks:
　General Delivery 99701
　See street listings in
　official ZIP code directory.
False Pass 99583
Farewell 99695
Fire Cove 99950
Flat 99584
Fort Richardson 99505
Fort Wainwright 99703
Fort Yukon 99740
Fortuna Ledge 99585
Funter Bay 99850
Gakona 99586
Galena 99741
Gambell 99742
Girdwood 99587
Glennallen 99588
Gold Creek 99695
Golovin 99762
Goodnews Bay 99589
Grayling 99590
Gulkana 99695
Gustavus 99826
Haines 99827
Halibut Cove 99603
Happy Harbor 99950
Hawk Inlet 99850
Healy 99743
Holy Cross 99602
Homer 99603
Hoonah 99829
Hooper Bay 99604
Hope 99605
Houston 99694
Hughes 99745
Huslia 99746
Hydaburg 99922
Hyder 99923
Icy Bay 99695
Igiugig 99613
Iliamna 99606
Indian 99540
Ivanoff Bay 99695
Juneau:
　General Delivery 99801
　See street listings in
　official ZIP code directory.
Kake 99830
Kaktovik 99747
Kalskag 99607
Kaltag 99748
Karluk 99608
Kasaan 99950
Kasigluk 99609
Kasilof 99610
Kasitsna Bay 99695
Kenai 99611
Kenny Cove 99695
Ketchikan 99901
Kiana 99749
King Cove 99612
King Salmon 99613
Kipnuk 99614
Kitoi Bay 99697
Kivalina 99750
Klawock 99925
Kobuk 99751
Kodiak ....■99615
Kokhanok 99606
Koliganek 99576
Kongiganak 99559
Kotlik 99620
Kotzebue ....■99752

Koyuk 99753
Koyukuk 99754
Kwethluk 99621
Kwigillingok 99622
Lab Bay 99950
Lake Minchumina 99757
Larsen Bay 99624
Levelock 99625
Lime Village 99695
Little Diomede 99762
Long Island 99950
Loring 99950
Lower Kalskag 99626
Manley Hot Springs 99756
Manokotak 99628
May Creek 99695
McCarthy 99695
McGrath 99627
McKinley Park (see Denali
　National Park)
Mekoryuk 99630
Mentasta Lake 99780
Metlakatla ....■99926
Meyers Chuck 99903
Minto 99758
Moose Pass 99631
Moser Bay 99697
Mountain Village 99632
Naknek 99633
Napakiak 99634
Napaskiak 99559
Neets Cove 99950
Nelson Lagoon 99551
Nenana 99760
New Stuyahok 99636
Newtok 99559
Nickolaevsk 99556
Nightmute 99690
Nikiski 99635
Nikolai 99691
Nikolski 99638
Ninilchik 99639
Noatak 99761
Nome 99762
Nondalton 99640
Noorvik 99763
North Pole 99705
Northway 99764
Noyes Island 99950
Nuiqsut 99789
Nulato 99765
Nunapitchuk 99641
Nyac 99642
Old Harbor 99643
Olga Bay 99697
Ophir Bay 99695
Ouzinkie 99644
Palmer 99645
Paxson 99737
Pedro Bay 99647
Pelican 99832
Perryville 99648
Petersburg 99833
Pilot Point 99649
Pilot Station 99650
Platinum 99651
Point Baker 99927
Point Hope 99766
Point Lay 99759
Pope Vancy Landing 99695
Port Alexander 99836
Port Alice 99950
Port Alsworth 99653
Port Ashton 99695
Port Bailey 99697
Port Clarence 99790
Port Graham 99603
Port Heiden 99549
Port Johnson 99950
Port Lions ....■99550
Port Moller 99695
Port Protection 99950
Port San Juan 99695
Port Walter 99850
Port William 99697

Portage Creek 99695
Prudhoe Bay 99734
Quinhagak 99655
Rampart 99767
Red Devil 99656
Red Mountain 99695
Rowan Bay 99850
Ruby 99768
Russian Mission 99657
Saint George Island 99591
Saint Marys 99658
Saint Michael 99659
Saint Paul Island 99660
Salcha 99714
Sand Point 99661
Savoonga 99769
Scammon Bay 99662
Seal Bay 99697
Selawik 99770
Seldovia 99663
Seward ....■99664
Shageluk 99665
Shaktoolik 99771
Sheldon Point 99666
Shishmaref 99772
Shungnak 99773
Sitka 99835
Skagway 99840
Skwentna 99667
Slana 99586
Sleetmute 99668
Soldotna 99669
Solomon 99790
South Naknek 99670
Sparrevohn 99502
Stebbins 99671
Sterling 99672
Stevens Village 99774
Stony River 99557
Sutton 99674
Takotna 99675
Talkeetna 99676
Tanacross 99776
Tanana 99777
Tatitlek 99677
Telida 99695
Teller 99778
Tenakee Springs 99841
Terror Bay 99697
Tetlin 99779
Thorne Bay 99919
Togiak 99678
Tok 99780
Tokeen 99950
Toksook Bay 99637
Trapper Creek 99683
Tuluksak 99679
Tuntutuliak 99680
Tununak 99681
Twin Hills 99576
Tyonek 99682
Uganik Bay 99697
Ugashik 99695
Unalakleet 99684
Unalaska 99685
Utopia 99790
Uyak 99697
Valdez ....■99686
Venetie 99781
View Cove 99950
Wainwright 99782
Wales 99783
Ward Cove 99928
Wasilla 99687
Waterfall 99950
West Point 99697
Whale Pass 99950
White Mountain 99784
Whittier 99693
Willow 99688
Wiseman 99790
Wrangell 99929
Yakutat 99689
Yes Bay 99950
ZackarBay 99697

INDEX OF PLACE NAMES

Communities, Highways, National Parks (NP), National Wildlife Refuges (NWR) and other attractions. *A detailed map is included.*